# JUSTICE SYSTEM

TRIAL
ACQUITTED
CONVICTED
APPEAL
GUILTY PLEA
SENTENCING
INTERMEDIATE SANCTIONS

HABEAS CORPUS
CAPITAL PUNISHMENT
PARDON & CLEMENCY

PROBATION
REVOCATION
PRISON
REVOCATION
PAROLE

OUT OF SYSTEM

JAIL
REVOCATION
PROBATION
OUT OF SYSTEM

TRIAL
ACQUITTED
CONVICTED
GUILTY PLEA
SENTENCING

DEFENDANT    DISTRICT ATTORNEY    LAWYER    JUDGE

LAW ENFORCEMENT    CONVICT    OUT OF SYSTEM

# Welcome to the 9th Edition!

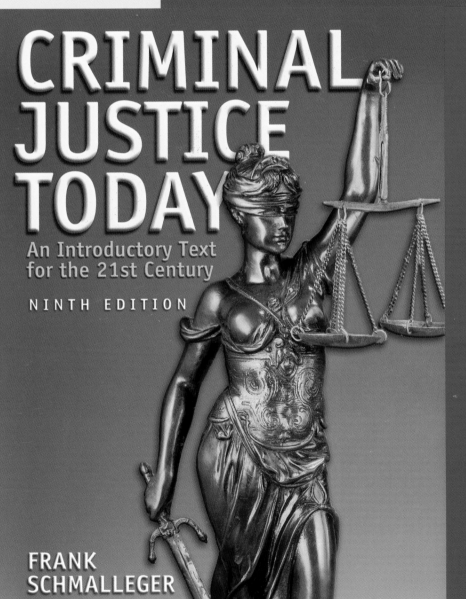

CRIMINAL JUSTICE TODAY

An Introductory Text for the 21st Century

NINTH EDITION

FRANK SCHMALLEGER

The following pages will introduce you to what's new in the 9th edition as well as to the hallmark features that have made *Criminal Justice Today* the most widely used introduction to criminal justice textbook in America today.

# What's New

## CJ Ethics and Professionalism Boxes

**Enhanced emphasis on ethics, stressing the importance of ethical behavior for the criminal justice professional**

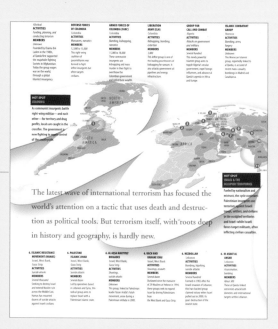

## Terrorism and the Criminal Justice System

**Global approach to the problem of terrorism, including its broad impact on American policing, corrections, and courts**

## Coverage of Today's Issues

The new U.S. Supreme Court Chief Justice

The case of the BTK killer

## CD Extras

**Additional in-depth coverage of important issues and background material found in the text, and full opinions of important U.S. Supreme Court cases found in the text**

# Theme

The always-evolving theme of individual rights versus public order has been a hallmark feature of *Criminal Justice Today* since the first edition, and it is more important now than ever before. The theme builds on the highest goal of the American criminal justice system, which is to achieve a just and orderly society in which people are free to pursue personal interests while remaining safe and secure.

**Effective law enforcement helps maintain social order and fills a critical need in the face of the widespread social disorganization that sometimes follows natural disasters or large-scale terrorist attacks.**

## FREEDOM OR SAFETY? YOU DECIDE.

On July 1, 2004, the New York City Commission on Human Rights ordered reinstatement of a New York Police Department (NYPD) officer who had quit the force in 2002 because supervisors would not allow him to wear a turban while working. Jasjit Jaggi is a Sikh, whose religion mandates the wearing of turbans and beards by adult males as a sign of their faith. The order, compelling the police department to grant a Sikh employee a religious accommodation, was the first such ruling in the nation issued to a law enforcement agency.

Although turbaned correctional officers are a rarity, some observers have pointed to the possibility of similar lawsuits in the corrections arena. One way for agencies and businesses to avoid legal action comes from the resolution of a religious bias claim brought against United Airlines by a turban-wearing Sikh employee in 2001. Although airline regulations banned the wearing of headgear by employees while indoors, company officials were able to avoid civil liability by offering the man six alternative jobs where he could wear a turban.

### YOU DECIDE

How might dress codes relate to public safety? Should agencies have the authority to enforce dress codes without fear of civil liability if those codes enhance public safety? What if they merely enforce uniformity of appearance? How do these ideas apply to correctional agencies?

Jasjit Jaggi directs traffic headed towards the Brooklyn Bridge in New York City in 2004. Jaggi, a devout Sikh, quit the NYPD in 2002 because his supervisors would not allow him to wear a turban. His reinstatement by the New York City Commission on Human Rights highlights the clash of cultures for all justice system workers, including corrections officers.
*Todd Maisel, New York Daily News*

**Some people fear that the use of profiling techniques holds the potential to unfairly discriminate against members of certain racial and ethnic groups. Others suggest that the careful use of profiling can provide an important advantage in an age of scarce resources. Which perspective appeals to you?**

# Timeliness

## Homeland Security in Our Post-9/11 Society

| Era | Political Era | Reform Era | Community Era | Homeland Security Era |
|---|---|---|---|---|
| **Time Period** | 1840s–1930 | 1930–1970s | 1970s–Today | 2001–Today |
| **Characteristics** | Close ties between the police and public officials.<br><br>Uniformed officers in paramilitary-style organizations serving the interests of the politically powerful. | Pride in professional crime fighting.<br><br>An emphasis on solving "traditional" crimes and capturing offenders. | Police departments work to identify and serve the needs of their communities.<br><br>Envisions a partnership between local police agencies and their communities. | Policing to secure the homeland; emphasis on terrorism prevention.<br><br>Builds on partnerships with the community to gather actionable intelligence to circumvent threats of terrorism. |
| **Catalyst** | The need for social order and security in a dynamic and rapidly changing society. | Citizen calls for reform and the development of police professionalism.<br><br>The removal of politics from policing. | The realization that effective community partnerships can help prevent and solve crimes. | The terrorist attacks of September 11, 2001, and ongoing threats to the safety and security of all Americans. |
| **Example** | Police departments and officers were closely tied to their city's political system.<br><br>Local "ward politicians" hired officers for their own purposes. | "G-men" and the crackdown on organized crime.<br><br>Progressive policing, led by men like August Vollmer and O. W. Wilson. | A focus on quality-of-life offenses as a crime-reduction and peacekeeping strategy.<br><br>The broken windows model of policing. | Creation of counterterrorism divisions and offices within departments.<br><br>Collaboration between police agencies and the sharing of information needed to identify threats. |

*Historical Eras in American Policing*

## The War on Terror

Policing strategies across the United States have been significantly affected by the threat of terrorism and the need for a rapid and effective response to attacks.

## AMBER Alert

With 50 statewide Amber plans now in place, AMBER Alerts have already helped police save hundreds of children's lives across the country.

# Technology

## High-Tech Policing

### The FBI's New Information Technology Tools

Since 9/11 the FBI has recognized that the ability to assemble, analyze, and disseminate information both internally and with other intelligence and law enforcement agencies is essential to the nation's success in the war on terrorism. Consequently, it has made modernization of its information technology (IT) systems a top priority.

According to FBI director Robert S. Mueller III, the agency has recently taken a coordinated, strategic approach to IT, building a strategic IT plan and creating an internal system for managing IT projects at each stage of their life cycle.

IT modernization is occurring under a multiphased program code-named Trilogy. As a result of Trilogy, the FBI has:

1. Deployed a high-speed, secure network that enables personnel in FBI offices around the country to share data, including audio, video, and image files.
2. Provided its agents and intelligence analysts with more than 30,000 new desktop computers running modern software applications, along with 3,700 printers, 1,600 scanners, 465 servers, and 1,400 routers.
3. Developed an IT infrastructure that provides for secure communication with FBI intelligence community partners.

The third phase of Trilogy included the Virtual Case File (VCF) system, which was intended to give the bureau's agents nearly instant access to all needed information in the agency's databases. VCF, however, encountered technical problems, some of which were related to requirements involving the sharing of information

with other law enforcement and national security organizations. Consequently, the VCF system was scrapped in 2005, and the FBI announced plans to use mostly off-the-shelf products that will allow agents to easily share information. The replacement system, called Sentinel, is based on a problem-solving framework known as the Federal Investigative Case Management Solution (FICMS).

Separate from the Trilogy/Sentinel program, the FBI has successfully deployed a number of new investigative and information-sharing capabilities, including the following:

- *Investigative Data Warehouse (IDW)*. IDW offers agents and analysts the technology needed to perform intelligent link analysis to uncover potential relationships that might exist between suspects, physical and information resources, and anticipated threats. IDW provides FBI users with a single access point to more than 47 sources of counterterrorism data, including information from FBI files, other government agency data, and open source news feeds, that were previously available only through separate proprietary information systems and laborious data-gathering efforts.
- *FBI Automated Messaging System (FAMS)*. FAMS began operations in December 2004 and now provides more than 30,000 FBI agents and intelligence analysts with the capability to send and receive critical organizational message traffic to any of the 40,000+ addresses on the Defense Messaging System.
- *FBI Intelligence Information Reports Dissemination System (FIDS)*. FIDS is a Web-based software application that allows all FBI personnel with access to the FBI's internal intranet to create and disseminate standardized intelligence information reports quickly and efficiently to FBI agents and other law enforcement officers.

References: Testimony of Robert S. Mueller, III, Director, Federal Bureau of Investigation, before the Committee on Intelligence of the United States Senate, February 16, 2005; and Linda Rosencrance, "It's Official: FBI Scraps $170 million Virtual Case File Project," *Computerworld*, March 9, 2005.

## High-Tech Legislation

### Identity Theft: A New Kind of Larceny

In 2005, ChoicePoint, a personal-information clearinghouse with huge stores of private data on millions of Americans, announced that it had been the victim of a fraud perpetrated by thieves posing as legitimate business customers.[1] The firm quickly notified more than 145,000 people nationwide that critical personal information, including credit scores, Social Security numbers, street addresses, and more, had been stolen in what looked like a massive identity theft scheme. Later that year, more than 100,000 Bank of America and Wachovia customers were notified that their financial records might have been stolen.[2] MasterCard reported that 40 million credit card accounts had been compromised by a security breach at a payment processing center.[3]

**Identity theft**, which involves obtaining credit, merchandise, or services by fraudulent personal representation, is a special kind of larceny. According to a recent Federal Trade Commission survey, identity theft directly impacts as many as 10 million victims annually, although most do not report the crime.[4] Identity theft became a federal crime in 1998 with the passage of the Identity Theft and Assumption Deterrence Act.[5] The law makes it a crime whenever anyone "knowingly transfers or uses, without lawful authority, a means of identification of another person with the intent to commit, or to aid or abet, any unlawful activity that constitutes a violation of federal law, or that constitutes a felony under any applicable state or local law."

The 2004 Identity Theft Penalty Enhancement Act[6] added years to federal prison sentences for criminals convicted of using stolen credit card numbers and other personal data to commit crimes. It also prescribed prison sentences for those who use identity theft to commit other crimes, including terrorism, and it increased penalties for defendants who exceed or abuse the authority of their position in unlawfully obtaining or using means of personal identification.

Anyone can fall prey to identity theft—even celebrities. In 2000, for example, golfer Tiger Woods learned that his identity had been stolen and that credit cards taken out in his name had been used to steal $17,000 worth of merchandise, including a 70-inch TV, stereos, and a used luxury car. In 2001, a thief, 30-year-old Anthony Lemar Taylor, who looks nothing like Woods, was convicted of falsely obtaining a driver's license using the name of Eldrick T. Woods (Tiger's given name), Woods's Social Security number, and his birth date. Because Taylor already had 20 previous convictions of all sorts on his record, he was sentenced to 200 years in prison under California's three-strikes law.[7] Like Woods, most victims of identity theft do not even know that their identities have been stolen until they receive bills for merchandise they didn't purchased.

According to the National White Collar Crime Center, identity thieves use several common techniques. Some engage in "Dumpster diving," going through trash bags, cans, or Dumpsters to get copies of checks, credit card and bank statements, credit card applications, or other records that typically bear identifying information. Others use a technique called "shoulder surfing." It involves simply looking over the victim's shoulder as he or she enters personal information into a computer or on a written form. Eavesdropping is another simple, yet effective, technique that identity thieves often use. Eavesdropping can occur when the victim is using an ATM machine, giving credit card or other personal information over the phone, or dialing the number for their telephone calling card. Criminals can also obtain personal identifying information from potential victims through "spam" (unsolicited e-mail) that promises them all sorts of attractive benefits while requesting identifying data, such as checking account or credit card numbers and expiration dates, along with the victim's name and address.[8] Identity theft perpetrated through the use of high technology depends on the fact that a person's legal and economic identity in contemporary society is largely "virtual" and supported by technology.

Learn more about identity thieves and how they operate via Web Extra 2-7 and Library Extra 2-5 at cjtoday.com.

World-renowned professional golfer Tiger Woods. In 2000, Woods became the victim of identity theft when 29-year-old Anthony Lemar Taylor of Sacramento, California, used Woods's identity to charge $17,000 on the golfer's charge cards.
*AP Wide World Photos*

*(continued)*

## High-Tech Technology

### Multistate Anti-TeRrorism Information EXchange (MATRIX)

*MATRIX Project* — a pilot effort to increase and enhance the exchange of sensitive terrorism and other criminal activity information between local, state, and federal law enforcement agencies.

**The home page of the Multistate Anti-Terrorism Information Exchange (MATRIX), a pilot project in boundaryless policing and interagency information sharing.**

**Identix Corporation's CEO Joseph Atick, demonstrates use of a digital handprint scanner.**

# Criminal Justice Today

## An Introductory Text for the Twenty-First Century

### Ninth Edition

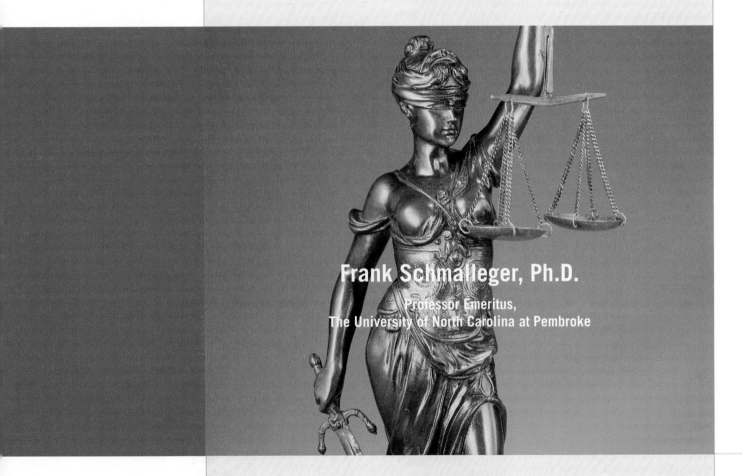

**Frank Schmalleger, Ph.D.**

Professor Emeritus,
The University of North Carolina at Pembroke

PEARSON

Prentice
Hall

Upper Saddle River, New Jersey 07458

**Library of Congress Cataloging-in-Publication Data**

Schmalleger, Frank.
    Criminal justice today : an introductory text for the twenty-first century / Frank
Schmalleger.—9th ed.
      p. cm.
    Includes bibliographical references and indexes.
    ISBN 0-13-171950-5
    1. Criminal justice, Administration of—United States. I. Title.
HV9950.S35 2006
364.973—dc22

2005052319

**Executive Editor:** Frank Mortimer, Jr.
**Associate Editor:** Sarah Holle
**Marketing Manager:** Adam Kloza
**Editorial Assistant:** Kelly Krug
**Managing Editor:** Mary Carnis
**Production Liaison:** Barbara Marttine Cappuccio
**Production Editor:** Janet Bolton
**Director of Manufacturing and Production:** Bruce Johnson
**Manufacturing Manager:** Ilene Sanford
**Manufacturing Buyer:** Cathleen Petersen
**Director, Image Resource Center:** Melinda Reo
**Manager, Rights and Permissions:** Zina Arabia
**Manager, Visual Research:** Beth Brenzel
**Manager, Cover Visual Research & Permissions:** Karen Sanatar
**Image Permission Coordinator:** Cynthia Vincenti
**Photo Researcher:** Alexandra Truitt and Jerry Marshall
**Manager of Media Production:** Amy Peltier
**Media Production Project Manager:** Lisa Rinaldi
**Creative Director:** Cheryl Asherman
**Cover Design:** Cheryl Asherman
**Cover Image:** Corbis
**Interior Design:** Amanda Kavanagh
**Electronic Art Creation:** Carlisle Publishing Services
**Composition:** Carlisle Publishing Services
**Printing and Binding:** Courier, Kendallville
**Proofreader:** Maine Proofreading Services
**Copy Editor:** Loretta Palagi

**Part Opening Photo Credits:** Corbis Royalty Free; Nick Koudis/PhotoDisc/Getty Images; Don Farrall/Photodisc/Getty Images, Inc.; Scott Goldsmith/Stone/Getty Images; Raymond Allbritton/Stone/Getty Images.
**Chapter Opening Photo Credits (right page):** Getty Images, Inc.—Comstock Images, Royalty Free; Koopman, Corbis/Bettmann; Jeremy Woodhouse, Photodisc, Getty Images, Inc.; Michael Kelley, Stone, Getty Images, Inc.; Getty Images, Inc.—Photodisc.
**Chapter Opening Photo Credits (left page):** AP Wide World Photos; Dwayne Newton, PhotoEdit; Edouard Berne, Getty Images, Inc.—Stone Allstock; David Young-Wolff, PhotoEdit; Monica Graff, The Image Works; AP Wide World Photos; David McNew, Getty Images, Inc.—Hulton Archive Photos; AP Wide World Photos; Annette Coolidge, PhotoEdit; © brt Photo/Mira.com; Michael Newman, PhotoEdit; A. Ramey, Stock Boston; AP Wide World Photos; Bob Daemmrich, The Image Works; Jim Corwin, Getty Images, Inc.—Stone Allstock; © Owen Franken, CORBIS; Ian Waldie, Reuters NewMedia, Inc.—Corbis/Bettmann; AP Wide World Photos.

Pearson Education LTD.
Pearson Education Australia PTY, Limited
Pearson Education Singapore, Pte. Ltd.
Pearson Education North Asia Ltd.
Pearson Education Canada, Ltd.
Pearson Educacion de Mexico, S.A. de C.V.
Pearson Education—Japan
Pearson Education Malaysia, Pte. Ltd.
Pearson Education, Upper Saddle River, New Jersey

10 9 8 7 6 5 4 3 2 1
ISBN 0-13-171950-5
ISBN 0-13-171965-3

For Harmonie Star-Schmalleger,
my beautiful wife and other self

# BRIEF CONTENTS

**Part 1**    Crime in America

Chapter 1    **What Is Criminal Justice?**
Chapter 2    **The Crime Picture**
Chapter 3    **The Search for Causes**
Chapter 4    **Criminal Law**

**Part 2**    Policing

Chapter 5    **Policing: History and Structure**
Chapter 6    **Policing: Purpose and Organization**
Chapter 7    **Policing: Legal Aspects**
Chapter 8    **Policing: Issues and Challenges**

**Part 3**    Adjudication

Chapter 9    **The Courts: Structure and Participants**
Chapter 10    **Pretrial Activities and the Criminal Trial**
Chapter 11    **Sentencing**

**Part 4**    Corrections

Chapter 12    **Probation, Parole, and Community Corrections**
Chapter 13    **Prisons and Jails**
Chapter 14    **Prison Life**

**Part 5**    Special Issues

Chapter 15    **Juvenile Justice**
Chapter 16    **Drugs and Crime**
Chapter 17    **Terrorism and Multinational Criminal Justice**
Chapter 18    **The Future of Criminal Justice**

# CONTENTS

Preface  xxiii
To the Student  xxiv
Acknowledgments  xxv
About the Author  xxx

**Part 1  Crime in America  2**

Chapter 1  **What Is Criminal Justice?**  4
INTRODUCTION  6
A BRIEF HISTORY OF CRIME IN AMERICA  7
THE THEME OF THIS BOOK  10

FREEDOM OR SAFETY? YOU DECIDE.  Giuliani Says: "Freedom Is about Authority"  11

SOCIAL JUSTICE  12

CJ NEWS  Chicago Plans Advanced Camera Surveillance  13

AMERICAN CRIMINAL JUSTICE: SYSTEM AND FUNCTIONS  15
   The Consensus Model  15
   The Conflict Model  16
AMERICAN CRIMINAL JUSTICE: THE PROCESS  16
   Investigation and Arrest  17
   Pretrial Activities  17
   Adjudication  19
   Sentencing  19
   Corrections  20
DUE PROCESS AND INDIVIDUAL RIGHTS  21

CJ CAREERS  Why Study Criminal Justice?  22

   The Role of the Courts in Defining Rights  22
   The Ultimate Goal: Crime Control through Due Process  22

CJ CAREERS  U.S. Federal Government 2005 General Schedule Pay  23

THE ROLE OF RESEARCH IN CRIMINAL JUSTICE  23

CJ FUTURES  The National Law Enforcement and Corrections Technology Center  24

MULTICULTURALISM AND DIVERSITY IN CRIMINAL JUSTICE  24

CJ NEWS  Border Incident Angers Muslims  26

SUMMARY  27
DISCUSSION QUESTIONS  28
WEB QUEST  29
NOTES  29

# CONTENTS

**Chapter 2   The Crime Picture   32**

**INTRODUCTION   34**

Crime Data and Social Policy   34

The Collection of Crime Data   35

**THE UNIFORM CRIME REPORTS   36**

Development of the UCR Program   36

**CJ NEWS   Lost Police Reports Hint at Problems   37**

Historical Trends   38

UCR Terminology   40

**FREEDOM OR SAFETY? YOU DECIDE.   A Dress Code for Bank Customers?   40**

Part I Offenses   42

**MULTICULTURALISM AND DIVERSITY   Race and the Criminal Justice System   47**

**CJ TODAY EXHIBIT 2–1   Identity Theft: A New Kind of Larceny   51**

Part II Offenses   53

NIBRS: The New UCR   54

**THE NATIONAL CRIME VICTIMIZATION SURVEY   56**

**COMPARISONS OF THE UCR AND THE NCVS   57**

Problems with the UCR and the NCVS   57

**SPECIAL CATEGORIES OF CRIME   59**

Crime Against Women   59

**MULTICULTURALISM AND DIVERSITY   Gender Issues in Criminal Justice   61**

Crime Against the Elderly   62

Hate Crime   63

Corporate and White-Collar Crime   63

Organized Crime   65

Gun Crime   66

Drug Crime   67

High-Technology and Computer Crime   67

**CJ TODAY EXHIBIT 2–2   Gun Control   68**

Terrorism   69

**CJ NEWS   Hunting Cybercrooks   70**

**SUMMARY   71**

**DISCUSSION QUESTIONS   72**

**WEB QUEST   73**

**NOTES   73**

# CONTENTS

Chapter 3   The Search for Causes   78

**INTRODUCTION   80**

**CRIMINOLOGICAL THEORY   82**

**THE CLASSICAL SCHOOL   86**

Cesare Beccaria: Crime and Punishment   86

Jeremy Bentham: Hedonistic Calculus   86

The Neoclassical Perspective   86

Social Policy and Classical Theories   87

**BIOLOGICAL THEORIES   87**

Franz Joseph Gall: Phrenology   87

Cesare Lombroso: Atavism   88

Criminal Families   90

William Sheldon: Somatotypes   90

Social Policy and Biological Theories   90

**PSYCHOBIOLOGICAL THEORIES   91**

Chromosome Theory   91

Biochemical Factors and Imbalances   91

Heredity and Other Physical Factors   92

Social Policy and Psychobiological Theories   93

**PSYCHOLOGICAL THEORIES   93**

Behavioral Conditioning   93

Freudian Psychoanalysis   93

Psychopathology and Crime   94

The Psychotic Offender   95

Psychological Profiling   96

Social Policy and Psychological Theories   96

**SOCIOLOGICAL THEORIES   96**

Social Ecology Theory   97

Anomie Theory   97

Subcultural Theory   98

CJ FUTURES   The Physical Environment and Crime   99

Social Policy and Sociological Theories   100

**SOCIAL PROCESS THEORIES   101**

Differential Association Theory   101

Restraint Theories   102

Labeling Theory   103

The Life Course Perspective   104

**CONFLICT THEORIES   106**

Radical Criminology   107

Peacemaking Criminology   107

Social Policy and Conflict Theories   108

# CONTENTS

**EMERGENT PERSPECTIVES** 109

    Feminist Criminology   109

    Constitutive Criminology   111

    Postmodern Criminology   111

**SUMMARY**   111

**DISCUSSION QUESTIONS**   112

**WEB QUEST**   112

**NOTES**   112

Chapter 4   **Criminal Law**   118

**INTRODUCTION**   120

**THE NATURE AND PURPOSE OF LAW**   120

**THE RULE OF LAW**   121

**TYPES OF LAW**   122

    Criminal Law   122

    Civil Law   123

**FREEDOM OR SAFETY? YOU DECIDE.**   The Lawsuits of Madison County   124

    Administrative Law   126

    Case Law   126

    Procedural Law   126

**CJ NEWS**   $1B Judgment Against Spammers   127

**GENERAL CATEGORIES OF CRIME**   128

    Felonies   128

    Misdemeanors   128

    Offenses   129

    Treason and Espionage   129

    Inchoate Offenses   130

**GENERAL FEATURES OF CRIME**   130

    The Criminal Act (*Actus Reus*)   130

    A Guilty Mind (*Mens Rea*)   131

    Concurrence   132

    Other Features of Crime   132

**ELEMENTS OF A SPECIFIC CRIMINAL OFFENSE**   134

    The Example of Murder   134

**CJ CAREERS**   U.S. Secret Service Uniformed Division   135

    The *Corpus Delicti* of a Crime   136

**TYPES OF DEFENSES TO A CRIMINAL CHARGE**   137

    Alibi   138

    Justifications   138

    Excuses   140

# CONTENTS

CJ NEWS **Courts Asked to Consider Culture  141**

   Procedural Defenses  149

SUMMARY  152

DISCUSSION QUESTIONS  152

WEB QUEST  153

NOTES  153

## Part 2  Policing  156

### Chapter 5  Policing: History and Structure  158

INTRODUCTION  160

HISTORICAL DEVELOPMENT OF THE POLICE  161

   English Roots  161

   The Early American Experience  163

   The Last Half of the Twentieth Century  165

   Scientific Police Management  166

AMERICAN LAW ENFORCEMENT TODAY: FROM THE FEDERAL TO THE LOCAL LEVEL  170

FEDERAL AGENCIES  170

   The Federal Bureau of Investigation  170

CJ CAREERS **Federal Bureau of Investigation  172**

   The FBI and Counterterrorism  174

STATE AGENCIES  175

CJ FUTURES **The FBI's New Information Technology Tools  176**

CJ NEWS **Don't Even Ask About Extra Credit  178**

LOCAL AGENCIES  179

FREEDOM OR SAFETY? YOU DECIDE.  **The Conch Republic  181**

PRIVATE PROTECTIVE SERVICES  181

ETHICS AND PROFESSIONALISM  **ASIS International Code of Ethics  183**

   Integrating Public and Private Security  185

SUMMARY  186

DISCUSSION QUESTIONS  187

WEB QUEST  187

NOTES  187

### Chapter 6  Policing: Purpose and Organization  190

INTRODUCTION  192

THE POLICE MISSION  192

   Enforcing the Law  192

# CONTENTS

Apprehending Offenders   193

Preventing Crime   194

Preserving the Peace   195

**CJ NEWS   Crime-Fighting by Computer   196**

Providing Services   198

**OPERATIONAL STRATEGIES   198**

Preventive Patrol   198

Routine Incident Response   198

Emergency Response   200

Criminal Investigation   200

Problem Solving   202

Support Services   203

**MANAGING POLICE DEPARTMENTS   203**

Police Organization and Structure   203

Chain of Command   203

**POLICING STYLES   204**

The Watchman Style of Policing   207

The Legalistic Style of Policing   207

The Service Style of Policing   207

**FREEDOM OR SAFETY? YOU DECIDE.   Watch Out: You're on Police TV   208**

Police–Community Relations   208

Critique of Community Policing   212

**TERRORISM'S IMPACT ON POLICING   214**

Intelligence-Led Policing and Antiterrorism   216

**CJ NEWS   Police Tactic Against Terror: Let's Network   217**

Community Policing and Antiterrorism   219

Information Sharing and Antiterrorism   219

**DISCRETION AND THE INDIVIDUAL OFFICER   221**

**PROFESSIONALISM AND ETHICS   223**

**ETHICS AND PROFESSIONALISM   The Law Enforcement Code of Ethics   223**

Education and Training   224

**CJ CAREERS   Policing: Average Base Starting Pay   226**

Recruitment and Selection   226

**ETHNIC AND GENDER DIVERSITY IN POLICING   228**

Women as Effective Police Officers   230

Increasing the Number of Minorities and Women in Police Work   230

# CONTENTS

SUMMARY 231
DISCUSSION QUESTIONS 231
WEB QUEST 232
NOTES 232

Chapter 7   Policing: Legal Aspects 238
INTRODUCTION 240
THE ABUSE OF POLICE POWER 240
    A Changing Legal Climate 242
INDIVIDUAL RIGHTS 243
    Due Process Requirements 244
SEARCH AND SEIZURE 244
    The Exclusionary Rule 244

FREEDOM OR SAFETY? YOU DECIDE.   Liberty Is a Double-Edged Sword 246

    The Warren Court (1953–1969) 246
    The Burger Court (1969–1986) and Rehnquist Court (1986–2005) 248
ARREST 253

CJ NEWS   Court Permits Speedy Drug Raid 255

    Searches Incident to Arrest 256

CJ TODAY EXHIBIT 7–1   Plain-View Requirements 258

    Emergency Searches of Persons 258
    Vehicle Searches 259

CJ CAREERS   Bureau of Immigration and Customs Enforcement (ICE) 260

    Suspicionless Searches 263

CJ NEWS   Legal Issues Being Raised on Searches in Subways 265

    High-Technology Searches 266
THE INTELLIGENCE FUNCTION 267
    Informants 267
    Police Interrogation 268
    The Right to a Lawyer at Interrogation 270

CJ TODAY EXHIBIT 7–2   The Miranda Warnings 271

    Suspect Rights: The Miranda Decision 271
    Gathering Special Kinds of Nontestimonial Evidence 275

CJ TODAY EXHIBIT 7–3   Miranda Update 276

    Electronic Eavesdropping 277

CJ TODAY EXHIBIT 7–4   The USA PATRIOT Act of 2001 280

# CONTENTS

SUMMARY  282

DISCUSSION QUESTIONS  283

WEB QUEST  283

NOTES  283


Chapter 8    Policing: Issues and Challenges  288

INTRODUCTION  290

POLICE PERSONALITY AND CULTURE  290

CORRUPTION AND INTEGRITY  291

MULTICULTURALISM AND DIVERSITY  Policing a Multicultural Society  292

Money—The Root of Police Evil?  295

Building Police Integrity  296

ETHICS AND PROFESSIONALISM    The Law Enforcement Oath of Honor  297

Drug Testing of Police Employees  297

THE DANGERS OF POLICE WORK  298

Violence in the Line of Duty  299

Risk of Disease and Infected Evidence  300

Stress and Fatigue among Police Officers  302

POLICE USE OF FORCE  303

FREEDOM OR SAFETY? YOU DECIDE.   Protecting Public Places  304

Deadly Force  306

CJ CAREERS  Bureau of Alcohol, Tobacco, Firearms, and Explosives  308

Less-Lethal Weapons  309

RACIAL PROFILING AND BIASED POLICING  309

CJ NEWS   As Shocks Replace Bullets, Questions Arise  310

Racially Biased Policing  313

MULTICULTURALISM AND DIVERSITY  Investigating Crime in a Multicultural Setting  314

POLICE CIVIL LIABILITY  314

Common Sources of Civil Suits  315

Federal Lawsuits  317

SUMMARY  319

DISCUSSION QUESTIONS  319

WEB QUEST  319

NOTES  320

# CONTENTS

## Part 3 Adjudication 324

### Chapter 9 The Courts: Structure and Participants 326

**INTRODUCTION** 328

**HISTORY AND STRUCTURE OF THE AMERICAN COURT SYSTEM** 329

**THE STATE COURT SYSTEM** 330

   The Development of State Courts 330

   State Court Systems Today 332

**THE FEDERAL COURT SYSTEM** 336

   U.S. District Courts 336

   U.S. Courts of Appeal 337

   The U.S. Supreme Court 338

**THE COURTROOM WORK GROUP** 340

**PROFESSIONAL COURTROOM PARTICIPANTS** 341

   The Judge 341

   The Prosecuting Attorney 343

   The Defense Counsel 346

**CJ TODAY EXHIBIT 9–1** *Gideon* v. *Wainwright* and Indigent Defense 350

**ETHICS AND PROFESSIONALISM** American Bar Association Model Code of Professional Responsibility 352

   The Bailiff 353

   Local Court Administrators 353

   The Court Reporter 353

**CJ CAREERS** U.S. Marshals Service 354

   The Clerk of Court 354

   Expert Witnesses 355

**NONPROFESSIONAL COURTROOM PARTICIPANTS** 356

   Lay Witnesses 356

   Jurors 357

**CJ NEWS** "CSI Effect" Has Juries Wanting More Evidence 358

   The Victim 360

   The Defendant 361

   Spectators and the Press 361

**SUMMARY** 363

**DISCUSSION QUESTIONS** 363

**WEB QUEST** 364

**NOTES** 364

# CONTENTS

Chapter 10  Pretrial Activities and the Criminal Trial  368

INTRODUCTION  370

PRETRIAL ACTIVITIES  371

The First Appearance  371

The Grand Jury  376

The Preliminary Hearing  376

CJ TODAY EXHIBIT 10–1  Nonjudicial Pretrial Release Decisions  377

Arraignment and the Plea  378

Plea Bargaining  378

THE CRIMINAL TRIAL  380

Nature and Purpose of the Criminal Trial  380

STAGES OF A CRIMINAL TRIAL  381

Trial Initiation: The Speedy Trial Act  382

Jury Selection  383

CJ TODAY EXHIBIT 10–2  Peremptory Challenges and Race  385

Opening Statements  387

The Presentation of Evidence  387

CJ TODAY EXHIBIT 10–3  Pretrial and Posttrial Motions  388

Closing Arguments  391

The Judge's Charge to the Jury  392

Jury Deliberations and the Verdict  392

IMPROVING THE ADJUDICATION PROCESS  393

CJ FUTURES  Courtrooms of the Future  394

SUMMARY  395

MULTICULTURALISM AND DIVERSITY  The Bilingual Courtroom  396

DISCUSSION QUESTIONS  397

WEB QUEST  397

NOTES  397


Chapter 11  Sentencing  400

INTRODUCTION  402

THE PHILOSOPHY AND GOALS OF CRIMINAL SENTENCING  403

Retribution  403

Incapacitation  404

Deterrence  404

Rehabilitation  404

Restoration  405

# CONTENTS

**INDETERMINATE SENTENCING  406**

Critiques of Indeterminate Sentencing  407

**STRUCTURED SENTENCING  408**

Federal Sentencing Guidelines  409

**CJ TODAY EXHIBIT 11–1  Aggravating and Mitigating Circumstances  410**

**CJ NEWS  Supreme Court Transforms Federal Sentencing Guidelines  411**

The Legal Environment of Structured Sentencing  413

Mandatory Sentencing  414

**CJ TODAY EXHIBIT 11–2  Three Strikes and You're Out: A Brief History of the "Get Tough on Crime" Movement  416**

**INNOVATIONS IN SENTENCING  418**

Questions about Alternative Sanctions  418

**THE PRESENTENCE INVESTIGATION  418**

**CJ FUTURES  Is Chemical Castration a Valid Sentencing Option?  419**

**THE VICTIM—FORGOTTEN NO LONGER  420**

**CJ TODAY EXHIBIT 11–3  President Bush Calls for Victims' Rights Amendment  421**

Victim Impact Statements  423

**MODERN SENTENCING OPTIONS  423**

Fines  425

**DEATH: THE ULTIMATE SANCTION  426**

*Habeas Corpus* Review  427

**FREEDOM OR SAFETY? YOU DECIDE.  What Are the Limits of Genetic Privacy?  429**

Opposition to Capital Punishment  429

**CJ NEWS  DNA Tests for Guilty Jam System  432**

Justifications for Capital Punishment  434

The Courts and the Death Penalty  434

The Future of the Death Penalty  437

**CJ NEWS  Death Penalty Gains Unusual Defenders  438**

**SUMMARY  441**

**DISCUSSION QUESTIONS  441**

**WEB QUEST  442**

**NOTES  442**

# CONTENTS

## Part 4 Corrections 448

### Chapter 12 Probation, Parole, and Community Corrections 450
INTRODUCTION 452
WHAT IS PROBATION? 453
The Extent of Probation 453

CJ NEWS Getting Tough on Paroled Sex Offenders 454

Probation Conditions 456

MULTICULTURALISM AND DIVERSITY Culturally Skilled Probation Officers 458

WHAT IS PAROLE? 458
The Extent of Parole 459
Parole Conditions 460
Federal Parole 460
PROBATION AND PAROLE: THE PLUSES AND MINUSES 460
Advantages of Probation and Parole 460
Disadvantages of Probation and Parole 461
THE LEGAL ENVIRONMENT 462
THE JOB OF PROBATION AND PAROLE OFFICERS 464

CJ CAREERS Probation Officer 465

The Challenges of the Job 466
INTERMEDIATE SANCTIONS 466
Split Sentencing 467
Shock Probation and Shock Parole 467
Shock Incarceration 467
Mixed Sentencing and Community Service 468

ETHICS AND PROFESSIONALISM American Probation and Parole Association Code of Ethics 469

Intensive Supervision 469
Home Confinement and Remote Location Monitoring 470
THE FUTURE OF PROBATION AND PAROLE 472
Reinventing Parole 473
Reinventing Probation 474

CJ FUTURES Probation Kiosks: High-Tech Supervision 475

SUMMARY 476
DISCUSSION QUESTIONS 476
WEB QUEST 476
NOTES 477

# CONTENTS

Chapter 13 **Prisons and Jails** **480**

**INTRODUCTION** **482**

**EARLY PUNISHMENTS** **482**

Flogging 483

Mutilation 483

Branding 484

Public Humiliation 484

Workhouses 484

Exile 484

**THE EMERGENCE OF PRISONS** **485**

The Penitentiary Era (1790–1825) 485

The Mass Prison Era (1825–1876) 487

**CJ TODAY EXHIBIT 13–1** **Chaplain James Finley's Letter from the Ohio Penitentiary, 1850** **488**

The Reformatory Era (1876–1890) 488

**CJ TODAY EXHIBIT 13–2** **An Early Texas Prison** **489**

The Industrial Era (1890–1935) 490

The Punitive Era (1935–1945) 492

The Treatment Era (1945–1967) 492

The Community-Based Era (1967–1980) 493

The Warehousing Era (1980–1995) 494

The Just Deserts Era (1995–Present) 496

**PRISONS TODAY** **498**

Overcrowding 499

Security Levels 502

Prison Classification Systems 503

The Federal Prison System 504

**CJ CAREERS** **Federal Bureau of Prisons** **507**

Recent Improvements 507

**JAILS** **507**

Women and Jail 508

**CJ NEWS** **Federal Prisons to End Boot-Camp Programs** **509**

The Growth of Jails 510

Direct-Supervision Jails 511

Jails and the Future 513

**ETHICS AND PROFESSIONALISM** **American Jail Association Code of Ethics for Jail Officers** **514**

**PRIVATE PRISONS** **514**

**CJ FUTURES** **Jails and the Future** **515**

**CJ TODAY EXHIBIT 13–3** **Arguments For and Against the Privatization of Prisons** **517**

# CONTENTS

SUMMARY  517

DISCUSSION QUESTIONS  518

WEB QUEST  518

NOTES  518


Chapter 14   Prison Life   524

INTRODUCTION  526

   Research on Prison Life—Total Institutions  526

THE MALE INMATE'S WORLD  527

CJ TODAY EXHIBIT 14–1   Prison Argot: The Language of Confinement  528

   Prison Subcultures  528

   The Functions of Prison Subcultures  529

   Prison Lifestyles and Inmate Types  530

   Homosexuality in Prison  532

THE FEMALE INMATE'S WORLD  533

   Gender Responsiveness  536

   Institutions for Women  536

   Social Structure in Women's Prisons  537

   Types of Female Inmates  538

   Violence in Women's Prisons  539

THE STAFF WORLD  539

FREEDOM OR SAFETY? YOU DECIDE.   Dress Codes and Public Safety  541

ETHICS AND PROFESSIONALISM   American Correctional Association Code of Ethics  542

   The Professionalization of Correctional Officers  542

PRISON RIOTS  543

   Causes of Riots  544

   Stages in Riots and Riot Control  544

PRISONERS' RIGHTS  545

   The Legal Basis of Prisoners' Rights  546

   Precedents in Prisoners' Rights  547

CJ NEWS   Inmates versus Outsourcing  552

CJ TODAY EXHIBIT 14–2   Federal Oversight of the Texas Prison System: A Timeline  556

   A Return to the Hands-Off Doctrine?  557

ISSUES FACING PRISONS TODAY  559

   AIDS  559

CJ CAREERS   U.S. Customs and Border Protection (CBP)  560

   Geriatric Offenders  561

# CONTENTS

CJ NEWS   **Death Row Population Is Graying   562**

CJ FUTURES   **Technocorrections   564**

  Mentally Ill and Mentally Deficient Inmates   565

FREEDOM OR SAFETY? YOU DECIDE.   **Censoring Prison Communications   566**

  Terrorism   566

CJ FUTURES   **The Commission on Safety and Abuse in America's Prisons   568**

SUMMARY   569
DISCUSSION QUESTIONS   569
WEB QUEST   570
NOTES   570


**Part 5   Special Issues   576**

Chapter 15   Juvenile Justice   578
INTRODUCTION   580
JUVENILE JUSTICE THROUGHOUT HISTORY   582
  Earliest Times   582
  Juveniles in Early America   583
  The Institutional Era   584
  The Juvenile Court Era   585
THE PROBLEMS OF CHILDREN TODAY   588
  Drug and Alcohol Abuse   588
  Violence   590
  Gangs   591

CJ NEWS   **Mean Streets Once Again: Gang Activity Surging   592**

CJ TODAY EXHIBIT 15–1   **What Is a Gang?   595**

  Runaways   595
  Sexual Abuse   596
  Other Forms of Abuse   597

CJ TODAY EXHIBIT 15–2   **Parents on Trial   598**

THE LEGAL ENVIRONMENT   599
  *Kent* v. *U.S.* (1966)   599
  *In re Gault* (1967)   599
  *In re Winship* (1970)   601
  *McKeiver* v. *Pennsylvania* (1971)   601
  *Breed* v. *Jones* (1975)   602
  *Schall* v. *Martin* (1984)   602

# CONTENTS

*Illinois* v. *Montanez* (1996)   602

Legislation Concerning Juvenile Justice   603

The Legal Rights of Juveniles   604

**THE JUVENILE JUSTICE PROCESS TODAY   604**

**CJ TODAY EXHIBIT 15–3   The Juvenile Justice System versus Criminal Case Processing   606**

Adult and Juvenile Justice Compared   606

How the System Works   606

**CJ TODAY EXHIBIT 15–4   Juvenile Courts versus Adult Courts   610**

**THE POST–JUVENILE COURT ERA   614**

**SUMMARY   615**

**DISCUSSION QUESTIONS   615**

**WEB QUEST   616**

**NOTES   616**


Chapter 16   Drugs and Crime   620

**INTRODUCTION   622**

Drug Abuse: More Than an Individual Choice   622

**WHAT IS A DRUG?   623**

Alcohol Abuse   624

**A HISTORY OF DRUG ABUSE IN AMERICA   626**

Drug Use and Social Awareness   627

Antidrug Legislation   628

**CJ CAREERS   Drug Enforcement Administration   631**

The Investigation of Drug Abuse and Manufacturing   632

**FREEDOM OR SAFETY? YOU DECIDE.   Drug-Related Criminal Activity and Public Housing   633**

**CJ TODAY EXHIBIT 16–1   Drugs: What's in a Name?   634**

**THE MOST COMMON DRUGS—AND WHO IS USING THEM   634**

Drug Trafficking   636

Marijuana   637

Cocaine   639

Heroin   640

**CJ NEWS   Club Drugs Sending More Young People to Hospitals   641**

Club Drugs   641

**COSTS OF ABUSE   644**

The Indirect Costs of Abuse   644

Drug-Related Crime   644

# CONTENTS

**SOLVING THE DRUG PROBLEM   647**

   Strict Enforcement   647

   Asset Forfeiture   648

   Interdiction   649

   Crop Control   650

   Prevention and Treatment   650

   Legalization and Decriminalization   652

**SUMMARY   654**

**DISCUSSION QUESTIONS   655**

**WEB QUEST   655**

**NOTES   655**


**Chapter 17   Terrorism and Multinational Criminal Justice   660**

**INTRODUCTION   662**

   Ethnocentrism and the Study of Criminal Justice   662

   Problems with Data   663

**ISLAMIC CRIMINAL JUSTICE   664**

   The *Hudud* Crimes   665

   The *Tazir* Crimes   666

   Islamic Courts   667

**INTERNATIONAL CRIMINAL JUSTICE ORGANIZATIONS   667**

   The Role of the United Nations in Criminal Justice   668

**CJ TODAY EXHIBIT 17–1   Vienna Declaration on Crime and Justice   670**

   INTERPOL and Europol   671

   The International Criminal Court   672

**TRANSNATIONAL CRIME   673**

   Globalization and Crime   673

**TERRORISM   674**

**CJ TODAY EXHIBIT 17–2   What Is Terrorist Activity?   675**

   Types of Terrorism   675

**CJ NEWS   Domestic Terrorism: New Trouble at Home   677**

**FREEDOM OR SAFETY? YOU DECIDE.   Should Violent Speech Be Free Speech?   681**

**CJ NEWS   Intelligence Chiefs: Terrorists Intent on U.S. Attack   682**

   Causes of Terrorism   683

   Combating Terrorism   684

   Antiterrorism Committees and Reports   685

**CJ TODAY EXHIBIT 17–3   The USA PATRIOT Act of 2001   686**

# CONTENTS

**CJ TODAY EXHIBIT 17–4**   The Report of the National Commission on Terrorist Attacks upon the United States   687

    Foreign Terrorist Organizations   691

    The Future of International Terrorism   693

**SUMMARY**   696

**DISCUSSION QUESTIONS**   697

**WEB QUEST**   697

**NOTES**   697

Chapter 18   **The Future of Criminal Justice**   702

**INTRODUCTION**   704

**TECHNOLOGY AND CRIME**   704

    Biocrime   705

    Cybercrime   706

**CJ NEWS**   Terrorists' Use of the Internet Spreads   711

    Terrorism and Technology   712

**TECHNOLOGY AND CRIME CONTROL**   713

    Leading Technical Organizations in Criminal Justice   714

**CRIMINALISTICS: PAST, PRESENT, AND FUTURE**   715

**CJ CAREERS**   Criminalist   718

    New Technologies in Criminalistics   720

**CJ NEWS**   Study: Untested DNA Allows Crime   724

    On the Horizon   727

    Problems in Implementing New Technologies   729

**FREEDOM OR SAFETY? YOU DECIDE.**   Religion and Public Safety   731

    Secure Identity Management   732

**FREEDOM OR SAFETY? YOU DECIDE.**   A National ID: An Idea Whose Time Has Come?   733

**TECHNOLOGY AND INDIVIDUAL RIGHTS**   734

**SUMMARY**   735

**DISCUSSION QUESTIONS**   736

**WEB QUEST**   736

**NOTES**   736

**THE BILL OF RIGHTS**   B-1

**LIST OF ACRONYMS**   A-1

**GLOSSARY**   G-1

**CASE INDEX**   I-1

**NAME INDEX**   I-4

**SUBJECT INDEX**   I-14

# PREFACE

The attacks of September 11, 2001, changed our nation's course and tested the moral fiber of Americans everywhere. Nowhere outside the armed forces has the terrorist threat been felt more keenly than in the criminal justice area. The 2001 attacks led many to look to our system of justice, and to the people who serve it, for protection and reassurance—protection from threats both internal and external and reassurance that a justice system rooted in the ideals of democracy will continue to offer fairness and equality to all who come before the law.

In the years since September 11, strict new laws have been enacted, security efforts have been greatly enhanced, and practitioners of American criminal justice (especially those in law enforcement agencies) have recognized their important role as the first line of defense against threats to the American way of life. As a consequence, the study of criminal justice is more relevant today than ever before.

For many, personal involvement in the criminal justice field has become a way of serving our nation and helping to protect our communities. I understand that motivation and applaud it—partially because of the heroism and personal sacrifice it involves, but also because it adds to the important "moral sense" of what we, as Americans, are all about. The justice profession's service role has expanded to include college and university students who, in ever greater numbers, are declaring majors in criminal justice. Participation in the criminal justice system, and in the study of criminal justice, offers students a way of personally and meaningfully contributing to our society. It allows those who meet the challenging criteria for successful studies and employment to give something back to the nation and to the communities that nurtured them, and it reaffirms the American way of life by reinforcing the social values on which it is based.

Many students are also attracted to criminal justice because it provides a focus for the tension that exists within our society between individual rights and freedoms, on the one hand, and the need for public safety, security, and order, on the other. That tension—between individual rights and public order—is the theme around which all editions of this textbook have been built. That same theme is all the more relevant today, because the important question that we have all been asking ourselves in recent years is "How much personal freedom are we willing to sacrifice to achieve a solid sense of security?"

While there are no easy answers to this question, this textbook guides criminal justice students in the struggle to find a satisfying balance between freedom and security. True to its origins, the ninth edition focuses directly on the crime picture in America and on the three traditional elements of the criminal justice system: police, courts, and corrections. This edition has been enhanced by additional Freedom or Safety boxes, which time and again question the viability of our freedoms in a world grown increasingly more dangerous. This edition also asks students to evaluate the strengths and weaknesses of the American justice system as it struggles to adapt to an increasingly multicultural society and to a society in which the rights of a few can threaten the safety of many.

It is my hope that this book will ground students in the important issues that continue to evolve from the tension between the struggle for justice and the need for safety. For it is on that bedrock that the American system of criminal justice stands, and it is on that foundation that the future of the justice system—and of this country—will be built.

**Frank Schmalleger, Ph.D.**
Professor Emeritus,
The University of North Carolina at Pembroke

## Exploring Criminal Justice Today

Anyone using this book is encouraged to visit the award-winning *Criminal Justice Today* site on the World Wide Web. This book's Companion Website provides a broad range of materials of relevance to the study of criminal justice and has links to a vast number of other criminal justice–related sites. Through the many "Web Extras" and "Library Extras" that are built into this text, and via the "Web Quests" found at the end of every chapter, the Companion Website provides substantially enhanced learning opportunities.

**Audio Extras** let you hear the author introduce each chapter and provide a summary of important topics. Audio chapter introductions require Real Player™ or Windows Media Player™ software.

Keep up with the latest news and pressing justice-related issues in the **CJToday Blogspace**, with links to active blogs in criminal law, policing, the courts, sentencing, and corrections.

**Library Extras** provide access to selected documents from the Bureau of Justice Statistics, the National Institute of Justice, the Bureau of Justice Assistance, the Federal Bureau of Investigation, and other important criminal justice agencies.

**Web Extras** provide virtual criminal justice tours of the Internet, with visits to significant police, courts, and corrections sites on the Web.

Found on the CD at the back of this book, **CJ Extras** supplement the text and provide historical information on important crime and justice issues.

Join our **E-mail Discussion List** at http://groups.yahoo.com/group/CJToday, and stay abreast of what other students using this textbook are talking about.

The feature-rich **Research Navigator** Website, which is available only if your instructor has chosen this option, provides enhanced access to academic journals and popular writings in the criminal justice area.

# ACKNOWLEDGMENTS

My thanks to all who assisted in so many different ways in the development of this textbook. The sacrifice of time made by my wife, Harmonie, as I worked endlessly in my office is very much appreciated. Thanks also to Cheryl Asherman, Barbara Cappuccio, Mary Carnis, Sarah Holle, John Jordan, Kelly Krug, Craig Marcus, Jerry Marshall, Amy Peltier, Cathleen Petersen, Lisa Rinaldi, Joe Saba, Ilene Sanford, and all the past and present Prentice Hall staff with whom I have worked. They are true professionals and have made the task of manuscript development enjoyable.

A very special thank-you goes to Robin Baliszewski, David Gesell, and Vern Anthony for their stewardship and support, and to my editor and friend Frank Mortimer (aka "Krazy Elvis") and marketing manager Adam Kloza for their invaluable insights, perseverance, and dedication to this project.

I am grateful to my supplements authors for their support of this new edition: Steve Chermak for the Student Study Guide; Sandy Boyd, Instructor's Resource Guide; Carolyn Dennis, Companion Website; Kay Henriksen, TestGen and Test Item File; and Carolyn D'Argenio, PowerPoints. Thanks also to production coordinator Janet Bolton and personal assistant Laura Joyce for their very capable handling of numerous details. The keen eye of copy editor Lorretta Palagi is beyond compare, and this book is much richer for her efforts. I am grateful, as well, to the manuscript reviewers involved in this and previous editions for holding me to the fire when I might have opted for a less rigorous coverage of some topics—especially Darl Champion of Methodist College, Jim Smith at West Valley College, Cassandra L. Renzi of Keiser College, and Bryan J. Vila at the National Institute of Justice, for their insightful suggestions as this book got under way.

Manuscript reviewers who have contributed to the development of *Criminal Justice Today* include

Howard Abadinsky
St. Johns University
Jamaica, NY

Reed Adams
Elizabeth City State University
Elizabeth City, NC

Kevin Barrett
Palomar College
San Marcos, CA

Larry Bassi
State University of New York (SUNY)–
Brockport
Brockport, NY

Richard Becker
North Harris College
Houston, TX

Michael Blankenship
Boise State University
Boise, ID

W. Garret Capune
California State University–Fullerton
Fullerton, CA

Mike Carlie
Southwest Missouri State University
Springfield, MO

Geary Chlebus
James Sprunt Community College
Kenansville, NC

Jon E. Clark
Temple University
Philadelphia, PA

Lora C. Clark, J.D.
Pitt Community College
Greenville, NC

Warren Clark
California State University–Bakersfield
Bakersfield, CA

Ellen G. Cohn
Florida International University
Miami, FL

Gary Colboth
California State University–Long Beach
Long Beach, CA

Jannette O. Domingo
John Jay College of Criminal Justice
New York, NY

Vicky Doworth
Montgomery College
Rockville, MD

Steven Egger
University of Houston–Clearlake
Houston, TX

Ron Fagan
Pepperdine University
Malibu, CA

Michael Gray
Wor-Wic Community College
Salisbury, MD

Alex Greenberg
Niagara County Community College
Sanborn, NY

Julia Hall
Drexel University
Philadelphia, PA

Ed Heischmidt
Rend Lake College
Ina, IL

Dennis Hoffman
University of Nebraska at Omaha
Omaha, NE

Michael Hooper
California Department of Justice
Sacramento, CA

William D. Hyatt
Western Carolina University
Cullowhee, NC

Nicholas H. Irons
County College of Morris
Randolph, NJ

Galan M. Janeksela
University of Tennessee at Chattanooga
Chattanooga, TN

Terry L. Johnson
Owens Community College
Toledo, OH

David M. Jones
University of Wisconsin–Oshkosh
Oshkosh, WI

Victor Kappeler
Eastern Kentucky State University
Richmond, KY

P. Ray Kedia
Grambling State University
Grambling, LA

Debra Kelly
Longwood University
Farmville, VA

Lloyd Klein
Louisiana State University–Shreveport
Shreveport, LA

Sylvia Kuennen
Briar Cliff College
Sioux City, IA

Karel Kurst-Swanger
Oswego State University of New York
Oswego, NY

Hamid R. Kusha
Texas A&M International University
Laredo, TX

Joan Luxenburg
University of Central Oklahoma
Edmond, OK

Michael Lyman
Columbia College
Columbia, MO

Richard H. Martin
Elgin Community College
Elgin, IL

David C. May
Eastern Kentucky University
Richmond, KY

# ACKNOWLEDGMENTS

G. Larry Mays
New Mexico State University
Las Cruces, NM

Thomas P. McAninch
Scott Community College
Bettendorf, IA

Susan S. McGuire
San Jacinto College North
Houston, TX

Robert J. Meadows
California Lutheran University
Thousand Oaks, CA

Jim Mezhir
Niagara County Community College
Sanborn, NY

Rick Michelson
Grossmont College
El Cajon, CA

Harvey Morley
California State University–Long Beach
Long Beach, CA

Roslyn Muraskin
C. W. Post Campus of Long Island University
Brookville, NY

Charles Myles
California State University–Los Angeles
Los Angeles, CA

Bonnie Neher
Harrisburg Area Community College
Harrisburg, PA

David Neubauer
University of New Orleans–Lakefront
New Orleans, LA

P. J. Ortmier
Grossmont College
El Cajon, CA

David F. Owens
Onondaga Community College
Syracuse, NY

Michael J. Palmiotto
Wichita State University
Wichita, KS

Lance Parr
Grossmont College
El Cajon, CA

William H. Parsonage
Penn State University
University Park, PA

Ken Peak
University of Nevada–Reno
Reno, NV

Joseph M. Pellicciotti
Indiana University Northwest
Gary, IN

Roger L. Pennel
Central Missouri State University
Warrensburg, MO

Joseph L. Peterson
University of Illinois at Chicago
Chicago, IL

Morgan Peterson
Palomar College
San Marcos, CA

Gary Prawel
Keuka College
Keuka Park, NY

Philip J. Reichel
University of Northern Colorado
Greely, CO

Albert Roberts
Rutgers University
New Brunswick, NJ

Carl E. Russell
Scottsdale Community College
Scottsdale, AZ

Benson Schaffer
IVAMS Arbitration and Mediation Services
Pomona, CA

# ACKNOWLEDGMENTS

Stephen J. Schoenthaler
California State University–Stanislaus
Turlock, CA

Jeff Schrink
Indiana State University
Terre Haute, IN

Judith M. Sgarzi
Mount Ida College
Newton, MA

Ira Silverman
University of South Florida
Tampa, FL

Loretta J. Stalans
Loyola University–Chicago
Chicago, IL

Z. G. Standing Bear
University of Colorado
Colorado Springs, CO

Mark A. Stetler
Montgomery College
Conroe, TX

B. Grant Stitt
University of Nevada–Reno
Reno, NV

Robert W. Taylor
University of North Texas
Denton, TX

Lawrence F. Travis III
University of Cincinnati
Cincinnati, OH

Ron Vogel
California State University–Long Beach
Long Beach, CA

John Vollmann, Jr.
Florida Metropolitan University
Ft. Lauderdale, FL

David Whelan
Western Carolina University
Cullowhee, NC

Lois Wims
Salve Regina University
Newport, RI

L. Thomas Winfree, Jr.
New Mexico State University
Las Cruces, NM

John M. Wyant
Illinois Central College
East Peoria, IL

My thanks to everyone! I would also like to extend a special thanks to the following individuals for their invaluable comments and suggestions along the way: Gordon Armstrong, Avon Burns, Kathy Cameron-Hahn, Gene Evans, Joe Graziano, Donald J. Melisi, Phil Purpura, John Robich, Barry Schreiber, Ted Skotnicki, Bill Tafoya, Tom Thackery, Joe Trevalino, Howard Tritt, Bill Tyrrell, Tim Veiders, and Bob Winslow.

Thanks are also due everyone who assisted in artistic arrangements, including Sergeant Michael Flores of the New York City Police Department's Photo Unit, Michael L. Hammond of the Everett (Washington) Police Department, Mikael Karlsson of Arresting Images, Assistant Chief James M. Lewis of the Bakersfield (California) Police Department, Tonya Matz of the University of Illinois at Chicago, and Monique Smith of the National Institute of Justice—all of whom were especially helpful in providing a wealth of photo resources. I am especially indebted to University of Illinois Professor Joseph L. Peterson for assistance with sections on scientific evidence and to George W. Knox of the National Gang Crime Research Center for providing valuable information on gangs and gang activity.

I'd also like to acknowledge Chief J. Harper Wilson and Nancy Carnes of the FBI's Uniform Crime Reporting Program; Mark Reading of the Drug Enforcement Administration's Office of Intelligence; Kristina Rose at the National Institute of Justice; Marilyn Marbrook and Michael Rand at the Office of Justice Programs; Wilma M. Grant of the U.S. Supreme Court's Project Hermes; Ken Kerle at the American Jail Association; Lisa Bastian, survey statistician with the National Crime Victimization Survey Program; Steve Shackelton with the U.S. Parks Service; Ronald T. Allen, Steve Chaney, Bernie Homme, and Kenneth L. Whitman, all with the California Peace Officer Standards and Training Commission; Dianne Martin at the Drug En-

# ACKNOWLEDGMENTS

forcement Administration; and George J. Davino of the New York City Police Department for their help in making this book both timely and accurate.

Last, but by no means least, Taylor Davis, H. R. Delaney, Jannette O. Domingo, Al Garcia, Rodney Hennigsen, Norman G. Kittel, Robert O. Lampert, and Joseph M. Pellicciotti should know that their writings, contributions, and valuable suggestions at the earliest stages of manuscript development continue to be very much appreciated. Thank you, everyone!

**Frank Schmalleger, Ph.D.**

Frank Schmalleger, Ph.D., is Professor Emeritus at the University of North Carolina at Pembroke. He holds degrees from the University of Notre Dame and Ohio State University, having earned both a master's (1970) and a doctorate in sociology (1974) from Ohio State University with a special emphasis in criminology. From 1976 to 1994, he taught criminology and criminal justice courses at the University of North Carolina at Pembroke. For the last 16 of those years, he chaired the university's Department of Sociology, Social Work, and Criminal Justice. The university named him Distinguished Professor in 1991.

Schmalleger is also the Director of the Justice Research Association, a private consulting firm and think tank focusing on issues of crime and justice. The Justice Research Association (JRA) serves the needs of the nation's civil and criminal justice planners and administrators through workshops, conferences, and grant-writing and program-evaluation support. JRA also sponsors the Criminal Justice Distance Learning Consortium, which resides on the Web at http://www.cjdlc.org.

Schmalleger has taught in the online graduate program of the New School for Social Research, helping to build the world's first electronic classrooms in support of distance learning through computer telecommunications. As an adjunct professor with Webster University in St. Louis, Missouri, Schmalleger helped develop the university's graduate program in security administration and loss prevention. He taught courses in that curriculum for more than a decade. An avid Web surfer, Schmalleger is also the creator of a number of award-winning World Wide Web sites, including one that supports this textbook (http://www.cjtoday.com).

Frank Schmalleger is the author of numerous articles and more than 30 books, including the widely used *Criminal Justice: A Brief Introduction* (Prentice Hall, 2006), *Criminology Today* (Prentice Hall, 2006), and *Criminal Law Today* (Prentice Hall, 2006).

Schmalleger is also founding editor of the journal *Criminal Justice Studies.* He has served as editor for the Prentice Hall series *Criminal Justice in the Twenty-First Century* and as imprint adviser for Greenwood Publishing Group's criminal justice reference series.

Schmalleger's philosophy of both teaching and writing can be summed up in these words: "In order to communicate knowledge we must first catch, then hold, a person's interest—be it student, colleague, or policymaker. Our writing, our speaking, and our teaching must be relevant to the problems facing people today, and they must in some way help solve those problems." Visit the author's website at http://www.schmalleger.com.

Justice is truth in action!

—Benjamin Disraeli (1804–1881)

Injustice anywhere is a threat
to justice everywhere.

—Martin Luther King, Jr. (1929–1968)

# PART 1

# Crime in America

## GOALS OF THE CRIMINAL JUSTICE SYSTEM

Common law, constitutional, statutory, and humanitarian rights of the accused:

- Justice for the individual
- Personal liberty
- Dignity as a human being
- The right to due process

These individual rights must be effectively balanced against these community concerns:

- Social justice
- Equality before the law
- The protection of society
- Freedom from fear

How does our system of justice work toward balance?

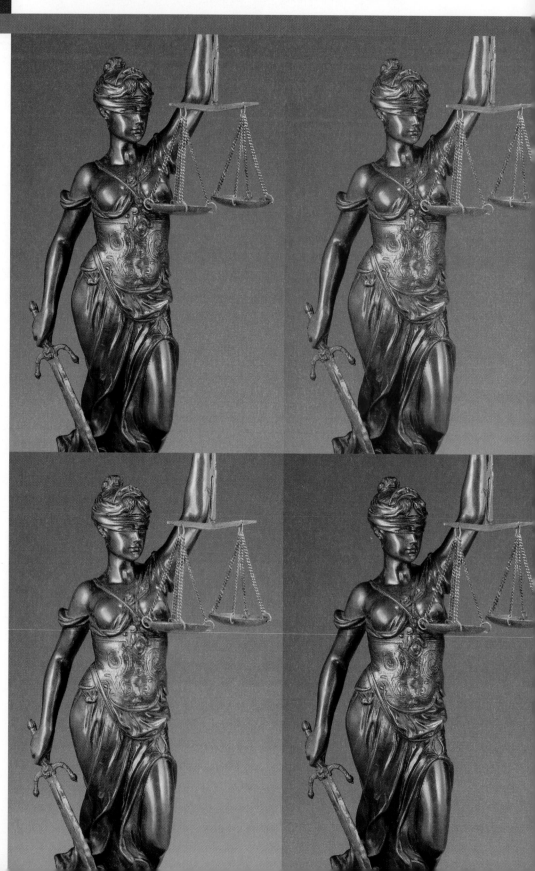

## The Will of the People Is the Best Law

The great American statesman and orator Daniel Webster (1782–1852) once wrote, "Justice is the great interest of man on earth. It is the ligament which holds civilized beings and civilized nations together." Although Webster lived in a relatively simple time with few problems and many shared rules, justice has never been easily won. Unlike Webster's era, society today is highly complex and populated by groups with a wide diversity of interests. It is within this challenging context that the daily practice of American criminal justice occurs.

The criminal justice system has three central components: police, courts, and corrections. The history, the activities, and the legal environment surrounding the police are discussed in Part 2 of this book. Part 3 describes the courts, and Part 4 deals with prisons, probation, and parole. Part 5 provides a guide to the future of the justice system and describes how the threat of terrorism has impacted enforcement agencies. We begin here in Part 1, however, with an overview of that grand ideal that we call *justice,* and we consider how the justice ideal relates to the everyday practice of criminal justice in the United States today. To that end, in the four chapters that make up this section, we will examine how and why laws are made. We will look at the wide array of interests that impinge upon the justice system, and we will examine closely the dichotomy that distinguishes citizens who are primarily concerned with individual rights from those who emphasize the need for individual responsibility and social accountability. In the pages that follow, we will see how justice can mean protection from the power of the state to some people, and vengeance to others. In this section, we will also lay the groundwork for the rest of the text by painting a picture of crime in America today, suggesting possible causes for it, and showing how policies for dealing with crime have evolved.

As you read about the complex tapestry that is the practice of criminal justice in America today, you will learn of a system in flux, perhaps less sure of its purpose than at any time in its history. You may also catch the sense, however, that very soon a new and reborn institution of justice may emerge from the ferment that now exists. Whatever the final outcome, it can only be hoped that *justice,* as proffered by the American system of criminal justice, will be sufficient to hold our civilization together—and to allow it to prosper well into the twenty-first century and beyond.

**1**
**What Is Criminal Justice?**

**2**
**The Crime Picture**

**3**
**The Search for Causes**

**4**
**Criminal Law**

# CHAPTER 1

# What Is Criminal Justice?

## OUTLINE

- Introduction
- A Brief History of Crime in America
- The Theme of This Book
- Social Justice
- American Criminal Justice: System and Functions
- American Criminal Justice: The Process
- Due Process and Individual Rights
- The Role of Research in Criminal Justice
- Multiculturalism and Diversity in Criminal Justice

## LEARNING OBJECTIVES

After reading this chapter, you should be able to:

- Identify the theme on which this textbook builds.
- Highlight the differences between the individual-rights and public-order perspectives.
- Explain society's need for a system of order maintenance, and detail the role of law within that system.
- Describe the personal sacrifices necessitated by public order.
- Expound upon the relationship of criminal justice to social justice and other wider notions of equity and fairness.
- Explain the structure of the criminal justice system in terms of its major components.
- Describe the differences between the consensus and conflict models of the criminal justice system.
- Describe the process of American criminal justice, including the stages of criminal case processing.
- Explain the meaning of due process of law, and identify where due process guarantees can be found in the American legal system.
- Explain how multiculturalism and diversity present special challenges to, and opportunities for, the American system of criminal justice.

*The rights guaranteed to criminal suspects, defendants, offenders, and prisoners were not included in the Bill of Rights for the benefit of criminals. They are fundamental political rights that protect all Americans from governmental abuse of power. These rights are found in the Fourth, Fifth, Sixth, Eighth, and Fourteenth Amendments. They include the guarantee against unreasonable search and seizure, the right to reasonable bail, the right to due process of law, and the right to be free from cruel and unusual treatment. This "bundle of rights" is indispensable to a free society.*

—American Civil Liberties Union[1]

*The Constitution is not a suicide pact.*

—Former Secretary of State Warren Christopher,
after terrorists destroyed the World Trade Center
in New York City in 2001[2]

## KEY CONCEPTS

### TERMS

administration of justice
arraignment
bail
booking
civil justice
concurrent sentence
conflict model
consensus model
crime
crime-control model

criminal justice
criminal justice system
criminology
due process
due process model
grand jury
indictment
individual rights
individual-rights advocate
information
justice

multiculturalism
preliminary hearing
probable cause
public-order advocate
social control
social justice
trial
USA PATRIOT Act of 2001
warrant

# Introduction

Hear the author discuss
this chapter at
**cjtoday.com**

On June 13, 2005, hundreds of onlookers waiting outside the Santa Maria, California, courtroom witnessed the American justice system in action as they listened to loudspeakers blaring a series of not guilty verdicts on each of ten criminal charges that had been brought against pop music superstar Michael Jackson. As the verdicts were read, people across the country paused to hear the trial's outcome. Hundreds gathered in New York's Times Square, where a giant screen heralded Jackson's acquittal, and a pilot broke in on a New York-to-California flight shortly before landing to relay news of the verdicts to passengers.[3] Following a trial that lasted 14 weeks, a jury of four men and eight women had acquitted the performer of charges that he sexually molested a 13-year-old cancer survivor who visited his Neverland Ranch in 2003.[4] Prosecutors had also alleged that Jackson conspired to imprison the boy and his family at his sprawling estate.

Trial testimony included appearances by former child star Macaulay Culkin and comedian Jay Leno—who spoke of Jackson's good character. Other witnesses, however, alleged that Jackson had had improper relationships with young boys for years. Had he been convicted, Jackson could have been sentenced to serve more than 20 years in prison. Transcripts of the Jackson trial can be viewed at Library Extra 1–1 at cjtoday.com, and a fan-sponsored website detailing events in the trial is accessible at Web Extra 1–1 at cjtoday.com.

Michael Jackson critic Bobby Bible confronts a fan from Switzerland in front of the Santa Barbara County (California) Courthouse as not-guilty verdicts are announced in the superstar's 2005 child molestation trial. The American justice system, while it determines guilt or innocence in individual cases, also reflects society's wider concerns with morality, fairness, and equity.
*AP Wide World Photos*

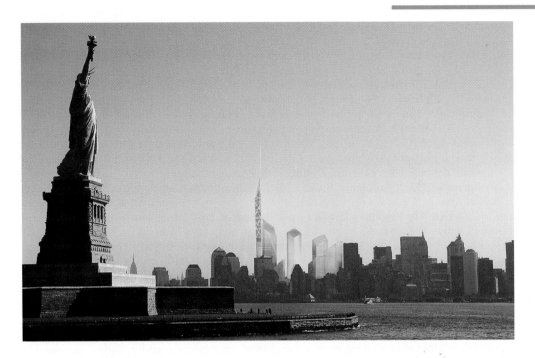

An artist's rendition of the New York City skyline as it will look once buildings envisioned by renowned architect Daniel Libeskind are constructed on the 16-acre World Trade Center site. The plan includes one soaring "Freedom Tower" that stands 1,776 feet tall, several other towers, and a memorial to the nearly 3,000 people who were killed in the terrorist attacks that demolished the city's World Trade Center twin towers in 2001.

*AP Wide World Photos*

A very different kind of criminal event thrust itself on American society and our justice system with the September 11, 2001, terrorist attacks that targeted New York City's World Trade Center and the Pentagon. Those attacks, including one on an airliner that crashed in the Pennsylvania countryside, left nearly 3,000 people dead and caused billions of dollars in property damage. They have since been classified as the most destructive criminal activity ever to have been perpetrated on U.S. soil. The resulting "war on terrorism" changed the face of world politics and ushered in a new era in American society. Before the attacks, most Americans lived relatively secure lives largely unfettered by fear of random personal attack. Following September 11, however, a heated debate has taken place between those wanting to enforce powerful crime-prevention and security measures and others seeking to preserve the individual rights and freedoms that have long been characteristic of American life. This issue, which has continued to feed TV talk shows and newspaper editorials nationwide, asks Americans to determine which rights, freedoms, and conveniences (if any) they are willing to sacrifice to increase personal and public safety. It also anticipates the theme on which this book is based—and which is discussed at length later in this chapter.

Regardless of your personal position in the ongoing debate between freedom and safety, it is important to recognize that terrorism is a potentially horrendous **crime.** Many states and the federal government have statutes outlawing terrorism, although terrorism itself can involve many other kinds of crimes. In the case of the World Trade Center and Pentagon attacks, for example, the crimes committed included murder, kidnapping, hijacking, grand theft, felonious assault, battery, conspiracy, and arson.

> You're looking now not only at a rescue operation, but a gigantic crime scene.
>
> —Newscaster, ABC Nightly News, commenting on the World Trade Center site a few days after the September 11, 2001, attacks[i]

**crime**

Conduct in violation of the criminal laws of a state, the federal government, or a local jurisdiction, for which there is no legally acceptable justification or excuse.

# A Brief History of Crime in America

What we call *criminal activity* has undoubtedly been with us since the dawn of history, and crime control has long been a primary concern of politicians and government leaders worldwide. Still, the American experience with crime during the last half century has been especially influential in shaping the criminal justice system of today. In this country, crime waves have come and gone, including an 1850–1880 crime epidemic, which was apparently related to social upheaval caused by large-scale immigration.[5] A spurt of widespread organized criminal activity was associated with the Prohibition years of the early twentieth century. Following World War II, however, American crime rates remained relatively stable until the 1960s.

The 1960s and 1970s saw a burgeoning concern for the rights of ethnic and racial minorities, women, people with physical and mental challenges, and many other groups. The civil rights movement of the period emphasized equality of opportunity and respect for individuals, regardless of

> Crime does more than expose the weakness in social relationships; it undermines the social order itself, by destroying the assumptions on which it is based.
>
> —James Q. Wilson, UCLA[ii]

race, color, creed, gender, or personal attributes. As new laws were passed and suits filed, court involvement in the movement grew. Soon a plethora of hard-won individual rights and prerogatives, based on the U.S. Constitution, the Bill of Rights, and new federal and state legislation, were recognized and guaranteed. By the 1980s, the civil rights movement had profoundly affected all areas of social life—from education through employment to the activities of the criminal justice system.

This emphasis on **individual rights** was accompanied by a dramatic increase in reported criminal activity. While some researchers doubted the accuracy of official accounts, reports by the FBI of "traditional" crimes such as murder, rape, and assault increased considerably during the 1970s and into the 1980s. Many theories were advanced to explain this leap in observed criminality. Some analysts of American culture, for example, suggested that the combination of newfound freedoms and long-pent-up hostilities of the socially and economically deprived worked to produce social disorganization, which in turn increased criminality.

By the mid-1980s the dramatic increase in the sale and use of illicit drugs threatened the foundation of American society. Cocaine, and later laboratory-processed "crack," spread to every corner of America. The country's borders were inundated with smugglers intent on reaping quick fortunes. Large cities became havens for drug gangs, and many inner-city areas were all but abandoned to highly armed and well-financed drug racketeers. Cities experienced dramatic declines in property values, and residents wrestled with an eroding quality of life.

By the close of the 1980s, neighborhoods and towns were fighting for their communal lives. Huge rents had been torn in the national social fabric, and the American way of life, long taken for granted, was under the gun. Traditional values appeared in danger of going up in smoke along with the "crack" being consumed openly in some parks and resorts. Looking for a way to stem the tide of increased criminality, many took up the call for "law and order." In response, President Ronald Reagan created a "drug czar" cabinet-level position to coordinate the "war on drugs." Careful thought was given at the highest levels to using the military to patrol the sea-lanes and air corridors through which many of the illegal drugs entered the country. President George H. W. Bush, who followed Reagan into office, quickly embraced and expanded the government's antidrug efforts.

In 1992, the videotaped beating of Rodney King, an African-American motorist, at the hands of Los Angeles–area police officers splashed across TV screens throughout the country and shifted the public's focus onto issues of police brutality and the effective management of law enforcement personnel. As the King incident seemed to show, when racial minorities come face to face with agents of the American criminal justice system, something less than justice may be the result. Although initially acquitted by a California jury—which contained no black members—two of the officers who beat King were convicted in a 1993 federal courtroom of violating his civil rights.[6] The King incident and associated trials are described in more detail in Chapter 7.

Then, the very next year, law enforcement agencies were again criticized when agents of the Bureau of Alcohol, Tobacco, and Firearms (ATF) and the Federal Bureau of Investigation (FBI) faced off with David Koresh and members of his Branch Davidian cult in Waco, Texas. The con-

---

**individual rights**

The rights guaranteed to all members of American society by the U.S. Constitution (especially those found in the first ten amendments to the Constitution, known as the *Bill of Rights*). These rights are particularly important to criminal defendants facing formal processing by the criminal justice system.

---

**The current crisis in criminal and juvenile justice is fueled by the public's conviction that the system no longer represents an effective response to the problem of crime.**

—Reinventing Probation Council

---

A street-corner drug deal. By the mid-1980s, the American criminal justice system had become embroiled in a war against illicit drugs, filling the nation's prisons and jails with drug dealers, traffickers, and users.

*Brand X Pictures, Robertstock.com*

flict began when ATF agents assaulted Koresh's fortress-like compound, leaving four agents and six cult members dead. It ended 51 days later with the fiery deaths of Koresh and 71 of his followers, many of whom were children. The event led to a congressional investigation and charges that the ATF and the FBI had been ill prepared to deal successfully with large-scale domestic resistance and had reacted more out of alarm and frustration than wisdom. Attorney General Janet Reno refused to blame agents for misjudging Koresh's intentions, although 11 Davidians were later acquitted of charges that they had murdered the federal agents.

Soon afterward, a few spectacular crimes that received widespread coverage in the news media fostered a sense among the American public that crime in the United States was out of hand and that strict new measures were needed to combat it. One such crime was the 1996 bombing of the Alfred P. Murrah Federal Building in Oklahoma City by antigovernment extremists. Another was the 1999 Columbine High School massacre in Colorado that left 12 students and one teacher dead.[7]

The public's perception that crime rates were growing, coupled with a belief that offenders frequently went unpunished or received only a judicial slap on the wrist, led to a burgeoning emphasis on responsibility and punishment. By the late 1990s, a strong shift away from the claimed misdeeds of the criminal justice system was well underway, and a newfound emphasis on individual accountability began to blossom among an American public fed up with crime and fearful of their own victimization. Growing calls for enhanced responsibility quickly began to replace the previous emphasis on individual rights. As a juggernaut of conservative opinion made itself felt on the political scene, Senator Phil Gramm of Texas observed that the public wants to "grab violent criminals by the throat, put them in prison [and] stop building prisons like Holiday Inns."[8]

Then, in an event that changed the course of our society, public tragedy became forever joined with private victimization in our collective consciousness after a series of highly destructive and well-coordinated terrorist attacks on New York City and Washington, D.C., on September 11, 2001. Those attacks resulted in the collapse and total destruction of the twin 110-story towers of the World Trade Center and a devastating explosion at the Pentagon. Thousands of people perished, and many were injured. Although law enforcement and security agencies were unable to prevent the September 11 attacks, many have since moved from a reactive to a proactive posture in the fight against terrorism—a change that is discussed in more detail in Chapter 6.

An especially important new tool in the law enforcement arsenal is the federal **USA PATRIOT Act of 2001**,[9] enacted as a legislative response to terrorism. The law is officially known as the Uniting and Strengthening America by Providing Appropriate Tools Required to Intercept and Obstruct Terrorism Act of 2001 (from which the acronym *USA PATRIOT* is derived). The law dramatically increases the investigatory authority of federal, state, and local police agencies, although sometimes only temporarily. The expanded police powers created under the legislation are not limited to investigations of terrorist activity but apply to many different criminal offenses. Terrorism is discussed in more detail in Chapter 17. As that chapter points out, terrorism is a criminal act, and preventing terrorism and investigating terrorist incidents after they occur are highly important roles for local, state, and federal law enforcement agencies.

A different kind of offending, corporate and white-collar crime, took center stage in 2002 and 2003 as President George W. Bush called on Congress to stiffen penalties for unscrupulous business executives who knowingly falsify their company's financial reports.[10] The president's request came amidst declining stock market values, shaken investor confidence, and threats to the viability of employee pension plans in the wake of a corporate crime wave involving criminal activities that had been planned and undertaken by executives at a number of leading corporations. In an effort to restore order to American financial markets, President Bush signed the Sarbanes-Oxley Act on July 30, 2002.[11] The law, which has been called "the single most important piece of legislation affecting corporate governance, financial disclosure and the practice of public accounting since the US securities laws of the early 1930s,"[12] is intended to deter corporate fraud and to hold business executives accountable for their actions. White-collar crime continues to be a focus of federal prosecutors, and in 2004 homemaking queen Martha Stewart was convicted of conspiracy, obstruction of justice, and making false statements to investigators in an insider stock trading scandal and was sentenced to five months in prison and fined $30,000. White-collar crime is discussed in more detail in Chapter 2.

For a detailed look at crimes that have shaped the past hundred years, see Web Extra 1–2 at cjtoday.com. Library Extra 1–2 at cjtoday.com also describes the changing nature of crime in America.

> If you break the law, we're going to hold you accountable, and there will be tough consequences for your actions.
>
> —North Carolina Governor Jim Hunt[iii]

> People expect both safety and justice and do not want to sacrifice one for the other.
>
> —Christopher Stone, President and Director, Vera Institute of Justice

**USA PATRIOT Act of 2001**

A federal law (Public Law 107-56) enacted in response to terrorist attacks on the World Trade Center and the Pentagon on September 11, 2001. The law, officially titled the Uniting and Strengthening America by Providing Appropriate Tools Required to Intercept and Obstruct Terrorism Act, substantially broadened the investigative authority of law enforcement agencies throughout America and is applicable to many crimes other than terrorism.

A Brief History of Crime in America

**CJ BLOG**

See the rights versus safety Web logs available in the cjtoday.com blogspace.

# The Theme of This Book

This book examines the American system of criminal justice and the agencies and processes that constitute it. It builds on a theme that is especially valuable for studying criminal justice today: *individual rights versus public order*. This theme draws on historical developments that have shaped our legal system and our understandings of crime and justice. It is one of the primary determinants of the nature of contemporary criminal justice—including criminal law, police practice, sentencing, and corrections.

A strong emphasis on individual rights rose to the forefront of American social thought during the 1960s and 1970s, a period known as the *civil rights era.* The civil rights era led to the recognition of fundamental personal rights that had previously been denied illegally to many people on the basis of race, ethnicity, gender, sexual preference, or disability. The civil rights movement soon expanded to include the rights of many other groups, including criminal suspects, parolees and probationers, trial participants, prison and jail inmates, and victims. As the emphasis on civil rights grew, new laws and court decisions broadened the rights available to many.

The treatment of criminal suspects was afforded special attention by those who argued that the purpose of any civilized society should be to secure rights and freedoms for each of its citizens—including those suspected and convicted of crimes. Rights advocates feared unnecessarily restrictive government action and viewed it as an assault on basic human dignity and individual liberty. They believed that at times it was necessary to sacrifice some degree of public safety and predictability to guarantee basic freedoms. Hence criminal rights activists demanded a justice system that limits police powers and that holds justice agencies accountable to the highest procedural standards.

During the 1960s and 1970s, the dominant philosophy in American criminal justice focused on guaranteeing the rights of criminal defendants while seeking to understand the root causes of crime and violence. The past 25 years, however, have witnessed increased interest in an ordered society, in public safety, and in the rights of crime victims. This change in attitudes was likely brought about by national frustration with the perceived inability of our society and its justice system to prevent crimes and to consistently hold offenders to heartfelt standards of right and wrong. Increased conservatism in the public-policy arena was given new life by the September

> I would rather be exposed to the inconveniences attending too much liberty than to those attending too small a degree of it.
>
> —Thomas Jefferson

## FREEDOM OR SAFETY? YOU DECIDE.

### Giuliani Says: "Freedom Is about Authority"

As we move through the early years of the twenty-first century, the challenge for the criminal justice system, it seems, is to balance individual rights and personal freedoms with social control and respect for legitimate authority. Years ago, during the height of what was then a powerful movement to win back control of our nation's cities and to rein in skyrocketing crime rates, the *New York Post* sponsored a conference on crime and civil rights. The keynote speaker at that conference was New York City Mayor Rudolph W. Giuliani. In his speech, Giuliani identified the tension between personal freedoms and individual responsibilities as the crux of the crime problem then facing his city and the nation. We mistakenly look to government and elected officials, Giuliani said,

to assume responsibility for solving the problem of crime when, instead, each individual citizen must become accountable for fixing what is wrong with our society. "We only see the oppressive side of authority. . . . What we don't see is that freedom is not a concept in which people can do anything they want, be anything they can be. Freedom is about authority. Freedom is about the willingness of every single human being to cede to lawful authority a great deal of discretion about what you do."

### YOU DECIDE

What did Giuliani mean when he said, "What we don't see is that freedom is not a concept in which people can do anything they want, be anything they can be"? How can we, as a society, best balance individual rights and personal freedoms with social control and respect for legitimate authority?

*Reference:* Philip Taylor, "Civil Libertarians: Giuliani's Efforts Threaten First Amendment," Freedom Forum Online. Web posted at http://www.freedomforum.org.

---

11, 2001, terrorist attacks and by recent instances of corporate fraud. It continues to be sustained by the many widely publicized stories of violent victimization that seem to be the current mainstay of the American media.

Today, public perspectives have largely shifted away from seeing the criminal as an unfortunate victim of poor social and personal circumstances who is inherently protected by fundamental human and constitutional rights, to seeing him or her as a dangerous social predator who usurps the rights and privileges of law-abiding citizens. Reflecting the "get tough on crime" attitudes of today, many Americans demand to know how offenders can better be held accountable for violations of the criminal law.

Nonetheless, the tension between individual rights and social responsibility still forms the basis for most policy-making activity in the criminal justice arena. Those who fight for individual rights continue to carry the banner of civil and criminal rights for the accused and the convicted, while public-order activists loudly proclaim the rights of the victimized and call for an increased emphasis on social responsibility and criminal punishment for convicted criminals. In keeping with these realizations, the theme of this book can be stated as follows:

> There is widespread recognition in contemporary society of the need to balance (1) the freedoms and privileges of our nation's citizens and the respect accorded the rights of individuals faced with criminal prosecution against (2) the valid interests that society has in preventing future crimes, in public safety, and in reducing the harm caused by criminal activity. While the personal freedoms guaranteed to law-abiding citizens as well as to criminal suspects by the Constitution, as interpreted by the U.S. Supreme Court, must be closely guarded, so too the urgent social needs of communities for controlling unacceptable behavior and protecting law-abiding citizens from harm must be recognized. Still to be adequately addressed are the needs and interests of victims and the fear of crime and personal victimization that is often prevalent in the minds of many law-abiding citizens.

Figure 1–1 represents our theme and shows that most people today who intelligently consider the criminal justice system assume one of two viewpoints. We will refer to those who seek to protect personal freedoms and civil rights within society, and especially within the criminal justice process, as **individual-rights advocates.** Those who suggest that under certain circumstances involving criminal threats to public safety, the interests of society (especially crime control and social order) should take precedence over individual rights will be called **public-order advocates.** Recently, U.S. Supreme Court Justice Sandra Day O'Connor summed up the differences between these two perspectives by asking, "At what point does the cost to civil liberties from legislation designed to prevent terrorism [and crime] outweigh the added security that that legislation provides?"[13] In this book, we seek to look at ways that the individual-rights and public-order

> We must not defeat our liberties in trying to defend them.
>
> —Former National Security Adviser Anthony Lake[iv]

**individual-rights advocate**
One who seeks to protect personal freedoms within the process of criminal justice.

**public-order advocate**
One who believes that under certain circumstances involving a criminal threat to public safety, the interests of society should take precedence over individual rights.

**The theme of this book.**

Balancing the concern for individual rights with the need for public order through the administration of criminal justice is the theme of this book.

perspectives can be balanced to serve both sets of needs. Hence you will find our theme discussed throughout this text, within "Freedom or Safety" boxes, and highlighted in many of the Web Quest sections at the end of each chapter.

# Social Justice

When you know both the accuser and the accused, as we so often do, the conflict between civil rights and victims' rights is seldom completely black or white. And it is the gray areas in between that make the debate so difficult.

—Columnist Vicki Williams, writing on crime in a small American town

On September 20, 2001, in the immediate aftermath of the attacks on the World Trade Center and the Pentagon, President Bush delivered a televised address to the American people. In his rallying cry to a nation about to embark on a war against world terrorism, Bush said, "We will bring our enemies to justice; or we will bring justice to our enemies."[14] The word *justice* is powerful, and the president's choice of words spoke to all Americans.

The reality, however, is that *justice* is an elusive term. In the new "war on terrorism," for example, no one who heard the president's speech knew exactly what justice might mean and what form it might eventually take. Even to those living within the same society, *justice* means different things. And just as *justice* can be an ambiguous term for politicians, even in times of war, it

Demonstrators gather on the steps of New York City's Federal Hall to protest provisions of the USA PATRIOT Act. Federal Hall served as the venue for President George Washington's inauguration in 1789 and was the meeting place of the First Congress, which wrote our nation's Bill of Rights. The PATRIOT Act was passed by Congress with little debate just 45 days after the terrorist attacks of September 11, 2001. Rights advocates claim that the act unfairly restricts individual liberties.

*AP Wide World Photos*

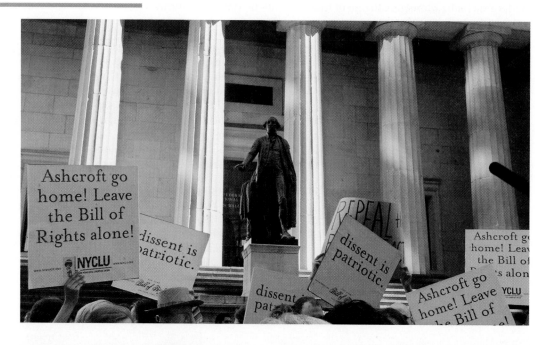

## CJ NEWS

### Chicago Plans Advanced Camera Surveillance

A surveillance system that uses 2,000 remote-control cameras and motion-sensing software to spot crimes or terrorist acts as they happen is being planned for the city of Chicago.

If that sounds a little like Big Brother is watching, he might be.

"Cameras are the equivalent of hundreds of sets of eyes," Mayor Richard Daley said Thursday. "They are the next best thing to having police officers stationed at every potential trouble spot."

The system would exceed existing projects in how it would tie cameras to emergency operations, said Ron Huberman, executive director of the city's Office of Emergency Management.

Neither the courts nor the American Civil Liberties Union has objected to cameras in public places, saying there is no expectation of privacy on a city street.

"We live in a video world," said Ed Yohnka of the ACLU of Illinois.

The high-definition, motorized cameras can rotate 360 degrees and include night-vision capability. They will be mounted on buildings and utility poles across the city.

Most are already in use—30 by the police department and 1,000 at O'Hare International Airport. Other cameras are on elevated train platforms and the city's 600 schools. An additional 250 cameras yet to be installed will raise the number to more than 2,000.

The city is also considering allowing private companies to join the network, for a fee. Officials said the system size is nearly limitless.

The linchpin in the network—paid for with a $5 million grant from the U.S. Department of Homeland Security and scheduled to be up by March 2006—is software designed to detect "suspicious" activity.

For instance, if someone left a suitcase in a stairwell, the software would engage any camera within range and alert a worker at the emergency operations center. It would do the same if an individual rushed up to another and dragged him away. A series of cameras could track fleeing criminals, and 911 operators would be able to give police descriptions of suspects.

Huberman said the cameras will also allow city departments to be more vigilant. Public works will be able to spot a broken water main instantly, or the transportation department can see traffic jams developing.

"It really adds a whole new tool to public safety," Huberman said. "It gives us a tremendous early warning and detection capacity."

A Chicago Police Department surveillance camera system (PODSS) and microphone unit positioned high above the street. This surveillance system includes a PTZ camera, high bandwith wireless communication, a strobe light, and a gunshot recognition system, all in a bullet proof enclosure. The city is installing the PODSS system to spot crimes or terrorist activity.

*Safety Dynamics*

Chicago is the first U.S. city to install such a network.

Officials here said they studied systems used by Las Vegas hotels and casinos, as well as the Pentagon and the city of London, where it's said that the average resident is scrutinized by 300 cameras a day.

Baltimore is trying to build a network with around-the-clock surveillance cameras. Other cities have used them during big events.

Police in Tampa tried the cameras, using a mug shot database and facial-recognition software to identify criminals on the street. It abandoned the effort after two years because it never identified a wanted criminal.

Huberman said Chicago considered face-recognition technology but rejected it as inefficient and immature. But, he said, it's a possibility in the future.

"Chicago has a history of pioneering 911 operations," Huberman said. "Now, we're stepping off in the direction where 911 operation is going to be in the future."

For the latest in crime and justice news, visit the Talk Justice news feed at http://www. crimenews.info.

*Author's Note:* Security cameras, like those described here, played an important role in identifying the perpetrators of the 2005 London subway bombings. Police in London have access to over 500,000 cameras in public places.
*Source:* Debbie Howlett, "Chicago Plans Advanced Surveillance: Emergency Services Would Be Linked to 2,000 Cameras," *USA Today,* September 10, 2004, p. 3A. Copyright © 2004, *USA Today.* Reprinted with permission.

The crowd reacts outside the San Mateo County courthouse as guilty verdicts are returned in the 2005 California murder trial of Scott Peterson. Criminal justice and social justice are concepts that are closely tied in most people's minds.

*AP Wide World Photos*

**justice**

The principle of fairness; the ideal of moral equity.

**social justice**

An ideal that embraces all aspects of civilized life and that is linked to fundamental notions of fairness and to cultural beliefs about right and wrong.

**civil justice**

The civil law, the law of civil procedure, and the array of procedures and activities having to do with private rights and remedies sought by civil action. Civil justice cannot be separated from social justice because the kind of justice enacted in our nation's civil courts is a reflection of basic American understandings of right and wrong.

**criminal justice**

In the strictest sense, the criminal (penal) law, the law of criminal procedure, and the array of procedures and activities having to do with the enforcement of this body of law. Criminal justice cannot be separated from social justice because the kind of justice enacted in our nation's criminal courts is a reflection of basic American understandings of right and wrong.

**administration of justice**

The performance of any of the following activities: detection, apprehension, detention, pretrial release, post-trial release, prosecution, adjudication, correctional supervision, or rehabilitation of accused persons or criminal offenders.[v]

is not always clear how justice can be achieved in the criminal justice system. For example, is "justice for all" a reasonable expectation of today's—or tomorrow's—system of criminal justice? The answer is unclear because individual interests and social needs often diverge. From the perspective of a society or an entire nation, justice can look very different than it does from the perspective of an individual or a small group of people. Because of this dilemma, we now turn our attention to the nature of justice.

British philosopher and statesman Benjamin Disraeli (1804–1881) defined **justice** as "truth in action." A popular dictionary defines it as "the principle of moral rightness, or conformity to truth."[15] **Social justice** is a concept that embraces all aspects of civilized life. It is linked to notions of fairness and to cultural beliefs about right and wrong. Questions of social justice can arise about relationships between individuals, between parties (such as corporations and agencies of government), between the rich and the poor, between the sexes, between ethnic groups and minorities—about social connections of all sorts. In the abstract, the concept of social justice embodies the highest personal and cultural ideals.

**Civil justice,** one component of social justice, concerns itself with fairness in relationships between citizens, government agencies, and businesses in private matters, such as those involving contractual obligations, business dealings, hiring, and equality of treatment. **Criminal justice,** on the other hand, refers to the aspects of social justice that concern violations of the criminal law. As mentioned earlier, community interests in the criminal justice sphere demand the apprehension and punishment of law violators. At the same time, criminal justice ideals extend to the protection of the innocent, the fair treatment of offenders, and fair play by the agencies of law enforcement, including courts and correctional institutions.

Criminal justice, ideally speaking, is "truth in action" within the process that we call the **administration of justice.** It is therefore vital to remember that justice, in the truest and most satisfying sense of the word, is the ultimate goal of criminal justice—and of the day-to-day practices and challenges that characterize the American criminal justice system. Reality, unfortunately, typically falls short of the ideal and is severely complicated by the fact that justice seems to wear different guises when viewed from diverse vantage points. To some people, the criminal justice system and criminal justice agencies often seem biased in favor of the powerful. The laws they enforce seem to emanate more from well-financed, organized, and vocal interest groups than they do from any idealized sense of social justice. As a consequence, disenfranchised groups, those who do not feel as though they share in the political and economic power of society, are often wary of the agencies of justice, seeing them more as enemies than as benefactors.

On the other hand, justice practitioners, including police officers, prosecutors, judges, and corrections officials, frequently complain that their efforts to uphold the law garner unfair public criticism. The realities of law enforcement and of "doing justice," they say, are often overlooked by critics of the system who have little experience in dealing with offenders and victims. We must rec-

**FIGURE 1–2**

The core components of the American criminal justice system.

### The Police

- Enforce the law
- Investigate crimes
- Apprehend offenders
- Reduce and prevent crime
- Maintain public order
- Ensure community safety
- Provide emergency and related community services
- Protect the fundamental rights and freedoms of individuals

**Police**

**Courts**

**Corrections**

### Correctional Agencies

- Carry out sentences imposed by the courts
- Provide safe and humane custody and supervision of offenders
- Protect the community
- Rehabilitate, reform, and reintegrate convicted offenders back into the community
- Respect the legal and human rights of the convicted

### Criminal Courts

- Conduct fair and impartial trials
- Decide criminal cases
- Ensure due process
- Determine guilt or innocence
- Impose sentences on the guilty
- Uphold the law
- Require fairness throughout the justice process
- Protect the rights and freedoms of anyone facing processing by the justice system
- Provide a check on the exercise of power by other justice system agencies*

*Fairness, professionalism, integrity, and impartiality are expected of all criminal justice personnel at every stage of criminal case processing, and it is a special duty of the courts to ensure that these expectations are met.

ognize, practitioners often tell us, that those accused of violating the criminal law face an elaborate process built around numerous legislative, administrative, and organizational concerns. Viewed realistically, the criminal justice process, while it can be fine-tuned to take into consideration the interests of ever-larger numbers of people, rarely pleases everyone. The outcome of the criminal justice process in any particular case is a social product, and like any product that is the result of group effort, it must inevitably be a patchwork quilt of human emotions, reasoning, and concerns.

Whichever side we choose in the ongoing debate over the nature and quality of criminal justice in America, it is vital that we recognize the plethora of pragmatic issues involved in the administration of justice while also keeping a clear focus on the justice ideal.[16] Was justice done, for example, in the criminal trial of O. J. Simpson, in the trials of the Los Angeles police officers accused of beating Rodney King, or in the arrest and lengthy detention of hundreds of Muslims after September 11, 2001?[17] While answers to such questions may reveal a great deal about the American criminal justice system, they also have much to say about the perspectives of those who provide them.

# American Criminal Justice: System and Functions

## The Consensus Model

So far, we have described a **criminal justice system**[18] consisting of the component agencies of police, courts, and corrections. Each of these components can, in turn, be described in terms of its functions and purpose (Figure 1–2).

The systems perspective on criminal justice is characterized primarily by its assumption that the various parts of the justice system work together by design to achieve the wider purpose we

**criminal justice system**

The aggregate of all operating and administrative or technical support agencies that perform criminal justice functions. The basic divisions of the operational aspects of criminal justice are law enforcement, courts, and corrections.

**consensus model**

A criminal justice perspective that assumes that the system's components work together harmoniously to achieve the social product we call *justice*.

have been calling *justice.* Hence the systems perspective on criminal justice generally encompasses a point of view called the **consensus model.** The consensus model assumes that each of the component parts of the criminal justice system strives toward a common goal and that the movement of cases and people through the system is smooth due to cooperation between the various components of the system.

The systems model of criminal justice is more an analytic tool than a reality, however. An analytic model, whether in the hard sciences or in the social sciences, is simply a convention chosen for its explanatory power. By explaining the actions of criminal justice officials (such as arrest, prosecution, and sentencing) as though they were systematically related, we are able to envision a fairly smooth and predictable process (which is described in more detail later in this chapter).

The systems model has been criticized for implying a greater level of organization and cooperation among the various agencies of justice than actually exists. The word *system* calls to mind a near-perfect form of social organization. The modern mind associates the idea of a system with machine-like precision in which the problems of wasted effort, redundancy, and conflicting actions are quickly corrected. In practice, the justice system has nowhere near this level of perfection, and the systems model is admittedly an oversimplification. Conflicts among and within agencies are rife; individual actors within the system often do not share immediate goals; and the system may move in different directions depending on political currents, informal arrangements, and personal discretion.

> If we do not maintain Justice,
> Justice will not maintain us.
>
> —Francis Bacon

## The Conflict Model

**conflict model**

A criminal justice perspective that assumes that the system's components function primarily to serve their own interests. According to this theoretical framework, justice is more a product of conflicts among agencies within the system than it is the result of cooperation among component agencies.

The **conflict model** provides another approach to the study of American criminal justice. The conflict model says that the interests of criminal justice agencies tend to make actors within the system self-serving. According to this model, the goals of individual agencies often conflict, and pressures for success, promotion, pay increases, and general accountability fragment the efforts of the system as a whole, leading to a criminal justice *non*system.[19]

A classic study of clearance rates by Jerome H. Skolnick provides support for the idea of a criminal justice nonsystem.[20] Clearance rates are a measure of crimes solved by the police. The more crimes the police can show they have solved, the better they look to the public they serve. Skolnick discovered an instance in which a burglar was caught red-handed during the commission of a burglary. After his arrest, the police suggested that he confess to many unsolved burglaries that they knew he had not committed. In effect they said, "Help us out, and we will try to help you out!" The burglar did confess—to more than 400 other burglaries. Following the confession, the police were satisfied because they could say they had "solved" many burglaries, and the suspect was pleased as well because the police and prosecutor agreed to speak on his behalf before the judge.

Both models have something to tell us. Agencies of justice with a diversity of functions (police, courts, and corrections) and at all levels (federal, state, and local) are linked closely enough for the term *system* to be meaningfully applied to them. On the other hand, the very size of the criminal justice undertaking makes effective cooperation between component agencies difficult. The police, for example, have an interest in seeing offenders put behind bars. Prison officials, on the other hand, are often working with extremely overcrowded facilities. They may favor early-release programs for certain categories of offenders, such as those judged to be nonviolent. Who wins out in the long run might just be a matter of internal politics and quasi-official wrangling. Everyone should be concerned, however, when the goal of justice is affected, and sometimes even sacrificed, because of conflicts within the system.

## American Criminal Justice: The Process

> Justice cannot be for one side alone, but must be for both.
>
> —Eleanor Roosevelt

Whether part of a system or a nonsystem, the agencies of criminal justice must process the cases that come before them. An analysis of criminal justice case processing provides both a useful guide to this book and a "road map" to the criminal justice system itself. Beginning with the investigation of reported crimes, the figure in the front of this book illustrates the processing of a criminal case through the federal justice system. The process in most state systems is similar. See Web Extra 1–3 at cjtoday.com for more information about the process shown in the figure.

# Investigation and Arrest

The modern justice process begins with investigation. After a crime has been discovered, evidence is gathered at the scene when possible, and a follow-up investigation attempts to reconstruct the sequence of activities. Although a few offenders are arrested at the scene of the crime, most are apprehended later. In such cases, an arrest **warrant** issued by a judge provides the legal basis for an apprehension by police.

An arrest, in which a person is taken into custody, limits the arrestee's freedom. Arrest is a serious step in the process of justice and involves a discretionary decision made by the police seeking to bring criminal sanctions to bear. Most arrests are made peacefully, but if a suspect tries to resist, a police officer may need to use force. Only about half of all people arrested are eventually convicted, and of those, only about a quarter are sentenced to a year or more in prison.

During arrest and prior to questioning, defendants are usually advised of their constitutional rights, as enumerated in the U.S. Supreme Court decision of *Miranda* v. *Arizona*.[21] Defendants are told:

(1) "You have the right to remain silent." (2) "Anything you say can and will be used against you in court." (3) "You have the right to talk to a lawyer for advice before we ask you any questions, and to have him with you during questioning." (4) "If you cannot afford a lawyer, one will be appointed for you before any questioning if you wish." (5) "If you decide to answer questions now without a lawyer present, you will still have the right to stop answering at any time. You also have the right to stop answering at any time and may talk with a lawyer before deciding to speak again." (6) "Do you wish to talk or not?" and (7) "Do you want a lawyer?"[22]

Although television dramas about the criminal justice system nearly always show an offender being given a rights advisement at the time of arrest, the *Miranda* decision requires only that police advise a person of his rights prior to questioning. An arrest without questioning can occur in the absence of any warning. When an officer interrupts a crime in progress, public-safety considerations may make it reasonable for the officer to ask a few questions prior to a rights advisement. Many officers, however, feel they are on sound legal ground only by advising suspects of their rights immediately after arrest. Investigation and arrest are discussed in detail in Chapter 7, "Policing: Legal Aspects."

## Booking

Following arrest, suspects are booked. During **booking,** pictures are taken, fingerprints are made, and personal information such as address, date of birth, weight, and height is gathered. Details of the charges are recorded, and an administrative record of the arrest is created. At this time suspects are again advised of their rights and are asked to sign a form on which each right is written. The written form generally contains a statement acknowledging the advisement of rights and attesting to the fact that the suspect understands them.

# Pretrial Activities

## First Appearance

Within hours of arrest, suspects must be brought before a magistrate (a judicial officer) for an initial appearance. The judge will tell them of the charges against them, will again advise them of their rights, and may sometimes provide the opportunity for **bail.**

Most defendants are released on recognizance into their own care or the care of another, or are given the chance to post a bond during their first appearance. A bond may take the form of a cash deposit or a property bond in which a house or other property serves as collateral against flight. Those who flee may be ordered to forfeit the posted cash or property. Suspects who are not afforded the opportunity for bail because their crimes are very serious or who do not have the needed financial resources are taken to jail to await the next stage in the justice process.

If a defendant doesn't have a lawyer, one will be appointed at the first appearance. To retain a court-appointed lawyer, the defendant may have to demonstrate financial hardship. The names

**warrant**

In criminal proceedings, a writ issued by a judicial officer directing a law enforcement officer to perform a specified act and affording the officer protection from damages if he or she performs it.

> Everywhere across the nation, we are more concerned with ensuring that criminal activity does not repeat itself, rather than keeping criminal activity from occurring in the first place.
>
> —Tony Fabelo, Executive Director, Texas Criminal Justice Policy Council

> While the federal government occasionally may make a great advance in the direction of civil liberties, they can also make a very disastrous reversal. . . .
>
> —Supreme Court Justice Robert H. Jackson[vi]

**booking**

A law enforcement or correctional administrative process officially recording an entry into detention after arrest and identifying the person, the place, the time, the reason for the arrest, and the arresting authority.

**bail**

The money or property pledged to the court or actually deposited with the court to effect the release of a person from legal custody.

of assigned lawyers are usually drawn off the roster of practicing defense attorneys in the county. Some jurisdictions use public defenders to represent indigent defendants.

All aspects of the first appearance, including bail bonds and possible pretrial release, are discussed in detail in Chapter 10, "Pretrial Activities and the Criminal Trial."

## Preliminary Hearing

**preliminary hearing**

A proceeding before a judicial officer in which three matters must be decided: (1) whether a crime was committed, (2) whether the crime occurred within the territorial jurisdiction of the court, and (3) whether there are reasonable grounds to believe that the defendant committed the crime.

The primary purpose of a **preliminary hearing,** also sometimes called a *preliminary examination,* is to establish whether sufficient evidence exists against a person to continue the justice process. At the preliminary hearing, the hearing judge will seek to determine whether there is **probable cause** to believe that (1) a crime has been committed and (2) the defendant committed it. The decision is a judicial one, but the process provides the prosecutor with an opportunity to test the strength of the evidence at his or her disposal.

The preliminary hearing also allows defense counsel the chance to assess the strength of the prosecution's case. As the prosecution presents evidence, the defense is said to "discover" what it is. Hence, the preliminary hearing serves a discovery function for the defense. If the defense attorney thinks the evidence is strong, he or she may suggest that a plea bargain be arranged. All defendants, including those who are indigent, have a right to be represented by counsel at the preliminary hearing.

**probable cause**

A set of facts and circumstances that would induce a reasonably intelligent and prudent person to believe that a particular other person has committed a specific crime. Also, reasonable grounds to make or believe an accusation. Probable cause refers to the necessary level of belief that would allow for police seizures (arrests) of individuals and full searches of dwellings, vehicles, and possessions.

## Information or Indictment

**information**

A formal, written accusation submitted to a court by a prosecutor, alleging that a specified person has committed a specified offense.

In some states, the prosecutor may seek to continue the case against a defendant by filing an **information** with the court. An information, which is a formal written accusation, is filed on the basis of the outcome of the preliminary hearing.

Other states require that an **indictment** be returned by a **grand jury** before prosecution can proceed. The grand jury hears evidence from the prosecutor and decides whether a case should go to trial. In effect, the grand jury is the formal indicting authority. It determines whether probable cause exists to charge a defendant formally with a crime. Grand juries can return an indictment on less than a unanimous vote.

**indictment**

A formal, written accusation submitted to the court by a grand jury, alleging that a specified person has committed a specified offense, usually a felony.

The grand jury system has been criticized because it is one-sided. The defense has no opportunity to present evidence; the grand jury is led only by the prosecutor, often through an appeal to emotions or in ways that would not be permitted in a trial. At the same time, the grand jury is less bound by specific rules than a trial jury. For example, a grand jury member once told the author that a rape case had been dismissed because the man had taken the woman to dinner first. Personal ignorance and cultural biases are far more likely to play a role in grand jury hearings than in criminal trials. In defense of the grand jury system, however, defendants who are clearly innocent will likely not be indicted. A grand jury's refusal to indict can save the system considerable time and money by preventing cases lacking in evidence from further processing by the criminal justice system.

**grand jury**

A group of jurors who have been selected according to law and have been sworn to hear the evidence and to determine whether there is sufficient evidence to bring the accused person to trial, to investigate criminal activity generally, or to investigate the conduct of a public agency or official.

## Arraignment

The **arraignment** is "the first appearance of the defendant before the court that has the authority to conduct a trial."[23] At arraignment, the accused stands before a judge and hears the information, or indictment, against him as it is read. Defendants are again notified of their rights and are asked to enter a plea. Acceptable pleas generally include (1) not guilty, (2) guilty, and (3) no contest (*nolo contendere*), which may result in conviction but which can't be used later as an admission of guilt in civil proceedings. Civil proceedings, or private lawsuits, while not covered in detail in this book, provide an additional avenue of relief for victims or their survivors. Convicted offenders increasingly face suits brought against them by victims seeking to collect monetary damages.

The Federal Rules of Criminal Procedure specify that "arraignment shall be conducted in open court and shall consist of reading the indictment or information to the defendant or stating to him the substance of the charge and calling on him to plead thereto. He shall be given a copy of the indictment or information before he is called upon to plead."[24]

Guilty pleas are not always accepted by the judge. If the judge believes a guilty plea is made under duress or is due to a lack of knowledge on the part of the defendant, the plea will be rejected and a plea of "not guilty" will be substituted for it. Sometimes defendants "stand mute"; that is, they refuse to speak or to enter a plea of any kind. In that case, the judge will enter a plea of "not guilty" on their behalf.

The arraignment process is discussed in detail in Chapter 10, "Pretrial Activities and the Criminal Trial."

# Adjudication

Under the Sixth Amendment to the U.S. Constitution, every criminal defendant has a right to a **trial** by jury. The U.S. Supreme Court, however, has held that petty offenses are not covered by the Sixth Amendment guarantee and that the seriousness of a case is determined by the way in which "society regards the offense." For the most part, "offenses for which the maximum period of incarceration is six months or less are presumptively petty."[25] In *Blanton* v. *City of North Las Vegas* (1989), the Court held that "a defendant can overcome this presumption and become entitled to a jury trial, only by showing that . . . additional penalties [such as fines and community service] viewed together with the maximum prison term, are so severe that the legislature clearly determined that the offense is a serious one."[26] The *Blanton* decision was further reinforced in the case of *U.S.* v. *Nachtigal* (1993).[27]

In most jurisdictions, many criminal cases never come to trial. The majority are "pleaded out," that is, they are dispensed of as the result of a bargained plea, or they are dismissed for one of a variety of reasons. Studies have found that as many as 82% of all sentences are imposed in criminal cases because of guilty pleas rather than trials.[28]

In cases that do come to trial, the procedures governing the submission of evidence are tightly controlled by procedural law and precedent. *Procedural law* specifies the type of evidence that may be submitted, the credentials of those allowed to represent the state or the defendant, and what a jury is allowed to hear.

*Precedent* refers to understandings built up through common usage and also to decisions rendered by courts in previous cases. Precedent in the courtroom, for example, requires that lawyers request permission from the judge before approaching a witness. It also can mean that excessively gruesome items of evidence may not be used or must be altered in some way so that their factual value is not lost in the strong emotional reactions they may create.

Some states allow trials for less serious offenses to occur before a judge if defendants waive their right to a trial by jury. This is called a *bench trial.* Other states require a jury trial for all serious criminal offenses.

Trials are expensive and time-consuming. They pit defense attorneys against prosecutors. Regulated conflict is the rule, and jurors are required to decide the facts and apply the law as the judge explains it to them. In some cases, however, a jury may be unable to decide. Such a jury is said to be *deadlocked,* and the judge declares a mistrial. The defendant may be tried again when a new jury is impaneled.

The criminal trial and its participants are described fully in Chapter 9, "The Courts: Structure and Participants," and Chapter 10, "Pretrial Activities and the Criminal Trial."

# Sentencing

Once a person has been convicted, it becomes the responsibility of the judge to impose some form of punishment. The sentence may take the form of supervised probation in the community, a fine, a prison term, or some combination of these. Defendants will often be ordered to pay the costs of court or of their own defense if they are able.

Prior to sentencing, a sentencing hearing may be held in which lawyers on both sides present information concerning the defendant. The judge may also ask a probation or parole officer to compile a presentence report, which contains information on the defendant's family and business situation, emotional state, social background, and criminal history. This report helps the judge make an appropriate sentencing decision.

Judges traditionally have had considerable discretion in sentencing, although new state and federal laws now place limits on judicial discretion in some cases, requiring that a sentence "presumed" by law be imposed. Judges still retain enormous discretion, however, in specifying whether sentences on multiple charges are to run consecutively or concurrently. Offenders found guilty of more than one charge may be ordered to serve one sentence after another is completed,

---

**arraignment**

Strictly, the hearing before a court having jurisdiction in a criminal case, in which the identity of the defendant is established, the defendant is informed of the charge and of his or her rights, and the defendant is required to enter a plea. Also, in some usages, any appearance in criminal court prior to trial.

**trial**

In criminal proceedings, the examination in court of the issues of fact and relevant law in a case for the purpose of convicting or acquitting the defendant.

Criminal justice cannot be achieved in the absence of social justice.

—American Friends' Service Committee, *Struggle for Justice*

The criminal justice system is composed of a sprawling bureaucracy with many separate agencies that are largely autonomous and independent.

—Gary LaFree, Ph.D., University of New Mexico

**consecutive sentence**

One of two or more sentences imposed at the same time, after conviction for more than one offense, and served in sequence with the other sentence. Also, a new sentence for a new conviction, imposed upon a person already under sentence for a previous offense, which is added to the previous sentence, thus increasing the maximum time the offender may be confined or under supervision.

**concurrent sentence**

One of two or more sentences imposed at the same time, after conviction for more than one offense, and served at the same time. Also, a new sentence for a new conviction, imposed upon a person already under sentence for a previous offense, served at the same time as the previous sentence.

African-American men comprise less than 6% of the U.S. population and almost one-half of its criminal prisoners.

—Bureau of Justice Statistics

called a **consecutive sentence,** or may be told that their sentences will run at the same time, which is called a **concurrent sentence.**

Many convictions are appealed. The appeals process can be complex and can involve both state and federal judiciaries. An appeal is based on the defendant's claim that rules of procedure were not followed properly at some earlier stage in the justice process or that the defendant was denied the rights guaranteed by the U.S. Constitution.

Chapter 11, "Sentencing," outlines modern sentencing practices and describes the many modern alternatives to imprisonment.

# Corrections

Once an offender has been sentenced, the corrections stage begins. Some offenders are sentenced to prison, where they "do time" for their crimes. Once in the correctional system, they are classified according to local procedures and are assigned to confinement facilities and treatment programs. Newer prisons today bear little resemblance to the massive bastions of the past, which isolated offenders from society behind huge stone walls. Many modern prisons, however, still suffer from a "lock psychosis" (a preoccupation with security) among top- and mid-level administrators as well as a lack of significant rehabilitation programs.

Chapter 13, "Prisons and Jails," discusses the philosophy behind prisons and sketches their historical development. Chapter 14, "Prison Life," portrays life on the inside and delineates the social structures that develop in response to the pains of imprisonment.

## Probation and Parole

Not everyone who is convicted of a crime and sentenced ends up in prison. Some offenders are ordered to prison only to have their sentences suspended and a probationary term imposed. They may also be ordered to perform community-service activities as a condition of their probation. During the term of probation, these offenders are required to submit to supervision by a probation officer and to meet other conditions set by the court. Failure to do so results in revocation of probation and imposition of the original prison sentence.

Offenders who have served a portion of their prison sentences may be freed on parole. They are supervised by a parole officer and assisted in their readjustment to society. As in the case of probation, failure to meet the conditions of parole may result in parole revocation and a return to prison.

A criminal defendant at a preliminary hearing. Everyone facing criminal prosecution in the United States is guaranteed a constitutional right to due process, meaning that defendants must be afforded a fair opportunity to participate in every stage of criminal proceedings.

*AP Wide World Photos*

Chapter 11, "Sentencing," and Chapter 12, "Probation, Parole, and Community Corrections," deal with the practice of probation and parole and with the issues surrounding it. Learn more about the criminal justice process at Library Extra 1–3 at cjtoday.com. For a critical look at the justice system, visit Web Extra 1–4 at cjtoday.com.

# Due Process and Individual Rights

The U.S. Constitution requires that criminal justice case processing be conducted with fairness and equity; this requirement is referred to as **due process.** Simply put, *due process* means procedural fairness.[29] It recognizes the individual rights of criminal defendants facing prosecution by a state or the federal government. Under the due process standard, rights violations may become the basis for the dismissal of evidence or of criminal charges, especially at the appellate level. Table 1–1 outlines the basic rights to which defendants in criminal proceedings are generally entitled.

Due process underlies the first ten amendments to the Constitution, which are collectively known as the *Bill of Rights.* It is specifically guaranteed by the Fifth, Sixth, and Fourteenth Amendments and is succinctly stated in the Fifth, which reads, "No person shall be . . . deprived of life, liberty, or property, without due process of law." The Fourteenth Amendment makes due process binding on the states; that is, it requires individual states to respect the due process rights of U.S. citizens who come under their jurisdiction.

The courts, and specifically the U.S. Supreme Court, have interpreted and clarified the guarantees of the Bill of Rights. The due process standard was set in the 1960s by the Warren Court (1953–1969), following a number of far-reaching Supreme Court decisions that affected criminal procedure. Led by Chief Justice Earl Warren, the Warren Court is remembered for its concern with protecting the innocent against the massive power of the state in criminal proceedings.[30] As a result of its tireless efforts to institutionalize the Bill of Rights, the daily practice of modern American criminal justice is now set squarely upon the due process standard.

**due process**

A right guaranteed by the Fifth, Sixth, and Fourteenth Amendments of the U.S. Constitution and generally understood, in legal contexts, to mean the due course of legal proceedings according to the rules and forms established for the protection of individual rights. In criminal proceedings, due process of law is generally understood to include the following basic elements: a law creating and defining the offense, an impartial tribunal having jurisdictional authority over the case, accusation in proper form, notice and opportunity to defend, trial according to established procedure, and discharge from all restraints or obligations unless convicted.

| INDIVIDUAL RIGHTS GUARANTEED BY THE BILL OF RIGHTS[1] |
|---|
| A right to be assumed innocent until proven guilty |
| A right against unreasonable searches of person and place of residence |
| A right against arrest without probable cause |
| A right against unreasonable seizure of personal property |
| A right against self-incrimination |
| A right to fair questioning by the police |
| A right to protection from physical harm throughout the justice process |
| A right to an attorney |
| A right to trial by jury |
| A right to know the charges |
| A right to cross-examine prosecution witnesses |
| A right to speak and present witnesses |
| A right not to be tried twice for the same crime |
| A right against cruel or unusual punishment |
| A right to due process |
| A right to a speedy trial |
| A right against excessive bail |
| A right against excessive fines |
| A right to be treated the same as others, regardless of race, sex, religious preference, and other personal attributes |

TABLE 1–1

[1]As interpreted by the U.S. Supreme Court.

## CJ CAREERS

### WHY STUDY CRIMINAL JUSTICE?

As this chapter points out, criminal justice, as an academic area, is one of the fastest-growing disciplines in the United States. While the discipline has been expanding for more than a decade, much job growth is still to come, as the table in this box shows.

#### PROJECTED OCCUPATION GROWTH 2002–2012

| Occupation | Federal Workforce (%) | Civilian Labor Force (%) |
| --- | --- | --- |
| Criminal investigators | 42.7 | 22.4 |
| Management analysts | 22.0 | 30.4 |
| Biological scientists | 20.8 | 19.0 |
| Lawyers | 10.7 | 17.0 |
| Computer specialists | 10.2 | 35.8 |
| Production occupations | –4.2 | 3.2 |
| Office clerks | –11.4 | 10.4 |
| Secretaries | –17.2 | 4.5 |

*Source:* Bureau of Labor Statistics, *Career Guide to Industries, 2004–2005;* Bureau of Labor Statistics, *Occupational Projections and Training Data, 2004–2005.*

The events of September 11, 2001, have made the study of criminal justice more relevant than ever, and many of today's students use their criminal justice major as a path to fulfilling jobs serving the nation and helping to protect local communities. A criminal justice career offers students a way of contributing to society, and it permits them to give something back to the country and to the community that nurtured them. For many, a criminal justice career reaffirms the American way of life by supporting the values on which it is based.

Other students are attracted to the study of criminal justice because it facilitates exploration of the tension that exists within American society between individual rights and freedoms, on the one hand, and the need for public safety and security, on the other. That tension—between individual rights and public order—forms the theme upon which this textbook is built, and it is discussed in detail elsewhere in this chapter.

For more information on the rapidly expanding criminal justice careers area, read *Where the Jobs Are: The Continuing Growth of Federal Job Opportunities,* available on the Web at http://www.justicestudies.com/jobs.htm.

**WHAT WOULD YOU DO?**

The CD-ROM scenario for this chapter builds on the concept of proper police behavior when interrogating suspects who have just been taken into custody. It is derived from a real-life incident in which a young woman was raped by a man who then fled into a supermarket, where he was arrested. The real-life case eventually found its way to the U.S. Supreme Court, with favorable consequences for the on-the-scene officers. Use the CD-ROM found in your textbook to work through this scenario to learn why responding officers acted the way they did.

# The Role of the Courts in Defining Rights

Although the U.S. Constitution is the basis for our rights as citizens, many modern rights exist *in practice* due to U.S. Supreme Court decisions. For example, it was *Gideon* v. *Wainwright* (1963)[31] that led the Court to embrace the Sixth Amendment's guarantee of a right to a lawyer to all criminal defendants, and to mandate that states provide lawyers for defendants who are unable to pay for them. Prior to *Gideon* (which is discussed in detail in Chapter 9), it was rare that courts appointed attorneys for defendants unable to afford their own counsel, except in capital cases and in some federal courts. After the *Gideon* decision, court-appointed counsel became commonplace, and measures were instituted in jurisdictions across the nation to select attorneys fairly for indigent defendants. It is important to note, however, that while the Sixth Amendment specifically says, among other things, that "in all criminal prosecutions, the accused shall enjoy the right . . . to have the Assistance of Counsel for his defence," it does not say, in so many words, that the state is *required* to provide counsel. It is the U.S. Supreme Court, interpreting the amendment, which has said that.

The U.S. Supreme Court is very powerful, and its decisions often have far-reaching consequences. The decisions rendered by the justices in cases like *Gideon* become, in effect, the law of the land. For all practical purposes, such decisions often carry as much weight as legislative action. For this reason, some writers speak of "judge-made law" (rather than legislated law) in describing judicial precedents that affect the process of justice.

Rights that have been recognized by court decisions are often subject to continual refinement, and although the process of change is usually very slow, new interpretations may broaden or narrow the scope of applicability accorded to constitutional guarantees.

The Study of Criminal Justice:
A Brief History

# The Ultimate Goal: Crime Control through Due Process

Two primary principles were identified in our discussion of this book's theme: (1) the need to enforce the law and to maintain public order and (2) the need to protect individuals from injustice—especially at the hands of the criminal justice system. Two contrasting models of criminal justice

## CJ CAREERS

### U.S. FEDERAL GOVERNMENT 2005 GENERAL SCHEDULE PAY

Throughout this book, you will find a number of CJ Careers boxes showcasing job opportunities with various federal criminal justice agencies, such as the FBI, DEA, U.S. Secret Service, U.S. Marshals, and Bureau of Prisons. Those boxes describe agency-specific job requirements and list the federal pay levels at which successful applicants might expect to be employed.

Basic pay under the federal General Schedule (GS) pay plan is shown in the following table. Annual salaries for federal law enforcement officers, which are higher than for most other federal employees in the same grade, are also indicated.

For additional federal employment information, visit http://www.usajobs.opm.gov, the official U.S. government website for job and employment information.

| Salary Grade | Most Federal Employees | Federal Law Enforcement Personnel | Salary Grade | Most Federal Employees | Federal Law Enforcement Personnel | Salary Grade | Most Federal Employees |
|---|---|---|---|---|---|---|---|
| GS-1 | $16,016 | NA | GS-6 | $27,507 | **$32,092** | GS-11 | $45,239 |
| GS-2 | 18,007 | NA | GS-7 | 30,567 | **34,643** | GS-12 | 54,221 |
| GS-3 | 19,647 | **$23,577** | GS-8 | 33,852 | **36,108** | GS-13 | 64,478 |
| GS-4 | 22,056 | **26,466** | GS-9 | 37,390 | **38,636** | GS-14 | 76,193 |
| GS-5 | 24,677 | **30,438** | GS-10 | 41,175 | **42,548** | GS-15 | 89,625 |

*Note:* GS pay is adjusted geographically, and most federal jobs pay a higher salary than that shown in the table. Locality payments in the continental United States range from 8.6% to 19%. Pay rates outside the continental United States are 10% to 25% higher. Also, certain hard-to-fill jobs, usually in the scientific, technical, and medical fields, may have higher starting salaries. Exact pay information can be found in federal position vacancy announcements. To view the most recent federal pay scale and locality pay charts, go to http://www.usdoj.gov/marshals/careers/benefits.htm.

are built on these principles. The first values the efficient arrest and conviction of criminal offenders. It is often called the **crime-control model** of justice. This model was first described by Herbert Packer in his analysis of the state of criminal justice in the late 1960s.[32] For this reason, it is sometimes referred to as *Packer's crime-control model.*

The second model is called the **due process model** because of its emphasis on individual rights. Due process is intended to ensure that innocent people are not convicted of crimes; it is a fundamental part of American criminal justice. It requires a careful and informed consideration of the facts of each individual case. Under the due process model, police are required to recognize the rights of suspects during arrest, questioning, and handling. Similarly, prosecutors and judges must recognize constitutional and other guarantees during trial and the presentation of evidence.

The dual goals of crime control and due process are often assumed to be opposing goals. Indeed, some critics of American criminal justice argue that the practice of justice is too often concerned with crime control at the expense of due process. Other analysts of the American scene maintain that our type of justice coddles offenders and does too little to protect the innocent. While it is impossible to avoid ideological conflicts like these, it is also realistic to think of the American system of justice as representative of *crime control through due process*—that is, as a system of **social control** that is fair to those whom it processes. This model of *law enforcement infused with the recognition of individual rights* provides a workable conceptual framework for understanding the American system of criminal justice.

# The Role of Research in Criminal Justice

The study of criminal justice as an academic discipline began in this country in the late 1920s, when August Vollmer (1876–1955), the former police chief of the Los Angeles Police Department (LAPD), persuaded the University of California to offer courses on the subject.[33] Vollmer was joined by his for-

**crime-control model**
A criminal justice perspective that emphasizes the efficient arrest and conviction of criminal offenders.

**due process model**
A criminal justice perspective that emphasizes individual rights at all stages of justice system processing.

**social control**
The use of sanctions and rewards within a group to influence and shape the behavior of individual members of that group. Social control is a primary concern of social groups and communities, and it is their interest in the exercise of social control that leads to the creation of both criminal and civil statutes.

## CJ FUTURES

### The National Law Enforcement and Corrections Technology Center

You will encounter a number of CJ Futures boxes in this book. These boxes illustrate a subtheme of your textbook: the future of crime and justice, including social issues and changing technology.

A major source of information about the impact of technology on the criminal justice system is the National Law Enforcement and Corrections Technology Center (NLECTC). This network of regional centers and specialty offices located across the country offers no-cost assistance in helping law enforcement and corrections agencies implement current and emerging technology. The system is composed of a national center located in Rockville, Maryland, and five regional centers in Rome, New York; Charleston, South Carolina; Denver, Colorado; El Segundo, California; and Anchorage, Alaska.

The NLECTC system also includes the Border Research and Technology Center in San Diego, California; the Office of Law Enforcement Standards in Gaithersburg, Maryland; the Office of Law Enforcement Technology Commercialization in Wheeling, West Virginia; and the Rural Law Enforcement Technology Center in Hazard, Kentucky.

NLECTC is supported by the National Institute of Justice (NIJ), an arm of the U.S. Department of Justice. It is overseen by the Office of Science and Technology within NIJ.

David G. Boyd, director of NIJ's Office of Science and Technology, is convinced of the important role that technology will continue to play in the fight against crime. According to Boyd, "The technological revolution that has swept society as a whole in recent years has also affected the criminal justice system. Some technologies that not long ago seemed advanced—vests that can stop bullets and electronic monitoring of probationers—today seem commonplace. But the revolution continues apace, with ever more spectacular advances now being made, or in the testing stages, or on the drawing board."

NLECTC provides a wealth of online information for anyone interested in technology assessment as applied to criminal justice. The agency's free newsletter, *TechBeat*, is published four times each year, both on paper and in electronic format. To request a subscription, e-mail asknlectc@nlectc.org. You can visit NLECTC on the Web via Web Extra 1–5 at cjtoday.com.

**WEB EXTRA**

*Reference:* National Law Enforcement and Corrections Technology Center, a program of the National Institute of Justice, November 2002.

---

> Liberty is the perfection of civil society, but still authority must be acknowledged essential to its very existence.
>
> —David Hume

**criminology**
The scientific study of the causes and prevention of crime and the rehabilitation and punishment of offenders.

mer student Orlando W. Wilson (1900–1972) and by William H. Parker (who later served as chief of the LAPD from 1950 to 1966) in calling for increased professionalism in police work through better training.[34] Largely as a result of Vollmer's influence, early criminal justice education was practice oriented; it was a kind of extension of on-the-job training for working practitioners. Hence, in the early days of the discipline, criminal justice students were primarily focused on the application of general management principles to the administration of police agencies. Criminal justice came to be seen as a practical field of study concerned largely with issues of organizational effectiveness.

By the 1960s, however, students of criminal justice were beginning to apply the techniques of social scientific research—many of them borrowed from sister disciplines like **criminology**, sociology, psychology, and political science—to the study of all aspects of the justice system. Scientific research into the operation of the criminal justice system was encouraged by the 1967 President's Commission on Law Enforcement and Administration of Justice, which influenced passage of the Safe Streets and Crime Control Act of 1968. The Safe Streets Act led to the creation of the National Institute of Law Enforcement and Criminal Justice, which later became the National Institute of Justice (NIJ). As a central part of its mission, NIJ continues to support research in the criminal justice field through substantial funding for scientific explorations into all aspects of the discipline, and it funnels much of the $3 billion spent annually by the Department of Justice to help local communities fight crime. Scientific research has since become a major element in the increasing professionalization of criminal justice, both as a career field and as a field of study, and can be expected to play an ever-wider role in years to come.

# Multiculturalism and Diversity in Criminal Justice

In late 2001, Tom Green, a 52-year-old Mormon with five wives, another five former wives, and 29 known children, was sentenced to five years in a Utah prison after being convicted of four counts of polygamy.[35] A year later he was sentenced to another five years for child rape that

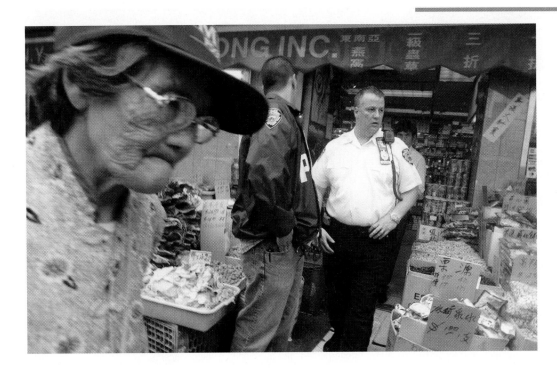

NYPD officers respond to a call for service in New York City's Chinatown. American society is a multicultural society, composed of a wide variety of racial and ethnic heritages, diverse religions, incongruous values, disparate traditions, and distinct languages.

*Ting-Li Want,* The New York Times

occurred when he married a 12-year-old girl in 1986. The Church of Jesus Christ of Latter-day Saints brought plural marriage to Utah in the early nineteenth century, but the state legislature banned the practice more than 100 years ago. Today, the church officially excommunicates polygamists.

Green was the first polygamist prosecuted in Utah in almost 50 years. The last major prosecution occurred in 1953, when the federal government raided the polygamous town of Short Creek, on the Utah–Arizona border. Images of children being torn away from their parents during that raid led to a public outcry. Since then, the government has mostly ignored practitioners of plural marriage. Green's supporters claimed that it was because of the upcoming 2002 Winter Olympics to be held in Salt Lake City that polygamists, including Green, were targeted. (Two years before the Olympics, the Utah legislature appropriated monies for the hiring of a specialist in polygamy prosecutions. The "polygamy czar" was supposed to assist the state's counties in ferreting out crimes in small towns and "closed societies.") While the exact number of polygamists in Utah and elsewhere is unknown, the existence of such alternative family lifestyles is just one indicator that the United States is indeed a multicultural and diverse society.

**Multiculturalism** describes a society that is home to a multitude of different cultures, each with its own set of norms, values, and routine behaviors. While American society today is truly a multicultural society, composed of a wide variety of racial and ethnic heritages, diverse religions, incongruous values, disparate traditions, and distinct languages, multiculturalism in America is not new. For thousands of years before Europeans arrived in the Western Hemisphere, tribal nations of Native Americans each spoke their own language, were bound to customs that differed significantly from one another, and practiced a wide range of religions. European immigration, which began in earnest in the seventeenth century, led to greater diversity still. Successive waves of immigrants, along with the slave trade of the early and mid-nineteenth century,[36] brought a diversity of values, beliefs, and patterns of behavior to American shores that frequently conflicted with prevailing cultures. Differences in languages and traditions fed the American melting pot of the late nineteenth and early twentieth centuries and made effective communication between groups difficult.

The face of multiculturalism in America today is quite different than it was in the past, due largely to relatively high birthrates among some minority populations and the significant but relatively recent immigration of Spanish-speaking people from Mexico, Cuba, Central America, and South America. Part of that influx consists of substantial numbers of undocumented immigrants who have entered the country illegally and who, because of experiences in their

---

**multiculturalism**

The existence within one society of diverse groups that maintain unique cultural identities while frequently accepting and participating in the larger society's legal and political systems.[vii] *Multiculturalism* is often used in conjunction with the term *diversity* to identify many distinctions of social significance.

---

***E Pluribus Unum* (Out of Many, One)**

## CJ NEWS

### Border Incident Angers Muslims

The Department of Homeland Security is examining the detentions and interrogations of dozens of Muslims who were stopped at border crossings in Upstate New York while returning to the United States from Canada in December 2004, said DHS spokeswoman Kristi Clemens.

The moves by the DHS's civil rights and inspector general's offices come after an emotional meeting in Buffalo between members of the local Muslim Public Affairs Council and Michael Battle, the U.S. attorney there.

Khalid Qazi, president of the Muslim group, said several Buffalo-area Muslims complained that they were unnecessarily held, fingerprinted and questioned by border agents for more than four hours. He said it was "degrading, humiliating and dishonorable."

The DHS inquiries will examine whether U.S. border agents incorrectly detained the Muslims by misusing a government database that is aimed at identifying potential terrorism suspects and violent gang members.

The list, which is kept by the FBI and is known as the Violent Gang and Terrorist Organization File (VGTOF), is part of a network of databases that have been compiled by U.S. agencies since the Sept. 11 attacks to monitor traffic at border crossings and airports.

The VGTOF list includes hundreds of names. It has been expanded during the past three years to include "associates" of suspected terrorists and gang leaders. The FBI acknowledges that in some cases, people have been flagged for increased scrutiny only because their names are similar to someone who has been targeted for surveillance, or because they unwittingly have had contact with the targets.

Under federal guidelines, such "associates" are not supposed to be detained or questioned. U.S. agents who come across them are merely supposed to make note of them as possible contacts in investigations.

But recently, the FBI has received complaints that people with no apparent links to terrorism or gangs are being held for hours with little or no explanation at border crossings in Buffalo and Niagara Falls, N.Y.

Clemens said that when the December detentions occurred, agents were acting on new intelligence reports that indicated crossings in the Buffalo area might be used by associates of potential terrorists to smuggle fake travel documents into the USA. Clemens said the reports also suggested the crossings could be used by those traveling to Canada to raise funds for terrorism.

The Buffalo area has been the focus of counterterrorism efforts before. In the past two years, six men from nearby Lackawanna who trained at an al-Qaeda camp pleaded guilty to

U.S. Customs and Border Protection agents patrol at the U.S.–Canadian border. In late 2004, several Muslims in the Buffalo, New York, area complained that they were unnecessarily detained, fingerprinted, and questioned by border agents.
*Photo by Charles Lewis,* The Buffalo News

providing material support to terrorists. They got prison terms of seven to 10 years.

Qazi, a Buffalo physician, said that as many as 50 members of the area's Muslim community were detained at the border in December. He said many were stopped while returning from a conference called Reviving the Islamic Spirit, held Dec. 25–26 in Toronto.

Karema Atassi said she was detained along with her husband, Tamer Osman, and 7-month-old son, Ismail. She said the three, all U.S. citizens, were held from 11:30 P.M. on Dec. 26 until 4:30 the next morning.

When they got to the border station, Atassi said, there were "25 to 30 Muslims" there, waiting to be processed. At one point, Atassi said, her husband was interrogated in a separate room.

"We all demanded why we were being held and what were they looking for," Atassi said in a written statement offered at last week's meeting. "No answer was ever given. Our only sin was being Muslim and attending (a convention) . . . about peace, unity and understanding."

Battle, the U.S. attorney, said that after the meeting he sought help from DHS. "We're very aware of the concerns," he said. "These were American citizens delayed at the border, and when they made inquiries about why, they weren't getting answers. We want to . . . bring closure to this."

For the latest in crime and justice news, visit the Talk Justice news feed at http://www.crimenews.info.

home countries, may have a special fear of police authority and a general distrust for the law. Such fears make members of this group hesitant to report being victimized, and their undocumented status makes them easy prey for illegal scams such as extortion, blackmail, and documentation crimes. Learn more about immigration and crime via Library Extra 1–4 at cjtoday.com.

Diversity characterizes both immigrant and U.S.-born individuals. U.S. Census Bureau statistics show that people identifying themselves as white account for 71% of the U.S. population—a percentage that has been dropping steadily for at least the past 40 years. People of Hispanic origin constitute approximately 12% of the population and are the fastest-growing group in the country. Individuals identifying themselves as African-American make up another 12% of the population, and people of Asian and Pacific Island origin make up almost 4% of the total. Native Americans, including American Indians, Eskimos, and Aleuts, account for slightly less than 1% of all Americans.[37] Statistics like these, however, are only estimates, and their interpretation is complicated by the fact that surveyed individuals may be of mixed race. Nonetheless, it is clear that American society today is ethnically and racially quite diverse.

*Race* and *ethnicity* are only buzzwords that people use when they talk about multiculturalism. After all, neither race nor ethnicity determines a person's values, attitudes, or behavior. Just as there is no uniquely identifiable "white culture" in American society, it is a mistake to think that all African-Americans share the same values or that everyone of Hispanic descent honors the same traditions or even speaks Spanish.

Multiculturalism, as the term is used today, is but one form of *diversity*. Taken together, these two concepts—multiculturalism and diversity—encompass many distinctions of social significance. The broad brush of contemporary multiculturalism and social diversity draws attention to variety along racial, ethnic, subcultural, generational, faith, economic, and gender lines. Lifestyle diversity is also important. The fact that influential elements of the wider society are less accepting of some lifestyles than others doesn't mean that such lifestyles aren't recognized from the viewpoint of multiculturalism. It simply means that at least for now, some lifestyles are accorded less official acceptability than others. As a result, certain lifestyle choices, even within a multicultural society that generally respects and encourages diversity, may still be criminalized, as in the case of polygamy.

Multiculturalism and diversity will be discussed in various chapters throughout this textbook. For now, it is sufficient to recognize that the diverse values, perspectives, and behaviors characteristic of various groups within our society have a significant impact on the justice system. Whether it is the confusion that arises from a police officer's commands to a non-English-speaking suspect, the need for interpreters in the courtroom, a deep-seated distrust of the police in some minority communities, a lack of willingness among some immigrants to report crime, the underrepresentation of women in criminal justice agencies, or some people's irrational suspicions of Arab-Americans after the September 11, 2001, attacks, diversity and multiculturalism present special challenges to the everyday practice of criminal justice in America. Finally, as we shall see, the demands and expectations placed on justice agencies in multicultural societies involve a dilemma that is closely associated with the theme of this text: how to respect important cultural differences and traditions while ensuring social control and the safety and security of the public.

LIBRARY EXTRA

America, known the world over as the land of the free, was founded on the principle of liberty and justice for all. . . . Yet, at the same time, some 2 million of our citizens are denied their freedom. . . . At some point we must ask ourselves: What is the moral price we pay as a nation for locking up our youth rather than lifting them up?

—Reverend Jesse L. Jackson, Sr.[viii]

Without security, government cannot deliver, nor can the people enjoy, the prosperity and opportunities that flow from freedom and democracy.

—U.S. Attorney General Alberto Gonzales[ix]

## SUMMARY

In this chapter, we described the process of American criminal justice as a system with three major components: police, courts, and corrections. As we warned, however, a systems viewpoint is useful primarily for the simplification that it provides. A more realistic approach to understanding criminal justice may be the nonsystem approach. As a nonsystem, criminal justice is depicted as a fragmented activity in which individuals and agencies within the process have interests and goals that at times coincide but often conflict.

Defendants processed by the justice system come into contact with numerous workers whose duty it is to enforce the law but who also have a stake in the agencies employing them and who hold their own personal interests and values. As defendants wend their way through the system, they may be held accountable to the law, but in the process they will also be buf-

It is commonly assumed that these three components—law enforcement (police, sheriffs, marshals), the judicial process (judges, prosecutors, defense lawyers), and corrections (prison officials, probation, and parole officers)—add up to a "system" of criminal justice. A system implies some unity of purpose and organized interrelationship among component parts. In the typical American city and state, and under federal jurisdiction as well, no such relationship exists. There is, instead, a reasonably well-defined criminal process, a continuum through which each accused offender may pass: from the hands of the police, to the jurisdiction of the courts, behind the walls of a prison, then back onto the street.

—National Commission on the Causes and Prevention of Violence

feted by the personal whims of "officials" as well as by the practical needs of the system itself. A complete view of American criminal justice must recognize that the final outcome of any encounter with the criminal justice system will be a consequence not just of decisions made at the legislative level, but of the day-to-day activities undertaken by everyone in the system. Hence, the quality of justice is determined just as much by pressures on the system as by idealistic notions of right and wrong.

Multiculturalism, an idea that was introduced near the end of this chapter, complicates the practice of American criminal justice still further since there is rarely universal agreement in our society about what is right or wrong or about what constitutes "justice."

An alternative way of viewing the practice of criminal justice is in terms of its two goals: crime control and due process. The crime-control perspective urges rapid and effective enforcement of the law and calls for the stiff punishment of lawbreakers. Due process, on the other hand, requires a recognition of the defendant's rights and holds the agents of justice accountable for any actions that might contravene those rights. The goals of crime control and due process often conflict, and some people may consider them mutually exclusive. As we describe the agencies of justice in the chapters that follow, the goals of crime control and due process will appear again and again. They will often be phrased in terms of the theme of this book, which contrasts the need to balance the rights of individuals against other valid social interests, especially the need for public order.

Our central theme is represented by two opposing groups: individual-rights advocates and public-order advocates. As we shall see, the fundamental challenge facing the practice of American criminal justice is achieving efficient enforcement of the laws while recognizing and supporting the legal rights of suspects and the legitimate personal differences and prerogatives of individuals. This goal is made all the more difficult by changing social values and by rapid advances in the kinds of technology available to criminals. Nonetheless, the American mandate of crime control through due process ensures that criminal justice will remain an exciting and ever-evolving undertaking well into the twenty-first century and beyond.

## DISCUSSION QUESTIONS

1. What is the theme on which this textbook builds? How does the theme facilitate the study of criminal justice?

2. Describe the individual-rights and public-order perspectives. What are the central features of each? How do they differ?

3. Why is public order necessary? Do we have enough public order or too little? How can we tell? What might a large, complex society like ours be like without laws and without a system of criminal justice? Would you want to live in such a society? Why or why not?

4. What must we, as individuals, sacrifice to facilitate public order? Do we ever give up too much in the interest of public order? If so, when?

5. What is justice? What aspects of justice does this chapter discuss? How does criminal justice relate to social justice and to other wider notions of equity and fairness?

6. What are the main components of the criminal justice system? How do they interrelate? How might they conflict?

7. This chapter describes two models of the criminal justice system. What are they, and how do they differ? Which model do you think is more useful? Which is more accurate? Why?

8. List the stages of case processing that characterize the American system of criminal justice, and describe each stage.

**9.** What is meant by "due process of law"? Where in the American legal system are guarantees of due process found?

**10.** What is multiculturalism? What is social diversity? What impact do multiculturalism and diversity have on the practice of criminal justice in contemporary American society?

Familiarize yourself with the *Criminal Justice Today* Companion Website and with its many features. To get there, point your browser to http://www.cjtoday.com. Once you've opened the site, you'll be able to read the latest crime and justice news, join the *Criminal Justice Today* e-mail discussion list, and research a wide variety of criminal justice topics. You can learn about your textbook's chapter objectives, practice with online review questions, preview chapter summaries, submit electronic homework to your instructor, and enjoy many Web-based criminal justice projects. (If your instructor decides to use the electronic homework feature of the site, it's always a good idea to keep a copy of any materials that you submit.) The site also allows you to listen to the author introduce each chapter.

Unique Web Extras and book-specific Library Extras substantially enhance the learning opportunities your text offers. Web Extras bring the justice system to life by providing a wealth of links to relevant and informative sites. Library Extras help you learn more about important topics in the justice field via the textbook's electronic library. Library Extras include the latest reports and bulletins from the Bureau of Justice Statistics, the National Institute of Justice, the Bureau of Justice Assistance, the FBI, the Department of Homeland Security, and other agencies. Each report has been selected by the author to complement the textbook and to enhance your learning experience.

One Web resource of special importance is the Prentice Hall Criminal Justice Cybrary (*Cybrary* means "cyber-library"). Known to justice professionals as "the world's crime and justice directory," the Cybrary contains annotated links to more than 12,000 crime and justice sites throughout the nation and around the world. Because it is continually updated and fully searchable, the Cybrary can be an invaluable tool as you write term papers or do Web-based research on crime and justice. You can reach the Cybrary directly by going to http://www.cybrary.info.

Another important Web-based resource is Prentice Hall's Research Navigator™. Research Navigator, which can be found on the Web at http://www.researchnavigator.com, provides an easy way to research an assignment or term paper topic. Complete with extensive help on the research process and three comprehensive databases of credible and reliable source material (the EBSCO Academic Journal and Abstract Database, the *New York Times* Search by Subject Archive, and the "Best of the Web" Link Library), Research Navigator helps users quickly and efficiently make the most of their research time. If your instructor has selected Research Navigator for use with your textbook, you should have received a copy of *The Prentice Hall Guide to Evaluating On-line Resources with Research Navigator: Criminal Justice.* Before you can begin exploring the Research Navigator site, you must register using your personal Research Navigator access code, which is printed in the guide.

To complete this Web Quest online, go to the Web Quest module in Chapter 1 of the *Criminal Justice Today* Companion Website at cjtoday.com.

**NOTES**

**i.** ABC News, September 16, 2001, 7:08 P.M.

**ii.** Quoted in Charles E. Silberman, *Criminal Violence, Criminal Justice* (New York: Random House, 1978), p. 12.

**iii.** Quoted in *Criminal Justice Newsletter,* September 16, 1997, p. 1.

**iv.** ABC News, September 11, 2001.

**v.** Adapted from U.S. Code, Title 28, Section 20.3 (2[d]). Title 28 of the U.S. Code defines the term *administration of criminal justice.*

**vi.** Philip B. Kurland, "Robert H. Jackson," in Leon Friedman and Fred L. Israel, eds., *The Justices of the United States Supreme Court 1789–1969: Their Lives and Major Opinions,* Vol. 4 (New York: Chelsea House, 1969), p. 2565.

vii. Adapted from Robert M. Shusta et al., *Multicultural Law Enforcement,* 2d ed. (Upper Saddle River, NJ: Prentice Hall, 2002), p. 443.

viii. Reverend Jesse L. Jackson, Sr., "Liberty and Justice for Some: Mass Incarceration Comes at a Moral Cost to Every American," July 10, 2001. Web posted at http://www.motherjones .com/prisons/print_liberty.html (accessed January 22, 2002).

ix. Prepared remarks of U.S. Attorney General Alberto Gonzales, Address to the National Association of Counties Legislative Conference, Washington, D.C., March 7, 2005.

1. American Civil Liberties Union website, http://www.aclu.org/issues/criminal/iscj.html (accessed January 22, 2002).

2. ABC News, September 11, 2001. Christopher was repeating a phrase generally attributed to former U.S. Supreme Court Justice Arthur Goldberg.

3. John M. Broder and Nick Madigan, "Michael Jackson Cleared after 14-Week Child Molesting Trial," *The New York Times,* June 14, 2005, p. 1A.

4. "Jackson Website Hails Verdict," *USA Today,* June 14, 2005, p. 1A.

5. For a thorough discussion of immigration as it relates to crime, see Ramiro Martinez, Jr., and Matthew T. Lee, "On Immigration and Crime," in National Institute of Justice, *Criminal Justice 2000, Volume 1: The Nature of Crime— Continuity and Change* (Washington, DC: U.S. Department of Justice, Office of Justice Programs, 2000).

6. "Cries of Relief," *Time,* April 26, 1993, p. 18; and "King II: What Made the Difference?" *Newsweek,* April 26, 1993, p. 26.

7. "Inside Columbine," *The Rocky Mountain News.* Web posted at http://www. rockymountainnews.com/drmn/columbine (accessed July 4, 2005).

8. "Cries of Relief."

9. Public Law 107–56.

10. Laurence McQuillan, "Bush to Urge Jail for Execs Who Lie," *USA Today,* July 9, 2002. Web posted at http://www.usatoday.com/news/ washdc/2002/07/09/bush-business.htm (accessed July 9, 2002).

11. Sarbanes-Oxley Act of 2002 (officially known as the Public Company Accounting Reform and Investor Protection Act), Pub. L. 107–204, 116 Stat. 745 (July 30, 2002).

12. PricewaterhouseCoopers, "The Sarbanes-Oxley Act." Web posted at http://www.pwcglobal .com/Extweb/NewCoAtWork.nsf/docid/ D0D7F79003C6D64485256CF30074D66C (accessed July 8, 2005).

13. Ibid.

14. George W. Bush, "Presidential Address to the Nation," September 20, 2001.

15. *The American Heritage Dictionary on CD-ROM* (Boston: Houghton Mifflin, 1991).

16. For a good overview of the issues involved, see Judge Harold J. Rothwax, *Guilty: The Collapse of Criminal Justice* (New York: Random House, 1996).

17. For one perspective on the detention of Muslims following September 11, 2001, see the plaintiff's motion to stay proceedings on defendant's summary judgment motion pending discovery, in *Center for National Security Studies* v. *U.S. Department of Justice,* U.S. District Court for the District of Columbia (Civil Action No. 01–2500; January 2002). Web posted at http://www.aclu.org/ court/ cnssjan22.pdf (accessed September 24, 2005).

18. The systems model of criminal justice is often attributed to the frequent use of the term *system* by the 1967 Presidential Commission in its report *The Challenge of Crime in a Free Society* (Washington, DC: U.S. Government Printing Office, 1967).

19. One of the first published works to use the nonsystem approach to criminal justice was the American Bar Association's *New Perspective on Urban Crime* (Washington, DC: ABA Special Committee on Crime Prevention and Control, 1972).

20. Jerome H. Skolnick, *Justice without Trial* (New York: John Wiley, 1966), p. 179.

21. *Miranda* v. *Arizona,* 384 U.S. 436, 16 L.Ed.2d 694, 86 S.Ct. 1602 (1966).

22. North Carolina Justice Academy, *Miranda Warning Card* (Salemburg, NC).

23. John M. Scheb and John M. Scheb II, *American Criminal Law* (St. Paul, MN: West, 1996), p. 32.

24. Federal Rules of Criminal Procedure, 10.

25. *Blanton* v. *City of North Las Vegas,* 489 U.S. 538, 103 L.Ed.2d 550, 109 S.Ct. 1289 (1989).

26. Ibid.

27. *U.S.* v. *Nachtigal,* 122 L.Ed.2d 374, 113 S.Ct. 1072, 1073 (1993), *per curiam.*

28. Barbara Borland and Ronald Sones, *Prosecution of Felony Arrests* (Washington, DC: Bureau of Justice Statistics, 1991).

29. "The Defendants' Rights at a Criminal Trial." Web posted at http://www.mycounsel.com/ content/arrests/court/rights.html (accessed February 10, 2005).

30. For a complete and now-classic analysis of the impact of decisions made by the Warren Court, see Fred P. Graham, *The Due Process Revolution: The Warren Court's Impact on Criminal Law* (New York: Hayden Press, 1970).

31. *Gideon* v. *Wainwright,* 372 U.S. 353 (1963).

32. Herbert Packer, *The Limits of the Criminal Sanction* (Stanford, CA: Stanford University Press, 1968).

33. For an excellent history of policing in the United States, see Edward A. Farris, "Five Decades of American Policing: 1932–1982," *Police Chief* (November 1982), pp. 30–36.

34. Gene Edward Carte, "August Vollmer and the Origins of Police Professionalism," *Journal of Police Science and Administration,* Vol. 1, No. 1 (1973), pp. 274–281.

35. See Patrick O'Driscoll, "Utah Steps Up Prosecutions of Polygamists," *USA Today,* May 14, 2001, p. 5A, from which some of the wording in this paragraph is adapted.

36. On March 22, 1794, the U.S. Congress barred American citizens from transporting slaves from the United States to another nation or between foreign nations. On January 1, 1808, the importation of slaves into the United States became illegal, and Congress charged the U.S. Revenue Cutter Service (now known as the U.S. Coast Guard) with enforcing the law on the high seas. Although some slave ships were seized, the importation of Africans for sale as slaves apparently continued in some southern states until the early 1860s. See U.S. Coast Guard, "U.S. Coast Guard in Illegal Immigration (1794–1971)." Web posted at http://www.uscg.mil/hq/g-o/g-opl/mle/ amiohist.htm (accessed October 13, 2004).

37. U.S. Census Bureau website at http://www.census.gov (accessed March 22, 2005). Population statistics are estimates because race is a difficult concept to define, and Census Bureau interviewers allow individuals to choose more than one race when completing census forms.

# CHAPTER 2

# The Crime Picture

## OUTLINE

- Introduction
- The Uniform Crime Reports
- The National Crime Victimization Survey
- Comparisons of the UCR and the NCVS
- Special Categories of Crime

## LEARNING OBJECTIVES

After reading this chapter, you should be able to:

- Name and compare the two major national crime data–gathering programs in the United States today.
- Explain what crime statistics can tell us about crime in America.
- Discuss some of the limitations inherent in statistical reports of crime.
- Describe the FBI's Crime Index, and list the eight major crimes that make up the index.
- Explain why crime statistics are generally expressed as rates instead of simple numerical tabulations.
- Describe the two major categories of Part I offenses in the Uniform Crime Reports.
- Explain the hierarchy rule, and discuss how it affects crime reporting.
- Discuss the meaning of the term *clearance rate.*
- Explain how the National Incident-Based Reporting System operates, and describe how it differs from the traditional Uniform Crime Reporting Program.
- Identify the special categories of crime discussed in this chapter.

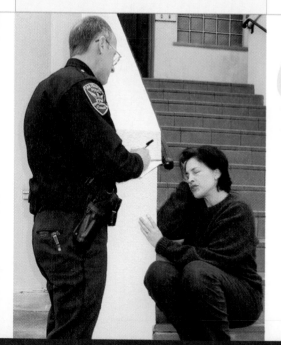

*It may turn out that a free society cannot really prevent crime. Perhaps its causes are locked so deeply into the human personality, the intimate processes of family life, and the subtlest aspects of the popular culture that coping is the best that we can hope for.*

—James Q. Wilson, University of California, Los Angeles[1]

*No one way of describing crime describes it well enough.*
—President's Commission on Law Enforcement
and Administration of Justice

# KEY CONCEPTS

## TERMS

| | | |
|---|---|---|
| aggravated assault | date rape | Part II offenses |
| arson | forcible rape | property crime |
| assault | hate crime | rape |
| Bureau of Justice Statistics (BJS) | identity theft | robbery |
| burglary | larceny-theft | sexual battery |
| clearance rate | motor vehicle theft | stalking |
| computer crime | murder | transnational organized crime |
| corporate crime | National Crime Victimization Survey (NCVS) | Uniform Crime Reports (UCR) |
| Crime Index | National Incident-Based Reporting | violent crime |
| crime typology | System (NIBRS) | white-collar crime |
| cyberstalking | organized crime | |
| dark figure of crime | Part I offenses | |

# Introduction

Hear the author discuss
this chapter at
**cjtoday.com**

According to broadcast ratings guru *MediaWeek,* the most popular show on television today is the CBS crime drama *CSI: Crime Scene Investigation.*[2] The series' top ranking would seem to be no small feat for a "cop show" that has to compete with the likes of widely watched offerings such as *American Idol, Desperate Housewives, ER, Survivor,* and *Lost.* Until, that is, one realizes that the American public is fascinated with hard-hitting crime dramas. And that helps to explain the success of shows like the *CSI* spin-offs, *CSI: Miami* and *CSI: New York,* as well as to explain why the NBC-TV show *Law and Order* is the longest-running drama on television today. Like *CSI,* the *Law and Order* series has generated its own spin-offs, including *Law and Order: Criminal Intent* and *Law and Order: Special Victims' Unit.* Some other crime and justice shows on TV today include *Blind Justice* (ABC), *Cold Case* (CBS), *The District* (CBS), *Numb3rs* (CBS), *Hack* (CBS), *JAG* (CBS), *NCIS* (CBS), *The Shield* (FX), *The Wire* (HBO), *Wanted* (TNT), and *Without a Trace* (CBS). Like this textbook, many of today's television shows deliver content across a variety of media. View the on-line CSI crime labs at Web Extra 2–1 and see some real-life crime prevention links sponsored by *Law and Order: SVU* at Web Extra 2–2. Visit a real cold case squad via Web Extra 2–3.

This chapter has a dual purpose. First, it provides a statistical overview of crime in contemporary America by examining information on reported and discovered crimes. Second, it identifies special categories of crime that are of particular interest today, including crimes against women, crimes against the elderly, hate crimes, corporate and white-collar crime, organized crime, gun crime, drug crime, high-technology and computer crime, and terrorism.

Although we will look at many crime statistics in this chapter, it is important to remember that statistical aggregates of reported crime, whatever their source, do not reveal the lost lives, human suffering, lessened productivity, and reduced quality of life that crime causes. Unlike the fictional characters on TV crime shows, real-life crime victims as well as real-life offenders lead intricate lives—they have families, hold jobs, and dream dreams. As we examine the crime statistics, we must not lose sight of the people behind the numbers.

We can have as much or as little
crime as we please; depending
on what we choose to count as
criminal.

—Herbert L. Packer

# Crime Data and Social Policy

Crime statistics provide an overview of criminal activity. If used properly, a statistical picture of crime can serve as a powerful tool for creating social policy. Decision makers at all levels, including legislators, other elected officials, and administrators throughout the criminal justice system, rely on crime data to analyze and evaluate existing programs, to fashion and design new crime-control initiatives, to develop funding requests, and to plan new laws and crime-control legislation. Many "get tough" policies, such as the three-strikes movement that swept the country during the 1990s, have been based in large part on the measured ineffectiveness of existing programs to reduce the incidence of repeat offending.

However, some people question just how objective—and therefore how useful—crime statistics are. Social events, including crime, are complex and difficult to quantify. Even the decision

The cast of the NBC-TV show *CSI*. The American public has long been enthralled with crime shows, and since the terrorist attacks of 2001, the public's concern with personal safety has surged.

*CBS, Landov LLC*

of which crimes should be included and which excluded in statistical reports is itself a judgment reflecting the interests and biases of policymakers. Moreover, public opinion about crime is not always realistic. As well-known criminologist Norval Morris points out, the news media do more to influence public perceptions of crime than any official data do.[3] During a four-year period (in the mid-1990s) covered by Morris's study, for example, the frequency of crime stories reported in the national media increased fourfold. During the same time period, crime was at the top of the list in subject matter covered in news stories at both the local and national levels. The irony, says Morris, is that "the grossly increasing preoccupation with crime stories came at a time of steadily declining crime and violence." However, as Morris adds, "aided and abetted by this flood of misinformation, the politicians, federal and state and local, fostered the view that the public demands our present 'get tough' policies."

## The Collection of Crime Data

Nationally, crime statistics come from two major sources: (1) the Uniform Crime Reporting Program of the Federal Bureau of Investigation (FBI), which produces the **Uniform Crime Reports** (known simply as the **UCR**, but also referred to by its official subtitle, *Crime in the United States*); and (2) the **National Crime Victimization Survey (NCVS)** of the **Bureau of Justice Statistics (BJS)**. The most widely quoted numbers purporting to describe crime in America today probably come from the UCR, the statistics of which are based on reports to the police by victims of crime.

A third source of crime data is offender self-reports based on surveys that ask respondents to reveal any illegal activity in which they have been involved. Offender self-reports are not discussed in detail in this chapter because surveys utilizing them are not national in scope. Moreover, offenders are often reluctant to accurately report ongoing or recent criminal involvement, making information derived from these surveys somewhat unreliable and less than current. However, the available information from offender self-reports reveals that serious criminal activity is considerably more widespread than most "official" surveys show (Figure 2–1).

Finally, other regular publications contribute to our knowledge of crime patterns throughout the nation. The *Sourcebook of Criminal Justice Statistics* is an annual compilation of national information on crime and on the criminal justice system. The *Sourcebook* is published by the BJS,

**Uniform Crime Reports (UCR)**

An annual FBI publication that summarizes the incidence and rate of reported crimes throughout the United States.

**National Crime Victimization Survey (NCVS)**

An annual survey of selected American households conducted by the Bureau of Justice Statistics to determine the extent of criminal victimization—especially unreported victimization—in the United States.

**Bureau of Justice Statistics (BJS)**

A U.S. Department of Justice agency responsible for the collection of criminal justice data, including the annual National Crime Victimization Survey.

**FIGURE 2–1**

**The criminal justice funnel.**

*Source:* Derived from Gerard Rainville and Brian Reaves, *Felony Defendants in Large Urban Countries, 2000* (Washington, DC: Bureau of Justice Statistics, 2003).

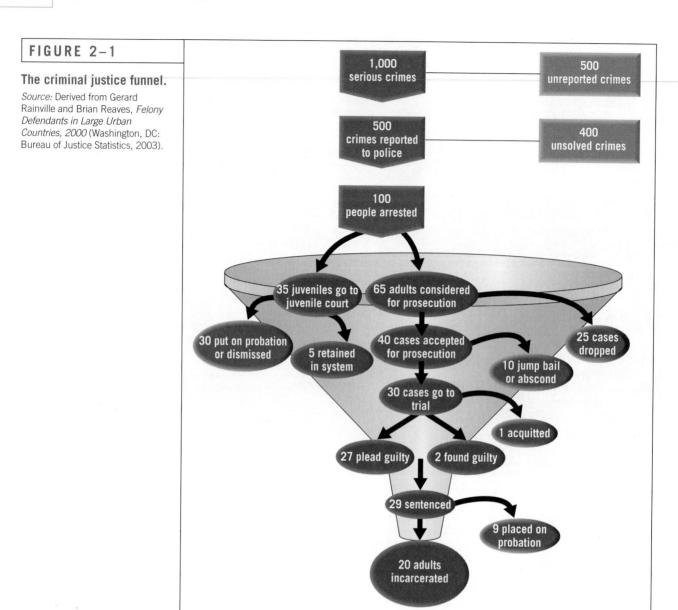

and a Web-based version of the *Sourcebook* is continually updated as data become available. The National Institute of Justice (NIJ), which is the primary research arm of the U.S. Department of Justice, the Office of Juvenile Justice and Delinquency Prevention (OJJDP), the Federal Justice Statistics Resource Center, and the National Victim's Resource Center provide still more information on crime patterns. Visit Web Extra 2–4 at cjtoday.com for an overview of the many sources of crime data. See Library Extra 2–1 at cjtoday.com to learn more about the measurement and analysis of crime.

# The Uniform Crime Reports
## Development of the UCR Program

In 1930, Congress authorized the U.S. attorney general to survey crime in America, and the FBI was designated to implement the program. In short order, the bureau built on earlier efforts by the International Association of Chiefs of Police (IACP) to create a national system of uniform crime statistics. As a practical measure, IACP had recommended the use of readily available information, and so it was that citizens' crime reports to the police became the basis of the FBI's plan.[4]

## Lost Police Reports Hint at Problems

Not accounting for 22,000 crimes can definitely improve a city's crime rate.

That was the case in Atlanta, where police recently revealed they were missing that many crime reports from a single year.

While the underreporting shocked many civilians, it was no surprise for those in law enforcement, who are well aware that agencies across the country lose or alter crime reports to burnish their widely reported crime statistics.

In New York, a police captain was accused of routinely downgrading crime reports so he'd look good in the eyes of his superiors. Philadelphia's Sex Crimes Unit dismissed as non-crimes several thousand reports of rape in 1999. And in Baltimore, an information technology worker quit in December over claims the city's crime reporting was wildly inaccurate.

"It's been a chronic problem," said Samuel Walker, a criminal justice professor at the University of Nebraska at Omaha who runs the Web site www.policeaccountability.org. "But then again, no one knows exactly how serious it is. There's no real accounting, no real auditing."

Police and experts say crime rates never are all that accurate, since the job of crime reporting is mostly left to the police themselves—and police are under constant pressure to show crime rates are dropping.

Even the FBI's national crime reports are known to be only vaguely accurate, since they too rely on reports from police.

"Criminologists have known for years that crime statistics are not reliable," said Robert Friedmann, a criminal justice professor at Georgia State University.

The problem, Friedmann said, can be caused by pressure from politicians who want to put a good face on crime, or by officers who fear for their jobs. The solution may involve more independent assessments like Atlanta's.

For the most part, the public would only find out if crimes are being downgraded—or if incidents are tucked into a dark corner—when there's a scandal.

The exception is a department such as Atlanta's, which ordered an independent audit to come clean on its misreporting problem. Only a few other cities—including Boston and New Orleans—have done the same.

Atlanta's audit said the city underreported crimes for years to help land the 1996 Olympics and pump up tourism. In 2002 alone, there were more than 22,000 missing police reports, 4,281 of which could have been counted as violent offenses.

Despite the distorted figures, Atlanta ranked No. 1 or No. 2 in violent crimes such as rape and murder in nine of the last 10 years, according to FBI crime data, which is compiled from reports submitted by police departments.

"Soon after coming here, I discovered that the systems and practice of the Atlanta police department were essentially broken," Chief Richard Pennington said in the audit.

Pennington has proposed a number of reforms, including accounting for crimes from the time a 911 call is made.

In Broward County, Fla., which includes Fort Lauderdale, the state attorney's office is investigating reports that deputies cooked crime statistics so evaluations of the department would go more smoothly.

"Crimes are reclassified every day. If someone has a broken window, they may dial 911 and say their house was robbed. It may turn out it was a burglary, perhaps it was criminal mischief," said sheriff's spokesman Jim Leljedal.

Sometimes, as in Baltimore's case, the crime statistics were simply miscategorized, said police spokesman Matt Jablow.

"In no case did we find that any allegations of rape were uninvestigated," Jablow said. "No one came forward and said, 'No one investigated my rape.'"

So crime reporting often comes down to the integrity and ethics of police officers.

In New York, 70 sergeants rallied in front of a Queens station house with a 15-foot inflatable rat this month as they demanded the ouster of Capt. Sheldon Howard, who they say reduces the severity of crimes so his statistics look better than they are.

"If Howard's numbers are good, he doesn't get called up and he looks like a star," said Sergeants Benevolent Association President Ed Mullins. "It's a regular pattern and practice that exists in that precinct."

New York police spokeswoman Chris Filipazzo would not comment because of an ongoing investigation.

In Atlanta, meanwhile, police believe the audit may have overstated its case. The accounting of the problem could have been exaggerated because crimes get repeatedly recategorized in different computers, said Sgt. John Quigley.

"If there were a lot of reports missing, I would have thought letters to the editor would have reflected the frustration of the citizenry," he said.

For the latest in crime and justice news, visit the Talk Justice news feed at http://www.crimenews.info.

During its first year of operation, the FBI's Uniform Crime Reporting Program received reports from 400 cities in 43 states. Twenty million people were covered by that first comprehensive survey. Today, approximately 16,000 law enforcement agencies provide crime information for the program, with data coming from city, county, and state departments. To ensure uniformity in reporting, the FBI has developed standardized definitions of offenses and terminologies used in the program. A number of publications, including the *Uniform Crime Reporting Handbook* and the *Manual of Law Enforcement Records,* are supplied to participating agencies, and training for effective reporting is available through FBI-sponsored seminars and instructional literature.

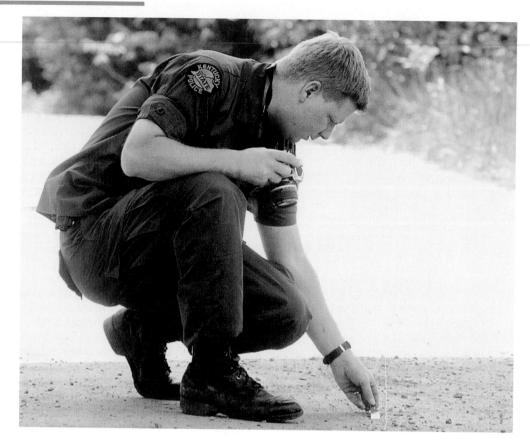

A Kentucky State Police photographer recording a crime scene. Uniform Crime Reports (UCR) data become statistics when crimes are reported or discovered.

*AP Wide World Photos*

### Crime Index

An inclusive measure of the violent and property crime categories, or Part I offenses, of the Uniform Crime Reports. The Crime Index has been a useful tool for geographic (state-to-state) and historical (year-to-year) comparisons because it employs the concept of a crime rate (the number of crimes per unit of population). However, the addition of arson as an eighth index offense and the new requirements with regard to the gathering of hate-crime statistics could result in new Crime Index measurements that provide less-than-ideal comparisons.

Crime is like cutting grass. Just because you cut it down doesn't mean it's going to stay there.

—Senator Joseph R. Biden, Jr. (D—Delaware)[i]

Following IACP recommendations, the original UCR Program was designed to permit comparisons over time through construction of a **Crime Index**. The index summed the occurrences of seven major offenses—murder, forcible rape, robbery, aggravated assault, burglary, larceny-theft, and motor vehicle theft—and expressed the result as a crime rate based on population. In 1979, by congressional mandate, an eighth offense—arson—was added to the index. Although UCR categories today parallel statutory definitions of criminal behavior, they are not legal classifications, only conveniences created for statistical-reporting purposes. Because many of the definitions of crime used in this textbook are derived from official UCR terminology, it is important to remember that UCR terminology may differ from statutory definitions of crime.

## Historical Trends

Most UCR information is reported as a rate of crime. Rates are computed as the number of crimes *per* some unit of population. National reports generally make use of large units of population, such as 100,000 people. Hence, the rate of rape reported by the UCR for 2004 was 32.2 forcible rapes per every 100,000 inhabitants of the United States.[5] Rates allow for a meaningful comparison over areas and across time. The rate of reported rape for 1960, for example, was only about 10 per 100,000. We expect the number of crimes to increase as population grows, but rate increases are cause for concern because they indicate that reports of crime are increasing faster than the population is growing. Rates, however, require interpretation. Since the FBI definition of rape includes only female victims, for example, the rate of victimization might be more meaningfully expressed in terms of every 100,000 female inhabitants. Similarly, although there is a tendency to judge an individual's risk of victimization based on rates, such judgments tend to be inaccurate since they are based purely on averages and do not take into consideration individual life circumstances, such as place of residence, wealth, and educational level. While rates may tell us about aggregate conditions and trends, we must be very careful when applying them to individual cases.

Since the UCR Program began, there have been three major shifts in crime rates—and we now seem to be witnessing the beginning of a fourth. The first occurred during the early 1940s, when crime decreased sharply due to the large number of young men who entered military service during World War II. Young males make up the most "crime-prone" segment of the population, and their deployment overseas did much to lower crime rates at home. From 1933 to 1941, the Crime Index declined from 770 to 508 offenses per every 100,000 members of the American population.[6]

The second noteworthy shift in offense statistics was a dramatic increase in most forms of crime between 1960 and the early 1990s. Several factors contributed to the increase in reported crime during this period. One was also linked to World War II. With the end of the war and the return of millions of young men to civilian life, birthrates skyrocketed between 1945 and 1955, creating a postwar baby boom. By 1960, the first baby boomers were teenagers—and had entered a crime-prone age. This disproportionate number of young people produced a dramatic increase in most major crimes.

Other factors contributed to the increase in reported crime during the same period. Modified reporting requirements made it less stressful for victims to file police reports, and the publicity associated with the rise in crime sensitized victims to the importance of reporting. Crimes that might have gone undetected in the past began to figure more prominently in official statistics. Similarly, the growing professionalization of some police departments resulted in greater and more accurate data collection, making some of the most progressive departments appear to be associated with the largest crime increases.[7]

The 1960s were tumultuous years. The Vietnam War, a vibrant civil rights struggle, the heady growth of secularism, a dramatic increase in the divorce rate, diverse forms of "liberation," and the influx of psychedelic and other drugs all combined to fragment existing institutions. Social norms were blurred, and group control over individual behavior declined substantially. The "normless" quality of American society in the 1960s contributed greatly to the rise in crime.

From 1960 to 1980, crime rates rose from 1,887 to 5,950 offenses per every 100,000 U.S. residents. In the early 1980s when postwar boomers began to age out of the crime-prone years and American society emerged from the cultural drift that had characterized the previous 20 years, crime rates leveled out briefly. Soon, however, an increase in drug-related criminal activity led crime rates—especially violent crime rates—to soar once again. Crime rates peaked during the early 1990s.

A third major shift came with the significant declines in the rate of most major crimes being reported between 1991 and 2004. During these years, the Crime Index dropped from 5,897 to 3,982 offenses per every 100,000 residents—sending it down to levels not seen since 1975. The U.S. Department of Justice suggests various reasons for the decline, including[8]

- A coordinated, collaborative, and well-funded national effort to combat crime, beginning with the Safe Streets Act of 1968 and continuing through the USA PATRIOT Act of 2001

- Stronger, better-prepared criminal justice agencies, resulting from increased spending by federal and state governments on crime-control programs

- Growth in the popularity of innovative police programs, such as community policing (discussed in detail in Chapter 6)

- An aggressive approach to gun control, including the Brady Handgun Violence Prevention Act (discussed later in this chapter)

- A strong victims' movement and enactment of the 1984 federal Victims of Crime Act (see Chapter 11) and the 1994 Violence Against Women Act (discussed later in this chapter), which established the Office for Victims of Crime in the U.S. Department of Justice

- Sentencing reform, including various "get tough on crime" initiatives (see Chapter 11)

- A substantial growth in the use of incarceration (see Chapter 13) due to changes in sentencing law practice (see Chapter 11)

- The "war on drugs," begun in the 1970s,[9] which resulted in stiff penalties for drug dealers and repeat drug offenders

- Increased use of the death penalty (see Chapter 11)

- Advances in forensic science and enforcement technology, including the increased use of real-time communications, the growth of the Internet, and the advent of DNA evidence (see Chapter 11)

More important than new strict laws, an expanded justice system and police funding, or changes in crime-fighting technologies, however, may have been influential economic and demographic factors that were largely beyond the control of policymakers but that combined to produce substantial decreases in rates of crime—including economic expansion and a significant shift in demographics caused by an aging of the population. During the 1990s, unemployment decreased by 36% in the United States, while the number of people aged 20 to 34 declined by 18%.

> The great 1990s crime drop ended with the 1990s. The new millennium brings a different picture.
>
> —James Alan Fox, Northeastern University[ii]

## FIGURE 2-2

**Actual and projected rates of crime in the United States per 100,000 inhabitants, 1950–2010.**

*Source:* Federal Bureau of Investigation, *Uniform Crime Reports: Crime in the United States* (Washington, DC: U.S. Government Printing Office, various years); and James Alan Fox, *Trends in Juvenile Violence: A Report to the United States Attorney General on Current and Future Rates of Offending* (Washington, DC: Bureau of Justice Statistics, 1996).

Hence, it may have been the ready availability of jobs combined with demographic shifts in the population—not the official efforts of policymakers—that produced a noteworthy decrease in crime during the 1990s. Read noted criminologist Alfred Blumstein's analysis of crime's decline in Library Extra 2–2 at cjtoday.com to learn more about why crime rates fell during the 1990s.

A fourth shift in crime trends may be starting now. Some think that recent economic uncertainty, an increased jobless rate among unskilled workers, the growing number of ex-convicts who are now back on the streets, the recent growth in the teenage population in this country, and the lingering social disorganization brought on by natural disasters like Hurricane Katrina in 2005, may lead to sustained increases in crime.[10] "We're probably done seeing declines in crime rates for some time to come," says Jack Riley, director of the Public Safety and Justice Program at RAND Corporation in Santa Monica, California. "The question," says Riley, "is how strong and how fast will those rates [rise], and what tools do we have at our disposal to get ahead of the curve."[11] Some authorities forecast a crime wave that will peak around 2010.[12] Figure 2–2 shows historical rates of crime and projected rates through the end of this decade.

## UCR Terminology

Figure 2–3 shows the FBI crime clock, which is calculated yearly as a shorthand way of diagramming crime frequency in the United States. Note that crime clock data imply a regularity to crime that, in reality, does not exist.[13] Also, although the crime clock is a useful diagrammatic tool, it is not a rate-based measure of criminal activity and does not allow easy comparisons over

# FREEDOM OR SAFETY? YOU DECIDE.

### A Dress Code for Bank Customers?

Dark glasses, a hooded sweatshirt, and a hat have been called the "uniform of choice" for bank robbers. In July 2002, in an effort to thwart a dramatic increase in robberies, some Massachusetts banks began posting requests for customers to remove hats, hoods, and sunglasses before entering financial establishments.

Not all banks, however, posted the signs. "I think what you have to weigh is convenience to customers versus the added benefits in terms of identifying suspects with a measure like this," said Melodie Jackson, spokeswoman for Citizens Bank of Massachusetts. "We're taking a very close look at things."

Banks in other parts of the country soon followed suit. By October 2002, 26 banks and credit unions with 141 locations in and around Springfield, Missouri, had posted signs asking visitors to remove sunglasses, hats, and anything that might hide their faces.

**YOU DECIDE**

Are bank "dress codes" asking too much of customers? How would you feel about doing business with a bank that posts requests like those described here?

*References:* Michael S. Rosenwald and Emily Ramshaw, "Banks Post Dress Code to Deter Robbers," *Boston Globe,* July 13, 2002; and "Missouri Banks Attempt Unmasking Robbers," *Police Magazine* online, October 25, 2002, Web posted at http://www.policemag.com/t_newspick.cfm?rank=71952.

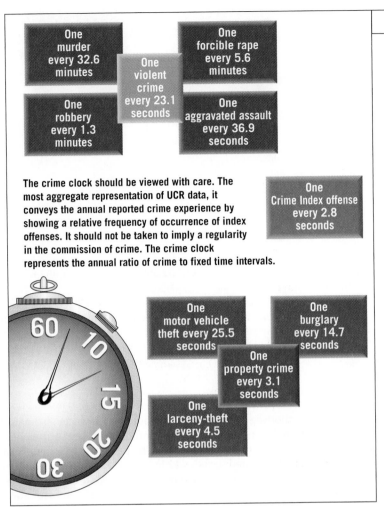

**FIGURE 2–3**

**The FBI crime clock, which shows the frequency of major crime commission in 2004.**

*Source:* Adapted from Federal Bureau of Investigation, *Uniform Crime Reports: Crime in the United States, 2004* (Washington, DC: U.S. Government Printing Office, 2005).

time. Seven Part I offenses, or major crimes, are included in the figure: (1) murder, (2) forcible rape, (3) robbery, (4) aggravated assault, (5) burglary, (6) larceny-theft, and (7) motor vehicle theft. The sum total of all Part I offenses, divided by the nation's population, comprises the UCR's widely reported Crime Index. Arson, the eighth major crime, added as a Part I offense relatively late in the history of the UCR Program, is typically excluded from the crime clock.

The crime clock distinguishes between two categories of Part I offenses: **violent crime** and **property crime**. The violent, or personal, crimes are murder, forcible rape, robbery, and aggravated assault. The property crimes, as Figure 2–3 shows, are burglary, larceny-theft, and motor vehicle theft. Other than the use of this simple dichotomy, UCR data do not provide a clear measure of the severity of the crimes they cover.

Like most UCR statistics, crime clock data are based on crimes reported to (or discovered by) the police. For a few offenses, the numbers reported are probably close to the numbers that actually occur. Murder, for example, is a crime that is difficult to conceal because of its seriousness. Even where the crime is not immediately discovered, the victim is often quickly missed by family members, friends, and associates, and someone files a "missing persons" report with the police. Auto theft is another crime that is reported in numbers similar to its actual rate of occurrence, probably because insurance companies require that the victim file a police report before they will pay the claim.

Built into the UCR's traditional reporting system is the hierarchy rule, which is a way of "counting" crime reports such that only the most serious out of a series of events is scored. If a man and a woman go on a picnic, for example, and their party is set upon by a criminal who kills the man, rapes the woman, steals the couple's car, and later burns the vehicle, the hierarchy rule dictates that only one crime will be reported in official statistics—the murder. The offender, if apprehended, may later be charged with each of the offenses listed, but only one report of murder will appear in UCR data.

A commonly used term in today's UCR is **clearance rate**, which refers to the proportion of reported crimes that have been "solved." Clearances are judged primarily on the basis of arrests and do not involve judicial disposition. Once an arrest has been made, a crime is regarded as

---

**violent crime**

A UCR offense category that includes murder, rape, robbery, and aggravated assault.

---

**property crime**

A UCR offense category that includes burglary, larceny-theft, motor vehicle theft, and arson.

---

**clearance rate**

A traditional measure of investigative effectiveness that compares the number of crimes reported or discovered to the number of crimes solved through arrest or other means (such as the death of the suspect).

| MAJOR CRIMES KNOWN TO THE POLICE, 2004 (UCR PART I OFFENSES) | | | |
|---|---|---|---|
| Offense | Number | Rate per 100,000 | Clearance Rate |
| **Personal/Violent Crimes** | | | |
| Murder | 16,137 | 5.5 | 62.6% |
| Forcible rape | 94,635 | 32.2 | 41.8 |
| Robbery | 401,326 | 136.7 | 26.2 |
| Aggravated assault | 854,911 | 291.1 | 55.6 |
| **Property Crimes** | | | |
| Burglary | 2,143,456 | 729.9 | 12.9 |
| Larceny-theft | 6,947,685 | 2,365.9 | 18.3 |
| Motor vehicle theft | 1,237,114 | 421.3 | 13.0 |
| Arson[1] | 68,245 | 32.4 | 17.1 |
| **U.S. total** | **11,763,509** | **3,982.6** | **19.8** |

[1]Arson can be classified as either a property crime or a violent crime, depending on whether personal injury or loss of life results from its commission. It is generally classified as a property crime, however. Arson statistics are incomplete for 2004.

*Source:* Adapted from Federal Bureau of Investigation, *Uniform Crime Reports: Crime in the United States, 2004* (Washington, DC: U.S. Government Printing Office, 2005).

"cleared" for reporting purposes. Exceptional clearances (sometimes called *clearances by exceptional means*) can result when law enforcement authorities believe they know who committed a crime but cannot make an arrest. The perpetrator may, for example, have fled the country, committed suicide, died, or been killed.

For data-gathering and reporting purposes, the UCR Program divides the country into four geographic regions: Northeast, West, South, and Midwest. Unfortunately, no real attempt has been made to create divisions with nearly equal populations or similar demographic characteristics, and it is difficult to meaningfully compare one region of the country to another.

**WEB EXTRA**

Table 2–1 summarizes UCR statistics for 2004. For a detailed overview of the most recent UCR data, see Web Extra 2–5 at cjtoday.com.

# Part I Offenses

## Murder

**murder**

The unlawful killing of a human being. *Murder* is a generic term that in common usage may include first- and second-degree murder, manslaughter, involuntary manslaughter, and other similar offenses.

**Murder** is the unlawful killing of one human being by another.[14] UCR statistics on murder describe the yearly incidence of all willful and unlawful homicides within the United States. Included in the count are all cases of nonnegligent manslaughter that have been reported to or discovered by the police. Not included in the count are suicides, justifiable homicides (that is, those committed in self-defense), deaths caused by negligence or accident, and murder attempts. In 2004, some 16,137 murders came to the attention of police departments across the United States. First-degree murder is a criminal homicide that is planned. Second-degree murder is an intentional and unlawful killing but one that is generally unplanned and that happens "in the heat of the moment."

Murder is the smallest numerical category in the **Part I offenses.** The 2004 murder rate was 5.5 homicides for every 100,000 residents of the United States. Generally, murder rates peak in the warmest months; in 2004 the greatest number of murders occurred in July. Geographically, murder is most common in the southern states. However, because those states are also the most populous, a meaningful comparison across regions of the country is difficult.

Age is no barrier to murder. Statistics for 2004 reveal that 176 infants (children under the age of one) were victims of homicide, as were 299 people aged 75 and over.[15] Young adults between 20 and 24 were the most likely to be murdered. Murder perpetrators were also most common in this age group.

Firearms are the weapon used most often to commit murder. In 2004, guns were used in 70.3% of all killings. Handguns outnumbered shotguns almost 15 to 1 in the murder statistics, with rifles used

**Part I offenses**

A set of UCR categories used to report murder, rape, robbery, aggravated assault, burglary, larceny-theft, motor vehicle theft, and arson, as defined under the FBI's Uniform Crime Reporting Program.

Self-confessed serial killers Gary L. Ridgway (left) and Dennis Rader (right). Fifty-four-year-old Ridgway, known as the Green River strangler, is said to be the nation's worst captured serial killer. In 2003, Ridgway admitted to killing 48 women over a 20-year period in the Pacific Northwest and is now serving life in prison without possibility of parole. Rader, the 59-year-old infamous BTK ("bind, torture, and kill") strangler confessed in 2005 to ten killings that were committed between 1974 and 1986 in the Wichita, Kansas, area. He was sentenced to serve ten consecutive life prison terms.

*Elaine Thompson/Reuters, Landov LLC*

almost as often as shotguns. Knives were used in approximately 14% of all murders. Other weapons included explosives, poison, narcotics overdose, blunt objects like clubs, and hands, feet, and fists.

Only 12.9% of all murders in 2004 were perpetrated by offenders classified as "strangers." In 44.1% of all killings, the relationship between the parties had not yet been determined. The largest category of killers was officially listed as "acquaintances," which probably includes a large number of former friends. Arguments cause most murders (44.4%), but murders also occur during the commission of other crimes, such as robbery, rape, and burglary. Homicides that follow from other crimes are more likely to be impulsive rather than planned.

Murders may occur in sprees, which "involve killings at two or more locations with almost no time break between murders."[16] John Allen Muhammad, 41, part of the "sniper team" that terrorized the Washington, D.C., area in 2002, was arrested along with 17-year-old Jamaican immigrant Lee Boyd Malvo in the random shootings of 13 people in Maryland, Virginia, and Washington over a three-week period. Ten of the victims died.[17] In 2003, Muhammad and Malvo were convicted of capital murder; Muhammad was sentenced to die. Malvo was given a second sentence of life without the possibility of parole in 2004, after he struck a deal with prosecutors in an effort to avoid the death penalty.[18]

In contrast to spree killing, mass murder entails "the killing of four or more victims at one location, within one event."[19] Recent mass murderers have included Timothy McVeigh (the antigovernment Oklahoma City bomber) and Mohammed Atta and the terrorists whom he led in the September 11, 2001, attacks against American targets.

Yet another kind of murder, serial murder, happens over time and officially "involves the killing of several victims in three or more separate events."[20] In cases of serial murder, days, months, or even years may elapse between killings.[21] Some of the more infamous serial killers of recent years are confessed Wichita BTK[22] murderer Dennis Rader; Jeffrey Dahmer, who received 936 years in prison for the murders of 15 young men (and who was himself later murdered in prison); Ted Bundy, who killed many college-aged women; Henry Lee Lucas, now in a Texas prison, who confessed to 600 murders but later recanted (yet was convicted of 11 murders and linked to at least 140 others)[23]; Ottis Toole, Lucas's partner in crime; cult leader Charles Manson, still serving time for ordering followers to kill seven Californians, including famed actress Sharon Tate; Andrei Chikatilo, the Russian "Hannibal Lecter," who killed 52 people, mostly schoolchildren[24]; David Berkowitz, also known as the "Son of Sam," who killed six people on lovers' lanes around New York City; Theodore Kaczynski, the Unabomber, who perpetrated a series of bomb attacks on "establishment" figures; Seattle's Green River killer, Gary Leon Ridgway, a 54-year-old painter who in 2003 confessed to killing 48 women in the 1980s; and the infamous "railroad killer" Angel Maturino Resendiz. Although Resendiz was convicted of only one murder—that of Dr. Claudia Benton, which occurred in 1998—he is suspected of many more.[25]

> The public is properly obsessed with safety. Of industrialized countries, the U.S. has the highest rate of violent crime.
>
> —Bob Moffitt, Heritage Foundation

> If people here were not getting killed on the job in homicides, we would have quite a low rate of fatalities.
>
> —Samuel Ehrenhalt, former Labor Department official, commenting on findings that show murder to be the top cause of on-the-job deaths in New York City

**FIGURE 2-4**

**Crimes cleared by arrest, 2004.**

*Source:* Federal Bureau of Investigation, *Uniform Crime Reports: Crime in the United States, 2004* (Washington, DC: U.S. Government Printing Office, 2005).

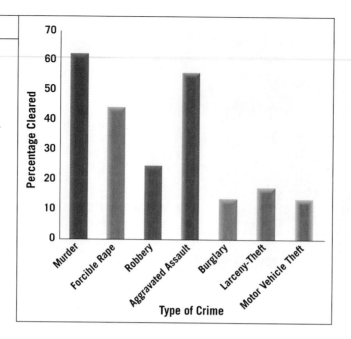

The typical mass murderer is extraordinarily ordinary.

—James Alan Fox,
Northeastern University

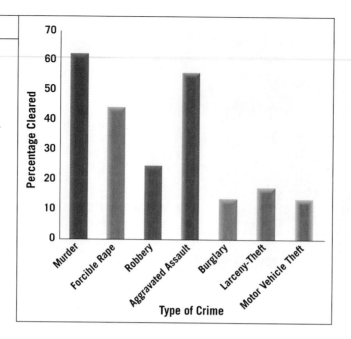

**rape**

Unlawful sexual intercourse, achieved through force and without consent. Broadly speaking, the term *rape* has been applied to a wide variety of sexual attacks and may include same-sex rape and the rape of a male by a female. Some jurisdictions refer to same-sex rape as *sexual battery.*

**forcible rape (UCR)**

The carnal knowledge of a female forcibly and against her will. For statistical reporting purposes, the FBI defines *forcible rape* as "unlawful sexual intercourse with a female, by force and against her will, or without legal or factual consent." Statutory rape differs from forcible rape in that it generally involves nonforcible sexual intercourse with a minor.

Federal homicide laws changed in 2004, when President George Bush signed the Unborn Victims of Violence Act.[26] The act, which passed the Senate by only one vote, made it a separate federal crime to "kill or attempt to kill" a fetus "at any stage of development" during an assault on a pregnant woman. The fetal homicide statute, better known as "Laci and Conner's Law," after homicide victims Laci Peterson and her unborn son (whom she had planned to name Conner), specifically prohibits the prosecution of "any person for conduct relating to an abortion for which the consent of the pregnant woman, or a person authorized by law to act on her behalf, has been obtained. . . . "

Because murder is such a serious crime, it consumes substantial police resources. Consequently, over the years the offense has shown the highest clearance rate of any index crime. Nearly 63% of all homicides were cleared in 2004. Figure 2–4 shows clearance rates for all Part I offenses except arson. Learn more about homicide trends in the United States at Library Extra 2–3.

## Forcible Rape

The term **rape** is often applied to a wide variety of sexual attacks including same-sex rape and the rape of a male by a female. For statistical-reporting purposes, however, the term **forcible rape** has a specific and somewhat different meaning. The Uniform Crime Reports define *forcible rape* as "the carnal knowledge of a female forcibly and against her will."[27] By definition, rapes reported under the UCR Program are always of females. Although today our society acknowledges that males can be the victims of sexual assault, the *Uniform Crime Reporting Handbook,* which serves as a statistical-reporting guide for law enforcement agencies, says, "Sex attacks on males are excluded [from the crime of forcible rape] and should be classified as assaults or 'other sex offenses,' depending on the nature of the crime and the extent of the injury."[28] While it is not part of official UCR terminology, some jurisdictions refer to same-sex rape as **sexual battery.** Incidents of sexual battery are not included in the UCR tally of reported rapes. Statutory rape, where no force is involved but the victim is younger than the age of consent, is not included in rape statistics, but attempts to commit rape by force or the threat of force are.

Forcible rape is the least reported of all violent crimes. Estimates are that only one out of every four forcible rapes is reported to the police. An even lower figure was reported by a 1992 government-sponsored study, which found that only 16% of rapes were reported.[29] The victim's fear of embarrassment was the most commonly cited reason for nonreports. In the past, reports of rapes were often handled in ways that made victims feel further victimized. Information was usually taken by desk sergeants or male detectives who were typically insensitive to victims' needs, and the physical examination victims had to endure was often a traumatizing experience in itself. Also, many states routinely permitted the woman's past sexual history to be revealed in detail in the courtroom if a trial ensued. But the past few decades have seen many changes designed to facilitate accurate reporting of rape and other sex offenses. Trained female detectives often interview the victims, physicians have become better educated in handling the psychological needs of victims, and sexual histories are no longer regarded as relevant in most trials.

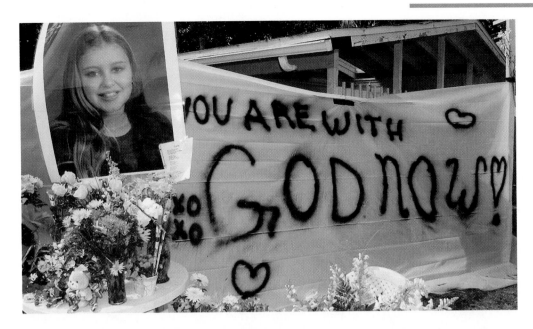

A makeshift memorial to 11-year-old Carlie Brucia who authorities say was abducted and killed by 37-year-old Joseph Smith, in Florida in 2004. Smith had been arrested at least 13 times in the ten years before the murder, and was caught on camera leading the girl away prior to the discovery of her body. Random personal violence is the type of crime that Americans fear the most.

*AP Wide World Photos*

UCR statistics show 94,635 reported forcible rapes for 2004, a slight increase over the number of offenses reported for the previous year. Rape reports have generally increased, even in years when reports of other violent crimes have been on the decline. Figure 2–5 shows the rate of reported rape per 100,000. The offense of rape follows homicide in its seasonal variation. The greatest number of forcible rapes in 2004 was reported in the hot summer months, while the lowest number of reports was recorded in January, February, November, and December.

Rape is frequently committed by a man known to the victim, as in the case of **date rape**. Victims may be held captive and subjected to repeated assaults.[30] In the crime of heterosexual rape, any female—regardless of age, appearance, or occupation—is a potential victim. Through personal violation, humiliation, and physical battering, rapists seek a sense of personal aggrandizement and dominance. Victims of rape often experience a lessened sense of personal worth; feelings of despair, helplessness, and vulnerability; a misplaced sense of guilt; and a lack of control over their personal lives.

Contemporary wisdom holds that forcible rape is often a planned violent crime that serves the offender's need for power rather than sexual gratification.[31] The "power thesis" has its origins in

---

**sexual battery**

Intentional and wrongful physical contact with a person, without his or her consent, that entails a sexual component or purpose.

---

**date rape**

Unlawful forced sexual intercourse with a female against her will that occurs within the context of a dating relationship. Date rape, or acquaintance rape, is a subcategory of rape that is of special concern today.

---

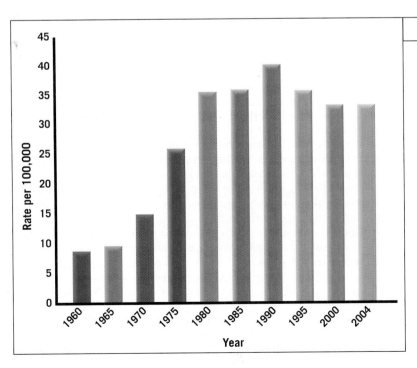

**FIGURE 2–5**

**Rate of reported rape, 1960–2004.**

*Source:* Federal Bureau of Investigation, *Uniform Crime Reports: Crime in the United States* (Washington, DC: U.S. Government Printing Office, various years).

A crime in progress? Date rape is unlawful sexual intercourse with a female against her will that occurs within the context of a dating relationship. "Date rape drugs," like Rohypnol, are sometimes secretly placed in women's drinks, rendering them unable to resist.

*Peter Dokus, Getty Images Inc.— Stone Allstock*

the writings of Susan Brownmiller, who argued in 1975 that the primary motivation leading to rape is the male desire to "keep women in their place" and to preserve sexual role inequality through violence.[32] Although many writers on the subject of forcible rape have generally accepted the power thesis, at least one study has caused some to rethink it. In a 1995 survey of imprisoned serial rapists, for example, Dennis J. Stevens found that "lust" was reported most often (41%) as "the primary motive for predatory rape."[33]

Statistically speaking, most rapes are committed by acquaintances of the victims and often betray a trust or friendship. Date rape, which falls into this category, appears to be far more common than previously believed. Recently, the growing number of rapes perpetrated with the use of the "date rape drug" Rohypnol have alarmed law enforcement personnel. Rohypnol, which is discussed in Chapter 16, is an illegal pharmaceutical substance that is virtually tasteless. Available on the black market, it dissolves easily in drinks and can leave anyone who consumes it unconscious for hours, making them vulnerable to sexual assault.

Rape within marriage, which has not always been recognized as a crime, is a growing area of concern in American criminal justice, and many laws have been enacted during the past few decades to deter it. Similarly, even though UCR statistics report only the rape or attempted rape of females, some state statutes criminalize the rape of a male by a female. When it occurs, this offense is typically statutory rape. In 1997, for example, sixth-grade schoolteacher Mary Kay Le-Tourneau, a 35-year-old married mother of four, pleaded guilty in Burien, Washington, to second-degree child rape after having a child by one of her students, a 13-year-old boy named Vili Fualuaau. LeTourneau had known the boy since he was in the second grade.[34] She was sentenced to six months in jail and was banned from seeing the boy or their child. Following her release after a brief jail stay, LeTourneau became known as "America's most famous pedophile" after she had a second child by her teenage lover. In 1998, she was sentenced to a seven-and-a-half-year prison term for violating probation.[35] She was released from prison in 2004, and she and her former student have since gotten married.

Learn more about the crime of rape and about what people can do to protect themselves at Web Extra 2–6 at cjtoday.com. Read about statistical measures relating to the sexual victimization of women at Library Extra 2–4.

## Robbery

**Robbery** is a personal crime and involves a face-to-face confrontation between victim and perpetrator. It is often confused with burglary, which is primarily a property crime. (We'll examine burglary later.) Weapons may be used in robbery, or strong-arm robbery may occur through

---

**robbery (UCR)**

The unlawful taking or attempted taking of property that is in the immediate possession of another by force or violence and/or by putting the victim in fear. Armed robbery differs from unarmed, or strong-arm, robbery with regard to the presence of a weapon. Contrary to popular conceptions, highway robbery does not necessarily occur on a street—and rarely in a vehicle. The term *highway robbery* applies to any form of robbery that occurs outdoors in a public place.

# MULTICULTURALISM AND DIVERSITY

## Race and the Criminal Justice System

Several years ago, Professor Lani Guinier of the University of Pennsylvania School of Law was interviewed on *Think Tank,* a public television show. Guinier was asked by Ben Wattenberg, the program's moderator, "When we talk about crime, crime, crime, are we really using a code for black, black, black?" Guinier responded this way: "To a great extent, yes, and I think that's a problem, not because we shouldn't deal with the disproportionate number of crimes that young black men may be committing, but because if we can't talk about race, then when we talk about crime, we're really talking about other things, and it means that we're not being honest in terms of acknowledging what the problem is and then trying to deal with it."[1]

Crimes, of course, are committed by individuals of all races. The link between crime—especially violent, street, and predatory crimes—and race, however, shows a striking pattern. In most crime categories, arrests of African-American offenders equal or exceed arrests of whites. In any given year, arrests of blacks account for more than 50% of all arrests for violent crimes. Blacks, however, comprise only 12% of the U.S. population. When *rates* (which are based upon the relative proportion of racial groups) are examined, the statistics are even more striking. The murder rate among African-Americans, for example, is ten times that of whites. Similar rate comparisons, when calculated for other violent crimes, show that far more blacks than whites are involved in other street crimes, such as assault, burglary, and robbery. Related studies show that 30% of all young black men in America are under correctional supervision on any given *day*—a far greater percentage than for members of any other race in the country.[2]

The real question for anyone interested in the justice system is how to explain such huge race-based disparities. Some authors maintain that racial differences in arrests and in rates of imprisonment are due to the differential treatment of African-Americans at the hands of a discriminatory criminal justice system. Marvin D. Free, Jr., for example, says that the fact that African-Americans are underrepresented as criminal justice professionals results in their being overrepresented in arrest and confinement statistics.[3] Some police officers, says Free, are more prone to arrest blacks than whites, frequently arrest blacks without sufficient evidence to support criminal charges, and overcharge in criminal cases involving black defendants—resulting in misleading statistical tabulations that depict blacks as being responsible for a greater proportion of crime than is, in fact, the case.

Other writers disagree. In *The Myth of a Racist Criminal Justice System,* for example, William Wilbanks claims that while the practice of American criminal justice may have been significantly racist in the past, and while some vestiges of racism may indeed remain, the system today is by and large objective in its processing of criminal defendants.[4] Using statistical data, Wilbanks shows that "at every point from arrest to parole there is little or no evidence of an overall racial effect, in that the percentage outcomes for blacks and whites are not very different."[5] Wilbanks claims to have reviewed "all the available studies that have examined the possible existence of racial discrimination from arrest to parole." In essence, he says, "this examination of the available evidence indicates that support for the 'discrimination thesis' is sparse, inconsistent, and frequently contradictory."

Wilbanks is careful to counter arguments advanced by those who continue to suggest that the system is racist. He writes, for example, "Perhaps the black/white gap at arrest is a product of racial bias by the police in that the police are more likely to select and arrest black than white offenders. The best evidence on this question comes from the National Crime Survey which interviews 130,000 Americans each year about crime victimization. . . . The percent of offenders described by victims as being black is generally consistent with the percent of offenders who are black according to arrest figures."

A fundamental critique of Wilbanks's thesis comes from Coramae Richey Mann, who says that his overreliance on quantitative or statistical data fails to capture the reality of racial discrimination within the justice system.[6] White victims, says Mann, tend to overreport being victimized by black offenders because they often misperceive Hispanic and other minority offenders as black. Similarly, she says, black victims are sometimes reluctant to report victimization—especially at the hands of whites.

Mann's arguments are discounted by those who point out that the statistics appear to be overwhelming. *If* they are accurate, then another question emerges: Why do blacks commit more crimes? Wilbanks says, "The assertion that the criminal justice system is not racist does not address the reasons why blacks appear to offend at higher rates than whites before coming into contact with the criminal justice system. . . . It may be that racial discrimination in American society has been responsible for conditions (for example, discrimination in employment, housing, and education) that lead to higher rates of offending by blacks."

Marvin Free, Jr., suggests that African-Americans are still systematically denied equal access to societal resources that would allow for full participation in American society—resulting in a higher rate of law violation. In a work that considers such issues in great detail, John Hagan and Ruth D. Peterson acknowledge the reality of higher crime rates among ethnic minorities and attribute them to (1) concentrated poverty, (2) joblessness, (3) family disruption, and (4) racial segregation.[7]

The question of *actual* fairness of the justice system can be quite different from one of *perceived* fairness. As University of Maryland Professor Katheryn K. Russell points out, "Study after study has shown that blacks and whites hold contrary views on the fairness of the criminal justice system's operation; blacks tend to be more cautious in their praise and frequently view the system as unfair and racially biased; by contrast whites have a favorable impression of the justice system. . . . The point is not that whites are completely satisfied with the justice system, but rather that, relative to blacks, they have faith in the system."[8] One reason for such differences may be that African-Americans are more likely to be victims of police harassment and brutality or may know someone who has been.

*(continued)*

## MULTICULTURALISM AND DIVERSITY *(continued)*

Even if blacks do engage in more criminal activity than whites, says noted criminologist Thomas J. Bernard, higher rates of offending may be due, at least in part, to their perception that members of their group have historically been treated unfairly by agents of social control—resulting in anger and defiance, which express themselves in criminal activity.[9] Hence, says Bernard, crime—at least crime committed by minority group members—becomes a kind of protest against a system that is perceived as fundamentally unfair.

According to Russell, inequities in the existing system may propel African-Americans into crime and combine with stereotypical images in the popular media to perpetuate what she calls the *criminalblackman* myth. The criminalblackman myth, says Russell, is a stereotypical portrayal of black men as *inherently* more sinister, evil, and dangerous than their white counterparts. The myth of the criminalblackman, adds Russell, is self-perpetuating, resulting in continued frustration, more crime, and growing alienation among African-Americans.

[1]Quoted in "For the Record," *Washington Post* wire service, March 3, 1994.
[2]Marvin D. Free, Jr., *African-Americans and the Criminal Justice System* (New York: Garland, 1996).
[3]Ibid.
[4]William Wilbanks, *The Myth of a Racist Criminal Justice System* (Monterey, CA: Brooks/Cole, 1987).
[5]William Wilbanks, "The Myth of a Racist Criminal Justice System," *Criminal Justice Research Bulletin,* Vol. 3, No. 5 (Huntsville, TX: Sam Houston State University, 1987), p. 2.
[6]Coramae Richey Mann, "The Reality of a Racist Criminal Justice System," in Barry W. Hancock and Paul M. Sharp, eds., *Criminal Justice in America: Theory, Practice, and Policy* (Upper Saddle River, NJ: Prentice Hall, 1996), pp. 51–59.
[7]John Hagan and Ruth D. Peterson, *Crime and Inequality* (Stanford, CA: Stanford University Press, 1995).
[8]Katheryn K. Russell, "The Racial Hoax as Crime: The Law as Affirmation," *Indiana Law Journal,* Vol. 71 (1996), pp. 593–621.
[9]Thomas J. Bernard, "Angry Aggression among the 'Truly Disadvantaged,'" *Criminology,* Vol. 28, No. 1 (1990), pp. 73–96.

intimidation. Purse snatching and pocket picking are not classified as robbery by the UCR Program but are included under the category of larceny-theft.

In 2004, individuals were the most common target of robbers. Banks, gas stations, convenience stores, and other businesses were the second most common target, with residential robberies accounting for only 13.8% of the total. In 2004, 401,326 robberies were reported to the police. Of that number, 42.8% were highway robberies, meaning that the crime occurred outdoors, most commonly as the victim was walking. Strong-arm robberies, in which the victim was intimidated but no weapon was used, accounted for 41.1% of the total robberies reported. Guns were used in 40.6% of all robberies, and knives were used in 8.9%. Armed robbers are dangerous; guns are actually discharged in 20% of all robberies.[36]

When a robbery occurs, the UCR Program scores the event as one robbery, even when a number of victims were robbed during the event. With the move toward incident-driven reporting (discussed later in this chapter), however, the UCR will soon make data available on the number of individuals robbed in each incident. Because statistics on crime show only the most serious offense that occurred during a particular episode, robberies are often hidden when they occur in conjunction with more serious crimes. For example, 3% of robbery victims are also raped, and a large number of homicide victims are robbed.[37]

Robbery is primarily an urban offense, and most arrestees are young male minorities. The robbery rate in cities in 2004 was 158.3 per every 100,000 inhabitants, whereas it was only 15.5 in rural areas. Eighty-nine percent of those arrested for robbery in 2004 were male, 60% were under the age of 25, and 55% were minorities.[38]

## Aggravated Assault

In December 2004, police charged five Indiana Pacers basketball players and seven Detroit Piston fans after a mass brawl erupted during a game. The fight, which aired on national television, was sparked by a dispute over a foul.[39] Pacers teammates Jermaine O'Neal, Ron Artest, David Harrison, Anthony Johnson, and Stephen Jackson were all charged with misdemeanor assault and battery. Detroit fan John Green was charged with two counts of simple assault for throwing cups and ice at Artest, while another fan, Bryant Jackson, was charged with felony assault for throwing a chair into the crowd. In September 2005, Artest, O'Neil, and Jackson were each sentenced to one year probation and ordered to complete 60 hours of community service.

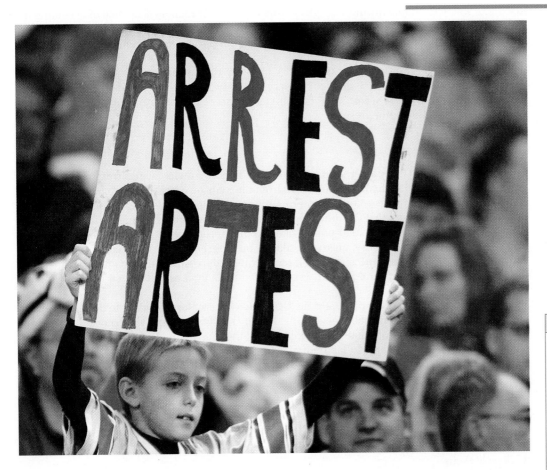

A young fan holds a sign reading "Arrest Artest"—a reference to Indiana Pacers basketball player Ron Artest who, along with others, was charged by police with misdemeanor assault and battery after a brawl involving players erupted at a game between the Pacers and the Detroit Pistons in 2004. The fight, which aired on national television, was sparked by a dispute over a foul.

© Tom Pidgeon, Getty Images, Inc.

---

**assault (UCR)**

An unlawful attack by one person upon another. Historically, *assault* meant only the attempt to inflict injury on another person; a completed act constituted the separate offense of battery. Under modern statistical usage, however, attempted and completed acts are grouped together under the generic term *assault*.

---

**aggravated assault**

The unlawful, intentional inflicting, or attempted or threatened inflicting, of serious injury upon the person of another. While *aggravated assault* and *simple assault* are standard terms for reporting purposes, most state penal codes use labels like *first-degree* and *second-degree* to make such distinctions.

---

**burglary (UCR)**

The unlawful entry of a structure to commit a felony or a theft (excludes tents, trailers, and other mobile units used for recreational purposes). For the UCR, the crime of burglary can be reported if (1) an unlawful entry of an unlocked structure has occurred, (2) a breaking and entering (of a secured structure) has taken place, or (3) a burglary has been attempted.

---

**Assaults** are of two types: simple (misdemeanor) and aggravated (felonious). For statistical-reporting purposes, simple assaults typically involve pushing and shoving. While simple assault may also at times include fistfights, the correct legal term to describe such incidents is *battery*. **Aggravated assaults** are distinguished from simple assaults in that either a weapon is used or the assault victim requires medical assistance. When a deadly weapon is employed, an aggravated assault may be charged as attempted murder even if no injury results.[40] In some cases, the UCR Program scores these attempted assaults as aggravated assault, because of the potential for serious consequences.

In 2004, 854,911 cases of aggravated assault were reported to law enforcement agencies in the United States. Assault reports were most frequent in summer months and least frequent in February, November, December and January. Most aggravated assaults were committed with blunt objects or objects near at hand (35.6%), while hands, feet, and fists were also commonly used (26.6%). Less frequently used were knives (18.5%) and firearms (19.3%). Because those who commit assaults are often known to their victims, aggravated assaults are relatively easy to solve. Slightly more than 55% of all aggravated assaults reported to the police in 2004 were cleared by arrest.

## Burglary

Although it may involve personal and even violent confrontation, **burglary** is primarily a property crime. Burglars are interested in financial gain and usually fence (that is, illegally sell) stolen items, recovering a fraction of their cash value. About 2.1 million burglaries were reported to the police in 2004. Dollar losses to burglary victims totaled $3.5 billion, with an average loss per offense of $1,642.

The UCR Program employs three classifications of burglary: (1) forcible entry, (2) unlawful entry where no force is used, and (3) attempted forcible entry. In most jurisdictions, force need not be employed for a crime to be classified as burglary. Unlocked doors and open windows are invitations to burglars, and the legal essence of burglary consists not so much of a forcible entry as it does of the intent to trespass and steal. In 2004, 61.4% of all burglaries were forcible entries, 32.4% were unlawful entries, and 6.2% were attempted forcible entries.[41] The most dangerous burglaries were those in which a household member was home (about 10% of all burglaries).[42]

Residents who were home during a burglary suffered a greater than 30% chance of becoming the victim of a violent crime.[43] However, while burglary may evoke images of dark-clothed strangers breaking into houses in which families lie sleeping, burglaries more often are of unoccupied homes and take place during daylight hours.

The clearance rates for burglary, as for other property crimes that we'll look at later, are generally low. In 2004 the clearance rate for burglary was only 12.9%. Burglars usually do not know their victims, and in cases where they do, burglars conceal their identity by committing their crime when the victim is not present.

## Larceny-Theft

In 2002, 25-year-old Thad Roberts and 22-year-old Tiffany Fowler were arrested in Orlando, Florida, and charged with stealing moon rocks from the Johnson Space Center in Houston, Texas. Roberts had been working as a student intern at the center, and Fowler was a Space Center employee.[44] Officials realized that the lunar samples, along with a number of meteorites, were missing when they discovered that a 600-pound safe had disappeared from the Houston facility. They had been alerted to the loss by messages placed on a website run by a mineralogy club in Antwerp, Belgium, offering "priceless moon rocks collected by Apollo astronauts" for sale for up to $5,000 per gram. Roberts and Fowler were arrested by federal agents pretending to be potential purchasers.

*Larceny* is another name for theft, and the UCR uses the term **larceny-theft** to describe theft offenses. Some states distinguish between simple larceny and grand larceny, categorizing the crime based on the dollar value of what is stolen. Larceny-theft, as defined by the UCR Program, includes theft of valuables of any dollar amount. The reports specifically list the following offenses as types of larceny (listed here in order of declining frequency):

- Thefts from motor vehicles
- Shoplifting
- Thefts from buildings
- Thefts of motor vehicle parts and accessories
- Bicycle thefts
- Thefts from coin-operated machines
- Purse snatching
- Pocket picking

> **larceny-theft (UCR)**
>
> The unlawful taking or attempted taking, carrying, leading, or riding away of property, from the possession or constructive possession of another. Motor vehicles are excluded. Larceny is the most common of the eight major offenses, although probably only a small percentage of all larcenies are actually reported to the police because of the small dollar amounts involved.

Thefts of farm animals (known as *rustling*) and thefts of most types of farm machinery also fall into the larceny category. In fact, larceny is such a broad category that it serves as a kind of catchall in the UCR. In 1995, for example, Yale University officials filed larceny charges against 25-year-old student Lon Grammer, claiming that he had fraudulently obtained university funds.[45] The university maintained that Grammer had stolen his education by forging college and high school transcripts and concocting letters of recommendation prior to admission. Grammer's alleged misdeeds, which Yale University officials said misled them into thinking that Grammer, a poor student before attending Yale, had an exceptional scholastic record, permitted him to receive $61,475 in grants and loans during the time he attended the school. Grammer was expelled.

Reported thefts vary widely, in terms of both the objects stolen and their value. They range from stolen pocket change to the stealing of a $100 million aircraft. For reporting purposes, crimes entailing embezzlement, con games, forgery, and worthless checks are specifically excluded from the count of larceny. Because larceny has traditionally been considered a crime that requires physical possession of the item appropriated, some computer crimes, including thefts engineered through online access or thefts of software and information, have not been scored as larcenies unless computer equipment, electronic circuitry, or computer media were actually stolen. In 2004, however, the FBI confirmed that it was working with Cisco Systems, Inc., to investigate the possible theft of some of the company's intellectual property.[46] The theft involved approximately 800 megabytes of proprietary software code used to control the company's Internet routers. Since hardware manufactured by Cisco Systems accounts for more than 60% of all routers used on the Internet,[47] officials feared that the lost software could represent a major security threat for the entire Internet.

> **identity theft**
>
> A crime in which an imposter obtains key pieces of information, such as Social Security and driver's license numbers, to obtain credit, merchandise, and services in the name of the victim. The victim is often left with a ruined credit history and the time-consuming and complicated task of repairing the financial damages.[iii]

From a statistical standpoint, the most common form of larceny in recent years has been theft of motor vehicle parts, accessories, and contents. Tires, wheels, hubcaps, radar detectors, stereos, CD players, cassette tapes, compact discs, and cellular phones account for many of the items reported stolen.

**CJ TODAY EXHIBIT 2-1**

## Identity Theft: A New Kind of Larceny

In 2005, ChoicePoint, a personal-information clearinghouse with huge stores of private data on millions of Americans, announced that it had been the victim of a fraud perpetrated by thieves posing as legitimate business customers.[1] The firm quickly notified more than 145,000 people nationwide that critical personal information, including credit scores, Social Security numbers, street addresses, and more, had been stolen in what looked like a massive identity theft scheme. Later that year, more than 100,000 Bank of America and Wachovia customers were notified that their financial records might have been stolen.[2] MasterCard reported that 40 million credit card accounts had been compromised by a security breach at a payment processing center.[3]

**Identity theft**, which involves obtaining credit, merchandise, or services by fraudulent personal representation, is a special kind of larceny. According to a recent Federal Trade Commission survey, identity theft directly impacts as many as 10 million victims annually, although most do not report the crime.[4] Identity theft became a federal crime in 1998 with the passage of the Identity Theft and Assumption Deterrence Act.[5] The law makes it a crime whenever anyone "knowingly transfers or uses, without lawful authority, a means of identification of another person with the intent to commit, or to aid or abet, any unlawful activity that constitutes a violation of federal law, or that constitutes a felony under any applicable state or local law."

The 2004 Identity Theft Penalty Enhancement Act[6] added two years to federal prison sentences for criminals convicted of using stolen credit card numbers and other personal data to commit crimes. It also prescribed prison sentences for those who use identity theft to commit other crimes, including terrorism, and it increased penalties for defendants who exceed or abuse the authority of their position in unlawfully obtaining or misusing means of personal identification.

Anyone can fall prey to identity theft—even celebrities. In 2000, for example, golfer Tiger Woods learned that his identity had been stolen and that credit cards taken out in his name had been used to steal $17,000 worth of merchandise, including a 70-inch TV, stereos, and a used luxury car. In 2001, the thief, 30-year-old Anthony Lemar Taylor, who looks nothing like Woods, was convicted of falsely obtaining a driver's license using the name of Eldrick T. Woods (Tiger's given name), Woods' Social Security number, and his birth date. Because Taylor already had 20 previous convictions of all kinds on his record, he was sentenced to 200 years in prison under California's three-strikes law.[7] Like Woods, most victims of identity theft do not even know that their identities have been stolen until they receive bills for merchandise they haven't purchased.

According to the National White Collar Crime Center, identity thieves use several common techniques. Some engage in "Dumpster diving," going through trash bags, cans, or Dumpsters to get copies of checks, credit card and bank statements, credit card applications, or other records that typically bear identifying information. Others use a technique called "shoulder surfing." It involves simply looking over the victim's shoulder as he or she enters personal information into a computer or on a written form. Eavesdropping is another simple, yet effective, technique that identity thieves often use. Eavesdropping can occur when the victim is using an ATM machine, giving credit card or other personal information over the phone, or dialing the number for their telephone calling card. Criminals can also obtain personal identifying information from potential victims through the Internet. Some Internet users, for example, reply to "spam" (unsolicited e-mail) that promises them all sorts of attractive benefits while requesting identifying data, such as checking account or credit card numbers and expiration dates, along with the victim's name and address.[8] Identity theft perpetrated through the use of high technology depends on the fact that a person's legal and economic identity in contemporary society is largely "virtual" and supported by technology.

Learn more about identity thieves and how they operate via Web Extra 2–7 and Library Extra 2–5 at cjtoday.com.

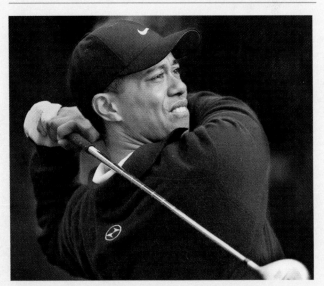

World-renowned professional golfer Tiger Woods. In 2000, Woods became the victim of identity theft when 29-year-old Anthony Lemar Taylor of Sacramento, California, used Woods's identity to charge $17,000 on the golfer's charge cards.

*AP Wide World Photos*

*(continued)*

## CJ TODAY EXHIBIT 2–1 *(continued)*

[1]John Waggoner, "ID Theft Scam Spreads Across USA," *USA Today*, February 22, 2005, p. 1A.
[2]Paul Nowell, "Info on 100,000 Bank Users Possibly Stolen," *USA Today*, May 24, 1005, p. B6.
[3]Eric Dash and Tom Zeller, "MasterCard Says 40 Million Files Put at Risk," *The New York Times*, June 18, 2005, p. A1.
[4]Christine Dugas, "Federal Survey: Identity Theft Hits 1 in 4 U.S. Households; Scope of Crime Much Worse Than Previously Thought," *USA Today*, September 4, 2003, p. B10.
[5]18 U.S.C. Section 1028.
[6]HR 1731 (2004).
[7]"Three Strikes, He's Out: Woods' Identity Thief Gets 200 Years-to-Life," Associated Press wire service, April 28, 2001.
[8]Much of the information in this paragraph is adapted from National White Collar Crime Center, "WCC Issue: Identity Theft," Web posted at http://www.nw3c.org/papers/Identity_Theft.pdf.

Reports to the police in 2004 showed 6,947,685 larcenies nationwide, with the total value of property stolen placed at $5.1 billion. Larceny-theft is the most frequently reported major crime, according to the UCR. It may also be the UCR's most underreported crime category because small thefts rarely come to the attention of the police. The average value of items reported stolen in 2004 was about $727.

### Motor Vehicle Theft

For record-keeping purposes, the UCR Program defines *motor vehicles* as self-propelled vehicles that run on the ground and not on rails. Included in the definition are automobiles, motorcycles, motor scooters, trucks, buses, and snowmobiles. Excluded are trains, airplanes, bulldozers, most farm and construction machinery, ships, boats, and spacecraft; the theft of these would be scored as larceny-theft.[48] Vehicles that are temporarily taken by individuals who have lawful access to

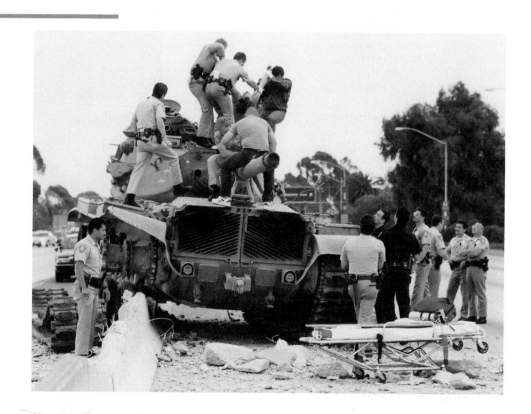

Motor vehicle theft or larceny? Even members of the FBI's Education and Training Services Unit in Washington, D.C., were unsure of how to classify the 1995 theft of this M-60 tank by Shawn Nelson, a former Army tank operator. Nelson drove the tank through the streets of San Diego before being shot and killed by police, who jumped on the tank and cut the hatch open with bolt cutters. In this photo, Nelson's body is being removed from the tank shortly after he was shot.

*David McNew, Corbis/Sygma*

them are not thefts. Hence spouses who jointly own all property may drive the family car, even though one spouse may think of the vehicle as his or her exclusive personal property.

As we said earlier, because most insurance companies require police reports before they will reimburse car owners for their losses, most occurrences of **motor vehicle theft** are reported to law enforcement agencies. Some reports of motor vehicle thefts, however, may be false. People who have damaged their own vehicles in solitary crashes or who have been unable to sell them may try to force insurance companies to "buy" them through reports of theft.

In 2004, 1,237,114 motor vehicles were reported stolen. The average value per stolen vehicle was $6,143, making motor vehicle theft an $7.6 billion crime. The clearance rate for motor vehicle theft was only 13% in 2004. Large city agencies reported the lowest rates of clearance (9.4%), while rural counties had the highest rate (26%). Many stolen vehicles are quickly disassembled and the parts resold, since auto parts are much more difficult to identify and trace than are intact vehicles. In some parts of the country, chop shops—which take stolen vehicles apart and sell their components—operate like big businesses, and one shop may strip a dozen or more cars per day.

Motor vehicle theft can turn violent, as in cases of carjacking—a crime in which offenders usually force the car's occupants onto the street before stealing the vehicle. For example, in February 2000, Christy Robel watched helplessly as her six-year-old son Jake was dragged to his death after a man jumped behind the wheel of her car and sped off.[49] Robel had left the car running with the boy inside as she made a brief stop at a Kansas City sandwich shop. The carjacker, 35-year-old Kim L. Davis, tried to push Jake from the car as he made his escape, but the boy became entangled in his seat belt and was dragged for five miles at speeds of more than 80 mph. In October 2001, Davis was convicted of murder and was sentenced to spend the rest of his life in prison without possibility of parole.[50] The Bureau of Justice Statistics estimates that around 34,000 carjackings occur annually and account for slightly more than 1% of all motor vehicle thefts.[51]

Arrest reports for motor vehicle theft show that the typical offender is a young male. Sixty-seven percent of all arrestees in 2004 were under the age of 25, and 83.6% were male.

## Arson

The UCR Program received crime reports from more than 16,000 law enforcement agencies in 2004.[52] Of these, only 13,286 submitted **arson** data. Even fewer agencies provided complete data as to the type of arson (the nature of the property burned), the estimated monetary value of the property, the ownership, and so on. Arson data include only the fires that are determined through investigation to have been willfully or maliciously set. Fires of unknown or suspicious origin are excluded from arson statistics.[53]

The intentional and unlawful burning of structures (houses, storage buildings, manufacturing facilities, and so on) was the type of arson reported most often in 2004 (28,202 instances). The arson of vehicles was the second most common category, with 18,070 such burnings reported. The average dollar loss per instance of arson in 2004 was $12,017, and total nationwide property damage was placed at close to $1 billion.[54] As with most property crimes, the clearance rate for arson was low—only 17.1% nationally.

The crime of arson exists in a kind of statistical limbo. In 1979, Congress ordered that it be added as an eighth index offense. To date, however, the UCR Program has been unable to successfully integrate statistics on arson into the yearly Crime Index. The problem is twofold: (1) Many law enforcement agencies have not yet begun making regular reports to the FBI on arson offenses in their jurisdiction, and (2) any change in the number of index offenses threatens the usefulness of the Crime Index because it does not facilitate meaningful comparisons over time. The Crime Index will allow useful comparisons over time and between jurisdictions only as long as it retains definitional consistency. Adding another offense to the index, or substantially changing the definition of any of its categories, still provides a measure of crime, but it changes the meaning of the term.

Some of these difficulties have been resolved through the Special Arson Program, authorized by Congress in 1982. In conjunction with the National Fire Data Center, the FBI now operates a Special Arson Reporting System, which focuses on fire departments across the nation. The reporting system is designed to provide data to supplement yearly UCR arson tabulations.[55]

# Part II Offenses

The Uniform Crime Reports also include information on what the FBI calls **Part II offenses**. Part II offenses, which are generally less serious than those that make up the Crime Index, include a number of social-order, or so-called victimless, crimes. The statistics on Part II offenses are for recorded

---

**motor vehicle theft (UCR)**

The theft or attempted theft of a motor vehicle. *Motor vehicle* is defined as a self-propelled road vehicle that runs on land surface and not on rails. The stealing of trains, planes, boats, construction equipment, and most farm machinery is classified as larceny under the UCR Program, not as motor vehicle theft.

**arson (UCR)**

The burning or attempted burning of property, with or without the intent to defraud. Some instances of arson result from malicious mischief, some involve attempts to claim insurance monies, and some are committed in an effort to disguise other crimes, such as murder, burglary, or larceny.

**Part II offenses**

A set of UCR categories used to report arrests for less serious offenses.

| UCR PART II OFFENSES, 2004 | |
|---|---|
| **Offense Category** | **Number of Arrests** |
| Simple assault | 1,285,501 |
| Forgery and counterfeiting | 119,410 |
| Fraud | 282,884 |
| Embezzlement | 17,386 |
| Stolen property (i.e., receiving) | 129,280 |
| Vandalism | 276,543 |
| Weapons (i.e., carrying) | 177,330 |
| Prostitution and related offenses | 90,231 |
| Sex offenses (i.e., statutory rape) | 91,395 |
| Drug-law violations | 1,745,715 |
| Gambling | 10,916 |
| Offenses against the family (i.e., nonsupport) | 125,955 |
| Driving under the influence | 1,432,524 |
| Liquor-law violations | 613,922 |
| Public drunkenness | 550,795 |
| Disorderly conduct | 683,850 |
| Vagrancy | 36,082 |
| Curfew violation/loitering | 138,685 |
| Runaways | 118,966 |

*Source:* Adapted from Federal Bureau of Investigation, *Uniform Crime Reports: Crime in the United States, 2004* (Washington, DC: U.S. Government Printing Office, 2005), p. 280.

TABLE 2-2

What NIBRS Records
on Each Criminal Incident

arrests, not for crimes reported to the police. The logic inherent in this form of scoring is that most Part II offenses would never come to the attention of the police were it not for arrests. Part II offenses are shown in Table 2–2, with the number of estimated arrests made in each category for 2004.

A Part II arrest is counted each time a person is taken into custody. As a result, the statistics in Table 2–2 do not report the number of suspects arrested, but rather the number of arrests made. Some suspects were arrested more than once.

## NIBRS: The New UCR

The Uniform Crime Reporting Program is undergoing significant changes in the way in which data are gathered and reported. Whereas the original UCR system was "summary based," the newly enhanced UCR, called the **National Incident-Based Reporting System (NIBRS)**, is incident driven (Table 2–3). Under NIBRS, city, county, state, and federal law enforcement agencies throughout the country furnish detailed data on crime and arrest activities at the incident level either to the individual state incident-based reporting programs or directly to the federal NIBRS program.

The goals of NIBRS are to enhance the quantity, quality, and timeliness of crime data collection by law enforcement and to improve the methodology used for compiling, analyzing, auditing, and publishing the collected data. A major advantage of NIBRS, beyond the increase in data collected, is the ability to break down and combine crime offense data into specific information.[56]

The old UCR system depended on statistical tabulations of crime data that were often little more than frequency counts. Under the new system, many details are being gathered about each criminal incident. Included among them are information on place of occurrence, weapon used, type and value of property damaged or stolen, the personal characteristics of the offender and the victim, the nature of any relationship between the two, and the disposition of the complaint.

NIBRS replaces the old Part I and Part II offenses with 22 general offenses: arson, assault, bribery, burglary, counterfeiting, embezzlement, extortion, forcible sex offenses, fraud, gambling, homicide, kidnapping, larceny, motor vehicle theft, narcotics offenses, nonforcible sex offenses, pornography, prostitution, receiving stolen property, robbery, vandalism, and weapons violations. Other offenses on which NIBRS data are being gathered include bad checks, vagrancy, disorderly conduct, driving

**National Incident-Based Reporting System (NIBRS)**

An incident-based reporting system that collects data on every single crime occurrence. NIBRS data will soon supersede the kinds of traditional data provided by the FBI's Uniform Crime Reports.

> Those who insist that crime never pays have never met an identity thief. Identity theft not only pays, it pays extremely well.
>
> —Jonathan Turley[iv]

## DIFFERENCES BETWEEN THE UCR AND NIBRS

TABLE 2-3

| Uniform Crime Reports | National Incident-Based Reporting System |
|---|---|
| Consists of monthly aggregate crime counts | Consists of individual incident records for the eight index crimes and 38 other offenses, with details on offense, victim, offender, and property involved |
| Records one offense per incident, as determined by the hierarchy rule, which suppresses counts of lesser offenses in multiple-offense incidents | Records each offense occurring in an incident |
| Does not distinguish between attempted and completed crimes | Distinguishes between attempted and completed crimes |
| Records rape of females only | Records rape of males and females |
| Collects assault information in five categories | Restructures definition of assault |
| Collects weapon information for murder, robbery, and aggravated assault | Collects weapon information for all violent offenses |
| Provides counts on arrests for the eight index crimes and 21 other offenses | Provides details on arrests for the eight index crimes and 49 other offenses |

*Source:* Adapted from *Effects of NIBRS on Crime Statistics,* BJS Special Report (Washington, DC: Bureau of Justice Statistics, 2000), p. 1.

under the influence, drunkenness, nonviolent family offenses, liquor-law violations, "Peeping Tom" activity, runaways, trespass, and a general category of all "other" criminal law violations.

NIBRS also eliminates the need for the hierarchy rule (because multiple types of crimes can be reported within a single incident) and collects an expanded array of attributes involved in the commission of offenses, including whether the offender is suspected of using alcohol, drugs or narcotics, or a computer in the commission of the offense.

The FBI began accepting crime data in NIBRS format in January 1989. Although the bureau intended to have NIBRS fully in place by 1999, delays have been routine and the NIBRS format has not yet been fully adopted. A study by the National Consortium for Justice Information and Statistics (SEARCH) concluded that for many law enforcement agencies, "the costs of implementing changes in reporting practices to make their systems NIBRS-compliant (for example, revising offense reporting forms, department-wide training, and software reprogramming), compounded by concerns over the impact NIBRS will have on the department's reported crime rate and a lack of understanding on how the data will be used at state and federal levels, create formidable impediments to NIBRS implementation."[57]

A sample of NIBRS data can be viewed at Web Extra 2–8 at cjtoday.com. To learn more about the effects of NIBRS on crime statistics, including comparisons of UCR data and NIBRS data, see Web Extra 2–9. Finally, the Bureau of Justice Statistics provides an NIBRS information website, which can be accessed via Web Extra 2–10.

Another change in crime reporting was brought about by the 1990 Crime Awareness and Campus Security Act, which requires colleges to publish annual security reports.[58] Most campuses share crime data with the FBI, increasing the reported national incidence of a variety of offenses. The U.S. Department of Education reported that 395 murders and 3,982 forcible sex offenses occurred on and around college campuses in 2000. Also reported were 12,894 robberies, 18,761 aggravated assaults, 68,486 burglaries, and 31,056 motor vehicle thefts.[59] Although these numbers may seem high, it is important to realize that, except for the crimes of rape and sexual assault, college students experience violence at average annual rates that are lower than those for nonstudents in the same age group.[60] Rates of rape and sexual assault do not differ statistically between students and nonstudents. For the latest campus crime statistics, see Web Extra 2–11 at cjtoday.com. Library Extra 2–6 provides statistical information on the sexual victimization of college women.

WEB EXTRA

WEB EXTRA

LIBRARY EXTRA

# The National Crime Victimization Survey

As mentioned earlier, a second major source of statistical data about crime in the United States is the National Crime Victimization Survey, which is based on victim self-reports rather than on police reports. The NCVS is designed to estimate the occurrence of all crimes, whether reported or not.[61] The NCVS began operation in 1972. It built on efforts in the late 1960s by both the National Opinion Research Center and the President's Commission on Law Enforcement and the Administration of Justice to uncover what some had been calling the **dark figure of crime.** This term refers to those crimes that are not reported to the police and that remain unknown to officials. Prior to the development of the NCVS, little was known about such unreported and undiscovered offenses.

> **dark figure of crime**
>
> Crime that is not reported to the police and that remains unknown to officials.

Early data from the NCVS changed the way criminologists thought about crime in the United States. The use of victim self-reports led to the discovery that crimes of all types were more prevalent than UCR statistics indicated. Many cities were shown to have victimization rates that were more than twice the rate of reported offenses. Others, like Saint Louis, Missouri, and Newark, New Jersey, were found to have rates of victimization that very nearly approximated reported crime. New York, often thought of as a high-crime city, was discovered to have one of the lowest rates of self-reported victimization.

NCVS data are gathered by the Bureau of Justice Statistics through a cooperative arrangement with the U.S. Census Bureau.[62] NCVS interviewers work with a national sample of more than 149,000 people 12 years of age or older, living in 84,360 households. Household lists are completely revised every few years. BJS statistics are published in annual reports entitled *Criminal Victimization* and *Crime and the Nation's Households.*

Using definitions similar to those employed by the UCR Program, the NCVS includes data on the national incidence of rape, sexual assault, robbery, assault, burglary, personal and household larceny, and motor vehicle theft. Not included are murder, kidnapping, and victimless crimes (crimes that, by their nature, tend to involve willing participants). Commercial robbery and the burglary of businesses were dropped from NCVS reports in 1977. The NCVS employs a hierarchical counting system similar to that of the pre-NIBRS system: It counts only the most "serious" incident in any series of criminal events perpetrated against the same individual. Both completed and attempted offenses are counted, although only people 12 years of age and older are included in household surveys.

Highlights of NCVS statistics for recent years reveal the following:

- Approximately 15% of American households are touched by crime every year.
- About 24 million victimizations occur each year.
- City residents are almost twice as likely as rural residents to be victims of crime.
- About half of all violent crimes, and slightly more than one-third of all property crimes, are reported to police.[63]
- Victims of crime are more often men than women.
- Younger people are more likely than the elderly to be victims of crime.
- Blacks are more likely than whites or members of other racial groups to be victims of violent crimes.
- Violent victimization rates are highest among people in lower-income families.

Offense Definitions
by Reporting Program

A report by the Bureau of Justice Statistics found that in 2004, NCVS crime rates had reached their lowest level since the survey began.[64] Declines began in the mid-1990s, with violent crime rates dropping 57% between 1993 and 2004.[65] While these statistics indicate that in recent years crime rates have declined, UCR statistics, which go back almost another 40 years, show that today's crime rate is still many times what it was in the early and middle years of the twentieth century.[66] A comparison of UCR and NCVS data for 2004 can be found in Table 2–4. Explore the latest NCVS data via Web Extra 2–12 at cjtoday.com.

Many researchers accept NCVS data over those provided by the UCR Program because they believe that self-reports provide a more accurate gauge of criminal incidents than do police reports. Learn more about the use of self-report surveys in the measurement of crime and delinquency via Library Extras 2–7 and 2–8 at cjtoday.com.

| COMPARISON OF UCR AND NCVS DATA, 2004 | | |
| --- | --- | --- |
| Offense | Uniform Crime Reports | National Crime Victimization Survey[1] |
| **Personal/Violent Crimes** | | |
| Homicide | 16,137 | — |
| Forcible rape[2] | 94,635 | 209,880 |
| Robbery | 401,326 | 501,820 |
| Aggravated assault | 854,911 | 1,030,080 |
| **Property Crimes** | | |
| Burglary[3] | 2,143,456 | 3,427,690 |
| Larceny | 6,947,685 | 14,211,940 |
| Motor vehicle theft | 1,237,114 | 1,014,770 |
| Arson[4] | 68,245 | — |
| **Total of all crimes recorded** | **11,763,509** | **24,061,140**[5] |

TABLE 2-4

[1]NCVS data cover "households touched by crime," not absolute numbers of crime occurrences. More than one victimization may occur per household, but only the number of households in which victimizations occur enters the tabulations.

[2]NCVS statistics include both rape and sexual assault.

[3]NCVS statistics include only household burglary and attempts.

[4]Arson data are incomplete in the UCR and are not reported by the NCVS.

[5]Includes other forms of victimization, such as simple assault.

*Source:* Compiled from U.S. Department of Justice, *Criminal Victimization, 2004* (Washington, DC: Bureau of Justice Statistics, 2005); and Federal Bureau of Investigation, *Uniform Crime Reports: Crime in the United States, 2004* (Washington, DC: U.S. Government Printing Office, 2005).

# Comparisons of the UCR and the NCVS

Table 2–5 summarizes the differences between the UCR and the NCVS. Both provide estimates of crime in America. Both are limited by the types of crimes they measure and those they exclude and by the methods they use to gather crime data.

As mentioned earlier in this chapter, crime statistics from the UCR and the NCVS reveal crime patterns that are often the bases for social policies created to deter or reduce crime. These policies also build on explanations for criminal behavior found in more elaborate interpretations of the statistical information. Unfortunately, however, researchers too often forget that statistics, which are merely descriptive, can be weak in explanatory power. For example, NCVS data show that "household crime rates" are highest for households (1) headed by blacks, (2) headed by younger people, (3) with six or more members, (4) headed by renters, and (5) located in central cities.[67] Such findings, combined with statistics that show that most crime occurs among members of the same race, have led some researchers to conclude that values among certain black subcultural group members both propel them into crime and make them targets of criminal victimization. The truth may be, however, that crime is more a function of inner-city location than of culture. From simple descriptive statistics, it is difficult to know which is the case. Learn more about the UCR and the NCVS, and see how they compare, by viewing Web Extra 2–13 at cjtoday.com.

WEB EXTRA

## Problems with the UCR and the NCVS

Like most statistical data-gathering programs in the social sciences, the UCR and the NCVS are not without problems. Because UCR data are based primarily on citizens' crime reports to the police, there are several inherent difficulties. First, not all people report when they are victimized. Some victims are afraid to contact the police, while others may not believe that the police can do

TABLE 2-5

### HOW THE UCR AND THE NCVS COMPARE

| Uniform Crime Reports | National Crime Victimization Survey |
|---|---|
| **Offenses Measured** | |
| Homicide | |
| Rape | Rape |
| Robbery (personal and commercial) | Robbery (personal) |
| Assault (aggravated) | Assault (aggravated and simple) |
| Burglary (commercial and household) | Burglary (household) |
| Larceny (commercial and household) | Larceny (personal and household) |
| Motor vehicle theft | Motor vehicle theft |
| Arson | |
| **Scope** | |
| Crimes reported to police in most jurisdictions | Crimes both reported and not reported to police; all data are available for a few large geographic areas |
| **Collection Method** | |
| Police departments report to the FBI or to centralized state agencies that then report to the FBI | Survey interviews; periodically measures the total number of crimes committed by asking a national sample of 50,000 households encompassing more than 100,000 people aged 12 and older about their experiences as victims of crime during a specified period |
| **Kinds of Information** | |
| In addition to offense counts, provides information on crime clearances, persons arrested, persons charged, law enforcement officers killed and assaulted, and characteristics of homicide victims | Provides details about victims (such as age, race, sex, education, income, and whether the victim and offender were related to each other) and about crimes (such as time and place of occurrence, whether reported to police, use of weapons, occurrence of injury, and economic consequences) |
| **Sponsor** | |
| U.S. Department of Justice; Federal Bureau of Investigation | U.S. Department of Justice; Bureau of Justice Statistics |

*Source:* Bureau of Justice Statistics, *Report to the Nation on Crime and Justice,* 2nd ed. (Washington, DC: U.S. Department of Justice, 1988), p. 11.

anything about the offense. Second, certain kinds of crimes are reported rarely, if at all. These include victimless crimes, also known as *social-order offenses,* such as drug use, prostitution, and gambling. Similarly, white-collar and high-technology offenses, such as embezzlement and computer crime—because they often go undiscovered—probably enter the official statistics only rarely. Third, victims' reports may not be entirely accurate. A victim's memory may be faulty, he may feel the need to impress or please the police, or he may be under pressure from others to misrepresent the facts. Finally, all reports are filtered through a number of bureaucratic levels, which increases the likelihood that inaccuracies will enter the data. As noted methodologist Frank Hagan points out, "The government is very keen on amassing statistics. They collect them, add to them, raise them to the nth power, take the cube root, and prepare wonderful diagrams. But what you must never forget is that every one of these figures comes in the first instance from the *chowty dar* [village watchman], who puts down what he damn pleases."[68]

In contrast to the UCR's dependence on crimes reported by victims who seek out the police, the National Crime Victimization Survey relies on door-to-door surveys and personal interviews for its data. Survey results are skewed for several reasons. First, survey respondents provide their personal interpretations and descriptions of what may or may not have been a criminal event. Second, by its very nature, the survey includes only information from those willing to talk to surveyors; more reclusive people are less likely to respond regardless of the level of victimization they may have suffered. Also, some victims are afraid to report crimes even to nonpolice interviewers, while others may invent victimizations for the interviewer's sake. As the first page of the NCVS report admits, "Details about the crimes come directly from the victims, and no attempt is made to validate the information against police records or any other source."[69]

Finally, because both the UCR and the NCVS are human artifacts, they contain only data that their creators think appropriate. UCR statistics for 2001, for example, do not include a tally of those who perished in the September 11, 2001, attacks on the World Trade Center and the Pentagon because FBI officials concluded that the events were too "unusual" to count. Although the 2001 UCR acknowledges "the 2,830 homicides reported as a result of the events of September 11, 2001," it goes on to say that "these figures have been removed" from the reported data.[70] Crimes that result from an anomalous event, but are excluded from reported data, highlight the arbitrary nature of the data-collection process itself.

> In a field like criminal justice, where sensitive issues abound, none is more sensitive than the issue of race and gender bias.
>
> —Gary LaFree, University of New Mexico

# Special Categories of Crime

A **crime typology** is a classification scheme used in the study and description of criminal behavior. There are many typologies, all of which have an underlying logic. The system of classification that derives from any particular typology may be based on legal criteria, offender motivation, victim behavior, the characteristics of individual offenders, or the like. Criminologists Terance D. Miethe and Richard C. McCorkle note that crime typologies "are designed primarily to simplify social reality by identifying homogeneous groups of crime behaviors that are different from other clusters of crime behaviors."[71] Hence one common but simple typology contains only two categories of crime: violent and property. In fact, many crime typologies contain overlapping or nonexclusive categories—just as violent crimes may involve property offenses, and property offenses may lead to violent crimes. Thus no one typology is likely to capture all of the nuances of criminal offending.

Social relevance is a central distinguishing feature of any meaningful typology, and it is with that in mind that the remaining sections of this chapter briefly highlight crimes of special importance today. They are crime against women, crime against the elderly, hate crime, corporate and white-collar crime, organized crime, gun crime, drug crime, high-technology and computer crime, and terrorism.

**crime typology**

A classification of crimes along a particular dimension, such as legal categories, offender motivation, victim behavior, or the characteristics of individual offenders.

# Crime Against Women

The victimization of women is a special area of concern, and both the NCVS and the UCR contain data on gender as it relates to victimization. Statistics show that women are victimized less frequently than men in every major personal crime category other than rape.[72] The overall U.S. rate of violent victimization is about 25 per 1,000 males age 12 or older, and 18 per 1,000 females.[73] When women become victims of violent crime, however, they are more likely than men to be injured (29% versus 22%, respectively).[74] Moreover, a larger proportion of women than men make modifications in the way they live because of the threat of crime.[75] Women, especially those living in cities, have become increasingly careful about where they travel and the time of day they leave their homes—particularly if they are unaccompanied—and in many settings are often wary of unfamiliar males.

Date rape, familial incest, spousal abuse, **stalking**, and the exploitation of women through social-order offenses such as prostitution and pornography are major issues facing American society today. Testimony before Congress tagged domestic violence as the largest cause of injury to American women.[76] Former Surgeon General C. Everett Koop once identified violence against women by their partners as the number one health problem facing women in America.[77] Findings from the National Violence Against Women Survey (NVAWS) reveal the following[78]:

- Physical assault is widespread among American women. Fifty-two percent of surveyed women said that they had been physically assaulted as a child or as an adult.
- Approximately 1.9 million women are physically assaulted in the United States each year.

**stalking**

Repeated harassing and threatening behavior by one individual against another, aspects of which may be planned or carried out in secret. Stalking might involve following a person, appearing at a person's home or place of business, making harassing phone calls, leaving written messages or objects, or vandalizing a person's property. Most stalking laws require that the perpetrator make a credible threat of violence against the victim or members of the victim's immediate family.

Offline versus Online Stalking: A Comparison

**LIBRARY** EXTRA

**WEB** EXTRA

- Eighteen percent of women experienced a completed or attempted rape at some time in their lives.

- Of those reporting rape, 22% were under 12 years old, and 32% were between 12 and 17 years old when they were first raped.

- Native American and Alaska Native women were most likely to report rape and physical assault, while Asian/Pacific Islander women were least likely to report such victimization. Hispanic women were less likely to report rape than non-Hispanic women.

- Women report significantly more partner violence than men. Twenty-five percent of surveyed women, and only 8% of surveyed men, said they had been raped or physically assaulted by a current or former spouse, cohabiting partner, or date.

- Violence against women is primarily partner violence. Seventy-six percent of the women who had been raped or physically assaulted since age 18 were assaulted by a current or former husband, cohabiting partner, or date, compared with 18% of the men.

- Women are significantly more likely than men to be injured during an assault. Thirty-two percent of the women and 16% of the men who had been raped since age 18 were injured during their most recent rape; 39% of the women and 25% of the men who were physically assaulted since age 18 were injured during their most recent physical assault.

- Eight percent of surveyed women and 2% of surveyed men said they had been stalked at some time in their lives. According to survey estimates, approximately 1 million women and 371,000 men are stalked annually in the United States.

A detailed BJS analysis found that women who are victims of violent crime are twice as likely to be victimized by strangers as by people whom they know.[79] However, they are far more likely than men to be victimized by a current or former intimate partner. When the perpetrators are known to them, women are most likely to be violently victimized by ex-husbands, boyfriends, and spouses (in descending order of incidence). The BJS study also found that separated or divorced women are six times more likely to be victims of violent crime than widows, four and a half times more likely than married women, and three times more likely than widowers and married men. Other findings indicate that (1) women living in central-city areas are considerably more likely to be victimized than women residing in the suburbs; (2) suburban women, in turn, are more likely to be victimized than women living in rural areas; (3) women from low-income families experience the highest amount of violent crime; (4) the victimization of women falls as family income rises; (5) unemployed women, female students, and those in the armed forces are the most likely of all women to experience violent victimization; (6) black women are victims of violent crime more frequently than are women of any other race; (7) Hispanic women are victimized more frequently than white women; and (8) women in the age range of 20 to 24 are most at risk for violent victimization, while those age 16 to 19 make up the second most likely group of victims. Learn more about violence against women via Library Extra 2–9 at cjtoday.com.

Survey findings like these show that more must be done to alleviate the social conditions that result in the victimization of women. Suggestions already under consideration call for expansion in the number of federal and state laws designed to control domestic violence, a broadening of the federal Family Violence Prevention and Services Act, federal help in setting up state advocacy offices for battered women, increased funding for battered women's shelters, and additional funds for prosecutors and courts to develop spousal abuse units. The federal Violent Crime Control and Law Enforcement Act of 1994 was designed to meet many of these needs through a subsection entitled the Violence Against Women Act (VAWA). That act signified a major shift in our national response to domestic violence, stalking (which is often part of the domestic violence continuum), and sexual assault crimes. For the first time in our nation's history, violent crimes against women were addressed in relation to the more general problem of gender inequality.

The VAWA seeks to eradicate violence against women at all levels, and the act allocated $1.6 billion to fight violence against women. Included are funds to (1) educate police, prosecutors, and judges about the special needs of female victims; (2) encourage pro-arrest policies in cases of domestic abuse; (3) provide specialized services for female victims of crime; (4) fund battered women's shelters across the country; and (5) support rape education in a variety of settings nationwide. The law also extends "rape shield law" protections to civil cases and to all criminal cases in order to bar irrelevant inquiries into a victim's sexual history. VAWA was reauthorized by Congress in 2000. Read the text of the original VAWA legislation at Web Extra 2–14 at cjtoday.com.

## MULTICULTURALISM AND DIVERSITY

### Gender Issues in Criminal Justice

The Violent Crime Control and Law Enforcement Act of 1994 included significant provisions intended to enhance gender equality throughout the criminal justice system. Title IV of the Violent Crime Control and Law Enforcement Act, known as the Violence Against Women Act (VAWA) of 1994, contains the Safe Streets for Women Act. This act increases federal penalties for repeat sex offenders and requires mandatory restitution for sex crimes, including costs related to medical services (including physical, psychiatric, and psychological care); physical and occupational therapy or rehabilitation; necessary transportation, temporary housing, and child-care expenses; lost income; attorneys' fees, including any costs incurred in obtaining a civil protection order; and any other losses suffered by the victim as a result of the offense. The act also requires that compliance with a restitution order be made a condition of probation or supervised release (if such a sentence is imposed by the court) and provides that violation of the order will result in the offender's imprisonment.

Chapter 2 of VAWA provides funds for grants to combat violent crimes against women. The purpose of funding is to assist states and local governments to "develop and strengthen effective law enforcement and prosecution strategies to combat violent crimes against women, and to develop and strengthen victim services in cases involving violent crimes against women." The law also provides funds for the "training of law enforcement officers and prosecutors to more effectively identify and respond to violent crimes against women, including the crimes of sexual assault and domestic violence"; for "developing, installing, or expanding data collection and communication systems, including computerized systems, linking police, prosecutors, and courts or for the purpose of identifying and tracking arrests, protection orders, violations of protection orders, prosecutions, and convictions for violent crimes against women, including the crimes of sexual assault and domestic violence"; and for developing and strengthening "victim services programs, including sexual assault and domestic violence programs."

The act also creates the crime of crossing state lines in violation of a protection order and the crime of crossing state lines to commit assault on a domestic partner. It sets out federal penalties for the latter offense of up to life in prison in cases where death results.

Chapter 3 of the act provides funds to increase the "safety for women in public transit and public parks." It authorizes up to $10 million in grants through the Department of Transportation to enhance lighting, camera surveillance, and security telephones in public transportation systems used by women.

Chapter 5 of VAWA provides for the creation of hot lines, educational seminars, informational materials, and training programs for professionals who provide assistance to victims of sexual assault. Another portion of the law, titled the Safe Homes for Women Act, increases grants for battered women's shelters, encourages arrest in cases of domestic violence, and provides for the creation of a national domestic violence hot line to provide counseling, information, and assistance to victims of domestic violence. The act also orders that any protection order issued by a state court must be recognized by the other states and by the federal government and must be enforced "as if it were the order of the enforcing state."

Section 40401, known as the Equal Justice for Women in the Courts Act of 1994, provides funds "for the purpose of developing, testing, presenting, and disseminating model programs" to be used by states in training judges and court personnel in the laws "on rape, sexual assault, domestic violence, and other crimes of violence motivated by the victim's gender." The goal of the training is to help participants recognize the underreporting of rape, sexual assault, and child sexual abuse; the physical, psychological, and economic impact of rape and sexual assault on the victim; and the psychology of sex offenders, their high rate of recidivism, and implications for sentencing.

In 2000, VAWA was reauthorized by Congress, which provided $3.3 billion in additional funding over a five-year period. Much of the money was earmarked for programs that coordinate the work of victims' advocates, police, and prosecutors in the fight against domestic violence. Congressional reauthorization is again pending as this book goes to press. Learn more about VAWA and efforts at reauthorization at http://www.vawa2005.org.

A battered woman posing for police photographers who are documenting her injuries. Intimate partner violence is a problem of special concern to the criminal justice system, and violence against women is an area that is receiving legislative attention, as evidenced by the federal Violence Against Women Act.

*Michael Newman, PhotoEdit*

Finally, the passage of antistalking legislation by all 50 states and the District of Columbia provides some measure of additional protection to women (since women comprise 80% of all stalking victims[80]). On the federal level, the seriousness of stalking was addressed when Congress passed the interstate stalking law in 1996.[81] The law[82] also addresses **cyberstalking**, or the use of the Internet by perpetrators seeking to exercise power and control over their victims

**cyberstalking**

The use of the Internet, e-mail, and other electronic communication technologies to stalk another person.[vi]

by threatening them directly or by posting misleading and harassing information about them. Cyberstalking can be especially insidious, because it does not require that the perpetrator and the victim be in the same geographic area. Similarly, electronic communication technologies lower the barriers to harassment and threats; a cyberstalker does not need to confront the victim physically.[83]

# Crime Against the Elderly

Relative to other age groups, older victims rarely appear in the crime statistics. Criminal victimization seems to decline with age, suggesting that older people are only infrequently targeted by violent and property criminals. Moreover, older people are more likely than younger individuals to live in secure areas and to have the financial means to provide for their own personal security.

Victimization data pertaining to older people come mostly from the NCVS, which, for such purposes, looks at people age 65 and older. The elderly generally experience the lowest rate of victimization of any age group in both violent and property crime categories.[84] Some aspects of crime against older people are worth noting. In general, elderly crime victims are more likely than younger victims to

- Be victims of property crime—nine out of ten crimes committed against the elderly are property crimes, compared to fewer than four in ten crimes against people between 12 and 24
- Face offenders who are armed with guns
- Be victimized by strangers
- Be victimized in or near their homes during daylight hours
- Report their victimization to the police, especially when they fall victim to violent crime
- Be physically injured

In addition, elderly people are less likely to attempt to protect themselves when they are victims of violent crime. Only 49% of elderly victims attempt to protect themselves versus 70% of younger victims.

Elderly people are victimized disproportionately. Relative to their numbers, black men are more often victims, and separated or divorced people and urban residents have higher rates of victimization than do other elderly people. Even though their risk of victimization is considerably less, older people fear crime more than younger people; however, they are less likely to take crime-prevention measures than any other age group. Only 6% of households headed by people older than age 65 have an alarm, and only 16% of such households report engraving their valuables (versus a 25% national average).

The elderly face special kinds of victimizations that only rarely affect younger adults, such as physical abuse at the hands of caregivers. Criminal physical abuse of the elderly falls into two categories: domestic and institutional. Domestic abuse often occurs at the hands of caregivers who are related to their victims; institutional abuse occurs in residential settings such as retirement centers, nursing homes, and hospitals. Both forms of elder abuse may also involve criminal sexual victimization. To learn more about domestic and institutional elder abuse, visit the National Center on Elder Abuse (NCEA) via Web Extra 2–15 at cjtoday.com.

The elderly are also more often targeted by con artists. Confidence schemes center on commercial and financial fraud (including telemarketing fraud), charitable donation fraud, funeral and cemetery fraud, real estate fraud, caretaker fraud, automobile and home repair fraud, living trust fraud, health care fraud (e.g., promises of "miracle cures") and health provider fraud (overbilling and unjustified repeat billing by otherwise legitimate health care providers). "False friends" may intentionally isolate elderly targets from others in the hopes of misappropriating money through short-term secret loans or outright theft. Similarly, a younger person may feign romantic involvement with an elderly victim or pretend to be devoted to the senior in order to solicit money or receive an inappropriate gift or inheritance. The U.S. Senate's Special Committee on Aging provides additional information on such crimes at its Elder Justice Center website, which can be accessed via Web Extra 2–16 at cjtoday.com.

Finally, crime against the elderly will likely undergo a significant increase as baby boomers enter their retirement years. Not only will the elderly comprise an increasingly larger segment of the population as boomers age, but it is anticipated that they will be wealthier than any preceding generation of retirees, making them attractive targets for scam artists and property criminals.[85]

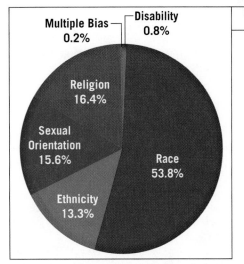

**FIGURE 2–6**

**Motivation of hate crime offenders, 2004.**

*Source:* Federal Bureau of Investigation, *Uniform Crime Reports: Crime in the United States, 2004* (Washington, DC: U.S. Government Printing Office, 2005).

# Hate Crime

A significant change in crime-reporting practices resulted from the Hate Crime Statistics Act,[86] signed into law by President George Bush in 1990. The act mandates a statistical tally of **hate crimes**; data collection under the law began in 1991. Congress defined *hate crime* as an offense "in which the defendant's conduct was motivated by hatred, bias, or prejudice, based on the actual or perceived race, color, religion, national origin, ethnicity, gender, or sexual orientation of another individual or group of individuals."[87] In 2004, police agencies reported a total of 7,649 hate-crime incidents, including 19 murders, across the country. As Figure 2–6 shows, approximately 16% of the incidents were motivated by religious bias, 53.8% were caused by racial hatred, and 13.3% were driven by prejudice against ethnicity or national origin. Another 15.6% of all hate crimes were based on sexual orientation, most committed against males believed by their victimizers to be homosexuals.[88] A relatively small number of hate crimes targeted people with physical or mental disabilities.

Following the terrorist attacks of September 11, 2001, authorities in some jurisdictions reported a dramatic shift in the nature of hate crime, with race-motivated crimes declining and crimes motivated by religion or ethnicity increasing sharply.[89] Islamic individuals, in particular, became the target of many such crimes.

Most hate crimes consist of intimidation, although vandalism, simple assault, and aggravated assault also account for a number of hate-crime offenses. A few robberies and rapes were also classified as hate crimes in 2004.

One particularly heinous and widely publicized hate crime culminated in death sentences for John William King, 24, and Lawrence Russell Brewer, 32, two white residents of Jasper County, Texas.[90] In separate 1999 trials, King and Brewer were found guilty of first-degree murder in the death of James Byrd, Jr., a 49-year-old black man. Using a chain, King and Brewer lashed Byrd to a pickup truck and dragged him over three miles of rural Texas asphalt to his death. If executed, King or Brewer will become only the second white person ever put to death in Texas for killing a black person. A third white supremacist, 24-year-old Shawn Allen Berry, was found guilty of participating in the crime and was sentenced to life in prison.

Although hate crimes are popularly conceived of as crimes motivated by racial enmity, the Violent Crime Control and Law Enforcement Act of 1994 created a new category of "crimes of violence motivated by gender." Congress defined this crime as "a crime of violence committed because of gender or on the basis of gender, and due, at least in part, to an animus based on the victim's gender." The 1994 act did not establish separate penalties for gender-motivated crimes, anticipating that they would be prosecuted as felonies under existing laws. The 1994 act also mandated that crimes motivated by biases against people with disabilities be considered hate crimes.

Hate crimes are sometimes called *bias crimes.* One form of bias crime that bears special mention is homophobic homicide. This term refers to the murder of homosexuals by those opposed to their lifestyles. Learn more about hate crimes and what can be done to address them via **Library Extras 2–10** and **2–11** at cjtoday.com.

**hate crime**

A criminal offense in which the motive is "hatred, bias, or prejudice, based on the actual or perceived race, color, religion, national origin, ethnicity, gender, or sexual orientation of another individual or group of individuals."[vii]

> With each arrest, indictment and prosecution, we sent this clear, unmistakable message: corrupt corporate executives are no better than common thieves.
>
> —U.S. Attorney General John Ashcroft, commenting on the arrests of former WorldCom executives[viii]

# Corporate and White-Collar Crime

Recently, a record number of corporations and their executives and former executives have faced high-profile criminal investigations and fraud charges. Between 2001 and 2003, accounting fraud and the ensuing bankruptcies of energy broker Enron Corporation and telecommunications giant

Convicted killer John William King (left photo) being escorted from the Jasper County (Texas) Courthouse in 1999. King, along with two other men, was convicted of the pickup truck dragging death of James Byrd, Jr. (right). King received the death penalty.

*AP Wide World Photos (left) and Buck Kelly, Getty Images, Inc.—Liaison (right)*

WorldCom, Inc., reduced the holdings of investment and retirement accounts across the country and around the world, wiping out hundreds of billions of dollars' worth of investor equity and taking a significant toll on the wealth of many Americans. Other publicly traded companies that have recently faced investigation include cable services provider Adelphia Communications Corporation; French-based media conglomerate Vivendi Universal; national discount retailer Kmart; fiber optics giant Global Crossing; multinational conglomerate Tyco International, Ltd.; accounting firm Arthur Andersen, LLP (whose employees served as auditors and accountants for bankrupt Enron); Metabolife, a leading seller of products containing the herbal stimulant ephedrine, which faced a criminal investigation by the U.S. Justice Department into whether the company had lied about drug safety[91]; and London-based auction house Sotheby's. In 2004, Adelphia Communications Corporation founder John Rigas and his son, former Adelphia chief financial officer Timothy Rigas, were found guilty of 18 counts of securities and bank fraud, of conspiring to loot the cable company of millions of dollars, and of misleading its investors.[92] Rigas, 80, was sentenced to 15 years in prison, while his son received a 20-year sentence.[93] In 2005, in a case that came to epitomize corporate greed, former Tyco CEO L. Dennis Kozlowski and former Tyco finance chief Mark H. Swartz were convicted of looting their former company of nearly $600 million.[94]

Under the American system of criminal justice, corporations can be treated as separate legal entities and can be convicted of violations of the criminal law under a legal principle known as the *identification doctrine.* In 2002, for example, a federal jury convicted global accounting firm Arthur Andersen of obstruction of justice after its employees shredded documents related to Enron's bankruptcy in an effort to impede an investigation by securities regulators. The conviction (which was overturned by a unanimous U.S. Supreme Court in 2005[95]) capped the firm's demise, and it ended U.S. operations in August 2002.[96]

Although corporations may be convicted of a crime, the human perpetrators of **corporate crime** are business executives known as *white-collar criminals.* **White-collar crime** was first defined in 1939 by Edwin H. Sutherland in his presidential address to the American Sociological Society.[97] Sutherland proposed that "crime in the suites" (a reference to corporate offices) rivaled the importance of street crime in its potential impact on American society.

In July 2002, President George W. Bush unveiled plans to create a new Corporate Fraud Task Force within the federal government and proposed a new law providing criminal penalties for corporate fraud. He addressed corporate leaders on Wall Street saying, "At this moment, America's greatest economic need is higher ethical standards—standards enforced by strict laws and upheld by responsible business leaders."[98] A few months later, the president signed into law the Sarbanes-Oxley Act.[99] The new law created tough provisions designed to deter and punish corporate and accounting fraud and corruption and to protect the interests of workers and share-

---

**corporate crime**

A violation of a criminal statute by a corporate entity or by its executives, employees, or agents acting on behalf of and for the benefit of the corporation, partnership, or other form of business entity.[ix]

**white-collar crime**

Violations of the criminal law committed by a person of respectability and high social status in the course of his or her occupation. Also, nonviolent crime for financial gain utilizing deception and committed by anyone who has special technical and professional knowledge of business and government, irrespective of the person's occupation.

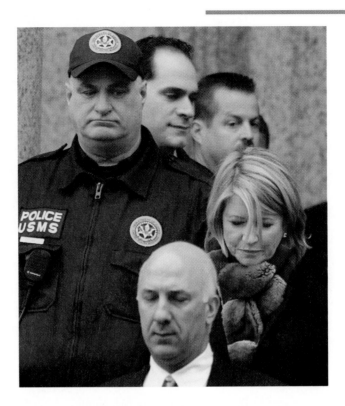

Home-decorating mogul Martha Stewart leaving the federal courthouse in New York City in 2004 after being found guilty on charges of conspiracy, obstruction of justice, and making false statements to federal investigators over a stock deal. Stewart served five months in prison before being released under home confinement. Her conviction signaled a new "get tough" attitude toward white-collar criminals in this country.

*AP Wide World Photos*

holders. Under the Sarbanes-Oxley Act, corporate officials (chief executive officers and chief financial officers) must personally vouch for the truth and accuracy of their companies' financial statements, and federal penalties for obstructing justice and, specifically, for shredding or destroying documents that might aid in a criminal investigation of business practices are substantially increased. Learn more about corporate and white-collar crime at the National White Collar Crime Center (NWCCC) via Web Extra 2–17 at cjtoday.com.

Established in 1992, the NWCCC provides a national support system for the prevention, investigation, and prosecution of multijurisdictional economic crimes. Learn more about how corporations can be held accountable from CorpWatch via Web Extra 2–18 at cjtoday.com.

**WEB** EXTRA

**WEB** EXTRA

# Organized Crime

For many people, the term **organized crime** conjures up images of the Mafia (also called the *Cosa Nostra*) or the hit HBO TV series *The Sopranos*. Although organized criminal activity is decidedly a group phenomenon, the groups involved in such activity in the United States today display a great deal of variation. During the past few decades in the United States, the preeminence of traditional Sicilian-American criminal organizations has fallen to such diverse criminal associations as the Black Mafia, the Cuban Mafia, the Haitian Mafia, the Colombian cartels, and the Asian criminal groups such as Chinese Tongs and street gangs, Japanese *yakuza*, and Vietnamese gangs. Included here as well might be inner-city gangs, the best known of which are probably the Los Angeles Crips and Bloods and the Chicago Vice Lords, international drug rings, outlaw motorcycle gangs such as the Hell's Angels and the Pagans, and other looser associations of small-time thugs, prison gangs, and drug dealers. Noteworthy among these groups—especially for their involvement in the lucrative drug trade—are the Latino organized bands, including the Dominican, Colombian, Mexican, and Cuban importers of cocaine, heroin, marijuana, and other controlled substances.

The unlawful activities of organized groups that operate across national boundaries are especially significant. Such activity is referred to as **transnational organized crime**. Transnational criminal associations worthy of special mention are the Hong Kong–based Triads, the South American cocaine cartels, the Italian Mafia, the Japanese *yakuza*, the Russian *Mafiya*, and the West African crime groups—each of which extends its reach well beyond its home country. In some parts of the world, close links between organized crime and terrorist groups involve money laundering, which provides cash to finance the activities of terrorist cells and to finance paramilitary efforts to overthrow established governments.

**organized crime**

The unlawful activities of the members of a highly organized, disciplined association engaged in supplying illegal goods and services, including gambling, prostitution, loan-sharking, narcotics, and labor racketeering, and in other unlawful activities.[x]

**transnational organized crime**

Unlawful activity undertaken and supported by organized criminal groups operating across national boundaries.

Actor James Gandolfini (Tony Soprano) from HBO's hit series *The Sopranos*. The show explores the life of fictionalized organized crime figures in New Jersey. The popularity of shows like *The Sopranos* demonstrates America's fascination with organized crime and with the lives of organized crime figures.

*HBO, Picture Desk, Inc./Kobal Collection*

Former CIA Director R. James Woolsey points out that "while organized crime is not a new phenomenon today, some governments find their authority besieged at home and their foreign policy interests imperiled abroad. Drug trafficking, links between drug traffickers and terrorists, smuggling of illegal aliens, massive financial and bank fraud, arms smuggling, potential involvement in the theft and sale of nuclear material, political intimidation, and corruption all constitute a poisonous brew—a mixture potentially as deadly as what we faced during the cold war."[100] The challenge for today's criminal justice student is to recognize that crime does not respect national boundaries. Crime is global, and what happens in one part of the world could affect us all.[101]

## Gun Crime

> I'm signing a good bill. . . . It says loud and clear to corporate America, we expect you to be responsible, we expect you to be responsible with the people's money. We expect you to be responsible for the shareholders and your employees and if you're not, we're going to investigate you, arrest you and prosecute you.
>
> —President George W. Bush, at the signing of the Sarbanes-Oxley Act of 2002[xi]

Constitutional guarantees of the right to bear arms have combined with historical circumstances to make ours a well-armed society. Guns are used in many types of crimes. Each year, approximately 1 million serious crimes—including homicide, rape, robbery, and assault—involve the use of a handgun. In a typical year, approximately 10,000 murders are committed in the United States with firearms. A recent report by the Bureau of Justice Statistics found that 18% of state prison inmates and 15% of federal inmates were armed at the time they committed the crime for which they were imprisoned.[102] Nine percent of those in state prisons said they fired a gun while committing the offense for which they were serving time.[103]

Both federal and state governments have responded to the public concern over the ready availability of handguns. In 1994, Congress passed the Brady Handgun Violence Prevention Act, which President Bill Clinton signed into law. The law was named for former Press Secretary James Brady, who was shot and severely wounded in an attempt on President Ronald Reagan's life on March 30, 1981. The law mandated a five-day waiting period before the purchase of a handgun, and it established a national instant criminal background check system that firearms dealers must use before selling a handgun. Under the system, licensed importers, manufacturers, and dealers are required to verify the identity of a firearm purchaser using a valid photo ID (such as a driver's license); must submit the purchaser's application to ensure that the applicant's receipt or possession of a handgun would not violate federal, state, or local law[104]; and must contact the system to receive a unique identification number authorizing the purchase before they transfer the handgun.

While the Brady Law may limit retail purchases of handguns by felons, a BJS study found that most offenders obtain weapons from friends or family members or "on the street" without attempting to purchase them at retail establishments.[105] In 2001, undercover congressional investigators were able to show that applicants using fake forms of identification, such as counterfeit driver's licenses with fictitious names, could easily circumvent Brady law provisions.[106] More-over, according to these studies, an ever-growing number of violent criminals are now carrying handguns.

In Congress, debate continues about whether to require gun manufacturers to create and retain "ballistic fingerprints" (the marks left on a bullet by the barrel of the gun from which it was fired) of each weapon they produce. Although a national ballistics fingerprinting requirement may still be years away, two states—Maryland and New York—already require that a record be kept of the "fingerprint" characteristics of each new handgun sold.[107] Learn more about promising strategies to reduce gun violence via Library Extra 2–12 at cjtoday.com. For the latest information on gun violence and gun laws, visit the Brady Center to Prevent Gun Violence via Web Extra 2–19.

## Drug Crime

Drug-law violations do not figure into Crime Index calculations. Unlike index crimes, however, drug-related crime continues to rise, lending support to the belief that the United States is experiencing more crime than traditional index tabulations show. The relentless increase in drug violations largely accounts for the continued growth in America's prison populations, even when official crime rates (that is, index offenses) have been declining. Chapter 16 discusses illicit drugs and drug-law violations in detail. As that chapter shows, the rate of drug-related crime commission has more than doubled in the United States since 1975.

Alone, drug-law violations are themselves criminal, but more and more studies are linking drug abuse to other serious crimes. An early study by the RAND Corporation found that most of the "violent predators" among prisoners had extensive histories of heroin abuse, often in combination with alcohol and other drugs.[108] Some cities reported that a large percentage of their homicides were drug related.[109] More recent studies also link drug abuse to other serious crimes. Community leaders perceive, and data analyses confirm, that crack cocaine profoundly impacts violent crime, with homicide rates closely tracking cocaine use levels among adult male arrestees.[110] Prisoner survey data show that 19% of state inmates and 16% of federal prisoners reported committing their current offense to obtain money for drugs.[111] A 1998 study found that 13.3% of convicted jail inmates said that they had committed their offense to get money for drugs.[112]

Criminal justice system costs associated with the handling of drug offenders have increased substantially in recent years. Between 1984 and 2002, for example, the annual number of defendants charged with a drug offense in federal courts increased from 11,854 to more than 30,000.[113] Similarly, between 1984 and 2002, drug offenses accounted for an increased proportion of the federal criminal caseload, even when charges weren't brought. During 1984, 18% of referrals to U.S. attorneys were drug related, compared to 31% during 2002.[114] Some of the increase stems from changes in federal drug laws. Whatever the cause, the drug–crime link is costly to society and shows few signs of abating.

## High-Technology and Computer Crime

**Computer crimes**, sometimes called *cybercrimes* or *information-technology crimes,* use computers and computer technology as tools in crime commission. Computer criminals manipulate the information stored in computer systems in ways that violate the law. (Thefts of computer equipment, although sometimes spectacular, are not computer crimes but are instead classified as larcenies.)

Many crimes committed via the Internet, such as prostitution, drug sales, theft, and fraud, are not new forms of offending. Rather, they are traditional offenses that use technology in their commission, or which build on the possibilities for criminal activity that new technologies make possible. In 2004, for example, police and real estate agents in Australia and New Zealand issued warnings to people who had been using Web-based virtual tours to sell their houses.[115] Burglars "down under" had been using the tours, which provide 360-degree views of a home's interior, to target expensive houses, locate valuables, and identify and disarm security devices.

U.S. Customs and Border Protection Senior Special Agent Donald Daufenbach, an international expert in child pornography and the Internet, points out that "the Internet is like anything else: It can be bent or perverted for nefarious purposes. . . . The Internet has absolutely changed the way people communicate with each other, changed the way people conduct commerce, changed the way people do research, changed the way people entertain themselves and changed the way people break the law. . . . People are catching on pretty quick, but law enforcement is lagging behind miserably in this whole endeavor."[116]

> **computer crime**
> Any crime perpetrated through the use of computer technology. Also, any violation of a federal or state computer-crime statute. Also called *cybercrime.*

## CJ TODAY EXHIBIT 2-2

# Gun Control

The Second Amendment to the U.S. Constitution reads, "A well regulated Militia, being necessary to the security of a free State, the right of the people to keep and bear Arms, shall not be infringed." For many years, the official position of the U.S. Justice Department had been that the Second Amendment merely gives states the collective right to organize and arm militias in order to protect the public interest and that it does not mean that individual citizens have a constitutional right to own firearms. On May 7, 2002, however, in two briefs filed with the U.S. Supreme Court by U.S. Solicitor General Theodore B. Olson, the Justice Department officially reversed course, declaring, "The current position of the United States . . . is that the Second Amendment more broadly protects the rights of individuals, including persons who are not members of any militia or engaged in active military service or training, to possess and bear their own firearms, subject to reasonable restrictions designed to prevent possession . . . of types of firearms that are particularly suited to criminal misuse."[1] Although the government's briefs did not ask the justices to take any action, they were seen by many as representing a significant victory for advocates of private gun ownership, such as the National Rifle Association (NRA). Nonetheless, few imagine that the apparent change in policy will lead to significant modifications in existing gun-control legislation, much of which was passed in the 1990s.

One of those laws, the Violent Crime Control and Law Enforcement Act of 1994,[2] regulated the sale of firearms within the United States and originally banned the manufacture of 19 military-style assault weapons, including those with specific combat features, such as high-capacity ammunition clips capable of holding more than ten rounds. The ban on assault weapons ended in 2004, however, when it was not renewed by Congress. The 1994 law also prohibited the sale or transfer of a gun to a juvenile, as well as the possession of a gun by a juvenile, and it prohibits gun sales to, and possession by, people subject to family violence restraining orders.

The 1996 Domestic Violence Offender Gun Ban[3] prohibits individuals convicted of misdemeanor domestic violence offenses from owning or using firearms. Soon after the law was passed, however, it became embroiled in controversy when hundreds of police officers across the country who had been convicted of domestic violence offenses were found to be in violation of the ban. A number of officers lost their jobs, while others were placed in positions that did not require them to carry firearms. While some legislators pushed to exempt police officers and military personnel from the ban's provisions, others ar-

gued that they should be included. Feminist Majority President Eleanor Smeal was angered. "Rather than trying to seek an exemption for police officers and military personnel who are abusers, we should be concerned with why we are recruiting so many abusers for these positions," she said.[4]

Following the 1999 Columbine High School shooting, a number of states moved to tighten controls over handguns and assault weapons. The California legislature, for example, restricted gun purchases to one per month and tightened a ten-year-old ban on assault weapons. Similarly, Illinois passed a law requiring that gun owners lock their weapons away from anyone under age 14.

In 2004, at the urging of major police organizations, the U.S. Senate scuttled plans for a gun industry protection bill. The bill, which was revived in 2005 and is before congress as this book goes to press, would grant gunmakers and most gun dealers immunity from lawsuits brought by victims of gun crimes and their survivors. The proposed law has been a priority of the NRA and the White House. NRA spokespeople claim that the legislation is necessary to protect the gun industry, which, they say, is being sued out of existence for manufacturing and marketing a legal product.[5]

---

**Assault Weapons: A Primer**

**Legal Definition**
A weapon that can accept a magazine, or bullet chamber, that can easily be removed. It has at least two "assault" features, such as a flash suppressor (which suppresses the light when the weapon is fired) or a protruding pistol grip (which allows it to be held like a pistol).

**Well-Known Types**

**Intratec TEC-9/DC-9**
Made in the USA. Semiautomatic version of the automatic pistol. Can handle magazines with up to 50 rounds.

**Colt AR-15**
Made in the USA. Semiautomatic version of the M-16 military rifle. Holds 9 rounds standard, more with "high-capacity" magazines. Has a pistol grip and flash suppressor.

**Streetsweeper**
U.S.-made version of the Striker-12 shotgun that is made in South Africa. Police often have cited its use among gangs. Holds 12 rounds in a rotating chamber.

**Beretta AR-70**
Made in Italy. Assault rifle that initially was used by Italian special forces. Can fire 650 rounds per minute; its magazine can hold 30 rounds. Comes with pistol grips.

**Norinco MAK-90**
Made in China. Semiautomatic version of the AK-47. Has a 30-round magazine but can handle larger magazines.

*Note:* Firearms not to scale.

*Karl Gelles,* USA Today

---

[1]"Justice Department Reverses Second-Amendment Interpretation." Web posted at http://www.jointogether.org/gv/news/summaries/reader/0,2061,550836,00.html (accessed August 27, 2002).

[2]PL 103–322, 108 Stat. 1796 (codified as amended in scattered sections of 18, 21, 28, 42, etc., U.S.).

[3]PL 104–208. An amendment to Section 921(a) of Title 18, U.S.C. Also known as the Lautenberg Amendment.

[4]Jacob R. Clark, "Police Careers May Take a Beating from Fed Domestic-Violence Law," *Law Enforcement News,* Vol. 23, No. 461 (February 14, 1997), p. 1.

[5]"Senate Shoots Down Gun Industry Immunity," MSNBC.com. March 2, 2004. Web posted at http://www.msnbc.msn.com/id/4429245 (accessed June 5, 2004).

Chapter 18 provides additional information about cybercrime, including computer viruses, software piracy, and the law enforcement technologies used to fight it. Learn more about cybercrime and efforts to combat it via Web Extra 2–20 at cjtoday.com.

**WEB** EXTRA

# Terrorism

Following the September 11, 2001, attacks on the World Trade Center and the Pentagon, terrorism and its prevention became primary concerns of American justice system officials. Before 9/11, however, terrorism was far from unknown. In 2001, for example, terrorist attacks totaled 864 worldwide—down from the 1,106 reported a year earlier.[117]

The great blackout of 2003, which affected as many as 50 million people in the United States and Canada, demonstrated the fragility of the nation's energy grid—another potential terrorist target. To assist in developing protection for the nation's critical infrastructure, the Homeland Security Act of 2002 created the Department of Homeland Security and made its director a Cabinet member. Similarly, in an effort to protect vital interests from future acts of terrorism, the U.S. government is building a whole new Internet of its own. Dubbed GOVNET, the service will provide secure voice and data communication by remaining physically and electronically separate from existing Internet routers and gateways.[118] Visit the Department of Homeland Security via Web Extra 2–21 at cjtoday.com. Terrorism and efforts to combat it are discussed in detail in Chapter 17.

**WEB** EXTRA

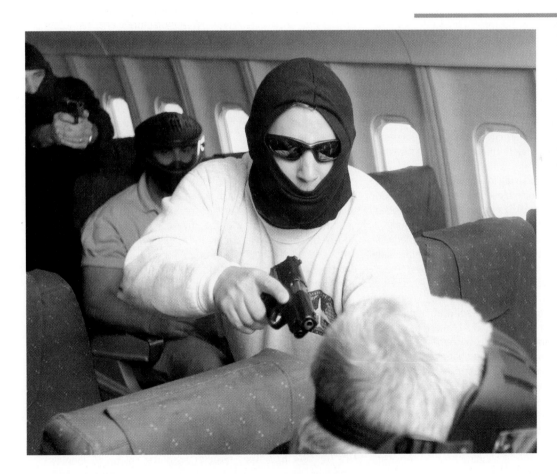

A pistol-wielding FAA sky marshal running between seats during a simulated hijacking aboard a retired L-1011 aircraft at the FAA training facility in Pomona, New Jersey. The FAA began hiring many additional sky marshals following the September 11, 2001, terrorist attacks on national landmarks.

© Tim Shaffer, Reuters NewMedia, Inc./CORBIS

## Hunting Cybercrooks

The cybersleuths who helped smoke out some of the biggest crooks online can be as reclusive as their prey.

Tucked inside an inconspicuous office in a business park on the banks of the Monongahela River near Pittsburgh, two dozen employees of the National Cyber-Forensics & Training Alliance quietly peck away at PCs in small cubicles. Here, the nation's cyberequivalent of *CSI* relies on a computer lab that simulates Internet attacks and diagnostic tools that extract clues from tainted PCs and suspicious Web sites. Yet few people are aware of the non-profit group.

"I chuckle whenever people complain nothing is being done to stop cybercrime," says investigator Sarah Patrick, who—like a dozen other college students—monitors Web sites and chat rooms from a desktop computer in a small, unadorned cubicle. "What have I been doing the past nine months?"

That was abundantly clear in August, when a Justice Department sting led to 160 arrests, including dozens of spammers and online fraudsters. Key evidence came from NCFTA, whose discoveries could fetch more arrests. "We're at the start—not the end—of a major crackdown on digital crime," FBI Special Agent Tom Grasso says. As consumer losses to online fraud mount, the FBI has identified cybercrime as one of its top priorities, behind terrorism and counterintelligence.

### LAB WORK

The rugged mountains of western Pennsylvania seem more suited for deer hunting than for hunting the Internet's most wanted criminals.

But Pittsburgh is considered a digital epicenter by federal officials. It is also home to Carnegie Mellon University's CERT Coordination Center and near the FBI's Internet Crime Complaint Center (IC3) and finger-printing facility, both in West Virginia.

NCFTA was established in 2002 as an extension of the Pittsburgh High Tech Crimes Task Force, a team of federal, state and local law enforcement officials. The federal government, private industry and academia underwrite NCFTA's annual budget of about $750,000.

Microsoft recently donated $46,000 in software and lent an analyst, Liz Christopher.

Security experts compare NCFTA to a teaching hospital, where cases are treated and employees share research and training. NCFTA, they say, could be the template for how tech companies work with government agencies to tackle cybercrime. "It's a spectacular idea to have the learning take place in the context of real-world cases," says Alan Paller, director of SANS Institute, an Internet security think tank and training center.

The NCFTA's deathly quiet office resembles a college study hall or a library more than it does a bustling hospital. Analysts methodically peck away at PCs, looking for leads in areas in which they specialize. What they find they share with other analysts and law enforcement officials who also work in the office. Patrick, for example, scours Russian Web sites to follow the exploits of organized crime groups. She routinely engages in online chats for clues.

Microsoft technical analysts Bryan McDoweel (rear) and Liz Christopher (left), and FBI agents Dan Larkin and Tom Grasso work to train students at the National Cyber-Forensics & Training Alliance in Pittsburgh, Pennsylvania.
© 2004 Jason Cohn/Photo by www.jasoncohn.com

She says online misdeeds are soaring there because the post–Soviet Union lacks civil and criminal code, the area is economically depressed, and there is a high degree of engineering talent among the young, who view the Internet as an ideal vehicle for stealing. "There is a cultural mind-set that it's OK to gouge rich Americans," says Patrick, a University of Pittsburgh graduate student who in August presented a paper on Internet crime in Russia. Behind Patrick, a private room with five workstations is home to a lab, where another investigator sifts through the computer hard drives and disks of a suspected spammer. Special software lets investigators view files, e-mail and Web searches—including those deleted—on a hard drive. The cybersleuths also sift through criminal files and the IC3 database of criminal activity to spot links between suspected spammers and crooks.

Digital evidence is shared among a coterie of NCFTA partners—the FBI, the National White Collar Crime Center, Carnegie Mellon, West Virginia University, Microsoft and others—to understand who is behind digital attacks and track them down. "As much as we've been trained in cybercrime, the reality is we need the tech industry's expertise to target the bad guys," says Dan Larkin, unit chief of IC3 and founder of NCFTA. Larkin recently barnstormed Silicon Valley to recruit tech companies as partners.

"We have a lot of resources law enforcement doesn't. We're on the front line," says Stirling McBride, senior investigator in Microsoft's digital-integrity group, which shares information with NCFTA. "We have trap (e-mail) accounts set up to identify spammers. We collect data (spam) they need to present a case."

When Microsoft, America Online and others develop cases, rather than try to find law enforcement interested in them—as they sometimes did before—they hand information to NCFTA. It, in turn, goes to the proper law-enforcement agency to build a case and pursue charges.

## CJ NEWS *(continued)*

During Justice's recent investigation, the NCFTA discovered through industry experts that hundreds of powerful computers at the Defense Department and U.S. Senate were hijacked by hackers, who used them to send spam e-mail. It is unclear how long the computers were compromised or how much spam was sent, investigators say. Authorities are in the process of repairing the computers.

Investigators also came across new spam and phishing schemes that incorporate digital images to deceive consumers and elude computer defenses. Phishing scams use e-mail to trick consumers into surrendering personal information on bogus Web sites. Christopher, the Microsoft investigator lent to the NCFTA, concentrates on passing phishing-related data from Microsoft. "We see her as a conduit to get information from Microsoft," Grasso says.

### A TOUGH TASK

Although federal authorities have made strides in digital gumshoeing, they are more accustomed to chasing bank robbers than computer nerds. Hunting high-tech high jinks requires extensive training and a new crime-fighting approach, admits Bruce Townsend, who coordinates cybercrime investigations for the U.S. Secret Service.

Complicating matters, the few computer crime laws on the books are poorly written and a Bush administration strategy on cybersecurity lacks government regulations and funding, critics say. Historically, private sector–government partnerships sputter and have little impact.

There can be jurisdictional snags with foreign governments when trying to extradite suspects, many of whom strike with impunity from Europe and Asia. Spammers, for example, increasingly are establishing operations in China and South Korea, security experts say.

The challenge can be as daunting as getting President Bush and Sen. John Kerry to share a podium in Ohio to swap Vietnam War stories. Tech companies are loath to share sensitive information with anyone, and investigators are reluctant to have companies wade into law-enforcement matters. "Many companies don't have the know-how or resources to investigate, and the cops don't have the expertise," says John Frazzini, a former Secret Service agent who now is a computer-security consultant.

By necessity, authorities often rely on old-fashioned crime-fighting methods besides cyberforensics. Private investigators at Microsoft and AOL supply information to cops.

And, if all else fails, authorities offer cash rewards. Microsoft last year created a $5 million reward fund for information leading to the arrest and conviction of writers of viruses and worms. A $250,000 slice of the fund led to the May arrest of Sven Jaschan, a German teenager who confessed to writing the Sasser and Netsky worms, which infected millions of computers worldwide this year.

Still, the crime-busting exploits of NCFTA and others are an encouraging start, says Howard Schmidt, chief information security officer at eBay, which has shared information with NCFTA.

"The problem is nearly overwhelming," says U.S. Rep. Mac Thornberry, R–Texas, chairman of the cybersecurity subcommittee of the Select Committee on Homeland Security. But groups such as NCFTA are "good and reasonable efforts."

For the latest in crime and justice news, visit the Talk Justice news feed at http://www.crimenews.info.

*Source:* Jon Swartz, "Shhh, They're Hunting Cybercrooks," *USA Today,* September 20, 2004. Copyright © 2004 *USA Today.* Reprinted with permission.

## SUMMARY

Two comprehensive national programs gather crime statistics in the United States today: the FBI's Uniform Crime Reporting Program and the Bureau of Justice Statistics' National Crime Victimization Survey. These programs provide a picture of victim characteristics through self-reports (the NCVS) and reports to the police (the UCR). Both programs also permit historical comparisons in crime rates and may allow for some degree of predictability as to trends in crime. It is important to realize, however, that all statistics, including crime statistics, are inherently limited by the way in which they are gathered. Statistics can only portray the extent of crime according to the categories they are designed to measure and in terms understood by those who provide the information.

Lacking in most of the crime statistics that are reported today is any realistic appraisal of the human costs of crime, and it is important to remember that statistical aggregates of reported crime, whatever their source, do not reveal the lost lives, human suffering, lessened productivity, and reduced quality of life that crime causes. Unlike the fictional characters on TV crime shows, real-life crime victims lead intricate lives—and it is too easy to lose sight of the people behind the numbers. On the other side of the balance sheet, crime statistics also fail to adequately identify the social costs suffered by offenders and their families. The social deprivation that may lead to crime, the fragmentation of private lives following conviction, and the loss of individuality that comes with confinement are all costs in which society must share, just as they are the culturally imposed consequences of crime and failure. Today's data-gathering strategies fall far short of gauging the human suffering and wasted human potential that both cause and follow crime.

Statistical pictures of crime can serve as powerful tools for creating social policy. Decision makers at all levels, including legislators, other elected officials, and administrators throughout the criminal justice system, rely on crime data to analyze and evaluate existing programs, to fashion and design new crime-control initiatives, to develop funding requests, and to plan new laws and crime-control legislation. Many "get tough" policies, such as the three-strikes movement that swept the country during the 1990s, have been based in large part on the measured ineffectiveness of existing programs to reduce the incidence of repeat offending.

Crimes can be categorized into useful groupings, or typologies, that are relevant for particular purposes. The categories within crime typologies, although they serve as useful analytic conventions, sometimes overlap. For example, corporate crime, which is discussed in this chapter, is also a type of white-collar crime and can be a kind of property crime. Moreover, corporate crime may be perpetrated with the use of computer technology and so can be considered a form of cybercrime. Crimes against women and the elderly, hate crime, corporate and white-collar crime, organized crime, gun crime, drug crime, high-technology and computer crime, and terrorism are all special forms of crime that this chapter discusses.

This chapter points out that there have been three major shifts in crime rates since the gathering of crime statistics began in earnest in this country. The first occurred during the early 1940s, when crime decreased sharply due to the large number of young men who entered military service during World War II. The second noteworthy shift in offense statistics was a dramatic increase in most forms of crime between 1960 and the early 1990s, brought about in part by population demographics—specifically the large numbers of young men in their crime-prone years who had been born following the Second World War. A third major shift came with the significant declines in the rate of most major crimes being reported between 1991 and 2004. A fourth shift in crime trends may be starting now, and some think that recent economic uncertainty, an increased jobless rate among unskilled workers, the growing number of ex-convicts who are back on the streets, and recent growth in the teenage population in this country may lead to sustained increases in crime.

## DISCUSSION QUESTIONS

1. What are the two major crime data–gathering programs in the United States today? How do they differ? How are they alike?

2. What can crime statistics tell us about the crime picture in America? How has that picture changed over time?

3. What are the potential sources of error in the major reports on crime? Can you think of some popular usage of those statistics that might be especially misleading?

4. What is the Crime Index, and how is it computed? What crimes make up the Crime Index? Why is it difficult to add offenses to (or remove them from) the index without reducing its value as a comparative tool?

5. Why are many crime statistics expressed as rates? How does the use of crime rates instead of simple numerical tabulations improve the reporting of crime data?

6. What are the two major categories of Part I offenses in the Uniform Crime Reports? Do some property crimes have a violent aspect? Are there any personal crimes that could be nonviolent? If so, what might they be?

7. What is the hierarchy rule used in crime-reporting programs? What purpose does it serve? What do you think of the modifications in the hierarchy rule that are occurring today under the National Incident-Based Reporting System?

8. What is a clearance rate? What does it mean to say that a crime has been "cleared"? In what ways can a crime be cleared?

**9.** What is the National Incident-Based Reporting System? How does it differ from the traditional Uniform Crime Reporting Program?

**10.** What are the special categories of crime discussed in this chapter? Why are they important?

Visit the Prentice Hall Cybrary of Criminal Justice Links on the Web at http://www .cybrary. info, and familiarize yourself with the Cybrary's features. Note that a number of general categories are listed on the home page. (Click "Show All Categories" at the bottom of the page to see more.) The power of the Cybrary lies in its advanced search capabilities.

Practice using the Cybrary's search feature. Once you have become familiar with how the search feature works, use it to find links to the Uniform Crime Reports (*Hint:* Look for the FBI's home page), the *Sourcebook of Criminal Justice Statistics,* and the Bureau of Justice Statistics.

Visit all three sites to gather information on the crime of rape. Compare the availability of information on rape at these three sites. Compare the sites in other ways. Which do you find most useful? Why? Submit your answers to your instructor if asked to do so.

To complete this Web Quest online, go to the Web Quest module in Chapter 2 of the *Criminal Justice Today* Companion Website at cjtoday.com.

**NOTES**

**i.** Dan Eggen, "Major Crimes in U.S. Increase: 2001 Rise Follows Nine Years of Decline," *Washington Post,* June 23, 2002, p. A1.

**ii.** Ibid.

**iii.** Identity Theft Resource Center website at http://www.idtheftcenter.org (accessed April 4, 2002).

**iv.** Jonathan Turley, "Arrest Me . . . Before I Strike Again," *USA Today,* February 22, 2005, p. 13A.

**v.** Violence Against Women Office, *Stalking and Domestic Violence: Report to Congress* (Washington, DC: U.S. Department of Justice, 2001), p. 5.

**vi.** Ibid.

**vii.** H.R. 4797, 102d Cong. 2d Sess. (1992).

**viii.** Andrew Backover, "Two Former WorldCom Execs Charged," *USA Today* Online, August 1, 2002. Web posted at http://www.usatoday.com/ money/industries/telecom/2002–08–01- worldcom-execs-surrender_x.htm (accessed August 2, 2002).

**ix.** Michael L. Benson, Francis T. Cullen, and William J. Maakestad, *Local Prosecutors and Corporate Crime* (Washington, DC: National Institute of Justice, 1992), p. 1.

**x.** The Organized Crime Control Act of 1970.

**xi.** Suzanne Malveaux, "Bush to CEO's: No More Fudging the Books," CNN.com, July 3, 2002. Web posted at http://www.cnn.com/2002/ ALLPOLITICS/07/03/bush.corporate.reform (accessed July 30, 2002).

**1.** James Q. Wilson, "Point of View," *Chronicle of Higher Education,* June 10, 1992, p. A40.

**2.** "The Programming Insider," *MediaWeek,* February 22, 2005. See, also, Bill Keveney, "Crime Pays for 'CSI' Franchise," *USA Today,* September 16, 2004, p. D1.

**3.** Norval Morris, "Crime, the Media, and Our Public Discourse," National Institute of Justice, Perspectives on Crime and Justice video series, recorded May 13, 1997.

**4.** Federal Bureau of Investigation, *Uniform Crime Reports: Crime in the United States, 1987* (Washington, DC: U.S. Government Printing Office, 1988), p. 1.

**5.** Federal Bureau of Investigation, *Uniform Crime Reports: Crime in the United States, 2004* (Washington, DC: U.S. Government Printing Office, 2005).

**6.** The President's Commission on Law Enforcement and Administration of Justice, *The Challenge of Crime in a Free Society* (Washington, DC: U.S. Government Printing Office, 1967). The commission relied on Uniform Crime Reports data. The other crime statistics reported in this section come from Uniform Crime Reports for various years.

**7.** Frank Hagan, *Research Methods in Criminal Justice and Criminology* (New York: Macmillan, 1982).

**8.** U.S. Department of Justice, *Fiscal Years 2000–2005 Strategic Plan* (Washington, DC: U.S. Government Printing Office, 2000).

**9.** The war on drugs, and the use of that term, can be traced back to the Nixon administration. See Dan Baum, *Smoke and Mirrors: The War on Drugs and the Politics of Failure,* reprint ed. (Boston: Little, Brown, 1997).

**10.** John J. DiIulio, Jr., "The Question of Black Crime," *Public Interest* (Fall 1994), pp. 3–12.

11. Quoted in Dan Eggen, "Major Crimes in U.S. Increase: 2001 Rise Follows Nine Years of Decline," *Washington Post,* June 23, 2002, p. A1.

12. See, for example, James Alan Fox, *Trends in Juvenile Violence: A Report to the United States Attorney General on Current and Future Rates of Juvenile Offending* (Washington, DC: Bureau of Justice Statistics, 1996); and David G. Savage, "Urban Crime Resurges after Decade Drop," *Los Angeles Times,* November 25, 2001, in which Fox continues to predict a rise in crime.

13. That is, while crime clock data may imply that one murder occurs every half hour or so, most murders actually occur during the evening, and only a very few take place around sunrise.

14. Most offense definitions in this chapter are derived from those used by the UCR Program and are taken from the FBI's *Uniform Crime Reports: Crime in the United States, 2004,* or from the Bureau of Justice Statistics, *Criminal Justice Data Terminology,* 2nd ed. (Washington, DC: Bureau of Justice Statistics, 1981).

15. These and other statistics in this chapter are derived primarily from the FBI's *Uniform Crime Reports: Crime in the United States, 2004.*

16. Bureau of Justice Statistics, *Report to the Nation on Crime and Justice,* 2nd ed. (Washington, DC: U.S. Government Printing Office, 1988), p. 4.

17. "Feds Deny Thwarting Sniper Suspect's Confession," CNN.com, October 31, 2002. Web posted at http://www.cnn.com/2002/US/10/30/snipers.interrogation/index.html (accessed October 31, 2002).

18. "Sniper Malvo Given Second Life Sentence," *USA Today,* October 27, 2004, p. 3A.

19. BJS, *Report to the Nation on Crime and Justice,* p. 4.

20. Ibid.

21. For excellent coverage of serial killers, see Steven Egger, *The Killers among Us: An Examination of Serial Murder and Its Investigation* (Upper Saddle River, NJ: Prentice Hall, 1998); Steven A. Egger, *Serial Murder: An Elusive Phenomenon* (Westport, CT: Praeger, 1990); and Stephen J. Giannangelo, *The Psychopathology of Serial Murder: A Theory of Violence* (New York: Praeger, 1996).

22. "BTK" stands for "Bind, Torture, and Kill," an acronym that Rader applied to himself in letters he sent to the media during the 1970s.

23. Several years ago, Lucas recanted all of his confessions, saying that he had never killed anyone—except possibly his mother, a killing he said he didn't remember. See "Condemned Killer Admits Lying, Denies Slayings," *Washington Post,* October 1, 1995.

24. Chikatilo was executed in 1994.

25. See Mark Babineck, "Railroad Killer Gets Death Penalty," Associated Press wire service, May 22, 2000. Web posted at http://cnews.tribune.com/news/tribune/story/0,1235,tribune-nation-37649,00.html (accessed March 3, 2002).

26. Public Law 108-212.

27. FBI, *Uniform Crime Reports: Crime in the United States, 2004.*

28. Federal Bureau of Investigation, *Uniform Crime Reporting Handbook* (Washington, DC: FBI, 1984), p. 10.

29. "Study: Rape Vastly Underreported," Associated Press wire service, April 26, 1992.

30. Ronald Barri Flowers, *Women and Criminality: The Woman as Victim, Offender, and Practitioner* (Westport, CT: Greenwood Press, 1987), p. 36.

31. A. Nichols Groth, *Men Who Rape: The Psychology of the Offender* (New York: Plenum Press, 1979).

32. Susan Brownmiller, *Against Our Will: Men, Women, and Rape* (New York: Simon and Schuster, 1975).

33. Dennis J. Stevens, "Motives of Social Rapists," *Free Inquiry in Creative Sociology,* Vol. 23, No. 2 (November 1995), pp. 117–126.

34. "Teen: Teacher's Pregnancy Planned," Associated Press wire service, August 22, 1997.

35. *Washington v. LeTourneau,* Court TV online, March 18, 1998. Web posted at http://www.courttv.com/trials/letourneau/031898.html (accessed February 20, 2000).

36. BJS, *Report to the Nation on Crime and Justice,* p. 5.

37. Ibid.

38. FBI, *Uniform Crime Reports: Crime in the United States, 2004.* For UCR reporting purposes, *minorities* are defined as African-Americans, Native Americans, Asians, Pacific Islanders, and Alaskan Natives.

39. Details for this story come from "5 Pacers, 7 Fans Charged in Detroit Brawl," Associated Press, December 8, 2004. Web posted at http://abcnews.go.com/Sports/wireStory?id=313524.

40. This offense is sometimes called *assault with a deadly weapon with intent to kill* (AWDWWITK).

41. FBI, *Uniform Crime Reports: Crime in the United States, 2004.*

**42.** BJS, *Report to the Nation on Crime and Justice,* p. 6.

**43.** Ibid.

**44.** "Four Arrested for Stealing Moon Rocks," Associated Press online, July 23, 2002; and Sheena McFarland, "U. Student Arrested for Moon Rock Theft," *Daily Utah Chronicle* online. Web posted at http://www. dailyutahchronicle.com/main.cfm/include/ detail/storyid/259076.html (accessed August 22, 2002).

**45.** "Yale Says Student Stole His Education," *USA Today,* April 12, 1995, p. 3A.

**46.** Steven J. Vaughan-Nichols, "Cisco Source Code Reportedly Stolen," *eWeek,* May 18, 2004. Web posted at http://www.eweek .com/article2/0,1759,1593862,00.asp.

**47.** Ibid.

**48.** FBI, *Uniform Crime Reporting Handbook,* p. 28.

**49.** Matt Stearns and Donald Bradley, "Boy's Last Moments of Life Are Frozen in Mother's Memory," *Kansas City Star,* February 23, 2000.

**50.** "Jury Recommends Life Term in Dragging Death Wednesday," Associated Press wire service, October 3, 2001.

**51.** Patsy Klaus, *Carjacking, 1993–2002* (Washington, DC: Bureau of Justice Statistics, July 2004).

**52.** FBI, *Uniform Crime Reports: Crime in the United States, 2004.*

**53.** As indicated in the UCR definition of *arson.* See Federal Bureau of Investigation, *Uniform Crime Reports: Crime in the United States, 1998* (Washington, DC: U.S. Government Printing Office, 1999).

**54.** FBI, *Uniform Crime Reports: Crime in the United States, 2004.*

**55.** Ibid.

**56.** See the FBI's UCR/NIBRS website at http://www.fbi.gov/hq/cjisd/ucr.htm (accessed August 27, 2005).

**57.** "NIBRS Overview," SEARCH Project website at http://www.nibrs.search.org (accessed February 10, 2000).

**58.** The 1990 Crime Awareness and Campus Security Act (Public Law 101-542) required college campuses to commence publishing annual security reports beginning in September 1992.

**59.** FBI, *Uniform Crime Reports: Crime in the United States, 2004.*

**60.** Katrina Baum and Patsy Klaus, *Violent Victimization of College Students, 1995–2002*

(Washington, DC: Bureau of Justice Statistics, 2005).

**61.** "Trends in Crime and Victimization," *Criminal Justice Research Reports,* Vol. 2, No. 6 (July/August 2001), p. 83.

**62.** For additional information, see Shannan M. Catalano, *Criminal Victimization, 2004* (Washington, DC: Bureau of Justice Statistics, 2005); and Patsy A. Klaus, *Crime and the Nation's Households, 2004* (Washington, DC: Bureau of Justice Statistics, 2005).

**63.** Klaus, *Crime and the Nation's Households, 2004.*

**64.** Catalano, *Criminal Victimization, 2004.*

**65.** Ibid., p. 1.

**66.** See, for example, President's Commission on Law Enforcement and Administration of Justice, *The Challenge of Crime in a Free Society,* pp. 22–23.

**67.** BJS, *Report to the Nation on Crime and Justice,* p. 27.

**68.** Hagan, *Research Methods in Criminal Justice and Criminology,* p. 89.

**69.** Bureau of Justice Statistics, *Criminal Victimization in the United States, 1985* (Washington, DC: U.S. Government Printing Office, 1987), p. 1.

**70.** FBI, *Uniform Crime Reports: Crime in the United States, 2001,* preliminary data. Web posted at http://www.fbi.gov./ucr/ 01prelim.pdf (accessed August 27, 2002).

**71.** Terance D. Miethe and Richard C. McCorkle, *Crime Profiles: The Anatomy of Dangerous Persons, Places, and Situations* (Los Angeles: Roxbury, 1998), p. 19.

**72.** The definition of *rape* employed by the UCR Program, however, automatically excludes crimes of homosexual rape such as might occur in prisons and jails. As a consequence, the rape of males is excluded from the official count for crimes of rape.

**73.** Catalano, *Criminal Victimization, 2004,* p. 6.

**74.** Thomas Simon et al., *Injuries from Violent Crime, 1992–98* (Washington, DC: Bureau of Justice Statistics, 2001), p. 5.

**75.** See, for example, Elizabeth Stanko, "When Precaution Is Normal: A Feminist Critique of Crime Prevention," in Loraine Gelsthorpe and Allison Morris, eds., *Feminist Perspectives in Criminology* (Philadelphia: Open University Press, 1990).

**76.** For more information, see Eve S. Buzawa and Carl G. Buzawa, *Domestic Violence: The Criminal Justice Response* (Thousand Oaks, CA: Sage, 1996).

**77.** "Battered Women Tell Their Stories to the Senate," *Charlotte (N.C.) Observer,* July 10, 1991, p. 3A.

**78.** Patricia Tjaden and Nancy Thoennes, *Full Report of the Prevalence, Incidence, and Consequences of Violence Against Women: Findings from the National Violence Against Women Survey* (Washington, DC: National Institute of Justice, 2000).

**79.** Caroline Wolf Harlow, *Female Victims of Violent Crime* (Washington, DC: Bureau of Justice Statistics, 1991).

**80.** Violence Against Women Office, *Stalking and Domestic Violence: Report to Congress* (Washington, DC: U.S. Department of Justice, 2001).

**81.** 18 U.S.C., Section 2261A.

**82.** As modified through VAWA 2000.

**83.** Violence Against Women Office, *Stalking and Domestic Violence.*

**84.** Much of the data in this section come from Bureau of Justice Statistics, *Crimes Against Persons Age 65 or Older, 1993–2002* (Rockville, MD: BJS, 2005).

**85.** Lamar Jordan, "Law Enforcement and the Elderly: A Concern for the Twenty-First Century," *FBI Law Enforcement Bulletin,* May 2002, pp. 20–23.

**86.** Public Law 101–275.

**87.** H.R. 4797, 102d Cong. 2d Sess. (1992).

**88.** FBI, *Uniform Crime Reports: Crime in the United States, 2004.*

**89.** "Sept. 11 Attacks Cited in Nearly 25 Percent Increase in Florida Hate Crimes," Associated Press wire service, August 30, 2002.

**90.** "Dragging Death Still Haunts Family," APB News, June 7, 1999. Web posted at http://www.apbnews.com/newscenter/breakingnews/1999/06/07/byrd060701.html (accessed January 2, 2000).

**91.** Rita Rubin, "Justice Investigates Metabolife," *USA Today,* August 16–18, 2002, p. 1A.

**92.** Brooke A. Masters and Ben White, "Adelphia Founder, Son Convicted of Fraud," *Washington Post,* July 9, 2004, p. E1.

**93.** Dionne Searcey and Li Yuan, "Adelphia's John Rigas Gets 15 Years," *Wall Street Journal,* June 21, 2005, p. A3.

**94.** Samuel Maull, "Ex-Tyco Execs Convicted in Second Trial," Washington Post.com, June 18, 2005. Web posted at http://www.washingtonpost.com/wp-dyn/content/article/2005/06/17/AR2005061700863.html.

**95.** *Andersen* v. *U.S.,* U.S. Supreme Court, No. 04-368 (decided May 31, 2005).

**96.** Public Broadcasting System, "Enron: After the Collapse." Web posted at http://www.pbs.org/newshour/bb/business/enron/player6.html (accessed August 27, 2002).

**97.** Edwin H. Sutherland, "White-Collar Criminality," *American Sociological Review* (February 1940), p. 12.

**98.** Scott Lindlaw, "Bush to Propose Crackdown on Corporate Abuses: President's Own Business Dealings Come under Scrutiny," Associated Press wire service, July 9, 2002. Web posted at http://www.washingtonpost.com/wp-dyn/articles/A43384-2002Jul9.html.

**99.** Public Law 107–204.

**100.** R. James Woolsey, as quoted on the Transnational Threats Initiative home page of the Center for Strategic and International Studies (CSIS). Web posted at http://www.csis.org/tnt/index.htm (accessed August 22, 2002).

**101.** These ideas were originally expressed by Assistant U.S. Attorney General Laurie Robinson, in an address given at the Twelfth International Congress on Criminology, Seoul, Korea, August 28, 1998.

**102.** Caroline Wolf Harlow, *Firearm Use by Offenders* (Washington, DC: Bureau of Justice Statistics, 2001).

**103.** Ibid., p. 1.

**104.** 18 U.S.C., Section 922(q)(1)(A).

**105.** Harlow, *Firearm Use by Offenders.*

**106.** *Firearms Purchased from Federal Firearm Licensees Using Bogus Identification* (Washington, DC: General Accounting Office, 2001).

**107.** Sarah Brady, "Statement on the Sniper Shootings," October 8, 2002. Web posted at http://www.bradycampaign.org/press/release.asp?Record=429 (accessed October 16, 2002).

**108.** J. M. Chaiken and M. R. Chaiken, *Varieties of Criminal Behavior* (Santa Monica, CA: RAND Corporation, 1982).

**109.** D. McBride, "Trends in Drugs and Death," paper presented at the annual meeting of the American Society of Criminology, Denver, 1983.

**110.** National Criminal Justice Reference Service, *The Micro Domain: Behavior and Homicide,* p. 140. Online at http://www.ncjrs.org/pdffiles/167262-3.pdf (accessed February 23, 2002).

**111.** Bureau of Justice Statistics, *Substance Abuse and Treatment: State and Federal Prisoners* (Washington, DC: U.S. Department of Justice, January 1999).

**112.** Bureau of Justice Statistics, *Drug Use, Testing, and Treatment in Jails* (Washington, DC: U.S. Department of Justice, May 2000).

113. Information in this paragraph comes from John Scalia, *Federal Drug Offenders, 1999, with Trends, 1984–99* (Washington, DC: Bureau of Justice Statistics, 2001); and Bureau of Justice Statistics, *Federal Criminal Case Processing, 2002—With Trends 1982–2002* (Washington, DC: BJS, 2005).

114. Ibid.

115. Rachel Grunwell, "Burglars Benefit from Virtual Tour," *Stuff,* August 22, 2004. Web posted at http://www.stuff.co.nz/stuff/0.2106.3010824a11.00.html.

116. Ibid.

117. Emergency Response and Research Institute, *Summary of Emergency Response and Research Institute Terrorism Statistics: 2000 and 2001.* Web posted at http://www.emergency.com/2002/terroris00-01.pdf (accessed August 22, 2002).

118. "U.S. Plans New Secure Government Internet," Associated Press wire service, October 11, 2001.

# CHAPTER 3

# The Search for Causes

## OUTLINE

- Introduction
- Criminological Theory
- The Classical School
- Biological Theories
- Psychobiological Theories
- Psychological Theories
- Sociological Theories
- Social Process Theories
- Conflict Theories
- Emergent Perspectives

## LEARNING OBJECTIVES

**After reading this chapter, you should be able to:**

- List the various categories of theoretical approaches used to explain crime.
- Describe the basic features of biological theories of crime causation.
- Describe the basic features of psychological explanations for crime.
- Describe the basic features of sociological theories of crime causation.
- Identify two emergent theories of crime causation.

*During the last several years, violent crime in America has been decreasing. And all Americans are grateful. . . . But, unfortunately, American society is still far too violent. The violent crime rate in the United States remains among the highest in the industrialized world.*

—President George W. Bush[1]

*I could kill everyone without blinking an eye!*
—Charlie Manson[2]

*Congress of*

*begun and hel*

*Wednesday the Fourth of*

THE Con

RESOL

or abuse of its powers, that further declaratory and restrictive claus

concurring that the following Articles be proposed to the Legisl

said Legislatures, to be valid to all intents and purposes

of the several States, pursuant to the fifth Article

*Article the first....* After the first enumeration required

which, the proportion shall be se

until the number of Represen

nor more than one Represen

*Article the second....* No law, varying the comp

*Article the third....* Congress shall make no

assemble, and to petiti

*Article the fourth....* A well regulated

*Article the fifth....* No soldier shall

*Article the sixth....* The right f

*Article the seventh....* No person

militia

*Article the eighth....* In

*Article the ni*

*Article the te*

# KEY CONCEPTS

## TERMS

anomie
atavism
behavioral conditioning
Biological School
broken windows thesis
Chicago School
Classical School
conflict perspective
constitutive criminology
containment
dangerousness
deconstructionist theory
defensible space theory
deviance
feminist criminology

hypothesis
interdisciplinary theory
labeling theory
life course perspective
moral enterprise
neoclassical criminology
peacemaking criminology
phrenology
Positivist School
postmodern criminology
psychoanalysis
psychological profiling
Psychological School
psychopath
psychopathology

psychosis
radical criminology
rational choice theory
reaction formation
research
routine activities theory
schizophrenic
social development theory
social disorganization
social learning theory
social process theory
somatotyping
subculture of violence
supermale
theory

## NAMES

Freda Adler
Cesare Beccaria
Howard Becker
Jeremy Bentham
Ernest Burgess
Meda Chesney-Lind
Hervey Cleckley
Albert Cohen
Lawrence Cohen
Kathleen Daly
Marcus Felson

Sigmund Freud
Franz Joseph Gall
Stuart Henry
Richard Herrnstein
John H. Laub
Cesare Lombroso
Henry McKay
Sarnoff Mednick
Robert Merton
Walter Miller
Dragan Milovanovic

Robert Park
Harold Pepinsky
Richard Quinney
Walter Reckless
Robert J. Sampson
Clifford Shaw
William Sheldon
Rita Simon
Edwin Sutherland
James Q. Wilson
Marvin Wolfgang

# Introduction

Hear the author discuss
this chapter at
**cjtoday.com**

In April 2000, hip-hop artist Curtis "50 Cent" Jackson, a rising star in the world of hard-core rap music, was shot nine times in front of his grandmother's home in New York City.[3] One of the bullets hit him in the face. "50," as the singer is known to his fans, survived the shooting but spent months recovering. Two years later, 50 was back on the music scene, having recorded a top-selling album, *Get Rich or Die Tryin,* propelled by his hit song "In Da Club." In 2002 rumors linked 50 to the fatal shooting of legendary Run-DMC DJ Jam Master Jay (born Jason Mizell), and he made headlines when he was arrested for illegal possession of a handgun on New Year's Eve, 2002.[4] 50 told fans that he'd had a bulletproof jacket made for his six-year-old son. In 2005, 50 released the album *The Massacre,* which quickly went Platinum, and his songs "Disco Inferno," "Candy Shop," and "P.I.M.P." led the hip-hop charts. Shortly afterward, rumors circulated that 50 had lost his left hand when a door on his Cadillac slammed shut unexpectedly. The rumors turned out to be false.[5]

As 50's story illustrates, violent crime is no stranger to the hard-core rap world. Murdered rap greats include Tupac Shakur, Notorious B.I.G., Big L., and the Lost Boyz's hip-hop hype man Raymond "Freaky Tah" Rogers. Whether rap music merely reflects the social conditions under which its artists come of age or whether it is a direct cause of the violence that surrounds them is a question to which we will return in a few paragraphs.

No discussion of crime and of the criminal justice system would be complete without considering the *causes* of crime and **deviance**. Criminologists search for answers to the fundamental questions about what causes crime: Why do people commit crime? What are the root causes of violence and aggression? Are people basically good, or are they motivated only by self-interest? More precisely, we might ask, "Why does a particular person commit a particular crime on a given occasion and under specific circumstances?"

**deviance**

A violation of social norms defining appropriate or proper behavior under a particular set of circumstances. Deviance often includes criminal acts.

Rapper 50 Cent performs in Moline, Illinois, in 2003. In 2000, 50 was shot nine times in front of his grandmother's house in New York City. He survived and went on to record dozens of hit songs. Some people think that violent crimes are glorified and encouraged by certain kinds of rap music, especially "gangsta rap," and by some forms of hip-hop.

*AP Wide World Photos*

In this chapter we will look at the causes of crime. Before we begin, however, some brief definitions are in order. *Crime,* as noted in Chapter 1, is a violation of the criminal law without acceptable legal justification,[6] while *deviant behavior* is a violation of social norms that specify appropriate or proper behavior under a particular set of circumstances. Deviant behavior is a broad category that often includes crime.

Many theories have been advanced to explain all sorts of rule-violating behavior. Some observers of the contemporary scene, for example, blame much of today's crime on commonplace episodes of violence in the American media—especially on television, in music, and on film. Experts who study the media estimate that the average American child watches 8,000 murders and 100,000 acts of violence while growing up.[7] At an international conference, Suzanne Stutman, president of the Institute for Mental Health Initiatives, a nonprofit organization in Washington, D.C., reported that studies consistently show that the extent of exposure to television violence in childhood is a good predictor of future criminal behavior.[8] One particular study, released in 2002, found that watching just one hour of television a day can make a person more violent toward others.[9] The study, which was conducted over a 25-year period at New York's Columbia University, used police records to confirm that 45% of young men who had watched three or more hours of television a day went on to commit at least one aggressive act against another person, compared to 9% of young men who had watched for less than one hour per day.

Robert Brown, executive director of the Washington, D.C., Children's Trust Neighborhood Initiative, lays much of the blame for contemporary violence on rap music, especially "gangsta rap" and some forms of hip-hop. "So many of our young men," says Brown, "have accepted false icons of manhood for themselves . . . because the popular culture of videos and rap—Snoop Doggy Dogg and the rest—reinforces that this is the correct way to be. Guys . . . try to exude an aura that says, 'I am so bad that I am not afraid to take your life or to offer mine up in the process.'"[10]

An African-American critic of gangsta rap puts it this way: "The key element is aggression—in rappers' body language, tone, and witty rhymes—that often leaves listeners hyped, on edge, angry about . . . something. Perhaps the most important element in gangsta rap is its messages, which center largely around these ideas: that women are no more than 'bitches and hos,' disposable playthings who exist merely for men's abusive delight; that it's cool to use any means necessary to get the material things you want; and most importantly, it's admirable to be cold-blooded and hard."[11] The Reverend Arthur L. Cribbs, Jr., an African-American social critic, agrees. Cribbs calls gangsta rap "nothing but modern-day violence and vulgarity wrapped and packaged in blackface."[12]

Most people agree that media violence harms society. According to one recent survey, "57% of the public thinks violence in the media is a major factor in real-life violence" of all kinds.[13] But it is less than clear whether violence in the media and aggressive themes in popular music are indeed a cause of crime, as many believe, or merely a reflection of the social conditions that exist

The political right believes that the root cause of violent crime is bad genes or bad morals. Not so, says the left. The root cause of violent crime is bad housing or dead-end jobs. And I tell you that while doing something about the causes of violence surely requires a political ideology, the only way we can determine what those causes are in the first place is to check our ideologies at the door and to try to keep our minds open as wide, and for as long, as we can bear.

—John Monahan, speaking at the U.S. Sentencing Commission's Inaugural Symposium on Crime and Punishment in many American communities today. Findings from studies on the effect of television viewing, for example, may be inadvertently spotlighting existing criminal tendencies among lower-class undereducated teenagers with enough time on their hands for extensive TV viewing. Hence, getting legislators to address the issue of violence in the media is difficult. For example, a proposed labeling system for video games and other forms of entertainment was advanced some years ago by Representatives Zach Wamp (R–Tenn.) and Bart Stupak (D–Mich.). They argued that the government requires warning labels on food, alcohol, and tobacco and should do likewise on sources of violence, but the proposal was voted down 266–161.[14]

# Criminological Theory

It is easy to understand why the entertainment industry and the media are often targeted as the cause of crime and criminal violence. However, many other types of explanations for crime are also viable, such as genetic abnormalities, individual psychological differences, or variations in patterns of early socialization that may predispose people to crime and violence. Likewise, it is prudent to examine social institutions such as the family, schools, and churches for their role in reducing or enhancing the likelihood of criminality among people.

One thing is certain: There is no single cause of crime; it is rooted in a diversity of causal factors and takes a variety of forms, depending on the situation in which it occurs. Nonetheless, some theories of human behavior help us understand why certain people engage in acts that society defines as criminal or deviant, while others do not. A **theory** is a kind of model. Theories posit relationships, often of a causal sort, between events and things under study. Formally, a complete theory consists of a series of interrelated propositions that attempt to describe, explain, predict, and ultimately control some class of events. A theory's explanatory power derives primarily from its inherent logical consistency, and theories are tested by how well they describe and predict reality. In other words, a good theory provides relatively complete understanding of the phenomenon under study, and carefully made observations support predictions based on the theory. A good theory fits the facts, and it stands up to continued scrutiny. Figure 3–1 uses the association between poverty and crime as an example to diagram the important aspects of theory creation in the social sciences.

History is rife with theories purporting to explain rule-violating behavior. For example, an old Roman theory, based on ancient observations that more crime and deviance occur on nights with a full moon, proposed that the moon causes a kind of temporary insanity, or *lunacy*. According to this theory, deviant behavior isn't random; it waxes and wanes in cadence with the lunar cycle. Although modern statisticians have noted an association between phases of the moon and crime rates, the precise mechanism by which the moon influences behavior—if it does—has never been adequately explained.

As mentioned, a complete theory attempts to flesh out all of the causal links between phenomena that are associated or "correlated." For example, some comprehensive theories of lunacy suggest that light from the full moon stimulates the reticular-activating system (RAS) in the limbic portion of the human brain, which makes people more excitable and hyperactive—and thus more likely to behave in deviant ways and to commit crime. Others have suggested, quite simply, that people commit more crimes when the moon is full because it is easier to see.

Theories, once created, must be tested to determine whether they are valid, and modern criminology has become increasingly scientific.[15] Theory testing usually involves the development of **hypotheses** based on what the theory under scrutiny would predict. A theory of lunacy, for example, might be tested in a variety of ways, including (1) observing rates of crime and deviance on nights when the light of the full moon is obscured by clouds (we would expect no rise in crime rates if the RAS or visibility explanations are correct); and (2) examining city crime rates on full-moon nights—especially in well-lit city areas where the light of the moon hardly increases visibility. If the predictions made by a theory are validated by careful observation, the theory gains greater acceptability.

Generally accepted research designs—coupled with careful data-gathering strategies and statistical techniques for data analysis—have yielded considerable confidence in certain explanations for crime, while at the same time disproving others. Theories of crime causation that have met rigorous scientific tests for acceptability give policymakers the intellectual basis they need to create informed crime-control strategies. The ultimate goal of **research** and theory building in criminology is to provide models that permit a better understanding of criminal behavior and that enhance the development of strategies intended to address the problem of crime.

While we will use the word *theory* in describing various explanations for crime throughout this chapter, it should be recognized that the word is only loosely applicable to some of the perspectives we will discuss. As noted, many social scientists insist that to be considered "theories," explanations must consist of sets of clearly stated, logically interrelated, and measurable propo-

**theory**

A set of interrelated propositions that attempt to describe, explain, predict, and ultimately control some class of events. A theory gains explanatory power from inherent logical consistency and is "tested" by how well it describes and predicts reality.

**hypothesis**

An explanation that accounts for a set of facts and that can be tested by further investigation. Also, something that is taken to be true for the purpose of argument or investigation.[i]

**research**

The use of standardized, systematic procedures in the search for knowledge.

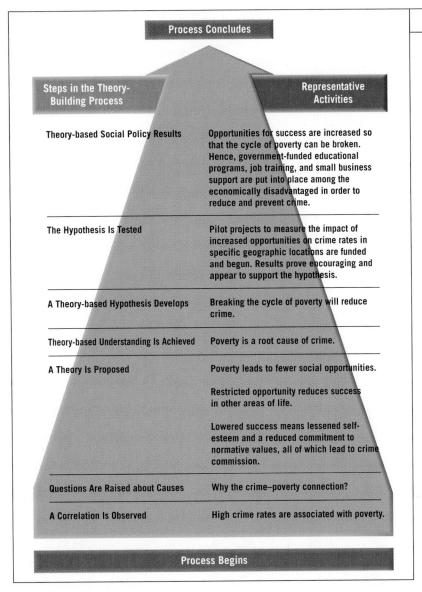

**FIGURE 3–1**

Steps in criminal justice theory building and social policy creation.

**Process Concludes**

| Steps in the Theory-Building Process | Representative Activities |
|---|---|
| Theory-based Social Policy Results | Opportunities for success are increased so that the cycle of poverty can be broken. Hence, government-funded educational programs, job training, and small business support are put into place among the economically disadvantaged in order to reduce and prevent crime. |
| The Hypothesis Is Tested | Pilot projects to measure the impact of increased opportunities on crime rates in specific geographic locations are funded and begun. Results prove encouraging and appear to support the hypothesis. |
| A Theory-based Hypothesis Develops | Breaking the cycle of poverty will reduce crime. |
| Theory-based Understanding Is Achieved | Poverty is a root cause of crime. |
| A Theory Is Proposed | Poverty leads to fewer social opportunities. Restricted opportunity reduces success in other areas of life. Lowered success means lessened self-esteem and a reduced commitment to normative values, all of which lead to crime commission. |
| Questions Are Raised about Causes | Why the crime–poverty connection? |
| A Correlation Is Observed | High crime rates are associated with poverty. |

**Process Begins**

sitions. The fact that few of the "theories" that follow rise above the level of organized conjecture, and that many others are not readily amenable to objective scrutiny through scientific testing, is one of the greatest failures of social science today.

Also, many contemporary theories of deviant and criminal behavior are far from complete, offering only limited ideas rather than complete explanations for the behavior in question. Moreover, when we consider the wide range of behaviors regarded as criminal—from murder to drug use to white-collar crime—it is difficult to imagine a theory that can explain them all.

For our purposes, explanations of criminal behavior fall into eight general categories:

- Classical
- Biological
- Psychobiological
- Psychological
- Sociological
- Social process
- Conflict
- Emergent

The differences among these approaches are summarized in Table 3–1. A ninth category could be **interdisciplinary theories**. These approaches integrate a variety of theoretical viewpoints in an

**interdisciplinary theory**

An approach that integrates a variety of theoretical viewpoints in an attempt to explain crime and violence.

**TABLE 3–1**

## TYPES OF CRIMINOLOGICAL THEORY

| Type | Theorists | Characteristics |
|---|---|---|
| **Classical and Neoclassical** | | |
| Free will theories | Beccaria | Crime is caused by the individual exercise of free will. Prevention is possible through swift and certain punishment that offsets any gains to be had through criminal behavior. |
| Hedonistic calculus | Bentham | |
| Rational choice theory | Cohen & Felson | |
| Routine activities theory | | |
| **Biological** | | |
| Phrenology | Gall | "Criminal genes" cause deviant behavior. Criminals are identifiable through physical characteristics or genetic makeup. Treatment is generally ineffective, but aggression may be usefully redirected. |
| Atavism | Lombroso | |
| Criminal families | Dugdale | |
| | Goddard | |
| Somatotypes | Sheldon | |
| **Psychobiological** | | |
| Chromosome theory | Jacobs | Human DNA, environmental contaminants, nutrition, hormones, physical trauma, and body chemistry play important and interwoven roles in producing human cognition, feeling, and behavior— including crime. |
| Biochemical approaches | | |
| Heredity | Mednick; Wilson & Herrnstein | |
| **Psychological** | | |
| Behavioral conditioning | Pavlov | Crime is the result of inappropriate behavioral conditioning or a diseased mind. Treatment necessitates extensive behavioral therapy. |
| Psychoanalysis | Freud | |
| Psychopathology | Cleckley | |
| **Sociological** | | |
| Social disorganization | Park & Burgess; Shaw & McKay | The structure of society and its relative degree of organization or disorganization are important actors contributing to the prevalence of criminal behavior. Group dynamics, group organization, and subgroup relationships form the causal nexus out of which crime develops. Effective social policy may require basic changes in patterns of socialization and an increase in accepted opportunities for success. |
| Anomie | Durkheim; Merton | |
| Subcultures | Cohen | |
| Focal concerns | Miller | |
| Subculture of violence | Wolfgang & Ferracuti | |

## TYPES OF CRIMINOLOGICAL THEORY *(continued)*

TABLE 3–1

**Social Process**

| | | |
|---|---|---|
| Differential association | Sutherland | Crime results from the failure of self-direction, inadequate social roles, or association with defective others. Social policy places responsibility for change on the offender. |
| Social learning | Burgess & Akers | |
| Containment | Reckless | |
| Social control | Hirschi | |
| Neutralization | Sykes & Matza | |
| Labeling | Becker | The source of criminal behavior is unknown, but an understanding of crime requires recognition that the definition of crime is imposed on behavior by the wider society. Individuals defined as "criminal" may be excluded by society from "normal" opportunities. Therapy requires a total reorientation of the offender. |
| Social development theory Life course perspective | Sampson & Laub | Human development occurs simultaneously on many levels, including psychological, biological, familial, interpersonal, cultural, societal, and ecological. The life course perspective notes that criminal behavior tends to follow an identifiable pattern throughout a person's life cycle. |

**Conflict**

| | | |
|---|---|---|
| Radical criminology | Turk; Vold; Chambliss | Conflict is fundamental to social life. Crime is a natural consequence of social, political, and economic inequities. |
| Peacemaking criminology | Pepinsky; Quinney | Fundamental changes to the structure of society are needed to eliminate crime. |

**Emergent**

| | | |
|---|---|---|
| Feminist criminology | Adler; Simon; Daly & Chesney-Lind | Feminist criminology emphasizes the need for gender awareness in the criminological enterprise. |
| Constitutive criminology | Henry & Milovanovic | Crime is a social phenomenon and, as such, is socially constructed. |
| Postmodern criminology | Henry & Milovanovic | Deconstructionist approaches challenge existing theories in order to replace them with perspectives more relevant to the modern era. |

attempt to explain crime and violence. Harvard University's Project on Human Development in Chicago Neighborhoods is one example of an ongoing interdisciplinary study of the causes of crime. Described in more detail later in this chapter, the Harvard project is examining the roles of personality, school, and community as they contribute to juvenile delinquency and criminal behavior. See Web Extra 3–1 at cjtoday.com for more information on the project. Web Extra 3–2 leads to more information on the general categories of criminological theory mentioned here, and Library Extra 3–1 at cjtoday.com discusses recent theoretical developments in the field of criminological theory.

# The Classical School

**Classical School**

An eighteenth-century approach to crime causation and criminal responsibility that grew out of the Enlightenment and that emphasized the role of free will and reasonable punishments. Classical thinkers believed that punishment, if it is to be an effective deterrent, has to outweigh the potential pleasure derived from criminal behavior.

Theories of the **Classical School** of crime causation dominated criminological thought for much of the late eighteenth and early nineteenth centuries. These theories represented a noteworthy advance over previous thinking about crime because they moved beyond superstition and mysticism as explanations for deviance. As noted criminologist Stephen Schafer puts it, "In the eighteenth-century individualistic orientation of criminal law, the act was judged and the man made responsible."[16] A product of the Enlightenment then sweeping through Europe, the Classical School demanded recognition of rationality and the ability to exercise informed choice in human social life.

Most classical theories of crime causation, both old and new, make certain basic assumptions. Among them are these:

- Crime is caused by the individual exercise of free will. Human beings are fundamentally rational, and most human behavior is the result of free will coupled with rational choice.
- Pain and pleasure are the two central determinants of human behavior.
- Crime erodes the bond that exists between individuals and society and is therefore an immoral form of behavior.
- Punishment, a necessary evil, is sometimes required to deter law violators from repeating their crime and to serve as an example to others who would also violate the law.
- Crime prevention is possible through swift and certain punishment that offsets any gains to be had through criminal behavior.

**neoclassical criminology**

A contemporary version of classical criminology that emphasizes deterrence and retribution and that holds that human beings are essentially free to make choices in favor of crime and deviance or conformity.

## Cesare Beccaria: Crime and Punishment

In 1764, Cesare Beccaria (1738–1794) published his *Essays on Crimes and Punishment*. The book was an immediate success and stirred a hornet's nest of controversy over the treatment of criminal offenders. Beccaria proposed basic changes in the criminal laws of his day to make them more "humanitarian." He called for the abolition of physical punishment and an end to the death penalty. Beccaria is best remembered for his suggestion that punishment should be just sufficient to deter criminal behavior but should never be excessive. Because Beccaria's writings stimulated many other thinkers throughout the eighteenth and early nineteenth centuries, he is referred to today as the founder of the Classical School of criminology.

**rational choice theory**

A perspective on crime causation that holds that criminality is the result of conscious choice. Rational choice theory predicts that individuals will choose to commit crime when the benefits of doing so outweigh the costs of disobeying the law.

## Jeremy Bentham: Hedonistic Calculus

Among those influenced by Beccaria was the Englishman Jeremy Bentham (1748–1832). Bentham devised a "hedonistic calculus," which essentially said that the exercise of free will would cause an individual to avoid committing a crime as long as the punishment for committing that crime outweighed the benefits to be derived from committing it. Bentham termed this philosophy of social control *utilitarianism*. Both Bentham and Beccaria agreed that punishment had to be "swift and certain"—as well as just—to be effective. Learn more about Jeremy Bentham at Web Extra 3–3 at cjtoday.com.

## The Neoclassical Perspective

A contemporary theory with roots in the Classical School, **neoclassical criminology** is a perspective that owes much to the early classical thinkers. Although classical criminology focuses primarily on pleasure and pain as motivators of human behavior, neoclassical criminology places greater emphasis on rationality and cognition. Central to such perspectives is **rational choice theory**, a point of view that holds that criminality is largely the result of conscious choices that people make.

According to the theory, offenders choose to violate the law when they believe that the benefits of doing so outweigh the costs.

Rational choice theory is represented by a somewhat narrower perspective called **routine activities theory**. Routine activities theory was first proposed by Lawrence Cohen and Marcus Felson in 1979.[17] Cohen and Felson argued that lifestyles significantly affect both the volume and type of crime found in any society, and they noted that "the risk of criminal victimization varies dramatically among the circumstances and locations in which people place themselves and their property."[18] Lifestyles that contribute to criminal opportunities are likely to result in crime because they increase the risk of potential victimization.[19] For example, a person who routinely uses an automated teller machine late at night in an isolated location is far more likely to be preyed on by robbers than is someone who stays home after dark. Rational choice theorists concentrate on "the decision-making process of offenders confronted with specific contexts" and have shifted "the focus of the effort to prevent crime . . . from broad social programs to target hardening, environmental design or any impediment that would [dissuade] a motivated offender from offending."[20]

Central to the routine activities approach is the claim that crime is likely to occur when a motivated offender and a suitable target come together in the absence of a *capable guardian.* Capable guardians are those who effectively discourage crime and prevent it from occurring. Members of neighborhood watch groups, for example, might be capable guardians. Capable guardians do not necessarily have to confront would-be offenders directly but might be people who have completed classes in crime prevention and who have taken steps to reduce their chances of victimization.

| **routine activities theory** |
| :--- |
| A neoclassical perspective that suggests that lifestyles contribute significantly to both the volume and the type of crime found in any society. |

> [Television] poisons the minds of our young people . . . with destructive messages of casual violence and even more casual sex.
>
> —**Bob Dole, former Republican presidential candidate**

## Social Policy and Classical Theories

Much of the practice of criminal justice in America today is built on concepts provided by Classical School theorists. Many contemporary programs designed to prevent crime, for example, have their philosophical roots in the classical axioms of deterrence and punishment. Modern heirs of the Classical School see punishment as central to criminal justice policy, use evidence of high crime rates to argue that punishment is a necessary crime preventive, and believe punishment is a natural and deserved consequence of criminal activity. Such thinkers call for greater prison capacity and new prison construction. In Chapter 1, we used the term *public-order advocates,* which can be applied to modern-day proponents of classical theory who frequently seek stiffer criminal laws and greater penalties for criminal activity. The emphasis on punishment as an appropriate response to crime, however, whether founded on principles of deterrence or revenge, has left many contemporary criminal justice policy initiatives foundering in overcrowded prisons and packed courtrooms.

# Biological Theories

Biological theories of crime causation, which had fallen into disrepute during the past few decades, are beginning to experience something of a contemporary resurgence. Most early theories of the **Biological School** of crime causation, which built on inherited or bodily characteristics and features, made certain fundamental assumptions. Among them are these:

| **Biological School** |
| :--- |
| A perspective on criminological thought that holds that criminal behavior has a physiological basis. |

- Basic determinants of human behavior, including criminal tendencies, are constitutionally or genetically based.

- The basic determinants of human behavior, including criminality, may be passed on from generation to generation. In other words, a penchant for crime may be inherited.

- At least some human behavior is the result of biological propensities inherited from more primitive developmental stages in the evolutionary process. Some human beings may be further along the evolutionary ladder than others, and their behavior may reflect it.

## Franz Joseph Gall: Phrenology

The idea that the quality of a person can be judged by a study of the person's face is as old as antiquity. Even today, we often judge people on their looks, saying, "He has an honest face" or "She has tender eyes." Horror movies play on unspoken cultural themes to shape the way a "maniac" might look. Jack Nicholson's portrayal of a crazed killer in *The Shining* and Anthony Hopkins' role as a serial killer in *Silence of the Lambs* turned that look into fortunes at the box office.

Cesare Lombroso (left), who has been dubbed "the father of modern criminology," posing with friend Louis Lombard in a rare photograph from 1909.
*Culver Pictures, Inc.*

Franz Joseph Gall (1758–1828) was one of the first thinkers to theorize about the idea that bodily constitution might reflect personality. Gall was writing at a time when it was thought that organs throughout the body determined one's mental state and behavior. People were said to be "hard-hearted" or to have a "bad spleen" that filled them with bile. Gall focused on the head and the brain and called his approach *cranioscopy*. It can be summarized in four propositions:

> **Biological explanations shaped criminology at its inception, and today they are reemerging with fresh vigor and increased potential.**
>
> —Nicole Rafter, Northeastern University[ii]

- The brain is the organ of the mind.
- The brain consists of localized faculties or functions.
- The shape of the skull reveals the underlying development (or lack of development) of areas within the brain.
- The personality can be revealed by a study of the skull.

Gall never systematically "tested" his theory in a way that would meet contemporary scientific standards. Even so, his approach to predicting behavior, which came to be known as **phrenology**, quickly spread throughout Europe. Gall's student, Johann Gaspar Spurzheim (1776–1853), brought phrenology to America in a series of lectures and publications on the subject. By 1825, 29 phrenological journals were being produced in the United States and Britain.[21] Until the turn of the twentieth century, phrenology remained popular in some American circles where it was used in some diagnostic schemes to classify new prisoners.

**phrenology**

The study of the shape of the head to determine anatomical correlates of human behavior.

## Cesare Lombroso: Atavism

Gall's theory was "deterministic" in the sense that it left little room for choice. What a person did depended more on the shape of the skull than on the exercise of free will. Other biological theories would soon build on that premise. One of the best known is that created by the Italian psychologist Cesare Lombroso (1835–1909).

Lombroso began his criminal anthropology with a postmortem evaluation of famous criminals, including one by the name of Vilella. Before Vilella died, Lombroso had the opportunity to interview him on a number of occasions. After Vilella's death, Lombroso correlated earlier observations of personality traits with measurable physical abnormalities. As a result of this and other studies, Lombroso concluded that criminals were atavistic human beings—throwbacks to earlier stages of evolution who were not sufficiently mentally advanced for successful life in the modern world. **Atavism** was identifiable in suspicious individuals, Lombroso suggested, through measures designed to reveal "primitive" physical characteristics.

In the late nineteenth century, Charles Darwin's theory of evolution was rapidly being applied to a wide range of fields. It was not surprising, therefore, that Lombroso linked evolution and criminality. What separated Lombroso from his predecessors, however, was that he continually refined his theory through ongoing observation. Based on studies of known offenders, whom he compared to conformists, Lombroso identified a large number of atavistic traits, which, he claimed, characterized criminals. Among them were long arms, large lips, crooked noses, an abnormally large amount of body hair, prominent cheekbones, two eyes of different colors, and ears that lacked clearly defined lobes.

Atavism implies that certain people are born criminals. Throughout his life, Lombroso grappled with the task of determining what proportion of the total population of offenders were born criminals. His estimates ranged at different times between 70% and 90%. Career criminals and those who committed crimes of opportunity without atavistic features he termed *criminaloids,* and he recognized the potential causative roles of greed, passion, and circumstance in their behavior.

Today, Lombroso is known as the founder of the **Positivist School** of criminology because of the role observation played in the formulation of his theories. Stephen Schafer calls Lombroso "the father of modern criminology"[22] because most contemporary criminologists follow in the tradition that Lombroso began—scientific observation and a comparison of theory with fact.

## The Evidence for and Against Atavism

After Lombroso died, two English physicians, Charles Goring and Karl Pearson, conducted a test of atavism, studying more than 3,000 prisoners and comparing them along physiological criteria to an army detachment known as the Royal Engineers. No significant differences were found between the two groups, and Lombroso's ideas rapidly began to fall into disrepute.

A further study of atavism was published in 1939 by Earnest A. Hooton, a distinguished Harvard University anthropologist. Hooton spent 12 years constructing anthropometric profiles—profiles based on human body measurements—of 13,873 male convicts in ten different American states. He measured each inmate in 107 different ways and compared them to 3,203 volunteers from National Guard units, firehouses, beaches, and hospitals. Surprisingly, Hooton did find some basis for Lombroso's beliefs, and he concluded that the inmate population in his study demonstrated a decided physical "inferiority."

However, Hooton never recognized that the prisoners he studied were only a subgroup of the population of all offenders throughout the country. They were, in fact, the least successful offenders—the ones who had been caught and imprisoned. Hooton may have unknowingly measured other criminals—the ones who had avoided capture—among his "conformist" population. Hence the "inferiority" Hooton observed may have been an artificial product of a process of selection (arrest) by the justice system.

**atavism**

A condition characterized by the existence of features thought to be common in earlier stages of human evolution.

**Positivist School**

An approach to criminal justice theory that stresses the application of scientific techniques to the study of crime and criminals.

The Bertillion system of identification being applied to a subject in the years prior to the development of fingerprinting. The theory of atavism, based on the ideas of Charles Darwin, supported the use of physical anthropology in the identification of offenders.

*Courtesy of the Library of Congress*

# Criminal Families

The concept of biological inheritance has been applied to "criminal families" as well as to individuals. The idea of mental degeneration as an inherited contributor to crime was first explored by Richard Dugdale.[23] Dugdale used the family tree method to study a family he called the Jukes, publishing his findings in 1877. The Juke lineage had its beginning in America with "Max" (whose last name is unknown), a descendant of Dutch immigrants to New Amsterdam in the early eighteenth century. Two of Max's sons married into the notorious "Juke family of girls," six sisters, all of whom were illegitimate. Male Jukes were reputed to have been "vicious," while Ada, one of the sisters, had an especially bad reputation and eventually came to be known as "the mother of criminals."

Dugdale found that, during the next 75 years, Ada's heirs included 1,200 people, most of whom were "social degenerates." Only a handful of socially productive progeny could be identified. In 1915, Dugdale's study of the Jukes was continued by Arthur A. Estabrook, who extended the line to include 2,094 descendants and found just as few conformists.

A similar study was published by Henry Goddard in 1912.[24] Goddard examined the Kallikak family, which contained two clear lines of descent. One emanated from an affair that Revolutionary War soldier Martin Kallikak had with a "feebleminded" barmaid. She bore a son, and the line eventually produced 480 identifiable descendants. After the war, Kallikak returned home and married a "virtuous" Quaker woman in Philadelphia. This legitimate line produced 496 offspring by 1912, of whom only three were abnormal; not one was criminal. The illegitimate group, however, contained over half "feebleminded" or deviant progeny.

The underlying suppositions of these studies are that degenerate and feebleminded people are produced and propagated through bad genetic material, and that crime is an outlet for degenerate urges. However, these studies fail to recognize any effect that socialization and life circumstances have on the development of criminal behavior.

# William Sheldon: Somatotypes

"Constitutional" theories of crime causation refer to the *physical constitution,* or bodily characteristics, of offenders. The last of the famous constitutional theorists was William Sheldon (1893–1977), who developed the idea of **somatotyping**.

**somatotyping**

The classification of human beings into types according to body build and other physical characteristics.

Sheldon studied 200 juvenile delinquents between the ages of 15 and 21 at the Hayden Goodwill Institute in Boston, Massachusetts, and decided that the young men possessed one of three somatotypes (or body types). The types of bodies described by Sheldon were (in his words):

- *Mesomorphs* with a relative predominance of muscle, bone, and connective tissue
- *Endomorphs* with a soft roundness throughout the various regions of the body; short tapering limbs; small bones; and soft, smooth, velvety skin
- *Ectomorphs* characterized by thinness, fragility, and delicacy of body

Sheldon developed a system of measurements by which an individual's physique could be expressed as a combination of three numbers, such as 4.0–4.0–3.5 (the representation of an average male). The numbers represented the degree of mesomorphy, endomorphy, and ectomorphy present in the individual on a scale of 0 to 7, where 0 indicates a complete lack of features of one category. American females were said to average 5.0–3.0–3.5 on the scale. Sheldon wrote that each somatotype was possessed of a characteristic personality, and believed that predominantly mesomorphic individuals were most prone to aggression, violence, and delinquency.[25]

# Social Policy and Biological Theories

Because traditional biological theories of crime causation attribute the cause of crime to fundamental physical characteristics that are not easily modified, they suggest the need for extreme social policies. During the 1920s and early 1930s, for example, biological theories of crime causation, especially those focusing on inherited mental degeneration, led to the eugenics movement, under which mentally handicapped women were sometimes sterilized to prevent them from bearing offspring. The eugenics movement was institutionalized by the 1927 U.S. Supreme Court case of *Buck* v. *Bell,* in which Justice Oliver Wendell Holmes, Jr., writing in support of a Virginia statute permitting sterilization, said, "It is better for all the world, if instead of waiting to execute degenerate offspring for crime, or to let them starve for their imbecility, society can prevent those persons who are manifestly unfit from continuing their kind."[26] Visit Web Extra 3–4 at cjtoday.com to learn more about biological theories of crime and violence.

**WEB EXTRA**

# Psychobiological Theories

During the past few decades, researchers have taken a sophisticated approach to biological theorizing about the causes of crime. Contemporary biochemical and physiological perspectives are sometimes termed *psychobiology*. The psychobiology of crime highlights the role of human DNA, environmental contaminants, nutrition, hormones, physical trauma (especially to the brain), and body chemistry in human cognition, feeling, and behavior.

## Chromosome Theory

The ongoing mapping of human DNA and recent advances in the field of recombinant DNA have rekindled interest in genetic correlates of deviant behavior. More sophisticated than their historical counterparts, the biological theories of today often draw on the latest medical advances or build on popular health concerns.

The links between chromosome patterns and crime were first explored in the 1960s. A normal female has a chromosome structure often diagrammed as "XX" because of how the sex-determining gene pair looks in an electron microscope. A male has a Y chromosome in place of the second X, for a typical male XY pattern. Although it had been known for some time that a few people have abnormal patterns that include "extra" chromosomes (such as XXX females, XXY males with Klinefelter's syndrome, and XXYY "double males"), it wasn't until 1965 that the respected English journal *Nature* reported on the work of Patricia Jacobs, who identified **supermales**—men with an extra Y chromosome whose chromosome structure is diagrammed XYY. Jacobs found that supermales were more common in prisons than in the general population.[27]

| **supermale** |
| --- |
| A human male displaying the XYY chromosome structure. |

Other early studies claimed that the XYY male was more aggressive than other males and that he possessed a number of specific physical and psychological traits, such as height (taller than 6 feet, 1 inch), thinness, acne, a tendency toward homosexuality, a somewhat low IQ, and "a marked tendency to commit a succession of apparently motiveless property crimes."[28] Later studies disputed many of these findings, and the significance of the XYY pattern for behavioral prediction is in doubt today.

## Biochemical Factors and Imbalances

Research in the area of nutrition has produced some limited evidence that the old maxim "You are what you eat!" may contain more than a grain of truth. *Biocriminology* is a field of study that links violent or disruptive behavior to eating habits, vitamin deficiencies, genetics, and other conditions that affect body tissues.

One of the first studies to focus on chemical imbalances in the body as a cause of crime was reported in the British medical journal *Lancet* in 1943.[29] Authors of the study linked murder to hypoglycemia (low blood sugar), which is caused by too much insulin in the blood or by near-starvation diets. Some researchers believe that hypoglycemia reduces the mind's capacity to reason effectively or to judge the long-term consequences of behavior.

Allergic reactions to common foods have been reported as the cause of violence and homicide in a number of studies.[30] Foods said to produce allergic reactions in sensitive individuals, leading to a swelling of the brain and brain stem, include milk, citrus fruit, chocolate, corn, wheat, and eggs. Involvement of the central nervous system in such allergies, it has been suggested, reduces the amount of learning that occurs during childhood and may contribute to delinquency as well as to adult criminal behavior. Some studies have implicated food additives, such as monosodium glutamate, dyes, and artificial flavorings, in producing criminal behavior.[31]

Other research has found that the amount of coffee and sugar consumed by inmates is considerably greater than in the outside population.[32] Theorists have suggested that high blood levels of caffeine and sugar produce antisocial behavior.[33] It is unclear whether inmates consume more coffee due to boredom or whether those with "excitable" personalities need the kind of stimulation coffee drinking produces. On the other hand, habitual coffee drinkers in nonprison populations have not been linked to crime, and other studies, such as that conducted by Mortimer Gross of the University of Illinois, show no link between the amount of sugar consumed and hyperactivity.[34] Similarly, studies "have not yielded evidence that a change in diet will result in [a] significant reduction in aggressive or antisocial behavior" among inmate populations.[35] Nonetheless, some prison programs have limited the intake of dietary stimulants through nutritional management and the substitution of artificial sweeteners for refined sugar.

Vitamins have also been examined for their impact on delinquency. Abram Hoffer found that disruptive children consumed far less than the optimum levels of vitamins $B_3$ and $B_6$ than did nonproblem youths.[36] He claimed that the addition of these vitamins to the diets of children who were deficient in them could control unruly behavior and improve school performance.

Overall, the role of food and diet in producing criminal behavior has not been well established. The American Dietetic Association and the National Council against Health Fraud have concluded that no convincing scientific relationship between crime and diet has yet been demonstrated.[37] Both groups are concerned that poor nutrition may result from programs that reduce or modify diets in an effort to affect behavior.

Hormones have also come under scrutiny as potential behavioral determinants. The male sex hormone, testosterone, has been linked to aggressiveness in males. Some studies of blood-serum levels of testosterone have shown a direct relationship[38] between the amount of chemical present and the degree of violence used by sex offenders,[39] and steroid abuse among bodybuilders has been linked to destructive urges and psychosis.[40] One 1998 study found that high levels of testosterone, especially when combined with low socioeconomic status, produced antisocial personalities, resulting in deviance and criminality.[41]

Some studies of brain chemistry have led researchers to conclude that low levels of certain neurotransmitters, especially serotonin, are directly related to a person's inability to control aggressive impulses.[42] The presence of adequate serotonin levels in the human brain buffers irritating experiences that might otherwise result in anger and aggression. Low serotonin levels may result from the ingestion of toxic pollutants, such as the metals lead and manganese, according to one study.[43] Reduced serotonin levels, say other researchers, is sometimes found in men with an extra Y chromosome.[44]

A malfunctioning endocrine system has also been implicated by researchers as a cause of physical abuse, antisocial behavior, and psychopathology. A Swedish study published in 1999 focused on variations in blood-serum levels of two thyroid hormones: triiodothyronine ($T_3$) and thyroxine ($FT_4$).[45] Researchers found that elevated $T_3$ levels were related to alcoholism and criminality. Serum levels of $FT_4$ were found to be negatively correlated to such behavior.

## Heredity and Other Physical Factors

Other physical factors have been shown to play a role in an individual's inclination toward criminality. Sarnoff Mednick, for example, found some basis for the claim that the autonomic nervous system (ANS) predisposes certain individuals toward criminality by limiting their ability to learn quickly.[46] He claims that those with a slow ANS are unable to inhibit antisocial behavior quickly enough to avoid punishment and stigmatization.[47] Physical trauma, especially brain injury, has also been shown to at times induce severe personality changes, including aggression and violent behavior in people with a previous behavioral history of neither.[48] Similarly, people born with certain abnormalities of the brain, especially frontal lobe dysfunction, may display a penchant for violence.[49] Frontal lobe dysfunction is sometimes caused by reduced cerebral blood flow.

Studies have shown that the behavior of biological children of criminals who are adopted at birth tends to reflect the criminality of biological parents, independent of the environment in which the children were raised.[50] Also, identical twins exhibit a greater similarity in behavior than do nonidentical (or "fraternal") twins, and a number of studies have shown that identical twins are more alike in patterns and degree of criminal involvement than are fraternal twins.[51]

Perhaps the best known of modern-day biological perspectives on crime was proposed by James Q. Wilson and Richard Herrnstein in their book *Crime and Human Nature,*[52] published in 1985. Wilson and Herrnstein argue that inherited traits, such as maleness, aggressiveness, mesomorphic body type, and low intelligence, combine with environmental influences, including poor schools and strained family life, to produce crime. Although the authors reject a firm determinism, asserting that it is the interaction between genetics and environment that determines behavior, they do claim that children who will eventually grow up to be criminals can sometimes be identified early in their lives. The most important factor in the diversion of potential offenders from lives of crime, according to Wilson and Herrnstein, is a healthy family life in which affection for others and conscience can develop.[53] Wilson and Herrnstein also use cross-cultural data from Japan, where crime rates are very low, to suggest that tendencies toward introversion among the Japanese result in fewer serious crimes than in the United States. The Wilson–Herrnstein thesis has been criticized for failing to explain crime that extends beyond "traditional lower-class street crime" and for failing to recognize the political nature of criminal definitions.[54]

> The word needs to go out on the street. We have had it with violence. We have had it with violent people. We're tired of being told to try to understand their childhood or understand their past.
>
> —Newt Gingrich, former Speaker of the House[iii]

# Social Policy and Psychobiological Theories

Psychobiological theories often suggest modifying body chemistry to produce desirable behavioral changes. Hence, just as cancer researchers look for a "magic bullet" that might target defective chromosomes in the human immune system that allow for the growth of cancerous tissue, psychobiologists concerned with crime and its causes envision the day when similar techniques can be applied to the prevention and control of crime. If a gene for crime can be found, such researchers suggest, it might be turned off. In the meantime, psychobiologists have to be content with medicinal approaches to the treatment of crime and violence, such as employing tranquilizers, antipsychotic medications, mood-altering substances, and other drugs.

Studies show that drug treatments fashioned after psychobiological perspectives control aggressive and criminal behavior temporarily, but there is little evidence to suggest that they produce lasting results. In 1993, all biologically based theories of crime and violence were called into question by the National Academy of Sciences, whose review of hundreds of studies on the relationship among biology, violence, and crime concluded that "no patterns precise enough to be considered reliable biological markers for violent behavior have yet been identified."[55] The study did, however, find what it called "promising leads for future research."

# Psychological Theories

Theories of the **Psychological School** of crime causation have an increasingly significant place in the criminological literature. Most psychological theories of crime make certain fundamental assumptions. Among them are these:

- The individual is the primary unit of analysis.
- Personality is the major motivational element within individuals, since it is the source of drives and motives.
- Crimes result from inappropriately conditioned behavior or from abnormal, dysfunctional, or inappropriate mental processes within the personality.
- Defective or abnormal mental processes may have a variety of causes, including a diseased mind and inappropriate learning or improper conditioning—often occurring in early childhood.

**Psychological School**

A perspective on criminological thought that views offensive and deviant behavior as the product of dysfunctional personalities. Psychological thinkers identify the conscious, and especially the subconscious, contents of the human psyche as major determinants of behavior.

# Behavioral Conditioning

A twin thread was woven through early psychological theories. One emphasized **behavioral conditioning**, while the other focused mostly on personality disturbances and diseases of the mind. Taken together, these two foci constituted the early field of psychological criminology. Conditioning is a psychological principle that holds that the frequency of any behavior, including criminal or deviant behavior, can be increased or decreased through reward, punishment, and association with other stimuli. The concept of conditioned behavior was popularized through the work of the Russian physiologist Ivan Pavlov (1849–1936), whose work with dogs won him the Nobel Prize in physiology and medicine in 1904. Similarly, behavioral psychologists suggest that criminal behavior, which may be inherently rewarding under many circumstances, tends to be more common in those who are able to avoid punishment when involved in rule-breaking behavior.

**behavioral conditioning**

A psychological principle that holds that the frequency of any behavior can be increased or decreased through reward, punishment, and association with other stimuli.

# Freudian Psychoanalysis

The name most widely associated with the field of psychology is that of Sigmund Freud (1856–1939). Freudian theory posits the existence of an id, an ego, and a superego within the personality.[56] The id is the source of drives, which are seen as primarily sexual. The ego is a rational mental entity, which outlines paths through which the desires of the id can be fulfilled. The ego is often called the *reality principle* because of the belief that it relates desires to practical behavioral alternatives. The superego is a guiding principle, often compared to conscience, which judges the quality of the alternatives presented by the ego according to the standards of right and wrong acquired by the personality of which it is a part. Freud wrote very little about crime, but his followers, who developed the school of Freudian **psychoanalysis**, believe that crime can result from at least three conditions.

**psychoanalysis**

A theory of human behavior, based on the writings of Sigmund Freud, that sees personality as a complex composite of interacting mental entities.

A battered woman turning away from her husband. When a woman is victimized, it is often at the hands of an "intimate other," such as a spouse or a boyfriend. Sigmund Freud suggested that a male batterer acts out a deep-seated resentment toward women that resulted from his childhood relationship with his mother. However, this kind of theoretical perspective is rarely given credence by criminologists today.

*Francisco Cruz, SuperStock, Inc.*

> I really truly tried to stop—but I couldn't.
>
> —Henry Louis Wallace, convicted killer of nine women, in a tape-recorded interview with police

The first possible source of criminal behavior is a weak superego, which cannot responsibly control the drives that emanate from the id. Sex crimes, crimes of passion, murder, and other violent crimes are thought to follow inadequate superego development. People who lack fully developed superegos are often called *psychopaths* or *sociopaths* to indicate that they cannot see beyond their own interests. Canadian criminologist Gwynn Nettler observes that "civilization is paid for through development of a sense of guilt."[57]

Freud also created the concept of sublimation to explain the process by which one thing is symbolically substituted for another. He believed that sublimation was necessary when the direct pursuit of one's desires was not possible. Freud suggested, for example, that many children learned to sublimate negative feelings about their mothers. In the society in which Freud developed his theories, mothers closely controlled the lives of their children, and Freud saw the developing child as continually frustrated in seeking freedom to act on his or her own. The strain produced by this conflict could not be directly expressed by the child because the mother also controlled rewards and punishments. Hence, dislike for one's mother (which Freud thought was especially strong in boys) might show itself symbolically later in life. Crimes against women could then be explained as being committed by men expressing a symbolic hatred.

A final Freudian explanation for criminality is based on the death wish, or Thanatos, which Freud believed each of us carries. Thanatos is the often-unrecognized desire of animate matter to return to the inanimate. Potentially self-destructive activities, including smoking, speeding, skydiving, bad diets, "picking fights," and so on, can be explained by Thanatos. The self-destructive wish may also motivate offenders to commit crimes that are themselves dangerous or self-destructive—such as burglary, assault, murder, prostitution, and drug use—or it may result in unconscious efforts to be caught. Criminals who leave evidence behind may be responding to some basic need for apprehension and punishment.

## Psychopathology and Crime

From a psychiatric point of view, crime might also occur because of a diseased mind or a disordered personality—conditions that may collectively be referred to as *psychopathy*. The study of psychopathic mental conditions is called **psychopathology**. The role of a disordered personality in crime causation was central to early psychiatric theorizing. In 1944, for example, the well-known psychiatrist David Abrahamsen wrote, "When we seek to explain the riddle of human conduct in general and of antisocial behavior in particular, the solution must be sought in the personality."[58] Later, some psychiatrists went so far as to claim that criminal behavior itself is only a symptom of a more fundamental psychiatric disorder.[59]

**psychopathology**

The study of pathological mental conditions—that is, mental illness.

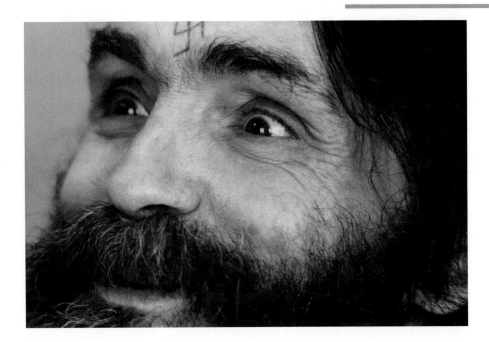

Charles Manson, one of the most photographed criminal offenders of all time, 20 years after he and his "family" shocked the world with their gruesome crimes.

*Grey Villet, Black Star*

By the 1930s, psychiatrists had begun to develop the concept of a psychopathic personality. This personality type, which by its very definition is asocial, was fully developed by Hervey Cleckley in his 1941 book, *The Mask of Sanity*.[60] Cleckley described the **psychopath**, also called a *sociopath,* as a "moral idiot" whose central defining characteristic is the inability to accurately imagine how others think and feel. Hence, it becomes possible for a psychopath to inflict pain and engage in cruelty without appreciation for the victim's suffering. Charles Manson, for example, whom some have called a psychopath, once told a television reporter, "I could take this book and beat you to death with it, and I wouldn't feel a thing. It'd be just like walking to the drugstore." According to Cleckley, psychopathic indicators appear early in life, often in the teenage years. They include lying, fighting, stealing, and vandalism. Even earlier signs may be found, according to some authors, in bed-wetting, cruelty to animals, sleepwalking, and fire setting.[61]

While the terms *psychopath* and *criminal* are not synonymous, individuals manifesting characteristics of a psychopathic personality are likely, sooner or later, to run afoul of the law. As one writer says, "The impulsivity and aggression, the selfishness in achieving one's own immediate needs, and the disregard for society's rules and laws bring these people to the attention of the criminal justice system."[62]

Although much studied, the causes of psychopathy are unclear. Somatogenic causes, or those that are based on physiological aspects of the human organism, include (1) a malfunctioning central nervous system characterized by a low state of arousal, which drives the sufferer to seek excitement, and (2) brain abnormalities, which may be present in most psychopaths from birth. Psychogenic causes, or those rooted in early interpersonal experiences, include the inability to form attachments to parents or other caregivers early in life, sudden separation from the mother during the first six months of life, and other forms of insecurity during the first few years of life. In short, a lack of love or the sensed inability to unconditionally depend on one central loving figure (typically the mother in most psychological literature) immediately following birth is often posited as a major psychogenic factor contributing to psychopathic development. Learn more about psychopathology and crime at Library Extra 3–2 at cjtoday.com. Read more about the Manson murders at Web Extra 3–5 at cjtoday.com.

| **psychopath** |
| --- |
| A person with a personality disorder, especially one manifested in aggressively antisocial behavior, which is often said to be the result of a poorly developed superego. |

## The Psychotic Offender

Another form of mental disorder is called **psychosis**. Psychotic people, according to psychiatric definitions, are out of touch with reality in some fundamental way. They may suffer from hallucinations, delusions, or other breaks with reality. For example, a psychotic may believe that she is a famous historical figure or may see spiders crawling on a bare wall. Psychoses may be either organic (that is, caused by physical damage to, or abnormalities in, the brain) or functional (that is, with no known physical cause). Psychotic people have also been classified as schizophrenic

| **psychosis** |
| --- |
| A form of mental illness in which sufferers are said to be out of touch with reality. |

**schizophrenic**

A mentally ill individual who suffers from disjointed thinking and possibly from delusions and hallucinations.

or paranoid schizophrenic. **Schizophrenics** are characterized by disordered or disjointed thinking, in which the types of logical associations they make are atypical of other people. Paranoid schizophrenics suffer from delusions and hallucinations.

Psychoses may lead to crime in a number of ways. Following the Vietnam War, for example, a number of former American soldiers suffering from a kind of battlefield psychosis killed friends and family members, thinking they were enemy soldiers. These men, who had been traumatized by battlefield experiences in Southeast Asia, relived their past on American streets.

# Psychological Profiling

**psychological profiling**

The attempt to categorize, understand, and predict the behavior of certain types of offenders based on behavioral clues they provide.

**Psychological profiling** is the attempt to derive a composite picture of an offender's social and psychological characteristics from the crime she committed and from the manner in which it was committed. Psychological profiling began during World War II as an effort by William Langer (1896–1977), a government psychiatrist hired by the Office of Strategic Services, to predict Adolf Hitler's actions.[63] Profiling in criminal investigations is based on the belief that criminality, because it is a form of behavior, can be viewed as symptomatic of the offender's personality. Psychological evaluations of crime scenes, including the analysis of evidence, are used to re-create the offender's frame of mind during the commission of the crime. A profile of the offender is then constructed to help in the investigation of suspects.

During the 1980s, the Federal Bureau of Investigation led the movement toward psychological profiling[64] through its focus on violent sex offenses[65] and arson.[66] FBI profilers described what they termed *lust murderers* and serial arsonists. Often depicted as loners with an aversion to casual social contact, lust murderers were shown to rarely arouse suspicions in neighbors or employers. Other personality types became the focus of police efforts to arrest such offenders through a prediction of what they might do next.

New areas for psychological profiling include hostage negotiation[67] and international terrorism.[68] Right-wing terrorist groups in the United States have also been the subject of profiling efforts.

# Social Policy and Psychological Theories

Crime-control policies based on psychological perspectives are primarily individualistic. They are oriented toward individualized treatment, characteristically exposing the individual offender to various forms of therapy intended to overcome the person's propensity for criminality.

**dangerousness**

The likelihood that a given individual will later harm society or others. Dangerousness is often measured in terms of recidivism, or the likelihood of additional crime commission within five years following arrest or release from confinement.

Most crime-control strategies based on psychological theories emphasize assessing personal **dangerousness**, through psychological testing and other efforts to identify personality-based characteristics that predict interpersonal aggression. Although the ability to accurately predict future dangerousness is of great concern to today's policymakers, definitions of *dangerousness* are fraught with difficulty. As some authors have pointed out, "Dangerousness is not an objective quality like obesity or brown eyes; rather it is an ascribed quality like trustworthiness."[69] Hence dangerousness is not necessarily a personality trait that is stable or easily identifiable. Even if it were, some studies of criminal careers show that involvement in crime decreases with age.[70] As one author puts it, if "criminality declines more or less uniformly with age, then many offenders will be 'over the hill' by the time they are old enough to be plausible candidates for preventive incarceration."[71]

Before crime-control policies can be based on present understandings of dangerousness, research must answer several questions: Can past behavior predict future behavior? Do former instances of criminality foretell additional ones? Are there other identifiable characteristics that violent offenders might manifest that could serve as warning signs to criminal justice decision makers faced with the dilemma of whether to release convicted felons?

**Chicago School**

A sociological approach that emphasizes demographics (the characteristics of population groups) and geographics (the mapped location of such groups relative to one another) and that sees the social disorganization that characterizes delinquency areas as a major cause of criminality and victimization.

# Sociological Theories

Sociological theories are largely an American contribution to the study of crime causation. In the 1920s and 1930s, the famous **Chicago School** of sociology explained criminality as a product of society's impact on the individual. The structure of prevailing social arrangements, the interaction between individuals and groups, and the social environment were all seen as major determinants of criminal behavior.

Sociological perspectives on crime causation are quite diverse. Most, however, build on certain fundamental assumptions. Among them are these:

Lyman Faris, the 34-year-old Columbus, Ohio, long-haul truck driver and naturalized U.S. citizen, who admitted to authorities in 2003 that he had scoped out New York City's famed Brooklyn Bridge for al-Qaeda. Faris, who had hoped to find a way to collapse the span, was born in Kashmir but had been living in the United States since the early 1990s. Some criminal offenders, including terrorist "sleeper cell" operatives like Faris, are motivated by "causes"—whether real or imaginary.

*AP Wide World Photos*

- Social groups, social institutions, the arrangements of society, and social roles all provide the proper focus for criminological study.
- Group dynamics, group organization, and subgroup relationships form the causal nexus out of which crime develops.
- The structure of society and the relative degree of social organization or **social disorganization** are important factors contributing to the prevalence of criminal behavior.

All sociological perspectives on crime share the foregoing characteristics, but particular theories may give greater or lesser weight to the following aspects of social life:

- The clash of norms and values among variously socialized groups
- Socialization and the process of association between individuals
- The existence of subcultures and varying types of opportunities

**social disorganization**

A condition said to exist when a group is faced with social change, uneven development of culture, maladaptiveness, disharmony, conflict, and lack of consensus.

## Social Ecology Theory

In the 1920s, during the early days of sociological theorizing, the University of Chicago brought together such thinkers as Robert Park, Ernest Burgess,[72] Clifford Shaw, and Henry McKay.[73] Park and Burgess recognized that Chicago, like most cities, could be mapped according to its social characteristics. Their map resembled a target with a bull's-eye in the center. Shaw and McKay adapted these concentric zones to the study of crime when they realized that the zones nearest the center of the city had the highest crime rates. In particular, zone 2 (one removed from the center) consistently showed the highest crime rate over time, regardless of the groups or nationalities inhabiting it. This "zone of transition"—so called because new immigrant groups moved into it as earlier ones became integrated into American culture and moved out—demonstrated that crime was dependent to a considerable extent on aspects of the social structure of the city itself. Structural elements identified by Shaw and McKay included poverty, illiteracy, lack of schooling, unemployment, and illegitimacy. In combination, these elements were seen to lead to social disorganization, which in turn produced crime.

## Anomie Theory

The French word **anomie** has been loosely translated as a condition of "normlessness." Anomie entered the literature as a sociological concept with the writings of Émile Durkheim (1858–1917) in the late nineteenth century.[74] Robert Merton (1910–2003) applied anomie to criminology in 1938 when he used the term to describe a disjunction between socially acceptable goals and means in American society.[75]

**anomie**

A socially pervasive condition of normlessness. Also, a disjunction between approved goals and means.

TABLE 3-2

## MERTON'S ANOMIE THEORY AND IMPLIED TYPES OF CRIMINALITY

| Category | Goals | Means | Examples |
|---|---|---|---|
| Conformist | + | + | Law-abiding behavior |
| Innovator | + | − | Property offenses |
|  |  |  | White-collar crimes |
| Retreatist | − | − | Drug use/addiction, vagrancy, some "victimless" crimes |
| Ritualist | − | + | A repetitive and mundane lifestyle |
| Rebel | ± | ± | Political crime (for example, environmental activists who violate the law, violence-prone antiabortionists) |

*Source:* Adapted with the permission of the Free Press, a Division of Simon & Schuster Adult Publishing Group, from *Social Theory and Social Structure,* Revised and Enlarged Edition by Robert K. Merton. Copyright © 1967, 1968 by Robert K. Merton. All rights reserved.

---

> If we are ever to reduce the tragic toll of crime in society, we must compare the measured benefits of incarceration to less costly and more productive crime prevention strategies— especially those programs aimed at helping high-risk families and young people escape the hopelessness that surrounds their lives.
>
> —Barry Krisberg, President, National Council on Crime and Delinquency

**defensible space theory**

The belief that an area's physical features may be modified and structured so as to reduce crime rates in that area and to lower the fear of victimization that residents experience.

**broken windows thesis**

A perspective on crime causation that holds that physical deterioration in an area leads to higher crime rates and an increased concern for personal safety among residents.

Merton believed that while the same goals and means are held out by society as desirable for everyone, they are not equally available to all. Socially approved goals in American society, for example, include wealth, status, and political power. The acceptable means to achieve these goals are education, wise investment, and hard work. Unfortunately, however, opportunities are not equally distributed throughout society, and some people turn to illegitimate means to achieve the goals they are pressured to reach. Still others reject both acceptable goals and legitimate means of reaching them.

Merton represented his theory with a chart, shown in Table 3–2. *Conformists* accept both the goals and means that society holds out as legitimate, while *innovators* accept the goals but reject the means, and use illegal means to gain money, power, and success. It is innovators whom Merton identified as criminal. The inherent logic of the model led Merton to posit other social types. *Ritualists* are those who reject success goals but still perform their daily tasks in conformity with social expectations. They might hold regular jobs but lack the desire to advance in life. *Retreatists* reject both the goals and the means and usually drop out of society by becoming derelicts, drug users, hermits, or the like. *Rebels* constitute a special category. Their desire to replace the existing system of socially approved goals and means with some other system more to their liking makes them the revolutionaries of the theory.

Merton believed that categories are not intentionally selected by the individuals who occupy them but rather are imposed on people by structural aspects of society. Where people live, how wealthy their family is, and what ethnic background they come from are all significant determinants of the "box" into which people are placed.

Modern writers on anomie recognize that normlessness is not likely to be expressed as criminality unless people who experience it also feel that they are capable of doing something to change their lives. As Catherine Ross and John Mirowsky put it, "A person who has high levels of normlessness and powerlessness is less likely to get in trouble with the law than a person who has a high level of normlessness and a high level of instrumentalism."[76]

Merton's anomie theory drew attention to the lack of equality of opportunity that existed in society at the time he was writing. While considerable efforts have been made to eradicate it, much of that inequality continues today.

## Subcultural Theory

Another sociological contribution to criminological theory is the idea of a subculture. A subculture is a group of people who participate in a shared system of values and norms that are at variance with those of the larger culture. Subcultural explanations of crime posit the existence of group values that support criminal behavior. Subcultures were first recognized in the enclaves formed by immigrants who came to America during the early part of the twentieth century. Statistics have shown that certain immigrant groups had low crime rates.[77] Among them were the Scandinavians, Chinese, Dutch, Germans, and Japanese. Other immigrant groups, including Italians, Mexicans, Puerto Ricans, and Africans, demonstrated a significantly greater propensity for involvement in crime.[78]

## CJ FUTURES

### The Physical Environment and Crime

Social ecology theory—an outgrowth of the Chicago School of sociological thought, which flourished during the 1920s and 1930s—posited a link between physical location and crime. A modern perspective, called *crime prevention through environmental design* (CPTED), bears a strong resemblance to earlier ecological theories. CPTED, which was first formulated in the 1960s and 1970s, focuses on the settings in which crimes occur and on techniques for reducing vulnerability within those settings. Because defensible space concepts are being increasingly applied to the design of physical facilities, including housing, parking garages, public buildings, and even entire neighborhoods, it is highly likely that applications of CPTED will accelerate throughout the twenty-first century.

Second-generation **defensible space theory**, upon which contemporary CPTED is built, developed around 1980 and considered more carefully how the impact of physical features on fear and victimizations depends on other social and cultural features in the setting. Second-generation defensible space theory employed the **broken windows thesis**, which holds that physical deterioration and an increase in unrepaired buildings lead to increased concerns for personal safety among area residents. Heightened concerns, in turn, lead to further decreases in maintenance and repair and to increased delinquency, vandalism, and crime among local residents, which spawn even further deterioration in both a sense of safety and in the physical environment. Offenders from other neighborhoods are then increasingly attracted by the area's perceived vulnerability.

Research on CPTED has shown environmental design to be effective in lowering crime and crime-related public-order prob-

lems. Effective use of CPTED to alter features of the physical environment can affect potential offenders' perceptions about a possible crime site, their evaluations of the opportunities associated with that site, and the availability and visibility of one or more natural guardians at or near the site. CPTED is based on the belief that offenders decide whether to commit a crime in a particular location after they evaluate the area's features, including (1) the ease of entry to the area, (2) the visibility of the target to others—that is, the chance of being seen, (3) the attractiveness or vulnerability of the target, (4) the likelihood that criminal behavior will be challenged or thwarted if discovered, and (5) the ease of egress—that is, the ability to quickly and easily leave the area once the crime has been committed.

According to the National Institute of Justice, CPTED suggests four approaches to making a location more resistant to crime and to crime-related public-order problems:

- *Housing design or block layout*—making it more difficult to commit crimes by (1) reducing the availability of crime targets, (2) removing barriers that prevent easy detection of potential offenders or of an offense in progress, and (3) increasing physical obstacles to committing a crime.
- *Land use and circulation patterns*—creating safer use of neighborhood space by reducing routine exposure of potential offenders to crime targets. This can be accomplished through careful attention to walkways, paths, streets, traffic patterns, and locations and hours of operation of public spaces and facilities. Street closings or revised traffic patterns that decrease vehicular volume may, under some conditions, encourage residents to better maintain the sidewalks and streets in front of their houses.

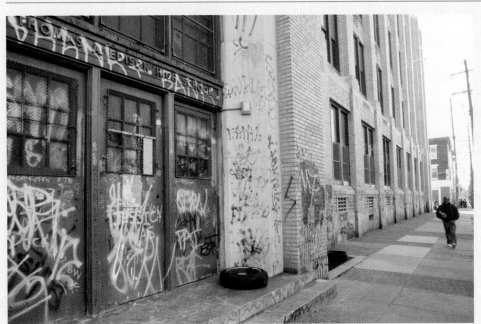

A run-down city street. To explain crime, criminologists sometimes use the "broken windows" approach, which says that neighborhood deterioration leads to rising crime rates. Similarly, poverty, unemployment, a relative lack of formal education, and low skill levels, which often characterize inner-city populations, seem to be linked to criminality.

*Peter Byron, PhotoEdit*

*(continued)*

CJ FUTURES *(continued)*

■ *Territorial features*—encouraging the use of territorial markers or fostering conditions that will lead to more extensive marking to indicate that the block or site is occupied by vigilant residents. Sponsoring cleanup and beautification contests and creating controllable, semiprivate outdoor locations may encourage such activities. This strategy focuses on small-scale, private, and semipublic sites, usually within predominantly residential locales. It is most relevant at the street-block level and below. It enhances the chances that residents themselves will generate semifixed features that demonstrate their involvement in and watchfulness over a particular delimited location.

■ *Physical maintenance*—controlling physical deterioration to reduce offenders' perceptions that areas are vulnerable to crime and that residents are so fearful they would do nothing to stop a crime. Physical improvements may reduce the signals of vulnerability and increase commitment to joint protective activities. Physical deterioration, in all probability, not only influences the cognition and behavior of potential offenders but also shapes how residents behave and what they think about other residents.

For additional information on CPTED via the Crime Mapping Research Center, see Web Extra 3–6 at cjtoday.com.

WEB EXTRA

*References:* Derek J. Paulsen and Matthew B. Robinson, *Spatial Aspects of Crime: Theory and Practice* (Boston, MA: Allyn & Bacon, 2004); Oscar Newman, *Defensible Space* (New York: Macmillan, 1972); Oscar Newman, *Creating Defensible Space* (Washington, DC: Office of Housing and Urban Development, 1996); James Q. Wilson and George Kelling, "Broken Windows," *Atlantic Monthly,* March 1982; Dan Fleissner and Fred Heinzelmann, *Crime Prevention through Environmental Design and Community Policing* (Washington, DC: National Institute of Justice, 1996); Ralph B. Taylor and Adele V. Harrell, *Physical Environment and Crime* (Washington, DC: National Institute of Justice, 1996); Mary S. Smith, *Crime Prevention through Environmental Design in Parking Facilities* (Washington, DC: National Institute of Justice, 1996); and Corey L. Gordon and William Brill, *The Expanding Role of Crime Prevention through Environmental Design in Premises Liability* (Washington, DC: National Institute of Justice, 1996).

**reaction formation**

The process whereby a person openly rejects that which he or she wants or aspires to but cannot obtain or achieve.

Albert Cohen (b. 1918) coined the term **reaction formation** to encompass the rejection of middle-class values by status-seeking lower-class youths who find they are not permitted access to approved opportunities for success.[79] In Cohen's eyes, reaction formation leads to the development of gangs and perpetuates the existence of subcultures. Walter Miller described the focal concerns of subcultural participants in terms of "trouble," "toughness," "excitement," "smartness," "fate," and "autonomy."[80] It is a focus on such concerns, Miller suggested, that leads members of criminal subcultures into violations of the law. Richard Cloward and Lloyd Ohlin proposed the existence of an illegitimate opportunity structure that permits delinquent youths to achieve in ways that are outside of legitimate avenues to success.[81]

During the 1950s, Marvin Wolfgang and Franco Ferracuti examined homicide rates in Philadelphia and found that murder was a way of life among certain groups.[82] They discovered a "wholesale" and a "retail" price for murder—which depended on who was killed and who did the killing. Killings that occurred within violent subgroups were more likely to be partially excused than those that happened elsewhere. The term **subculture of violence** has come to be associated with their work and has since been applied to other locations across the country.

**subculture of violence**

A cultural setting in which violence is a traditional and often accepted method of dispute resolution.

Critiques of subcultural theory have been numerous. A major difficulty for these theories lies in the fact that studies involving self-reports of crime commission have shown that much violence and crime occur outside of "criminal" subcultures. Many middle- and upper-class lawbreakers are able to avoid the justice system and therefore do not enter the "official" crime statistics. Hence, criminal subcultures may be those in which crime is more visible rather than more prevalent.

## Social Policy and Sociological Theories

Theoretical approaches that fault the social environment as the root cause of crime point to social action as a panacea. A contemporary example of intervention efforts based on sociological theories can be found in Targeted Outreach,[83] a program operated by the Boys and Girls Clubs of America. The program's philosophy is based on studies undertaken at the University of Colorado that showed that at-risk youths could be effectively diverted from the juvenile justice system through the provision of positive alternatives. The program recruits at-risk youngsters—many as young as seven years old—and diverts them into activities that are intended to promote a sense of belonging, competence, usefulness, and power. Social programs like Targeted Outreach are intended to change the cultural conditions and societal arrangements that are thought to lead people into crime.

# Social Process Theories

While psychological approaches to crime causation seek to uncover aspects of the personality hidden even from the mind in which they reside, and while sociological theories look to institutional arrangements in the social world to explain crime, social process approaches focus on the interaction between individuals and society. Most **social process theories** highlight the role of social learning. They build on the premise that behavior—both "good" and "bad"—is learned, and they suggest that "bad" behavior can be unlearned. Social process theories are often the most attractive to contemporary policymakers because they demand that responsibility be placed on the offender for actively participating in rehabilitation efforts and because they are consistent with popular cultural and religious values centered on teaching right from wrong.

**social process theory**
A perspective on criminological thought that highlights the process of interaction between individuals and society. Most social process theories highlight the role of social learning.

## Differential Association Theory

In 1939, Edwin Sutherland (1883–1950) published the third edition of his *Principles of Criminology*. It contained, for the first time, a formalized statement of his theory of differential association, a perspective that Sutherland based on the "laws of imitation" described by Gabriel Tarde (1843–1904), a French sociologist.

The theory of differential association explains crime as a natural consequence of the interaction with criminal lifestyles. Sutherland suggested that children raised in crime-prone environments were often isolated and unable to experience the values that would otherwise lead to conformity. Differential association provides the basis for much research in modern criminology.[84] Even popular stories of young drug pushers, for instance, often refer to the fact that inner-city youths imitate what they see. Some residents of poverty-ridden ghettos learn quickly that fast money can be made in the illicit drug trade, and they tend to follow the examples of material "success" that they see around them.

Differential association views crime as the product of socialization and sees it as being acquired by criminals according to the same principles that guide the learning of law-abiding behavior in conformists. Differential association removes criminality from the framework of the abnormal and places it squarely within a general perspective applicable to all behavior. In the 1947 edition of his text, Sutherland wrote, "Criminal behavior is a part of human behavior, has much in common with non-criminal behavior, and must be explained within the same general framework as any other human behavior."[85] A study of the tenets of differential association (listed in Table 3–3) shows that Sutherland believed that even the sources of behavioral motivation are much the same for conformists and criminals; that is, both groups strive for money and success but choose different paths to the same goal.

| SUTHERLAND'S PRINCIPLES OF DIFFERENTIAL ASSOCIATION |
| --- |
| 1. Criminal behavior is learned. |
| 2. Criminal behavior is learned in interaction with others in a process of communication. |
| 3. The principal part of the learning of criminal behavior occurs within intimate personal groups. |
| 4. When criminal behavior is learned, the learning includes (a) techniques of committing the crime, which are sometimes very complicated, sometimes very simple, and (b) the specific direction of motives, drives, rationalizations, and attitudes. |
| 5. The specific direction of motives and drives is learned from definitions of the legal codes as favorable or unfavorable. |
| 6. A person becomes delinquent because of an excess of definitions favorable to violations of law over definitions unfavorable to violations of law. |
| 7. Differential associations may vary in frequency, duration, priority, and intensity. |
| 8. The process of learning criminal behavior by association with criminal and anticriminal patterns involves all the mechanisms that are involved in any other learning. |
| 9. Although criminal behavior is an expression of general needs and values, it is not explained by those general needs and values since noncriminal behavior is an expression of the same needs and values. |

TABLE 3–3

*Source:* Edwin Sutherland, *Principles of Criminology,* 4th ed. (Chicago: J. B. Lippincott, 1947), pp. 6–7.

However, differential association theory fails to explain why people have the associations they do and why some associations affect certain individuals more than others. Why, for example, are most prison guards unaffected by their constant association with offenders, while a few take advantage of their position to smuggle contraband? The theory has also been criticized for being so general and imprecise as to allow for little testing.[86] Complete testing of the theory would require that all of the associations a person has ever had be recorded and analyzed from the standpoint of the individual—a clearly impossible task.

Other theorists continue to build on Sutherland's early work. Robert Burgess and Ronald Akers, for example, have constructed a differential association–reinforcement theory that seeks to integrate Sutherland's original propositions with the work of American psychologist B. F. Skinner's work on conditioning.[87] Burgess and Akers suggest that although values and behavior patterns are learned in association with others, the primary mechanism through which such learning occurs is operant conditioning. Reinforcement is the key, they say, to understanding any social learning as it takes place. The name **social learning theory** has been widely applied to the work of Burgess and Akers. It is somewhat of a misnomer, however, since the term can easily encompass a wide range of approaches and should not be limited to one specific combination of the ideas found in differential association and reinforcement theory.

> **social learning theory**
>
> A psychological perspective that says that people learn how to behave by modeling themselves after others whom they have the opportunity to observe.

# Restraint Theories

As we have seen throughout this chapter, most criminological theories posit a cause of crime.[88] Some theories, however, focus less on causes than on constraints—those forces that keep people from committing a crime. These theories are called *restraint theories*. However, since they focus primarily on why people do not break the law, restraint theories provide only one-half of the causal picture. They are especially weak in identifying the social-structural sources of motivations to commit crimes.[89] Also, the ways in which bonds with different institutions interact with one another and with personal attributes, as well as the variety of bonds that operate throughout the life cycle, have yet to be clarified.[90]

## Containment Theory

*Containment theory,* a type of restraint theory offered by Walter Reckless (1899–1988), assumes that all of us are subject to inducements to crime.[91] Some of us resist these "pushes" toward criminal behavior, while others do not. The difference, according to Reckless, can be found in forces that contain, or control, behavior.

> **containment**
>
> The aspects of the social bond and of the personality that act to prevent individuals from committing crimes and that keep them from engaging in deviance.

Reckless described two types of **containment**: outer and inner. Outer containment depends on social roles and the norms and expectations that apply to them. People who occupy significant roles in society find themselves insulated from deviant tendencies. A corporate executive, for example, is less apt to hold up a liquor store than is a drifter. The difference, according to Reckless, is not due solely to income, but also to the pressure the executive feels to conform.

Inner containment involves a number of factors, such as conscience, a positive self-image, a tolerance for frustration, and aspirations that are in line with reality. Reckless believed that inner containment is more powerful than outer containment; inner containment functions even in secret. For example, an inner-directed person who comes across a lost purse feels compelled to locate its rightful owner and return it. If theft or greed crosses the mind of an inner-directed person, he will say to himself, "I'm not that kind of person. That would be wrong."

Reckless studied small, close-knit societies—including the Hutterites, Mennonites, and Amish—in developing his theory. He realized that the "containment of behavior . . . is . . . maximized under conditions of isolation and homogeneity of culture, class, and population."[92] Hence its applicability to modern American society, with its considerable heterogeneity of values and perspectives, is questionable.

## Social Control Theory

Travis Hirschi emphasized the bond between individuals and society as the primary operative mechanism in his *social control theory.*[93] Hirschi identified four components of that bond: (1) emotional attachments to significant others, (2) a commitment to appropriate lifestyles, (3) involvement or immersion in conventional values, and (4) a belief in the "correctness" of social obligations and the rules of the larger society. These components act as social controls on deviant and criminal behavior; as they weaken, social control suffers, and the likelihood of crime and deviance increases. Using self-reports of delinquency from high school students in California, Hirschi concluded that youngsters who were less attached to teachers and parents and who had few positive attitudes about their own accomplishments were more likely to engage in crime and deviance than were others.[94]

## Neutralization Techniques

Complementing restraint theory is the *neutralization approach* of Gresham Sykes and David Matza.[95] The neutralization approach centers on rationalizations that allow offenders to shed feelings of guilt and responsibility for their behavior. Sykes and Matza believed that most people drift into and out of criminal behavior but will not commit a crime unless they have available to them techniques of neutralization. Their study primarily concerned juveniles for whom, they suggested, neutralization techniques provided only a temporary respite from guilt. That respite, however, lasted long enough to avoid the twinges of conscience while a crime was being committed. Neutralization techniques include the following:

- Denial of responsibility ("I'm a product of my background.")
- Denial of injury ("No one was really hurt.")
- Denial of the victim ("They deserved it.")
- Condemnation of the condemners ("The cops are corrupt.")
- Appeal to higher loyalties ("I did it for my friends.")

Like containment theory, restraint theories tend to depend on a general agreement as to values, or they assume that offenders are simply conformists who suffer temporary lapses. Neutralization techniques, by definition, are only needed when the delinquent has been socialized into middle-class values or where conscience is well developed. Even so, neutralization techniques do not in themselves explain crime. Such techniques are available to us all, if we make only a slight effort to conjure them up. The real question is why some people readily allow proffered neutralizations to affect their behavior, while others effortlessly discount them.

## Labeling Theory

As we saw earlier in this chapter, the worth of any theory of behavior is proved by how well it reflects the reality of the social world. In practice, however, theoretical perspectives find acceptance in the academic environment via a number of considerations. **Labeling theory**, for example, became fashionable in the 1960s. Its popularity may have been due more to the cultural environment into which it was introduced rather than to any inherent quality of the theory itself.

Labeling theory was first introduced by Frank Tannenbaum (1893–1969) in 1938 under the rubric of *tagging*.[96] He wrote, "The young delinquent becomes bad because he is defined as bad and because he is not believed if he is good." He went on to say, "The process of making the criminal, therefore, is a process of tagging. . . . It becomes a way of stimulating . . . and evolving the very traits that are complained of. . . . The person becomes the thing he is described as being."[97] Tannenbaum focused on society's power to *define* an act or an individual as bad and drew attention to the group need for a scapegoat in explaining crime. The search for causes inherent in individuals was not yet exhausted, however, and Tannenbaum's theory fell mostly on deaf ears.

By the 1960s, the social and academic environments in America had changed, and the issue of responsibility was seen more in terms of the group than the individual. In his book *Outsiders*, published in 1963, Howard Becker pointed out that criminality is not a quality inherent in an act or in a person. Crime, said Becker, results from a social definition, through law, of unacceptable behavior. That definition arises through **moral enterprise**, by which groups on both sides of an issue debate and eventually legislate their notion of what is moral and what is not. Becker wrote, "The central fact about deviance [is that] it is created by society. . . . Social groups create deviance by making the rules whose infraction constitutes deviance."[98]

The criminal label, however, produces consequences for labeled individuals that may necessitate continued criminality. In describing the criminal career, Becker wrote, "To be labeled a criminal one need only commit a single criminal offense. . . . Yet the word carries a number of connotations specifying auxiliary traits characteristic of anyone bearing the label."[99] The first time a person commits a crime, the behavior is called *primary deviance* and may be a merely transitory form of behavior.

However, in the popular mind, a "known" criminal is not to be trusted, should not be hired because of the potential for crimes on the job, and would not be a good candidate for the military, marriage, or any position requiring responsibility. Society's tendency toward such thinking, Becker suggested, closes legitimate opportunities, ensuring that the only new behavioral

**labeling theory**

A social process perspective that sees continued crime as a consequence of the limited opportunities for acceptable behavior that follow from the negative responses of society to those defined as offenders.

**moral enterprise**

The process undertaken by an advocacy group to have its values legitimated and embodied in law.

An honest and fully professional police community would acknowledge in its police education the root causes of crime—poverty, unemployment, underemployment, racism, poor health care, bad housing, weak schools, mental illness, alcoholism, addiction, single-parent families, teenage pregnancy, and a society of selfishness and greed.

—Patrick V. Murphy, former New York City Police Commissioner

alternatives available to the labeled criminal are deviant ones. Succeeding episodes of criminal behavior are seen as a form of secondary deviance that eventually becomes stabilized in the behavioral repertoire and self-concept of the labeled person.[100]

Labeling theory can be critiqued along a number of dimensions. First, it is not really a "theory" in that labeling does not uncover the genesis of criminal behavior. It is more useful in describing how such behavior continues than in explaining how it originates. Second, labeling theory does not recognize the possibility that the labeled individual may make successful attempts at reform and may shed the negative label. Finally, the theory does not provide an effective way of dealing with offenders. Should people who commit crimes not be arrested and tried, so as to avoid the consequences of negative labels? It would be exceedingly naive to suggest that all repeat criminal behavior would cease, as labeling theory might predict, if people who commit crimes are not officially "handled" by the system.

## The Life Course Perspective

**social development theory**

An integrated view of human development that points to the process of interaction among and between individuals and society as the root cause of criminal behavior.

**life course perspective**

An approach to explaining crime and deviance that investigates developments and turning points in the course of a person's life over time.

Some of the most recent perspectives on crime causation belong to a subcategory of social process thought called **social development theory**. According to the social development perspective, human development occurs simultaneously on many levels, including the psychological, biological, familial, interpersonal, cultural, societal, and ecological levels. Hence, social development theories tend to be integrated theories—that is, theories that combine various points of view on the process of development. Theories that fall into this category, however, highlight the process of interaction between individuals and society as the root cause of criminal behavior. In particular, they emphasize that a critical period of transition occurs in a person's life as he or she moves from childhood to adulthood.

One social development perspective of special significance is the **life course perspective**. According to Robert J. Sampson and John H. Laub,[101] who named the life course perspective in 1993, criminal behavior typically follows an identifiable pattern throughout a person's life cycle. In the lives of those who eventually become criminal, crime-like or deviant behavior is relatively rare during early childhood, tends to begin as sporadic instances during early adolescence, becomes more common during the late-teen and early-adult years, and then gradually diminishes as the person gets older.

Sampson and Laub also used the idea of *transitions* in the life course, or turning points that identify significant events in a person's life and represent the opportunity for people to turn either away from or toward deviance and crime. An employer who gives an employee a second chance, for example, may provide a unique opportunity that helps determine the future course of that person's life. Similarly, the principle of *linked lives,* also common to life course theories, highlights the fact that no one lives in isolation. Events in the life course are constantly being influenced by family members, friends, acquaintances, employers, teachers, and so on. Not only might such influences determine the life course of any given individual, but they are active throughout the life course. Figure 3–2 diagrams some of the life course influences experienced by most adolescents. Also shown in the diagram are desired outcomes and positive and negative indicators of development.

In 1986, the federal Office of Juvenile Justice and Delinquency Prevention (OJJDP) began funding a study of life pathways as they lead to criminality. *The Program of Research on the Causes and Correlates of Delinquency* continues to produce results.[102] Researchers have been examining how delinquency, violence, and drug use develop within and are related to various social contexts, including the family, peer groups, schools, and the surrounding community. To date, the study has identified three distinct pathways to delinquency, which are shown in Figure 3–3. These pathways are not mutually exclusive and can sometimes converge:

- The *authority conflict pathway,* along which children begin to move during their early years (as early as three or four years old), involves stubborn behavior and resistance to parental authority. Defiance of authority begins around age 11, and authority avoidance (that is, truancy, running away) begins about the same time.

- The *covert pathway,* which starts around age ten with minor covert acts such as shoplifting and lying, quickly progresses to acts of vandalism involving property damage. Moderate to severe delinquency frequently begins a year or two later.

- The *overt pathway* is marked by minor aggression, such as bullying, that develops around age 11 or 12. The overt pathway leads to fighting and physical violence during the teenage years and tends to eventuate in serious violent criminality that may include rape, robbery, and assault.

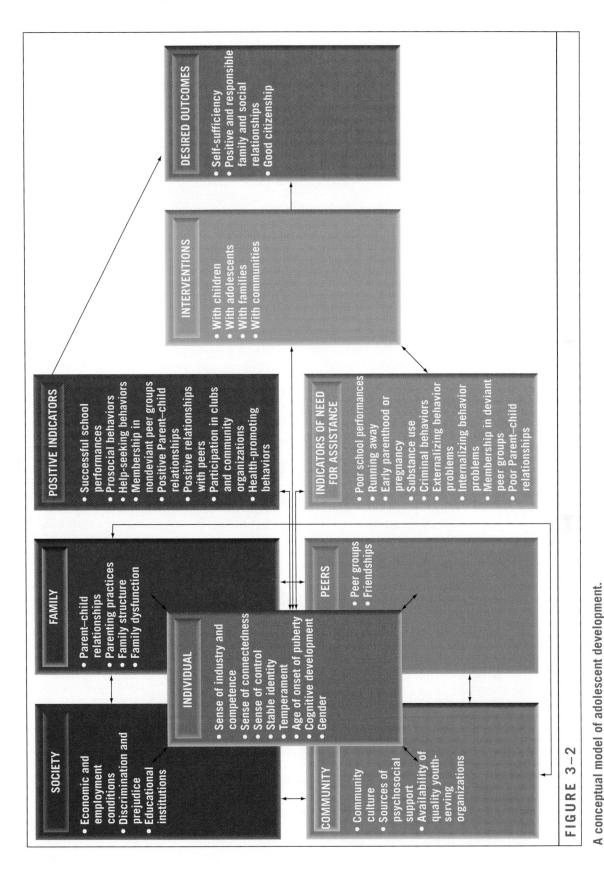

**FIGURE 3–2**

**A conceptual model of adolescent development.**

*Source:* Family and Youth Services Bureau, *Understanding Youth Development: Promoting Positive Pathways of Growth* (Washington, DC: U.S. Department of Health and Human Services, 2000).

FIGURE 3–3

**Three pathways to disruptive behavior and delinquency.**

*Source:* Barbara Tatem Kelley, Rolf Loeber, Kate Keenan, and Mary DeLamatre, *Developmental Pathways in Boys' Disruptive and Delinquent Behavior* (Washington, DC: Office of Juvenile Justice and Delinquency Prevention, 1997).

**conflict perspective**

A theoretical approach that holds that crime is the natural consequence of economic and other social inequities. Conflict theorists highlight the stresses that arise among and within social groups as they compete with one another for resources and for survival. The social forces that result are viewed as major determinants of group and individual behavior, including crime.

A similar study is underway at the Project on Human Development in Chicago Neighborhoods (PHDCN), mentioned earlier in this chapter. PHDCN researchers are "tracing how criminal behavior develops from birth to age 32."[103] Participating researchers come from a variety of scientific backgrounds and include psychiatrists, developmental psychologists, sociologists, criminologists, physicians, educators, statisticians, and public health officials. The study focuses on the influence of communities, peers, families, and health-related, cognitive, and emotional factors to decipher the lines along which crime and delinquency are likely to develop. Learn more about the OJJDP's causes and correlates study via Web Extra 3–7 at cjtoday.com; find out more about the PHDCN project via Web Extra 3–1 and Library Extra 3–3; and read about the possible effects of childhood victimization on later criminality at Library Extra 3–4.

# Conflict Theories

Basic to the **conflict perspective** is the belief that conflict is a fundamental aspect of social life and can never be fully resolved. From the conflict point of view, formal agencies of social control at best merely coerce the unempowered or the disenfranchised to comply with the rules established by those in power. Laws become tools of the powerful, tools that are useful in keeping others from wresting control over important social institutions. Social order, rather than being the result of any consensus or process of dispute resolution, rests on the exercise of power through law. The conflict perspective can be described in terms of four key elements[104]:

■ Society is composed of diverse social groups, and diversity is based on distinctions that people hold to be significant, such as gender, sexual orientation, and social class.

- Conflict among groups is unavoidable because of differing interests and differing values. Hence, conflict is inherent in social life.

- The fundamental nature of group conflict centers on the exercise of political power. Political power is the key to the accumulation of wealth and to other forms of power.

- Laws are the tools of power and further the interests of those powerful enough to make them. Laws allow those in control to gain what they define (through the law) as legitimate access to scarce resources and to deny (through the law) such access to the politically disenfranchised.

# Radical Criminology

Criminological theory took a new direction during the 1960s and 1970s, brought about in part by the turmoil that characterized American society during that period. **Radical criminology** placed the blame for criminality and deviant behavior squarely on officially sanctioned cultural and economic arrangements. The distribution of wealth and power in society was held to be the primary cause of criminal behavior, especially among those who were disenfranchised. Poverty and discrimination were seen to lead to frustration and pent-up hostilities that were expressed through murder, rape, theft, and other crimes.

Radical criminology had its roots in early conflict theories and in the thought of Dutch criminologist Willem Bonger. Some authors have distinguished between conflict theory and radical criminology by naming them "conservative conflict theory" and "radical conflict theory" respectively.[105] The difference between the two theories, however, is mostly in the rhetoric of the times. Conservative conflict theories held that conflict was a natural part of any society and that struggles for power and control would always occur. "Losers" of conflicts were defined as "criminal," and constraints on their behavior would be legislated. Characteristic of this perspective are the approaches of Austin Turk[106] (b. 1934) and George Vold (1896–1967). An even earlier conflict perspective can be found in the culture conflict notions of Thorsten Sellin, who was concerned with the clash of immigrant values and traditions with those of established American culture.[107]

Radical criminology went a step further. It recognized that the struggle to control resources is central to society, and it encompassed the notion that the law is a tool of the powerful. The focus of radical criminology, however, was capitalism and the evils that capitalism was believed to entail. The ideas of Karl Marx (1818–1883) entered the field of criminology through the writings of William Chambliss[108] (b. 1933) and Richard Quinney[109] (b. 1934). According to Marx, the labor of the lower classes provides the basis for the accumulated wealth of the upper classes, and the lower classes are always exploited by the "owners" in society. The poor were trained to believe that capitalism was in their best interests and the working classes suffered under the consequences of a "false class consciousness" perpetrated by the powerful. Marx believed that only when the exploited workers realized their exploitation would they rebel and change society for the better.

American radical criminology built on the ideals of the 1960s and charged that the "establishment," controlled by the upper classes, perverted justice through the unequal application of judicial sanctions. As David Greenberg observed, "Many researchers attributed the overrepresentation of blacks and persons from impoverished family backgrounds in arrest and conviction statistics to the discriminatory practices of the enforcement agencies. It was not that the poor stole more, but rather that when they did, the police were more likely to arrest them."[110] Conflict theories of criminality face the difficulty of realistic implementation. Radical criminology, in particular, is flawed by its narrow emphasis on capitalist societies. It fails to recognize adequately the role of human nature in the creation of social classes and in the perpetuation of the struggle for control of resources. Radical criminology implies that a utopian social arrangement—perhaps communism—would eliminate most crime. Such a belief is contrary to historical experience: A close look at any contemporary communist society will reveal both social conflict and crime.

# Peacemaking Criminology

**Peacemaking criminology**, which some theorists see as a mature expression of earlier conflict theories, holds that crime-control agencies and the citizens they serve should work together to alleviate social problems and human suffering and thus reduce crime.[111] Criminology as peacemaking has its roots in ancient Christian and Eastern philosophies, as well as in traditional conflict theory. Peacemaking criminology, which includes the notion of service and has also been

---

**radical criminology**

A conflict perspective that sees crime as engendered by the unequal distribution of wealth, power, and other resources, which adherents believe is especially characteristic of capitalist societies.

Log on to ResearchNavigator.com, and choose "Criminal Justice" under EBSCO's Content Select™ section. Enter the words "crime" and "causation" (without the quotation marks) in the search box, and click "Go." Select five of the articles that appear, and classify each according to where it might fit within this chapter's eight general categories of explanations for criminal behavior. If an article does not clearly fit with any of the categories, choose another article. Send the titles of the articles and your classification of each, along with source information (that is, author, journal, date of publication), to your instructor if asked to do so. *Note:* This feature is available only if your instructor has chosen the Research Navigator option available with a new textbook.

**peacemaking criminology**

A perspective that holds that crime-control agencies and the citizens they serve should work together to alleviate social problems and human suffering and thus reduce crime.

A homeless man passes by an expensive home. Radical criminologists claim that the inequitable distribution of wealth in society produces frustrations and pent-up hostilities that lead to criminality. According to radical criminology, the criminal law is a tool used by the powerful to maintain their place in the social world.

*Joel Stettenheim, Corbis/Bettmann*

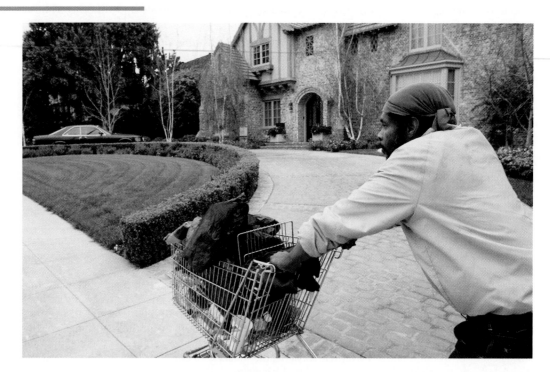

called *compassionate criminology,* suggests that "compassion, wisdom, and love are essential for understanding the suffering of which we are all a part, and for practicing a criminology of nonviolence."[112] Peacemaking criminology also holds that official agents of social control need to work with both the victimized and the victimizers to achieve a new world order that is more just and fair to all who live in it. In a fundamental sense, peacemaking criminologists exhort their colleagues to transcend personal dichotomies to end the political and ideological divisiveness that separates people. "If we ourselves cannot know peace . . . how will our acts disarm hatred and violence?" they ask.[113]

Peacemaking criminology was popularized by the works of Harold Pepinsky[114] and Richard Quinney[115] beginning in 1986. Both Pepinsky and Quinney restate the problem of crime control from one of "how to stop crime" to one of "how to make peace" within society and among citizens and criminal justice agencies. Peacemaking criminology draws attention to many issues, among them the perpetuation of violence through the continuation of social policies based on dominant forms of criminological theory, the role of education in peacemaking, "commonsense theories of crime," crime control as human rights enforcement, and conflict resolution within community settings.[116]

## Social Policy and Conflict Theories

Because radical and conflict criminologists view social inequality as the cause of crime, many suggest that the only way to achieve real change in the rate of crime is through revolution. Revolution—because it holds the promise of greater equality for underrepresented groups and because it mandates a redistribution of wealth and power—is thought necessary for any lasting reduction in crime.

Some contemporary writers on radical criminology, however, have attempted to address the issue of what can be done under our current system, because they recognize that a sudden and total reversal of existing political arrangements within the United States is highly unlikely. Hence, they have begun to focus on promoting "middle-range policy alternatives" to the present system, including "equal justice in the bail system, the abolition of mandatory sentences, prosecution of corporate crimes, increased employment opportunities, and promoting community alternatives to imprisonment."[117] Likewise, programs to reduce prison overcrowding, efforts to highlight injustices within the current system, the elimination of racism and other forms of inequality in the handling of both victims and offenders, growing equality in criminal justice system employment, and the like are all frequently mentioned as mid-range strategies for bringing about a justice system that is fairer and closer to the radical ideal.

When internal cultures conflict, it can be as destructive as a collision between an iceberg and an ocean liner. Misunderstanding between two cultural groups can lead to conflict and, taken to the extreme, physical confrontations.

—Sherman Block, Los Angeles County Sheriff

Raymond Michalowski summarizes the policy directions envisioned by today's radical criminologists when he says, "We cannot be free from the crimes of the poor until there are no more poor; we cannot be free from domination of the powerful until we reduce the inequalities that make domination possible; and we cannot live in harmony with others until we begin to limit the competition for material advantage over others that alienates us from one another."[118]

# Emergent Perspectives

A number of new and developing criminological perspectives deserve special mention. They include feminist criminology, constitutive criminology, and postmodern criminology. We will briefly discuss each in the sections that follow.

## Feminist Criminology

As some writers in the developing field of **feminist criminology** have observed, "Women have been virtually invisible in criminological analysis until recently and much theorizing has proceeded as though criminality is restricted to men."[119] Another puts it this way: "[Traditional] criminological theory assumes a woman is like a man."[120] Feminist criminologists are now working to change long-cherished notions of crime and of criminal justice so that the role of women in both crime causation and crime control might be better appreciated.[121]

One of the first writers to attempt a definitive explanation of the criminality of women was Otto Pollak. Pollak's book, *The Criminality of Women*,[122] written in 1950, suggested that women commit the same number of offenses as men but that most of their criminality is hidden. Pollak claimed that women's roles at the time, primarily those of homemaker and mother, served to disguise their criminal undertakings. He also proposed that chivalrous treatment by a male-dominated justice system acted to bias every stage of criminal justice processing in favor of women. Hence, according to Pollak, although women are just as criminal as men, they are rarely arrested, tried, or imprisoned. In fact, although the criminality of women may approach or exceed that of men in selected offense categories, today it is safe to say that Pollak was incorrect in his assessment of the degree of female criminality; overall women commit far fewer crimes than men.

Early works in the field of feminist criminology include Freda Adler's *Sisters in Crime*[123] and Rita Simon's *Women and Crime*.[124] Both books were published in 1975, and in them the authors claimed that the existing divergences in crime rates between men and women were due primarily to socialization rather than biology. Women, claimed these authors, were taught to believe in personal limitations, faced reduced socioeconomic opportunities, and, as a result, suffered from lowered aspirations. As gender equality increased, they said, it could be expected that male and female criminality would take on similar characteristics. More recent researchers, however, have not found this to be true, with substantial differences between the criminality of men and women remaining, even as gender equality grows.[125]

Contemporary feminist thinking in criminology is represented by the works of writers like Kathleen Daly and Meda Chesney-Lind.[126] Daly and Chesney-Lind emphasize the need for a "gender-aware" criminology and stress the usefulness of applying feminist thinking to criminological analysis. Gender, say these writers, is a central organizing principle of contemporary life. Feminist criminology suggests that theories of crime causation and prevention must include women, and that more research on gender-related issues in the field is badly needed. Additionally, some authors say, "Criminologists should begin to appreciate that their discipline and its questions are a product of white, economically privileged men's experiences."[127] They suggest that rates of female criminality, which are lower than those of males, may show that criminal behavior is not as "normal" as once thought. Because modern-day criminological perspectives were mostly developed by white middle-class males, the propositions and theories they advance fail to take into consideration women's "ways of knowing."[128] Hence, the fundamental challenge posed by feminist criminology is this: Do existing theories of crime causation apply as well to women as they do to men? Or, as Daly and Chesney-Lind put it, given the current situation in theory development, "Do theories of men's crime apply to women?"[129] Read some of Chesney-Lind's recent work via Library Extra 3–5 at cjtoday.com.

Recent perspectives on female criminality stress the fact "that a key to understanding and responding to women as offenders is understanding their status as crime victims."[130] Psychologist Cathy Spatz Widom, for example, examined the life cycle of female offenders, looking for links between childhood abuse and neglect and later criminality. Widom suggested that the successful

> **feminist criminology**
> A developing intellectual approach that emphasizes gender issues in criminology.

TABLE 3-4

## MALE AND FEMALE INVOLVEMENT IN CRIME: OFFENSE PATTERNS, 2004

| | Percentage of All Arrests | |
| --- | --- | --- |
| UCR Index Crime | Males | Females |
| Murder and nonnegligent manslaughter | 88.4% | 11.6% |
| Rape | 98.5 | 1.5 |
| Robbery | 89.0 | 11.0 |
| Aggravated assault | 79.3 | 20.7 |
| Burglary | 85.7 | 14.3 |
| Larceny-theft | 61.7 | 38.3 |
| Motor vehicle theft | 82.9 | 17.1 |
| Arson | 83.5 | 16.5 |

**Gender Differences**

- Men are more likely than women to be arrested for serious crimes, such as murder, rape, robbery, and burglary.
- Arrest, jail, and prison data all suggest that more women than men who commit crimes are involved in property crimes, such as larceny, forgery, fraud, and embezzlement, and in drug offenses.

*Source:* Federal Bureau of Investigation, *Uniform Crime Reports: Crime in the United States, 2004* (Washington, DC: U.S. Government Printing Office, 2005).

socialization of girls can be "derailed" by early victimization through mechanisms such as "running away, deficits in cognitive ability and achievement, growing up without traditional social controls, engaging in relationships with deviant or delinquent individuals, and failing to learn the social and psychological skills necessary for successful adult development."[131]

Contemporary statistics tell us that although females make up 51% of the population of the United States, they are arrested for only 17.8% of all violent crimes and 31.9% of property crimes. The relatively limited involvement of women in the FBI's eight major crimes can be seen in Table 3–4. Data show that the number of women committing crimes is increasing faster than the number of male offenders, however. Between 1970 and 2000, the number of crimes committed by men grew by 46%, while crimes committed by women increased 144%. Violent crimes by men increased 82% during the period; by women, 260%. Property crimes perpetrated by men grew by 3%; by women, 85%.[132]

Relative increases in the FBI's Part II offenses tell a similar story. Arrests of women for embezzlement, for example, increased by more than 228% between 1970 and 2000, versus only 8.5% for men—reflecting women's increased entry into areas of financial responsibility. Arrests of women for drug abuse grew by 289%, and liquor-law violations by women increased 285% (versus 96% for men).[133] In two officially reported categories—prostitution and runaways—women outnumber men in the volume of offenses committed.[134] Other crimes in which significant numbers of women (relative to men) are involved include larceny-theft (where 38.5% of reported crimes are committed by women), forgery and counterfeiting (39.8%), fraud (44.9%), and embezzlement (50.4%).[135] Nonetheless, as Table 3–4 shows, female offenders still account for only a small proportion of all reported crimes. Statistics on female criminality are difficult to interpret since reports of increasing female criminality may reflect the greater equality of treatment accorded women in contemporary society more than they do actual increases in criminal activity. In the past, when women committed crimes, they were dealt with less officiously than is likely to be the case today.

When women do commit serious crimes, they are more often followers than leaders. A study of women in correctional settings, for example, found that women are far more likely to assume "secondary follower roles during criminal events" than "dominant leadership roles."[136] Only 14% of women surveyed played primary roles, but those who did "felt that men had little influence in initiating or leading them into crime." African-American women were found to be more likely to play "primary and equal crime roles" with men or with female accomplices than were white or Hispanic women. Statistics such as these dispel the myth that the female criminal in America has taken her place alongside the male offender—in terms of either leadership roles or the absolute number of crimes committed.

WHAT WOULD YOU DO?

The CD-ROM scenario for Chapter 3 builds on the Bill of Rights and constitutional guarantees against illegal searches and seizures. In doing so, it prepares you for the chapters that follow. Use the CD-ROM found in your textbook to work through this scenario.

# Constitutive Criminology

In the early 1900s, George Herbert Mead[137] (1863–1931) set forth a theory called *symbolic interaction,* in which he demonstrated how people give meaning to the things around them and to their lives. About the same time, William Thomas[138] (1863–1947) explained that the significance of any human behavior is relative to the intentions behind it and to the situation in which it is interpreted. Hence, behavior that in one place or at one time is seen as acceptable, in another place or time may be perceived as deviant or even criminal. From this viewpoint, crime, like any other social phenomenon, is more a definition imposed by society on a particular type of activity than it is a quality inherent in the behavior itself. As a consequence, crime may mean different things to different people and is, no doubt, variously interpreted by the offender, by the victim, and by agents of social control. Seen this way, the significance of criminal behavior depends on one's interests in the crime and one's point of view and is ultimately knowable only to those who participate in it. Central to this way of thinking are the following principles:

- The significance of any behavior depends on a social consensus about what that behavior "means."
- Crime is the product of an active process of interpretation and social definition.
- Continued criminal activity may be more a consequence of the limited opportunities for acceptable behavior that are imposed on individuals defined as "criminal" than it is a product of choice.

Contemporary criminologists Stuart Henry and Dragan Milovanovic use the term **constitutive criminology** to refer to the process by which human beings create "an ideology of crime that sustains it as a concrete reality."[139] A central feature of constitutive criminology is its assertion that individuals shape their world while also being shaped by it. Constitutive criminology claims that crime and crime control are not "object-like entities," but constructions produced through a social process in which offender, victim, and society are all involved.[140] "We are concerned with the ways in which human agents actively coproduce that which they take to be crime," write Henry and Milovanovic. For these theorists, the idea of crime itself is a social construction, and researchers, they say, should recognize that criminals and victims are also "emergent realities." In short, constitutive criminology focuses on the social process by which crime and criminology become cultural realities.[141] Read some of Milovanovic's work via **Library Extra 3–6** at cjtoday.com.

> **constitutive criminology**
>
> The study of the process by which human beings create an ideology of crime that sustains the notion of crime as a concrete reality.

> **postmodern criminology**
>
> A branch of criminology that developed after World War II and that builds on the tenets inherent in postmodern social thought.

# Postmodern Criminology

Before concluding this chapter, it is important to note that **postmodern criminology** is a term applied to a wide variety of novel perspectives that have developed in recent decades. It encompasses evolving paradigms with such intriguing names as *chaos theory, discourse analysis, topology theory, critical theory, realist criminology, constitutive theory,* and *anarchic criminology.*[142] Postmodern criminology builds on the belief that past criminological approaches have failed to realistically assess the true causes of crime and have therefore failed to offer workable solutions for crime control—or if they have, that such theories and solutions may have been appropriate at one time but no longer apply to the postmodern era. Because postmodern criminology challenges and debunks existing perspectives, it is referred to as *deconstructionist,* and such theories are sometimes called **deconstructionist theories**.

> **deconstructionist theory**
>
> One of the emerging approaches that challenges existing criminological perspectives to debunk them and that works toward replacing them with concepts more applicable to the postmodern era.

**SUMMARY**

This chapter describes theoretical explanations for crime. Most of the perspectives discussed are grounded in biology, psychology, or sociology. Biological theories posit a genetic or a physiological basis for deviant and criminal behavior. The notion of a "weak" gene that might predispose certain individuals toward criminal activity has recently been expanded to include the impact of environmental contaminants, poor nutrition, and food additives on behavior. Studies of fraternal twins and chromosome structure have helped to lead biological theories into the modern day.

Psychological explanations of crime are individualistic. Some psychoanalytical theories see offenders as sick; other psychological theories claim merely that criminal behavior is a type of conditioned response. The stimulus–response model depicts criminal behavior as the consequence of a conditioning process that extends over the entire life span of an individual.

Sociological theories, which hold that the individual is a product of the environment, constitute today's perspective of choice. These theories emphasize the role of social structure, inequality, and socialization in generating criminality. The danger of most sociological approaches, however, is that they tend to deny the significance of any influences beyond those that are mediated through social interaction.

An integrated perspective that recognizes that human behavior results from a mix of biology, mental processes, and acquired traits holds much future promise. As a consequence, our understanding of crime causation is headed toward a unified theory of conduct drawn on many explanations to interpret the whole range of human behavior—including crime.

## DISCUSSION QUESTIONS

1. This chapter describes various categories of theoretical approaches used to explain crime. What are they?

2. Describe the basic features of biological theories of crime causation. What are the shortcomings of this perspective? Do you think that biological theories have much explanatory power? Why or why not?

3. Describe the basic features of psychological explanations for crime. What are the shortcomings of this perspective? Do you think that psychological theories have much explanatory power? Why or why not?

4. Describe the basic features of sociological theories of crime causation. What are the shortcomings of this perspective? Do you think that sociological theories have much explanatory power? Why or why not?

5. What is meant by "emergent theories"? Identify two emergent theories of crime causation.

## WEB QUEST

One of the most informative criminal justice–related sites on the Web is the National Criminal Justice Reference Service (NCJRS). Visit the NCJRS at ncjrs.org, or use the Cybrary to locate the NCJRS. Once you have found NCJRS, explore each of the major informational categories it provides: Corrections, Courts, Crime, Crime Prevention, Drugs, Justice System, Juvenile Justice, Law Enforcement, and Victims.

Visit each category, and make a note of the features available. View at least one document from each category. Write a summary of each document (you should have a total of nine), and submit the summaries to your instructor if asked to do so.

Reenter each NCJRS category, and make a note of the websites referenced there. Visit at least three sites under each category, and write a brief description of each site (you should have a total of 27). Submit the descriptions to your instructor if asked to do so.

To complete this Web Quest online, go to the Web Quest module in Chapter 3 of the *Criminal Justice Today* Companion Website at cjtoday.com.

## NOTES

i. *The American Heritage Dictionary and Electronic Thesaurus on CD-ROM* (Boston: Houghton Mifflin, 1987).

ii. Nicole Rafter, "Earnest A. Hooton and the Biological Tradition in American Criminology," *Criminology*, Vol. 42, No. 3 (2004), p. 735.

iii. "Gingrich Says Felons Should Be Tracked by Satellite," Reuters wire service, March 4, 1995.

1. "Remarks by the President on Project Safe Neighborhoods," Pennsylvania Convention Center, Philadelphia, Pennsylvania, May 14, 2001. Web posted at http://www.whitehouse.gov/news/releases/2001/05/20010514-1.html (accessed April 2, 2002).

2. Quoted in Gwynn Nettler, *Killing One Another* (Cincinnati, OH: Anderson, 1982), p. 194.

3. "50 Cent." Web posted at http://www.who2.com/50cent.html (accessed August 28, 2005).

4. Jason Birchmeier, "50 Cent: Bio," *All Music Guide*. Web posted at http://www.mtv.com/bands/az/50_cent/bio.jhtml (accessed August 30, 2005).

5. "Rumor Has It: 50 Cent Piece," Snopes.com. Web posted at http://www.snopes.com/inboxer/hoaxes/50cent.asp (accessed August 30, 2005).

6. As we will see in Chapter 4, behavior that violates the criminal law may not be "crime" if accompanied by an acceptable legal justification or excuse. Justifications and excuses that are recognized by the law may serve as defenses to a criminal charge.

7. This and many of the statistics in these opening paragraphs come from Jonathan Wright, "Media Are Mixed Blessing, Criminologists Say," Reuters wire service, May 2, 1995.

8. See "Comments of James T. Hamilton before the Federal Communications Commission, in the Matter of Industry Proposal for Rating Video Programming," May 23, 1997, citing Suzanne Stutman, Joanne Cantor, and Victoria Duran, *What Parents Want in a Television Rating System: Results of a National Survey* (Madison: University of Wisconsin, 1996); Wes Shipley and Gary Cavender, "Murder and Mayhem at the Movies," *Journal of Criminal Justice and Popular Culture*, Vol. 9, No. 1 (2001), pp. 1–14; and Suzanne Stutman, Joanne Cantor, and Victoria Duran, "What Parents Want in a Television Rating System: Results of a National Survey (Washington, DC: National PTA, 2002). Web posted at http://www.pta.org/ptacommunity/tvreport.asp (accessed August 21, 2005).

9. Jeffrey Johnson, "Television Viewing and Aggressive Behavior during Adolescence and Adulthood," *Science*, Vol. 295 (2002), pp. 2468–2471.

10. Wright, "Media Are Mixed Blessing, Criminologists Say."

11. Nathan McCall, "My Rap against Rap," *Washington Post* wire service, November 14, 1993.

12. Arthur L. Cribbs, Jr., "Gangsta Rappers Sing White Racists' Tune," *USA Today*, December 27, 1993, p. 9A.

13. U.S. News/UCLA Survey on the Media and Violence, reported in "Hollywood: Right Face," *U.S. News & World Report*, May 15, 1995, p. 71.

14. See "Congress Hopes Ten Commandments Curb Violence," APB Online, June 17, 1999. Web posted at http://www.apbonline.com/911/1999/06/17/congress0617 01.html (accessed March 1, 2000).

15. The word *scientific* is used here to refer to the application of generally accepted research strategies designed to reject explanations that rival the one under study.

16. Stephen Schafer, *Theories in Criminology* (New York: Random House, 1969), p. 109.

17. L. E. Cohen and Marcus Felson, "Social Change and Crime Rate Trends: A Routine Activity Approach," *American Sociological Review*, Vol. 44, No. 4 (August 1979), pp. 588–608. Also see Marcus Felson and L. E. Cohen, "Human Ecology and Crime: A Routine Activity Approach," *Human Ecology*, Vol. 8, No. 4 (1980), pp. 389–406; Marcus Felson, "Linking Criminal Choices, Routine Activities, Informal Control, and Criminal Outcomes," in Derek B. Cornish and Ronald V. Clarke, eds., *The Reasoning Criminal: Rational Choice Perspectives on Offending* (New York: Springer-Verlag, 1986), pp. 119–128; and Ronald V. Clarke and Marcus Felson, eds., *Advances in Criminological Theory: Routine Activity and Rational Choice* (New Brunswick, NJ: Transaction, 1993).

18. Cohen and Felson, "Social Change and Crime Rate Trends," p. 595.

19. For a test of routine activities theory as an explanation for victimization in the workplace, see John D. Wooldredge, Francis T. Cullen, and Edward J. Latessa, "Victimization in the Workplace: A Test of Routine Activities Theory," *Justice Quarterly*, Vol. 9, No. 2 (June 1992), pp. 325–335.

20. Werner Einstadter and Stuart Henry, *Criminological Theory: An Analysis of Its Underlying Assumptions* (Fort Worth, TX: Harcourt Brace, 1995), p. 70.

21. For a modern reprint of a widely read nineteenth-century work on phrenology, see Orson Squire Fowler and Lorenzo Niles Fowler, *Phrenology: A Practical Guide to Your Head* (New York: Chelsea House, 1980).

22. Schafer, *Theories in Criminology*, p. 123.

23. Richard Louis Dugdale, *The Jukes: A Study in Crime, Pauperism, Disease, and Heredity*, 3rd ed. (New York: G. P. Putnam's Sons, 1985).

24. Henry Herbert Goddard, *The Kallikak Family: A Study in the Heredity of Feeblemindedness* (New York: Macmillan, 1912).

25. For more information, see Richard Herrnstein, "Crime File: Biology and Crime," a study guide (Washington, DC: National Institute of Justice, no date).

26. *Buck* v. *Bell*, 274 U.S. 200, 207 (1927).

27. Patricia Jacobs et al., "Aggressive Behavior, Mental Subnormality, and the XYY Male," *Nature*, Vol. 208 (1965), pp. 1351–1352.

28. Schafer, *Theories in Criminology*, p. 193.

29. D. Hill and W. Sargent, "A Case of Matricide," *Lancet*, Vol. 244 (1943), pp. 526–527.

30. See, for example, A. R. Mawson and K. J. Jacobs, "Corn Consumption, Tryptophan, and Cross-National Homicide Rates," *Journal of Orthomolecular Psychiatry,* Vol. 7 (1978), pp. 227–230; and A. Hoffer, "The Relation of Crime to Nutrition," *Humanist in Canada,* Vol. 8 (1975), p. 8.

31. See, for example, C. Hawley and R. E. Buckley, "Food Dyes and Hyperkinetic Children," *Academy Therapy,* Vol. 10 (1974), pp. 27–32; and Alexander Schauss, *Diet, Crime, and Delinquency* (Berkeley, CA: Parker House, 1980).

32. "Special Report: Measuring Your Life with Coffee Spoons," *Tufts University Diet and Nutrition Letter,* Vol. 2, No. 2 (April 1984), pp. 3–6.

33. See, for example, "Special Report: Does What You Eat Affect Your Mood and Actions?" *Tufts University Diet and Nutrition Letter,* Vol. 2, No. 12 (February 1985), pp. 4–6.

34. See *Tufts University Diet and Nutrition Letter,* Vol. 2, No. 11 (January 1985), p. 2; and "Special Report: Why Sugar Continues to Concern Nutritionists," *Tufts University Diet and Nutrition Letter,* Vol. 3, No. 3 (May 1985), pp. 3–6.

35. Diana H. Fishbein and Susan E. Pease, "Diet, Nutrition, and Aggression," in Marc Hillbrand and Nathaniel J. Pallone, eds., *The Psychobiology of Aggression: Engines, Measurement, Control* (New York: Haworth Press, 1994), pp. 114–117.

36. A. Hoffer, "Children with Learning and Behavioral Disorders," *Journal of Orthomolecular Psychiatry,* Vol. 5 (1976), p. 229.

37. "Special Report: Does What You Eat Affect Your Mood and Actions?" p. 4.

38. See, for example, R. T. Rada, D. R. Laws, and R. Kellner, "Plasma Testosterone Levels in the Rapist," *Psychomatic Medicine,* Vol. 38 (1976), pp. 257–268.

39. Later studies, however, have been less than clear. See, for example, J. M. Dabbs, Jr., "Testosterone Measurements in Social and Clinical Psychology," *Journal of Social and Clinical Psychology,* Vol. 11 (1992), pp. 302–321.

40. "The Insanity of Steroid Abuse," *Newsweek,* May 23, 1988, p. 75.

41. E. G. Stalenheim et al., "Testosterone as a Biological Marker in Psychopathy and Alcoholism," *Psychiatry Research,* Vol. 77, No. 2 (February 1998), pp. 79–88.

42. For a summary of such studies, see Serena-Lynn Brown, Alexander Botsis, and Herman M. Van Praag, "Serotonin and Aggression," in Marc Hillbrand and Nathaniel J. Pallone, eds., *The Psychobiology of Aggression: Engines, Measurement, Control* (New York: Haworth Press, 1994), pp. 28–39.

43. Roger D. Masters, Brian Hone, and Anil Doshi, "Environmental Pollution, Neurotoxicity, and Criminal Violence," in J. Rose, ed., *Environmental Toxicology* (London and New York: Gordon and Breach, 1997).

44. B. Bioulac et al., "Serotonergic Functions in the XYY Syndrome," *Biological Psychiatry,* Vol. 15 (1980), pp. 917–923.

45. E. G. Stalenheim, L. von Knorring, and L. Wide, "Serum Levels of Thyroid Hormones as Biological Markers in a Swedish Forensic Psychiatric Population," *Biological Psychiatry,* Vol. 43, No. 10 (May 15, 1998), pp. 755–761.

46. Sarnoff Mednick and Jan Volavka, "Biology and Crime," in Norval Morris and Michael Tonry, eds., *Crime and Justice* (Chicago: University of Chicago Press, 1980), pp. 85–159.

47. Sarnoff Mednick and S. Gloria Shaham, eds., *New Paths in Criminology* (Lexington, MA: D. C. Heath, 1979).

48. For a good survey of studies in this area, see Laurence Miller, "Traumatic Brain Injury and Aggression," in Marc Hillbrand and Nathaniel J. Pallone, eds., *The Psychobiology of Aggression: Engines, Measurement, Control* (New York: Haworth Press, 1994), pp. 91–103.

49. For an excellent overview of such studies, see Shari Mills and Adrian Raine, "Neuroimaging and Aggression," in Marc Hillbrand and Nathaniel J. Pallone, eds., *The Psychobiology of Aggression: Engines, Measurement, Control* (New York: Haworth Press, 1994), pp. 145–158.

50. R. B. Cattell, *The Inheritance of Personality and Ability: Research Methods and Findings* (New York: Academic Press, 1982).

51. Karl Christiansen, "A Preliminary Study of Criminality among Twins," in Sarnoff Mednick and Karl O. Christiansen, eds., *Biosocial Bases of Criminal Behavior* (New York: Gardner Press, 1977).

52. James Q. Wilson and Richard J. Herrnstein, *Crime and Human Nature* (New York: Simon and Schuster, 1985).

53. "Criminals Born and Bred," *Newsweek,* September 16, 1985, p. 69.

54. William J. Chambliss, *Exploring Criminology* (New York: Macmillan, 1988), p. 202.

55. A. Reiss and J. Roth, eds., *Understanding and Preventing Violence* (Washington, DC: National Academy Press, 1993).

56. Sigmund Freud, *A General Introduction to Psychoanalysis* (New York: Boni and Liveright, 1920).

57. Nettler, *Killing One Another,* p. 79.

58. David Abrahamsen, *Crime and the Human Mind* (reprint, Montclair, NJ: Patterson Smith, 1969), p. 23.

59. See Adrian Raine, *The Psychopathology of Crime: Criminal Behavior as a Clinical*

*Disorder* (Orlando, FL: Academic Press, 1993).

60. Hervey M. Cleckley, *The Mask of Sanity: An Attempt to Reinterpret the So-Called Psychopathic Personality* (St. Louis, MO: Mosby, 1941).

61. Nettler, *Killing One Another,* p. 179.

62. Albert I. Rabin, "The Antisocial Personality—Psychopathy and Sociopathy," in Hans Toch, ed., *Psychology of Crime and Criminal Justice* (Prospect Heights, IL: Waveland Press, 1979), p. 330.

63. Richard L. Ault and James T. Reese, "A Psychological Assessment of Crime Profiling," *FBI Law Enforcement Bulletin* (March 1980), pp. 22–25.

64. John E. Douglas and Alan E. Burgess, "Criminal Profiling: A Viable Investigative Tool against Violent Crime," *FBI Law Enforcement Bulletin* (December 1986), pp. 9–13.

65. Robert R. Hazelwood and John E. Douglass, "The Lust Murderer," *FBI Law Enforcement Bulletin* (April 1980), pp. 18–22.

66. A. O. Rider, "The Firesetter—A Psychological Profile," *FBI Law Enforcement Bulletin* (June 1980), pp. 4–11.

67. M. Reiser, "Crime-Specific Psychological Consultation," *Police Chief* (March 1982), pp. 53–56.

68. Thomas Strentz, "A Terrorist Psychosocial Profile: Past and Present," *FBI Law Enforcement Bulletin* (April 1988), pp. 13–19.

69. Jill Peay, "Dangerousness—Ascription or Description," in M. P. Feldman, ed., *Violence,* Vol. 2 of *Developments in the Study of Criminal Behavior* (New York: John Wiley, 1982), p. 211, citing N. Walker, "Dangerous People," *International Journal of Law and Psychiatry,* Vol. 1 (1978), pp. 37–50.

70. See, for example, Michael Gottfredson and Travis Hirschi, *A General Theory of Crime* (Stanford, CA: Stanford University Press, 1990); and Travis Hirschi and Michael Gottfredson, "Age and the Explanation of Crime," *American Journal of Sociology,* Vol. 89 (1983), pp. 552–584.

71. David F. Greenberg, "Modeling Criminal Careers," *Criminology,* Vol. 29, No. 1 (1991), p. 39.

72. Robert E. Park and Ernest Burgess, *Introduction to the Science of Sociology,* 2nd ed. (Chicago: University of Chicago Press, 1924); and Robert E. Park, ed., *The City* (Chicago: University of Chicago Press, 1925).

73. Clifford R. Shaw and Henry D. McKay, "Social Factors in Juvenile Delinquency," in Vol. 2 of the *Report on the Causes of Crime,* National Commission on Law Observance and Enforcement Report No. 13 (Washington, DC: U.S. Government Printing Office, 1931); and

Clifford R. Shaw, *Juvenile Delinquency in Urban Areas* (Chicago: University of Chicago Press, 1942).

74. Émile Durkheim, *Suicide* (reprint, New York: Free Press, 1951).

75. Robert K. Merton, "Social Structure and Anomie," *American Sociological Review,* Vol. 3 (1938), pp. 672–682.

76. Catherine E. Ross and John Mirowsky, "Normlessness, Powerlessness, and Trouble with the Law," *Criminology,* Vol. 25, No. 2 (May 1987), p. 257.

77. See Nettler, *Killing One Another,* p. 58.

78. This is not to say that all members of these groups engaged in criminal behavior, but rather that statistics indicated higher average crime rates for these groups than for certain others immediately after immigration to the United States.

79. Albert K. Cohen, *Delinquent Boys: The Culture of the Gang* (Glencoe, IL: Free Press, 1958).

80. Walter B. Miller, "Lower Class Culture as a Generating Milieu of Gang Delinquency," *Journal of Social Issues,* Vol. 14 (1958), pp. 5–19.

81. Richard Cloward and Lloyd Ohlin, *Delinquency and Opportunity: A Theory of Delinquent Gangs* (New York: Free Press, 1960).

82. Marvin Wolfgang, *Patterns in Criminal Homicide* (Philadelphia: University of Pennsylvania Press, 1958). See also Marvin Wolfgang and Franco Ferracuti, *The Subculture of Violence: Toward an Integrated Theory in Criminology* (London: Tavistock, 1967).

83. "Gang Prevention through Targeted Outreach—Boys and Girls Clubs of America." Web posted at http://ojjdp.ncjrs.org/pubs/ gun_ violence/sect08-k.html (accessed April 10, 2005).

84. See, for example, James D. Orcutt, "Differential Association and Marijuana Use: A Closer Look at Sutherland (with a Little Help from Becker)," *Criminology,* Vol. 25, No. 2 (1987), pp. 341–358.

85. Edwin Sutherland, *Principles of Criminology,* 4th ed. (Chicago: J. B. Lippincott, 1947), p. 4.

86. John E. Conklin, *Criminology,* 3rd ed. (New York: Macmillan, 1989), p. 278.

87. Robert L. Burgess and Ronald L. Akers, "A Differential Association—Reinforcement Theory of Criminal Behavior," *Social Problems,* Vol. 14 (fall 1996), pp. 128–147.

88. Some theories are multicausal and provide explanations for criminal behavior that include a diversity of "causes."

89. For a more elaborate criticism of this sort, see Conklin, *Criminology,* p. 260.

90. Ibid.

91.  Walter C. Reckless, *The Crime Problem,* 4th ed. (New York: Appleton-Century-Crofts, 1961).

92.  Ibid., p. 472.

93.  Travis Hirschi, *Causes of Delinquency* (Berkeley: University of California Press, 1969).

94.  Ibid., p. 472.

95.  Gresham Sykes and David Matza, "Techniques of Neutralization: A Theory of Delinquency," *American Sociological Review,* Vol. 22 (1957), pp. 664–670.

96.  Many of the concepts used by Howard Becker in explicating his theory of labeling were, in fact, used previously not only by Frank Tannenbaum, but also by Edwin M. Lemert. Lemert wrote of "societal reaction" and "primary and secondary deviance" and even used the word *labeling* in his book *Social Pathology* (New York: McGraw-Hill, 1951).

97.  Frank Tannenbaum, *Crime and the Community* (Boston: Ginn, 1938), pp. 19–20.

98.  Howard Becker, *Outsiders: Studies in the Sociology of Deviance* (New York: Free Press, 1963), pp. 8–9.

99.  Ibid.

100. Ibid., p. 33.

101. Robert J. Sampson and John H. Laub, *Crime in the Making: Pathways and Turning Points through the Life Course* (Cambridge, MA: Harvard University Press, 1993).

102. Katharine Browning et al., "Causes and Correlates of Delinquency Program," *OJJDP Fact Sheet* (Washington, DC: U.S. Department of Justice, April 1999).

103. MacArthur Foundation, "The Project on Human Development in Chicago Neighborhoods." Web posted at http://www.macfound.org/research/hcd/hcd_5.htm (accessed January 5, 2001).

104. Adapted from Raymond Michalowski, "Perspectives and Paradigm: Structuring Criminological Thought," in Robert F. Meier, ed., *Theory in Criminology* (Beverly Hills, CA: Sage, 1977).

105. See George B. Vold, *Theoretical Criminology* (New York: Oxford University Press, 1986).

106. Austin T. Turk, *Criminality and the Legal Order* (Chicago: Rand McNally, 1969).

107. Thorsten Sellin, *Culture Conflict and Crime* (New York: Social Science Research Council, 1938).

108. William J. Chambliss and Robert B. Seidman, *Law, Order, and Power* (Reading, MA: Addison-Wesley, 1971).

109. Richard Quinney, *The Social Reality of Crime* (Boston: Little, Brown, 1970).

110. David F. Greenberg, *Crime and Capitalism* (Palo Alto, CA: Mayfield, 1981), p. 3.

111. For examples of how this might be accomplished, see F. H. Knopp, "Community Solutions to Sexual Violence: Feminist/Abolitionist Perspectives," in Harold E. Pepinsky and Richard Quinney, eds., *Criminology as Peacemaking* (Bloomington: Indiana University Press, 1991), pp. 181–193; and S. Caringella-MacDonald and D. Humphries, "Sexual Assault, Women, and the Community: Organizing to Prevent Sexual Violence," in Pepinsky and Quinney, eds., *Criminology as Peacemaking,* pp. 98–113.

112. Richard Quinney, "Life of Crime: Criminology and Public Policy as Peacemaking," *Journal of Crime and Justice,* Vol. 16, No. 2 (1993), pp. 3–9.

113. Ram Dass and P. Gorman, *How Can I Help? Stories and Reflections on Service* (New York: Alfred A. Knopf, 1985), p. 165, as cited in Richard Quinney and John Wildeman, *The Problem of Crime: A Peace and Social Justice Perspective,* 3rd ed. (Mayfield, CA: Mountain View Press, 1991), p. 116, originally published as *The Problem of Crime: A Critical Introduction to Criminology* (New York: Bantam, 1977).

114. See, for example, Harold E. Pepinsky, "This Can't Be Peace: A Pessimist Looks at Punishment," in W. B. Groves and G. Newman, eds., *Punishment and Privilege* (Albany, NY: Harrow and Heston, 1986); Harold E. Pepinsky, "Violence as Unresponsiveness: Toward a New Conception of Crime," *Justice Quarterly,* Vol. 5 (1988), pp. 539–563; and Pepinsky and Quinney, eds., *Criminology as Peacemaking.*

115. See, for example, Richard Quinney, "Crime, Suffering, Service: Toward a Criminology of Peacemaking," *Quest,* Vol. 1 (1988), pp. 66–75; Richard Quinney, "The Theory and Practice of Peacemaking in the Development of Radical Criminology," *Critical Criminologist,* Vol. 1, No. 5 (1989), p. 5; and Quinney and Wildeman, *The Problem of Crime.*

116. All of these themes are addressed, for example, in Pepinsky and Quinney, eds., *Criminology as Peacemaking.*

117. Michael J. Lynch and W. Byron Groves, *A Primer in Radical Criminology,* 2nd ed. (Albany, NY: Harrow and Heston, 1989), p. 128.

118. Raymond J. Michalowski, *Order, Law, and Crime: An Introduction to Criminology* (New York: Random House, 1985), p. 410.

119. Don C. Gibbons, *Talking about Crime and Criminals: Problems and Issues in Theory Development in Criminology* (Englewood Cliffs, NJ: Prentice Hall, 1994), p. 165, citing Loraine Gelsthorpe and Alison Morris, eds., *Feminist Perspectives in Criminology* (Bristol: Open University Press, 1990).

120. Sally S. Simpson, "Feminist Theory, Crime, and Justice," *Criminology,* Vol. 27, No. 4 (1989), p. 605.

121. For an excellent overview of feminist theory in criminology and for a comprehensive review of research regarding female offenders, see Joanne Belknap, *The Invisible Woman: Gender Crime and Justice* (Belmont, CA: Wadsworth, 1996).

122. Otto Pollak, *The Criminality of Women* (Philadelphia: University of Pennsylvania Press, 1950).

123. Freda Adler, *Sisters in Crime: The Rise of the New Female Criminal* (New York: McGraw-Hill, 1975).

124. Rita J. Simon, *Women and Crime* (Lexington, MA: Lexington Books, 1975).

125. See, for example, Darrell J. Steffensmeir, "Sex Differences in Patterns of Adult Crime, 1965–1977: A Review and Assessment," *Social Forces,* Vol. 58 (1980), pp. 1098–1099.

126. See, for example, Kathleen Daly and Meda Chesney-Lind, "Feminism and Criminology," *Justice Quarterly,* Vol. 5, No. 5 (December 1988), pp. 497–535.

127. Ibid., p. 506.

128. Ibid.

129. Ibid., p. 514.

130. Cathy Spatz Widom, "Childhood Victimization and the Derailment of Girls and Women to the Criminal Justice System," in Beth E. Richie et al., eds., *Research on Women and Girls in the Justice System* (Washington, DC: National Institute of Justice, 2000), p. iii.

131. Ibid., pp. 27–36.

132. Federal Bureau of Investigation, *Uniform Crime Reports: Crime in the United States, 1970* (Washington, DC: U.S. Government Printing Office, 1971); and Federal Bureau of Investigation, *Uniform Crime Reports: Crime in the United States, 2000* (Washington, DC: U.S. Government Printing Office, 2001).

133. Ibid.

134. FBI, *Uniform Crime Reports: Crime in the United States, 2000.*

135. Federal Bureau of Investigation, *Uniform Crime Reports: Crime in the United States, 2004* (Washington DC: U.S. Government Printing Office, 2005).

136. Leanne Fiftal Alarid et al., "Women's Roles in Serious Offenses: A Study of Adult Felons," *Justice Quarterly,* Vol. 13, No. 3 (September 1996), pp. 432–454.

137. George Herbert Mead and Charles W. Morris, eds., *Mind, Self, and Society* (Chicago: University of Chicago Press, 1934).

138. William I. Thomas and Florian Znaneicki, *The Polish Peasant in Europe and America* (Chicago: University of Chicago Press, 1918).

139. Stuart Henry and Dragan Milovanovic, "Constitutive Criminology: The Maturation of Critical Theory," *Criminology,* Vol. 29, No. 2 (May 1991), p. 293.

140. Dragan Milovanovic, *Postmodern Criminology* (Hamden, CT: Garland, 1997).

141. See also Stuart Henry and Dragan Milovanovic, *Constitutive Criminology: Beyond Postmodernism* (London: Sage, 1996).

142. For an excellent and detailed discussion of many of these approaches, see Milovanovic, *Postmodern Criminology.*

# CHAPTER 4

# Criminal Law

## OUTLINE

- Introduction
- The Nature and Purpose of Law
- The Rule of Law
- Types of Law
- General Categories of Crime
- General Features of Crime
- Elements of a Specific Criminal Offense
- Types of Defenses to a Criminal Charge

## LEARNING OBJECTIVES

**After reading this chapter, you should be able to:**

- Explain the impact of common law on contemporary American criminal justice.
- Discuss the nature of the rule of law, and describe its purpose in Western democracies.
- Identify the various types of law, and explain the purpose of each.
- List the five categories of criminal law violations.
- List the eight general features of crime.
- Explain the concept of *corpus delicti.*
- Discuss the four broad categories of criminal defenses that our legal system recognizes.
- Explain the legal concept of insanity, and distinguish it from psychiatric explanations of mental illness.

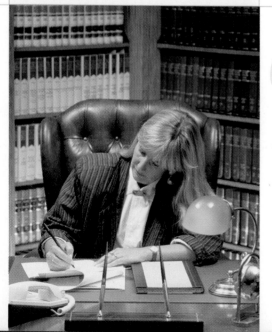

*Law is the art of the good and the fair.*

—Ulpian, Roman judge (circa A.D. 200)

*Every law is an infraction of liberty.*

—Jeremy Bentham (1748–1832)

Law should be like death, which spares no one.
—Montesquieu (1689–1755)

## KEY CONCEPTS

### TERMS

*actus reus*
alibi
alter ego rule
attendant circumstances
case law
civil law
class-action lawsuit
common law
compensatory damages
concurrence
*corpus delicti*
criminal law
criminal negligence
cultural defense
defense (to a criminal charge)
diminished capacity
double jeopardy
element (of a crime)

entrapment
espionage
*ex post facto*
excuse
felony
gross negligence
guilty but mentally ill (GBMI)
inchoate offense
incompetent to stand trial
infraction
insanity defense
jurisprudence
justification
law
legal cause
*mens rea*
misdemeanor
M'Naghten rule

motive
offense
penal code
precedent
procedural defense
procedural law
punitive damages
reasonable force
reckless behavior
rule of law
self-defense
*stare decisis*
statutory law
strict liability
substantive criminal law
tort
treason

### CASES

*Ake* v. *Oklahoma*
*The Crown* v. *Dudly & Stephens*
*Durham* v. *U.S.*

*Ford* v. *Wainwright*
*Foucha* v. *Louisiana*

*U.S.* v. *Brawner*
*U.S.* v. *Felix*

The original full-text court opinion for each of these cases is available on the CD-ROM that accompanies this book.

# Introduction

Hear the author discuss this chapter at **cjtoday.com**

In 2003, after the American military had toppled the regime of Saddam Hussein, but before the establishment of a new Iraqi government, soldiers of the U.S. Third Infantry Division had to release a man who had taken his beaten and bloodied wife to a Baghdad hospital for treatment and continued to beat her while waiting for doctors to arrive.[1] When soldiers restrained the man, he exclaimed that he was exercising his marital rights under Islamic tradition and was beating his wife because she had interfered with his attempts to have intercourse with the couple's 14-year-old daughter. "The sad thing is there was nothing we could do," said Sergeant First Class Michael Shirley of Hinesville, Georgia, "apart from separate them and send her to her mother's house in a taxi, because there are no laws against domestic violence here. The women have to respect their husband's decisions. We can't get involved with religious or cultural beliefs."[2]

> The greatest happiness of the greatest number is the foundation of morals and legislation.
>
> —Jeremy Bentham

In contrast to prewar Iraq, modern postindustrial societies like the United States have developed highly formalized secular legal systems. Laws govern many aspects of our lives, and we are expected to know both what the law *says* as it applies to our daily lives, and to follow it. But do we really know what **law** *is?* The job of this chapter is to discuss the law both as a product of rule creation and as a guide for behavior. We will also examine criminal law in some detail, and we will discuss defenses commonly used by defendants charged with violations of the criminal law.

**law**

A rule of conduct, generally found enacted in the form of a statute, that proscribes or mandates certain forms of behavior.

# The Nature and Purpose of Law

Imagine a society without laws. Without civil law people would not know what to expect from one another, nor would they be able to plan for the future with any degree of certainty. Without criminal law people wouldn't feel safe because the more powerful could forcibly take what they wanted from the less powerful. Without constitutional law people could not exercise the basic

| WHAT DO LAWS DO? |
| --- |

- Laws maintain order in society.
- Laws regulate human interaction.
- Laws enforce moral beliefs.
- Laws define the economic environment.
- Laws enhance predictability.
- Laws support the powerful.
- Laws promote orderly social change.
- Laws sustain individual rights.
- Laws redress wrongs.
- Laws identify wrongdoers.
- Laws mandate punishment and retribution.

**TABLE 4–1**

rights that are available to them as citizens of a free nation. A society needs laws to uphold fairness and to prevent the victimization of innocents.

Practically speaking, laws regulate relationships between people and also between parties, such as government agencies and individuals. They channel and simultaneously constrain human behavior, and they empower individuals while contributing to public order. Laws also serve other purposes. They ensure that the philosophical, moral, and economic perspectives of their creators are protected and made credible. They maintain values and uphold established patterns of social privilege. They sustain existing power relationships, and finally, they support a system for the punishment and rehabilitation of offenders. (See Table 4–1.) Modifications of the law, when gradually induced, promote orderly change in the rest of society.

Our laws are found in statutory provisions and constitutional enactments,[3] as well as in hundreds of years of rulings by courts at all levels. According to the authoritative *Black's Law Dictionary,* the word *law* "generally contemplates both statutory and case law."[4] **Statutory law** is "the law on the books." It results from legislative action and is often thought of as "the law of the land." Written laws exist in both criminal and civil areas and are called *codes.* Once laws have been written down in organized fashion, they are said to be *codified.* Federal statutes are compiled in the U.S. Code (U.S.C.), which is available online in its entirety via Library Extra 4–1 at cjtoday.com. State codes and municipal ordinances are also readily available in written, or statutory, form. The written form of the criminal law is called the **penal code. Case law**, which we will discuss in detail a bit later, is the law that results from judicial decisions.

But the laws of our country are not unambiguous. If all of "the law" could be found in written legal codes, it would be plain to nearly everyone, and we would need far fewer lawyers than are practicing today. But some laws—the precedents established by courts—do not exist "on the books," and even those that do are open to interpretation. This is where common law comes into play. **Common law** is the traditional body of unwritten historical precedents created from everyday social customs, rules, and practices, many of which were supported by judicial decisions during early times. Common law principles are still used to interpret many legal issues in quite a few states. Hence, it is not uncommon to hear of jurisdictions within the United States referred to as "common law jurisdictions" or "common law states."

# The Rule of Law

The social, economic, and political stability of any society depends largely on the development and institutionalization of a predictable system of laws. Western democratic societies adhere to the **rule of law**, which is sometimes also referred to as the *supremacy of law.* The rule of law centers on the belief that an orderly society must be governed by established principles and known codes that are applied uniformly and fairly to all of its members. Under this tenet, no one is above the law, and those who make or enforce the law must also abide by it. The principle was well illustrated in 2002 when U.S. Representative James Traficant, a Democrat from Ohio, was expelled from Congress by fellow lawmakers after he was convicted in federal court of ten counts of bribery, tax evasion, and racketeering.[5] He was later sentenced to eight years in prison. Other formerly powerful politicians who have recently served time in prison include former four-term South Dakota governor Bill Janklow and former Connecticut governor John G. Rowland.

**statutory law**

Written or codified law; the "law on the books," as enacted by a government body or agency having the power to make laws.

**penal code**

The written, organized, and compiled form of the criminal laws of a jurisdiction.

**case law**

The body of judicial precedent, historically built on legal reasoning and past interpretations of statutory laws, that serves as a guide to decision making, especially in the courts.

**common law**

Law originating from usage and custom rather than from written statutes. The term refers to an unwritten body of judicial opinion, originally developed by English courts, that is based on nonstatutory customs, traditions, and precedents that help guide judicial decision making.

**rule of law**

The maxim that an orderly society must be governed by established principles and known codes that are applied uniformly and fairly to all of its members.

> The law isn't justice. It's a very imperfect mechanism. If you press exactly the right buttons and are also lucky, justice may show up in the answer. A mechanism is all the law was ever intended to be.
>
> —Raymond Chandler[i]

The rule of law has been called the greatest political achievement of our culture. Without it, few other human achievements—especially those that require the coordinated efforts of a large number of people—would be possible. President John F. Kennedy eloquently explained the rule of law, saying, "Americans are free to disagree with the law, but not to disobey it; for [in] a government of laws and not of men, no man, however prominent and powerful, no mob, however unruly or boisterous, is entitled to defy a court of law."[6]

The American Bar Association notes that the rule of law includes these elements[7]:

- Freedom from private lawlessness provided by the legal system of a politically organized society
- A relatively high degree of objectivity in the formulation of legal norms and a like degree of evenhandedness in their application
- Legal ideas and juristic devices for the attainment of individual and group objectives within the bounds of ordered liberty
- Substantive and procedural limitations on governmental power in the interest of the individual for the enforcement of which there are appropriate legal institutions and machinery

**jurisprudence**

The philosophy of law. Also, the science and study of the law.

**Jurisprudence** is the philosophy of law or the science and study of the law, including the rule of law. To learn more about the rule of law, visit Web Extra 4–1 at cjtoday.com.

WEB EXTRA

# Types of Law

Criminal and civil law are the best-known types of modern law. However, there are several other categories of law; their distinctions rest on the source, intent, and application of laws. Laws in modern societies can be usefully described in terms of the following groups:

- Criminal law
- Civil law
- Administrative law
- Case law
- Procedural law

This typology is helpful in understanding and thinking about the law. We will now discuss each type of law in some detail.

## Criminal Law

**criminal law**

The body of rules and regulations that define and specify the nature of and punishments for offenses of a public nature or for wrongs committed against the state or society. Also called *penal law*.

Fundamental to the concept of **criminal law** is the assumption that criminal acts injure not just individuals, but society as a whole. Hence, we can define *criminal law* as the body of rules and regulations that define and specify the nature of and punishments for offenses of a public nature or for wrongs committed against the state or society. Criminal law is also called *penal law*.

Public order is compromised whenever a criminal act occurs. In old England, from which much of American legal tradition stems, offenders were said to have violated the "king's peace" when they committed a crime. They not only offended their victims but also contravened the peaceful order established under the rule of the monarch. It is for this reason that in criminal cases the state, as the injured party, begins the official process of bringing the offender to justice. Even if the victim is dead and has no one to speak on his behalf, the agencies of justice will investigate the crime and file charges against the offender. Because crimes injure the fabric of society, the state—not the individual victim—becomes the plaintiff in criminal proceedings. Criminal court cases reflect this by being cited as follows: *State of New York* v. *Smith* (where state law has been violated) or *U.S.* v. *Smith* (where the federal government is the injured party).

Those found guilty of violating the criminal law are punished. Punishment is philosophically justified by the fact that the criminal *intended* the harm and is responsible for it. When punishment is imposed in a criminal case, it is for one basic reason: to express society's fundamental displeasure with the offensive behavior and to hold the offender accountable for it. Punishment serves a variety of other purposes too, which we will discuss in Chapter 11. Criminal law, which is built on constitutional principles and which operates within an established set of procedures applicable to the criminal justice system, is composed of both statutory and case law.

**substantive criminal law**

The part of the law that defines crimes and specifies punishments.

Written law is of two types: substantive and procedural. **Substantive criminal law** describes what constitutes particular crimes, such as murder, rape, robbery, and assault, and specifies the

As the loss of political office suffered by former Connecticut governor John G. Rowland and U.S. Representatives Bill Janklow (R–South Dakota) and James Traficant (D–Ohio) demonstrates, the *rule of law* means that no one is above the law—not even those who make it. Traficant (left) was expelled from Congress in 2002 following his conviction on a number of federal crimes, including bribery, tax evasion, and racketeering. He is currently serving eight years in federal prison. Janklow (bottom left) was convicted of manslaughter in 2003 after he was involved in a traffic accident that killed a motorcyclist. A former four-term South Dakota governor, Janklow sped through a stop sign, causing the accident. He was forced to resign from Congress and was sentenced to serve 100 days in jail. Rowland (bottom right) entered federal prison in 2005 following a corruption conviction.

*Summit County Jail, Getty Images, Inc. and AP Wide World Photos*

appropriate punishment for each particular offense. We can study the differences in substantive laws from state to state because each offense and the punishments associated with it are available in written form in the substantive criminal law. **Procedural laws** specify the rules that determine how those who are accused of crimes are dealt with in the judicial system, including the issuance of warrants, the gathering of evidence, and the conduct of a criminal trial. Learn more about the evolution of American criminal law via **Library Extra 4–2** at cjtoday.com. Online criminal law journals may be accessed via **Library Extras 4–3** and **4–4**.

**procedural law**

The part of the law that specifies the methods to be used in enforcing substantive law.

**LIBRARY** **EXTRA**

## Civil Law

**Civil law** governs relationships between parties. It provides a formal means for regulating noncriminal relationships between people, businesses and other organizations, and agencies of government. Civil law contains rules for contracts, divorce, child support and custody, the creation of wills, property transfers, negligence, libel, unfair practices in hiring, the manufacture and sale of consumer goods with hidden hazards for the user, and many other contractual and social obligations. When the civil law is violated, a civil suit may follow.

Typically, civil suits seek compensation in the form of property or monetary damages. They may also be filed to achieve an injunction, or a kind of judicial cease-and-desist order. A violation of the civil law is not a crime. It may be a contract violation or a **tort**—a wrongful act, damage, or injury not involving a breach of contract. A tort involving, say, an automobile accident may give rise to civil liability under which the injured party may sue the person or entity that caused the injury and ask that the offending party be ordered to pay damages directly to her. Because a

**civil law**

The branch of modern law that governs relationships between parties.

**tort**

A wrongful act, damage, or injury not involving a breach of contract. Also, a private or civil wrong or injury.

## FREEDOM OR SAFETY? YOU DECIDE.

### The Lawsuits of Madison County

In 2005, President George Bush made Madison County, Illinois, ground zero in his party's campaign to reign in what many saw as excesses in civil litigation. The locale, made famous in the battle over tort reform as a little county with a reputation for big lawsuits, had been blasted by the American Tort Reform Association (ATRA), which dubbed it the nation's top "judicial hellhole." The ATRA claimed that Madison County has a reputation for allowing junk lawsuits that would be thrown out elsewhere, and for handing out huge and sometimes unjustified awards. The ATRA noted that defendants had been dragged into Madison County civil courts from across the country by attorneys shopping for sympathetic local courts, even though plaintiffs who lend their names to the lawsuits frequently don't live in Illinois.

A total of 179 **class-action lawsuits** were filed in the county in 2003 and 2004, and more than 1,400 asbestos-related cases were filed during the same period. In 2004, a single Madison County judge ordered Philip Morris to pay $10.1 billion for marketing light cigarettes as being less harmful than regular cigarettes.

During his Madison County stop, President Bush told those gathered to hear him speak that class-action lawsuit abuse is a tactic employed by unscrupulous and greedy lawyers seeking to enrich themselves. Attorneys who win such cases can keep up to one-half of the court award as their fee. Defendants, he suggested, are often intimidated by the possibility of having to pay huge awards and may end up settling out of court rather than risking unpredictable trials, even when cases against them are not very strong. The president's supporters called the resulting agreements "extortionate settlements."

Lending credence to the view that lawsuit abuse has reached a crisis point are findings from an independent consulting firm that tracks the national costs of civil litigation—including damage awards, out-of-court settlements, and attorneys' fees. Findings show that the 2002 cost of tort litigation throughout the United States totaled $233 billion, an amount that is typically passed on to consumers in the form of higher prices for goods and services. According to the Department of Treasury, this annual "tort tax" amounts to $809 for every American and totals more than $3,200 for a family of four.

Making matters worse is the fact that damage awards in class-action suits can enrich lawyers but often don't reach class members. A 1996 false advertising suit against computer chip maker Intel Corporation, for example, awarded 500,000 people the right to claim a $50 discount off the purchase price of a new processor. Only 150, or 0.0003% of class members, took advantage of the judgment—while the attorneys who filed the suit received $1.5 million in fees that the company had to pay.

The first legislative milestone on the road to the administration's goal of tort reform was reached in 2005, when President Bush signed the Class Action Fairness Act (CAFA; S. 274) into law. The CAFA funnels most large, interstate class-action lawsuits into federal courts and away from state courts. It is also designed to ensure that plaintiffs in class-action lawsuits are treated fairly, and it requires that settlements and rulings be explained in plain English so that class members fully understand their rights.

The Class Action Fairness Act is the first plank in a broader White House campaign to impose rules designed to limit what administration staffers describe as a glut of meritless lawsuits seeking billions of dollars. Many believe that the administration is likely to seek limits on other civil suits, such as the one exemplified by a $4.9 billion award by a California civil jury to six people injured in a 1999 case brought against General Motors. The case, *Anderson* v. *General Motors Corp.,* involved an exploding gas tank on a 1979 Chevrolet Malibu, a problem that General Motors apparently knew about but didn't fix. The judgment was the biggest personal-injury award in U.S. history. Although only $107 million of the judgment was awarded for compensatory damages, the other $4.8 billion, which was later reduced on appeal, consisted entirely of punitive damages.

Current administration proposals would limit punitive damage claims in civil suits brought in federal and state courts to a maximum of $250,000 or three times the plaintiff's economic damages from such things as lost income and medical expenses, whichever is greater. Compensatory damages could be awarded only for the amount of damages the plaintiff could prove were actually incurred.

Opponents of the administration's efforts to limit awards in civil suits argue that such limits are inherently unfair and claim that federal restrictions on suits filed in state courts illegally preempt state authority over such matters. Limiting punitive damage awards, they say, can only encourage irresponsibility at all levels of American society.

### YOU DECIDE

Do you agree with the administration's efforts to funnel class-action lawsuits through federal rather than state courts, and to limit punitive damage awards in civil suits? What do you see as the pros and cons of such a position?

*Note:* You can visit the American Tort Reform Association on the Web at http://www.atra.org, and download its report, *Judicial Hellholes,* at http://www.atra.org/reports/hellholes.
*References:* Jim VandeHei and John F. Harris, "Bush to Seek Limits on Lawsuits: Fierce Battle over Curbs Is Expected," *Washington Post,* January 5, 2005, p. A3; "Bush to Highlight Tort Reform in Illinois," *USA Today,* January 4, 2005; Mike France, "Special Report: How to Fix the Tort System," *Business Week,* March 14, 2005, pp. 70–78; "Jury Awards $4.9 Billion in Suit against GM," *USA Today,* July 7, 1999; Dick Armey, "The Lawsuits of Madison County," Freedom Works, March 23, 2004. Web posted at http://www.freedomworks.org/informed/issues_ template.php?issue_id51719; John F. Harris, "Victory for Bush on Suits," *Washington Post,* February 18, 2005.

tort is a personal wrong, however, it is left to the aggrieved individual to set the machinery of the court in motion—that is, to bring a suit.

In 2005, for example, attorney Jack Thompson filed a $600 million lawsuit against video game maker Take-Two Interactive Software, claiming that the company's products, *Grand Theft Auto III* and *Grand Theft Auto: Vice City*, led to the shooting deaths of two Alabama police officers and a police dispatcher in 2003.[8] The lawsuit, which also named retailers Wal-Mart and Gamestop, which sold the games, alleges that 17-year-old Devin Thompson was mirroring violent acts that he had learned from the software when he grabbed an officer's gun, started firing, and then stole a patrol car. Thompson, an avid player of the games which depict police killings and other violent acts, had originally been taken into custody by officers on suspicion of driving a stolen automobile. According to press reports, Thompson, who has been charged with murder, told authorities who captured him, "Life is a video game. You gotta die sometime."

Civil law is more concerned with assessing liability than it is with intent. For example, civil suits arising from automobile accidents do not allege that the driver intended to inflict bodily harm. Nor do they claim that it was the intent of the driver to damage either vehicle. However, when someone is injured or when property damage occurs, even in an accident, civil procedures make it possible to gauge responsibility and to assign liability to one party or the other. The parties to a civil suit are referred to as the *plaintiff,* who seeks relief, and the *defendant,* against whom relief is sought. Civil suits are also sometimes brought by crime victims against those whose criminal intent is clear. Once the perpetrator of a crime has been convicted, his victim may decide to seek monetary compensation from him through our system of civil laws.

**Compensatory damages** are awarded to compensate the victim or her survivors for actual losses and for the dollar amount that can be ascribed to pain, suffering, lost quality of life, and so on. Currently, many states also award **punitive damages,** which are often intended to compensate for mental anguish, degradation, shame, or hurt feelings suffered by the plaintiff, when jurors determine that the chances were better than 50% that the defendant acted with **gross negligence**. According to a 2005 Bureau of Justice Statistics report, 12,000 tort, contract, and real property cases were disposed of in state civil courts by bench or jury trial in the nation's 75 largest counties in 2001.[9] Six percent of the 6,504 civil trials with plaintiff winners resulted in damage awards totaling $4 billion in 2001.[10] Amounts awarded to plaintiff winners ranged from under $10 to $454 million. Punitive damages estimated at $1.2 billion were awarded to 6% of plaintiffs who won their cases. In contrast, federal district courts handled 512,000 civil cases in 2002–2003.[11] Although punitive damage awards may be relatively rare, some involve large dollar amounts. As the Freedom or Safety box in this chapter points out,

---

**class-action lawsuit**

A lawsuit filed by one or more people on behalf of themselves and a larger group of people "who are similarly situated."[ii]

---

**compensatory damages**

Damages recovered in payment for an actual injury or economic loss.

---

**punitive damages**

Damages requested or awarded in a civil lawsuit when the defendant's willful acts were malicious, violent, oppressive, fraudulent, wanton, or grossly reckless.[iii]

---

**gross negligence**

The intentional failure to perform a manifest duty in reckless disregard of the consequences as affecting the life or property of another.[iv]

---

Patricia Anderson posing with her daughter, Alisha Parker, at their attorney's office. In 1999, Anderson, her four children, and a family friend were awarded $4.9 billion by a Los Angeles civil jury in a suit against General Motors. The suit stemmed from a 1993 Beverly Hills accident in which the plaintiffs were burned when the gas tank of their 1979 Chevrolet Malibu exploded in flames. The huge personal-injury award was the largest in U.S. history. It was reduced to $1.1 billion on appeal.

*Reuters, Fred Prouser, Getty Images, Inc.—Hulton Archive Photos* the threat of huge punitive damage awards may lead defendants to settle out of court rather than risk a jury trial even when they feel they have done no wrong.

An offender's criminal action may be grounds for a civil suit by the offender. For example, in June 2001, drug maker GlaxoSmith-Kline, Inc., was on the losing end of a civil suit when a U.S. district court panel in Wyoming awarded $8 million to the surviving family of an oil field worker who went on a murderous rampage in 1998 after taking the antidepressant Paxil.[12] Donald Schell killed his wife, daughter, infant granddaughter, and himself almost immediately after beginning therapy involving the drug. The court apparently accepted the plaintiff's claim that the drug can trigger inner turmoil and agitation called *akathisia,* leading to violence.

## Administrative Law

*Administrative law* is the body of regulations that governments create to control the activities of industry, business, and individuals. Tax laws, health codes, restrictions on pollution and waste disposal, vehicle registration laws, and building codes are examples of administrative law. Other administrative laws cover practices in the areas of customs (imports and exports), immigration, agriculture, product safety, and most areas of manufacturing.

Administrative agencies will sometimes arrange settlements that fall short of court action but that are considered binding on individuals or groups that have not lived up to the intent of federal or state regulations. Settlements have been made in areas such as education, environmental protection, and discriminatory hiring practices.

For the most part, a breach of the administrative law is not a crime. However, criminal law and administrative regulations may overlap. For instance, organized criminal activity is on the rise in the area of toxic waste disposal—an area covered by many administrative regulations—which has led to criminal prosecutions in several states. The intentional and systematic denial of civil rights in areas generally thought to be administrative in nature, such as hiring, employment, and job compensation, may also lead to criminal sanctions through the federal system of laws.

## Case Law

**precedent**

A legal principle that ensures that previous judicial decisions are authoritatively considered and incorporated into future cases.

Case law comes from judicial decisions and is also referred to as the law of **precedent**. It represents the accumulated wisdom of trial and appellate courts (courts that hear appeals) in criminal, civil, and administrative law cases over the years. Once a court decision is rendered, it is written down. At the appellate level, the reasoning behind the decision is recorded as well. Under the law of precedent, this reasoning should then be taken into consideration by other courts in settling similar future cases.

Appellate courts have considerable influence on new court decisions at the trial level. The court with the greatest influence, of course, is the U.S. Supreme Court. The precedents it establishes are incorporated as guidelines into the process of legal reasoning by which lower courts reach conclusions.

**stare decisis**

A legal principle that requires that in subsequent cases on similar issues of law and fact, courts be bound by their own earlier decisions and by those of higher courts having jurisdiction over them. The term literally means "standing by decided matters."

The principle of recognizing previous decisions as precedents to guide future deliberations, called **stare decisis**, forms the basis for our modern law of precedent. Lief H. Carter, professor of political science at Colorado College, has pointed out that precedent operates along two dimensions, which he calls the *vertical* and the *horizontal.*[13] A vertical rule requires that decisions made by a higher court be taken into consideration by lower courts in their deliberations. Under this rule, state appellate courts, for example, are expected to follow the spirit of decisions rendered by the state supreme court. The horizontal dimension means that courts on the same level should be consistent in their interpretation of the law. The U.S. Supreme Court, operating under the horizontal rule, for example, should not be expected to change its ruling in cases similar to those it has already decided. *Stare decisis* makes for predictability in the law. Defendants walking into a modern courtroom are represented by lawyers who are trained in legal precedents as well as procedure. As a consequence, defendants have a good idea of what to expect about the manner in which their trial will proceed.

## Procedural Law

Procedural law is another kind of statutory law. It is a body of rules that determine the proceedings by which legal rights are enforced. The law of criminal procedure regulates the gathering of evidence and the processing of offenders by the criminal justice system. General rules of evidence, search and seizure, procedures to be followed in an arrest, trial procedures, and other

## CJ NEWS

# $1B Judgment Against Spammers

A federal judge has awarded an Internet service provider more than $1 billion in what is believed to be the largest judgment ever against spammers.

Robert Kramer, whose company provides e-mail service for about 5,000 subscribers in eastern Iowa, filed suit against 300 spammers after his inbound mail servers received up to 10 million spam e-mails a day in 2000, according to court documents.

Kramer said he was called away almost daily to repair downed e-mail servers that should run months without interruption.

U.S. District Judge Charles Wolle filed default judgments Friday against three of the defendants under the federal Racketeer Influenced and Corrupt Organizations Act (RICO) and the Iowa Ongoing Criminal Conduct Act.

AMP Dollar Savings of Mesa, Ariz., was ordered to pay $720 million, and Cash Link Systems of Miami was ordered to pay $360 million. The third company, Florida-based TEI Marketing Group, was ordered to pay $140,000.

"It's definitely a victory for all of us that open up our e-mail and find lewd and malicious and fraudulent e-mail in our boxes every day," Kramer told the *Quad-City Times* after the ruling. Kramer's attorney, Kelly Wallace, said he is unlikely to ever collect the judgment, which was made possible by an Iowa law that allows plaintiffs to claim damages of $10 per spam message. The judgments were then tripled under RICO.

"We hope to recover at least his costs," Wallace said.

Kramer's lawsuit was originally filed in October 2003 against 300 defendants then known only as John Does. There were no telephone listings for the three companies in Arizona and Florida. Nobody replied to an e-mail sent Saturday to Cash Link Systems.

According to court documents, no attorneys for the defendants were present during a bench trial in November.

The lawsuit continues against other named defendants.

Kramer's problems are linked to a CD-ROM sold to spammers that is called Bulk Mailing 4 Dummies, which includes a guide for sending spam and a large number of mainly fictitious e-mail addresses for some of the largest Internet providers in the nation, the judgment states.

While most of the addresses were for large providers such as America Online, Microsoft Network, Hotmail and EarthLink, Kramer's company—CIS Internet Services in Clinton—somehow had 2.8 million addresses entered on the CD-ROM, Wallace said.

Laura Atkins, president of SpamCon Foundation, an anti-spamming organization based in Palo Alto, Calif., said she believed it was the largest judgment ever in an anti-spam lawsuit. "This is just incredible," she said. "I'm not aware of anything that's been over $100 million."

For the latest in crime and justice news, visit the Talk Justice news feed at http://www.crimenews.info.

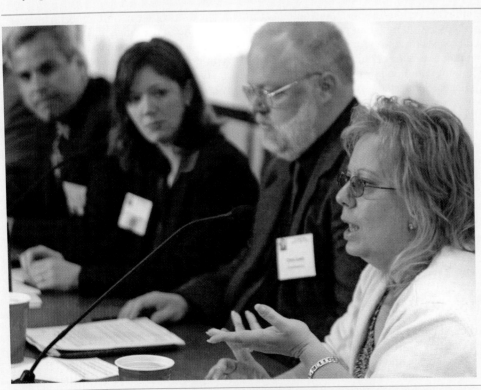

Laura Betterly, president of Data Resource Consulting, right, speaks at the Federal Trade Commission's Spam Forum in Washington, D.C., on May 1, 2003. Also pictured (from left to right) are Al DiGuido, CEO of Bigfoot Interactive, Lisa Pollock Mann, senior director of messaging at Yahoo! Inc., and Chris Lewis, security architect at Nortel Networks. The three-day forum explored possible government and business responses to spam.

*AP Wide World Photos*

...ich the justice system operates are all contained in procedural law. Each ...riminal procedure laws, as does the federal government. Florida laws of ...xample, specify that a police officer making an arrest by a warrant "shall ...arrested of the cause of arrest and that a warrant has been issued, except ...r forcibly resists before the officer has an opportunity to inform the per-...e information will imperil the arrest." Florida law goes on to say that "the ...the warrant in his or her possession at the time of arrest but on request of ...all show it to the person as soon as practicable."[14]

...ecognize that procedural laws are intended to protect the rights of criminal ...lishing a clear-cut series of formal proceedings through which the substan-...n be enforced. In short, rules of criminal procedure balance a suspect's rights ...terests in the speedy and efficient processing of criminal defendants. Florida ...ocedure are available online at **Library Extra 4–5** at cjtoday.com. View federal ...e laws, known as the Federal Rules of Criminal Procedure and the Federal ... at **Library Extras 4–6** and **4–7** at cjtoday.com.

## General Categories of Crime

Violations of the *criminal* law can be of many different types and can vary in severity. We will look at five categories of violations:

- Felonies
- Misdemeanors
- Offenses
- Treason and espionage
- Inchoate offenses

## Felonies

**felony**

A criminal offense punishable by death or by incarceration in a prison facility for at least one year.

**Felonies** are serious crimes; they include murder, rape, aggravated assault, robbery, burglary, and arson. Today, many felons receive prison sentences, although the range of potential penalties includes everything from probation and a fine to capital punishment in many jurisdictions. Under common law, felons could be sentenced to death, could have their property confiscated, or both. Following common law tradition, people who are convicted of felonies today usually lose certain privileges. Some states, for example, make a felony conviction and incarceration grounds for uncontested divorce. Others prohibit offenders from running for public office or owning a firearm and exclude them from some professions, such as medicine, law, and police work.

The federal government and many states have moved to a scheme of classifying the seriousness of felonies, using a number or letter designation. For purposes of criminal sentencing, for example, the federal system assigns a score of 43 to first-degree murder, while the crime of theft is only rated a "base offense level" of 4.[15] Attendant circumstances and the criminal history of the offender are also taken into consideration in sentencing decisions.

Because of differences among the states, a crime classified as a felony in one part of the country may be a misdemeanor in another, while in still other areas it may not even be a crime at all! This is especially true of some drug-law violations and of certain other public-order offenses, such as homosexuality, prostitution, and gambling, which in a number of jurisdictions are perfectly legal, although such activity may still be subject to certain administrative regulations.

## Misdemeanors

**misdemeanor**

An offense punishable by incarceration, usually in a local confinement facility, for a period whose upper limit is prescribed by statute in a given jurisdiction, typically one year or less.

**Misdemeanors** are relatively minor crimes, consisting of offenses such as petty theft, which is the theft of items of little value; simple assault, in which the victim suffers no serious injury and in which none was intended; breaking and entering; disorderly conduct; disturbing the peace; filing a false crime report; and writing bad checks, although the amount for which the check is written may determine the classification of this offense.

In general, misdemeanors are any crime punishable by a year or less in prison. In fact, most misdemeanants receive suspended sentences involving a fine and supervised probation. If an "active sentence" is given for a misdemeanor violation of the law, it may involve time spent in a local jail, perhaps on weekends, rather than imprisonment in a long-term confinement facility. Alternatively, some misdemeanants are sentenced to perform community-service activities, such as washing school buses, painting local government buildings, and cleaning parks and other public areas.

Normally, a police officer cannot arrest a person for a misdemeanor unless the crime was committed in the officer's presence. If this requirement is not met, the officer must seek an arrest warrant from a magistrate or other judicial officer. Once a warrant has been issued, the officer may then proceed with the arrest.

> One has not only a legal but a moral responsibility to obey just laws. Conversely, one has a moral responsibility to disobey unjust laws.
>
> —Martin Luther King, Jr.[vi]

## Offenses

A third category of crime is the **offense**. Although strictly speaking all violations of the criminal law can be called *criminal offenses*, the term *offense* is also used specifically to refer to minor violations of the law that are less serious than misdemeanors. In this sense, the term refers to such things as jaywalking, spitting on the sidewalk, littering, and committing certain traffic violations, including the failure to wear a seat belt. Another word used to describe such minor law violations is **infraction**. People committing infractions are typically ticketed and released, usually on a promise to appear later in court. Court appearances may often be waived through payment of a small fine.

## Treason and Espionage

Felonies, misdemeanors, offenses, and the people who commit them constitute the daily work of the justice system. However, special categories of crime do exist and should be recognized. They include treason and espionage, two felonies that are often regarded as the most serious of crimes. **Treason** has been defined as "a U.S. citizen's actions to help a foreign government overthrow, make war against, or seriously injure the United States."[16] In addition to being a federal offense, treason is also a crime under the laws of most states, either through legislation or through state constitutions. Hence, treason can be more generally defined as the attempt to overthrow the government of the society of which one is a member.

**Espionage**, an offense akin to treason, but which can be committed by noncitizens, is the "gathering, transmitting, or losing"[17] of information related to the national defense in such a manner that the information becomes available to enemies of the United States and may be used to their advantage. In 1999, for example, one of the most significant espionage cases ever came to light. It involved the theft of highly classified American nuclear weapons secrets by spies working for the People's Republic of China. Over at least three decades, beginning in the 1960s, Chinese spies apparently stole enough weapons-related information to advance China's nuclear weapons program into the modern era. Were it not for the missile and bomb information gathered by the spies, congressional officials said, China's nuclear weapons technology might still be where America's was in the 1950s. See Web Extra 4–2 and Library Extra 4–8 at cjtoday.com for additional information on this very serious incident.

Another example of espionage is the crime committed by former FBI agent Robert Hanssen. In July 2001 he pleaded guilty in U.S. District Court in Alexandria, Virginia, to 15 counts of espionage and conspiracy against the United States.[18] Hanssen admitted to having passed U.S. secrets to Moscow from about 1979 until 2001, when undercover investigators caught him leaving a package for his Russian handlers under a wooden footbridge in a Virginia park. The 25-year agency veteran had accepted more than $1.4 million in cash and diamonds from the Russians in return for disclosing secret and highly sensitive information, including U.S. nuclear warfare plans, advanced eavesdropping technology, and the identities of U.S. spies working overseas. Government officials feared that the information Hanssen provided had resulted in the deaths of a number of U.S. agents working in Russia. Prosecutors described the damage done to national security by Hanssen's spying as extremely grave. In return for his full cooperation in assessing the damage he had caused, Hanssen was spared the death penalty. Instead, he was sentenced to life in prison without possibility of parole. Learn more about Robert Hanssen and the crimes he committed at Web Extra 4–3 at cjtoday.com.

Yet a third contemporary example of espionage was committed by a former Air Force intelligence analyst. In March 2003, Brian P. Regan was convicted of trying to sell classified documents to prewar Iraq and China.[19] Prior to sentencing, Regan made a deal with prosecutors to accept a sentence of life in prison in exchange for an agreement not to prosecute his wife, whom authorities claimed obstructed justice to help her husband. Prosecutors, who parlayed the impending war with Iraq into a background that emphasized the seriousness of the charges against Regan, had originally sought the death penalty.

**offense**

A violation of the criminal law. Also, in some jurisdictions, a minor crime, such as jaywalking, that is sometimes described as *ticketable*.

**infraction**

A minor violation of state statute or local ordinance punishable by a fine or other penalty or by a specified, usually limited, term of incarceration.

**treason**

A U.S. citizen's actions to help a foreign government overthrow, make war against, or seriously injure the United States.[vii] Also, the attempt to overthrow the government of the society of which one is a member.

**espionage**

The "gathering, transmitting, or losing"[viii] of information related to the national defense in such a manner that the information becomes available to enemies of the United States and may be used to their advantage.

Self-confessed FBI spy Robert Hanssen being arraigned before U.S. Magistrate Judge Theresa Buchanan in 2001. From left are Assistant U.S. Attorney Randy Bellows, defense attorney Plato Cacheris, Robert Hanssen, and defense attorney Preston Burton.

*AP Wide World Photos*

## Inchoate Offenses

**inchoate offense**

An offense not yet completed. Also, an offense that consists of an action or conduct that is a step toward the intended commission of another offense.

Another special category of crime is called *inchoate*. The word *inchoate* means "incomplete or partial," and **inchoate offenses** are those that have not been fully carried out. Conspiracies are an example. When a person conspires to commit a crime, any action undertaken in furtherance of the conspiracy is generally regarded as a sufficient basis for arrest and prosecution. For instance, a woman who intends to kill her husband may make a phone call to find a hit man to carry out her plan. The call itself is evidence of her intent and can result in her imprisonment for conspiracy to murder.

Another type of inchoate offense is the attempt to commit a crime, which occurs when an offender is unable to complete a crime. For example, homeowners may arrive just as a burglar is entering their residence, causing the burglar to run. In most jurisdictions, this frustrated burglar can be arrested and charged with attempted burglary.

# General Features of Crime

From the perspective of Western jurisprudence, all crimes share certain features, and the notion of crime itself rests on such general principles. Taken together, these features, which are described in this section, make up the legal essence of the concept of crime. Conventional legal wisdom holds that the essence of crime consists of three elements: (1) the criminal act, which in legal parlance is termed the *actus reus,* (2) a culpable mental state or *mens rea,* and (3) a concurrence of the two. Hence, as we shall see in the following pages, the essence of criminal conduct consists of a combination of a criminal act with a culpable mental state.

## The Criminal Act *(Actus Reus)*

**actus reus**

An act in violation of the law. Also, a guilty act.

A necessary first feature of any crime is some act in violation of the criminal law. Such an act is termed the **actus reus** of a crime. The term means "guilty act." Generally, a person must commit some voluntary act before he is subject to criminal sanctions. To *be something* is not a crime; to *do something* may be. For example, someone who is caught using drugs can be arrested, while someone who simply admits that he is a drug user (on a TV talk show, for instance) cannot be arrested on that basis. Police who hear the drug user's admission might begin gathering evidence to prove some specific law violation in that person's past, or perhaps they might watch that individual for future behavior in violation of the law. An arrest that occurred then would be based on a specific action in violation of the law pertaining to controlled substances.

Vagrancy laws, popular in the early part of the twentieth century, have generally been invalidated by the courts because they did not specify what act violated the law. In fact, the less a person did, the more vagrant he or she was. An omission to act, however, may be criminal where the person in question is required by law to do something. Child-neglect laws, for example, focus on parents and child guardians who do not live up to their responsibilities of caring for their children.

Threatening to act can be a criminal offense. For example, threatening to kill someone can result in an arrest for the offense of communicating threats. Such threats against the president of the United States are taken seriously by the Secret Service, and individuals are arrested for boasting about planned violence directed at the president. Attempted criminal activity is also illegal. An attempt to murder or rape, for example, is a serious crime, even when the planned act is not accomplished.

Conspiracies, mentioned earlier in this chapter, are another criminal act. When a conspiracy unfolds, the ultimate act that it aims to bring about does not have to occur for the parties to the conspiracy to be arrested. When people plan to bomb a public building, for example, they can be legally stopped before the bombing. As soon as they take steps to "further" their plan, they have met the requirement for an act. Buying explosives, telephoning one another, and drawing plans of the building may all be actions in "furtherance of the conspiracy." But not all conspiracy statutes require actions in furtherance of the "target crime" before an arrest can be made. Technically speaking, crimes of conspiracy can be seen as entirely distinct from the target crimes that the conspirators are contemplating. For example, in 1994 the U.S. Supreme Court upheld the drug-related conviction of Reshat Shabani when it ruled that in the case of certain antidrug laws,[20] "it is presumed that Congress intended to adopt the common law definition of conspiracy, which does not make the doing of any act other than the act of conspiring a condition of liability."[21] Hence according to the Court, "The criminal agreement itself," even in the absence of actions directed toward realizing the target crime, can be grounds for arrest and prosecution.

Similar to conspiracy statutes are many newly enacted antistalking laws, which are intended to prevent harassment and intimidation, even when no physical harm occurs. Antistalking statutes, however, still face the constitutional hurdle of attempting to prevent people not otherwise involved in criminal activity from walking and standing where they wish and from speaking freely. Ultimately, the U.S. Supreme Court will probably have to decide the legitimacy of such statutes.

> Justice is incidental to law and order.
>
> —J. Edgar Hoover[ix]

# A Guilty Mind (*Mens Rea*)

*Mens rea* is the second component of crime. The term, which literally means "guilty mind," refers to the defendant's specific mental state at the time the behavior in question occurred. The importance of *mens rea* as a component of crime cannot be overemphasized. In fact some courts have held that "[a]ll crime exists primarily in the mind."[22] The extent to which a person can be held criminally responsible for her actions generally depends on the nature of the mental state under which she was laboring at the time of the offense.

Four levels, or types, of *mens rea* can be distinguished: (1) purposeful (or intentional), (2) knowing, (3) reckless, and (4) negligent. Purposeful or intentional action is that which is undertaken to achieve some goal. Sometimes the harm that results from intentional action may be unintended; however, this does not reduce criminal liability. The doctrine of *transferred intent,* for example, which operates in all U.S. jurisdictions, holds a person guilty of murder if he took aim and shot at an intended victim but missed, killing another person instead. The philosophical notion behind the concept of transferred intent is that the killer's intent to kill, which existed at the time of the crime, transferred from the intended victim to the person who was struck by the bullet and died.

Knowing behavior is action undertaken with awareness. A person who acts purposefully always acts knowingly, but a person may act in a knowingly criminal way but for a purpose other than criminal intent. For example, an airline captain who allows a flight attendant to transport cocaine aboard an airplane may do so to gain sexual favors from the attendant, but without the purpose of drug smuggling. Knowing behavior involves near certainty. In this scenario, if the airline captain allows the flight attendant to carry cocaine aboard the plane, it *will* be transported, and the pilot knows it. In another example, if an HIV-infected individual has unprotected sexual intercourse with another person, the partner *will* be exposed to the virus.

**Reckless behavior** is activity that increases the risk of harm. In contrast to knowing behavior, knowledge may be part of recklessness, but it exists more in the form of probability than certainty. As a practical example, reckless driving is a frequent charge in many jurisdictions; it is generally brought when a driver engages in risky activity that endangers others.

**mens rea**

The state of mind that accompanies a criminal act. Also, a guilty mind.

**reckless behavior**

Activity that increases the risk of harm.

**criminal negligence**

Behavior in which a person fails to reasonably perceive substantial and unjustifiable risks of dangerous consequences.

**motive**

A person's reason for committing a crime.

**strict liability**

Liability without fault or intention. Strict liability offenses do not require *mens rea*.

**concurrence**

The coexistence of (1) an act in violation of the law and (2) a culpable mental state.

Nevertheless, *mens rea* is said to be present when a person should have known better, even if the person did not directly intend the consequences of his or her action. A person who acts negligently and thereby endangers others may be found guilty of **criminal negligence** when harm occurs, even though no negative consequences were intended. For example, a mother who leaves her 12-month-old child alone in the tub can be prosecuted for negligent homicide if the child drowns.[23] It should be emphasized, however, that negligence in and of itself is not a crime. Negligent conduct can be evidence of crime only when it falls below some acceptable standard of care. That standard is applied today in criminal courts through the fictional creation of a *reasonable person*. The question to be asked in a given case is whether a reasonable person, in the same situation, would have known better and acted differently than the defendant. The reasonable person criterion provides a yardstick for juries faced with thorny issues of guilt or innocence.

It is important to note that *mens rea,* even in the sense of intent, is not the same thing as motive. A **motive** refers to a person's reason for committing a crime. While evidence of motive may be admissible during a criminal trial to help prove a crime, motive itself is not an essential element of a crime. As a result, we cannot say that a bad or immoral motive makes an act a crime.

*Mens rea* is a tricky concept. Not only is it philosophically and legally complex, but a person's state of mind during the commission of an offense can rarely be known directly unless the person confesses. Hence, *mens rea* must generally be inferred from a person's actions and from all the circumstances surrounding those actions. Pure accident, however, which involves no recklessness or negligence, cannot serve as the basis for either criminal or civil liability. "Even a dog," the famous Supreme Court Justice Oliver Wendell Holmes once wrote, "distinguishes between being stumbled over and being kicked."[24]

### Strict Liability and *Mens Rea*

A special category of crimes, called **strict liability** offenses, requires no culpable mental state and presents a significant exception to the principle that all crimes require a concurrence of *actus reus* and *mens rea*. Strict liability offenses, also called *absolute liability offenses,* make it a crime simply to *do* something, even if the offender has no intention of violating the law. Strict liability is philosophically based on the presumption that causing harm is in itself blameworthy, regardless of the actor's intent.

Routine traffic offenses are generally considered strict liability offenses. Driving 65 miles per hour in a 55-mph zone is a violation of the law, even though the driver may be listening to music, thinking, or simply going with the flow of traffic, entirely unaware that his or her vehicle is exceeding the posted speed limit. Statutory rape is another example of strict liability.[25] This crime generally occurs between two consenting individuals; it requires only that the offender have sexual intercourse with a person under the age of legal consent. Statutes describing the crime routinely avoid any mention of a culpable mental state. In many jurisdictions, it matters little whether the "perpetrator" knew the exact age of the "victim" or whether the "victim" lied about his or her age or had given consent, since statutory rape laws are "an attempt to prevent the sexual exploitation of persons deemed legally incapable of giving consent."[26]

## Concurrence

The concurrence of an unlawful act and a culpable mental state provides the third basic component of crime. **Concurrence** requires that the act and the mental state occur together in order for a crime to take place. If one precedes the other, the requirements of the criminal law have not been met. A person may intend to kill a rival, for example. He drives to the intended victim's house, gun in hand, fantasizing about how he will commit the murder. Just as he nears the victim's home, the victim crosses the street on the way to the grocery store. If the two accidentally collide and the intended victim dies, there has been no concurrence of act and intent.

## Other Features of Crime

Some scholars contend that the three features of crime that we have just outlined—*actus reus, mens rea,* and concurrence—are sufficient to constitute the essence of the legal concept of crime. Other scholars, however, see modern Western law as more complex. They argue that recognition of five additional principles is necessary to fully appreciate contemporary understandings of crime. These five principles are (1) causation, (2) a resulting harm, (3) the principle of legality, (4) the principle of punishment, and (5) necessary attendant circumstances. We will now discuss each of these additional features in turn.

# Causation

*Causation* refers to the fact that the concurrence of a guilty mind and a criminal act may cause harm. While some statutes criminalize only conduct, others require that the offender *cause* a particular result before criminal liability can be incurred. Sometimes, however, a causal link is unclear. For example, let's consider a case of assault with a deadly weapon with intent to kill. A person shoots another, and the victim is seriously injured but is not immediately killed. The victim, who remains in the hospital, survives for more than a year. The victim's death occurs due to a blood clot that forms from lack of activity. In such a case, it is likely that defense attorneys will argue that the defendant did not cause the death; rather, the death occurred because of disease. If a jury agrees with the defense's claim, the shooter may go free or be found guilty of a lesser charge, such as assault.

To clarify the issue of causation, the American Law Institute suggests use of the term **legal cause** to emphasize the notion of a legally recognizable cause and to preclude any assumption that such a cause must be close in time and space to the result it produces. Legal causes can be distinguished from those causes that may have produced the result in question but do not provide the basis for a criminal prosecution because they are too complex, too indistinguishable from other causes, not knowable, or not provable in a court of law.

> **legal cause**
>
> A legally recognizable cause. A legal cause must be demonstrated in court in order to hold an individual criminally liable for causing harm.

# Harm

A harm occurs in any crime, although not all harms are crimes. When a person is murdered or raped, harm can be clearly identified. Some crimes, however, can be said to be *victimless.* Perpetrators maintain that in committing such crimes they harm no one but themselves. Rather, they say, the crime is pleasurable. Prostitution, gambling, and drug use are commonly classified as "victimless." What these offenders fail to recognize, say legal theorists, is the social harm caused by their behavior. In areas afflicted with chronic prostitution, drug use, and illegal gambling, property values fall, family life disintegrates, and other, more traditional crimes increase as money is sought to support the "victimless" activities. Law-abiding citizens flee the area.

In a criminal prosecution, however, it is rarely necessary to prove harm as a separate element of a crime, since it is subsumed under the notion of a guilty act. In the crime of murder, for example, the "killing of a human being" brings about a harm but is, properly speaking, an act. When committed with the requisite *mens rea,* it becomes a crime. A similar type of reasoning applies to the criminalization of *attempts* that cause no harm. A scenario commonly raised to illustrate this dilemma is one in which vandals throw rocks at a blind person, but because of bad aim, the rocks hit no one, and the intended target remains unaware that anyone is trying to harm him. In such a case, should throwing rocks provide a basis for criminal liability? As one authority on the subject observes, "Criticism of the principle of harm has . . . been based on the view that the harm actually caused may be a matter of sheer accident and that the rational thing to do is to base the punishment on the *mens rea,* and the action, disregarding any actual harm or lack of harm or its degree."[27] This observation also shows why we have said that the essence of crime consists only of three things: (1) *actus reus,* (2) *mens rea,* and (3) the concurrence of an illegal act and a culpable mental state.

# Legality

The principle of legality is concerned with the fact that a behavior cannot be criminal if no law exists that defines it as such. For example, as long as you are of drinking age, it is all right to drink beer because there is no statute on the books prohibiting it. During Prohibition, of course, the situation was quite different. (In fact, some parts of the United States are still "dry," and the purchase or public consumption of alcohol can be a law violation regardless of age.) The principle of legality also includes the notion that **ex post facto** laws are not binding, which means that a law cannot be created tomorrow that will hold a person legally responsible for something she does today. Rather, laws are binding only from the date of their creation or from some future date at which they are specified as taking effect.[28]

> **ex post facto**
>
> Latin for "after the fact." The Constitution prohibits the enactment of *ex post facto* laws, which make acts committed before the laws in question were passed punishable as crimes.

# Punishment

The principle of punishment holds that no crime can be said to occur where punishment has not been specified in the law. Larceny, for example, would not be a crime if the law simply said, "It is illegal to steal." Punishment for the crime must be specified so that if a person is found guilty of violating the law, sanctions can be lawfully imposed.

## Necessary Attendant Circumstances

**attendant circumstances**

The facts surrounding an event.

Finally, statutes defining some crimes specify that additional elements, called **attendant circumstances**, must be present for a conviction to be obtained. Generally speaking, attendant circumstances are the "facts surrounding an event"[29] and include such things as time and place. Attendant circumstances that are specified by law as necessary elements of an offense are sometimes called *necessary attendant circumstances,* indicating that the existence of such circumstances is necessary, along with the other elements included in the relevant statute, for a crime to have been committed. Florida law, for example, makes it a crime to "[k]nowingly commit any lewd or lascivious act in the presence of any child under the age of 16 years."[30] In this case, the behavior in question might not be a crime if committed in the presence of someone who is older than 16.

Sometimes attendant circumstances increase the degree, or level of seriousness, of an offense. Under Texas law, for example, the crime of burglary has two degrees, defined by state law as follows: Burglary is a "(1) state jail felony if committed in a building other than a habitation; or (2) felony of the second degree [that is, a more serious crime] if committed in a habitation." Hence, the degree of the offense of burglary depends on the nature of the place burglarized.

Circumstances surrounding a crime can also be classified as aggravating or mitigating and may, by law, increase or lessen the penalty that can be imposed on a convicted offender. Aggravating and mitigating circumstances are not elements of an offense, however, since they are primarily relevant at the sentencing stage of a criminal prosecution. They are discussed in Chapter 11.

# Elements of a Specific Criminal Offense

**element (of a crime)**

In a specific crime, one of the essential features of that crime, as specified by law or statute.

Now that we have identified the principles that constitute the *general* notion of crime, we can examine individual statutes to see what particular statutory **elements** constitute a *specific* crime. Written laws specify exactly what conditions are necessary for a person to be charged in a given instance of criminal activity. Elements of a crime are specific legal aspects of a criminal offense that the prosecution must prove to obtain a conviction. In almost every jurisdiction in the United States, for example, the crime of first-degree murder involves four distinct elements:

1. An unlawful killing
2. Of a human being
3. Intentionally
4. With planning (or "malice aforethought")

The elements of any specific crime are the statutory minimum without which that crime cannot be said to have occurred. Because statutes differ between jurisdictions, the specific elements of a particular crime may vary. To convict a defendant of a particular crime, prosecutors must prove to a judge or jury that all the required statutory elements are present[31] and that the accused was responsible for producing them.[32] If even one element of an offense cannot be established beyond a reasonable doubt, criminal liability will not have been demonstrated, and the defendant will be found not guilty.

## The Example of Murder

Every statutory element of a crime serves a purpose. As mentioned, the crime of first-degree murder includes an *unlawful killing* as one of its required elements. Not all killing is unlawful. In a wartime situation, for instance, human beings are killed. These killings are committed with planning and sometimes with "malice." They are certainly intentional. Yet killing in war is not unlawful as long as the belligerents wage war according to international conventions.

The second element of first-degree murder specifies that the killing must be *of a human being.* People kill all the time. They kill animals for meat, they hunt, and they practice euthanasia on aged and injured pets. Even if the killing of an animal is planned and involves malice (perhaps a vendetta against a neighborhood dog that overturns trash cans), it does not constitute first-degree murder. Such a killing, however, may violate statutes pertaining to cruelty to animals.

The third element of first-degree murder, *intentionality,* is the basis for the defense of accident. An unintentional or nonpurposeful killing is not first-degree murder, although it may violate some other statute.

## CJ CAREERS

# U.S. SECRET SERVICE UNIFORMED DIVISION

**Name:** Kevin S. Simpson

**Position:** Deputy Chief/White House Branch, U.S. Secret Service Uniformed Division

**City:** Washington, D.C.

**College Attended:** 1 year from completing associate's degree in criminal justice, with future plans to attend George Mason University.

**Year Hired:** 1988

*"The U.S. Secret Service is recognized throughout the world as an elite law enforcement agency. As a member of this organization, I can assure you that the U.S. Secret Service offers a wide range of career opportunities that are both rewarding and fulfilling."*

### TYPICAL POSITION

*Uniformed Division officer.* Secret service agents provide personal protection for the president, vice president, president-elect, vice president-elect, and their immediate families; former presidents, their spouses, and minor children until the age of 16; visiting heads of foreign states and their spouses; major presidential and vice presidential candidates and their spouses; and others designated by law. They also work to suppress the counterfeiting of U.S. currency and to curtail financial crimes relating to banks, financial access devices (including credit and debit cards), computers, telecommunications, and telemarketing. In addition, Uniformed Division officers provide protection for the White House complex, the vice president's residence, the Main Treasury Building and Annex, and foreign diplomatic missions and embassies in the Washington, D.C., area. They travel in support of government missions of the president, vice president, and foreign heads of state, and they are responsible for the enforcement of mandated protective responsibilities as described under Title 3, U.S. Code, Section 202.

### EMPLOYMENT REQUIREMENTS

An applicant for the position of Uniformed Division officer must (1) be a U.S. citizen, (2) be between the ages of 21 and 37 at the time of appointment, (3) hold a high school diploma or the equivalent, (4) be in excellent health and physical condition, and (5) have uncorrected vision no worse than 20/60 binocular, correctable to 20/20 in each eye. (Lasik, ALK, RK, and PRK corrective eye surgeries are acceptable provided that applicants pass specific visual tests one year after surgery. Applicants who have undergone Lasik surgery may have visual tests three months after the surgery.) In addition, applicants are required to complete interviews, pass a written test, and undergo comprehensive background investigations, including a driving record check, drug screening, and medical and polygraph examinations. Male applicants born after December 31, 1959, must certify that they have registered with the Selective Service System or are exempt from having to do so under Selective Service law. Positions are available only in Washington, D.C.; reasonable moving expenses are paid for out-of-area hires. The position of Uniformed Division officer is designated as a key position in accordance with Department of Defense Directive 1200.7. As such, employees occupying this position will have their military status changed to either Retired Reserve or Standby Reserve or may be discharged, as appropriate.

### OTHER REQUIREMENTS

The position of Uniformed Division officer entails the following additional requirements: (1) long work hours in undesirable conditions on short notice, (2) frequent travel, and (3) the carrying of a firearm while on duty and the maintenance of firearms proficiency. Newly appointed Uniformed Division officers receive approximately eight weeks of intensive training at the Federal Law Enforcement Training Center (FLETC) in Glynco, Georgia, or Artesia, New Mexico. Upon successful completion of training at FLETC, they receive approximately 11 weeks of specialized instruction at the James J. Rowley Training Center in Laurel, Maryland.

### SALARY

The starting salary is $42,129 per year.

### BENEFITS

Benefits include (1) 13 days of sick leave annually, (2) two and a half to five weeks of paid vacation and ten paid federal holidays each year, (3) federal health and life insurance, (4) a comprehensive retirement program, (5) uniforms and equipment, (6) credit for prior federal civilian and military service, and (7) the opportunity for overtime work.

### DIRECT INQUIRIES TO:

U.S. Secret Service
Personnel Division
950 H Street N.W., Suite 912
Washington, DC 20223

Phone: (888)813-USSS

Website: http://www.secretservice.gov

To learn about the Secret Service's special agent, special officer, administrative, technical, and professional support positions, call (888)813-USSS, visit http://www.secretservice.gov, or contact the nearest U.S. Secret Service field office.

For additional information on employment opportunities in the criminal justice field, view the careers portion of the CD-ROM included with this book.

Sarah Miller taking part in a San Francisco candlelight vigil held in memory of her friend and lacrosse teammate Diane Whipple. Whipple, 33, was mauled to death by neighbors' dogs in the hallway of her apartment building in January 2001. A year after Whipple's death, the dogs' owners, attorneys Marjorie Knoller, 47, and Robert Noel, 61, were convicted of involuntary manslaughter and were sentenced to four years in prison. Prosecutors argued that the owners knew that the dogs were dangerous and that they couldn't control them.

*AP Wide World Photos*

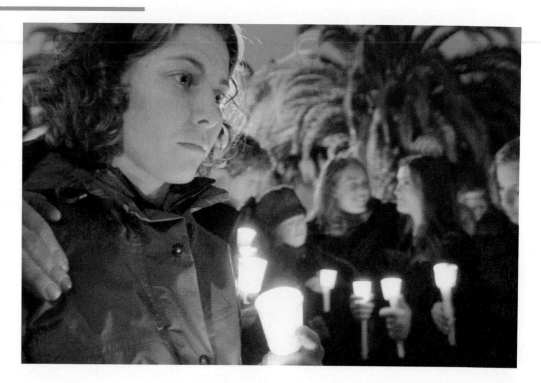

Finally, murder has not been committed unless *malice* is involved. There are different kinds of malice. An extreme form of malice is necessary for a finding of first-degree murder, which is sometimes called *malice aforethought.* This severe kind of malice can be demonstrated by showing that planning was involved in the commission of the murder. Often, first-degree murder is described as "lying in wait," a practice that shows that thought and planning went into the illegal killing.

A charge of second-degree murder in most jurisdictions necessitates proving that an intentional killing of a human being took place—although without the degree of malice necessary for it to be classified as first degree. A crime of passion is an example of second-degree murder. In a crime of passion, the malice felt by the perpetrator is hatred or spite, which is considered less severe than malice aforethought. Manslaughter, or third-degree murder, another type of homicide, can be defined simply as the unlawful killing of a human being. Not only is malice lacking in third-degree murder cases, but so is intention; in fact the killer may not have intended that *any* harm come to the victim.

Manslaughter charges are often brought when a defendant acted in a negligent or reckless manner. The 2001 sentencing of 21-year-old Nathan Hall to 90 days in jail on charges of criminally negligent homicide following a fatal collision with another ski racer on Vail Mountain near Eagle, Colorado, provides such an example.[33] Hall had been tried on a more serious charge of reckless manslaughter, which carries a sentence of up to 16 years under Colorado law, but the jury convicted him of the lesser charge.

Manslaughter statutes, however, frequently necessitate some degree of negligence on the part of the killer. When a wanton disregard for human life is present—legally defined as "gross negligence"—some jurisdictions permit the offender to be charged with a more serious count of murder.

## The *Corpus Delicti* of a Crime

**corpus delicti**

The facts that show that a crime has occurred. The term literally means "the body of the crime."

The term **corpus delicti** literally means "the body of the crime." One way to understand the concept of *corpus delicti* is to realize that a person cannot be tried for a crime unless it can first be shown that the offense has, in fact, occurred. In other words, to establish the *corpus delicti* of a crime, the state has to demonstrate that a criminal law has been violated and that someone violated it. This term is often confused with the statutory elements of a crime, and sometimes the concept is mistakenly thought to mean the *body of a murder victim* or some other physical result of criminal activity. It actually means something quite different.

There are two aspects to the *corpus delicti* of an offense: (1) that a certain result has been produced and (2) that a person is criminally responsible for its production. For example, the crime of larceny requires proof that the property of another has been stolen—that is, unlawfully taken by someone whose intent it was to permanently deprive the owner of its possession.[34] Hence, evidence offered to prove the *corpus delicti* in a trial for larceny is insufficient if it fails to prove that any property was stolen or if property found in a defendant's possession cannot be identified as having been stolen. Similarly, "[i]n an arson case, the *corpus delicti* consists of (1) a burned building or other property, and (2) some criminal agency which caused the burning. . . . In other words, the *corpus delicti* includes not only the fact of burning, but it must also appear that the burning was by the willful act of some person, and not as a result of a natural or accidental cause."[35]

We should note that the identity of the perpetrator is not an element of the *corpus delicti* of an offense. Hence, the fact that a crime has occurred can be established without having any idea who committed it or even why it was committed. This principle was clearly enunciated in a Montana case when that state's supreme court held that "the identity of the perpetrator is not an element of the corpus delicti." In *State* v. *Kindle* (1924),[36] the court said, "We stated that '[i]n a prosecution for murder, proof of the *corpus delicti* does not necessarily carry with it the identity of the slain nor of the slayer.' . . . The essential elements of the *corpus delicti* are . . . establishing the death and the fact that the death was caused by a criminal agency, nothing more." *Black's Law Dictionary* puts it another way: "The *corpus delicti* [of a crime] is the fact of its having been actually committed."[37]

# Types of Defenses to a Criminal Charge

When a person is charged with a crime, she typically offers some defense. A **defense** consists of evidence and arguments offered by a defendant and her attorneys to show why she should not be held liable for a criminal charge. Our legal system generally recognizes four broad categories of defenses: (1) **alibi**, (2) **justifications**, (3) **excuses**, and (4) **procedural defenses**. An alibi, if shown to be valid, means that the defendant could not have committed the crime in question because he or she was somewhere else (and generally with someone else) at the time of the crime. When a defendant offers a justification as a defense, he or she admits committing the act in question but claims that it was necessary to avoid some greater evil. A defendant who offers an excuse as a defense, on the other hand, claims that some personal condition or circumstance at the time of the act was such that he or she should not be held accountable under the criminal law. Procedural defenses make the claim that the defendant was in some significant way discriminated against in the justice process or that some important aspect of official procedure was not properly followed in the investigation or prosecution of the crime charged. Table 4–2 lists the types of defenses that fall into our four categories. Each will be discussed in the pages that follow.

See the Criminal Law Web logs available in the cjtoday.com blogspace.

**defense (to a criminal charge)**
Evidence and arguments offered by a defendant and his or her attorney to show why the defendant should not be held liable for a criminal charge.

**alibi**
A statement or contention by an individual charged with a crime that he or she was so distant when the crime was committed, or so engaged in other provable activities, that his or her participation in the commission of that crime was impossible.

**justification**
A legal defense in which the defendant admits to committing the act in question but claims it was necessary in order to avoid some greater evil.

| TYPES OF DEFENSES |  |
|---|---|
| **Alibi** | |
| A claim of alibi | |
| **Justifications** | |
| Self-defense | Necessity |
| Defense of others | Consent |
| Defense of home and property | Resisting unlawful arrest |
| **Excuses** | |
| Duress | Provocation |
| Age | Insanity |
| Mistake | Diminished capacity |
| Involuntary intoxication | Mental incompetence |
| Unconsciousness | |
| **Procedural Defenses** | |
| Entrapment | Denial of a speedy trial |
| Double jeopardy | Prosecutorial misconduct |
| *Collateral estoppel* | Police fraud |
| Selective prosecution | |

TABLE 4–2

**excuse**

A legal defense in which the defendant claims that some personal condition or circumstance at the time of the act was such that he or she should not be held accountable under the criminal law.

**procedural defense**

A defense that claims that the defendant was in some significant way discriminated against in the justice process or that some important aspect of official procedure was not properly followed in the investigation or prosecution of the crime charged.

# Alibi

A reference book for criminal trial lawyers says, "Alibi is different from all of the other defenses . . . because . . . it is based upon the premise that the defendant is truly innocent."[38] The defense of alibi denies that the defendant committed the act in question. All of the other defenses grant that the defendant committed the act, but they deny that he or she should be held criminally responsible. While justifications and excuses may produce findings of "not guilty," the defense of alibi claims outright innocence.

Alibi is best supported by witnesses and documentation. A person charged with a crime can use the defense of alibi to show that he or she was not present at the scene when the crime was alleged to have occurred. Hotel receipts, eyewitness identification, and participation in social events have all been used to prove alibis.

# Justifications

As defenses, justifications claim a kind of moral high ground. Justifications may be offered by people who face a choice between a "lesser of two evils." Generally speaking, conduct that a person believes is necessary to avoid harm to himself or to another is justifiable if the harm he is trying to avoid is greater than the harm the law defining the offense seeks to avoid. For example, a firefighter might set a controlled fire to create a firebreak to head off a conflagration threatening a community. While intentionally setting a fire might constitute arson, destroying property to save a town by creating a firebreak may be justifiable behavior in the eyes of the community and in the eyes of the law. Included under the broad category of justifications are (1) self-defense, (2) defense of others, (3) defense of home and property, (4) necessity, (5) consent, and (6) resisting unlawful arrest.

## Self-Defense

**self-defense**

The protection of oneself or of one's property from unlawful injury or from the immediate risk of unlawful injury. Also, the justification that the person who committed an act that would otherwise constitute an offense reasonably believed that the act was necessary to protect self or property from immediate danger.

**Self-defense** makes the claim that it was necessary to inflict harm on another to ensure one's own safety in the face of near-certain injury or death. A person who harms an attacker can generally use this defense. However, the courts have held that where a "path of retreat" exists for a person being attacked, it should be taken. In other words, the safest use of self-defense is only when cornered, with no path of escape.

The amount of defensive force used must be proportional to the amount of force or the perceived degree of threat that one is seeking to defend against. Hence, **reasonable force** is the degree of force that is appropriate in a given situation and that is not excessive. Reasonable force can also be thought of as the minimum degree of force necessary to protect oneself, one's property, a third party, or the property of another in the face of a substantial threat. Deadly force, the highest degree of force, is considered reasonable only when used to counter an immediate threat of death or great bodily harm. Deadly force cannot be used against nondeadly force.

**reasonable force**

A degree of force that is appropriate in a given situation and is not excessive. Also, the minimum degree of force necessary to protect oneself, one's property, a third party, or the property of another in the face of a substantial threat.

*Force,* as the term is used within the context of self-defense, means physical force and does not extend to emotional, psychological, economic, psychic, or other forms of coercion. A person who turns the tables on a robber and assaults him during a robbery attempt, for example, may be able to claim self-defense, but a businessperson who physically assaults a financial rival to prevent a hostile takeover of her company will have no such recourse.

Self-defense has been claimed in killings of abusive spouses. A jury is likely to accept as justified a killing that occurs while the physical abuse is in progress, especially where a history of such abuse can be shown. On the other hand, wives who suffer repeated abuse but coldly plan the killing of their husbands have not fared well in court.

## Defense of Others

**alter ego rule**

In some jurisdictions, a rule of law that holds that a person can only defend a third party under circumstances and only to the degree that the third party could act on his or her own behalf.

The use of force to defend oneself has generally been extended to permit the use of reasonable force to defend others who are or who appear to be in imminent danger. The defense of others, sometimes called *defense of a third person,* is circumscribed in some jurisdictions by the **alter ego rule**. The alter ego rule holds that a person can only defend a third party under circumstances and only to the degree that the third party could act. In other words, a person who aids a person whom he sees being attacked may become criminally liable if that person initiated the attack or if the assault is a lawful one—for example, an assault made by a law enforcement officer conducting a lawful arrest of a person who is resisting. A few jurisdictions, however, do not recognize the alter ego rule and allow a person to act in defense of another if the actor reasonably believes that his or her intervention is immediately necessary to protect the third person.

Defense of others cannot be claimed by an individual who joins an illegal fight merely to assist a friend or family member. Likewise, one who intentionally aids an offender in an assault, even though the tables have turned and the offender is losing the battle, cannot claim defense of others. Under the law, defense of a third person always requires that the defender be free from fault and that he act to aid an innocent person who is in the process of being victimized. The same restrictions that apply to self-defense also apply to the defense of a third party. Hence, a defender may act only in the face of an immediate threat to another person, cannot use deadly force against nondeadly force, and must act only to the extent and use only the degree of force needed to repel the attack.

## Defense of Home and Property

In most jurisdictions, the owner of property can justifiably use reasonable, *nondeadly* force to prevent others from unlawfully taking or damaging it. As a general rule, the preservation of human life outweighs the protection of property, and the use of deadly force to protect property is not justified unless the perpetrator of the illegal act may intend to commit, or is in the act of committing, a violent act against another human being. A person who shoots an unarmed trespasser, for example, could not claim "defense of property" to avoid criminal liability. However, a person who shoots and kills an armed robber while being robbed can make such a claim.[39]

The use of mechanical devices to protect property is a special area of law. Because deadly force is usually not permitted in defense of property, the setting of booby traps, such as spring-loaded shotguns, electrified gates, and explosive devices, is generally not permitted to protect property that is unattended and unoccupied. If an individual is injured as a result of a mechanical device intended to cause death or injury in the protection of property, criminal charges may be brought against the person who set the device.

On the other hand, acts that would otherwise be criminal may carry no criminal liability if undertaken to protect one's home. For purposes of the law, one's "home" is one's dwelling, whether owned, rented, or merely borrowed. Hotel rooms, rooms aboard vessels, and rented rooms in houses belonging to others are all considered, for purposes of the law, one's home. The retreat rule that requires a person under attack to retreat when possible before resorting to deadly force is subject to what some call the *castle exception*. The castle exception can be traced to the writings of the sixteenth-century English jurist Sir Edward Coke, who said, "A man's house is his castle—for where shall a man be safe if it be not in his house?"[40] The castle exception generally recognizes that a person has a fundamental right to be in his or her home and that the home is a final and inviolable place of retreat (that is, the home offers a place of retreat from which a person can be expected to retreat no farther). Hence, it is not necessary for one to retreat from one's home in the face of an immediate threat, even where such retreat is possible, before resorting to deadly force in protection of the home. A number of court decisions have extended the castle exception to include one's place of business, such as a store or an office.

## Necessity

Necessity, or the claim that some illegal action was needed to prevent an even greater harm, is a useful defense in cases that do not involve serious bodily harm. A famous but unsuccessful use of this defense occurred in *The Crown* v. *Dudly & Stephens* in the late nineteenth century.[41] This British case involved a shipwreck in which three sailors and a cabin boy were set adrift in a lifeboat. After a number of days at sea without food, two of the sailors decided to kill and eat the cabin boy. At their trial, they argued that it was necessary to do so, or none of them would have survived. The court, however, reasoned that the cabin boy was not a direct threat to the survival of the men and rejected this defense. Convicted of murder, they were sentenced to death, although they were spared the gallows by royal intervention. Although cannibalism is usually against the law, courts have sometimes recognized the necessity of consuming human flesh where survival was at issue. Those cases, however, involved only "victims" who had already died of natural causes.

## Consent

The defense of consent claims that whatever harm was done occurred only after the injured person gave his or her permission for the behavior in question. In the late 1980s, for example, Robert Chambers pleaded guilty to first-degree manslaughter in the killing of 18-year-old Jennifer Levin. In what was dubbed the "Preppy Murder Case,"[42] Chambers had claimed that Levin died as a result of "rough sex," during which she had tied his hands behind his back and injured his testicles. Other cases, some involving sexual asphyxia (partial suffocation designed to heighten erotic pleasures) and bondage, culminated in a headline in *Time* heralding the era of the "rough-sex defense."[43]

In the "Condom Rapist Case," Joel Valdez was found guilty of rape in 1993 after a jury in Austin, Texas, rejected his claim that the act became consensual once he complied with his victim's request to use a condom. Valdez, who was drunk and armed with a knife at the time of the offense, claimed that his victim's request was a consent to sex. After that, he said, "we were making love."[44]

## Resisting Unlawful Arrest

All jurisdictions make resisting arrest a crime. Resistance, however, may be justifiable, especially if the arresting officer uses excessive force. Some justifications have statutory provisions detailing the limits imposed on such resistance and the conditions under which it can be used. Such laws generally state that a person may use a reasonable amount of force, other than deadly force, to resist an arrest or an unlawful search by a law enforcement officer if the officer uses or attempts to use greater force than necessary to make the arrest or search. Such laws are inapplicable in cases where the defendant is the first to resort to force. Deadly force to resist arrest is never justified unless the law enforcement officer resorts to deadly force when it is not called for.

# Excuses

In contrast to a justification, an excuse does not claim that the conduct in question is justified by the situation or that it is moral. An excuse claims, rather, that the actor who engaged in the unlawful behavior was, at the time, not legally responsible for his or her actions and should not be held accountable under the law. For example, a person who assaults a police officer, thinking that the officer is really a disguised space alien who has come to abduct him, may be found "not guilty" of the charge of assault and battery by reason of insanity. Actions for which excuses are offered do not morally outweigh the wrong committed, but criminal liability may still be negated on the basis of some personal disability of the actor or because of some special circumstances that characterize the situation. Excuses recognized by the law include (1) duress, (2) age, (3) mistake, (4) involuntary intoxication, (5) unconsciousness, (6) provocation, (7) insanity, (8) diminished capacity, and (9) mental incompetence.

## Duress

The defense of duress depends on an understanding of the situation. *Duress* has been defined as "any unlawful threat or coercion used by a person to induce another to act (or to refrain from acting) in a manner he or she otherwise would not (or would)."[45] A person may act under duress if, for example, he or she steals an employer's payroll to meet a ransom demand for kidnappers holding the person's children. Should the person later be arrested for larceny or embezzlement, the person can claim that he or she felt compelled to commit the crime to help ensure the safety of the children. Duress is generally not a useful defense when the crime committed involves serious physical harm, since the harm committed may outweigh the coercive influence in the minds of jurors and judges. Duress is sometimes also called *coercion*.

## Age

Age offers another kind of excuse to a criminal charge, and the defense of "infancy"—as it is sometimes known in legal jargon—has its roots in the ancient belief that children cannot reason logically until around the age of seven. Early doctrine in the Christian church sanctioned that belief by declaring that rationality develops around that age. As a consequence, only older children could be held responsible for their crimes.

The defense of infancy today has been expanded to include young people well beyond the age of seven. Many states set the sixteenth birthday as the age at which a person becomes an adult for purposes of criminal prosecution. Others use the age of 17, and still others 18. When a person younger than the age required for adult prosecution commits a "crime," it is termed a *juvenile offense*. He or she is not guilty of a criminal violation of the law by virtue of youth.

In most jurisdictions, children younger than seven cannot be charged even with juvenile offenses, no matter how serious their actions. However, in a rather amazing 1994 case, prosecutors in Cincinnati, Ohio, charged a 12-year-old girl with murder after she confessed to drowning her toddler cousin ten years earlier. The cousin, 13-month-old Lamar Howell, drowned in 1984 in a bucket of bleach mixed with water. Howell's drowning had been ruled an accidental death

**cultural defense**

A defense to a criminal charge in which the defendant's culture is taken into account in judging his or her culpability.

## CJ NEWS

### Courts Asked to Consider Culture

Santeria priest Ernesto Pichardo thought it was a good thing when fellow members of the Church of the Lukumi Babalu Aye began to leave the bodies of sacrificed chickens near the trees and bushes of Hialeah, Florida, the congregation's hometown, during the 1980s.

Others did not. The City Council in the city of 240,000 people, 11 miles northwest of Miami, rejected the church's contention that the ritual scatterings were a vital part of the Santeria religion and of the Afro-Cuban culture on which it is based. The city prosecuted the church under a law banning animal sacrifices that stood until 1993, when the U.S. Supreme Court struck it down as religious discrimination.

The sacrifices continue, although Pichardo says church members still are occasionally hassled by authorities.

"I learned one thing," says Pichardo, who as an orite, or special priest, is empowered to conduct the sacrifices. "When you bring something forward that is outside the Judeo-Christian tradition, the dominant culture is going to cause you problems."

Immigrants with roots in Africa, Asia and other non-Western cultures are winding up in America's courts after being charged with crimes for acts that would not be offenses in their home countries. In recent years, U.S. courts have been asked to decide the fates of defendants involved in animal sacrifices, ritual mutilations and other customs of foreign cultures.

Some legal analysts and academics say the phenomenon should lead U.S. courts to allow defendants from non-Western backgrounds to raise a **cultural defense** when they are charged with certain crimes. Legal traditionalists blanch at the idea, and courts here traditionally have been reluctant to allow such defenses.

"We say that as a society we welcome diversity, and in fact that we embrace it," says Alison Dundes Renteln, a political science professor at the University of Southern California and author of *The Cultural Defense,* a book that examines the influence of such cases on U.S. courts. "In practice, it's not that easy."

Recent cases bear that out:

- In Fresno in 1995, Thai Chia Moua, a Hmong shaman originally from Laos, ordered a German shepherd puppy beaten to death on his front porch while he chanted over its body. Moua later explained that he wanted the puppy's soul to hunt down an evil spirit that was tormenting his wife. He pleaded guilty to animal cruelty. He was sentenced to probation and community service.
- In San Mateo, Calif., in 2000, Taufui Piutau was arrested for driving under the influence of kava tea, a mild euphoric popular in his native Tonga. A hung jury led to a mistrial.
- Chewers of khat, a leaf grown in East Africa and Yemen that produces a caffeine-like stimulant buzz, have been prosecuted in Michigan, New York, Georgia, Connecticut and Minnesota since the mid-1990s. Khat is legal in Great Britain, but the U.S. government classifies it as a controlled substance in the same category as LSD and Ecstasy.

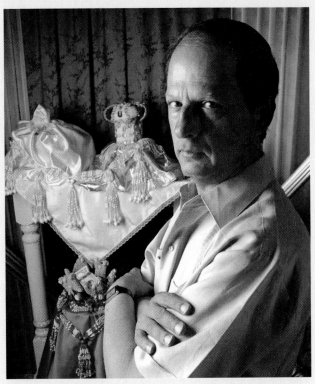

Santeria priest Ernesto Pichardo. The practice of animal sacrifice in Pichardo's Hialeah, Florida–based Church of the Lukumi Babalu Aye is protected under a U.S. Supreme Court decision and highlights the possibility of raising cultural defenses against certain criminal charges. Cultural defenses have become especially important in recent years as immigrants with roots in Africa, Asia, and other non-Western cultures are being increasingly charged in the United States with crimes for acts that would not be against the law in their home countries.

*Eliot J. Schechter, EJS Photo.Com, Inc.*

- In Sanford, N.C., in 2003, city officials banned the slaughter of goats and other farm animals. Mexican agricultural workers who had settled in the town had begun killing goats for backyard barbecues and nailing their heads to nearby trees.
- In Lawrenceville, Ga., in March, Ethiopian immigrant Khalid Adem was charged with child cruelty after his 4-year-old daughter was found to have undergone female circumcision. The practice, in which portions of the female genitals are removed, is condemned by the United Nations and is banned under a 1995 U.S. law, but it is common in some African cultures.

### CIVIL LAWSUITS

Culture clashes also are producing civil lawsuits that run in the other direction: Recently arrived immigrants have filed claims against airlines and fast-food restaurants over conduct that was offensive in the immigrants' cultures.

*(continued)*

## CJ NEWS *(continued)*

In 1988, the parents of Jasbir Singh, a Sikh, won $400,000 in court from Air Illinois after Singh, 26, was killed in a plane crash. An Illinois court ruled that the family was entitled to a larger-than-usual amount because Sikh custom would have required Singh to care for them in their old age.

Cultural claims have worked on occasion. In 1999, Mukesh Rai, a Carpenteria, Calif., pharmacist who is a vegetarian, accepted an undisclosed sum from Taco Bell after he mistakenly was served a beef burrito. Rai, a Hindu who had sued for $144,000, claimed that he was offended on cultural and religious grounds. He said the incident led him to consult a psychiatrist and to journey to India for a purifying bath in the Ganges River. Similar lawsuits by non-religious vegetarians usually fail, legal analysts say.

U.S. courts have dealt with similar pressures before.

In the early 20th century, Renteln says, Orthodox Jewish immigrants from Eastern Europe and Catholics from Italy brought religious and cultural practices that clashed with U.S. customs. Practices such as contracted or underage marriages, she says, were not protected under U.S. law and largely were eliminated.

Renteln wants courts to recognize what she calls America's "evolving definition of diversity." She says cultural defenses should be considered when determining guilt. But she does not say that those who commit culture-based crimes should always be found not guilty.

"Courts can judge on a case-by-case basis," Renteln says. "For instance, they could rule that it's OK for a Sikh man to wear a *kirpan* (a ceremonial dagger worn on or under the clothes) without endorsing female genital mutilation."

Legal traditionalists reject that notion. Michael Rushford, president of the Criminal Justice Legal Foundation, a conservative group, says that permitting cultural defenses would lead to a "legal relativism" in which "what's a crime for one person isn't for his neighbor. . . . The system we have is the best we can do to allow cultural differences without beating down basic human rights."

### RELIGIOUS ASPECT IMPORTANT

Courts have long been reluctant to accept cultural defenses. Exceptions have come when groups have been able to argue that their religious as well as cultural rights have been violated.

In a case now before a U.S. appeals court, Albuquerque-based adherents of Uniao de Vegetal, a Brazilian religion, are claiming that restricting their access to the ayahuasca root violates a 1993 U.S. law that protects exotic religious practices. Tea brewed from the root produces a dreamlike state that is essential to their religion, the adherents say. The group won in federal trial court; the U.S. government has appealed.

Occasionally, lawyers have persuaded judges to go easy on defendants from other cultures.

In Brooklyn, N.Y., in 1989, Chinese-born Dong Lu Chen received probation for beating his wife to death with a claw hammer after she confessed to adultery. Chen's attorney, Stewart Orden, argued that the shame Chen felt was the result of his Chinese upbringing, and that it fed his frenzy.

"It was as much of a cultural explanation as cultural defense," says Orden, who says he has not used the strategy since the Chen case.

"Culture may not excuse (a crime), but it can certainly shed light on things we may have difficulty understanding. Why shouldn't a court listen?"

For the latest in crime and justice news, visit the Talk Justice news feed at http://www.crimenews.info.

*Source:* Richard Willing, "Courts Asked to Consider Culture," *USA Today,* May 25, 2004, p. 3A. Copyright © 2004 *USA Today.* Reprinted with permission.

---

until his cousin came forward. In discussing the charges with the media, Hamilton (Ohio) County Prosecutor Joe Deters admitted that the girl could not be prosecuted successfully. "Frankly," he said, "anything under seven cannot be an age where you form criminal intent."[46] The prosecution's goal, claimed one of Deters's associates, was simply to "make sure she gets the counseling she needs."

## Mistake

Two types of mistake can serve as a defense. One is mistake of law, and the other is mistake of fact. Rarely is mistake of law held to be an acceptable defense. Most people realize that it is their responsibility to know the law as it applies to them. "Ignorance of the law is no excuse" is an old dictum still heard today. On occasion, however, cases do arise in which such a defense is accepted by authorities. For example, an elderly woman raised marijuana plants because they could be used to make a tea that relieved her arthritis pain. When her garden was discovered, she was not arrested but was advised as to how the law applied to her.

Mistake of fact is a much more useful form of the mistake defense. In 2000, for example, the statutory rape conviction of 39-year-old Charles Ballinger of Bradley County, Tennessee, was reversed by Tennessee's Court of Criminal Appeals at Knoxville on a mistake-of-fact claim.[47] Ballinger admitted that he had had sex with his 15-year-old neighbor, who was under the age of legal consent at the time of the act. In his defense, however, Ballinger claimed that he had had good reason to mistake the girl's age.

## Involuntary Intoxication

The claim of involuntary intoxication may form the basis for another excuse defense. Either drugs or alcohol may produce intoxication. Voluntary intoxication is rarely a defense to a criminal charge because it is a self-induced condition. It is widely recognized in Western legal tradition that an altered mental condition that is the product of voluntary activity cannot be used to exonerate guilty actions that follow from it. Some state statutes formalize this general principle of law and specifically state that voluntary intoxication cannot be offered as a defense to a charge of criminal behavior.[48]

Involuntary intoxication, however, is another matter. A person can be tricked into consuming an intoxicating substance. Secretly "spiked" punch, popular aphrodisiacs, or LSD-laced desserts can be ingested unknowingly. In the mid-1990s, for example, the Drug Enforcement Administration reported that a powerful sedative manufactured by Hoffmann-LaRoche Pharmaceuticals and sold under the brand name Rohypnol had become popular with college students and with "young men [who] put doses of Rohypnol in women's drinks without their consent in order to lower their inhibitions."[49] Other behavioral effects of the drug are unknown. On the street, Rohypnol is known as *roples, roche, ruffles, roofies,* and *rophies.*

Because the effects and taste of alcohol are so widely known in our society, the defense of involuntary intoxication due to alcohol consumption can be difficult to demonstrate.

## Unconsciousness

A very rarely used excuse is unconsciousness. An individual cannot be held responsible for anything he or she does while unconscious. Because unconscious people rarely do anything at all, this defense is almost never seen in the courts. However, cases of sleepwalking, epileptic seizure, and neurological dysfunction may result in injurious, although unintentional, actions by people so afflicted. Under such circumstances, a defense of unconsciousness might be argued with success.

## Provocation

Provocation recognizes that a person can be emotionally enraged by another who intends to elicit just such a reaction. Should the person then strike out at the tormentor, some courts have held, he or she may not be guilty of criminality or may be guilty of a lesser degree of criminality than might otherwise be the case. The defense of provocation is commonly used in cases arising from barroom brawls, although most states don't look favorably on verbal provocation alone. This defense has also been used recently in some spectacular cases where wives have killed their husbands, or children their fathers, citing years of verbal and physical abuse. In these instances, perhaps because the degree of physical harm inflicted—the death of husband or father—appears to be out of proportion to the abuse suffered by the wife or the child, the courts have not readily accepted the defense of provocation. As a rule, this defense is generally more acceptable in minor offenses than in serious violations of the law.

## Insanity

From the point of view of the criminal law, *insanity* has a legal definition and not a medical one. This legal definition often has very little to do with psychological or psychiatric understandings of mental illness; rather, it is a concept developed to enable the judicial system to assign guilt or innocence to particular defendants. As a consequence, medical conceptions of mental illness do not always fit well into the legal categories of mental illness created by courts and legislatures. The differences between psychiatric and legal conceptualizations of insanity often lead to disagreements among expert witnesses who, in criminal court, may provide conflicting testimony as to the sanity of a defendant.

Consider, for example, the sad story of Andrea Pia Yates. The Texas mother was convicted in 2002 of the drowning murders of her five young children and ordered to serve life in prison. Evidence presented to the jury during Yates' trial established that she methodically killed the children one at a time and that she did so because she believed that it was the only way she could

Convicted child killer Andrea Pia Yates in Texas Department of Criminal Justice photos made after her arrival at the Woodman State Jail in Gatesville, Texas. Yates confessed to drowning her five children in a bathtub. She was convicted in 2002 on two counts of capital murder and sentenced to life in prison. In 2005, however, her conviction was overturned and a new trial ordered.

*AP Wide World Photos*

> What Yates knew is that others would deem her actions wrong. But as for herself, she was right. Her children were not "righteous." She was saving them from eternal damnation by sending them to heaven.
>
> —Richard Cohen[xi]

**insanity defense**

A legal defense based on claims of mental illness or mental incapacity.

save them from the devil. Prior to the killings, Yates had attempted suicide twice and had been hospitalized several times for mental illness. She had been diagnosed as schizophrenic and was known to be suffering from postpartum depression following the birth of her last child. Both the prosecution and the defense in her trial agreed that she was severely mentally ill, and jurors were aware of the details of her mental illness. Nonetheless, given the differences between the psychiatric definition of mental illness and legal definition of insanity, Yates's attorneys could not convince the jury that their client was not guilty by reason of insanity. The jurors reasoned that Yates must have known her actions were wrong because she called the police immediately after she killed her children. Because the legal definition of insanity asks what a person knew or did not know at the time of the crime, they found her guilty.

Critics of the Yates decision have pointed out that while Andrea Yates may have known that society and the justice system would view her actions as "wrong," she may have believed that they were "right" and even necessary. In 2005, in what many saw as partial vindication of such a view, Yates' conviction was overturned by a Texas appeals court and a new trial was ordered. The court found that false testimony by a prosecution psychiatrist had been instrumental in persuading the jury to reject Yates' claim of insanity. The testimony, by California psychiatrist Park Dietz, included a false assertion that he had consulted for an episode of the TV show *Law and Order* about a fictional case like that involving Yates. University of Texas law professor George Dix said that Yates' conviction had been vacated because of difficulties with proving insanity under Texas law. "I'm persuaded," said Dix, "that the reason the court found this reversible error is because it's such a difficult and screwed-up case."[50]

The **insanity defense** is given a lot of play in the entertainment industry—movies and televisions regularly employ it because it makes for good drama. In practice, however, the defense of insanity is rarely raised. According to an eight-state study funded by the National Institute of Mental Health, the insanity defense was used in less than 1% of the cases that came before county-level courts.[51] The study showed that only 26% of all insanity pleas were argued successfully and that 90% of those who employed the defense had been previously diagnosed with a mental illness. As the American Bar Association says, "The best evidence suggests that the mental nonresponsibility defense is raised in less than one percent of all felony cases in the United States and is successful in about a fourth of these."[52] Even so, there are several rules that guide the legal definition of insanity.

**The M'Naghten Rule**   The insanity defense, as we know it today, was nonexistent prior to the nineteenth century. Up to then, insane people who committed crimes were punished in the same way as other law violators. It was Daniel M'Naghten (sometimes spelled McNaughten or M'Naughten), a woodworker from Glasgow, Scotland, who, in 1844, became the first person to be found not guilty of a crime by reason of insanity. M'Naghten had tried to assassinate Sir Robert

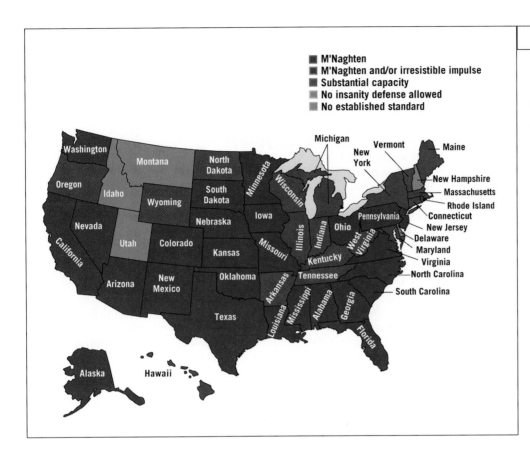

**FIGURE 4–1**

**Standards for insanity determinations by jurisdiction.**

*Source:* Adapted from Bureau of Justice Statistics, *State Court Organization 1998* (Washington, DC: U.S. Department of Justice, 2000), pp. 257–259.

Peel, the British prime minister. He mistook Edward Drummond, Peel's secretary, for Peel himself and killed Drummond instead. At his trial, defense attorneys argued that M'Naghten suffered from vague delusions centered on the idea that the Tories, a British political party, were persecuting him. Medical testimony at the trial supported the defense's assertion that he didn't know what he was doing at the time of the shooting. The jury accepted M'Naghten's claim, and the insanity defense was born. Later, the House of Lords defined the criteria necessary for a finding of insanity. The **M'Naghten rule**, as it is called, holds that *a person is not guilty of a crime if, at the time of the crime, the person either didn't know what he or she was doing or didn't know that what he or she was doing was wrong.* The inability to distinguish right from wrong must be the result of some mental defect or disability.

Today, the M'Naghten rule is still followed in many U.S. jurisdictions (Figure 4–1). In those states, the burden of proving insanity falls on the defendant. Just as defendants are assumed to be innocent, they are also assumed to be sane at the outset of any criminal trial. Learn more about the M'Naghten rule via Web Extra 4–4 at cjtoday.com.

**M'Naghten rule**

A rule for determining insanity, which asks whether the defendant knew what he or she was doing or whether the defendant knew that what he or she was doing was wrong.

**Irresistible Impulse** The M'Naghten rule worked well for a time. Eventually, however, some cases arose in which defendants clearly knew what they were doing, and they knew it was wrong. Even so, they argued in their defense that they couldn't stop doing what they knew was wrong. Such people are said to suffer from an *irresistible impulse,* and in several states today, they may be found not guilty by reason of this particular type of insanity. Some states that do not use the irresistible impulse test in determining insanity may still allow the successful demonstration of such an impulse to be considered in sentencing decisions.

In a spectacular 1994 Virginia trial, Lorena Bobbitt successfully employed the irresistible impulse defense against charges of malicious wounding stemming from an incident in which she cut off her husband's penis with a kitchen knife as he slept. In the case, which made headlines around the world, Bobbitt's defense attorney told the jury, "What we have is Lorena Bobbitt's life juxtaposed against John Wayne Bobbitt's penis. The evidence will show that in her mind it was his penis from which she could not escape, that caused her the most pain, the most fear, the most humiliation."[53] The impulse to sever the organ, said the lawyer, became irresistible.

The irresistible impulse test has been criticized on a number of grounds. Primary among them is the belief that all of us suffer from compulsions. Most of us, however, learn to control them. If we give in to a compulsion, the critique goes, then why not just say it was unavoidable so as to escape any legal consequences?

**The Durham Rule** Another rule for gauging insanity is called the *Durham rule.* Originally created in 1871 by a New Hampshire court, it was later adopted by Judge David Bazelon in 1954 when he decided the case of *Durham* v. *U.S.* for the court of appeals in the District of Columbia.[54] The Durham rule states that *a person is not criminally responsible for his or her behavior if the person's illegal actions were the result of some mental disease or defect.*

Courts that follow the Durham rule typically hear from an array of psychiatric specialists as to the mental state of the defendant. Their testimony is inevitably clouded by the need to address the question of cause. A successful defense under the Durham rule necessitates that jurors be able to see the criminal activity in question as the *product* of mental deficiencies harbored by the defendant. However, most people who suffer from mental diseases or defects never commit crimes, and low IQ, mental retardation, and lack of general mental capacity are not allowable excuses for criminal behavior. Because the Durham rule is especially vague, it provides fertile ground for conflicting claims.

**The Substantial Capacity Test** Nineteen states follow another guideline—the substantial capacity test—as found in the Model Penal Code (MPC) of the American Law Institute (ALI).[55] Also called the *ALI rule* or the *MPC rule,* it suggests that insanity should be defined as the lack of a substantial capacity to control one's behavior. This test requires a judgment to the effect that the defendant either had, or lacked, "the mental capacity needed to understand the wrongfulness of his act or to conform his behavior to the requirements of the law."[56] The substantial capacity test is a blending of the M'Naghten rule with the irresistible impulse standard. "Substantial capacity" does not require total mental incompetence, nor does the rule require the behavior in question to live up to the criterion of total irresistibility. However, the problem of establishing just what constitutes "substantial mental capacity" has plagued this rule from its conception.

**The Brawner Rule** Judge Bazelon, apparently dissatisfied with the application of the Durham rule, created a new criterion for gauging insanity in the 1972 case of *U.S.* v. *Brawner.*[57] The *Brawner rule,* as it is called, places responsibility for deciding insanity squarely with the jury. Bazelon suggested that the jury should be concerned with whether the defendant could be justly held responsible for the criminal act in the face of any claims of insanity. Under this proposal, juries are left with few rules to guide them other than their own sense of fairness.

**The Insanity Defense and Social Reaction** The insanity defense originated as a way to recognize the social reality of mental disease. However, the history of this defense has been rife with difficulty and contradiction. First, psychiatric testimony is expensive, and "expert" witnesses often are at odds with one another. Another difficulty with this defense is society's acceptance of it. When not guilty due to insanity findings have been made, the public has not always been satisfied that justice has been served. Dissatisfaction with the jumble of rules defining legal insanity peaked in 1982, when John Hinckley was acquitted of trying to assassinate then-President Ronald Reagan. At his trial, Hinckley's lawyers claimed that a series of delusions brought about by a history of schizophrenia left him unable to control his behavior. Government prosecutors were unable to counter defense contentions of insanity. The resulting acquittal shocked the nation and resulted in calls for a review of the insanity defense.

One response has been to ban the insanity defense from use at trial. A ruling by the U.S. Supreme Court in support of a Montana law allows states to prohibit defendants from claiming that they were insane at the time they committed their crimes. In 1994, without comment, the high court let stand a Montana Supreme Court ruling that held that eliminating the insanity defense does not violate the U.S. Constitution. Currently, only three states—Montana, Idaho, and Utah—bar use of the insanity defense.[58]

**Guilty but Mentally Ill** Another response to public frustration with the insanity and responsibility issue is the **guilty but mentally ill (GBMI)** verdict, now possible in at least 11 states. (In a few states the finding is "guilty but insane.") A GBMI verdict means that a person can be held responsible for a specific criminal act even though a degree of mental incompetence may be present in his or her personality. In most GBMI jurisdictions, a jury must return a finding of "guilty but mentally ill" if (1) every element necessary for a conviction has been proved beyond a reasonable doubt, (2) the defendant is found to have been *mentally ill* at the time the crime was committed, and (3) the defendant was *not* found to have been *legally insane* at the time the crime was committed. The difference between mental illness and legal insanity is a crucial one, since a defendant can be mentally ill by standards of the medical profession but sane for purposes of the law.

**guilty but mentally ill (GBMI)**

A verdict, equivalent to a finding of "guilty," that establishes that the defendant, although mentally ill, was in sufficient possession of his or her faculties to be morally blameworthy for his or her acts.

Upon return of a GBMI verdict, a judge may impose any sentence possible under the law for the crime in question. Mandated psychiatric treatment, however, is often part of the commitment order. Once cured, the offender is usually placed in the general prison population to serve any remaining sentence.

In 1997, Pennsylvania multimillionaire John E. du Pont was found guilty but mentally ill in the shooting death of former Olympic gold medalist David Schultz during a delusional episode. Although defense attorneys were able to show that du Pont sometimes saw Nazis in his trees, heard the walls talking, and had cut off pieces of his skin to remove bugs from outer space, he was held criminally liable for Schultz's death and was sentenced to 13 to 30 years in confinement.

As some authors have observed, the "guilty but mentally ill" finding has three purposes: "first, to protect society; second, to hold some offenders who were mentally ill accountable for their criminal acts; [and] third, to make treatment available to convicted offenders suffering from some form of mental illness."[59] The U.S. Supreme Court case of *Ford* v. *Wainwright* recognized an issue of a different sort.[60] The 1986 decision specified that prisoners who become insane while incarcerated cannot be executed. Hence, although insanity may not always be a successful defense to criminal prosecution, it can later become a block to the ultimate punishment.

**Temporary Insanity** Temporary insanity is another possible defense against a criminal charge. Widely used in the 1940s and 1950s, temporary insanity means that the offender claims to have been insane only at the time of the commission of the offense. If a jury agrees, the defendant goes free. The defendant is not guilty of the criminal action by virtue of having been insane at the time, yet he or she cannot be ordered to undergo psychiatric counseling or treatment because the insanity is no longer present. This type of plea has become less popular as legislatures have regulated the circumstances under which it can be made.

**The Insanity Defense under Federal Law** Yet another response to the public's concern with the insanity defense and responsibility issues is the federal Insanity Defense Reform Act (IDRA). In 1984, Congress passed this act, which created major revisions in the federal insanity defense. Insanity under the law is now defined as a condition in which the defendant can be shown to have been suffering under a "severe mental disease or defect" and, as a result, "was unable to appreciate the nature and quality or the wrongfulness of his acts."[61] This definition of insanity comes close to that set forth in the old M'Naghten rule.

The act also places the burden of proving the insanity defense squarely on the defendant—a provision that has been challenged a number of times since the act was passed. The Supreme Court supported a similar requirement prior to the act's passage. In 1983, in the case of *Jones* v. *U.S.*,[62] the Court ruled that defendants can be required to prove their insanity when it becomes an issue in their defense. Shortly after the act became law, the Court held, in *Ake* v. *Oklahoma* (1985),[63] that the government must ensure access to a competent psychiatrist whenever a defendant indicates that insanity will be an issue at trial.

**Consequences of an Insanity Ruling** The insanity defense today is not an "easy way out" of criminal prosecution, as some people assume. Once a verdict of "not guilty by reason of insanity" is returned, the judge may order the defendant to undergo psychiatric treatment until cured. Because psychiatrists are reluctant to declare any potential criminal "cured," such a sentence may result in more time spent in an institution than would have been spent in a prison. In *Foucha* v. *Louisiana* (1992),[64] however, the U.S. Supreme Court held that a defendant found not guilty by reason of insanity in a criminal trial could not thereafter be institutionalized indefinitely without a showing that he or she was either dangerous or mentally ill.

## Diminished Capacity

**Diminished capacity**, or *diminished responsibility,* is a defense available in some jurisdictions. In 2003, the U.S. Sentencing Commission issued a policy statement saying that *diminished capacity* may mean that "the defendant, although convicted, *has a significantly impaired ability* [italics added] to (A) understand the wrongfulness of the behavior comprising the offense or to exercise the power of reason; or (B) control behavior that the defendant knows is wrongful."[65] Still, "the terms 'diminished responsibility' and 'diminished capacity' do not have a clearly accepted meaning in [many] courts."[66] Some defendants who offer diminished capacity defenses do so in recognition of the fact that such claims may be based on a mental condition that would not qualify as mental disease or mental defect nor be sufficient to support the defense of insanity but that might still lower criminal culpability. According to Peter Arenella, professor of law at UCLA, "the defense [of diminished capacity] was first recognized by Scottish common law courts to reduce the punishment of the 'partially insane' from murder to culpable homicide, a non-capital offense."[67]

**diminished capacity**
A defense based on claims of a mental condition that may be insufficient to exonerate the defendant of guilt but that may be relevant to specific mental elements of certain crimes or degrees of crime.

> No person shall be . . . twice put in jeopardy of life or limb.
>
> —Fifth Amendment to the U.S. Constitution

The diminished capacity defense is similar to the defense of insanity in that it depends on a showing that the defendant's mental state was impaired at the time of the crime. As a defense, diminished capacity is most useful when it can be shown that because of some defect of reason or mental shortcoming, the defendant's capacity to form the *mens rea* required by a specific crime was impaired. Unlike an insanity defense, however, which can result in a finding of "not guilty," a diminished capacity defense is built on the recognition that "[m]ental condition, though insufficient to exonerate, may be relevant to specific mental elements of certain crimes or degrees of crime."[68] For example, a defendant might present evidence of mental abnormality in an effort to reduce first-degree murder to second-degree murder, or second-degree murder to manslaughter, when a killing occurs under extreme emotional disturbance. Similarly, in some jurisdictions, very low intelligence will, if proved, serve to reduce first-degree murder to manslaughter.[69]

As is the case with the insanity defense, some jurisdictions have entirely eliminated the diminished capacity defense. The California Penal Code, for example, abolished the defense of diminished capacity,[70] stating that "[a]s a matter of public policy there shall be no defense of diminished capacity, diminished responsibility, or irresistible impulse in a criminal action or juvenile adjudication hearing."[71]

## Mental Incompetence

In a July 2001 ruling that he later reversed, Jefferson County (Alabama) Circuit Court Judge James Garrett interrupted the prosecution of 72-year-old Bobby Frank Cherry, declaring him mentally **incompetent to stand trial**.[72] Cherry, a former Ku Klux Klansman, was the last living defendant in the bombing case of an African-American church in Birmingham, Alabama, in 1963. Four children were killed in the basement of the 16th Street Baptist Church when the bomb went off. Cherry had been suspected of involvement in the bombing since shortly after the explosion.

Following six rounds of psychiatric evaluations, Judge Garrett made an initial determination that Cherry's dementia was too severe for him to help his lawyers. The judge's decision was strongly influenced by Alabama law, which requires the prosecution to show "clear, unequivocal and convincing evidence" that a defendant is competent to stand trial once the defendant has shown that he or she is incompetent. In Cherry's case, both a defense psychologist and a court-appointed psychiatrist asserted that he was incompetent after brain scans indicated that he suffered from vascular dementia, a physical deterioration of the brain caused by a series of small strokes.

Cherry was ordered to undergo an intensive psychological evaluation at Alabama's Taylor Hardin Secure Medical Facility, where he was sent for ten weeks following the judge's initial finding of incompetency. Following the evaluation, and at the request of prosecutors, Judge Garrett reopened the inquiry into Cherry's competency, and he was declared competent to stand trial. In May 2002, Cherry was found guilty of first-degree murder and was sentenced to life in prison.[73] He died of cancer in an Alabama prison in 2004.

**incompetent to stand trial**

In criminal proceedings, a finding by a court that as a result of mental illness, defect, or disability, a defendant is incapable of understanding the nature of the charges and proceedings against him or her, of consulting with an attorney, and of aiding in his or her own defense.

Former Ku Klux Klansman Bobby Frank Cherry, 72, appearing in court in 2002. Cherry was tried and convicted of first-degree murder in the 1963 bombing of an African-American church in Birmingham, Alabama, in which four young girls were killed. A year earlier, Cherry had been found mentally incompetent, delaying his trial until the finding was reversed. He was sentenced to life in prison and died behind bars in 2004.

*Charles Nesbit, Birmingham News, Corbis/Sygma*

In contrast to Alabama law, federal law requires a much lower level of proof of competency, one that depends on a mere preponderance of the evidence. While insanity refers to an assessment of the offender's mental condition at the time the crime was committed, mental incompetence refers to his or her condition immediately before prosecution.

# Procedural Defenses

Procedural defenses make the claim either that the justice process discriminated in some way against the defendant or that some important aspect of official procedure was not properly followed and that, as a result, the defendant should be released from any criminal liability. The procedural defenses we will discuss here are (1) entrapment, (2) double jeopardy, (3) *collateral estoppel,* (4) selective prosecution, (5) denial of a speedy trial, (6) prosecutorial misconduct, and (7) police fraud.

## Entrapment

**Entrapment** is an improper or illegal inducement to crime by enforcement agents. Entrapment defenses argue that enforcement agents effectively created a crime where there would otherwise have been none. For entrapment to occur, the idea for the criminal activity must originate with official agents of the criminal justice system. Entrapment can also result when overzealous undercover police officers convince a defendant that the contemplated law-violating behavior is not a crime. To avoid claims of entrapment, officers must not engage in activity that would cause a person to commit a crime that he or she would not otherwise commit. Merely providing an opportunity for a willing offender to commit a crime, however, is not entrapment.

One of the best known entrapment cases of the twentieth century involved automaker John DeLorean. DeLorean was arrested in 1982 by federal agents near the Los Angeles airport.[74] An FBI

**entrapment**

An improper or illegal inducement to crime by agents of law enforcement. Also, a defense that may be raised when such inducements have occurred.

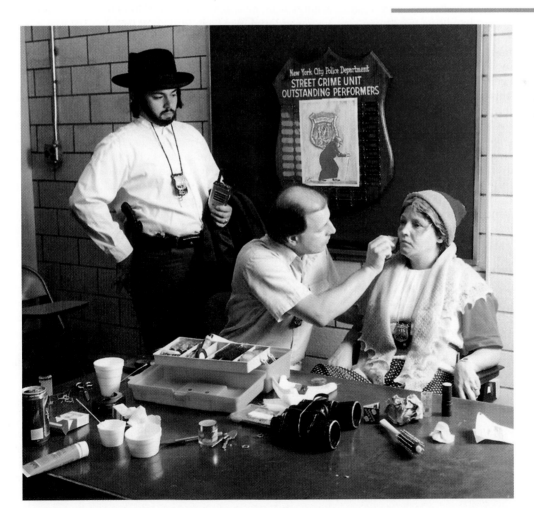

Members of the New York City Police Department's Street Crimes Unit preparing for a day's work. Entrapment will likely not be an effective defense for muggers who attack these decoys.

*Courtesy of the New York City Police Department*

videotape, secretly made at the scene, showed him allegedly "dealing" with undercover agents and holding packets of cocaine, which he said were "better than gold." DeLorean was charged with narcotics smuggling violations involving a large amount of drugs.

At his 1984 trial, DeLorean claimed that he had been set up by the police to commit a crime that he would not have been involved in were it not for their urging. DeLorean's auto company had fallen on hard times, and he was facing heavy debts. Federal agents, acting undercover, proposed to DeLorean a plan whereby he could make a great deal of money through drugs. Because the idea originated with the police, not with DeLorean, and because DeLorean was able to demonstrate successfully that he was repeatedly threatened by a police informant not to pull out of the deal, the jury returned a "not guilty" verdict.

The concept of entrapment is well summarized in a statement made by DeLorean's defense attorney to *Time* magazine before the trial: "This is a fictitious crime. Without the Government there would be no crime. This is one of the most insidious and misguided law-enforcement operations in history."[75]

## Double Jeopardy

The Fifth Amendment to the U.S. Constitution makes it clear that no person may be tried twice for the same offense. People who have been acquitted or found innocent may not again be "put in jeopardy of life or limb" for the same crime. The same is true of those who have been convicted: They cannot be tried again for the same offense. Cases that are dismissed for a lack of evidence also come under the double jeopardy rule and cannot result in a new trial. The U.S. Supreme Court has ruled that "the Double Jeopardy Clause protects against three distinct abuses: a second prosecution for the same offense after acquittal; a second prosecution for the same offense after conviction; and multiple punishments for the same offense."[76]

**double jeopardy**

A common law and constitutional prohibition against a second trial for the same offense.

**Double jeopardy** does not apply in cases of trial error. Hence, convictions that are set aside because of some error in proceedings at a lower court level (for example, inappropriate instructions to the jury by the trial court judge) will permit a retrial on the same charges. Similarly, when a defendant's motion for a mistrial is successful, or when members of the jury cannot agree on a verdict (resulting in a "hung jury"), a second trial may be held.

Defendants, however, may be tried in both federal and state courts without necessarily violating the principle of double jeopardy. For example, 33-year-old Rufina Canedo pleaded guilty to possession of 50 kilograms of cocaine in 1991 and received a six-year prison sentence from a California court.[77] Federal prosecutors, however, indicted her again—this time under a federal law—for the same offense. They offered her a deal: Testify against your husband, or face federal prosecution and the possibility of 20 years in a federal prison. Because state and federal statutes emanate from different jurisdictions, the Supreme Court has held this kind of dual prosecution to be constitutional. To prevent abuse, the U.S. Justice Department acted in 1960 to restrict federal prosecution in such cases to situations involving a "compelling federal interest," such as civil rights violations. However, in the face of soaring drug-law violations in recent years, the restriction has been relaxed.

In 1992, in another drug case, the Supreme Court ruled that the double jeopardy clause of the U.S. Constitution "only prevents duplicative prosecution for the same offense" but that "a substantive offense and a conspiracy to commit that offense are not the same offense for double jeopardy purposes." In that case, *U.S.* v. *Felix* (1992),[78] a Missouri man was convicted in that state of manufacturing methamphetamine and was then convicted again in Oklahoma of the "separate crime" of conspiracy to manufacture a controlled substance—in part based on his activities in Missouri.

Generally, because civil and criminal law differ as to purpose, it is possible to try someone in civil court to collect damages for a possible violation of civil law, even if they were found "not guilty" in criminal court, without violating the principle of double jeopardy. The well-known 1997 California civil trial of O. J. Simpson on grounds of wrongful death resulted in widespread publicity of just such a possibility. In cases where civil penalties are "so punitive in form and effect as to render them criminal,"[79] however, a person sanctioned by a court in a civil case may not be tried in criminal court.

**WHAT WOULD YOU DO?**

The CD-ROM scenario for this chapter builds on the concept of entrapment and reinforces the discussion of the entrapment defense. It is derived from a real-life incident involving police investigation of a child-pornography suspect. The real-life case eventually found its way to the U.S. Supreme Court, with unfavorable consequences for investigating officers and the prosecutors. Use the CD-ROM found in your textbook to work through this scenario, and see if you can make better decisions than the investigating officers did.

## *Collateral Estoppel*

*Collateral estoppel* is similar to double jeopardy, but it applies to facts that have been determined by a "valid and final judgment."[80] Such facts cannot become the object of new litigation. For example, if a defendant has been acquitted of a murder charge by virtue of an alibi, it would not be permissible to try that person again for the murder of a second person killed along with the first.

## Selective Prosecution

The procedural defense of selective prosecution is based on the Fourteenth Amendment's guarantee of "equal protection of the laws." This defense may be available where two or more individuals are suspected of criminal involvement, but not all are actively prosecuted. Selective prosecution based fairly on the strength of available evidence is not the object of this defense. But when prosecution proceeds unfairly on the basis of some arbitrary and discriminatory attribute, such as race, sex, friendship, age, or religious preference, this defense may offer protection. In 1996, however, in a case that reaffirmed reasonable limits on claims of selective prosecution, the U.S. Supreme Court ruled that for a defendant to successfully "claim that he was singled out for prosecution on the basis of his race, he must make a . . . showing that the Government declined to prosecute similarly situated suspects of other races."[81]

## Denial of a Speedy Trial

> In all criminal prosecutions, the accused shall enjoy the right to a speedy and public trial, by an impartial jury.
>
> —Sixth Amendment to the U.S. Constitution

The Sixth Amendment to the Constitution guarantees a right to a speedy trial. The purpose of the guarantee is to prevent unconvicted and potentially innocent people from languishing in jail. The federal government[82] and most states have laws (generally referred to as *speedy trial acts*) that define the time limit necessary for a trial to be "speedy." They generally set a reasonable period, such as 90 or 120 days following arrest. Excluded from the total number of days are delays that result from requests by the defense to prepare the defendant's case. If the limit set by law is exceeded, the defendant must be set free, and no trial can occur.

Speedy trial claims were raised unsuccessfully by defense attorneys in the case of Byron De La Beckwith, the unrepentant 75-year-old white supremacist who was convicted in 1994 of the murder of black civil rights leader Medgar Evers in Mississippi. The killing took place in 1963. More than 30 years after the murder, Beckwith was sentenced to life in prison, but only after two previous trials had ended in hung juries. In 1998, the Mississippi Supreme Court denied a request that Beckwith's case be reviewed on claims that he had not received a speedy trial.

## Prosecutorial Misconduct

Another procedural defense is prosecutorial misconduct. Generally speaking, legal scholars use the term *prosecutorial misconduct* to describe actions undertaken by prosecutors that give the government an unfair advantage or that prejudice the rights of a defendant or a witness. Prosecutors are expected to uphold the highest ethical standards in the performance of their roles. When they knowingly permit false testimony, when they hide information that would clearly help the defense, or when they make unduly biased statements to the jury in closing arguments, the defense of prosecutorial misconduct may be available to the defendant.

The most famous instance of prosecutorial misconduct may have occurred during a convoluted 17-year-long federal case against former Cleveland autoworker John Demjanjuk. Demjanjuk, who was accused of committing war crimes as the notorious Nazi guard "Ivan the Terrible," was extradited in 1986 by the federal government to Israel to face charges there. In late 1993, however, the Sixth U.S. Circuit Court of Appeals in Cincinnati, Ohio, ruled that federal prosecutors, working under what the court called a "win-at-any-cost" attitude, had intentionally withheld evidence that might have exonerated Demjanjuk. Demjanjuk was stripped of his U.S. citizenship when extradited but later returned to the United States after the Supreme Court of Israel overturned his sentence there.[83]

## Police Fraud

During the 1995 double-murder trial of O. J. Simpson, defense attorneys suggested that evidence against Simpson had been concocted and planted by police officers with a personal dislike of the defendant. In particular, defense attorneys pointed a finger at Los Angeles Police Detective Mark Fuhrman, suggesting that he had planted a bloody glove at the Simpson estate and had tampered with bloodstain evidence taken from Simpson's Ford Bronco. To support allegations that Fuhrman was motivated by racist leanings, defense attorneys subpoenaed tapes Fuhrman had made over a ten-year period with a North Carolina screenwriter who had been documenting life within the Los Angeles Police Department.

As one observer put it, however, the defense of police fraud builds on extreme paranoia about the government and police agencies. This type of defense, said Francis Fukuyama,

Log on to ResearchNavigator .com, and choose "All" under the *New York Times* subject archive section. Enter the word "insanity" (without the quotation marks) in the search box, and click "Go." Ignore any non-law-related "hits" on the results page, and select two articles that you find interesting. (If there are no results, or none that you find interesting, choose a different word that is related to the chapter, for instance, "justification.") Write a summary of each article, including complete source information— that is, article title, author (if available), date of publication, and source (in this case, the *New York Times*). Submit what you have written to your instructor if asked to do so. *Note:* This feature is available only if your instructor has chosen the Research Navigator option available with a new textbook.

Innovative Defenses

Legal Authority
and the Criminal Law

carries "to extremes a distrust of government and the belief that public authorities are in a vast conspiracy to violate the rights of individuals."[84] It can also be extremely unfair to innocent people, because a strategy of this sort subjects otherwise well-meaning public servants to intense public scrutiny, effectively shifting attention away from criminal defendants and onto the police officers—sometimes with disastrous personal results. Anthony Pellicano, a private investigator hired by Fuhrman's lawyers, put it this way: "[Fuhrman's] life right now is in the toilet. He has no job, no future. People think he's a racist. He can't do anything to help himself. He's been ordered not to talk. His family and friends, he's told them not to get involved. . . . Mark Fuhrman's life is ruined. For what? Because he found a key piece of evidence."[85] The 43-year-old Fuhrman retired from police work before the Simpson trial concluded and has since written two books.

## SUMMARY

Law are rules of conduct, usually found enacted in the form of statutes, that regulate relationships between people and also between parties. Hence, one of the primary functions of the law is the maintenance of public order. Generally speaking, laws reflect the values held by the society that created them, and legal systems throughout the world reflect the experience of the society of which they are a part. The emphasis placed by any law on individual rights, personal property, and criminal reformation and punishment can tell us much about the cultural and philosophical basis of the society that created it.

The rule of law, the principle that an orderly society must be governed by established principles and known codes that are applied uniformly and fairly to all of its members, is regarded as a vital underpinning of fairness in modern democratic societies. The rule of law holds that no one is above the law, even those who make it.

This chapter identified various types of law, including criminal law, civil law, administrative law, case law, and procedural law. It is concerned primarily, however, with criminal law, which is the form of the law that defines and specifies punishments for offenses of a public nature or for wrongs committed against the state or the society. American criminal law generally distinguishes between serious crimes (felonies) and those that are less grave (misdemeanors). Guilt can be demonstrated, and criminal offenders convicted, only if all of the statutory elements of a particular crime can be proved in court.

Our legal system recognizes a number of defenses to a criminal charge. Primary among them are justifications and excuses. One form of excuse, the insanity defense, has been widely criticized recently, and efforts to reduce its application have been under way for more than a decade.

## DISCUSSION QUESTIONS

1. What is common law? What impact does common law have on contemporary American criminal justice?

2. What is the rule of law? What is its purpose in Western democracies? What does it mean to say that "nobody is above the law"?

3. What types of law does this chapter discuss? What purpose does each serve?

4. What five categories of criminal law violations does this chapter discuss? Describe each, and rank the categories in terms of seriousness.

5. List and describe the eight general features of crime that this chapter discusses. What are the "three conjoined elements" that comprise the legal essence of the concept of crime?

6. What is meant by the *corpus delicti* of a crime? How does the *corpus delicti* of a crime differ from the statutory elements that must be proved to convict a particular defendant of committing that crime?

7. What four broad categories of criminal defenses does our legal system recognize? Under what circumstances might each be employed?

8. How does the legal concept of insanity differ from psychiatric explanations of mental illness? Does the insanity defense serve a useful function today? If you could create your own rule for determining insanity in criminal trials, what would it be? How would it differ from existing rules?

Use the Cybrary (http://www.cybrary.info) to locate websites containing state criminal codes. Choose a state, and locate the statutes pertaining to the FBI's eight major crimes. (Remember that the terminology may be different. Whereas the FBI uses the term *rape,* for example, the state you've selected may use *sexual assault.*) After studying the statutes, describe the *corpus delicti* of each major offense, that is, list the elements of each offense that a prosecutor must prove in court to obtain a conviction. Now choose a second state, preferably from a different geographic region of the country. Again, list the elements of each major offense. Compare the way in which those elements are described with the terminology used by the first state you chose. What differences, if any, exist? Submit your findings to your instructor if asked to do so.

To complete this Web Quest online, go to the Web Quest module in Chapter 4 of the *Criminal Justice Today* Companion Website at cjtoday.com.

**NOTES**

i. World of Quotes.com. Web posted at http://www.worldofquotes.com/author/Raymond-Chandler/1/index.html (accessed January 10, 2006).

ii. Gerald Hill and Kathleen Hill, *The Real Life Dictionary of the Law* (Santa Monica, CA: General Publishing Group, 2000). Web posted at http://dictionary.law.com/lookup2.asp (accessed February 21, 2002).

iii. Hill and Hill, *The Real Life Dictionary of the Law.*

iv. Henry Campbell Black, Joseph R. Nolan, and Jacqueline M. Nolan-Haley, *Black's Law Dictionary,* 6th ed. (St. Paul, MN: West, 1990), p. 1003.

v. Office of the White House Press Secretary, "President Signs Class-Action Fairness Act of 2005," February 18, 2005. Web posted at http://www.whitehouse.gov/news/releases/2005/02/20050218-11.html (accessed January 10, 2006).

vi. Martin Luther King, Jr., "Letter from Birmingham Jail," in *Why We Can't Wait* (Minneapolis, MN: Econ-Clad Books, 2000). Web posted at http://quotations.about.com/library/weekly/aa010103a.htm (accessed July 22, 2002).

vii. Daniel Oran, *Oran's Dictionary of the Law* (St. Paul, MN: West, 1983), p. 306.

viii. Black, Nolan, and Nolan-Haley, *Black's Law Dictionary,* p. 24.

ix. The 'Lectric Law Library. Web posted at http://www.lectlaw.com/ref.html (accessed July 28, 2003).

x. "Yates Sentence Set to Be Formalized," Associated Press Online, March 18, 2002.

xi. Richard Cohen, "Are We Insane?" *Washington Post,* March 14, 2002, p. A27.

1. The details for this story come from Maureen Fan, "Iraqi Legal System in Transition: U.S. Occupiers Trying to Re-establish Order Even without Laws," *San Jose Mercury News,* June 7, 2003. Web posted at http://www.bayarea.com/mld/mercurynews/news/world/6036097.htm (accessed June 8, 2003).

2. Ibid.

3. Henry Campbell Black, Joseph R. Nolan, and Jacqueline M. Nolan-Haley, *Black's Law Dictionary,* 6th ed. (St. Paul, MN: West, 1990), p. 884.

4. Ibid.

5. "Traficant Faces Sentencing on Corruption Charges," CNN.com, July 30, 2002. Web posted at http://www.cnn.com/2002/LAW/07/30/traficant.trial.ap/index.html (accessed July 30, 2002).

6. John F. Kennedy, *Profiles in Courage* (New York: Harper and Row, 1956).

7. American Bar Association Section of International and Comparative Law, *The Rule of Law in the United States* (Chicago: American Bar Association, 1958).

8. "'Grand Theft Auto' Led Teen to Kill, Lawyer Claims," MSNBC News, February 15, 2005. Web posted at http://www.msnbc.msn.com/id/6976676.

9. Thomas H. Cohen, *Tort Trials and Verdicts in Large Counties, 2001* (Washington, DC: Bureau of Justice Statistics, 2005).

10. Thomas H. Cohen, *Punitive Damage Awards in Large Counties, 2001* (Washington, DC: Bureau of Justice Statistics, 2005).

11. Thomas H. Cohen, *Federal Tort Trials and Verdicts, 2002–2003* (Washington, DC: Bureau of Justice Statistics, 2005).

12. See Emily Heller, "Paxil Maker Hit with $8 Million Verdict," *National Law Journal* (June 2001).

13. Lief H. Carter, *Reason in Law,* 4th ed. (New York: HarperCollins, 1994).

14. Florida Statutes, Title XLVII, Section 901.16

15. U.S. Sentencing Commission, *Federal Sentencing Guidelines Manual* (St. Paul, MN: West, 1987).

16. Daniel Oran, *Oran's Dictionary of the Law* (St. Paul, MN: West, 1983), p. 306.

17. Black, Nolan, and Nolan-Haley, *Black's Law Dictionary*, p. 24.

18. Much of the information in this paragraph comes from "Hanssen Pleads Guilty to Spying for Moscow," CNN.com Law Center, July 8, 2001. Web posted at http://www.cnn.com/2001/LAW/07/06/hanssen/index.html (accessed September 22, 2001).

19. Jerry Markon, "Convicted Spy Accepts Life Sentence," *Washington Post,* March 21, 2003. Web posted at http://www.washingtonpost.com/wp-dyn/articles/A1276-2003Mar20.html (accessed May 14, 2003); and "Jury Pool in Espionage Trial Asked Thoughts about Death Penalty," CNN.com, January 13, 2003. Web posted at http://www.cnn.com/2003/LAW/01/13/espionage.trial.ap/index.html (accessed May 14, 2003).

20. Specifically, 21 U.S.C. §846.

21. *U.S.* v. *Shabani,* 510 U.S. 1108 (1994).

22. *Gordon* v. *State,* 52 Ala. 3008, 23 Am. Rep. 575 (1875).

23. But not for a more serious degree of homicide, since leaving a young child alone in a tub of water, even if intentional, does not necessarily mean that the person who so acts intends the child to drown.

24. O. W. Holmes, *The Common Law,* Vol. 3 (Boston: Little, Brown, 1881).

25. There is disagreement among some jurists as to whether the crime of statutory rape is a strict liability offense. Some jurisdictions treat it as such and will not accept a reasonable mistake about the victim's age. Others, however, do accept such a mistake as a defense.

26. *State* v. *Stiffler,* 763 P.2d 308 (Idaho App. 1988).

27. John S. Baker, Jr., et al., *Hall's Criminal Law,* 5th ed. (Charlottesville, VA: Michie, 1993), p. 138.

28. The same is not true for procedures within the criminal justice system, which can be modified even after a person has been sentenced and, hence, become retroactive. See, for example, the U.S. Supreme Court case of *California Department of Corrections* v. *Morales,* 514 U.S. 499 (1995), in which the Court allowed changes in the length of time between parole hearings, even though those changes applied to offenders who had already been sentenced.

29. Black, Nolan, and Nolan-Haley, *Black's Law Dictionary*, p. 127.

30. The statute also says, "A mother's breastfeeding of her baby does not under any circumstance violate this section."

31. Common law crimes, of course, are not based on statutory elements.

32. Common law crimes, of course, are not based on statutory elements.

33. *People* v. *Hall* Final Analysis, SkiSafety.com. Web posted at http://www.skisafety.com/amicuscases-hall2.html (accessed August 28, 2005).

34. See *Maughs* v. *Commonwealth,* 181 Va. 117, 120, 23 S.E.2d 784, 786 (1943).

35. *State* v. *Stephenson,* Opinion No. 24403 (South Carolina, 1996). See also *State* v. *Blocker,* 205 S.C. 303, 31 S.E.2d 908 (1944).

36. *State* v. *Kindle,* 71 Mont. 58, 64, 227 (1924).

37. Black, Nolan, and Nolan-Haley, *Black's Law Dictionary*, p. 343.

38. Patrick L. McCloskey and Ronald L. Schoenberg, *Criminal Law Deskbook* (New York: Matthew Bender, 1988), Section 20.03[13].

39. The exception, of course, is that of a trespasser who trespasses in order to commit a more serious crime.

40. Sir Edward Coke, 3 *Institute,* 162.

41. *The Crown* v. *Dudly & Stephens,* 14 Q.B.D. 273, 286, 15 Cox C. C. 624, 636 (1884).

42. "The Rough-Sex Defense," *Time,* May 23, 1988, p. 55.

43. Ibid.

44. "Jury Convicts Condom Rapist," *USA Today,* May 14, 1993, p. 3A.

45. Black, Nolan, and Nolan-Haley, *Black's Law Dictionary*, p. 504.

46. "Girl Charged," Associated Press wire service, northern edition, February 28, 1994.

47. *State of Tennessee* v. *Charles Arnold Ballinger,* No. E2000-01339-CCA-R3-CD (Tenn.Crim.App. 01/09/2000).

48. See, for example, *Montana* v. *Egelhoff,* 116 S.Ct. 2013, 135 L.Ed.2d 361 (1996).

49. "'Rophies' Reported Spreading Quickly throughout the South," *Drug Enforcement Report,* June 23, 1995, pp. 1–5.

50. Laura Parker, "Yates' Murder Conviction Tossed," *USA Today,* January 7, 2005, p. 3A.

51. L. A. Callahan et al., "The Volume and Characteristics of Insanity Defense Pleas: An Eight-State Study," *Bulletin of the American Academy of Psychiatry and the Law,* Vol. 19, No. 4 (1991), pp. 331–338.

52. American Bar Association Standing Committee on Association Standards for Criminal Justice, *Proposed Criminal Justice Mental Health Standards* (Chicago: American Bar Association, 1984).

53. "Mrs. Bobbitt's Defense 'Life Worth More Than Penis,'" Reuters wire service, January 10, 1994.

54. *Durham* v. *U.S.,* 214 F.2d 867, 875 (D.C. Cir. 1954).

55. American Law Institute, *Model Penal Code: Official Draft and Explanatory Notes* (Philadelphia: American Law Institute, 1985).

56. Ibid.

**57.** *U.S.* v. *Brawner,* 471 F.2d 969, 973 (D.C. Cir. 1972).

**58.** See Joan Biskupic, "Insanity Defense: Not a Right; In Montana Case, Justices Give States Option to Prohibit Claim," *Washington Post* wire service, March 29, 1994.

**59.** Ibid.

**60.** *Ford* v. *Wainwright,* 477 U.S. 399, 106 S.Ct. 2595, 91 L.Ed.2d 335 (1986).

**61.** 18 U.S.C. §401.

**62.** *Jones* v. *U.S.,* U.S. Sup. Ct., 33 CrL 3233 (1983).

**63.** *Ake* v. *Oklahoma,* 470 U.S. 68, 105 S.Ct. 1087, 84 L.Ed.2d 53 (1985).

**64.** *Foucha* v. *Louisiana,* 504 U.S. 71 (1992).

**65.** U.S. Sentencing Commission, "Supplement to the 2002 Federal Sentencing Guidelines: Section 5K2.13. Diminished Capacity (Policy Statement)," April 30, 2003. Web posted at http://www.ussc.gov/2002suppb/5K2_13.htm.

**66.** *U.S.* v. *Pohlot,* 827 F.2d 889 (1987).

**67.** Peter Arenella, "The Diminished Capacity and Diminished Responsibility Defenses: Two Children of a Doomed Marriage," *Columbia Law Review,* Vol. 77 (1977), p. 830.

**68.** *U.S.* v. *Brawner,* 471 F.2d 969 (1972).

**69.** Black, Nolan, and Nolan-Haley, *Black's Law Dictionary,* p. 458.

**70.** California Penal Code, §25(a).

**71.** Ibid., §28(b).

**72.** Kevin Sack, "Church Bombing Figure Found to Be Incompetent," *New York Times,* July 17, 2001.

**73.** "Ex-Klansman Guilty in 1963 Church Blast," *USA Today,* May 23, 2002, p. 3A.

**74.** *Time,* March 19, 1984, p. 26.

**75.** Ibid.

**76.** *U.S.* v. *Halper,* 490 U.S. 435 (1989).

**77.** "Dual Prosecution Can Give One Crime Two Punishments," *USA Today,* March 29, 1993, p. 10A.

**78.** *U.S.* v. *Felix,* 112 S.Ct. 1377 (1992).

**79.** See, for example, *Hudson* v. *U.S.,* 18 S.Ct. 488 (1997); and *U.S.* v. *Ursery,* 518 U.S. 267 (1996).

**80.** McCloskey and Schoenberg, *Criminal Law Deskbook,* Section 20.02[4].

**81.** *U.S.* v. *Armstrong,* 116 S.Ct. 1480, 134 L.Ed.2d 687 (1996).

**82.** Speedy Trial Act, 18 U.S.C. §3161. Significant cases involving the U.S. Speedy Trial Act are those of *U.S.* v. *Carter,* 476 U.S. 1138, 106 S.Ct. 2241, 90 L.Ed.2d 688 (1986); and *Henderson* v. *U.S.,* 476 U.S. 321, 106 S.Ct. 1871, 90 L.Ed.2d 299 (1986).

**83.** See Jim McGee, "Judges Increasingly Question U.S. Prosecutors' Conduct," *Washington Post* wire service, November 23, 1993.

**84.** Francis Fukuyama, "Extreme Paranoia about Government Abounds," *USA Today,* August 24, 1995, p. 17A.

**85.** Lorraine Adams, "Simpson Trial Focus Shifts to Detective with Troubling Past," *Washington Post* wire service, August 22, 1995.

# PART 2

# Policing

**RIGHTS OF THE ACCUSED UNDER INVESTIGATION**

Common law, constitutional, statutory, and humanitarian rights of the accused:

- A right against unreasonable searches
- A right against unreasonable arrest
- A right against unreasonable seizures of property
- A right to fair questioning by authorities
- A right to protection from personal harm

These individual rights must be effectively balanced against these community concerns:

- The efficient apprehension of offenders
- The prevention of crimes

How does our system of justice work toward balance?

## To Protect and to Serve

Famed police administrator and former New York City Police Commissioner Patrick V. Murphy once said, "It is a privilege to be a police officer in a democratic society." While Murphy's words still ring true, many of today's law enforcement officers might hear in them only the echo of a long-dead ideal, unrealistic for today's times.

America's police officers form the front line in the unending battle against crime—a battle that seems to get more sinister and more demanding with each passing day. It is the police who are called when a crime is in progress or when one has been committed. The police are expected to objectively and impartially investigate law violations, gather evidence, solve crimes, and make arrests resulting in the successful prosecution of suspects—all the while adhering to strict due process standards set forth in the U.S. Constitution and enforced by the courts. The chapters in this section of *Criminal Justice Today* provide an overview of the historical development of policing; describe law enforcement agencies at the federal, state, and local levels; explore issues related to police administration; and discuss the due process and legal environments surrounding police activity.

As you will see, although the police are ultimately charged with protecting the public, they often believe that members of the public do not accord them the respect they deserve, and they feel that the distance between the police and the public is not easily bridged. Within the last few decades, however, an image of policing has emerged that may do much to heal that divide. This model, known as *community policing*, goes well beyond traditional conceptions of the police as mere law enforcers and encompasses the idea that police agencies should take counsel from the communities they serve. Under this model, the police are expected to prevent crime, as well as solve it, and to help members of the community deal with other pressing social issues.

5

**Policing:
History
and Structure**

6

**Policing:
Purpose
and
Organization**

7

**Policing:
Legal
Aspects**

8

**Policing:
Issues
and
Challenges**

# CHAPTER 5

# Policing: History and Structure

## OUTLINE

- Introduction
- Historical Development of the Police
- American Law Enforcement Today: From the Federal to the Local Level
- Federal Agencies
- State Agencies
- Local Agencies
- Private Protective Services

## LEARNING OBJECTIVES

**After reading this chapter, you should be able to:**

- Summarize the historical development of policing in America, including the impact of the Prohibition era on American policing.
- Describe the nature of scientific police studies, and explain the significance they hold for law enforcement practice today.
- Describe the three major levels of public law enforcement in the United States today.
- Describe the nature and extent of private protective services in the United States today, and describe the role these services might play in the future.
- Explain the relationship between private security and public policing in America today.

*The police in the United States are not separate from the people. They draw their authority from the will and consent of the people, and they recruit their officers from them. The police are the instrument of the people to achieve and maintain order; their efforts are founded on principles of public service and ultimate responsibility to the public.*

—National Advisory Commission on Criminal Justice Standards and Goals

"Unlike the soldier fighting a war on foreign soil, police officers, who provide for our safety at home, have never been given the honor that was their due."

—Hubert Williams, President, The Police Foundation[1]

## KEY CONCEPTS

### TERMS

bobbies
Bow Street Runners
*comes stabuli*
directed patrol
evidence-based policing
Exemplary Projects Program
federal law enforcement agency

Kansas City experiment
Law Enforcement Assistance
    Administration (LEAA)
municipal police department
new police
night watch
private protective services

scientific police management
sheriff
Statute of Winchester
sworn officer
vigilantism
Wickersham Commission

### NAMES

Henry Fielding
Richard Mayne

Patrick V. Murphy
Robert Peel

Charles Rowan

# Introduction

Hear the author discuss
this chapter at
**cjtoday.com**

If you want the present to be
different from the past, study the
past.

—Baruch Spinoza (1632–1677)

Many of the techniques used by today's police differ quite a bit from those employed in days gone by. Listen to how a policeman, writing in the mid-1800s, describes the way pickpockets were caught in London 200 years ago: "I walked forth the day after my arrival, rigged out as the very model of a gentleman farmer, and with eyes, mouth, and pockets wide open, and a stout gold-headed cane in my hand, strolled leisurely through the fashionable thoroughfares, the pump-rooms, and the assembly-rooms, like a fat goose waiting to be plucked. I wore a pair of yellow gloves well wadded, to save me from falling, through a moment's inadvertency, into my own snare, which consisted of about fifty fish-hooks, large black hackles, firmly sewn barb downward, into each of the pockets of my brand new leather breeches. The most blundering 'prig' alive might have easily got his hand to the bottom of my pockets, but to get it out again, without tearing every particle of flesh from the bones, was a sheer impossibility. . . . I took care never to see any of my old customers until the convulsive tug at one or other of the pockets announced the capture of a thief. I then coolly linked my arm in that of the prisoner, [and] told him in a confidential whisper who I was."[2]

British "bobbies." Today's uniformed English police officers have a recognizable appearance rooted in the time of Sir Robert Peel.

*Comstock Images*

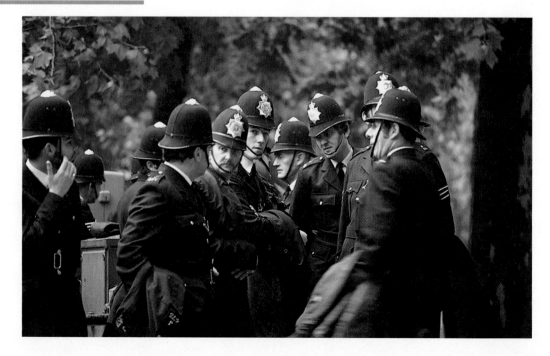

# Historical Development of the Police

Police tactics and strategy have changed substantially since historical times, and many different kinds of police agencies—some of them highly specialized—function within the modern criminal justice system. This chapter describes the development of organized policing in Western culture and discusses the function of contemporary American police forces at the federal, state, and local levels. Agency examples are given at each level. The promise held by private protective services, the recent rapid growth of private security organizations, and the quasi-private system of justice are also discussed.

## English Roots

The rise of the police as an organized force in the Western world coincided with the evolution of strong centralized governments. Although police forces have developed throughout the world, often in isolation from one another, the historical growth of the English police is of special significance to students of criminal justice in America, for it was on the British model that much of early American policing was based.

Efforts at law enforcement in early Britain, except for military intervention in the pursuit of bandits and habitual thieves, were not well organized until around the year A.D. 1200.[3] When a person committed an offense and could be identified, he or she was usually pursued by an organized posse. All able-bodied men who could hear a victim's cry for help were obligated to join the posse in a common effort to apprehend the offender. The posse was led by the shire reeve (the leader of the county) or by a mounted officer (the **comes stabuli**). Our modern words *sheriff* and *constable* are derived from these early terms. The *comites stabuli* (the plural form of the term) were not uniformed, nor were they numerous enough to perform all the tasks we associate today with law enforcement. This early system, employing a small number of mounted officers, depended for its effectiveness on the ability to organize and direct the efforts of citizens toward criminal apprehension.

The offender, cognizant of a near-certain end at the hands of the posse, often sought protection from trusted friends and family. As a consequence, feuds developed among organized groups of citizens, some seeking revenge and some siding with the offender. Suspects who lacked the shelter of a sympathetic group might flee into a church and invoke the time-honored custom of sanctuary. Sanctuary was rarely an ideal escape, however, as pursuers could surround the church and wait out the offender, preventing food and water from being carried inside. The offender, once caught, became the victim. Guilt was usually assumed, and trials were rare. Public executions, often involving torture, typified this early justice and served to provide a sense of communal solidarity as well as group retribution.

The development of law enforcement in English cities and towns grew out of an early reliance on bailiffs, or watchmen. Bailiffs were assigned the task of maintaining a **night watch**, primarily to detect fires and spot thieves. While too few in number to handle most emergencies, bailiffs were able to rouse the sleeping population, which could then deal with whatever crisis was at hand. Larger cities expanded the idea of bailiffs by creating both a night watch and a day ward.

British police practices became codified in the **Statute of Winchester**, written in 1285. The statute (1) specified the creation of the watch and the ward in cities and towns; (2) mandated the draft of eligible males to serve those forces; (3) institutionalized the use of the *hue and cry,* making citizens who disregarded a call for help subject to criminal penalties; and (4) required that citizens maintain weapons in their home for answering the call to arms.

Some authors have attributed the growth of modern police forces to the gin riots that plagued London and other European cities in the eighteenth and nineteenth centuries. The invention of gin around 1720 provided, for the first time, a potent and inexpensive alcoholic drink readily available to the massed populations gathered in the early industrial ghettos of eighteenth-century cities. Seeking to drown their troubles, huge numbers of people, far beyond the ability of the bailiffs to control, began binges of drinking and rioting. During the next hundred years, these gin riots created an immense social problem for British authorities. By this time, the bailiff system had broken down and was staffed by groups of woefully inadequate substitutes, hired by original draftees to perform duties in their stead. Incompetent and unable to depend on the citizenry for help in enforcing the laws, bailiffs became targets of mob violence and were often attacked and beaten for sport.

**comes stabuli**

A nonuniformed mounted law enforcement officer of medieval England. Early police forces were small and relatively unorganized but made effective use of local resources in the formation of posses, the pursuit of offenders, and the like.

**night watch**

An early form of police patrol in English cities and towns.

**Statute of Winchester**

A law, written in 1285, that created a watch and ward system in English cities and towns and that codified early police practices.

**Bow Street Runners**

An early English police unit formed under the leadership of Henry Fielding, magistrate of the Bow Street region of London.

**new police**

A police force formed in 1829 under the command of Sir Robert Peel. It became the model for modern-day police forces throughout the Western world.

**bobbies**

The popular British name given to members of Sir Robert (Bob) Peel's Metropolitan Police Force.

## The Bow Street Runners

The early eighteenth century saw the emergence in London of a large criminal organization led by Jonathan Wild. Wild ran a type of fencing operation built around a group of loosely organized robbers, thieves, and burglars who would turn their plunder over to him. Wild would then negotiate with the legitimate owners for a ransom of their possessions.

The police response to Wild was limited by disinterest and corruption. However, change began when Henry Fielding, a well-known writer, became the magistrate of the Bow Street region of London. Fielding attracted a force of dedicated officers, dubbed the **Bow Street Runners**, who soon stood out as the best and most disciplined enforcement agents that London had to offer. Fielding's personal inspiration and his ability to communicate what he saw as the social needs of the period may have accounted for his success.

In February 1725, Wild was arrested and arraigned on the following charges: "(1) that for many years past he had been a confederate with great numbers of highwaymen, pick-pockets, house-breakers, shop-lifters, and other thieves, (2) that he had formed a kind of corporation of thieves, of which he was the head or director . . . , (3) that he had divided the town and country into so many districts, and appointed distinct gangs for each, who regularly accounted with him for their robberies . . . , (4) that the persons employed by him were for the most part felon convicts . . . , (5) that he had, under his care and direction, several warehouses for receiving and concealing stolen goods, and also a ship for carrying off jewels, watches, and other valuable goods, to Holland, where he had a superannuated thief for his benefactor, and (6) that he kept in his pay several artists to make alterations, and transform watches, seals, snuff-boxes, rings, and other valuable things, that they might not be known."[4] Convicted of these and other crimes, Wild attempted suicide by drinking a large amount of laudanum, an opium compound. The drug merely rendered him senseless, and he was hanged the following morning, having only partially recovered from its effects.

In 1754, Henry Fielding died. His brother John took over his work and occupied the position of Bow Street magistrate for another 25 years. The Bow Street Runners remain famous to this day for quality police work.

## The New Police

In 1829, Sir Robert Peel, who later became prime minister of England, formed what many have hailed as the world's first modern police force. Passage of the Metropolitan Police Act that same year allocated the resources for Peel's force of 1,000 handpicked men. The London Metropolitan Police Force, also known as the **new police** or more simply the "Met," soon became a model for police forces around the world.

Members of the Metropolitan Police were quickly dubbed **bobbies**, after their founder. London's bobbies were organized around two principles: the belief that it was possible to discourage crime, and the practice of preventive patrol. Peel's police patrolled the streets by walking beats. Their predecessors, the watchmen, had occupied fixed posts throughout the city, awaiting a public outcry. The new police were uniformed, resembling a military organization, and adopted a military administrative style.

Judge Roy Bean (seated on barrel) holding court in Langtry, Texas, circa 1900.

*Culver Pictures, Inc.*

London's first two police commissioners were Colonel Charles Rowan, a career military officer, and Richard Mayne, a lawyer. Rowan believed that mutual respect between the police and the citizenry would be crucial to the success of the new force. As a consequence, early bobbies were chosen for their ability to reflect and inspire the highest personal ideals among young men in early-nineteenth-century Britain.

The new police were not immediately well received. Some elements of the population saw them as an occupying army, and open battles between the police and the citizenry ensued. The tide of sentiment turned, however, when an officer was viciously killed in the Cold Bath Fields riot of 1833. A jury, considering a murder charge against the killer, returned a verdict of "not guilty," inspiring a groundswell of public support for the much-maligned force.

# The Early American Experience

Early American law enforcement efforts were based to some degree on the British experience. Towns and cities in colonial America depended on modified versions of the night watch and the day ward, but the unique experience of the American colonies quickly differentiated the needs of colonists from those of the masses remaining in Europe. Huge expanses of uncharted territory, vast wealth, a widely dispersed population engaged mostly in agriculture, and a sometimes ferocious frontier all combined to mold American law enforcement in a distinctive way. Recent writers on the history of the American police have observed that policing in America was originally "decentralized," "geographically dispersed," "idiosyncratic," and "highly personalized."[5]

## The Frontier

One of the major factors determining the development of American law enforcement was the frontier, which remained vast and wild until late in the nineteenth century. The backwoods areas provided a natural haven for outlaws and bandits. Henry Berry Lowery, a famous outlaw of the Carolinas, the James Gang, and many lesser-known desperadoes felt at home in the unclaimed swamps and forests.

Only the boldest of settlers tried to police the frontier. Among them was Charles Lynch, a Virginia farmer of the late eighteenth century. Lynch and his associates tracked and punished offenders, often according to the dictates of the still well-known lynch law, or vigilante justice, which they originated. Citizen posses and vigilante groups were often the only law available to settlers on the western frontier. Judge Roy Bean ("the Law West of the Pecos"), "Wild Bill" Hickok, Bat Masterson, Wyatt Earp, and Pat Garrett were other popular figures of the nineteenth century who took it upon themselves, sometimes in semiofficial capacities, to enforce the law on the books as well as the standards of common decency.

Although today **vigilantism** has a negative connotation, most of the original vigilantes of the American West were honest men and women trying to forge an organized and predictable lifestyle out of the challenging situations that they encountered. Often faced with unscrupulous, money-hungry desperadoes, they did what they could to bring the standards of civilization, as they understood them, to bear in their communities.

| **vigilantism** |
| --- |
| The act of taking the law into one's own hands. |

## Policing America's Early Cities

Small-scale, organized law enforcement came into being quite early in America's larger cities. In 1658, paid watchmen were hired by the city of New York to replace drafted citizens.[6] By 1693, the first uniformed officer was employed by the city, and in 1731, the first neighborhood station, or precinct, was constructed. Boston, Cincinnati, and New Orleans were among the American communities to follow the New York model and hire a force of watchmen in the early nineteenth century.

In 1829, American leaders closely watched as Sir Robert Peel created London's new police. One year later, Stephen Girard, a wealthy manufacturer, donated a considerable amount of money to the city of Philadelphia to create a capable police force. The city hired 120 men to staff a night watch and 24 to perform similar duties during the day.

In 1844, New York's separate day and night forces were combined into the New York City Police Department. Boston followed suit in 1855. Further advances in American policing were precluded by the Civil War. Southern cities captured in the war came under martial law and were subject to policing by the military.

The coming of the twentieth century, coinciding as it did with numerous technological advances and significant social changes, brought a flood of reform. The International Association of Chiefs of Police (IACP) was formed in 1902; it immediately moved to create a nationwide clearinghouse for

A New York City police officer "mugging" a prisoner in the early days of police photography.

*Courtesy of the Library of Congress*

criminal identification. In 1915, the Fraternal Order of Police (FOP) initiated operations. It was patterned after labor unions but prohibited strikes; it accepted personnel of all ranks, from patrol officer to chief. In 1910, Alice Stebbins Wells became the first policewoman in the world, serving with the Los Angeles Police Department.[7] Prior to Wells's appointment, women had served as jail matrons, and widows had sometimes been carried on police department payrolls after their officer-husbands had died in the line of duty, but they had not been fully "sworn" with carrying out the duties of a police officer. Wells became an outspoken advocate for the hiring of more policewomen, and police departments across the country began to hire female officers, especially to provide police services to children and to women and to "protect male officers from delicate and troublesome situations"[8]—such as the need to physically restrain female offenders.

In 1915, the U.S. Census reported that 25 cities employed policewomen. In that year, coinciding with the creation of the FOP, the International Association of Policewomen (now the International Association of Women Police) was formed in the city of Baltimore. In 1918, Ellen O'Grady became the first woman to hold a high administrative post in a major police organization when she was promoted to the rank of deputy police commissioner for the city of New York. As Dorothy Moses Schulz, a contemporary commentator on women's entry into policing, has observed, "The Policewomen's movement was not an isolated phenomenon, but was part of women's movement into other newly created or newly professionalized fields."[9]

During the early twentieth century, telephones, automobiles, and radios all had their impact on the American police. Teddy Roosevelt, the twenty-sixth president of the United States, began his career by serving as a police commissioner in New York City from 1895 to 1897. While there, he promoted the use of a call-box system of telephones, which allowed citizens to report crimes rapidly and made it possible for officers to quickly call for assistance. As president, Roosevelt helped to organize the Bureau of Investigation, which later became the Federal Bureau of Investigation (FBI). Federal law enforcement already existed in the form of U.S. marshals, created by an act of Congress in 1789, and in the form of postal inspectors, authorized by the U.S. Postal Act of 1829. The FBI became a national investigative service designed to quickly identify and apprehend offenders charged with a growing list of federal offenses. Automobiles created an era of affordable, rapid transportation and gave police forces far-reaching powers and high mobility. Telephones and radios provided the ability to maintain regular communication with central authorities. State police agencies arose to counter the threat of the mobile offender, with Massachusetts and Pennsylvania leading the way to statewide forces.

## Prohibition and Police Corruption

A dark period for American law enforcement agencies began in 1920 with the passage of a constitutional prohibition against all forms of alcoholic beverages. Until Prohibition was repealed in 1933, most parts of the country were rife with criminal activity, much of it supporting the trade

Detroit police officers inspecting equipment found in an illegal underground brewery during the Prohibition era. The constitutional prohibition against alcoholic beverages during the 1920s and early 1930s had a significant impact on police operations throughout America and opened the door for potential corruption of law enforcement personnel.
*© CORBIS*

in bootlegged liquor. Bootleggers earned huge sums of money, and some of them became quite wealthy. Massive wealth in the hands of law violators greatly increased the potential for corruption among police officials, some of whom were "paid off" to support bootlegging operations.

In 1931, the **Wickersham Commission**, officially called the National Commission on Law Observance and Enforcement, and led by former U.S. Attorney General George W. Wickersham, recognized that Prohibition was unenforceable and reported that it carried a great potential for police corruption.[10] The commission, which released a number of reports, also established guidelines for enforcement agencies, which directed many aspects of American law enforcement until the 1970s. The most influential of the Wickersham Commission reports was entitled *Report on the Enforcement of the Prohibition Laws of the United States.* That report, the release of which became one of the most important events in the history of American policing, can be read in its entirety at **Library Extra 5–1** at cjtoday.com.

## The Last Half of the Twentieth Century

The rapid cultural change that took place throughout America in the 1960s and 1970s forever altered the legal and social environment in which the police must work. During that period, in conjunction with a burgeoning civil rights movement, the U.S. Supreme Court frequently enumerated constitutionally based personal rights for those facing arrest, investigation, and criminal prosecution. Although a "chipping away" at those rights, which some say is continuing today, may have begun in the 1980s, the earlier emphasis placed on the rights of defendants undergoing criminal investigation and prosecution will have a substantial impact on law enforcement activities for many years to come.

The 1960s and 1970s were also a period of intense examination of police operations, from day-to-day enforcement decisions to administrative organization and police–community relations. In 1967, the President's Commission on Law Enforcement and Administration of Justice issued its report, *The Challenge of Crime in a Free Society,* which found that the police were often isolated from the communities they served.[11] In 1969, the **Law Enforcement Assistance Administration (LEAA)** was formed to assist police forces across the nation in acquiring the latest in technology and in adopting new enforcement methods. In 1973, the National Advisory Commission on Criminal Justice Standards and Goals issued a comprehensive report detailing strategies for combating and preventing crime and for improving the quality of law enforcement efforts at all levels.[12] Included in the report was a call for greater participation in police work by women and ethnic minorities and the recommendation that a college degree be made a basic prerequisite for police employment by the 1980s. The creation of a third major commission, the National Commission on Crime Prevention and Control, was authorized by the federal Violent Crime Control and Law

**Wickersham Commission**

The National Commission on Law Observance and Enforcement. In 1931, the commission issued a report stating that Prohibition was unenforceable and carried a great potential for police corruption.

**LIBRARY EXTRA**

**Law Enforcement Assistance Administration (LEAA)**

A now-defunct federal agency established under Title I of the Omnibus Crime Control and Safe Streets Act of 1968 to funnel federal funding to state and local law enforcement agencies.

WEB EXTRA

Enforcement Act of 1994, but the commission never saw the light of day.[13] Read about the crime commission that never was at Web Extra 5–1 at cjtoday.com.

# Scientific Police Management

**scientific police management**

The application of social science techniques to the study of police administration for the purpose of increasing effectiveness, reducing the frequency of citizen complaints, and enhancing the efficient use of available resources.

In 1969, with the passage of the Omnibus Crime Control and Safe Streets Act, the U.S. Congress created the Law Enforcement Assistance Administration. LEAA was charged with combating crime through the expenditure of huge amounts of money in support of crime-prevention and crime-reduction programs. Some have compared the philosophy establishing LEAA to that which supported the American space program's goal of landing people on the moon: Put enough money into any problem, and it will be solved! Unfortunately, the crime problem was more difficult to address than the challenge of a moon landing; even after the expenditure of nearly $8 billion, LEAA had not come close to its goal. In 1982, LEAA expired when Congress refused it further funding.

The legacy of LEAA is an important one for police managers, however. The research-rich years of 1969 to 1982, supported largely through LEAA funding, have left a plethora of scientific findings relevant to police administration and, more importantly, have established a tradition of program evaluation within police management circles. This tradition, which is known as **scientific police management**, is a natural outgrowth of LEAA's insistence that every funded program contain a plan for its evaluation. *Scientific police management* refers to the application of social science techniques to the study of police administration for the purpose of increasing effectiveness, reducing the frequency of citizen complaints, and enhancing the efficient use of available resources. The heyday of scientific police management occurred in the 1970s, when federal monies were far more readily available than they are today to support such studies.

LEAA was not alone in funding police research during the 1970s. On July 1, 1970, the Ford Foundation announced the establishment of a Police Development Fund totaling $30 million, to be spent during the following five years to support major crime-fighting strategies of police departments. This funding led to the establishment of the Police Foundation, which continues to exist today with the mission of "foster[ing] improvement and innovation in American policing."[14] Police Foundation–sponsored studies during the past 20 years have added to the growing body of scientific knowledge about policing.

Today, federal support for criminal justice research and evaluation continues under the National Institute of Justice (NIJ) and the Bureau of Justice Statistics (BJS), both part of the Office of Justice Programs (OJP). OJP, created by Congress in 1984, provides federal leadership in developing the nation's capacity to prevent and control crime. The National Criminal Justice Reference Service (NCJRS), a part of NIJ, assists researchers nationwide in locating information applicable to their research projects. "Custom searches" of the NCJRS computer database can be done online and can yield voluminous information in most criminal justice subject areas. NIJ also publishes a series of informative periodic reports such as the *NIJ Journal* and *NIJ Research in Review*, which serve to keep criminal justice practitioners and researchers informed about recent findings. View the NIJ online publication list at Web Extra 5–2 at cjtoday.com.

WEB EXTRA

## Exemplary Projects

**Exemplary Projects Program**

An initiative, sponsored by the Law Enforcement Assistance Administration, designed to recognize outstanding innovative efforts to combat crime and to provide assistance to crime victims.

In 1973, LEAA established the **Exemplary Projects Program**, which was designed to recognize outstanding innovative efforts to combat crime and to provide assistance to crime victims so that such initiatives might serve as models for the nation. One project that won exemplary status early in the program was the Street Crimes Unit (SCU) of the New York City Police Department. The SCU disguised officers as potential mugging victims and put them in areas where they were most likely to be attacked. In its first year, the SCU made nearly 4,000 arrests and averaged a successful conviction rate of around 80%. Perhaps the most telling statistic was the "average officer days per arrest." The SCU invested only 8.2 days in each arrest, whereas the department average for all uniformed officers was 167 days per arrest.[15]

Many other programs were supported and evaluated. The Hidden Cameras Project in Seattle, Washington, for example, utilized cameras hidden in convenience stores, which were triggered when a "trip" bill in the cash register drawer was removed. The clearance rate for robberies of businesses with hidden cameras was twice that of other similar businesses. The conviction rate for photographed robbers was more than twice that of suspects arrested for robbing stores without cameras. Commercial robbery in Seattle decreased by 38% in the first year of the project.

# The Kansas City Experiment

By far the most famous application of social research principles to police management was the Kansas City preventive patrol experiment.[16] Sponsored by the Police Foundation, the year-long **Kansas City experiment** had its results published in 1974. The study divided the southern part of Kansas City into 15 areas. Five of these "beats" were patrolled in the usual fashion. Another five beats experienced a doubling of patrol activities by having twice the normal number of patrol officers assigned to them. The final third of the beats received a novel "treatment" indeed: No patrols were assigned to them, and no uniformed officers entered that part of the city unless they were called. The program was kept secret, and citizens were unaware of the difference between the patrolled and unpatrolled parts of the city.

The results of the Kansas City experiment were surprising. Records of "preventable crimes," those toward which the activities of patrol were oriented—such as burglary, robbery, auto theft, larceny, and vandalism—showed no significant differences in rate of occurrence among the three experimental beats. Similarly, citizens didn't seem to notice the change in patrol patterns in the two areas where patrol frequency was changed. Surveys conducted at the conclusion of the experiment showed no difference in citizens' fear of crime before and after the study. The 1974 study can be summed up in the words of the author of the final report: "The whole idea of riding around in cars to create a feeling of omnipresence just hasn't worked. . . . Good people with good intentions tried something that logically should have worked, but didn't."[17] This study has been credited with beginning the now-established tradition of scientific studies of policing.

A second Kansas City study focused on "response time."[18] It found that even consistently fast police response to citizen reports of crime had little effect on citizen satisfaction with the police or on the arrest of suspects. The study uncovered the fact that most reports made to the police came only after a considerable amount of time had passed. Hence, the police were initially handicapped by the timing of the report, and even the fastest police response was not especially effective.

Scientific studies of special significance to law enforcement are summarized in Table 5–1.

## Effects of the Kansas City Studies

The Kansas City studies greatly affected managerial assumptions about the role of preventive patrol and traditional strategies for responding to citizen calls for assistance. As Joseph Lewis, then director of evaluation at the Police Foundation, said, "I think that now almost everyone would agree that almost anything you do is better than random patrol."[19]

While the Kansas City studies called into question some basic assumptions about patrol, patrol remains the backbone of police work. New patrol strategies for the effective utilization of human resources have led to various kinds of **directed patrol** activities. One form of directed patrol varies the number of officers involved in patrolling according to the time of day or the frequency

**Kansas City experiment**

The first large-scale scientific study of law enforcement practices. Sponsored by the Police Foundation, it focused on the practice of preventive patrol.

**directed patrol**

A police management strategy designed to increase the productivity of patrol officers through the scientific analysis and evaluation of patrol techniques.

Members of the Kansas City (Missouri) Police Department being briefed on security measures for a planned city tour by President George W. Bush. Scientific police management was given early credence by studies of preventive patrol undertaken in Kansas City in 1974.

*Courtesy of the Media Office of the Kansas City, Missouri, Police Department*

TABLE 5–1

## SELECTED SCIENTIFIC STUDIES IN LAW ENFORCEMENT

| Year | Study Name | Focus |
|---|---|---|
| 2002 | Reducing Gun Violence (Indianapolis) | Targeted police patrols to reduce gun crime and violence |
| 2001 | Boston's Operation Ceasefire Evaluation | Citywide effort to reduce gun violence, especially gang-related homicides |
| 1999 | National Evaluation of Weed-and-Seed Programs | Weed-and-seed programs in eight states |
| 1998 | Community Policing in Action (Indianapolis) | Police and citizen cooperation and neighborhood security |
| 1994 | Kansas City Gun Experiment | Supplemental police patrol to reduce gun crime |
| 1992 | New York City Police Department's Cadet Corps Study | Level of education among officers and hiring of minority officers |
| 1992 | Metro-Dade Spouse Abuse Experiment Replication (Florida) | Replication of a 1984 Minneapolis study |
| 1991 | Quality Policing in Madison, Wisconsin | Community policing and participatory police management |
| 1990 | Minneapolis "Hot Spot" Patrolling | Intensive patrol of problem areas |
| 1987 | Newport News Problem-Oriented Policing (Virginia) | Police solutions to community crime problems |
| 1986 | Crime Stoppers: A National Evaluation | Media crime-reduction programs |
| 1986 | Reducing Fear of Crime in Houston and Newark | Strategies for fear reduction among urban populations |
| 1984 | Minneapolis Domestic Violence Experiment | Effective police action in domestic violence situations |
| 1981 | Newark Foot Patrol Experiment | Costs versus benefits of foot patrol |
| 1977 | Cincinnati Team Policing Experiment | Team versus traditional policing |
| 1977 | Patrol Staffing in San Diego | One- versus two-officer units |
| 1976 | Police Response Time (Kansas City) | Citizen satisfaction with police response |
| 1976 | Police and Interpersonal Conflict | Police intervention in domestic and other disputes |
| 1976 | Managing Investigations | Detective/patrol officer teams |
| 1976 | Kansas City Peer Review Panel | Improvement in police behavior |
| 1974 | Kansas City Preventive Patrol Experiment | Effectiveness of police patrol |

of reported crimes within an area, so as to put the most officers on the street where and when crime is most prevalent. Wilmington, Delaware, was one of the first cities to make use of split-force patrol, in which only a part of the patrol force performs routine patrol.[20] The remaining officers respond to calls for service, take reports, and conduct investigations.

In response to the Kansas City study on response time, some cities have prioritized calls for service,[21] ordering a quick police response only when crimes are in progress or when serious crimes have occurred. Less significant offenses, such as minor larcenies and certain citizen complaints, are handled through the mail or by having citizens come to the police station to make a report.

## Recent Studies

Early scientific studies of policing, such as the Kansas City patrol experiment, were designed to identify and probe some of the basic assumptions that guided police work throughout the twentieth century. The initial response to many such studies was "Why should we study that? Everybody knows the answer already!" As in the case of the Kansas City experiment, however, it soon became obvious that conventional wisdom was not always correct. The value of applying evaluative techniques to police work can also be seen in the following, more recent, studies:

- A study was conducted in 2002 of directed police patrols in Indianapolis that were targeted at reducing gun violence. The study found that targeted patrols can effectively reduce gun crime and that they can produce substantially better results than routine policing.[22]

- The 2001 evaluation of Boston's gun project, known as Operation Ceasefire, determined that the project, a problem-oriented policing initiative targeting homicide victimization among the city's youths, was successful in its implementation.[23]

- A national evaluation of weed-and-seed programs was conducted in eight states in 1999. The weed-and-seed program is a community-based anticrime approach that links intensified geographically targeted law enforcement efforts by police and prosecutors with local neighborhood-improvement initiatives and human services programs. It found that the effectiveness of the weed-and-seed philosophy varied considerably. The programs that worked best were those that relied on bottom-up, participatory decision-making approaches, especially when combined with efforts to build capacity and partnerships among local organizations.[24] Learn more about the national weed-and-seed evaluation at Library Extra 5–2 at cjtoday.com. You can also read about neighborhood attitudes toward crime and how they affect the police at Library Extra 5–3.

LIBRARY EXTRA

- The 1994 Kansas City Gun Experiment was designed to "learn whether vigorous enforcement of existing gun laws could reduce gun crime." The Kansas City Police Department's weed-and-seed program targeted areas designated as "hot spots" within the city. These were locations identified by computer analysis as having the most gun-related crimes within the metropolitan area. A special gun-detection unit was assigned to the area, and guns were removed from citizens following searches incident to arrest for other, non-gun-related crimes, at traffic stops, and as the result of other legal stop-and-frisk activities. While the program was in operation, gun crimes declined by 49% in the target area, while they increased slightly in a comparison area. Drive-by shootings, which dropped from seven (in the six months prior to the program) to only one following implementation of the program, were particularly affected.[25] Learn more about the Kansas City Gun Experiment at Library Extra 5–4 at cjtoday.com.

LIBRARY EXTRA

- The 1984 Minneapolis Domestic Violence Experiment was the first scientifically engineered social experiment to test the impact of arrest (versus alternative forms of disposition) on crime.[26] In this case, the crime in focus was violence in the home. Investigators found that offenders who were arrested were less likely to commit repeat offenses than were those who were handled in some other fashion. A Police Foundation–sponsored study of domestic violence in the Metro-Dade (Florida) area in 1992 reinforced the Minneapolis findings but found that the positive effect of arrest applied almost solely to those who were employed.

- In the late 1980s, the police in Newport News, Virginia, decided to test traditional incident-driven policing against a new approach called *problem-oriented policing*.[27] Incident-driven policing mobilizes police forces to respond to complaints and offenses reported by citizens. It is what the Newport News police called "the standard method for delivering police services." Problem-oriented policing, on the other hand, was developed in Newport News to identify critical crime problems in the community and to effectively address the underlying causes of crime. For example, one identified problem was thefts from vehicles parked in the Newport News shipbuilding yard. As many as 36,000 cars were parked in those lots during the day. Applying the principles of problem-oriented policing, Newport News officers explored the dimensions of the problem. After identifying theft-prone lots and a small group of frequent offenders, officers arrested one suspect in the act of breaking into a vehicle. That suspect provided the information police were seeking: It turned out that drugs were the real target of the car thieves. The thieves looked for "muscle cars," rock music bumper stickers, and other indicators to identify the cars with the highest potential for yielding drugs. The police learned that what seemed to be a simple problem of thefts from automobiles was really a search for drugs by a small group of hard-core offenders. Strategies to address the problem were developed, including wider efforts to reduce illicit drug use throughout the city.

> Of all the ideas in policing, one stands out as the most powerful force for change: Police practices should be based on scientific evidence about what works best.
>
> —Lawrence W. Sherman[i]

These and other studies have established a sound basis for the use of scientific evaluation in police work today. The accumulated wisdom of police management studies was summed up by

Patrick V. Murphy, who, as director of the Police Foundation in 1985, stated five tenets for guiding American policing into the future[28]:

1. Neighborhood policing programs of all kinds need to be developed, improved, and expanded.

2. More police officers need college- and graduate-level education.

3. Police departments should hire more civilians. Civilian specialists can help with department operations and release **sworn officers** for police duties.

4. Departments must continue to become more representative of the communities they serve by recruiting more women and minorities.

5. Restraint in the use of force, especially deadly force, must be increased.

### Evidence-Based Policing

In recent years, scientific studies of policing have culminated in a sustained push toward what noted police researcher Lawrence W. Sherman calls **evidence-based policing**. Evidence-based policing, says Sherman, "is the use of best available research on the outcomes of police work to implement guidelines and evaluate agencies, units, and officers."[29] In other words, evidence-based policing uses research into everyday police procedures to evaluate current practices and to guide officers and police executives in future decision making. In any discussion of evidence-based policing, it is important to remember that the word *evidence* refers to scientific evidence, and not criminal evidence. "The basic premise of evidence-based practice," says Sherman, "is that we are all entitled to our own opinions, but not to our own facts."[30] Our own facts, or our beliefs about the way things should be done, says Sherman, often turn out to be wrong. During the civil rights movement of the 1960s and 1970s, for example, police executives in many areas took a heavy-handed approach in an attempt to control demonstrators. Images of tear-gas-filled streets, the use of high-pressure fire hoses on marchers, and police dogs biting fleeing demonstrators are burned into the minds of many who lived through that era and still appear in televised histories of the period. The heavy-handed approach had unintended consequences and served to inflame protesters. Situations that might have otherwise been contained with simple crowd-control tactics and the use of physical barriers became largely uncontrollable. Sherman reminds us that "the mythic power of subjective and unstructured wisdom holds back every field and keeps it from systematically discovering and implementing what works best in repeated tasks."

# American Law Enforcement Today: From the Federal to the Local Level

The organization of American law enforcement has been called the most complex in the world. Three major legislative and judicial jurisdictions exist in the United States—federal, state, and local—and each has created a variety of police agencies to enforce its laws. Unfortunately, there has been little uniformity among jurisdictions as to the naming, function, or authority of enforcement agencies. The matter is further complicated by the rapid growth of private security firms, which operate on a for-profit basis and provide services that have traditionally been regarded as law enforcement activities.

# Federal Agencies

Dozens of **federal law enforcement agencies** are distributed among 11 U.S. government services (Table 5–2). In addition to the enforcement agencies listed in the table, many other federal government offices are involved in enforcement through inspection, regulation, and control activities. The Federal Bureau of Investigation, one of the best-known federal law enforcement agencies, is described in the paragraphs that follow.

Visit the home pages of many federal law enforcement agencies via Web Extra 5–3 at cjtoday.com. Learn more about staffing levels of federal criminal justice agencies at Library Extra 5–5.

## The Federal Bureau of Investigation

The Federal Bureau of Investigation may be the most famous law enforcement agency in the country and in the world. The FBI has traditionally been held in high regard by many Americans, who think of it as an example of what a law enforcement organization should be and who believe that

---

**sworn officer**

A law enforcement officer who is trained and empowered to perform full police duties, such as making arrests, conducting investigations, and carrying firearms.[ii]

---

**evidence-based policing**

The use of best available research on the outcomes of police work to implement guidelines and evaluate agencies, units, and officers.[iii]

---

**federal law enforcement agency**

A U.S. government agency or office whose primary functional responsibility is the enforcement of federal criminal laws.

---

**TABLE 5-2**

## AMERICAN POLICING: FEDERAL LAW ENFORCEMENT AGENCIES

**Department of Agriculture**
U.S. Forest Service

**Department of Commerce**
Bureau of Export Enforcement
National Marine Fisheries Administration

**Department of Defense**
Air Force Office of Special Investigations
Army Criminal Investigation Division
Defense Criminal Investigative Service
Naval Investigative Service

**Department of Homeland Security**
Federal Law Enforcement Training Center
Federal Protective Service
Transportation Security Administration
U.S. Coast Guard
U.S. Customs and Border Protection (CBP; includes U.S. Border Patrol)
U.S. Immigration and Customs Enforcement (ICE)
U.S. Secret Service

**Department of the Interior**
Bureau of Indian Affairs
Bureau of Land Management
Fish and Wildlife Service
National Park Service
U.S. Park Police

**Department of Justice**
Bureau of Alcohol, Tobacco, Firearms, and Explosives
Bureau of Prisons
Drug Enforcement Administration
Federal Bureau of Investigation
U.S. Marshals Service

**Department of Labor**
Office of Labor Racketeering

**Department of State**
Diplomatic Security Service

**Department of Transportation**
Federal Air Marshals Program

**Department of the Treasury**
Internal Revenue Service–Criminal Investigation Division
Treasury Inspector General for Tax Enforcement

**U.S. Postal Service**
Postal Inspection Service

**Other Offices with Enforcement Personnel**
AMTRAK Police
Bureau of Engraving and Printing Police
Department of Energy
Environmental Protection Agency–Criminal Investigations Division
Food and Drug Administration
Tennessee Valley Authority
U.S. Capitol Police
U.S. Mint
U.S. Supreme Court Police
Washington, D.C., Metropolitan Police Department

*Note:* Virtually every cabinet-level federal agency has its own Office of the Inspector General, with enforcement authority.

---

FBI agents are exemplary police officers. William Webster, former director of the FBI, reflected this sentiment when he said, "Over the years the American people have come to expect the most professional law enforcement from the FBI. Although we use the most modern forms of management and technology in the fight against crime, our strength is in our people—in the character of the men and women of the FBI. For that reason we seek only those who have demonstrated that they can perform as professional people who can, and will, carry on our tradition of fidelity, bravery, and integrity."[31]

The history of the FBI spans almost 100 years. It began as the Bureau of Investigation in 1908, when it was designed to serve as the investigative arm of the U.S. Department of Justice. The creation of the bureau was motivated, at least in part, by the inability of other agencies to stem the rising tide of American political and business corruption.[32]

The official purpose of today's FBI is succinctly stated in the agency's mission statement: "The Mission of the FBI is to protect and defend the United States against terrorist and foreign intelligence threats, uphold and enforce the criminal laws of the United States; and to provide leadership and law enforcement assistance to federal, state, local, and international agencies and partners."[33]

**Fidelity, bravery, and integrity.**

—Motto of the Federal Bureau of Investigation

It remains the FBI's overriding priority to predict and prevent terrorist attacks. The threat posed by international terrorism, and in particular from Al Qaeda and related groups, continues to be the gravest we face.

—FBI Director Robert S. Mueller, III[iv]

## CJ CAREERS

### FEDERAL BUREAU OF INVESTIGATION

**Name:** Kevin Kendrick

**Position:** Section Chief, Executive Development and Selection Program, Administrative Services Division

**City:** Washington, D.C.

**College Attended:** Wayne State University

**Year Hired:** 1981

*"Seeing the good work that officers were doing when I was in school at Wayne State opened my eyes to the possibility of a career in law enforcement. I saw this as a wonderful opportunity to do something positive. Every day at the FBI is different. I can honestly say this is the greatest part of the job: the variety of assignments, the interaction with other agencies and the community. It's an incredible way to get things done. We do something that means something. We are having an impact on people's lives."*

### TYPICAL POSITIONS

Special agent, crime laboratory technician, ballistics technician, computer operator, fingerprint specialist, explosives examiner, document expert, and other nonagent technical positions. FBI activities include investigations into organized crime, white-collar crime, public corruption, financial crime, fraud against the government, bribery, copyright matters, civil rights violations, bank robbery, extortion, kidnapping, air piracy, terrorism, foreign counterintelligence, interstate criminal activity, fugitive and drug trafficking matters, and other violations of federal statutes. The FBI also works with other federal, state, and local law enforcement agencies in investigating matters of joint interest and in training law enforcement officers from around the world.

### EMPLOYMENT REQUIREMENTS

General employment requirements include (1) an age of between 23 and 37; (2) excellent physical health; (3) uncorrected vision of not less than 20/200, correctable to 20/20 in one eye and at least 20/40 in the other eye; (4) good hearing; (5) U.S. citizenship; (6) a valid driver's license; (7) successful completion of a comprehensive background investigation; (8) a law degree or a bachelor's degree from an accredited college or university; (9) successful completion of an initial written examination; (10) an intensive formal interview; and (11) urinalysis. A polygraph examination may also be required.

### OTHER REQUIREMENTS

Special-agent entry programs exist in the areas of law, accounting, languages, engineering/science, and a general "diversified" area. They require a minimum of three years of full-time work experience, preferably with a law enforcement agency. Candidates who otherwise meet entry requirements and who possess one or more of the following critical skills are currently deemed essential to address the agency's increasingly complex responsibilities and will be given priority in the hiring process: (1) computer science and other information technology specialties; (2) engi-

neering; (3) physical sciences (physics, chemistry, biology, and so on); (4) foreign language proficiency (Arabic, Farsi, Pashtu, Urdu, Chinese [all dialects], Japanese, Korean, Russian, Spanish, and Vietnamese); (5) foreign counterintelligence; (6) counterterrorism; and (7) military intelligence experience. The FBI emphasizes education and especially values degrees in law, graduate studies, and business and accounting. Most nonagent technical career paths also require bachelor's or advanced degrees and U.S. citizenship.

### SALARY

Special agents enter the bureau at Government Service (GS) grade 10 on the federal government's pay scale and earned $40,419 in the summer of 2004 while undergoing training at the FBI Academy. Upon graduation, agents' pay rises to between $53,743 and $58,235, including locality and special availability pay. Special agents can advance to GS-13 in field assignments and to GS-15 or higher in supervisory and management positions.

### BENEFITS

Benefits include (1) 13 days of sick leave annually, (2) two and a half to five weeks of paid vacation and ten paid federal holidays each year, (3) federal health and life insurance, and (4) a comprehensive retirement program.

### DIRECT INQUIRIES TO:

Federal Bureau of Investigation
J. Edgar Hoover Building
935 Pennsylvania Avenue, N.W.
Washington, DC 20535–0001

Phone: (202)324–3000, or check your local telephone book

Website: http://www.fbi.gov, or visit http://fbijobs.com

For additional information on employment opportunities in the criminal justice field, view the careers portion of the CD-ROM included with this book.

FBI headquarters are located in the J. Edgar Hoover Building on Pennsylvania Avenue in Washington, D.C. Special agents and support personnel who work at the agency's headquarters organize and coordinate FBI activities throughout the country and around the world. Headquarters staff determines investigative priorities, oversee major cases, and manage the organization's resources, technology, and personnel.

The daily work of the FBI is done through 56 field offices and 400 satellite offices (known as *resident agencies*). A special agent in charge oversees each field office, except for the largest field offices in Washington, D.C.; Los Angeles; and New York City; each of which is headed by an assistant director.

The FBI also operates "legal attaché offices" (called Legats) in a number of major cities around the world, including London and Paris. Such offices allow the international coordination of enforcement activities and facilitate the flow of law enforcement–related information between the FBI and police agencies in host countries. In 1995, a few years after the end of the cold war, the FBI opened a legal attaché office in Moscow. The Moscow office assists Russian police agencies in the growing battle against organized crime in that country and helps American officials track suspected Russian criminals operating in the United States. Also in 1995, an Eastern European version of the FBI Academy, known as the International Law Enforcement Academy (ILEA), opened in Budapest, Hungary. Its purpose is to train police administrators from all of Eastern Europe in the latest crime-fighting techniques.[34]

A little over a decade ago, the FBI formed the National Computer Crime Squad (NCCS) to investigate violations of the federal Counterfeit Access Device and Computer Fraud and Abuse Act of 1984, the Computer Fraud and Abuse Act of 1986 (CFAA),[35] and other federal computer-crime laws. NCCS focuses on computer crimes such as (1) intrusions of public switched networks (telephone company networks), (2) major computer network intrusions, (3) network integrity violations, (4) privacy violations, (5) industrial espionage, (6) pirated computer software, and (7) other crimes in which a computer is centrally involved. In recent years, the FBI has created individual computer-crime investigation teams in each of its field offices within the United States.

The FBI also operates the Combined DNA Index System (CODIS), a computerized forensic database of DNA "profiles" of offenders convicted of serious crimes (such as rape, other sexual assaults, murder, and certain crimes against children), as well as DNA profiles from unknown offenders.[36] CODIS, now a part of the National DNA Index System (NDIS), was formally authorized by the federal DNA Identification Act of 1994.[37] It is being enhanced daily through the work of federal, state, and local law enforcement agencies that take DNA samples from biological evidence gathered at crime scenes and from offenders themselves. The computerized CODIS can rapidly identify a perpetrator when it finds a match between an evidence sample and a stored profile. By 1998, every state had enacted legislation establishing a CODIS database and requiring that DNA from offenders convicted of certain serious crimes be entered into the system. Today the CODIS database, which continues to grow, holds 1.7 million DNA profiles.[38]

The History of the FBI

The CD-ROM scenario for Chapter 5 is a Fourth Amendment case. It involves an unsuccessful search of a residence during which law enforcement officers were accompanied by newspaper reporters and photographers. The scenario is derived from a real-life incident involving a raid by deputy U.S. marshals on a residence thought to be the home of a wanted suspect. The real-life case eventually found its way to the U.S. Supreme Court, with negative consequences for the officers and for the practice of bringing news reporters along during the execution of a warrant that involves the search of a home. Use the CD-ROM found in your textbook to work through this scenario.

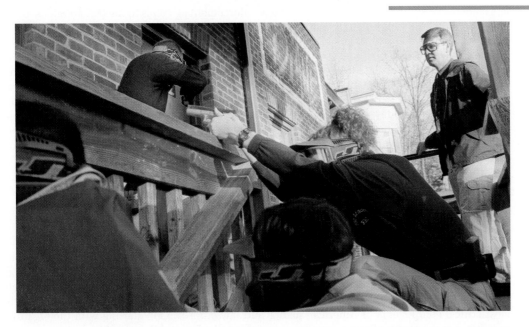

FBI agents taking part in an apartment arrest training exercise at the FBI Academy in Quantico, Virginia, as an instructor looks on. Student agents chosen for the course receive classroom and shooting-range instruction and act out crime and arrest scenarios at a mock-up town called Hogan's Alley. The academy, which began operations in 1935 in Washington, D.C., covers more than 300 acres and has produced more than 30,000 graduates.

*AP Wide World Photos*

FBI Director Robert S. Mueller III explaining his agency's shift in priorities following the 2001 terrorist attacks on the World Trade Center and the Pentagon.

*AP Wide World Photos*

**FBI Priorities**

1. Protect the United States from terrorist attack
2. Protect the United States against foreign intelligence operations and espionage
3. Protect the United States against cyber-based attacks and high-technology crimes
4. Combat public corruption at all levels
5. Protect civil rights
6. Combat transnational and national o̶r̶g̶... and enterprises
7. Combat major white-collar crime
8. Combat significant violent crime
9. Support federal, state, local and international partners
10. Upgrade technology to successfully perform the FBI's mission

As the FBI has grown, some of its functions have become geographically dispersed. Headquartered in Clarksburg, West Virginia, the Criminal Justice Information Services (CJIS) Division serves as the central repository for criminal justice information services in the FBI. The FBI describes the division as "a customer-driven organization providing state-of-the-art identification and information services to local, state, federal, and international criminal justice communities." In support of these activities, CJIS has developed an advisory process that involves sharing management and policy-making decisions with local, state, and federal criminal justice agencies. The CJIS Division includes the Fingerprint Identification Program, the National Crime Information Center Program, the Uniform Crime Reporting Program, and the Integrated Automated Fingerprint Identification System (IAFIS)—a computer-based system that can store, process, analyze, and retrieve millions of fingerprints in a relatively short period of time. The FBI Laboratory Division, located in Quantico, Virginia, operates one of the largest and most comprehensive crime laboratories in the world. It provides services related to the scientific solution and prosecution of crimes throughout the country. It is also the only full-service federal forensic laboratory in the United States. Laboratory activities include crime-scene searches, special surveillance photography, latent-fingerprint examinations, forensic examinations of evidence (including DNA testing), court testimony by laboratory personnel, and other scientific and technical services. The FBI offers laboratory services, free of charge, to all law enforcement agencies in the United States. Learn more about the FBI's administrative divisions, including the activities of each, via Web Extra 5–4 at cjtoday.com.

The FBI also runs a National Academy Program, which is part of its Training Division. The program offered its first class in 1935 and had 23 students. It was then known as the FBI National Police Training School. In 1940, the school moved from Washington, D.C., to the U.S. Marine Amphibious Base at Quantico, Virginia. In 1972, the facility expanded to 334 acres, and the FBI Academy, as we know it today, officially opened.[39] According to the most recent statistics available, the academy program has produced 37,990 graduates since it began operations. This includes 2,475 international graduates from 151 countries and 328 graduates from U.S. territories and possessions. More than 220 sessions have been offered since inception of the training program. Visit the FBI Academy on the Web via Web Extra 5–5 at cjtoday.com.

## The FBI and Counterterrorism

The FBI's counterterrorism efforts became especially important following the September 11, 2001, attacks on American targets. Two months after the attacks, U.S. Attorney General John Ashcroft announced a major "reorganization and mobilization" of the FBI and other federal agencies, such as the Immigration and Naturalization Service. Speaking at a press conference in Washington, D.C., Ashcroft said, "Our strategic plan mandates fundamental change in several of the most critical components of American justice and law enforcement, starting with the organization that is at the center of our counterterrorism effort, the Federal Bureau of Investigation. In its

**WEB** EXTRA

**WEB** EXTRA

history, the FBI has been many things: the protector of our institutions when they were under assault from organized crime; the keeper of our security when it was threatened by international espionage; and the defender of our civil rights when they were denied to some Americans on the basis of their race, color or creed. Today the American people call upon the Federal Bureau of Investigation to put prevention of terrorism at the center of its law-enforcement and national-security efforts."[40]

Following the attorney general's lead, the FBI reshaped its priorities to focus on preventing future terrorist attacks. This effort is managed by the Counterterrorism Division at FBI headquarters and is emphasized at every field office, resident agency, and Legat. Headquarters administers a national threat warning system that allows the FBI to instantly distribute important terrorism-related bulletins to law enforcement agencies and public-safety departments throughout the country. "Flying Squads" provide specialized counterterrorism knowledge and experience, language capabilities, and analytic support as needed to FBI field offices and Legats. To combat terrorism, the FBI's Counterterrorism Division collects, analyzes, and shares information and critical intelligence with various federal agencies and departments—including the Central Intelligence Agency (CIA), the National Security Agency (NSA), and the Department of Homeland Security (DHS)—and with law enforcement agencies throughout the country. An essential weapon in the FBI's battle against terrorism is the Joint Terrorism Task Force (JTTF). A national JTTF, located at the FBI's Washington headquarters, includes representatives from the Department of Defense, the Department of Energy, the Federal Emergency Management Agency, the Central Intelligence Agency, the Customs Service, the Secret Service, and U.S. Immigration and Customs Enforcement. In addition, through 66 local JTTFs, representatives from federal agencies, state and local law enforcement personnel, and first responders coordinate efforts to track down terrorists and to prevent acts of terrorism in the United States.

In testimony before Congress in 2005, FBI Director Robert S. Mueller III identified three areas of special concern relative to the bureau's ongoing antiterrorism efforts. First, said Mueller, "is the threat from covert operatives who may be inside the U.S. who have the intention to facilitate or conduct an attack."[41] The very nature of trained covert operatives, said the director, is that they are difficult to detect. "I remain very concerned about what we are *not* seeing," said Mueller. Second, Mueller identified a concern "with the growing body of sensitive reporting that continues to show Al-Qaeda's clear intention to obtain and ultimately use some form of chemical, biological, radiological, nuclear or high-energy explosives (CBRNE) material in its attacks against America." Finally, said Mueller, "we remain concerned about the potential for Al-Qaeda to . . . exploit radical American converts and other indigenous extremists." Read more about Director Mueller's vision for the future of the FBI in the FBI's *Strategic Plan for 2004–2009* at Library Extra 5–6.

> Law enforcement can ill afford to continue its traditional policy of isolating and even ignoring the activities of private security.
>
> —National Institute of Justice, *Crime and Protection in America*

> Every day [as a police officer] you get to be a different person. In that regard it is the best job in the world. You get to play many roles: rabbi, lawyer, social worker, psychiatrist.
>
> —New York Police Officer Salvatore Maniscalco

**CJ BLOG**

See the Policing Web logs available in the CJToday.com blogspace.

**LIBRARY EXTRA**

# State Agencies

Most state police agencies were created in the late nineteenth or early twentieth century to meet specific needs. The Texas Rangers, created in 1835 before Texas attained statehood, functioned as a military organization responsible for patrolling the republic's borders. The apprehension of Mexican cattle rustlers was one of the main concerns.[42] Massachusetts, which focused on vice control, was the second state to create a law enforcement agency. Today, a wide diversity of state policing agencies exists. Table 5–3 provides a list of typical state-sponsored law enforcement

**AMERICAN POLICING: STATE LAW ENFORCEMENT AGENCIES**

| | | |
|---|---|---|
| Alcohol law enforcement agencies | Port authorities | State police |
| Fish and wildlife agencies | State bureaus of investigation | State university police |
| Highway patrol | State park services | Weigh station operations |

TABLE 5–3

## CJ FUTURES

### The FBI's New Information Technology Tools

Since 9/11 the FBI has recognized that the ability to assemble, analyze, and disseminate information both internally and with other intelligence and law enforcement agencies is essential to the nation's success in the war on terrorism. Consequently, it has made modernization of its information technology (IT) systems a top priority.

According to FBI director Robert S. Mueller III, the agency has recently taken a coordinated, strategic approach to IT, building a strategic IT plan and creating an internal system for managing IT projects at each stage of their life cycle.

IT modernization is occurring under a multiphased program code-named Trilogy. As a result of Trilogy, the FBI has:

1. Deployed a high-speed, secure network that enables personnel in FBI offices around the country to share data, including audio, video, and image files.
2. Provided its agents and intelligence analysts with more than 30,000 new desktop computers running modern software applications, along with 3,700 printers, 1,600 scanners, 465 servers, and 1,400 routers.
3. Developed an IT infrastructure that provides for secure communication with FBI intelligence community partners.

The third phase of Trilogy included the Virtual Case File (VCF) system, which was intended to give the bureau's agents nearly instant access to all needed information in the agency's databases. VCF, however, encountered technical problems, some of which were related to requirements involving the sharing of information

with other law enforcement and national security organizations. Consequently, the VCF system was scrapped in 2005, and the FBI announced plans to use mostly off-the-shelf products that will allow agents to easily share information. The replacement system, called Sentinel, is based on a problem-solving framework known as the Federal Investigative Case Management Solution (FICMS).

Separate from the Trilogy/Sentinel program, the FBI has successfully deployed a number of new investigative and information-sharing capabilities, including the following:

- *Investigative Data Warehouse (IDW).* IDW offers agents and analysts the technology needed to perform intelligent link analysis to uncover potential relationships that might exist between suspects, physical and information resources, and anticipated threats. IDW provides FBI users with a single access point to more than 47 sources of counterterrorism data, including information from FBI files, other government agency data, and open source news feeds, that were previously available only through separate proprietary information systems and laborious data-gathering efforts.
- *FBI Automated Messaging System (FAMS).* FAMS began operations in December 2004 and now provides more than 300 FBI agents and intelligence analysts with the capability to send and receive critical organizational message traffic to any of the 40,000+ addresses on the Defense Messaging System.
- *FBI Intelligence Information Reports Dissemination System (FIDS).* FIDS is a Web-based software application that allows all FBI personnel with access to the FBI's internal intranet to create and disseminate standardized intelligence information reports quickly and efficiently to FBI agents and other law enforcement officers.

*References:* Testimony of Robert S. Mueller III, Director, Federal Bureau of Investigation, before the Committee on Intelligence of the U.S. Senate, February 16, 2005; and Linda Rosencrance, "It's Official: FBI Scraps $170 Million Virtual Case File Project," *Computerworld,* March 9, 2005.

agencies. Figure 5–1 shows that the number of personnel employed by state law enforcement agencies is significantly less than the level of employment in local police departments.

State law enforcement agencies are usually organized after one of two models. In the first, a centralized model, the tasks of major criminal investigations are combined with the patrol of state highways. Centralized state police agencies generally do the following:

- Assist local law enforcement departments in criminal investigations when asked to do so.
- Operate identification bureaus.
- Maintain a centralized criminal records repository.
- Patrol the state's highways.
- Provide select training for municipal and county officers.

The Pennsylvania Constabulary, known today as the Pennsylvania State Police, was the first modern force to combine these duties and has been called the "first modern state police agency."[43] Michigan, New Jersey, New York, Vermont, and Delaware are a few of the states that patterned their state-level enforcement activities after the Pennsylvania model.

The second state model, the decentralized model of police organization, characterizes operations in the southern United States but is also found in the Midwest and in some western states. The model draws a clear distinction between traffic enforcement on state highways and

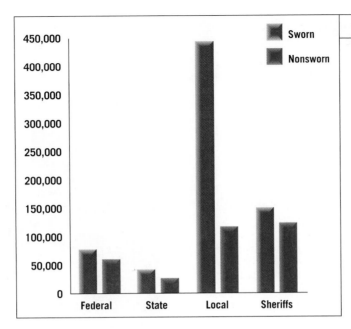

**FIGURE 5–1**

**Federal, state, and local law enforcement employment in the United States, 2000.**

*Source:* Brian A. Reaves, *Census of State and Local Law Enforcement Agencies, 2000* (Washington, DC: Bureau of Justice Statistics, 2002); Brian A. Reaves and Timothy C. Hart, *Federal Law Enforcement Officers, 2000* (Washington, DC: Bureau of Justice Statistics, 2002); and Matthew J. Hickman and Brian A. Reaves, *Local Police Departments, 2000* (Washington, DC: Bureau of Justice Statistics, 2003).

other state-level law enforcement functions by creating at least two separate agencies. North Carolina, South Carolina, and Georgia are a few of the many states that employ both a highway patrol and a state bureau of investigation. The names of the respective agencies may vary, however, even though their functions are largely the same. In North Carolina, for example, the two major state-level law enforcement agencies are the North Carolina Highway Patrol and the State Bureau of Investigation. Georgia fields a highway patrol and the Georgia Bureau of Investigation, and South Carolina operates a highway patrol and the South Carolina Law Enforcement Division.

States that use the decentralized model usually have a number of other adjunct state-level law enforcement agencies. North Carolina, for example, has created a State Wildlife Commission with enforcement powers, a Board of Alcohol Beverage Control with additional agents, and a separate Enforcement and Theft Bureau for enforcing certain motor vehicle and theft laws. Learn more about state-level law enforcement agencies by visiting Web Extra 5–6 and Library Extra 5–7 at cjtoday.com.

A group of Texas Rangers providing additional security during a scheduled execution at Huntsville, Texas, in 2000. The Texas Rangers have long been held in high regard among state police agencies.

*Bob Daemmrich, Stock Boston*

## CJ NEWS

### Don't Even Ask About Extra Credit

They could be students in a classroom anywhere. The pupils sit in rows of chairs with fold-out desktops, taking and passing notes, eyeing wristwatches and cellphones. They laugh despite themselves when a classmate misreads the text aloud, substituting "pubic area" for "public area." They tap their feet impatiently and pass around packs of gum. Sometimes a tiny detail betrays them: a dull gleam of gunmetal at the hip, or a spoken reference to time on the 24-hour clock.

"If he were to say, 'I'm a Goodyear auto mechanic, and I'll fix your car in exchange for whatever sexual act,' I'd say yes," lectures Detective Jeffrey Etheridge, one of the instructors. As the giggling dies down, he adds, "This is more for academic discussion. This is never going to happen out on the street."

Call them the newest recruits for the oldest profession. The students—over a hundred of them, many female in their mid-20's—are all New York police officers who have volunteered to walk, or even strut, to the rhythm of an unusual beat. Hailing from precincts across the city, they've convened for a common purpose: to learn the tricks of the prostitute's trade and go undercover in a citywide sting called Operation Losing Proposition.

Their education is a single seven-hour session, traditionally offered twice or three times annually at the Police Academy on East 20th Street. The program began about a decade ago, and after a year's hiatus because of personnel and budget concerns, a pair of classes were taught late last year, preparing more than 200 new officers to walk the streets.

Some will tackle neighborhoods with the busiest corners in town, rough-and-tumble places like Hunts Point in the Bronx or Queens Plaza; the intersection of Weehawken and Christopher Streets in the West Village, popular among transvestites; or a notorious industrial strip in East New York, Brooklyn, between Flatlands Avenue and Linden Boulevard, that the police call the Pennsylvania Track.

But even in the busiest areas, busting a bona fide john is no easy task.

"You're going to get some very unusual requests: kissing, hugging, talking, medical procedures," Detective James Held of the Vice Division told his November class, adding that none of those requests was a crime. He offered an example: "What if someone comes up to you and says: 'Do you know what I want you to do? I want you to dress up like a girl and I want to go back to a hotel room, and I want you to paint my toenails. I'll pay you a thousand dollars for the hour.'"

"I'll bring the nail polish!" called out Tisjé Golden, an officer from the 25th Precinct in East Harlem. Laughter rippled outward from her seat and spread through the audience.

Still, Detective Held clarified, that's not a crime. Prostitution is not like a game of horseshoes. Close isn't good enough. To determine whether a suspect's behavior is illegal, officers must consult a rigorous recipe. The first ingredient is a sexual act, whether promised or performed. The latter, joked Detective Etheridge, who works in the Police Department's legal bureau, "is something you're not going to worry about, because you're not going to have sex, at least not on company time."

NYPD officers undergoing in-service tactical training in a Bronx classroom.

*Photo by New York Police Department Photographic Unit*

The second component is money, goods or services, including anything from a vial of crack to a ride across town. The final touch is an agreement, verbal or otherwise (a simple nod of the head will do, the courts have concluded), to bind the service and fee together in a consensual exchange. To gather these elements, an experienced decoy will choreograph a suggestive verbal ballet, getting a john to articulate what he wants without being too pushy. Any aggressive or overly eager behavior, like offering repeated discounts or chasing down a customer, can be dismissed as entrapment.

Patronizing a prostitute is a Class B misdemeanor, punishable by up to three months in prison and a fine not to exceed $500. In certain cases, the police may even seize a john's car.

"Remember, as police, our role is to detect crime, not create crime," Detective Held gently reminded his charges. As the students listened, some thumbed through copies of a 46-page handbook that included a brief glossary of the prostitute's vernacular, a Kama Sutra of sexual slang. The lexicon included phrases like "john jams," or "lines of cars with tricks/johns to be serviced." It also named different types of prostitutes, from the "lot lizard," whose habitat is a truck stop, to the "bubble gum prostitute," who will sell herself for anything, accepting drugs, alcohol, or cigarettes in lieu of cash.

The curriculum also included tactics and equipment. Conversations with customers are recorded using a remote audio system called a Kel set. Before hitting the streets, students learned, a decoy hitches up to a transmitter, roughly the size of a pack of cigarettes, and snakes a microphone wire up the inside of his or her shirt. Sgt. Dan Farrell, an equipment expert, cautioned his students against leaning into the window of a john's vehicle while wearing a wire. It's a sloppy move that not only makes decoys vulnerable to getting grabbed by the hair, but also threatens to expose the wire.

Students learned how other officers play supporting roles, from the arrest team waiting nearby in unmarked cars, to the

## CJ NEWS (*continued*)

"ghost," an undercover officer who fades into the surroundings, ready to help a decoy in distress. Depending on the situation, a ghost may choose to pose as a pimp, a wino or a junkie.

Assuming a role in Operation Losing Proposition is strictly voluntary. That said, it is also equal-opportunity.

"The decoy officer may be male or female," Detective Held announced, eliciting a chorus of groans and protests from the roughly 20 men in the class. "Sorry, guys. I used to say that, too," he quipped, "and then I was up on 43rd Street, shaking what mama gave me."

Officer Gamaliel Torres, 32, a broad-shouldered, soft-spoken officer from the Homeless Outreach Unit, said he was ribbed by colleagues when they heard he had signed up for the class. "I got a little hazing for it," he admitted.

Officer Taralee Gugliociello, 30, a former preschool teacher from a family of male police officers, said she was excited to try on the prostitute's role. "I'll be doing something my brothers can't do," she announced proudly, then reddened a bit. "I don't think they'd want to see," she confided. "My brothers would be like, 'Put some clothes on.'"

Not everyone shares the officers' ready spirit. "Is this really what our police department should be doing?" said Norman Siegel, a prominent civil rights lawyer and the former executive director of the New York Civil Liberties Union. "Look at the consensual nature of the crime, the fact that they're arresting the john—that's problematic in and of itself—and then seizing cars

as a deterrent. It's disproportionate to the crime. History shows that it's very hard to deter this kind of activity."

Since the mid-1990's, precincts have conducted Operation Losing Proposition sporadically, usually in response to neighbors' complaints. Some complain more loudly than others. Detective Kevin Mannion, an instructor from the vice squad, told the class about an eccentric woman whose cruel habit—dumping a pot of scalding water from her window to disperse the prostitutes below—once misfired and splashed a cluster of undercover officers.

For the police, taking lumps is a part of getting into the act. "We're all actors or actresses in a way," mused Sgt. Joanne Riggs, who coordinates the training classes. "You've gotta be."

At the very least, undercover prostitution busts are more colorful than routine traffic stops.

"It breaks the monotony and it gives them great stories; cops love great stories," offered Eugene O'Donnell, an assistant professor of police studies at John Jay College of Criminal Justice. "What's a more bizarre way to make a living than standing out on a corner and talking to some guy in a limo?"

Toward the end of the class, Officer Golden offered her own take on getting into character. With a laugh and a slight shimmy, she suggested a sly motive. "Every woman," she said, "has a little prostitute in her."

For the latest in crime and justice news, visit the Talk Justice news feed at http://www.crimenews.info.

*Source:* Jessica Bruder, "Don't Even Ask About Extra Credit," *The New York Times* online, February 13, 2005. Copyright © 2005 by the New York Times Co. Reprinted with permission.

# Local Agencies

Local police agencies, including city and county agencies, represent a third level of law enforcement activity in the United States. The term *local police* encompasses a wide variety of agencies. Municipal departments, rural sheriff's departments, and specialized groups like campus police and transit police can all be grouped under the "local" rubric. Large municipal departments are highly visible because of their vast size, huge budgets, and innovative programs. The nation's largest law enforcement agency, the New York City Police Department (NYPD), for example, has about 45,000 full-time employees, including about 39,000 full-time sworn officers.[44]

Far greater in number, however, are small-town and county sheriff's departments. There are approximately 12,700 **municipal police departments** and 3,100 sheriff's departments in the United States.[45] Every incorporated municipality in the country has the authority to create its own police force. Some very small communities hire only one officer, who fills the roles of chief, investigator, and night watch—as well as everything in between. The majority of local agencies employ fewer than ten full-time officers, and about three in eight agencies (more than 7,000 in all) employ fewer than five full-time officers. These smaller agencies include 2,245 (or 12%) with just one full-time officer and 1,164 (or 6%) with only part-time officers.[46] A few communities contract with private security firms for police services, and still others have no active police force at all, depending instead on local sheriff's departments to deal with law violators.

City police chiefs are typically appointed by the mayor or selected by the city council. Their departments' jurisdictions are limited by convention to the geographic boundaries of their communities. **Sheriffs**, on the other hand, are elected public officials whose agencies are responsible for law enforcement throughout the counties in which they function. Sheriff's deputies mostly patrol the "unincorporated" areas of the county, or those that lie between municipalities. They

**municipal police department**

A city- or town-based law enforcement agency; also known as *local police*.

**sheriff**

The elected chief officer of a county law enforcement agency. The sheriff is usually responsible for law enforcement in unincorporated areas and for the operation of the county jail.

A Daytona Beach, Florida, police officer ticketing a driver for a seat belt violation. Local police agencies, including city and county agencies, represent a third level of law enforcement activity in the United States.

*AP Wide World Photos*

> The most fundamental weakness in crime control is the failure of federal and state governments to create a framework for local policing. Much of what is wrong with the police is the result of the absurd, fragmented, unworkable nonsystem of more than 17,000 local departments.
>
> —Patrick V. Murphy, former New York City Police Commissioner

do, however, have jurisdiction throughout the county, and in some areas they routinely work alongside municipal police to enforce laws within towns and cities.

Sheriff's departments are generally responsible for serving court papers, including civil summonses, and for maintaining security within state courtrooms. Sheriffs also run county jails and are responsible for more detainees awaiting trial than any other type of law enforcement department in the country. For example, the Los Angeles (L.A.) County Jail System, operated by the L.A. County Sheriff's Department (LASD), is the largest in the world.[47] In 2003, with eight separate facilities, it had an average daily population of 18,423 inmates—considerably larger than the number of inmates held in many state prison systems. More than 2,200 uniformed officers and 1,265 civilian employees work in the Custody Division of the L.A. County Sheriff's Department, and that division alone operates with a yearly budget in excess of $200 million.[48]

Sheriff's departments remain strong across most of the country, although in parts of New England, deputies mostly function as court agents with limited law enforcement duties. One report found that most sheriff's departments are small, with nearly two-thirds of them employing fewer than 25 sworn officers.[49] Only 12 departments employ more than 1,000 officers. Even so, southern and western sheriffs are still considered the "chief law enforcement officers" in their counties. A list of conventional police agencies found at the local level is shown in Table 5–4. For information on selected local law enforcement agencies, view Web Extra 5–7 at cjtoday.com. Visit Library Extra 5–8 to learn more about staffing levels at local police agencies. Sheriff's departments are described in Library Extra 5–9.

| TABLE 5-4 | AMERICAN POLICING: LOCAL LAW ENFORCEMENT AGENCIES | | |
|---|---|---|---|
| | Campus police | Housing authority agencies | Sheriff's departments |
| | City/county agencies | Marine patrol agencies | Transit police |
| | Constables | Municipal police departments | Tribal police |
| | Coroners or medical examiners | | |

## FREEDOM OR SAFETY? YOU DECIDE.

### The Conch Republic

The citizens of the tiny island town of Key West, Florida, have always prided themselves on being different. Hence, it should have come as no surprise when, on April 23, 1982, the island's mayor issued a proclamation seceding from the United States and declaring Key West a new nation named the "Conch Republic." The decision to withdraw from the Union came in reaction to a 19-mile-long traffic jam created when authorities from the Task Force on South Florida Crime set up a checkpoint on U.S. 1—the only highway traversing the Florida Keys. Law enforcement officers used the checkpoint to examine the driver's licenses of travelers leaving the Keys and meticulously searched vehicles looking for contraband and illegal immigrants. At the time of the roadblock, at least one law enforcement official estimated that up to 80% of all marijuana and cocaine entering the nation was coming through south Florida, and Key West was said to be the "drug-smuggling capital of America."

In 1982, as today, the primary legal industry in Key West was tourism, and island officials feared that long delays at police roadblocks would keep visitors away. Protests about the roadblock were lodged with the White House, the Florida governor's office, and with U.S. congressional offices—all to no avail. Then-Vice President George H. W. Bush's press secretary issued a statement saying, "You have illegal immigrants and crime on the streets. . . . There's going to be some inconvenience. I think most people would want a little inconvenience compared to having grocery stores held up and senior citizens mugged in the streets."

Island officials, however, didn't agree and hired an attorney to seek an injunction against the roadblock, arguing that it violated the Fourth Amendment's restriction against unreasonable search and seizure. "Unless they see the hand of a Haitian sticking out of the trunk or marijuana wafting out of the car, they don't have probable cause," said David Horan, the town's attorney. When the roadblock remained in place, island leaders issued a secession proclamation and promptly applied to the U.S. government for foreign aid.

For its part, the U.S. government ignored the secession movement, but the roadblock was quietly removed two months after it was put in place. Island residents, however, still celebrate April 23 as the day when, as one former Key West mayor put it, "the brave men and women of the Conch Republic gave up their lunch hour to secede from the United States."

### YOU DECIDE

Although Key West's secession was never taken very seriously by the people involved in it 25 years ago, it illustrates an undeniable tension between freedom and security that continues to characterize American society today. How would you describe that tension in your own words? Are Americans today more or less willing to sacrifice some of their personal rights and freedoms in the interest of safety than they were 25 years ago?

*Reference:* Cynthia Crossen, "To Fight Car Searches, A Florida City Declared Itself a Foreign Nation," *Wall Street Journal* online, January 19, 2005. Web posted at http://online.wsj.com/article_print/0, SB110609219909929528, 00.html.

# Private Protective Services

**Private protective services** constitute a fourth level of enforcement activity in the United States today. While public police are employed by the government and enforce public laws, private security personnel work for corporate employers and secure private interests.

Private security has been defined as "those self-employed individuals and privately funded business entities and organizations providing security-related services to specific clientele for a fee, for the individual or entity that retains or employs them, or for themselves, in order to protect their persons, private property, or interests from various hazards."[50] The growth in the size of private security in recent years has been phenomenal. In 2002, for example, $212.7 million was spent for security arrangements at the Olympic winter games in Salt Lake City, Utah—leading to the employment of more than 40,000 private security personnel in association with the event.[51] Only two years later, in 2004, however, official estimates put the total amount spent to secure the Olympic Games in Athens at $1.5 billion—or $283 per paid ticket.[52] Given Greece's geopolitical situation, and its proximity to the Balkans and the Middle East, officials in Athens wanted to be sure they could prevent terrorist attacks.

ASIS International, with more than 33,000 members, is the preeminent international organization for private security professionals.[53] ASIS International membership includes corporate security managers and directors, as well as architects, attorneys, and federal, state, and local law enforcement personnel. Founded in 1955, ASIS International, formerly known as the American Society for Industrial Security, is dedicated to increasing the effectiveness and productivity of security professionals by developing educational and certification programs and training materials

**private protective services**

Independent or proprietary commercial organizations that provide protective services to employers on a contractual basis.

The Development of Private Policing

that address the needs of the security profession. ASIS also actively promotes the value of security management to business, the media, governmental entities, and the public. The organization publishes the industry-leading magazine, *Security Management*.

With 204 chapters worldwide, ASIS administers three certifications programs: (1) the Certified Protection Professional (CPP) program, which provides for board certification in security management; (2) the Physical Security Professional (PSP) program, which provides a technical certification opportunity for specialists in physical plant security; and (3) the Professional Certified Investigator (PCI) program. Holders of PCI certification have satisfactorily demonstrated significant education and/or experience in the fields of case management, evidence collection, and case presentation. ASIS also promotes the importance of ethical standards in the private security sector. The ASIS International Code of Ethics can be found in the CJ Ethics and Professionalism box in this chapter. ASIS can be reached online at Web Extra 5–8, and the ASIS Security Toolkit, consisting of advisories, guidelines, case studies, information, news, and advice in the area of private security, can be seen at Web Extra 5–9.

**WEB EXTRA**

A report released by the National Institute of Justice in 2001, entitled *The New Structure of Policing,* found that "policing is being transformed and restructured in the modern world" in ways that were unanticipated only a few decades ago.[54] Much of the change is due to the development of private protective services as an important adjunct to public law enforcement activities in the United States and throughout much of the rest of the world. The NIJ report says that "the key to [understanding] the transformation is that policing, meaning the activity of making societies safe, is no longer carried out exclusively by governments" and that the distinction between private and public police has begun to blur. According to the NIJ, "gradually, almost imperceptibly, policing has been 'multilateralized,'" meaning that "a host of nongovernmental agencies have undertaken to provide security services." As a result, the NIJ report says, "policing has entered a new era, an era characterized by a transformation in the governance of security." The report concludes the following:

■ In most countries, certainly in the democratic world, private police outnumber public police.

■ In these same countries, people spend more time in their daily lives in places where visible crime prevention and control are provided by nongovernmental groups rather than by governmental police agencies.

■ The reconstruction of policing is occurring worldwide despite differences in wealth and economic systems.

**LIBRARY EXTRA**

View the NIJ report in its entirety via Library Extra 5–10 at cjtoday.com.

Private security guards aiming at targets during a training exercise in Israel. The privatization of policing has become a major issue facing governments and public justice agencies everywhere.

*Ed Kashi, Corbis/Bettmann*

# ETHICS AND PROFESSIONALISM

## ASIS International Code of Ethics

### PREAMBLE

Aware that the quality of professional security activity ultimately depends upon the willingness of practitioners to observe special standards of conduct and to manifest good faith in professional relationships, the American Society for Industrial Security adopts the following Code of Ethics and mandates its conscientious observance as a binding condition of membership in or affiliation with the Society:

### CODE OF ETHICS

1. A member shall perform professional duties in accordance with the law and the highest moral principles.
2. A member shall observe the precepts of truthfulness, honesty, and integrity.
3. A member shall be faithful and diligent in discharging professional responsibilities.
4. A member shall be competent in discharging professional responsibilities.
5. A member shall safeguard confidential information and exercise due care to prevent its improper disclosure.
6. A member shall not maliciously injure the professional reputation or practice of colleagues, clients, or employers.

### Article I

A member shall perform professional duties in accordance with the law and the highest moral principles.

#### Ethical Considerations

1. A member shall abide by the law of the land in which the services are rendered and perform all duties in an honorable manner.
2. A member shall not knowingly become associated in responsibility for work with colleagues who do not conform to the law and these ethical standards.
3. A member shall be just and respect the rights of others in performing professional responsibilities.

### Article II

A member shall observe the precepts of truthfulness, honesty, and integrity.

#### Ethical Considerations

1. A member shall disclose all relevant information to those having the right to know.
2. A right to know is a legally enforceable claim or demand by a person for disclosure of information by a member. Such a right does not depend upon prior knowledge by the person of the existence of the information to be disclosed.
3. A member shall not knowingly release misleading information nor encourage or otherwise participate in the release of such information.

### Article III

A member shall be faithful and diligent in discharging professional responsibilities.

#### Ethical Considerations

1. A member is faithful when fair and steadfast in adherence to promises and commitments.
2. A member is diligent when employing best efforts in an assignment.
3. A member shall not act in matters involving conflicts of interest without appropriate disclosure and approval.
4. A member shall represent services or products fairly and truthfully.

### Article IV

A member shall be competent in discharging professional responsibilities.

#### Ethical Considerations

1. A member is competent who possesses and applies the skills and knowledge required for the task.
2. A member shall not accept a task beyond the member's competence nor shall competence be claimed when not possessed.

### Article V

A member shall safeguard confidential information and exercise due care to prevent its improper disclosure.

#### Ethical Considerations

1. Confidential information is nonpublic information, the disclosure of which is restricted.
2. Due care requires that the professional must not knowingly reveal confidential information, or use a confidence to the disadvantage of the principal or to the advantage of the member or a third person, unless the principal consents after full disclosure of all the facts. This confidentiality continues after the business relationship between the member and his principal has terminated.
3. A member who receives information and has not agreed to be bound by confidentiality is not bound from disclosing it. A member is not bound by confidential disclosures made of acts or omissions which constitute a violation of the law.
4. Confidential disclosures made by a principal to a member are not recognized by law as privileged in a legal proceeding. The member may be required to testify in a legal proceeding to the information received in confidence from his principal over the objection of his principal's counsel.
5. A member shall not disclose confidential information for personal gain without appropriate authorization.

*(continued)*

## ETHICS AND PROFESSIONALISM (*continued*)

### Article VI

A member shall not maliciously injure the professional reputation or practice of colleagues, clients, or employers.

### Ethical Considerations

1. A member shall not comment falsely and with malice concerning a colleague's competence, performance, or professional capabilities.
2. A member who knows, or has reasonable grounds to believe, that another member has failed to conform to the Society's Code of Ethics shall present such information to the Ethical Standards Committee in accordance with Article VIII of the Society's bylaws.

*Source:* ASIS International. Reprinted with permission.

### THINKING ABOUT ETHICS

1. The ASIS code of ethics says that "A member shall observe the precepts of truthfulness, honesty, and integrity." Why are these qualities important in a security professional?
2. Why is it important for security personnel to "safeguard confidential information and exercise due care to prevent its improper disclosure"? What might happen if they didn't?

The Private System of Justice

According to the National Center for Policy Analysis, private security personnel outnumber public law enforcement officers in the United States by nearly three to one.[55] The widely cited *Hallcrest Report II*,[56] another important document describing the private security industry, says that employment in the field of private security is anticipated to continue to expand by around 4% per year, whereas public police agencies are expected to grow by only 2.8% per year for the foreseeable future. Still faster growth is predicted in private security industry revenues, which are expected to increase about 7% per year, a growth rate almost three times greater than that projected for the gross national product. Table 5–5 lists the ten largest private security agencies in business today and some of the services they offer.

Private agencies provide tailored policing funded by the guarded organization rather than through the expenditure of public monies. Experts estimate that the money spent on private security in this country exceeds the combined budgets of all law enforcement agencies—local, state, and federal.[57] Contributing to this vast expenditure is the federal government, which is itself a major employer of private security personnel, contracting for services that range from guards to highly specialized electronic snooping and computerized countermeasures at military installations and embassies throughout the world.

| TABLE 5–5 | AMERICAN POLICING: PRIVATE SECURITY AGENCIES | | |
|---|---|---|---|
| | **The Largest Private Security Agencies in the United States** | | |
| | Advance Security, Inc. | Globe Security | Security Bureau, Inc. |
| | Allied Security, Inc. | Guardsmark, Inc. | Wackenhut Corp. |
| | American Protective Services | Pinkerton's, Inc. | Wells Fargo Guard Services |
| | Burns International Security Services | | |
| | **Private Security Services** | | |
| | Airport security | Computer/information security | Nuclear facility security |
| | Automated teller machine (ATM) services | Executive protection | Railroad detectives |
| | Bank guards | Hospital security | School security |
| | Company guards | Loss-prevention specialists | Store/mall security |

*Source:* Adapted from William C. Cunningham, John J. Strauchs, and Clifford W. Van Meter, *The Hallcrest Report II: Private Security Trends, 1970–2000* (McLean, VA: Hallcrest Systems, 1990).

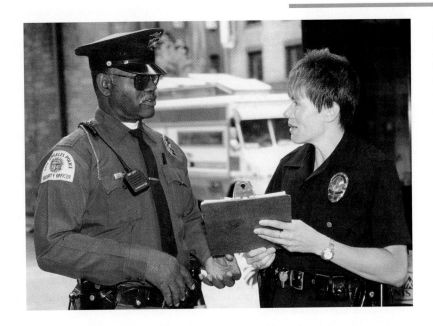

A private security officer conferring with a sworn public law enforcement officer. Cooperation among private security agencies and public law enforcement offices can help solve and prevent crimes.
*Michael Newman, PhotoEdit*

Major reasons for the quick growth of the American proprietary security sector include "(1) an increase in crimes in the workplace, (2) an increase in fear (real or perceived) of crime and terrorism, (3) the fiscal crises of the states, [which have] limited public protection, and (4) an increased public and business awareness and use of . . . more cost-effective private security products and services."[58]

There are indications that private security activities are rapidly growing beyond traditional guard services to encompass dedicated efforts at security-related intelligence gathering. In August 2004, for example, the Department of Homeland Security warned that terrorists might be actively targeting Citigroup, Prudential, the New York Stock Exchange, and other large financial institutions on the U.S. East Coast. At the same time, however, Austin-based Stratfor Inc., a low-profile private intelligence agency run by former CIA officers, was quietly assuring its clients that such an attack was very unlikely, saying that "Al Qaeda has never attacked into an alert."[59]

According to security investment firm Morgan Keegan, overall spending on corporate security, including intelligence, will amount to around $50 billion in 2005.[60] The total includes spending on physical security, Internet safeguards, staff screening and training, and terrorist and related intelligence analysis.

# Integrating Public and Private Security

As the private security field grows, its relationship to public law enforcement continues to evolve. Some argue that "today, a distinction between public and private policing is increasingly meaningless."[61] As a result, the focus has largely shifted from an analysis of competition between the sectors to the recognition that each form of policing can help the other.

One government-sponsored report makes the following policy recommendations, which are designed to maximize the cooperative crime-fighting potential of existing private and public security resources[62]:

1. The resources of proprietary and contract security should be brought to bear in cooperative, community-based crime prevention and security awareness programs.

2. An assessment should be made of (1) the basic police services the public is willing to support financially, (2) the types of police services most acceptable to police administrators and the public for transfer to the private sector, and (3) which services might be performed for a lower unit cost by the private sector with the same level of community satisfaction.

3. With special police powers, security personnel could resolve many or most minor criminal incidents prior to police involvement. State statutes providing such powers could also provide for standardized training and certification requirements, thus assuring uniformity and precluding abuses. . . . Ideally, licensing and regulatory requirements would be the same for all states, with reciprocity for firms licensed elsewhere.

The Professionalization of Private Security

Log on to ResearchNavigator.com, and choose "Criminal Justice" under ContentSelect's Academic Journal Database. Enter the phrase "private security" (with the quotation marks to indicate that you wish to search for a phrase) in the search box, and click "Go." Search again using the phrase "private policing." Which articles from the search results page usefully add to this chapter's discussion of private security? Write a summary of each of those articles, including complete source information—that is, article title, author (if available), date of publication, and source. In some cases, only abstracts (and not the entire article) may be available. If that's the case, then base your written summary on the information provided in the abstract (otherwise, use the full article). Submit what you have written to your instructor if asked to do so. *Note:* This feature is available only if your instructor has chosen the Research Navigator option available with a new textbook.

> Without close scrutiny, it has become difficult to tell whether policing is being done by a government using sworn personnel, by a government using a private security company, by a private security company using civilian employees, by a private company using public police, or by a government employing civilians.
>
> —David H. Bayley and Clifford D. Shearing[v]

4. Law enforcement agencies should be included in the crisis-management planning of private organizations. . . . Similarly, private security should be consulted when law enforcement agencies are developing SWAT [special weapons and tactics] and hostage-negotiation teams. The federal government should provide channels of communication with private security with respect to terrorist activities and threats.

5. States should enact legislation permitting private security firms access to criminal history records in order to improve the selection process for security personnel and also to enable businesses to assess the integrity of key employees.

6. Research should . . . attempt to delineate the characteristics of the private justice system; identify the crimes most frequently resolved; assess the types and amount of unreported crime in organizations; quantify the redirection of [the] public criminal justice workload . . . and examine [the] . . . relationships between private security and . . . components of the criminal justice system.

7. A federal tax credit for security expenditures, similar to the energy tax credit, might be a cost-effective way to reduce police workloads.

One especially important policy area involves building private security/public policing partnerships to prevent terrorism and to respond to threats of terrorism. A 2004 national policy summit report, jointly authored by the International Association of Chiefs of Police and the 30,000-member ASIS International, says that despite similar interests in protecting people and property in the United States, public police and private security agencies have rarely collaborated.[63] The report notes, however, that as much as 85% of the nation's critical infrastructure is protected by private security. It goes on to say that "the need for complex coordination, extra staffing, and special resources" in the light of possible terror attacks, "coupled with the significant demands of crime prevention and response, absolutely requires boosting the level of partnership between public policing and private security."[64] The full national policy summit report is available at cjtoday.com as Library Extra 5–11.

## SUMMARY

Today's police departments owe a considerable historical legacy to Sir Robert Peel and the London Metropolitan Police Force. The "Met," begun in 1829 under Peel's leadership, was the world's first modern police force. It was organized around the practice of preventive patrol by uniformed officers.

Early American law enforcement efforts were based to some degree on the British experience, but the unique character of the American frontier led to the growth of a decentralized form of policing throughout the United States. American police agencies function to enforce the statutes created by law-making bodies, and differing types and levels of legislative authority are reflected in the diversity of police forces in our country today. Consequently, American policing presents a complex picture that is structured along federal, state, and local lines. Each federal agency empowered by Congress to enforce specific statutes has its own enforcement arm, and tasks deemed especially significant by state legislatures, such as patrol of the highways, have resulted in the creation of specialized law enforcement agencies under state jurisdiction. For many of today's local law enforcement agencies, patrol retains a central role—with investigation, interrogation, and numerous support roles rounding out an increasingly specialized profession.

Studies sponsored by the Police Foundation and the Law Enforcement Assistance Administration during the 1970s and 1980s brought scientific scrutiny to bear on many of the guiding assumptions of police work. One of the most important early scientific studies of policing was the Kansas City preventive patrol experiment, which brought into question long-standing assumptions about the effectiveness of routine police patrol. The contemporary notion of evidence-based policing represents a push to apply scientific studies of policing to everyday police practice.

Private policing, represented by the recent tremendous growth of for-hire security agencies, adds another dimension to American policing. Private security is now undergoing many of the changes that have already occurred in other law enforcement areas. Heightened training requirements, legislative regulation, court-mandated changes, and college-level educational programs in private security are all leading to increased professionalism within the security profession. Recognizing the pervasiveness of today's private security operations, many municipal departments have begun concerted efforts to involve security organizations in their crime-detection and crime-prevention efforts.

1. Describe the historical development of policing in America. What impact did the Prohibition era have on the development of American policing?

2. What is scientific police management? What assumptions about police work have scientific studies of law enforcement called into question? What other assumptions made about police work today might be similarly questioned or studied?

3. What are the three levels of public law enforcement described in this chapter? Why do we have so many different types of enforcement agencies in the United States? What problems, if any, do you think are created by such a diversity of agencies?

4. Describe the nature and extent of private protective services in the United States today. Contrast the current deployment of private security personnel with the number of public law enforcement personnel. What do you think will be the future role of private protective services in the United States? How can the quality of private security services be ensured?

5. What is the relationship between private security and public policing in America today? How might the nature of that relationship be expected to change over time? Why?

Visit at least four of the federal law enforcement agencies listed under Web Extra 5–3 at cjtoday.com. Use the online information that each site provides to describe each agency in terms of its history, organization, and mission. Do the same with at least four of the state-level law enforcement agencies listed under Web Extra 5–6 and with at least four of the local law enforcement agencies listed under Web Extra 5–7. If you would like to use federal, state, or local agencies other than those listed at cjtoday.com, you can find many such sites in the Cybrary at http://www.cybrary.info.

i. Lawrence W. Sherman, *Evidence-Based Policing* (Washington, DC: Police Foundation, 1998), p. 2.

ii. Adapted from Darl H. Champion and Michael K. Hooper, *Introduction to American Policing* (New York: McGraw-Hill, 2003), p. 166.

iii. Lawrence W. Sherman, *Evidence-Based Policing* (Washington, DC: Police Foundation, 1998), p. 3.

iv. In testimony before the Senate Committee on Intelligence of the U.S. Senate, February 16, 2005.

v. David H. Bayley and Clifford D. Shearing, *The New Structure of Policing: Description, Conceptualization, and Research Agenda* (Washington, DC: National Institute of Justice, 2001), p. 5.

1. Police Foundation, *Annual Report 1991* (Washington, DC: Police Foundation, 1992).

2. "A Reminiscence of a Bow-Street Officer," *Harper's New Monthly Magazine*, Vol. 5, No. 28 (September 1852), p. 484.

3. For a good discussion of the development of the modern police, see Sue Titus Reid, *Criminal Justice: Procedures and Issues* (St. Paul, MN: West, 1987), pp. 110–115; and

Henry M. Wrobleski and Karen M. Hess, *Introduction to Law Enforcement and Criminal Justice,* 4th ed. (St. Paul, MN: West, 1993), pp. 3–51.

4. Camdem Pelham, *Chronicles of Crime*, Vol. 1 (London: T. Miles, 1887), p. 59.

5. Gary Sykes, "Street Justice: A Moral Defense of Order Maintenance Policing," *Justice Quarterly*, Vol. 3, No. 4 (December 1986), p. 504.

6. Law Enforcement Assistance Administration, *Two Hundred Years of American Criminal Justice: An LEAA Bicentennial Study* (Washington, DC: U.S. Government Printing Office, 1976), p. 15.

7. For an excellent discussion of the history of policewomen in the United States, see Dorothy Moses Schulz, *From Social Worker to Crimefighter: Women in United States Municipal Policing* (Westport, CT: Praeger, 1995); and Dorothy Moses Schulz, "Invisible No More: A Social History of Women in U.S. Policing," in Barbara R. Price and Natalie J. Sokoloff, eds., *The Criminal Justice System and Women: Offender, Victim, Worker,* 2nd ed. (New York: McGraw Hill, 1995), pp. 372–382.

8. Schulz, *From Social Worker to Crimefighter,* p. 25.

9. Ibid., p. 27.

10. National Commission on Law Observance and Enforcement, *Wickersham Commission Reports,* 14 vols. (Washington, DC: U.S. Government Printing Office, 1931).

11. President's Commission on Law Enforcement and Administration of Justice, *The Challenge of Crime in a Free Society* (Washington, DC: U.S. Government Printing Office, 1967).

12. National Advisory Commission on Criminal Justice Standards and Goals, *A National Strategy to Reduce Crime* (Washington, DC: U.S. Government Printing Office, 1973).

13. Enacted as Title 42, U.S. Code, Chapter 136, Subchapter XII.

14. Thomas J. Deakin, "The Police Foundation: A Special Report," *FBI Law Enforcement Bulletin* (November 1986), p. 2.

15. National Institute of Justice, *The Exemplary Projects Program* (Washington, DC: U.S. Government Printing Office, 1982), p. 11.

16. George L. Kelling et al., *The Kansas City Patrol Experiment* (Washington, DC: Police Foundation, 1974).

17. Kevin Krajick, "Does Patrol Prevent Crime?" *Police Magazine* (September 1978), quoting Dr. George Kelling.

18. William Bieck and David Kessler, *Response Time Analysis* (Kansas City, MO: Board of Police Commissioners, 1977). See also J. Thomas McEwen et al., *Evaluation of the Differential Police Response Field Test: Executive Summary* (Alexandria, VA: Research Management Associates, 1984); and Lawrence Sherman, "Policing Communities: What Works?" in Michael Tonry and Norval Morris, eds., *Crime and Justice: An Annual Review of Research,* Vol. 8 (Chicago: University of Chicago Press, 1986).

19. Krajick, "Does Patrol Prevent Crime?"

20. Ibid.

21. Ibid.

22. Edmund F. McGarrell, Steven Chermak, and Alexander Weiss, *Reducing Gun Violence: Evaluation of the Indianapolis Police Department's Directed Patrol Project* (Washington, DC: National Institute of Justice, 2002).

23. David M. Kennedy et al., *Reducing Gun Violence: The Boston Gun Project's Operation Ceasefire* (Washington, DC: National Institute of Justice, 2001).

24. Terence Dunworth and Gregory Mills, *National Evaluation of Weed and Seed* (Washington, DC: National Institute of Justice, 1999).

25. Lawrence W. Sherman, Dennis P. Rogan, and James W. Shaw, "The Kansas City Gun Experiment—NIJ Update," *Research in Brief* (November 1994).

26. Lawrence W. Sherman and Richard A. Berk, *Minneapolis Domestic Violence Experiment,* Police Foundation Report 1 (Washington, DC: Police Foundation, April 1984).

27. National Institute of Justice, *Newport News Tests Problem-Oriented Policing,* National Institute of Justice Reports (Washington, DC: U.S. Government Printing Office, January/February 1987).

28. Adapted from Deakin, "The Police Foundation."

29. Lawrence W. Sherman, *Evidence-Based Policing* (Washington, DC: Police Foundation, 1998), p. 3.

30. Sherman, *Evidence-Based Policing,* from which much of the material in this section is taken.

31. U.S. Department of Justice, *A Proud History . . . a Bright Future: Careers with the FBI,* pamphlet (October 1986), p. 1.

32. Much of the information in this section comes from U.S. Department of Justice, *The FBI: The First Seventy-Five Years* (Washington, DC: U.S. Government Printing Office, 1986).

33. Some of the information in this section is adapted from Federal Bureau of Investigation, "Facts and Figures 2003." Web posted at http://www.fbi.gov/priorities/priorities.htm (accessed January 5, 2006).

34. Telephone conversation with FBI officials, April 21, 1995.

35. Public Laws 98-473 and 99-474.

36. Information in this section comes from Christopher H. Asplen, "National Commission Explores Its Future," *NIJ Journal* (January 1999), pp. 17–24.

37. The DNA Identification Act is Section 210301 of the Violent Crime Control and Law Enforcement Act of 1994.

38. As reported in "DNA Profiles Face Delays before Reaching FBI Database," Associated Press, November 15, 2004.

39. Much of the information in this paragraph comes from the FBI Academy website at http://www.fbi.gov/hq/td/academy/academy.htm (accessed January 3, 2006).

40. "Attorney General Ashcroft and Deputy Attorney General Thompson Announce Reorganization and Mobilization of the Nation's Justice and Law Enforcement Resources," U.S. Department of Justice press release, November 8, 2001.

41. Testimony of Robert S. Mueller III, director of the Federal Bureau of Investigation, before the Senate Committee on Intelligence of the U.S. Senate, February 16, 2005.

42. Henry M. Wrobleski and Karen M. Hess, *Introduction to Law Enforcement and Criminal Justice,* 4th ed. (St. Paul, MN: West, 1993), p. 34.

43. Ibid., p. 35.

44. New York City Police Department website, http://www.nyc.gov/html/nypd (accessed June 11, 2005).

45. Brian A. Reaves and Matthew J. Hickman, *Census of State and Local Law Enforcement Agencies, 2000* (Washington, DC: Bureau of Justice Statistics, 2002).

46. Ibid.

47. Note, however, that New York City jails may have daily populations that, on a given day, exceed those of Los Angeles County.

48. The Police Assessment Resource Center, *The Los Angeles County Sheriff's Department—17th Semiannual Report* (Los Angeles: LASD, 2003); and telephone communication with Deputy Ethan Marquez, L.A. County Sheriff's Department, Custodial Division, January 24, 2002.

49. Reaves and Hickman, *Census of State and Local Law Enforcement Agencies, 2000.*

50. *Private Security: Report of the Task Force on Private Security* (Washington, DC: U.S. Government Printing Office, 1976), p. 4.

51. "Olympic Committee to Review Salt Lake Security in Wake of Terror Attacks," Associated Press, September 17, 2001.

52. "Securing the Olympic Games: $142,857 Security Cost per Athlete in Greece," *Wall Street Journal,* August 22, 2004. Web posted at http://www.mindfully.org/Reform/2004/Olympic-Games-Security22aug04.htm.

53. The information and some of the wording in this paragraph come from the ASIS International website at http://www.asisonline.org (accessed August 5, 2005).

54. David H. Bayley and Clifford D. Shearing, *The New Structure of Policing: Description, Conceptualization, and Research Agenda* (Washington, DC: National Institute of Justice, 2001).

55. National Center for Policy Analysis, *Using the Private Sector to Deter Crime* (Washington, DC: NCPA, 2001).

56. William C. Cunningham, John J. Strauchs, and Clifford W. Van Meter, *The Hallcrest Report II: Private Security Trends, 1970–2000* (McLean, VA: Hallcrest Systems, 1990).

57. See http://www.spyandsecuritystore.com .conex.html (accessed June 5, 2005).

58. Cunningham, Strauchs, and Van Meter, *The Hallcrest Report II,* p. 236.

59. Peter Lewis, "Companies Turn to Private Spies," *Fortune,* August 9, 2004, p. 24.

60. Ibid.

61. Bayley and Shearing, *The New Structure of Policing,* p. 15.

62. NIJ, *Crime and Protection in America,* pp. 59–72.

63. International Association of Chiefs of Police, *National Policy Summit: Building Private Security/Public Policing Partnerships to Prevent and Respond to Terrorism and Public Disorder: Vital Issues and Policy Recommendations 2004* (Washington, DC: U.S. Department of Justice, 2004).

64. Ibid, p. 1.

# CHAPTER 6

# Policing: Purpose and Organization

## OUTLINE

- Introduction
- The Police Mission
- Operational Strategies
- Managing Police Departments
- Policing Styles
- Terrorism's Impact on Policing
- Discretion and the Individual Officer
- Professionalism and Ethics
- Ethnic and Gender Diversity in Policing

## LEARNING OBJECTIVES

**After reading this chapter, you should be able to:**

- Explain the basic purposes of policing in democratic societies.
- List and discuss the five core operational strategies of today's police departments.
- Define the term *police management,* and describe the different types of organizational structures typical of American police departments.
- Identify the three styles of policing, and discuss differences in these approaches.
- Describe community policing, and explain how it differs from traditional policing.
- Describe the changed role of American police in the post-9/11 environment.
- Explain police discretion and how it affects the practice of contemporary law enforcement.
- Demonstrate why professionalism is important in policing today.
- Identify some of the issues related to ethnic and gender diversity in policing, and suggest ways of addressing them.

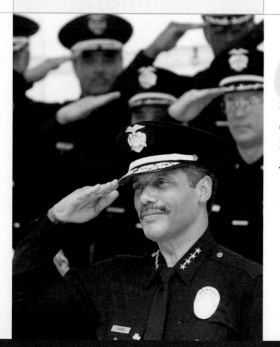

> *The purpose of the police service is to uphold the law fairly and firmly; to prevent crime; to pursue and bring to justice those who break the law; to keep the . . . peace; to protect, help and reassure the community; and to be seen to do this with integrity, common sense and sound judgment.*
>
> —United Kingdom Police Service, Statement of Common Purpose

*The tragedies of September 11, 2001, have forever changed the roles of traditional law enforcement in this country.*

—Major Cities Chiefs Association[1]

## KEY CONCEPTS

### TERMS

chain of command
community policing
CompStat
crime prevention
crime scene
crime-scene investigator
criminal intelligence
criminal investigation
intelligence-led policing
legalistic style
line operations

MATRIX
peace officer standards and training
(POST) program
police–community relations (PCR)
police discretion
police ethics
police management
police professionalism
police subculture
preliminary investigation

problem-solving policing
quality-of-life offense
response time
service style
solvability factor
span of control
staff operations
strategic policing
team policing
watchman style

# Introduction

Hear the author discuss
this chapter at
**cjtoday.com**

In mid-November 2003, thousands of demonstrators protesting the proposed creation of the Free Trade Area of the Americas (FTAA) clashed with hundreds of Miami police officers equipped with riot gear. The protesters were targeting a meeting by foreign trade ministers to express concern that the creation of the 34-nation FTAA would send thousands of U.S. jobs overseas, exploit cheap labor, and waste natural resources.[2]

Although most demonstrators paraded peacefully and avoided confrontations, some pulled down crowd-control barriers with grappling hooks and scuffled with officers who were trying to maintain order. Before the melee ended, officers had to use batons, plastic shields, concussion grenades, pepper spray, and stun guns to regain control over the unruly protesters. Armored personnel carriers stood ready to move into hot spots. "We're basically trying to maintain the peace downtown," said police spokesperson Jorge Pino, as demonstrators advanced on police lines.[3] By the time the event ended, 74 people had been arrested and 42 protesters were injured, including 10 who had to be hospitalized. Three police officers were also hurt. As the Miami riots demonstrate, the maintenance of social order is an important part of police work today.

# The Police Mission

The basic purposes of policing in democratic societies are to (1) enforce and support the laws of the society of which the police are a part, (2) investigate crimes and apprehend offenders, (3) prevent crime, (4) help ensure domestic peace and tranquility, and (5) provide the community with needed enforcement-related services. Simply put, as Sir Robert Peel, founder of the British system of policing, explained in 1822, "The basic mission for which the police exist is to reduce crime and disorder."[4]

In the paragraphs that follow, we turn our attention to these five basic elements of the police mission.

It shall be the mission of the Bradley County Sheriff's Office to consistently meet the public safety needs of all the people we serve, with integrity, respect, and fairness, within the resources allocated to us for this purpose. We shall strive to meet or exceed the expectations of those we serve, while enforcing the spirit of the law, and by always doing what is right.

—Mission statement,
Bradley County (Tennessee)
Sheriff's Office[i]

# Enforcing the Law

The police operate under an official public mandate that requires them to enforce the law. Collectively speaking, police agencies are the primary enforcers of federal, state, and local criminal laws. Not surprisingly, police officers see themselves as crime fighters, a view shared by the public and promoted by the popular media.

Although it is the job of the police to enforce the law, it is not their *only* job. Practically speaking, most officers spend the majority of their time answering nonemergency public-service calls,[5] controlling traffic, or writing tickets. Most are not involved in intensive, ongoing crime-fighting activities. Research shows that only about 10% to 20% of all calls to the police involve situations that actually require a law enforcement response, that is, situations that might lead to arrest and eventual prosecution.[6]

Miami riot police advancing through burning trash to control demonstrators protesting a meeting of foreign delegates who were attempting to negotiate an international free-trade agreement in 2003. Order maintenance is an important part of the police mission.

*AP Wide World Photos*

Even when the police are busy enforcing laws, they can't enforce them all. Police resources, including labor, vehicles, and investigative assets, are limited, causing officers to focus more on certain types of law violations than on others. Old laws prohibiting minor offenses such as spitting on the sidewalk hold little social significance today and are typically relegated to the dustbin of statutory history. Even though they are still "on the books," few officers, if any, even think about enforcing such laws. Police tend to tailor their enforcement efforts to meet the contemporary concerns of the populace they serve.[7] For example, if a community is upset about a "massage parlor" operating in its neighborhood, the local police department may bring enforcement efforts to bear that lead to the relocation of such a business. However, while community interests significantly influence the enforcement practices of police agencies, individual officers take their cue on enforcement priorities from their departments, their peers, and their supervisors. Learn more about how police supervisory styles influence patrol officer behavior at **Library Extra 6–1** at cjtoday.com.

The police are expected not only to enforce the law but also to support it. The personal actions of law enforcement personnel should inspire others to respect and obey the law. Off-duty officers who speed down the highway or smoke marijuana at a party, for example, do a disservice to the police profession and engender disrespect for all agents of enforcement and for the law itself. Hence, in an important sense, we can say that respect for the law begins with the personal and public behavior of law enforcement officers.

## Apprehending Offenders

Some offenders are apprehended during the commission of a crime or immediately afterward. Fleeing Oklahoma City bomber Timothy McVeigh, for example, was stopped by an Oklahoma Highway Patrol officer on routine patrol only 90 minutes after the destruction of the Alfred P. Murrah federal building[8] for driving a car with no license plate. When the officer questioned McVeigh about a bulge in his jacket, McVeigh admitted that it was a gun. The officer then took McVeigh into custody for carrying a concealed weapon. Typically, McVeigh would then have made an immediate appearance before a judge and have been released on bail. As fate would have it, however, the judge assigned to see McVeigh was involved in a protracted divorce case. The longer jail stay proved to be McVeigh's undoing. As the investigation into the bombing progressed, profiler Clinton R. Van Zandt of the Federal Bureau of Investigation's Behavioral Science Unit concluded that the bomber was likely a native-born white male in his twenties who had been in the military and was probably a member of a fringe militia group—all of which were true of McVeigh.[9] Working together, the FBI and the Oklahoma State Police realized that McVeigh was a

A warning sign amidst the destruction left by Hurricane Katrina in 2005 telling looters to stay away from a flood-damaged home in Biloxi, Mississippi. Effective law enforcement helps maintain social order and fills a critical need in the face of the widespread social disorganization that sometimes follows natural disasters or large-scale terrorist attacks.

*Win McNamee, Getty Images, Inc.*

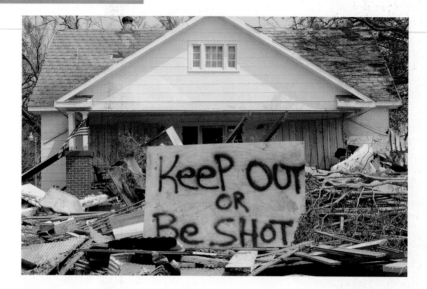

likely suspect and questioned him. While McVeigh's capture was the result of a bit of good luck, many offenders are only caught as the result of extensive police work involving a painstaking investigation. (Investigation is described in more detail later in this chapter.)

# Preventing Crime

**crime prevention**

The anticipation, recognition, and appraisal of a crime risk and the initiation of action to eliminate or reduce it.

**Crime prevention** is a proactive approach to the problem of crime; it is "the anticipation, recognition and appraisal of a crime risk and initiation of action to remove or reduce it."[10] In preventing crime, police agencies act before a crime happens, thus preventing victimization from occurring. Although the term *crime prevention* is relatively new, the idea is not. Securing valuables, limiting access to sensitive areas, and monitoring the activities of suspicious people are techniques used long before Western police forces were established in the 1800s.

Modern crime-prevention efforts aim not only to reduce crime and criminal opportunities and to lower the potential rewards of criminal activity, but also to lessen the public's fear of crime.[11] Law enforcement–led crime-prevention efforts include both techniques and programs. Crime-prevention techniques include controlling access, including barriers to entryways and exits; surveillance, such as video surveillance; theft-deterrence devices such as locks, alarms, and tethers; lighting; and visibility landscaping. Crime-prevention *programs* are organized efforts that focus resources on reducing a specific form of criminal threat. The Philadelphia Police Department's Operation Identification, for example, is designed to discourage theft and to help recover stolen property.[12] The program educates citizens on the importance of identifying, marking, and listing their valuables to deter theft (because marked items are more difficult to sell) and to aid in their recovery. Through Operation Identification, the police department provides engraving pens, suggests ways of photographing valuables, and provides window decals and car bumper stickers that identify citizens as participants in the program. Other crime-prevention programs typically target school-based crime, gang activity, drug abuse, violence, domestic abuse, identity theft, vehicle theft, or neighborhood crimes, such as burglary.

Today's crime-prevention programs depend on community involvement and education and effective interaction between enforcement agencies and the communities they serve. For example, "neighborhood watch" programs build on active observation by homeowners and businesspeople on the lookout for anything unusual. Crime Stoppers International and Crime Stoppers USA are examples of privately sponsored programs that accept tips about criminal activity that they pass on to the appropriate law enforcement organization. Crime Stoppers International can be accessed at Web Extra 6–1, and the National Crime Prevention Council can be found at Web Extra 6–2 at cjtoday.com.

> Unlike the soldier fighting a war on foreign soil, police officers, who provide for our safety at home, have never been given the honor that was their due.
>
> —Hubert Williams, President, The Police Foundation[ii]

**WEB EXTRA**

## Predicting Crime

Law enforcement's ability to prevent crimes relies in part on the ability of police planners to predict when and where crimes will occur. Effective prediction means that limited police resources can be correctly assigned to the areas with the greatest need. One technique for predicting criminal activity is **CompStat**.[13] While CompStat may sound like a software program, it is actually a process of crime analysis and police management developed by the New York City Police Department in the mid-1990s[14] to help police managers better assess their performance and foresee the potential for crime. The CompStat process involves first collecting and analyzing the information received from 9-1-1 calls and officer reports.[15] Then, this detailed and timely information is mapped using special software developed for the purpose. The resulting map sequences, generated over time, reveal the time and place of crime patterns and identify "hot spots" of ongoing criminal activity. The maps also show the number of patrol officers active in an area, ongoing investigations, arrests made, and so on, thus helping commanders see which anticrime strategies are working.

CrimeStat, a Windows®-based spatial statistics-analysis software program for analyzing crime-incident locations, is a second technique for predicting criminal activity and produces results similar to CompStat's.[16] Developed by Ned Levine and Associates with grants from the National Institute of Justice (NIJ), CrimeStat provides statistical tools for crime mapping and analysis—including identification of crime hot spots, spatial distribution of incidents, and distance analysis—which help crime analysts target offenses that might be related to one another. CrimeStat software is available online via Web Extra 6–3, and Web Extra 6–4 provides a link to chicagocrime.org, which overlays crime statistics on maps of the city.

| **CompStat** |
| --- |
| A crime-analysis and police-management process built on crime mapping that was developed by the New York City Police Department in the mid-1990s. |

**WEB** EXTRA

# Preserving the Peace

Enforcing the law, apprehending offenders, and preventing crime are all daunting tasks for police departments, because there are many laws and numerous offenders. Still, crimes are clearly defined by statute and are therefore limited in number. Peacekeeping, however, is a virtually limitless police activity involving not only activities that violate the law (and hence the community's peace) but many others as well. Law enforcement officers who supervise parades, public demonstrations, and picketing strikers, for example, attempt to ensure that the behavior of everyone involved remains "civil" so that it does not disrupt community life.

Robert H. Langworthy, who has written extensively about the police, says that keeping the peace is often left up to individual officers.[17] Basically, he says, departments depend on patrol officers "to define the peace and decide how to support it," and an officer is doing a good job when his or her "beat is quiet, meaning there are no complaints about loiterers or traffic flow, and commerce is supported."

Many police departments focus on quality-of-life offenses as a crime-reduction and peacekeeping strategy. **Quality-of-life offenses** are minor law violations, sometimes called *petty crimes,* that demoralize residents and businesspeople by creating disorder. Examples of petty crimes include excessive noise, graffiti, abandoned cars, and vandalism. Other quality-of-life offenses

| **quality-of-life offense** |
| --- |
| A minor violation of the law (sometimes called a *petty crime*) that demoralizes community residents and businesspeople. Quality-of-life offenses involve acts that create physical disorder (for example, excessive noise or vandalism) or that reflect social decay (for example, panhandling and prostitution). |

Chief Deputy Paula Townsend of the Watauga County, North Carolina, Sheriff's Department carries 11-month-old Breanna Chambers to safety in 2005 after the capture of the child's parents. The parents, who were already wanted on charges related to methamphetamine manufacture, were charged with additional counts of child abduction, felonious restraint, and assault with a gun after they abducted Breanna and her two-year-old brother, James Paul Chambers, from a foster home. Today's police officers are expected to enforce the law while meeting the needs of the community.
*AP Wide World Photos*

# CJ NEWS

## Crime-Fighting by Computer

New York City's renowned CompStat crime-fighting program, originally created to measure and map serious crime in city neighborhoods, has grown into a sweeping data-collection machine that traces hundreds of factors, many of which appear distant from the nuts and bolts of police work.

The system, introduced in 1994 to focus largely on the seven major crime categories, has changed in ways both substantial and subtle, and now records 734 of what officials call indicators: everything from concentrations of prostitutes to police overtime, allegations of abuse by officers and how often police commanders meet with community leaders.

The expansion reflects an acknowledgment that fighting crime is not just about finding criminals and arresting them, but about enlisting the support of communities and finding a way to do it economically.

In effect, CompStat has become an intricate map of the city and its ills—the annoying and the deadly—and an abacus upon which officials can calculate how the Police Department is working to alleviate them.

Gone are the days when murder, rape, robbery, assault, burglary, grand larceny and auto theft were the central focus of searing CompStat meetings in a cavernous room on the eighth floor of 1 Police Plaza.

Under the current commissioner, Raymond W. Kelly, CompStat has further evolved, focusing also on minor offenses that can have a major impact on the quality of city life: panhandling, squeegee men, loud parties and barking dogs. And the weekly meetings have become more collegial, with an atmosphere, Mr. Kelly said, in which commanders are often put on the spot but spared the abuse that many glumly suffered in years past.

"It's been broadened, and again, it is more collaborative, in the sense that we're trying to share information as to what was done by other commands to address problems," said Mr. Kelly, who took over the force in January in his second tour as commissioner.

CompStat has long been admired nationally and internationally; the system has been used by cities like Baltimore, and Caracas, Venezuela, plans to use it. The concept has also been copied in its hometown, where it has been brought into other agencies like the Sanitation and Correction Departments, and where Mayor Michael R. Bloomberg is considering using it to measure the effectiveness of other city agencies.

The innovation was created and developed under William J. Bratton, the police commissioner from 1994 to 1996, the first two years of Mayor Rudolph W. Giuliani's administration; one of the primary architects of the program was Jack Maple, Mr. Bratton's deputy commissioner for crime control strategies. Mr. Maple died of cancer last summer.

Mr. Bratton used CompStat to direct swift deployments of officers to areas with high concentrations of crime and to hold commanders accountable for crime problems in their precincts.

His approach turned into a police philosophy that changed the way departments across America and in other parts of the world serve their communities, drawing a nonstop procession of police commanders and government officials from as far away as China and Chile.

A screen capture of a COPLINK® search results page. COPLINK, proprietary software that has been described as "Google for Cops," links together crime records from many different databases. Shown here is the COPLINK visualizer component, which allows investigators to rapidly identify relationships and to detect patterns that generate solid leads to solve crimes faster than conventional tools. Some suggest that the software, which is catching on quickly with police departments throughout the nation, may soon become more popular than CompStat crime-mapping software.

*Courtesy of Knowledge Computing Corporation*

## CJ NEWS *(continued)*

Soon after it was introduced, it became part of the culture at 1 Police Plaza: twice-weekly meetings in which local commanders were pushed, prodded and sometimes humiliated by senior officials who pinpointed crime problems on their streets and broadcast their failings.

Mr. Bratton defended the aggressive nature of the sessions in the early days, arguing that precinct commanders were making $80,000 a year. "If they can't deal with the pressure of that room, you can be damn sure they can't deal with pressure out there on the street," he said.

Mr. Kelly, however, said he felt that commanders, who are each running what he called the equivalent of a $30 million to $40 million business, "shouldn't be abused, they should be treated with dignity and respect, while held accountable for what happens on their watch."

Eli B. Silverman, a professor at the John Jay College of Criminal Justice and the author of "NYPD Battles Crime: Innovative Strategies in Policing," said a certain amount of pressure was required in the program's early days. "My own view was that in the beginning it needed to be very forceful because you were starting something very different," he said.

Mr. Kelly, who has made upgrading department technology a priority, says he hopes to use teleconferencing to broadcast the now weekly meetings to officials in boroughs beyond the one under scrutiny each week.

And, it seems, there is much to learn. Mr. Kelly said the meetings now focused on the number of precinct arrests that were made by officers on overtime patrols, part of an effort to reduce costs and ensure that enforcement is driven by crime rather than an officer's desire for more overtime.

CompStat now also measures emergency response time, conditions in police station houses and how many police cars are available for patrol and how quickly those in need of repairs are turned around in the department's shops.

The system also records the number of corruption allegations and civilian complaints of police abuse in each precinct, which along with community relations are important indicators of how a department serves the people, according to Mark H. Moore, a professor of criminal justice policy and management at the Kennedy School of Government at Harvard University. Professor Moore, who has been studying methods to measure police performance for five years, contends that crime reductions alone provide an incomplete picture of a police department.

He maintains that a police force's performance—or "profits"—can be accurately gauged only by factoring in the "costs" of police operations: not only the financial costs, but the toll that police operations take on community relations, or how the department's use of authority impinges on citizens' liberties.

"The degree that people feel alienated by the police is the degree to which they are reluctant to cooperate with them, something that makes the work of the police more difficult," he said.

For the latest in crime and justice news, visit the Talk Justice news feed at http://www.crimenews.info.

*Source:* William K. Rashbaum, "Crime-Fighting by Computer Widens Scope," *The New York Times,* March 24, 2002. Copyright © 2002 by the New York Times Co. Reprinted with permission.

reflect social decay and include panhandling and aggressive begging, public urination, prostitution, roaming youth gangs, public consumption of alcohol, and street-level substance abuse.[18] Homelessness, while not necessarily a violation of the law unless it involves some form of trespass,[19] is also typically addressed under quality-of-life programs. Through police interviews, many of the homeless are relocated to shelters or hospitals or are arrested for some other offense. Some researchers claim that reducing the number of quality-of-life offenses in a community can restore a sense of order, reduce the fear of crime, and lessen the number of serious crimes that occur. However, quality-of-life programs have been criticized by those who say that the police should not be taking a law enforcement approach to social and economic problems.[20]

A similar approach to keeping the peace can be found in the broken windows model of policing.[21] This thesis (which is also discussed in the CJ Futures box in Chapter 3) is based on the notion that physical decay in a community, such as litter and abandoned buildings, can breed disorder and lead to crime by signaling that laws are not being enforced.[22] Such decay, the theory postulates, pushes law-abiding citizens to withdraw from the streets, which then sends a signal that lawbreakers can operate freely.[23] The broken windows thesis suggests that by encouraging the repair of rundown buildings and controlling disorderly behavior in public spaces, police agencies can create an environment in which serious crime cannot easily flourish.[24]

While desirable, public order has its own costs. Noted police author Charles R. Swanson says, "The degree to which any society achieves some amount of public order through police action depends in part upon the price that society is willing to pay to obtain it."[25] Swanson goes on to describe the price to be paid in terms of (1) police resources paid for by tax dollars and (2) "a reduction in the number, kinds, and extent of liberties" that are available to members of the public.

Log on to ResearchNavigator .com, and choose "All" under the *New York Times* subject archive section. Enter the word "COMPSTAT" (without the quotation marks) in the search box, and click "Go." Select two articles that you find interesting from the results page. Write a summary of each article, including complete source information—that is, article title, author (if available), date of publication, and source (in this case, the *New York Times*). Submit what you have written to your instructor if asked to do so. *Note:* This feature is available only if your instructor has chosen the Research Navigator option available with a new textbook.

# Providing Services

As writers for the National Institute of Justice observe, "any citizen from any city, suburb, or town across the United States can mobilize police resources by simply picking up the phone and placing a direct call to the police."[26] "Calling the cops" has been described as the cornerstone of policing in a democratic society. About 70% of the millions of daily calls to 9-1-1 systems across the country are directed to the police, although callers can also request emergency medical and fire services. Calls received by 9-1-1 operators are prioritized and then relayed to patrol officers, specialized field units, or other emergency personnel. For example, the Hastings (Minnesota) Police Department handled a total of 12,895 calls for service in 2001.[27] A breakdown of those calls shows that there were 1,837 calls related to serious crimes such as arson, assault, auto theft, burglary, larceny, rape, and robbery. The remaining 11,058 calls were nonemergency calls about lost and found articles, minor motor vehicle accidents, barking dogs, suspicious persons, and parking and traffic law violation reports. Numbers like these have led some cities to adopt nonemergency "Citizen Service System" call numbers in addition to 9-1-1. More than a dozen metropolitan areas, including Baltimore, Dallas, Detroit, Las Vegas, New York, and San Jose, now staff 3-1-1 nonemergency systems around the clock. Plans are afoot in some places to adopt the 3-1-1 system statewide.

# Operational Strategies

The police mission offers insight into general law enforcement goals, which help shape the various operational strategies that departments employ.[28] There are five core operational strategies—preventive patrol, routine incident response, emergency response, criminal investigation, and problem solving—and one ancillary operational strategy—support services.[29] The first four core strategies constitute the conventional way in which police have worked, at least since the 1930s; problem solving is relatively new. Each strategy has unique features, and each represents a particular way to approach situations that the police encounter. Operational strategies can be discussed along a number of dimensions. Table 6–1 describes each strategy in different ways, including the objectives, performance standards, and processes involved.

## Preventive Patrol

Preventive patrol is the dominant operational policing strategy[30] and has been the backbone of police work since the time of Sir Robert Peel. Routine patrol activities, which place uniformed police officers on the street in the midst of the public, consume most of the resources of most local and state-level police agencies.

The purpose of patrol is fourfold: to deter crimes, to interrupt crimes in progress, to position officers for quick response to emergency situations, and to increase the public's feelings of safety and security. Patrol is the operational mode uniformed officers are expected to work in when not otherwise involved in answering calls for service. Most departments use a computer-assisted dispatch (CAD) system to prioritize incoming service calls into different categories and to record dispatches issued, time spent on each call, the identities of responding personnel, and so on.

The majority of patrol activity is *interactive* because officers on patrol commonly interact with the public. Some forms of patrol, however, involve more interaction than others. The many types of patrol include foot, automobile, motorcycle, mounted, bicycle, boat, K-9, and aerial. Although some scientific studies of policing have questioned the effectiveness of preventive patrol in reducing crime (discussed in Chapter 5), most citizens expect police to patrol.

## Routine Incident Response

Police officers on patrol frequently respond to routine incidents, such as minor traffic accidents. Routine incident responses comprise the second most common activity of patrol officers.[31] Officers responding to routine incidents must collect information and, typically, file a written report. As noted by the National Institute of Justice, "the specific police objective will . . . vary depending on the nature of the situation, but generally, the objective is to restore order, document information or otherwise provide some immediate service to the parties involved."[32]

TABLE 6-1

## OPERATIONAL STRATEGIES OF POLICE WORK

| Operational Strategy | Work Unit | Objectives | Record System | Reporting Requirements | Performance Standards | Specialized Training | Processes | Accountability |
|---|---|---|---|---|---|---|---|---|
| Preventive patrol | None—ongoing | Prevent and detect offenses, promote general feelings of security | Daily activity reports, patrol vehicle mileage | Daily activity reports | Absence of crime, low levels of citizen fear, high rates of police detection of certain types of offenses (e.g., commercial burglary) | Patrol methods (random, directed) | Limited—some officers use systematic area coverage patterns and plans | Limited—some expectation that officers will detect certain offenses on their beats, some command accountability for absence of citizen complaints about police presence |
| Routine incident response | Call | Record incident, resolve dispute, provide or take information | Dispatch records | Report or coded disposition | Complainant satisfaction, response time, fair treatment of parties, proper completion of report | Special training by type of incident | Procedures according to call type, reporting requirements | Code out call, file report, accountability rests with officer assigned and shift supervisor |
| Emergency response | Critical incident | Save life, interrupt crime, protect property, minimize injury | Dispatch records, after-action reports | Critical incident report | No deaths, minimal injuries, order restored | Vehicle operation, first aid, hostage rescue, SWAT, defensive tactics | First aid procedures, critical incident procedures, triage | Primary officer or scene commander, until incident ends (handed off, if necessary) |
| Criminal investigation | Case | Establish culpability, make prosecutable case, apprehend offender, clear case | Case files | Case report and file | Case filed by prosecutor, suspect apprehended | Death investigation, crime-scene analysis, forensics, interviewing | Criminal investigative procedures | Case file deadlines, case management (handed off, if necessary), rests with detective assigned, unit supervisor |
| Problem solving | Problem or project | Reduce harm, reduce incidence, eliminate problem, improve response | Project files | Sometimes none, project report | Significant reduction in harm, caused by intervention, for reasonable period of time | Problem-solving methods | SARA, CAPRA (see text) | Rests with police chief, district commander, supervisor, and officer |
| Support services | Program or procedure | Provide service, enhance police legitimacy | Program reports | Program or budget reports | Use/popularity of service | Specific procedures | Written procedure or curriculum | Fiscal |

Source: Adapted from Michael S. Scott, *Problem-Oriented Policing: Reflections on the First 20 Years* (Washington, DC: U.S. Department of Justice, Office of Community Oriented Policing Services, 2000), p. 89.

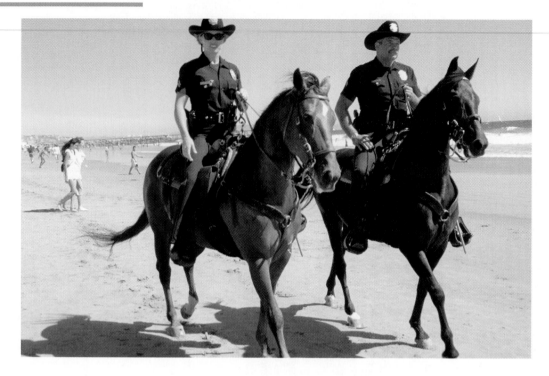

Patrol, a typical police function, can take a variety of forms. Here, mounted Los Angeles Police Department officers patrol a beach within the city limits.

*A. Ramey, PhotoEdit*

---

**response time**

A measure of the time that it takes for police officers to respond to calls for service.

---

One important measure of police success that is strongly linked to citizen satisfaction is **response time**—the time it takes for police officers to respond to calls for service. It is measured from the time a call for service is received by a dispatcher until an officer arrives on the scene. In 2001, for example, police response time in New York City averaged 7.2 minutes for all types of calls, 29% faster than the previous year and the quickest response time in a decade.[33] Average response time for critical calls in New York City decreased 20%, to 4.8 minutes. Response times in 2001 were cut by an average of nearly three minutes over the previous year, even in the face of an increased number of calls and budget cutbacks that resulted in fewer officers on patrol.

## Emergency Response

The spectacular and horrific nature of the September 11 terrorist attacks and the massive devastation and loss of life that they wrought have ushered in a new era of policing in the United States.

—International Association of Chiefs of Police[iv]

In May 2003, Pomona, California, police officers on routine patrol responded to a dispatcher's instructions to assist in an emergency at a local coin-operated laundry.[34] On arrival, they found a two-year-old girl trapped inside an industrial-size washing machine. The officers used their batons to smash the locked glass-paned door. The girl, unconscious and nearly drowned when pulled from the machine, was taken to a local hospital where she was expected to recover. Her mother, 35-year-old Erma Osborne, was arrested at the scene and charged with child endangerment when the on-site video surveillance cameras showed her placing her daughter in the machine and shutting the door.

Although police respond to emergencies far less frequently than to routine incidents,[35] emergency response is a vital aspect of what police agencies do. Emergency responses, often referred to as *critical incidents,* are used for crimes in progress, traffic accidents with serious injuries, natural disasters, incidents of terrorism, officer requests for assistance, and other situations in which human life may be in jeopardy. Emergency responses take priority over all other police work, and until an emergency situation is secured and some order restored, the officers involved will not turn to other tasks. An important part of police training involves emergency response techniques, including first aid, hostage rescue, and the physical capture of suspects.

---

**criminal investigation**

"The process of discovering, collecting, preparing, identifying, and presenting evidence to determine *what happened and who is responsible*"[v] when a crime has occurred.

---

## Criminal Investigation

The fourth operational strategy, criminal investigation, dominates media depictions of police work. Although central to the mission of the police, investigations actually constitute a relatively small proportion of police work. A **criminal investigation** is "the process of discovering, collect-

**FIGURE 6–1**

**The crime-scene investigation process.**

*Source:* Courtesy of the Massachusetts State Police.

The Arson and Explosives Unit receives evidence recovered from crime scenes involving suspicious fires and explosions. The unit identifies ignitable liquid evidence recovered from a fire scene that may have been intentionally used to propagate a fire. The unit also identifies explosives or explosive residues recovered from a bombing scene and can reconstruct devices to assist investigators in identifying perpetrators and the source(s) of device components.

The Drug Unit analyzes all contraband seized by state police agencies and some local and federal agencies in Massachusetts. The most common substances analyzed at the laboratory are marijuana, cocaine, and heroin. To perform these analyses, the unit utilizes sensitive and selective instrumentation. This instrumentation allows the unit to identify and measure a wide range of illegal substances that have been seized.

The Massachusetts State Police Crime Laboratory's DNA Unit processes forensic casework samples for STR (short tandem repeat) fragment analysis using a Perkin-Elmer 310 Genetic Analyzer. Thirteen specific locations on the molecule are tested for comparative DNA analysis of biological stains. DNA evidence is crucial to protect the unjustly accused and convict the guilty. Blood, such as that found on the rock in the mock crime scene, would be analyzed by the DNA Lab. Other biological materials—including saliva, semen, skin tissue, hair roots, and sweat— also contain nuclear DNA, which may lead to STR DNA profiles.

The Ballistics Section is responsible for conducting scientific examination, comparison, and identification of firearms and firearms-related evidence. Weapon operability must be demonstrated to support the successful prosecution of weapons-related offenses. Members respond to crime scenes to assist in determining what role, if any, a firearm has played in the commission of a crime. The section is also responsible for the destruction of firearms and ammunition as ordered by the court.

A victim's clothing would be logged in by the Evidence Control Unit. Clothing could also be of interest to the Criminalistics Unit and Trace Analysis Unit.

*Note:* This is not a real crime scene. This picture was fabricated by the Massachusetts State Police Crime Lab staff for demonstrative purposes.

ing, preparing, identifying, and presenting evidence to determine *what happened and who is responsible*"[36] when a crime occurs.

Criminal investigators are often referred to as *detectives,* and it is up to them to solve most crimes and to produce the evidence needed for the successful prosecution of suspects. But any police officer can be involved in the initial stages of the investigative process, especially those responding to critical incidents. First-on-the-scene officers, or first responders, can play a critical role in providing emergency assistance to the injured and in capturing suspects. First responders, however, also have an important responsibility to secure the crime scene, a duty that can later provide the basis for a successful criminal investigation. A **crime scene** is the physical area in which a crime is thought to have occurred and in which evidence of the crime is thought to reside (Figure 6–1). Securing the crime scene is particularly crucial, for when a crime takes place,

**crime scene**

The physical area in which a crime is thought to have occurred and in which evidence of the crime is thought to reside.

especially a violent one, confusion often results. People at the scene and curious onlookers may unwittingly (and sometimes intentionally) destroy physical evidence, obliterating important clues like tire tracks, fingerprints, or footprints.

The preliminary investigation is an important part of the investigatory process. An effective preliminary investigation is the foundation on which the entire criminal investigation process is built.[37] The Florida Highway Patrol's policy manual provides a broad definition of a **preliminary investigation**, saying that it refers to all of the activities undertaken by a police officer who responds to the scene of a crime.[38] Those activities include the following:

1. Responding to immediate needs and rendering aid to the injured
2. Noting such facts as the position of victims or injured subjects, recording spontaneous statements, noting unusual actions or activities, and notifying headquarters with an assessment of the scene
3. Determining that a crime has been committed
4. Initiating enforcement action, such as arresting or pursuing the offender or dispatching apprehension information
5. Securing the crime scene and protecting evidence, including limiting access, identifying and isolating witnesses, and protecting all evidence, especially short-lived evidence (such as impressions in sand or mud)
6. Determining the need for investigative specialists and arranging for their notification
7. Compiling a thorough and accurate report of activities

A preliminary investigation begins when the call to respond has been received. Even before they arrive at the crime scene, officers may observe important events related to the offense, such as fleeing vehicles or the presence of suspicious people nearby. After they arrive, first responders begin collecting information through observation and possibly through conversations with others who are already at the scene. Typically, it is at this point that officers determine whether there are sufficient grounds to believe that a crime has actually occurred. Even in suspected homicides, for example, it is important to rule out accidental death, suicide, and death by natural causes before the investigation can proceed beyond the preliminary stage.

Next, specially trained crime-scene investigators arrive, and the detailed examination of a crime scene begins. **Crime-scene investigators** are expert in the use of specific forensics techniques, such as gathering DNA evidence, collecting fingerprints, photographing the scene, making sketches to show the position of items at the scene, and interviewing witnesses.

Crime-scene investigators are commonly promoted to their posts internally, after at least a few years of patrol work. However, large local police departments and those at the state and federal levels may employ civilian crime-scene investigators. Follow-up investigations, based on evidence collected at the scene, are conducted by police detectives. Important to any investigation are solvability factors. A **solvability factor** is information about a crime that can provide a basis for determining the perpetrator's identity. If few solvability factors exist, a continuing investigation is unlikely to lead to an arrest. Learn more about crime-scene investigation at Library Extra 6–2 at cjtoday.com.

## Problem Solving

The fifth operational strategy of police work is problem solving. Also called *problem-oriented policing,* problem solving seeks to reduce chronic offending in a community. NIJ authors note that "historically, it is the least well-developed by the police profession. While the police have always used the mental processes of problem-solving, problem-solving as a formal operational strategy of police work has gained some structure and systematic attention only in the past 20 years."[39]

The methodology of police problem solving is known by acronyms such as SARA (scanning, analysis, response, and assessment) or CAPRA (clients, acquired/analyzed, partnerships, respond, assess). CAPRA was developed by the Royal Canadian Mounted Police, who built on the earlier SARA process. This is the CAPRA process[40]:

■ The police begin by communicating with the *clients* most affected by community problems.
■ Information is *acquired* and *analyzed* to determine the problem's causes.
■ Solutions are developed through community *partnerships.*

**preliminary investigation**
All of the activities undertaken by a police officer who responds to the scene of a crime, including determining whether a crime has occurred, securing the crime scene, and preserving evidence.

**crime-scene investigator**
An expert trained in the use of forensics techniques, such as gathering DNA evidence, collecting fingerprints, photography, sketching, and interviewing witnesses.

**solvability factor**
Information about a crime that forms the basis for determining the perpetrator's identity.

LIBRARY EXTRA

The expectations of law enforcement as first responder for homeland security have put an almost unachievable burden on local law enforcement.

—Judith Lewis, Captain (retired), Los Angeles County Sheriff's Department

- Police *respond* with a workable plan.
- After plan implementation, the police periodically *assess* the situation to ensure progress.

Learn more about problem analysis in policing via Library Extra 6–3 at cjtoday.com.

## Support Services

Support services constitute the sixth operational strategy found in police organizations. They include such activities as dispatch, training, human resources management, property and evidence control, and record keeping. Support services keep police agencies running and help deliver the equipment, money, and resources necessary to support law enforcement officers in the field.

# Managing Police Departments

**Police management** entails administrative activities that control, direct, and coordinate police personnel, resources, and activities in an effort to prevent crime, apprehend criminals, recover stolen property, and perform a variety of regulatory and helping services.[41] Police managers include sworn law enforcement personnel with administrative authority, from the rank of sergeant to captain, chief, or sheriff, and civilians such as police commissioners, attorneys general, state secretaries of crime control, and public-safety directors.

> **police management**
> The administrative activities of controlling, directing, and coordinating police personnel, resources, and activities in the service of preventing crime, apprehending criminals, recovering stolen property, and performing regulatory and helping services.[vi]

## Police Organization and Structure

Almost all American law enforcement organizations are formally structured among divisions and along lines of authority. Roles within police agencies generally fall into one of two categories: line and staff. **Line operations** are field or supervisory activities directly related to daily police work. **Staff operations** include support roles, such as administration. In organizations that have line operations only, authority flows from the top down in a clear, unbroken line[42]; no supporting elements (media relations, training, fiscal management divisions, and so on) exist. All line operations are directly involved in providing field services. Because almost all police agencies need support, only the smallest departments have only line operations.

> **line operations**
> In police organizations, the field activities or supervisory activities directly related to day-to-day police work.

Most police organizations include both line and staff operations. In such organizations, line managers are largely unencumbered with staff operations such as budgeting, training, the scientific analysis of evidence, legal advice, shift assignments, and personnel management. Support personnel handle these activities, freeing line personnel to focus on the day-to-day requirements of providing field services.

> **staff operations**
> In police organizations, activities (such as administration and training) that provide support for line operations.

In a line and staff agency, divisions are likely to exist within both line operations and staff operations. For example, field services, a line operation, may be broken down into enforcement and investigation. Administrative services, a staff operation, may be divided into human resources management, training and education, materials supply, finance management, and facilities management.. The line and staff structure easily accommodates functional areas of responsibility within line and staff divisions. The organizational chart of the Elk Grove (California) Police Department shows this type of organization (Figure 6–2). A similar organizational chart showing the line and staff structure of the Los Angeles County Sheriff's Department (LASD)—the largest sheriff's department in the world[43]—is shown in Figure 6–3.

## Chain of Command

The organizational chart of any police agency shows a hierarchical **chain of command**, or the order of authority within the department. The chain of command clarifies who reports to whom. Usually, the chief of police or sheriff is at the top of the command chain, although his or her boss may be a police commissioner, city council, or mayor, followed by the subordinate leaders of each division. In the Elk Grove Police Department's chain of command (see Figure 6–2), for example, one assistant chief answers to the chief of police and oversees each of the department's divisions; a sergeant heads the administration division; and a lieutenant heads the other two divisions—field operations and investigations. Because field operations provides services 24 hours each day,

> **chain of command**
> The unbroken line of authority that extends through all levels of an organization, from the highest to the lowest.

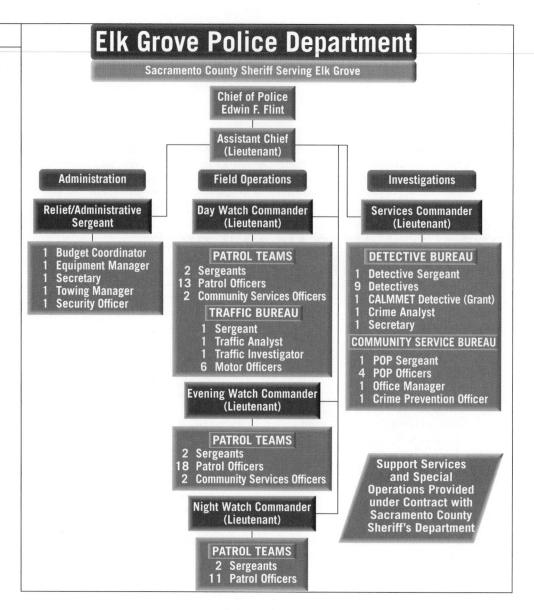

a number of lieutenants are assigned to it, each in charge of an 8-hour shift. Within that division, the day watch is staffed by 26 enforcement personnel, while the night watch routinely has only 13 officers on duty (two sergeants and 11 patrol officers).

Because police departments employ a quasi-military chain-of-command structure, the titles assigned to personnel (captain, lieutenant, sergeant) are similar to those used by the military. It is important for individual personnel to know who is in charge; hence, unity of command is an important principle that must be firmly established within the department. When unity of command exists, every individual has only one supervisor to whom she answers and from whom, under normal circumstances, she takes orders. **Span of control** refers to the number of police personnel or the number of units supervised by a particular commander. For example, one sergeant may be in charge of five or six officers; they represent the sergeant's span of control.

**span of control**

The number of police personnel or the number of units supervised by a particular commander.

# Policing Styles

The history of American policing can be divided into four epochs,[44] each distinguishable by the relative dominance of a particular approach to police operations (Figure 6–4). The first period, the political era, was characterized by close ties between police and public officials. It began in the 1840s and ended around 1930. Throughout the period, American police agencies tended to serve the interests of powerful politicians and their cronies, providing public-order-maintenance

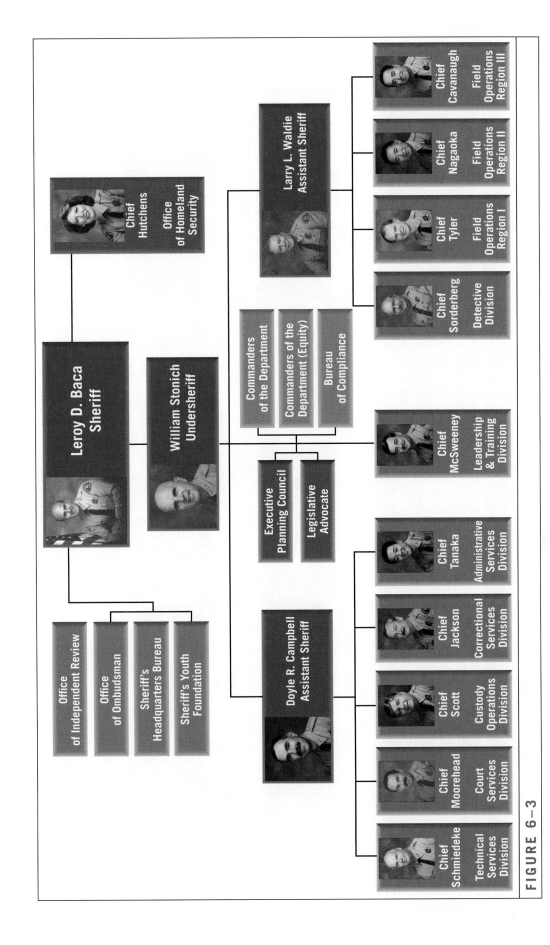

**FIGURE 6–3**

**Organizational chart of the Los Angeles County Sheriff's Department.**

*Source:* Los Angeles County Sheriff's Department. Reprinted with permission.

| Era | Political Era | Reform Era | Community Era | Homeland Security Era |
|---|---|---|---|---|
| Time Period | 1840s–1930 | 1930–1970s | 1970s–Today | 2001–Today |
| Characteristics | Close ties between the police and public officials.<br><br>Uniformed officers in paramilitary-style organizations serving the interests of the politically powerful. | Pride in professional crime fighting.<br><br>An emphasis on solving "traditional" crimes and capturing offenders. | Police departments work to identify and serve the needs of their communities.<br><br>Envisions a partnership between local police agencies and their communities. | Policing to secure the homeland; emphasis on terrorism prevention.<br><br>Builds on partnerships with the community to gather actionable intelligence to circumvent threats of terrorism. |
| Catalyst | The need for social order and security in a dynamic and rapidly changing society. | Citizen calls for reform and the development of police professionalism.<br><br>The removal of politics from policing. | The realization that effective community partnerships can help prevent and solve crimes. | The terrorist attacks of September 11, 2001, and ongoing threats to the safety and security of all Americans. |
| Example | Police departments and officers were closely tied to their city's political system.<br><br>Local "ward politicians" hired officers for their own purposes. | "G-men" and the crackdown on organized crime.<br><br>Progressive policing, led by men like August Vollmer and O. W. Wilson. | A focus on quality-of-life offenses as a crime-reduction and peacekeeping strategy.<br><br>The broken windows model of policing. | Creation of counterterrorism divisions and offices within departments.<br><br>Collaboration between police agencies and the sharing of information needed to identify threats. |

FIGURE 6–4

Historical eras in American policing.

services almost as an afterthought. The second period, the reform era, began in the 1930s and lasted until the 1970s. It was characterized by pride in professional crime fighting. Police departments during this period focused most of their resources on solving "traditional" crimes, such as murder, rape, and burglary, and on capturing offenders. The third period, and the one that continues to characterize much of contemporary policing in America today, is the community policing era—an approach to policing that stresses the service role of police officers and envisions a partnership between police agencies and their communities.

The fourth period, policing to secure the homeland, is quite new and continues to evolve.[45] The homeland security era grew out of national concerns with terrorism prevention born of the terrorist attacks of September 11, 2001. As police scholar Gene Stephens explains it, "the twenty-first century has put policing into a whole new milieu—one in which the causes of crime and disorder often lie outside the immediate community, demanding new and innovative approaches."[46] A decline in street crime, says Stephens, has been replaced by concern with new and more insidious types of offending, including terrorism and Internet-assisted crimes. These new kinds of crimes, says Stephens, while they threaten the integrity of local communities, often involve offenders thousands of miles away. Nonetheless, as we shall see later in this chapter, the homeland security era builds substantially upon the community policing philosophy with which it coexists.

The influence of each of the first three historical phases survives today in what noted social commentator and Presidential Medal of Freedom recipient James Q. Wilson[47] calls "policing styles."[48] A style of policing describes how a particular agency sees its purpose and chooses the methods it uses to fulfill that purpose. Wilson's three policing styles—which he does not link to any particular historical era—are (1) the watchman (characteristic of the political era), (2) the legalistic (professional crime fighting of the reform era), and (3) the service (which is becoming more common today). These three styles characterize nearly all municipal law enforcement agencies now operating in the United States, although some departments are a mixture of two or more styles.

## The Watchman Style of Policing

Police departments marked by the **watchman style** are chiefly concerned with achieving what Wilson calls "order maintenance" through control of illegal and disruptive behavior. Compared to the legalistic style, the watchman style uses discretion liberally. Watchman-style departments keep order through informal police "intervention," which may include persuasion, threats, or even "roughing up" disruptive people. Some authors condemn this style of policing, suggesting that it is typically found in lower- or lower-middle-class communities, especially where interpersonal relations include a fair amount of violence or physical abuse.

The watchman style was typified by the Los Angeles police officers who took part in the infamous beating of Rodney King. After the ensuing riots, the Christopher Commission, the independent commission on the Los Angeles Police Department (LAPD), found that the Los Angeles police "placed greater emphasis on crime control over crime prevention, a policy that distanced cops from the people they serve."[49]

## The Legalistic Style of Policing

Departments operating under the **legalistic style** enforce the letter of the law. For example, an officer who tickets a person going 71 mph in a 70-mph speed zone may be enforcing the law, but she is likely a member of a department that adheres to the legalistic style of policing. Conversely, legalistic departments routinely avoid community disputes arising from violations of social norms that do not break the law. Police expert Gary Sykes calls this enforcement style "laissez-faire policing" in recognition of its hands-off approach to behaviors that are simply bothersome or inconsiderate of community principles.[50]

## The Service Style of Policing

In service-oriented departments, which strive to meet the needs of the community and serve its members, the police see themselves more as helpers than as soldiers in a war on crime. This type of department works with social services and other agencies to provide counseling for minor offenders and to assist community groups in preventing crimes and solving problems. Prosecutors may support the **service style** by agreeing not to prosecute law violators who seek psychiatric help or who voluntarily participate in programs like Alcoholics Anonymous, family counseling,

**watchman style**
A style of policing marked by a concern for order maintenance. Watchman policing is characteristic of lower-class communities where police intervene informally into the lives of residents to keep the peace.

**legalistic style**
A style of policing marked by a strict concern with enforcing the precise letter of the law. Legalistic departments may take a hands-off approach to disruptive or problematic behavior that does not violate the criminal law.

**service style**
A style of policing marked by a concern with helping rather than strict enforcement. Service-oriented police agencies are more likely to use community resources, such as drug-treatment programs, to supplement traditional law enforcement activities than are other types of agencies.

## FREEDOM OR SAFETY? YOU DECIDE.

### Watch Out: You're on Police TV

Patrol cars equipped with video cameras have been on the nation's highways since the late 1980s, and the footage they've produced has been a staple of real-life police TV shows for years. In 2002, following the nationally televised airing of what appeared to be the physical abuse of a teenage suspect by an Inglewood, California, arresting officer, Inglewood Mayor Roosevelt Dorn called for cameras to be installed in all of his city's patrol cars. The alleged abuse had been videotaped by a bystander.

Many people believe that camera-equipped cars will lead to a reduction in police abuses while serving to capture evidence of illegal behavior by suspects. Video footage can also be used for identification purposes and might be coupled with software, allowing officers to quickly identify individuals who are wanted on other charges.

Some, however, fear that the combination of video images and face-recognition software will lead to the creation of a suspect database that will inevitably include many otherwise innocent people.

Since 2000, the Justice Department's Office of Community-Oriented Policing Services has provided $15 million to state law enforcement agencies to equip 3,563 cruisers with cameras, and in mid-2002, a Senate Appropriations subcommittee approved $1 million to install digital video cameras in the Seattle Police Department's 224 patrol cars. By 2003, across the country 17,500 state police vehicles were equipped with in-car cameras. A 2005 study by the International Association of Chiefs of Police surveyed 47 state law enforcement agencies that received federal grants to buy in-car cameras and concluded that such cameras substantially improved public trust in the police and protected officers against unfounded lawsuits.

#### YOU DECIDE

Do you think that equipping all patrol cars with video cameras is a good idea? What negative impact, if any, might this initiative have on personal freedoms in our society?

*References:* International Association of Chiefs of Police, *The Impact of Video Evidence on Modern Policing* (Alexandria, VA: IACP, 2005); Patrick McMahon, "Increased Clamor for Cameras in Cop Cars," *USA Today,* July 18, 2002.

or drug treatment. The service style is supported in part by citizens who seek to avoid the embarrassment that might result from a public airing of personal problems, thereby reducing the number of criminal complaints filed, especially in minor disputes. While the service style of policing may seem more appropriate to wealthy communities or small towns, it can also exist in cities whose police departments actively seek citizen involvement in identifying issues that the police can help address.

## Police–Community Relations

The 1960s were fraught with riots, unrest, and student activism as the war in Vietnam, civil rights concerns, and other social movements produced large demonstrations and marches. The police, generally inexperienced in crowd control, were all too often embroiled in tumultuous encounters—even pitched battles—with citizen groups that viewed the police as agents of "the establishment." To manage these new challenges, the legalistic style of policing, so common in America until then, began to yield to the newer service-oriented policing.

As social disorganization increased, police departments across the nation, seeking to understand and better cope with the problems they faced, created **police–community relations (PCR)** programs. PCR programs represented a movement away from an exclusive emphasis on the apprehension of law violators toward an effort to increase the level of positive police–citizen interaction. At the height of the PCR movement, city police departments across the country opened storefront centers where citizens could air complaints and interact easily with police representatives. As police scholar Egon Bittner recognized in 1976, PCR programs need to reach to "the grassroots of discontent," where citizen dissatisfaction with the police exists,[51] if they are to be truly effective.

In many contemporary PCR programs, public-relations officers are appointed to provide an array of services, such as "neighborhood watch" programs, drug-awareness workshops, "Project ID"—using police equipment and expertise to mark valuables for identification in the event of theft—and victims' assistance programs. Modern PCR programs, however, often fail to achieve their goal of increased community satisfaction with police services because they focus on servicing groups already well satisfied with the police. PCR initiatives that do reach disaffected community groups are difficult to manage and may even alienate participating officers from the

**police–community relations (PCR)**

An area of police activity that recognizes the need for the community and the police to work together effectively and that is based on the notion that the police derive their legitimacy from the community they serve. Many police agencies began to explore PCR in the 1960s and 1970s.

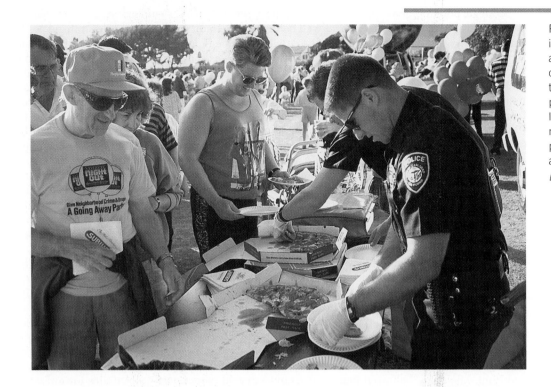

Police officers serving food during an anticrime rally to encourage citizen involvement in crime fighting. Activities like this help foster the community policing ideal through which law enforcement officers and members of the public become partners in controlling crime and keeping communities safe.

*Dale Stockton*

communities they are assigned to serve. Thus, as Bittner noted, "while the first approach fails because it leaves out those groups to which the program is primarily directed, the second fails because it leaves out the police department."

## Team Policing

During the 1960s and 1970s, some communities experimented with **team policing**, which rapidly became an extension of the PCR movement. With team policing, officers were assigned semipermanently to particular neighborhoods, where it was expected they would become familiar with the inhabitants and with their problems and concerns. Patrol officers were given considerable authority in processing complaints, from receipt through resolution. Crimes were investigated and solved at the local level, with specialists called in only if the resources needed to continue an investigation were not available locally. Some authors called team policing a "technique to deliver total police services to a neighborhood."[52] Others, however, dismissed it as "little more than an attempt to return to the style of policing that was prevalent in the United States over a century ago."[53]

> **team policing**
>
> The reorganization of conventional patrol strategies into "an integrated and versatile police team assigned to a fixed district."[vii]

## Community Policing

During the past 20 years, the role of the police in police–community relations has changed considerably. Originally, the PCR model was based on the fact that many police administrators saw police officers as enforcers of the law who were isolated from, and often in opposition to, the communities they policed. As a result, PCR programs were often a shallowly disguised effort to overcome public suspicion and community hostility.

Today, increasing numbers of law enforcement administrators embrace the role of service provider. Modern departments frequently help citizens solve a vast array of personal problems, many of which involve no law-breaking activity. For example, officers regularly aid sick or distraught people, organize community crime-prevention efforts, investigate domestic disputes, regulate traffic, and educate children and teens about drug abuse. Because service calls far exceed calls directly related to law violations, most officers more often make referrals for interpersonal problems to agencies such as Alcoholics Anonymous, domestic violence centers, and drug-rehabilitation programs rather than make an arrest.

In contemporary America, some say, police departments function a lot like corporations. According to Harvard University's Executive Session on Policing, three generic kinds of "corporate strategies" guide American policing: (1) strategic policing, (2) problem-solving policing, and (3) community policing.[54]

**strategic policing**

A type of policing that retains the traditional police goal of professional crime fighting but enlarges the enforcement target to include nontraditional kinds of criminals, such as serial offenders, gangs and criminal associations, drug-distribution networks, and sophisticated white-collar and computer criminals. Strategic policing generally makes use of innovative enforcement techniques, including intelligence operations, undercover stings, electronic surveillance, and sophisticated forensic methods.

**problem-solving policing**

A type of policing that assumes that crimes can be controlled by uncovering and effectively addressing the underlying social problems that cause crime. Problem-solving policing makes use of community resources, such as counseling centers, welfare programs, and job-training facilities. It also attempts to involve citizens in crime prevention through education, negotiation, and conflict management.

**community policing**

"A collaborative effort between the police and the community that identifies problems of crime and disorder and involves all elements of the community in the search for solutions to these problems."[viii]

**Strategic policing**, something of a holdover from the reform era, "emphasizes an increased capacity to deal with crimes that are not well controlled by traditional methods."[55] Strategic policing retains the traditional police goal of professional crime fighting but enlarges the enforcement target to include nontraditional kinds of criminals, such as serial offenders, gangs and criminal associations, drug-distribution networks, and sophisticated white-collar and computer criminals. To meet its goals, strategic policing generally makes use of innovative enforcement techniques, including intelligence operations, undercover stings, electronic surveillance, and sophisticated forensic methods. The other two strategies give greater recognition to Wilson's service style. **Problem-solving** (or problem-oriented) **policing** takes the view that many crimes are caused by existing social conditions in the communities. To control crime, problem-oriented police managers attempt to uncover and effectively address these underlying social problems. Problem-solving policing makes thorough use of community resources, such as counseling centers, welfare programs, and job-training facilities. It also attempts to involve citizens in crime prevention through education, negotiation, and conflict management. For example, police may ask residents of poorly maintained housing areas to clean up litter, install better lighting, and provide security devices for their houses and apartments in the belief that clean, well-lighted, secure areas are a deterrent to criminal activity.

The third and newest strategy, **community policing** (sometimes called *community-oriented policing*), goes a step beyond the other two. It has been described as "a philosophy based on forging a partnership between the police and the community, so that they can work together on solving problems of crime, [and] fear of crime and disorder, thereby enhancing the overall quality of life in their neighborhoods."[56] This approach addresses the causes of crime to reduce the fear of crime and social disorder through problem-solving strategies and police–community partnerships.

The community policing concept evolved from the early works of police researchers George Kelling and Robert Trojanowicz. Their studies of foot-patrol programs in Newark, New Jersey,[57] and Flint, Michigan,[58] showed that "police could develop more positive attitudes toward community members and could promote positive attitudes toward police if they spent time on foot in their neighborhoods."[59] Trojanowicz's *Community Policing*, published in 1990,[60] may be the definitive work on this topic.

Community policing seeks to actively involve citizens in the task of crime control by creating an effective working partnership between them and the police.[61] Under the community policing ideal, the public and the police share responsibility for establishing and maintaining peaceful neighborhoods.[62] As a result, community members participate more fully than ever before in defining the police role. Police expert Jerome Skolnick says community policing is "grounded on the notion that, together, police and public are more effective and more humane coproducers of safety and public order than are the police alone."[63] According to Skolnick, community policing involves at least one of four elements: (1) community-based crime prevention, (2) the reorientation of patrol activities to emphasize the importance of nonemergency services, (3) increased police accountability to the public, and (4) a decentralization of command, including a greater use of civilians at all levels of police decision making.[64] As one writer explains it, "Community policing seeks to integrate what was traditionally seen as the different law enforcement, order maintenance and social service roles of the police. Central to the integration of these roles is a working partnership with the community in determining what neighborhood problems are to be addressed, and how."[65] Table 6–2 highlights the differences between traditional and community policing.

Community policing is a two-way street. It requires not only police awareness of community needs but also both involvement and crime-fighting action on the part of citizens themselves. As Detective Tracie Harrison of the Denver Police Department explains, "When the neighborhood takes stock in their community and they're serious they don't want crime, then you start to see crime go down. . . . They're basically fed up and know the police can't do it alone."[66]

Police departments throughout the country continue to join the community policing bandwagon. A 2001 report by the Bureau of Justice Statistics (BJS) showed that state and local law enforcement agencies across the United States had nearly 113,000 full-time sworn personnel regularly engaged in community policing activities.[67] BJS noted that only about 21,000 officers would have been so categorized in 1997. At the time of the report, 64% of local police departments serving 86% of all residents had full-time officers engaged in some form of community policing activity, compared to 34% of departments serving 62% of all residents in 1997.

The Chicago Police Department launched its comprehensive community policing program, called Chicago's Alternative Policing Strategy (CAPS), in 1993. The development of a strategic plan for "reinventing the Chicago Police Department," from which CAPS evolved, included significant contributions by Mayor Richard M. Daley, who noted that community policing "means doing more than responding to calls for service and solving crimes. It means transforming the

## TRADITIONAL VERSUS COMMUNITY POLICING

| Question | Traditional Policing | Community Policing |
|---|---|---|
| Who are the police? | The police are a government agency principally responsible for law enforcement. | The police are the public, and the public are the police. Police officers are paid to give full-time attention to the duties of every citizen. |
| What is the relationship of the police force to other public-service departments? | Priorities often conflict. | The police are one department among many responsible for improving the quality of life. |
| What is the role of the police? | To solve crimes. | To solve problems. |
| How is police efficiency measured? | By detection and arrest rates. | By the absence of crime and disorder. |
| What are the highest priorities? | Crimes that are high value (for example, bank robberies) and those involving violence. | Whatever problems disturb the community most. |
| What do police deal with? | Incidents. | Citizens' problems and concerns. |
| What determines the effectiveness of police? | Response times. | Public cooperation. |
| What view do police take of service calls? | They deal with them only if there is no "real" police work to do. | They view them as a vital function and a great opportunity. |
| What is police professionalism? | Providing a swift, effective response to serious crime. | Keeping close to the community. |
| What kind of intelligence is most important? | Crime intelligence (study of particular crimes or series of crimes). | Criminal intelligence (information about the activities of individuals or groups). |
| What is the essential nature of police accountability? | Highly centralized; governed by rules, regulations, and policy directives; accountable to the law. | Local accountability to community needs. |
| What is the role of headquarters? | To provide the necessary rules and policy directives. | To preach organizational values. |
| What is the role of the press liaison department? | To keep the "heat" off operational officers so they can get on with the job. | To coordinate an essential channel of communication with the community. |
| How do the police regard prosecutions? | As an important goal. | As one tool among many. |

**TABLE 6–2**

*Source:* William R. Parks II, "Community Policing: A Foundation for Restorative Justice." Web posted at http://www.realjustice.org/Pages/t2000papers/t2000_wparks.html (accessed March 5, 2002). Originally printed in Malcolm K. Sparrow, *Implementing Community Policing* (Washington, DC: National Institute of Justice, 1988), pp. 8–9.

Department to support a new, proactive approach to preventing crimes before they occur. It means forging new partnerships among residents, business owners, community leaders, the police, and City services to solve long-range community problems."[68] Read the mayor's original report, written in conjunction with the Chicago Police Department, at Library Extra 6–4 at cjtoday.com.

Today, CAPS functions on a department-wide basis throughout the city. Learn more about CAPS via Web Extra 6–5 at cjtoday.com. A review of Chicago's experience with community policing is available at Library Extra 6–5.

Although community policing efforts began in metropolitan areas, the community engagement and problem-solving spirit of these programs have spread to rural regions. Sheriff's departments operating community policing programs sometimes refer to them as "neighborhood-oriented policing" in recognition of the decentralized nature of rural communities. A Bureau of Justice Assistance (BJA) report on neighborhood-oriented policing notes that "the stereotypical view is that police officers in rural areas naturally work more closely with the public than do officers in metropolitan areas."[69] This view, warns the BJA, may not be entirely accurate, and rural departments would do well "to recognize that considerable diversity exists among rural communities and rural law enforcement agencies." Hence, as in metropolitan areas, effective community policing requires the involvement of all members of the community in identifying and solving problems.

The emphasis on community policing continues to grow. Title I of the Violent Crime Control and Law Enforcement Act of 1994, known as the Public Safety Partnership and Community Policing Act of 1994, highlighted community policing's role in combating crime and funded (among other things) "increas[ing] the number of law enforcement officers involved in activities that are focused on interaction with members of the community on proactive crime control and prevention by redeploying officers to such activities." The avowed purposes of the Community Policing Act were to (1) substantially increase the number of law enforcement officers interacting directly with the public (through a program known as Cops on the Beat); (2) provide additional and more effective training to law enforcement officers to enhance their problem-solving, service, and other skills needed in interacting with community members; (3) encourage development and implementation of innovative programs to permit community members to assist local law enforcement agencies in the prevention of crime; and (4) encourage development of new technologies to assist local law enforcement agencies in reorienting their emphasis from reacting to crime to preventing crime.

In response to the 1994 law, the U.S. Department of Justice created the Office of Community Oriented Policing Services (COPS). The COPS Office administered the funds necessary to add 100,000 community policing officers to our nation's streets—the number originally targeted by law. In 1999, the U.S. Department of Justice and COPS reached an important milestone by funding the 100,000th officer ahead of schedule and under budget. Although the Community Policing Act originally provided COPS funding only through 2000, Congress has continued to fund COPS, making another $500 million available for the hiring of an additional 50,000 officers.[70] In 2002, the COPS Office adopted the theme "Homeland Security through Community Policing," which emphasizes the local police officers' crucial role in gathering information on terrorist suspects—a topic that is discussed later in this chapter. The federal COPS Office can be found at Web Extra 6–6.

About the same time that the Violent Crime Control and Law Enforcement Act was passed, the Community Policing Consortium, based in Washington, D.C., began operations. Administered and funded by the U.S. Department of Justice's BJA, the consortium provides a forum for training and information exchange in the area of community policing. Members of the consortium include the International Association of Chiefs of Police, the National Sheriff's Association, the Police Executive Research Forum, the Police Foundation, and the National Organization of Black Law Enforcement Executives. Visit the Community Policing Consortium via Web Extra 6–7 at cjtoday.com.

## Critique of Community Policing

As some authors have noted, "Community policing has become the dominant theme of contemporary police reform in America,"[71] yet problems have plagued the movement since its inception.[72] For one thing, the range, complexity, and evolving nature of community policing programs make their effectiveness difficult to measure.[73] Moreover, "citizen satisfaction" with police performance can be difficult to conceptualize and quantify. Most early studies examined citizens' attitudes developed through face-to-face interaction with individual police officers. They generally found a far higher level of dissatisfaction with the police among African-Americans than among most other groups. Recent findings continue to show that the attitudes of African-Americans toward the police remain poor. The wider reach of these studies, however,

Los Angeles police bike patrol officers conferring with a supervisor. The community policing concept requires that officers become an integral part of the communities they serve.

*Michael Newman, PhotoEdit*

led evaluators to discover that this dissatisfaction may be rooted in overall quality of life and type of neighborhood.[74] Since, on average, African-Americans continue to experience a lower quality of life than most other U.S. citizens, and because they often live in neighborhoods characterized by economic problems, drug trafficking, and street crime, recent studies conclude that it is these conditions of life, rather than race, that are most predictive of citizen dissatisfaction with the police.

Those who study community policing have often been stymied by ambiguity surrounding the concept of community.[75] Sociologists, who sometimes define a community as "any area in which members of a common culture share common interests,"[76] tend to deny that a community needs to be limited geographically. Police departments, on the other hand, tend to define communities "within jurisdictional, district or precinct lines, or within the confines of public or private housing developments."[77] Robert Trojanowicz cautioned police planners that "the impact of mass transit, mass communications and mass media have widened the rift between a sense of community based on geography and one [based] on interest."[78]

Researchers who follow the police definition of *community* recognize that there may be little consensus within and between members of a local community about community problems and appropriate solutions. Robert Bohm and colleagues at the University of Central Florida have found, for example, that while there may be some "consensus about social problems and their solutions . . . the consensus may not be community-wide." It may, in fact, exist only among "a relatively small group of 'active' stakeholders who differ significantly about the seriousness of most of the problems and the utility of some solutions."[79]

Finally, there is continuing evidence that not all police officers or managers are willing to accept nontraditional images of police work. One reason is that the goals of community policing often conflict with standard police performance criteria (such as arrests), leading to a perception among officers that community policing is inefficient at best and, at worst, a waste of time.[80] Similarly, many officers are loathe to take on new responsibilities as service providers whose role is more defined by community needs and less by strict interpretation of the law.

Some authors have warned that **police subculture** is so committed to a traditional view of police work, which is focused almost exclusively on crime fighting, that efforts to promote community policing can demoralize an entire department, rendering it ineffective at its basic tasks.[81] As the Christopher Commission found following the Rodney King riots, "Too many . . . patrol officers view citizens with resentment and hostility; too many treat the public with rudeness and disrespect."[82] Some analysts warn that only when the formal values espoused by today's innovative police administrators begin to match those of rank-and-file officers can any police agency begin to perform well in terms of the goals espoused by community policing reformers.[83]

> In the 21st Century the community policing philosophy is well positioned to take a central role in preventing and responding to terrorism and in efforts to reduce citizen fear.
>
> —Matthew C. Scheider,
> Office of Community Oriented Policing Services[ix]

**police subculture**

A particular set of values, beliefs, and acceptable forms of behavior characteristic of American police. Socialization into the police subculture begins with recruit training and continues thereafter.

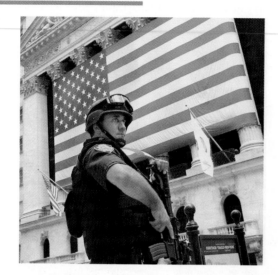

A New York City police officer with a semiautomatic weapon stands guard outside the New York Stock Exchange. Policing strategies across the United States have been significantly affected by the threat of terrorism and the need for a rapid and effective response to attacks.

*AP Wide World Photos*

Some public officials, too, are unwilling to accept community policing. Ten years ago, for example, New York City Mayor Rudolph W. Giuliani criticized the police department's Community Police Officer Program (CPOP), saying that it "has resulted in officers doing too much social work and making too few arrests."[84] Similarly, many citizens are not ready to accept a greater involvement of the police in their personal lives. Although the turbulent, protest-prone years of the 1960s and early 1970s are long gone, some groups remain suspicious of the police. No matter how inclusive community policing programs become, it is doubtful that the gap between the police and the public will ever be entirely bridged. The police role of restraining behavior that violates the law will always produce friction between police departments and some segments of the community. Learn more about measures of police effectiveness, including those related to community policing, at Library Extra 6–6 at cjtoday.com.

**LIBRARY** EXTRA

# Terrorism's Impact on Policing

In April 2005, three British nationals were charged with plotting to bomb five financial buildings in New York City, New Jersey, and Washington, D.C. The men, Dhiren Barot, 32, Nadeem Tarmohamed, 26, and Qaisar Shaffi, 25, allegedly served as al-Qaeda scouts and performed reconnaissance on the buildings.[85] The three had been arrested by British authorities in August 2004, and information gathered during the arrest led homeland security officials to convene a press conference at the Citigroup tower in Midtown Manhattan. The nation was told that known al-Qaeda operatives had conducted surveillance at several large New York financial centers, including the New York Stock Exchange.[86] Officials said that the terrorists may have been planning to use truck bombs targeting Wall Street in an effort to disrupt world financial markets. Outgoing Homeland Security Secretary Tom Ridge stressed the seriousness of the threat when he told reporters who had gathered for the briefing that "This is the most significant, detailed piece of information about any particular region that we have come across in a long, long time, perhaps ever."[87] In response to the announcement, the New York City Police Department set up barricades and vehicle checkpoints and mobilized heavily armed officers specially trained in antiterrorism tactics to patrol the financial district. Downtown city streets took on the embattled look of a city at war.

The incident made clear the changed role of American police agencies in a new era of international terrorism that began with the September 11, 2001, attacks on American targets. While the core mission of American police departments has not changed, law enforcement agencies at all levels now devote an increased amount of time and other resources to preparing for possible terrorist attacks and to gathering the intelligence necessary to thwart them.

Local police departments play an especially important role in responding to the challenges of terrorism. They must help prevent attacks and respond when attacks occur, offering critical evacuation, emergency medical, and security functions to help stabilize communities following an incident. A recent survey of 250 police chiefs by the Police Executive Research Forum (PERF) found

To deal effectively with the threat of domestic terrorism, the police must be able to manage and coordinate different sources of data and intelligence, and then process them in such a way as to provide an enhanced understanding of actual or potential criminal activity.

—COPS Office[x]

that the chiefs strongly believe that their departments can make valuable contributions to terrorism prevention by using community-policing networks to exchange information with citizens and to gather intelligence.[88] Read the results of the PERF survey online at Library Extra 6–7 at cjtoday.com.

The Council on Foreign Relations, headquartered in New York City and Washington, D.C., agrees with PERF that American police departments can no longer assume that federal counterterrorism efforts alone will be sufficient to protect the communities they serve. Consequently, says the council, many police departments have responded by[89]

- Strengthening liaisons with federal, state, and local agencies, including fire departments and other police departments

- Refining their training and emergency response plans to address terrorist threats, including attacks with weapons of mass destruction

- Increasing patrols and shoring up barriers around landmarks, places of worship, ports of entry, transit systems, nuclear power plants, and so on

- More heavily guarding public speeches, parades, and other public events

- Creating new counterterrorism divisions and reassigning officers to counterterrorism from other divisions, such as drug enforcement

- Employing new technologies, such as X-ray-like devices, to scan containers at ports of entry and sophisticated sensors to detect a chemical, biological, or radiological attack

The extent of local departments' engagement in such preventive activities depends substantially on budgetary considerations and is strongly influenced by the assessed likelihood of attack. The New York City Police Department (NYPD), for example, which has firsthand experience in responding to terrorist attacks (23 of its officers were killed when the World Trade Center towers collapsed), has created a special bureau headed by a deputy police commissioner responsible for counterterrorism training, prevention, and investigation.[90] One thousand officers have been reassigned to antiterrorism duties, and the department is training its entire 39,000-member force in how to respond to biological, radiological, and chemical attacks.[91] The NYPD has assigned detectives to work abroad with law enforcement agencies in Canada, Israel, Southeast Asia, and the Middle East to track terrorists who might target New York City,[92] and it now employs officers with a command of the Pashtun, Farsi, and Urdu languages of the Middle East to monitor foreign television, radio, and Internet communications. The department has also invested heavily in new hazardous materials protective suits, gas masks, and portable radiation detectors.

In November 2004, in an effort to provide the law enforcement community and policy makers with guidance on critical issues related to antiterrorism planning and critical incident response, the International Association of Chiefs of Police (IACP) announced its *Taking Command Initiative*. The IACP describes the initiative as "an aggressive project to assess the current state of homeland security efforts in the United States and to develop and implement the actions necessary to protect our communities from the specter of both crime and terrorism."[93] Initial deliberations under the initiative led the IACP to conclude that "the current homeland security strategy is handicapped by a fundamental flaw: It was developed without sufficiently seeking or incorporating the advice, expertise, or consent of public safety organizations at the state, tribal or local level."[94] Building on that premise, the IACP identified five key principles that it says must form the basis of any effective national homeland security strategy[95]:

- Homeland security proposals must be developed in a local context, acknowledging that local, not federal, authorities have the primary responsibility for preventing, responding to, and recovering from terrorist attacks.

- Prevention, not just response and recovery, must be paramount in any national, state, or local security strategy. For too long, federal strategies have minimized the importance of prevention, focusing instead on response and recovery.

- Because of their daily efforts to combat crime and violence in their communities, state and local law enforcement officers are uniquely situated to identify, investigate, and apprehend suspected terrorists.

- Homeland security strategies must be coordinated nationally, not federally.

- A truly successful national strategy must recognize, embrace, and value the vast diversity among state and local law enforcement and public safety agencies. A one-size-fits-all approach will fail to secure our homeland.

Learn more about the ongoing IACP initiative as its leaders work to "transform the concept of a locally designed, nationally coordinated homeland security strategy into a reality" at Web Extra 6–8.

LIBRARY EXTRA

It is very important that our first line of defense against terrorism—the seven hundred thousand officers on the street—be given adequate training and background information on terrorism, the methods and techniques of the terrorists, and the likelihood of an imminent attack.

—Major Cities Chiefs Association[xi]

WEB EXTRA

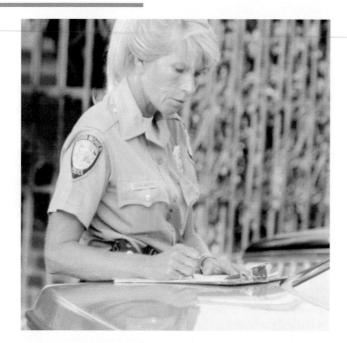

An officer writing a traffic ticket. Police officers wield a great amount of discretion, and an individual officer's decision to enforce a particular law or to effect an arrest is based not just on the law's applicability to a particular set of circumstances but also on the officer's subjective judgment about the nature of appropriate enforcement activity.

*David Young-Wolff, PhotoEdit*

As the IACP recognizes, workable antiterrorism programs at the local level require effective sharing of critical information between agencies. FBI-sponsored Joint Terrorism Task Forces (JTTFs) facilitate this by bringing together federal and local law enforcement personnel to focus on specific threats. The FBI currently has established or authorized JTTFs in each of its 56 field offices. In addition to the JTTFs, the FBI has created Regional Terrorism Task Forces (RTTFs) to share information with local enforcement agencies. Through the RTTFs, FBI special agents assigned to terrorism prevention and investigation meet twice a year with their federal, state, and local counterparts for common training, discussion of investigations, and intelligence sharing. The FBI says that "the design of this non-traditional terrorism task force provides the necessary mechanism and structure to direct counterterrorism resources toward localized terrorism problems within the United States."[96] Six RTTFs are currently in operation: the Inland Northwest, South Central, Southeastern, Northeast Border, Deep South, and Southwest.

Given the changes that have taken place in American law enforcement since the terrorist attacks of September 11, 2001, some say that traditional distinctions between crime, terrorism, and war are fading and that, at least in some instances, military action and civil law enforcement are becoming integrated. The critical question for law enforcement administrators in the near future may be one of discerning the role that law enforcement is to play in the emerging global context.

## Intelligence-Led Policing and Antiterrorism

**intelligence-led policing**

The collection and analysis of information to produce an intelligence end product designed to inform police decision making at both the tactical and strategic levels.[xii]

**criminal intelligence**

Information compiled, analyzed, and/or disseminated in an effort to anticipate, prevent, or monitor criminal activity.[xiii]

In 2005 the U.S. Department of Justice embraced the concept of **intelligence-led policing** (ILP) as an important technique to be employed by American law enforcement agencies in the battle against terrorism.[97] Intelligence is information that has been analyzed and integrated into a useful perspective. The information used in the development of effective intelligence is typically gathered from many sources, such as newspapers, surveillance, covert operations, financial records, electronic eavesdropping, interviews, and interrogations. Law enforcement intelligence, or **criminal intelligence**, is the result of a "process that evaluates information collected from diverse sources, integrates the relevant information into a cohesive package, and produces a conclusion or estimate about a criminal phenomenon by using the scientific approach to problem solving."[98] While criminal investigation is typically part of the intelligence-gathering process, the intelligence function of a police department is more exploratory and more broadly focused than a single criminal investigation.[99]

ILP (also known as *intelligence-driven policing*) is the use of criminal intelligence to guide policing. A detailed description of ILP and its applicability to American law enforcement agencies is provided in the Department of Justice–funded document *Law Enforcement Intelligence: A*

## Police Tactic Against Terror: Let's Network

In January, their mission was to speak before a mosquito sprayers' convention in Harrisburg, Pennsylvania. In April, the detectives attended a meeting of self-storage business owners in Atlanta. This summer, they were in Naples, Florida, mingling with propane gas vendors at their trade association's annual conference.

These are, admittedly, not the sort of assignments that investigators envision when they join the New York Police Department. But such missions, however mundane, have become as much a part of police counterterrorism efforts as the posting of detectives in places like Tel Aviv and Singapore, the planning for a bioterror attack or the identification of Arab speakers on the force.

Involving more grunt work than glamour, the city's counterterrorism effort has largely been built atop a nuts-and-bolts program of cultivating contacts with the businesses that might become unwitting parts of the next terror plot. Detectives visit scuba shops and hardware stores. They talk to parking garage attendants and plastic surgeons, hotel managers and tool rental companies, bulk fuel dealers and trade schools.

Police officials acknowledge that the program, which grew out of an effort two years ago to contact businesses that sold explosives, is something of a needle-in-a-haystack approach to stopping an attack or tracking down terrorist cells that may be plotting one. But in the post-9/11 world, in light of the failure of government agencies to act on a range of clues in the weeks and months before the attacks, they argue that no effort to develop this kind of early-warning system is wasted.

Called Operation Nexus, the program has focused on particular types of businesses based on intelligence that the department has culled from sources like an Al Qaeda manual for terrorist operatives and debriefings of some of the group's leaders and foot soldiers, said David Cohen, the deputy commissioner for intelligence.

Those debriefings and other evidence have suggested, among other things, that Al Qaeda has at least considered, if not plotted, using scuba divers to blow up bridges, riding in tourist helicopters for surveillance, turning trucks and limousines into rolling bombs and using special torches to cut the cables of the Brooklyn Bridge.

And Mr. Cohen noted that Al Qaeda members are trained to avoid the police.

"The next Mohamed Atta is far more likely to intersect with someone in the private sector than a law enforcement officer," he said, referring to the leader of the September 11 plot.

Mr. Cohen, a former deputy director of the Central Intelligence Agency, who oversees the program, said it is based on personal contact with people and repeated visits to various businesses. "If you take the time to talk to people, it leaves an imprint," he said.

The effort is focused largely in and around New York City, where six or so detectives have made close to 20,000 visits,

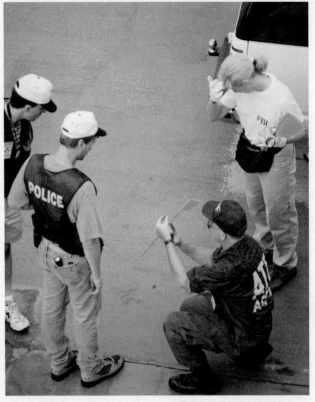

Atlanta police officers, an FBI agent, and an ATF agent search for evidence while investigating an Atlanta-area bombing. The fight against terrorism has enhanced the realization that law enforcement agencies at all levels need to work together.

© Wally McNamee, Corbis

returning to some businesses time and again to leave their business cards and the department's terrorism hot line number. The detectives are encouraged to spend time with the businesses, leaving an outline of what they describe as possibly suspicious activity tailored for each type of business: more than 60 altogether, said Lt. Christopher S. Higgins, whom police officials credit with developing the program from concept to reality.

At an agricultural or mosquito-spraying business, which the authorities fear could be used to spread a biological agent like anthrax, the detectives cite possible warning signs like the loss, theft or attempted theft of equipment or machine components. They tell business owners to call if they encounter evasive customers who inquire about equipment but seem to lack previous experience in the industry.

Businesses that offer used emergency vehicles for sale are told to watch for requests to buy fire or police vehicles with radios or other equipment intact. Army-Navy and uniform stores are warned to watch for people who say they are in the military or civil service but who make statements suggesting their stories are false.

*(continued)*

## CJ NEWS *(continued)*

"We're going to have eyeball-to-eyeball contact with that individual who may be approached by someone who wants to do harm to our city," Mr. Cohen said, noting that the business owners themselves can best spot an anomaly.

Police Commissioner Raymond W. Kelly, who instituted the program, said it quickly expanded from its initial focus on explosives and marinas, at a time when there was heightened concern about terrorists using boats in attacks, to a wide range of other businesses. They include chemical and insecticide companies, livery car businesses, truck and van rentals, travel agencies and self-storage businesses, where the authorities fear terrorists could store explosives or radioactive materials for a dirty bomb.

"We're looking for anything that with a little thought could be used by a terrorist," Mr. Kelly said. Glenn Martin, a vice president of Helicopter Applications Inc., an agricultural spraying company in Pennsylvania, said that in a presentation to the Northeast Agricultural Aviation Association in Harrisburg this year, two Nexus detectives provided companies that do mosquito-spraying and crop dusting with some insight into what they should look for. "It just drove the point home, basically," he said in a telephone interview. "We have to be more vigilant."

Other jurisdictions, including the Metropolitan Police in London, have studied New York's program and are trying to use it as a model in some fashion, Lieutenant Higgins said. The New York State Office of Public Security recently put in place a mirror image of the city's program across the state.

In at least one instance, though, the New York City detectives have raised the hackles of law enforcement authorities elsewhere. Last year, to test the program's effectiveness, detectives called scuba shops in New Jersey without identifying themselves and made several suspicious requests, seeking to pay cash for diving lessons and to avoid the required paperwork.

The store owners called the New Jersey authorities, who were unaware of the New York detectives' actions and were annoyed that they had not been notified, an official said.

Over all, the program has won high marks. Many current and former counterterrorism analysts say an aggressive approach, devised to provide an early warning that operatives or their supporters are already at work in this country, is critical to any antiterrorism effort.

"In today's day and age, where the ramifications of terrorism are so great, you've got to prevent," said Larry Mefford, who oversaw the FBI's counterterrorism and counterintelligence programs until he retired last year. "You can't wait for the attack, especially when you're talking about the future and the possible use of weapons of mass destruction.

"If you don't have a system like this, you're saying by default, 'They'll never get through our defenses,' and we obviously know from our past experience that that's not realistic."

As high as the stakes are, the work itself can be grindingly dull, visiting business after business and trying to remain energized. "This is the part of the business that is unrelenting and unglamorous," Mr. Cohen said.

Lieutenant Higgins said he usually fields three teams of two detectives each day, and they are expected to visit more than a dozen sites a day. Each visit is recorded in an extensive database that tracks the contacts, listing the detective assigned, the type of business, hours of operation, those who were spoken to, and whether they have any security equipment, like video cameras, that can capture images of people who come in.

Mr. Cohen said the program is a crucial part of the city's shield even if it is hard to quantify its effectiveness. For one thing, it is hard to know whether an attack has been prevented, officials noted.

For another, callers to the terrorism hot line do not generally identify whether their call was prompted by a Nexus visit.

"The risk is the farther we get from 9/11, complacency sets in, and we simply won't let that happen," Mr. Cohen said. "So we start out the day knowing that we are the bull's-eye. So how many have we stopped, we don't know. We do know a couple of things: We know we've been attacked; we know they have said very clearly they want to come back; we know we are high on the target list."

For the latest in crime and justice news, visit the Talk Justice news feed at http://www.crimenews.info.

*Guide for State, Local, and Tribal Law Enforcement Agencies,* by David L. Carter in Michigan State University's school of criminal justice. The 14-part document is available in its entirety at cjtoday.com as **Library Extra 6–8.**

According to Carter, criminal intelligence "is a synergistic product intended to provide meaningful and trustworthy direction to law enforcement decision makers about complex criminality, criminal enterprises, criminal extremists, and terrorists." Carter goes on to point out that law enforcement intelligence consists of two types: tactical and strategic. Tactical intelligence "includes gaining or developing information related to threats of terrorism or crime and using this information to apprehend offenders, harden targets, and use strategies that will eliminate or mitigate the threat." Strategic intelligence, in contrast, provides information to decision makers about the changing nature of threats for the purpose of "developing response strategies and reallocating resources" to accomplish effective prevention.

Not every agency, especially small ones, has the staff or resources needed to create a dedicated intelligence unit. Even without an intelligence unit, however, a law enforcement organization should have the ability to effectively utilize the information and intelligence products that are developed and disseminated by organizations at all levels of government. In other words, even though a police agency may not have the resources necessary to analyze all the information it acquires, it should still be able to mount an effective response to credible threat information that it receives. Learn more about the law enforcement intelligence function and intelligence-led policing at Library Extra 6–9 at cjtoday.com.

LIBRARY EXTRA

# Community Policing and Antiterrorism

Carter says that "a common concern expressed by police executives is that the shift toward increased counterterrorism responsibilities may require a shift of resources away from community policing."[100] That concern, he says, is misdirected because community policing provides a natural conduit for information gathering and the development of counterterrorism intelligence. Information gathered by state and local police departments can be funneled to federal agencies, especially the FBI, that have been charged with developing national security intelligence. Carter notes that the "increased social tension" resulting from the current concern with terrorism has led to a greater need "to maintain a close, interactive dialogue between law enforcement and the community."

The importance of community policing in the fight against terrorism was reflected in comments made by FBI Director Robert Mueller during the summer of 2004. While pointing to photographs of seven terror suspects believed to be in the United States, Mueller said: "We need the support of the American people . . . to cooperate when called upon, as agents will be reaching out to many across the nation to help gather information and intelligence . . . to be aware of your surroundings and report anything suspicious . . . to "BOLO" [Be On the LookOut] for those pictured above. . . . Have you seen them in your communities? Have you heard that someone might be helping them to hide? Do you have any idea where they might be? If so, we need you to come forward."[101]

Members of the U.S. Department of Justice's Global Intelligence Working Group (GIWG) also recognized the importance of community-oriented policing efforts when developing the national intelligence sharing plan, described in the next section of this chapter. "Over the past decade," members noted, "thousands of community policing officers have been building close and productive relationships with the citizens they serve."[102] Community policing officers, they observed, "have immediate and unfettered access to local, neighborhood information as it develops. Citizens are aware of and seek out [community policing] officers to provide them with new information that may be useful to criminal interdiction or long-term problem solving. The positive nature of police/citizen relationships promotes a continuous and reliable transfer of information from one to the other. It is time to maximize the potential for community policing efforts to serve as a gateway of locally based information to prevent terrorism, and all other crimes."[103]

The Office for Domestic Preparedness (ODP) of the U.S. Department of Homeland Security describes the roles community policing can play in the intelligence process to include the following[104]:

- Provide materials to community policing contacts that may aid in the recognition of terrorism-related activities in order to make members of the community aware of suspicious actions, behaviors, and events.

- Organize community meetings to emphasize prevention strategies, vigilance, and public awareness.

- Ensure that members of the community are aware of the means of and processes for relaying information to police officers and police organizations.

- Encourage crime prevention, proactive policing, and close working relationships between the police and the community.

In any successful police–community interaction, information flows both ways. Consequently, while community policing efforts seek information from the public about offenders, police departments can also communicate critical information to the public in order to aid in crime prevention and fear reduction.

# Information Sharing and Antiterrorism

The need to effectively share criminal intelligence across jurisdictions and between law enforcement agencies nationwide became apparent with the tragic events of September 11, 2001. Consequently, governments at all levels are today working toward the creation of a fully integrated

Cooperation of police at all levels along with coordination with other agencies will be necessary to cope with crime that is increasingly cross-jurisdictional.

—Bud Levin, Blue Ridge Community College

criminal justice information system. According to a recent task force report, a fully integrated criminal justice information system is "a network of public safety, justice and homeland security computer systems which provides to each agency the information it needs, at the time it is needed, in the form that it is needed, regardless of the source and regardless of the physical location at which it is stored."[105] The information that is provided should be complete, accurate, and formatted in whatever way is most useful for the agency's tasks. In a fully integrated criminal justice information system, information would be made available at the practitioner's workstation, whether that workstation is a patrol car, desk, laptop, or a judge's bench. Within such a system, each agency shares information not only with other agencies in its own jurisdiction but with multiple justice agencies on the federal, state, and local levels. In such an idealized justice information system, accurate information is also available to nonjustice agencies with statutory authority and a legal obligation to check criminal histories before licensing, employment, weapons purchase, and so on.

Although a nationwide fully integrated criminal justice information system does not yet exist, efforts to create one found their beginning in the 2003 National Criminal Intelligence Sharing Plan (NCISP). The NCISP was developed under the auspices of the U.S. Department of Justice's Global Justice Information Sharing Initiative and authored by its GIWG.[106] Federal, local, state, and tribal law enforcement representatives all had a voice in the development of the plan. The NCISP provides specific steps that can be taken by law enforcement agencies to participate in the sharing of critical law enforcement and terrorism prevention information.

Plan authors note that not every agency has the staff or resources needed to create a formal intelligence unit. Even without a dedicated intelligence unit, however, the plan says that every law enforcement organization needs to have the ability to effectively consume the intelligence available from a wide range of organizations at all levels of government.[107] The NCISP is available in its entirety at cjtoday.com as Library Extra 6–10.

**LIBRARY** **EXTRA**

The home page of the Multistate Anti-Terrorism Information Exchange (MATRIX), a pilot project in boundaryless policing and interagency information sharing. MATRIX ceased operation in 2005 after fielding almost 2 million queries from law enforcement investigators during the two years it was in existence.

© 2005 Institute of Intergovernmental Research®. All rights reserved.

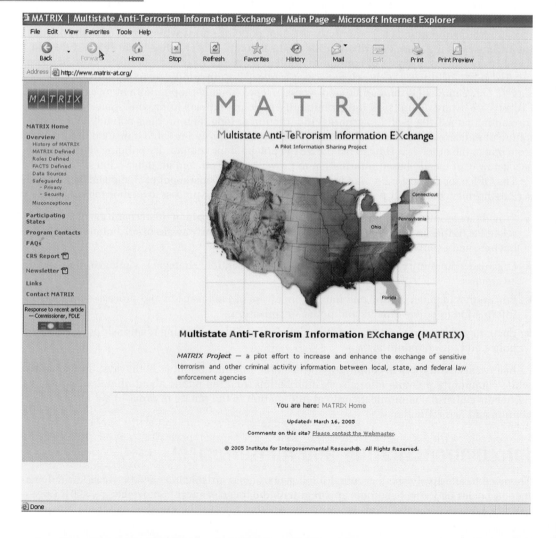

Efforts to share crime and terrorism-related intelligence can result in what some have called *boundaryless policing*.[108] Examples of boundaryless policing can be found today in the Regional Information Sharing Systems Anti-Terrorism Information Exchange (RISS ATIX) Program, and the State and Local Anti-Terrorism Training (SLATT) Program, both of which are supported through grants from the Bureau of Justice Assistance.[109] A similar program, the Multistate Anti-Terrorism Information Exchange (**MATRIX**), ceased operation in 2005 after fielding almost 2 million queries from law enforcement investigators during the two years it was in existence.[110]

RISS, a nationwide communications and information-sharing network, serves more than 6,300 law enforcement member agencies from the 50 states, the District of Columbia, the U.S. territories, Canada, Australia, and England. A private, secure intranet (riss.net) connects six RISS centers and their participating law enforcement member agencies.[111] The RISS ATIX, a special aspect of the RISS program, began operating in 2003. RISS ATIX allows for the secure exchange of information between government and nongovernment officials who are responsible for planning and implementing terrorism-related prevention, response, mitigation, and recovery efforts.

The MATRIX project was an Internet-based proof-of-concept pilot program, funded by the Department of Justice and the Department of Homeland Security, to increase and enhance the exchange of sensitive information about terrorism and other criminal activity between enforcement agencies at the local, state, and federal levels. MATRIX used the Factual Analysis Criminal Threat Solution (FACTS) software application, which provides a technology-based investigative tool to facilitate free-form searches of available state and public records. FACTS analyzes and integrates disparate data from many different types of storage systems.[112] The MATRIX system combined data from various sources to which agencies already had access into a single searchable database of 4 billion records. Available records included criminal histories, driver's license data, vehicle registration data, prison/corrections records, digitized photographs, and public data. Using FACTS, investigators were able to conduct searches using incomplete information, such as a portion of a vehicle license number. At the conclusion of the MATRIX pilot program, a number of participating states continued to use the FACTS application.[113]

Finally, the federally funded SLATT Program provides specialized training for active state and local law enforcement personnel in combating terrorism and extremist criminal activity.[114] The SLATT Program has been central to antiterrorism research and training since the bombing of the Alfred P. Murrah federal building in Kansas City in 1996. SLATT focuses on the prevention of terrorism by training state and local law enforcement officers to understand, detect, deter, and investigate acts of terrorism in the United States by both international and domestic terrorists. Following the attacks of September 11, 2001, SLATT increased its training in the area of foreign-inspired terrorism.

| **MATRIX** |
| --- |
| An acronym for the Multistate Anti-Terrorism Information Exchange, an Internet-based proof-of-concept pilot program funded by the Department of Justice and the Department of Homeland Security to increase and enhance the exchange of sensitive information about terrorism and other criminal activity between enforcement agencies at the local, state, and federal levels. |

# Discretion and the Individual Officer

Even as law enforcement agencies struggle to adapt to the threats posed by international terrorism, individual officers continue to retain considerable discretion in terms of their actions. **Police discretion** refers to the exercise of choice by law enforcement officers in the decision to investigate or apprehend, the disposition of suspects, the carrying out of official duties, and the application of sanctions. As one author has observed, "Police authority can be, at once, highly specific and exceedingly vague."[115] Decisions to stop and question someone, arrest a suspect, and perform many other police tasks are made solely by individual officers and must often be made quickly and in the absence of any close supervision. Kenneth Culp Davis, who pioneered the study of police discretion, says, "The police make policy about what law to enforce, how much to enforce it, against whom, and on what occasions."[116] To those who have contact with the police, the discretionary authority exercised by individual officers is of greater significance than all the department manuals and official policy statements combined.

Patrolling officers often decide against a strict enforcement of the law, preferring instead to handle situations informally. Minor law violations, crimes committed out of the officer's presence where the victim refuses to file a complaint, and certain violations of the criminal law where the officer suspects that sufficient evidence to obtain a conviction is lacking may all lead to discretionary action short of arrest. The widest exercise of discretion is in routine situations involving relatively less serious violations of the law, but serious criminal behavior may occasionally result in discretionary decisions not to make an arrest. Drunk driving, possession of controlled substances, and assault are examples of crimes in which on-the-scene officers may choose warnings or referrals over arrest.

| **police discretion** |
| --- |
| The opportunity of law enforcement officers to exercise choice in their daily activities. |

Studies of police discretion have found that a number of factors influence the discretionary decisions of individual officers. Here are some of these factors:

- *Background of the officer.* Law enforcement officers bring their life experience to the job. Values shaped through early socialization and attitudes acquired from ongoing socialization influence an officer's decisions. For example, if an officer learned prejudice against certain ethnic groups, that prejudice will likely manifest itself in enforcement decisions; an officer who values the nuclear family may handle spousal or child abuse and domestic disputes in predetermined ways.

- *Characteristics of the suspect.* Characteristics of a suspect that may influence police decisions include gender, demeanor, style of dress, and grooming.[117] Some officers treat men and women differently. Belligerent suspects are often seen as "asking for it" and as challenging police authority. Well-dressed suspects are likely to be treated with deference, but poorly groomed suspects can expect less respectful treatment. Suspects sporting personal styles with a message—biker's attire, unkempt beards, outlandish haircuts, gang-style clothes, and other nonconformist styles—are more likely to be arrested than are others.

- *Department policy.* Official policy rarely controls discretion, but it does influence it. For example, if department supervisors adhere to strict enforcement guidelines and closely monitor dispatches and other communications, individual officers will be less likely to release suspects at their own discretion.

- *Community interest.* Public attitudes toward certain crimes will increase the likelihood of arrest for suspected offenders. Contemporary attitudes toward crimes involving children—including child sex abuse, the sale of drugs to minors, domestic violence involving children, and child pornography—have all led to increased and strict enforcement of laws governing such offenses. Communities may identify specific problems affecting them and ask law enforcement to respond. Fayetteville, North Carolina, was plagued some years ago by a downtown area notorious for prostitution and massage parlors. Once the community voiced its concern over the problem and its economic impact on the city, the police responded with a series of highly effective arrests that eliminated massage parlors within the city limits. Departments that require officers to live in the areas they police recognize that community interests affect citizens and officers alike.

- *Pressure from victims.* Victims of certain crimes, such as spousal abuse and assaults on customers of prostitutes, commonly refuse to file a complaint. When victims refuse to cooperate, there is often little that police can do. However, some victims demand that their victimization be recognized and dealt with. Victims' assistance groups, such as People Assisting Victims and the Victim's Assistance Network, have sought to keep pressure on police departments and individual investigators to ensure the arrest and prosecution of suspects.

- *Disagreement with the law.* Some behaviors that are crimes in one area are not crimes in other jurisdictions. For example, gambling is now legal in many states, aboard cruise ships, and on some Native American reservations; many states have legalized homosexuality and most forms of consensual adult sexual behavior; prostitution is legal in portions of Nevada; and some drug offenses have been "decriminalized," with offenders being ticketed rather than arrested.

  Some laws lack a popular consensus, such as laws relating to many victimless offenses. Unpopular laws are not likely to get much attention from law enforcement officers. Sometimes such crimes are regarded as just "part of the landscape," or the law is thought to have not kept pace with a changing society. When an arrest does occur, it is often because individuals being investigated for more serious offenses were caught violating an unpopular statute. For example, drug offenders arrested in the middle of the night may be caught performing an illegal sexual act when the police break in. Charges may then include "crime against nature," as well as possession or sale of drugs.

  In some cases, discretionary police activity may take the form of "street justice" and may approach vigilantism. For example, certain lawful, even protected, behaviors may be annoying, offensive, or disruptive by the normative standards of a community or the personal standards of an officer. In these cases, the officer makes a personal decision about how to handle the disruption. Or, an officer investigating a clear violation of the law may discover that he knows the guilty party. In these cases, an officer has been known to render unusable the evidence needed for a conviction in court. Noted law enforcement scholar Gary Sykes, in recognizing these possibilities, says, "One of the major ambiguities of the police task is that officers are caught between two profoundly compelling moral systems: justice as due process . . . and conversely, justice as righting a wrong as part of defining and maintaining community norms."[118]

- *Available alternatives.* An officer's awareness of alternatives to arrest can influence discretion. Officers looking to avoid official action may turn to community treatment programs such as outpatient drug or alcohol counseling and domestic dispute-resolution centers.

- *Personal practices of the officer.* Some officers view the violation of particular laws less seriously than other officers. The police officer who smokes an occasional marijuana cigarette may deal less harshly with minor drug offenders than nonusing officers, and officers who routinely speed while driving the family car may be more lenient with speeders encountered while on duty.

# Professionalism and Ethics

A profession is an organized undertaking characterized by a body of specialized knowledge acquired through extensive education[119] and by a well-considered set of internal standards and ethical guidelines that hold members of the profession accountable to one another and to society. Contemporary policing has many of the attributes of a profession.

**Police professionalism** requires that today's police officers have a great deal of specialized knowledge and that they adhere to the standards and ethics set out by the profession. Specialized knowledge in policing includes an understanding of criminal law, laws of procedure, constitutional guarantees, and relevant Supreme Court decisions; a working knowledge of weapons, hand-to-hand tactics, driving skills, vehicle maintenance, and radio communications; report-writing abilities; interviewing techniques; and media and human relations skills. Other specialized knowledge may include Breathalyzer operation, special weapons skills, polygraph operation, conflict resolution, and hostage negotiation. Supervisory personnel require an even wider range of skills, including administrative skills, management techniques, and strategies for optimum utilization of resources.

Police professionalism also places important limits on the discretionary activities of individual enforcement personnel. Police work is guided by an ethical code developed in 1956 by the Peace Officer's Research Association of California (PORAC) in conjunction with Dr. Douglas M. Kelley of Berkeley's School of Criminology.[120] The Law Enforcement Code of Ethics is reproduced in a CJ Ethics and Professionalism box in this chapter.

Ethics training has been integrated into most basic law enforcement training programs, and calls for expanded training in **police ethics** are being heard from many corners. A comprehensive resource for enhancing awareness of law enforcement ethics, called the "Ethics Toolkit," is available from the International Association of Chiefs of Police (IACP) and the federal Office of Community Oriented Policing Services via Web Extra 6–9.

---

**police professionalism**

The increasing formalization of police work and the accompanying rise in public acceptance of the police.

---

**police ethics**

The special responsibility to adhere to moral duty and obligation that is inherent in police work.

WEB EXTRA

---

## ETHICS AND PROFESSIONALISM

### The Law Enforcement Code of Ethics

As a Law Enforcement Officer, my fundamental duty is to serve mankind; to safeguard lives and property; to protect the innocent against deception, the weak against oppression or intimidation, and the peaceful against violence or disorder; and to respect the Constitutional rights of all men to liberty, equality, and justice.

I will keep my private life unsullied as an example to all; maintain courageous calm in the face of danger, scorn, or ridicule; develop self-restraint; and be constantly mindful of the welfare of others. Honest in thought and deed in both my personal and official life, I will be exemplary in obeying the laws of the land and the regulations of my department. Whatever I see or hear of a confidential nature or that is confided to me in my official capacity will be kept secret unless revelation is necessary in the performance of my duty.

I will never act officiously or permit personal feelings, prejudices, animosities, or friendships to influence my decisions.

With no compromise for crime and with relentless prosecution of criminals, I will enforce the law courteously and appropriately without fear or favor, malice or ill will, never employing unnecessary force or violence and never accepting gratuities.

I recognize the badge of my office as a symbol of public faith, and I accept it as a public trust to be held so long as I am true to the ethics of the police service. I will constantly strive to achieve these objectives and ideals, dedicating myself before God to my chosen profession . . . law enforcement.

#### THINKING ABOUT ETHICS

1. Why does the Law Enforcement Code of Ethics ask law enforcement officers "to respect the Constitutional rights of all men to liberty, equality, and justice"? Does such respect further the goals of law enforcement? Why or why not?

2. Why is it important for a law enforcement officer to "keep my private life unsullied as an example to all"? What are the potential consequences of *not* doing so?

*Source:* International Association of Chiefs of Police. Reprinted with permission.

Many professional associations are associated with police work. One such organization, the Arlington, Virginia–based International Association of Chiefs of Police, has done much to raise professional standards in policing and continually strives for improvements in law enforcement nationwide. In like manner, the Fraternal Order of Police (FOP) is one of the best-known organizations of public service workers in the United States. The FOP is the world's largest organization of sworn law enforcement officers, with more than 318,000 members in more than 2,100 lodges.

Accreditation is another avenue toward police professionalism. The Commission on Accreditation for Law Enforcement Agencies (CALEA) was formed in 1979. Police departments seeking accreditation through the commission must meet hundreds of standards in areas as diverse as day-to-day operations, administration, review of incidents involving the use of a weapon by officers, and evaluation and promotion of personnel. As of March 15, 2005, nearly 580 (3.3%) of the nation's 17,784 law enforcement agencies were accredited,[121] while a number of others were undergoing the accreditation process. However, many accredited agencies are among the nation's largest; as a result, 25% of full-time law enforcement officers in the United States at the state and local levels are members of CALEA-accredited programs.[122] Although accreditation makes possible the identification of high-quality police departments, it is often not valued by agency leaders because it offers few incentives. Accreditation does not guarantee a department any rewards beyond that of peer recognition. Visit CALEA online via Web Extra 6–10 at cjtoday.com.

**WEB EXTRA**

# Education and Training

**WEB EXTRA**

Basic law enforcement training requirements were established in the 1950s by the state of New York and through a voluntary **peace officer standards and training (POST) program** in California. (Information on California's POST programs can be accessed via Web Extra 6–11 at cjtoday.com.) Today, every jurisdiction mandates POST-like requirements, although these requirements vary considerably. Modern police education generally involves training in subjects as varied as human relations, firearms and weapons, communications, legal aspects of policing, patrol, criminal investigations, administration, report writing, and criminal justice systems. According to a 1999 Bureau of Justice Statistics report, the median number of hours of classroom training required of new officers is 823 in state police agencies, 760 in county departments, 640 in municipal departments, and 448 in sheriff's departments.[123] Standards continue to be modified. In 2002, for example, the California Commission on POST responded to statewide concerns over racial profiling by adding material to the police-training curriculum to ensure that all California law enforcement officers receive training "that reinforces the fact that racial profiling has a profound negative impact on communities and cannot be tolerated."[124]

**peace officer standards and training (POST) program**

The official program of a state or legislative jurisdiction that sets standards for the training of law enforcement officers. All states set such standards, although not all use the term *POST*.

Federal law enforcement agents receive schooling at the Federal Law Enforcement Training Center (FLETC) in Glynco, Georgia. The center provides training for about 60 federal law enforcement agencies, excluding the FBI and the Drug Enforcement Administration (DEA), which have their own training academies in Quantico, Virginia. FLETC also offers advanced training to state and local police organizations through the National Center for State and Local Law Enforcement Training, located on the FLETC campus. Specialized schools, such as Northwestern University's Traffic Institute, are also credited with raising the level of police practice from purely operational concerns to a more professional level.

In 1987, in a move to further professionalize police training, the American Society for Law Enforcement Trainers was formed at the Ohio Peace Officer Training Academy. Now known as the American Society for Law Enforcement Training (ASLET), the Frederick, Maryland–based agency works to ensure quality in peace officer training and confers the title Certified Law Enforcement Trainer (CLET) on police-training professionals who meet its high standards. ASLET also works with the Police Training Network (online at Web Extra 6–12 at cjtoday.com) to provide an ongoing and comprehensive nationwide calendar of law enforcement training activities.

**WEB EXTRA**

A recent innovation in law enforcement training is the Police Training Officer (PTO) program, whose development was funded by the COPS Office starting in 1999.[125] The PTO program was designed by the Reno (Nevada) Police Department, in conjunction with the Police Executive Research Forum, as an alternative model for police field training. In fact, it represents the first new postacademy field training program for law enforcement agencies in more than 30 years. PTO uses contemporary methods of adult education and a version of problem-based learning that is specifically adapted to the police environment. It incorporates community policing and problem-solving principles and, according to the COPS Office, fosters "the foundation for life-long learning that prepares new officers for the complexities of policing today and in the future." Learn more about PTO at Library Extra 6–11 at cjtoday.com.

**LIBRARY EXTRA**

As the concern for quality policing builds, increasing emphasis is also being placed on the formal education of police officers. As early as 1931, the National Commission on Law Observance and Enforcement (the Wickersham Commission) highlighted the importance of a well-educated police force by calling for "educationally sound" officers.[126] In 1967, the President's Commission on Law Enforcement and Administration of Justice voiced the belief that "the ultimate aim of all police departments should be that all personnel with general enforcement powers have baccalaureate degrees."[127] At the time, the average educational level of police officers in the United States was 12.4 years—slightly beyond a high school degree. In 1973, the National Advisory Commission on Criminal Justice Standards and Goals made the following rather specific recommendation: "Every police agency should, no later than 1982, require as a condition of initial employment the completion of at least four years of education . . . at an accredited college or university."[128]

However, recommendations do not always translate into practice. A 1999 report found that 16% of state police agencies require a two-year college degree, and 4% require a four-year degree. County police are the next most likely to require either a two-year (13%) or four-year (3%) degree.[129] Among sheriff's departments, 6% require a degree, including 1% with a four-year degree requirement.[130] A 2002 report on police departments in large cities found that the percentage requiring new officers to have at least some college rose from 19% in 1990 to 37% in 2000, and the percentage requiring a two-year or four-year degree grew from 6% to 14% over the same period.[131] A Dallas Police Department[132] policy requiring a minimum of 45 semester hours of successful college-level study for new recruits was upheld in 1985 by the Fifth U.S. Circuit Court of Appeals in the case of *Davis v. Dallas*.[133]

An early survey of police departments by the Police Executive Research Forum found that police agencies that hire educated officers accrue these benefits[134]: (1) better written reports, (2) enhanced communications with the public, (3) more effective job performance, (4) fewer citizen complaints, (5) greater initiative, (6) wiser use of discretion, (7) heightened sensitivity to racial and ethnic issues, and (8) fewer disciplinary problems. However, there are drawbacks to having more educated police forces. Educated officers are more likely to leave police work, question orders, and request reassignment more frequently than noneducated officers.

Finally, most federal agencies require college degrees for entry-level positions. Among them are the FBI, the DEA, the Bureau of Alcohol, Tobacco, Firearms, and Explosives (ATF), the Secret Service, the Bureau of Customs and Border Protection, and the Bureau of Immigration and Customs Enforcement (ICE).[135]

> **A good cop stays a rookie at heart, excited by every shift.**
>
> —A Nashville, Tennessee, police officer

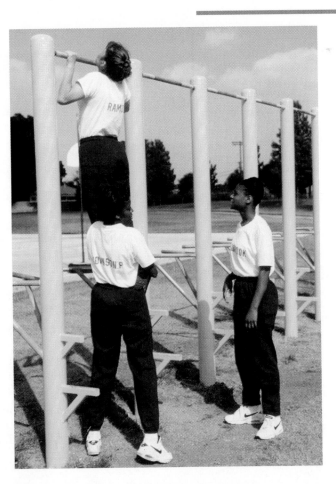

Policewomen trainees helping one another during physical training at the Los Angeles Police Academy's Parker Center. Rigorous training and high performance standards in all areas of police responsibility are crucial to effective law enforcement operations.

*Michael Newman, PhotoEdit*

## CJ CAREERS

### POLICING: AVERAGE BASE STARTING PAY

The below figures show the starting salary for police officers in midsize to large municipal police agencies and sheriff's departments in the United States averaged between $32,000 and $34,000 in 2000. Smaller departments, as seen in the figures below, paid less. The figures also show that very little change in base pay occurred between 1990 and 2000.

For additional information on employment opportunities in the criminal justice field, view the careers portion of the CD-ROM included with this book.

**Average base starting salary for entry-level officers in local police agencies and sheriff's departments, 1990 and 2000.**

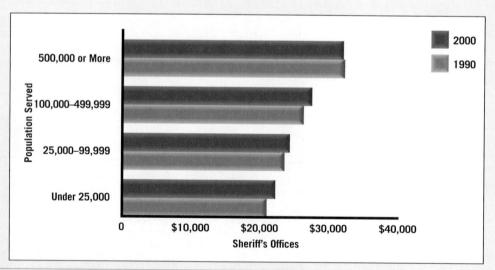

*References:* Matthew J. Hickman and Brian A. Reaves, *Local Police Departments, 2000* (Washington, DC: Bureau of Justice Statistics, 2003), p. 5; and Matthew J. Hickman and Brian A. Reaves, *Sheriff's Offices, 2000* (Washington, DC: Bureau of Justice Statistics, 2003), p. 8.

# Recruitment and Selection

All professions need informed, dedicated, and competent personnel. In its 1973 report on the police, the National Advisory Commission on Criminal Justice Standards and Goals bemoaned the fact that "many college students are unaware of the varied, interesting, and challenging assign-

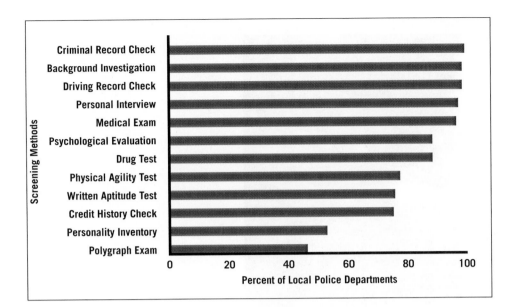

**FIGURE 6–5**

**Percentage of local police departments using various recruit-screening methods, 2000.**

*Source:* Matthew J. Hickman and Brian A. Reaves, *Local Police Departments, 2000* (Washington, DC: Bureau of Justice Statistics, 2003), p. 5.

ments and career opportunities that exist within the police service."[136] Today, police organizations consider education an important recruiting criterion, and they actively recruit new officers from two- and four-year colleges and universities, technical institutions, and professional organizations. The national commission report stressed the setting of high standards for police recruits and recommended a strong emphasis on minority recruitment, elimination of the requirement that new officers live in the area they were hired to serve, decentralized application and testing procedures, and various recruiting incentives.

A 2003 Bureau of Justice Statistics study found that local police departments use a variety of applicant-screening methods.[137] Nearly all use personal interviews, and a large majority use basic skills tests, physical agility measurements, medical exams, drug tests, psychological evaluations, and background investigations into the personal character of applicants (see Figure 6–5). Among departments serving 25,000 or more residents, about eight in ten use physical agility tests and written aptitude tests, more than half check credit records, and about half use personality inventories and polygraph exams. After training, successful applicants are typically placed on probation for one year. The probationary period in police work has been called the "first true job-related test . . . in the selection procedure,"[138] providing the opportunity for supervisors to gauge the new officer's response to real-life situations.

Effective policing, however, may depend more on innate personal qualities than on educational attainment or credit history. One of the first people to attempt to describe the personal attributes necessary in a successful police officer, famed 1930s police administrator August Vollmer, said that the public expects police officers to have "the wisdom of Solomon, the courage of David, the strength of Samson, the patience of Job, the leadership of Moses, the kindness of the Good Samaritan, the strategic training of Alexander, the faith of Daniel, the diplomacy of Lincoln, the tolerance of the Carpenter of Nazareth, and finally, an intimate knowledge of every branch of the natural, biological, and social sciences."[139] More practically, Orlando (O. W.) Wilson, the well-known police administrator of the 1940s and 1950s, once enumerated some "desirable personal qualities of patrol officers"[140]: (1) initiative; (2) responsibility; (3) the ability to deal alone with emergencies; (4) the capacity to communicate effectively with people from diverse social, cultural, and ethnic backgrounds; (5) the ability to learn a variety of tasks quickly; (6) the attitude and ability necessary to adapt to technological changes; (7) the desire to help people in need; (8) an understanding of others; (9) emotional maturity; and (10) sufficient physical strength and endurance.

High-quality police recruits, an emphasis on training with an eye toward ethical aspects of police performance, and higher levels of education are beginning to raise police pay, which has traditionally been low. The acceptance of police work as a true profession should contribute to significantly higher rates of pay in coming years.

**WHAT WOULD YOU DO?**

The CD-ROM scenario for Chapter 6 focuses on police hiring practices. This scenario is derived from an actual incident involving hiring practices by the Dallas (Texas) Police Department in which the department's standards were contested. The real-life case eventually found its way to the Fifth U.S. Circuit Court of Appeals. Use the CD-ROM found in your textbook to work through this scenario.

An advertisement for police professionals to work in Iraq. The acceptance of police work as a true profession will mean high pay and benefits—both at home and abroad—for those who embrace the professional ideals of training, education, and ethics.

*Courtesy of DynCorp International, LLC*

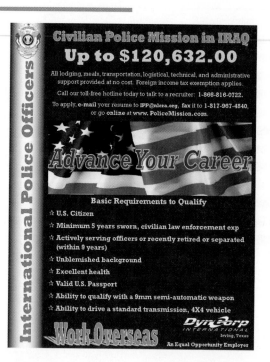

# Ethnic and Gender Diversity in Policing

In 2003, Annetta W. Nunn took the reins of the Birmingham (Alabama) Police Department. For many, Nunn, a 44-year-old African-American mother and Baptist choir singer, symbolizes the changes that have taken place in American policing during the past few decades. The new chief sits in a chair once occupied by Eugene "Bull" Connor, an arch segregationist and a national symbol of the South's fight against integration who jailed thousands of civil rights demonstrators during the 1960s. A 23-year veteran of the department, Nunn heads a force of 838 men and women.

Birmingham, Alabama, Chief of Police Annetta Nunn. Nunn's appointment in 2003 is indicative of expanded opportunities in policing for women and minorities. Nunn, who holds a bachelor's degree in criminal justice from the University of Alabama, was four years old in 1963 when thousands of civil rights demonstrators in Birmingham were beaten and arrested on orders of Police Chief Eugene "Bull" Connor.

*Birmingham Police Department*

African-American and Hispanic police officers in Los Angeles. Ethnic minorities, while still underrepresented in the criminal justice field, have many opportunities for employment throughout the system.

*David R. Frazier, Photolibrary, Photo Researchers, Inc.*

Today, through dedicated recruitment efforts, many departments have dramatically increased their complement of officers from underrepresented groups. The Metropolitan Detroit Police Department, for example, now has a force that is more than 30% black. Nationwide, racial and ethnic minorities comprised 22.7% of full-time sworn police personnel in 2000, up from 17.0% in 1990.[141] From 1990 to 2000, the number of African-American local police officers increased by 13,300, or 35%; and the number of Hispanic officers increased by 17,600, or 93%.

Although ethnic minorities are now employed in policing in numbers that approach their representation in the American population, women are still significantly underrepresented. The 2000 Status of Women in Policing Survey, conducted by the National Center for Women and Policing (NCWP), found that women fill only 13% of all sworn law enforcement positions nationwide.[142] On the other hand, the NCWP notes that women account for 46.5% of employed people over the age of 16 nationwide, meaning that they are "strikingly under-represented within the field of sworn law enforcement."[143] Key findings from the survey show the following[144]:

■ Women currently fill about 13% of all sworn law enforcement positions among municipal, county, and state agencies in the United States with 100 or more sworn officers. Women of color hold 4.9% of these positions.

■ Between 1990 and 2000, the representation of women in sworn law enforcement ranks has increased from 9% to 13%—a gain of only 4%, or less than 0.5% each year.

■ If the slow growth rate of women in policing holds, women will not achieve equal representation within the police profession for another 70 years, and many experts caution that time alone may not be sufficient to substantially increase the number of female officers.

■ Women hold 7.3% of sworn top command law enforcement positions, 10.3% of supervisory positions, and 13.7% of line operation positions. Women of color hold 1.7% of sworn top command positions, 3.2% of supervisory positions, and 5.3% of line operation positions.

■ Fifty-seven percent of the agencies surveyed reported no women in top command positions, and 88% of the agencies reported no women of color in their highest ranks.

■ State agencies trail municipal and county agencies by a wide margin in hiring and promoting women. Specifically, 6.8% of the sworn law enforcement officers in state agencies are women, which is significantly lower than the percentage reported by municipal agencies (14.5%) and county agencies (13.5%).

■ Consent decrees mandating the hiring and promotion of women and minorities significantly affected the gains women have made in law enforcement. Of the 25 agencies with the highest percentage of sworn women, ten are subject to such decrees. This contrasts sharply with just four of the 25 agencies with the lowest percentage of sworn women operating under consent decrees.

- On average, in agencies without a consent decree mandating the hiring and promotion of women and minorities, women comprise 9.7% of sworn personnel, whereas those agencies with a consent decree in force average 14.0% women in their ranks. The percentage of women of color is 6.3% in agencies without a consent decree and 11.7% in agencies operating under one.

It is unclear just how many women actually *want* to work in policing. Nonetheless, many departments aggressively recruit and retain women because they understand the benefits of having more women as sworn officers. Because female officers tend to use less physical force than male officers, for example, they are less likely to be accused of using excessive force. Female officers are also better at defusing and deescalating potentially violent confrontations; often possess better communications skills than their male counterparts; and are better able to facilitate the cooperation and trust required to implement a community policing model. Moreover, the NCWP says that "female officers often respond more effectively to incidents of violence against women—crimes that represent one of the largest categories of calls to police departments. Increasing the representation of women on the force is also likely to address another costly problem for police administrators—the pervasive problem of sex discrimination and sexual harassment—by changing the climate of modern law enforcement agencies."[145] Finally, "because women frequently have different life experiences than men, they approach policing with a different perspective, and the very presence of women in the field will often bring about changes in policies and procedures that benefit both male and female officers."[146] Additional information on how police departments can recruit and retain female officers can be found at Library Extra 6–12 at cjtoday.com.

## Women as Effective Police Officers

One research report on female police officers in Massachusetts found that female officers (1) are "extremely devoted to their work," (2) "see themselves as women first, and then police officers," and (3) are more satisfied when working in nonuniformed capacities.[147] The researcher identified two groups of female officers: (1) those who felt themselves to be well integrated into their departments and were confident in their jobs and (2) those who experienced strain and on-the-job isolation. The officers' children were cited as a significant influence on their perceptions of self and their jobs. The demands of child rearing in contemporary society were found to be a major factor contributing to the resignation of female officers. The study also found that the longer female officers stayed on the job, the greater the stress and frustration they tended to experience, primarily because of the uncooperative attitudes of male officers. Some of the female officers identified networking as a potential solution to the stresses encountered by female officers but also said that when women get together to solve problems, they are seen as "crybabies" rather than professionals. Said one of the women in the study, "We've lost a lot of good women who never should have left the job. If we had helped each other, maybe they wouldn't have left."[148]

Some studies found that female officers are often underutilized and that many departments hesitate to assign women to patrol and other potentially dangerous field activities.[149] Consequently, some policewomen experience frustration and a lack of job satisfaction. An analysis of the genderization of the criminal justice workplace by Susan Ehrlich Martin and Nancy Jurik, for example, points out that gender inequality is part of a historical pattern of entrenched forms of gender interaction relating to the division of labor, power, and culture.[150] Martin and Jurik contend that women working in the justice system are viewed in terms of such historically developed filters, causing them to be judged and treated according to normative standards developed for men. As a result, formal and informal social controls continue to disenfranchise women who wish to work in the system and make it difficult to recognize the specific contributions that they make as women.

## Increasing the Number of Minorities and Women in Police Work

To increase the representation of ethnic minorities and women in police work, the Police Foundation recommends (1) involving underrepresented groups in departmental affirmative action and long-term planning programs, (2) encouraging the development of an open promotion system whereby women can feel free to apply for promotion and in which qualified individuals of any race or gender will face equity in the promotion process, and (3) periodic audits to ensure that female officers are not being underutilized by ineffective tracking into clerical and support positions.[151]

Networking is quickly taking root among the nation's female police officers, as attested to by the growth of organizations like the International Association of Women Police. Networks support female officers and help them deal with dilemmas on the job. Mentoring, another method for introducing women to police work,[152] creates semiformal relationships between experienced female officers and rookies through which problems can be addressed, and experienced officers can guide junior partners through the maze of formal and informal expectations of policing.

Women today have entered the ranks of police administration. The 2,000-member International Association of Women Police estimates that there are more than 100 female chiefs of police throughout the country. The Women's Police Chief Association offers networking opportunities to women seeking and holding high rank in departments nationwide.[153] And the National Center for Women and Policing, a project of the Feminist Majority Foundation, provides a nationwide resource for law enforcement agencies, community leaders, and public officials seeking to increase the numbers of female police officers in their communities.

Barriers to diversity continue to fall. In 1979, for example, San Francisco became the first city in the world to actively recruit homosexuals for its police force. That action reduced the fear of reporting crimes among many homosexuals, who for years had been victims of organized assaults by bikers and street gangs. During the Clinton administration, Attorney General Janet Reno ordered all Justice Department agencies to end hiring discrimination based on sexual orientation.

## SUMMARY

The face of policing in America was forever changed by the events of September 11, 2001. Local law enforcement agencies, many of which saw community protection and peacekeeping as their primary roles, are now being called upon to protect against potential terrorist threats with international roots. Even with this new focus on terrorism prevention and response, however, the fundamental mission of American policing remains essentially unchanged from what it has always been. Law enforcement agencies are charged with (1) enforcing the law (especially the criminal law), (2) investigating crimes and apprehending offenders, (3) preventing crime, (4) helping to ensure domestic peace and tranquility, and (5) providing the community with needed enforcement-related services.

Law enforcement agencies employ operational strategies to meet their goals. This chapter presents five core strategies: preventive patrol, routine incident response, emergency response, criminal investigation, and problem solving. Support, an ancillary operational strategy, is also discussed. Police management and the organizational structure of law enforcement agencies provide two additional dimensions of police administration. Distinctions between line and staff operations are critical to understanding agency organization.

Three policing styles are identified in this chapter: (1) the watchman style, (2) the legalistic style, and (3) the service style. The style of policing that characterizes a community tends to flow from the lifestyles of those who live there. While the watchman style of policing, with its emphasis on order maintenance, was widespread during the mid-twentieth century, the service style, which is embodied in the community policing model, is commonplace today. Community policing is built on the principle that police departments and the communities they serve can work together effectively as partners in the fight against crime.

American policing continues to evolve, and the contemporary emphasis on terrorism prevention alongside the need for a rapid response to threats of terrorism has led to what some see as a new era of policing to secure the homeland. Homeland security policing builds upon the established framework of community policing for the purpose of intelligence gathering to prevent terrorism. The jury is still out as to whether the nature of policing will change dramatically in this new era or whether community policing will prevail as the preferred philosophy with relatively minor changes to fight terrorism at home.[154]

## DISCUSSION QUESTIONS

1. What are the basic purposes of policing in democratic societies? How are they consistent with one another? In what ways might they be inconsistent?

2. What are the five core operational strategies that police departments use today?

3. Define the term *police management,* and describe the different types of organizational structures typical of American police departments.

4. What are the three styles of policing described in this chapter? How do they differ? Which one characterizes the community in which you live?

5. What is community policing? How does it differ from traditional policing? Does community policing offer an opportunity to improve policing services in the United States? Why or why not?

6. What new responsibilities have American police agencies assumed since the 9/11 terrorist attacks? What new challenges are they facing?

7. What is meant by *police discretion?* How does the practice of discretion by today's officers affect their departments and the policing profession as a whole?

8. What is police professionalism? How can you tell when police action is professional? Why is professionalism important in policing today?

9. What issues related to gender and ethnicity are important in American policing? How can existing problems be addressed?

**WEB QUEST**

Use the Web to find the home pages of three police departments (other than those described in this chapter) that have posted organizational charts showing their agency structure. The departments you find should include one big-city agency, a smaller town police department, and a sheriff's office. Compare the three organizational charts to see how they differ and how they are the same. Describe the differences and the similarities that you find, and submit your findings to your instructor if asked to do so.

To complete this Web Quest online, go to the Web Quest module in Chapter 6 of the *Criminal Justice Today* Companion Website at cjtoday.com.

**NOTES**

i. Jim Hodgson, "Living the Bradley County Sheriff's Mission Statement." Web posted at http://www.bradleysheriff.com/majorthoughts.htm (accessed February 22, 2002).

ii. Police Foundation, *Annual Report, 1991* (Washington, DC: Police Foundation, 1992).

iii. From Michael S. Scott, *Problem-Oriented Policing: Reflections on the First 20 Years* (Washington, DC: U.S. Department of Justice, Office of Community Oriented Policing Services, 2000), p. 88. Web posted at http://www.cops.usdoj.gov/Default.asp?Item=311 (accessed May 25, 2003).

iv. International Association of Chiefs of Police, *From Hometown Security to Homeland Security: IACP's Principles for a Locally Designed and Nationally Coordinated Homeland Security Strategy* (Alexandria, VA: IACP, 2005).

v. Wayne W. Bennett and Karen M. Hess, *Criminal Investigation,* 6th ed. (Belmont, CA: Wadsworth, 2001), p. 3. Italics in original.

vi. This definition draws on the classic work by O. W. Wilson, *Police Administration* (New York: McGraw-Hill, 1950), pp. 2–3.

vii. Sam S. Souryal, *Police Administration and Management* (St. Paul, MN: West, 1977), p. 261.

viii. Community Policing Consortium, *What Is Community Policing?* (Washington, DC: Community Policing Consortium, 1995).

ix. Matthew C. Scheider, Robert E. Chapman, and Michael F. Seelman, *Border and Transportation Security: Connecting the Dots for a Proactive Approach* (Washington, DC: U.S. Department of Justice, 2004), p. 162.

x. Robert Chapman et al., *Local Law Enforcement Responds to Terrorism: Lessons in Prevention and Preparedness* (Washington, DC: U.S. Department of Justice, Office of Community Oriented Policing Services, 2002), p. 2.

xi. Major Cities Chiefs Association, *Terrorism: The Impact on State and Local Law Enforcement,* Intelligence Commanders Conference Report, June 2002. Web posted at http://www.neiassociates.org/mccintelligencereport.pdf (accessed September 30, 2002).

xii. Angus Smith, ed., *Intelligence-Led Policing* (Richmond, VA: International Association of Law Enforcement Intelligence Analysts, 1997), p. 1.

xiii. Office of Justice Programs, *The National Criminal Intelligence Sharing Plan* (Washington, DC: U.S. Department of Justice, 2005), p. 27.

1. Major Cities Chiefs Association, *Terrorism: The Impact on State and Local Law Enforcement,* Intelligence Commanders Conference Report,

June 2002. Web posted at http://www
.neiassociates.org/mccintelligencereport.pdf
(accessed September 30, 2002).

2. "Police, Protestors Clash Near Miami Trade
Talks," CNN.com, November 20, 2003. Web
posted at http://www.cnn.com/2003/US/South/
11/20/miami.protests (accessed June 3, 2004).

3. "Demonstrators, Police Clash during Free
Trade Talks," *USA Today,* November 20, 2003.
Web posted at http://www.usatoday.com/
news/nation/2003–11–20-miami-
protests_x.htm (accessed June 3, 2004).

4. Andrew P. Sutor, *Police Operations: Tactical
Approaches to Crimes in Progress* (St. Paul,
MN: West, 1976), p. 68, citing Peel.

5. C. D. Hale, *Police Patrol: Operations and
Management* (Englewood Cliffs, NJ: Prentice
Hall, 1994).

6. Victor Kappeler et al., *The Mythology of Crime
and Criminal Justice* (Prospect Heights, IL:
Waveland Press, 1996).

7. Darl H. Champion and Michael K. Hooper,
*Introduction to American Policing* (New York:
McGraw-Hill, 2003), p. 133.

8. Details for this story come from Ted Ottley,
"Bad Day Dawning," Court TV's Crime Library.
Web posted at http://www.crimelibrary.com/
serial_killers/notorious/mcveigh/dawning_1
.html (accessed June 22, 2003).

9. Ibid.

10. This definition has been attributed to the
National Crime Prevention Institute (see http://
www.lvmpd.com/community/crmtip25.htm).

11. See Steven P. Lab, *Crime Prevention at a
Crossroads* (Cincinnati, OH: Anderson, 1997).

12. See the Philadelphia Police Department's
Operation Identification website at http://
www.ppdonline.org/ppd4_home_opid.htm.

13. The term *CompStat* is sometimes interpreted
to mean computer statistics, comparative
statistics, or computer comparative statistics,
although, as the CJ News box in this chapter
shows, it is generally accorded no specific
meaning.

14. Learn more about CompStat from Vincent E.
Henry, *The COMPSTAT Paradigm:
Management Accountability in Policing,
Business, and the Public Sector* (Flushing, NY:
Looseleaf Law Publications, 2002).

15. Much of the information in this section comes
from the Philadelphia Police Department, "The
COMPSTAT Process." Web posted at http://
www.ppdonline.org/ppd_compstat.htm
(accessed May 28, 2003).

16. See Ned Levine, *CrimeStat: A Spatial Statistics
Program for the Analysis of Crime Incident
Locations,* version 2.0 (Houston, TX: Ned
Levine and Associates; Washington, DC:
National Institute of Justice, May 2002).

17. Robert H. Langworthy and Lawrence P. Travis
III, *Policing in America: A Balance of Forces,*
2nd ed. (Upper Saddle River, NJ: Prentice Hall,
1999), p. 194.

18. Adapted from Bronx County (New York) District
Attorney's Office, "Quality of Life Offenses,"
December 24, 2002. Web posted at
http://www.bronxda.net/fighting_crime/quality_
of_life_offenses.html (accessed June 20, 2003).

19. Other violations may be involved, as well. On
December 29, 2000, for example, Judge John S.
Martin, Jr., of the Federal District Court in
Manhattan, ruled that homeless persons in
New York City could be arrested for sleeping
in cardboard boxes in public. Judge Martin
held that a city Sanitation Department
regulation barring people from abandoning
cars or boxes on city streets could be applied
to the homeless who were sleeping in boxes.

20. Norman Siegel, executive director of the New
York Civil Liberties Union, as reported in
"Quality of Life Offenses Targeted," *Western
Queens Gazette,* November 22, 2000. Web
posted at http://www.qgazette.com/News/
2000/1122/Editorial_pages/e01.html (accessed
June 12, 2003).

21. The broken windows thesis was first suggested
by George L. Kelling and James Q. Wilson in
"Broken Windows: The Police and
Neighborhood Safety," *Atlantic Monthly,*
March 1982. The article is available online at
http://www.theatlantic.com/politics/crime/
windows.htm.

22. For a critique of the broken windows thesis,
see Bernard E. Harcourt, *Illusion of Order:
The False Promise of Broken Windows
Policing* (Cambridge, MA: Harvard University
Press, 2001).

23. Peter Schuler, "Law Professor Harcourt
Challenges Popular Policing Method, Gun
Violence Interventions," *Chicago Chronicle,*
Vol. 22, No. 12 (March 20, 2003).

24. George L. Kelling, Catherine M. Coles, and
James Q. Wilson, *Fixing Broken Windows:
Restoring Order and Reducing Crime in Our
Communities,* reprint (New York: Touchstone,
1998).

25. Charles R. Swanson, Leonard Territo, and
Robert W. Taylor, *Police Administration:
Structures, Processes, and Behavior,* 4th ed.
(Upper Saddle River, NJ: Prentice Hall,
1998), p. 1.

26. Lorraine Mazerolle et al., *Managing Citizen
Calls to the Police: An Assessment of
Nonemergency Call Systems* (Washington, DC:
National Institute of Justice, 2001), p. 1–1.

27. The Hastings (Minnesota) Police Department
Web page at http://www.ci.hastings.mn.us/
Police/deptnews.htm (accessed May 24,
2003).

28. The term *operational strategies* is taken from
Michael S. Scott, *Problem-Oriented Policing:
Reflections on the First 20 Years* (Washington,
DC: U.S. Department of Justice, Office of
Community Oriented Policing Services, 2000),

p. 85. Web posted at http://www.cops.usdoj .gov/Default.asp?Item5311 (accessed May 25, 2003).

29. Ibid., from which some of the wording and much of the material in this section is adapted.

30. Ibid., p. 86.

31. Ibid., from which much of this material is adapted.

32. Ibid., p. 86.

33. William K. Rashbaum, "Response Time to Police Calls Is 29% Faster," *New York Times*, September 26, 2002, p. B1.

34. Details for this story come from Kurt Streeter, "Girl, 2, Rescued from Washer," *Los Angeles Times*, May 26, 2003. Web posted at http:// www.latimes.com/news/local/ la-me-laundry 26may26,1,7334286.story (accessed May 27, 2003).

35. See Scott, *Problem-Oriented Policing*, from which much of this material is adapted.

36. Wayne W. Bennett and Karen M. Hess, *Criminal Investigation*, 6th ed. (Belmont, CA: Wadsworth, 2001), p. 3. Italics in original.

37. Chief Gordon F. Urlacher and Lieutenant Robert J. Duffy, Rochester (New York) Police Department, "The Preliminary Investigation Process." Web posted at http://www.surviveall .net/preliminary_investigation_proces.htm (no date) (accessed May 27, 2003).

38. Florida Highway Patrol, "Policy Number 22.01," *Policy Manual*, February 1, 1996. Web posted at http://www.fhp.state.fl.us/html/ Manuals/fh22–01.pdf (accessed June 1, 2003).

39. Scott, *Problem-Oriented Policing*, p. 88.

40. Adapted from Michigan State Police, *Annual Report 2000*, p. 12.

41. This definition draws on the classic work by O. W. Wilson, *Police Administration* (New York: McGraw-Hill, 1950), pp. 2–3.

42. Charles R. Swanson, Leonard Territo, and Robert W. Taylor, *Police Administration: Structures, Processes, and Behavior* (Upper Saddle River, NJ: Prentice Hall, 1998), p. 167.

43. Los Angeles County Sheriff's Department, "About LASD." Web posted at http://www .lasd.org/aboutlasd/about.html (accessed June 25, 2003).

44. For more information on the first three categories, see Francis X. Hartmann, "Debating the Evolution of American Policing," *Perspectives on Policing*, No. 5 (Washington, DC: National Institute of Justice, 1988).

45. Willard M. Oliver, "The Homeland Security Juggernaut: The End of the Community Policing Era," *Crime and Justice International*, Vol. 20, No. 79 (2004), pp. 4–10. See also Willard M. Oliver, "The Era of Homeland Security: September 11, 2001 to . . . ," *Crime and Justice International*, Vol. 21, No. 85 (2005), pp. 9–17.

46. Gene Stephens, "Policing the Future: Law Enforcement's New Challenges," *The Futurist*, March/April 2005, pp. 51–57.

47. To learn more about Wilson, see "Presidential Medal of Freedom Recipient James Q. Wilson." Web posted at http://www.medaloffreedom .com/JamesQWilson.htm (accessed January 5, 2006).

48. James Q. Wilson, *Varieties of Police Behavior: The Management of Law and Order in Eight Communities* (Cambridge, MA: Harvard University Press, 1968).

49. Independent Commission on the Los Angeles Police Department, *Report of the Independent Commission on the Los Angeles Police Department* (Los Angeles: The Commission, 1991).

50. Gary W. Sykes, "Street Justice: A Moral Defense of Order Maintenance Policing," *Justice Quarterly*, Vol. 3, No. 4 (December 1986), p. 505.

51. Egon Bittner, "Community Relations," in Alvin W. Cohn and Emilio C. Viano, eds., *Police Community Relations: Images, Roles, Realities* (Philadelphia: J. B. Lippincott, 1976), pp. 77–82.

52. Paul B. Weston, *Police Organization and Management* (Pacific Palisades, CA: Goodyear, 1976), p. 159.

53. Hale, *Police Patrol*.

54. Mark H. Moore and Robert C. Trojanowicz, "Corporate Strategies for Policing," *Perspectives on Policing*, No. 6 (Washington, DC: National Institute of Justice, 1988).

55. Ibid., p. 6.

56. Community Policing Consortium, *Community Policing Is Alive and Well* (Washington, DC: Community Policing Consortium, 1995), p. 1.

57. George L. Kelling, *The Newark Foot Patrol Experiment* (Washington, DC: Police Foundation, 1981).

58. Robert C. Trojanowicz, "An Evaluation of a Neighborhood Foot Patrol Program," *Journal of Police Science and Administration*, Vol. 11 (1983).

59. Bureau of Justice Assistance, *Understanding Community Policing: A Framework for Action* (Washington, DC: Bureau of Justice Statistics, 1994), p. 10.

60. Robert C. Trojanowicz and Bonnie Bucqueroux, *Community Policing* (Cincinnati, OH: Anderson, 1990).

61. Moore and Trojanowicz, "Corporate Strategies for Policing," p. 8.

62. S. M. Hartnett and W. G. Skogan, "Community Policing: Chicago's Experience," *National Institute of Justice Journal* (April 1999), pp. 2–11.

63. Jerome H. Skolnick and David H. Bayley, *Community Policing: Issues and Practices*

*around the World* (Washington, DC: National Institute of Justice, 1988).

64. Ibid.

65. William L. Goodbody, "What Do We Expect New-Age Cops to Do?" *Law Enforcement News,* April 30, 1995, pp. 14, 18.

66. Sam Vincent Meddis and Desda Moss, "Many 'Fed-Up' Communities Cornering Crime," *USA Today,* May 22, 1995, p. 8A.

67. Matthew J. Hickman and Brian A. Reaves, *Community Policing in Local Police Departments, 1997 and 1999,* Bureau of Justice Statistics Special Report (Washington, DC: Department of Justice, 2001).

68. Richard M. Daley and Matt L. Rodriguez, *Together We Can: A Strategic Plan for Reinventing the Chicago Police Department* (Chicago: Chicago Police Department, 1993). Web posted at http://www.ci.chi.il.us/ CommunityPolicing/Statistics/Reports/TWC .pdf (accessed March 5, 2002).

69. Bureau of Justice Assistance, *Neighborhood-Oriented Policing in Rural Communities: A Program Planning Guide* (Washington, DC: Bureau of Justice Statistics, 1994), p. 4.

70. See the COPS Office website at http://www .usdoj.gov/cops (accessed January 22, 2000).

71. Jihong Zhao, Nicholas P. Lovrich, and Quint Thurman, "The Status of Community Policing in American Cities: Facilitators and Impediments Revisited," *Policing,* Vol. 22, No. 1 (1999), p. 74.

72. For a good critique and overview of community policing, see Geoffrey P. Alpert et al., *Community Policing: Contemporary Readings* (Prospect Heights, IL: Waveland Press, 1998).

73. Jack R. Greene, "Community Policing in America: Changing the Nature, Structure, and Function of the Police," in U.S. Department of Justice, *Criminal Justice 2000,* Vol. 3 (Washington, DC: Department of Justice, 2000).

74. Michael D. Reisig and Roger B. Parks, "Experience, Quality of Life, and Neighborhood Context: A Hierarchical Analysis of Satisfaction with Police," *Justice Quarterly,* Vol. 17, No. 3 (2000), p. 607.

75. Mark E. Correla, "The Conceptual Ambiguity of Community in Community Policing: Filtering the Muddy Waters," *Policing,* Vol. 23, No. 2 (2000), pp. 218–233.

76. Adapted from Donald R. Fessler, *Facilitating Community Change: A Basic Guide* (San Diego: San Diego State University, 1976), p. 7.

77. Daniel W. Flynn, *Defining the "Community" in Community Policing* (Washington, DC: Police Executive Research Forum, 1998).

78. Robert C. Trojanowicz and Mark H. Moore, *The Meaning of Community in Community Policing* (East Lansing: Michigan State University's National Neighborhood Foot Patrol Center, 1988).

79. Robert M. Bohm, K. Michael Reynolds, and Stephen T. Holms, "Perceptions of Neighborhood Problems and Their Solutions: Implications for Community Policing," *Policing,* Vol. 23, No. 4 (2000), p. 439.

80. Ibid., p. 442.

81. Malcolm K. Sparrow, "Implementing Community Policing," *Perspectives on Policing,* No. 9 (Washington, DC: National Institute of Justice, 1988).

82. "L. A. Police Chief: Treat People Like Customers," *USA Today,* March 29, 1993, p. 13A.

83. Robert Wasserman and Mark H. Moore, "Values in Policing," *Perspectives in Policing,* No. 8 (Washington, DC: National Institute of Justice, 1988), p. 7.

84. "New York City Mayor Sparks Debate on Community Policing," *Criminal Justice Newsletter,* Vol. 25, No. 2 (January 18, 1994), p. 1.

85. Toni Locy, "Three Men Indicted on Terror Charges," *USA Today,* April 13, 2005, p. 1A.

86. Details for this story are taken from Thor Valdmanis, "Wall Street Stays on Guard Against Terror Attacks," *USA Today,* August 23, 2004. Web posted at http://www.usatoday .com/money/markets/us/2004-08-03-wall -street_x.htm (accessed January 10, 2006).

87. Ibid.

88. Police Executive Research Forum, *Local Law Enforcement's Role in Preventing and Responding to Terrorism* (Washington, DC: PERF, October 2, 2001). Web posted at http://www.policeforum.org/terrorismfinal.doc (accessed June 1, 2003).

89. Council on Foreign Relations, "Terrorism Questions and Answers: Police Departments." Web posted at http://www.terrorismanswers .com/security/police.html (accessed April 19, 2003).

90. Ibid.

91. Michael Weissenstein, "NYPD Shifts Focus to Terrorism, Long Considered the Turf of Federal Agents," Associated Press, March 21, 2003. Web posted at http://www.nj.com/newsflash/ national/index.ssf?/cgi-free/getstory_ ssf.cgi?a0801_BC_NYPD-Counterterror &&news&newsflash-national (accessed May 25, 2003).

92. Ibid.

93. International Association of Chiefs of Police, *From Hometown Security to Homeland Security: IACP's Principles for a Locally Designed and Nationally Coordinated Homeland Security Strategy* (Alexandria, VA: IACP, 2005).

94. Ibid.

95. Joseph G. Estey, "President's Message: Taking Command Initiative—An Update" (Washington, DC: International Association of

Chiefs of Police, 2005). Web posted at http://www.theiacp.org/documents/index.cfm?fuseaction=document&document_id=697 (accessed July 25, 2005).

96. Robert J. Jordan (FBI), Congressional Statement on Information Sharing before the U.S. Senate Committee on the Judiciary, Subcommittee on Administrative Oversight and the Courts, Washington, DC, April 17, 2002. Web posted at http://www.fbi.gov/ congress/congress02/jordan041702.htm (accessed April 19, 2003).

97. The concept of intelligence-led policing appears to have been first fully articulated in Angus Smith, ed., *Intelligence-Led Policing* (Richmond, VA: International Association of Law Enforcement Intelligence Analysts, 1997).

98. David L. Carter, *Law Enforcement Intelligence: A Guide for State, Local, and Tribal Law Enforcement Agencies* (Washington, DC: U.S. Department of Justice, 2004), p. 7.

99. Much of the information and some of the wording in this section is taken from Carter, *Law Enforcement Intelligence.*

100. Ibid., p. 39.

101. FBI, Press BOLO for US, "Protecting America from Terrorist Attacks," May 26, 2004. Web posted at http://www.fbi.gov/page2/may04/bolo052604.htm (accessed August 28, 2005).

102. Office of Justice Programs, *The National Criminal Intelligence Sharing Plan* (Washington, DC: U.S. Department of Justice, 2005), p. 4.

103. International Association of Chiefs of Police, *Recommendations from the IACP Intelligence Summit, Criminal Intelligence Sharing: A National Plan for Intelligence-Led Policing at the Local, State and Federal Levels* (Alexandria, VA: IACP, 2002), p. 2.

104. Office for Domestic Preparedness, *Guidelines for Homeland Security* (Washington, DC: U.S. Department of Homeland Security, 2003).

105. Governor's Commission on Criminal Justice Innovation, *Final Report* (Boston, MA: The Commission, 2004), p. 57, from which much of the wording in the rest of this paragraph is taken.

106. The plan was an outgrowth of the IACP Criminal Intelligence Sharing Summit held in Alexandria, VA, in March 2002. Results of the summit are documented in International Association of Chiefs of Police, *Recommendations from the IACP Intelligence Summit, Criminal Intelligence Sharing.*

107. Office of Justice Programs, *The National Criminal Intelligence Sharing Plan* (Washington, DC: U.S. Department of Justice, 2003).

108. The term comes from Bud Levin, as quoted in Gene Stephens, "Policing the Future: Law Enforcement's New Challenges," *The Futurist,* March/April 2005, p. 55.

109. Much of the information in this section comes from Bureau of Justice Assistance, *Promoting Partnerships for Public Safety, Annual Report FY 2002* (Washington, DC: December 2003). Web posted at http://www.ncjrs.org/html/bja/200252/sec2_b.html (accessed January 5, 2006).

110. MATRIX, "Background Information for Press Releases/Inquiries," press release, April 2005.

111. Visit RISS at http://www.iir.com/riss/RISS_centers.htm.

112. MATRIX, "FACTS Defined." Web posted at http://www.matrix-at.org/FACTS_ defined.htm (accessed March 14, 2005).

113. MATRIX, "Background Information for Press Releases/Inquiries."

114. See "About SLATT" at http://www.iir.com/slatt (accessed March 14, 2005).

115. Howard Cohen, "Overstepping Police Authority," *Criminal Justice Ethics* (Summer/Fall 1987), pp. 52–60.

116. Kenneth Culp Davis, *Police Discretion* (St. Paul, MN: West, 1975).

117. See, for example, Robert Shepard Engel, James J. Sobol, and Robert E. Worden, "Further Exploration of the Demeanor Hypothesis: The Interaction of Effects of Suspects' Characteristics and Demeanor on Police Behavior," *Justice Quarterly,* Vol. 17, No. 2 (2000), p. 235.

118. Sykes, "Street Justice," p. 505.

119. Michael Siegfried, "Notes on the Professionalization of Private Security," *Justice Professional* (Spring 1989).

120. See Edward A. Farris, "Five Decades of American Policing, 1932–1982: The Path to Professionalism," *Police Chief* (November 1982), p. 34.

121. E-mail correspondence with Janice Dixon at the Commission on Accreditation for Law Enforcement Agencies, March 16, 2005. Agency estimates are from Brian A. Reaves and Matthew J. Hickman, *Census of State and Local Law Enforcement Agencies, 2000* (Washington, DC: Bureau of Justice Statistics, 2002).

122. *CALEA Update,* No. 81 (February 2003). Web posted at http://www.calea.org/newweb/newsletter/No81/81index.htm (accessed May 21, 2003).

123. Brian A. Reaves and Andrew L. Goldberg, *Law Enforcement Management and Administrative Statistics, 1997: Data for Individual State and Local Law Enforcement Agencies with 100 or More Officers* (Washington, DC: Bureau of Justice Statistics, 1999).

124. California Commission on POST, "California Responds to Racial Profiling." Web posted at http://www.post.ca.gov/surveys/racialprofile.htm (accessed March 3, 2002).

125. Information in this paragraph comes from "PTO Program," COPS Office, U.S. Department of Justice (no date). Web posted at http://www.cops.usdoj.gov/print.asp?Item_461 (accessed June 3, 2005).

126. National Commission on Law Observance and Enforcement, *Report on Police* (Washington, DC: U.S. Government Printing Office, 1931).

127. President's Commission on Law Enforcement and Administration of Justice, *The Challenge of Crime in a Free Society* (Washington, DC: U.S. Government Printing Office, 1967).

128. National Advisory Commission on Criminal Justice Standards and Goals, *Report on the Police* (Washington, DC: U.S. Government Printing Office, 1973).

129. Reaves and Goldberg, *Law Enforcement Management and Administrative Statistics, 1997.*

130. Ibid.

131. Brian A. Reaves and Matthew J. Hickman, *Police Departments in Large Cities, 1990–2000* (Washington, DC: Bureau of Justice Statistics, 2002), p. 1.

132. "Dallas PD College Rule Gets Final OK," *Law Enforcement News,* July 7, 1986, pp. 1, 13.

133. *Davis* v. *Dallas,* 777 F.2d 205 (5th Cir. 1985).

134. David L. Carter, Allen D. Sapp, and Darrel W. Stephens, *The State of Police Education: Policy Direction for the Twenty-First Century* (Washington, DC: Police Executive Research Forum, 1989), pp. xxii–xxiii.

135. The latter two were formerly part of the Immigration and Naturalization Service until its reorganization under the Homeland Security Act of 2002.

136. National Advisory Commission on Criminal Justice Standards and Goals, *Report on the Police,* p. 238.

137. Hickman and Reaves, *Community Policing,* p. 5.

138. Ibid., p. 270.

139. August Vollmer, *The Police and Modern Society* (Berkeley: University of California Press, 1936), p. 222.

140. O. W. Wilson and Roy Clinton McLaren, *Police Administration,* 4th ed. (New York: McGraw-Hill, 1977), p. 259.

141. Hickman and Reaves, *Community Policing.*

142. National Center for Women and Policing, *Equality Denied: The Status of Women in Policing, 2000* (Los Angeles: NCWP, 2001), p. 1.

143. Ibid.

144. Ibid., p. 3, from which some of the wording in the list is taken.

145. National Center for Women and Policing, *Recruiting and Retaining Women: A Self-Assessment Guide for Law Enforcement* (Los Angeles: NCWP, 2001), p. 22.

146. Ibid.

147. C. Lee Bennett, "Interviews with Female Police Officers in Western Massachusetts," paper presented at the annual meeting of the Academy of Criminal Justice Sciences, Nashville, TN, March 1991.

148. Ibid., p. 9.

149. Carole G. Garrison, Nancy K. Grant, and Kenneth L. J. McCormick, "Utilization of Police Women," *The Police Chief,* Vol. 32, No. 7 (September 1998).

150. Susan Ehrlich Martin and Nancy C. Jurik, *Doing Justice, Doing Gender: Women in Law and Criminal Justice Occupations* (Thousand Oaks, CA: Sage, 1996).

151. Police Foundation, *On the Move: The Status of Women in Policing* (Washington, DC: Police Foundation, 1990).

152. See, for example, Pearl Jacobs, "Suggestions for the Greater Integration of Women into Policing," paper presented at the annual meeting of the Academy of Criminal Justice Sciences, Nashville, TN, March 1991; and Cynthia Fuchs Epstein, *Deceptive Distinctions: Sex, Gender, and the Social Order* (New Haven, CT: Yale University Press, 1988).

153. See Sara Roen, "The Longest Climb," *Police* (October 1996), pp. 44–46, 66.

154. See editor's query, "The Homeland Security Era of Policing," *Crime and Justice International,* Vol. 21, No. 85 (2005), p. 2, from which the wording in this sentence is adapted.

# CHAPTER 7

# Policing: Legal Aspects

## OUTLINE

- Introduction
- The Abuse of Police Power
- Individual Rights
- Search and Seizure
- Arrest
- The Intelligence Function

## LEARNING OBJECTIVES

After reading this chapter, you should be able to:

- Explain how the Bill of Rights and democratically inspired legal restraints on the police help ensure personal freedoms in our society.
- Describe the nature of due process and the specific constitutional amendments on which due process guarantees are based.
- Explain the importance of the exclusionary rule and the fruit of the poisoned tree doctrine.
- Define *arrest,* and describe how popular depictions of the arrest process may not be consistent with legal understandings of the term.
- Describe the circumstances under which police officers may search vehicles and the extent to which such searches are permissible.
- Explain how the need to ensure public safety justifies certain suspicionless searches.
- Recite the *Miranda* warnings, and describe in detail recent U.S. Supreme Court cases that have affected *Miranda* warning requirements.
- Describe the nature of electronic evidence, and explain how first-on-the-scene law enforcement personnel should handle it.

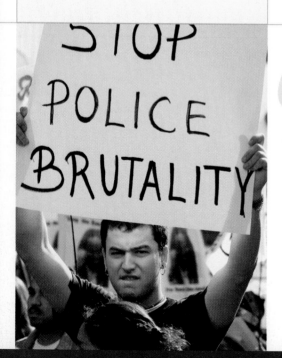

*The touchstone of the Fourth Amendment is reasonableness. The Fourth Amendment does not proscribe all state-initiated searches and seizures. It merely proscribes those which are unreasonable.*

—*Florida* v. *Jimeno*, 500 U.S. 248 (1991)

'Yeah,' the detective mumbled. 'Fifteen guys. You might want to think about that. Only two of us . . . ' He shook his head. 'Sneaking a bunch of cops into a neighborhood like this is going to be like trying to sneak the sun past a rooster. . . . ' As he started up the stairs, Angelo reached not for his gun but for his wallet. He took out a Chase Manhattan calendar printed on a supple but firm slip of plastic. He flicked the card at Rand. 'I'll open the door with this. You step in and freeze them.'

'Jesus Christ, Angelo,' the agent almost gasped. 'We can't do that. We haven't got a warrant.'

'Don't worry about it, kid,' Angelo said, drawing up to the second door on the right on the second floor. 'It ain't a perfect world.'

—Larry Collins and Dominique Lapierre[1]

## KEY CONCEPTS

### TERMS

arrest
Bill of Rights
compelling interest
digital criminal forensics
Electronic Communications Privacy Act (ECPA)
electronic evidence
emergency search
exclusionary rule

fleeting-targets exception
fruit of the poisoned tree doctrine
good-faith exception
illegally seized evidence
inherent coercion
interrogation
landmark case
latent evidence
*Miranda* triggers

*Miranda* warnings
plain view
probable cause
psychological manipulation
reasonable suspicion
search incident to an arrest
"sneak and peek" search
suspicionless search
writ of *certiorari*

### CASES

*Alabama* v. *White*
*Arizona* v. *Fulminante*
*Brecht* v. *Abrahamson*
*Brown* v. *Mississippi*
*California* v. *Hodari D.*
*Carroll* v. *U.S.*
*Chimel* v. *California*
*Dickerson* v. *U.S.*
*Escobedo* v. *Illinois*
*Florida* v. *Bostick*

*Horton* v. *California*
*Illinois* v. *Perkins*
*Indianapolis* v. *Edmond*
*Kyllo* v. *U.S.*
*Mapp* v. *Ohio*
*Minnick* v. *Mississippi*
*Miranda* v. *Arizona*
*Nix* v. *Williams*
*Richards* v. *Wisconsin*
*Silverthorne Lumber Co.* v. *U.S.*

*Smith* v. *Ohio*
*Terry* v. *Ohio*
*U.S. Dept. of Justice* v. *Landano*
*U.S.* v. *Drayton*
*U.S.* v. *Patane*
*U.S.* v. *Robinson*
*Weeks* v. *U.S.*
*Wilson* v. *Arkansas*

The original full-text court opinion for each of these cases is available on the CD-ROM that accompanies this book.

# Introduction

Hear the author discuss this chapter at **cjtoday.com**

In 2004, New York City officials agreed to pay $3 million to surviving family members of 22-year-old West African immigrant Amadou Diallo.[2] Diallo, who was black, died in a barrage of police bullets in 1999 when four white New York City Police Department (NYPD) officers opened fire on him as he stood in the doorway of his apartment building. The officers were searching for a rape suspect and said that they fired when Diallo reached for his pocket after they had yelled, "Freeze." Nineteen of 41 bullets fired by the officers struck Diallo. Diallo's shocked friends later said that he spoke little English and may have been reaching for his identification.

WEB EXTRA

Charges of second-degree murder were brought against the officers involved. In 2000, however, a state jury found the officers innocent of any criminal wrongdoing, and in 2001, the U.S. Department of Justice found that the shooting entailed no violation of Diallo's civil rights. Read more about the Diallo case at Web Extra 7–1 at cjtoday.com.

# The Abuse of Police Power

> There is more law at the end of the policeman's nightstick than in all the decisions of the Supreme Court.
>
> —Alexander "Clubber" Williams, late-nineteenth-century New York police officer

National publicity surrounding the Diallo incident was considerably less than that of the 1991 videotaped beating of motorist Rodney King by Los Angeles Police Department (LAPD) officers. King, an unemployed 25-year-old African-American man, was stopped by LAPD officers for an alleged violation of motor vehicle laws. Police said King had been speeding and had refused to stop for a pursuing patrol car. Officers claimed to have clocked King's 1988 Hyundai at 115 miles per hour on suburban Los Angeles's Foothill Freeway—even though the car's manufacturer later said the vehicle was not capable of speeds over 100 mph.

Eventually King did stop, but then officers of the LAPD appeared to attack him, shocking him twice with electronic stun guns and striking him with nightsticks and fists. Kicked in the stomach, face, and back, King was left with 11 skull fractures, missing teeth, a crushed cheekbone, and a broken ankle. A witness told reporters that she heard King begging officers to stop the beating

Protesters demonstrating in New York City in 1999 following the shooting of 22-year-old West African immigrant Amadou Diallo. Unarmed and innocent of any crime, Diallo was shot 19 times by four white undercover New York police officers as he stood in the doorway of his apartment building. The officers later said that they thought Diallo was reaching for a weapon when they opened fire.
*Stephen Ferry, Getty Images, Inc.*

but that they "were all laughing, like they just had a party."[3] King eventually underwent surgery for brain injuries. Officers involved in the beating claimed that King, at 6 feet 3 inches and 225 pounds, appeared strung out on PCP and that he and his two companions made the officers feel threatened.[4]

The entire incident was captured on videotape by an amateur photographer on a nearby balcony who was trying out his new night-sensitive video camera. The two-minute videotape was repeatedly broadcast over national television and was picked up by hundreds of local TV stations. The furor that erupted over the tape led to the ouster of LAPD Chief Daryl Gates and initiated a Justice Department review of law enforcement practices across the country.[5]

In 1992, a California jury found four police defendants not guilty—a verdict that resulted in days of rioting across Los Angeles. A year later, however, in the spring of 1993, two of the officers, Sergeant Stacey Koon and Officer Laurence Powell, were found guilty in federal court of denying King his constitutional right "not to be deprived of liberty without due process of law, including the right to be . . . free from the intentional use of unreasonable force."[6] Later that year, both were sentenced to two and a half years in prison, far less than might have been expected under federal sentencing guidelines. They were released from prison in December 1995, and a three-year court battle over whether federal sentencing guidelines were violated was resolved in the officers' favor the next year. Officers Theodore Briseno and Timothy Wind were exonerated at the federal level.

In 1994, King settled a civil suit against the city of Los Angeles for a reported $3.8 million. Observers later concluded that King himself was not a model citizen. At the time of the beating, he was on parole after having served time in prison for robbery. Since then he has been arrested on a variety of other charges, including battery, assault, drug use, and indecent exposure.[7] Regardless, King's 1991 beating continues to serve as a rallying point for individual-rights activists who want to ensure that citizens remain protected from the abuse of police power in an increasingly conservative society. Learn more about the Rodney King incident and its ramifications at Web Extra 7–2 at cjtoday.com.

This chapter shows how no one is above the law—even the police. It describes the legal environment surrounding police activities, from search and seizure through arrest and the interrogation of suspects. As we shall see throughout, democratically inspired legal restraints on the police help ensure individual freedoms in our society and prevent the development of a police state in America. Like anything else, however, the rules by which the police are expected to operate are in constant flux, and their continuing development forms the meat of this chapter. For a police perspective on these issues, visit Web Extra 7–3 at cjtoday.com.

**WEB** EXTRA

**WEB** EXTRA

Former Indiana police officer Mandell Gathright prays before a rally at the Police Memorial Building in Jacksonville, Florida, in 2005. The rally, in which approximately 200 people participated, was held to protest the deaths of three black men in police custody. Protesters believed that the deaths, which occurred over a span of two years, were caused by excessive force. The abuse of police power remains a critical issue in policing.

*Don Burk,* Florida Times-Union

# A Changing Legal Climate

**Bill of Rights**

The popular name given to the first ten amendments to the U.S. Constitution, which are considered especially important in the processing of criminal defendants.

The Constitution of the United States is designed—especially in the **Bill of Rights**—to protect citizens against abuses of police power (Table 7–1). However, the legal environment surrounding the police in modern America is much more complex than it was just 45 years ago. Up until that time, the Bill of Rights was largely given only lip service in criminal justice proceedings around the country. In practice, law enforcement, especially on the state and local levels, revolved around tried-and-true methods of search, arrest, and interrogation that sometimes left little room for recognition of individual rights. Police operations during that period were often far more informal than they are today, and investigating officers frequently assumed that they could come and go as they pleased, even to the extent of invading someone's home without a search warrant. Interrogations could quickly turn violent, and the infamous "rubber hose," which was reputed to leave few marks on the body, was widely used during the questioning of suspects. Similarly, "doing things by the book" sometimes meant using thick telephone books to beat suspects, since the books spread out the force of blows and left few visible bruises. Although these abuses were not day-to-day practices in all police agencies, and characterized just a small proportion of all officers, such conduct pointed to the need for greater control over police activities so that even the potential for abuse could be curtailed.

In the 1960s, the U.S. Supreme Court, under the direction of Chief Justice Earl Warren (1891–1974), accelerated the process of guaranteeing individual rights in the face of criminal prosecution. Warren Court rulings bound the police to strict procedural requirements in the areas of investigation, arrest, and interrogation. Later rulings scrutinized trial court procedure and enforced humanitarian standards in sentencing and punishment. The Warren Court also seized on the Fourteenth Amendment and made it the basis for judicial mandates requiring that both state and federal criminal justice agencies adhere to the Court's interpretation of the Constitution. The apex of the individual-rights emphasis in Supreme Court decisions was reached in the 1966

| CONSTITUTIONAL AMENDMENTS OF SPECIAL SIGNIFICANCE TO THE AMERICAN SYSTEM OF JUSTICE | |
|---|---|
| **This Right Is Guaranteed** | **By This Amendment** |
| The right against unreasonable searches and seizures | Fourth |
| The right against arrest without probable cause | Fourth |
| The right against self-incrimination | Fifth |
| The right against "double jeopardy" | Fifth |
| The right to due process of law | Fifth, Sixth, Fourteenth |
| The right to a speedy trial | Sixth |
| The right to a jury trial | Sixth |
| The right to know the charges | Sixth |
| The right to cross-examine witnesses | Sixth |
| The right to a lawyer | Sixth |
| The right to compel witnesses on one's behalf | Sixth |
| The right to reasonable bail | Eighth |
| The right against excessive fines | Eighth |
| The right against cruel and unusual punishments | Eighth |
| The applicability of constitutional rights to all citizens, regardless of state law or procedure | Fourteenth |

TABLE 7–1

case of *Miranda* v. *Arizona*,[8] which established the famous requirement of a police "rights advisement" of suspects. In wielding its brand of idealism, the Warren Court (which held sway from 1953 until 1969) accepted that a few guilty people would go free in order that the rights of the majority of Americans would be protected.

In the decades since the Warren Court, a new conservative Court philosophy has resulted in Supreme Court decisions that have brought about what some call a "reversal" of Warren-era advances in the area of individual rights. By creating exceptions to some of the Warren Court's rules and restraints, and by allowing for the emergency questioning of suspects before they are read their rights, a changed Supreme Court has recognized the realities attending day-to-day police work and the need to ensure public safety.

# Individual Rights

The Constitution of the United States provides for a system of checks and balances among the legislative, judicial, and executive (presidential) branches of government. By this we mean that one branch of government is always held accountable to the other branches. The system is designed to ensure that no one individual or agency can become powerful enough to usurp the rights and freedoms guaranteed under the Constitution. Accountability rules out the possibility of a police state in which the power of law enforcement is absolute and is related more to political considerations and personal vendettas than to objective considerations of guilt or innocence.

Under our system of government, courts are the arena for dispute resolution, not just between individuals but between citizens and the agencies of government. People who feel they have not received the respect and dignity from the justice system that are due them under the law can appeal to the courts for redress. Such appeals are usually based on procedural issues and are independent of more narrow considerations of guilt or innocence in a particular case.

In this chapter, we focus on cases that are important for having clarified constitutional guarantees concerning individual liberties within the criminal justice arena. They involve issues that most of us have come to call *rights*. Rights are concerned with procedure, that is, with how police and other actors in the criminal justice system handle each part of the process of dealing with suspects. Rights violations have often become the basis for the dismissal of charges, the acquittal of defendants, or the release of convicted offenders after an appeal to a higher court.

> [The police] are not perfect; we don't sign them up on some far-off planet and bring them into police service. They are products of society, and let me tell you, the human product today often is pretty weak.
>
> —Former Los Angeles Police Chief Daryl Gates

An officer patting down a suspect. The legal environment in which the police work helps ensure proper official conduct. In a search like this, inappropriate behavior on the part of the officer can later become the basis for civil or criminal action against the officer and the police department.

*John Boykin, PhotoEdit*

# Due Process Requirements

As you may recall from Chapter 1, the Fifth, Sixth, and Fourteenth Amendments to the U.S. Constitution require due process, which mandates that justice system officials respect the rights of accused individuals throughout the criminal justice process. Most due process requirements of relevance to the police pertain to three major areas: (1) evidence and investigation (often called *search* and *seizure*), (2) arrest, and (3) interrogation. Each of these areas has been addressed by a plethora of landmark U.S. Supreme Court decisions. **Landmark cases** produce substantial changes both in the understanding of the requirements of due process and in the practical day-to-day operations of the justice system. Landmark cases significantly clarify the "rules of the game"— the procedural guidelines by which the police and the rest of the justice system must abide.

The three areas we will discuss have been well defined by decades of court precedent. Keep in mind, however, that judicial interpretations of the constitutional requirement of due process are always evolving. As new decisions are rendered and as the composition of the Court itself changes, major changes and additional refinements may occur.

**landmark case**

A precedent-setting court decision that produces substantial changes in both the understanding of the requirements of due process and in the practical day-to-day operations of the justice system.

# Search and Seizure

The Fourth Amendment to the U.S. Constitution declares that people must be secure in their homes and in their persons against unreasonable searches and seizures. This right reads, "The right of the people to be secure in their persons, houses, papers, and effects, against unreasonable searches and seizures, shall not be violated, and no Warrants shall issue, but upon probable cause, supported by Oath or affirmation, and particularly describing the place to be searched, and the persons or things to be seized." This amendment, a part of the Bill of Rights, was adopted by Congress and became effective on December 15, 1791.

The language of the Fourth Amendment is familiar to all of us. "Warrants," "probable cause," and other phrases from the amendment are frequently cited in editorials, TV news shows, and daily conversation about **illegally seized evidence**. It is the interpretation of these phrases over time by the U.S. Supreme Court, however, that has given them the impact they have on the justice system today.

**illegally seized evidence**

Evidence seized without regard to the principles of due process as described by the Bill of Rights. Most illegally seized evidence is the result of police searches conducted without a proper warrant or of improperly conducted interrogations.

# The Exclusionary Rule

The first landmark case concerning search and seizure was *Weeks* v. *U.S.* (1914).[9] Freemont Weeks was suspected of using the U.S. mail to sell lottery tickets, a federal crime. Weeks was arrested, and federal agents went to his home to conduct a search. Since at the time investigators did not routinely use warrants, the agents had no search warrant. Still, they confiscated many incriminating items of evidence, as well as some of the suspect's personal possessions, including clothes, papers, books, and even candy.

Prior to trial, Weeks's attorney asked that the personal items be returned, claiming that they had been illegally seized under Fourth Amendment guarantees. A judge agreed and ordered the materials returned. On the basis of the evidence that was retained, however, Weeks was convicted in federal court and was sentenced to prison. He appealed his conviction through other courts, and his case eventually reached the U.S. Supreme Court. There, his lawyer reasoned that if some of his client's belongings had been illegally seized, then all were taken improperly. The Court agreed and overturned Weeks's earlier conviction.

The *Weeks* case forms the basis of what is now called the **exclusionary rule**, which holds that evidence illegally seized by the police cannot be used in a trial. The rule acts as a control over police behavior and specifically focuses on the failure of officers to obtain warrants authorizing them either to conduct searches or to make arrests, especially where arrest may lead to the acquisition of incriminating statements or to the seizure of physical evidence. The decision of the Supreme Court in the *Weeks* case was binding, at the time, only on federal officers because it was federal agents who were involved in the illegal seizure. Learn more about *Weeks* v. *U.S.* at **Library Extra 7–1** at cjtoday.com.

## Problems with Precedent

The *Weeks* case demonstrates the Supreme Court's power to enforce the "rules of the game," as well as the much more significant role that it plays in rule creation. Until the *Weeks* case was decided, federal law enforcement officers had little reason to think they were violating due process, because they were not required to obtain a warrant before conducting searches. The rule that resulted from *Weeks* was new, and it would forever alter the enforcement activities of federal officers.

The *Weeks* case reveals that the present appeals system, focusing as it does on the "rules of the game," presents a ready-made channel for the guilty to go free. There is little doubt that Freemont Weeks had violated federal law. A jury had convicted him. Yet he escaped punishment because of the illegal behavior of the police—behavior that, until the Court ruled, had been widely regarded as legitimate. Even if the police knowingly violate the principles of due process, which they sometimes do, our sense of justice is compromised when the guilty go free. Famed Supreme Court Justice Benjamin Cardozo (1870–1938) once complained, "The criminal is to go free because the constable has blundered."

Analysts of the criminal justice system have long considered three possible solutions to this problem. The first suggests that rules of due process, especially when newly articulated by the courts, should be applied only to future cases, not to the initial case in which they are stated. The justices in the *Weeks* case, for example, might have said, "We are creating the 'exclusionary rule' based on our realization in this case. Law enforcement officers are obligated to use it as a guide in all future searches. However, insofar as the guilt of Mr. Weeks was decided by a jury under rules of evidence existing at the time, we will let that decision stand."

A second solution would punish police officers or other actors in the criminal justice system who act illegally but would not allow the guilty defendant to escape punishment. This would allow the application of established precedent in cases where officers and officials had the benefit of clearly articulated rules and should have known better. Under this arrangement, any officer who intentionally violates due process guarantees might be suspended, be reduced in rank, lose pay, or be fired. Some authors have suggested that the decertification of police officers might serve as "an alternative to traditional remedies for police misconduct."[10] Because officers in every state except Hawaii[11] must meet the certification requirements of state boards in order to hold employment, some authors argue that decertification would have a much more personal (and therefore more effective) impact on individual officers than the exclusionary rule ever could.[12]

A third possibility would allow the Supreme Court to address theoretical questions involving issues of due process. Concerned supervisors and officials could ask how the Court would rule "if. . . ." As things now work, the Court can only address real cases and does so on a **writ of *certiorari***, in which the Court orders the record of a lower court case to be prepared for review.

The difficulty with these solutions, however, is that they would substantially reduce the potential benefits available to defendants through the appeals process, effectively eliminating the process itself.

## The Fruit of the Poisoned Tree Doctrine

The Court continued to build on the rules concerning evidence with its ruling in *Silverthorne Lumber Co.* v. *U.S.* (1920).[13] In 1918, Frederick Silverthorne and his sons operated a lumber

A Note on Double Jeopardy

**exclusionary rule**

The understanding, based on U.S. Supreme Court precedent, that incriminating information must be seized according to constitutional specifications of due process or it will not be allowed as evidence in a criminal trial.

**LIBRARY** EXTRA

**writ of *certiorari***

A writ issued from an appellate court for the purpose of obtaining from a lower court the record of its proceedings in a particular case. In some states, this writ is the mechanism for discretionary review. A request for review is made by petitioning for a writ of *certiorari,* and the granting of review is indicated by the issuance of the writ.

## FREEDOM OR SAFETY? YOU DECIDE.

### Liberty Is a Double-Edged Sword

This chapter builds on the following theme: For police action to be "just," it must recognize the rights of individuals while holding them accountable to the social obligations defined by law. It is important to realize that many democratically inspired legal restraints on the police stem from the Bill of Rights, which comprises the first ten amendments to the U.S. Constitution. Such restraints help ensure individual freedoms in our society and prevent the development of a "police state" in America.

In police work and elsewhere, the principles of individual liberty and social justice are cornerstones on which the American way of life rests. Ideally, the work of police agencies, as well as the American system of criminal justice, is to ensure justice while guarding liberty. The liberty–justice issue is the dual thread that holds the tapestry of the justice system to-

gether—from the simplest daily activities of police officers on the beat to the often complex and lengthy renderings of the U.S. Supreme Court.

For the criminal justice system as a whole, the question becomes, How can individual liberties be maintained in the face of the need for official action, including arrest, interrogation, incarceration, and the like? The answer is far from simple, but it begins with the recognition that liberty is a double-edged sword, entailing obligations as well as rights.

**YOU DECIDE**

What does it mean to say that "for police action to be 'just,' it must recognize the rights of individuals while holding them accountable to the social obligations defined by law"? How can police agencies accomplish this? What can individual officers do to help their agencies in this regard?

---

company and were accused of avoiding payment of federal taxes. When asked to turn over the company's books to federal investigators, the Silverthornes refused, citing their Fifth Amendment privilege against self-incrimination.

Shortly thereafter, federal agents descended on the lumber company and, without a search warrant, seized the company's books. The Silverthornes' lawyer appeared in court and asked that the materials be returned, citing the need for a search warrant, as had been established in the *Weeks* case. The prosecutor agreed, and the books were returned to the Silverthornes.

The Silverthornes came to trial thinking they would be acquitted because the evidence against them was no longer in the hands of prosecutors. In a surprise move, however, the prosecution introduced photographic copies of incriminating evidence, which they had made before returning the books. The Silverthornes were convicted in federal court. Their appeal eventually reached the U.S. Supreme Court. The Court ruled that just as illegally seized evidence cannot be used in a trial, neither can evidence be used that *derives* from an illegal seizure.[14] The conviction of the Silverthornes was overturned, and they were set free.

The *Silverthorne* case articulated a new principle of due process that today we call the **fruit of the poisoned tree doctrine**. This doctrine is potentially far-reaching. Complex cases developed after years of police investigative effort may be ruined if defense attorneys are able to demonstrate that the prosecution's case was originally based on a search or seizure that violated due process. In such cases, it is likely that all evidence will be declared "tainted" and will become useless.

**fruit of the poisoned tree doctrine**

A legal principle that excludes from introduction at trial any evidence later developed as a result of an illegal search or seizure.

## The Warren Court (1953–1969)

Before the 1960s, the U.S. Supreme Court intruded only occasionally on the overall operation of the criminal justice system at the state and local levels. As one author observed, however, the 1960s were a time of idealism, and "without the distraction of a depression or world war, individual liberties were examined at all levels of society."[15] Hence, while the exclusionary rule became an overriding consideration in federal law enforcement from the time of its creation in 1914, it was not until 1961 that the Court, under Chief Justice Earl Warren, decided a case that changed the face of American law enforcement forever. Beginning with the now-famous *Mapp* v. *Ohio* (1961)[16] case, the Warren Court charted a course that would guarantee nationwide recognition of individual rights, as it understood them, by agencies at all levels of the criminal justice system.

### Application of the Exclusionary Rule to the States

The public safety exception [to the exclusionary rule] was intended to protect the police, as well as the public, from danger.

—*U.S. v. Brady*, 819 F.2d 884 (1987)

*Mapp* v. *Ohio* (1961) made the exclusionary rule applicable to criminal prosecutions at the state level. Dolree Mapp was suspected of harboring a fugitive wanted in a bombing. When Ohio police officers arrived at her house, she refused to admit them. Eventually, they forced their way in.

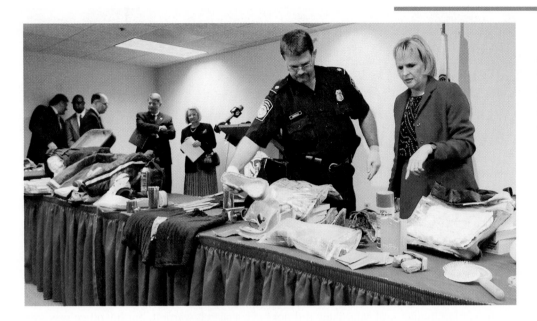

Police officers examining suspected controlled substances after a drug raid. The exclusionary rule means that illegally gathered evidence cannot be used later in court, requiring that police officers pay close attention to how they gather and handle evidence.

*AP Wide World Photos*

During the search that ensued, pornographic materials were uncovered. Mapp was arrested and eventually convicted under a state law that made possession of such materials illegal.

Because of prior decisions by the U.S. Supreme Court, including *Wolf* v. *Colorado* (1949),[17] officers believed that the exclusionary rule did not apply to agents of state and local law enforcement. However, in a wide-reaching and precedent-setting decision, Mapp's conviction was overturned on appeal by a majority of Warren Court justices who decided that the U.S. Constitution, under the Fourteenth Amendment's due process guarantee, mandates that state and local law enforcement officers be held to the same standards of accountability as federal officers. The justices said that since the evidence against Mapp had been illegally obtained, it could not be used against her in any court of law in the United States. The precedent established in *Mapp* v. *Ohio* firmly applied the principles developed in *Weeks* and *Silverthorne* to trials in state courts, making police officers at all levels accountable to the rule of law, which, as embodied in the words of the Fourteenth Amendment, reads, "No State shall . . . deprive any person of life, liberty, or property, without due process of law; nor deny to any person within its jurisdiction the equal protection of the laws." Learn more about the case of *Mapp* v. *Ohio* at Library Extra 7–2 at cjtoday.com.

**LIBRARY EXTRA**

## Searches Incident to Arrest

Another important Warren-era case, *Chimel* v. *California* (1969),[18] involved both arrest and search activities by local law enforcement officers. Ted Chimel was convicted of the burglary of a coin shop based on evidence gathered at his home, where he was arrested. Officers, armed with an arrest warrant but not a search warrant, took Chimel into custody when they arrived at his residence and proceeded with a search of his entire three-bedroom house, including the attic, a small workshop, and the garage. Although officers realized that the search might be challenged in court, they justified it by claiming that it was conducted not so much to uncover evidence but as part of the arrest process. Searches that are conducted incident to arrest, they argued, are necessary for the officers' protection and should not require a search warrant. Coins taken from the burglarized coin shop were found in various places in Chimel's residence, including the garage, and were presented as evidence against him at trial.

Chimel's appeal eventually reached the U.S. Supreme Court, which ruled that the search of Chimel's residence, although incident to arrest, became invalid when it went beyond the person arrested and the area subject to that person's "immediate control." The thrust of the Court's decision was that searches during arrest can be made to protect arresting officers but that without a search warrant, their scope must be strongly circumscribed. The legal implications of *Chimel* v. *California* are summarized in Table 7–2.

The decision in the *Chimel* case built on the 1950 U.S. Supreme Court case of *U.S.* v. *Rabinowitz* (1950).[19] Rabinowitz, a stamp collector, had been arrested and charged by federal agents with selling altered postage stamps in order to defraud other collectors. Employing a valid arrest

| | IMPLICATIONS OF *CHIMEL* V. *CALIFORNIA* (1969) |
|---|---|
| **TABLE 7–2** | **What Arresting Officers May Search** |
| | The defendant<br>The physical area within easy reach of the defendant |
| | **Valid Reasons for Conducting a Search** |
| | To protect the arresting officers<br>To prevent evidence from being destroyed<br>To keep the defendant from escaping |
| | **When a Search Becomes Illegal** |
| | When it goes beyond the defendant and the area within the defendant's immediate control<br>When it is conducted for other than a valid reason |

warrant, officers arrested Rabinowitz at his place of employment and then proceeded to search his desk, file cabinets, and safe. They did not have a search warrant, but his office was small—only one room—and the officers conducted the search with a specific object in mind, the illegal stamps. Eventually, 573 altered postage stamps were seized in the search, and Rabinowitz was convicted in federal court of charges related to selling altered stamps.

Rabinowitz's appeal to the U.S. Supreme Court, based on the claim that the warrantless search of his business was illegal, was denied. The Court ruled that the Fourth Amendment provides protection against *unreasonable* searches but that the search in this case followed legally from the arrest of the suspect. In the language used by the Court, "It is not disputed that there may be reasonable searches, incident to arrest, without a search warrant. Upon acceptance of this established rule that some authority to search follows from lawfully taking the person into custody, it becomes apparent that such searches turn upon the reasonableness under all the circumstances and not upon the practicability of procuring a search warrant, for the warrant is not required."

Since the early days of the exclusionary rule, other court decisions have highlighted the fact that "the Fourth Amendment protects people, not places."[20] In other words, people can reasonably expect privacy in their *homes*—even if those homes are not houses. "Homes" including apartments, duplex dwellings, motel rooms—even the cardboard boxes or makeshift tents of the homeless—can all become protected places under the Fourth Amendment. In *Minnesota* v. *Olson* (1990),[21] for example, the U.S. Supreme Court extended the protection against warrantless searches to overnight guests residing in the home of another. The capacity to claim the protection of the Fourth Amendment, said the Court, depends on whether the *person* who makes that claim has a legitimate expectation of privacy in the place searched.

In 1998, in the case of *Minnesota* v. *Carter*,[22] the Court held that for a defendant to be entitled to Fourth Amendment protection, "he must demonstrate that he personally has an expectation of privacy in the place searched, and that his expectation is reasonable." The Court noted that "the extent to which the Amendment protects people may depend upon where those people are. While an overnight guest may have a legitimate expectation of privacy in someone else's home . . . one who is merely present with the consent of the householder may not." Hence, an appliance repair person visiting a residence is unlikely to be accorded privacy protections while on the job.

## The Burger Court (1969–1986) and Rehnquist Court (1986–2005)

During the 1980s and 1990s, the United States experienced a swing toward conservatism, giving rise to a renewed concern with protecting the interests—financial and otherwise—of those who live within the law. The Reagan-Bush years, and the popularity of the two presidents who many thought embodied "old-fashioned" values, reflected the tenor of a nation seeking a return to "simpler," less volatile times.

Throughout the late 1980s, the U.S. Supreme Court mirrored the nation's conservative tenor by distancing itself from some earlier decisions of the Warren Court. While the Warren Court embodied the individual rights heyday in Court jurisprudence, Court decisions beginning in the 1970s were generally supportive of a "greater good era"—one in which the justices increasingly acknowledge the importance of social order and communal safety. Under Chief Justice Warren E. Burger, the new Court adhered to the principle that criminal defendants who claimed violations of their due process rights needed to bear most of the responsibility of showing that police went beyond the law in the performance of their duties. This tenet is still held by the Court today.

## Good-Faith Exceptions to the Exclusionary Rule

The Burger Court, which held sway from 1969 until 1986, "chipped away" at the strict application of the exclusionary rule originally set forth in the *Weeks* and *Silverthorne* cases. In the 1984 case of *U.S.* v. *Leon*,[23] the Court recognized what has come to be called the **good-faith exception** to the exclusionary rule. In this case, the Court modified the exclusionary rule to allow evidence that officers had seized in "reasonable good faith" to be used in court, even though the search was later ruled illegal. The suspect, Alberto Leon, was placed under surveillance for drug trafficking following a tip from a confidential informant. Burbank (California) Police Department investigators applied for a search warrant based on information gleaned from the surveillance, believing they were in compliance with the Fourth Amendment requirement that "no Warrants shall issue, but upon probable cause." **Probable cause** is a tricky but important concept. Its legal criteria are based on facts and circumstances that would cause a reasonable person to believe that a particular other person has committed a specific crime. Before a warrant can be issued, police officers must satisfactorily demonstrate probable cause in a written affidavit to a magistrate[24]—a low-level judge who ensures that the police establish the probable cause needed for warrants to be obtained. Upon a demonstration of probable cause, the magistrate will issue a warrant authorizing law enforcement officers to effect an arrest or conduct a search.

In *U.S.* v. *Leon,* a warrant was issued, and a search of Leon's three residences yielded a large amount of drugs and other evidence. Although Leon was convicted of drug trafficking, a later ruling in a federal district court resulted in the suppression of evidence against him on the basis that the original affidavit prepared by the police had not, in the opinion of the reviewing court, been sufficient to establish probable cause.

The federal government petitioned the U.S. Supreme Court to consider whether evidence gathered by officers acting in good faith as to the validity of a warrant should be fairly excluded at trial. The good-faith exception was presaged in the first sentences of the Court's written decision: "This case presents the question whether the Fourth Amendment exclusionary rule should be modified so as not to bar the use in the prosecution's case-in-chief of evidence obtained by officers acting in reasonable reliance on a search warrant issued by a detached and neutral magistrate but ultimately found to be unsupported by probable cause." The Court continued, "When law enforcement officers have acted in objective good faith or their transgressions have been minor, the magnitude of the benefit conferred on such guilty defendants offends basic concepts of the criminal justice system." Reflecting the renewed conservatism of the Burger Court, the justices found for the government and reinstated Leon's conviction.

In that same year, the Supreme Court case of *Massachusetts* v. *Sheppard* (1984)[25] further reinforced the concept of good faith. In the *Sheppard* case, officers executed a search warrant that failed to accurately describe the property to be seized. Although they were aware of the error, a magistrate had assured them that the warrant was valid. After the seizure was complete and a conviction had been obtained, the Massachusetts Supreme Judicial Court reversed the finding of the trial court. Upon appeal, the U.S. Supreme Court reiterated the good-faith exception and reinstated the original conviction.

The cases of *Leon* and *Sheppard* represented a clear reversal of the Warren Court's philosophy, and the trend continued with the 1987 case of *Illinois* v. *Krull.*[26] In *Krull,* the Court, now under the leadership of Chief Justice Rehnquist, held that the good-faith exception applied to a warrantless search permitted by an Illinois law related to automobile junkyards and vehicular parts sellers even though the state statute was later found to violate the Fourth Amendment. And, in a case similar to Sheppard, another 1987 Supreme Court case, *Maryland* v. *Garrison,*[27] supported the use of evidence obtained with a search warrant that was inaccurate in its specifics. In *Garrison,* officers had procured a warrant to search an apartment, believing it was the only dwelling on the building's third floor. After searching the entire floor, they discovered that it housed more than one apartment. Even so, evidence acquired in the search was held to be admissible based on the reasonable mistake of the officers.

The 1990 case of *Illinois* v. *Rodriguez*[28] further diminished the scope of the exclusionary rule. In *Rodriguez,* a badly beaten woman named Gail Fischer complained to police that she had been assaulted in a Chicago apartment. Fischer led police to the apartment—which she indicated she

### good-faith exception

An exception to the exclusionary rule. Law enforcement officers who conduct a search or who seize evidence on the basis of good faith (that is, when they believe they are operating according to the dictates of the law) and who later discover that a mistake was made (perhaps in the format of the application for a search warrant) may still use the seized evidence in court.

### probable cause

A set of facts and circumstances that would induce a reasonably intelligent and prudent person to believe that a particular other person has committed a specific crime. Also, reasonable grounds to make or believe an accusation. Probable cause refers to the necessary level of belief that would allow for police seizures (arrests) of individuals and full searches of dwellings, vehicles, and possessions.

shared with the defendant—produced a key, and opened the door to the dwelling. Inside, investigators found the defendant, Edward Rodriguez, asleep on a bed, with drug paraphernalia and cocaine spread around him. Rodriguez was arrested and charged with assault and possession of a controlled substance.

Upon appeal, Rodriguez demonstrated that Fischer had not lived with him for at least a month and argued that she could no longer be said to have legal control over the apartment. Hence, the defense claimed, Fischer had no authority to provide investigators with access to the dwelling. According to arguments made by the defense, the evidence, which had been obtained without a warrant, had not been properly seized. The Supreme Court disagreed, ruling that "even if Fischer did not possess common authority over the premises, there was no Fourth Amendment violation if the police *reasonably believed* at the time of their entry that Fischer possessed the authority to consent."

In 1995, in the case of *Arizona* v. *Evans,* the U.S. Supreme Court created a "computer errors exception" to the exclusionary rule. In *Evans,* the Court held that a traffic stop that led to the seizure of marijuana was legal even though officers conducted the stop based on an arrest warrant that should have been deleted from their computer database. The arrest warrant reported to the officers by their computer had actually be quashed a few weeks earlier, but due to an oversight, a court employee had never removed it from the database.

In reaching its decision, the high court reasoned that police officers could not be held responsible for a clerical error made by a court worker and concluded that the arresting officers had acted in good faith. In addition, the majority opinion said that "the rule excluding evidence obtained without a warrant was intended to deter police misconduct, not mistakes by court employees."

Legal scholars have suggested that the exclusionary rule may undergo even further modification in the near future. Some analysts of the contemporary scene point to the fact that "the Court's majority is [now] clearly committed to the idea that the exclusionary rule is not directly part of the Fourth Amendment (and Fourteenth Amendment due process), but instead is an evidentiary device instituted by the Court to effectuate it."[29] In other words, if the Court should be persuaded that the rule is no longer effective or that some other strategy would better achieve the aim of protecting individual rights, the rule could be abandoned entirely. A general listing of established exceptions to the exclusionary rule, along with other investigative powers created by court precedent, is provided in Table 7–3.

During Rehnquist's tenure as chief justice, the Court invoked a characteristically conservative approach to many important criminal justice issues—from limiting the exclusionary rule[30] and generally broadening police powers, to sharply limiting the opportunities for state prisoners to bring appeals in federal courts.[31] Preventive detention, "no knock" police searches,[32] the death penalty,[33] and habitual offender statutes[34] (often known as *three-strikes laws*) all found decisive support under Chief Justice Rehnquist.[35] The particular cases in which the Court addressed these issues are discussed elsewhere in this text.

Following Rehnquist's death in 2005, President Bush nominated Judge John G. Roberts, Jr., to become the nation's seventeenth Chief Justice. Roberts, who had previously served as a judge on the United States Court of Appeals for the District of Columbia Circuit, was easily confirmed and assumed the bench in October, 2005—in time for the Court's new term. Court watchers predict that Roberts is likely to continue the Rehnquist Court's conservative ways.

## The Plain-View Doctrine

Police officers have the opportunity to begin investigations or to confiscate evidence, without a warrant, based on what they find in **plain view** and open to public inspection. The plain-view doctrine was succinctly stated in the U.S. Supreme Court case of *Harris* v. *U.S.* (1968),[36] in which a police officer inventorying an impounded vehicle discovered evidence of a robbery.[37] In the *Harris* case, the Court ruled that "objects falling in the plain view of an officer who has a right to be in the position to have that view are subject to seizure and may be introduced in evidence."[38]

The plain-view doctrine is applicable in common situations such as crimes in progress, fires, accidents, and other emergencies. For example, a police officer who enters a residence responding to a call for assistance and finds drugs or other contraband in plain view is within his legitimate authority to confiscate the materials and to effect an arrest if the owner of the substance can be identified. However, the plain-view doctrine applies only to sightings by the police under legal circumstances—that is, in places where the police have a legitimate right to be and, typically, only if the sighting was coincidental. Similarly, the incriminating nature of the evidence seized must have been "immediately apparent" to the officers making the seizure.[39] If officers conspired to avoid the necessity for a search warrant by helping to create a plain-view situation through surveillance, duplicity, or other means, the doctrine likely would not apply.

| This Police Power | Is Supported By |
|---|---|
| Arrest based on computer error made by clerk | *Arizona* v. *Evans* (1995) |
| Authority to enter and/or search an "open field" without a warrant | *U.S.* v. *Dunn* (1987)<br>*Oliver* v. *U.S.* (1984)<br>*Hester* v. *U.S.* (1924) |
| Authority to search incident to arrest and/or to conduct a protective sweep in conjunction with an in-home arrest | *Maryland* v. *Buie* (1990)<br>*U.S.* v. *Edwards* (1974)<br>*Chimel* v. *California* (1969) |
| Gathering of incriminating evidence during interrogation in noncustodial circumstances | *Yarborough* v. *Alvarado* (2004)<br>*Thompson* v. *Keohane* (1996)<br>*Stansbury* v. *California* (1994)<br>*U.S.* v. *Mendenhall* (1980)<br>*Beckwith* v. *U.S.* (1976) |
| Gathering of incriminating evidence during *Miranda*-less custodial interrogation | *U.S.* v. *Patane* (2004) |
| Inevitable discovery of evidence | *Nix* v. *Williams* (1984) |
| "No-knock" searches or quick entry | *U.S.* v. *Barnes* (2003)<br>*Richards* v. *Wisconsin* (1997)<br>*Wilson* v. *Arkansas* (1995) |
| Prompt action in the face of threat to public or personal safety or destruction of evidence | *U.S.* v. *Banks* (2004)<br>*Borchardt* v. *U.S.* (1987)<br>*New York* v. *Quarles* (1984)<br>*Warden* v. *Hayden* (1967) |
| Seizure of evidence in good faith, even in the face of some exclusionary rule violations | *Illinois* v. *Krull* (1987)<br>*U.S.* v. *Leon* (1984) |
| Seizure of evidence in plain view | *Horton* v. *California* (1990)<br>*Coolidge* v. *New Hampshire* (1971)<br>*Harris* v. *U.S.* (1968) |
| Stop and frisk/request personal identification | *Hiibel* v. *Sixth Judicial District Court of Nevada* (2004)<br>*Terry* v. *Ohio* (1968) |
| Use of police informants in jail cells | *Arizona* v. *Fulminante* (1991)<br>*Illinois* v. *Perkins* (1990)<br>*Kuhlmann* v. *Wilson* (1986) |
| Warrantless naked-eye aerial observation of open areas and/or greenhouses | *Florida* v. *Riley* (1989)<br>*California* v. *Ciraolo* (1986) |
| Warrantless search incident to a lawful arrest | *U.S.* v. *Rabinowitz* (1950) |
| Warrantless seizure of abandoned materials and refuse | *California* v. *Greenwood* (1988) |
| Warrantless vehicle search where probable cause exists to believe that the vehicle contains contraband and/or that the occupants have been lawfully arrested | *Thornton* v. *U.S.* (2004)<br>*Ornelas* v. *U.S.* (1996)<br>*California* v. *Acevedo* (1991)<br>*California* v. *Carney* (1985)<br>*U.S.* v. *Ross* (1982)<br>*New York* v. *Belton* (1981)<br>*Carroll* v. *U.S.* (1925) |

The plain-view doctrine was restricted by later federal court decisions. In the 1982 case of *U.S. v. Irizarry,*[40] the First Circuit Court of Appeals held that officers could not move objects to gain a view of evidence otherwise hidden from view. In the U.S. Supreme Court case of *Arizona* v. *Hicks* (1987),[41] the requirement that evidence be in plain view, without requiring officers to move or dislodge objects, was reiterated. In the *Hicks* case, officers responded to a shooting; a bullet fired in a second-floor apartment had gone through the floor, injuring a man in the apartment below. When they entered, officers found the second-floor apartment in considerable disarray. While looking for the person who fired the weapon, they discovered and confiscated a number of guns and a stocking mask, like those used in robberies. Two expensive stereo sets lay in a corner of the apartment. Suspecting that the stereos were stolen, an officer looked over the equipment and was able to read the serial number of one of the components from where it rested. The other serial numbers, however, were not clearly visible, and the investigating officer moved some of the equipment in order to read them. When he called the numbers in to headquarters, he was told that the stereos indeed had been stolen. They were seized, and James Hicks, who lived in the apartment, was arrested. Hicks was eventually convicted on a charge of armed robbery, based on the evidence seized.

Upon appeal, the *Hicks* case reached the Supreme Court, which ruled that the officer's behavior had become illegal when he moved the stereo equipment to record the serial numbers. The Court held that people have a "reasonable expectation to privacy,"[42] which means that officers lacking a search warrant, even when invited into a residence, must act more like guests than inquisitors.

Most evidence seized under the plain-view doctrine is discovered "inadvertently"—that is, by accident.[43] However, in 1990, the U.S. Supreme Court ruled in the case of *Horton* v. *California*[44] that "even though inadvertence *is* a characteristic of most legitimate 'plain view' seizures, it is not a necessary condition."[45] In the *Horton* case, a warrant was issued authorizing the search of Terry Brice Horton's home for stolen jewelry. The affidavit, completed by the officer who requested the warrant, alluded to an Uzi submachine gun and a stun gun—weapons purportedly used in the jewelry robbery. It did not request that those weapons be listed on the search warrant. Officers searched the defendant's home but did not find the stolen jewelry. They did, however, seize a number of weapons, among them an Uzi, two stun guns, and a .38-caliber revolver. Horton was convicted of robbery in a trial in which the seized weapons were introduced into evidence. He appealed his conviction, claiming that officers had reason to believe that the weapons were in his home at the time of the search and were therefore not seized inadvertently. His appeal was rejected by the Court. As a result of the *Horton* case, inadvertence is no longer considered a condition necessary to ensure the legitimacy of a seizure that results when evidence other than that listed in a search warrant is discovered.

Latasha Smith (shown here sitting on a curb), who was arrested for failing to appear in court for a previous misdemeanor violation. Although the concept of plain view is difficult to define, Smith provides a personal example of the concept. After Dallas narcotics officers searched the house behind her for crack cocaine, they turned their attention to Smith and discovered the outstanding charges.

*AP Wide World Photos*

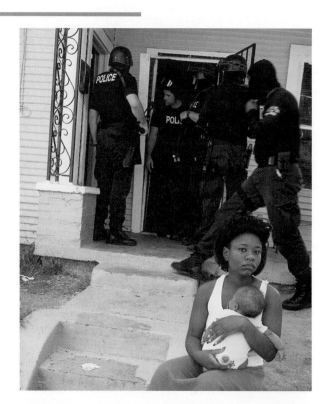

## Emergency Searches of Property

Certain emergencies may justify a police officer's search of premises, even without a warrant. Such activities are termed *exigent circumstances searches* or **emergency searches**. According to the Legal Counsel Division of the Federal Bureau of Investigation (FBI), there are three threats that "provide justification for emergency warrantless action."[46] They are clear dangers (1) to life, (2) of escape, and (3) of the removal or destruction of evidence. When emergencies necessitate a quick search of premises, however, law enforcement officers must demonstrate that a dire situation existed that justified their actions. Failure to do so successfully in court will, of course, taint any seized evidence and make it unusable.

The U.S. Supreme Court first recognized the need for emergency searches in 1967 in the case of *Warden* v. *Hayden*.[47] In that case, the Court approved the warrantless search of a residence following reports that an armed robber had fled into the building. In *Mincey* v. *Arizona* (1978),[48] the Supreme Court held that "the Fourth Amendment does not require police officers to delay in the course of an investigation if to do so would gravely endanger their lives or the lives of others."[49]

A 1990 decision, rendered in the case of *Maryland* v. *Buie*,[50] extended the authority of police to search locations in a house where a potentially dangerous person could hide while an arrest warrant is being served. The *Buie* decision was meant primarily to protect investigators from potential danger and can apply even when officers lack a warrant, probable cause, or reasonable suspicion.

In 1995, in the case of *Wilson* v. *Arkansas*,[51] the U.S. Supreme Court ruled that police officers generally must knock and announce their identity before entering a dwelling or other premises, even when armed with a search warrant. Under certain emergency circumstances, however, exceptions may be made, and officers may not need to knock or to identify themselves before entering.[52] In *Wilson*, the Court added that the Fourth Amendment requirement that searches be reasonable "should not be read to mandate a rigid rule of announcement that ignores countervailing law enforcement interests." Hence, officers need not announce themselves, the Court said, when suspects may be in the process of destroying evidence, officers are pursuing a recently escaped arrestee, or officers' lives may be endangered by such an announcement. Because the *Wilson* case involved an appeal from a drug dealer who was apprehended by police officers who entered her unlocked house while she was flushing marijuana down a toilet, some say that it establishes a "drug-law exception" to the knock-and-announce requirement.

In 1997, however, in *Richards* v. *Wisconsin*,[53] the Supreme Court clarified its position on "no knock" exceptions, saying that individual courts have the duty in each case to "determine whether the facts and circumstances of the particular entry justified dispensing with the requirement." The Court went on to say that "[a] 'no knock' entry is justified when the police have a reasonable suspicion that knocking and announcing their presence, under the particular circumstances, would be dangerous or futile, or that it would inhibit the effective investigation of the crime. This standard strikes the appropriate balance," said the Court, "between the legitimate law enforcement concerns at issue in the execution of search warrants and the individual privacy interests affected by no knock entries."

In 2001, in the case of *Illinois* v. *McArthur*,[54] the U.S. Supreme Court ruled that police officers with probable cause to believe that a home contains contraband or evidence of criminal activity may reasonably prevent a suspect found outside the home from reentering it while they apply for a search warrant; and in 2003, in a case involving drug possession, the Court held that a 15- to 20-second wait after officers knocked, announced themselves, and requested entry before breaking open a door was sufficient to satisfy Fourth Amendment requirements.[55]

# Arrest

Officers seize not only property but people as well—a process referred to as *arrest.* While many people think of arrest in terms of what they see on popular TV crime shows—the suspect is chased, subdued, and "cuffed" after committing a loathsome act in view of the camera—most arrests are far more mundane.

In technical terms, an **arrest** occurs whenever a law enforcement officer restricts a person's freedom to leave. There may be no yelling, "You're under arrest!" No *Miranda* warnings may be offered, and in fact, the suspect may not even consider himself or herself to be in custody. Some arrests, and the decision to enforce them, evolve as a conversation between the officer and the suspect develops. Only when the suspect tries to leave and tests the limits of the police response may the suspect discover that he or she is really in custody. In the 1980 case of

**emergency search**
A search conducted by the police without a warrant, which is justified on the basis of some immediate and overriding need, such as public safety, the likely escape of a dangerous suspect, or the removal or destruction of evidence.

**arrest**
The act of taking an adult or juvenile into physical custody by authority of law for the purpose of charging the person with a criminal offense, a delinquent act, or a status offense, terminating with the recording of a specific offense. Technically, an arrest occurs whenever a law enforcement officer curtails a person's freedom to leave.

*U.S.* v. *Mendenhall,*[56] Justice Potter Stewart set forth the "free to leave" test for determining whether a person has been arrested. Stewart wrote, "A person has been 'seized' within the meaning of the Fourth Amendment only if in view of all the circumstances surrounding the incident, a reasonable person would have believed that he was not free to leave." The "free to leave" test "has been repeatedly adopted by the Court as the test for a seizure."[57] In 1994, in the case of *Stansbury* v. *California,*[58] the Court once again used such a test in determining the point at which an arrest had been made. In *Stansbury,* where the focus was on the interrogation of a suspected child molester and murderer, the Court ruled, "In determining whether an individual was in custody, a court must examine all of the circumstances surrounding the interrogation, but the ultimate inquiry is simply whether there [was] a formal arrest or restraint on freedom of movement of the degree associated with a formal arrest."

Youth and inexperience do not automatically undermine a reasonable person's ability to assess when they are free to leave. Hence, in the 2004 case of *Yarborough* v. *Alvarado,*[59] the U.S. Supreme Court found that a 17-year-old boy's two-hour interrogation in a police station without a *Miranda* advisement was not custodial, even though the boy confessed to his involvement in a murder and consequently was later arrested. The boy, said the Court, had not actually been in police custody even though he was in a building used by the police for questioning, because actions taken by the interviewing officer indicated that the juvenile had been free to leave. Whether a person is actually free to leave, said the Court, can only be determined by examining the totality of the circumstances surrounding the interrogation.[60]

Arrests that follow the questioning of a suspect are probably the most common type. When the decision to arrest is reached, the officer has come to the conclusion that a crime has been committed and that the suspect is probably the one who committed it. The presence of these elements constitutes the probable cause needed for an arrest. Probable cause is the basic minimum necessary for an arrest under any circumstances.

Arrests may also occur when the officer comes upon a crime in progress. Although such situations sometimes require apprehension of the offender to ensure the safety of the public, most arrests made during crimes in progress are for misdemeanors rather than felonies. In fact, many states do not allow arrest for a misdemeanor unless it is committed in the presence of an officer, since visible crimes in progress clearly provide the probable cause necessary for an arrest. In 2001, in a case that made headlines nationwide,[61] the U.S. Supreme Court upheld a warrantless arrest made by a Largo Vista, Texas, police officer for a seat belt violation. In what many saw as an unfair exercise of discretion, Patrolman Bart Turek stopped, then arrested, Gail Atwater, a young local woman whom he observed driving a pickup truck in which she and her two small children (ages three and five) were unbelted. Facts in the case showed that Turek verbally berated the woman after stopping her vehicle and that he handcuffed her, placed her in his squad car, and drove her to the local police station, where she was made to remove her shoes, jewelry, and eyeglasses and empty her pockets. Officers took her "mug shot" and placed her alone in a jail cell for about an hour, after which she was taken before a magistrate and released on $310 bond. Atwater was charged with a misdemeanor violation of Texas seat belt law. She later pleaded no contest and paid a $50 fine. Soon afterward, she and her husband filed a Section 1983 lawsuit against the officer, his department, and the police chief, alleging that the actions of the officer violated Atwater's Fourth Amendment right to be free from unreasonable seizures. The Court, however, concluded that "the Fourth Amendment does not forbid a warrantless arrest for a minor criminal offense, such as a misdemeanor seatbelt violation punishable only by a fine."

Most jurisdictions allow arrest for a felony without a warrant when a crime is not in progress, as long as probable cause can be established.[62] In jurisdictions that do require a warrant, arrest warrants are issued by magistrates when police officers can demonstrate probable cause. Magistrates will usually require that the officers seeking an arrest warrant submit a written affidavit outlining their reason for the arrest. In the case of *Payton* v. *New York* (1980),[63] the U.S. Supreme Court ruled that unless the suspect gives consent or an emergency exists, an arrest warrant is necessary if an arrest requires entry into a suspect's private residence.[64] In *Payton,* the justices held that "[a]bsent exigent circumstances," the "firm line at the entrance to the house . . . may not reasonably be crossed without a warrant." The Court reiterated its *Payton* holding in the 2002 case of *Kirk* v. *Louisiana.*[65] In Kirk, which involved an anonymous complaint about drug sales said to be taking place in the apartment of Kennedy Kirk, the justices reaffirmed their belief that "[t]he Fourth Amendment to the United States Constitution has drawn a firm line at the entrance to the home, and thus, the police need both probable cause to either arrest or search, and exigent circumstances to justify a nonconsensual warrantless intrusion into private premises."

# CJ NEWS

## Court Permits Speedy Drug Raid

Police may knock down the door of a suspected drug dealer after waiting only 15 to 20 seconds for him to answer, the Supreme Court ruled on November 30, 2003, in a decision that was a victory for law enforcement.

The unanimous decision marks the first time that the Court has defined the amount of time that officers serving narcotics warrants must wait after knocking on a suspect's door and announcing their presence.

It's the latest in a series of rulings since 1995 in which the Court has clarified what police who serve warrants must do to avoid violating the Fourth Amendment's prohibition against unreasonable searches and seizures of evidence. Generally, the justices have given police latitude in deciding when and how to serve warrants.

In their ruling in the Nevada case, the justices agreed with the Justice Department's argument that a "prolonged delay" by police in such instances could allow suspects to destroy evidence—in this case, crack cocaine—and expose officers to "undue danger" from "violent, armed" criminals.

"What matters is the opportunity to get rid of cocaine, which a prudent dealer will keep near a commode or kitchen sink," Justice David Souter wrote for the Court. "And 15 to 20 seconds does not seem an unrealistic guess about the time someone would need to . . . rid his quarters of cocaine."

The Court's decision reinstated the narcotics conviction of Lashawn Banks, arrested at his apartment in north Las Vegas on a July afternoon in 1998. Police and FBI agents, who had a search warrant for drugs, found 11 ounces of crack cocaine and three guns in the apartment.

Officers testified that they had knocked and announced a "police warrant search," then waited 15 to 20 seconds before concluding that the occupants, if any, would not open the door. Police used a battering ram to knock it down.

Banks, who was taking a shower, claimed that he had not heard the knock. He argued that the officers did not give him enough time to reach the door, making the search "unreasonable" and thus a violation of the Fourth Amendment.

Banks was convicted and sentenced to 11 years in prison. But his conviction was overturned in 2002 by the 9th Circuit Court of Appeals.

In his opinion, Souter said that Banks' arguments missed the point. The key, Souter wrote, is what police officers reasonably expect in such a situation. Based on the "totality" of the circumstances—the time of day, the small size of Banks' apartment—it was reasonable for police to suspect that Banks could have disposed of the drugs if officers had waited any longer, Souter said.

The Court made clear that the 15- to 20-second guideline might not apply to searches in cases that do not involve drugs. "Police seeking a stolen piano may be able to spend more time to make sure they really need a battering ram," Souter wrote.

Banks, now 26, faces possible resentencing. He had served four years of his sentence before he was released after the appeals court ruling.

Randall Roske, Banks' attorney, said the high court's ruling would encourage police misconduct. "Police are going to read this as, 'Knock and announce and kick the door in,'" he said.

Mark Dobson, a criminal law specialist at Nova Southeastern University Law Center in Fort Lauderdale, said it was "significant that the court, for the first time, has given officers a time period to work with when they serve warrants. It's in keeping with the trend that the court is giving guidance to officers, and that it puts a lot of weight on their judgment."

Learn more about court requirements related to speedy drug raids at Library Extra 7–3 at cjtoday.com.

**LIBRARY** EXTRA

For the latest in crime and justice news, visit the Talk Justice news feed at http://www. crimenews.info.

Kansas City, Missouri, police officers using a battering ram to gain entry to the house of a suspected drug dealer. According to the 2003 U.S. Supreme Court case of *U.S.* v. *Banks,* officers serving a search warrant need wait only 15 to 20 seconds after knocking and requesting entry before forcibly entering a residence in drug-related cases.

Arresting officers patting down a drug suspect. The courts have generally held that to protect themselves and the public, officers have the authority to search suspects being arrested.
*Craig Filipacchi, Getty Images, Inc.*

**search incident to an arrest**

A warrantless search of an arrested individual conducted to ensure the safety of the arresting officer. Because individuals placed under arrest may be in possession of weapons, courts have recognized the need for arresting officers to protect themselves by conducting an immediate search of arrestees without obtaining a warrant.

**reasonable suspicion**

The level of suspicion that would justify an officer in making further inquiry or in conducting further investigation. Reasonable suspicion may permit stopping a person for questioning or for a simple pat-down search. Also, a belief, based on a consideration of the facts at hand and on reasonable inferences drawn from those facts, that would induce an ordinarily prudent and cautious person under the same circumstances to conclude that criminal activity is taking place or that criminal activity has recently occurred. Reasonable suspicion is a *general* and reasonable belief that a crime is in progress or has occurred, whereas probable cause is a reasonable belief that a *particular* person has committed a *specific* crime.

# Searches Incident to Arrest

The U.S. Supreme Court has established that police officers, to protect themselves from attack, have the right to conduct a search of a person being arrested regardless of gender, and to search the area under the arrestee's immediate control. This rule regarding **search incident to an arrest** was created in the *Rabinowitz* and *Chimel* cases discussed earlier. It became firmly established in other cases involving personal searches, such as the 1973 case of *U.S.* v. *Robinson*.[66] After Robinson had been stopped for a traffic violation, it was learned that his driver's license had expired. He was arrested for operating a vehicle without a valid license. Officers subsequently searched the defendant to be sure he wasn't carrying a weapon and discovered a substance that later proved to be heroin. He was convicted of drug possession but appealed. When Robinson's appeal reached the U.S. Supreme Court, the Court upheld an officer's right to conduct a search without a warrant for purposes of personal protection and to use the fruits of the search when it turns up contraband. In the words of the Court, "A custodial arrest of a suspect based upon probable cause is a reasonable intrusion under the Fourth Amendment; that intrusion being lawful, a search incident to the arrest requires no additional jurisdiction."[67]

The Court's decision in *Robinson* reinforced an earlier ruling in *Terry* v. *Ohio* (1968),[68] involving a seasoned officer who conducted a pat-down search of two men whom he suspected were casing a store, about to commit a robbery. The arresting officer was a 39-year veteran of police work who testified that the men "did not look right." When he approached them, he suspected they were armed. Fearing for his life, he quickly spun the men around, put them up against a wall, patted down their clothing, and found a gun on one of the men. The man, Terry, was later convicted in Ohio courts of carrying a concealed weapon.

Terry's appeal was based on the argument that the suspicious officer had no probable cause to arrest him and therefore no cause to search him. The search, he argued, was illegal, and the evidence obtained should not have been used against him. The Supreme Court disagreed, saying, "In view of these facts, we cannot blind ourselves to the need for law enforcement officers to protect themselves and other prospective victims of violence in situations where they may lack probable cause for an arrest."

The *Terry* case set the standard for a brief stop and frisk based on reasonable suspicion. Attorneys refer to such brief encounters as *Terry-type stops*. **Reasonable suspicion** can be defined as a belief, based on a consideration of the facts at hand and on reasonable inferences drawn from those facts, which would induce an ordinarily prudent and cautious person under the same circumstances to conclude that criminal activity is taking place or that criminal activity has recently occurred. It is the level of suspicion needed to justify an officer in making further inquiry or in conducting further investigation. Reasonable suspicion, which is a *general* and reasonable belief that a crime is in progress or has occurred, should be differentiated from probable cause. Probable cause, as noted earlier, is a reasonable belief that a *particular* person has committed a *specific* crime. It is important to note that the *Terry* case, for all the authority it conferred on officers, also made it clear that officers must have reasonable grounds for any stop and frisk that they conduct. Read more about the case of *Terry* v. *Ohio* at **Library Extra 7–4** at cjtoday.com.

In 1989, in the case of *U.S.* v. *Sokolow,*[69] the Supreme Court clarified the basis on which law enforcement officers, lacking probable cause to believe that a crime has occurred, may stop and briefly detain a person for investigative purposes. In *Sokolow,* the Court ruled that the legitimacy of such a stop must be evaluated according to a "totality of circumstances" criterion—in which all aspects of the defendant's behavior, taken in concert, may provide the basis for a legitimate stop based on reasonable suspicion. In this case, the defendant, Andrew Sokolow, appeared suspicious to police because, while traveling under an alias from Honolulu, he had paid $2,100 in $20 bills (from a large roll of money) for two airplane tickets after spending a surprisingly small amount of time in Miami. In addition, the defendant was obviously nervous and checked no luggage. A warrantless airport investigation by Drug Enforcement Administration (DEA) agents uncovered more than 1,000 grams of cocaine in the defendant's belongings. In upholding Sokolow's conviction, the Court ruled that although no single behavior was proof of illegal activity, taken together his behaviors created circumstances under which suspicion of illegal activity was justified.

In 2002, the Court reinforced the *Sokolow* decision in *U.S.* v. *Arvizu* when it ruled that the "balance between the public interest and the individual's right to personal security"[70] "tilts in favor of a standard less than probable cause in brief investigatory stops of persons or vehicles . . . if the officer's action is supported by reasonable suspicion to believe that criminal activity may be afoot."[71] In the words of the Court, "This process allows officers to draw on their own experiences and specialized training to make inferences from and deductions about the cumulative information available."[72]

In 1993, in the case of *Minnesota* v. *Dickerson,*[73] the U.S. Supreme Court placed new limits on an officer's ability to seize evidence discovered during a pat-down search conducted for protective reasons when the search itself was based merely on suspicion and failed to immediately reveal the presence of a weapon. In this case, Timothy Dickerson, who was observed leaving a building known for cocaine trafficking, was stopped by Minneapolis police officers after they noticed him acting suspiciously. The officers investigated further and ordered Dickerson to submit to a pat-down search. The search revealed no weapons, but the officer conducting it testified that he felt a small lump in Dickerson's jacket pocket, believed it to be a lump of crack cocaine after examining it with his fingers, and then reached into Dickerson's pocket and retrieved a small bag of cocaine. Dickerson was arrested, tried, and convicted of possession of a controlled substance. His appeal, which claimed that the pat-down search had been illegal, eventually made its way to the U.S. Supreme Court. The high court ruled that "if an officer lawfully pats down a suspect's outer clothing and feels an object whose contour or mass makes its identity immediately apparent, there has been no invasion of the suspect's privacy beyond that already authorized by the officer's search for weapons." However, in *Dickerson,* the justices ruled, "the officer never thought that the lump was a weapon, but did not immediately recognize it as cocaine." The lump was determined to be cocaine only after the officer "squeezed, slid, and otherwise manipulated the pocket's contents." Hence, the Court held, the officer's actions in this case did not qualify under what might be called a "plain feel" exception. In any case, said the Court, the search in *Dickerson* went far beyond what is permissible under *Terry,* where officer safety was the crucial issue. The Court summed up its ruling in *Dickerson* this way: "While *Terry* entitled [the officer] to place his hands on respondent's jacket and to feel the lump in the pocket, his continued exploration of the pocket after he concluded that it contained no weapon was unrelated to the sole justification for the search under *Terry*" and was therefore illegal.

Just as arrest must be based on probable cause, officers may not stop and question an unwilling citizen whom they have no reason to suspect of a crime. In the case of *Brown* v. *Texas* (1979),[74] two Texas law enforcement officers stopped the defendant and asked for identification. Ed Brown, they later testified, had not been acting suspiciously, nor did they think he might have a weapon. The stop was made simply because officers wanted to know who he was. Brown was arrested under a Texas statute that required a person to identify himself properly and accurately when asked to do so by peace officers. Eventually, his appeal reached the U.S. Supreme Court, which ruled that under the circumstances of the *Brown* case, a person "may not be punished for refusing to identify himself."

In the 2004 case of *Hiibel* v. *Sixth Judicial District Court of Nevada,*[75] however, the Court upheld Nevada's "stop and identify" law that requires a person to identify himself to police if they encounter him under circumstances that reasonably indicate that he "has committed, is committing or is about to commit a crime." The *Hiibel* case was an extension of the reasonable suspicion doctrine set forth earlier in *Terry.*

LIBRARY EXTRA

## CJ TODAY EXHIBIT 7–1

### Plain-View Requirements

Following the opinion of the U.S. Supreme Court in the case of *Horton* v. *California* (1990), items seized under the plain-view doctrine may be admissible as evidence in a court of law if both of the following conditions are met:

1. The officer who seized the evidence was in the viewing area lawfully.
2. The officer had probable cause to believe that the evidence was somehow associated with criminal activity.

In *Smith* v. *Ohio* (1990),[76] the Court held that an individual has the right to protect his or her belongings from unwarranted police inspection. In *Smith,* the defendant was approached by two officers in plain clothes who observed that he was carrying a brown paper bag. The officers asked him to "come here a minute" and, when he kept walking, identified themselves as police officers. The defendant threw the bag onto the hood of his car and attempted to protect it from the officers' intrusion. Marijuana was found inside the bag, and the defendant was arrested. Since there was little reason to stop the suspect in this case and because control over the bag was not thought necessary for the officers' protection, the Court found that the Fourth Amendment protects both "the traveler who carries a toothbrush and a few articles of clothing in a paper bag" and "the sophisticated executive with the locked attaché case."[77]

The following year, however, in what some Court observers saw as a turnabout, the Court ruled in *California* v. *Hodari D.* (1991)[78] that suspects who flee from the police and throw away evidence as they retreat may later be arrested based on the incriminating nature of the abandoned evidence. The significance of *Hodari* for future police action was highlighted by California prosecutors who pointed out that cases like *Hodari* occur "almost every day in this nation's urban areas."[79]

In 2000, the Court decided the case of William Wardlow.[80] Wardlow had fled upon seeing a caravan of police vehicles converge on an area of Chicago known for narcotics trafficking. Officers caught him and, searching for weapons, conducted a pat-down search of his clothing. After discovering a handgun, the officers arrested Wardlow on weapons charges, but his lawyer argued that police had acted illegally in stopping him since they did not have reasonable suspicion that he had committed an offense. The Illinois Supreme Court agreed with Wardlow's attorney, holding that "sudden flight in a high crime area does not create a reasonable suspicion justifying a *Terry* stop because flight may simply be an exercise of the right to 'go on one's way.'"[81] The case eventually reached the U.S. Supreme Court, which overturned the Illinois court, finding, instead, that the officers' actions did not violate the Fourth Amendment. In the words of the Court, "This case, involving a brief encounter between a citizen and a police officer on a public street, is governed by *Terry,* under which an officer who has a reasonable, articulable suspicion that criminal activity is afoot may conduct a brief, investigatory stop. While 'reasonable suspicion' is a less demanding standard than probable cause, there must be at least a minimal level of objective justification for the stop. An individual's presence in a 'high crime area,' standing alone, is not enough to support a reasonable, particularized suspicion of criminal activity, but a location's characteristics are relevant in determining whether the circumstances are sufficiently suspicious to warrant further investigation. . . . In this case, moreover, it was also Wardlow's unprovoked flight that aroused the officers' suspicions. Nervous, evasive behavior is another pertinent factor in determining reasonable suspicion . . . and headlong flight is the consummate act of evasion."[82]

## Emergency Searches of Persons

Situations in which officers have to search people based on quick decisions do arise. An emergency search of a person may be warranted when, for example, he matches the description of an armed robber, he is found unconscious, or he has what appears to be blood on his clothes. Such searches can save lives by disarming fleeing felons or by uncovering a medical reason for an emergency situation. They may also prevent criminals from escaping or destroying evidence.

Emergency searches of persons, like those of premises, fall under the exigent circumstances exception to the warrant requirement of the Fourth Amendment. In the 1979 case of *Arkansas* v. *Sanders,*[83] the Supreme Court recognized the need for such searches "where the societal costs of

Police work is the only profession that gives you the test first, then the lesson.

—Anonymous

obtaining a warrant, such as danger to law officers or the risk of loss or destruction of evidence, outweigh the reasons for prior recourse to a neutral magistrate."[84]

The 1987 case of *U.S.* v. *Borchardt,*[85] decided by the Fifth Circuit Court of Appeals, held that Ira Eugene Borchardt could be prosecuted for heroin uncovered during medical treatment, even though the defendant had objected to the treatment. Borchardt was a federal inmate when he was found unconscious in his cell. He was taken to a hospital, where tests revealed heroin in his blood. His heart stopped, and he was revived using cardiopulmonary resuscitation (CPR). Borchardt was given three doses of Narcan, a drug used to counteract the effects of heroin, and he improved, regaining consciousness. The patient refused requests to pump his stomach but began to become lethargic, indicating the need for additional Narcan. Eventually, he vomited nine plastic bags full of heroin, along with two bags that had burst. The heroin was turned over to federal officers, and Borchardt was eventually convicted of heroin possession. Attempts to exclude the heroin from evidence were unsuccessful, and the appeals court ruled that the necessity of the emergency situation overruled the defendant's objections to search his person.

The Legal Counsel Division of the FBI provides the following guidelines for conducting emergency warrantless searches of individuals, where the possible destruction of evidence is at issue.[86] (Keep in mind that there may be no probable cause to *arrest* the individual being searched.) All four conditions must apply:

1. At the time of the search there was probable cause to believe that evidence was concealed on the person searched.

2. At the time of the search there was probable cause to believe an emergency threat of destruction of evidence existed.

3. The officer had no prior opportunity to obtain a warrant authorizing the search.

4. The action was no greater than necessary to eliminate the threat of destruction of evidence.

# Vehicle Searches

Vehicles present a special law enforcement problem. They are highly mobile, and when a driver or an occupant is arrested, the need to search the vehicle may be immediate.

The first significant Supreme Court case involving an automobile was *Carroll* v. *U.S.*[87] in 1925, in which a divided Court ruled that a warrantless search of an automobile or other vehicle is valid if it is based on a reasonable belief that contraband is present. In 1964, however, in the case of *Preston* v. *U.S.,*[88] the limits of warrantless vehicle searches were defined. Preston was arrested for vagrancy and taken to jail. His vehicle was impounded, towed to the police garage, and later searched. Two revolvers were uncovered in the glove compartment, and more incriminating evidence was found in the trunk. Preston, convicted on weapons possession and other charges, eventually appealed to the U.S. Supreme Court. The Court held that the warrantless search of Preston's vehicle had occurred while the automobile was in secure custody and had therefore been illegal. Time and circumstances would have permitted acquisition of a warrant to conduct the search, the Court reasoned.

When the search of a vehicle occurs after it has been impounded, however, that search may be legitimate if it is undertaken for routine and reasonable purposes. In the case of *South Dakota* v. *Opperman* (1976),[89] for example, the Court held that a warrantless search undertaken for purposes of inventorying and safekeeping the personal possessions of the car's owner was not illegal. The intent of the search, which turned up marijuana, had not been to discover contraband but to secure the owner's belongings from possible theft. Again, in *Colorado* v. *Bertine* (1987),[90] the Court supported the right of officers to open closed containers found in a vehicle while conducting a routine search for inventorying purposes. In the words of the Court, such searches are "now a well-defined exception in the warrant requirement." In 1990, however, in the precedent-setting case of *Florida* v. *Wells,*[91] the Court agreed with a lower court's suppression of marijuana evidence discovered in a locked suitcase in the trunk of a defendant's impounded vehicle. In *Wells*, the Court held that standardized criteria authorizing the search of a vehicle for inventorying purposes were necessary before such a discovery could be legitimate. Standardized criteria, said the Court, could take the form of department policies, written general orders, or established routines.

Generally speaking, where vehicles are concerned, an investigatory stop is permissible under the Fourth Amendment if supported by reasonable suspicion,[92] and a warrantless search of a stopped car is valid if it is based on probable cause.[93] Reasonable suspicion can expand into probable cause when the facts in a given situation so warrant. In the 1996 case of *Ornelas* v. *U.S.,*[94] for example, two experienced Milwaukee police officers stopped a car with California license plates

## CJ CAREERS

# BUREAU OF IMMIGRATION AND CUSTOMS ENFORCEMENT (ICE)

**Name:** Tamara N. Johnson

**Position:** Immigration Enforcement Agent

**City:** Dallas

**College Attended:** Northwestern State University

**Year Hired:** 2000

*I pursued a career in criminal justice because I believed that the criminal justice system lacked an effective form of rehabilitation. I wanted to make a difference and have an impact on repeat offenders in minority neighborhoods by establishing a form of rehabilitation that would not perpetuate criminal behavior. Recruiters [from the Immigration and Naturalization Service] came to my university and did a presentation. I applied and took the test.*

The greatest challenge of my job is being impartial, offering unbiased information and treating each detainee equally, regardless of their ethnicity, age, sex, or offense. It is also challenging working in a male-dominated career. Although I'm a female, I'm expected to respond to situations and provide backup for my male counterpart.

The greatest reward of my job has been the opportunity to travel throughout the world. I've been exposed to many different cultures and customs. I've ridden a camel over the Sahara Desert and walked along the Nile River. I've learned survival skills and to always be prepared. The experiences and opportunities I have gained as an immigration enforcement officer have been priceless.

### TYPICAL POSITIONS

Criminal investigator (special agent), immigration enforcement agent, detention enforcement agent, and deportation officer. The Bureau of Immigration and Customs Enforcement (ICE), a part of the Department of Homeland Security, focuses on the enforcement of immigration and customs laws within the United States, the protection of specified federal buildings, and air and marine enforcement.

### EMPLOYMENT REQUIREMENTS

The applicant must be a U.S. citizen between 21 and 36 years of age, must be in good medical condition, and must possess a valid driver's license. General employment requirements include (1) a comprehensive written exam, (2) a structured employment interview, and (3) a background investigation. Appointment at the GS-5 level requires (1) a bachelor's degree from an accredited college or university; (2) three years of progressively responsible experience that demonstrates the ability to (a) analyze problems to identify

significant factors, gather pertinent data, and recognize solutions, (b) plan and organize work, and (c) communicate effectively orally and in writing; or (3) an equivalent combination of education and experience.

### OTHER REQUIREMENTS

Applicants are required to submit to urinalysis to screen for illegal drug use prior to appointment and will be subject to random testing after being hired. Selected candidates will attend basic training at the Immigration Officer Academy in Glynco, Georgia.

### SALARY

Successful candidates are typically hired at the GS-5 or GS-7 level, depending on education and work experience.

### BENEFITS

Benefits include (1) 13 days of sick leave annually, (2) two and a half to five weeks of paid vacation and ten paid federal holidays each year, (3) federal health and life insurance, and (4) a comprehensive retirement program.

### DIRECT INQUIRIES TO:

Department of Homeland Security
Twin Cities Hiring Center, Recruitment Unit
One Federal Drive
Fort Snelling, MN 55111-4055

Phone: (612)725-3496

Website: http://www.bice.gov

For additional information on employment opportunities in the criminal justice field, view the careers portion of the CD-ROM included with this book.

*Source:* Bureau of Immigration and Customs Enforcement.

that had been spotted in a motel parking lot known for drug trafficking after the Narcotics and Dangerous Drugs Information System (NADDIS) identified the car's owner as a known or suspected drug trafficker. One of the officers noticed a loose panel above an armrest in the vehicle's backseat and then searched the car. A package of cocaine was found beneath the panel, and the driver and a passenger were arrested. Following conviction, the defendants appealed to the U.S. Supreme Court, claiming that no probable cause to search the car existed at the time of the stop. The majority opinion, however, noted that in the view of the court that originally heard the case, "the model, age, and source-State origin of the car, and the fact that two men traveling together checked into a motel at 4 o'clock in the morning without reservations, formed a drug-courier profile and . . . this profile together with the [computer] reports gave rise to a reasonable suspicion of drug-trafficking activity. . . . [I]n the court's view, reasonable suspicion became probable cause when [the deputy] found the loose panel."[95] Probable cause permits a warrantless search of a vehicle because it is able to quickly leave a jurisdiction. This exception to the exclusionary rule is called the **fleeting-targets exception**.[96]

Warrantless vehicle searches can extend to any area of the vehicle if officers have probable cause to conduct a purposeful search or if officers have been given permission to search the vehicle. In the 1991 case of *Florida* v. *Jimeno*,[97] arresting officers stopped a motorist who gave them permission to search his car. A bag on the floor of the car was found to contain cocaine and the defendant was later convicted on a drug charge. On appeal to the U.S. Supreme Court, however, he argued that the permission given to search his car did not extend to bags and other items within the car. In a decision that may have implications beyond vehicle searches, the Court held that "[a] criminal suspect's Fourth Amendment right to be free from unreasonable searches is not violated when, after he gives police permission to search his car, they open a closed container found within the car that might reasonably hold the object of the search. The amendment is satisfied when, under the circumstances, it is objectively reasonable for the police to believe that the scope of the suspect's consent permitted them to open the particular container."[98]

In *U.S.* v. *Ross* (1982),[99] the Court found that officers had not exceeded their authority in opening a bag in the defendant's trunk which was found to contain heroin. The search was held to be justifiable on the basis of information developed from a search of the passenger compartment. The Court said, "If probable cause justifies the search of a lawfully stopped vehicle, it justifies the search of every part of the vehicle and its contents that may conceal the object of the search."[100] Moreover, according to the 1996 U.S. Supreme Court decision in *Whren* v. *U.S.*,[101] officers may stop a vehicle being driven suspiciously and then search it once probable cause has developed, even if their primary assignment centers on duties other than traffic enforcement or "if a reasonable officer would not have stopped the motorist absent some additional law enforcement objective" (which in the case of *Whren* was drug enforcement).

Motorists and their passengers may be ordered out of stopped vehicles in the interest of officer safety, and any evidence developed as a result of such a procedure may be used in court.[102] In 1997, for example, in the case of *Maryland* v. *Wilson*,[103] the U.S. Supreme Court overturned a decision by a Maryland court that held that crack cocaine found during a traffic stop was seized illegally when it fell from the lap of a passenger ordered out of a stopped vehicle by a Maryland state trooper. The Maryland court reasoned that the police should not have authority to order seemingly innocent passengers out of vehicles—even vehicles that have been stopped for legitimate reasons. The Supreme Court cited concerns for officer safety in overturning the Maryland court's ruling and held that the activities of passengers are subject to police control.

In 1998, however, the U.S. Supreme Court placed clear limits on warrantless vehicle searches. In the case of *Knowles* v. *Iowa*,[104] an Iowa policeman stopped Patrick Knowles for speeding, issued him a citation, but did not make a custodial arrest. The officer then conducted a full search of his car without Knowles's consent and without probable cause. Marijuana was found, and Knowles was arrested. At the time, Iowa state law gave officers authority to conduct full-blown automobile searches when issuing only a citation. The Supreme Court found, however, that while concern for officer safety during a routine traffic stop may justify the minimal intrusion of ordering a driver and passengers out of a car, it does not by itself justify what it called "the considerably greater intrusion attending a full field-type search." Hence, while a search incident to arrest may be justifiable in the eyes of the Court, a search incident to citation clearly is not.

In the 1999 case of *Wyoming* v. *Houghton*,[105] the Court ruled that police officers with probable cause to search a car may inspect any passengers' belongings found in the car that are capable of concealing the object of the search. *Thornton* v. *U.S.* (2004) established the authority of arresting officers to search a car without a warrant even if the driver had previously exited the vehicle.[106]

**fleeting-targets exception**

An exception to the exclusionary rule that permits law enforcement officers to search a motor vehicle based on probable cause but without a warrant. The fleeting-targets exception is predicated on the fact that vehicles can quickly leave the jurisdiction of a law enforcement agency.

In this case, we hold that this common-law "knock and announce" principle forms a part of the reasonableness inquiry under the Fourth Amendment.

—*Wilson* v. *Arkansas*, 514 U.S. 927 (1995)

A police officer searching a vehicle in San Diego, California. Warrantless vehicle searches, where the driver is suspected of a crime, have generally been justified by the fact that vehicles are highly mobile and can quickly leave police jurisdiction.

*David R. Frazier, Photolibrary, Inc.*

> Every U.S. law enforcement officer takes an oath to defend and protect the Constitution. . . . We exist to protect the rights of the public. We are the first line of defense in protection of the Constitution and the Bill of Rights.
>
> —Chief Joe Grebmeier, Greenfield (California) Police Department[i]

In 2005, in the case of *Illinois* v. *Caballes,*[107] the Court held that the use of a drug-sniffing dog during a routine and lawful traffic stop is permissible and may not even be a search within the meaning of the Fourth Amendment. In writing for the majority, Justice John Paul Stevens said that "the use of a well-trained narcotics-detection dog—one that does not expose noncontraband items that otherwise would remain hidden from public view—during a lawful traffic stop generally does not implicate legitimate privacy interests."

## Roadblocks and Motor Vehicle Checkpoints

The Fourth and Fourteenth Amendments to the U.S. Constitution guarantee liberty and personal security to all people residing within the United States. Courts have generally held that police officers have no legitimate authority to detain or arrest people who are going about their business in a peaceful manner, in the absence of probable cause to believe that a crime has been committed. In a number of instances, however, the U.S. Supreme Court has decided that community interests may necessitate a temporary suspension of personal liberty, even when probable cause is lacking. One such case is *Michigan Dept. of State Police* v. *Sitz* (1990),[108] which involved the legality of highway sobriety checkpoints, including those at which nonsuspicious drivers are subjected to scrutiny. In *Sitz,* the Court ruled that such stops are reasonable insofar as they are essential to the welfare of the community as a whole. That the Court reached its conclusion based on pragmatic social interests is clear from the words used by Chief Justice Rehnquist: "No one can seriously dispute the magnitude of the drunken driving problem or the States' interest in eradicating it. Media reports of alcohol-related death and mutilation on the Nation's roads are legion. Drunk drivers cause an annual death toll of over 25,000 and in the same time span cause nearly one million personal injuries and more than five billion dollars in property damage. . . . [T]he balance of the State's interest in preventing drunken driving, the extent to which this system can reasonably be said to advance that interest, and the degree of intrusion upon individual motorists who are briefly stopped, weighs in favor of the state program."[109]

In a second case, *U.S.* v. *Martinez-Fuerte* (1976),[110] the Court upheld brief, suspicionless seizures at a fixed international checkpoint designed to intercept illegal aliens. The Court noted that "to require that such stops always be based on reasonable suspicion would be impractical because the flow of traffic tends to be too heavy to allow the particularized study of a given car necessary to identify it as a possible carrier of illegal aliens. Such a requirement also would largely eliminate any deterrent to the conduct of well-disguised smuggling operations, even though smugglers are known to use these highways regularly."[111]

In 2000, however, in what some people saw as a change in direction, the Court struck down a narcotics checkpoint program established by the Indianapolis Police Department in 1998. Under the program, stopped drivers were told that they were at a drug checkpoint, and officers examined each driver's license and registration while visually assessing the driver for signs of impairment. Drug-sniffing dogs were then walked around the vehicle's exterior. On average, motorists were stopped for three minutes. In ruling the program illegal, the justices held that the Fourth Amendment prohibits even a brief "seizure" of a motorist "under a program whose primary purpose is ultimately indistinguishable from the general interest in crime control." The Court's written opinion in this case, *Indianapolis* v. *Edmond*,[112] indicated that similar programs with the purpose of verifying driver's licenses and vehicle registrations would continue to be permissible because they were not intended to "detect evidence of ordinary criminal wrongdoing."

In fact, in 2004, in the case of *Illinois* v. *Lidster*,[113] the Court held that information-seeking highway roadblocks are permissible. In distinguishing this kind of stop from that in *Edmond*, the Court said that *Edmond*-type stops targeted motorists and were intended to determine whether a vehicle's occupants were committing a crime when stopped. The stop in *Lidster*, said the Court, was different because its intent was merely to solicit motorists' help in solving a crime. "The law," said the Court, "ordinarily permits police to seek the public's voluntary cooperation in a criminal investigation."

## Watercraft and Motor Homes

The 1983 case of *U.S.* v. *Villamonte-Marquez*[114] widened the *Carroll* decision (the first U.S. Supreme Court case involving a vehicle that was discussed earlier) to include watercraft. The case involved an anchored sailboat occupied by Villamonte-Marquez, which was searched by a U.S. Customs officer after one of the crew members appeared unresponsive to being hailed. The officer thought he smelled burning marijuana after boarding the vessel and, through an open hatch, saw burlap bales that he suspected might be contraband. A search proved him correct, and the ship's occupants were arrested. Their conviction was overturned on appeal, but the U.S. Supreme Court reversed the appellate court. The Court reasoned that a vehicle on the water can easily leave the jurisdiction of enforcement officials, just as a car or truck can.

In *California* v. *Carney* (1985),[115] the Court extended police authority to conduct warrantless searches of vehicles to include motor homes. Earlier arguments had been advanced that a motor home, because it is more like a permanent residence than a vehicle, should not be considered a vehicle for purposes of search and seizure. In a 6–3 decision, the Court rejected those arguments, reasoning that a vehicle's appointments and size do not alter its basic function of providing transportation.

Houseboats were brought under the automobile exception to the Fourth Amendment warrant requirement in the 1988 Tenth Circuit Court case of *U.S.* v. *Hill*.[116] In this case, DEA agents believed that methamphetamine was being manufactured aboard a houseboat traversing Lake Texoma in Oklahoma. Because a storm warning had been issued for the area, agents decided to board and to search the boat prior to obtaining a warrant. During the search, an operating methamphetamine laboratory was discovered, and the boat was seized. In an appeal, the defendants argued that the houseboat search had been illegal because agents lacked a warrant to search their home. The appellate court, in rejecting the claims of the defendants, ruled that a houseboat, because it is readily mobile, may be searched without a warrant when probable cause exists to believe that a crime has been or is being committed.

## Suspicionless Searches

In two 1989 decisions, the U.S. Supreme Court ruled for the first time in its history that there may be instances when the need to ensure public safety provides a **compelling interest** that negates the rights of any individual to privacy, permitting **suspicionless searches**—those that occur when a person is not suspected of a crime. In the case of *National Treasury Employees Union* v. *Von Raab* (1989),[117] the Court, by a 5–4 vote, upheld a program of the U.S. Customs Service that required mandatory drug testing for all workers seeking promotions or job transfers involving drug interdiction and the carrying of firearms. The Court's majority opinion read, "We think the government's need to conduct the suspicionless searches required by the Customs program outweighs the privacy interest of employees engaged directly in drug interdiction, and of those who otherwise are required to carry firearms."

**compelling interest**
A legal concept that provides a basis for suspicionless searches when public safety is at issue. (Urinalysis tests of train engineers are an example.) It is the concept on which the U.S. Supreme Court cases of *Skinner* v. *Railway Labor Executives' Association* (1989) and *National Treasury Employees Union* v. *Von Raab* (1989) turned. In those cases, the Court held that public safety may sometimes provide a sufficiently compelling interest to justify limiting an individual's right to privacy.

**suspicionless search**
A search conducted by law enforcement personnel without a warrant and without suspicion. Suspicionless searches are permissible only if based on an overriding concern for public safety.

In terms that apply equally to seizures of property and to seizures of persons, the Fourth Amendment has drawn a firm line at the entrance to the house. Absent exigent circumstances, that threshold may not reasonably be crossed without a warrant.

—*Payton* v. *New York*, 445 U.S. 573, 590 (1980)

The second case, *Skinner* v. *Railway Labor Executives' Association* (1989),[118] was decided on the same day. In *Skinner,* the justices voted 7 to 2 to permit the mandatory testing of railway crews for the presence of drugs or alcohol following serious train accidents. The *Skinner* case involved evidence of drugs in a 1987 train wreck outside of Baltimore, Maryland, in which 16 people were killed and hundreds were injured.

The 1991 Supreme Court case of *Florida* v. *Bostick,*[119] which permitted warrantless "sweeps" of intercity buses, moved the Court deeply into conservative territory. The *Bostick* case came to the attention of the Court as a result of the Broward County (Florida) Sheriff's Department's routine practice of boarding buses at scheduled stops and asking passengers for permission to search their bags. Terrance Bostick, a passenger on one of the buses, gave police permission to search his luggage, which was found to contain cocaine. Bostick was arrested and eventually pleaded guilty to charges of drug trafficking. The Florida Supreme Court, however, found merit in Bostick's appeal, which was based on a Fourth Amendment claim that the search of his luggage had been unreasonable. The Florida court held that "a reasonable passenger in [Bostick's] situation would not have felt free to leave the bus to avoid questioning by the police," and it overturned the conviction.

The state appealed to the U.S. Supreme Court, which held that the Florida Supreme Court had erred in interpreting Bostick's *feelings* that he was not free to leave the bus. In the words of the Court, "Bostick was a passenger on a bus that was scheduled to depart. He would not have felt free to leave the bus even if the police had not been present. Bostick's movements were 'confined' in a sense, but this was the natural result of his decision to take the bus." In other words, Bostick was constrained not so much by police action as by his own feelings that he might miss the bus were he to get off. Following this line of reasoning, the Court concluded that warrantless, suspicionless "sweeps" of buses, "trains, planes, and city streets" are permissible as long as officers (1) ask individual passengers for permission before searching their possessions, (2) do not coerce passengers to consent to a search, and (3) do not convey the message that citizen compliance with the search request is mandatory. Passenger compliance with police searches must be voluntary for the searches to be legal.

In contrast to the tone of Court decisions more than two decades earlier, the justices did not require officers to inform passengers that they were free to leave nor that they had the right to deny officers the opportunity to search (although Bostick himself was so advised by Florida officers). Any reasonable person, the Court ruled, should feel free to deny the police request. In the words of the Court, "The appropriate test is whether, taking into account all of the circumstances surrounding the encounter, a reasonable passenger would feel free to decline the officers' requests or otherwise terminate the encounter." The Court continued, "Rejected, however, is Bostick's argument that he must have been seized because no reasonable person would freely consent to a search of luggage containing drugs, since the 'reasonable person' test presumes an innocent person."

Critics of the decision saw it as creating new "gestapo-like" police powers in the face of which citizens on public transportation will feel compelled to comply with police requests for search authority. Dissenting Justices Harry Blackmun, John Paul Stevens, and Thurgood Marshall held that "the bus sweep at issue in this case violates the core values of the Fourth Amendment." The Court's majority, however, defended its ruling by writing, "[T]he Fourth Amendment proscribes unreasonable searches and seizures; it does not proscribe voluntary cooperation." In mid-2000, however, in the case of *Bond* v. *U.S.,*[120] the Court ruled that physical manipulation of a carry-on bag in the possession of a bus passenger without the owner's consent violates the Fourth Amendment's proscription against unreasonable searches.

In the case of *U.S.* v. *Drayton* (2002),[121] the U.S. Supreme Court reiterated its position that police officers are not required to advise bus passengers of their right to refuse to cooperate with officers conducting searches or of their right to refuse to be searched. In *Drayton,* the driver of a bus allowed three police officers to board the bus as part of a routine drug and weapons interdiction effort. One officer knelt on the driver's seat, facing the rear of the bus, while another officer stayed in the rear, facing forward. A third officer, named Lang, worked his way from back to front, speaking with individual passengers as he went. To avoid blocking the aisle, Lang stood next to or just behind each passenger with whom he spoke. He later testified that passengers who declined to cooperate or who chose to exit the bus at any time would have been allowed to do so without argument; that most people were willing to cooperate; that in his experience, passengers often leave buses for a cigarette or a snack while officers are on board; and that although he sometimes informed passengers of their right to refuse to cooperate, he did not do so on the day in question. As Lang approached Christopher Drayton and Clifton Brown, Jr., who were seated together, he held up his badge long enough for them to identify him as an officer. Speaking just loud enough for the two to hear, he declared that the police were looking for drugs and weapons and asked if respondents had any bags. When both of them pointed to a bag overhead, Lang asked if they minded if he checked it. Brown agreed, and a search of the bag revealed no contraband.

## CJ NEWS

## Legal Issues Being Raised on Searches in Subways

Even more than security experts and intelligence analysts, one group of employees has become central to the new program of bag searches in the transit networks of the New York region: lawyers.

The decision in July 2005 to have police officers inspect the belongings of thousands of subway riders has opened a thicket of legal and constitutional issues, involving criminal procedure, transit security and concerns about potential misuse of the new tactic.

Donna Lieberman, the executive director of the New York Civil Liberties Union, said the organization had begun work on a federal lawsuit, which could be filed soon. Such a challenge will most likely claim that the policy violates the Fourth Amendment's prohibition against "unreasonable searches and seizures."

And at a news conference in Brooklyn, Capt. Eric Adams, the president of a group of black police officers, said its members were worried that riders of Middle Eastern, African or Asian descent would be disproportionately targeted in the searches, despite official assurances to the contrary.

New Jersey Transit and the Port Authority of New York and New Jersey started random searches on their trains and in their buses and stations, joining the city police and the Metropolitan Transportation Authority in conducting searches.

The four agencies have tried to sidestep a potential legal minefield by carefully specifying the limits and objectives of the policies, but the legality of the searches could well rest on subtle distinctions in the way they are carried out.

"It is by no means a foregone conclusion that these searches will be found reasonable under the Fourth Amendment," said Tracey Maclin, a law professor at Boston University. "The number of people involved, the nature and severity of the intrusions and the uncertain duration of the searches all make this fundamentally very different from anything we have seen before."

At least three United States Supreme Court cases will probably influence any judge assessing the searches.

In 1979, in *Delaware* v. *Prouse,* the court held that random traffic stops, left to the discretion of police officers, were unconstitutional. In 1990, in *Michigan* v. *Sitz,* the court upheld the legality of sobriety checkpoints in which a consistent proportion of drivers was stopped. The court ruled that such roadblocks were permitted as a way to prevent drunken driving.

The court has set limits on those roadblocks, however. In 2000, in *Indianapolis* v. *Edmond,* it struck down the use of traffic checkpoints to stop drivers so that trained dogs could sniff the vehicles for narcotics. Unlike checkpoints to make sure that drivers were sober or had valid licenses and registrations, the court said, roadblocks for general law enforcement were unconstitutional.

David D. Cole, a law professor at Georgetown University, said the government was likely to succeed in demonstrating a special need for the current searches in New York.

A judge evaluating a legal challenge, he said, would probably look at three factors: whether the searches are truly random or use standardized criteria; whether riders were given advance notice or provided their consent to the searches; and the degree of intrusiveness. "It's very hard to predict how these cases will turn out, because it's such an open-ended balancing test," he said.

According to a two-page directive sent to all police commanders following the July 2005 subway bombings in London, the searches were begun "to increase deterrence and detection of potential terrorist activity and to give greater protection to the mass transit-riding public." The directive authorized the police to inspect "backpacks, containers and other carry-on items which are capable of containing explosive devices."

The policy includes several provisions that could help in defending the new searches from court challenges.

First, although Mayor Michael R. Bloomberg and Police Commissioner Raymond W. Kelly have described the searches as "random," they should rely on a precise frequency that is not subject to officers' discretion, according to the directive.

A supervisor at each checkpoint is supposed to determine the frequency of searches—1 in every 5, 12 or 20 passengers, for example—based on the volume of passengers, the number of officers available and the "flow of commuter traffic."

Second, extensive steps were taken to notify the public about the searches. At subway stations and train terminals, megaphone and public-address systems were used. Notices were handwritten on dry-erase boards in the booths in most subway stations. At many checkpoints, the police have set up signs on easels near the turnstiles.

The directive states that individuals who refuse to be searched can leave the subway system, and that such a refusal "shall not constitute probable cause for an arrest or reasonable suspicion for a forcible stop."

The degree of intrusiveness could become a thorny issue. The directive provides that officers may open a package and "physically inspect and manipulate the contents to ensure it does not contain an explosive device." Leaving aside the issue of illegal drugs or weapons, some riders have already voiced misgivings about having the police examine sensitive possessions, like medications and personal hygiene products.

Lawyers have been used extensively in writing the search policies. The deputy police commissioner for legal matters, S. Andrew Schaffer, formerly the general counsel for New York University, joined Mr. Kelly and top police commanders in completing their plans for the searches.

Similarly, Catherine A. Rinaldi, the general counsel for the Metropolitan Transportation Authority, was "intimately involved" in plans for searches on the Long Island Rail Road and Metro-North Commuter Railroad, according to Tom Kelly, a spokesman for the authority.

Ronald Susswein, an assistant attorney general in New Jersey, said that the New Jersey Transit searches would not be conducted arbitrarily. "This is not a criminal enforcement procedure," he said. "We're not trying to catch anyone. We're trying to deter terrorism."

*(continued)*

## CJ NEWS *(continued)*

While the majority of riders interviewed since the searches began said they supported the searches, a few have expressed concerns.

"For a split second, I thought that because of my skin complexion, they picked me," said James Hamilton, 38, whose attaché case was searched at Herald Square. "I'm not sure if I had brown hair and blue eyes, that that would have happened." He has black hair, dark brown eyes and a dark complexion.

Charles Wilson, 35, a schoolteacher whose bag was searched at Fulton Street in Lower Manhattan, said, "This is not going to make things better between the police and people of color." Mr. Wilson is black.

Captain Adams, whose organization, 100 Blacks in Law Enforcement Who Care, held a news conference immediately after the searches began, said he believed that discrimination was likely in practice, if not intent. "You can say 'no profiling,' but when you have a police department that has a history of profiling, it is going to practice what it knows," he said.

A police spokesman, Paul J. Browne, said he strongly disagreed. "These inspections are being conducted in a constitutional manner and have been met with enthusiastic cooperation by the overwhelming majority of riders we've come into contact with," he said.

*Source:* Sewell Chan and Kareem Fahim, "Legal Issues Being Raised on Searches in Subways," *The New York Times,* July 24, 2005. Web posted at http://query.nytimes.com/mem/tnt.html?emc-tnt&tntget-2005/07/24/nyregion/ 24subways.html&tntemail (accessed July 26, 2005). Copyright © 2005 by the New York Times Co. Reprinted with permission.

Lang then asked Brown whether he minded if the officer checked his person. Brown agreed, and a pat-down search revealed hard objects similar to drug packages in both of Brown's thigh areas, resulting in his arrest. Lang then asked Drayton, "Mind if I check you?" When Drayton agreed, a pat-down revealed objects similar to those found on Brown, and Drayton was also arrested. A further search of the two men revealed that Drayton and Brown had taped cocaine between their legs. Both were charged with federal drug crimes. In court, their attorneys moved to suppress the cocaine as evidence, arguing that their consent to the pat-down searches was invalid. In denying the motions, the federal district court determined that the police conduct was not coercive and that the defendants' consent to the search had been voluntary. The Eleventh Circuit Court, however, reversed that finding based on the belief that bus passengers do not feel free to disregard officers' requests to search in the absence of some positive indication that consent may be refused.

In 2004, the Court made it clear that suspicionless searches of vehicles at our nation's borders are permitted, even when the searches are extensive. In the case of *U.S.* v. *Flores-Montano,*[122] customs officials disassembled the gas tank of a car belonging to a man entering the country from Mexico and found that it contained 37 kilograms of marijuana. Although the officers admitted that their actions were not motivated by any particular belief that the search would reveal contraband, the Court held that Congress has always granted "plenary authority to conduct routine searches and seizures at the border without probable cause or a warrant. . . . " In the words of the Court, "the Government's authority to conduct suspicionless inspections at the border includes the authority to remove, disassemble and reassemble a vehicles' fuel tank."

## High-Technology Searches

The burgeoning use of high technology to investigate crime and to uncover violations of the criminal law is forcing courts throughout the nation to evaluate the applicability of constitutional guarantees in light of high-tech searches and seizures. In 1996, the California appellate court decision in *People* v. *Deutsch*[123] presaged the kinds of issues that are likely to be encountered as American law enforcement expands its use of cutting-edge technology. In *Deutsch,* judges faced the question of whether a warrantless scan of a private dwelling with a thermal-imaging device constitutes an unreasonable search within the meaning of the Fourth Amendment. Such devices (also called *forward-looking infrared [FLIR] systems*) measure radiant energy in the radiant heat portion of the electromagnetic spectrum[124] and display their readings as thermographs. The "heat picture" that a thermal imager produces can be used, as it was in the case of Dorian Deutsch, to reveal unusually warm areas or rooms that might be associated with the cultivation of drug-bearing plants, such as marijuana. Two hundred cannabis plants, which were being grown hydroponically under high-wattage lights in two walled-off portions of Deutsch's home, were seized following an exterior thermal scan of her home by a police officer who drove by the residence at 1:30 in the morning. Because

A photo created by a thermal-imaging device. The photo shows "hot spots" in a suspected marijuana grower's home that might be produced by lights used to grow the plants indoors. In *Kyllo* v. *U.S.* (2001), the U.S. Supreme Court held that the police may not use such devices without a search warrant.

*Image compliments of Spi–www.x20.org*

no entry of the house was anticipated during the search, the officer had acted without a search warrant. The California court ruled that the scan was an illegal search because "society accepts a reasonable expectation of privacy" surrounding "nondisclosed activities within the home."[125]

In a similar case, *Kyllo* v. *U.S* (2001),[126] the U.S. Supreme Court reached much the same conclusion. Based on the results of a warrantless search conducted by officers using a thermal-imaging device, investigators applied for a search warrant of Kyllo's home. The subsequent search uncovered more than 100 marijuana plants that were being grown under bright lights. In overturning Kyllo's conviction on drug-manufacturing charges, the Court held, "Where, as here, the Government uses a device that is not in general public use, to explore details of a private home that would previously have been unknowable without physical intrusion, the surveillance is a Fourth Amendment 'search,' and is presumptively unreasonable without a warrant."[127] Learn more about the issues surrounding search and seizure at Web Extra 7–4 at cjtoday.com.

**WEB** EXTRA

# The Intelligence Function

The need for information leads police investigators to question both suspects and informants, and even more often, potentially knowledgeable citizens who may have been witnesses or victims. Data gathering is a crucial form of intelligence; without it, enforcement agencies would be virtually powerless to plan and effect arrests.

The importance of gathering information in police work cannot be overstressed. Studies have found that the one factor most likely to lead to arrest in serious crimes is the presence of a witness who can provide information to the police. Undercover operations, "neighborhood watch" programs, "crime stopper" groups, and organized detective work all contribute this vital information.

## Informants

Information gathering is a complex process, and many ethical questions have been raised about the techniques police use to gather information. The use of paid informants, for example, is an area of concern to ethicists who believe that informants are often paid while getting away with minor crimes that investigators are willing to overlook. The police practice (endorsed by some prosecutors) of agreeing not to charge one offender out of a group if he or she will "talk" and testify against others is another concern.

As we have seen, probable cause is an important aspect of both police searches and legal arrests. The successful use of informants in supporting requests for a warrant depends on the demonstrable reliability of their information. The case of *Aguilar* v. *Texas* (1964)[128] clarified the use of informants and established a two-pronged test. The U.S. Supreme Court ruled that informant information could establish probable cause if both of the following criteria are met:

- The source of the informant's information is made clear.
- The police officer has a reasonable belief that the informant is reliable.

The two-pronged test of *Aguilar* v. *Texas* was intended to prevent the issuance of warrants on the basis of false or fabricated information. The case of *U.S.* v. *Harris* (1971)[129] provided an exception to the two-pronged *Aguilar* test. The *Harris* court recognized the fact that when an informant provides information that is damaging to him or her, it is probably true. In *Harris*, an informant told police that he had purchased non-tax-paid whiskey from another person. Since the information also implicated the informant in a crime, it was held to be accurate, even though it could not meet the second prong of the *Aguilar* test. "Admissions of crime," said the Court, "carry their own indicia of credibility—sufficient at least to support a finding of probable cause to search."[130]

In 1983, in the case of *Illinois* v. *Gates*,[131] the Court adopted a totality-of-circumstances approach, which held that sufficient probable cause for issuing a warrant exists where an informant can be reasonably believed on the basis of everything that the police know. The *Gates* case involved an anonymous informant who provided incriminating information about another person through a letter to the police. Although the source of the information was not stated and the police were unable to say whether the informant was reliable, the overall sense of things, given what was already known to police, was that the information supplied was probably valid.

In the 1990 case of *Alabama* v. *White*,[132] the Supreme Court ruled that an anonymous tip, even in the absence of other corroborating information about a suspect, could form the basis for an investigatory stop if the informant accurately predicted the *future* behavior of the suspect. The Court reasoned that the ability to predict a suspect's behavior demonstrates a significant degree of familiarity with the suspect's affairs. In the words of the Court, "Because only a small number of people are generally privy to an individual's itinerary, it is reasonable for the police to believe that a person with access to such information is likely to also have access to reliable information about that individual's illegal activities."[133]

In 2000, in the case of *Florida* v. *J.L.*,[134] the Court held that an anonymous tip that a person is carrying a gun does not, without more, justify a police officer's stop and frisk of that person. Ruling that such a search is invalid under the Fourth Amendment, the Court rejected the suggestion of a firearm exception to the general stop-and-frisk rule.[135]

The identity of informants may be kept secret only if sources have been explicitly assured of confidentiality by investigating officers or if a reasonably implied assurance of confidentiality has been made. In *U.S. Dept. of Justice* v. *Landano* (1993),[136] the U.S. Supreme Court required that an informant's identity be revealed through a request made under the federal Freedom of Information Act. In that case, the FBI had not specifically assured the informant of confidentiality, and the Court ruled that "the government is not entitled to a presumption that all sources supplying information to the FBI in the course of a criminal investigation are confidential sources."

The right of the people to be secure in their persons, houses, papers, and effects, against unreasonable searches and seizures, shall not be violated, and no Warrants shall issue, but upon probable cause, supported by Oath or affirmation, and particularly describing the place to be searched, and the persons or things to be seized.

—Fourth Amendment to the U.S. Constitution

# Police Interrogation

In 2003, Illinois became the first state in the nation to require the electronic recording of police interrogations and confessions in homicide cases.[137] State lawmakers hoped that the use of recordings would reduce the incidence of false confessions as well as the likelihood of convictions based on such confessions. Under the law, police interrogators must create videotape or audiotape recordings on any questions involving suspects. The law prohibits the courtroom introduction of statements and confessions that have not been taped. Proponents of the law say that it will prevent the police intimidation of murder suspects and will put an end to coerced confessions.

The U.S. Supreme Court has defined **interrogation** as any behaviors by the police "that the police should know are reasonably likely to elicit an incriminating response from the suspect."[138] Hence, interrogation may involve activities that go well beyond mere verbal questioning, and the Court has held that interrogation may include "staged lineups, reverse lineups, positing guilt, minimizing the moral seriousness of crime, and casting blame on the victim or society." The Court has also held that "police words or actions normally attendant to arrest and custody do not constitute interrogation" unless they involve pointed or directed questions. Hence, an arresting officer may instruct a suspect on what to do and may chitchat with him or her without engaging in interrogation within the meaning of the law. Once police officers make inquiries intended to elicit information about the crime in question, however, interrogation has begun. The interrogation of suspects, like other areas of police activity, is subject to constitutional limits as interpreted by the courts, and a series of landmark decisions by the U.S. Supreme Court has focused on police interrogation.

> **interrogation**
>
> The information-gathering activity of police officers that involves the direct questioning of suspects.

## Physical Abuse

The first in a series of significant cases regarding police interrogation was *Brown* v. *Mississippi*,[139] decided in 1936. The *Brown* case began with the robbery of a white store owner in Mississippi in 1934 during which the store owner was killed. A posse formed and went to the home of a local African-American man rumored to have been one of the perpetrators. They dragged the suspect from his home, put a rope around his neck, and hoisted and lowered him from a tree a number of times, hoping to get a confession from the man, but failing. The posse was headed by a deputy sheriff who then arrested other suspects in the case and laid them over chairs in the local jail and whipped them with belts and buckles until they "confessed." These confessions were used in the trial that followed, and all three defendants were convicted of murder. Their convictions were upheld by the Mississippi Supreme Court. In 1936, however, the case was reviewed by the U.S. Supreme Court, which overturned all of the convictions, saying that it was difficult to imagine techniques of interrogation more "revolting" to the sense of justice than those used in this case.

## Inherent Coercion

Interrogation need not involve physical abuse for it to be contrary to constitutional principles. In the case of *Ashcraft* v. *Tennessee* (1944)[140] the U.S. Supreme Court found that interrogation involving **inherent coercion** was not acceptable. Ashcraft had been charged with the murder of his wife, Zelma. He was arrested on a Saturday night and interrogated by relays of skilled interrogators until Monday morning, when he purportedly made a statement implicating himself in the murder. During questioning he had faced a blinding light but was not physically mistreated. Investigators later testified that when the suspect requested cigarettes, food, or water, they "kindly" provided them. The Court's ruling, which reversed Ashcraft's conviction, made it plain that the Fifth Amendment guarantee against self-incrimination excludes any form of official coercion or pressure during interrogation.

> **inherent coercion**
>
> The tactics used by police interviewers that fall short of physical abuse but that nonetheless pressure suspects to divulge information.

A similar case, *Chambers* v. *Florida,* was decided in 1940.[141] In that case, four African-American men were arrested without warrants as suspects in the robbery and murder of an aged white man. After several days of questioning in a hostile atmosphere, the men confessed to the murder. The confessions were used as the primary evidence against them at the trial that ensued, and all four were sentenced to die. On appeal, the U.S. Supreme Court held that "the very circumstances surrounding their confinement and their questioning without any formal charges having been brought, were such as to fill petitioners with terror and frightful misgivings."[142] Learn more about the case of *Chambers* v. *Florida* at Library Extra 7–5 at cjtoday.com.

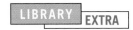

## Psychological Manipulation

Not only must interrogation be free of coercion and hostility, but it also cannot involve sophisticated trickery designed to ferret out a confession. Interrogators do not necessarily have to be scrupulously honest in confronting suspects, and the expert opinions of medical and psychiatric practitioners may be sought in investigations. However, the use of professionals skilled in **psychological manipulation** to gain confessions was banned by the Court in the case of *Leyra* v. *Denno*[143] in 1954, during the heyday of psychiatric perspectives on criminal behavior.

In the *Leyra* case, detectives employed a psychiatrist to question Camilo Leyra, who had been charged with the hammer slayings of his parents. Leyra had been led to believe that the medical doctor to whom he was introduced in an interrogation room had actually been sent to help him

> **psychological manipulation**
>
> Manipulative actions by police interviewers, designed to pressure suspects to divulge information, that are based on subtle forms of intimidation and control.

with a sinus problem. Following a period of questioning, including subtle suggestions by the psychiatrist that he would feel better if he confessed to the murders, Leyra did indeed confess.

The Supreme Court, on appeal, ruled that the defendant had been effectively and improperly duped by the police. In the words of the Court, "Instead of giving petitioner the medical advice and treatment he expected, the psychiatrist by subtle and suggestive questions simply continued the police effort of the past days and nights to induce petitioner to admit his guilt. For an hour and a half or more the techniques of a highly trained psychiatrist were used to break petitioner's will in order to get him to say he had murdered his parents."[144]

In 1991, in the case of *Arizona* v. *Fulminante*,[145] the U.S. Supreme Court further curtailed the use of sophisticated techniques to gain a confession. Oreste Fulminante was an inmate in a federal prison when he was approached by a fellow inmate who was an FBI informant. The informant told Fulminante that other inmates were plotting to kill him because of a rumor that he had killed a child. The informant offered to protect Fulminante if Fulminante divulged the details of his crime. Fulminante then described his role in the murder of his 11-year-old stepdaughter. Fulminante was charged with that murder, tried, and convicted.

On appeal to the U.S. Supreme Court, Fulminante's lawyers argued that their client's confession had been coerced because of the threat of violence communicated by the informant. The Court agreed that the confession had been coerced and ordered a new trial at which the confession could not be admitted into evidence. Simultaneously, however, the Court found that the admission of a coerced confession should be considered a harmless "trial error" that need not necessarily result in reversal of a conviction if other evidence still proves guilt. The decision was especially significant because it partially reversed the Court's earlier ruling, in *Chapman* v. *California* (1967),[146] where it was held that forced confessions were such a basic form of constitutional error that they automatically invalidated any conviction to which they related. Fulminante was again convicted at his second trial where his confession was not entered into evidence, and he was sentenced to die. The Arizona Supreme Court, however, overturned his conviction, ruling that testimony describing statements the victim had made about fearing for her life prior to her murder, and which had been entered into evidence, were hearsay and had prejudiced the jury.[147]

## The Right to a Lawyer at Interrogation

In 1964, in the case of *Escobedo* v. *Illinois*,[148] the Supreme Court recognized the right to have legal counsel present during police interrogation. Danny Escobedo was arrested for the murder of his brother-in-law. During the interrogation that followed, officers told him that they "had him cold" and that he should confess. Escobedo asked to see his lawyer but was told that an interrogation was in progress and that he couldn't see his lawyer. Soon the lawyer arrived and asked to see Escobedo. Police told him that his client was being questioned and could be seen after questioning concluded. Escobedo later claimed that while he repeatedly asked for his lawyer, he was told, "Your lawyer doesn't want to see you." Eventually, Escobedo confessed and was convicted at trial on the basis of his confession. Upon appeal, the U.S. Supreme Court overturned Escobedo's conviction, ruling that counsel is necessary at police interrogations to protect the rights of the defendant and should be provided when the defendant desires.

In 1981, the case of *Edwards* v. *Arizona*[149] established a "bright-line rule" (that is, specified a criterion that cannot be violated) for investigators to use in interpreting a suspect's right to counsel. In *Edwards,* the Supreme Court reiterated its *Miranda* concern that once a suspect who is in custody and is being questioned requests the assistance of counsel, all questioning must cease until an attorney is present. In 1990, the Court refined the rule in *Minnick* v. *Mississippi*,[150] when it held that after the suspect has had an opportunity to consult his or her lawyer, interrogation may not resume unless the lawyer is present. Similarly, according to *Arizona* v. *Roberson* (1988),[151] the police may not avoid the suspect's request for a lawyer by beginning a new line of questioning, even if it is about an unrelated offense. In 1994, however, in the case of *Davis* v. *U.S.*,[152] the Court "put the burden on custodial suspects to make unequivocal invocations of the right to counsel." In the *Davis* case, a man being interrogated in the death of a sailor waived his *Miranda* rights but later said, "Maybe I should talk to a lawyer." Investigators asked the suspect clarifying questions, and he responded, "No, I don't want a lawyer." He appealed his conviction, claiming that interrogation should have ceased when he mentioned a lawyer. The Court, in affirming the conviction, stated that "it will often be good police practice for the interviewing officers to clarify whether or not [the suspect] actually wants an attorney."

While every person is entitled to stand silent, it is more virtuous for the wrongdoer to admit his offense and accept the punishment he deserves. . . . It is wrong, and subtly corrosive of our criminal justice system, to regard an honest confession as a mistake.

—Justice Antonin Scalia, dissenting in *Minnick* v. *Mississippi*, 498 U.S. 146 (1990)

## CJ TODAY EXHIBIT 7-2

### The *Miranda* Warnings

#### ADULT RIGHTS WARNING

Suspects 18 years old or older who are in custody must be advised of the following rights before any questioning begins:

1. You have the right to remain silent.
2. Anything you say can be used against you in a court of law.
3. You have the right to talk to a lawyer and to have a lawyer present while you are being questioned.
4. If you want a lawyer before or during questioning but cannot afford to hire a lawyer, one will be appointed to represent you at no cost before any questioning.
5. If you answer questions now without a lawyer here, you still have the right to stop answering questions at any time.

#### WAIVER OF RIGHTS

After reading and explaining the rights of a person in custody, an officer must also ask for a waiver of those rights before any questioning. The following waiver questions must be answered affirmatively, either by express answer or by clear implication. Silence alone is not a waiver.

1. Do you understand each of these rights I have explained to you? (Answer must be YES.)
2. Having these rights in mind, do you now wish to answer questions? (Answer must be YES.)
3. Do you now wish to answer questions without a lawyer present? (Answer must be YES.)
   The following question must be asked of juveniles ages 14, 15, 16, and 17:
4. Do you now wish to answer questions without your parents, guardians, or custodians present? (Answer must be YES.)

*Source:* North Carolina Justice Academy. Reprinted with permission.

# Suspect Rights: The *Miranda* Decision

In the area of suspect rights, no case is as famous as *Miranda* v. *Arizona* (1966),[153] which established the well-known ***Miranda* warnings**. Many people regard *Miranda* as the centerpiece of the Warren Court due process rulings.

The case involved Ernesto Miranda, who was arrested in Phoenix, Arizona, and was accused of having kidnapped and raped a young woman. At police headquarters, he was identified by the victim. After being interrogated for two hours, Miranda signed a confession that formed the basis of his later conviction on the charges.

On appeal, the U.S. Supreme Court rendered what some regard as the most far-reaching opinion to have affected criminal justice in the last half-century. The Court ruled that Miranda's conviction was unconstitutional because "[t]he entire aura and atmosphere of police interrogation without notification of rights and an offer of assistance of counsel tends to subjugate the individual to the will of his examiner."

The Court continued, saying that the suspect "must be warned prior to any questioning that he has the right to remain silent, that anything he says can be used against him in a court of law, that he has the right to the presence of an attorney, and that if he cannot afford an attorney one will be appointed for him prior to any questioning if he so desires. Opportunity to exercise these rights must be afforded to him throughout the interrogation. After such warnings have been given, and such opportunity afforded him, the individual may knowingly and intelligently waive these rights and agree to answer the questions or make a statement. But unless and until such warnings and waiver are demonstrated by the prosecution at the trial, no evidence obtained as a result of interrogation can be used against him."

To ensure that proper advice is given to suspects at the time of their arrest, the now-famous *Miranda* rights are read before any questioning begins. These rights, as they appear on a *Miranda* warning card commonly used by police agencies, appear in CJ Today Exhibit 7–2.

Once suspects have been advised of their *Miranda* rights, they are commonly asked to sign a paper that lists each right, in order to confirm that they were advised of their rights and that they understand each right. Questioning may then begin, but only if suspects waive their rights not to talk and to have a lawyer present during interrogation.

In 1992, *Miranda* rights were effectively extended to illegal immigrants living in the United States. In a settlement of a class-action lawsuit reached in Los Angeles with the Immigration and

**_Miranda_ warnings**

The advisement of rights due criminal suspects by the police before questioning begins. *Miranda* warnings were first set forth by the U.S. Supreme Court in the 1966 case of *Miranda* v. *Arizona.*

Naturalization Service, U.S. District Court Judge William Byrne, Jr., approved the printing of millions of notices in several languages to be given to arrestees. The approximately 1.5 million illegal aliens arrested each year must be told they may (1) talk with a lawyer, (2) make a phone call, (3) request a list of available legal services, (4) seek a hearing before an immigration judge, (5) possibly obtain release on bond, and (6) contact a diplomatic officer representing their country.[154] This was "long overdue," said Roberto Martinez of the American Friends Service Committee's Mexico-U.S. border program. "Up to now, we've had total mistreatment of civil rights of undocumented people."

When the *Miranda* decision was originally handed down, some hailed it as ensuring the protection of individual rights guaranteed under the Constitution. To guarantee those rights, they suggested, no better agency is available than the police themselves, since the police are present at the initial stages of the criminal justice process. Critics of *Miranda,* however, argued that the decision put police agencies in the uncomfortable and contradictory position not only of enforcing the law but also of having to offer defendants advice on how they might circumvent conviction and punishment. Under *Miranda,* the police partially assume the role of legal adviser to the accused.

In 1999, however, in the case of *U.S.* v. *Dickerson,*[155] the Fourth Circuit U.S. Court of Appeals upheld an almost-forgotten law that Congress had passed in 1968 with the intention of overturning *Miranda.* That law, Section 3501 of Chapter 223, Part II of Title 18 of the U.S. Code, says that "a confession . . . shall be admissible in evidence if it is voluntarily given." On appeal in 2000, the U.S. Supreme Court upheld its original *Miranda* ruling by a 7–2 vote and found that *Miranda* is a constitutional rule (that is, a fundamental right inherent in the U.S. Constitution) that cannot be dismissed by an act of Congress. "*Miranda* and its progeny," the majority wrote in *Dickerson* v. *U.S.* (2000), will continue to "govern the admissibility of statements made during custodial interrogation in both state and federal courts."[156]

Read the full text of the original *Miranda* decision, the text of Section 3501 of the U.S. Code, the Fourth Circuit Court's 1999 opinion in *Dickerson,* and the final U.S. Supreme Court majority and dissenting opinions at the *Miranda* Revisited website via Web Extra 7–5 at cjtoday.com.

WEB EXTRA

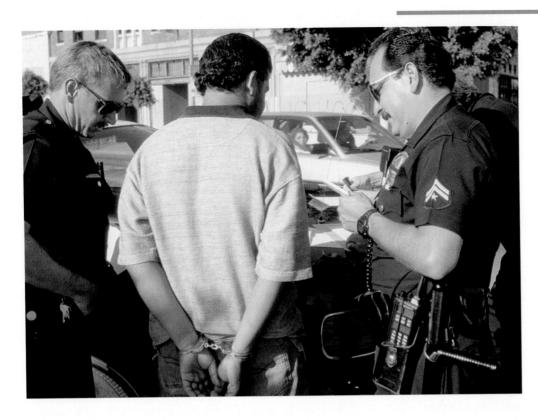

A suspect being read his *Miranda* rights immediately after arrest. Officers often read *Miranda* rights from a card to preclude the possibility of mistake.

*Michael Newman, PhotoEdit*

## Waiver of *Miranda* Rights by Suspects

Suspects in police custody may legally waive their *Miranda* rights through a *voluntary* "knowing and intelligent" waiver. A *knowing waiver* can only be made if a suspect is advised of his or her rights and is in a condition to understand the advisement. A rights advisement made in English to a Spanish-speaking suspect, for example, cannot produce a knowing waiver. Likewise, an *intelligent waiver* of rights requires that the defendant be able to understand the consequences of not invoking the *Miranda* rights. In the case of *Moran* v. *Burbine* (1986),[157] the U.S. Supreme Court defined an intelligent and knowing waiver as one "made with a full awareness both of the nature of the right being abandoned and the consequences of the decision to abandon it." Similarly, in *Colorado* v. *Spring* (1987),[158] the Court held that an intelligent and knowing waiver can be made even though a suspect has not been informed of all the alleged offenses about which he or she is about to be questioned.

## Inevitable-Discovery Exception to *Miranda*

The case of Robert Anthony Williams provides a good example of the change in the U.S. Supreme Court philosophy, alluded to earlier in this chapter, from an individual-rights perspective toward a public-order perspective. It epitomizes what many consider a slow erosion of the advances in defendant rights, which reached their apex in *Miranda*. This case began in 1969, at the close of the Warren Court era. Williams was apprehended as a suspect in the murder of ten-year-old Pamela Powers around Christmas time and advised of his rights. Later, as Williams rode in a car with detectives who were searching for the girl's body, one of the detectives made what has since become known as the "Christian burial speech." The detective told Williams that since Christmas was almost upon them, it would be "the Christian thing to do" to see to it that Pamela had a decent burial rather than having to lie in a field somewhere. Williams confessed and led detectives to the body. However, because Williams had not been reminded of his right to have a lawyer present during his conversation with the detective, the Supreme Court in *Brewer* v. *Williams* (1977)[159] overturned Williams's conviction, saying that the detective's remarks were "a deliberate eliciting of incriminating evidence from an accused in the absence of his lawyer."

In 1977, Williams was retried for the murder, but his remarks in leading detectives to the body were not entered into evidence. The discovery of the body was used, however, and Williams was

The CD-ROM scenario for Chapter 7 builds on the concepts of reasonable suspicion and probable cause. It is derived from a real-life incident involving a Cleveland, Ohio, police officer's on-the-street interrogation of two suspicious-looking individuals. The real-life case eventually found its way to the U.S. Supreme Court, with favorable consequences for the officer and his department. Use the CD-ROM found in your textbook to work through this scenario.

convicted, prompting another appeal to the Supreme Court based on the argument that the body should not have been used as evidence since it was discovered due to the illegally gathered statements. This time, in the 1984 case of *Nix* v. *Williams*,[160] the Supreme Court affirmed Williams's second conviction, holding that the body would have been found anyway, since detectives were searching in the direction where it lay when Williams revealed its location. This ruling came during the heyday of the Burger Court and clearly demonstrates a tilt by the Court away from suspects' rights and an acknowledgment of the imperfect world of police procedure. The *Williams* case, as it was finally resolved, is said to have created the *inevitable-discovery exception* to the *Miranda* requirements. The inevitable-discovery exception means that evidence, even if it was otherwise gathered inappropriately, can be used in a court of law if it would have invariably turned up in the normal course of events.

## Public-Safety Exception to *Miranda*

Also in 1984, the U.S. Supreme Court established what has come to be known as the *public-safety exception* to the *Miranda* rule. The case of *New York* v. *Quarles*[161] centered on a rape in which the victim told police her assailant had a gun and had fled into a nearby supermarket. Two police officers entered the store and apprehended the suspect. One officer immediately noticed that the man was wearing an empty shoulder holster and, fearing that a child might find the discarded weapon, quickly asked, "Where's the gun?" Quarles was convicted of rape but appealed his conviction, requesting that the weapon be suppressed as evidence because officers had not advised him of his *Miranda* rights before asking him about it. The Supreme Court disagreed, stating that considerations of public safety were overriding and negated the need for rights advisement prior to limited questioning that focused on the need to prevent further harm.

The U.S. Supreme Court has also held that in cases when the police issue *Miranda* warnings, a later demonstration that a person may have been suffering from mental problems does not necessarily negate a confession. *Colorado* v. *Connelly* (1986)[162] involved a man who approached a Denver police officer and said he wanted to confess to the murder of a young girl. The officer immediately informed him of his *Miranda* rights, but the man waived them and continued to talk. When a detective arrived, the man was again advised of his rights and again waived them. After being taken to the local jail, the man began to hear "voices" and later claimed that it was these voices that had made him confess. At the trial, the defense moved to have the earlier confession negated on the basis that it was not voluntarily or freely given because of the defendant's mental condition. On appeal, the U.S. Supreme Court disagreed, saying that "no coercive government conduct occurred in this case." Hence "self-coercion," due to either a guilty conscience or faulty thought processes, does not bar prosecution based on information revealed willingly by a suspect.

The 1986 case of *Kuhlmann* v. *Wilson*[163] represents another refinement of *Miranda*. In this case, the Court upheld a police informant's lawful ability to gather information for use at a trial from a defendant while the two were placed together in a jail cell. The passive gathering of information was judged to be acceptable, provided that the informant did not make attempts to elicit information.

In the case of *Illinois* v. *Perkins* (1990),[164] the Court expanded its position to say that under appropriate circumstances, even the active questioning of a suspect by an undercover officer posing as a fellow inmate does not require *Miranda* warnings. In *Perkins*, the Court found that, lacking other forms of coercion, the fact that the suspect was not aware of the questioner's identity as a law enforcement officer ensured that his statements were freely given. In the words of the Court, "The essential ingredients of a 'police-dominated atmosphere' and compulsion are not present when an incarcerated person speaks freely to someone that he believes to be a fellow inmate."

## *Miranda* and the Meaning of Interrogation

Modern interpretations of the applicability of *Miranda* warnings turn on an understanding of *interrogation*. The *Miranda* decision, as originally rendered, specifically recognized the need for police investigators to make inquiries at crime scenes to determine facts or to establish identities. As long as the individual questioned is not yet in custody and as long as probable cause is lacking in the investigator's mind, such questioning can proceed without *Miranda* warnings. In such cases, interrogation, within the meaning of *Miranda,* has not yet begun.

The case of *Rock* v. *Zimmerman* (1982)[165] provides a different sort of example—one in which a suspect willingly made statements to the police before interrogation began. The suspect had burned his own house and shot and killed a neighbor. When the fire department arrived, he began shooting again and killed the fire chief. Cornered later in a field, the defendant, gun in hand, spontaneously shouted at police, "How many people did I kill? How many people are dead?"[166] This spontaneous statement was held to be admissible evidence at the suspect's trial.

It is also important to recognize that in the *Miranda* decision, the Supreme Court required that officers provide warnings only in those situations involving *both* arrest and custodial interrogation—what some call the **Miranda triggers.** In other words, it is generally permissible for officers to take a suspect into custody and listen without asking questions while he talks. Similarly, they may ask questions without providing a *Miranda* warning, even within the confines of a police station house, as long as the person questioned is not a suspect and is not under arrest.[167] Warnings are required only when officers begin to actively and deliberately elicit responses from a suspect whom they know has been indicted or who is in custody.

Officers were found to have acted properly in the case of *South Dakota* v. *Neville* (1983)[168] when they informed a man suspected of driving while intoxicated (DWI), without reading him his rights, that he would stand to lose his driver's license if he did not submit to a Breathalyzer test. When the driver responded, "I'm too drunk. I won't pass the test," his answer became evidence of his condition and was permitted at trial.

A third-party conversation recorded by the police after a suspect has invoked the *Miranda* right to remain silent may be used as evidence, according to a 1987 ruling in *Arizona* v. *Mauro*.[169] In *Mauro,* a man who willingly conversed with his wife in the presence of a police tape recorder, even after invoking his right to keep silent, was held to have effectively abandoned that right.

When a waiver is not made, however, in-court references to a defendant's silence following the issuing of *Miranda* warnings are unconstitutional. In the 1976 case of *Doyle* v. *Ohio*,[170] the U.S. Supreme Court definitively ruled that "a suspect's [post-*Miranda*] silence will not be used against him." Even so, according to the Court in *Brecht* v. *Abrahamson* (1993),[171] prosecution efforts to use such silence against a defendant may not invalidate a finding of guilt by a jury unless the "error had substantial and injurious effect or influence in determining the jury's verdict."[172]

Of course, when a person is *not* a suspect and is *not* charged with a crime, *Miranda* warnings need not be given. Such logic led to what some have called a "fractured opinion"[173] in the 2003 case of *Chavez* v. *Martinez*.[174] The case involved Oliverio Martinez, who was blinded and paralyzed in a police shooting after he grabbed an officer's weapon during an altercation. An Oxnard, California, police officer named Chavez persisted in questioning Martinez while he was awaiting treatment despite his pleas to stop and the fact that he was obviously in great pain. The Court held that "police questioning in [the] absence of *Miranda* warnings, even questioning that is overbearing to [the] point of coercion, does not violate constitutional protections against self-incrimination, as long as no incriminating statements are introduced at trial."[175] Nonetheless, the Court found that Martinez could bring a civil suit against Chavez and the Oxnard Police Department for violation of his constitutional right to due process.

***Miranda* triggers**

The dual principles of custody and interrogation, both of which are necessary before an advisement of rights is required.

# Gathering Special Kinds of Nontestimonial Evidence

The role of law enforcement is complicated by the fact that suspects are often privy to special evidence of a nontestimonial sort. Nontestimonial evidence is generally physical evidence, and most physical evidence is subject to normal procedures of search and seizure. A special category of nontestimonial evidence, however, includes very personal items that may be within or part of a person's body, such as ingested drugs, blood cells, foreign objects, medical implants, and human DNA. Also included in this category are fingerprints and other kinds of biological residue. The gathering of such special kinds of nontestimonial evidence is a complex area rich in precedent. The Fourth Amendment guarantee that people be secure in their homes and in their persons has generally been interpreted by the courts to mean that the improper seizure of physical evidence of any kind is illegal and will result in exclusion of that evidence at trial. When very personal kinds of nontestimonial evidence are considered, however, the issue becomes more complicated.

## The Right to Privacy

Two 1985 cases, *Hayes* v. *Florida*[176] and *Winston* v. *Lee*,[177] provide examples of limits the courts have placed on the seizure of very personal forms of nontestimonial evidence. The *Hayes* case established the right of suspects to refuse to be fingerprinted when probable cause necessary to

# CJ TODAY EXHIBIT 7-3

## *Miranda* Update

On June 28, 2004, the U.S. Supreme Court handed down two important decisions—*U.S.* v. *Patane*[1] and *Missouri* v. *Seibert*[2]—in a continuing refinement of its original 1966 ruling in *Miranda* v. *Arizona.*[3]

As described elsewhere in this chapter, *Miranda* created a presumption of coercion in all custodial interrogations. Generally speaking, only a demonstration that *Miranda* warnings have been provided to a suspect has been sufficient to counter that presumption and allow legal proceedings based on the fruits of an interrogation to move forward. Consequently, some scholars were surprised by *Patane,* in which the Court found that "a mere failure to give *Miranda* warnings does not, by itself, violate a suspect's constitutional rights or even the *Miranda* rule."

The *Patane* case began with the arrest of a convicted felon after a federal agent told officers that the man owned a handgun illegally. At the time of arrest, the officers tried to advise the defendant of his rights, but he interrupted them, saying that he already knew his rights. The officers then asked him about the pistol, and he told them where it was. After the weapon was recovered, the defendant was charged with illegal possession of a firearm by a convicted felon.

At first glance, *Patane* appears to contradict the fruit of the poisoned tree doctrine established by the Court in the 1920 case of *Silverthorne Lumber Co.* v. *U.S.*[4] and made applicable by *Wong Sun* v. *U.S.* (1963)[5] to verbal evidence derived immediately from an illegal search and seizure. An understanding of *Patane,* however, requires recognition of the fact that the *Miranda* rule is based on the self-incrimination clause of the Fifth Amendment to the U.S. Constitution. According to the Court in *Patane,* "that Clause's core protection is a prohibition on compelling a criminal defendant to testify against himself at trial." It cannot be violated, the Court said, "by the introduction of nontestimonial evidence obtained as a result of voluntary statements." In other words, according to the Court, only (1) coerced statements and (2) those voluntary statements made by

a defendant that might directly incriminate him or her at a later trial are precluded by a failure to read a suspect his or her *Miranda* rights. Such voluntary statements would, of course, include such things as an outright confession.

Significantly, however, oral statements must be distinguished, the Court said, from the "physical fruits of the suspect's unwarned but voluntary statements." In other words, if an unwarned suspect is questioned by police officers and tells the officers where they can find an illegal weapon or a weapon that has been used in a crime, the weapon can be recovered and later introduced as evidence at the suspect's trial. If the same unwarned suspect, however, tells police that he committed a murder, then his confession will not be allowed into evidence at trial. The line drawn by the court is against the admissibility of *oral statements* made by an unwarned defendant, not the *nontestimonial physical evidence* resulting from continued police investigation of such statements. Under *Patane,* the oral statements themselves cannot be admitted, but the physical evidence derived from them can be. "Thus," wrote the justices in *Patane,* "admission of nontestimonial physical fruits (the pistol here) does not run the risk of admitting into trial an accused's coerced incriminating statements against himself."

The *Seibert* case addressed a far different issue: that of the legality of a two-step police interrogation technique in which suspects were questioned and—if they made incriminating statements—were then advised of their *Miranda* rights and questioned again. The justices found that such a technique could not meet constitutional muster, writing, "When the [*Miranda*] warnings are inserted in the midst of coordinated and continuing interrogation, they are likely to mislead and deprive a defendant of knowledge essential to his ability to understand the nature of his rights and the consequences of abandoning them. . . . And it would be unrealistic to treat two spates of integrated and proximately conducted questioning as independent interrogations . . . simply because *Miranda* warnings formally punctuate them in the middle.

[1]*U.S.* v. *Patane,* U.S. Supreme Court, No. 02-1183 (decided June 28, 2004).
[2]*Missouri* v. *Seibert,* U.S. Supreme Court, No. 02-1371 (decided June 28, 2004).
[3]*Miranda* v. *Arizona,* 384 U.S. 436 (1966).
[4]*Silverthorne Lumber Co.* v. *U.S.,* 251 U.S. 385 (1920).
[5]*Wong Sun* v. *U.S.,* 371 US 471 (1963).

effect an arrest does not exist. *Winston* demonstrated the inviolability of the body against surgical and other substantially invasive techniques that might be ordered by authorities against a suspect's will.

In the *Winston* case, Rudolph Lee, Jr., was found a few blocks from the scene of a robbery with a gunshot wound in his chest. The robbery had involved an exchange of gunshots by the store owner and the robber, with the owner noting that the robber had apparently been hit by a bullet. At the hospital, the store owner identified Lee as the robber. The prosecution sought to have Lee submit to surgery to remove the bullet in his chest, arguing that the bullet would provide physical evidence linking him to the crime. Lee refused the surgery, and in *Winston* v. *Lee,* the U.S. Supreme Court ruled that Lee could not be ordered to undergo surgery because such a magnitude of intrusion into his body was unacceptable under the right to privacy guaranteed by the Fourth

Amendment. The *Winston* case was based on precedent established in *Schmerber* v. *California* (1966).[178] The *Schmerber* case turned on the extraction against the defendant's will of a blood sample to be measured for alcohol content. In *Schmerber,* the Court ruled that warrants must be obtained for bodily intrusions unless fast action is necessary to prevent the destruction of evidence by natural physiological processes.

## Body-Cavity Searches

In early 2005, officers of the Suffolk County (New York) Police Department arrested 36-year-old Terrance Haynes and charged him with marijuana possession.[179] After placing him in the back of a patrol car, Haynes appeared to choke and had difficulty breathing. Soon his breathing stopped, prompting officers to use the Heimlich maneuver, which dislodged a plastic bag from Haynes's windpipe. The bag contained eleven packets of cocaine. Although Haynes survived the ordeal, he now faces up to 25 years in prison.

While some suspects might literally "cough up" evidence, some are more successful at hiding it *in* their bodies. Body-cavity searches are among the most problematic types of searches for police today. "Strip" searches of convicts in prison, including the search of body cavities, have generally been held to be permissible.

The 1985 Supreme Court case of *U.S.* v. *Montoya de Hernandez*[180] focused on the issue of "alimentary canal smuggling," in which the offender typically swallows condoms filled with cocaine or heroin and waits for nature to take its course to recover the substance. In the *Montoya* case, a woman known to be a "balloon swallower" arrived in the United States on a flight from Colombia. She was detained by customs officials and given a pat-down search by a female agent. The agent reported that the woman's abdomen was firm and suggested that X-rays be taken. The suspect refused and was given the choice of submitting to further tests or taking the next flight back to Colombia. No flight was immediately available, however, and the suspect was placed in a room for 16 hours, where she refused all food and drink. Finally, a court order for an X-ray was obtained. The procedure revealed "balloons," and the woman was detained another four days, during which time she passed numerous cocaine-filled plastic condoms. The Court ruled that the woman's confinement was not unreasonable, based as it was on the supportable suspicion that she was "body-packing" cocaine. Any discomfort she experienced, the Court ruled, "resulted solely from the method that she chose to smuggle illicit drugs."[181]

# Electronic Eavesdropping

Modern technology makes possible increasingly complex forms of communication. One of the Supreme Court decisions involving electronic communications was the 1928 case of *Olmstead* v. *U.S.*[182] In *Olmstead,* bootleggers used their home telephones to discuss and transact business. Agents tapped the lines and based their investigation and ensuing arrests on conversations they overheard. The defendants were convicted and eventually appealed to the high court, arguing that the agents had in effect seized information illegally without a search warrant in violation of the defendants' Fourth Amendment right to be secure in their homes. The Court ruled, however, that telephone lines were not an extension of the defendant's home and therefore were not protected by the constitutional guarantee of security. However, subsequent federal statutes have substantially modified the significance of *Olmstead.*

Recording devices carried on the body of an undercover agent or an informant were ruled to produce admissible evidence in *On Lee* v. *U.S.* (1952)[183] and *Lopez* v. *U.S.* (1963).[184] The 1967 case of *Berger* v. *New York*[185] permitted wiretaps and "bugs" in instances where state law provided for the use of such devices and where officers obtained a warrant based on probable cause.

The Court appeared to undertake a significant change of direction in the area of electronic eavesdropping when it decided the case of *Katz* v. *U.S.* in 1967.[186] Federal agents had monitored a number of Katz's telephone calls from a public phone using a device separate from the phone lines and attached to the glass of the phone booth. The Court, in this case, stated that a warrant is required to unveil what a person makes an effort to keep private, even in a public place. In the words of the Court, "The government's activities in electronically listening to and recording the petitioner's words violated the privacy upon which he justifiably relied while using the telephone booth and thus constituted a 'search and seizure' within the meaning of the Fourth Amendment."

Prosecutors and police perform the balancing test every day between individual rights and the right of citizens to be free of crime in their homes and neighborhoods, and they are watched over closely by our courts. For all in law enforcement, this balancing of rights is not an academic exercise, but a real test, where the consequence of being wrong is that a killer may go free, or even worse, an innocent man may be convicted.

—Cape Cod prosecutor Michael O'Keefe[ii]

How much of our freedom must we surrender in the name of preserving it?

—Letter to the editor, *The New York Times,* July 28, 2005.

In 1968, with the case of *Lee* v. *Florida,*[187] the Court applied the Federal Communications Act[188] to telephone conversations that might be the object of police investigation and held that evidence obtained without a warrant could not be used in state proceedings if it resulted from a wiretap. The only person who has the authority to permit eavesdropping, according to that act, is the sender of the message.

The Federal Communications Act, originally passed in 1934, does not specifically mention the potential interest of law enforcement agencies in monitoring communications. Title III of the Omnibus Crime Control and Safe Streets Act of 1968, however, mostly prohibits wiretaps but does allow officers to listen to electronic communications when (1) an officer is one of the parties involved in the communication, (2) one of the parties is not the officer but willingly decides to share the communication with the officer, or (3) officers obtain a warrant based on probable cause. In the 1971 case of *U.S.* v. *White,*[189] the Court held that law enforcement officers may intercept electronic information when one of the parties involved in the communication gives her consent, even without a warrant.

In 1984, the Supreme Court decided the case of *U.S.* v. *Karo,*[190] in which DEA agents had arrested James Karo for cocaine importation. Officers placed a radio transmitter inside a 50-gallon drum of ether purchased by Karo for use in processing the cocaine. The device was placed inside the drum with the consent of the seller of the ether but without a search warrant. The shipment of ether was followed to the Karo house, and Karo was arrested and convicted of cocaine-trafficking charges. Karo appealed to the U.S. Supreme Court, claiming that the radio beeper had violated his reasonable expectation of privacy inside his premises and that, without a warrant, the evidence it produced was tainted. The Court agreed and overturned his conviction.

## Minimization Requirement for Electronic Surveillance

The Supreme Court established a minimization requirement pertinent to electronic surveillance in the 1978 case of *U.S.* v. *Scott.*[191] *Minimization* means that officers must make every reasonable effort to monitor only those conversations, through the use of phone taps, body bugs, and the like, that are specifically related to the criminal activity under investigation. As soon as it becomes obvious that a conversation is innocent, then the monitoring personnel are required to cease their invasion of privacy. Problems arise if the conversation occurs in a foreign language, if it is "coded," or if it is ambiguous. It has been suggested that investigators involved in electronic surveillance maintain logbooks of their activities that specifically show monitored conversations, as well as efforts made at minimization.[192]

## The Electronic Communications Privacy Act of 1986

**Electronic Communications Privacy Act (ECPA)**

A law passed by Congress in 1986 establishing the due process requirements that law enforcement officers must meet in order to legally intercept wire communications.

Passed by Congress in 1986, the **Electronic Communications Privacy Act (ECPA)**[193] brought major changes in the requirements law enforcement officers must meet to intercept wire communications (those involving the human voice). The ECPA deals specifically with three areas of communication: (1) wiretaps and bugs, (2) pen registers, which record the numbers dialed from a telephone, and (3) tracing devices, which determine the number from which a call emanates. The act also addresses the procedures to be followed by officers in obtaining records relating to communications services, and it establishes requirements for gaining access to stored electronic communications and records of those communications. The ECPA basically requires that investigating officers must obtain wiretap-type court orders to eavesdrop on *ongoing communications*. The use of pen registers and recording devices, however, is specifically excluded by the law from court order requirements.[194]

A related measure, the Communications Assistance for Law Enforcement Act (CALEA) of 1994,[195] appropriated $500 million to modify the U.S. phone system to allow for continued wiretapping by law enforcement agencies. The law also specifies a standard-setting process for the redesign of existing equipment that would permit effective wiretapping in the face of coming technological advances. In the words of the FBI's Telecommunications Industry Liaison Unit, "This law requires telecommunications carriers, as defined in the Act, to ensure law enforcement's ability, pursuant to court order or other lawful authorization, to intercept communications notwithstanding advanced telecommunications technologies."[196] In 2003, federal and state judges approved 1,442 wiretap requests, and approximately 4.3 million conversations were intercepted by law enforcement agencies throughout the country.[197] Approximately one-third of all intercepted conversations were classified as "incriminating."

## The Telecommunications Act of 1996

Title V of the Telecommunications Act of 1996[198] made it a federal offense for anyone engaged in interstate or international communications to knowingly use a telecommunications device "to create, solicit, or initiate the transmission of any comment, request, suggestion, proposal, image, or other communication which is obscene, lewd, lascivious, filthy, or indecent, with intent to annoy, abuse, threaten, or harass another person." The law also provided special penalties for anyone who "makes a telephone call . . . without disclosing his identity and with intent to annoy, abuse, threaten, or harass any person at the called number or who receives the communication" or who "makes or causes the telephone of another repeatedly or continuously to ring, with intent to harass any person at the called number; or makes repeated telephone calls" for the purpose of harassing a person at the called number.

A section of the law, known as the Communications Decency Act (CDA),[199] criminalized the transmission to minors of "patently offensive" obscene materials over the Internet or other computer telecommunications services. Portions of the CDA, however, were invalidated by the U.S. Supreme Court in the case of *Reno* v. *ACLU* (1997).[200]

## The USA PATRIOT Act of 2001

The USA PATRIOT Act of 2001, which is also discussed in CJ Today Exhibit 7–4, made it easier for police investigators to intercept many forms of electronic communications. Under previous federal law, for example, investigators could not obtain a wiretap order to intercept *wire* communications for violations of the Computer Fraud and Abuse Act.[201] In several well-known investigations, however, hackers had stolen teleconferencing services from telephone companies and then used those services to plan and execute hacking attacks.

The act[202] added felony violations of the Computer Fraud and Abuse Act to Section 2516(1) of Title 18 of the U.S. Code—the portion of federal law that lists specific types of crimes for which investigators may obtain a wiretap order for wire communications. The change is only a temporary one, however, but faces likely renewal by Congress.

The USA PATRIOT Act also modified that portion of the ECPA that governs law enforcement access to stored electronic communications such as e-mail to include stored wire communications, such as voice mail. Before the modification, law enforcement officers needed to obtain a wiretap order rather than a search warrant to obtain unopened voice communications. Because today's e-mail messages may contain digitized voice "attachments," investigators were sometimes required to obtain both a search warrant and a wiretap order to learn the contents of a specific message. Under the act, the same rules now apply to both stored wire communications and stored electronic communications. Wiretap orders, which are often much more difficult to obtain than search warrants, are now only required to intercept real-time telephone conversations. This provision will also expire unless renewed by Congress.

Before passage of the USA PATRIOT Act, federal law allowed investigators to use an administrative subpoena (that is, a subpoena authorized by a federal or state statute or by a federal or state grand jury or trial court) to compel Internet service providers to provide a limited class of information, such as a customer's name, address, length of service, and means of payment. Also under previous law, investigators could not subpoena certain records, including credit card numbers or details about other forms of payment for Internet service. Such information, however, can be very useful in determining a suspect's true identity because, in many cases, users provide Internet service providers with false names.

Previous federal law[203] was also technology specific, relating primarily to telephone communications. Local and long-distance telephone billing records, for example, could be subpoenaed, but not billing information for Internet communications or records of Internet session times and durations. Similarly, previous law allowed the government to use a subpoena to obtain the customer's "telephone number or other subscriber number or identity" but did not define what that phrase meant in the context of Internet communications.

The USA PATRIOT Act amended portions of this federal law[204] to update and expand the types of records that law enforcement authorities may obtain with a subpoena. "Records of session times and durations," as well as "any temporarily assigned network address" may now be gathered. Such changes should make the process of identifying computer criminals and tracing their Internet communications faster and easier. Unlike some other parts of the law, this section is not slated to expire.

Log on to ResearchNavigator .com, and choose "Criminal Justice" under ContentSelect's Academic Journal Database. Enter the names of some of the parties to the cases discussed in this chapter: Escobedo, Dickerson, Bostick, Fulminante, Hodari, Miranda (without the commas) one at a time in the search box, and click "Go." Which articles from the search results page usefully add to this chapter's discussion of the legal environment of policing? Write a summary of each of those articles, including complete source information—that is, article title, author (if available), date of publication, and source. In some cases, only abstracts may be available. If that's the case, then base your written summary on the information provided in the abstract (otherwise, use the full article). Submit what you have written to your instructor if asked to do so. *Note:* This feature is available only if your instructor has chosen the Research Navigator option available with a new textbook.

**"sneak and peek" search**

A search that occurs in the suspect's absence and without his or her prior knowledge. Also known as a *delayed notification search.*

## CJ TODAY EXHIBIT 7-4

### The USA PATRIOT Act of 2001

On October 26, 2001, President George W. Bush signed into law the USA PATRIOT Act, also known as the Uniting and Strengthening America by Providing Appropriate Tools Required to Intercept and Obstruct Terrorism Act. The law, which was drafted in response to the September 11, 2001, terrorist attacks on the World Trade Center and the Pentagon, substantially increased the investigatory authority of federal, state, and local police agencies. The act permits longer jail terms for certain suspects arrested without a warrant, broadens **"sneak and peek" search** authority (searches conducted without prior notice and in the absence of the suspect), and enhances the power of prosecutors. The law also increases the ability of federal authorities to tap phones (including wireless devices), share intelligence information, track Internet usage, crack down on money laundering, and protect U.S. borders. Many of the crime-fighting powers created under the legislation are not limited to acts of terrorism but apply to many different kinds of criminal offenses. The new law has led individual-rights advocates to question whether the government unfairly expanded police powers at the expense of civil liberties.

Major provisions of the law relevant to law enforcement investigations in general are shown in this box. Some of the law's provisions will "sunset," or expire unless periodically renewed by Congress.

One Hundred Seventh Congress
of the
United States of America
AT THE FIRST SESSION
*Begun and held at the City of Washington on Wednesday, the third day of January, two thousand and one*
An Act
To deter and punish terrorist acts in the United States and around the world, to enhance law enforcement investigatory tools,
and for other purposes.
*Be it enacted by the Senate and House of Representatives of the
United States of America in Congress assembled,*

### SECTION 1. SHORT TITLE AND TABLE OF CONTENTS.
(a) SHORT TITLE—This Act may be cited as the "Uniting and Strengthening America by Providing Appropriate Tools Required to Intercept and Obstruct Terrorism (USA PATRIOT Act) Act of 2001."

### TITLE II—ENHANCED SURVEILLANCE PROCEDURES

### SEC. 203. AUTHORITY TO SHARE CRIMINAL INVESTIGATIVE INFORMATION.
(b) AUTHORITY TO SHARE ELECTRONIC, WIRE, AND ORAL INTERCEPTION INFORMATION.—
(1) LAW ENFORCEMENT.—Section 2517 of title 18, United States Code, is amended by inserting at the end the following:

"(6) Any investigative or law enforcement officer, or attorney for the Government, who by any means authorized by this chapter, has obtained knowledge of the contents of any wire, oral, or electronic communication, or evidence derived therefrom, may disclose such contents to any other Federal law enforcement, intelligence, protective, immigration, national defense, or national security official to the extent that such contents include foreign intelligence or counterintelligence (as defined in section 3 of the National Security Act of 1947 (50 U.S.C. 401a)), or foreign intelligence information (as defined in subsection 19 of section 2510 of this title), to assist the official who is to receive that information in the performance of his official duties. Any Federal official who receives information pursuant to this provision may use that information only as necessary in the conduct of that person's official duties subject to any limitations on the unauthorized disclosure of such information."

### SEC. 213. AUTHORITY FOR DELAYING NOTICE OF THE EXECUTION OF A WARRANT.
Section 3103a of title 18, United States Code, is amended—
(1) by inserting "(a) IN GENERAL.—" before "In addition"; and
(2) by adding at the end the following:
"(b) DELAY.—With respect to the issuance of any warrant or court order under this section, or any other rule of law, to search for and seize any property or material that constitutes evidence of a criminal offense in violation of the laws of the United States, any notice required, or that may be required, to be given may be delayed if—
"(1) the court finds reasonable cause to believe that providing immediate notification of the execution of the warrant may have an adverse result (as defined in section 2705);
"(2) the warrant prohibits the seizure of any tangible property, any wire or electronic communication (as defined in section 2510), or, except as expressly provided in chapter 121, any stored wire or electronic information, except where the court finds reasonable necessity for the seizure; and
"(3) the warrant provides for the giving of such notice within a reasonable period of its execution, which period may thereafter be extended by the court for good cause shown."

### What This Means
The USA PATRIOT Act amends Title 18, Section 3103, of the U.S. Code to create a uniform standard authorizing courts to delay notification if the court finds "reasonable cause" to believe that providing immediate notification of the execution of the warrant may have an "adverse result" (such as endangering the life or physical safety of an individual, flight from prosecution, evidence tampering, or witness intimidation) or might otherwise seriously jeopardize an investigation or unduly delay a trial. This section of the USA PATRIOT Act is primarily designed to authorize delayed notice of *searches* rather than delayed notice of *seizures*.

## CJ TODAY EXHIBIT 7–4 *(continued)*

### SEC. 216. MODIFICATION OF AUTHORITIES RELATING TO USE OF PEN REGISTERS AND TRAP AND TRACE DEVICES.

(b) ISSUANCE OF ORDERS.—

(1) IN GENERAL.—Section 3123(a) of title 18, United States Code, is amended to read as follows:

"(a) IN GENERAL.—

"(1) ATTORNEY FOR THE GOVERNMENT.—Upon an application made under section 3122(a)(1), the court shall enter an *ex parte* order authorizing the installation and use of a pen register or trap and trace device anywhere within the United States, if the court finds that the attorney for the Government has certified to the court that the information likely to be obtained by such installation and use is relevant to an ongoing criminal investigation."

### What This Means

Although Congress enacted a pen/trap statute in 1986 (which made possible the collection of noncontent traffic information associated with communications, such as the phone number dialed from a particular telephone), it could not anticipate the dramatic expansion in electronic communications that would occur in the next 15 years, including communications over computer networks.

Section 216 of the USA PATRIOT Act updates the pen/trap statute in three important ways: (1) The amendments clarify that law enforcement may use pen/trap orders to trace communications on the Internet and other computer networks; (2) pen/trap orders issued by federal courts now have nationwide effect; and (3) law enforcement authorities must file a special report with the court whenever they use a pen/trap order to install their own monitoring device on computers belonging to a public provider.

### SEC. 219. SINGLE-JURISDICTION SEARCH WARRANTS FOR TERRORISM.

Rule 41(a) of the Federal Rules of Criminal Procedure is amended by inserting after "executed" the following: "and (3) in an investigation of domestic terrorism or international terrorism (as defined in section 2331 of title 18, United States Code), by a Federal magistrate judge in any district in which activities related to the terrorism may have occurred, for a search of property or for a person within or outside the district."

### What This Means

Under prior law, Rule 41(a) of the Federal Rules of Criminal Procedure required that a search warrant be obtained within a district for searches within that district. The only exception was for cases in which property or a person within the district might leave the district before the warrant could be executed. The rule created what some saw as unnecessary delays and burdens in the investigation of terrorist activities and networks that spanned a number of districts, because warrants had to be obtained separately in each district. Section 219 purports to solve that problem by providing that, in domestic or international terrorism cases, a search warrant may be issued by a magistrate judge in any district in which activities related to the terrorism have occurred for a search of property or persons located within or outside of the district.

### SEC. 224. SUNSET.

(a) IN GENERAL.—Except as provided in subsection (b), this title and the amendments made by this title (other than sections 203(a), 203(c), 205, 208, 210, 211, 213, 216, 219, 221, and 222, and the amendments made by those sections) shall cease to have effect [unless renewed by Congress].

### What This Means

Only Section 203(b), as discussed in this box, is slated to expire unless renewed by Congress.

### CIVIL RIGHTS IMPLICATIONS

While many aspects of the USA PATRIOT Act have been criticized as potentially unconstitutional, Section 213, which authorizes delayed notice of the execution of a warrant, may be most vulnerable to challenge. The American Civil Liberties Union (ACLU) maintains that under this section, law enforcement agents could enter a house, apartment, or office with a search warrant while the occupant is away, search through his or her property, and take photographs without having to tell the suspect about the search until later.[1] The ACLU also believes that this provision is illegal because the Fourth Amendment to the Constitution protects against unreasonable searches and seizures and requires the government to obtain a warrant and to give notice to the person whose property will be searched before conducting the search. The notice requirement enables the suspect to assert his or her Fourth Amendment rights.

Read the entire USA PATRIOT Act of 2001 via Library Extra 7–6 at cjtoday.com. Title 18 of the U.S. Code is available at Library Extra 7–7.

**LIBRARY EXTRA**

---

*References:* U.S. Department of Justice, *Field Guidance on Authorities (Redacted) Enacted in the 2001 Anti-Terrorism Legislation* (Washington, DC: Author, no date). Web posted at http://www.epic.org/terrorism/DOJ guidance.pdf; USA PATRIOT Act, 2001 (Public Law 107-56); American Civil Liberties Union, *How the Anti-Terrorism Bill Expands Law Enforcement "Sneak and Peek" Warrants.* Web posted at http://www.aclu.org/congress/1102301b.html; and American Civil Liberties Union, *How the Anti-Terrorism Bill Limits Judicial Oversight of Telephone and Internet Surveillance.* Web posted at http://www.aclu.org/congress/1102301g.html.
[1] Much of the information in this paragraph is taken from American Civil Liberties Union, *How the Anti-Terrorism Bill Expands Law Enforcement "Sneak and Peek" Warrants.* Web posted at http://www.aclu.org/congress/1102301b.html (accessed February 12, 2005).

Finally, the USA PATRIOT Act facilitates the use of roving, or multipoint, wiretaps. Roving wiretaps, issued with court approval, target a specific individual and not a particular telephone number or communications device. Hence, law enforcement agents armed with an order for a multipoint wiretap can follow the flow of communications engaged in by a person as he switches from one cellular phone to another, or to a wired telephone. Learn more about electronic surveillance and wiretapping in criminal cases via Web Extra 7–6 at cjtoday.com.

## Gathering Electronic Evidence

The Internet, computer networks, and automated data systems present many new opportunities for committing criminal activity.[205] Computers and other electronic devices are increasingly being used to commit, enable, or support crimes perpetrated against people, organizations, and property. Whether the crime involves attacks against computer systems or the information they contain or more traditional offenses like murder, money laundering, trafficking, or fraud, **electronic evidence** is increasingly important.

Electronic evidence is "information and data of investigative value that is stored in or transmitted by an electronic device."[206] Such evidence is often acquired when physical items, such as computers, removable disks, CDs, DVDs, magnetic tape, flash memory chips, cellular telephones, personal digital assistants, and other electronic devices, are collected from a crime scene or are obtained from a suspect.

Electronic evidence has special characteristics: (1) It is latent; (2) it can transcend national and state borders quickly and easily; (3) it is fragile and can easily be altered, damaged, compromised, or destroyed by improper handling or improper examination; (4) it may be time sensitive. Like DNA or fingerprints, electronic evidence is **latent evidence** because it is not readily visible to the human eye under normal conditions. Special equipment and software are required to "see" and evaluate electronic evidence. In the courtroom, expert testimony may be needed to explain the acquisition of electronic evidence and the examination process used to interpret it.

In 2002, in recognition of the special challenges posed by electronic evidence, the Computer Crime and Intellectual Property Section of the Criminal Division of the U.S. Department of Justice released a how-to manual for law enforcement officers called *Searching and Seizing Computers and Obtaining Electronic Evidence in Criminal Investigations.*[207] The manual, which is a how-to in **digital criminal forensics**, can be accessed via Library Extra 7–8 at cjtoday.com.

About the same time, the Technical Working Group for Electronic Crime Scene Investigation (TWGECSI) released a detailed guide for law enforcement officers to use in gathering electronic evidence. The manual, *Electronic Crime Scene Investigation: A Guide for First Responders,*[208] grew out of a partnership formed in 1998 between the National Cybercrime Training Partnership, the Office of Law Enforcement Standards, and the National Institute of Justice. The working group was asked to identify, define, and establish basic criteria to assist federal and state agencies in handling electronic investigations and related prosecutions.

TWGECSI guidelines say that law enforcement must take special precautions when documenting, collecting, preserving, and examining electronic evidence to maintain its integrity. The guidelines also note that the first law enforcement officer on the scene should take steps to ensure the safety of everyone at the scene and to protect the integrity of all evidence, both traditional and electronic.

The entire TWGECSI guide, which includes many practical instructions for investigators working with electronic evidence, is available at Library Extra 7–9 at cjtoday.com.

---

**WEB EXTRA**

**electronic evidence**

Information and data of investigative value that are stored in or transmitted by an electronic device.[iii]

**latent evidence**

Evidence of relevance to a criminal investigation that is not readily seen by the unaided eye.

**LIBRARY EXTRA**

**digital criminal forensics**

The lawful seizure, acquisition, analysis, reporting, and safeguarding of data from digital devices that may contain information of evidentiary value to the trier of fact in criminal events.[iv]

**LIBRARY EXTRA**

---

## SUMMARY

This chapter describes the legal environment surrounding police activities, from the search for and seizure of evidence through the arrest and interrogation of suspects. The Constitution of the United States—especially the Bill of Rights—is designed to protect citizens against abuses of police power. It does so by guaranteeing due process of law for every suspect and by ensuring the availability of constitutional rights to all citizens, regardless of state law or procedure. Within the context of criminal case processing, due process requirements mandate that justice system officials respect the rights of accused individuals throughout the criminal justice process.

From 1953 to 1969, the U.S. Supreme Court was known as the Warren Court because it was presided over by Chief Justice Earl Warren. The Warren Court was instrumental in expanding due process requirements so that they applied to the states as well as to the federal government. The Burger Court (1969–1986), headed by Chief Justice Warren E. Burger, began a movement away from Warren-era precedents and adhered to the principle that criminal defendants who claim violations of their due process rights must bear most of the responsibility of showing that the police acted outside of the law. The trend begun by the Burger Court continues today.

1. How do the Bill of Rights and democratically inspired legal restraints on the police help ensure personal freedoms in our society?

2. What is due process? On what constitutional amendments are due process guarantees based? Can we ensure due process in our legal system without substantially increasing the risk of criminal activity?

3. What is the exclusionary rule? What is the fruit of the poisoned tree doctrine? What is their importance in American criminal justice?

4. What is arrest, and when does it occur? How do legal understandings of the term differ from popular depictions of the arrest process?

5. Under what circumstances may police officers search vehicles? What limits, if any, are there on such searches? What determines such limits?

6. What are suspicionless searches? How does the need to ensure public safety justify certain suspicionless searches?

7. List each of the *Miranda* warnings. Which recent U.S. Supreme Court cases have affected *Miranda* warning requirements?

8. What is electronic evidence? How should first-on-the-scene law enforcement personnel handle such evidence?

**WEB QUEST**

Create a list of every U.S. Supreme Court decision discussed in this chapter. Group the cases by subject (that is, vehicle searches, searches following arrest, interrogation, and so on), and list them in order by year of decision. Use the Web to collect full-text opinions from the Court for as many of these cases as you can find. Visit the Legal Information Institute at Cornell University at http://www.law.cornell.edu for some of the best Supreme Court information available anywhere. (*Hint:* A number of full-text opinions can be found on the CD in the back of this book.) Submit the materials you find to your instructor if asked to do so.

*Note:* This is a large project, and your instructor may ask you to work with just one area (such as vehicle searches) or may assign the entire project to your class, asking individual students or groups of students to be responsible for separate subjects.

To complete this Web Quest online, go to the Web Quest module in Chapter 7 of the *Criminal Justice Today* Companion Website at cjtoday.com.

**NOTES**

i. Quoted in Gene Stephens, "Policing the Future: Law Enforcement's New Challenges," *The Futurist,* March–April 2005, p. 57.

ii. Michael O'Keefe, "Sweep Can Solve Crime," *USA Today,* January 19, 2005, p. 10A.

iii. Adapted from Technical Working Group for Electronic Crime Scene Investigation, *Electronic Crime Scene Investigation: A Guide for First Responders* (Washington, DC: National Institute of Justice, 2001), p. 2.

iv. Adapted from Larry R. Leibrock, "Overview and Impact on 21st Century Legal Practice:

Digital Forensics and Electronic Discovery," no date. Web posted at http://www.courtroom21.net/FDIC.pps (accessed July 5, 2005).

1. Larry Collins and Dominique Lapierre, *The Fifth Horseman* (New York: Simon and Schuster, 1980).

2. "NYC to Pay Diallo Family $3 Million," National Public Radio, January 7, 2004. Web posted at http://www.npr.org/templates/story/story.php?storyId=1586791 (accessed April 5, 2005).

3. "Police Brutality!" *Time,* March 25, 1991, p. 18.

4. "Police Charged in Beating Case Say They Feared for Their Lives," *Boston Globe,* May 22, 1991, p. 22.

5. Ibid., pp. 16–19.

6. "Cries of Relief," *Time,* April 26, 1993, p. 18.

7. "Rodney King Slams SUV into House, Breaks Pelvis," CNN.com, April 16, 2003. Web posted at http://www.cnn.com/2003/US/West/04/15/rodney.king.ap/index.html (accessed August 5, 2005).

8. *Miranda* v. *Arizona,* 384 U.S. 436 (1966).

9. *Weeks* v. *U.S.,* 232 U.S. 383 (1914).

10. Roger Goldman and Steven Puro, "Decertification of Police: An Alternative to Traditional Remedies for Police Misconduct," *Hastings Constitutional Law Quarterly,* Vol. 15 (1988), pp. 45–80.

11. Hawaii police departments set their own training requirements. The Honolulu Police Department, for example, requires six and a half months of student officer training and another 14 weeks of postgraduation field training. See the Honolulu Police Department's website at http://www.honolulupd .org/main/index.html (accessed March 27, 2000).

12. Goldman and Puro, "Decertification of Police."

13. *Silverthorne Lumber Co.* v. *U.S.,* 251 U.S. 385 (1920).

14. Ibid.

15. Clemmens Bartollas, *American Criminal Justice* (New York: Macmillan, 1988), p. 186.

16. *Mapp* v. *Ohio,* 367 U.S. 643 (1961).

17. *Wolf* v. *Colorado,* 338 U.S. 25 (1949).

18. *Chimel* v. *California,* 395 U.S. 752 (1969).

19. *U.S.* v. *Rabinowitz,* 339 U.S. 56 (1950).

20. *Katz* v. *U.S.,* 389 U.S. 347, 88 S.Ct. 507 (1967).

21. *Minnesota* v. *Olson,* 110 S.Ct. 1684 (1990).

22. *Minnesota* v. *Carter,* 525 U.S. 83 (1998).

23. *U.S.* v. *Leon,* 468 U.S. 897, 104 S.Ct. 3405, 82 L.Ed.2d 677, 52 U.S.L.W. 5155 (1984).

24. Judicial titles among/between jurisdictions. Many lower-level state judicial officers are called *magistrates.* Federal magistrates, however, generally have a significantly higher level of judicial authority.

25. *Massachusetts* v. *Sheppard,* 104 S.Ct. 3424 (1984).

26. *Illinois* v. *Krull,* 107 S.Ct. 1160 (1987).

27. *Maryland* v. *Garrison,* 107 S.Ct. 1013 (1987).

28. *Illinois* v. *Rodriguez,* 110 S.Ct. 2793 (1990).

29. William H. Erickson, William D. Neighbors, and B. J. George, Jr., *United States Supreme Court Cases and Comments* (New York: Matthew Bender, 1987), Section 1.13[7].

30. See *California* v. *Acevedo,* 500 U.S. 565 (1991); *Ornelas* v. *U.S.,* 517 U.S. 690 (1996); and others.

31. See *Edwards* v. *Balisok,* 520 U.S. 641 (1997); *Booth* v. *Churner,* 532 U.S. 731 (2001); and *Porter* v. *Nussle,* 534 U.S. 516 (2002).

32. See *Wilson* v. *Arkansas,* 115 S.Ct. 1914 (1995); and *Richards* v. *Wisconsin,* 117 S.Ct. 1416 (1997).

33. See *McCleskey* v. *Kemp,* 481 U.S. 279, 107 S.Ct. 1756, 95 L.Ed.2d 262 (1987); *McCleskey* v. *Zant,* 499 U.S. 467, 493–494 (1991); *Coleman* v. *Thompson,* 501 U.S. 722 (1991); *Schlup* v. *Delo,* 115 S.Ct. 851, 130 L.Ed.2d 808 (1995); *Felker* v. *Turpin, Warden,* 117 S.Ct. 30, 135 L.Ed.2d 1123 (1996); *Boyde* v. *California,* 494 U.S. 370 (1990); and others.

34. See *Ewing* v. *California,* 538 U.S. 11 (2003); and *Lockyer* v. *Andrade,* 538 U.S. 63 (2003).

35. Richard Lacayo and Viveca Novak, "How Rehnquist Changed America," *Time,* June 30, 2003, pp. 20–25.

36. *Harris* v. *U.S.,* 390 U.S. 234 (1968).

37. The legality of plain-view seizures was also confirmed in earlier cases, including *Ker* v. *California,* 374 U.S. 23, 42–43 (1963); *U.S.* v. *Lee,* 274 U.S. 559 (1927); *U.S.* v. *Lefkowitz,* 285 U.S. 452, 465 (1932); and *Hester* v. *U.S.,* 265 U.S. 57 (1924).

38. As cited in Kimberly A. Kingston, "Look but Don't Touch: The Plain View Doctrine," *FBI Law Enforcement Bulletin,* December 1987, p. 18.

39. *Horton* v. *California,* 496 U.S. 128 (1990).

40. *U.S.* v. *Irizarry,* 673 F.2d 554, 556–67 (1st Cir. 1982).

41. *Arizona* v. *Hicks,* 107 S.Ct. 1149 (1987).

42. See *Criminal Justice Today,* North Carolina Justice Academy (Fall 1987), p. 24.

43. Inadvertence, as a requirement of legitimate plain-view seizures, was first cited in the U.S. Supreme Court case of *Coolidge* v. *New Hampshire,* 403 U.S. 443, 91 S.Ct. 2022 (1971).

44. *Horton* v. *California,* 496 U.S. 128 (1990).

45. Ibid.

46. John Gales Sauls, "Emergency Searches of Premises," Part 1, *FBI Law Enforcement Bulletin,* March 1987, p. 23.

47. *Warden* v. *Hayden,* 387 U.S. 294 (1967).

48. *Mincey* v. *Arizona,* 437 U.S. 385, 392 (1978).

49. Sauls, "Emergency Searches of Premises," p. 25.

50. *Maryland* v. *Buie,* 110 S.Ct. 1093 (1990).

51. *Wilson* v. *Arkansas,* 514 U.S. 927, 115 S.Ct. 1914 (1995).

52. For additional information, see Michael J. Bulzomi, "Knock and Announce: A Fourth Amendment Standard," *FBI Law Enforcement Bulletin,* May 1997, pp. 27–31.

53. *Richards* v. *Wisconsin,* 117 S.Ct. 1416 (1997), syllabus.

54. *Illinois* v. *McArthur,* 531 U.S. 326, 330 (2001).

55. *U.S.* v. *Banks,* U.S. Supreme Court, No. 02-473 (decided December 2, 2003).

56. *U.S.* v. *Mendenhall,* 446 U.S. 544 (1980).

57. A. Louis DiPietro, "Voluntary Encounters or Fourth Amendment Seizures," *FBI Law Enforcement Bulletin,* January 1992, pp. 28–32 at note 6.

58. *Stansbury* v. *California,* 114 S.Ct. 1526, 1529, 128 L.Ed.2d 293 (1994).

59. *Yarborough* v. *Alvarado,* U.S. Supreme Court, No. 02-1684 (decided June 1, 2004).

60. *Thompson* v. *Keohane,* 516 U.S. 99, 112 (1996).

61. *Atwater* v. *Lago Vista,* 532 U.S. 318 (2001).

62. In 1976, in the case of *Watson* v. *U.S.* (432 U.S. 411), the U.S. Supreme Court refused to impose a warrant requirement for felony arrests that occur in public places.

63. *Payton* v. *New York,* 445 U.S. 573, 590 (1980).

64. In 1981, in the case of *U.S.* v. *Steagald* (451 U.S. 204), the Court ruled that a search warrant is also necessary when the planned arrest involves entry into a third party's premises.

65. *Kirk* v. *Louisiana,* 122 S.Ct. 2458, 153 L.Ed.2d 599 (2002).

66. *U.S.* v. *Robinson,* 414 U.S. 218 (1973).

67. Ibid.

68. *Terry* v. *Ohio,* 392 U.S. 1 (1968).

69. *U.S.* v. *Sokolow,* 109 S.Ct. 1581 (1989).

70. The Court was quoting from *U.S.* v. *Brignoni-Ponce,* 422 U.S. 873, 878 (1975).

71. *U.S.* v. *Arvizu,* 534 U.S. 266 (2002).

72. Ibid.

73. *Minnesota* v. *Dickerson,* 113 S.Ct. 2130, 124 L.Ed.2d 334 (1993).

74. *Brown* v. *Texas,* 443 U.S. 47 (1979).

75. *Hiibel* v. *Sixth Judicial District Court of Nevada,* U.S. Supreme Court, No. 03-5554 (decided June 21, 2004).

76. *Smith* v. *Ohio,* 110 S.Ct. 1288 (1990).

77. Ibid., at 1289.

78. *California* v. *Hodari* D., 111 S.Ct. 1547 (1991).

79. *Criminal Justice Newsletter,* May 1, 1991, p. 2.

80. *Illinois* v. *Wardlow,* 528 U.S. 119 (2000).

81. Ibid., syllabus. Web posted at http://supct.law .cornell.edu/supct/html/98-1036.ZS.html (accessed April 1, 2002).

82. Ibid.

83. *Arkansas* v. *Sanders,* 442 U.S. 753 (1979).

84. Ibid.

85. *U.S.* v. *Borchardt,* 809 F.2d 1115 (5th Cir. 1987).

86. *FBI Law Enforcement Bulletin,* January 1988, p. 28.

87. *Carroll* v. *U.S.,* 267 U.S. 132 (1925).

88. *Preston* v. *U.S.,* 376 U.S. 364 (1964).

89. *South Dakota* v. *Opperman,* 428 U.S. 364 (1976).

90. *Colorado* v. *Bertine,* 479 U.S. 367, 107 S.Ct. 741 (1987).

91. *Florida* v. *Wells,* 110 S.Ct. 1632 (1990).

92. *Terry* v. *Ohio,* 392 U.S. 1 (1968).

93. *California* v. *Acevedo,* 500 U.S. 565 (1991).

94. *Ornelas* v. *U.S.* 517 U.S. 690, 696 (1996).

95. Ibid.

96. The phrase is usually attributed to the 1991 U.S. Supreme Court case of *California* v. *Acevedo* (500 U.S. 565 [1991]). See Devallis Rutledge, "Taking an Inventory," *Police,* November 1995, pp. 8–9.

97. *Florida* v. *Jimeno,* 111 S.Ct. 1801 (1991).

98. Ibid., syllabus. Web posted at http://laws .findlaw.com/us/500/248.html (accessed March 2, 2002).

99. *U.S.* v. *Ross,* 456 U.S. 798 (1982).

100. Ibid.

101. *Whren* v. *U.S.,* 517 U.S. 806 (1996).

102. See *Pennsylvania* v. *Mimms,* 434 U.S. 106 (1977).

103. *Maryland* v. *Wilson,* 117 S.Ct. 882 (1997).

104. *Knowles* v. *Iowa,* 525 U.S. 113 (1998).

105. *Wyoming* v. *Houghton,* 526 U.S. 295 (1999).

106. *Thornton* v. *United States,* U.S. Supreme Court, No. 03-5165 (decided May 24, 2004).

107. *Illinois* v. *Caballes,* U.S. Supreme Court, No. 03-923 (decided January 24, 2005).

108. *Michigan Dept. of State Police* v. *Sitz,* 110 S.Ct. 2481 (1990).

109. Ibid.

110. *U.S.* v. *Martinez-Fuerte,* 428 U.S. 543 (1976).

111. Ibid., syllabus.

112. *Indianapolis* v. *Edmond,* 531 U.S. 32 (2000). Web posted at http://supct.law.cornell.edu/ supct/html/99-1030.ZS.html (accessed April 2, 2002).

113. *Illinois* v. *Lidster,* U.S. Supreme Court, No. 02-1060 (decided January 13, 2004).

114. *U.S.* v. *Villamonte-Marquez,* 462 U.S. 579 (1983).

115. *California* v. *Carney,* 471 U.S. 386, 105 S.Ct. 2066, 85 L.Ed.2d 406, 53 U.S.L.W. 4521 (1985).

116. *U.S.* v. *Hill,* 855 F.2d 664 (10th Cir. 1988).

117. *National Treasury Employees Union* v. *Von Raab,* 489 U.S. 656 (1989).

118. *Skinner* v. *Railway Labor Executives' Association,* 489 U.S. 602 (1989).

119. *Florida* v. *Bostick,* 111 S.Ct. 2382 (1991).

120. *Bond* v. *U.S.,* 529 U.S. 334 (2000). Web posted at http://supct.law.cornell.edu/supct/ html/ 98-9349.ZS.html (accessed January 10, 2002).

121. *U.S.* v. *Drayton*, 122 S.Ct. 2105 (2002).

122. *U.S.* v. *Flores-Montano*, U.S. Supreme Court, No. 02-1794 (decided March 30, 2004).

123. *People* v. *Deutsch*, 96 C.D.O.S. 2827 (1996).

124. The thermal imager differs from infrared devices (such as night-vision goggles) in that infrared devices amplify the infrared spectrum of light, whereas thermal imagers register solely the portion of the infrared spectrum that we call *heat*.

125. *People* v. *Deutsch*, 96 C.D.O.S. 2827 (1996).

126. *Kyllo* v. *U.S.*, 533 U.S. 27 (2001).

127. Ibid.

128. *Aguilar* v. *Texas*, 378 U.S. 108 (1964).

129. *U.S.* v. *Harris*, 403 U.S. 573 (1971).

130. Ibid. at 584.

131. *Illinois* v. *Gates*, 426 U.S. 213 (1983).

132. *Alabama* v. *White*, 110 S.Ct. 2412 (1990).

133. Ibid., at 2417.

134. *Florida* v. *J.L.*, 529 U.S. 266 (2000).

135. Some of the wording in this paragraph is adapted from the *LII Bulletin*, "End of Term Wrap-Up," June 29, 2000 (e-mail bulletin of the Legal Information Institute, Cornell University School of Law).

136. *U.S. Dept. of Justice* v. *Landano*, 113 S.Ct. 2014, 124 L.Ed.2d 84 (1993).

137. Richard Willing, "Third Law First to Order Taping Murder Confessions," *USA Today*, July 18, 2003, p. 3A.

138. *South Dakota* v. *Neville*, 103 S.Ct. 916 (1983).

139. *Brown* v. *Mississippi*, 297 U.S. 278 (1936).

140. *Ashcraft* v. *Tennessee*, 322 U.S. 143 (1944).

141. *Chambers* v. *Florida*, 309 U.S. 227 (1940).

142. Ibid.

143. *Leyra* v. *Denno*, 347 U.S. 556 (1954).

144. Ibid.

145. *Arizona* v. *Fulminante*, 111 S.Ct. 1246 (1991).

146. *Chapman* v. *California*, 386 U.S. 18 (1967).

147. *State* v. *Fulminante*, No. CR-95-0160.

148. *Escobedo* v. *Illinois*, 378 U.S. 478 (1964).

149. *Edwards* v. *Arizona*, 451 U.S. 477, 101 S.Ct. 1880, 68 L.Ed.2d 378 (1981).

150. *Minnick* v. *Mississippi*, 498 U.S. 146 (1990).

151. *Arizona* v. *Roberson*, 486 U.S. 675, 108 S.Ct. 2093 (1988).

152. *Davis* v. *U.S.*, 114 S.Ct. 2350 (1994).

153. *Miranda* v. *Arizona*, 384 U.S. 436 (1966).

154. "Immigrants Get Civil Rights," *USA Today*, June 11, 1992, p. 1A.

155. *U.S.* v. *Dickerson*, 166 F.3d 667 (1999).

156. *Dickerson* v. *U.S.*, 530 U.S. 428 (2000). Web posted at http://supct.law.cornell.edu/supct/ html/99-5525.ZS.html (accessed May 10, 2002).

157. *Moran* v. *Burbine*, 475 U.S. 412, 421 (1986).

158. *Colorado* v. *Spring*, 479 U.S. 564, 107 S.Ct. 851 (1987).

159. *Brewer* v. *Williams*, 430 U.S. 387 (1977).

160. *Nix* v. *Williams*, 104 S.Ct. 2501 (1984).

161. *New York* v. *Quarles*, 104 S.Ct. 2626, 81 L.Ed.2d 550 (1984).

162. *Colorado* v. *Connelly*, 107 S.Ct. 515, 93 L.Ed.2d 473 (1986).

163. *Kuhlmann* v. *Wilson*, 477 U.S. 436 (1986).

164. *Illinois* v. *Perkins*, 495 U.S. 292 (1990).

165. *Rock* v. *Zimmerman*, 543 F.Supp. 179 (M.D. Pa. 1982).

166. Ibid.

167. See *Oregon* v. *Mathiason*, 429 U.S. 492, 97 S.Ct. 711 (1977).

168. *South Dakota* v. *Neville*, 103 S.Ct. 916 (1983).

169. *Arizona* v. *Mauro*, 107 S.Ct. 1931, 95 L.Ed.2d 458 (1987).

170. *Doyle* v. *Ohio*, 426 U.S. 610 (1976).

171. *Brecht* v. *Abrahamson*, 113 S.Ct. 1710, 123 L.Ed.2d 353 (1993).

172. Citing *Kotteakos* v. *U.S.*, 328 U.S. 750 (1946).

173. See Linda Greenhouse, "The Supreme Court: Supreme Court Roundup—Police Questioning Allowed to the Point of Coercion," *New York Times*, May 28, 2003, p. A18.

174. *Chavez* v. *Martinez*, 538 U.S. 760 (2003).

175. Ibid.

176. *Hayes* v. *Florida*, 470 U.S. 811, 105 S.Ct. 1643 (1985).

177. *Winston* v. *Lee*, 470 U.S. 753, 105 S.Ct. 1611 (1985).

178. *Schmerber* v. *California*, 384 U.S. 757 (1966).

179. "Man Coughs Up Cocaine While in Custody," *Police Magazine* online, March 4, 2005. Web posted at http://www.policemag.com/ t_newspick.cfm?rank=74703 (accessed January 4, 2006).

180. *U.S.* v. *Montoya de Hernandez*, 473 U.S. 531, 105 S.Ct. 3304 (1985).

181. Ibid.

182. *Olmstead* v. *U.S.*, 277 U.S. 438 (1928).

183. *On Lee* v. *U.S.*, 343 U.S. 747 (1952).

184. *Lopez* v. *U.S.*, 373 U.S. 427 (1963).

185. *Berger* v. *New York*, 388 U.S. 41 (1967).

186. *Katz* v. *U.S.*, 389 U.S. 347 (1967).

187. *Lee* v. *Florida*, 392 U.S. 378 (1968).

188. Federal Communications Act of 1934, 47 U.S.C. 151.

189. *U.S.* v. *White*, 401 U.S. 745 (1971).

190. *U.S.* v. *Karo*, 468 U.S. 705 (1984).

191. *U.S.* v. *Scott,* 436 U.S. 128 (1978).

192. For more information, see *FBI Law Enforcement Bulletin,* June 1987, p. 25.

193. Electronic Communications Privacy Act of 1986, Public Law 99-508.

194. For more information on the ECPA, see Robert A. Fiatal, "The Electronic Communications Privacy Act: Addressing Today's Technology," *FBI Law Enforcement Bulletin,* April 1988, pp. 24–30.

195. Communications Assistance for Law Enforcement Act of 1994, Public Law 103-414.

196. U.S. Department of Justice, Office of the Inspector General, *Implementation of the Communications Assistance for Law Enforcement Act by the Federal Bureau of Investigation* (Washington, DC: USDOJ, 2004).

197. Administrative Office of the United States Courts, *2003 Wiretap Report.* Web posted at http://www.uscourts.gov/wiretap03/contents .html (accessed January 4, 2006).

198. Telecommunications Act of 1996, Public Law 104, 110 Statute 56.

199. Title 47, U.S.C.A., Section 223(a)(1)(B)(ii) (Supp. 1997).

200. *Reno* v. *ACLU,* 117 S.Ct. 2329 (1997).

201. 18 U.S.C. §1030.

202. Section 202.

203. 18 U.S.C. §2703(c).

204. Ibid.

205. Adapted from Technical Working Group for Electronic Crime Scene Investigation, *Electronic Crime Scene Investigation: A Guide for First Responders* (Washington, DC: National Institute of Justice, 2001), from which much of the information in this section is taken.

206. Ibid., p. 2.

207. Computer Crime and Intellectual Property Section, U.S. Department of Justice, *Searching and Seizing Computers and Obtaining Electronic Evidence in Criminal Investigations* (Washington, DC: U.S. Department of Justice, 2002). Web posted at http://www.usdoj.gov/ criminal/cybercrime/s&smanual2002.htm (accessed August 4, 2003).

208. Technical Working Group, *Electronic Crime Scene Investigation,* p. 2.

# CHAPTER 8

# Policing: Issues and Challenges

## OUTLINE

- Introduction
- Police Personality and Culture
- Corruption and Integrity
- The Dangers of Police Work
- Police Use of Force
- Racial Profiling and Biased Policing
- Police Civil Liability

## LEARNING OBJECTIVES

After reading this chapter, you should be able to:

- Describe the police working personality, and relate it to police culture.
- List and describe different types of police corruption, and discuss possible methods for building police integrity.
- Explain the dangers of police work, and discuss what can be done to reduce those dangers.
- Describe the situations in which police officers are most likely to use force, and provide some guidelines for determining when too much force has been used.
- Describe racial profiling, and explain why it has become a significant issue in policing today.
- Describe the civil liability issues associated with policing, and identify common sources of civil suits against the police.

*Respect and appreciation for diversity relating to gender, race, victims, and people with special needs are central to recognizing human rights. Police agencies that understand and value diverse communities create structures and systems that reach outward, enjoining and empowering police officers and citizens to collaborate in problem-solving on issues of crime and disorder.*

—Police Executive Research Forum[1]

*The police at all times should maintain a relationship with the public that gives reality to the historic tradition that the police are the public and that the public are the police.*

—Sir Robert Peel, 1829[2]

## KEY CONCEPTS

### TERMS

| | | |
|---|---|---|
| 1983 lawsuit | excessive force | police use of force |
| biological weapon | internal affairs | police working personality |
| *Bivens* action | Knapp Commission | problem police officer |
| civil liability | less-lethal weapon | racial profiling |
| deadly force | police corruption | |

### CASES

| | | |
|---|---|---|
| *Biscoe* v. *Arlington County* | *Graham* v. *Connor* | *Malley* v. *Briggs* |
| *Bivens* v. *Six Unknown Federal Agents* | *Hunter* v. *Bryant* | *Tennessee* v. *Garner* |
| *City of Canton, Ohio* v. *Harris* | *Idaho* v. *Horiuchi* | |

The original full-text court opinion for each of these cases is available on the CD-ROM that accompanies this book.

# Introduction

Hear the author discuss
this chapter at
**cjtoday.com**

Today's police officers and administrators face many complex issues. Some concerns, such as corruption, on-the-job dangers, and the use of deadly force, derive from the very nature of police work. Others, like racial profiling and exposure to civil liability, have arisen due to common practices, characteristic police values, public expectations, legislative action, and ongoing societal change. Certainly one of the most significant challenges facing American law enforcement today is policing a multicultural society. All of these issues are discussed in the pages that follow. We begin, however, with the police recruit socialization process. It is vital to understand this process because the values and expectations learned through it not only contribute to the nature of many important police issues but also determine how the police view and respond to those issues.

# Police Personality and Culture

New police officers learn what is considered appropriate police behavior by working with seasoned veterans. Through conversations with other officers in the locker room, in a squad car, or over a cup of coffee, a new recruit is introduced to the value-laden subculture of police work. A definition of *police subculture* was given in Chapter 6. It can also be understood as "the set of informal values which characterize the police force as a distinct community with a common identity."[3] This process of informal socialization plays a much bigger role than formal police academy training in determining how rookies come to see police work. Through it, new officers gain a shared view of the world that can best be described as "streetwise." Streetwise cops know what official department policy is, but they also know the most efficient way to get a job done. By the time rookie officers become streetwise, they know which of the various informal means of accomplishing the job are acceptable to other officers. The police subculture creates few real mavericks, but it also produces few officers who view their jobs exclusively in terms of public mandates and official dictums.

In the 1960s, renowned criminologist Jerome Skolnick described what he called the **police working personality** of police officers.[4] He asserted that this personality has at least six recognizable characteristics. Additional writers have identified others.[5] Taken in concert, they create the picture of the police personality shown in Table 8–1.

Some characteristics of the police working personality are essential for survival and effectiveness. For example, because officers are often exposed to highly emotional and potentially threatening confrontations with belligerent people, they must develop *efficient, authoritarian* strategies for gaining control over others. Similarly, a suspicious nature makes for a good police officer, especially during interrogations and investigations.

However, other characteristics of the police working personality are not so advantageous. For example, many officers are cynical and some can be hostile toward members of the public who

**police working
personality**

All aspects of the traditional values and patterns of behavior evidenced by police officers who have been effectively socialized into the police subculture. Characteristics of the police personality often extend to the personal lives of law enforcement personnel.

| THE POLICE PERSONALITY | | |
|---|---|---|
| Authoritarian | Honorable | Loyal |
| Conservative | Hostile | Prejudiced |
| Cynical | Individualistic | Secret |
| Dogmatic | Insecure | Suspicious |
| Efficient | | |

TABLE 8–1

may not share their conservative values. These traits result from regular interaction with suspects, most of whom, even when they are clearly guilty in the eyes of the police, deny any wrongdoing. Eventually, personal traits that result from typical police work become firmly ingrained, setting the cornerstone of the police working personality.

There are at least two sources of the police personality. On the one hand, it may be that components of the police personality already exist in some individuals and draw them toward police work.[6] Supporting this view are studies that indicate that police officers who come from conservative backgrounds view themselves as defenders of middle-class morality.[7] On the other hand, some aspects of the police personality can be attributed to the socialization into the police subculture that rookie officers experience when they are inducted into police ranks.

Researchers have reported similar elements in police subculture throughout the United States. They have concluded that like all cultures, police subculture is a relatively stable collection of beliefs and values that is unlikely to change from within. Police subculture may, however, be changed through external pressures, such as new hiring practices, investigations into police corruption or misuse of authority, and commission reports that create pressures for police reform. Learn more about police subculture and police behavior at Web Extra 8–1 at cjtoday.com.

WEB EXTRA

# Corruption and Integrity

Although most police officers perform their duties responsibly, some do not. In 2004, for example, former Maryland State Police Superintendent Edward T. Norris, 43, pleaded guilty to federal felony charges of tax evasion and corruption.[8] Norris, who had also served as police

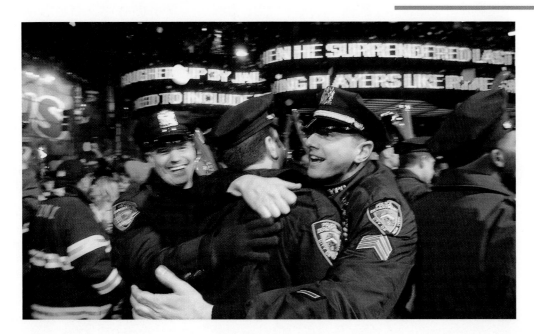

New York City police officers celebrate after the completion of a training ceremony. The police working personality has been characterized as authoritarian, suspicious, and conservative. Much of that personality is formed through informal socialization like this.

*AP Wide World Photos*

## MULTICULTURALISM AND DIVERSITY

### Policing a Multicultural Society

Members of some social groups have backgrounds, values, and perspectives that, while not directly supportive of law breaking, contrast sharply with those of many police officials. Robert M. Shusta, a well-known writer on multicultural law enforcement, says that police officers "need to recognize the fact of poor police—minority relations historically, including *unequal* treatment under the law."[1] Moreover, says Shusta, "many officers and citizens are defensive with each other because their contact is tinged with negative historical 'baggage.'"

In other words, even though discrimination in the enforcement of the criminal law may not be commonplace today, it *was* in the past—and perceptions built on past experience are often difficult to change. Moreover, if the function of law enforcement is to "protect and serve" law-abiding citizens from all backgrounds, then it becomes vital for officers to understand and respect differences in habits, customs, beliefs, patterns of thought, and traditions.[2] Hence, as Shusta says, "the acts of approaching, communicating, questioning, assisting, and establishing trust with members of different groups require special knowledge and skills that have nothing to do with the fact that 'the law is the law' and must be enforced equally. Acquiring sensitivity, knowledge, and skills leads to [an increased appreciation for the position of others] that will contribute to improved communications with members of all groups."[3]

How can police officers acquire greater sensitivity to the issues involved in policing a diverse multicultural society? Some researchers suggest that law enforcement officers of *all* backgrounds begin by exploring their own prejudices. Prejudices, which are judgments or opinions formed before facts are known and which usually involve negative or unfavorable thoughts about groups of people, can lead to discrimination. Most peo-ple, including police officers, are able to reduce their tendency to discriminate against those who are different by exploring and uprooting their own personal prejudices.

One technique for identifying prejudices is cultural awareness training. As practiced in some police departments today, cultural awareness training explores the impact of culture on human behavior—and especially law-breaking behavior. Cultural awareness training generally involves four stages[4]:

- *Clarifying the relationship between cultural awareness and police professionalism.* As Shusta explains it, "The more professional a police officer is, the more sophisticated he or she is in responding to people of all backgrounds and the more successful he or she is in cross-cultural contact."[5]
- *Recognizing personal prejudices.* In the second stage of cultural awareness training, participating officers are asked to recognize and identify their own personal prejudices and biases. Once prejudices have been identified, trainers strive to show how they can affect daily behavior.
- *Acquiring sensitivity to police–community relations.* In this stage of training, participating officers learn about historical and existing community perceptions of the police. Training can often be enhanced through the use of carefully chosen and well-qualified guest speakers or participants from minority communities.
- *Developing interpersonal relations skills.* The goal of this last stage of training is to assist with the development of the positive verbal and nonverbal communications skills necessary for successful interaction with community members. Many trainers believe that basic skills training will result in the continuing development of such skills because officers will quickly begin to see the benefits (in terms of lessened interpersonal conflict) of effective interpersonal skills.

[1]Robert M. Shusta et al., *Multicultural Law Enforcement: Strategies for Peacekeeping in a Diverse Society,* 2nd ed. (Upper Saddle River, NJ: Prentice Hall, 2002), p. 4.
[2]Ibid., p. 16.
[3]Ibid., p. 4.
[4]Ibid., pp. 104–106.
[5]Ibid., p. 4.

> Good cops always seem to be able to identify causes of problems and to come up with the least troublesome ways of solving them.
>
> —Jerome Skolnick

commissioner in Baltimore before taking the head job at the state police, admitted to conspiring to misuse money from a supplemental city police fund and lying about his taxes. Court records show that Norris used the money to pay for extramarital affairs with several women while disguising the expenditures as legitimate business expenses. Prosecutors said that Norris sometimes sent officers under his command to scout hotels for video cameras and other security devices that might record their boss's visit to the women's rooms.

The kind of corruption seen in Norris's case pales alongside that of two retired New York City police detectives arrested in 2005 and charged with having led double lives as Mafia hitmen.[9] Federal prosecutors allege that retired police investigator Louis Eppolito, 56, and his former partner, Stephen Caracappa, 63, gave confidential information to mob leaders and kidnapped and killed rival gangsters. As this book goes to press, each has been charged with eight murders, two attempted murders, murder conspiracy, drug distribution, money laundering, and obstruction of justice. The men are said to have worked for organized crime for more than a decade, and to have killed in retaliation for an assassination attempt on the life of Luchese family underboss Anthony

"Gaspipe" Casso. Caracappa was known for helping to create the New York Police Department's Organized Crime Homicide Unit and has been described as "a gatekeeper of information about Mafia killings investigated by police."

**Police corruption** has been a problem in American society since the early days of policing. The combination of power, authority, and discretion in police work produces great potential for abuse. In today's society, the personal and financial benefits of having the police "on your side" are greater than ever. Police officers face temptations that range from a small restaurant owner's offer of a free cup of coffee in exchange for the officer's future goodwill, perhaps for something as simple as a traffic ticket, to a drug dealer's huge monetary bribe to guarantee that the officer will look the other way when a shipment of cocaine arrives. As noted criminologist Carl B. Klockars says, policing, by its very nature, "is an occupation that is rife with opportunities for misconduct. Policing is a highly discretionary, coercive activity that routinely takes place in private settings, out of the sight of supervisors, and in the presence of witnesses who are often regarded as unreliable."[10]

The effects of police corruption are far-reaching. As Michael Palmiotto of Wichita State University notes, "Not only does misconduct committed by an officer personally affect that officer, it also affects the community, the police department that employs the officer and every police department and police officer in America. Frequently, negative police actions caused by inappropriate police behavior reach every corner of the nation, and at times, the world."[11]

Exactly what constitutes corruption is not always clear. Ethicists say that police corruption ranges from minor offenses to serious violations of the law. In recognition of what some have called corruption's "slippery slope,"[12] most police departments now explicitly prohibit officers from accepting even minor gratuities in the belief that their acceptance can lead an officer to more readily take larger bribes.

Thomas Barker and David Carter, who have studied police corruption in depth, make the distinction between "occupational deviance," which is motivated by the desire for personal benefit, and "abuse of authority, which occurs most often to further the organizational goals of law enforcement, including arrest, ticketing, and the successful conviction of suspects."[13]

FBI Special Agent Frank Perry, former chief of the bureau's ethics unit, distinguishes between police deviance and police corruption. Police deviance, according to Perry, consists of "unprofessional on- and off-duty misconduct, isolated instances of misuse of position, improper relationships with informants or criminals, sexual harassment, disparaging racial or sexual comments, embellished/falsified reporting, time and attendance abuse, insubordination, nepotism, cronyism, and noncriminal unauthorized disclosure of information."[14] Deviance, says Perry, is a precursor to individual and organizational corruption. Unless police supervisors and internal affairs units are alert to it, deviance can lead to corruption.

**police corruption**

The abuse of police authority for personal or organizational gain.[i]

Nearly all men can stand adversity, but if you want to test a man's character, give him power.

—Abraham Lincoln

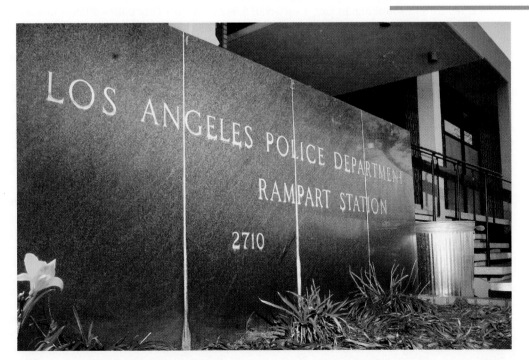

The Los Angeles Police Department's Rampart Station office, where a corruption scandal occurred in 2000 and 2001. A number of officers assigned to the Rampart Division were investigated on charges ranging from falsifying evidence to the theft and sale of illegal drugs. In what some have called "the biggest police scandal case in Los Angeles history," many criminal cases had to be dismissed.

*David McNew, Liaison, Getty Images, Inc.*

**FIGURE 8–1**

Types and examples
of police corruption.

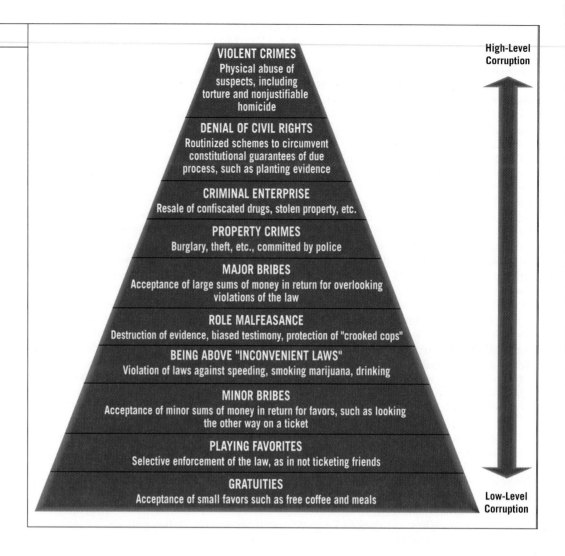

VIOLENT CRIMES
Physical abuse of
suspects, including
torture and nonjustifiable
homicide

DENIAL OF CIVIL RIGHTS
Routinized schemes to circumvent
constitutional guarantees of due
process, such as planting evidence

CRIMINAL ENTERPRISE
Resale of confiscated drugs, stolen property, etc.

PROPERTY CRIMES
Burglary, theft, etc., committed by police

MAJOR BRIBES
Acceptance of large sums of money in return for overlooking
violations of the law

ROLE MALFEASANCE
Destruction of evidence, biased testimony, protection of "crooked cops"

BEING ABOVE "INCONVENIENT LAWS"
Violation of laws against speeding, smoking marijuana, drinking

MINOR BRIBES
Acceptance of minor sums of money in return for favors, such as looking
the other way on a ticket

PLAYING FAVORITES
Selective enforcement of the law, as in not ticketing friends

GRATUITIES
Acceptance of small favors such as free coffee and meals

High-Level
Corruption

Low-Level
Corruption

Figure 8–1 sorts examples of police corruption in levels of seriousness, though not everyone would agree with this ranking. In fact, a survey of 6,982 New York City police officers found that 65% did not classify excessive force, which we define later in this chapter, as a corrupt behavior.[15] Likewise, 71% of responding officers said that accepting a free meal is not a corrupt practice. Another 15% said that personal use of illegal drugs by law enforcement officers should not be considered corruption.

In the early 1970s, Frank Serpico made headlines when he testified before the **Knapp Commission** on police corruption in New York City.[16] Serpico, an undercover operative within the police department, revealed a complex web of corruption in which money and services routinely changed hands in "protection rackets" created by unethical officers. The authors of the Knapp Commission report distinguished between two types of corrupt officers, which they termed "grass eaters" and "meat eaters."[17] "Grass eating," the more common form of police corruption, was described as illegitimate activity that occurs from time to time in the normal course of police work. It involves mostly small bribes or relatively minor services offered by citizens seeking to avoid arrest and prosecution. "Meat eating" is a much more serious form of corruption, involving an officer's actively seeking illicit moneymaking opportunities. Meat eaters solicit bribes through threat or intimidation, whereas grass eaters commit the less serious offense of failing to refuse bribes that are offered.

In 1993, during 11 days of corruption hearings reminiscent of the Knapp Commission era, a parade of crooked New York police officers testified before a commission headed by former judge and Deputy Mayor Milton Mollen. Among the many revelations, officers spoke of dealing drugs, stealing confiscated drug funds, stifling investigations, and beating innocent people. Officer Michael Dowd, for example, told the commission that he had run a cocaine ring out of his station house in Brooklyn and had bought three homes on Long Island and a Corvette with the money he made. Most shocking of all, however, were allegations that high-level police officials attempted

**Knapp Commission**

A committee that investigated police corruption in New York City in the early 1970s.

to cover up embarrassing incidents and that many officials may have condoned unprofessional and even criminal practices by the officers under their command. Honest officers, including internal affairs investigators, described how higher authorities had resisted their efforts to end corruption among their colleagues.

Repercussions from the Mollen Commission hearings continue to be felt. In 2004, for example, a New York State judge ruled that the city of New York must pay special disability benefits to former police officer Jeffrey W. Baird, who served as an informer for the commission. Baird helped uncover corruption while working as an internal affairs officer but suffered from posttraumatic stress disorder after fellow officers threatened him, vandalized his work area, and sent obscene materials to his home.[18]

Corruption in the Los Angeles Police Department's (LAPD) Rampart Division was slated to be fictionalized in a planned Franchise Pictures 2005 movie, *Rampart Scandal*.[19] The movie, starring Sylvester Stallone as an LAPD detective, suggests that rappers Biggie Smalls (aka Notorious B.I.G.) and Tupac Shakur were killed as part of a conspiracy involving the police, gang members, and officials from the music industry. The true Rampart scandal, although it involved widespread and significant police corruption, was a somewhat more mundane affair. The scandal began in mid-2000, when the LAPD became embroiled in accusations of corruption that centered on the Rampart Division's antigang unit, known as CRASH (Community Resources Against Street Hoodlums).[20] Many of the unit's officers were accused of operating like a criminal organization to frame hundreds of people through threats and beatings, by planting evidence, and by committing perjury. They and other officers were alleged to be running a drug ring, while eliminating competition from civilian dealers by framing them and seeing them sent to prison.[21] Seven shootings and at least two killings, said to be perpetrated by police officers, were among the illegal activities allegedly committed by officers. The scandal came to light after LAPD officer Rafael Perez was caught stealing $1 million worth of cocaine from an evidence room. In exchange for an offer of leniency, Perez turned informant and cooperated with prosecutors. Perez, who was also accused of murder by a former girlfriend, provided investigators with details about ongoing corruption in the Rampart area.[22] As events unfolded, prosecutors accused LAPD Chief Bernard Parks of withholding critical information needed to build a case against the accused officers. According to prosecutors, the LAPD, under the direction of Chief Parks, "failed to provide arrest reports, witness statements and background information." The prosecutors claimed that "on several occasions, the LAPD ... actually hindered the progress of the investigation."[23] Parks was replaced as chief by William J. Bratton in 2002.

By 2005, more than 100 falsely obtained convictions had been thrown out, and 20 LAPD officers had left active duty.[24] Another seven officers were convicted of conspiring to frame innocent people, but a judge overturned three of the convictions on procedural grounds. The remaining four officers received sentences of up to five years in prison.[25] The Los Angeles City Attorney agreed to pay a total of $70.2 million to settle approximately 214 lawsuits stemming from the corruption scandal. At the time of the settlement, the *Los Angeles Times* complained that much of the money, averaging $400,000 per settlement, went to "drug dealers, gang members and other criminals who said they had been framed, shot, beaten or otherwise mistreated by police."[26] The largest settlement, $15 million, went to former gang member Javier Francisco Ovando who had been paralyzed by a police shooting. In responding to critics, Cindy Miscikowski, chairwoman of Los Angeles city council's Public Safety Committee, pointed out that "regardless of who the plaintiffs were, there was evidence of wrongdoing. That's what we had to recognize. . . . Civil rights are civil rights," Miscikowski said, "and they apply to everyone across the board."[27]

The LAPD is now operating under a consent decree, a legally binding agreement with the U.S. Department of Justice that calls for major reforms. The decree requires the department to install a computer system to track complaints and disciplinary actions against LAPD officers; to collect data on the racial makeup of citizens stopped for traffic violations; and to create a special unit within the department to investigate shootings and beatings by police officers to determine whether excessive force was used.[28] Rafael Perez, sentenced to five years in prison, warned young officers as he was sentenced that "whoever chases monsters must see that he not become a monster himself."[29] Continuing criminal and civil trials and other repercussions from the Rampart scandal are expected to last for years. Learn more about the Rampart scandal at Web Extra 8–2 at cjtoday.com.

## Money—The Root of Police Evil?

Years ago, Edwin Sutherland applied the concept of *differential association* (discussed in Chapter 3) to the study of deviant behavior.[30] Sutherland suggested that frequent, continued association of one person with another makes the associates similar. Of course, Sutherland was talking about criminals, not police officers. Consider, however, the dilemma of average officers: Their job

Log on to ReseachNavigator.com, and choose "Criminal Justice" under ContentSelect's Academic Journal Database. Enter the phrase "police culture" (with the quotation marks to indicate that you wish to search for a phrase) in the search box, and click "Go." Which articles from the search results page usefully add to this chapter's discussion of police personality and culture? Write a summary of each of those articles, including complete source information—that is, article title, author (if available), date of publication, and source. In some cases, only abstracts may be available. If that's the case, then base your written summary on the information provided in the abstract (otherwise, use the full article). Submit what you have written to your instructor if asked to do so.

*Note:* This feature is available only if your instructor has chosen the Research Navigator option available with a new textbook.

If you can't apply the rule of law to police, who does it apply to?

—Former U.S. Attorney General Ramsey Clark[ii]

Iowa Governor Tom Vilsack presents Governor's Awards of Valor to Mills County deputy Eugene Goos (left) and Glenwood police officer Gary Chambers (center) at the Statehouse in Des Moines, Iowa, in 2002. The officers were given the award for their arrest of an armed gunman in a Glenwood shooting. The appropriate and timely recognition of outstanding and professional police activity can go a long way toward building police integrity and offsetting possible temptations for individual officers to engage in inappropriate behavior.

*AP Wide World Photos*

entails issuing traffic citations to citizens who try to talk their way out of a ticket, dealing with prostitutes who feel hassled by police, and arresting drug users who think it should be their right to do what they want as long as "it doesn't hurt anyone." Officers regularly encounter personal hostility and experience consistent and often quite vocal rejection of society's formalized norms. They receive relatively low pay, which indicates to them that their work is not really valued. By looking at the combination of these factors, it is easy to understand how officers often develop a jaded attitude toward the society they are sworn to protect.

Police officers' low pay may be a critical ingredient of the corruption mix. Salaries paid to police officers in this country have been notoriously low compared to that of other professions that require personal dedication, extensive training, high stress, and the risk of bodily harm. As police work becomes more professional, many police administrators hope that salaries will rise. However, no matter how much police pay increases, it will never be able to compete with the staggering amounts of money to be made through dealing in contraband. Unenforceable laws provide the basis for criminal profit. During Prohibition, the Wickersham Commission warned of the potential for official corruption inherent in the legislative taboos on alcohol. The immense demand for drink called into question the wisdom of the law while simultaneously providing vast resources designed to circumvent it. Today's drug scene bears similarities to the Prohibition era. As long as there is a market for illegal drugs, the financial as well as societal pressures on the police to profit from the drug trade will remain substantial.

## Building Police Integrity

The difficulties of controlling corruption can be traced to several factors, including the reluctance of police officers to report corrupt activities by their fellow officers, the reluctance of police administrators to acknowledge the existence of corruption in their agencies, the benefits of corrupt transactions to the parties involved, and the lack of immediate victims willing to report corruption. However, high moral standards embedded in the principles of the police profession and effectively communicated to individual officers through formal training and peer-group socialization can raise the level of integrity in any department. Some law enforcement training programs are increasingly determined to reinforce the high ideals many recruits bring to police work and to encourage veteran officers to retain their commitment to the highest professional standards. As one Federal Bureau of Investigation (FBI) publication explains it, "Ethics training must become an integral part of academy and in-service training for new and experienced officers alike."[31]

Ethics training, which was discussed in Chapter 6, is part of a "reframing" strategy that emphasizes integrity to target police corruption. In 1997, for example, the National Institute of Justice (NIJ) released a report entitled *Police Integrity: Public Service with Honor.*[32] The report, based

**Nothing's so sacred as honor.**

—Inscription on Wyatt Earp's headstone

## ETHICS AND PROFESSIONALISM

### The Law Enforcement Oath of Honor

**LAW ENFORCEMENT OATH OF HONOR**

On my honor, I will never
Betray my badge, my integrity,
My character or the public trust.
I will always have the courage to hold
Myself and others accountable for our actions.
I will always uphold the Constitution,
My community, and the agency I serve.

*Honor* means that one's word is given as a guarantee.
*Betray* is defined as breaking faith with the public trust.
*Badge* is the symbol of your office.
*Integrity* is being the same person in both private and public life.

*Character* means the qualities that distinguish an individual.
*Public trust* is a charge of duty imposed in faith toward those you serve.
*Courage* is having the strength to withstand unethical pressure, fear or danger.
*Accountability* means that you are answerable and responsible to your oath of office.
*Community* is the jurisdiction and citizens served.

**THINKING ABOUT ETHICS**

1. How is the Law Enforcement Oath of Honor similar to the Law Enforcement Code of Ethics found in Chapter 6? How does it differ? How do the two support one another?

*Source:* Adopted at the 107th International Association of Chiefs of Police Annual Conference, November 15, 2000. Reprinted with permission.

---

on recommendations made by participants in a national symposium on police integrity, suggested (1) integrating ethics training into the programs offered by newly funded Regional Community Policing Institutes throughout the country, (2) broadening research activities in the area of ethics through NIJ-awarded grants for research on police integrity, and (3) conducting case studies of departments that have an excellent track record in the area of police integrity.

The NIJ report was followed in 2001 by a U.S. Department of Justice document entitled *Principles for Promoting Police Integrity.*[33] The foreword to that document states, "For . . . policing to be successful, and crime reduction efforts to be effective, citizens must have trust in the police. All of us must work together to address the problems of excessive use of force and racial profiling, and—equally important—the perceptions of many minority residents that law enforcement treats them unfairly, if we are to build the confidence in law enforcement necessary for continued progress. Our goal must be professional law enforcement that gives all citizens of our country the feeling that they are being treated fairly, equally and with respect." The report covered such topics as the use of force; complaints and misconduct investigations; accountability and effective management; training; nondiscriminatory policing; and recruitment, hiring, and retention. Read the full report, which provides examples of promising police practices and policies that promote integrity, at Library Extra 8–1 at cjtoday.com.

In 2000, the International Association of Chiefs of Police (IACP), in an effort to reinforce the importance of ethical standards in policing, adopted the Law Enforcement Oath of Honor, shown in an Ethics and Professionalism box in this chapter. The IACP suggests that the Law Enforcement Oath of Honor should be seen by individual officers as a statement of commitment to ethical behavior. It is meant to reinforce the principles embodied in the Law Enforcement Code of Ethics, which is printed in an Ethics and Professionalism box in Chapter 6.

Most large city law enforcement agencies have their own **internal affairs** divisions, which are empowered to investigate charges of wrongdoing made against officers. Where necessary, state police agencies may be called on to examine reported incidents. Federal agencies, including the FBI and the Drug Enforcement Administration (DEA), get involved when corruption violates federal statutes. The U.S. Department of Justice (DOJ), through various investigative offices, has the authority to examine possible violations of civil rights resulting from the misuse of police authority. The DOJ is often supported in these endeavors by the American Civil Liberties Union (ACLU), the National Association for the Advancement of Colored People (NAACP), and other watchdog groups.

> To introduce and implement new police ideas is not easy, but it is possible. More than that, it is essential if we are to achieve elementary public safety in American cities and confidence in the police by those who are being policed.
>
> —Jerome H. Skolnick and David H. Bayley[iii]

LIBRARY EXTRA

**internal affairs**

The branch of a police organization tasked with investigating charges of wrongdoing involving members of the department.

## Drug Testing of Police Employees

On November 17, 2000, the U.S. Court of Appeals for the Fourth Circuit found that the chief of police in Westminster, Maryland, had acted properly in asking a doctor to test an officer's urine for the presence of heroin without the officer's knowledge.[34] Westminster police officer Eric Carroll had gone to the local hospital complaining of tightness in his chest and fatigue. The doctor who examined Carroll diagnosed him as suffering from high blood pressure. Carroll was placed on disability leave for three days. While Carroll was gone, the police chief received a call from someone who said that the officer was using heroin. The chief verified the caller's identity and then called the department doctor and asked him to test Carroll for drugs—but directed that the officer not be informed of the test. When Carroll returned to the physician for a follow-up visit, the doctor took a urine sample, saying that it was to test for the presence of blood. Although no blood was found in Carroll's urine, it did test positive for heroin. As a consequence, Officer Carroll's employment with the department was terminated. He then sued in federal court, alleging conspiracy, defamation, and violations of his constitutional rights. The Fourth Circuit Court of Appeals, however, determined that the chief's actions were reasonable because, among other things, Carroll had signed a preemployment waiver that permitted the department to conduct drug tests at any time, with or without cause.[35]

The widespread potential for police corruption created by illicit drugs has led to focused efforts to combat drug use by officers. Drug-testing programs in local police departments are an example of such efforts. The IACP has developed a model drug-testing policy for police managers. The policy, designed to meet the needs of local departments, suggests the following[36]:

- Testing all applicants and recruits for drug or narcotics use
- Testing current employees when performance difficulties or documentation indicates a potential drug problem
- Testing current employees when they are involved in the use of excessive force or when they suffer or cause on-duty injury
- Routine testing of all employees assigned to special "high-risk" areas, such as narcotics and vice

The courts have supported drug testing based on a reasonable suspicion that drug abuse has been or is occurring (*Maurice Turner* v. *Fraternal Order of Police,* 1985),[37] although random testing of officers was banned by the New York State Supreme Court in the case of *Philip Caruso, President of P.B.A.* v. *Benjamin Ward, Police Commissioner* (1986).[38] Citing overriding public interests, a 1989 decision by the U.S. Supreme Court upheld the testing of U.S. Customs personnel applying for transfer into drug-law enforcement positions or into those positions requiring a firearm.[39] Many legal issues surrounding employee drug testing remain to be resolved in court, however.

Complicating this issue is the fact that drug and alcohol addictions are "handicaps" protected by the Federal Rehabilitation Act of 1973. As such, federal law enforcement employees, as well as those working for agencies with federal contracts, are entitled to counseling and treatment before action can be taken toward termination.

Employee drug testing in police departments, as in many other agencies, is a sensitive subject. Some claim that existing tests for drug use are inaccurate, yielding a significant number of "false positives." Repeated testing and high threshold levels for narcotic substances in the blood may eliminate many of these concerns. Less easy to address, however, is the belief that drug testing intrudes on the personal rights and professional dignity of individual employees. Learn more about employee drug-testing policies in police departments at Web Extra 8–3 at cjtoday.com, and discover more about corruption and the continuing drive toward police integrity with Library Extras 8–2 and 8–3.

WEB EXTRA

LIBRARY EXTRA

# The Dangers of Police Work

On October 15, 1991, the National Law Enforcement Officers' Memorial was unveiled in Washington, D.C. The memorial contained the names of 12,561 law enforcement officers killed in the line of duty, including U.S. Marshals Service Officer Robert Forsyth, who in 1794 was the nation's first law enforcement officer killed. More than 4,100 names have been added since opening day.[40] At the memorial, an interactive video system provides visitors with brief biographies and photographs of officers who have died. Tour the memorial by visiting Web Extra 8–4 at cjtoday.com.

As the memorial proves, police work is, by its very nature, dangerous. Although many officers never once fire their weapons in the line of duty, many die while performing their jobs. On-the-job police deaths occur from stress, training accidents, and auto crashes. However, it is violent death at the hands of criminal offenders that police officers and their families fear most.

Pallbearers carry a flag-draped casket to a waiting hearse and past a second flag-draped casket following a memorial service for Detroit police officers Jennifer Fettig and Matthew Bowens at Greater Grace Temple in Detroit on February 20, 2004. Fettig, 26, and Bowens, 21, were killed during an early-morning traffic stop. Police officers risk their lives in the performance of their duties, and even what appear to be routine incidents can sometimes disguise mortal threats.

*AP Wide World Photos*

## Violence in the Line of Duty

In February 2004, two Detroit police officers were shot dead during what initially seemed like a routine traffic stop.[41] After returning to their cruiser, Officers Jennifer Fettig, 26, and Matthew Bowens, 21, were killed about 2 A.M. by the motorist, who got out of his pickup truck and fired at the officers as they sat in their police cruiser. Investigators found the shooter's driver's license in the police car and arrested 23-year-old Eric Marshall, who was charged with two counts of first-degree murder, two counts of felony murder, and one count of felonious use of a firearm. Convicted of double first-degree murder in 2005, Marshall was sentenced to life in prison without parole.[42] As was the case with Officers Fettig and Bowens, most officers who are shot are killed by lone suspects armed with a single weapon.

In 2004, 154 American law enforcement officers were killed in the line of duty.[43] Figure 8–2 shows the number of officers killed in different types of incidents. In 2001, the attacks on the World Trade Center resulted in the greatest ever annual loss of life of on-duty law enforcement officers when 72 police officers perished.[44]

A study by the FBI found that, generally, slain officers were good natured and conservative in the use of physical force, "as compared to other law enforcement officers in similar situations. They were also perceived as being well-liked by the community and the department, friendly to everyone, laid

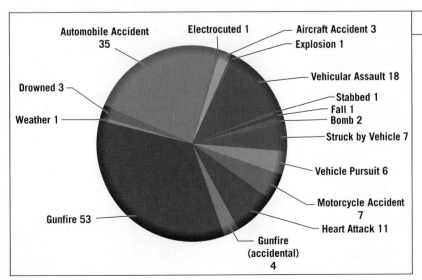

Automobile Accident 35 — Electrocuted 1 — Aircraft Accident 3 — Explosion 1 — Vehicular Assault 18 — Drowned 3 — Stabbed 1 — Fall 1 — Bomb 2 — Weather 1 — Struck by Vehicle 7 — Vehicle Pursuit 6 — Motorcycle Accident 7 — Heart Attack 11 — Gunfire 53 — Gunfire (accidental) 4

**FIGURE 8–2**

**U.S. law enforcement officers killed in the line of duty, 2004.**

*Source:* Based on data from the Officer Down Memorial Page website: http://www.odmp.org.

back, and easy going."[45] Finally, the study, which was published before the September 11, 2001, terrorist attacks, also found that most officers who were killed failed to wear protective vests.

For statistics on police killings to have meaning beyond the personal tragedy they entail, it is necessary to place them within a larger framework. There are approximately 730,000 state and local (full- and part-time) sworn police employees in this country,[46] and another 88,000 federal agents.[47] Such numbers demonstrate that the rate of violent death among law enforcement officers in the line of duty is small indeed.

# Risk of Disease and Infected Evidence

**biological weapon**

A biological agent used to threaten human life (for example, anthrax, smallpox, or any infectious disease).[iv]

Dangers other than violence also threaten enforcement officers. The increase in serious diseases that can be transmitted by blood and other body fluids, the possible planned release of active **biological weapons** such as anthrax or smallpox, and the fact that crime and accident scenes are inherently dangerous combine to make *caution* a necessary watchword among investigators and first responders. Routine criminal and accident investigations hold the potential for infection through minor cuts and abrasions resulting from contact with the broken glass and torn metal of a wrecked vehicle, the sharp edges of knives found at the scene of an assault or murder, or drug implements such as razor blades and hypodermic needles secreted in vehicles, homes, and pockets. Such minor injuries, previously shrugged off by many police personnel, have become a focal point for warnings about the dangers of AIDS, hepatitis B, tuberculosis, and other diseases spread through contact with infected blood.

In 1988, in Sonoma County, California, Sheriff Dick Michaelson became the first law enforcement supervisor to announce a case of AIDS infection in an officer clearly caused by interaction with a suspect. A deputy in Michaelson's department had contracted AIDS a few years earlier when he was pricked by a hypodermic needle during a pat-down search.[48]

Infection can also occur from the use of breath alcohol instruments on infected persons, the handling of evidence of all types, seemingly innocuous implements such as staples, the emergency delivery of babies in squad cars, and the attack (especially bites) by infected individuals who are being questioned or who are in custody. Understandably, officers are concerned about how to handle the threat of AIDS and other bloodborne diseases. However, as a publication of the New York City Police Department reminds its officers, "Police officers have a professional responsibility to render assistance to those who are in need of our services. We cannot refuse to help. Persons with infectious diseases must be treated with the care and dignity we show all citizens."[49]

Of equal concern is the threat of biological agents. Although crime scenes and sites known to harbor (or that are suspected of harboring) dangerous active biological agents require a response by teams equipped with special protective equipment, all law enforcement officers should take reasonable precautions against exposure to the wide variety of infectious agents known to exist

The aftermath of a fiery truck crash on Interstate 95 in Connecticut in 2004. The intense heat caused part of the road to collapse. Law enforcement officers have a basic duty to render assistance to individuals in need of it and are often the first responders in emergencies.

*AP Wide World Photos*

## BIOLOGICAL INCIDENT LAW ENFORCEMENT CONCERNS

TABLE 8-2

| | |
|---|---|
| Suspicious material | Responding officers should not handle or come into close physical contact with suspicious material. If it is necessary to handle the material to evaluate it, officers should wear surgical gloves and masks and wash their hands thoroughly with soap and water after handling. |
| Human bites | The biter usually receives the victim's blood. Viral transmission through saliva is highly unlikely. If bitten by anyone, milk the wound to make it bleed, wash the area thoroughly, and seek medical attention. |
| Spitting | Viral has been transmission through saliva is highly unlikely. |
| Urine/feces | Virus isolated in only very low concentrations in urine, not at all in feces. No cases of AIDS or AIDS virus infection have been associated with either urine or feces. |
| Cuts/puncture wounds | Use caution in handling sharp objects and searching areas hidden from view. Needle-stick studies show risk of infection is very low. |
| CPR/first aid | To eliminate the already minimal risk associated with CPR, use masks/airways. Avoid blood-to-blood contact by keeping open wounds covered and wearing gloves when in contact with bleeding wounds. |
| Body removal | Observe crime-scene rules; do not touch anything. Those who must come in contact with blood or other body fluids should wear gloves. |
| Casual contact | No cases of AIDS or AIDS virus infection have been attributed to casual contact. |
| Any contact with blood or body fluids | Wear gloves if contact with blood or body fluids is considered likely. If contact occurs, wash thoroughly with soap and water; clean up spills with one part water to nine parts household bleach. |
| Contact with dried blood | No cases of infection have been traced to exposure to dried blood. The drying process itself appears to inactivate the virus. Despite low risk, however, caution dictates wearing gloves, a mask, and protective shoe coverings if exposure to dried blood particles is likely (for example, during a crime-scene investigation). |

*References:* Michigan Department of Community Health, *Anthrax (Bacillus anthracis) Information for Health Care Providers.* Web posted at http://www.michigan.gov/documents/Healthcare_provider_FAQ-anthrax_08-2004_104327_7.pdf (accessed June 1, 2005); Massachusetts Administrative Office of the Trial Court, *Personnel Policies and Procedures Manual,* Section 24.000 ("Statement of Policy and Procedures on AIDS"). Web posted at http://www.state.ma.us/courts/admin/hr/section24.html (accessed January 5, 2004); and "Collecting and Handling Evidence Infected with Human Disease-Causing Organisms," *FBI Law Enforcement Bulletin,* July 1987.

at even routine crime scenes. Emergency management agencies generally recommend a number of precautions to defend against exposure to infectious substances, as shown in Table 8–2.

To better combat the threat of infectious diseases among public-safety employees and health care professionals, the federal Bloodborne Pathogens Act of 1991[50] requires that police officers receive proper training in how to prevent contamination by bloodborne infectious agents. The act also requires that police officers undergo an annual refresher course on the topic.

Police departments will face an increasing number of legal challenges in the years to come in cases of infectious diseases such as AIDS and in cases involving the release of biological agents. Predictable areas of concern include (1) the need to educate officers and other police employees about AIDS, anthrax, and other serious infectious diseases; (2) the responsibility of police departments to prevent the spread of AIDS and other infectious diseases in police lockups; and (3) the necessity of effective and nondiscriminatory enforcement activities and lifesaving measures by police officers in environments contaminated with active biological agents. With regard to nondiscriminatory activities, the National Institute of Justice has suggested that legal claims in support of an officer's refusal to render assistance to people with AIDS would probably not be effective in court.[51] The reason is twofold: The officer has a basic duty to render assistance to individuals in need of it, and the possibility of AIDS transmission by casual contact has been scientifically established as extremely remote. A final issue of growing concern involves activities by police officers infected with the AIDS virus. Few statistics are currently available on the number of officers with AIDS, but public reaction to those officers may be a developing problem that police managers will soon need to address.

# Stress and Fatigue among Police Officers

Perhaps the most insidious and least visible of all threats facing law enforcement personnel today is debilitating stress. While some degree of stress can be a positive motivator, serious stress over long periods of time can be destructive, even life threatening.

Stress is a natural component of police work.[52] The American Institute of Stress, based in Yonkers, New York, ranks policing among the top ten stress-producing jobs in the country.[53] The Bureau of Justice Statistics points out that "exposure to violence, suffering, and death is inherent to the profession of the law enforcement officer. There are other sources of stress as well. Officers who deal with offenders on a daily basis may perceive the public's opinion of police performance to be unfavorable; they often are required to work mandatory, rotating shifts; and they may not have enough time to spend with their families. Police officers also face unusual, often highly disturbing, situations, such as dealing with a child homicide victim or the survivors of vehicle crashes."[54]

Some stressors in police work are particularly destructive. One is frustration brought on by the inability to be effective, regardless of the amount of personal effort expended. But arrests may not lead to convictions. Evidence available to the officer may not be allowed in court. Sentences that are imposed may seem too "light" to the arresting officer. The feelings of powerlessness that come from seeing repeat offenders back on the streets and from witnessing numerous injustices to innocent victims may greatly stress police officers and cause them to question the purpose of their professional lives. These feelings of frustration and powerlessness may also lead to desperate attempts to find relief. As one researcher observes, "The suicide rate of police officers is more than twice that of the general population."[55]

Another source of stress—that of living with constant danger—is incomprehensible to most of us, even to the family members of many officers. As one officer says, "I kick in a door and I've gotta talk some guy into putting a gun down. . . . And I go home, and my wife's upset because the lawn isn't cut and the kids have been bad. Now, to her that's a real problem."[56] Yet the support of family and friends is crucial for handling stress.

Stress is not unique to the police profession, but because of the "macho" attitude that is traditionally associated with police work, police officers deny that they feel stress more often than those in other occupations. Some individuals are more susceptible to the negative effects of stress than others. The Type A personality, popularized 30 years ago, is most likely to perceive life in terms of pressure and performance. Type B people are more laid back and less likely to suffer from the negative effects of stress. Police ranks, drawn as they are from the general population, are filled with both stress-sensitive and stress-resistant personalities.

## Stress Reduction

It is natural to want to reduce stress.[57] Humor helps, even if it's somewhat cynical. Health care professionals, for example, are noted for their ability to joke even though they are caring for patients who are seriously ill or even dying. At times, police officers use humor similarly to defuse their reactions to dark or threatening situations. Keeping an emotional distance from stressful events is another way of coping with them, although such distance is not always easy to maintain. Police officers who have had to deal with serious cases of child abuse often report that they experience emotional turmoil as a consequence.

Exercise, meditation, abdominal breathing, biofeedback, self-hypnosis, guided imaging, induced relaxation, subliminal conditioning, music, prayer, and diet have all been cited as useful techniques for stress reduction. Devices to measure stress levels are available in the form of handheld heart rate monitors, blood pressure devices, "biodots" (which change color according to the amount of blood flow in the extremities), and psychological inventories.

A new approach to managing stress among police officers holds that the amount of stress an officer experiences is directly related to her reactions to potentially stressful situations.[58] Officers who can filter out extraneous stimuli and who can distinguish between truly threatening situations and those that are benign are much less likely to report job-related stressors than those lacking these abilities. Because stress-filtering abilities are often closely linked to innate personality characteristics, some researchers suggest careful psychological screening of police applicants to better identify those who have a natural ability to cope with situations that others might perceive as stressful.[59]

A female NYPD officer shows obvious signs of fatigue while working at a traffic barrier. Stress and fatigue are common problems in police work and can result from long work hours, grueling investigations, traumatic experiences, or even boredom.

*Robert Brenner, PhotoEdit*

Police officers' family members often report feelings of stress that are directly related to the officer's work. As a result, some departments have developed innovative programs to allay family stress. The Collier County (Florida) Spousal Academy, for example, is a family support program that offers training to spouses and other domestic partners of deputies and recruits who are enrolled in the department's training academy. The ten-hour program deals directly with issues that are likely to produce stress and informs participants of department and community resources that are available to help them. Peer-support programs for spouses and life partners and for the adolescent children of officers are also beginning to operate nationwide. **Library Extra 8–4** at cjtoday.com provides a comprehensive overview of issues related to police officer stress.

**LIBRARY EXTRA**

## Officer Fatigue

Like stress, fatigue can affect a police officer's performance. As criminologist Bryan Vila points out, "Tired, urban street cops are a national icon. Weary from overtime assignments, shift work, night school, endless hours spent waiting to testify, and the emotional and physical demands of the job, not to mention trying to patch together a family and social life during irregular islands of off-duty time, they fend off fatigue with coffee and hard-bitten humor."[60] Vila found levels of police officer fatigue to be six times as high as those of shift workers in industrial and mining jobs.[61] As Vila notes, few departments set work-hour standards, and fatigue associated with the pattern and length of work hours may be expected to contribute to police accidents, injuries, and misconduct.

To address the problem, Vila recommends that police departments "review the policies, procedures, and practices that affect shift scheduling and rotation, overtime moonlighting, the number of consecutive work hours allowed, and the way in which the department deals with overly tired employees."[62] Vila also suggests controlling the work hours of police officers, "just as we control the working hours of many other occupational groups."[63]

# Police Use of Force

**Police use of force** is defined as the use of physical restraint by a police officer when dealing with a member of the public.[64] Law enforcement officers are authorized to use the amount of force that is reasonable and necessary given the circumstances. Most officers are trained in the

**police use of force**
The use of physical restraint by a police officer when dealing with a member of the public.[v]

## FREEDOM OR SAFETY? YOU DECIDE.

### Protecting Public Places

In October 2004, a three-judge panel of the 11th U.S. Circuit Court of Appeals held that protesters could not be required to pass through metal detectors at a planned rally against a school for Latin American soldiers at Ft. Benning in Columbus, Georgia. "In the absence of some reason to believe that international terrorists would target or infiltrate this protest, there is no basis for using September 11 as an excuse for searching the protesters," the court said. Protesters believe that the school, the Western Hemisphere Institute for Security Cooperation, teaches Latin American soldiers to violate the human rights of poor people in their home countries.

Fifteen thousand protesters routinely attend the annual vigil against the institute, which had previously been called the School of the Americas—and metal detectors had been used on the crowd in the past. Organizers claimed, however, that some security measures had been put in place merely to harass demonstrators and to keep people from participating in the protests.

The court seemed to agree. "We cannot simply suspend or restrict civil liberties until the War on Terror is over, because the War on Terror is unlikely ever to be truly over," said Judge Gerald Tjoflat, author of the 11th Circuit panel's opinion. "September 11, 2001, already a day of immeasurable tragedy, cannot be the day liberty perished in this country."

Columbus mayor Bob Poydasheff noted that his city would abide by the court's order but called it "unreasonable." "I can't go into the 11th Circuit Court of Appeals without being scanned and having my briefcase searched," the mayor said. "They have every right to do that, to make sure they're protected. And I have every right to make sure my police are protected, and the citizens and other protesters are protected."

### YOU DECIDE

Why did the court prohibit the use of metal detectors? Under what circumstances might the court allow their use? What do you think of Mayor Poydasheff's argument that city officials should have the same right to protect public areas under their jurisdiction that the court has to protect its courtrooms?

*Reference:* "Terrorism Fears Not Sufficient Reason to Search Protesters, Appellate Court Rules," Associated Press, October 17, 2004.

---

use of force and typically encounter numerous situations during their careers when the use of force is appropriate—for example, when making some arrests, restraining unruly combatants, or controlling a disruptive demonstration. Force may involve hitting; holding or restraining; pushing; choking; threatening with a flashlight, baton, or chemical or pepper spray; restraining with a police dog; or threatening with a gun. Some definitions of police use of force include handcuffing.

The National Institute of Justice estimates that over 45 million people nationwide have face-to-face contact with the police over a typical 12-month period and that approximately 1.5%, or about 500,000 of these people, become subject to the use of force or the threat of force.[65] When handcuffing is included in the definition of force, the number of people subjected to force increases to 1.2 million, or slightly more than 2.5% of those having contact with the police. Other studies show that police use weaponless tactics in approximately 80% of use-of-force incidents and that half of all use-of-force incidents involve merely grabbing or holding the suspect.[66]

Studies show that police use force in fewer than 20% of adult custodial arrests. Even in instances where force is used, the police primarily use weaponless tactics (Figure 8–3), and female officers are less likely to use physical force and firearms, and more likely to use chemical weapons (mostly pepper spray), than their male counterparts. Figure 8–4 shows the types of encounters in which the use of force is most likely to be employed.

A more complex issue is the use of excessive force. The International Association of Chiefs of Police defines **excessive force** as "the application of an amount and/or frequency of force greater than that required to compel compliance from a willing or unwilling subject."[67] When excessive force is employed, the activities of the police often come under public scrutiny and receive attention from the media and legislators. Police officers' use of excessive force can also result in lawsuits by members of the public who feel that they have been treated unfairly. Whether the use of excessive force is aberrant behavior on the part of an individual officer or is a practice of an entire law enforcement agency, both the law and public opinion generally condemn it.

**excessive force**

The application of an amount and/or frequency of force greater than that required to compel compliance from a willing or unwilling subject.[vi]

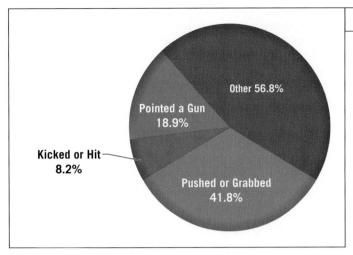

**FIGURE 8–3**

**Citizen reports of types of force used by police officers during adult custodial arrests involving force.**

*Source:* Matthew R. Durose et al., *Contacts between Police and Public* (Washington, DC: Bureau of Justice Statistics, February 2005), p. 17.

*Note:* Percents total more than 100 because some respondents reported more than one type of force.

Kenneth Adams, chair of the criminal justice faculty at Indiana University at Indianapolis and an expert in the use of force by police, notes that there is an important difference between the terms *excessive force,* such as shoving or pushing when simply grabbing a suspect would be adequate, and the *excessive use of force,* which refers to the phenomenon of force being used unacceptably, often on a department-wide basis. The term, says Adams, "deals with relative comparisons among police agencies, and there are no established criteria for judgment." *Use of excessive force* and the *excessive use of force* may be distinguished from the *illegal use of force,* which refers to situations in which the use of force by police violates a law or statute.[68]

In a study reported in 2001, Geoffrey Alpert and Roger Dunham found that the "force factor"— the level of force used by the police relative to the suspect's level of resistance—is a key element to consider in attempting to reduce injuries to both the police and suspects.[69] The force factor is calculated by measuring both the suspect's level of resistance and the officer's level of force on an equivalent scale and by then subtracting the level of resistance from the level of police force used. Results from the study indicate that, on average, the level of force that officers use is closely related to the type of training that their departments emphasize.

Excessive force can also be symptomatic of **problem police officers**. Problem police officers are those who exhibit problem behavior, as indicated by high rates of citizen complaints, frequent involvement in use-of-force incidents, and by other evidence.[70] The Christopher Commission, which studied the structure and operation of the Los Angeles Police Department in the wake of the Rodney King beating, found a number of "repeat offenders" on the LAPD

**problem police officer**

A law enforcement officer who exhibits problem behavior, as indicated by high rates of citizen complaints and use-of-force incidents and by other evidence.[vii]

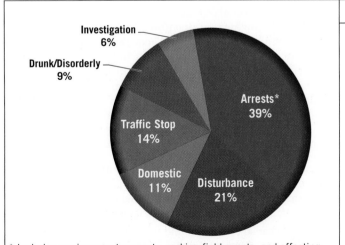

* Includes serving arrest warrants, making field arrests, and effecting other arrests.

**FIGURE 8–4**

**Police use of force by type of encounter.**

*Source:* International Association of Chiefs of Police, *Police Use of Force in America,* 2001 (Alexandria, VA: IACP, 2001), p. iii. Printed by permission of the International Association of Chiefs of Police.

force.[71] According to the commission, approximately 1,800 LAPD officers were alleged to have used excessive force or improper tactics between 1986 and 1990. Of these officers, more than 1,400 had only one or two allegations against them. Another 183 officers had four or more allegations, 44 had six or more, 16 had eight or more, and one had 16 such allegations. The commission also found that, generally speaking, the 44 officers with six complaints or more had received positive performance evaluations that failed to record "sustained" complaints or to discuss their significance.

Recent studies have found that problem police officers do not differ significantly in race or ethnicity from nonproblem officers, although they tend to be male and have disciplinary records that are more serious than those of other officers. Some departments are developing early-warning systems to allow police managers to identify potentially problematic officers and to reduce problem behavior. Learn more about police use of force, as well as force used against the police, from **Library Extras 8–5** and **8–6** at cjtoday.com.

# Deadly Force

Generally speaking, **deadly force** is likely to cause death or significant bodily harm. The FBI defines *deadly force* as "the intentional use of a firearm or other instrument resulting in a high probability of death."[72] According to a report released by the Bureau of Justice Statistics in 2001, the number of justifiable homicides by police averages "nearly 400 felons each year."[73]

The use of deadly force by law enforcement officers, especially when it is *not* considered justifiable, is one area of potential civil liability that has received considerable attention in recent years. Historically, the "fleeing felon rule" applied to most U.S. jurisdictions. It held that officers could use deadly force to prevent the escape of a suspected felon, even when that person represented no immediate threat to the officer or to the public.

The 1985 U.S. Supreme Court case of *Tennessee* v. *Garner*[74] specified the conditions under which deadly force could be used in the apprehension of suspected felons. Edward Garner, a 15-year-old suspected burglar, was shot to death by Memphis police after he refused their order to halt and attempted to climb over a chain-link fence. In an action initiated by Garner's father, who claimed that his son's constitutional rights had been violated, the Court held that the use of deadly force by the police to prevent the escape of a fleeing felon could be justified only where the suspect could reasonably be thought to represent a significant threat of serious injury or death to the public or to the officer and where deadly force is necessary to effect the arrest. In reaching its decision, the Court declared that "[t]he use of deadly force to prevent the escape of *all* felony suspects, whatever the circumstances, is constitutionally unreasonable."

In the 1989 case of *Graham* v. *Connor*,[75] the Supreme Court established the standard of "objective reasonableness." The Court said that whether deadly force has been used appropriately should be judged from the perspective of a reasonable officer on the scene and not with the benefit of "20/20 hindsight." The justices wrote, "The calculus of reasonableness must embody allowance for the fact that police officers are often forced to make split-second judgments—in circumstances that are tense, uncertain, and rapidly evolving—about the amount of force that is necessary in a particular situation."

In 1995, following investigations into the actions of federal agents at the deadly siege of the Branch Davidian compound at Waco, Texas, and the tragic deaths associated with a 1992 FBI assault on antigovernment separatists in Ruby Ridge, Idaho (a case that is detailed later in the chapter), the federal government announced that it was adopting an "imminent danger" standard for the use of deadly force by federal agents. The imminent danger standard restricts the use of deadly force to those situations in which the lives of agents or others are in danger. When the new standard was announced, federal agencies were criticized for taking so long to adopt them. The federal deadly force policy, as adopted by the FBI, contains the following elements[76]:

> The calculus of reasonableness must embody allowance for the fact that police officers are often forced to make split-second judgments—in circumstances that are tense, uncertain, and rapidly evolving—about the amount of force that is necessary in a particular situation.
>
> —*Graham* v. *Connor*, 490 U.S. 386, 396–397 (1989)

- *Defense of life.* Agents may use deadly force only when necessary—that is, only when they have probable cause to believe that the subject poses an imminent danger of death or serious physical injury to the agent or to others.

- *Fleeing subject.* Deadly force may be used to prevent the escape of a fleeing subject if there is probable cause to believe that the subject has committed a felony involving the infliction or threatened infliction of serious physical injury or death and that the subject's escape would pose an imminent danger of death or serious physical injury to the agents or to others.

- *Verbal warnings.* If feasible, and if doing so would not increase the danger to the agent or to others, a verbal warning to submit to the authority of the agent should be given prior to the use of deadly force.

- *Warning shots.* Agents may not fire warning shots.

- *Vehicles.* Agents may not fire weapons solely to disable moving vehicles. Weapons may be fired at the driver or other occupant of a moving motor vehicle only when the agent has probable cause to believe that the subject poses an imminent danger of death or serious physical injury to the agent or to others and when the use of deadly force does not create a danger to the public that outweighs the likely benefits of its use.

Studies of killings by the police have often focused on claims of discrimination—that is, that African-American and minority suspects are more likely to be shot than whites. But research has not provided solid support for such claims. While individuals shot by police are more likely to be minorities, an early study by James Fyfe found that police officers will generally respond with deadly force when mortally threatened and that minorities are considerably more likely to use weapons in assaults on officers than are whites.[77] Complicating the picture further, Fyfe's study showed that minority officers are involved in the shootings of suspects more often than other officers, a finding that may be due to the assignment of minority officers to inner-city and ghetto areas. However, a later study by Fyfe, which analyzed police shootings in Memphis, Tennessee, found that African-American property offenders were twice as likely as whites to be shot by police.[78]

Although relatively few police officers ever fire their weapons at suspects during the course of their careers, those who do may become embroiled in social, legal, and personal complications. It is estimated that in an average year, 600 suspects are killed by public police in America, while another 1,200 are shot and wounded, and 1,800 are shot at and missed.[79] The personal side of police shootings is well summarized in the title of an article that appeared in *Police Magazine.* The article, "I've Killed That Man Ten Thousand Times," demonstrates how police officers who have to use their weapons may be haunted by years of depression and despair.[80] Not long ago, according to author Anne Cohen, all departments did to help officers who had shot someone was to "give him enough bullets to reload his gun." The stress and trauma that police officers suffer from having shot someone are only now being realized, and many departments have yet to develop mechanisms for adequately dealing with them.[81]

Police officers have particular difficulty dealing with instances of "suicide by cop," in which individuals bent on dying engage in behavior that causes responding officers to resort to deadly force. On March 10, 2005, for example, John T. Garczynski, Jr., a father of two preteen boys, died in a hail of 26 police bullets fired by officers who had surrounded his vehicle in a Boca Raton, Florida, condominium parking lot.[82] Garczynski, a Florida Power and Light Company employee, had been separated from his wife months earlier and appeared to have been despondent over financial problems and the breakup of his marriage. The night before his death, Garczynski met his wife at a bowling alley and handed her a packet containing a suicide note, a typed obituary, and a eulogy to be read at his funeral. After he left, Garczysnki's wife called police, and officers used the help of a cell phone company to locate Garczynski. As deputies surrounded Garczynski's 2003 Ford Explorer, he attempted to start the vehicle. One of the officers yelled "Freeze," and then "Let me see your hands." It was at that point, deputies said, that Garczynski pointed a gun at them and they fired.

Rebecca Stincelli, author of the book *Suicide by Cop: Victims from Both Sides of the Badge,*[83] says an incident like that involving Garczynski can be devastating for police officers. "In the past, people have used rope, a gun, gas, jumped off a building. A police officer is just another method," said Stincelli. "They say it's nothing personal. [But] they are wrong. It's very personal" for the officers involved.[84] The FBI says that "Suicide-by-cop incidents are painful and damaging experiences for the surviving families, the communities, and all law enforcement professionals."[85]

A study of fatal shootings by Los Angeles police officers found that an astonishingly large number—more than 10%—could be classified as "suicide by cop."[86] Recently, researchers have identified three main "suicide by cop" categories: direct confrontations, in which suicidal subjects instigate attacks on police officers for the purpose of dying; disturbed interventions, in which potentially suicidal subjects take advantage of police intervention in their suicide attempt in order to die; and criminal interventions, in which criminal suspects prefer death to capture and arrest.[87]

> Everyone is a prisoner of his own experiences. No one can eliminate prejudices—just recognize them.
>
> —Edward R. Murrow

## CJ CAREERS

### BUREAU OF ALCOHOL, TOBACCO, FIREARMS, AND EXPLOSIVES

**Name:** Robert M. Young, Jr.

**Position:** Special Agent/Criminal Investigator

**City:** Lexington, Kentucky

**College Attended:** Rider University

**Year Hired:** 1998

*I pursued a career in criminal justice because I am not the type of person who enjoys working a nine-to-five office job. I like having a career where each day presents its own unique challenges. For instance, there are days when I may be in court testifying, days investigating an arson or explosive incident, or days in the field participating in an undercover operation. I believe it is this ever-changing work environment that attracts such a diverse and unique group of individuals to careers in law enforcement. . . .*

I believe the greatest challenge I have encountered in my job is the difficulty in trying to adequately balance the demands of the job with the demands of my personal life. . . . There is no greater reward for a law enforcement officer than that of seeing the look of appreciation on the face of a crime victim after the defendant has been convicted and sentenced for the crime that was investigated.

### TYPICAL POSITIONS

Special agent, explosives expert, criminal investigator, firearms specialist, bomb scene investigator, liquor law violations investigator, fingerprint identification specialist, intelligence research specialist, and forensic chemist. The Bureau of Alcohol, Tobacco, Firearms, and Explosives (ATF) has primary investigative jurisdiction among federal agencies for the investigation of international arms trafficking, illegal arms movement, and the illegal use of explosives.

### EMPLOYMENT REQUIREMENTS

GS-5 ATF special agent applicants must meet the same employment requirements as most other federal agents, including (1) successful completion of the Treasury Enforcement Agent Examination, (2) a field interview, (3) a full field background investigation leading to successful certification for a top-secret clearance, and (4) a bachelor's degree from an accredited college or university or three years of general experience, one of which must be equivalent to at least the GS-4 level.

### OTHER REQUIREMENTS

Other general requirements for employment as a federal officer apply. An applicant must (1) be a U.S. citizen, (2) be between 21 and 37 years old, (3) have good physical health, (4) hold a current, valid U.S. driver's license, (5) pass a polygraph examination, and (6) have eyesight of no less than 20/100 uncorrected, and corrected vision of at least 20/30 in one eye and 20/20 in the other. New agents undergo eight weeks of specialized training at the Federal Law Enforcement Training Center in Glynco, Georgia.

### SALARY

A bachelor's degree qualifies applicants for appointment at the GS-5 level, although appointments may be made at the GS-7 level for college graduates who are able to demonstrate superior academic achievement (that is, class standing in the upper third of their graduating class; a cumulative undergraduate grade point average of 2.95 or better; or membership in a national honor society recognized by the Association of College Honor Societies). GS-9 appointments require a master's degree, two full academic years of progressively higher-level graduate education, or one year of specialized experience equivalent to the next lower grade in the federal service. Depending on geographic area of assignment, this salary can be raised from 16% to 30% above the established base level.

### BENEFITS

Benefits include (1) 13 days of sick leave annually, (2) two and a half to five weeks of paid vacation and ten paid federal holidays each year, (3) federal health and life insurance, and (4) a comprehensive retirement program.

### DIRECT INQUIRIES TO:

Bureau of Alcohol, Tobacco, Firearms, and Explosives

Personnel Division

Room 4100

650 Massachusetts Avenue, N.W.

Washington, DC 20226

Phone: (202)927-5690

Website: http://atf.treas.gov

For additional information on employment opportunities in the criminal justice field, view the careers portion of the CD-ROM included with this book.

*Source:* Bureau of Alcohol, Tobacco, Firearms, and Explosives.

# Less-Lethal Weapons

**Less-lethal weapons** offer what may be a problem-specific solution to potential incidents of "suicide by cop," as well as a generic solution to at least some charges of use of excessive force. Less-lethal weapons are designed to disable, capture, or immobilize a suspect rather than kill him or her. Efforts to provide law enforcement officers with less-lethal weapons such as stun guns, Tasers, rubber bullets, beanbag projectiles, and pepper spray began in 1987.[88] More exotic types of less-lethal weapons, however, are on the horizon. They include snare nets fired from shotguns, disabling sticky foam that can be sprayed from a distance, microwave beams that heat the tissue of people exposed to them until they desist in their illegal or threatening behavior or lose consciousness, and high-tech guns that fire bolts of electromagnetic energy at a target, causing painful sensory overload and violent muscle spasms. The National Institute of Justice says, "The goal is to give line officers effective and safe alternatives to lethal force."[89]

As their name implies, however, less-lethal weapons are not always safe. On October 21, 2004, for example, 21-year-old Emerson College student Victoria Snelgrove died hours after being hit in the eye with a plastic pepper-spray-filled projectile that police officers fired at a rowdy crowd celebrating the Red Soxs' victory over the New York Yankees in the final game of the American League Championship Series in 2004. Witnesses said that officers fired the projectile into the crowd after a reveler near Fenway Park threw a bottle at a mounted Boston police officer.[90]

| less-lethal weapon |
|---|
| A weapon that is designed to disable, capture, or immobilize—but not kill—a suspect. Occasional deaths do result from the use of such weapons, however. |

# Racial Profiling and Biased Policing

**Racial profiling** first received national attention in the late 1990s. Racial profiling can be defined as any police action initiated on the basis of the race, ethnicity, or national origin of a suspect, rather than on the behavior of that individual or on information that leads the police to a particular individual who has been identified as being, or having been, engaged in criminal activity.[91]

The alleged use by police of racial profiling may take a number of forms. Minority accounts of disparate treatment at the hands of police officers include being stopped for being "in the wrong car" (for example, a police stop of an African-American youth driving an expensive late-model BMW); being stopped and questioned for being in the wrong neighborhood (that is, police stops of members of minority groups driving through traditionally white residential neighborhoods); and perceived harassment at the hands of police officers for petty traffic violations such as underinflated tires, failure to signal properly before switching lanes, vehicle equipment failures, driving less than 10 miles per hour above the speed limit, or having an illegible license plate.[92]

*Profiling* was originally intended to help catch drug couriers attempting to enter the country. The U.S. Customs Service and the Drug Enforcement Administration developed a number of "personal indicators" that seemed, from the agency's day-to-day enforcement experiences, to be associated with increased likelihood of law violation. Among the indicators were these: speaking Spanish; entering the United States on flights originating in particular Central and South American countries; being an 18- to 32-year-old male; having purchased tickets with cash; and having a short planned stay (often of only a day or two) in the United States. Federal agents frequently used these criteria in deciding which airline passengers to search and which bags to inspect.

Racial profiling has been derisively referred to as "driving while black" or "driving while brown," although it may also apply to situations other than those involving traffic violations. Racial profiling came to the attention of the public when police in New Jersey and Maryland were accused of unfair treatment of African-American motorists and admitted that race was a factor in traffic stops.

A 1999 report by the attorney general of New Jersey concluded that New Jersey state troopers *had* engaged in racial profiling along the New Jersey Turnpike.[93] The report, which tracked traffic stops between 1997 and 1998, found that people of color constituted 40.6% of the stops made on the turnpike. Although few stops resulted in a search, 77.2% of individuals searched were people of color. An analysis of these searches indicated that 10.5% of the searches that involved white motorists and 13.5% of the searches involving African-American motorists resulted in arrest or seizure.[94] An earlier racial profiling report, which had been compiled in support of a lawsuit against the state of New Jersey, showed that African-Americans comprised 13.5% of New Jersey Turnpike users and 15% of drivers who were speeding.[95] At the same time, blacks represented 35% of those stopped and 73.2% of those arrested. The lawsuit resulted in the suppression of evidence in many criminal cases involving black motorists who had been arrested on the turnpike.

In 2003, in response to widespread public outcry over the use of racial profiling, the U.S. Department of Justice banned its practice in all federal law enforcement agencies, except in cases

| racial profiling |
|---|
| "Any police-initiated action that relies on the race, ethnicity, or national origin, rather than [1] the behavior of an individual, or [2] . . . information that leads the police to a particular individual who has been identified as being, or having been, engaged in criminal activity."[ix] |

It is practically an article of faith among young, black males that they are more likely than whites to be stopped, frisked, spread-eagled, and arrested by the police, often on the flimsiest of charges.

—Hutchinson Report, July 2001

## CJ NEWS

### As Shocks Replace Bullets, Questions Arise

The police in Seattle have had their share of high-profile violent or deadly run-ins with protesters, mentally ill suspects and other lawbreakers. But in 2003, for the first time in 15 years, no one here was shot and killed by the police.

Miami, a city with a long history of police shootings and ensuing civil unrest, had no police shootings last year, fatal or otherwise, for the first time in 14 years. In Phoenix, where such shootings reached a level over the last several years that far outpaced the rate of much larger cities, deadly police shootings fell sharply in 2003, to their lowest rate in 14 years.

In these cities and in a fast-growing number of the nation's police departments, officers are carrying a slick new weapon, the Taser gun, which looks a lot like a pistol but does not shoot to kill.

Though officials say the Taser gun, which fires a stunning jolt of electricity, is not solely responsible for a decline in police killings, many departments say it has made a huge difference. Its supporters say the Taser is saving lives, protecting officers and suspects in standoffs that might otherwise have left someone dead or seriously injured.

"This is 100 percent more humane," said Officer Tom Burns, who has carried a Taser gun for the past two and a half years on bicycle patrol in Seattle.

But as the Taser spreads rapidly, it is raising questions about whether the weapon, which can also be applied directly to the skin as a stun gun, could be abused by the police. The Taser zaps suspects with 50,000 volts of electricity, disabling them for five seconds at a time. Critics say the weapon is ripe for abuse because the shock leaves no obvious mark, other than what looks like a small bee sting. Human rights groups in the United States and abroad have called Tasers potential instruments of torture.

They are now being used by more than 4,000 police departments. Roughly 170 new departments are buying the high-tech electro-shock guns every month, and the Army has begun using them in Iraq, according to Taser International, the Arizona company that makes them. More than one-third of Seattle's 600 patrol officers carry Tasers. In Miami, Phoenix and a growing number of cities, every officer has one.

Tasers have often been introduced in the wake of public outcry over deadly police shootings. That was the case in Seattle, Denver, Austin, Tex., and Portland, Ore., as part of an effort to reduce killings through the use of training programs and "less lethal" weapons.

"You have to think about the alternatives," said Officer Burns, who also carries pepper spray and a .40-caliber Glock pistol. He said he had used the Taser five times on suspects who seemed eager to attack or were difficult to control. "And without this technology you might have to break it down to very brutal methods."

Officer Burns was on the scene in 1999 when Seattle police shot and killed a mentally ill man, a widely publicized incident that led to soul-searching in the department and a plan that among other things involved the purchase of Tasers.

The newest Tasers are an advanced version of technology that was developed in the 1970's but was not considered by the police to be effective until recently. The electrical pulses travel from the gun through two 21-foot-long wires that look like a stretched-out Slinky tipped with barbed probes. If the probes pierce skin or a layer of clothing two inches thick or less, the jolt contracts the muscles and throws the suspect off balance. It makes the suspect unable to move and gives the police a full five seconds with every "tasing" to handcuff the suspect. The police say that 50,000 volts is a safe amount of electricity to absorb and that suspects shot with a Taser recover immediately.

A promotional photo showing the effects of Taser International's Advanced Taser®. This less-lethal weapon, intended for use in law enforcement and private security, incapacitates potential attackers by delivering an electrical shock to the person's nervous system. The technology is intended to reduce injury rates to both suspects and officers.

*TASER International (NASDAQ:TASR)*

## CJ NEWS *(continued)*

# Shocking force

Taser International Inc., the maker of stun weapons, has watched its stock soar amidst growing concerns about whether the weapons are as non-lethal as advertised. In a recent report, Amnesty International says stun guns are being abused by police.

A Taser's electrical current overrides the central nervous system for five seconds, temporarily paralyzing targets

**Dataport** stores date and time of Taser firing

**Disposable cartridge** uses compressed nitrogen to launch probes up to 21 feet

SOURCES: Amnesty International; Taser International

## Use of force incidents

At the Orange County, Florida, Sheriff's Office Tasers were the most prevalent force option, constituting 68 percent of all use-of-force incidents in 2002.

■ Taser
□ All other

600
500
400
300
200
100
0

0 — 1999
3 — 2000
201 / 228 — 2001
2002

**Insulated wires** transmit 50,000 volts of electricity through up to two inches of clothing

**ID tags** ejected like confetti when fired; printed with the serial number

**Probes** hook wires to target's skin or clothing

**Batteries** older models use eight AA batteries, newer models are rechargeable

*Source:* Dani Davies and Antigone Barton, "Jarring Death Rate Fuels Flap over Police Tasers: Despite 17 Florida Fatalities since 2000, Officers Back Their Use," *Palm Beach Post*, January 2, 2005, pages 1A and 10A. Used with permission of The Associated Press copyright © 2005. All rights reserved.

But critics and watchdog groups say the Taser could be used to torture suspects and prison inmates to extract confessions or taunt them, and Amnesty International has called for a ban on their use pending studies on their long-term effects. Human rights and civil liberties groups are also questioning whether the electro-shocks that Tasers deliver are potentially deadly.

"Surely it's better than being killed," said Dan Handelman, a founder of Portland Copwatch, a group that has been critical of that city's growing use of Tasers over the last year. "But it's not necessarily an acceptable replacement because it's not being used—at least in Portland—in place of lethal force; it's being used for compliance."

Across the country in recent months, several suspects who were shot with Tasers, sometimes repeatedly, have died. But officials said other health problems, like heart conditions and drug overdoses, were the cause.

The American Civil Liberties Union of Colorado urged the Denver Police Department two weeks ago to limit its use of

Tasers. The group cited a rising number of deaths nationally, saying 16 suspects in custody had died after being subdued with Tasers or stun guns in 2003, up from 10 in 2002 and 3 in 2001. But none of the deaths were officially attributed to the effect of the weapons.

In Las Vegas, William Lomax, 26, died last month after being arrested and, according to witnesses and the police, shot with a Taser four or five times, which critics of the Police Department said was an excessive use of force. Investigators said that Mr. Lomax had been under the influence of drugs, but that the cause of death was still under investigation.

Marsha Bell, 22, said she saw Mr. Lomax, her cousin, arrested on February 21 at her apartment complex, where he often visited his family. After he had a run-in with security guards, the police were called.

"He was on the ground," Ms. Bell said in a telephone interview. "He had two pairs of handcuffs on him, and I didn't know the Taser was being used until I heard him screaming. He kept screaming and screaming, saying, 'Oh God, Jesus,

*(continued)*

## CJ NEWS *(continued)*

please no.' He was screaming in pain; he was hurt and he didn't resist."

Lt. Tom Monahan of the Las Vegas Metropolitan Police Department, which bought several hundred Tasers last year, said that Mr. Lomax had struggled with officers, security guards and paramedics, and that the Taser was used while officers were trying to handcuff him.

Officer Thomas Miller, who conducts Taser training for the Las Vegas department, said that there were clear guidelines on when Tasers should be used.

"In the past, an officer would have to fight," Officer Miller said. "Now we have an option to stop that before it gets to that point, greatly reducing the risk to the officer and the suspect."

The police do say that a Taser would never replace lethal weapons if an officer felt his life was in imminent danger, like when a suspect is wielding a knife or a gun at close proximity, or when no other officer is available to provide "lethal cover" for an officer using the Taser. Most departments allow officers on the scene to make that judgment call.

In the New York City Police Department, supervisors and members of the large Emergency Service Unit, which helps patrol officers in violent situations, carry Tasers, but patrol officers do not, the police said.

The newest models cost $799 each, according to Taser International, the leading producer of the weapons. But company officials, who have seen their stock skyrocket over the last year, say the savings to police departments that might otherwise be sued over violent confrontations or shootings are potentially huge.

The police and other supporters of the new technology also say there are built-in safeguards to prevent abuse of the guns. Each Taser, which is powered by batteries, has a data port that records each shock and is used by police departments when they prepare incident reports, allowing supervisors to count how many times a Taser was fired.

Steve Tuttle, a spokesman for Taser International, which is based in Scottsdale, Ariz., said the company continually reviewed data and had found few instances among about 70,000 episodes so far of abuse or inappropriate use.

"If there's a bad apple out there, the technology we made will catch that bad apple," Mr. Tuttle said. "We've won the lottery in terms of great success, stock market-wise, but with that comes much more scrutiny."

Officer Burns of the Seattle department said the police could not deny that a misguided officer could abuse any weapon. But he said that there had been numerous instances in Seattle where officers had used the Taser instead of fists, nightsticks, guns or pepper spray, which can have much longer effects than Taser shocks, and that suspects had recovered immediately.

"Shooting someone is not a badge of honor," Officer Burns said. "It's something no one wants to do. No police officer in the world is paid to die; no police officer in the world is paid to get hurt."

For the latest in crime and justice news, visit the Talk Justice news feed at http://www.crimenews.info.

*Author's Update:* Amid continuing controversy over the safety of stun weapons, the two largest law enforcement divisions of the Department of Homeland Security, the bureaus of Immigration and Customs Enforcement (ICE) and Customs and Border Protection (CBP), recently rejected the use of stun guns for about 20,000 agents and officers.

*Source:* Sarah Kershaw, "As Shocks Replace Police Bullets, Deaths Fall but Questions Arise," *The New York Times,* March 7, 2004. Copyright © 2004 by the New York Times Co. Reprinted with permission.

that involve the possible identification of terrorist suspects.[96] According to the DOJ, "the guidance provides that in making routine law enforcement decisions—such as deciding which motorists to stop for traffic infractions—consideration of the driver's race or ethnicity is absolutely forbidden."[97]

Those who defend the use of racial profiling by the police argue that it is not a bigoted practice when based on facts (such as when a police department decides to increase patrols in a particular area because of exceptionally high crime rates) or when significant criminal potential exists among even a few members of a group. An example of the latter is the widespread public suspicions that focused on Arab-Americans (and other Arabs living in the United States or traveling through the country) following the terrorist attacks of September 11, 2001. As soon as it was publicly announced that the hijackers had been of Middle Eastern origin, some flight crews demanded that Arab-looking passengers be removed from their airplanes before takeoff, and passengers refused to fly with people who looked like Arabs.[98]

None of this is to say, of course, that race or ethnicity somehow inherently causes crime (or that it somehow causes poverty or increases the risk of victimization). If anything, race and ethnicity may simply display a significant correlation with certain types of crime, as they do with certain kinds of victimization. Hence, although the *real* causes of criminality may be socialization into criminal subcultures, economically deprived neighborhoods, a lack of salable job skills, and intergenerational poverty, and not race per se, to some law enforcement agencies race provides one more indicator of the likelihood of criminality. David Cole, a professor at Georgetown University's Law Center, for example, notes that in the minds of many police officials, "racial and ethnic disparities reflect not discrimination [or bigotry] but higher rates of offenses among minorities."[99] "Nationwide," says Cole, "blacks are 13 times more likely to be sent to state prisons for drug convictions than are whites, so it would seem rational for police to assume that all other things being equal, a black driver is more likely than a white driver to be carrying drugs." Statistics like this, of course, may further enhance police focus on minorities and may result in even more arrests, thereby reinforcing the beliefs on which racial profiling by enforcement agents is based. Such observations led esteemed sociologist Amitai Etzioni to declare in 2001 that racial profiling is not necessarily racist.[100] Moreover, warned Etzioni, an end to racial profiling "would penalize those African-American communities with high incidences of violent crime" because they would lose the levels of policing that they need to remain relatively secure.

Regardless of arguments offered in support of racial profiling as an enforcement tool, the practice has been widely condemned as being contrary to basic ethical principles. National public opinion polls conducted by the Gallup Organization in 1999, for example, showed that 81% of respondents were morally opposed to the practice of racial profiling by the police.[101] Those participating in the survey generally felt that profiling is wrong because it is a form of race-based discrimination. Findings from the poll might be interpreted to mean that most people believe that racial discrimination of any kind is inherently unethical and not permissible in a free society. Moreover, as Christopher Stone, known for his writings on racial justice, explains, "Most people of all races and ethnic groups are never convicted of a crime, but stereotypes can work to brand all members of some groups with suspicion . . . putting an undue burden on innocent members of these groups."[102]

From a more pragmatic viewpoint, however, racial profiling is unacceptable because it weakens the public's confidence in the police, thereby decreasing police–citizen trust and cooperation. As some authors explain, "Truly effective policing will only be achieved when police both protect their neighborhoods from crime and respect the civil liberties of all residents. When law enforcement practices are perceived to be biased, unfair, or disrespectful, communities of color are less willing to trust and confide in police officers, report crimes, participate in problem-solving activities, be witnesses at trials, or serve on juries."[103] These authors summarize the current situation with regard to racial profiling this way: "The challenge that confronts American police organizations is how to sustain the historic decline in rates of criminal activity while enhancing police legitimacy in the eyes of the communities they serve. Appropriately addressing allegations of racial profiling is central to this new mission."[104] Learn more about racial profiling and police management via Library Extra 8–7 at cjtoday.com.

## Racially Biased Policing

In 2001, the Police Executive Research Forum (PERF) released a detailed report entitled *Racially Biased Policing: A Principled Response*.[105] PERF researchers surveyed more than 1,000 police executives, analyzed material from more than 250 law enforcement agencies, and sought input from law enforcement agency personnel, community activists, and civil rights leaders about racial bias in policing. Researchers concluded that "the vast majority of law enforcement officers—of all ranks, nationwide—are dedicated men and women committed to serving all citizens with fairness and dignity."[106] Most police officers, said the report, share an intolerance for racially biased policing. The report's authors noted that some police behaviors may be misinterpreted as biased when, in fact, the officer is just doing his or her job. "The good officer continually scans the environment for anomalies to normalcy—for conditions, people and behavior that are unusual for that environment," they said. "In learning and practicing their craft, officers quickly develop a sense for what is normal and expected, and conversely, for what is not."[107] Hence, for officers of any race to take special notice of unknown young white males who unexpectedly appear in a traditionally African-American neighborhood, for example, might be nothing other than routine police procedure. Such an observation, however, is not in itself sufficient for an investigatory stop but might be used in conjunction with other trustworthy and relevant information already in the officer's possession—such as the officer's prior knowledge that young white men have been visiting a particular apartment complex in the neighborhood to purchase drugs—to justify such a stop.

The PERF report makes many specific recommendations to help police departments be free of bias. One recommendation, for example, says that "supervisors should monitor activity reports for

## MULTICULTURALISM AND DIVERSITY

### Investigating Crime in a Multicultural Setting

In the mid-1990s, the Washington, D.C.–based National Crime Prevention Council (NCPC) published an important guide for American law enforcement officers who work with multicultural groups. The principles it contains can be applied equally to most foreign-born individuals living in the United States and are especially important to patrol officers and criminal investigators.

The NCPC guide points out that it is important for well-intentioned newcomers to this country to learn that the law enforcement system in the United States is not a national police force but a series of local, state, and federal agencies that take seriously their obligation to "serve and protect" law-abiding residents. Newcomers need to know that police officers can teach them how to protect themselves and their families from crime. Many immigrants, especially political refugees, come from countries in which the criminal justice system is based on tyranny, repression, and fear.

The NCPC suggests that law enforcement officers and other members of the criminal justice system can help ease this transition by working not only to communicate with immigrants but also to understand them and the complexities of their native cultures. The mere absence of conflict in a neighborhood does not mean that residents of different cultures have found harmony and a cooperative working relationship, says the NCPC. True multicultural integration occurs when various cultures reach a comfortable day-to-day interaction marked by respect, interest, and caring.

Communities in which immigrants and law enforcement have established close positive ties benefit considerably, according to the NCPC. Immigrants gain greater access to police and other services, such as youth programs, victim assistance, parenting classes, medical assistance programs, business networking, and neighborhood groups. Crime decreases in communities where law enforcement officers help immigrants learn to protect themselves against crime.

For police officers working in communities in which "language is a serious barrier between cultures," the NCPC suggests the following pointers for communicating more effectively:

- Be patient when speaking with someone who does not clearly understand your language. Speak slowly and distinctly. Be willing to repeat words or phrases if necessary. Remember that shouting never helps a nonnative speaker understand better.
- Be careful with your choice of words, selecting those that are clear, straightforward, and simple to understand. Avoid colloquialisms and slang.
- Allow extra time for investigation when the people involved have not mastered English.
- Be sure that anyone who serves as an interpreter is fully qualified and has had experience. Interpreting under pressure is a difficult task; lack of training can lead to mistakes.
- Be candid about your ability to speak or understand a language. Trying to "fake it" just leads to confusion, misunderstanding, and misspent time.
- Never assume that someone is less intelligent just because he or she doesn't speak English well.

Visit the National Crime Prevention Council via Web Extra 8–5 at cjtoday.com.

*Reference:* Adapted from National Crime Prevention Council, *Building and Crossing Bridges: Refugees and Law Enforcement Working Together* (Washington, DC: NCPC, 1994).

evidence of improper practices and patterns. They should conduct spot-checks and regular sampling of in-car videotapes, radio transmissions, and in-car computer and central communications records to determine if both formal and informal communications are professional and free from racial bias and other disrespect."[108] Read the entire PERF report at Library Extra 8–8 at cjtoday.com.

# Police Civil Liability

In 1996, 51-year-old Richard Kelley filed suit in federal court against the Massachusetts State Police and the Weymouth (Massachusetts) Police Department.[109] The suit resulted from an incident during which, Kelley alleged, state troopers and Weymouth police officers treated him as a drunk rather than recognizing that he had just suffered a stroke while driving. According to Kelley, following a minor traffic accident caused by the stroke, officers pulled him from his car, handcuffed him, dragged him along the ground, and ignored his pleas for help—forcing him to stay at a state police barracks for seven hours before taking him for medical treatment. Drunk-driving charges against Kelley were dropped after medical tests failed to reveal the presence of any intoxicating substances in his body.

> We must strive to eliminate any racial, ethnic, or cultural bias that may exist among our ranks.
>
> —Sherman Block, Los Angeles County Sheriff

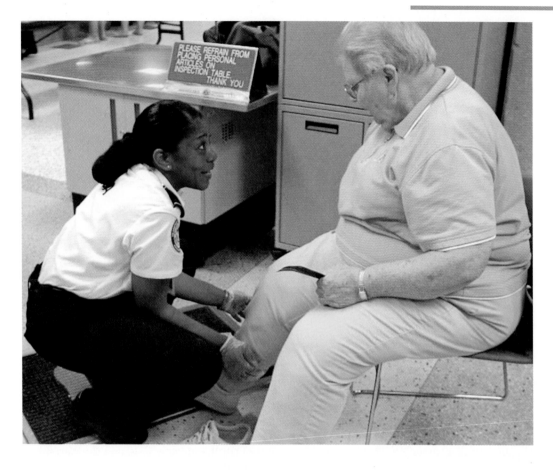

A female passenger is subjected to heightened security screening at Dallas-Forth Worth International Airport. Some people fear that the use of profiling techniques holds the potential to unfairly discriminate against members of certain racial and ethnic groups. Others suggest that the careful use of profiling can provide an important advantage in an age of scarce resources. Which perspective appeals to you?

USA Today, *Friday July 15, 2005, p. A4.*

**Civil liability** suits brought against law enforcement personnel are of two types: state and federal. Suits brought in state courts have generally been the more common form of civil litigation involving police officers. In recent years, however, an increasing number of suits have been brought in federal courts on the claim that the civil rights of the plaintiff, as guaranteed by federal law, were denied.

## Common Sources of Civil Suits

Police officers may become involved in a variety of situations that could result in civil suits against the officers, their superiors, and their departments. Major sources of police civil liability are listed in Table 8–3. Charles Swanson, an expert in police procedure, says that the most common sources of lawsuits against the police are "assault, battery, false imprisonment, and malicious prosecution."[110]

Of all complaints brought against the police, assault charges are the best known, being, as they are, subject to high media visibility. Less visible, but not uncommon, are civil suits charging the

**civil liability**

Potential responsibility for payment of damages or other court-ordered enforcement as a result of a ruling in a lawsuit. Civil liability is not the same as criminal liability, which means "open to punishment for a crime."[x]

| MAJOR SOURCES OF POLICE CIVIL LIABILITY | |
|---|---|
| Failure to protect property in police custody | Negligence in the care of suspects in police custody |
| Failure to render proper emergency medical assistance | Failure to prevent a foreseeable crime |
| Failure to aid private citizens | Lack of due regard for the safety of others |
| False arrest | False imprisonment |
| Inappropriate use of deadly force | Unnecessary assault or battery |
| Malicious prosecution | Violations of constitutional rights |
| Patterns of unfair and inequitable treatment | Racial profiling |

TABLE 8–3

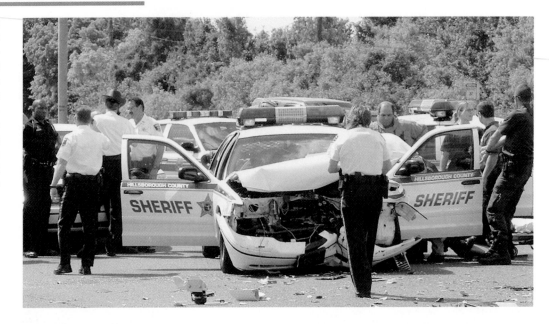

A police car destroyed during a high-speed chase. Research shows that most of the suspects chased by police are not violent criminals, and high-speed chases are especially dangerous because of their potential to injure innocent bystanders. When injuries do occur, a chase might provide a lawful basis for a civil suit against officers and their departments.

© Luis Santana, 911 Pictures

We depend on law enforcement officers to protect us. They have to make split-second decisions in the field. Would we want to put police officers in the position where they wouldn't (react) out of fear that three weeks later they'd be called a criminal?

—Florida defense attorney Michael Salnick, representing a police officer accused of manslaughter in the death of a fleeing suspect.[xi]

police with false arrest or false imprisonment. In the 1986 case of *Malley* v. *Briggs*,[111] the U.S. Supreme Court held that a police officer who effects an arrest or conducts a search on the basis of an improperly issued warrant may be liable for monetary damages when a reasonably well-trained officer, under the same circumstances, "would have known that his affidavit failed to establish probable cause and that he should not have applied for the warrant." Significantly, the Court ruled that an officer "cannot excuse his own default by pointing to the greater incompetence of the magistrate."[112] That is, the officer, rather than the judge who issued the warrant, is ultimately responsible for establishing the basis for pursuing the arrest or search.

When an officer makes an arrest without just cause or simply impedes an individual's right to leave the scene without good reason, he or she may also be liable for the charge of false arrest. Officers who "throw their weight around" are especially subject to this type of suit, grounded as it is on the abuse of police authority. Because generally employers may be sued for the negligent or malicious actions of their employees, many police departments are being named as codefendants in lawsuits today.

Civil suits are also brought against officers whose actions are deemed negligent. High-speed vehicle pursuits are especially dangerous because of the potential for injury to innocent bystanders (Figure 8–5). In the case of *Biscoe* v. *Arlington County* (1984),[113] for example, Alvin Biscoe was awarded $5 million after he lost both legs as a consequence of a high-speed chase while he was waiting to cross the street. Biscoe, an innocent bystander, was struck by a police car that went out of control. The officer driving the car had violated department policies prohibiting high-speed chases, and the court found that he had not been properly trained.

Departments may protect themselves to some degree through training combined with regulations limiting the authority of their personnel. One year after the *Biscoe* case was decided, for example, a Louisiana police officer, who had an accident while driving 75 mph in a 40-mph zone, was found to be negligent and was held liable for damages.[114] However, the department was not held liable because it had a policy limiting emergency driving to no more than 20 miles per hour over the posted speed limit and because officers were trained in that policy.

According to the FBI, "a traffic accident constitutes the most common terminating event in an urban pursuit."[115] Hence, some cities are actively replacing high-speed vehicle pursuits with surveillance technologies employing unmanned aerial vehicles (UAVs). Although helicopters have long been used in this capacity, the advent of UAV technology promises to make the tracking of fleeing suspects much quicker and far safer for all involved. UAVs in police service are discussed in greater detail in Chapter 18.

Law enforcement supervisors may be the object of lawsuits by virtue of the fact that they are responsible for the actions of their officers. If it can be shown that supervisors were negligent in hiring (as when someone with a history of alcoholism, mental problems, sexual deviance, or drug abuse is employed) or if supervisors failed in their responsibility to properly train officers before arming and deploying them, they may be found liable for damages.

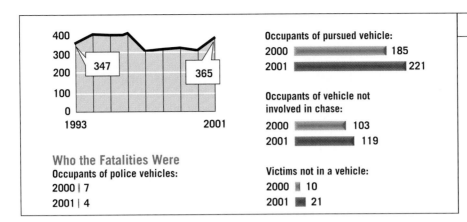

**FIGURE 8-5**

**U.S. deaths from high-speed police pursuits, 1993–2002.**

*Source:* National Highway Traffic Safety Administration.

In the 1989 case of the *City of Canton, Ohio* v. *Harris,*[116] the U.S. Supreme Court ruled that a "failure to train" can become the basis for legal liability on the part of a municipality where the "failure to train amounts to deliberate indifference to the rights of persons with whom the police come in contact."[117] In that case, Geraldine Harris was arrested and taken to the Canton, Ohio, police station. While at the station, she slumped to the floor several times. Officers left her on the floor and did not call for medical assistance. Upon release, Harris's family took her to a local hospital, where she was found to be suffering from several emotional ailments. Harris was hospitalized for a week and received follow-up outpatient treatment for the next year.

In the 1997 case of *Board of the County Commissioners of Bryan County, Oklahoma* v. *Brown,* however, the Supreme Court ruled that to establish liability, plaintiffs must show that "the municipal action in question was not simply negligent, but was taken with 'deliberate indifference' as to its known or obvious consequences."[118] In *Brown,* a deputy named Burns was hired by the sheriff of Bryan County, Oklahoma. Burns later used excessive force in arresting a woman, and the woman sued the county for damages, claiming that Deputy Burns had been hired despite his criminal record. In fact, some years earlier, Burns had pleaded guilty to various driving infractions and other misdemeanors, including assault and battery—a charge resulting from a college fight. At trial, a spokesperson for the sheriff's department admitted to receiving Burns's driving and criminal records but said he had not reviewed either in detail before the department decided to hire Burns. Nonetheless, the Supreme Court held that deliberate indifference on the part of the county had not been established because the plaintiff had not demonstrated that "Burns's background made his use of excessive force in making an arrest a plainly obvious consequence of the hiring decision." According to this decision, a municipality (in this case, a county) may not be held liable solely because it employs a person with an arrest record.

> The twenty-first century police candidate must be carefully chosen and then trained and mentored to fill the role of modern policing. Only then will policing become a true profession; and only then will police be able to deliver on their mission to protect and serve the citizenry.
>
> —Gene Stephens[xii]

# Federal Lawsuits

Civil suits alleging police misconduct that are filed in federal courts are often called **1983 lawsuits** because they are based on Section 1983 of Title 42 of the U.S. Code—an act passed by Congress in 1871 to ensure the civil rights of men and women of all races. That act requires due process of law before any person can be deprived of life, liberty, or property and specifically provides redress for the denial of these constitutional rights by officials acting under color of state law. It reads as follows:

> Every person who, under color of any statute, ordinance, regulation, custom, or usage, of any State or Territory, subjects, or causes to be subjected, any citizen of the United States or other person within the jurisdiction thereof to the deprivation of any rights, privileges, or immunities secured by the Constitution and laws, shall be liable to the party injured in an action at law, suit in equity, or other proper proceeding for redress.[119]

A 1983 suit may be brought, for example, against officers who shoot suspects under questionable circumstances, thereby denying them their right to life without due process. Similarly, an officer

**1983 lawsuit**

A civil suit brought under Title 42, Section 1983, of the U.S. Code against anyone who denies others their constitutional right to life, liberty, or property without due process of law.

**Bivens action**

A civil suit, based on the case of *Bivens* v. *Six Unknown Federal Agents,* brought against federal government officials for denying the constitutional rights of others.

The ability of the police to fulfill their sacred trust will improve as a lucid sense of ethical standards is developed.

—Patrick V. Murphy, former Commissioner, New York City Police Department

**WHAT WOULD YOU DO?**

The CD-ROM scenario for Chapter 8 builds on concepts of sovereign immunity and police civil liability. It is derived from a real-life incident involving a police officer's high-speed chase of a bank robbery suspect. The real-life case eventually found its way to the U.S. Supreme Court, with unfavorable consequences for the on-the-scene officer and his department. Use the CD-ROM found in your textbook to work through this scenario, and see if you can make better decisions than the responding officer did.

Background of the Ruby Ridge Incident

who makes an arrest based on accusations that he or she knows to be untrue may be subject to a 1983 lawsuit.

Another type of liability action, this one directed specifically at federal officials or enforcement agents, is called a **Bivens action**. The case of *Bivens* v. *Six Unknown Federal Agents* (1971)[120] established a path for legal action against agents enforcing federal laws, which is similar to that found in a 1983 suit. *Bivens* actions may be addressed against individuals but not against the United States or its agencies.[121] Federal officers have generally been granted a court-created qualified immunity and have been protected from suits where they were found to have acted in the belief that their action was consistent with federal law.[122]

In the past, the doctrine of sovereign immunity barred legal actions against state and local governments. Sovereign immunity was a legal theory that held that a governing body could not be sued because it made the law and therefore could not be bound by it. Immunity is a much more complex issue today. Some states have officially abandoned any pretext of immunity through legislative action. New York State, for example, has declared that public agencies are equally as liable as private agencies for violations of constitutional rights. Other states, for instance, California, have enacted statutory provisions that define and limit governmental liability.[123] A number of state immunity statutes have been struck down by court decision. In general, states are moving in the direction of setting dollar limits on liability and adopting federal immunity principles to protect individual officers, including "good faith" and "reasonable belief" rules.

At the federal level, the concept of sovereign immunity is embodied in the Federal Tort Claims Act (FTCA),[124] which grants broad immunity to federal government agencies engaged in discretionary activities. When a federal employee is sued for a wrongful or negligent act, the Federal Employees Liability Reform and Tort Compensation Act of 1988, commonly known as the Westfall Act, empowers the attorney general to certify that the employee was acting within the scope of his or her office or employment at the time of the incident. Upon certification, the employee is dismissed from the action, and the United States is substituted as defendant. The case then falls under the governance of the FTCA.

The U.S. Supreme Court has supported a type of qualified immunity for individual officers (as opposed to the agencies for which they work). This immunity "shields law enforcement officers from constitutional lawsuits if reasonable officers believe their actions to be lawful in light of clearly established law and the information the officers possess." The Supreme Court has also described qualified immunity as a defense "which shields public officials from actions for damages unless their conduct was unreasonable in light of clearly established law."[125] According to the Court, "[T]he qualified immunity doctrine's central objective is to protect public officials from undue interference with their duties and from potentially disabling threats of liability."[126] In the context of a warrantless arrest, the Court said in *Hunter* v. *Bryant* (1991),[127] "even law enforcement officials who reasonably but mistakenly conclude that probable cause is present are entitled to immunity."[128]

Criminal charges can also be brought against officers who appear to overstep boundaries or who act in violation of set standards. In 2001, for example, in the case of *Idaho* v. *Horiuchi,*[129] the Ninth U.S. Circuit Court of Appeals ruled that federal law enforcement officers are not immune from state prosecution where their actions violate state law "either through malice or excessive zeal." The case involved FBI sharpshooter Lon Horiuchi, who was charged with negligent manslaughter by prosecutors in Boundary County, Idaho, following the 1992 incident at Ruby Ridge.

Today, most police departments at both state and federal levels carry liability insurance to protect themselves against the severe financial damage that can result from the loss of a large civil suit. Some officers also acquire private policies that provide coverage in the event they are named as individuals in a civil suit. Both types of insurance policies generally cover legal fees up to a certain amount, regardless of the outcome of the case. Police departments that face civil prosecution because of the actions of an officer may find that legal and financial liability extends to supervisors, city managers, and the community itself. Where insurance coverage does not exist or is inadequate, city coffers may be nearly drained to meet the damages awarded.[130]

A 2001 study of a large sample of police chiefs throughout Texas found that most believed that lawsuits or the threat of civil litigation against the police makes it harder for individual officers to do their jobs. Most of the chiefs espoused the idea that adequate training, better screening of applicants, close supervision of officers, and "treating people fairly" all reduced the likelihood of lawsuits.[131]

Police today face many challenges. Among them are the informal pressures on officers by a powerful subculture that communicates select values in support of a police personality; public demands, including organized opposition to practices like racial profiling; and the real possibility of corruption and deviance, which some see as inherent in the very nature of authority.

Opposed to the illegitimate use of police authority, however, are increased calls for integrity and ethical awareness in police work and the continuing growth of professionalism. Professionalism, with its emphasis on education, training, high ethical values, and personal accountability, will lead to greater public recognition of the significance of police work and to higher police salaries. These, in turn, will do much to decrease corruption and deviance among law enforcement personnel.

Civil liability issues are very important in policing. They arise because officers and their agencies sometimes inappropriately use power to curtail the civil and due process rights of criminal suspects. High-speed chases gone wrong and allegations of unnecessary use of force provide the most visible instances of potential police civil liability today. Both police departments and individual police officers can be targeted by civil lawsuits. Supervisors can be named as defendants in lawsuits that claim that they failed to properly train their subordinates.

Federal suits based on claims that officers acted with disregard for an individual's right to due process are called *1983 lawsuits* because they are based on Section 1983 of Title 42 of the U.S. Code. Another type of civil suit that can be brought specifically against federal agents is known as a *Bivens* action. Although the doctrine of sovereign immunity barred legal action against state and local governments in the past, recent court cases and legislative activity have restricted the opportunity for law enforcement agencies and their officers to exercise claims of immunity.

**SUMMARY**

1. What is the police working personality? What are its central features? How does it develop? How does it relate to police culture?

2. What are the different types of police corruption? What themes run through the findings of the Knapp Commission and the Wickersham Commission? What innovative steps might police departments take to reduce or eliminate corruption among their officers?

3. What are the dangers of police work? What can be done to reduce those dangers?

4. In what kinds of situations are police officers most likely to use force? When has too much force been used?

5. What is racial profiling? Why has it become a significant issue in policing today?

6. What are some of the civil liability issues associated with policing? What are some of the common sources of civil suits against the police? How can civil liability be reduced?

**DISCUSSION QUESTIONS**

Visit the National Criminal Justice Reference Service (NCJRS) at http://www.ncjrs.org. Click on "Advanced Search" and then on "Hints on Searching the NCJRS website" to view tips on performing effective searches, modifying search queries, and interpreting search results. Write a description of the search techniques available in the NCJRS database, including wild-card, proximity, concept, Boolean, and pattern searching. What does the help text suggest you do if you find too much in your search? If you find too little?

Revisit the NCJRS advanced search page, and click on the "Library/Abstracts" tab. What is the NCJRS Abstracts Database? How does it differ from the NCJRS full-text collection?

After you have familiarized yourself with searching techniques, put your skills to use by conducting a search of the NCJRS site to identify documents on homeland security and policing. (*Note:* You may have to develop your own search strategy using other keywords in combination with "security" or "police" to narrow down the results of your search.) What kinds of documents did you find? What conclusions, if any, did you come to about the police role in homeland security after reading these documents?

To complete this Web Quest online, go to the Web Quest module in Chapter 8 of the *Criminal Justice Today* Companion Website at cjtoday.com.

**WEB QUEST**

## NOTES

**i.** Carl B. Klockars et al., *The Measurement of Police Integrity,* National Institute of Justice Research in Brief (Washington, DC: National Institute of Justice, 2000), p. 1.

**ii.** Kevin Johnson, "Court Says Idaho Can Prosecute FBI Agent," *USA Today,* June 6, 2001, p. 3A.

**iii.** Jerome H. Skolnick and David H. Bayley, *The New Blue Line: Police Innovation in Six American Cities* (New York: Free Press, 1986), p. 229.

**iv.** Technical Working Group on Crime Scene Investigation, *Crime Scene Investigation: A Guide for Law Enforcement* (Washington, DC: National Institute of Justice, 2000), p. 12.

**v.** National Institute of Justice, *Use of Force by Police: Overview of National and Local Data* (Washington, DC: National Institute of Justice, 1999).

**vi.** International Association of Chiefs of Police, *Police Use of Force in America 2001* (Alexandria, VA: Author, 2001), p. 1.

**vii.** Samuel Walker, Geoffrey P. Albert, and Dennis J. Kenney, *Responding to the Problem Police Officer: A National Study of Early Warning Systems* (Washington, DC: National Institute of Justice, 2000).

**viii.** Sam W. Lathrop, "Reviewing Use of Force: A Systematic Approach," *FBI Law Enforcement Bulletin,* October 2000, p. 18.

**ix.** Deborah Ramierz, Jack McDevitt, and Amy Farrell, *A Resource Guide on Racial Profiling Data Collection Systems: Promising Practices and Lessons Learned* (Washington, DC: U.S. Department of Justice, 2000), p. 3.

**x.** Adapted from Gerald and Kathleen Hill, *The Real Life Dictionary of the Law.* Web posted at http://www.law.com (accessed June 11, 2003).

**xi.** Jane Musgrave, "Charge Against Officer Likely, But Conviction Not, Lawyers Say," *Palm Beach Post,* April 22, 2005.

**xii.** Gene Stephens, "Policing the Future: Law Enforcement's New Challenges," *The Futurist,* March/April 2005, p. 57.

---

**1.** Lorie Fridell et al., *Racially Biased Policing: A Principled Response* (Washington, DC: Police Executive Research Forum, 2001), p. 41.

**2.** Quoted in Jim Helihy, "Issues Affecting Irish Policing, 1922–1932." Web posted at http://www.esatclear.ie/~garda/issues.html (accessed June 15, 2003).

**3.** The quotations in this paragraph are from Janine Rauch and Etienne Marasis, "Contextualizing the Waddington Report." Web posted at http://www.wits.ac.za/csvr/papers/papwadd.html (accessed January 5, 2002).

**4.** Jerome H. Skolnick, *Justice without Trial: Law Enforcement in a Democratic Society* (New York: John Wiley, 1966).

**5.** See, for example, Michael Brown, *Working the Street: Police Discretion and the Dilemmas of Reform* (New York: Russell Sage Foundation, 1981); and Christopher P. Wilson, *Cop Knowledge: Police Power and Cultural Narrative in Twentieth-Century America* (Chicago: University of Chicago Press, 2000). Wilson's book is about the production and influence of cultural knowledge about American policing.

**6.** Richard Bennett and Theodore Greenstein, "The Police Personality: A Test of the Predispositional Model," *Journal of Police Science and Administration,* Vol. 3 (1975), pp. 439–445.

**7.** James Teevan and Bernard Dolnick, "The Values of the Police: A Reconsideration and Interpretation," *Journal of Police Science and Administration* (1973), pp. 366–369.

**8.** Gail Gibson, "Norris Is Left to 'Pick Up the Pieces,'" Baltimoresun.com, March 9, 2004. Web posted at http://www.baltimoresun.com/news/local/balte.md.convicted09mar09,0,7577097.story?coll_bal-local-columnists (accessed July 5, 2004).

**9.** Details for this story come from "Retired Police Detectives Arrested for Suspected Mafia Killings," *USA Today,* March 11, 2005. Web posted at http://www.usatoday.com/news/nation/2005-03-10-mafia-police_x.htm (accessed July 30, 2005).

**10.** Carl B. Klockars et al., "The Measurement of Police Integrity," National Institute of Justice Research in Brief (Washington, DC: NIJ, 2000), p. 1.

**11.** Michael J. Palmiotto, ed., *Police Misconduct: A Reader for the Twenty-First Century* (Upper Saddle River, NJ: Prentice Hall, 2001), preface.

**12.** Tim Prenzler and Peta Mackay, "Police Gratuities: What the Public Thinks," *Criminal Justice Ethics* (Winter/Spring 1995), pp. 15–25.

**13.** Thomas Barker and David L. Carter, *Police Deviance* (Cincinnati, OH: Anderson, 1986). For a detailed overview of the issues involved in police corruption, see Victor E. Kappeler, Richard D. Sluder, and Geoffrey P. Alpert, *Forces of Deviance: Understanding the Dark Side of Policing,* 2nd ed. (Prospect Heights, IL: Waveland Press, 1998); Dean J. Champion, *Police Misconduct in America: A Reference Handbook* (Santa Barbara, CA: Abo-Clio, 2002); and Kim Michelle Lersch, ed., *Policing and Misconduct* (Upper Saddle River, NJ: Prentice Hall, 2002).

**14.** The quotations in this paragraph are from Frank L. Perry, "Repairing Broken Windows: Preventing Corruption within Our Ranks," *FBI Law Enforcement Bulletin,* February 2001, pp. 23–26.

**15.** "Nationline: NYC Cops—Excess Force Not Corruption," *USA Today,* June 16, 1995, p. 3A.

**16.** *Knapp Commission Report on Police Corruption* (New York: George Braziller, 1973).

**17.** Ibid.

**18.** Sabrina Tavernise, "Victory for Officer Who Aided Corruption Inquiry," *The New York Times,* April 3, 2004.

19. See "Plot Summary for *Notorious* (2004)." Web posted at http://yoursay.imdb.com/titlt/ tt00371115/plotsummary. The movie is said to be in production as this book goes to press. Its title may change when it is released, with some suggesting that it will be renamed *Notorious.*

20. See Erwin Chemerinsky, *An Independent Analysis of the Los Angeles Police Department's Board of Inquiry Report on the Rampart Scandal,* September 11, 2000. Web posted at http://www.usc.edu/dept/law/faculty/ chemerinsky/rampartfinalrep.html (accessed January 10, 2002).

21. Linda Deutsch, "Appeals Court Intercedes in LAPD Corruption Trial," Associated Press wire service, October 12, 2000. Web posted at http://www.newstimes.com/archive2000/ oct12/nah.htm (accessed January 20, 2002).

22. "Three LAPD Officers Convicted," *USA Today* online, November 15, 2000 (accessed July 16, 2001).

23. "Prosecutors: LAPD Hindering Police Corruption Trial," Associated Press wire service, October 6, 2000. Web posted at http:// www.newstimes.com/archive2000/oct06/ nac.htm (accessed February 2, 2002).

24. Scott Glover and Matt Lait, "LAPD Settling Abuse Scandal," *Los Angeles Times,* March 31, 2005.

25. "Three LAPD Officers Convicted" and "This Week's Corrupt Cop Story." Web posted at http://www.stopthedrugwar.org/chronicle/266/ copcorruption.shtml (accessed October 2, 2003).

26. Glover and Lait, "LAPD Settling Abuse Scandal."

27. Ibid.

28. Tina Daunt and Jim Newton, "Council OKs Police Reform Pact with Justice Department," *Los Angeles Times* online, November 3, 2000 (accessed May 20, 2001).

29. Scott Glover and Matt Lait, "A Tearful Perez Gets Five Years," *Los Angeles Times* online, February 26, 2000 (accessed August 28, 2001).

30. Edwin H. Sutherland and Donald Cressey, *Principles of Criminology,* 8th ed. (Philadelphia: J. B. Lippincott, 1970).

31. Tim R. Jones, Compton Owens, and Melissa A. Smith, "Police Ethics Training: A Three-Tiered Approach," *FBI Law Enforcement Bulletin,* June 1995, pp. 22–26.

32. Stephen J. Gaffigan and Phyllis P. McDonald, *Police Integrity: Public Service with Honor* (Washington, DC: National Institute of Justice, 1997).

33. U.S. Department of Justice, *Principles for Promoting Police Integrity: Examples of Promising Police Practices* (Washington, DC: DOJ, 2001).

34. *Carroll* v. *City of Westminster,* 4th Cir. No. 99-1556, November 17, 2000.

35. The material in this paragraph is adapted from Sharon Burrell, "Random Drug Testing

36. of Police Officers Upheld," *Legal Views* (Office of the County Attorney, Montgomery County, Maryland), Vol. 6, No. 2 (February 2001), p. 4.

36. International Association of Chiefs of Police, *Employee Drug Testing* (St. Paul, MN: IACP, 1999).

37. *Maurice Turner* v. *Fraternal Order of Police,* 500 A.2d 1005 (D.C. 1985).

38. *Philip Caruso, President of P.B.A.* v. *Benjamin Ward, Police Commissioner,* New York State Supreme Court, Pat. 37, Index no. 12632–86, 1986.

39. *National Treasury Employees Union* v. *Von Raab,* 489 U.S. 656, 659 (1989).

40. National Law Enforcement Officers' Memorial Fund website, http://www.nleomf.com (accessed March 25, 2005).

41. "Two Detroit Police Officers Shot Dead during Traffic Stop," *USA Today,* February 17, 2004. Web posted at www.usatoday.com/news/ nation/2004-02-17-officers-shot_x.htm (accessed February 17, 2004).

42. "Man Who Killed Two Detroit Police Officers Sentenced to Life Without Parole," Associated Press, January 5, 2005.

43. From the Officer Down Memorial Page on the Web, http://odmp.org/officer.php?oid515754 (accessed September 15, 2005).

44. Ibid., http://www.odmp.org/ yeardisp .php?year52001 (accessed January 16, 2001).

45. Anthony J. Pinizzotto and Edward F. Davis, "Cop Killers and Their Victims," *FBI Law Enforcement Bulletin,* December 1992, p. 10.

46. Brian A. Reaves, *Census of State and Local Law Enforcement Agencies, 2000* (Washington, DC: Bureau of Justice Statistics, 2002); and Matthew J. Hickman and Brian A. Reaves, *Local Police Departments, 2000* (Washington, DC: Bureau of Justice Statistics, 2003).

47. Brian A. Reaves and Timothy C. Hart, *Federal Law Enforcement Officers, 2000* (Washington, DC: Bureau of Justice Statistics, 2002).

48. As reported by the Headline News Network, April 26, 1988.

49. *AIDS and Our Workplace,* New York City Police Department pamphlet, November 1987.

50. See Occupational Safety and Health Administration, OSHA Bloodborne Pathogens Act of 1991 (29 CFR 1910.1030).

51. *National Institute of Justice Reports,* No. 206 (November/December 1987).

52. See "On-the-Job Stress in Policing: Reducing It, Preventing It," *National Institute of Justice Journal* (January 2000), pp. 18–24.

53. "Stress on the Job," *Newsweek,* April 25, 1988, p. 43.

54. "On-the-Job Stress in Policing," p. 19.

55. Kevin Barrett, "Police Suicide: Is Anyone Listening?" *Journal of Safe Management of*

*Disruptive and Assaultive Behavior* (Spring 1997), pp. 6–9.

56. Ibid.

57. For an excellent review of coping strategies among police officers, see Robin N. Haarr and Merry Morash, "Gender, Race, and Strategies of Coping with Occupational Stress in Policing," *Justice Quarterly,* Vol. 16, No. 2 (June 1999), pp. 303–336.

58. Mark H. Anshel, "A Conceptual Model and Implications for Coping with Stressful Events in Police Work," *Criminal Justice and Behavior,* Vol. 27, No. 3 (2000), p. 375.

59. Ibid.

60. Bryan Vila, "Tired Cops: Probable Connections between Fatigue and the Performance, Health, and Safety of Patrol Officers," *American Journal of Police,* Vol. 15, No. 2 (1996), pp. 51–92.

61. Bryan Vila et al., *Evaluating the Effects of Fatigue on Police Patrol Officers: Final Report* (Washington, DC: National Institute of Justice, 2000).

62. Bryan Vila and Dennis Jay Kenney, "Tired Cops: The Prevalence and Potential Consequences of Police Fatigue," *NIJ Journal,* No. 248 (2002), p. 19.

63. Bryan Vila and Erik Y. Taiji, "Fatigue and Police Officer Performance," paper presented at the annual meeting of the American Society of Criminology, Chicago, 1996.

64. Some of the material in this section is adapted or derived from National Institute of Justice, *Use of Force by Police: Overview of National and Local Data* (Washington, DC: NIJ, 1999).

65. Matthew R. Durose, Erica L. Schmitt, and Patrick A. Langan, *Contacts Between Police and the Public.* (Washington, DC: Bureau of Justice Statistics, 2005).

66. Joel H. Garner and Christopher D. Maxwell, "Measuring the Amount of Force Used by and against the Police in Six Jurisdictions," in National Institute of Justice, *Use of Force by Police,* p. 41.

67. International Association of Chiefs of Police, *Police Use of Force in America 2001* (Alexandria, VA: IACP, 2001), p. 1.

68. Ibid.

69. Geoffrey P. Alpert and Roger G. Dunham, *The Force Factor: Measuring Police Use of Force Relative to Suspect Resistance—A Final Report* (Washington, DC: National Institute of Justice, 2001).

70. Samuel Walker, Geoffrey P. Alpert, and Dennis J. Kenney, *Responding to the Problem Police Officer: A National Study of Early Warning Systems* (Washington, DC: National Institute of Justice, 2000).

71. See Human Rights Watch, "The Christopher Commission Report," from which some of the wording in this paragraph is adapted. Web posted at http://www.hrw.org/reports98/police/uspo73.htm (accessed March 30, 2002).

72. Sam W. Lathrop, "Reviewing Use of Force: A Systematic Approach," *FBI Law Enforcement Bulletin,* October 2000, p. 18.

73. Jodi M. Brown and Patrick A. Langan, *Policing and Homicide, 1976–98: Justifiable Homicide by Police, Police Officers Murdered by Felons* (Washington, DC: Bureau of Justice Statistics, 2001), p. iii.

74. *Tennessee* v. *Garner,* 471 U.S. 1 (1985).

75. *Graham* v. *Connor,* 490 U.S. 386, 396–397 (1989).

76. John C. Hall, "FBI Training on the New Federal Deadly Force Policy," *FBI Law Enforcement Bulletin,* April 1996, pp. 25–32.

77. James Fyfe, *Shots Fired: An Examination of New York City Police Firearms Discharges* (Ann Arbor, MI: University Microfilms, 1978).

78. James Fyfe, "Blind Justice? Police Shootings in Memphis," paper presented at the annual meeting of the Academy of Criminal Justice Sciences, Philadelphia, March 1981.

79. It is estimated that American police shoot *at* approximately 3,600 people every year. See William Geller, *Deadly Force* study guide, Crime File Series (Washington, DC: National Institute of Justice, no date).

80. Anne Cohen, "I've Killed That Man Ten Thousand Times," *Police Magazine,* July 1980.

81. For more information, see Joe Auten, "When Police Shoot," *North Carolina Criminal Justice Today,* Vol. 4, No. 4 (Summer 1986), pp. 9–14.

82. Details for this story come from Stephanie Slater, "Suicidal Man Killed by Police Fusillade," *Palm Beach Post,* March 11, 2005, p. 1A.

83. Rebecca Stincelli, *Suicide by Cop: Victims from Both Sides of the Badge* (Folsom, CA: Interviews & Interrogations Institute, 2004).

84. Slater, "Suicidal Man Killed by Police Fusillade."

85. Anthony J. Pinizzotto, Edward F. Davis, and Charles E. Miller III, "Suicide by Cop: Defining a Devastating Dilemma," *FBI Law Enforcement Bulletin,* Vol. 74, No. 2 (February 2005), p. 15.

86. "Ten Percent of Police Shootings Found to Be 'Suicide by Cop,'" *Criminal Justice Newsletter,* September 1, 1998, pp. 1–2.

87. Robert J. Homant and Daniel B. Kennedy, "Suicide by Police: A Proposed Typology of Law Enforcement Officer–Assisted Suicide," *Policing: An International Journal of Police Strategies and Management,* Vol. 23, No. 3 (2000), pp. 339–355.

88. David W. Hayeslip and Alan Preszler, "NIJ Initiative on Less-than-Lethal Weapons," NIJ Research in Brief (Washington, DC: National Institute of Justice, 1993).

89. Ibid.

90. Thomas Farragher and David Abel, "Postgame Police Projectile Kills an Emerson Student," *Boston Globe,* October 22, 2004. Web posted at http://www.boston.com/sports/baseball/redsox/articles/2004/10/22/postgame_police_projectile_kills_an_emerson_student (accessed July 25, 2005).

91. Adapted from Deborah Ramirez, Jack McDevitt, and Amy Farrell, *A Resource Guide on Racial Profiling Data Collection Systems: Promising Practices and Lessons Learned* (Washington, DC: U.S. Department of Justice, 2000), p. 3.

92. David Harris, *Driving While Black: Racial Profiling on Our Nation's Highways* (Washington, DC: American Civil Liberties Union, 1999).

93. Peter Verniero and Paul Zoubek, *New Jersey Attorney General's Interim Report of the State Police Review Team Regarding Allegations of Racial Profiling* (Trenton, NJ: Office of the New Jersey Attorney General, 1999).

94. This paragraph is adapted from Ramirez, McDevitt, and Farrell, *A Resource Guide on Racial Profiling Data Collection Systems,* pp. 7–8.

95. *State of New Jersey* v. *Pedro Soto et al.,* Superior Court of New Jersey, 734 A.2d 350, 1996.

96. "Justice Department Bars Race Profiling, with Exception for Terrorism," *Criminal Justice Newsletter,* July 15, 2003, pp. 6–7.

97. "Justice Department Issues Policy Guidance to Ban Racial Profiling," U.S. Department of Justice press release (No. 355), June 17, 2003.

98. Blaine Harden and Somini Sengupta, "Some Passengers Singled Out for Exclusion by Flight Crew," *New York Times,* September 22, 2001.

99. David Cole and John Lambreth, "The Fallacy of Racial Profiling," *New York Times* online, May 13, 2001. Web posted at http://college1.nytimes.com/buests/articles/2001/05/13/846196.xml (accessed August 28, 2001).

100. Amitai Etzioni, "Another Side of Racial Profiling," *USA Today,* May 21, 2001, p. 15A.

101. Gallup Poll Organization, *Racial Profiling Is Seen as Widespread, Particularly among Young Black Men* (Princeton, NJ: Gallup Poll Organization, December 9, 1999), p. 1.

102. Christopher Stone, "Race, Crime, and the Administration of Justice," *National Institute of Justice Journal* (April 1999), p. 28.

103. Ramirez, McDevitt, and Farrell, *A Resource Guide on Racial Profiling Data Collection Systems,* p. 3.

104. Ibid., p. 55.

105. Police Executive Research Forum, *Racially Biased Policing: A Principled Response* (Washington, DC: PERF, 2001).

106. Ibid., foreword.

107. Ibid., p. 39.

108. Ibid., p. 47.

109. "Stroke Victim Sues State over Arrest," Associated Press wire service, April 24, 1996.

110. Charles R. Swanson, Leonard Territo, and Robert W. Taylor, *Police Administration: Structures, Processes, and Behavior,* 2nd ed. (New York: Macmillan, 1988).

111. *Malley* v. *Briggs,* 475 U.S. 335, 106 S.Ct. 1092 (1986).

112. Ibid., at 4246.

113. *Biscoe* v. *Arlington County,* 238 U.S. App. D.C. 206, 738 F.2d 1352, 1362 (1984). See also 738 F.2d 1352 (D.C. Cir. 1984), cert denied; 469 U.S. 1159; and 105 S.Ct. 909, 83 L.E.2d 923 (1985).

114. *Kaplan* v. *Lloyd's Insurance Co.,* 479 So.2d 961 (La. App. 1985).

115. John Hill, "High-Speed Police Pursuits: Dangers, Dynamics, and Risk Reduction," *FBI Law Enforcement Bulletin,* July 2002, pp. 14–18.

116. *City of Canton, Ohio* v. *Harris,* 489 U.S. 378 (1989).

117. Ibid., at 1204.

118. *Board of the County Commissioners of Bryan County, Oklahoma* v. *Brown,* 520 U.S. 397 (1997).

119. Title 42, §1983, U.S. Code.

120. *Bivens* v. *Six Unknown Federal Agents,* 403 U.S. 388 (1971).

121. See *F.D.I.C.* v. *Meyer,* 510 U.S. 471 (1994), in which the U.S. Supreme Court reiterated its ruling under *Bivens,* stating that only government employees and not government agencies can be sued.

122. *Wyler* v. *U.S.,* 725 F.2d 157 (2d Cir. 1983).

123. California Government Code, §818.

124. Federal Tort Claims Act, 28 U.S.C. 1346(b), 2671–2680.

125. *Elder* v. *Holloway,* 114 S.Ct. 1019, 127 L.Ed.2d 344 (1994).

126. Ibid.

127. *Hunter* v. *Bryant,* 112 S.Ct. 534 (1991).

128. William U. McCormack, "Supreme Court Cases: 1991–1992 Term," *FBI Law Enforcement Bulletin,* November 1992, p. 30.

129. *Idaho* v. *Horiuchi,* No. 98-30149 (9th Cir. 06/05/2001).

130. For more information on police liability, see Daniel L. Schofield, "Legal Issues of Pursuit Driving," *FBI Law Enforcement Bulletin,* May 1988, pp. 23–29.

131. Michael S. Vaughn, Tab W. Cooper, and Rolando V. del Carmen, "Assessing Legal Liabilities in Law Enforcement: Police Chiefs' Views," *Crime and Delinquency,* Vol. 47, No. 1 (2001), p. 3.

# PART 3

# Adjudication

## RIGHTS OF THE ACCUSED BEFORE THE COURT

Common law, constitutional, statutory, and humanitarian rights of the accused:

- The right to a speedy trial
- The right to legal counsel
- The right against self-incrimination
- The right not to be tried twice for the same offense
- The right to know the charges
- The right to cross-examine witnesses
- The right against excessive bail

These individual rights must be effectively balanced against these community concerns:

- Conviction of the guilty
- Exoneration of the innocent
- The imposition of appropriate punishment
- The protection of society
- Efficient and cost-effective procedures
- Seeing justice done

How does our system of justice work toward balance?

## Equal Justice Under Law

The well-known British philosopher and statesman Benjamin Disraeli (1804–1881) once defined justice as "truth in action." The study of criminal case processing by courts at all levels provides perhaps the best opportunity available to us from within the criminal justice system to observe what should ideally be "truth in action." The courtroom search for truth, which is characteristic of criminal trials, pits the resources of the accused against those of the state. The ultimate outcome of such procedures, say advocates of our adversarial-based system of trial practice, should be both truth and justice.

Others are not so sure. British novelist William McIlvanney (1936– ) once wrote, "Who thinks the law has anything to do with justice? It's what we have because we can't have justice." Indeed, many critics of the present system claim that courts at all levels have become so concerned with procedure and with sets of formalized rules that they have lost sight of the truth. The chapters that make up this section of *Criminal Justice Today* provide an overview of American courts, including their history and present structure, and examine the multifaceted roles played by both professional and lay courtroom participants. Sentencing—the practice whereby juries recommend and judges impose sanctions on convicted offenders—is covered in the concluding chapter of this section. Whether American courts routinely uncover truth and therefore dispense justice, or whether they are merely locked into a pattern of hollow procedure that does little other than mock the justice ideal, will be for you to decide.

**9**
**The Courts: Structure and Participants**

**10**
**Pretrial Activities and the Criminal Trial**

**11**
**Sentencing**

# CHAPTER 9

# The Courts: Structure and Participants

## OUTLINE

- Introduction
- History and Structure of the American Court System
- The State Court System
- The Federal Court System
- The Courtroom Work Group
- Professional Courtroom Participants
- Nonprofessional Courtroom Participants

## LEARNING OBJECTIVES

After reading this chapter, you should be able to:

- Describe the development of the American court system.
- Explain the concept of the dual-court system in America.
- Identify some of the differences between the state and federal court systems.
- Identify and explain the roles of the professional members of the courtroom work group.
- Discuss indigent defense, and know what forms it takes in the United States.
- Identify and explain the roles of the nonprofessional courtroom participants.
- Explain the roles of expert and lay witnesses in a criminal trial, and describe how their testimony might differ.
- Explain how professional and nonprofessional courtroom participants work together to bring most criminal trials to a successful close.

*The criminal court is the central, crucial institution in the criminal justice system. It is the part of the system that is the most venerable, the most formally organized, and the most elaborately circumscribed by law and tradition. It is the institution around which the rest of the system has developed.*

—The President's Commission on Law Enforcement and Administration of Justice

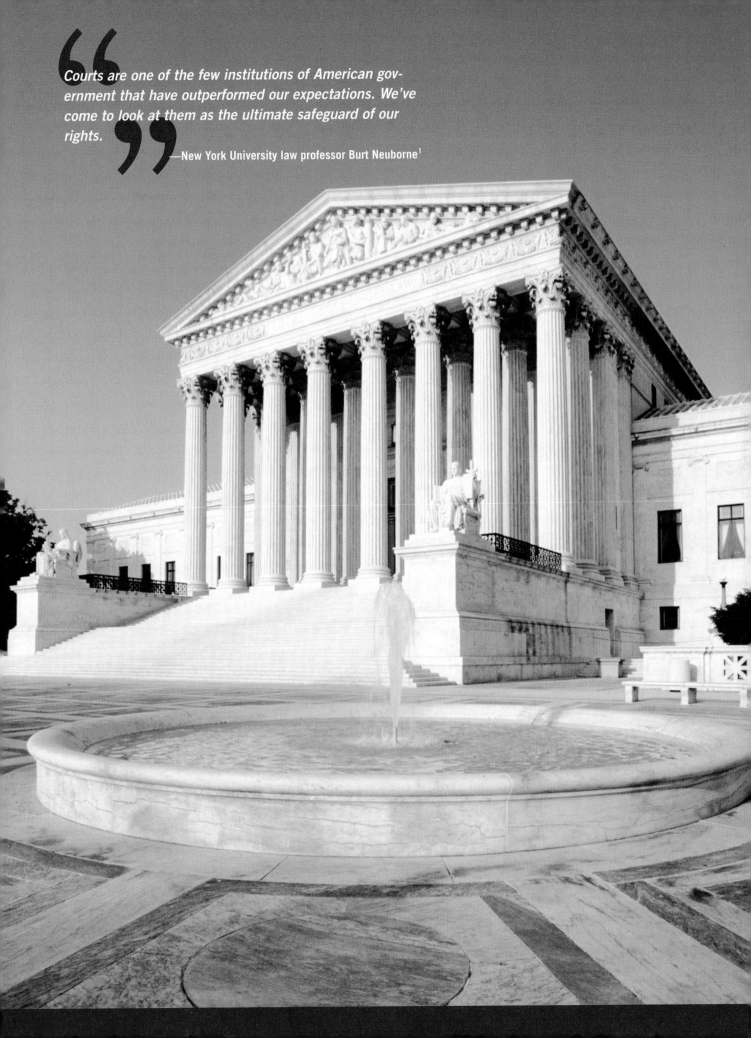

*Courts are one of the few institutions of American government that have outperformed our expectations. We've come to look at them as the ultimate safeguard of our rights.*

—New York University law professor Burt Neuborne[1]

# KEY CONCEPTS

## TERMS

| | | |
|---|---|---|
| appeal | expert witness | prosecutor |
| appellate jurisdiction | federal court system | prosecutorial discretion |
| bailiff | judge | public defender |
| change of venue | judicial review | state court administrator |
| community court | jurisdiction | state court system |
| court of last resort | juror | subpoena |
| courtroom work group | lay witness | trial *de novo* |
| defense counsel | original jurisdiction | victim-assistance program |
| dispute-resolution center | | |

## CASES

| | | |
|---|---|---|
| *Argersinger* v. *Hamlin* | *Gideon* v. *Wainwright* | *Keeney* v. *Tamayo-Reyes* |
| *Burns* v. *Reed* | *Herrera* v. *Collins* | *Marbury* v. *Madison* |
| *Crosby* v. *U.S.* | *Imbler* v. *Pachtman* | *Zafiro* v. *U.S.* |
| *Demarest* v. *Manspeaker et al.* | | |

The original full-text court opinion for each of these cases is available on the CD-ROM that accompanies this book.

# Introduction

Hear the author discuss this chapter at **cjtoday.com**

On March 11, 2005, rape suspect Brian Nichols grabbed a deputy's gun and shot her in the face as he was being prepared for transfer from a jail holding cell to an Atlanta courtroom.[2] Nichols, 33, then took the gun and crossed a pedestrian bridge into the courthouse area where he entered the eighth-floor courtroom in which his trial was scheduled to be held. Once inside, he shot and killed Superior Court Judge Rowland Barnes and court reporter Julie Ann Brandau. Both were in the midst of a civil hearing, with no police officers present. Nichols then fled down a stairwell, shooting and killing Fulton County Deputy Sheriff Hoyt Teasley whom he encountered along the way. Following several carjackings, Nichols came upon U.S. Customs Agent David Wilhelm as the agent worked on his house in Atlanta's Buckhead section. Nichols killed Wilhelm and took his truck, fleeing to the Atlanta suburb of Duluth. He became the focus of the largest manhunt in Georgia history before his capture a day later at a Gwinnett County condominium where he had been holding 26-year-old Ashley Smith captive.

Nichol's courthouse rampage came only a week after the husband and elderly mother of federal Judge Joan Humphrey Lefkow were found shot to death in the basement of the family's Chicago home.[3] A few days later the case seemed solved when 57-year-old Bart Ross shot himself to death during a Wisconsin traffic stop. Ross, stopped for having a burned-out taillight, left a suicide note saying that he had killed the judge's family. DNA from a cigarette butt found in the Lefkow house after the killings confirmed Ross's presence at the murder scene.[4] A medical malpractice case in which Ross had been the plaintiff, and which had earlier been dismissed by Judge Lefkow, apparently served as a motive in the killings.

Incidents like those in Atlanta and Chicago highlight the critical role that our nation's courts and the personnel who staff them play in the American system of justice. Breeches of courtroom security endanger courtroom participants and threaten the effective administration of justice. Without courts to decide guilt or innocence and to impose sentence on those convicted of crimes, the activities of law enforcement officials would become meaningless.

There are many different levels of courts in the United States, but they all dispense justice and work to ensure that officials in the justice system work within the law when carrying out their duties. At many points in this textbook and in three specific chapters (Chapter 7, "Policing: Legal Aspects"; Chapter 12, "Probation, Parole, and Community Corrections"; and Chapter 13, "Prisons and Jails"), we take a close look at court precedents that have defined the legality of enforcement efforts and correctional action. In Chapter 4, "Criminal Law," we explored the lawmaking function of courts. This chapter provides a picture of how courts work by describing the

A deputy is wheeled into a waiting ambulance (top left) in the aftermath of shootings at the Fulton County Courthouse in Atlanta, Georgia, in 2005. The deputy later died. Also killed in the shootings were Superior Court Judge Rowland Barnes (bottom) and court reporter Julie Ann Brandau. The shooter, rape suspect Brian Nichols (top right), grabbed a deputy's gun as he was being transferred from a holding cell. He escaped after the shootings, only to be captured the next day at a nearby condominium.

*AP Wide World Photos and Photo by Ben Gray*, Atlanta Journal—Constitution

American court system at both the state and federal levels. We will look at the roles of courtroom actors—from attorneys to victims and from jurors to judges. Then in Chapter 10, we will discuss pretrial activities and examine each of the steps in a criminal trial.

# History and Structure of the American Court System

Two types of courts function within the American criminal justice system: (1) state courts and (2) federal courts. Figure 9–1 outlines the structure of today's **federal court system**, and Figure 9–2 diagrams a typical **state court system**. This dual-court system is the result of general agreement among the nation's founders about the need for individual states to retain significant legislative authority and judicial autonomy separate from federal control. Under this concept, the United States developed as a relatively loose federation of semi-independent provinces. New states joining the union were assured of limited federal intervention into local affairs. State legislatures were free to create laws, and state court systems were needed to hear cases in which violations of those laws occurred.

In the last 200 years, states' rights have gradually waned relative to the power of the federal government, but the dual-court system still exists. Even today, state courts do not hear cases involving alleged violations of federal law, nor do federal courts get involved in deciding issues of state law unless there is a conflict between local or state statutes and federal constitutional guarantees. When such conflicts arise, claimed violations of federal due process guarantees—especially those found in the Bill of Rights—can provide the basis for appeals made to federal courts by offenders convicted in state court systems. Learn more about the dual-court system in America at **Library Extra 9–1** at cjtoday.com.

This chapter describes both federal and state court systems in terms of their historical development, **jurisdiction**, and current structure. Because it is within state courts that the large majority of criminal cases originate, we turn our attention first to them.

---

**federal court system**

The three-tiered structure of federal courts, comprising U.S. district courts, U.S. courts of appeal, and the U.S. Supreme Court.

---

**state court system**

A state judicial structure. Most states have at least three court levels: generally, trial courts, appellate courts, and a state supreme court.

---

**jurisdiction**

The territory, subject matter, or people over which a court or other justice agency may exercise lawful authority, as determined by statute or constitution.

---

**LIBRARY** EXTRA

**FIGURE 9–1**

The structure of the federal courts.

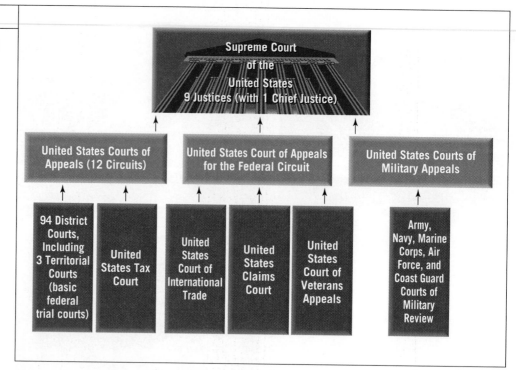

# The State Court System

## The Development of State Courts

Each of the original American colonies had its own court system for resolving disputes, both civil and criminal. As early as 1629, the Massachusetts Bay Colony created a General Court, composed of the governor, his deputy, 18 assistants, and 118 elected officials. The General Court was a combined legislature and court that made laws, held trials, and imposed sentences.[5] By 1639, as the colony grew, county courts were created, and the General Court took on the hearing of appeals as its primary job, retaining original jurisdiction only in cases involving "tryalls of life, limm, or banishment" and divorce.[6]

Pennsylvania began its colonial existence with the belief that "every man could serve as his own lawyer."[7] The Pennsylvania system utilized "common peacemakers" who served as referees in disputes. Parties to a dispute, including criminal suspects, could plead their case before a common peacemaker they had agreed on. The decision of the peacemaker was binding on the parties. Although the Pennsylvania referee system ended in 1766, lower-level judges are still referred to as *justices of the peace* in Pennsylvania and a few other states, though they are called *magistrates* in many other jurisdictions.

By 1776, all of the American colonies had established fully functioning court systems. The practice of law, however, was substantially inhibited by a lack of trained lawyers. A number of the early colonies even displayed a strong reluctance to recognize the practice of law as a profession. A Virginia statute enacted in 1645, for example, provided for the removal of "mercenary attorneys" from office and prohibited the practice of law for a fee. Most other colonies retained strict control over the number of authorized *barristers*—another name for lawyers—by requiring formal training in English law schools and appointment by the governor. New York, which provided for the appointment of "counselors at law," permitted a total of only 41 lawyers to practice law between 1695 and 1769[8]—in large part due to a widespread distrust of formally trained attorneys.

The tenuous status of lawyers in the colonies was highlighted by the 1735 trial of John Zenger in New York. Zenger was the editor of the newspaper *New York Journal* and was accused of slandering Governor William Cosby. When Cosby threatened to disbar any lawyer who defended Zenger, the editor hired Pennsylvania lawyer Andrew Hamilton, who was immune to the governor's threats because he was from out of state.[9]

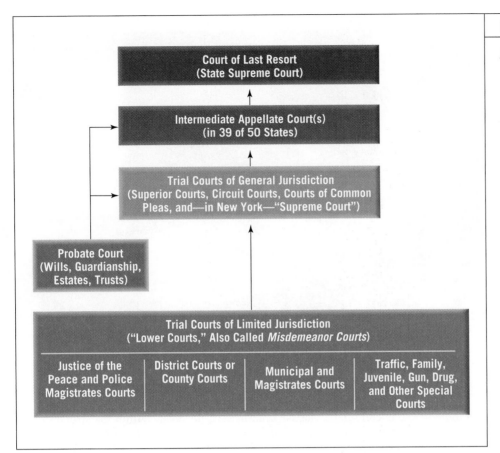

FIGURE 9–2

A typical state court system.

Following the American Revolution, colonial courts provided the organizational basis for the growth of fledgling state court systems. Since there had been considerable diversity in the structure of colonial courts, state courts were anything but uniform. Initially, most states made no distinction between **original jurisdiction**, the lawful authority of a court to hear cases that arise within a specified geographic area or that involve particular kinds of law violations, and **appellate jurisdiction**, the lawful authority of a court to review a decision made by a lower court. Many, in fact, had no provisions for appeal. Delaware, for example, did not allow appeals in criminal cases until 1897. States that did permit appeals often lacked any established appellate courts and sometimes used state legislatures for that purpose.

By the late nineteenth century, a dramatic increase in population, growing urbanization, the settlement of the West, and other far-reaching changes in the American way of life led to a tremendous increase in civil litigation and criminal arrests. Legislatures tried to keep pace with the rising tide of cases. States created a number of courts at the trial, appellate, and supreme court levels, calling them by a variety of names and assigning them functions that sometimes were completely different from those of similarly named courts in neighboring states. City courts, which were limited in their jurisdiction by community boundaries, arose to handle the special problems of urban life, such as disorderly conduct, property disputes, and the enforcement of restrictive and regulatory ordinances. Other tribunals, such as juvenile courts, developed to handle special kinds of problems or special clients. Some, like magistrate's courts or small-claims courts, handled only minor law violations and petty disputes. Still others, like traffic courts, were very narrow in focus. The result was a patchwork quilt of hearing bodies, some only vaguely resembling modern notions of a trial court.

State court systems developed by following several models. One was the New York State Field Code of 1848, which clarified jurisdictional claims and specified matters of court procedure. While many states copied the plan of the Field Code, it was later amended so extensively that its usefulness as a model dissolved. The federal Judiciary Act of 1789 and later the federal Reorganization Act of 1801 provided other models for state court systems. States that followed the federal model developed a three-tiered structure of (1) trial courts of limited jurisdiction, (2) trial courts of general jurisdiction, and (3) appellate courts.

**original jurisdiction**

The lawful authority of a court to hear or to act on a case from its beginning and to pass judgment on the law and the facts. The authority may be over a specific geographic area or over particular types of cases.

**appellate jurisdiction**

The lawful authority of a court to review a decision made by a lower court.

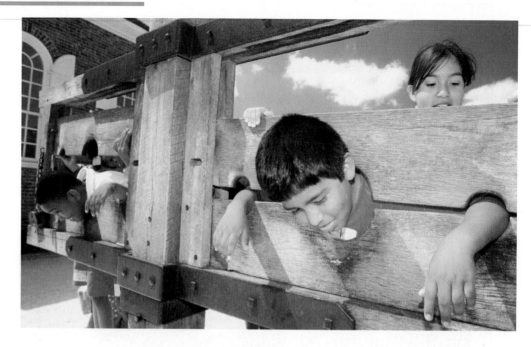

Junior high school children posing in the pillory in Williamsburg, Virginia. Just as criminal punishments have changed throughout the centuries, so too have criminal courts, which today provide civilized forums for exploring conflicting claims about guilt and innocence.

*Jeff Greenberg, PhotoEdit*

> **The power I exert on the Court depends on the power of my arguments, not on my gender.**
>
> —U.S. Supreme Court Justice
> Sandra Day O'Connor[i]

# State Court Systems Today

The three-tiered federal model was far from perfect, however. Within the structure it provided, many local and specialized courts proliferated. Traffic courts, magistrate's courts, municipal courts, recorder's courts, probate courts, and courts held by justices of the peace were but a few that functioned at the lower levels. In the early twentieth century, the American Bar Association and the American Judicature Society led the movement toward simplification of state court structures. Proponents of state court reform sought to unify redundant courts that held overlapping jurisdictions. Most reformers suggested a uniform model for all states that would build on (1) a centralized court structure composed of a clear hierarchy of trial and appellate courts, (2) the consolidation of numerous lower-level courts with overlapping jurisdictions, and (3) a centralized state court authority that would be responsible for budgeting, financing, and managing all courts within a state.

The court reform movement continues today. Although reformers have made substantial progress in many states, there are still many differences between and among state court systems. Reform states, which early on embraced the reform movement, are now characterized by streamlined judicial systems consisting of precisely conceived trial courts of limited and general jurisdiction, supplemented by one or two appellate court levels. Nonreform, or traditional, states retain judicial systems that are a conglomeration of multilevel and sometimes redundant courts with poorly defined jurisdictions. Even in nonreform states, however, most criminal courts can be classified within the three-tiered structure of two trial court echelons and an appellate tier.

## State Trial Courts

Trial courts are where criminal cases begin. The trial court conducts arraignments, sets bail, takes pleas, and conducts trials. (We will discuss each of these functions in more depth in the next chapter.) If the defendant pleads guilty or is found guilty, the trial court imposes sentence. Trial courts of limited, or special, jurisdiction are also called *lower courts*. Lower courts are authorized to hear only less serious criminal cases, usually involving misdemeanors, or to hear special types of cases, such as traffic violations, family disputes, and small claims. Courts of limited jurisdiction, which are depicted in TV shows like *Judge Judy* and *Joe Brown*, rarely hold jury trials, depending instead on the hearing judge to make determinations of both fact and law. At the lower-court level, a detailed record of the proceedings is not maintained. Case files will only include information on the charge, the plea, the finding of the court, and the sentence. All but six of the states make use of trial courts of limited jurisdiction.[10] These lower courts are much less formal than courts of general jurisdiction. In an intriguing analysis of court characteristics, Thomas Henderson, director of the National Center for State Courts, found that misdemeanor

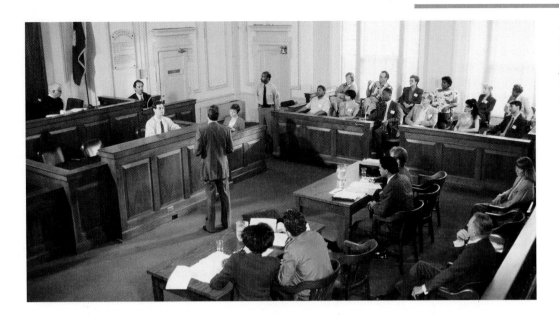

A criminal trial in progress. Courts have often been called "the fulcrum of the criminal justice system."

*Ron Chapple, Taxi, Getty Images, Inc.*

courts process cases according to a "decisional model."[11] The decisional model, said Henderson, is informal, personal, and decisive. It depends on the quick resolution of relatively uncomplicated issues of law and fact.

Trial courts of general jurisdiction—variously called *high courts, circuit courts,* or *superior courts*—are authorized to hear any criminal case. In many states, they also provide the first appellate level for courts of limited jurisdiction. In most cases, superior courts offer defendants whose cases originated in lower courts the chance for a new trial instead of a review of the record of the earlier hearing. When a new trial is held, it is referred to as **trial *de novo***.

Henderson describes courts of general jurisdiction according to a "procedural model."[12] Such courts, he says, make full use of juries, prosecutors, defense attorneys, witnesses, and all the other actors we usually associate with American courtrooms. The procedural model, which is far more formal than the decisional model, includes numerous court appearances to ensure that all of a defendant's due process rights are protected. The procedural model makes for a long, expensive, relatively impersonal, and highly formal series of legal maneuvers involving many professional participants—a fact clearly seen in the widely televised 1995 double-murder trial of famed athlete and media personality O. J. Simpson.

Trial courts of general jurisdiction operate within a fact-finding framework called the adversarial process. That process pits the interests of the state, represented by prosecutors, against the professional skills and abilities of defense attorneys. The adversarial process is not a free-for-all; rather, it is constrained by procedural rules specified in law and sustained through tradition. Take a virtual tour of California trial courts via Web Extra 9–1 at cjtoday.com.

## State Appellate Courts

Most states today have an appellate division where people can appeal a decision against them, consisting of an intermediate appellate court (often called the *court of appeals*) and a high-level appellate court (generally termed the *state supreme court*). High-level appellate courts are referred to as **courts of last resort**, indicating that a defendant can go no further with his appeal within the state court system once the high court rules on a case. All states have supreme courts, although only 39 have intermediate appellate courts.[13]

An **appeal** by a convicted defendant asks that a higher court review the actions of a lower court. Once they agree to review a decision, or accept an appeal, courts within the appellate division do not conduct a new trial. Instead, they review the case on the record, examining the written transcript of lower-court hearings to ensure that those proceedings were carried out fairly and in accordance with proper procedure and state law. These courts may also allow attorneys for both sides to make brief oral arguments and will generally consider other briefs or information filed by the appellant (the party initiating the appeal) or the appellee (the side opposed to the appeal). State statutes generally require that sentences of death or life imprisonment be automatically reviewed by the state supreme court.

---

**trial *de novo***

Literally, "new trial." The term is applied to cases that are retried on appeal, as opposed to those that are simply reviewed on the record.

**WEB EXTRA**

**court of last resort**

The court authorized by law to hear the final appeal on a matter.

**appeal**

Generally, the request that a court with appellate jurisdiction review the judgment, decision, or order of a lower court and set it aside (reverse it) or modify it.

Most convictions are affirmed on appeal. Occasionally, however, an appellate court will determine that the trial court erred in allowing certain kinds of evidence to be heard, that it failed to properly interpret the significance of a relevant statute, or that some other impropriety occurred. When that happens, the verdict of the trial court will be reversed, and the case may be sent back for a new trial, or *remanded*. When a conviction is overturned by an appellate court because of constitutional issues or when a statute is determined to be invalid, the state usually has recourse to the state supreme court, or when an issue of federal law is involved, as when a state court has ruled a federal law unconstitutional, to the U.S. Supreme Court.

Defendants who are not satisfied with the resolution of their case within the state court system may attempt an appeal to the U.S. Supreme Court. For such an appeal to have any chance of being heard, it must be based on claimed violations of the defendant's rights, as guaranteed under federal law or the U.S. Constitution. Under certain circumstances, federal district courts, which we will look at later in the chapter, may also provide a path of relief for state defendants who can show that their federal constitutional rights were violated. However, in the 1993 case of *Keeney* v. *Tamayo-Reyes,* the U.S. Supreme Court ruled that a "respondent is entitled to a federal evidentiary hearing [only] if he can show cause for his failure to develop the facts in the state-court proceedings and actual prejudice resulting from that failure, or if he can show that a fundamental miscarriage of justice would result from failure to hold such a hearing."[14] Justice Byron White, writing for the Court, said, "It is hardly a good use of scarce judicial resources to duplicate fact-finding in federal court merely because a petitioner has negligently failed to take advantage of opportunities in state-court proceedings."

Likewise, in *Herrera* v. *Collins* (1993),[15] the Court ruled that new evidence of innocence is no reason for a federal court to order a new state trial if constitutional grounds are lacking. In *Herrera,* where the defendant was under a Texas death sentence for the murder of two police officers, the Court said, "Where a defendant has been afforded a fair trial and convicted of the offense for which he was charged, the constitutional presumption of innocence disappears. . . . Thus, claims of actual innocence based on newly discovered evidence have never been held [to be] grounds for relief, absent an independent constitutional violation occurring in the course of the underlying state criminal proceedings. To allow a federal court to grant relief . . . would in effect require a new trial 10 years after the first trial, not because of any constitutional violation at the first trial, but simply because of a belief that in light of his new found evidence a jury might find him not guilty at a second trial." The *Keeney* and *Herrera* decisions have severely limited access by state defendants to federal courts. See Library Extra 9–2 at cjtoday.com for additional information on challenging state court criminal convictions within the federal court system.

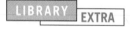

## State Court Administration

To function efficiently, courts require uninterrupted funding, adequate staffing, trained support personnel, a well-managed case flow, and coordination between levels and among jurisdictions. To oversee these and other aspects of judicial management, every state has its own mechanism for court administration. Most have **state court administrators** who manage these operational functions.

The following tasks are typical of state court administrators[16]:

- The preparation, presentation, and monitoring of a budget for the state court system
- The analysis of case flows and backlogs to determine where additional personnel, such as judges, prosecutors, and others, are needed
- The collection and publication of statistics describing the operation of state courts
- Efforts to streamline the flow of cases through individual courts and the system as a whole
- Service as a liaison between state legislatures and the court system
- The development or coordination of requests for federal and other outside funding
- The management of state court personnel, including promotions for support staff and the handling of retirement and other benefits packages for court employees
- The creation and coordination of plans for the training of judges and other court personnel (in conjunction with local chief judges and supreme court justices)
- The assignment of judges to judicial districts (especially in states that use rotating judgeships)
- The administrative review of payments to legal counsel for indigent defendants

State court administrators can receive assistance from the National Center for State Courts (NCSC) in Williamsburg, Virginia. The NCSC is an independent, nonprofit organization dedicated

**state court administrator**

A coordinator who assists with case-flow management, operating funds budgeting, and court docket administration.

Graduates of the Oakland County, Michigan, Community Dispute Resolution Center training program pose for a photo. Staffed largely by volunteers, dispute-resolution centers facilitate cooperative solutions to relatively low-level disputes in which minor criminal offenses might otherwise be charged.

*Photo courtesy of Oakland Mediation Center, Bloomfield Hills, Michigan*

to the improvement of the American court system. It was founded in 1971 at the behest of Chief Justice Warren E. Burger. The NCSC provides services to state courts, which include helping to

- Develop policies to enhance state courts.
- Advance state courts' interests within the federal government.
- Secure sufficient resources for state courts.
- Strengthen state court leadership.
- Facilitate state court collaboration.
- Provide a model for organizational administration.

You can visit the National Center for State Courts via Web Extra 9–2 at cjtoday.com.

At the federal level, the court system is administered by the Administrative Office of the United States Courts (AOUSC), in Washington, D.C. The AOUSC, created by Congress in 1939, prepares the budget and legislative agenda for federal courts. It also performs audits of court accounts, manages funds for the operation of federal courts, compiles and publishes statistics on the volume and type of business conducted by the courts, and recommends plans and strategies to efficiently manage court business. You can visit the Administrative Office of the United States Courts via Web Extra 9–3 at cjtoday.com.

WEB EXTRA

WEB EXTRA

## Dispute-Resolution Centers and Community Courts

Often, it is possible to resolve minor disputes (in which minor criminal offenses might otherwise be charged) without a formal court hearing. Some communities have **dispute-resolution centers**, which hear victims' claims of minor wrongs such as passing bad checks, trespassing, shoplifting, and petty theft. Today, more than 200 centers throughout the country,[17] frequently staffed by volunteer mediators, work to resolve disagreements without assigning blame. Dispute-resolution programs began in the early 1970s, with the earliest being the Community Assistance Project in Chester, Pennsylvania; the Columbus, Ohio, Night Prosecutor Program; and the Arbitration as an Alternative Program in Rochester, New York. Following the lead of these programs, the U.S. Department of Justice helped promote the development of three experimental Neighborhood Justice Centers in Los Angeles, Kansas City, and Atlanta. Each center accepted both minor civil and criminal cases.

Mediation centers are often closely integrated with the formal criminal justice process and may substantially reduce the caseload of lower-level courts. Some centers are, in fact, run by the courts and work only with court-ordered referrals. Others are semiautonomous but may be dependent on courts for endorsement of their decisions; others function with complete autonomy. Rarely, however, do dispute-resolution programs entirely supplant the formal criminal justice

**dispute-resolution center**

An informal hearing place designed to mediate interpersonal disputes without resorting to the more formal arrangements of a criminal trial court.

mechanism, and defendants who appear before a community mediator may later be charged with a crime. Community mediation programs have become a central feature of today's restorative-justice movement (discussed in more detail in Chapter 11).

Recently, the community-justice movement has led to the creation of innovative low-level courts in certain parts of the country. Unlike dispute-resolution centers, **community courts** are always *official* components of the formal justice system and can hand down sentences, including fines and jail time, without further judicial review. Community courts typically begin as grass-roots movements undertaken by community residents and local organizations seeking to build confidence in the way offenders are handled for less serious offenses. Community courts generally sentence convicted offenders to work within the community, "where neighbors can see what they are doing."[18] Like dispute-resolution centers, community courts focus on quality-of-life crimes that erode a neighborhood's morale, emphasize problem solving rather than punishment, and build on restorative principles such as community service and restitution.

Both mediation centers and community courts have been criticized because they typically work only with minor offenders and deny the opportunity for mediation to victims and offenders in more serious cases. They have also come under criticism because defendants may see them as just another form of criminal sanction rather than as a true alternative to processing by the criminal justice system.[19] Dispute-resolution centers, in particular, have been criticized for doing little more than providing a forum for shouting matches between the parties involved. Learn more about dispute-resolution centers and community courts via Library Extra 9–3 and Web Extra 9–4 at cjtoday.com.

**community court**

A low-level court that focuses on quality-of-life crimes that erode a neighborhood's morale, that emphasizes problem solving rather than punishment, and that builds on restorative principles such as community service and restitution.

Log on to ResearchNavigator .com, and choose "All" under the *New York Times* subject archive section. Enter the words "federal criminal court" (without the quotation marks) in the search box, and click "Go." Ignoring any "hits" that are not related to criminal justice, select five articles that you find interesting from the results page. Write a summary of each article, including complete source information—that is, article title, author (if available), date of publication, and source (in this case, the *New York Times*). Submit what you have written to your instructor if asked to do so. *Note:* This feature is available only if your instructor has chosen the Research Navigator option available with a new textbook.

# The Federal Court System

Whereas state courts evolved from early colonial arrangements, federal courts were created by the U.S. Constitution. Article III, Section 1, of the Constitution provides for the establishment of "one supreme Court, and . . . such inferior Courts as the Congress may from time to time ordain and establish." Article III, Section 2, specifies that such courts are to have jurisdiction over cases arising under the Constitution, federal laws, and treaties. Federal courts are also to settle disputes between states and to have jurisdiction in cases where one of the parties is a state.

Today's federal court system represents the culmination of a series of congressional mandates that have expanded the federal judicial infrastructure so that it can continue to carry out the duties envisioned by the Constitution. Notable federal statutes that have contributed to the present structure of the federal court system include the Judiciary Act of 1789, the Judiciary Act of 1925, and the Magistrate's Act of 1968.

As a result of constitutional mandates, congressional actions, and other historical developments, today's federal judiciary consists of three levels: (1) U.S. district courts, (2) U.S. courts of appeal, and (3) the U.S. Supreme Court. Each is described in turn in the following sections.

## U.S. District Courts

The U.S. district courts are the trial courts of the federal court system.[20] Within limits set by Congress and the Constitution, the district courts have jurisdiction to hear nearly all categories of federal cases, including both civil and criminal matters. There are 94 federal judicial districts, including at least one district in each state (some states, like New York and California, have as many as four), the District of Columbia, and Puerto Rico. Each district includes a U.S. bankruptcy court as a unit of the district court. Three territories of the United States—the Virgin Islands, Guam, and the Northern Mariana Islands—have district courts that hear federal cases, including bankruptcy cases. There are two special trial courts that have nationwide jurisdiction over certain types of cases. The Court of International Trade addresses cases involving international trade and customs issues. The U.S. Court of Federal Claims has jurisdiction over most claims for monetary damages against the United States, disputes over federal contracts, unlawful "takings" of private property by the federal government, and a variety of other claims against the United States.

Federal district courts have original jurisdiction over all cases involving alleged violations of federal statutes. A district may be divided into divisions and may have several places where the court hears cases. District courts were first authorized by Congress through the Judiciary Act of 1789, which allocated one federal court to each state. Because of population increases over the years, new courts have been added in many states.

Nearly 650 district court judges staff federal district courts. Because some courts are much busier than others, the number of district court judges varies from a low of 2 in some jurisdictions to a high of 27 in others. District court judges are appointed by the president and confirmed by the Senate, and they serve for life. An additional 369 full-time and 110 part-time magistrate judges (referred to as *U.S. magistrates* before 1990) serve the district court system and assist the federal judges. Magistrate judges have the power to conduct arraignments and may set bail, issue warrants, and try minor offenders.

U.S. district courts handle tens of thousands of cases per year. For the 12 months ending September 30, 2004, for example, 71,022 criminal cases[21] and 281,338 civil cases[22] were filed in U.S. district courts. Drug prosecution, especially in courts located close to the U.S.–Mexican border, has led to considerable growth in the number of cases filed. Federal drug prosecutions in the border states of California, Arizona, New Mexico, and Texas more than doubled between 1994 and 2000, from 2,864 to 6,116, and immigration prosecutions increased more than sevenfold, from 1,056 to 7,613.[23] During the past 20 years, the number of cases handled by the entire federal district court system has grown exponentially. The hiring of new judges and the creation of new courtroom facilities have not kept pace with the increase in caseload, and questions persist as to the quality of justice that overworked judges can deliver.

One of the most pressing issues facing district court judges is the fact that their pay, which at $154,700 in mid-2005[24] placed them in the top 1% of income-earning Americans, is low compared to what most could earn in private practice. Since 1992, the salaries of federal judges have remained relatively stagnant, leading many judges to leave the bench.[25] Learn more about the federal courts via **Library Extra 9–4** at cjtoday.com.

> Oyez, oyez, oyez! All persons having business before the honorable, the Supreme Court of the United States, are admonished to draw near and give their attention, for the court is now sitting. God save the United States and this honorable Court.
>
> —Marshal's cry at the opening of public sessions of the U.S. Supreme Court

# U.S. Courts of Appeal

The 94 judicial districts are organized into 12 regional circuits, each of which has a U.S. court of appeals.[26] A court of appeals hears appeals from the district courts located within its circuit, as well as appeals from decisions of federal administrative agencies. The Court of Appeals for the Federal Circuit has nationwide jurisdiction to hear appeals in special cases, such as those involving patent laws and cases decided by the Court of International Trade and the U.S. Court of Federal Claims.

The U.S. Court of Appeals for the Federal Circuit and the 12 regional courts of appeal are often referred to as *circuit courts.* Early in the nation's history, the judges of the first courts of appeal visited each of the courts in one region in a particular sequence, traveling by horseback and riding the "circuit." Today, the regional courts of appeal review matters from the district courts of their geographic regions, from the U.S. Tax Court, and from certain federal administrative agencies. A disappointed party in a district court usually has the right to have the case reviewed in the court of appeals for the circuit. The First through Eleventh Circuits all include three or more states, as illustrated in Figure 9–3.

Each court of appeals consists of six or more judges, depending on the caseload of the court. Circuit court judges are appointed for life by the president with the advice and consent of the Senate. The judge who has served on the court the longest and who is under 65 years of age is designated as the chief judge and performs administrative duties in addition to hearing cases. The chief judge serves for a maximum term of seven years. There are 167 judges on the 12 regional courts of appeals.

The U.S. Court of Appeals for the District of Columbia, which is often called the Twelfth Circuit, hears cases arising in the District of Columbia and has appellate jurisdiction assigned by Congress in legislation concerning many departments of the federal government. The U.S. Court of Appeals for the Federal Circuit (in effect, the Thirteenth Circuit) was created in 1982 by the merging of the U.S. Court of Claims and the U.S. Court of Customs and Patent Appeals. The court hears appeals in cases from the U.S. Court of Federal Claims, the U.S. Court of International Trade, the U.S. Court of Veterans Appeals, the International Trade Commission, the Board of Contract Appeals, the Patent and Trademark Office, and the Merit Systems Protection Board. The Federal Circuit Court also hears appeals from certain decisions of the secretaries of the Department of Agriculture and the Department of Commerce and cases from district courts involving patents and minor claims against the federal government.

Federal appellate courts have mandatory jurisdiction over the decisions of district courts within their circuits. Mandatory jurisdiction means that U.S. courts of appeal are required to hear the cases brought to them. Criminal appeals from federal district courts are usually heard by panels of three judges sitting on a court of appeals rather than by all the judges of each circuit.

**FIGURE 9-3**

Geographic boundaries of
the U.S. courts of appeal
and U.S. district courts.

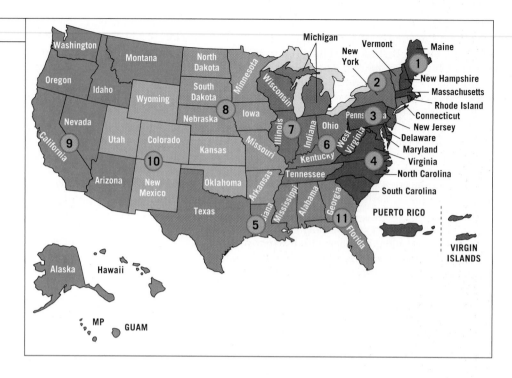

Federal appellate courts operate under the Federal Rules of Appellate Procedure, although each has also created its own separate Local Rules. Local Rules may mean that one circuit, such as the Second, will depend heavily on oral arguments, while others may substitute written summary depositions in their place. Appeals generally fall into one of three categories: (1) frivolous appeals, which have little substance, raise no significant new issues, and are generally disposed of quickly; (2) ritualistic appeals, which are brought primarily because of the demands of litigants, even though the probability of reversal is negligible; and (3) nonconsensual appeals, which entail major questions of law and policy and on which there is considerable professional disagreement among the courts and within the legal profession.[27] The probability of reversal is highest in the case of nonconsensual appeals.

Because the Constitution guarantees a right to an appeal, federal circuit courts face an ever-increasing workload. While the numbers of cases filed in both appellate courts and district courts have increased dramatically during the last 20 years, the number of federal judges has remained virtually unchanged. In 2005, the Judicial Conference of the United States, the primary policy-making arm of the federal courts, urged Congress to create 68 new federal judgeships in appellate and district courts.[28] The conference cited a need for 9 permanent and 3 temporary court of appeals judgeships, and 44 permanent and 12 temporary district judgeships.

Almost all appeals from federal district courts go to the court of appeals serving the circuit in which the case was first heard. A defendant's right to appeal, however, has been interpreted to mean the right to one appeal. Hence, the U.S. Supreme Court need not necessarily hear the appeals of defendants who are dissatisfied with the decision of a federal appeals court. Learn more about criminal appeals in federal courts via **Library Extra 9–5** at cjtoday.com.

## The U.S. Supreme Court

At the apex of the federal court system stands the U.S. Supreme Court. The Supreme Court is located in Washington, D.C., across the street from the U.S. Capitol. The Court consists of nine justices, eight of whom are associate justices. The ninth presides over the Court as the chief justice of the United States. Supreme Court justices are nominated by the president, are confirmed by the Senate, and serve for life. Lengthy terms of service are a tradition among justices. One of the earliest chief justices, John Marshall, served the Court for 34 years, from 1801 to 1835. The same was true of Justice Stephen J. Field, who sat on the bench between 1863 and 1897. Justice Hugo Black passed the 34-year milestone, serving an additional month, before he retired in 1971. Justice William O. Douglas set a record for longevity on the bench, retiring in 1975 after 36 years and six months of service. You can view the biographies of today's Supreme Court justices via **Web Extra 9–5** at cjtoday.com.

Protesters in front of the U.S. Supreme Court in 2004. Highlighting its importance as our nation's premier legal institution, the Court became the backdrop for a rally against the USA PATRIOT Act. Protesters claimed that the act unfairly denies foreign terror suspects the right to a quick and impartial hearing. The Court is often called on to balance individual rights and freedoms with the need for public safety and social order.

*© William Philpott, Corbis*

The Supreme Court of the United States wields immense power. The Court's greatest authority lies in its capacity for **judicial review** of lower-court decisions and state and federal statutes. By exercising its power of judicial review, the Court decides what laws and lower-court decisions keep with the intent of the U.S. Constitution. The power of judicial review is not explicit in the Constitution but was anticipated by its framers. In the *Federalist Papers,* which urged adoption of the Constitution, Alexander Hamilton wrote that through the practice of judicial review, the Court would ensure that "the will of the whole people," as grounded in the Constitution, would be supreme over the "will of the legislature," which might be subject to temporary whims.[29] It was not until 1803, however, that the Court forcefully asserted its power of judicial review. In an opinion written for the case of *Marbury* v. *Madison* (1803),[30] Chief Justice John Marshall established the Court's authority as final interpreter of the U.S. Constitution, declaring, "It is emphatically the province of the judicial department to say what the law is."

| judicial review |
| --- |
| The power of a court to review actions and decisions made by other agencies of government. |

## Increasing Complexity and the Supreme Court

The evolution of the U.S. Supreme Court provides one of the most dramatic examples of institutional development in American history. Sparsely described in the Constitution, the Court has grown from a handful of circuit-riding justices into a modern organization that wields tremendous legal power over all aspects of American life. Much of the Court's growth has been because it is increasingly willing to mediate fundamental issues of law and to act as a resort from arbitrary and capricious processing by the justice systems of the states and the national government.

The *Marbury* decision established the Court as a mighty force in the federal government by virtue of the power of judicial review. As we discussed in Chapter 7, the Court began to apply that power during the 1960s to issues of crime and justice at the state and local levels. You may recall that the Court signaled its change in orientation in 1961 with the case of *Mapp* v. *Ohio,*[31] which extended the exclusionary rule—which holds that evidence illegally seized by the police cannot be used in a trial—to the states. Such extension, combined with the near-simultaneous end of the hands-off doctrine that had previously exempted state prison systems from Court scrutiny (and which is discussed in Chapter 14), placed the authority of the Court squarely over the activities of state criminal justice systems. From that time forward, the Court's workload became increasingly heavy, and today it shows few signs of abatement.

## The Supreme Court Today

The Supreme Court reviews the decisions of lower courts and may accept cases from both U.S. courts of appeal and from state supreme courts. It has limited original jurisdiction and does not conduct trials except in disputes between states and in some cases of attorney disbarment. For a case to be heard, at least four justices must vote in favor of a hearing. When the Court agrees to

U.S. Supreme Court Chief Justice John G. Roberts, Jr., walks past an official portrait of his predecessor, former Chief Justice William H. Rehnquist—who died in office in 2005. Roberts, who served on the U.S. Court of Appeals for the District of Columbia Circuit prior to joining the nation's highest court, was nominated in 2005 by President George W. Bush to succeed Rehnquist. It is anticipated that Justice Roberts will play a key role in shaping the national debate on important issues for years to come.

*Charles Dharapak, Getty Images, Inc.*

hear a case, it will issue a writ of *certiorari* to a lower court, ordering it to send the records of the case forward for review. Once having granted *certiorari,* the justices can revoke the decision. In such cases, a writ is dismissed by ruling it improvidently granted.

The U.S. Supreme Court may review any decision appealed to it that it decides is worthy of review. In fact, however, the Court elects to review only cases that involve a substantial federal question. Of approximately 5,000 requests for review received by the Court yearly, only about 200 are heard.

A term of the Supreme Court begins, by statute, on the first Monday in October and lasts until early July. The term is divided among sittings, when cases will be heard, and time for the writing and delivering of opinions. Between 22 and 24 cases are heard at each sitting (which may last days), with each side allotted 30 minutes for arguments before the justices. Intervening recesses allow justices time to study arguments and supporting documentation and to work on their opinions.

Decisions rendered by the Supreme Court are rarely unanimous. Instead, the opinion that a majority of the Court's justices agree on becomes the judgment of the Court. Justices who agree with the Court's judgment write concurring opinions if they agree for a different reason or if they feel that they have some new light to shed on a legal issue in the case. Justices who do not agree with the decision of the Court write dissenting opinions, which may offer new possibilities for successful appeals of future cases. Visit the U.S. Supreme Court via Web Extra 9–6 at cjtoday.com, and learn more about the federal judiciary via Library Extra 9–6.

# The Courtroom Work Group

In March 2005, Scott Peterson became the 641st person on California's death row in San Quentin State Prison. Peterson, 32, had been sentenced to die by San Mateo (California) Superior Court Judge Alfred Delucchi following his conviction for the 2002 murders of his pregnant 27-year-old wife, Laci, and the couple's unborn son, Conner. Laci Peterson disappeared on December 24, 2002. Her badly decomposed body and that of her fetus washed ashore in San Francisco Bay four months later near the marina where Peterson said he had taken his boat on a fishing trip the day his wife disappeared. Peterson, a former fertilizer salesman, was found guilty by a jury of six men and six women that heard testimony from 184 witnesses, including massage therapist Amber Frey with whom Peterson had been having an affair. The trial lasted 23 weeks, during which two jurors had to be replaced with alternates. Peterson's attorney, Mark Geragos, indicated that he would make those dismissals the basis for an appeal to California's Supreme Court. The Peterson case captivated the country and made headlines worldwide. See a copy of the criminal indict-

Thurgood Marshall (1908–1993), the nation's first African-American U.S. Supreme Court justice.

*Collection of the Supreme Court of the United States*

ment against Scott Peterson at Library Extra 9–7 at cjtoday.com, and hear the verdicts against him being read at Web Extra 9–7 at cjtoday.com.

Like plays on a stage, criminal trials often entail quite a bit of drama and may involve many participants, each of whom has a different role to fill. Participants can be divided into two categories: professionals and outsiders. The professionals are the official courtroom actors and include judges, prosecuting attorneys, defense attorneys, public defenders, and others who earn a living serving the court. These professionals are called the **courtroom work group**. The courtroom work group is guided by statutory requirements and ethical considerations; members of the group also recognize informal rules of civility, cooperation, and shared goals.[32] Hence even within the adversarial framework of a criminal trial, the courtroom work group is dedicated to bringing the procedure to a successful close.[33]

In contrast, outsiders—those trial participants who are only temporarily involved with the court—are generally unfamiliar with courtroom organization and trial procedure. Outsiders include jurors and witnesses, as well as defendants and victims, even though they may have a greater personal investment in the outcome of the trial than anyone else. Learn more about professional and nonprofessional courtroom participants at Web Extra 9–8 at cjtoday.com.

**courtroom work group**

The professional courtroom actors, including judges, prosecuting attorneys, defense attorneys, public defenders, and others who earn a living serving the court.

# Professional Courtroom Participants

## The Judge

The trial **judge** has the primary duty of ensuring justice. The American Bar Association's *Standards for Criminal Justice* describes the duties of the trial judge as follows: "The trial judge has the responsibility for safeguarding both the rights of the accused and the interests of the public in the administration of criminal justice. . . . The only purpose of a criminal trial is to determine whether the prosecution has established the guilt of the accused as required by law, and the trial judge should not allow the proceedings to be used for any other purpose."[34]

In the courtroom, the judge holds ultimate authority, ruling on matters of law, weighing objections from both sides, deciding on the admissibility of evidence, and disciplining anyone who challenges the order of the court. In most jurisdictions, judges also sentence offenders after a verdict has been returned; in some states, judges serve to decide guilt or innocence for defendants who waive a jury trial. Most state jurisdictions have a chief judge who, besides serving as a trial judge, must also manage the court system. Management includes hiring staff, scheduling sessions of court, ensuring the adequate training of subordinate judges, and coordinating activities with other courtroom actors. Chief judges usually assume their position by virtue of seniority and rarely have any formal training in management. Hence, the managerial effectiveness of a chief judge is often a matter of personality and dedication more than anything else.

**judge**

An elected or appointed public official who presides over a court of law and who is authorized to hear and sometimes to decide cases and to conduct trials.

To hear patiently, to weigh deliberately and dispassionately, and to decide impartially; these are the chief duties of a judge.

—Albert Pike (1809–1891)

Scott Peterson with defense attorney Mark Geragos (left); Scott's wife, Laci (right); and Judge Alfred A. Delucchi (bottom left), who presided over Peterson's 2004 California murder trial. Peterson, 30, was convicted of killing his 27-year-old wife and their unborn son and was sentenced to die. Their bodies, which were dumped into San Francisco Bay on Christmas Eve of 2002, washed ashore four months later near the spot where Peterson said he had been fishing when Laci disappeared.

*AP Wide World Photos*

## Judicial Selection

As mentioned earlier, judges at the federal level are nominated by the president of the United States and take their place on the bench only after confirmation by the Senate. At the state level, things work somewhat differently. Depending on the jurisdiction, state judgeships are won either through popular election or by political (usually gubernatorial) appointment. The process of judicial selection at the state level is set by law.

Both judicial election and appointment have been criticized because each system allows politics to enter the judicial arena, although in somewhat different ways. Under the election system, judicial candidates must receive the endorsement of their parties, generate contributions, and manage an effective campaign. Under the appointment system, judicial hopefuls must be in favor with incumbent politicians to receive appointments. Because partisan politics plays a role in both systems, critics have claimed that sitting judges can rarely be as neutral as they should be. They carry to the bench with them campaign promises, personal indebtedness, and possible political agendas.

To counter some of these problems, a number of states have adopted the Missouri Plan (or the Missouri Bar Plan) for judicial selection,[35] which combines elements of both election and appointment. It requires candidates for judicial vacancies to undergo screening by a nonpartisan state judicial nominating committee. Candidates selected by the committee are reviewed by an arm of the governor's office, which selects a final list of names for appointment. Incumbent judges must face the electorate after a specified term in office. They then run unopposed in nonpartisan elections in which only their records may be considered. Voters have the choice of allowing a judge to continue in office or asking that another be appointed to take his or her place. Because the Missouri Plan provides for periodic public review of judicial performance, it is also called the *merit plan of judicial selection.*

## Judicial Qualifications

A few decades ago, many states did not require any special training, education, or other qualifications for judges. Anyone (even someone without a law degree) who won election or was appointed could assume a judgeship. Today, however, almost all states require that judges in general jurisdiction and appellate courts hold a law degree, be a licensed attorney, and be a member of their state bar association. Many states also require newly elected judges to attend state-sponsored training sessions on subjects such as courtroom procedure, evidence, dispute resolution, judicial writing, administrative record keeping, and ethics.

While most states provide instruction to meet the needs of trial judges, other organizations also provide specialized training. The National Judicial College, located on the campus of the University of Nevada at Reno, is one such institution. It was established in 1963 by the Joint Committee for the Effective Administration of Justice, chaired by Justice Tom C. Clark of the U.S. Supreme Court.[36] More than 32,000 judges have enrolled in courses since the college began operation.[37] Visit the National Judicial College via Web Extra 9–9 at cjtoday.com.

In some parts of the United States, lower-court judges, such as justices of the peace, local magistrates, and "district" court judges, may still be elected without educational and other professional requirements. Today, in 43 states, some 1,300 nonlawyer judges are serving in mostly rural courts of limited jurisdiction.[38] In New York, for example, of the 3,300 judges in the state's unified court system, approximately 65% are part-time town or village justices, and about 80% of town and village justices are not lawyers.[39] The majority of cases that come before New York lay judges involve alleged traffic violations, although they may also include misdemeanors, small-claims actions, and civil cases of up to $3,000.

Even though some have defended lay judges as being closer to the citizenry in their understanding of justice,[40] in most jurisdictions, the number of lay judges is declining. States that continue to use lay judges in lower courts do require that candidates for judgeships not have criminal records, and most states require that they attend special training sessions if elected.

## Judicial Misconduct

In June 1997, a bond hearing in West Virginia took a turn for the worse when Pleasant County Circuit Judge Joseph Troisi took off his robe, stepped to the front of the judge's bench, and bit defendant Bill Whittens on the nose. Whittens said the judge bit him after he directed a derogatory remark at him. Whittens's nose required medical treatment at a local hospital. The Federal Bureau of Investigation (FBI) was called in to investigate, and Judge Troisi later resigned.[41]

Most judges are highly professional in and out of the courtroom. However, occasionally a judge oversteps the limits of his authority; some unprofessional judicial behavior may even violate the law. In 2002, for example, two men who were sentenced to death in Arizona in the 1980s asked an appellate court to reverse their sentences, claiming that the judge who sentenced them suffered from impaired judgment because he had used marijuana.[42] The judge, former Phoenix Superior Court Judge Philip Marquardt, had bought marijuana by mail using office stationery—with the court's return address printed on it—to make the purchases. He was removed from the bench in 1991 and lost his license to practice law following a second drug conviction. The judge, now a 69-year-old retired ski instructor, recently conceded in an interview that he had used marijuana regularly during the years in which he sentenced Richard Michael Rossi and Warren Summerlin to death. Rossi, interviewed from prison, said, "There is a lot of irony here. We both had addiction problems. I acknowledged mine. He didn't acknowledge his."

At the federal level, the Judicial Councils Reform and Judicial Conduct and Disability Act, passed by Congress in 1980, specifies the procedures necessary to register complaints against federal judges and, in serious cases, to begin the process of impeachment, or forced removal from the bench.

## The Prosecuting Attorney

The **prosecutor**—called variously the *district attorney, state's attorney, county attorney, commonwealth attorney,* or *solicitor*—is responsible for presenting the state's case against the defendant. The prosecuting attorney is the primary representative of the people by virtue of the

> I left [the Supreme Court] . . . perfectly convinced that . . . a system so defective . . . would not obtain the energy, weight, and dignity which are essential to its affording due support to the national government, nor acquire the public confidence and respect which, as the last resort of the justice of the nation, it should possess.
>
> —John Jay, first Chief Justice of the United States, in a letter to John Adams, 1801

**WEB EXTRA**

**prosecutor**
An attorney whose official duty is to conduct criminal proceedings on behalf of the state or the people against those accused of having committed criminal offenses.

> When we have examined in detail the organization of the Supreme Court, and the entire prerogatives which it exercises, we shall readily admit that a more imposing judicial power was never constituted by any people.
>
> —Alexis de Tocqueville, *Democracy in America* (1835)

belief that violations of the criminal law are an affront to the public. Except for federal prosecutors (called *U.S. attorneys*) and solicitors in five states, prosecutors are elected and generally serve four-year terms with the possibility of continuing reelection.[43] Widespread criminal conspiracies, whether they involve government officials or private citizens, may require the services of a special prosecutor whose office can spend the time and resources needed for efficient prosecution.[44]

In many jurisdictions, because the job of prosecutor entails too many duties for one person to handle, prosecutors supervise a staff of assistant district attorneys who do most in-court work. Assistants are trained attorneys, usually hired directly by the chief prosecutor and licensed to practice law in the state where they work. Approximately 2,300 chief prosecutors, assisted by 24,000 deputy attorneys, serve the nation's counties and independent cities.[45]

Another prosecutorial role has traditionally been that of quasi-legal adviser to local police departments. Because prosecutors are sensitive to the kinds of information needed for conviction, they may help guide police investigations and will exhort detectives to identify credible witnesses, uncover additional evidence, and the like. This role is limited, however. Police departments are independent of the administrative authority of the prosecutor, and cooperation between them, although based on the common goal of conviction, is purely voluntary. Moreover, close cooperation between prosecutors and police may not always be legal. A 1998 federal law known as the McDade-Murtha Law,[46] for example, requires that federal prosecutors abide by all state bar ethics rules. In late 2000, in a reflection of the federal sentiment, the Oregon Supreme Court temporarily ended police–prosecutor collaboration in that state in instances involving potential deception by law enforcement officers.[47] The court, ruling in the Oregon State Bar disciplinary case of *In re Gatti,*[48] held that all lawyers within the state, including government prosecutors overseeing organized crime, child pornography, and narcotics cases, must abide by the Oregon State Bar's strictures against dishonesty, fraud, deceit, and misrepresentation.[49] Under the court's ruling, a prosecutor in Oregon who encourages an undercover officer or an informant to misrepresent himself or herself could be disbarred and prohibited from practicing law. As a result of the highly controversial ruling, the FBI and the Drug Enforcement Administration ended all big undercover operations in Oregon, and local police departments canceled many ongoing investigations. In 2002, the Oregon Supreme Court accepted an amendment to the state bar association's disciplinary rules to allow a lawyer to advise and to supervise otherwise lawful undercover investigations of violations of civil law, criminal law, or constitutional rights as long as the lawyer "in good faith believes there is a reasonable possibility that unlawful activity has taken place, is taking place or will take place in the foreseeable future."[50]

Once a trial begins, the job of the prosecutor is to vigorously present the state's case against the defendant. Prosecutors introduce evidence against the accused, steer the testimony of witnesses "for the people," and argue in favor of conviction. Because defendants are presumed innocent until proven guilty, the burden of demonstrating guilt beyond a reasonable doubt rests with the prosecutor.

Peterson prosecutors Rick Distaso and Dave Harris confer with one another in the Stanislaus County Courthouse in Modesto, California. The two men led the state's effort in 2004 to prove that Scott Peterson killed his pregnant wife, Laci.

*AP Wide World Photos*

# Prosecutorial Discretion

In August 2001, Miami prosecutors dropped domestic violence charges against Mayor Joe Carollo.[51] Carollo, who allegedly hit his wife on the head with a cardboard box of tea during an argument at their home, had been arrested after their daughter called 911 and reported, "My dad's hurting my mom." Charges against the mayor were dropped after he completed a counseling program for first-time domestic violence offenders. At a news conference held after the charges were dropped, Carollo told reporters, "The bottom line was that there was no crime committed. . . . It was an accident, and that is behind us now."

Whether or not Carollo's assertion about no crime having occurred is true, his case highlights the fact that American prosecutors occupy a unique position in the nation's criminal justice system by virtue of the considerable **prosecutorial discretion** they exercise. As U.S. Supreme Court Justice Robert H. Jackson noted in 1940, "The prosecutor has more control over life, liberty, and reputation than any other person in America."[52] Before a case comes to trial, the prosecutor may decide to accept a plea bargain, divert the suspect to a public or private social service agency, ask the suspect to seek counseling, or dismiss the case entirely for lack of evidence or for a variety of other reasons. Studies have found that the prosecution dismisses from one-third to one-half of all felony cases before trial or before a plea bargain is made.[53] Prosecutors also play a significant role before grand juries. States that use the grand jury system depend on prosecutors to bring evidence before the grand jury and to be effective in seeing indictments returned against suspects.

In preparation for trial, the prosecutor decides what charges are to be brought against the defendant, examines the strength of the incriminating evidence, and decides which witnesses to call. Two important U.S. Supreme Court decisions have held that it is the duty of prosecutors to make available any evidence in their possession to, in effect, help the defense build its case. In the first case, *Brady* v. *Maryland*[54] (1963), the Court held that the prosecution is required to disclose to the defense evidence that directly relates to claims of either guilt or innocence. The second and more recent case is that of *U.S.* v. *Bagley*,[55] decided in 1985. In *Bagley*, the Court ruled that the prosecution must disclose any evidence that the defense requests. The Court reasoned that to withhold evidence, even when it does not relate directly to issues of guilt or innocence, may mislead the defense into thinking that such evidence does not exist.

In 2004, in a decision predicated upon *Brady,* the U.S. Supreme Court intervened to stop the execution of 45-year-old Texan Delma Banks ten minutes before it was scheduled to begin. In finding that prosecutors had withheld vital exculpatory information during Banks's trial for the 1980 shooting death of a 16-year-old boy, the Court said "a rule declaring 'prosecutor may hide, defendant must seek,' is not tenable in a system constitutionally bound to accord defendants due process."[56] Banks had spent 24 years on death row.

One special decision that the prosecutor makes concerns the filing of separate or multiple charges. The decision to try a defendant simultaneously on multiple charges allows for the presentation of a considerable amount of evidence and permits an in-court demonstration of a complete sequence of criminal events. This strategy has additional practical advantages: It saves time and money by substituting one trial for what might otherwise be a number of trials if each charge were to be brought separately before the court. From the prosecutor's point of view, however, trying the charges one at a time carries the advantage of allowing for another trial on a new charge if a "not guilty" verdict is returned.

The activities of the prosecutor do not end with a finding of guilt or innocence. Following conviction, prosecutors are usually allowed to make sentencing recommendations to the judge. For example, they can argue that aggravating factors (discussed in Chapter 11), prior criminal record, or the especially heinous nature of the offense calls for strict punishment. When a convicted defendant appeals, prosecutors may need to defend their own actions and, in briefs filed with appellate courts, to argue that the conviction was properly obtained. Most jurisdictions also allow prosecutors to make recommendations when defendants they have convicted are being considered for parole or for early release from prison.

Until relatively recently, prosecutors generally enjoyed much the same kind of immunity against liability in the exercise of their official duties that judges do. The 1976 Supreme Court case *Imbler* v. *Pachtman*[57] provided the basis for immunity with its ruling that "state prosecutors are absolutely immune from liability . . . for their conduct in initiating a prosecution and in presenting the State's case." However, in the 1991 case of *Burns* v. *Reed*,[58] the Court held that "[a] state prosecuting attorney is absolutely immune from liability for damages . . . for participating in a probable cause hearing, but not for giving legal advice to the police." The *Burns* case involved Cathy Burns of Muncie, Indiana, who shot her sleeping sons while laboring under a multiple personality disorder. To explore the possibility of multiple personality further, the police asked the

## prosecutorial discretion

The decision-making power of prosecutors, based on the wide range of choices available to them, in the handling of criminal defendants, the scheduling of cases for trial, the acceptance of negotiated pleas, and so on. The most important form of prosecutorial discretion lies in the power to charge, or not to charge, a person with an offense.

I don't know if I ever want to try another case. I don't know if I ever want to practice law again.

—Los Angeles County Assistant Prosecutor Christopher Darden, expressing frustration over the O. J. Simpson case

> From the moment you walk into the courtroom, you are the defendant's only friend.
>
> —Austin defense attorney Michael E. Tigar

prosecuting attorney if it would be appropriate for them to hypnotize the defendant. The prosecutor agreed that hypnosis would be a permissible avenue for investigation, and the suspect confessed to the murders while hypnotized. She later alleged in her complaint to the Supreme Court "that [the prosecuting attorney] knew or should have known that hypnotically induced testimony was inadmissible" at trial.[59]

## The Abuse of Discretion

Because prosecutors have so much discretion in their decision making, there is considerable potential for abuse. Many types of discretionary decisions are always inappropriate. Examples include accepting guilty pleas to drastically reduced charges for personal considerations, deciding not to prosecute friends or political cronies, and the overzealous prosecution by district attorneys seeking heightened visibility to support political ambitions.

Administrative decisions such as case scheduling, which can wreak havoc with the personal lives of defendants and the professional lives of defense attorneys, can also be used by prosecutors to harass defendants into pleading guilty. Some forms of abuse may be unconscious. At least one study suggests that some prosecutors tend toward leniency where female defendants are concerned and tend to discriminate against minorities when deciding whether to prosecute.[60]

Although the electorate is the final authority to which prosecutors must answer, gross misconduct by prosecutors may be addressed by the state supreme court or by the state attorney general's office. Short of addressing *criminal* misconduct, however, most of the options available to the court and to the attorney general are limited.

## The Prosecutor's Professional Responsibility

As members of the legal profession, prosecutors are subject to the American Bar Association (ABA) Code of Professional Responsibility. Serious violations of the code may result in a prosecutor's disbarment from the practice of law. ABA Standard for Criminal Justice 3-1.1 describes the prosecutor's duty this way: "The duty of the prosecutor is to seek justice, not merely to convict." Hence, prosecutors are barred by the standards of the legal profession from advocating any fact or position that they know is untrue. Prosecutors can influence public policy that affects the safety of America's communities through the National District Attorneys Association (NDAA). Visit the NDAA via Web Extra 9–10 at cjtoday.com.

WEB EXTRA

# The Defense Counsel

**defense counsel**

A licensed trial lawyer hired or appointed to conduct the legal defense of a person accused of a crime and to represent him or her before a court of law.

The **defense counsel** is a trained lawyer who may specialize in the practice of criminal law. The task of the defense counsel is to represent the accused as soon as possible after arrest and to ensure that the defendant's civil rights are not violated during processing by the criminal justice system. Other duties of the defense counsel include testing the strength of the prosecution's case, taking part in plea negotiations, and preparing an adequate defense to be used at trial. In the preparation of a defense, criminal lawyers may enlist private detectives, experts, witnesses to the crime, and character witnesses. Some lawyers perform aspects of the role of private detective or of investigator themselves. Defense attorneys also review relevant court precedents to identify the best defense strategy.

Defense preparation often entails conversations between lawyer and defendant. Such discussions are recognized as privileged communications protected under the umbrella of attorney–client confidentiality. In other words, lawyers cannot be compelled to reveal information that their clients have confided to them.[61]

If the defendant is found guilty, the defense attorney will be involved in arguments at sentencing, may be asked to file an appeal, and may counsel the defendant and the defendant's family about any civil matters (payment of debts, release from contractual obligations, and so on) that must be arranged after sentence is imposed. Hence, the work of the defense attorney encompasses many roles, including attorney, negotiator, investigator, confidant, family and personal counselor, social worker, and, as we shall see, bill collector.

## The Criminal Lawyer

Three major categories of defense attorneys assist criminal defendants in the United States: (1) private attorneys, usually referred to as *retained counsel;* (2) *court-appointed counsel;* and (3) *public defenders.*

Private attorneys either have their own legal practices or work for law firms in which they are partners or employees. Private attorneys' fees can be high; most privately retained criminal lawyers charge from $100 to $250 per hour. Included in their bill is the time it takes to prepare for a case, as well as time spent in the courtroom. High-powered criminal defense attorneys who have a reputation for successfully defending their clients can be far more expensive. Fees charged by famous criminal defense attorneys can run into the hundreds of thousands of dollars—and sometimes exceed $1 million—for handling just one case!

Few law students choose to specialize in criminal law, even though the job of a criminal lawyer may appear glamorous. One reason may be that the collection of fees can be a significant source of difficulty for many defense attorneys. Most defendants are poor. Those who aren't are often reluctant to pay what they believe is an exorbitant fee, and woe be it to the defense attorney whose client is convicted before the fee has been paid! Visit the National Association of Criminal Defense Lawyers (NACDL) via Web Extra 9–11 and the Association of Federal Defense Attorneys (AFDA) via Web Extra 9–12 at cjtoday.com to learn more about the practice of criminal law.

> Even the intelligent and educated layman . . . requires the guiding hand of counsel at every step in the proceedings against him.
>
> —*Gideon* v. *Wainwright,* 372 U.S. 335, 344 (1963)

## Criminal Defense of the Poor

The Sixth Amendment to the U.S. Constitution guarantees criminal defendants the effective assistance of counsel. A series of U.S. Supreme Court decisions has established that defendants who are unable to pay for private criminal defense attorneys will receive adequate representation at all stages of criminal justice processing. In *Powell* v. *Alabama* (1932),[62] the Court held that the Fourteenth Amendment requires state courts to appoint counsel for defendants in capital cases who are unable to afford their own. In 1938, in *Johnson* v. *Zerbst,*[63] the Court overturned the conviction of an indigent federal inmate, holding that his Sixth Amendment due process right to counsel had been violated. The Court declared, "If the accused . . . is not represented by counsel and has not competently and intelligently waived his constitutional right, the Sixth Amendment stands as a jurisdictional bar to a valid conviction and sentence depriving him of his life or his liberty." The decision established the right of indigent defendants to receive the assistance of appointed counsel in all criminal proceedings in federal courts. The 1963 case of *Gideon* v. *Wainwright*[64] extended the right to appointed counsel to all indigent defendants charged with a felony in state courts. In *Argersinger* v. *Hamlin* (1972),[65] the Court required adequate legal representation for anyone facing a potential sentence of imprisonment. Juveniles charged with delinquent acts were granted the right to appointed counsel in the case of *In re Gault* (1967).[66]

In 2002, a closely divided U.S. Supreme Court expanded the Sixth Amendment right to counsel, ruling that defendants in state courts who are facing relatively minor charges must be provided with an attorney at government expense even when they face only the slightest chance of incarceration. The case, *Alabama* v. *Shelton,*[67] involved defendant LeReed Shelton who was convicted of third-degree assault after taking part in a fistfight with another motorist following a minor traffic accident. Shelton had been advised of his right to have an attorney represent him at trial, and the judge who heard his case repeatedly suggested that he should hire an attorney and warned him of the dangers of serving as his own attorney but at no time offered him assistance of counsel. Unable to afford an attorney, Shelton proceeded to represent himself and was convicted and sentenced to 30 days in the county jail. The sentence was suspended, and he was placed on two years of unsupervised probation, fined $500, and ordered to make restitution and to pay the costs of court. Shelton soon appealed on Sixth Amendment grounds, however, and the Alabama Supreme Court ruled in his favor, reasoning that a suspended sentence constitutes a "term of imprisonment" no matter how unlikely it is that the term will ever be served. On appeal by the state of Alabama, the case made its way to the U.S. Supreme Court, which agreed that "[a] suspended sentence is a prison term" and requires appointed counsel when an indigent defendant desires legal representation.

States have responded to the federal mandate for indigent defense in a number of ways. Most now use one of three systems to deliver legal services to criminal defendants who are unable to afford their own: (1) court-appointed counsel, (2) public defenders, and (3) contractual arrangements. Most systems are administered at the county level, although funding arrangements may involve state, county, and municipal monies—as well as federal grants and court fees.

Court-appointed defense attorneys, also called *assigned counsel,* are usually drawn from a roster of all practicing criminal attorneys within the jurisdiction of the trial court. Their fees are paid at a rate set by the state or local government. These fees are typically low, however, and may affect the amount of effort an assigned attorney puts into a case. In 2001, for example, New York's court-appointed attorneys were paid only $25 per hour for out-of-court preparation time and $40 an hour for time spent in the courtroom—a rate of pay that is 10 to 20 times less than what they normally earn for a private case.[68] So, although most attorneys assigned by the court to indigent defense take their jobs seriously, some feel only a loose commitment to their clients. Paying clients, in their eyes, deserve better service.

The second type of indigent defense, the **public defender** program, relies on full-time salaried staff. Staff members include defense attorneys, defense investigators, and office personnel. Defense investigators gather information in support of the defense effort. They may interview friends, family members, and employers of the accused, with an eye toward effective defense. Public defender programs have become popular in recent years, with approximately 64% of counties nationwide now funding them.[69] A 1996 Bureau of Justice Statistics report found that a public defender system is the primary method used to provide indigent counsel for criminal defendants and that 28% of state jurisdictions nationwide use public defender programs exclusively to provide indigent defense.[70] Critics charge that public defenders, because they are government employees, are not sufficiently independent from prosecutors and judges. For the same reason, clients may be suspicious of public defenders, viewing them as state functionaries. Finally, because of the huge caseloads typical of public defenders' offices, there is pressure to use plea bargaining excessively.

Through a third type of indigent defense, contract attorney programs, county and state officials arrange with local criminal lawyers to provide for indigent defense on a contractual basis. Individual attorneys, local bar associations, and multipartner law firms may all be tapped to provide services. Contract defense programs are the least widely used form of indigent defense at present, although their popularity is growing.

Critics of the current system of indigent defense point out that the system is woefully underfunded. Findings from the most recent National Survey of Indigent Defense Systems were published in 2001.[71] The survey found that states spent a total of $662,590,139 on indigent criminal defense in 1999. Most of the money ($337 million) went to fund public defender programs, while assigned counsel programs cost $191 million, and contract attorney fees totaled $53 million. New Jersey, the most populous of the states covered by the survey, spent the most money ($73 million) on indigent criminal defense. Although these figures may seem quite large, they total only about one-third the amount that states spend every year to prosecute criminal defendants. As a result, the report of the National Symposium on Indigent Defense proclaimed in 2000, "Indigent defense today, in terms of funding, caseloads, and quality, is in a chronic state of crisis."[72] Some question the quality of services available through public defender systems due to the fact that entry-level public defenders are paid poorly in comparison to what new attorneys entering private law firms might earn. In 2004, for example, Avoyelles Parish in Louisiana hired a part-time attorney with no previous criminal defense experience to handle all court-assigned juvenile and misdemeanor cases and to handle all felony arraignments. The attorney, whose work load included 1,088 misdemeanor and 256 juvenile cases, was paid $19,200.[73] In 2004 entry-level assistant public defenders in Massachusetts earned $35,000,[74] those in Georgia made $44,000, and those in Kentucky were paid $33,425; attorneys entering private practice can make much more. Moreover, the cost to the states for representing an indigent defendant averages around $490, while private attorney fees are generally much higher.[75]

As a consequence of such limited funding, many public defender's offices employ what critics call a "plead 'em and speed 'em through" strategy, which can often mean that attorneys meet their clients for the first time in courtrooms as trials are about to begin and use plea bargaining to move cases along. Mary Broderick of the National Legal Aid and Defender Association says, "We aren't being given the same weapons. . . . It's like trying to deal with smart bombs when all you've got is a couple of cap pistols."[76] Proposed enhancements to indigent defense systems are offered by the National Legal Aid and Defender Association (NLADA). You can visit the NLADA via **Web Extra 9–13** at cjtoday.com.

The entire 200-page report of the National Symposium on Indigent Defense is available as **Library Extra 9–8** at cjtoday.com, and the Bureau of Justice Statistics 2001 overview of the National Survey of Indigent Defense Systems can be found at **Library Extra 9–9. Library Extra 9–10** provides an overview of state-funded indigent defense services.

Although state indigent defense services are sometimes significantly underfunded, the same is not true of the federal system. The defense of indigent Oklahoma City bomber Timothy McVeigh, for example, cost taxpayers an estimated $13.8 million—which doesn't include the cost of his appeal or execution. McVeigh's expenses included $6.7 million for attorneys, $2 million for investigators, $3 million for expert witnesses, and approximately $1.4 million for office rent and secretarial assistance.[77]

In 2000, the Bureau of Justice Statistics (BJS) reported data on publicly financed counsel nationwide in two research reports that appear to conflict with the conclusions reached by the National Survey of Indigent Defense Systems.[78] BJS statisticians found that court-appointed defense attorneys represent 66% of federal felony defendants, as well as 82% of felony defendants in the nation's 75 most populous counties. The study also found that conviction rates for indigent de-

---

**public defender**

An attorney employed by a government agency or subagency, or by a private organization under contract to a government body, for the purpose of providing defense services to indigents, or an attorney who has volunteered such service.

WEB EXTRA

LIBRARY EXTRA

O Lord, look down upon these the multitudes, and spread strife and dissension, so that this, Thy servant, might prosper.

—Anonymous, "The Lawyer's Prayer"

fendants and those with their own lawyers were about the same in both federal and state courts. About 90% of the federal defendants and 75% of defendants in the most populous counties were found guilty regardless of the type of attorney they had. However, the study showed that those found guilty and represented by publicly financed attorneys were incarcerated at a higher rate than those defendants who paid for their own legal representation—88% compared to 77% in federal courts and 71% compared to 54% in the most populous counties. On average, however, prison sentences for defendants with publicly financed attorneys were shorter than were those with hired counsel. In federal district court, convicted defendants who had publicly financed attorneys were sentenced to less than five years on average, and those with private attorneys to just over five years. In large counties, those with publicly financed attorneys were sentenced to an average of two and a half years, and those with private attorneys to three years.

Of course, defendants need not accept any assigned counsel. Defendants may waive their right to an attorney and undertake their own defense—a right held to be inherent in the Sixth Amendment to the U.S. Constitution by the U.S. Supreme Court in the 1975 case of *Faretta* v. *California.*[79] Self-representation is uncommon, however, and only 1% of federal inmates and 3% of state inmates report having represented themselves.[80] Some famous and relatively recent instances of self-representation can be found in the 1995 trial of Long Island Rail Road commuter train shooter Colin Ferguson, the 1999 trial of Dr. Jack Kevorkian, and the 2002 federal competency hearings of Zacarias Moussaoui.

Defendants who are not pleased with the lawyer appointed to defend them are in a somewhat different situation. They may request, through the court, that a new lawyer be assigned to represent them, as Timothy McVeigh did following his conviction and death sentence in the Oklahoma City bombing case. However, unless there is clear reason for reassignment, such as an obvious personality conflict between defendant and attorney, few judges are likely to honor a request of this sort. Short of obvious difficulties, most judges will trust in the professionalism of appointed counselors.

State-supported indigent defense systems may also be called on to provide representation for clients upon appeal. An attorney who is appointed to represent an indigent defendant on appeal, however, may conclude that an appeal would be frivolous. If so, he or she may request that the appellate court allow him or her to withdraw from the case or that the court dispose of the case without requiring the attorney to file a brief arguing the merits of the appeal. In 1967, in the case of *Anders* v. *California,*[81] the U.S. Supreme Court found that to protect a defendant's constitutional right to appellate counsel, appellate courts must safeguard against the risk of accepting an attorney's negative assessment of a case where an appeal is not actually frivolous. The Court also found California's existing procedure for evaluating such requests to be inadequate, and the justices set forth an acceptable procedure. In 1979, in the case of *People* v. *Wende,*[82] the state of California adopted a new standardized procedure that, although not the same as the one put forth in *Anders,* was designed to protect the right of a criminal defendant to appeal.

The *Wende* standard was put to the test in the 2000 case of *Smith* v. *Robbins.*[83] The case began when convicted California murderer Lee Robbins told his court-appointed counsel that he wanted to file an appeal. His attorney concluded that the appeal would be frivolous and filed a brief with the state court of appeals to that effect. The court agreed with the attorney's assessment, and the appeal was not heard. The California Supreme Court denied further review of the case. After exhausting his state postconviction remedies, Robbins appealed to the federal courts, arguing that he had been denied effective assistance of appellate counsel because his counsel's brief did not comply with one of the requirements in *Anders*—specifically, the requirement that the brief must mention "anything in the record that might arguably support the appeal." A federal district court agreed, concluding that there were at least two issues that might have supported Robbins's appeal. The court found that the failure to include them in the brief deviated from the *Anders* procedure and thus amounted to deficient performance by counsel. The Ninth Circuit Court agreed, concluding that *Anders* established a mandatory procedure as a standard against which the performance of appointed counsel could be assessed. When the case finally reached the U.S. Supreme Court, the justices held that the *Anders* procedure is only one method of satisfying the Constitution's requirements for indigent criminal appeals and that the states are free to adopt different procedures as long as those procedures adequately safeguard a defendant's right to appellate counsel.

Finally, in 2001, in the case of *Texas* v. *Cobb,*[84] the Supreme Court ruled that the Sixth Amendment right to counsel is "offense specific" and applies only to the offense with which a defendant is charged—and not to other offenses, even if they are factually related to the charged offense. The case originated with the arrest of Raymond Cobb on charges of burglary. A woman and her 16-month-old daughter had disappeared from a house that had been burglarized, although it was unclear to investigators whether the burglary and the disappearances were related. Counsel was appointed to represent Cobb, who then confessed to the burglary but denied knowledge of the

> I truly believe he's innocent. And if I didn't convince 12 people of that, then I didn't do enough.
>
> —Scott Peterson's attorney Mark Geragos[ii]

## CJ TODAY EXHIBIT 9-1

### *Gideon* v. *Wainwright* and Indigent Defense

Today, about three-fourths of state-level criminal defendants and one-half of federal defendants are represented in court by publicly funded counsel.[1] As recently as 40 years ago, however, the practice of publicly funded indigent defense was uncommon. That changed in 1963 when, in the case of *Gideon* v. *Wainwright*,[2] the U.S. Supreme Court extended the right to legal counsel to indigent defendants charged with a criminal offense. The reasoning of the Court is well summarized in this excerpt from the majority opinion written by Justice Hugo Black:

> Governments, both state and federal, quite properly spend vast sums of money to establish machinery to try defendants accused of crime. Lawyers to prosecute are everywhere deemed essential to protect the public's in-

terest in an orderly society. Similarly, there are few defendants charged with crime, few indeed, who fail to hire the best lawyers they can get to prepare and present their defenses. That government hires lawyers to prosecute and defendants who have the money hire lawyers to defend are the strongest indications of the widespread belief that lawyers in criminal courts are necessities, not luxuries. The right of one charged with crime to counsel may not be deemed fundamental and essential to fair trials in some countries, but it is in ours. From the very beginning, our state and national constitutions and laws have laid great emphasis on procedural and substantive safeguards designed to assure fair trials before impartial tribunals in which every defendant stands equal before the law. This noble ideal cannot be realized if the poor man charged with crime has to face his accusers without a lawyer to assist him.

[1]Steven K. Smith and Carol J. DeFrances, *Indigent Defense* (Washington, DC: Bureau of Justice Statistics, 1996).
[2]*Gideon* v. *Wainwright*, 372 U.S. 335 (1963).

---

> We are under a Constitution, but the Constitution is what the judges say it is, and the judiciary is the safeguard of our liberty and of our property under the Constitution.
>
> —Charles Evans Hughes, eleventh Chief Justice of the United States, in a speech before the Elmira, New York, Chamber of Commerce, 1907

disappearance of the woman and child. While free on bond on the burglary charge, Cobb confessed to his father that he had killed the woman and child. His father then contacted the police, and Cobb was arrested. While in custody, Cobb waived his *Miranda* rights and confessed to the murders. He was later convicted of capital murder and was sentenced to death. On appeal to the Texas Court of Criminal Appeals, he argued that his confession should not have been admitted into evidence at his trial because it was obtained in violation of his Sixth Amendment right to counsel. That right, he claimed, stemmed from the fact that counsel had been appointed for him in the burglary case. The Texas court agreed with Cobb and reversed his conviction, finding that once the right to counsel attaches to the offense charged, it also attaches to any other offense that is very closely related factually to the offense charged. When the case reached the U.S. Supreme Court, however, the justices overturned the Texas court's ruling and held that the Sixth Amendment right to counsel is "offense specific" and does not necessarily extend to offenses that are "factually related" to those that have actually been charged.

## The Ethics of Defense

The job of defense counsel, as we have already mentioned, is to prepare and offer a vigorous defense on behalf of the accused at trial and to appeal cases that have merit. A proper defense at trial often involves the presentation of evidence and the examination of witnesses, both of which require careful thought and planning. Good attorneys may become emotionally committed to the outcomes of trials in which they are involved. Some lawyers, however, cross the line when they lose their professional objectivity and embrace the wider cause of their clients. That's what happened to Lynne Stewart, 65, who was convicted in 2005 of smuggling messages from her jailed client, the radical Egyptian sheik Omar Abdel-Rahman (aka the "blind sheik"), to his terrorist followers outside of prison.[85] Abdel-Rahman is serving life behind bars for his role in an unsuccessful 1993 plot to bomb New York City landmarks. Stewart, a 1960s-era radical, has often chosen to represent the most contemptible clients, believing that justice requires that everyone receive a vigorous defense. She was arrested, however, after she issued a public statement on behalf of the sheik expressing her client's withdrawal of support for a cease-fire involving his supporters in Egypt. Stewart had known in advance that making the statement violated an order to restrict the sheik's communications, but she later testified that she believed that violence is sometimes necessary to achieve justice. Other evidence showed that she had facilitated forbidden communications between Rahman and a translator by using prearranged cues such as tapping on a table, shaking a water bottle, and uttering key phrases like "chocolate" and "heart attack" during prison visits.

Defense attorney Lynne Stewart, 65, who was convicted in 2005 of smuggling messages from her jailed client, the radical Egyptian sheik Omar Abdel-Rahman (aka the "blind sheik"), to his terrorist followers outside of prison. Our adversarial system requires that attorneys sometimes defend unpopular clients, but the defense role is carefully prescribed by ethical and procedural considerations.
*AP Wide World Photos*

The nature of the adversarial process, fed by the emotions of the participants combined with the often privileged and extensive knowledge that defense attorneys have about their cases, is enough to tempt the professional ethics of some counselors. Because the defense counsel may often know more about the guilt or innocence of the defendant than anyone else prior to trial, the defense role is carefully prescribed by ethical and procedural considerations. Attorneys violate both law and the standards of their profession if they knowingly misrepresent themselves or their clients. As Michael Ratner, president of the Center for Constitutional Rights, put it when commenting on the Stewart case, "lawyers need to be advocates, but they don't need to be accomplices."[86]

To help attorneys understand what is expected of them, ethical standards abound. Four main groups of standards, each drafted by the American Bar Association (which you can visit via **Web Extra 9–14 at** cjtoday.com), are especially applicable to defense attorneys:

- Canons of Professional Ethics
- Model Code of Professional Responsibility
- Model Rules of Professional Conduct
- Standards for Criminal Justice

Each set of standards is revised periodically. The ABA Standards for Criminal Justice, Number 4–1.2, reads, in part,

> (e) Defense counsel, in common with all members of the bar, is subject to standards of conduct stated in statutes, rules, decisions of courts, and codes, canons, or other standards of professional conduct. Defense counsel has no duty to execute any directive of the accused which does not comport with law or such standards. Defense counsel is the professional representative of the accused, not the accused's alter ego.
>
> (f) Defense counsel should not intentionally misrepresent matters of fact or law to the court.
>
> (g) Defense counsel should disclose to the tribunal legal authority in the controlling jurisdiction [information] known to defense counsel to be directly adverse to the position of the accused and not disclosed by the prosecutor.
>
> (h) It is the duty of every lawyer to know and be guided by the standards of professional conduct as defined in codes and canons of the legal profession applicable in defense counsel's jurisdiction. Once representation has been undertaken, the functions and duties of defense counsel are the same whether defense counsel is assigned, privately retained, or serving in a legal aid or defender program.

**WEB** EXTRA

## ETHICS AND PROFESSIONALISM

### American Bar Association Model Code of Professional Responsibility

For most criminal trial lawyers, the intense effort of advocacy results in an emotional and personal investment in the outcome of a case. To strike a balance between zealous and effective advocacy, on the one hand, and just professional conduct within the bounds of the law, on the other, the American Bar Association has developed a Code of Professional Responsibility. It reads, in part,

In his representation of a client, a lawyer shall not:

- File a suit, assert a position, conduct a defense, delay a trial, or take other action on behalf of his client when he knows or when it is obvious that such action would serve merely to harass or maliciously injure another.
- Knowingly advance a claim or defense that is unwarranted under existing law.

- Conceal or knowingly fail to disclose that which he is required by law to reveal.
- Knowingly use perjured testimony or false evidence.
- Knowingly make a false statement of law or fact.
- Participate in the creation or preservation of evidence when he knows or it is obvious that the evidence is false.
- Counsel or assist his client in conduct that the lawyer knows to be illegal or fraudulent.

#### THINKING ABOUT ETHICS

1. What does the ABA's Code of Professional Responsibility require of a defense attorney who represents a client whom he or she knows to be guilty?
2. Would it be unethical for an attorney to refuse to represent such a client? Why or why not?

*Source:* Excerpted from American Bar Association, *Model Code of Professional Responsibility,* Disciplinary Rule 7–102. Reprinted by permission of the American Bar Association. All rights reserved. Copies of ABA Model Rules of Professional Responsibility, 2004 are available from Service Center, American Bar Association, 321 North Clark St., Chicago, IL 60610; 800-285-2221.

Even with these directives, defense attorneys are under no obligation to reveal information obtained from a client without the client's permission. However, all states permit defense lawyers to violate a client's confidentiality if they reasonably believe that doing so could prevent serious injury or death to another person. In 2004, with passage of a new evidence law broadening the state's evidence code, California joined the other 49 states in freeing attorneys to violate client confidentiality in such cases. California law makes disclosure discretionary, not mandatory. Kevin Mohr, a professor at Western State University College of Law in Fullerton, California, noted that the new law provides the first exception to the attorney–client privilege in California in more than 130 years. "A lawyer can now take action and intervene and prevent [a] criminal act from occurring," said Mohr.[87]

The California changes had been presaged by an action of the American Bar Association, which eased its secrecy rules surrounding attorney–client relationships in 2001.[88] Prior to that time, ABA rules permitted criminal defense attorneys to disclose incriminating information about a client only to prevent imminent death or substantial bodily harm. The 2001 rule change dispensed with the word *imminent,* allowing attorneys to reveal clients' secrets in order to stop future deaths or to prevent substantial bodily harm.

Somewhat earlier, the 1986 U.S. Supreme Court case of *Nix* v. *Whiteside*[89] clarified the duty of lawyers to reveal known instances of client perjury. The *Nix* case came to the Court upon the complaint of the defendant, Whiteside, who claimed that he was deprived of the assistance of effective counsel during his murder trial because his lawyer would not allow him to testify untruthfully. Whiteside wanted to testify that he had seen a gun or something metallic in his victim's hand before killing him. Before trial, however, Whiteside admitted to his lawyer that he had actually seen no weapon, but he believed that to testify to the truth would result in his conviction. The lawyer told Whiteside that, as a professional counselor, he would be forced to challenge Whiteside's false testimony if it occurred and to explain to the court the facts as he knew them. On the stand, Whiteside said only that he thought the victim was reaching for a gun but did not claim to have seen one. He was found guilty of second-degree murder and appealed to the Supreme Court on the claim of inadequate representation. The Court, recounting the development of ethical codes in the legal profession, held that a lawyer's duty to a client "is limited to legitimate, lawful conduct compatible with the very nature of a trial as a search for truth. . . . Counsel is precluded from taking steps or in any way assisting the client in presenting false evidence or otherwise violating the law."[90]

# The Bailiff

The **bailiff**, another member of the professional courtroom work group, is usually an armed law enforcement officer. The job of the bailiff, also called a *court officer*, is to ensure order in the courtroom, to announce the judge's entry into the courtroom, to call witnesses, and to prevent the escape of the accused (if the accused has not been released on bond). The bailiff also supervises the jury when it is sequestered and controls public and media access to jury members. Bailiffs in federal courtrooms are deputy U.S. marshals.

Courtrooms can be dangerous places—as the story that opened this chapter showed—and bailiffs play a critical role in courtroom security. In an event that led to tightened courtroom security nationwide, George Lott was sentenced to die in 1993 for a courtroom shooting in Tarrant County, Texas, which left two lawyers dead and three other people injured.[91] Lott was frustrated by the court's handling of his divorce and by child molestation charges that had been filed against him by his ex-wife. Following the Lott incident and others like it, most courts initiated the use of metal detectors, and many now require visitors to leave packages, cellular phones, and objects that might conceal weapons in lockers or to check them with personnel before entering the courtroom.

A comprehensive courthouse security plan must, of course, extend beyond individual courtrooms. In 2005, around the time of the courthouse shootings in Atlanta, the National Center for State Courts (NCSC) released a comprehensive plan for improving security in state courthouses.[92] The plan contained a list of ten essential elements for court safety that include the need to (1) assess existing and potential threats, (2) identify physical strengths and weaknesses of existing courts, (3) develop a comprehensive emergency response plan, (4) be aware of the latest technologies in court security, and (5) build strong and effective partnerships among state courts, law enforcement agencies, and county commissioners. The complete list of NCSC recommendations is available at **Library Extra 9–11**.

> **bailiff**
> The court officer whose duties are to keep order in the courtroom and to maintain physical custody of the jury.

> **LIBRARY EXTRA**

# Local Court Administrators

Many states now employ local court administrators whose job is to facilitate the smooth functioning of courts in a judicial district or area. A major impetus for hiring of local court administrators came from the 1967 President's Commission on Law Enforcement and Administration of Justice. Examining state courts, the report found "a system that treats defendants who are charged with minor offenses with less dignity and consideration than it treats those who are charged with serious crimes."[93] A few years later, the National Advisory Commission on Criminal Justice Standards and Goals recommended that all courts with five or more judges create the position of trial court administrator.[94]

Court administrators provide uniform court management, assuming many of the duties previously performed by chief judges, prosecutors, and court clerks. Where court administrators operate, the ultimate authority for running the court still rests with the chief judge. Administrators, however, are able to relieve the judge of many routine and repetitive tasks, such as record keeping, scheduling, case-flow analysis, personnel administration, space utilization, facilities planning, and budget management. They may also take the minutes at meetings of judges and their committees.

Juror management is another area in which trial court administrators are becoming increasingly involved. Juror utilization studies can identify problems such as the overselection of citizens for the jury pool and the reasons for excessive requests to be excused from jury service. They can also suggest ways to reduce the time jurors waste waiting to be called or impaneled.

Effective court administrators are able to track lengthy cases and identify bottlenecks in court processing. They then suggest strategies to make the administration of justice more efficient for courtroom professionals and more humane for lay participants.

# The Court Reporter

The role of the court reporter (also called the *court stenographer* or *court recorder*) is to create a record of all that occurs during a trial. Accurate records are very important in criminal trial courts because appeals may be based entirely on what went on in the courtroom. Especially significant are all verbal comments made in the courtroom, including testimony, objections, the judge's rulings, the judge's instructions to the jury, arguments made by lawyers, and the results of conferences between the lawyers and the judge. The official trial record, often taken on a stenotype machine or an audio recorder, may later be transcribed in manuscript form and will become the basis for any appellate review of the trial.

> Free and open access to justice requires a safe and secure environment in which all those who come to the courthouse are free from fear and intimidation. Judges, employees, and the public need to feel safe if they are to conduct themselves in a fair and impartial manner and in accordance with a sense of judicial decorum.
>
> —National Center for State Courts [iii]

## CJ CAREERS

### U.S. MARSHALS SERVICE

**Name:** Larry Harper

**Position:** Deputy U.S. Marshal, Operations Division

**City:** Albuquerque, New Mexico

**College Attended:** University of New Mexico

**Year Hired:** 2003

*I went into law enforcement because I wanted to do my part in making my community safe. Even when I was a child, I knew I wanted to go into law enforcement. When I saw the Marshals Service while doing an internship in college, I knew this was where I wanted to be. I enjoy the flexibility of the job. . . . It's not the same every day.*

#### TYPICAL POSITIONS

Deputy U.S. marshal. The mission of the U.S. Marshals Service is to protect the federal courts and to ensure the effective operation of the judicial system. Deputy U.S. marshals are involved in court security, fugitive investigations, witness security, transportation and custody of federal prisoners, management of seized assets, and special operations.

#### EMPLOYMENT REQUIREMENTS

The applicant must be a U.S. citizen between 21 and 36 years of age, must be in excellent physical condition, and must possess a valid driver's license and a good driving record. General employment requirements include (1) a comprehensive written exam, (2) a structured employment interview, and (3) a background investigation. Appointment at the GS-5 level requires (1) a bachelor's degree from an accredited college or university or (2) three years of "responsible volunteer or paid experience" or (3) an equivalent combination of education and experience.

#### OTHER REQUIREMENTS

Successful applicants must complete ten weeks of rigorous training at the U.S. Marshals Service Training Academy in Glynco, Georgia.

#### SALARY

Deputy U.S. marshals are typically hired at GS-5 or GS-7, depending on education and work experience.

#### BENEFITS

Benefits include (1) 13 days of sick leave annually, (2) two and a half to five weeks of paid vacation and ten paid federal holidays each year, (3) federal health and life insurance, and (4) a comprehensive retirement program.

#### DIRECT INQUIRIES TO:

U.S. Marshals Service
Human Resources Division—Law Enforcement Recruiting
Washington, DC 20530-1000

Phone: (202)307-9400

Website: http://www.usdoj.gov/marshals

For additional information on employment opportunities in the criminal justice field, view the careers portion of the CD-ROM included with this book.

*Source:* U.S. Department of Justice.

---

Today's court stenographers often employ computer-aided transcription (CAT) software, which translates typed stenographic shorthand into complete and readable transcripts. Court reporters may be members of the National Court Reporters Association, the United States Court Reporters Association, or the Association of Legal Administrators—all of which support the activities of these professionals. You can visit the National Court Reporters Association via Web Extra 9–15 at cjtoday.com.

WEB EXTRA

> The jury is such a cornerstone of justice and the democratic process, [but] the jury process needs to be brought into the 21st Century.
>
> —Robert Grey, President of the American Bar Association[iv]

## The Clerk of Court

The duties of the clerk of court (also known as the *county clerk*) extend beyond the courtroom. The clerk maintains all records of criminal cases, including all pleas and motions made both before and after the actual trial. The clerk also prepares a jury pool, issues jury summonses, and subpoenas witnesses for both the prosecution and the defense. During the trial, the clerk (or an

A ballistics expert testifying on the witness stand in a criminal trial as jurors view evidence on nearby computer displays. Expert witnesses may express opinions and draw conclusions; they need not limit their testimony to facts alone.
*© Royalty-Free, CORBIS*

assistant) marks physical evidence for identification as instructed by the judge and maintains custody of that evidence. The clerk also swears in witnesses and performs other functions as the judge directs. Some states allow the clerk limited judicial duties, such as the power to issue warrants, to handle certain matters relating to individuals declared mentally incompetent,[95] and to serve as judge of probate—overseeing wills and the administration of estates.

> From what I see in my courtroom every day, many American juries might as well be using Ouija boards.
>
> —Judge Harold J. Rothwax

# Expert Witnesses

Most of the "insiders" we've talked about so far either are employees of the state or have ongoing professional relationships with the court (as in the case of defense counsel). **Expert witnesses**, however, may not have that kind of status, although some do. Expert witnesses are recognized as having specialized skills and knowledge in an established profession or technical area. They must demonstrate their expertise through education, work experience, publications, and awards. Their testimony at trial provides an effective way of introducing scientific evidence in such areas as medicine, psychology, ballistics, crime-scene analysis, photography, and many other disciplines. Expert witnesses, like the other courtroom actors described in this chapter, are generally paid professionals. And like all other witnesses, they are subject to cross-examination. Unlike lay witnesses, they are allowed to express opinions and to draw conclusions, but only within their particular area of expertise.

**expert witness**

A person who has special knowledge and skills recognized by the court as relevant to the determination of guilt or innocence. Unlike lay witnesses, expert witnesses may express opinions or draw conclusions in their testimony.

One difficulty with expert testimony is that it can be confusing to the jury. Sometimes the trouble is due to the nature of the subject matter and sometimes to disagreements between the experts themselves. Often, however, it arises from the strict interpretation given to expert testimony by procedural requirements. The difference between medical and legal definitions of insanity, for example, points to a divergence in both history and purpose between the law and science. Courts that attempt to apply criteria like the M'Naghten rule (discussed in Chapter 4) in deciding claims of "insanity" are often faced with the testimony of psychiatric experts who refuse even to recognize the word. Such experts may prefer, instead, to speak in terms of *psychosis* and *neurosis*—words that have no place in legal jargon. Because of the uncertainties they create, legal requirements may pit experts against one another and may confound the jury.

Even so, most authorities agree that expert testimony is usually viewed by jurors as more trustworthy than other forms of evidence. In a study of scientific evidence, one prosecutor commented that if he had to choose between presenting a fingerprint or an eyewitness at trial, he would always go with the fingerprint.[96] As a consequence of the effectiveness of scientific evidence, the National Institute of Justice recommends that "prosecutors consider the potential utility of such information in all cases where such evidence is available."[97]

Some expert witnesses traverse the country and earn very high fees by testifying at trials. DNA specialist John Gerdes, for example, was paid $100 per hour for his work in support of the defense in the 1995 O. J. Simpson criminal trial, and New York forensic pathologist Michael Baden charged $1,500 per day for time spent working for Simpson in Los Angeles. Baden billed Simpson more than $100,000, and the laboratory for which Gerdes worked received more than $30,000 from Simpson's defense attorneys.[98]

# Nonprofessional Courtroom Participants

Defendants, victims, jurors, and most witnesses are usually unwilling or inadvertent participants in criminal trials. Although they are outsiders who lack the status of paid professional participants, these are precisely the people who provide the grist for the judicial mill. The press, a willing player in many criminal trials, makes up another group of outsiders. Let's look now at each of these courtroom actors.

## Lay Witnesses

**lay witness**

An eyewitness, character witness, or other person called on to testify who is not considered an expert. Lay witnesses must testify to facts only and may not draw conclusions or express opinions.

Nonexpert witnesses, also known as **lay witnesses**, may be called to testify by either the prosecution or the defense. Lay witnesses may be eyewitnesses who saw the crime being committed or who came upon the crime scene shortly after the crime had occurred. Another type of lay witness is the character witness, who frequently provides information about the personality,

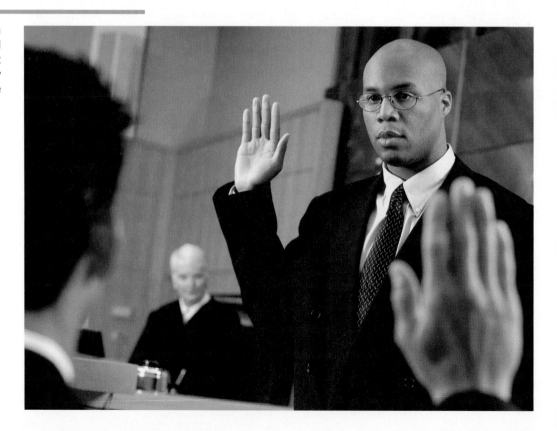

A lay witness being sworn in before testifying in a criminal trial. Nonexpert witnesses must generally limit their testimony to facts about which they have direct knowledge.
© Royalty-Free, CORBIS

family life, business acumen, and so on of the defendant in an effort to show that this is not the kind of person who would commit the crime with which she is charged. Of course, the victim may also be a witness, providing detailed and sometimes lengthy testimony about the defendant and the crime.

A written document called a **subpoena** officially notifies witnesses that they are to appear in court to testify. Subpoenas are generally served by an officer of the court or by a police officer, though they are sometimes mailed. Both sides in a criminal case may subpoena witnesses and might ask that individuals called to testify bring with them books, papers, photographs, videotapes, or other forms of physical evidence. Witnesses who fail to appear when summoned may face contempt-of-court charges.

The job of a witness is to provide accurate testimony concerning only those things of which he or she has direct knowledge. Normally, witnesses are not allowed to repeat things that others have told them unless they must do so to account for certain actions of their own. Since few witnesses are familiar with courtroom procedure, the task of testifying is fraught with uncertainty and can be traumatizing.

Everyone who testifies in a criminal trial must do so under oath, in which some reference to God is made, or after affirmation,[99] which is a pledge to tell the truth used by those who find either swearing or a reference to God objectionable.

All witnesses are subject to cross-examination, a process that will be discussed in the next chapter. Lay witnesses may be surprised to find that cross-examination can force them to defend their personal and moral integrity. A cross-examiner may question a witness about past vicious, criminal, or immoral acts, even when such matters have never been the subject of a criminal proceeding.[100] As long as the intent of such questions is to demonstrate to the jury that the witness is not credible, the judge will normally permit them.

Witnesses have traditionally been shortchanged by the judicial process. Subpoenaed to attend court, they have often suffered from frequent and unannounced changes in trial dates. A witness who promptly responds to a summons to appear may find that legal maneuvering has resulted in unanticipated delays. Strategic changes by either side may make the testimony of some witnesses entirely unnecessary, and people who have prepared themselves for the psychological rigors of testifying often experience an emotional letdown.

To compensate witnesses for their time and to make up for lost income, many states pay witnesses for each day that they spend in court. Payments range from $5 to $30 per day,[101] although some states pay nothing at all. In a 2004 Chicago murder case in which Oprah Winfrey served as a juror, for example, all jurors, including Winfrey—a billionaire—were paid $17.20 a day for their services.[102] The 1991 U.S. Supreme Court case of *Demarest* v. *Manspeaker et al.*[103] held that federal prisoners subpoenaed to testify are entitled to witness fees just as nonincarcerated witnesses would be.

In an effort to make the job of witnesses less onerous, 39 states and the federal government have laws or guidelines requiring that witnesses be notified of scheduling changes and cancellations in criminal proceedings.[104] In 1982, Congress passed the Victim and Witness Protection Act, which required the U.S. attorney general to develop guidelines to assist victims and witnesses in meeting the demands placed on them by the justice system. A number of **victim-assistance programs** (also called *victim/witness assistance programs*) have also taken up a call for the rights of witnesses and are working to make the courtroom experience more manageable.

## Jurors

The Cook County (Chicago) jury on which television diva Oprah Winfrey served convicted a man of first-degree murder in 2004. "It was an eye-opener for all of us," Winfrey said after the three-day trial ended. "It was not an easy decision to make."[105]

Article III of the U.S. Constitution requires that "[t]he trial of all crimes . . . shall be by jury." States have the authority to determine the size of criminal trial juries. Most states use juries composed of 12 people and one or two alternates designated to fill in for **jurors** who are unable to continue due to accident, illness, or personal emergency. Some states allow for juries of fewer than 12, and juries with as few as six members have survived Supreme Court scrutiny.[106]

Jury duty is regarded as a responsibility of citizenship. Other than juveniles and people in certain occupations, such as police personnel, physicians, members of the armed services on active duty, and emergency services workers, those who are called for jury duty must serve unless they can convince a judge that they should be excused for overriding reasons. Aliens, convicted felons, and citizens who have served on a jury within the past two years are excluded from jury service in most jurisdictions.

**subpoena**
A written order issued by a judicial officer or grand jury requiring an individual to appear in court and to give testimony or to bring material to be used as evidence. Some subpoenas mandate that books, papers, and other items be surrendered to the court.

**victim-assistance program**
An organized program that offers services to victims of crime in the areas of crisis intervention and follow-up counseling and that helps victims secure their rights under the law.

**juror**
A member of a trial or grand jury who has been selected for jury duty and is required to serve as an arbiter of the facts in a court of law. Jurors are expected to render verdicts of "guilty" or "not guilty" as to the charges brought against the accused, although they may sometimes fail to do so (as in the case of a hung jury).

## "CSI Effect" Has Juries Wanting More Evidence

Like viewers across the nation, folks in Galveston, Texas, watch a lot of TV shows about crime-scene investigators. Jury consultant Robert Hirschhorn couldn't be happier about that.

Hirschhorn was hired last year to help defense attorneys pick jurors for the trial of Robert Durst, a millionaire real estate heir who was accused of murdering and dismembering a neighbor, Morris Black. It was a case in which investigators never found Black's head. The defense claimed that wounds to the head might have supported Durst's story that he had killed Black in self-defense.

Hirschhorn wanted jurors who were familiar with shows such as *CSI: Crime Scene Investigation* to spot the importance of such a gap in the evidence. That wasn't difficult: In a survey of the 500 people in the jury pool, the defense found that about 70% were viewers of CBS's *CSI* or similar shows such as Court TV's *Forensic Files* or NBC's *Law & Order*.

Durst was acquitted in November. To legal analysts, his case seemed an example of how shows such as *CSI* are affecting action in courthouses across the USA by, among other things, raising jurors' expectations of what prosecutors should produce at trial.

Prosecutors, defense lawyers and judges call it "the *CSI* effect," after the crime-scene shows that are among the hottest attractions on television. The shows—*CSI* and *CSI: Miami,* in particular—feature high-tech labs and glib and gorgeous techies. By shining a glamorous light on a gory profession, the programs also have helped to draw more students into forensic studies.

But the programs also foster what analysts say is the mistaken notion that criminal science is fast and infallible and always gets its man. That's affecting the way lawyers prepare their cases, as well as the expectations that police and the public place on real crime labs. Real crime-scene investigators say that because of the programs, people often have unrealistic ideas of what criminal science can deliver.

Like Hirschhorn, many lawyers, judges and legal consultants say they appreciate how *CSI*-type shows have increased interest in forensic evidence.

"Talking about science in the courtroom used to be like talking about geometry—a real jury turnoff," says Hirschhorn, of Lewisville, Texas. "Now that there's this almost obsession with the (TV) shows, you can talk to jurors about (scientific evidence) and just see from the looks on their faces that they find it fascinating."

But some defense lawyers say *CSI* and similar shows make jurors rely too heavily on scientific findings and unwilling to accept that those findings can be compromised by human or technical errors.

Prosecutors also have complaints: They say the shows can make it more difficult for them to win convictions in the large majority of cases in which scientific evidence is irrelevant or absent.

"The lesson that both sides can agree on is, what's on TV does seep into the minds of jurors," says Paul Walsh, chief prosecutor in New Bedford, Mass., and president of the National District At-

Actors David Berman (as assistant coroner David Phillips), Robert David Hall (as coroner Al Robbins), and William Petersen (as Gil Grissom) examine a corpse in a scene from *CSI: Crime Scene Investigation*. Experts fear that popular TV crime dramas like *CSI* have led to unrealistic expectations among today's criminal jurors.

© Neal Preston, Corbis

torneys Association. "Jurors are going to have information, or what they think is information, in mind. That's the new state of affairs."

Lawyers and judges say the *CSI* effect has become a phenomenon in courthouses across the nation:

- In Phoenix last month, jurors in a murder trial noticed that a bloody coat introduced as evidence had not been tested for DNA. They alerted the judge. The tests hadn't been needed because the defendant had acknowledged being at the murder scene. The judge decided that TV had taught jurors about DNA tests, but not enough about when to use them.
- Three years ago in Richmond, Va., jurors in a murder trial asked the judge whether a cigarette butt found during the investigation could be tested for links to the defendant. Defense attorneys had ordered DNA tests but had not yet introduced them into evidence. The jury's hunch was correct—the tests exonerated the defendant, and the jury acquitted him.
- In Arizona, Illinois and California, prosecutors now use "negative evidence witnesses" to try to assure jurors that it is not unusual for real crime-scene investigators to fail to find DNA, fingerprints and other evidence at crime scenes.
- In Massachusetts, prosecutors have begun to ask judges for permission to question prospective jurors about their TV-watching habits. Several states already allow that.
- Last year in Wilmington, Del., federal researchers studying how juries evaluate scientific evidence staged dozens of simulated trials. At one point, a juror struggling with especially complicated DNA evidence lamented that such problems never come up "on *CSI*."

The *CSI* effect also is being felt beyond the courtroom. At West Virginia University, forensic science is the most popular undergraduate major for the second year in a row, attracting 13% of incoming freshmen this fall. In June, supporters of an Ohio library drew an overflow crowd of 200-plus to a luncheon speech on DNA by titling it "CSI: Dayton."

The Los Angeles County Sheriff's Department crime lab has seen another version of the *CSI* effect. Four technicians have left the lab for lucrative jobs as technical advisers to crime-scene programs. "They found a way to make science pay," lab director Barry Fisher says.

### SHOWS' POPULARITY SOARS

*CSI,* which recently began its fifth season, was America's second-most-popular TV program during the 2004 season, after the Tuesday edition of *American Idol.*

*CSI* and a spinoff, *CSI: Miami* (which is about to begin its third season), have drawn an average of more than 40 million viewers a week during the past TV season. *Law & Order,* whose plots sometimes focus on forensic evidence, has been the 13th-most-watched show during the 2003–04 season, averaging about 15 million viewers. On cable, the Discovery Channel, A&E and Court TV have programs that highlight DNA testing or the analysis of fingerprints, hair and blood-spatter patterns.

*CSI: NY,* set in New York City, premiered in September 2005. The *CSI* shows combine whiz-bang science with in-your-face interrogations to solve complex crimes. Some sample dialogue from actor David Caruso, the humorless monotone who plays investigator Horatio Caine on *CSI: Miami:* "He (the bad guy) doesn't know how evidence works, but you know what? He will."

The shows' popularity, TV historians say, is partly a result of their constant presence. Counting network and cable, at least one hour of crime-forensics programming airs in prime time six nights a week.

The stars of the shows often are the equipment—DNA sequencers, mass spectrometers, photometric fingerprint illuminators, scanning electron microscopes. But the technicians run a close second.

"It's 'geek chic,' the idea that kids who excel in science and math can grow up to be cool," says Robert Thompson, who teaches the history of TV programming at Syracuse University. "This is long overdue. . . . Cops and cowboys and doctors and lawyers have been done to death."

### DEPARTING FROM REALITY

Some of the science on *CSI* is state-of-the-art. Real lab technicians can, for example, lift DNA profiles from cigarette butts, candy wrappers and gobs of spit, just as their Hollywood counterparts do.

But some of what's on TV is far-fetched. Real technicians don't pour caulk into knife wounds to make a cast of the weapon. That wouldn't work in soft tissue. Machines that can identify cologne from scents on clothing are still in the experimental phase. A criminal charge based on "neuro-linguistic programming"—detecting lies by the way a person's eyes shift—likely would be dismissed by a judge.

But real scientists say *CSI*'s main fault is this: The science is always above reproach.

"You never see a case where the sample is degraded or the lab work is faulty or the test results don't solve the crime," says Dan Krane, president and DNA specialist at Forensic Bioinfor-

matics in Fairborn, Ohio. "These things happen all the time in the real world."

Defense lawyers say the misconception that crime-scene evidence and testing are always accurate helps prosecutors. "Jurors expect the criminal justice system to work better than it does," says Betty Layne DesPortes, a criminal defense lawyer in Richmond, Va., who has a master's degree in forensic science.

She notes that during the past 15 years, human errors and corruption have skewed test results in crime labs in West Virginia, Pennsylvania, California, Texas and Washington state.

But prosecutors say the shows help defense lawyers. Jurors who are regular viewers, they say, expect testable evidence to be present at all crime scenes.

In fact, they say, evidence such as DNA and fingerprints—the staple of *CSI* plots—is available in only a small minority of cases and can yield inconclusive results.

"Defense attorneys will get up there and bang the rail and say 'Where were the DNA tests?' to take advantage of the idea that's in the juror's mind," says Joshua Marquis, a prosecutor in Astoria, Ore. "You've got to do a lot of jury preparation to defeat that."

Some prosecutors have gone to great lengths to lower jurors' expectations about such evidence.

In Belleville, Ill., last spring, prosecutor Gary Duncan called on seven nationally recognized experts to testify about scientific evidence against a man accused of raping and murdering a 10-year-old girl. The witnesses included specialists in human and animal DNA, shoe-print evidence, population statistics and human mitochondrial DNA, genetic material that is inherited only from one's mother and that seldom is used in criminal cases. Duncan won a conviction.

"I wanted to be certain the jury was clear on the evidence and its meaning," he says. "These days, juries demand that."

*CSI* producers acknowledge that they take some liberties with facts and the capabilities of science, but they say it's necessary to keep their story lines moving.

Elizabeth Devine, a former crime-lab technician who writes and produces episodes of *CSI: Miami,* spoke at a training seminar for prosecutors last year in Columbia, S.C. She said that if the shows did not cut the time needed to perform DNA tests from weeks to minutes, a villain might not be caught before "episode five."

For all of *CSI*'s faults, some lab technicians say they have a soft spot for the TV version of their world. "It's great for getting people interested (in) careers" in forensic science, says Barbara Llewellyn, director of DNA analysis for the Illinois State Police.

Terry Melton, president of Mitotyping Technologies in State College, Pa., says the programs have made "jury duty something people now look forward to."

And Fisher says the shows have given "science types" like himself some unexpected cachet.

"When I tell someone what I do, I never have to explain it now," he says. "They know what a crime-scene (technician) does. At least, they think they do."

For the latest in crime and justice news, visit the Talk Justice news feed at http://www.crimenews.info.

---

*Source:* Richard Willing, "'CSI Effect' Has Juries Wanting More Evidence: People Expect Real Crime-solving to Be Like the Hit TV Show," *USA Today,* August 5, 2004, p. 1A. Copyright © 2004 *USA Today.* Reprinted with permission.

> No citizen possessing all other qualifications which are or may be prescribed by law shall be disqualified for service as grand or petit juror in any court of the United States, or of any State on account of race, color, or previous condition of servitude.
>
> —18 U.S.C. 243

The names of prospective jurors are often gathered from the tax register, motor vehicle records, or voter registration rolls of a county or municipality. Minimum qualifications for jury service include adulthood, a basic command of spoken English, citizenship, "ordinary intelligence," and local residency. Jurors are also expected to possess their "natural faculties," meaning that they should be able to hear, speak, see, move, and so forth. Some jurisdictions have recently allowed people with physical disabilities to serve as jurors, although the nature of the evidence to be presented in a case may preclude people with certain kinds of disabilities from serving.

Ideally, the jury should be a microcosm of society, reflecting the values, rationality, and common sense of the average person. The U.S. Supreme Court has held that criminal defendants have a right to have their cases heard before a jury of their peers.[107] Peer juries are those composed of a representative cross section of the community in which the alleged crime occurred and where the trial is to be held. The idea of a peer jury stems from the Magna Carta's original guarantee of jury trials for "freemen." Freemen in England during the thirteenth century, however, were more likely to be of similar mind than is a cross section of Americans today. Hence, although the duty of the jury is to deliberate on the evidence and, ultimately, to determine guilt or innocence, social dynamics may play just as great a role in jury verdicts as do the facts of a case.

In a 1945 case, *Thiel v. Southern Pacific Co.,*[108] the Supreme Court clarified the concept of a "jury of one's peers" by noting that while it is not necessary for every jury to contain representatives of every conceivable racial, ethnic, religious, gender, and economic group in the community, court officials may not systematically and intentionally exclude any juror solely because of his or her social characteristics.

In 2005 the American Bar Association released a set of 19 principles intended to guide jury reform.[109] ABA President Robert J. Grey, Jr., said that the principles were aimed at improving the courts' treatment of jurors and to "move jury service into the 21st Century." Some of the principles sounded like a juror's bill of rights and included provisions to protect jurors' privacy and personal information, to inform jurors of trial schedules, and to "vigorously promote juror understanding of the facts and the law." Courts should instruct jurors "in plain and understandable language," the ABA report said. When trials conclude, the report continued, jurors should be advised by judges that they have the right to talk to anyone, including members of the press, and that they also have the right to refuse to talk to anyone about their jury service. Practical recommendations included allowing jurors to take notes, educating jurors regarding the essential aspects of a jury trial, and providing them with identical notebooks containing the court's preliminary instructions and selected exhibits that have been ruled admissible. Read the ABA's entire report, *Principles for Juries and Jury Trials,* at Library Extra 9–12, and learn more about what it's like to serve on a jury in a criminal trial at Web Extra 9–16.

## The Victim

Not all crimes have clearly identifiable victims, and in a murder case, the victim does not survive. Where there is an identifiable surviving victim, however, he or she is often one of the most forgotten people in the courtroom. Although the victim may have been profoundly affected by the crime itself and is often emotionally committed to the proceedings and trial outcome, he or she may not even be permitted to participate directly in the trial process. Although a powerful movement to recognize the interests of victims is in full swing in this country, it is still not unusual for crime victims to be totally unaware of the final outcome of a case that intimately concerns them.[110]

Hundreds of years ago, the situation surrounding victims was far different. During the early Middle Ages in much of Europe, victims or their survivors routinely played a central role in trial proceedings and in sentencing decisions. They testified, examined witnesses, challenged defense contentions, and pleaded with the judge or jury for justice, honor, and often revenge. Sometimes they were even expected to carry out the sentence of the court by flogging the offender or by releasing the trapdoor used for hangings. This era ended with the consolidation of power into the hands of monarchs, who declared that vengeance was theirs alone.

Today, victims, like witnesses, experience many hardships as they participate in the criminal court process. These are a few of the rigors they endure:

- Uncertainties as to their role in the criminal justice process
- A general lack of knowledge about the criminal justice system, courtroom procedure, and legal issues

- Trial delays that result in frequent travel, missed work, and wasted time
- Fear of the defendant or of retaliation from the defendant's associates
- The trauma of testifying and of cross-examination

The trial process itself can make for a bitter experience. If victims take the stand, defense attorneys may test their memory, challenge their veracity, or even suggest that they were somehow responsible for their own victimization. After enduring cross-examination, some victims report feeling as though they, and not the offender, were portrayed as the criminal to the jury. The difficulties encountered by victims have been compared to a second victimization at the hands of the criminal justice system.

> The beauty of the jury is their morality. Tap into it.
>
> —San Francisco defense attorney Tony Serra

## The Defendant

Generally, defendants must be present at their trials. The Federal Rules of Criminal Procedure, like state rules, require that a defendant must be present at every stage of a trial, except that a defendant who is initially present may be voluntarily absent after the trial has commenced.[111] In *Crosby* v. *U.S.* (1993),[112] the U.S. Supreme Court held that a defendant may not be tried in absentia, even if he or she was present at the beginning of a trial, if his or her absence is due to escape or failure to appear. In a related issue, *Zafiro* v. *U.S.* (1993),[113] the justices held that, at least in federal courts, defendants charged with similar or related offenses may be tried together, even when their defenses differ substantially.

The majority of criminal defendants are poor, uneducated, and often alienated from the philosophy that undergirds the American justice system. Many are relatively powerless and are at the mercy of judicial mechanisms. However, experienced defendants, notably those who are career offenders, may be well versed in courtroom demeanor. As we discussed earlier, defendants in criminal trials may even choose to represent themselves, though such a choice may not be in their best interests.

Even without self-representation, every defendant who chooses to do so can substantially influence events in the courtroom. Defendants exercise choice in (1) selecting and retaining counsel, (2) planning a defense strategy in coordination with their attorney, (3) deciding what information to provide to (or withhold from) the defense team, (4) deciding what plea to enter, (5) deciding whether to testify personally, and (6) determining whether to file an appeal if convicted.

Nevertheless, even the most active defendants suffer from a number of disadvantages. One is the tendency of others to assume that anyone on trial must be guilty. Although a person is "innocent until proven guilty," the very fact that he or she is accused of an offense casts a shadow of suspicion that may foster biases in the minds of jurors and other courtroom actors. Another disadvantage lies in the often-substantial social and cultural differences that separate the offender from the professional courtroom staff. While lawyers and judges tend to identify with upper-middle-class values and lifestyles, few offenders do. The consequences of such a gap between defendant and courtroom staff may be insidious and far-reaching.

## Spectators and the Press

Spectators and the press are often overlooked because they do not have an official role in courtroom proceedings. Both spectators and media representatives may be present in large numbers at any trial. Spectators include members of the families of both victim and defendant, friends of either side, and curious onlookers—some of whom are avocational court watchers. Journalists, TV reporters, and other members of the press are apt to be present at "spectacular" trials (those involving an especially gruesome crime or a famous personality) and at those in which there is a great deal of community interest. The right of reporters and spectators to be present at a criminal trial is supported by the Sixth Amendment's requirement of a public trial.

Press reports at all stages of a criminal investigation and trial often create problems for the justice system. Significant pretrial publicity about a case may make it difficult to find jurors who have not already formed an opinion as to the guilt or innocence of the defendant. News reports from the courtroom may influence or confuse nonsequestered jurors who hear them, especially when they contain information brought to the bench but not heard by the jury.

In the 1976 case of *Nebraska Press Association* v. *Stuart*,[114] the U.S. Supreme Court ruled that trial court judges could not legitimately issue gag orders preventing the pretrial publication of

An artist's depiction of a portion of the 1995 South Carolina murder trial of Susan Smith. Federal courts and some state jurisdictions still restrict the use of cameras in the courtroom. Smith was convicted of drowning her two young children by rolling the car in which they were strapped into a lake. She was sentenced to life in prison.

*Yvonne Hemsey, Getty Images, Inc.*

**change of venue**

The movement of a trial or lawsuit from one jurisdiction to another or from one location to another within the same jurisdiction. A change of venue may be made in a criminal case to ensure that the defendant receives a fair trial.

information about a criminal case, as long as the defendant's right to a fair trial and an impartial jury could be ensured by traditional means.[115] These means include (1) a **change of venue**, whereby the trial is moved to another jurisdiction less likely to have been exposed to the publicity; (2) trial postponement, which would allow for memories to fade and emotions to cool; and (3) jury selection and screening to eliminate biased people from the jury pool. In 1986, the Court extended press access to preliminary hearings, which it said are "sufficiently like a trial to require public access."[116] In 1993, in the case of *Caribbean International News Corporation* v. *Puerto Rico*,[117] the Court effectively applied that requirement to territories under U.S. control.

Today, members of the press and their video, television, and still cameras are allowed into most state courtrooms. New York is one significant exception, and in 2004, a state court upheld the constitutionality of the 51-year-old law[118] prohibiting the use of cameras in that state's courts.[119] Forty-two states specifically allow cameras at most criminal trials,[120] although the majority require that permission be obtained from the judge before filming begins. Most states also impose restrictions on certain kinds of recording—of jurors or of juveniles, for example, or of conferences between an attorney and the defendant or between an attorney and the judge—although most states allow the filming of such proceedings without audio pickup. Only a few states ban television or video cameras outright. Indiana, Maryland, Mississippi, Nebraska, and Utah all prohibit audiovisual coverage of criminal trials. The District of Columbia prohibits cameras at trials and at appellate hearings.[121]

The U.S. Supreme Court has been far less favorably disposed to television coverage than have most state courts. In 1981, a Florida defendant appealed his burglary conviction to the Supreme Court,[122] arguing that the presence of television cameras at his trial had turned the court into a circus for attorneys and made the proceedings more a sideshow than a trial. The Supreme Court, recognizing that television cameras have an untoward effect on many people, found in favor of the defendant. In the words of the Court, "Trial courts must be especially vigilant to guard against any impairment of the defendant's right to a verdict based solely upon the evidence and the relevant law."

Cameras of all kinds have been prohibited in all federal district criminal proceedings since 1946 by Rule 53 of the Federal Rules of Criminal Procedure.[123] In 1972, the Judicial Conference of the United States adopted a policy opposing broadcast of civil proceedings in district courts, and that policy was incorporated into the Code of Conduct for United States Judges. Nonetheless, some district courts have local rules that allow photographs and filming during selected proceedings.

A three-year pilot project that allowed television cameras into six U.S. district courts and two appeals courts closed on December 31, 1994, when the Judicial Conference voted to end the project.

We have a criminal jury system which is superior to any in the world; and its efficiency is only marred by the difficulty of finding twelve men every day who don't know anything.

—Mark Twain

Conference members expressed concerns that cameras were a distracting influence and were having a "negative impact on jurors [and] witnesses"[124] by exposing them to possible harm by revealing their identities. Still, some federal appellate courts have created their own policy on the use of cameras and broadcast equipment in the courtroom. The official policy of the U.S. Court of Appeals for the Ninth Circuit, for example, permits cameras and media broadcasts that meet certain rules. The policy stipulates, "Three business days advance notice is required from the media of a request to be present to broadcast, televise, record electronically, or take photographs at a particular session. Such requests must be submitted to the Clerk of Court." The policy adds, "The presiding judge of the panel may limit or terminate media coverage, or direct the removal of camera coverage personnel when necessary to protect the rights of the parties or to assure the orderly conduct of the proceedings."[125]

Today's new personal technologies, however, which include cellular telephones with digital camera capabilities, streaming Web-based video, and miniaturized recording devices, all threaten courtroom room privacy. For more information on technology trends that might affect the use of cameras in courtrooms, see Library Extra 9–13 at cjtoday.com.

**LIBRARY EXTRA**

## SUMMARY

Throughout the United States, there are two judicial systems. One consists of state and local courts established under the authority of state governments. The other is the federal court system, created by Congress under the authority of the Constitution of the United States.

State courts have virtually unlimited power to decide nearly every type of case, subject only to the limitations of the U.S. Constitution, their own state constitutions, and state law. State and local courts, located in almost every town and county across the nation, are the courts with which citizens usually have contact. These courts handle most criminal matters and the great bulk of legal business concerning wills and inheritance, estates, marital disputes, real estate and land dealings, commercial and personal contracts, and other day-to-day matters.

State criminal courts present an intriguing contrast. On the one hand, they exude an aura of highly formalized judicial procedure, while on the other they demonstrate a surprising lack of organizational uniformity. Courts in one state may bear little resemblance to those in another. Court reform has not had an equal impact on all areas of the country and has, in some instances, exacerbated the differences between state court systems.

Federal courts, located principally in larger cities, decide only those cases over which the Constitution gives them authority. The highest federal court, the U.S. Supreme Court, is located in Washington, D.C., and hears cases only on appeal from lower courts.

This chapter also described professional and nonprofessional courtroom actors. In the professional category we find the judge, the prosecuting attorney, the defense counsel, the bailiff, local court administrators, the court reporter, the clerk of court, and expert witnesses. Nonprofessionals include lay witnesses, jurors, the victim, the defendant, and spectators and members of the press.

## DISCUSSION QUESTIONS

1. How did the American court system develop? What are some of the unique features of American court history?

2. What is the dual-court system? Why do we have a dual-court system in America?

3. What are some of the differences between the state and federal court systems?

4. Who are the professional members of the courtroom work group, and what are their roles?

5. What are the three forms of indigent defense used in the United States? Why might defendants prefer private attorneys over public counsel?

6. Who are the nonprofessional courtroom participants, and what are their roles?

7. What is an expert witness? What is a lay witness? How might their testimony differ? What are some of the issues involved in deciding whether a person is an expert for purposes of testimony?

8. How do the professional and nonprofessional courtroom participants work together to bring most criminal trials to a successful close? What do you think a "successful close" might mean to the judge? To the defense attorney? To the prosecutor? To the jury? To the defendant? To the victim?

**WEB QUEST**

Take a virtual tour of the U.S. Supreme Court Building via the multimedia Oyez Project, available on the Web at http://www.oyez.org/oyez/tour/. Once there, use the tour contents menu to help you navigate the site. Take a closer look at almost any area of the building, and get a 360-degree view of almost every room by clicking on the picture (hold the mouse button down and drag it). For this assignment, make use of all of the navigational features available at the Oyez Project site to move through the Supreme Court Building. As you tour the building, write down what you see, and print out images of each room you visit. Submit these descriptions and images to your instructor if asked to do so. *Note:* You must have Apple's QuickTime installed on your computer to view the images described here.

To complete this Web Quest online, go to the Web Quest module in Chapter 9 of the *Criminal Justice Today* Companion Website at cjtoday.com.

**NOTES**

i. "Sandra Day O'Connor: A Brief Biography of a Supreme Court Justice." Web posted at http://phoenix.about.com/library/weekly/aa081100a.htm (accessed July 22, 2002).

ii. "Fast Chat—Geragos: 'I Didn't Convince 12 People,'" *Newsweek,* March 21, 2005, p. 8.

iii. Don Hardenbergh, *Trends in 2004: The Future of Court Security* (Williamsburg, VA: National Center for State Courts, 2004). Web posted at http://www.ncsconline.org/wc/Publications/KIS_CtSecu_Trends04.pdf.

iv. Quoted in Richard Willing, "Courts Try to Make Jury Duty Less of a Choice," *USA Today,* March 17, 2005, p. 17A.

1. Quoted in Joan Biskupic, "Courts Can't Unravel All Election Snags," *USA Today,* September 17, 2000.

2. Details for this story come from "Nichols to Make Court Appearance Today," CNN.com, March 15, 2005. Web posted at http://www.cnn.com/2005/LAW/03/14/atlanta.shooting (accessed April 5, 2005).

3. Don Babwin, "Man Claims to Have Slain Judge's Family," ABC News, March 10, 2005. Web posted at http://abcnews.go.com/US/wireStory?id=568738 (accessed April 5, 2005).

4. "Police Match DNA from Lefkow Killings to Suicide Victim," WISCTV.com, March 10, 2005. Web posted at http://www.channel3000.com/news/4270937/detail.html (accessed July 5, 2005).

5. Law Enforcement Assistance Administration, *Two Hundred Years of American Criminal Justice* (Washington, DC: U.S. Government Printing Office, 1976), p. 31.

6. Ibid.

7. Ibid.

8. Ibid., p. 32.

9. Ibid.

10. David B. Rottman, Carol R. Flango, and R. Shedine Lockley, *State Court Organization, 1993* (Washington, DC: Bureau of Justice Statistics, 1995), p. 11.

11. Thomas A. Henderson et al., *The Significance of Judicial Structure: The Effects of Unification on Trial Court Operations* (Washington, DC: National Institute of Justice, 1984).

12. Ibid.

13. In 1957, only 13 states had permanent intermediate appellate courts. Now, all but 12 states have these courts, and North Dakota is operating one on a temporary basis to assist in handling the rising appellate caseload in that state. See Rottman, Flango, and Lockley, *State Court Organization, 1993,* p. 5.

14. *Keeney, Superintendent, Oregon State Penitentiary* v. *Tamayo-Reyes,* 113 S.Ct. 853, 122 L.Ed.2d 203 (1993).

15. *Herrera* v. *Collins,* 113 S.Ct. 853, 122 L.Ed.2d 203 (1993).

16. H. Ted Rubin, *The Courts: Fulcrum of the Justice System* (Pacific Palisades, CA: Goodyear, 1976), p. 198.

17. Martin Wright, *Justice for Victims and Offenders* (Bristol, PA: Open University Press, 1991), p. 56.

18. "Bridging the Gap between Communities and Courts." Web posted at http://www.communityjustice.org (accessed November 22, 2001).

19. Wright, *Justice for Victims and Offenders,* pp. 104, 106.

20. Most of the information and some of the wording in this section come from Administrative Office of the U.S. Courts, *Understanding the Federal Courts.* Web posted at http://www.uscourts.gov/UFC99.pdf (accessed April 2, 2005).

21. Administrative Office of the U.S. Courts, "U.S. District Courts—Criminal Cases Commenced, Terminated, and Pending during the 12-Month Periods Ending September 30, 2003 and 2004." Web posted at http://www.uscourts.gov/judbus2004/appendices/d.pdf (accessed May 11, 2005).

22. Administrative Office of the U.S. Courts, "U.S. District Courts—Civil Cases Filed by Origin, during the 12-Month Periods Ending September 30, 2000 through 2004." Web posted

at http://www.uscourts.gov/ judbus2004/ tables/s7.pdf (accessed May 11, 2005).

23. Administrative Office of the U.S. Courts, "U.S. District Courts—Criminal Cases Commenced, Terminated, and Pending."

24. Administrative Office of the U.S. Courts, "Comparison of Average Salaries of Deans and Senior Professors of Top Law Schools with U.S. District Court Judges," no date (accessed July 30, 2005).

25. Although the Ethics Reform Act of 1989 was supposed to allow for a cost-of-living increase in federal judicial salaries, Congress blocked the automatic increases from 1995 to 1999 because they also applied to the salaries of members of Congress and were seen as politically unpalatable.

26. Much of the information and some of the wording in this section come from Administrative Office of the U.S. Courts, "About the Federal Courts." Web posted at www.uscourts.gov/about.html (accessed October 4, 2001).

27. Stephen L. Wasby, *The Supreme Court in the Federal Judicial System,* 3rd ed. (Chicago: Nelson-Hall, 1988), p. 58.

28. Administrative Office of the U.S. Courts, "Judicial Conference Urges Congress to Create 68 New Federal Judgeships," March 15, 2005. Web posted at http://www.uscourts.gov/ newsroom/judconference68.htm (accessed May 5, 2005).

29. *The Supreme Court of the United States* (Washington, DC: U.S. Government Printing Office, no date), p. 4.

30. *Marbury* v. *Madison,* 1 Cranch 137 (1803).

31. Mapp v. *Ohio,* 367 U.S. 643 (1961).

32. See, for example, Jeffrey T. Ulmer, *Social Worlds of Sentencing: Court Communities under Sentencing Guidelines* (Ithaca: State University of New York Press, 1997); and Roy B. Flemming, Peter F. Nardulli, and James Eisenstein, *The Craft of Justice: Politics and Work in Criminal Court Communities* (Philadelphia: University of Pennsylvania Press, 1993).

33. See, for example, Edward J. Clynch and David W. Neubauer, "Trial Courts as Organizations," *Law and Policy Quarterly,* Vol. 3 (1981), pp. 69–94.

34. American Bar Association, *ABA Standards for Criminal Justice,* 2nd ed. (Chicago: ABA, 1980).

35. In 1940, Missouri became the first state to adopt a plan for the "merit selection" of judges based on periodic public review.

36. National Judicial College, "About the NJC." Web posted at http://www.judges.org/about (accessed February 2, 2000).

37. National Judicial College, "Judicial Education." Web posted at http://www. judges.org/educate (accessed January 30, 2000).

38. Doris Marie Provine, *Judging Credentials: Nonlawyer Judges and the Politics of Professionalism* (Chicago: University of Chicago Press, 1986).

39. Town and village justices in New York State serve part-time and may or may not be lawyers; judges of all other courts must be lawyers, whether or not they serve full-time. From New York State Commission on Judicial Conduct, *2001 Annual Report.* Web posted at http:// www.scjc.state.ny.us/annual.html (accessed March 10, 2002).

40. Ibid.

41. West Virginia Justice Watch, "Former Circuit Court Judge Joseph Troisi Made State and National Headlines for Biting the Nose of a Defendant (1997)." Web posted at http://www .wvjusticewatch.org/ethics/bite_nose.htm (accessed July 5, 2005).

42. Details for this story come from Adam Liptak, "Issue in Two Death Sentences: Judge's Drug Use," *New York Times,* May 16, 2002, p. 1A.

43. Bureau of Justice Statistics, *Report to the Nation on Crime and Justice: The Data* (Washington, DC: U.S. Department of Justice, 1983).

44. For a discussion of the resource limitations that district attorneys face in combating corporate crime, see Michael L. Benson et al., "District Attorneys and Corporate Crime: Surveying the Prosecutorial Gatekeepers," *Criminology,* Vol. 26, No. 3 (August 1988), pp. 505–517.

45. Carol J. DeFrances and Greg W. Steadman, *Prosecutors in State Courts, 1996* (Washington, DC: Bureau of Justice Statistics, 1998).

46. 28 U.S.C. 530A.

47. Some of the wording in this paragraph is adapted from Kim Murphy, "Prosecutors in Oregon Find 'Truth' Ruling a Real Hindrance," *Los Angeles Times,* August 5, 2001.

48. S45801, Oregon Supreme Court, August 17, 2000.

49. The ruling was based on Disciplinary Rule 1-102 of the Oregon State Bar, which says, in part, that it is professional misconduct for a lawyer to "engage in conduct involving dishonesty, fraud, deceit or misrepresentation." The rule also prohibits a lawyer from violating this dishonesty provision through the acts of another. Also at issue was Disciplinary Rule 7-102, which prohibits a lawyer from "knowingly making a false statement of law or fact."

50. Most of the information and some of the wording in this section come from Administrative Office of the U.S. Courts, *Understanding the Federal Courts.* Web posted at http://www.uscourts.gov/UFC99.pdf (accessed April 2, 2004).

51. "Nationline: Prosecutors Drop Charges against Mayor of Miami," *USA Today,* August 7, 2001, p. 3A.

52. Kenneth Culp Davis, *Discretionary Justice* (Baton Rouge: Louisiana State University Press, 1969), p. 190.

53. Barbara Borland, *The Prosecution of Felony Arrests* (Washington, DC: Bureau of Justice Statistics, 1983).

54. *Brady* v. *Maryland,* 373 U.S. 83 (1963).

55. *U.S.* v. *Bagley,* 473 U.S. 667 (1985).

56. *Banks* v. *Dretke,* 124 S.Ct. 1256, 1280 (2004).

57. *Imbler* v. *Pachtman,* 424 U.S. 409 (1976).

58. *Burns* v. *Reed,* 500 U.S. 478 (1991).

59. Ibid., complaint, p. 29.

60. Cassia Spohn, John Gruhl, and Susan Welch, "The Impact of the Ethnicity and Gender of Defendants on the Decision to Reject or Dismiss Felony Charges," *Criminology,* Vol. 25, No. 1 (1987), pp. 175–191.

61. The same is true under federal law, and in almost all of the states, of communications between defendants and members of the clergy, psychiatrists and psychologists, medical doctors, and licensed social workers in the course of psychotherapy. See, for example, *Jaffee* v. *Redmond,* 116 S.Ct. 1923 (1996).

62. *Powell* v. *Alabama,* 287 U.S. 45 (1932).

63. *Johnson* v. *Zerbst,* 304 U.S. 458 (1938).

64. *Gideon* v. *Wainwright,* 372 U.S. 335 (1963).

65. *Argersinger* v. *Hamlin,* 407 U.S. 25 (1972).

66. *In re Gault,* 387 U.S. 1 (1967).

67. *Alabama* v. *Shelton,* 535 U.S. 654 (2002).

68. Jane Fritsch, "Pataki Rethinks Promise of a Pay Raise for Lawyers to the Indigent," *New York Times,* December 24, 2001.

69. Steven K. Smith and Carol J. DeFrances, *Indigent Defense* (Washington, DC: Bureau of Justice Statistics, 1996).

70. Ibid.

71. Carol J. DeFrances, *State-Funded Indigent Defense Services, 1999* (Washington, DC: National Institute of Justice, 2001), from which the information in this paragraph is derived.

72. National Symposium on Indigent Defense, *Improving Criminal Justice Systems through Expanded Strategies and Innovative Collaborations* (Washington, DC: Office of Justice Programs, 2000).

73. National Association of Criminal Defense Lawyers, *In Defense of Public Access to Justice: An Assessment of Trial-Level Defense Services in Louisiana 40 Years after* Gideon (Washington, DC: NACDL, 2004).

74. David Exum, "Big Demand, Small Paychecks: State Struggles to Retain Public Defenders," *Jobfind* print edition, April 11, 2004.

75. DeFrances, *State-Funded Indigent Defense Services, 1999.*

76. Ibid.

77. "Nationline: McVeigh's Defense Cost Taxpayers $13.8 Million," *USA Today,* July 3, 2001, p. 3A.

78. Caroline Wolf Harlow, *Defense Counsel in Criminal Cases* (Washington, DC: Bureau of Justice Statistics, 2000); and Carol J. DeFrances and Marika F. X. Litras, *Indigent Defense Service in Large Counties, 1999* (Washington, DC: Bureau of Justice Statistics, 2000).

79. *Faretta* v. *California,* 422 U.S. 806 (1975).

80. Smith and DeFrances, *Indigent Defense,* pp. 2–3.

81. *Anders* v. *California,* 386 U.S. 738 (1967).

82. *People* v. *Wende,* 25 Cal.3d 436, 600 P.2d 1071 (1979).

83. *Smith* v. *Robbins,* 528 U.S. 259 (2000).

84. *Texas* v. *Cobb,* 532 U.S. 162 (2001).

85. Details for this story come from Chisun Lee, "Punishing Mmes. Stewart: The Parallel Universes of Martha and Lynne," The *Village Voice,* February 15, 2005. Web posted at http://www.refuseandresist.org/article-print .php?aid=1757 (accessed January 5, 2006).

86. "Lawyer Convicted of Terrorist Support," *USA Today,* February 11, 2005, p. 3A.

87. Mike McKee, "California State Bar to Allow Lawyers to Break Confidentiality," *The Recorder,* May 17, 2004. Web posted at http://www.law.com/jsp/article.jsp?id=10843 16038367 (accessed August 25, 2005).

88. "ABA Eases Secrecy Rules in Lawyer-Client Relationship," *USA Today,* August 7, 2001.

89. *Nix* v. *Whiteside,* 475 U.S. 157 (1986).

90. Ibid.

91. "Courtroom Killings Verdict," *USA Today,* February 15, 1993, p. 3A.

92. National Center for State Courts, "Improving Security in State Courthouses: Ten Essential Elements for Court Safety." Web posted at http://www.ncsconline.org/what'sNew/ TenPointPlan.htm (accessed October 20, 2005).

93. President's Commission on Law Enforcement and Administration of Justice, *The Challenge of Crime in a Free Society* (Washington, DC: U.S. Government Printing Office, 1967), p. 129.

94. National Advisory Commission on Criminal Justice Standards and Goals, *Courts* (Washington, DC: U.S. Government Printing Office, 1973), Standard 9.3.

95. See, for example, Joan G. Brannon, *The Judicial System in North Carolina* (Raleigh, NC: Administrative Office of the United States Courts, 1984), p. 14.

96. Joseph L. Peterson, "Use of Forensic Evidence by the Police and Courts," *Research in Brief*

(Washington, DC: National Institute of Justice, 1987), p. 3.

**97.** Ibid., p. 6.

**98.** Jennifer Bowles, "Simpson-Paid Experts," Associated Press wire service, August 12, 1995.

**99.** *California* v. *Green,* 399 U.S. 149 (1970).

**100.** Patrick L. McCloskey and Ronald L. Schoenberg, *Criminal Law Deskbook* (New York: Matthew Bender, 1988), Section 17, p. 123.

**101.** Bureau of Justice Statistics, *Report to the Nation on Crime and Justice,* 2nd ed. (Washington, DC: BJS, 1988), p. 82.

**102.** Anna Johnson, "Jury with Oprah Winfrey Convicts Man of Murder," Associated Press, August 19, 2004.

**103.** *Demarest* v. *Manspeaker et al.,* 498 U.S. 184, 111 S.Ct. 599, 112 L.Ed.2d 608 (1991).

**104.** Bureau of Justice Statistics, *Report to the Nation on Crime and Justice,* p. 82.

**105.** Johnson, "Jury with Oprah Winfrey Convicts Man of Murder."

**106.** *Williams* v. *Florida,* 399 U.S. 78, 90 S.Ct. 1893, 26 L.Ed.2d 446 (1970).

**107.** *Smith* v. *Texas,* 311 U.S. 128 (1940). That right does not apply when the defendants are facing the possibility of a prison sentence of less than six months in length or even when the potential aggregate sentence for multiple petty offenses exceeds six months (see *Lewis* v. *U.S.,* 518 U.S. 322 [1996]).

**108.** *Thiel* v. *Southern Pacific Co.,* 328 U.S. 217 (1945).

**109.** American Bar Association, *Principles for Juries and Jury Trials* (Chicago: ABA, 2005).

**110.** The author was himself the victim of a felony some years ago. His car was stolen in Columbus, Ohio, and recovered a year later in Cleveland. He was informed that the person who had taken it was in custody, but he never heard what happened to him, nor could he learn where or whether a trial was to be held.

**111.** Federal Rules of Criminal Procedure, Rule 43.

**112.** *Crosby* v. *U.S.,* 113 S.Ct. 748, 122 L.Ed.2d 25 (1993).

**113.** *Zafiro* v. *U.S.,* 113 S.Ct. 933, 122 L.Ed.2d 317 (1993).

**114.** *Nebraska Press Association* v. *Stuart,* 427 U.S. 539 (1976).

**115.** However, it is generally accepted that trial judges may issue limited gag orders aimed at trial participants.

**116.** *Press Enterprise Company* v. *Superior Court of California, Riverside County,* 478 U.S. 1 (1986).

**117.** *Caribbean International News Corporation* v. *Puerto Rico,* 508 U.S. 147 (1993).

**118.** N.Y. Civil Rights Law, Section 52.

**119.** Tom Perrotta, "New York Law Banning Cameras in State Courts Found Constitutional," *New York Law Journal,* May 23, 2004.

**120.** Charles L. Babcock et al., "Fifty-State Survey of the Law Governing Audio-Visual Coverage of Court Proceedings." Web posted at http://www.jw.com/articles/details.cfm?articlenum5120 (accessed October 10, 2001).

**121.** See Radio-Television News Directors Association, "Summary of State Camera Coverage Rules." Web posted at http://www.rtnda.org/issues/cameras—summary.htm (accessed February 9, 2000).

**122.** *Chandler* v. *Florida,* 499 U.S. 560 (1981).

**123.** Rule 53 of the Federal Rules of Criminal Procedure reads, "The taking of photographs in the court room during the progress of judicial proceedings or radio broadcasting of judicial proceedings from the court room shall not be permitted by the court."

**124.** Harry F. Rosenthal, "Courts-TV," Associated Press wire service, September 21, 1994. See also "Judicial Conference Rejects Cameras in Federal Courts," *Criminal Justice Newsletter,* September 15, 1994, p. 6.

**125.** Web posted at http://www.ce9.uscourts.gov/web/OCELibra.nsf/504ca249c786e20f85256284006da7ab/ba060a3e537d2866882569760067ac8e?OpenDocument (accessed September 16, 2005).

# CHAPTER 10

# Pretrial Activities and the Criminal Trial

## OUTLINE

- Introduction
- Pretrial Activities
- The Criminal Trial
- Stages of a Criminal Trial
- Improving the Adjudication Process

## LEARNING OBJECTIVES

**After reading this chapter, you should be able to:**

- List and explain the steps typically taken during pretrial activities.
- Explain plea bargaining, and discuss its impact on the criminal justice system.
- Describe the various stages of a criminal trial.
- Explain the hearsay rule, and identify recognized exceptions to it.
- Explain the possible benefits of a professional jury system.
- Describe methods that have been suggested for improving the adjudication process.

*Lives are lost and won in the courts, lost and won in the law—every day, everywhere. Most of us seldom really think about this. But in the jury room, the thought cannot be avoided, since there you learn that justice doesn't merely happen (neatly, reliably, like a crystal taking shape in a distant vacuum); justice is, rather, done, made, manufactured. Made by imperfect, wrangling, venal and virtuous human beings, using whatever means are at their disposal. In the jury room, you discover that the whole edifice of social order stands, finally, on handicraft—there is no magic, no mathematics, no science, no angelic fixer who checks our juridical homework. This is a frightening thing, not least because any one of us could be accused of a crime.*

—D. Graham Burnett, jury foreman[1]

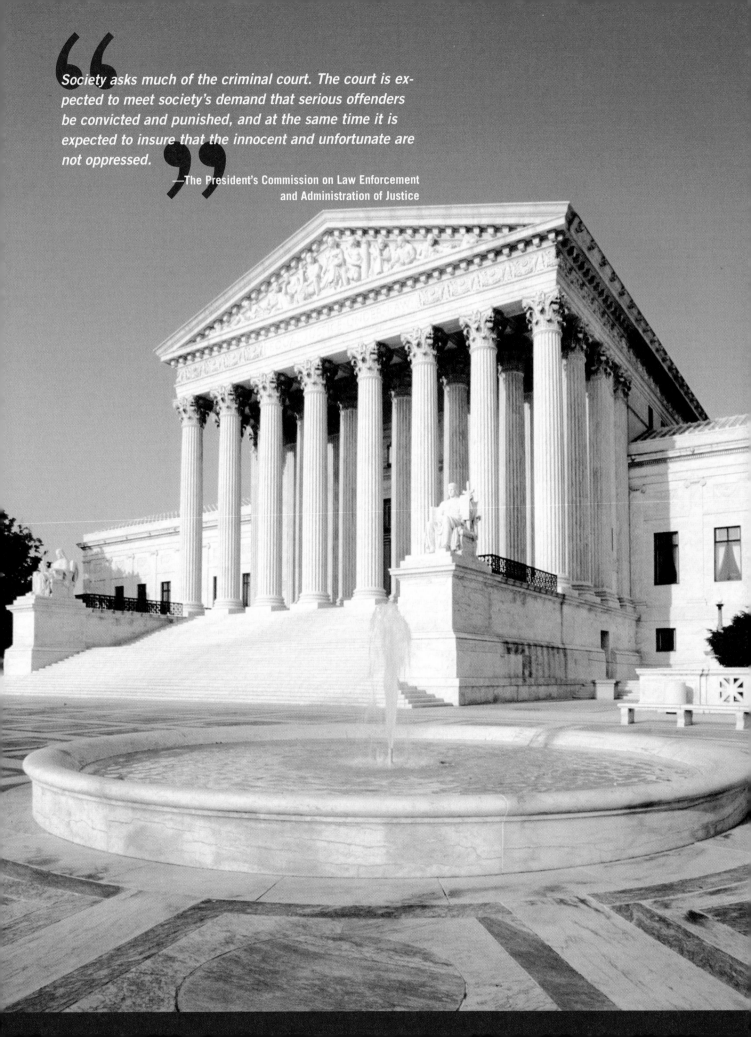

> "Society asks much of the criminal court. The court is expected to meet society's demand that serious offenders be convicted and punished, and at the same time it is expected to insure that the innocent and unfortunate are not oppressed."
>
> —The President's Commission on Law Enforcement and Administration of Justice

## KEY CONCEPTS

### TERMS

| | | |
|---|---|---|
| adversarial system | hearsay | probative value |
| bail bond | hearsay rule | property bond |
| circumstantial evidence | jury selection | real evidence |
| closing argument | *nolo contendere* | release on recognizance (ROR) |
| competent to stand trial | opening statement | rules of evidence |
| conditional release | peremptory challenge | scientific jury selection |
| danger law | perjury | sequestered jury |
| direct evidence | plea | Speedy Trial Act |
| evidence | plea bargaining | testimony |
| first appearance | pretrial release | verdict |

### CASES

| | | |
|---|---|---|
| *County of Riverside* v. *McLaughlin* | *Georgia* v. *McCollum* | *Miller-El* v. *Cockrell* |
| *Coy* v. *Iowa* | *Idaho* v. *Wright* | *Mu'Min* v. *Virginia* |
| *Doggett* v. *U.S.* | *Maryland* v. *Craig* | *Powers* v. *Ohio* |
| *Edmonson* v. *Leesville Concrete Co., Inc.* | *McNabb* v. *U.S.* | *U.S.* v. *Montalvo-Murillo* |
| *Fex* v. *Michigan* | *Michigan* v. *Lucas* | *White* v. *Illinois* |

The original full-text court opinion for each of these cases is available on the CD-ROM that accompanies this book.

# Introduction

Hear the author discuss
this chapter at
**cjtoday.com**

In 2005, following a 19-week trial that played out like pulp fiction,[2] 71-year-old Hollywood actor Robert Blake was acquitted of charges that he murdered his wife of six months, Bonny Lee Bakley. Blake had faced numerous counts, including charges that he had solicited two stuntmen to kill his wife. Prosecutors said Blake finally took matters into his own hands and shot his wife to death because he believed that Bakley, 44, had tricked him into marriage after she became pregnant with his child. They claimed that his hatred of Bakley, who had a shady past and who ran a mail-order porn business, was so intense that he would have done anything to keep her away from the couple's little girl, Rosie, who was three months old at the time of her mother's death.

Many of the facts in the case were not in dispute. On the evening of May 4, 2001, the couple had dinner at Blake's favorite Italian restaurant in Studio City, California. Following the meal, Blake walked his wife to their car, which was parked about a block and a half away. When he got to the car, Blake said, he realized that he had forgotten a .38-caliber revolver that he said he carried to protect his wife from shady characters in her past. Blake went back to the restaurant to retrieve the gun, and when he returned to the car, he said that he found his wife dying from gunshot wounds.

Although Blake's handgun was not the murder weapon, other evidence against Blake seemed strong. It included testimony by a former Los Angeles Police Department (LAPD) detective who said that Blake told him that he planned to "whack" his wife, and testimony from a stuntman who said that Blake had tried to hire him to kill Bakley for $10,000.[3]

The American criminal justice
system is theater to the world.

—Harvard University law professor
Alan Dershowitz

Following the trial, CNN legal analyst Jeffrey Toobin said he was "pretty surprised" by the not guilty verdicts and thought that prosecutors had presented a solid circumstantial case against Blake. "It sure seemed like he was the only person with the opportunity, the motive and the means to kill [Bakley]," Toobin said.[4] "But," he added, "there was no eyewitness. There was no murder weapon established. . . . The jury didn't buy it, and the jury didn't buy the whole prosecution's case." A juror later told reporters that the prosecution did not prove Blake committed the crimes. "We just didn't have enough evidence to say whether he did or if he didn't," she said.[5] Learn more about the Robert Blake case, including detailed information on the murder investigation, the preliminary hearing, pretrial maneuvering, jury selection, and witness testimony, via **Web Extra 10–1** at cjtoday.com.

Robert Blake (left), star of the 1970s TV detective drama *Baretta,* sobs in a Los Angeles courtroom after a jury acquitted him in 2005 of charges that he arranged his wife's murder. Jurors heard testimony that Blake tried to hire two men to kill his wife, Bonny Lee Bakley (right), but didn't feel that prosecutors had presented enough evidence for a conviction.

*Nick Ut, AP Wide World Photos and Spencer Tirey, Liaison, Getty Images, Inc.*

# Pretrial Activities

In this chapter, we will describe the criminal trial process, highlighting each important stage in the procedure. First, however, we look at the court-related activities that routinely take place *before* trial can begin. These activities (as well as the names given to them) vary among jurisdictions. They are described generally in the pages that follow.

# The First Appearance

Following arrest, most defendants do not come into contact with an officer of the court until their **first appearance** before a magistrate or a lower-court judge.[6] A first appearance, sometimes called an *initial appearance* or *magistrate's review,* occurs when defendants are brought before a judge (1) to be given formal notice of the charges against them, (2) to be advised of their rights, (3) to be given the opportunity to retain a lawyer or to have one appointed to represent them, and (4) perhaps to be afforded the opportunity for bail.

According to the procedural rules of all jurisdictions, defendants who have been taken into custody must be offered an in-court appearance before a magistrate "without unnecessary delay." The 1943 U.S. Supreme Court case of *McNabb* v. *U.S.*[7] established that any unreasonable delay in an initial court appearance would make confessions inadmissible if interrogating officers obtained them during the delay. Based on the *McNabb* decision, 48 hours following arrest became the standard maximum time by which a first appearance should be held.

The first appearance may also involve a probable cause hearing, although such hearings may be held separately since they do not require the defendant's presence. (In some jurisdictions, a probable cause hearing may be combined with the preliminary hearing, which we will look at later in this chapter.) Probable cause hearings are necessary when arrests are made without a warrant.[8] During a probable cause hearing, also called a *probable cause determination,* a judicial officer will review police documents and reports to ensure that probable cause supported the arrest. The review of the arrest proceeds in a relatively informal fashion, with the judge seeking to decide whether, at the time of apprehension, the arresting officer had reason to believe both (1) that a crime had been or was being committed and (2) that the defendant was the person who committed it. Most of the evidence presented to the judge comes either from the arresting officer or from the victim. If probable cause is not found, the suspect is released. As with a first appearance, a probable cause hearing should take place within 48 hours.

In 1991, in a class-action suit entitled *County of Riverside* v. *McLaughlin,*[9] the U.S. Supreme Court imposed a promptness requirement on probable cause determinations for in-custody

## first appearance

An appearance before a magistrate during which the legality of the defendant's arrest is initially assessed and the defendant is informed of the charges on which he or she is being held. At this stage in the criminal justice process, bail may be set or pretrial release arranged. Also called *initial appearance.*

A bail hearing in progress. Standing before the judge are Julie Barnes and Thomas Levesque, a homeless pair accused of accidentally starting a warehouse blaze that led to the deaths of six Worcester, Massachusetts, firefighters. Levesque's bail was set at $250,000 cash, or $2.5 million with surety; Barnes' bail was set at $75,000 cash, or $750,000 with surety. In 2002, the two agreed to a plea agreement, and each was sentenced to five years of probation for involuntary manslaughter.
*AP Wide World Photos*

arrestees. The Court held that "a jurisdiction that provides judicial determinations of probable cause within 48 hours of arrest will, as a general matter, comply with the promptness requirement." The Court specified, however, that weekends and holidays could not be excluded from the 48-hour requirement (as they had been in Riverside County, California) and that, depending on the specifics of the case, delays of fewer than two days may still be unreasonable.

During a first appearance, the suspect is not given an opportunity to present evidence, although the U.S. Supreme Court has held that defendants are entitled to representation by counsel at their first appearance.[10] Following a reading of the charges and an advisement of rights, counsel may be appointed to represent indigent defendants, and proceedings may be adjourned until counsel can be obtained. In cases where a suspect is unruly, intoxicated, or uncooperative, a judicial review may take place without the suspect's presence.

Some states waive a first appearance and proceed directly to arraignment (discussed later), especially when the defendant has been arrested on a warrant. In states that move directly to arraignment, the procedures undertaken to obtain a warrant are regarded as sufficient to demonstrate a basis for detention before arraignment.

## Pretrial Release

**pretrial release**

The release of an accused person from custody, for all or part of the time before or during prosecution, on his or her promise to appear in court when required.

**LIBRARY EXTRA**

A significant aspect of the first appearance hearing is the consideration of **pretrial release**. Defendants charged with very serious crimes, or those thought likely to escape or to injure others, are usually held in jail until trial. Such a practice is called *pretrial detention*. The majority of defendants, however, are afforded the opportunity for release. Many jurisdictions make use of pretrial service programs, which may also be called *early-intervention programs*.[11] Such programs, which are typically funded by the states or by individual counties, perform two critical functions: (1) They gather and present information about newly arrested defendants and about available release options for use by judicial officers in deciding what (if any) conditions are to be set for a defendant's release prior to trial, and (2) they supervise defendants released from custody during the pretrial period by monitoring their compliance with release conditions and by helping to ensure that they appear for scheduled court events. Learn more about pretrial services via Library Extra 10–1 at cjtoday.com.

The initial pretrial release/detention decision is usually made by a judicial officer or by a specially appointed hearing officer who considers background information provided by the pretrial service program, along with the representations made by the prosecutor and the defense attorney. In making this decision, judicial officers are concerned about two types of risk: (1) the risk of flight or nonappearance for scheduled court appearances and (2) the risk to public safety. In assessing these risks, judicial officers tend to focus on four key factors:

■ The seriousness of the current charge, as set forth in the complaint and the representations of the prosecutor

- The defendant's prior criminal record, which is widely viewed as relevant to assessing the risk to public safety that would be posed by a decision to release or to set a relatively low money bond amount

- Information about the defendant, including community and family ties; employment status; housing; existence and nature of any substance abuse problems; and (if the defendant had been arrested before) record of compliance with conditions of release set on previous occasions, including any failures to appear

- Information about available supervisory options if the defendant is released

## Bail

Bail is the most common release/detention decision-making mechanism in American courts. Bail serves two purposes: (1) It helps ensure reappearance of the accused, and (2) it prevents unconvicted individuals from suffering imprisonment unnecessarily.

Bail involves the posting of a bond as a pledge that the accused will return for further hearings. **Bail bonds** usually involve cash deposits but may be based on property or other valuables. A fully secured bond requires the defendant to post the full amount of bail set by the court. The usual practice, however, is for a defendant to seek privately secured bail through the services of a professional bail bondsman. The bondsman will assess a percentage (usually 10% to 15%) of the required bond as a fee, which the defendant will have to pay up front. Those who "skip bail" by hiding or fleeing will sometimes be ordered by the court to forfeit their bail. Forfeiture hearings must be held before a bond can be taken, and most courts will not order bail forfeited unless it appears that the defendant intends to avoid prosecution permanently. Bail forfeiture will often be reversed if the defendant later appears willingly to stand trial.

In many states, bondsmen are empowered to hunt down and bring back defendants who have fled. In some jurisdictions, bondsmen hold virtually unlimited powers and have been permitted by courts to pursue, arrest, and forcibly extradite their charges from foreign jurisdictions without concern for the due process considerations or statutory limitations that apply to law enforcement officers.[12] Recently, however, a number of states have enacted laws that eliminate for-profit bail bond businesses, replacing them instead with state-operated pretrial service agencies. Visit the Professional Bail Agents of the United States via Web Extra 10–2 at cjtoday.com to learn more about the job of a bail bondsman and to view the group's code of ethics.

> **bail bond**
> A document guaranteeing the appearance of a defendant in court as required and recording the pledge of money or property to be paid to the court if he or she does not appear, which is signed by the person to be released and anyone else acting on his or her behalf.

**WEB EXTRA**

## Alternatives to Bail

The Eighth Amendment to the U.S. Constitution does not guarantee the opportunity for bail but does state that "[e]xcessive bail shall not be required." Some studies, however, have found

A typical bail bond office. Bail bond offices like this one are usually found near courthouses where criminal trials are held.

*Mark Richards*

that many defendants who are offered the opportunity for bail are unable to raise the money. Thirty years ago, a report by the National Advisory Commission on Criminal Justice Standards and Goals found that as many as 93% of felony defendants in some jurisdictions were unable to make bail.[13]

To extend the opportunity for pretrial release to a greater number of nondangerous arrestees, many states and the federal government now offer various alternatives to the cash bond system, such as (1) release on recognizance, (2) property bond, (3) deposit bail, (4) conditional release, (5) third-party custody, (6) unsecured bond, and (7) signature bond.

**Release on Recognizance (ROR)** Release on recognizance (ROR) involves no cash bond, requiring as a guarantee only that the defendant agree in writing to return for further hearings as specified by the court. Release on recognizance was tested during the 1960s in a social experiment called the Manhattan Bail Project.[14] In the experiment, those arrested for serious crimes, including murder, rape, and robbery, and those with extensive prior criminal records were excluded from participating in the project. The rest of the defendants were scored and categorized according to a number of "ideal" criteria used as indicators of both dangerousness and the likelihood of pretrial flight. Criteria included (1) no previous convictions, (2) residential stability, and (3) a good employment record. Those likely to flee were not released.

Studies of the bail project revealed that it released four times as many defendants before trial as had been freed under the traditional cash bond system,[15] and that only 1% of those released fled from prosecution—the same percentage as for those set free on cash bond.[16] Later studies, however, were unclear as to the effectiveness of release on recognizance, with some finding a no-show rate as high as 12%.[17]

**Property Bonds** Property bonds substitute other items of value in place of cash. Land, houses, automobiles, stocks, and so on may be consigned to the court as collateral against pretrial flight.

**Deposit Bail** Deposit bail is an alternative form of cash bond available in some jurisdictions. Deposit bail places the court in the role of the bondsman, allowing the defendant to post a percentage of the full bail with the court. Unlike private bail bondsmen, court-run deposit bail pro-

---

**release on recognizance (ROR)**

The pretrial release of a criminal defendant on his or her written promise to appear in court as required. No cash or property bond is required.

---

**property bond**

The setting of bail in the form of land, houses, stocks, or other tangible property. In the event that the defendant absconds prior to trial, the bond becomes the property of the court.

---

Bounty hunter Duane "Dog" Chapman, owner of Bounty Hunter International and self-proclaimed "greatest bounty hunter in the world." Bounty hunters collect fees from bail bondsmen, who otherwise stand to forfeit money they have posted for clients who do not appear in court. Chapman, an ex-con born-again Christian, makes a living pursuing felons who fail to appear for their court dates after posting bail through a bondsman. He has more than 6,000 captures to his credit. Read more about him at http://www.dogthebountyhunter.com.

*Jim Ruymen, REUTERS, Corbis/Bettmann*

grams usually return the amount of the deposit except for a small administrative fee (perhaps 1%). If the defendant fails to appear for court, the entire amount of court-ordered bail is forfeited.

**Conditional Release**   Conditional release imposes requirements on the defendant such as participation in a drug-treatment program; staying away from specified others, such as potential witnesses; and attendance at a regular job. *Release under supervision* is similar to conditional release but adds the stipulation that defendants report to an officer of the court or to a police officer at designated times.

**Third-Party Custody**   Third-party custody is a bail bond alternative that assigns custody of the defendant to an individual or agency that promises to ensure his or her later appearance in court.[18] Some pretrial release programs allow attorneys to assume responsibility for their clients in this fashion. If a defendant fails to appear, the attorney's privilege to participate in the program may be ended.

**Unsecured Bonds**   Unsecured bonds are based on a court-determined dollar amount of bail. Like a credit contract, it requires no monetary deposit with the court. The defendant agrees in writing that failure to appear will result in forfeiture of the entire amount of the bond, which might then be taken in seizures of land, personal property, bank accounts, and so on.

**Signature Bonds**   Signature bonds allow release based on the defendant's written promise to appear. Signature bonds involve no particular assessment of the defendant's dangerousness or likelihood of later appearance in court. They are used only in cases of minor offenses like traffic law violations and some petty drug-law violations. Signature bonds may be issued by the arresting officer acting on behalf of the court.

## Pretrial Release and Public Safety

Pretrial release is common practice. Approximately 62% of all state-level felony criminal defendants[19] and 66% of all federal felony defendants[20] are released before trial (Figure 10–1). A growing movement, arguing that defendants released before trial may be dangerous to themselves or to others, seeks to reduce the number of defendants released under any conditions. Advocates of this conservative policy cite a number of studies documenting crimes committed by defendants released on bond. One study found that 16% of defendants released before trial were rearrested; of those, 30% were arrested more than once.[21] Another study determined that as many as 41% of those released before trial for serious crimes, such as rape and robbery, were rearrested before their trial date.[22] Not surprisingly, such studies generally find that the longer the time spent free on bail prior to trial, the greater the likelihood of misconduct.

In response to findings like these, some states have enacted **danger laws**, which limit the right to bail to certain kinds of offenders.[23] Other states, including Arizona, California, Colorado, Florida, and Illinois, have approved constitutional amendments restricting the use of bail.[24] Most

**conditional release**

The release by executive decision of a prisoner from a federal or state correctional facility who has not served his or her full sentence and whose freedom is contingent on obeying specified rules of behavior.

**danger law**

A law intended to prevent the pretrial release of criminal defendants judged to represent a danger to others in the community.

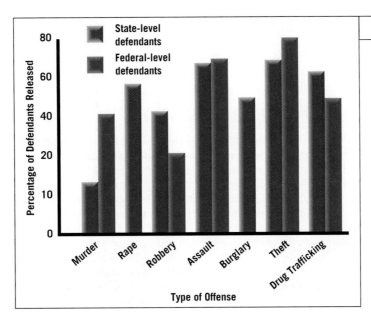

### FIGURE 10–1

**Proportion of state and federal felony defendants released before trial.**

*Sources:* Gerald Rainville and Brian A. Reaves, *Felony Defendants in Large Urban Counties, 2000* (Washington, DC: Bureau of Justice Statistics, 2003); Brian A. Reaves and Jacob Perez, *Pretrial Release of Felony Defendants, 1992* (Washington, DC: Bureau of Justice Statistics, 1994); and John Scalia, *Federal Pretrial Release and Detention, 1996* (Washington, DC: Bureau of Justice Statistics, 1999). *Note:* Federal pretrial release statistics are not available for the crimes of rape and burglary.

such provisions exclude defendants charged with certain crimes from being eligible for bail and demand that other defendants being considered for bail meet stringent conditions. Some states combine these strictures with tough release conditions designed to keep close control over defendants before trial.

The 1984 federal Bail Reform Act allows federal judges to assess the danger of an accused to the community and to deny bail to defendants who are thought to be dangerous. In the words of the act, a suspect held in pretrial custody on federal criminal charges must be detained if "after a hearing . . . he is found to pose a risk of flight and a danger to others or the community and if no condition of release can give reasonable assurances against these contingencies."[25] Defendants seeking bail must demonstrate a high likelihood of later court appearance. The act also requires that a defendant have a speedy first appearance and, if he or she is to be detained, that a *detention hearing* be held together with the initial appearance.

In the 1990 case of *U.S. v. Montalvo-Murillo*,[26] however, a defendant who was not provided with a detention hearing at the time of his first appearance and was subsequently released by an appeals court was found to have no "right" to freedom because of this "minor" statutory violation. The Supreme Court held that "unless it has a substantial influence on the outcome of the proceedings . . . failure to comply with the Act's prompt hearing provision does not require release of a person who should otherwise be detained" because "[a]utomatic release contravenes the statutory purpose of providing fair bail procedures while protecting the public's safety and assuring a defendant's appearance at trial."[27]

Court challenges to the constitutionality of pretrial detention legislation have not met with much success. The U.S. Supreme Court case of *U.S. v. Hazzard* (1984),[28] decided only a few months after enactment of federal bail reform, held that Congress was justified in providing for denial of bail to offenders who represent a danger to the community. Later cases have supported the presumption of flight, which federal law presupposes for certain types of defendants.[29]

## The Grand Jury

The federal government and about half of the states use grand juries as part of the pretrial process. Grand juries comprise private citizens (often 23 in number) who hear evidence presented by the prosecution. Grand juries serve primarily as filters to eliminate cases for which there is not sufficient evidence from further processing.

In early times, grand juries served a far different purpose. The grand jury system began in England in 1166 as a way of identifying law violators. Lacking a law enforcement agency with investigative authority, the government looked to the grand jury as a source of information on criminal activity in the community. Even today, grand juries in most jurisdictions may initiate prosecution independently of the prosecutor, although they rarely do.

Grand jury hearings are held in secret, and the defendant is generally not afforded the opportunity to appear.[30] Similarly, the defense has no opportunity to cross-examine prosecution witnesses. Grand juries have the power to subpoena witnesses and to mandate a review of books, records, and other documents crucial to their investigation.

After hearing the evidence, the grand jury votes on the indictment presented to it by the prosecution. The indictment is a formal listing of proposed charges. If the majority of grand jury members agree to forward the indictment to the trial court, it becomes a "true bill" on which further prosecution will turn.

## The Preliminary Hearing

States that do not use grand juries rely instead on a preliminary hearing "for charging defendants in a fashion that is less cumbersome and arguably more protective of the innocent."[31] In these jurisdictions, the prosecutor files an accusatory document called an *information,* or complaint, against the accused. A preliminary hearing is then held to determine whether there is probable cause to hold the defendant for trial. A few states, notably Tennessee and Georgia, use both the grand jury mechanism and a preliminary hearing as a "double check against the possibility of unwarranted prosecution."[32]

Although the preliminary hearing is not nearly as elaborate as a criminal trial, it has many of the same characteristics. The defendant is taken before a lower-court judge who summarizes the charges and reviews the rights to which all criminal defendants are entitled. The prosecution may present witnesses and will offer evidence in support of the complaint. The defendant is afforded the right to testify and may also call witnesses.

I have tried to minimize what I feel is one of the less desirable aspects of the job . . . that judges can become isolated from the people whose lives their decisions affect.

—U.S. Supreme Court Justice Stephen Breyer

# CJ TODAY EXHIBIT 10-1

## Nonjudicial Pretrial Release Decisions

In most American jurisdictions, judicial officers decide whether an arrested person will be detained or released. Some jurisdictions, however, allow others to make that decision. Some observers argue that the critical issue is not whether the decision maker is a judge, but whether there are clear and appropriate criteria for making the decision, whether the decision maker has adequate information, and whether he or she has been well trained in pretrial release/detention decision making.

Nonjudicial decision makers and release/detention mechanisms include the following:

■ *Police officers and desk appearance tickets.* Desk appearance tickets, or citations, are summonses given to defendants at the police station, usually for petty offenses or misdemeanor charges. The tickets can greatly reduce the use of pretrial detention and can save the court system a great deal of time by avoiding initial pretrial release or bail hearings in minor cases. However, because they are typically based only on the current charge (and sometimes on a computer search to check for outstanding warrants), high-risk defendants could be released without supervision or monitoring. As computerized access to criminal history information becomes more readily available, enabling rapid identification of individuals with prior records who pose a risk to the community, desk appearance tickets may be more widely used.

■ *Jail administrators.* In many jurisdictions, jail officials have the authority to release (or to refuse to book into jail) arrestees who meet certain criteria. In some localities, jail officials exercise this authority pursuant to a court order that specifies priorities with respect to the categories of defendants who can be admitted to the jail and those who are to be released when the jail population exceeds a court-imposed ceiling. The "automatic release" approach helps minimize jail crowding, but it does so at the risk of releasing some defendants who pose a high risk of becoming fugitives or committing criminal acts. To help minimize these risks, some sheriffs and jail administrators have developed their own pretrial services or "release on recognizance" units with staff who conduct risk assessments based on interviews with arrestees, information from references, and criminal history checks.

■ *Bail schedules.* These predetermined schedules set levels of bail (from release on recognizance to amounts of surety bond) based solely on the offense charged. Depending on local practices, release pursuant to a bail schedule may take place at a police station, at the local jail, or at court. This practice saves time for judicial officers and allows rapid release of defendants who can afford to post the bail amount. However, release determinations based solely on the current charge are of dubious value because there is no proven relationship between a particular charge and risk of flight or subsequent crime. Release pursuant to a bail schedule depends simply on the defendant's ability to post the amount of the bond. Moreover, when a defendant is released by posting bond, there is generally no procedure for supervision to minimize the risks of nonappearance and subsequent crime.

■ *Bail bondsmen.* When a judicial officer sets the amount of bond that a defendant must produce to be released, or when bond is set mechanically on the basis of a bail schedule, the real decision makers are often the surety bail bondsmen. If no bondsman will offer bond, the defendant without other sources of money remains in jail. The defendant's ability to pay a bondsman the 10% fee (and sometimes to post collateral) bears no relationship to his or her risk of flight or danger to the community.

■ *Pretrial service agencies.* In some jurisdictions, pretrial service agencies have the authority to release certain categories of defendants. The authority is usually limited to relatively minor cases, although agencies in a few jurisdictions can release some categories of felony defendants. Because the pretrial service agency can obtain information about the defendant's prior record, community ties, and other pending charges, its decision to release or detain is based on more extensive information and criteria than when the decision is based on a bail schedule. However, because these programs lack the independence that judicial officers are allowed, they can be targets of political and public pressure.

*References:* Adapted from Barry Mahoney et al., *Pretrial Services Programs: Responsibilities and Potential* (Washington, DC: National Institute of Justice, 2001).

---

The primary purpose of the preliminary hearing is to give the defendant an opportunity to challenge the legal basis for his or her detention. At this point, defendants who appear to be or claim to be mentally incompetent may be ordered to undergo further evaluation to determine whether they are **competent to stand trial**. Competence to stand trial, which was briefly discussed in Chapter 4, may become an issue when a defendant appears to be incapable of understanding the proceedings or is unable to assist in his or her own defense due to mental disease or defect.

In 2003, the U.S. Supreme Court placed strict limits on the government's power to forcibly medicate some mentally ill defendants to make them competent to stand trial.[33] In the case of *Sell* v. *U.S.*,[34] the Court ruled that the use of antipsychotic drugs on a nonviolent pretrial defendant who does not represent a danger while institutionalized must be in the defendant's best medical interest and be "substantially unlikely" to cause side effects that might compromise the fairness of the trial.

**competent to stand trial**

A finding by a court, when the defendant's sanity at the time of trial is at issue, that the defendant has sufficient present ability to consult with his or her attorney with a reasonable degree of rational understanding and that the defendant has a rational as well as factual understanding of the proceedings against him or her.

A grand jury in action. Grand jury proceedings are generally very informal, as this picture shows.

*David Young-Wolff, Getty Images, Inc.—Stone Allstock*

---

**plea**

In criminal proceedings, the defendant's formal answer in court to the charge contained in a complaint, information, or indictment that he or she is guilty of the offense charged, is not guilty of the offense charged, or does not contest the charge.

---

**nolo contendere**

A plea of "no contest." A no-contest plea is used when the defendant does not wish to contest conviction. Because the plea does not admit guilt, however, it cannot provide the basis for later civil suits that might follow a criminal conviction.

---

**plea bargaining**

The process of negotiating an agreement among the defendant, the prosecutor, and the court as to an appropriate plea and associated sentence in a given case. Plea bargaining circumvents the trial process and dramatically reduces the time required for the resolution of a criminal case.

---

Barring a finding of mental incompetence, all that is required for the wheels of justice to move forward is a demonstration "sufficient to justify a prudent man's belief that the suspect has committed or was committing an offense" within the jurisdiction of the court.[35] If the magistrate finds enough evidence to justify a trial, the defendant is bound over to the grand jury. In states that do not require grand jury review, the defendant is sent directly to the trial court. If the complaint against the defendant cannot be substantiated, he or she is released. A release is not a bar to further prosecution, however, and the defendant may be rearrested if further evidence comes to light.

## Arraignment and the Plea

Once an indictment has been returned or an information has been filed, the accused will be formally arraigned. Arraignment is "the first appearance of the defendant before the court that has the authority to conduct a trial."[36] Arraignment is generally a brief process with two purposes: (1) to once again inform the defendant of the specific charges against him or her and (2) to allow the defendant to enter a **plea**. The Federal Rules of Criminal Procedure allow for one of three types of pleas to be entered: guilty, not guilty, and *nolo contendere*. A **nolo contendere** (no-contest) plea is much the same as a guilty plea. A defendant who pleads "no contest" is immediately convicted and may be sentenced just as though he or she had pleaded guilty. A no-contest plea, however, is not an admission of guilt and provides one major advantage to defendants: It may not be used later as a basis for civil proceedings that seek monetary or other damages against the defendant.

Some defendants refuse to enter any plea and are said to "stand mute." Standing mute is a defense strategy that is rarely employed. Defendants who choose this alternative simply do not answer the request for a plea. However, for procedural purposes, a defendant who stands mute is considered to have entered a plea of not guilty.

## Plea Bargaining

Guilty pleas are often not straightforward and are typically arrived at only after complex negotiations known as *plea bargaining*. **Plea bargaining** is a process of negotiation that usually involves the defendant, the prosecutor, and the defense counsel. It is founded on the mutual interests of all involved. Defense attorneys and their clients will agree to a plea of guilty when they are unsure of their ability to win acquittal at trial. Prosecutors may be willing to bargain because the evidence they have against the defendant is weaker than they would like it to be. Plea bargaining offers prosecutors the additional advantage of a quick conviction without the need to commit the time and resources necessary for trial. Benefits to the accused include the possibility of reduced or combined charges, lower defense costs, and a shorter sentence than might otherwise be anticipated.

The U.S. Supreme Court has held that a guilty plea constitutes conviction.[37] To validate the conviction, negotiated pleas require judicial consent. Judges often accept pleas that are the result of a bargaining process because such pleas reduce the court's workload. Although few judges are willing to guarantee a sentence before a plea is entered, most prosecutors and criminal trial lawyers know what sentences to expect from typical pleas.

Bargained pleas are commonplace. Surveys have found that 90% of all criminal cases prepared for trial are eventually resolved through a negotiated plea.[38] In a study of 37 big-city prosecutors, the Bureau of Justice Statistics found that for every 100 adults arrested on a felony charge, half were eventually convicted of either a felony or a misdemeanor.[39] Of all convictions, fully 94% were the result of a plea. Only 6% of convictions were the result of a criminal trial.

After a guilty plea has been entered, it may be withdrawn with the consent of the court. In the case of *Henderson* v. *Morgan* (1976),[40] for example, the U.S. Supreme Court permitted a defendant to withdraw a plea of guilty nine years after it had been given. In that case, the defendant had originally entered a plea of guilty to second-degree murder but had attempted to withdraw it before trial. Reasons for wanting to withdraw the plea included the defendant's belief that he had not been completely advised as to the nature of the charge or the sentence he might receive as a result of the plea.

Some Supreme Court decisions, however, have enhanced the prosecutor's authority in the bargaining process by declaring that defendants cannot capriciously withdraw negotiated pleas.[41] Other rulings have supported discretionary actions by prosecutors in which sentencing recommendations were retracted even after bargains had been struck.[42] Some lower-court cases have upheld the government's authority to withdraw from a negotiated plea when the defendant fails to live up to certain conditions.[43] Conditions may include requiring the defendant to provide information on other criminals, criminal cartels, and the activities of smugglers.

While it is generally agreed that bargained pleas should relate in some way to the original charge, they do not always relate. Entered pleas may be chosen for the punishments likely to be associated with them rather than for their accuracy in describing the criminal offense in which the defendant was involved.[44] This is especially true when the defendant wants to minimize the socially stigmatizing impact of the offense. A charge of indecent liberties, for example, in which the defendant is accused of sexual misconduct, may be pleaded out as assault. Such a plea, which takes advantage of the fact that indecent liberties can be considered a form of sexual assault, would effectively disguise the true nature of the offense.

Even though the Supreme Court has endorsed plea bargaining, the public sometimes views it suspiciously. Law-and-order advocates, who generally favor harsh punishments and long jail terms, claim that plea bargaining results in unjustifiably light sentences. As a consequence, prosecutors who regularly engage in the practice rarely advertise it. Plea bargaining can be a powerful prosecutorial tool, but this power carries with it the potential for misuse. Because they circumvent the trial process, plea bargains can be abused by prosecutors and defense attorneys who are more interested in the speedy resolution of cases than they are in seeing justice done. Carried to the extreme, plea bargaining may result in defendants being convicted of crimes they did not commit. Although it is rare, innocent defendants (especially those with prior criminal records) who think a jury will convict them—for whatever reason—may plead guilty to reduced charges to avoid a trial. In an effort to protect defendants against hastily arranged pleas, the Federal Rules of Criminal Procedure require judges to (1) inform the defendant of the various rights he or she is surrendering by pleading guilty, (2) determine that the plea is voluntary, (3) require disclosure of any plea agreements, and (4) make sufficient inquiry to ensure there is a factual basis for the plea.[45]

Bargained pleas can take many forms and can be quite inventive. The case of Jeffrey Morse illustrates an unusual attempt at a bargained plea. In 1998, Morse, a convicted sex offender, petitioned courts in Illinois for permission to leave jail prior to sentencing for sexual assaults on two young girls so that he could undergo surgical castration. A judge agreed, and he was surgically castrated in a 45-minute outpatient procedure. Morse's mother noted that the surgery was done in an effort to avoid a long prison sentence. "He will cut whatever bodily part he has to be able to reduce his sentence," she said.[46] Two months later, however, Kane County Judge Donald C. Hudson refused to show leniency for Morse. Instead, Hudson sentenced Morse to 26 years in prison, saying that he wouldn't "place a seal of approval on trading body parts for a lesser sentence."[47]

Plea bargains can spare a defendant's life. Eric Rudolph, shown here in a police mug shot, pled guilty in 2005 to the deadly 1996 Atlanta Olympic park bombing, a fatal 1998 abortion clinic blast in Birmingham, and two other Atlanta-area bombings. Rudolph's deal with prosecutors spared him a possible death sentence, although he received four consecutive life prison terms. A follower of a white supremacist religion that is antiabortion, antigay, and anti-Semitic, Rudolph was on the FBI's 10 Most Wanted List for more than five years as he hid in the mountains of North Carolina before being apprehended by a lone officer as he scavenged for food in a garbage bin.

*AP Wide World Photos*

# The Criminal Trial

The criminal justice process is carefully choreographed in all aspects. Arresting officers must follow proper procedure when gathering evidence and arresting and questioning suspects. Magistrates, prosecutors, jailers, and prison officials are all subject to their own strictures. Nowhere, however, is the criminal justice process more closely circumscribed than it is at the criminal trial.

Procedures in a modern courtroom are highly formalized. **Rules of evidence**, which govern the admissibility of evidence, and other procedural guidelines determine the course of a criminal hearing and trial. While rules of evidence are partially based on tradition, all U.S. jurisdictions have formalized written rules of evidence. Criminal trials at the federal level generally adhere to the requirements of the Federal Rules of Evidence.

Trials are also circumscribed by informal rules and professional expectations. An important component of law school education is the teaching of rules that structure and define appropriate courtroom demeanor. In addition to statutory rules, law students are thoroughly exposed to the ethical standards of their profession as found in the American Bar Association standards and other writings.

> **rules of evidence**
>
> Court rules that govern the admissibility of evidence at criminal hearings and trials.

## Nature and Purpose of the Criminal Trial

In the remainder of this chapter, we will describe the chronology of a criminal trial and will explore some of the widely accepted rules of criminal procedure. Before we begin, however, it is good to keep two points in mind. One is that the primary purpose of any criminal trial is the determination of the defendant's guilt or innocence. In this regard, it is important to recognize the crucial distinction that scholars make between factual guilt and legal guilt. Factual guilt deals with the issue of whether the defendant is actually responsible for the crime of which he or she stands accused. If the defendant did it, then he or she is, in fact, guilty. Legal guilt is not as clear. Legal guilt is established only when the prosecutor presents sufficient evidence to convince the judge (where the judge determines the verdict) or the jury that the defendant is guilty as charged. The distinction between factual guilt and legal guilt is crucial because it points to the fact that the burden of proof rests with the prosecution, and it indicates the possibility that guilty defendants may, nonetheless, be found "not guilty."

The second point to remember is that criminal trials under our system of justice are built around an **adversarial system** and that central to this system is the advocacy model. Participating in the adversarial system are advocates for the state (the prosecutor or the district attorney) and for the defendant (the defense counsel, the public defender, and so on). The philosophy behind the adversarial system is that the greatest number of just resolutions in criminal trials will occur when both sides are allowed to argue their cases effectively and vociferously before a fair and impartial jury. The system requires that advocates for both sides do their utmost, within the boundaries set by law and professional ethics, to protect and advance the interests of their clients (that is, the defendant and the state). The advocacy model makes clear that it is not the job of the defense attorney or the prosecution to decide the guilt of any defendant. Hence, even defense attorneys who are convinced that their clients are guilty are still exhorted to offer the best possible defense and to counsel their clients as effectively as possible.

The adversarial system has been criticized by some thinkers who point to fundamental differences between law and science in the way the search for truth is conducted.[48] While proponents of traditional legal procedure accept the belief that truth can best be uncovered through an adversarial process, scientists adhere to a painstaking process of research and replication to acquire knowledge. Most of us would agree that scientific advances in recent years may have made factual issues less difficult to ascertain. For example, some of the new scientific techniques in evidence analysis, such as DNA fingerprinting, can now unequivocally link a suspect to criminal activity or even show that someone who was once thought guilty is actually innocent. At least 328 convictions have been overturned using DNA evidence since 1989, when Gary Dotson of Illinois became the first person exonerated through such evidence. (Read about Dotson's case in "The Rape That Wasn't" via **Library Extra 10–2** at cjtoday.com.) According to Samuel R. Gross and colleagues at the University of Michigan Law School, who published a comprehensive study of exonerations in 2004, those 328 persons ". . . had spent more than 3400 years in prison for crimes for which they never should have been convicted."[49] Exonerations occur more frequently in cases where DNA evidence is relatively easy to acquire, such as rape and murder cases. False conviction rates for other crimes, such as robbery, are much more difficult to assess using DNA. Hence, according to Gross, "The clearest and most important lesson from the recent spike in rape exonerations is that false convictions that come to light are the tip of the iceberg."[50]

Whether scientific findings should continue to serve a subservient role to the adversarial process is a question widely discussed. The answer will be determined by the results the two processes are able to produce. If the adversarial model results in the acquittal of too many demonstrably guilty people because of legal "technicalities" or if the scientific approach identifies too many suspects inaccurately, either could be restricted.

> **adversarial system**
>
> The two-sided structure under which American criminal trial courts operate that pits the prosecution against the defense. In theory, justice is done when the most effective adversary is able to convince the judge or jury that his or her perspective on the case is the correct one.

# Stages of a Criminal Trial

We turn now to a discussion of the steps in a criminal trial. As Figure 10–2 shows, trial chronology consists of eight stages:

1. Trial initiation
2. Jury selection
3. Opening statements
4. Presentation of evidence
5. Closing arguments
6. Judge's charge to the jury
7. Jury deliberations
8. Verdict

**FIGURE 10–2**

Stages in a criminal trial.

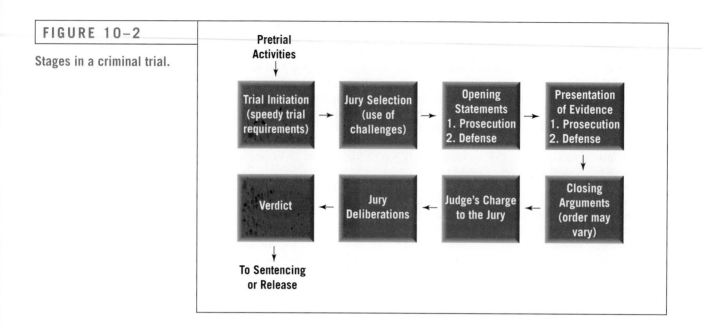

> There is no such thing as justice—in or out of court.
>
> —Clarence Darrow (1857–1938)[i]

Jury deliberations and the verdict are discussed jointly. If the defendant is found guilty, a sentence is imposed by the judge at the conclusion of the trial. Sentencing is discussed in the next chapter.

## Trial Initiation: The Speedy Trial Act

On September 14, 2000, in a move that raised a statewide outcry, the Oregon Supreme Court ordered that death-row inmate Scott Dean Harberts be freed and that charges against him be dismissed. Harberts had been convicted of aggravated murder, rape, and sodomy in the death of two-year-old Kristina Lynn Hornych, who died in 1989.[51] The court, however, found that a five-year delay between arrest and trial, resulting primarily from the prosecution's appeal of an earlier ruling concerning the admissibility of polygraph evidence,[52] violated the Oregon constitution's guarantee to a speedy trial.[53] Following his release in 2001, Harberts was convicted of a new crime involving sexual abuse of a child related to the girl he had killed and was ordered to serve a year in the Clackamas County jail.[54]

The U.S. Constitution contains a speedy trial provision in its Sixth Amendment, which guarantees that "[i]n all criminal prosecutions, the accused shall enjoy the right to a speedy and public trial." Clogged court calendars, limited judicial resources, and general inefficiency, however, often combine to produce what appears to many to be unreasonable delays in trial initiation. The attention of the U.S. Supreme Court was brought to bear on trial delays in three precedent-setting cases: *Klopfer* v. *North Carolina* (1967),[55] *Barker* v. *Wingo* (1972),[56] and *Strunk* v. *U.S.* (1973).[57] The *Klopfer* case involved a Duke University professor and focused on civil disobedience in a protest against segregated facilities. In ruling on Klopfer's long-delayed trial, the Court asserted that the right to a speedy trial is a fundamental guarantee of the Constitution. In the *Barker* case, the Court held that Sixth Amendment guarantees to a quick trial could be illegally violated even in cases where the accused did not explicitly object to delays. In *Strunk,* it found that the denial of a speedy trial should result in the dismissal of all charges.

In 1974, against the advice of the Justice Department, the U.S. Congress passed the federal **Speedy Trial Act**.[58] The act, which was phased in gradually and became fully effective in 1980, allows for the dismissal of federal criminal charges in cases in which the prosecution does not seek an indictment or information within 30 days of arrest (a 30-day extension is granted when the grand jury is not in session) or where a trial does not begin within 70 working days after indictment for defendants who plead "not guilty." If a defendant is not available for trial, or if witnesses cannot be called within the 70-day limit, the period may be extended up to 180 days. Delays brought about by the defendant, through requests for a continuance or because of escape, are not counted in the specified time periods. The Speedy Trial Act has been condemned by some as shortsighted. One federal judge, for example, wrote, "The ability of the criminal justice system to operate effectively and efficiently has been severely impeded by the Speedy Trial Act. Resources

**Speedy Trial Act**

A 1974 federal law requiring that proceedings against a defendant in a federal criminal case begin within a specified period of time, such as 70 working days after indictment. Some states also have speedy trial requirements.

are misdirected, unnecessary severances required, cases proceed to trial inadequately prepared, and in some indeterminate number of cases, indictments against guilty persons are dismissed."[59]

In an important 1988 decision, *U.S.* v. *Taylor*,[60] the U.S. Supreme Court applied the requirements of the Speedy Trial Act to the case of a drug defendant who had escaped following arrest. The Court made it clear that trial delays that derive from the willful actions of the defendant do not apply to the 70-day period. The Court also held that trial delays, even when they result from government action, do not necessarily provide grounds for dismissal if they occur "without prejudice." Delays without prejudice are those that are due to circumstances beyond the control of criminal justice agencies.

In 1993, an Indiana prisoner, William Fex, appealed a Michigan conviction on armed robbery and attempted murder charges, claiming that he had to wait 196 days after submitting a request to Indiana prison authorities for his Michigan trial to commence. In *Fex* v. *Michigan* (1993),[61] the U.S. Supreme Court ruled that "common sense compel[s] the conclusion that the 180-day period does not commence until the prisoner's disposition request has actually been delivered to the court and prosecutor of the jurisdiction that lodged the detainer against him." In Fex's case, Indiana authorities had taken 22 days to forward his request to Michigan.

However, in a 1992 case, *Doggett* v. *U.S.*,[62] the Court held that a delay of eight and a half years violated speedy trial provisions because it resulted from government negligence. In *Doggett*, the defendant was indicted on a drug charge in 1980 but left the country for Panama, where he lived until 1982, when he reentered the United States. He lived openly in the United States until 1988, when a credit check revealed him to authorities. He was arrested, tried, and convicted of federal drug charges stemming from his 1980 indictment. In overturning his conviction, the U.S. Supreme Court ruled, "[E]ven delay occasioned by the Government's negligence creates prejudice that compounds over time, and at some point, as here, becomes intolerable."[63]

The federal Speedy Trial Act is applicable only to federal courts. However, the *Klopfer* case effectively made constitutional guarantees of a speedy trial applicable to state courts. In keeping with the trend toward reduced delays, many states have since enacted their own speedy trial legislation. Most state legislation sets a limit of 90 or 120 days as a reasonable period of time for a trial to commence.

# Jury Selection

The Sixth Amendment guarantees the right to an impartial jury. An impartial jury is not necessarily an ignorant one. In other words, potential jurors will not always be excused from service on a jury if they have some knowledge of the case before them.[64] However, candidates who have already formed an opinion as to the guilt or innocence of the defendant are likely to be excused.

Some prospective jurors *try* to get excused, whereas others who would like to serve are excused because they are not judged to be suitable. Prosecution and defense attorneys use challenges to ensure the impartiality of the jury being impaneled. Three types of challenges are recognized in criminal courts: (1) challenges to the array, (2) challenges for cause, and (3) **peremptory challenges**.

Challenges to the array signify the belief, generally by the defense attorney, that the pool from which potential jurors are to be selected is not representative of the community or is biased in some significant way. A challenge to the array is argued before the hearing judge before **jury selection** begins.

During jury selection, both prosecution and defense attorneys question potential jurors in a process known as *voir dire* examination. Jurors are expected to be unbiased and free of preconceived notions of guilt or innocence. Challenges for cause, which may arise during *voir dire* examination, make the claim that an individual juror cannot be fair or impartial. A special issue of juror objectivity that has concerned the U.S. Supreme Court is whether jurors with philosophical opposition to the death penalty should be excluded from juries whose decisions might result in the imposition of capital punishment. In the case of *Witherspoon* v. *Illinois* (1968),[65] the Court ruled that a juror opposed to the death penalty could be excluded from such juries if it were shown that (1) the juror would automatically vote against conviction without regard to the evidence or (2) the juror's philosophical orientation would prevent an objective consideration of the evidence. The *Witherspoon* case left a number of issues unresolved, among them the concern that it is difficult to demonstrate how a juror would automatically vote, a fact that might not even be known to the juror before trial begins.

Another area of concern that the Supreme Court has addressed involves the potential that jurors could be influenced by pretrial news stories. In 1991, for example, the Court decided the case of *Mu'Min* v. *Virginia* (1991).[66] Dawud Majud Mu'Min was a Virginia inmate who was serving

---

**In all criminal prosecutions, the accused shall enjoy the right to a speedy and public trial, by an impartial jury . . . and to be informed of the nature and cause of the accusation; to be confronted with the witnesses against him; to have compulsory process for obtaining witnesses in his favor, and to have the Assistance of Counsel for his defence.**

—Sixth Amendment to the U.S. Constitution

---

**peremptory challenge**

The right to challenge a potential juror without disclosing the reason for the challenge. Prosecutors and defense attorneys routinely use peremptory challenges to eliminate from juries individuals who, although they express no obvious bias, are thought to be capable of swaying the jury in an undesirable direction.

---

**jury selection**

The process whereby, according to law and precedent, members of a trial jury are chosen.

time for first-degree murder. While accompanying a work detail outside the prison, he committed another murder. At the ensuing trial, 8 of the 12 jurors who were seated admitted that they had heard or read something about the case, although none indicated that he or she had formed an opinion in advance as to Mu'Min's guilt or innocence. Following his conviction, Mu'Min appealed to the Supreme Court, claiming that his right to a fair trial had been denied due to pretrial publicity. The Court disagreed and upheld his conviction, citing the jurors' claim not to be biased.

The third kind of challenge, the peremptory challenge, allows attorneys to remove potential jurors without having to give a reason. Peremptory challenges, used by both the prosecution and the defense, are limited in number. Federal courts allow each side up to 20 peremptory challenges in capital cases and as few as 3 in minor criminal cases.[67] States vary as to the number of peremptory challenges they permit.

A developing field that seeks to take advantage of peremptory challenges is **scientific jury selection**. Scientific jury selection uses correlational techniques from the social sciences to gauge the likelihood that a potential juror will vote for conviction or acquittal. It makes predictions based on the economic, ethnic, and other personal and social characteristics of each member of the juror pool. Such techniques generally remove potential jurors who have any knowledge or opinions about the case to be tried. Also removed are people who have been trained in the law or in criminal justice. Anyone working for a criminal justice agency or anyone who has a family member working for such an agency or for a defense attorney will likely be dismissed through peremptory challenges on the chance that they may be biased in favor of one side or the other. Additionally, scientific jury selection techniques may result in the dismissal of highly educated or professionally successful individuals to eliminate the possibility of such individuals exercising undue control over jury deliberations.

Critics of the jury selection process charge that the end result is a jury composed of people who are uneducated, uninformed, and generally inexperienced at making any type of well-considered decision. Some jurors may not understand the charges against the defendant or comprehend what is required for a finding of guilt or innocence. Likewise, some may not even possess the attention span needed to hear all the testimony that will be offered in a case. As a consequence, critics say, decisions rendered by such a jury may be based more on emotion than on findings of fact.

Another emerging technique is the use of "shadow juries" to assess the impact of a defense attorney's arguments. Shadow jurors are hired court observers who sit in the courtroom and listen to what both sides in a criminal trial have to say. They hear evidence as it is presented and listen as witnesses are examined and cross-examined. Unlike professional legal experts, shadow jurors are laypeople who are expected to give defense attorneys a feel for what the "real" jurors are thinking and feeling as a case progresses, allowing for ongoing modifications in defense strategy.[68]

**scientific jury selection**

The use of correlational techniques from the social sciences to gauge the likelihood that potential jurors will vote for conviction or for acquittal.

A pen-and-ink drawing, circa 1867, depicting one of the first jury trials on which both blacks and whites served.
*Courtesy of the Library of Congress*

## CJ TODAY EXHIBIT 10-2

### Peremptory Challenges and Race

A "peremptory challenge to a juror means that one side in a trial has been given the right to throw out a certain number of possible jurors before the trial without giving any reasons."[1] As this definition—borrowed from a legal dictionary—indicates, attorneys were once able to remove unwanted potential jurors from a criminal case during jury selection procedures through the use of a limited number of peremptory challenges without having to provide any reason whatsoever for the choices they made. (Challenges for cause, on the other hand, although not limited in number, require an acceptable rationale for juror removal.) The understanding of peremptory challenges was changed by the 1991 landmark U.S. Supreme Court case of *Powers* v. *Ohio*.[2] The *Powers* case dealt with a white defendant's desire to ensure a racially balanced jury. In *Powers,* the Supreme Court identified three reasons why peremptory challenges may not be issued if based on race[3]:

First, the discriminatory use of peremptory challenges causes the defendant cognizable injury, and he or she has a concrete interest in challenging the practice, because racial discrimination in jury selection casts doubt on the integrity of the judicial process and places the fairness of the criminal proceeding in doubt.

Second, the relationship between the defendant and the excluded jurors is such that . . . both have a common interest in eliminating racial discrimination from the courtroom. . . .

Third, it is unlikely that a juror dismissed because of race will possess sufficient incentive to set in motion the arduous process needed to vindicate his or her own rights.

The Court continued:

The very fact that [members of a particular race] are singled out and expressly denied . . . all right to participate in the administration of the law, as jurors, because of their color, though they are citizens, and may be in other respects fully qualified, is practically a brand upon them, affixed by the law, an assertion of their inferiority, and a stimulant to that race prejudice which is an impediment to securing to individuals of that race equal justice which the law aims to secure to all others.

Near the end of its 1991 term, in a move that surprised many Court watchers, the Supreme Court extended to civil cases its ban on racially motivated peremptory challenges. In *Edmonson* v. *Leesville Concrete Co., Inc.,*[4] the Court ruled,

The harms we recognized in *Powers* are not limited to the criminal sphere. A civil proceeding often implicates significant rights and interests. Civil juries, no less than their criminal counterparts, must follow the law and act as impartial fact-finders. And, as we have observed, their verdicts, no less than those of their criminal counterparts, become binding judgments of the court. Racial discrimination has no place in the courtroom, whether the proceeding is civil or criminal.

Following *Powers* and *Edmonson,* it is clear that neither prosecuting nor civil attorneys in the future will be able to exclude minority jurors consistently unless they are able to articulate clearly credible race-neutral rationales for their actions.

Even so, recent dissenting opinions indicate that considerable sentiment may exist among the justices that could lead to the return of a broader use of peremptory challenges. In a dissenting opinion in *J.E.B.* v. *Alabama* (1994),[5] Justices Antonin Scalia, William H. Rehnquist, and Clarence Thomas wrote, "[T]he core of the Court's reasoning [banning peremptory challenges based on gender] is that peremptory challenges on the basis of any group characteristic subject to heightened scrutiny are inconsistent with the guarantee of the Equal Protection Clause. . . . Since all groups are subject to the peremptory challenge . . . it is hard to see how any group is denied equal protection."

Read Library Extra 10–3 at cjtoday.com to learn more about the role of race in America's courtrooms today.

 **LIBRARY EXTRA**

---

[1] Daniel Oran, *Oran's Dictionary of the Law* (St. Paul, MN: West, 1983), p. 312.
[2] *Powers* v. *Ohio,* 499 U.S. 400 (1991).
[3] Ibid.
[4] *Edmonson* v. *Leesville Concrete Co., Inc.,* 500 U.S. 614, 111 S.Ct. 2077, 114 L.Ed.2d 660 (1991).
[5] *J.E.B.* v. *Alabama,* 114 S.Ct. 1419, 128 L.Ed.2d 89 (1994).

---

After wrangling over jury selection has run its course, the jury is sworn in, and alternate jurors are selected. Alternates may be called to replace jurors taken ill or dismissed from the jury because they don't conform to the requirements of jury service once trial has begun. At this point, the judge will decide whether the jury is to be sequestered during the trial. Members of **sequestered juries,** like those in the O. J. Simpson criminal trial, are not permitted to have contact with the public and are often housed in a motel or hotel until completion of the trial. Anyone who attempts to contact a sequestered jury or to influence members of a nonsequestered jury may be held accountable for jury tampering. Following jury selection, the stage is set for opening arguments[69] to begin.

**sequestered jury**

A jury that is isolated from the public during the course of a trial and throughout the deliberation process.

## Jury Selection and Race

Juries intentionally selected so that they are racially unbalanced may soon be a thing of the past. As long ago as 1880, the U.S. Supreme Court held that "a statute barring blacks from service on grand or petit juries denied equal protection of the laws to a black man convicted of murder by an all-white jury."[70] Even so, peremptory challenges continued to be used to strike racial imbalance on juries. In 1965, for example, an African-American defendant in Alabama was convicted of rape by an all-white jury. The local prosecutor had used his peremptory challenges to exclude blacks from the jury. The case eventually reached the Supreme Court, where the conviction was upheld.[71] At that time, the Court refused to limit the practice of peremptory challenges, reasoning that to do so would place these challenges under the same judicial scrutiny as challenges for cause.

However, in the 1986 case of *Batson* v. *Kentucky*,[72] following what many claimed was widespread abuse of peremptory challenges by prosecution and defense alike, the Supreme Court was forced to overrule its earlier decision. Batson, an African-American man, had been convicted of second-degree burglary and other offenses by an all-white jury. The prosecutor had used his peremptory challenges to remove all African-Americans from jury service at the trial. The Court agreed that the use of peremptory challenges for purposeful discrimination constitutes a violation of the defendant's right to an impartial jury.

The *Batson* decision laid out the requirements that defendants must prove when seeking to establish the discriminatory use of peremptory challenges. They include the need to prove that the defendant is a member of a recognized racial group that was intentionally excluded from the jury and the need to raise a reasonable suspicion that the prosecutor used peremptory challenges in a discriminatory manner. Justice Thurgood Marshall, writing a concurring opinion in *Batson*, presaged what was to come: "The inherent potential of peremptory challenges to destroy the jury process by permitting the exclusion of jurors on racial grounds should ideally lead the Court to ban them entirely from the criminal justice system."

A few years later, in *Ford* v. *Georgia* (1991),[73] the Court moved much closer to Justice Marshall's position when it remanded a case for a new trial because the prosecutor had misused peremptory challenges. The prosecutor had used nine of the ten peremptory challenges available under Georgia law to eliminate prospective African-American jurors. Following his conviction on charges of kidnapping, raping, and murdering a white woman, the African-American defendant, James Ford, argued that the prosecutor had demonstrated a systematic racial bias in other cases as well as his own. Specifically, Ford argued that his Sixth Amendment right to an impartial jury had been violated by the prosecutor's racially based method of jury selection. His appeal to the Supreme Court claimed that "the exclusion of members of the black race in the jury when a black accused is being tried is done in order that the accused will receive excessive punishment if found guilty, or to inject racial prejudice into the fact finding process of the jury."[74] While the Court did not find a basis for such a Sixth Amendment claim, it did determine that the civil rights of the jurors themselves had been violated under the Fourteenth Amendment due to a pattern of discrimination based on race.

In another 1991 case, *Powers* v. *Ohio*[75] (see CJ Today Exhibit 10–2), the Court found in favor of a white defendant who claimed that his constitutional rights had been violated by the intentional exclusion of African-Americans from his jury through the use of peremptory challenges. In *Powers*, the Court held that "[a]lthough an individual juror does not have the right to sit on any particular petit jury, he or she does possess the right not to be excluded from one on account of race."

In *Edmonson* v. *Leesville Concrete Co., Inc.* (1991),[76] a civil case with significance for the criminal justice system, the Court held that peremptory challenges in *civil* suits were not acceptable if based on race. Justice Anthony Kennedy, writing for the majority, said that race-based juror exclusions are forbidden in civil lawsuits because jury selection is a "unique governmental function delegated to private litigants" in a public courtroom.

In the 1992 case of *Georgia* v. *McCollum*,[77] the Court barred *criminal* defendants and their attorneys from using peremptory challenges to exclude potential jurors on the basis of race. In *McCollum*, Justice Harry Blackmun, writing for the majority, said, "Be it at the hands of the state or defense, if a court allows jurors to be excluded because of group bias, it is a willing participant in a scheme that could only undermine the very foundation of our system of justice—our citizens' confidence in it."

Soon thereafter, peremptory challenges based on gender were similarly restricted (*J.E.B.* v. *Alabama*, 1994[78]), although at the time of this writing the Court has refused to ban peremptory challenges that exclude jurors because of religious or sexual orientation.[79] Also, in 1996, the Court refused to review "whether potential jurors can be stricken from a trial panel because they are too fat."[80] The case involved Luis Santiago-Martinez, a drug defendant whose lawyer objected to the prosecution's use of peremptory challenges "because the government," he said, "had used such strikes to discriminate against the handicapped, specifically the obese." The attorney, who was himself obese, claimed that thin jurors might have been unfairly biased against his arguments.

Log on to ResearchNavigator.com, and choose "Criminal Justice" under ContentSelect's Academic Journal Database. Enter the word "pretrial" (without the quotation marks) in the search box, and click "Go." Which articles from the search results page usefully add to this chapter's discussion of pretrial activities? Write a summary of each of those articles, including complete source information—that is, article title, author (if available), date of publication, and source. In some cases, only abstracts may be available. If that's the case, then base your written summary on the information provided in the abstract (otherwise, use the full article). Submit what you have written to your instructor if asked to do so. *Note:* This feature is available only if your instructor has chosen the Research Navigator option available with a new textbook.

In the 1998 case of *Campbell* v. *Louisiana,*[81] the Court held that a white criminal defendant can raise equal protection and due process objections to discrimination against African-Americans in the selection of grand jurors. Attorneys for Terry Campbell, who was white, objected to an apparent pattern of discrimination in the selection of grand jury forepersons. The foreperson of the Evangeline Parish, Louisiana, grand jury that heard second-degree murder charges against him (in the killing of another white man) was white, as had been all such forepersons for the last 16 years. The Supreme Court reasoned that "regardless of skin color, an accused suffers a significant 'injury in fact' when the grand jury's composition is tainted by racial discrimination." The Court also said, "The integrity of the body's decisions depends on the integrity of the process used to select the grand jurors."

Finally, in the 2003 case of *Miller-El* v. *Cockrell,*[82] the Court found that a convicted capital defendant's constitutional rights had been violated by Dallas County, Texas, prosecutors who engaged in intentional efforts to remove eligible African-Americans from the pool of potential jurors. Ten out of 11 eligible African-Americans were excluded through the use of peremptory strikes. A relevant portion of the Court's majority opinion reads as follows: "In this case, debate as to whether the prosecution acted with a race-based reason when striking prospective jurors was raised by the statistical evidence demonstrating that 91% of the eligible African-Americans were excluded . . . ; and by the fact that three of the State's proffered race-neutral rationales for striking African Americans—ambivalence about the death penalty, hesitancy to vote to execute defendants capable of being rehabilitated, and the jurors' own family history of criminality—pertained just as well to some white jurors who were not challenged and who did serve on the jury."[83]

# Opening Statements

The presentation of information to the jury begins with **opening statements** made by the prosecution and the defense. The purpose of opening statements is to advise the jury of what the attorneys intend to prove and to describe how such proof will be offered. Evidence is not offered during opening statements. Eventually, however, the jury will have to weigh the evidence presented during the trial and decide which side made the more effective arguments. When a defendant has little evidence to present, the main job of the defense attorney will be to dispute the veracity of the prosecution's version of the facts. Under such circumstances, defense attorneys may choose not to present any evidence or testimony at all, focusing instead on the burden-of-proof requirement facing the prosecution. Such plans will generally be made clear during opening statements. At this time, the defense attorney is also likely to stress the human qualities of the defendant and to remind jurors of the awesome significance of their task.

Lawyers for both sides are bound by a "good-faith" ethical requirement in their opening statements. Attorneys may mention only the evidence that they believe actually can and will be presented as the trial progresses. Allusions to evidence that an attorney has no intention of offering are regarded as unprofessional and have been defined by the U.S. Supreme Court as "professional misconduct."[84] When material alluded to in an opening statement cannot, for whatever reason, later be presented in court, opposing counsel gains an opportunity to discredit the other side.

# The Presentation of Evidence

The crux of the criminal trial is the presentation of evidence. First the state is given the opportunity to present evidence intended to prove the defendant's guilt. After prosecutors have rested their case, the defense is afforded the opportunity to provide evidence favorable to the defendant.

## Types of Evidence

**Evidence** can be either direct or circumstantial. **Direct evidence**, if believed, proves a fact without requiring the judge or jury to draw inferences. For example, direct evidence may consist of the information contained in a photograph or a videotape. It might also consist of testimonial evidence provided by a witness on the stand. A straightforward statement by a witness, such as "I saw him do it!" is a form of direct evidence.

**Circumstantial evidence** is indirect. It requires the judge or jury to make inferences and to draw conclusions. At a murder trial, for example, a person who heard gunshots and moments later saw someone run by with a smoking gun in hand might testify to those facts. Even without an eyewitness to the actual homicide, the jury might conclude that the person seen with the gun was the one who pulled the trigger and committed the crime. Circumstantial evidence is sufficient to produce a conviction in a criminal trial. In fact, some prosecuting attorneys prefer to work entirely with circumstantial evidence, weaving a tapestry of the criminal act into their arguments to the jury.

**opening statement**

The initial statement of the prosecution or the defense, made in a court of law to a judge, or to a judge and jury, describing the facts that he or she intends to present during trial to prove the case.

**evidence**

Anything useful to a judge or jury in deciding the facts of a case. Evidence may take the form of witness testimony, written documents, videotapes, magnetic media, photographs, physical objects, and so on.

**direct evidence**

Evidence that, if believed, directly proves a fact. Eyewitness testimony and videotaped documentation account for the majority of all direct evidence heard in the criminal courtroom.

**circumstantial evidence**

Evidence that requires interpretation or that requires a judge or jury to reach a conclusion based on what the evidence indicates. From the proximity of the defendant to a smoking gun, for example, the jury might conclude that she pulled the trigger.

## CJ TODAY EXHIBIT 10-3

### Pretrial and Posttrial Motions

A *motion* is "an oral or written request made to a court at any time before, during, or after court proceedings, asking the court to make a specified finding, decision, or order."[1] Written motions are called *petitions*. This exhibit lists the most common motions made by both sides in a criminal case before and after trial.

**MOTION FOR DISCOVERY**

A motion for discovery, filed by the defense, asks the court to allow the defendant's lawyers to view the evidence that the prosecution intends to present at trial. Physical evidence, lists of witnesses, documents, photographs, and so on that the prosecution plans to introduce in court are usually made available to the defense as a result of a motion for discovery.

**MOTION TO SUPPRESS EVIDENCE**

The defense may file a motion to suppress evidence if it learns, in the preliminary hearing or through pretrial discovery, of evidence that it believes to have been unlawfully acquired.

**MOTION TO DISMISS CHARGES**

A variety of circumstances may result in the filing of a motion to dismiss charges. They include (1) an opinion, by defense counsel, that the indictment or information is not sound; (2) violations of speedy trial legislation; (3) a plea bargain with the defendant, which may require testimony against codefendants; (4) the death of an important witness or the destruction or disappearance of necessary evidence; (5) the confession, by a supposed victim, that the facts in the case were fabricated; and (6) the success of a motion to suppress evidence that effectively eliminates the prosecution's case.

**MOTION FOR CONTINUANCE**

This motion seeks a delay in the start of the trial. Defense motions for continuance are often based on an inability to locate important witnesses, the illness of the defendant, or a change in defense counsel immediately prior to trial.

**MOTION FOR CHANGE OF VENUE**

In well-known cases, pretrial publicity may lessen the opportunity for a case to be tried before an unbiased jury. A motion for a change in venue asks that the trial be moved to some other area where prejudice against the defendant is less likely to exist.

**MOTION FOR SEVERANCE OF OFFENSES**

Defendants charged with a number of crimes may ask to be tried separately on all or some of the charges. Although consol-

idating charges for trial saves time and money, some defendants believe that it is more likely to make them appear guilty.

**MOTION FOR SEVERANCE OF DEFENDANTS**

This request asks the court to try the accused separately from any codefendants. Motions for severance are likely to be filed when the defendant believes that the jury may be prejudiced against him or her by evidence applicable only to other defendants.

**MOTION TO DETERMINE PRESENT SANITY**

A lack of "present sanity," even though it may be no defense against the criminal charge, can delay trial. A person cannot be tried, sentenced, or punished while insane. If a defendant is insane at the time a trial is to begin, this motion may halt the proceedings until treatment can be arranged.

**MOTION FOR A BILL OF PARTICULARS**

This motion asks the court to order the prosecutor to provide detailed information about the charges that the defendant will be facing in court. Defendants charged with a number of offenses, or with a number of counts of the same offense, may make such a motion. They may, for example, seek to learn which alleged instances of an offense will become the basis for prosecution or which specific items of contraband allegedly found in their possession are held to violate the law.

**MOTION FOR A MISTRIAL**

A mistrial may be declared at any time, and a motion for a mistrial may be made by either side. Mistrials are likely to be declared in cases in which highly prejudicial comments are made by either attorney. Defense motions for a mistrial do not provide grounds for a later claim of double jeopardy.

**MOTION FOR ARREST OF JUDGMENT**

After the verdict of the jury has been announced, but before sentencing, the defendant may make a motion for arrest of judgment. With this motion, the defendant asserts that some legally acceptable reason exists as to why sentencing should not occur. Defendants who are seriously ill, who are hospitalized, or who have gone insane prior to judgment being imposed may file such a motion.

**MOTION FOR A NEW TRIAL**

After a jury has returned a guilty verdict, the court may entertain a defense motion for a new trial. Acceptance of such a motion is usually based on the discovery of new evidence that is of significant benefit to the defense and that will set aside the conviction.

[1]U.S. Department of Justice, *Dictionary of Criminal Justice Data Terminology,* 2nd ed. (Washington, DC: U.S. Government Printing Office, 1982).

---

**real evidence**

Evidence that consists of physical material or traces of physical activity.

**Real evidence**, which may be either direct or circumstantial, consists of physical material or traces of physical activity. Weapons, tire tracks, ransom notes, and fingerprints all fall into the category of real evidence. Real evidence, sometimes called *physical evidence,* is introduced in the trial by means of exhibits. *Exhibits* are objects or displays that, after having been formally accepted as evidence by the judge, may be shown to members of the jury. Documentary evidence, one type of real evidence, includes writings such as business records, journals, written confessions, and letters. Documentary evidence can extend beyond paper and ink to include stored computer data and video and audio recordings.

# The Evaluation of Evidence

One of the most significant decisions a trial court judge makes is which evidence can be presented to the jury. To make this determination, judges examine the relevance of the evidence to the case at hand. Relevant evidence has a bearing on the facts at issue. For example, decades ago, it was not unusual for a woman's sexual history to be brought out in rape trials. Under "rape shield statutes," most states today will not allow this practice, recognizing that these details have no bearing on the case. Rape shield statutes have been strengthened by recent U.S. Supreme Court decisions, including the 1991 case of *Michigan* v. *Lucas.*[85]

Colorado's rape shield law played a prominent role in the 2004 case of Kobe Bryant, a basketball superstar who was accused of sexually assaulting a 19-year-old Vail-area resort employee. Bryant admitted to having a sexual encounter with the defendant but claimed it was consensual. Defense attorneys sought to have the Colorado law declared unconstitutional in an effort to show that injuries to the woman were the result of her having had sexual intercourse with multiple partners before and after her encounter with Bryant. The defendant dropped the criminal case against Bryant and settled a civil suit against him in 2005.[86] Terms of the suit were not disclosed.

In evaluating evidence, judges must also weigh the **probative value** of an item of evidence against its potential inflammatory or prejudicial qualities. Evidence has probative value when it is useful and relevant, but even useful evidence, however, may unduly bias a jury if it is exceptionally gruesome or is presented in such a way as to imply guilt. For example, gory, color photographs may be withheld from the jury's eyes. In one recent case, a new trial was ordered when photos of the crime scene were projected on a wall over the head of the defendant as he sat in the courtroom. An appellate court found the presentation to have prejudiced the jury.

Sometimes evidence is found to have only limited admissibility. This means that the evidence can be used for a specific purpose but that it might not be accurate in other details. Photographs, for example, may be admitted as evidence for the narrow purpose of showing spatial relationships between objects under discussion, even if the photographs were taken under conditions that did not exist when the offense was committed (such as daylight).

When judges allow the use of evidence that may have been illegally or unconstitutionally gathered, there may be grounds for a later appeal if the trial concludes with a "guilty" verdict. Even when evidence is improperly introduced at trial, however, a number of Supreme Court decisions[87] have held that there may be no grounds for an effective appeal unless such introduction "had substantial and injurious effect or influence in determining the jury's verdict."[88] Called the *harmless error rule,* this standard places the burden on the prosecution to show that the jury's decision would most likely have been the same even in the absence of the inappropriate evidence. The rule is not applicable when a defendant's constitutional guarantees are violated by "structural defects in the constitution of the trial mechanism" itself[89]—as when a judge gives constitutionally improper instructions to a jury. (We'll discuss those instructions later in this chapter.)

**WHAT WOULD YOU DO?**

The CD-ROM scenario for Chapter 10 is built around a computer database error that results in a person's arrest. The scenario is based on an actual U.S. Supreme Court case. Work through the scenario using the CD-ROM found in your textbook to learn how computer errors can affect the work of both the police and the courts.

**probative value**

The degree to which a particular item of evidence is useful in, and relevant to, providing something important in a trial.

Los Angeles Lakers basketball star Kobe Bryant is surrounded by reporters and photographers after rape charges against him were dropped in 2004. The case had been slated to be tried in Colorado, where the state's stringent rape shield law played a prominent role in pretrial maneuvering.
*John Mablango, EPA, Landov LLC*

## The Testimony of Witnesses

Witness **testimony** is generally the chief means by which evidence is introduced at trial. Witnesses may include victims, police officers, the defendant, specialists in recognized fields, and others with useful information to provide. Some of these witnesses may have been present during the commission of the offense, while most will have had only a later opportunity to investigate the situation or to analyze evidence.

Before a witness is allowed to testify to any fact, the questioning attorney must establish the person's competence. Competence to testify requires that witnesses have personal knowledge of the information they will discuss and that they understand their duty to tell the truth.

One of the defense attorney's most critical decisions is whether to put the defendant on the stand. Defendants have a Fifth Amendment right to remain silent and to refuse to testify. In the precedent-setting case of *Griffin* v. *California* (1965),[90] the U.S. Supreme Court declared that if a defendant refuses to testify, prosecutors and judges are enjoined from even commenting on this fact, although the judge should instruct the jury that such a failure cannot be held to indicate guilt. In the 2001 case of *Ohio* v. *Reiner*,[91] the U.S. Supreme Court extended Fifth Amendment protections to witnesses who deny any and all guilt in association with a crime for which another person is being prosecuted.

Direct examination of a witness takes place when a witness is first called to the stand. If the prosecutor calls the witness, the witness is referred to as a *witness for the prosecution.* Where the direct examiner is a defense attorney, the witness is called a *witness for the defense.*

The direct examiner may ask questions that require a "yes" or "no" answer or may ask narrative questions that allow the witness to tell a story in his or her own words. During direct examination, courts generally prohibit the use of leading questions or those that suggest answers to the witness.[92]

Cross-examination is the questioning of a witness by someone other than the direct examiner. Anyone who offers testimony in a criminal court has the duty to submit to cross-examination.[93] The purpose of cross-examination is to test the credibility and the memory of the witness.

Most states and the federal government restrict the scope of cross-examination to material covered during direct examination. Questions about other matters, even though they may relate to the case before the court, are not allowed in most states, although a few states allow the cross-examiner to raise any issue as long as the court deems it relevant. Leading questions, generally disallowed in direct examination, are regarded as the mainstay of cross-examination. Such questions allow for a concise restatement of testimony that has already been offered and serve to focus efficiently on potential problems that the cross-examiner seeks to address.

Some witnesses commit **perjury**—that is, they make statements that they know are untrue. Reasons for perjured testimony vary, but most witnesses who lie on the stand do so in an effort to help friends accused of crimes. Witnesses who perjure themselves are subject to impeachment, in which either the defense or the prosecution demonstrates that a witness has intentionally offered false testimony. For example, previous statements made by the witness may be shown to be at odds with more recent declarations. When it can be demonstrated that a witness has offered inaccurate or false testimony, the witness has been effectively impeached. Perjury is a serious offense in its own right, and dishonest witnesses may face fines or jail time.

At the conclusion of the cross-examination, the direct examiner may again question the witness. This procedure is called *redirect examination* and may be followed by a recross-examination and so on, until both sides are satisfied that they have exhausted fruitful lines of questioning.

## Children as Witnesses

An area of special concern is the use of children as witnesses in a criminal trial, especially when the children are also victims. Currently, in an effort to avoid what may be traumatizing direct confrontations between child witnesses and the accused, 37 states allow the use of videotaped testimony in criminal courtrooms, and 32 permit the use of closed-circuit television, which allows the child to testify out of the presence of the defendant. In 1988, however, in the case of *Coy* v. *Iowa*,[94] the U.S. Supreme Court ruled that a courtroom screen, used to shield child witnesses from visual confrontation with a defendant in a child sex-abuse case, had violated the confrontation clause of the Constitution (found in the Sixth Amendment).

On the other hand, in the 1990 case of *Maryland* v. *Craig*,[95] the Court upheld the use of closed-circuit television to shield children who testify in criminal courts. The Court's decision was partially based on the realization that "a significant majority of States have enacted statutes to protect child witnesses from the trauma of giving testimony in child-abuse cases . . . [which] attests to the widespread belief in the importance of such a policy."

Although a face-to-face confrontation with a child victim may not be necessary in the courtroom, until 1992 the Supreme Court had been reluctant to allow into evidence descriptions of abuse and other statements made by children, even to child-care professionals, when those statements were made outside the courtroom. In *Idaho* v. *Wright* (1990),[96] the Court reasoned that such "statements [are] fraught with the dangers of unreliability which the Confrontation Clause is designed to highlight and obviate."

However, in *White* v. *Illinois* (1992),[97] the Court reversed its stance, ruling that in-court testimony provided by a medical provider and the child's baby-sitter, which repeated what the child had said to them concerning White's sexually abusive behavior, was permissible. The Court rejected White's claim that out-of-court statements should be admissible only when the witness is unavailable to testify at trial, saying instead, "A finding of unavailability of an out-of-court declarant is necessary only if the out-of-court statement was made at a prior judicial proceeding." Placing *White* within the context of generally established exceptions, the Court declared, "A statement that has been offered in a moment of excitement—without the opportunity to reflect on the consequences of one's exclamation—may justifiably carry more weight with a trier of fact than a similar statement offered in the relative calm of the courtroom. Similarly, a statement made in the course of procuring medical services, where the declarant knows that a false statement may cause misdiagnosis or mistreatment, carries special guarantees of credibility that a trier of fact may not think replicated by courtroom testimony."

## The Hearsay Rule

**Hearsay** is anything not based on the personal knowledge of a witness. A witness may say, for example, "John told me that Fred did it!" Such a witness becomes a hearsay declarant, and following a likely objection by counsel, the trial judge will have to decide whether the witness's statement will be allowed to stand as evidence. In most cases, the judge will instruct the jury to disregard the witness's comment, thereby enforcing the **hearsay rule**, which prohibits the use of "secondhand evidence."

Exceptions to the hearsay rule have been established by both precedent and tradition. One exception is the dying declaration. A dying declaration is a statement made by a person who is about to die. When heard by a second party, it may usually be repeated in court, provided that certain conditions have been met. A dying declaration is generally a valid exception to the hearsay rule when it is made by someone who knows that he or she is about to die and when the statement made relates to the cause and circumstances of the impending death.

Spontaneous statements provide another exception to the hearsay rule. A statement is considered spontaneous when it is made in the heat of excitement before the person has had time to make it up. For example, a defendant who was injured and is just regaining consciousness following a crime may say something that could later be repeated in court by those who heard it.

Out-of-court statements made by a witness, especially when they were recorded in writing or by some other means, may also become exceptions to the hearsay rule. The use of such statements usually requires the witness to testify that the statements were accurate at the time they were made. This "past recollection recorded" exception to the hearsay rule is especially useful in drawn-out court proceedings that occur long after the crime. Under such circumstances, witnesses may no longer remember the details of an event. Their earlier statements to authorities, however, can be introduced into evidence as past recollection recorded.

## Closing Arguments

At the conclusion of a criminal trial, both sides have the opportunity for a final narrative presentation to the jury in the form of a **closing argument**. This summation provides a review and analysis of the evidence. Its purpose is to persuade the jury to draw a conclusion favorable to the presenter. Testimony can be quoted, exhibits referred to, and attention drawn to inconsistencies in the evidence presented by the other side.

States vary as to the order of closing arguments. Nearly all allow the defense attorney to speak to the jury before the prosecution makes its final points. A few permit the prosecutor the first opportunity for summation. Some jurisdictions and the Federal Rules of Criminal Procedure[98] authorize a defense rebuttal. A rebuttal is a response to the closing argument of the other side.

Some specific issues may need to be addressed during summation. If, for example, the defendant has not taken the stand during the trial, the defense attorney's closing argument will inevitably stress that this failure to testify cannot be regarded as indicating guilt. Where the prosecution's case rests entirely on circumstantial evidence, the defense can be expected to stress the lack of any direct proof, and the prosecutor is likely to argue that circumstantial evidence can be stronger than direct evidence, since it is not as easily affected by human error or false testimony.

---

**hearsay**

Something that is not based on the personal knowledge of a witness. Witnesses who testify about something they have heard, for example, are offering hearsay by repeating information about a matter of which they have no direct knowledge.

**hearsay rule**

The long-standing precedent that hearsay cannot be used in American courtrooms. Rather than accepting testimony based on hearsay, the court will ask that the person who was the original source of the hearsay information be brought in to be questioned and cross-examined. Exceptions to the hearsay rule may occur when the person with direct knowledge is dead or is otherwise unable to testify.

**closing argument**

An oral summation of a case presented to a judge, or to a judge and jury, by the prosecution or by the defense in a criminal trial.

# The Judge's Charge to the Jury

After closing arguments, the judge charges the jury to "retire," select one of its number as a foreman, and deliberate on the evidence that has been presented until it has reached a verdict. The words of the judge's "charge" vary somewhat between jurisdictions and among judges, but all judges will remind members of the jury of their duty to consider objectively only the evidence that has been presented and of the need for impartiality. Most judges also remind jury members of the statutory elements of the alleged offense, of the burden of proof that rests on the prosecution, and of the need for the prosecution to have proved the defendant's guilt beyond a reasonable doubt before the jury can return a guilty verdict.

In their charge, many judges also provide a summary of the evidence presented, usually from notes they have taken during the trial, as a means of refreshing the jurors' memories of events. About half of all the states allow judges the freedom to express their own views as to the credibility of witnesses and the significance of evidence. Other states only permit judges to summarize the evidence in an objective and impartial manner.

Following the charge, the jury is removed from the courtroom and is permitted to begin its deliberations. In the absence of the jury, defense attorneys may choose to challenge portions of the judge's charge. If they feel that some oversight has occurred in the original charge, they may ask the judge to provide the jury with additional instructions or information. Such objections, if denied by the judge, often become the basis for an appeal when a conviction is returned.

# Jury Deliberations and the Verdict

In cases in which the evidence is either very clear or very weak, jury deliberations may be brief, lasting only a matter of hours or even minutes. Some juries, however, deliberate days or sometimes weeks, carefully weighing all the nuances of the evidence they have seen and heard. Many jurisdictions require that juries reach a unanimous **verdict**, although the U.S. Supreme Court has ruled that unanimous verdicts are not required in noncapital cases.[99] Even so, some juries are unable to agree on any verdict. When a jury is deadlocked, it is said to be a *hung jury*. When a unanimous decision is required, juries may be deadlocked by the strong opposition of several members or of only one member to a verdict agreed on by all the others.

In some states, judges are allowed to add a boost to nearly hung juries by recharging them under a set of instructions that the Supreme Court put forth in the 1896 case of *Allen* v. *U.S.*[100] The *Allen* charge, as it is known, urges the jury to vigorous deliberations and suggests to obstinate jurors that their objections may be ill founded if they make no impression on the other jurors.

> **verdict**
>
> The decision of the jury in a jury trial or of a judicial officer in a nonjury trial.

## Problems with the Jury System

Judge Harold J. Rothwax, a well-known critic of today's jury system, tells the tale of a rather startling 1991 case over which he presided. The case involved a murder defendant, a handsome young man who had been fired by a New York company that serviced automated teller machines (ATMs). After being fired, the defendant intentionally caused a machine in a remote area to malfunction. When two former colleagues arrived to fix it, he robbed them, stole the money inside the ATM, and shot both men repeatedly. One of the men survived long enough to identify his former coworker as the shooter. The man was arrested, and a trial ensued, but after three weeks of hearing the case, the jury deadlocked. Judge Rothwax later learned that the jury had voted 11 to 1 to convict the defendant, but the one holdout just couldn't believe that "someone so good-looking could . . . commit such a crime."[101]

Many routine cases as well as some highly publicized cases, like the murder trial of O. J. Simpson, which the whole world watched, have called into question the ability of the American jury system to do its job—that is, to sort through the evidence and to accurately determine the defendant's guilt or innocence. In a televised 1995 trial, Simpson was acquitted of the charge that he murdered his ex-wife Nicole Brown and her friend Ronald Goldman outside Brown's home in 1994. Many people believed that strong evidence tied Simpson to the crimes, and the criminal trial left many people feeling unsatisfied with the criminal justice system and with the criminal trial process. Later, a civil jury ordered Simpson to pay $33.5 million to the Goldman family and to Nicole Brown's estate.

Because jurors are drawn from all walks of life, many cannot be expected to understand modern legal complexities and to appreciate all the nuances of trial court practice. It is likely that even the best-intentioned jurors cannot understand and rarely observe some jury instructions.[102] In highly charged cases, emotions are often difficult to separate from fact, and during deliberations, some juries are dominated by one or two members with forceful personalities

Jurors may be less than effective in cases where they fear personal retaliation. In the state-level trial of the police officers accused in the infamous Rodney King beating, for example, jurors reported being afraid for their lives due to the riots in Los Angeles that broke out after their not-guilty verdict was announced. Some slept with weapons by their side, and others sent their children away to safe locations.[103] Because of the potential for harm that jurors faced in the 1993 federal trial of the same officers, U.S. District Judge John G. Davies ruled that the names of the jurors be forever kept secret. Members of the press called the secrecy order "an unprecedented infringement of the public's right of access to the justice system."[104] Similarly, in the 1993 trial of three African-American men charged with the beating of white truck driver Reginald Denny during the Los Angeles riots that followed the Rodney King verdict, Los Angeles Superior Court Judge John Ouderkirk ordered that the identities of the jurors not be released.

Opponents of the jury system have argued that it should be replaced by a panel of judges who would both render a verdict and impose sentence. Regardless of how well considered such a suggestion may be, such a change could not occur without modification of the Constitution's Sixth Amendment right to trial by jury.

An alternative suggestion for improving the process of trial by jury has been the call for professional jurors. Professional jurors would be paid by the government, as are judges, prosecutors, and public defenders. They would be expected to have the expertise to sit on any jury. Professional jurors would be trained to listen objectively and would be taught the kinds of decision-making skills they would need to function effectively within an adversarial context. They would hear one case after another, perhaps moving between jurisdictions in cases of highly publicized crimes.

A professional jury system offers these advantages:

1. *Dependability.* Professional jurors could be expected to report to the courtroom in a timely fashion and to be good listeners, since both would be required by the nature of the job.

2. *Knowledge.* Professional jurors would be trained in the law, would understand what a finding of guilt requires, and would know what to expect from other actors in the courtroom.

3. *Equity.* Professional jurors would understand the requirements of due process and would be less likely to be swayed by the emotional content of a case, having been schooled in the need to separate matters of fact from personal feelings.

A professional jury system would not be without difficulties. Jurors under such a system might become jaded, deciding cases out of hand as routines lead to boredom. They might categorize defendants according to whether they "fit the type" for guilt or innocence based on the jurors' previous experiences. Job requirements for professional jurors would be difficult to establish without infringing on the jurors' freedom to decide cases as they understand them. For the same reason, any evaluation of the job performance of professional jurors would be a difficult call. Finally, professional jurors might not truly be peer jurors, since their social characteristics might be skewed by education, residence, and politics.

# Improving the Adjudication Process

Courts today are coming under increasing scrutiny, and well-publicized trials, like those of Michael Jackson, Andrea Yates, Martha Stewart, Scott Peterson, O. J. Simpson, and John Allen Muhammad, have heightened awareness of problems with the American court system. One of today's most important issues is reducing the number of jurisdictions by unifying courts. The current multiplicity of jurisdictions frequently leads to what many believe are avoidable conflicts and overlaps in the handling of criminal defendants. In some states, problems are exacerbated by the lack of any centralized judicial authority that might resolve jurisdictional and procedural disputes.[105] Proponents of unification suggest the elimination of overlapping jurisdictions, the creation of special-purpose courts, and the formulation of administrative offices in order to achieve economies of scale.[106]

The number of court-watch citizens' groups is also rapidly growing. Such organizations focus on the trial court level, but they are part of a general trend toward seeking greater openness in government decision making at all levels.[107] Court-watch groups regularly monitor court proceedings and attempt to document and often publicize inadequacies. They frequently focus on the handling of indigents, fairness in the scheduling of cases for trial, unnecessary court delays, the reduction of waiting time, the treatment of witnesses and jurors, and the adequacy of rights advisements for defendants throughout judicial proceedings.

The statistical measurement of court performance is another area that is receiving increased attention. Research has looked at the efficiency with which prosecutors schedule cases for trial, the speed with which judges resolve issues, the amount of time judges spend on the bench, and the economic and other costs to defendants, witnesses, and communities involved in the judicial process.[108] Statistical studies of this type often attempt to measure elements of court performance

> In suits at common law, . . . the right of trial by jury shall be preserved, and no fact tried by a jury, shall be otherwise reexamined in any Court of the United States, than according to the rules of the common law.
>
> —Seventh Amendment to the U.S. Constitution

## CJ FUTURES

### Courtrooms of the Future

In the mid-1990s, the College of William and Mary, in conjunction with the National Center for State Courts (NCSC), unveiled Courtroom 21. At the time, it was the most technologically advanced courtroom in the United States. Courtroom 21, located in the McGlothlin Courtroom of the College of William and Mary, offers a glimpse at what American courtrooms might be like in the mid-twenty-first century. Courtroom 21 includes the following integrated capabilities:

1. *Automatic video recording of the proceedings, using ceiling-mounted cameras with voice-initiated switching.* A sophisticated voice-activation system directs cameras to record the person speaking and to record evidence as it is being presented.
2. *Recorded and televised evidence display with optical disk storage.* Documentary or real evidence can be presented to the judge and the jury through the use of a video "presenter," which also makes a video record of the evidence as it is being presented, so it can be used later.
3. *Remote two-way television.* The two-way television arrangement allows video and audio signals to be sent from the judge's bench to areas throughout the courtroom, including the jury box.
4. *Text-, graphics-, and video-capable jury computers.* Courtroom 21's jury box contains computers for information display and animation so that jury members can easily view documents, live or prerecorded video, and graphics, such as charts, diagrams, and pictures. Video-capable jury computers also allow for the remote appearance of witnesses—that is, for questioning witnesses who are unable or unwilling to appear in the courtroom—and for the display of crime-scene reenactments via computer animation.

5. *Access to online legal research databases for the judge and for counsel on both sides.* Available databases contain an extensive selection of state and federal statutes, case law, and other precedent, allowing the judge and the lawyers to find answers to unanticipated legal questions that arise during trial.
6. *Built-in video playback facilities for out-of-court testimony.* Because an increasing number of depositions are being videotaped by attorneys in preparation for trial, Courtroom 21 has capabilities for video playback. Video depositions can be played on courtroom monitors to present expert witness testimony or to impeach a witness.
7. *Information storage with software search capabilities.* Integrated software programs provide text-searching capabilities for courtroom participants. Previously transcribed testimony and precedent-setting cases from other courts can be searched and reviewed.
8. *Concurrent (real-time) court reporter transcription.* A court reporter uses a self-contained computerized writing machine for the real-time capture of testimony in the courtroom. While the reporter writes, the computer translates strokes into English transcripts, which are immediately distributed to the judge and counsel via their personal computers. Using this technology, the judge and attorneys can mark an individual copy of the day's testimony and take it with them on their laptop computer or on a floppy disk for later review and trial preparation.

The technology demonstrated in Courtroom 21 suggests many possibilities. For one thing, attorneys could use court video equipment for filing remote motions and for other types of hearings. As one of Courtroom 21's designers puts it, "Imagine the productivity gains if lawyers no longer need to travel across a city or county for a ten-minute appearance."

Fred Lederer, director of Courtroom 21 at the College of William and Mary law school in Williamsburg, Virginia, acting as a bailiff as he swears in a witness via the Internet. The witness, Hugh Selby, from the University of Canberra in Australia, was participating in a mock terrorism trial. The demonstration trial depended heavily on computer technology and the Internet to bring together attorneys, witnesses, defendants, jurors, and a judge.

*AP Wide World Photos*

## CJ FUTURES *(continued)*

Courtroom 21's designers also suggest that the innovative use of audio and video technology can preserve far more evidence and trial detail than written records, making a comprehensive review of cases easier for appellate judges. One study that has already been conducted by the NCSC showed that when a video record is available, an appellate court is less likely to reverse the original determination of the trial court. Video court records, analysts say, "might also improve the performance of attorneys and judges. By preserving matters not now apparent on a written record, such as facial expressions, voice inflections, body gestures, and the like, video records may cause trial participants to be more circumspect in their behavior than at present."

Advanced technology can also be expected to have a considerable impact on the trial itself. The technology built into Courtroom 21 facilitates computer animations and crime-scene reenactments. As one of the designers of Courtroom 21 says, "*Jurassic Park* quality computer reenactment may have enormous psychological impact" on jurors.

While Courtroom 21 shows what a typical courtroom of the near future may be like, it also raises questions about the appropriate use of innovative courtroom technologies. As Fred Lederer, one of Courtroom 21's designers, points out, "Modern technology holds enormous promise for our courts. We must recognize, however, that technology's utility often depends upon how people will use it. Although we must continue to improve our courts via technology, we must be sensitive to technology's impact and work to recognize and minimize any negative consequences it might have on our system of justice."

An even more intriguing vision of courtrooms of the future is offered by the Technology of Justice Task Force in its draft report to the Pennsylvania Futures Commission. The task force predicted that by the year 2020, "there will be 'virtual courtrooms,' where appropriate, to provide hearings without the need for people to come to a physical courthouse." The task force envisions trials via teleconferencing, public Internet access to many court documents, and payment of fines by credit card.

Visit Courtroom 21 on the Web at http://www.courtroom21.net, and take a virtual tour of its facilities at http://www.courtroom21.net/ctrm21_hires.ipx.

### DISCUSSION QUESTIONS

1. How might technologies like those discussed in this box affect the outcome of criminal trials, if at all?
2. Can you imagine types of criminal trials in which the use of high-technology courtrooms might not be appropriate? If so, describe them.

*References:* National Center for State Courts website at http://www.ncsc.us (from which some of the material in this box is taken); and Courtroom 21 website at http://www.courtroom21.net.

---

as diverse as sentence variation, charging accuracy, fairness in plea bargaining, evenhandedness, delays, and attitudes toward the court by lay participants. Visit **Library Extra 10–4** at cjtoday.com for more information on standards and measures in court performance.

## SUMMARY

This chapter described pretrial practices and the criminal trial process. Before trial, courts often act to shield the accused from the punitive power of the state through the use of pretrial release. In doing so, they must balance the rights of the unconvicted defendant against the potential for future harm that he or she represents. A significant issue facing pretrial decision makers is how to ensure that all defendants, rich and poor, black and white, male and female, are afforded the same degree of protection. This chapter identified the criminal trial as the hallmark of American criminal justice and discussed the activities characteristic of today's criminal courts. The criminal trial, which owes its legacy to the development of democratic principles in Western society, builds on an adversarial process that pits prosecution against defense. Trials have historically been viewed as peer-based fact-finding processes intended to protect the rights of the accused while disputed issues of guilt or innocence are resolved.

The adversarial system, which has served American courts for more than 200 years, is now being questioned. Well-publicized trials of the last decade or two have demonstrated apparent weaknesses in the trial process. Moreover, the plethora of recent social and technological changes might at least partially supplant the role of advocacy in the fact-finding process. In many cases, new technologies that the framers of our present system did not anticipate (such as DNA fingerprinting) hold the promise of closely linking suspects to criminal activity. Today's electronic media can rapidly and widely disseminate investigative findings, widening the meaning of the phrase "a trial by one's peers." Whether the current adversarial system can continue to serve the interests of justice in an information-rich and technologically advanced society will be a central question for the twenty-first century.

## MULTICULTURALISM AND DIVERSITY

### The Bilingual Courtroom

One of the central multicultural issues facing the criminal justice system today is the need for clear communication with recent immigrants and subcultural groups that have not been fully acculturated. Many such groups hold to traditions and values that differ from those held by the majority of Americans. Such differences influence the interpretation of things seen and heard. Even more basic, however, are language differences that might prevent effective communication with criminal justice system personnel.

Techniques that law enforcement officers can use in overcoming language differences were discussed in Chapter 8. This box focuses on the use of courtroom interpreters to facilitate effective and accurate communication. The role of the courtroom interpreter is to present neutral verbatim, or word-for-word, translations. Interpreters must provide true, accurate, and complete interpretation of the exact statements made by non-English-speaking defendants, victims, and witnesses—whether on the stand, in writing, or in court-related conferences. The Court Interpreters and Translators Association also requires, through its code of professional ethics, that translators remember their "absolute responsibility to keep all oral and written information gained completely confidential."

Although most court interpreters are actually present in the courtroom at the time of trial, telephone interpreting provides an alternative way for courts to reduce problems associated with the lack of access to qualified interpreters. Today, state court administrative offices in Florida, Idaho, New Jersey, and Washington sponsor programs through which qualified interpreters in metropolitan counties are made available to courts in rural counties by telephone.

The federal Court Interpreters Act of 1978[1] specifically provides for the use of interpreters in federal courts. It applies to both criminal and civil trials and hearings. The act reads, in part, as follows[2]:

> The presiding judicial officers . . . shall utilize [an interpreter] . . . in judicial proceedings instituted by the United States, if the presiding judicial officer determines on such officer's own motion or on the motion of a party that such party (including the defendant in a criminal case), or a witness who may present testimony in such judicial proceedings—
>
> (A) speaks only or primarily a language other than English; or
>
> (B) suffers from a hearing impairment . . . so as to inhibit such party's comprehension of the proceedings

or communication with counsel or the presiding officer, or so as to inhibit such witness's comprehension of questions and the presentation of such testimony.

As this extract from the statute shows, translators are also required for individuals with hearing impairments who communicate primarily through American Sign Language. The act does not require that an interpreter be appointed when a person has a speech impairment that is not accompanied by a hearing impairment. A court is not prohibited, however, from providing assistance to that person if it will aid in the efficient administration of justice.

Because it is a federal law, the Court Interpreters Act does not apply to state courts. Nonetheless, most states have enacted similar legislation. A few states are starting to introduce high-standard testing for court interpreters, although most states currently conduct little or no interpreter screening. The federal government and states with high standards for court interpreters generally require interpreter certification. To become certified, an interpreter must pass an oral examination, such as the federal court interpreter's examination or an examination administered by a state court or by a recognized international agency, such as the United Nations.

There is growing recognition among professional court interpreters of the need for standardized interstate testing and certification programs. To meet that need, the National Center for State Courts created the Consortium for State Court Interpreter Certification. The consortium works to pool state resources for developing and administering court interpreter testing and training programs. The consortium's founding states were Minnesota, New Jersey, Oregon, and Washington, although many other states have since joined.

Because certified interpreters are not always available, even by telephone, most states have created a special category of "language-skilled interpreters." To qualify as a language-skilled interpreter, a person must demonstrate to the court's satisfaction his or her ability to interpret court proceedings from English to a designated language and from that language to English. Many states require sign language interpreters to hold a Legal Specialist Certificate, or its equivalent, from the Registry of Interpreters for the Deaf, showing that they are certified in American Sign Language. Learn more about language interpretation in the courts from the National Association of Judiciary Interpreters and Translators via Web Extra 10–3 at cjtoday.com.

WEB EXTRA

---

[1] 28 U.S.C. §1827.
[2] Ibid., at §1827(d)(1).
*References:* The National Association of Judiciary Interpreters and Translators website at http://www.najit.org; Madelynn Herman and Anne Endress Skove, "State Court Rules for Language Interpreters," memorandum number IS 99.1242, National Center for State Courts, Knowledge Management Office, September 8, 1999; Madelynn Herman and Dot Bryant, "Language Interpreting in the Courts," National Center for State Courts. Web posted at http://www.ncsc.dni.us/KMO/Projects/Trends/99-00/articles/CtInterpreters.htm; and National Crime Prevention Council, *Building and Crossing Bridges: Refugees and Law Enforcement Working Together* (Washington, DC: Author, 1994).

1. What steps are typically taken during pretrial activities (that is, before the start of a criminal trial)?

2. What is plea bargaining, and what is its purpose? What impact does plea bargaining have on the criminal justice system? Given the issues associated with plea bargaining, do you believe that it is an acceptable practice? Explain.

3. What are the various stages of a criminal trial? Describe each one.

4. What is the hearsay rule? Under what circumstances might a dying declaration be a valid exception to the hearsay rule? What other exceptions to the hearsay rule have courts recognized?

5. Do you think the present jury system is outmoded? Why? How might a professional jury system be more effective than the present system of peer jurors?

6. How might the adjudication process be improved?

Visit Court TV on the Web by going to http://www.courttv.com. Once there, click on "Trial Coverage" and then on "Trials." Browse through some of the recent criminal cases displayed on the site. Which of the cases listed there do you find the most interesting? Why? Write down your answers along with a description of the cases you've chosen, and submit what you've written to your instructor if asked to do so.

To complete this Web Quest online, go to the Web Quest module in Chapter 10 of the *Criminal Justice Today* Companion Website at cjtoday.com.

i. Irving Stone, *Clarence Darrow for the Defense* (New York: Doubleday, 1941).

1. D. Graham Burnett, "Anatomy of a Verdict: The View from a Juror's Chair," *New York Times* magazine, August 26, 2001.

2. "Blake Found Not Guilty," Associated Press, March 16, 2005. Web posted at http://www.msnbc.msn.com/id/7211376 (accessed June 15, 2005).

3. Lisa Sweetingham, "Friend: Robert Blake Asked Me to Help Him 'Whack' His Wife," Court TV, January 20, 2005. Web posted at http://courttv.com/trials/blake/012005_ctv.html (accessed June 10, 2005).

4. "Blake Found Not Guilty in Wife's Killing," CNN.com, March 16, 2005. Web posted at http://www.cnn.com/2005/LAW/03/16/blake.case (accessed June 20, 2005).

5. Ibid.

6. *Arraignment* is another term used to describe an initial appearance, although we will reserve use of that word to describe a later court appearance following the defendant's indictment by a grand jury or the filing of an information by the prosecutor.

7. *McNabb* v. *U.S.,* 318 U.S. 332 (1943).

8. Because such arrests do not involve judicial determination of probable cause.

9. *County of Riverside* v. *McLaughlin,* 111 S.Ct. 1661 (1991).

10. *White* v. *Maryland,* 373 U.S. 59 (1963).

11. Much of the information in this section comes from Barry Mahoney et al., *Pretrial Services Programs: Responsibilities and Potential* (Washington, DC: National Institute of Justice, 2001).

12. *Taylor* v. *Taintor,* 83 U.S. 66 (1873).

13. National Advisory Commission on Criminal Justice Standards and Goals, *The Courts* (Washington, DC: U.S. Government Printing Office, 1973), p. 37.

14. C. Ares, A. Rankin, and H. Sturz, "The Manhattan Bail Project: An Interim Report on the Use of Pre-Trial Parole," *New York University Law Review,* Vol. 38 (January 1963), pp. 68–95.

15. H. Zeisel, "Bail Revisited," *American Bar Foundation Research Journal,* Vol. 4 (1979), pp. 769–789.

16. Ibid.

17. "Twelve Percent of Those Freed on Low Bail Fail to Appear," *New York Times,* December 2, 1983, p. 1.

18. Bureau of Justice Statistics, *Report to the Nation on Crime and Justice,* 2nd ed. (Washington, DC: U.S. Department of Justice, 1988), p. 76.

19. See Gerard Rainville and Brian A. Reaves, *Felony Defendants in Large Urban Counties, 2000* (Washington, DC: Bureau of Justice Statistics, 2003), p. iv.

20. John Scalia, *Federal Pretrial Release and Detention, 1996* (Washington, DC: Bureau of Justice Statistics, 1999), p. 1. Web posted at

http://www.ojp.usdoj.gov/bjs/pub/pdf/fprd96
.pdf (accessed January 25, 2002).

21. Donald E. Pryor and Walter F. Smith,
    "Significant Research Findings Concerning
    Pretrial Release," *Pretrial Issues*, Vol. 4, No. 1
    (Washington, DC: Pretrial Services Resource
    Center, February 1982). See also the Pretrial
    Services Resource Center on the Web at
    http://www.pretrial.org/mainpage.htm.

22. BJS, *Report to the Nation on Crime and
    Justice*, p. 77.

23. According to Joseph B. Vaughn and Victor E.
    Kappeler, the first such legislation was the
    1970 District of Columbia Court Reform and
    Criminal Procedure Act. See Vaughn and
    Kappeler, "The Denial of Bail: Pre-Trial
    Preventive Detention," *Criminal Justice
    Research Bulletin*, Vol. 3, No. 6 (Huntsville,
    TX: Sam Houston State University, 1987), p. 1.

24. Ibid.

25. Bail Reform Act of 1984, 18 U.S.C. 3142(e).

26. *U.S. v. Montalvo-Murillo*, 495 U.S. 711 (1990).

27. Ibid., syllabus.

28. *U.S. v. Hazzard*, 35 CrL 2217 (1984).

29. See, for example, *U.S. v. Motamedi*, 37 CrL
    2394, CA 9 (1985).

30. A few states now have laws that permit the
    defendant to appear before the grand jury.

31. John M. Scheb and John M. Scheb II,
    *American Criminal Law* (St. Paul, MN: West,
    1996), p. 31.

32. Ibid.

33. The information in this paragraph is adapted
    from Linda Greenhouse, "Supreme Court
    Limits Forced Medication of Some for Trial,"
    *New York Times*, June 16, 2003. Web posted at
    http://www.nytimes.com/2003/06/17/politics
    /17DRUG.html (accessed June 17, 2003).

34. *Sell v. U.S.*, 539 U.S. 166 (2003).

35. Federal Rules of Criminal Procedure, 5.1(a).

36. Scheb and Scheb, *American Criminal* Law,
    p. 32.

37. *Kercheval v. U.S.*, 274 U.S. 220, 223, 47 S.Ct.
    582, 583 (1927); *Boykin v. Alabama*, 395 U.S.
    238 (1969); and *Dickerson v. New Banner
    Institute, Inc.*, 460 U.S. 103 (1983).

38. Bureau of Justice Statistics, *The Prosecution
    of Felony Arrests* (Washington, DC: U.S.
    Government Printing Office, 1983).

39. Barbara Boland et al., *The Prosecution of
    Felony Arrests, 1987* (Washington, DC: U.S.
    Government Printing Office, 1990).

40. *Henderson v. Morgan*, 426 U.S. 637 (1976).

41. *Santobello v. New* York (1971).

42. *Mabry v. Johnson*, 467 U.S. 504 (1984).

43. *U.S. v. Baldacchino*, 762 F.2d 170 (1st Cir.
    1985); *U.S. v. Reardon*, 787 F.2d 512 (10th Cir.
    1986); and *U.S. v. Donahey*, 529 F.2d 831
    (11th Cir. 1976).

44. For a classic discussion of such considerations,
    see David Sudnow, "Normal Crimes:
    Sociological Features of the Penal Code in a
    Public Defender Office," *Social Problems*,
    Vol. 123, No. 3 (winter 1965), p. 255.

45. Federal Rules of Criminal Procedure, No. 11.

46. "A Desperate Act," *Prime Time Live*,
    ABCNews.com, January 28, 1998. Web
    posted at http://archive.abcnews.go.com/
    onair/ PTL/html—files/transcripts/ptl0128c
    .html (accessed July 21, 1999).

47. Dan Rozek, "Castration Doesn't Gain
    Leniency for Pedophile," *Chicago Sun-
    Times*, March 4, 1998.

48. Marc G. Gertz and Edmond J. True, "Social
    Scientists in the Courtroom: The Frustrations
    of Two Expert Witnesses," in Susette M.
    Talarico, ed., *Courts and Criminal Justice:
    Emerging Issues* (Beverly Hills, CA: Sage,
    1985), pp. 81–91.

49. Samuel R. Gross et al., *Exonerations in the
    United States, 1989 through 2003*, April 4,
    2004. Web posted at http://www.mindfully.org/
    Reform/2004/Prison-Exonerations-
    Gross19apr04.htm (accessed May 28, 2005).

50. Ibid.

51. *Oregon v. Harberts*, September 14, 2000. Web
    posted at http://www.publications.ojd.state.or
    .us/S41741.htm (accessed September 17, 2002).

52. The Daily Athenaeum Interactive, "Blind
    Justice." Web posted at http://www.da
    .wvu.edu/archives/001509/news/001509,04,01
    .html (accessed September 17, 2002).

53. Contained in Article I, Section 10.

54. Ron Obert, "Clackamas County Community
    Corrections Moves Scott Harberts to Work
    Center." Web posted at http://www.co
    .clackamas.or.us/press_releases/2001_Press_
    Releases/ 081301.htm (accessed
    September 17, 2002).

55. *Klopfer v. North Carolina*, 386 U.S. 213
    (1967).

56. *Barker v. Wingo*, 407 U.S. 514 (1972).

57. *Strunk v. U.S.*, 412 U.S. 434 (1973).

58. Speedy Trial Act, 18 U.S.C. 3161 (1974).

59. *U.S. v. Brainer*, 515 F.Supp. 627, 630 (D. Md.
    1981).

60. *U.S. v. Taylor*, 487 U.S. 326, 108 S.Ct. 2413,
    101 L.Ed.2d 297 (1988).

61. *Fex v. Michigan*, 113 S.Ct. 1085, 122 L.Ed.2d
    406 (1993).

62. *Doggett v. U.S.*, 112 S.Ct. 2686 (1992).

63. William U. McCormack, "Supreme Court
    Cases: 1991–1992 Term," *FBI Law
    Enforcement Bulletin*, November 1992,
    pp. 28–29.

64. See, for example, the U.S. Supreme Court's
    decision in the case of *Murphy v. Florida*, 410
    U.S. 525 (1973).

65. *Witherspoon v. Illinois*, 391 U.S. 510 (1968).

66. *Mu'Min* v. *Virginia,* 500 U.S. 415 (1991).

67. Federal Rules of Criminal Procedure, Rule 24(6).

68. Learn more about shadow juries from Molly McDonough, "Me and My Shadow: Shadow Juries Are Helping Litigators Shape Their Cases during Trial," *National Law Journal,* May 17, 2001.

69. Although the words *argument* and *statement* are sometimes used interchangeably to refer to opening remarks, defense attorneys are enjoined from drawing conclusions or "arguing" to the jury at this stage in the trial. Their task, as described in the section that follows, is simply to explain to the jury how the defense will be conducted.

70. Supreme Court majority opinion in *Powers* v. *Ohio,* 499 U.S. 400 (1991), citing *Strauder* v. *West Virginia,* 100 U.S. 303 (1880).

71. *Swain* v. *Alabama,* 380 U.S. 202 (1965).

72. *Batson* v. *Kentucky,* 476 U.S. 79, 106 S.Ct. 1712 (1986).

73. *Ford* v. *Georgia,* 498 U.S. 411 (1991), footnote 2.

74. Ibid.

75. *Powers* v. *Ohio,* 499 U.S. 400 (1991).

76. *Edmonson* v. *Leesville Concrete Co., Inc.,* 500 U.S. 614, 111 S.Ct. 2077, 114 L.Ed.2d 660 (1991).

77. *Georgia* v. *McCollum,* 505 U.S. 42 (1992).

78. *J.E.B.* v. *Alabama,* 114 S.Ct. 1419 (1994).

79. See, for example, *Davis* v. *Minnesota,* 511 U.S. 1115 (1994).

80. Michael Kirkland, "Court Rejects Fat Jurors Case," United Press International wire service, January 8, 1996. The case was *Santiago-Martinez* v. *U.S.,* No. 95–567 (1996).

81. *Campbell* v. *Louisiana,* 523 U.S. 392 (1998).

82. *Miller-El* v. *Cockrell,* 537 U.S. 322 (2003).

83. Ibid., syllabus.

84. *U.S.* v. *Dinitz,* 424 U.S. 600, 612 (1976).

85. *Michigan* v. *Lucas,* 500 U.S. 145 (1991).

86. Associated Press, "Suit Settlement Ends Bryant Saga," March 3, 2005. Web posted at http:// msnbc.msn.com/id/7019659 (accessed July 12, 2005).

87. *Kotteakos* v. *U.S.,* 328 U.S. 750 (1946); *Brecht* v. *Abrahamson,* 113 S.Ct. 1710, 123 L.Ed.2d 353 (1993); and *Arizona* v. *Fulminante,* 111 S.Ct. 1246 (1991).

88. The Court, citing *Kotteakos* v. *U.S.* (1946), in *Brecht* v. *Abrahamson,* 113 S.Ct. 1710, 123 L.Ed.2d 353 (1993).

89. *Sullivan* v. *Louisiana,* 113 S.Ct. 2078, 124 L.Ed.2d 182 (1993).

90. *Griffin* v. *California,* 380 U.S. 609 (1965).

91. *Ohio* v. *Reiner,* 123 S.Ct. 1252, 532 U.S. 17 (2001).

92. Leading questions may, in fact, be permitted for certain purposes, including refreshing a witness's memory, impeaching a hostile witness, introducing undisputed material, and helping a witness with impaired faculties.

93. *In re Oliver,* 333 U.S. 257 (1948).

94. *Coy* v. *Iowa,* 487 U.S. 1012, 108 S.Ct. 2798 (1988).

95. *Maryland* v. *Craig,* 497 U.S. 836, 845–847 (1990).

96. *Idaho* v. *Wright,* 497 U.S. 805 (1990).

97. *White* v. *Illinois,* 112 S.Ct. 736 (1992).

98. Federal Rules of Criminal Procedure, Rule 29.1.

99. See *Johnson* v. *Louisiana,* 406 U.S. 356 (1972); and *Apodaca* v. *Oregon,* 406 U.S. 404 (1972).

100. *Allen* v. *U.S.,* 164 U.S. 492 (1896).

101. Judge Harold J. Rothwax, *Guilty: The Collapse of Criminal Justice* (New York: Random House, 1996).

102. Amiram Elwork, Bruce D. Sales, and James Alfini, *Making Jury Instructions Understandable* (Charlottesville, VA: Michie, 1982).

103. "King Jury Lives in Fear from Unpopular Verdict," *Fayetteville (N.C.) Observer-Times,* May 10, 1992, p. 7A.

104. "Los Angeles Trials Spark Debate over Anonymous Juries," *Criminal Justice Newsletter,* February 16, 1993, pp. 3–4.

105. Some states have centralized offices called Administrative Offices of the Courts or something similar. Such offices, however, are often primarily data-gathering agencies with little or no authority over the day-to-day functioning of state or local courts.

106. See, for example, Larry Berkson and Susan Carbon, *Court Unification: Its History, Politics, and Implementation* (Washington, DC: U.S. Government Printing Office, 1978); and Thomas Henderson et al., *The Significance of Judicial Structure: The Effect of Unification on Trial Court Operators* (Alexandria, VA: Institute for Economic and Policy Studies, 1984).

107. See, for example, Thomas J. Cook et al., *Basic Issues in Court Performance* (Washington, DC: National Institute of Justice, 1982).

108. See, for example, Sorrel Wildhorn et al., *Indicators of Justice: Measuring the Performance of Prosecutors, Defense, and Court Agencies Involved in Felony Proceedings* (Lexington, MA: Lexington Books, 1977).

# CHAPTER 11

# Sentencing

## OUTLINE

- Introduction
- The Philosophy and Goals of Criminal Sentencing
- Indeterminate Sentencing
- Structured Sentencing
- Innovations in Sentencing
- The Presentence Investigation
- The Victim—Forgotten No Longer
- Modern Sentencing Options
- Death: The Ultimate Sanction

## LEARNING OBJECTIVES

After reading this chapter, you should be able to:

- Describe the five goals of contemporary criminal sentencing.
- Illustrate the difference between indeterminate and structured sentencing.
- Describe the different types of structured sentencing models in use today.
- Define mandatory sentencing, and explain how it came about.
- Describe truth in sentencing.
- Explain the importance of federal sentencing guidelines.
- Describe the nature and importance of the presentence investigation report.
- Describe the history of victims' rights and services, and discuss the growing role of the victim in criminal justice proceedings today.
- List the four traditional sentencing options.
- Outline the arguments for and against capital punishment.

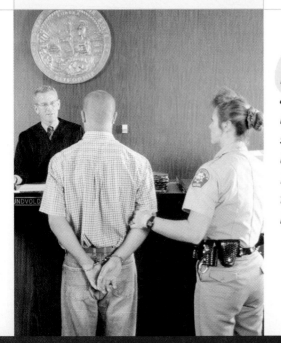

" *In sentencing, we have gone through determinate, indeterminate and back and forth in the last century. But in our time, life moves much faster. It took a hundred years from the peak of indeterminate sentencing, or the full realization of indeterminate sentencing values in the late 1870s to 1900 to wash away by the mid-1970s. . . . Is it possible that, with things happening so much faster, in just twenty or twenty-five years the cycle might once again be changing back in a different direction?* "

—Michael Tonry, Director, Institute of Criminology, Cambridge University[1]

*Developing a sentencing system that provides appropriate types and lengths of sentences for all offenders is a challenging task.*

—National Conference
of State Legislatures

## KEY CONCEPTS

### TERMS

| | | |
|---|---|---|
| aggravating circumstances | incapacitation | restorative justice |
| capital offense | indeterminate sentencing | retribution |
| capital punishment | just deserts | sentencing |
| determinate sentencing | mandatory sentencing | social debt |
| deterrence | mitigating circumstances | specific deterrence |
| diversion | presentence investigation | structured sentencing |
| equity | presumptive sentencing | truth in sentencing |
| gain time | proportionality | victim impact statement |
| general deterrence | rehabilitation | voluntary/advisory sentencing guidelines |
| good time | restoration | writ of *habeas corpus* |

### CASES

| | | |
|---|---|---|
| *Apprendi* v. *New Jersey* | *Furman* v. *Georgia* | *Ring* v. *Arizona* |
| *Atkins* v. *Virginia* | *Gregg* v. *Georgia* | *Schlup* v. *Delo* |
| *Blakely* v. *Washington* | *Harris* v. *U.S.* | *Schriro* v. *Summerlin* |
| *Coker* v. *Georgia* | *In re Kemmler* | *U.S.* v. *Booker* |
| *Coleman* v. *Thompson* | *McCleskey* v. *Zant* | *Wilkerson* v. *Utah* |
| *Deal* v. *U.S.* | *Mistretta* v. *U.S.* | *Woodson* v. *North Carolina* |

The original full-text court opinion for each of these cases is available on the CD-ROM that accompanies this book.

# Introduction

Hear the author discuss this chapter at **cjtoday.com**

To make punishments efficacious, two things are necessary. They must never be disproportioned to the offense, and they must be certain.

—William Sims (1806–1870)

**sentencing**

The imposition of a criminal sanction by a judicial authority.

On July 30, 2002, in what appeared to be an incident of vigilante justice, a small angry mob dragged two men from a crashed rental van and beat them to death with bricks and stones in a South Side Chicago neighborhood. The van had veered out of control and struck the front porch of a home, injuring three young women, one of them critically.[2] Witnesses said the vehicle appeared to accelerate wildly before hitting the women. "It all happened so fast, it seemed like he floored it or something," said witness Taquita Mixon, who saw the incident from her apartment window.[3] A bystander told reporters that one of the young men involved in the killings was the boyfriend of the critically injured woman.

While some in the neighborhood were ready to forgive the killers, others wanted them brought to trial. "It was an accident," one woman said of the beating. "I think emotions just got out of hand."[4] Another person disagreed, calling for those who participated in the killings to be arrested. "It's not going to bring them back, but it'll let them know you can't take the law in your own hands," she said.

In vigilante justice, a mob typically decides the fate of suspects before they can be fairly tried and formally sentenced. Under an organized system of criminal justice, **sentencing** is the imposition of a penalty on a person convicted of a crime following an impartial judicial proceeding during which criminal responsibility is ascertained. Most sentencing decisions are made by judges, although in some cases, especially where a death sentence is possible, juries may be involved in a special sentencing phase of courtroom proceedings. The sentencing decision is one of the most difficult made by any judge or jury. Not only does it affect the future of the defendant—and at times it is a decision about his or her life or death—but society looks to sentencing to achieve a diversity of goals, some of which may not be fully compatible with others.

This chapter examines sentencing in terms of both philosophy and practice. We will describe the goals of sentencing as well as the historical development of various sentencing models in the United States. This chapter contains a detailed overview of victimization and victims' rights in general, especially as they relate to courtroom procedure and to sentencing practice. Federal sentencing guidelines and the significance of presentence investigations are also described. For an overview of sentencing issues, visit the Sentencing Project via **Web Extra 11–1** at cjtoday.com.

WEB EXTRA

# The Philosophy and Goals of Criminal Sentencing

Traditional sentencing options have included imprisonment, fines, probation, and—for very serious offenses—death. Limits on the range of options available to sentencing authorities are generally specified by law. Historically, those limits have shifted as understanding of crime and the goals of sentencing have changed. Sentencing philosophies, or the justifications on which various sentencing strategies are based, are manifestly intertwined with issues of religion, morals, values, and emotions.[5] Philosophies that gained ascendancy at a particular point in history usually reflected more deeply held social values. Centuries ago, for example, it was thought that crime was due to sin and that suffering was the culprit's due. Judges were expected to be harsh. Capital punishment, torture, and painful physical penalties served this view of criminal behavior.

An emphasis on equitable punishments became prevalent around the time of the American and French Revolutions, brought about in part by Enlightenment philosophies. Offenders came to be seen as highly rational beings who intentionally and somewhat carefully chose their course of action. Sentencing philosophies of the period stressed the need for sanctions that outweighed the benefits to be derived from criminal activity. The severity of punishment became less important than quick and certain penalties.

Recent thinking has emphasized the need to limit offenders' potential for future harm by separating them from society. We also still believe that offenders deserve to be punished, and we have not entirely abandoned hope for their rehabilitation. Modern sentencing practices are influenced by five goals, which weave their way through widely disseminated professional and legal models, continuing public calls for sentencing reform, and everyday sentencing practice. Each goal represents a quasi-independent sentencing philosophy, since each makes distinctive assumptions about human nature and holds implications for sentencing practice. These are the five goals of contemporary sentencing:

- Retribution
- Incapacitation
- Deterrence
- Rehabilitation
- Restoration

> As a society we have at least in part created what we fear—a mass of convicts running loose through our society but unintegrated, hopeless, and hell-bent for reinstitutionalization, due in part to our focus on unrelenting lifelong punishment.
>
> —Bernard H. Levin, Blue Ridge Community College[i]

> If you want a small prison population, make punishment certain. If you want a large prison population, make punishment uncertain.
>
> —Former House Speaker Newt Gingrich

# Retribution

**Retribution** is a call for punishment based on a perceived need for vengeance. Retribution is the earliest known rationale for punishment. Most early societies punished all offenders who were caught. Early punishments were immediate—often without the benefit of a hearing—and they were often extreme, with little thought given to whether the punishment "fit" the crime. Death and exile, for example, were commonly imposed, even for relatively minor offenses. The Old Testament dictum of "an eye for an eye, a tooth for a tooth"—often cited as an ancient justification for retribution—was actually intended to reduce the severity of punishment for relatively minor crimes.

Today, retribution corresponds to the **just deserts** model of sentencing that holds that offenders are responsible for their crimes. When they are convicted and punished, they are said to have gotten their "just deserts." Retribution sees punishment as deserved, justified, and even required[6] by the offender's behavior. The primary sentencing tool of the just deserts model is imprisonment, but in extreme cases capital punishment (that is, death) becomes the ultimate retribution.

In both the public's view and in political policy making, retribution is still a primary goal of criminal sentencing. During the 1990s, as the public-order perspective with its emphasis on individual responsibility became dominant, public demands for retribution-based criminal punishments grew loud and clear. In the mid-1990s, for example, the Mississippi legislature, encouraged by then-Governor Kirk Fordice, voted to ban prison air-conditioning, remove privately owned television sets from prison cells and dormitories, and prohibit weight lifting by inmates. Governor Fordice sent a "get tough" proposal to the legislature, which was quickly dubbed the "Clint Eastwood Hang 'Em High Bill"[7] and which required inmates to wear striped uniforms with the word *CONVICT* stamped on the back. State Representative Mac McInnis explained the

**retribution**
The act of taking revenge on a criminal perpetrator.

**just deserts**
A model of criminal sentencing that holds that criminal offenders deserve the punishment they receive at the hands of the law and that punishments should be appropriate to the type and severity of the crime committed.

state's retribution-inspired fervor this way: "We want a prisoner to look like a prisoner, to smell like a prisoner."[8] As critics note, however, none of these measures is likely to deter crime, but that is beside the point. The goal of retribution, after all, is not deterrence, but satisfaction.[9]

## Incapacitation

**incapacitation**

The use of imprisonment or other means to reduce the likelihood that an offender will commit future offenses.

**Incapacitation**, the second goal of criminal sentencing, seeks to protect innocent members of society from offenders who might harm them if not prevented from doing so. In ancient times, mutilation and amputation of the extremities were sometimes used to prevent offenders from repeating their crimes. Modern incapacitation strategies separate offenders from the community to reduce opportunities for further criminality. Incapacitation, sometimes called the "lock 'em up approach," forms the basis for the modern movement toward prison "warehousing."

Unlike retribution, incapacitation requires only restraint—and not punishment. Hence, advocates of the incapacitation philosophy of sentencing are sometimes also active prison reformers, who want to humanize correctional institutions. Innovations in confinement offer new ways to achieve the goal of incapacitation without imprisonment. Remote location monitoring (discussed in Chapter 12) and biomedical intervention (such as "chemical castration") may offer alternatives to imprisonment.

## Deterrence

**deterrence**

A goal of criminal sentencing that seeks to inhibit criminal behavior through the fear of punishment.

**Deterrence** uses the example or threat of punishment to convince people that criminal activity is not worthwhile. Its overall goal is crime prevention. **Specific deterrence** seeks to reduce the likelihood of recidivism (repeat offenses) by convicted offenders, while **general deterrence** strives to influence the future behavior of people who have not yet been arrested and who may be tempted to turn to crime.

**specific deterrence**

A goal of criminal sentencing that seeks to prevent a particular offender from engaging in repeat criminality.

Deterrence is one of the more "rational" goals of sentencing, because it is an easily articulated goal and because it is possible to investigate objectively the amount of punishment required to deter. It is generally agreed today that harsh punishments can virtually eliminate many minor forms of criminality.[10] Few traffic tickets would have to be written, for example, if minor driving offenses were punishable by death. A free society like our own, of course, is not willing to impose extreme punishments on petty offenders, and even harsh punishments are not demonstrably effective in reducing the incidence of serious crimes, such as murder and drug running.

**general deterrence**

A goal of criminal sentencing that seeks to prevent others from committing crimes similar to the one for which a particular offender is being sentenced by making an example of the person sentenced.

Deterrence is compatible with the goal of incapacitation, since at least specific deterrence can be achieved through incapacitating offenders. Tufts University Professor Hugo Adam Bedau, however, points to significant differences between retribution and deterrence.[11] Retribution is oriented toward the past, says Bedau. It seeks to redress wrongs already committed. Deterrence, in contrast, is a strategy for the future. It aims to prevent new crimes. But as legal philosopher H. L. A. Hart observed, retribution can be the means through which deterrence is achieved.[12] By serving as an example of what might happen to others, punishment may have an inhibiting effect.

## Rehabilitation

**rehabilitation**

The attempt to reform a criminal offender. Also, the state in which a reformed offender is said to be.

**Rehabilitation** seeks to bring about fundamental changes in offenders and their behavior. As in the case of deterrence, the ultimate goal of rehabilitation is a reduction in the number of criminal offenses. Whereas deterrence depends on a fear of the consequences of violating the law, rehabilitation generally works through education and psychological treatment to reduce the likelihood of future criminality.

The term *rehabilitation,* however, is a misnomer for the kinds of changes that its supporters seek. Rehabilitation literally means to return a person to his or her previous condition, just as medical rehabilitation programs seek to restore functioning to atrophied limbs, to rejuvenate injured organs, and to mend shattered minds. In the case of criminal offenders, however, it is likely that in most cases restoring criminals to their previous state will result in nothing but a more youthful type of criminality.

In the late 1970s, the rehabilitative goal in sentencing fell victim to the "nothing-works doctrine." The nothing-works doctrine was based on studies of recidivism rates that consistently showed that rehabilitation was more an ideal than a reality.[13] With as many as 90% of former con-

Inmates in a California prison learning how to repair computer equipment. Skills acquired through such prison programs might translate into productive, noncriminal careers. Rehabilitation is an important, but infrequently voiced, goal of modern sentencing practices.
*Courtesy of Robert W. Winslow*

victed offenders returning to lives of crime following release from prison-based treatment programs, public sentiments in favor of incapacitation grew. Although the rehabilitation ideal has clearly suffered in the public arena, emerging evidence has begun to suggest that effective treatment programs do exist and may be growing in number.[14] See Library Extra 11–1 at cjtoday.com to read more about treatment programs that work.

## Restoration

Victims of crime and their families are frequently traumatized by their experiences. Some victims are killed, and others receive lasting physical or emotional injuries. For many, the world is never the same. The victimized may live in constant fear, be reduced in personal vigor, and be unable to form trusting relationships. **Restoration** is a sentencing goal that seeks to address this damage by making the victim and the community "whole again."

A U.S. Department of Justice report explains restoration this way: "Crime was once defined as a 'violation of the State.' This remains the case today, but we now recognize that crime is far more. It is—among other things—a violation of one person by another. While retributive justice may address the first type of violation adequately, **restorative justice** is required to effectively address the latter. . . . Thus [through restorative justice] we seek to attain a balance between the legitimate needs of the community, the . . . offender, and the victim."[15] The "healing" of all parties has many aspects, ranging from victim assistance initiatives to legislation supporting victims' compensation. See Table 11–1 for a comparison of retributive justice and restorative justice.

Sentencing options that seek to restore the victim have focused primarily on restitution payments that offenders are ordered to make, either to their victims or to a general fund, which may then go to reimburse victims for suffering, lost wages, and medical expenses. In support of these goals, the 1984 Federal Comprehensive Crime Control Act specifically requires that "If sentenced to probation, the defendant must also be ordered to pay a fine, make restitution, and/or work in community service."[16]

Vermont began a new Sentencing Options Program in 1995 built around the concept of reparative probation. According to state officials, the Vermont reparative options program, which "requires the offender to make reparations to the victim and to the community, marks the first time in the United States that the Restorative Justice model has been embraced by a state department of corrections and implemented on a statewide scale."[17] Vermont's reparative program builds on

BJS Guidelines for People Working in Restorative Justice

**restoration**

A goal of criminal sentencing that attempts to make the victim "whole again."

**restorative justice**

A sentencing model that builds on restitution and community participation in an attempt to make the victim "whole again."

**TABLE 11–1**

## DIFFERENCES BETWEEN RETRIBUTIVE AND RESTORATIVE JUSTICE

| Retributive Justice | Restorative Justice |
| --- | --- |
| Crime is an act against the state, a violation of a law, an abstract idea. | Crime is an act against another person or the community. |
| The criminal justice system controls crime. | Crime control lies primarily with the community. |
| Offender accountability is defined as taking punishment. | Offender accountability is defined as assuming responsibility and taking action to repair harm. |
| Crime is an individual act with individual responsibility. | Crime has both individual and social dimensions of responsibility. |
| Victims are peripheral to the process of resolving a crime. | Victims are central to the process of resolving a crime. |
| The offender is defined by deficits. | The offender is defined by the capacity to make reparation. |
| The emphasis is on adversarial relationships. | The emphasis is on dialogue and negotiation. |
| Pain is imposed to punish, deter, and prevent. | Restitution is a means of restoring both parties; the goal is reconciliation. |
| The community is on the sidelines, represented abstractly by the state. | The community is the facilitator in the restorative process. |
| The response is focused on the offender's past behavior. | The response is focused on harmful consequences of the offender's behavior; the emphasis is on the future and on reparation. |
| There is dependence on proxy professionals. | There is direct involvement by both the offender and the victim. |

*Source:* Adapted from Gordon Bazemore and Mark S. Umbreit, *Balanced and Restorative Justice: Program Summary* (Washington, DC: Office of Juvenile Justice and Delinquency Prevention, 1994), p. 7.

---

> The root of revenge is in the weakness of the Soul; the most abject and timorous are the most addicted to it.
>
> —Akhenaton (circa 1375 B.C.)

"community reparative boards" consisting of five or six citizens from the community where the crime was committed and requires face-to-face public meetings between the offender and board representatives. Keeping in mind the program's avowed goals of "making the victim(s) whole again" and having the offender "make amends to the community," board members determine the specifics of the offender's sentence. Options are restitution, community service work, victim–offender mediation, victim empathy programs, driver improvement courses, and the like.

Some advocates of the restoration philosophy of sentencing point out that restitution payments and work programs that benefit the victim can also have the added benefit of rehabilitating the offender. The hope is that such sentences will teach offenders personal responsibility through structured financial obligations, job requirements, and regularly scheduled payments. Learn more about restorative justice by visiting Library Extra 11–2 and Web Extra 11–2 at cjtoday.com.

# Indeterminate Sentencing

**indeterminate sentencing**

A model of criminal punishment that encourages rehabilitation through the use of general and relatively unspecific sentences (such as a term of imprisonment of from one to ten years).

While the *philosophy* of criminal sentencing is reflected in the goals of sentencing we have just discussed, different sentencing *practices* have been linked to each goal. During most of the twentieth century, for example, the rehabilitation goal was influential. Since rehabilitation required that individual offenders' personal characteristics be closely considered in defining effective treatment strategies, judges were generally permitted wide discretion in choosing from among sentencing options. Although incapacitation is increasingly becoming the sentencing strategy of choice today, many state criminal codes still allow judges to impose fines, probation, or widely varying prison terms, all for the same offense. These sentencing practices, characterized primarily by vast judicial choice, constitute an **indeterminate sentencing** model.

Indeterminate sentencing has both a historical and a philosophical basis in the belief that convicted offenders are more likely to participate in their own rehabilitation if participation will reduce the amount of time they have to spend in prison. Inmates on good behavior will be released early, while recalcitrant inmates will remain in prison until the end of their terms. For that reason, parole generally plays a significant role in states that employ the indeterminate sentencing model.

Indeterminate sentencing relies heavily on judges' discretion to choose among types of sanctions and to set upper and lower limits on the length of prison stays. Indeterminate sentences are typically imposed with wording like this: "The defendant shall serve not less than five and not more than twenty-five years in the state's prison, under the supervision of the state department of correction." Judicial discretion under the indeterminate model also extends to the imposition of concurrent or consecutive sentences when the offender is convicted on more than one charge. Consecutive sentences are served one after the other, while concurrent sentences expire simultaneously.

The indeterminate model was also created to take into consideration detailed differences in degrees of guilt. Under this model, judges can weigh minute differences among cases, situations, and offenders. All of the following can be considered before sentence is passed: (1) whether the offender committed the crime out of a need for money, for the thrill it afforded, out of a desire for revenge, or for the "hell of it"; (2) how much harm the offender intended; (3) how much the victim contributed to his or her own victimization; (4) the extent of the damages inflicted; (5) the mental state of the offender; (6) the likelihood of successful rehabilitation; and (7) the degree of the offender's cooperation with authorities. Under the indeterminate sentencing model, the inmate's behavior while incarcerated is the primary determinant of the amount of time served. State parole boards wield great discretion under this model, acting as the final arbiters of the actual sentence served.

A few states employ a partially indeterminate sentencing model. They allow judges to specify only the maximum amount of time to be served. Some minimum is generally implied by law but is not under the control of the sentencing authority. General practice is to set one year as a minimum for all felonies, although a few jurisdictions assume no minimum time at all, making offenders eligible for immediate parole.

# Critiques of Indeterminate Sentencing

Indeterminate sentencing is still the rule in many jurisdictions, including Georgia, Hawaii, Iowa, Kentucky, Massachusetts, Michigan, Nevada, New York, North Dakota, Oklahoma, Rhode Island, South Carolina, South Dakota, Texas, Utah, Vermont, West Virginia, and Wyoming.[18] By the 1970s, however, the model had come under fire for contributing to inequality in sentencing. Critics claimed that the indeterminate model allowed judges' personalities and personal philosophies to produce a too wide range of sentencing practices, from very lenient to very strict. The indeterminate model was also criticized for perpetuating a system under which offenders might be sentenced, at least by some judges, more on the basis of personal and social characteristics, such as race, gender, and social class, than on culpability.

Because of the personal nature of judicial decisions under the indeterminate model, offenders often depend on the advice and ploys of their attorneys to appear before a judge who is thought to be a good sentencing risk. Requests for delays are a common defense strategy in indeterminate sentencing states, where they are used to try to manipulate the selection of the judge involved in the sentencing decision.

Another charge leveled against indeterminate sentencing is that it tends to produce "dishonesty" in sentencing. Because of sentence cutbacks for good behavior and involvement in work and study programs, time served in prison is generally far less than sentences would seem to indicate. An inmate sentenced to five to ten years, for example, might actually be released in a couple of years after all **gain time, good time**, and other special allowances have been calculated. (Some of the same charges can be leveled against determinate sentencing schemes under which correctional officials can administratively reduce the time served by an inmate.) A recent survey by the Bureau of Justice Statistics found that even violent offenders released from state prisons during the study period served, on average, only 51% of the sentences they originally received.[19] Nonviolent offenders served even smaller portions of their sentences. Table 11–2 shows the percentage of an imposed sentence that an offender sentenced to state prison in 1996 could expect to serve.

To ensure long prison terms in indeterminate jurisdictions, some court officials have gone to extremes. In 1994, for example, Oklahoma judge Dan Owens sentenced convicted child molester

> Putting people in prison is the single most important thing we've done [to decrease crime].
>
> —James Q. Wilson, Professor Emeritus, University of California at Los Angeles[ii]

**gain time**

The amount of time deducted from time to be served in prison on a given sentence as a consequence of participation in special projects or programs.

**good time**

The amount of time deducted from time to be served in prison on a given sentence as a consequence of good behavior.

TABLE 11-2

| PERCENTAGE OF SENTENCE TO BE SERVED, BY NEW COURT COMMITMENTS TO STATE PRISON | |
| --- | --- |
| Offense Type | Percentage |
| Violent | 51 |
| Property | 46 |
| Drug | 46 |
| Public-order | 49 |
| Average for all felonies | 49 |

*Source:* Paula M. Ditton and Doris James Wilson, *Truth in Sentencing in State Prisons* (Washington, DC: Bureau of Justice Statistics, 1999).

**proportionality**

A sentencing principle that holds that the severity of sanctions should bear a direct relationship to the seriousness of the crime committed.

**equity**

A sentencing principle, based on concerns with social equality, that holds that similar crimes should be punished with the same degree of severity, regardless of the social or personal characteristics of the offenders.

**social debt**

A sentencing principle that holds that an offender's criminal history should objectively be taken into account in sentencing decisions.

**structured sentencing**

A model of criminal punishment that includes determinate and commission-created presumptive sentencing schemes, as well as voluntary/advisory sentencing guidelines.

**determinate sentencing**

A model of criminal punishment in which an offender is given a fixed term that may be reduced by good time or gain time. Under the model, for example, all offenders convicted of the same degree of burglary would be sentenced to the same length of time behind bars.

Charles Scott Robinson to 30,000 years in prison.[20] Judge Owens, complying with the jury's efforts to ensure that Robinson would spend the rest of his life behind bars, sentenced him to serve six consecutive 5,000-year sentences. Robinson had 14 previous felony convictions.

# Structured Sentencing

Until the 1970s, all 50 states used some form of indeterminate (or partially indeterminate) sentencing. Eventually, however, calls for equity and proportionality in sentencing, heightened by claims of racial disparity in the sentencing practices of some judges,[21] led many states to move toward greater control over their sentencing systems.

Critics of the indeterminate model called for the recognition of three fundamental sentencing principles: **proportionality, equity,** and **social debt.** Proportionality refers to the belief that the severity of sanctions should bear a direct relationship to the seriousness of the crime committed. Equity means that similar crimes should be punished with the same degree of severity, regardless of the social or personal characteristics of offenders. According to the principle of equity, for example, two bank robbers in different parts of the country, who use the same techniques and weapons, with the same degree of implied threat, should receive roughly the same sentence even though they are tried under separate circumstances. The equity principle needs to be balanced, however, against the notion of social debt. In the case of the bank robbers, the offender who has a prior criminal record can be said to have a higher level of social debt than the one-time robber, where all else is equal. Greater social debt, of course, suggests a more severe punishment or a greater need for treatment.

Beginning in the 1970s, a number of states addressed these concerns by developing a different model of sentencing, known as **structured sentencing**. One form of structured sentencing, called **determinate sentencing**, requires that a convicted offender be sentenced to a fixed term that may be reduced by good time or earned time. Determinate sentencing states eliminated the use of parole and created explicit standards to specify the amount of punishment appropriate for a given offense. Determinate sentencing practices also specify an anticipated release date for each sentenced offender.

In a 1996 report that traced the historical development of determinate sentencing, the National Council on Crime and Delinquency (NCCD) observed that "the term 'determinate sentencing' is generally used to refer to the sentencing reforms of the late 1970s." At that time, the legislatures of California, Illinois, Indiana, and Maine abolished the parole release decision and replaced indeterminate penalties with fixed (or flat) sentences that could be reduced by good-time provisions. In response to the then-growing determinate sentencing movement, a few states developed **voluntary/advisory sentencing guidelines** during the 1980s. These guidelines consist of recommended sentencing policies that are not required by law and are usually based on past sentencing practices and serve as guides to judges. Voluntary/advisory sentencing guidelines may build on either determinate or indeterminate sentencing structures. Florida, Maryland, Massachusetts, Michigan, Rhode Island, Utah, and Wisconsin all experimented with voluntary/advisory guidelines during the 1980s. Voluntary/advisory guidelines constitute a second form of structured sentencing.

A third model of structured sentencing employs what NCCD calls "commission-based presumptive sentencing guidelines." **Presumptive sentencing** became common in the 1980s as states began to experiment with sentencing guidelines developed by sentencing commissions. These models differed from both determinate and voluntary/advisory guidelines in three respects. First, presumptive sentencing guidelines were not developed by the state legislature but by a sentencing commission that often represented a diverse array of criminal justice and sometimes private interests. Second, presumptive sentencing guidelines were explicit and highly structured, typically relying on a quantitative scoring instrument to classify the offense for which a person was to be sentenced. Third, the guidelines were not voluntary/advisory in that judges had to adhere to the sentencing system or provide a written rationale for departures.

By 2005, the federal government and 16 states had established commission-based sentencing guidelines. Ten of the 16 states used presumptive sentencing guidelines. The remaining six relied on voluntary/advisory guidelines. As a consequence, with the advent of the twenty-first century, sentencing guidelines authored by legislatively created sentencing commissions had become the most popular form of structured sentencing. Learn more about the history of sentencing reform via Library Extras 11–3 and 11–4 at cjtoday.com.

Guideline jurisdictions, which specified a presumptive sentence for a given offense, generally allowed for "aggravating" or "mitigating" circumstances—indicating a greater or lesser degree of culpability—which judges could take into consideration when imposing a sentence somewhat at variance from the presumptive term. **Aggravating circumstances** call for a tougher sentence and may include especially heinous behavior, cruelty, injury to more than one person, and so on. **Mitigating circumstances**, which indicate that a lesser sentence is called for, are generally similar to legal defenses, although in this case they only reduce criminal responsibility, not eliminate it. Mitigating circumstances include such things as cooperation with the investigating authority, surrender, and good character. Common aggravating and mitigating circumstances are listed in CJ Today Exhibit 11–1.

# Federal Sentencing Guidelines

In 1984, with passage of the Comprehensive Crime Control Act, the federal government adopted presumptive sentencing for nearly all federal offenders.[22] The act also addressed the issue of **truth in sentencing.** Under the old federal system, on average, good-time credits and parole reduced time served to about one-third of the actual sentence.[23] At the time, the sentencing practices of most states reflected the federal model. While sentence reductions may have benefited offenders, they often outraged victims, who felt betrayed by the sentencing process. The 1984 act nearly eliminated good-time credits[24] and began the process of phasing out federal parole and eliminating the U.S. Parole Commission (read more about the commission in Chapter 12).[25] The emphasis on truth in sentencing created, in effect, a sentencing environment of "what you get is what you serve." Truth in sentencing, described as "a close correspondence between the sentence imposed upon those sent to prison and the time actually served prior to prison release,"[26] has become an important policy focus of many state legislatures and the U.S. Congress. The Violent Crime Control and Law Enforcement Act of 1994 set aside $4 billion in federal prison construction funds (called Truth in Sentencing Incentive Funds) for states that adopt truth-in-sentencing laws and are able to guarantee that certain violent offenders will serve 85% of their sentences.

Title II of the Comprehensive Crime Control Act, called the Sentencing Reform Act of 1984,[27] established the nine-member U.S. Sentencing Commission. The commission, which continues to function today, comprises presidential appointees, including three federal judges. The Sentencing Reform Act limited the discretion of federal judges by mandating the creation of federal sentencing guidelines, which federal judges were required to follow. The sentencing commission was given the task of developing structured sentencing guidelines to reduce disparity, promote consistency and uniformity, and increase fairness and equity in sentencing.

The guidelines established by the commission took effect in November 1987 but quickly became embroiled in a series of legal disputes, some of which challenged Congress's authority to form the Sentencing Commission. In January 1989, in the case of *Mistretta* v. *U.S.,*[28] the U.S. Supreme Court held that Congress had acted appropriately in establishing the Sentencing Commission and that the guidelines developed by the commission could be applied in federal cases nationwide. The federal Sentencing Commission continues to meet at least once a year to review the effectiveness of the guidelines it created. Visit the U.S. Sentencing Commission via Web Extra 11–3 at cjtoday.com.

## Federal Guideline Provisions

As originally established, federal sentencing guidelines specified a sentencing range from which judges had to choose. If a particular case had "atypical features," judges were allowed to depart

---

**voluntary/advisory sentencing guidelines**

Recommended sentencing policies that are not required by law.

**presumptive sentencing**

A model of criminal punishment that meets the following conditions: (1) The appropriate sentence for an offender convicted of a specific charge is presumed to fall within a range of sentences authorized by sentencing guidelines that are adopted by a legislatively created sentencing body, usually a sentencing commission. (2) Sentencing judges are expected to sentence within the range or to provide written justification for departure. (3) There is a mechanism for review, usually appellate, of any departure from the guidelines.

**aggravating circumstances**

Circumstances relating to the commission of a crime that make it more grave than the average instance of that crime.

**mitigating circumstances**

Circumstances relating to the commission of a crime that may be considered to reduce the blameworthiness of the defendant.

**truth in sentencing**

A close correspondence between the sentence imposed on an offender and the time actually served in prison.[iii]

## CJ TODAY EXHIBIT 11–1

### Aggravating and Mitigating Circumstances

Listed here are typical aggravating and mitigating circumstances that judges may consider in arriving at sentencing decisions in presumptive sentencing jurisdictions.

#### AGGRAVATING CIRCUMSTANCES

- The defendant induced others to participate in the commission of the offense.
- The offense was especially heinous, atrocious, or cruel.
- The defendant was armed with or used a deadly weapon during the crime.
- The defendant committed the offense to avoid or prevent a lawful arrest or to escape from custody.
- The offense was committed for hire.
- The offense was committed against a current or former law enforcement or correctional officer while engaged in the performance of official duties or because of the past exercise of official duties.
- The defendant took advantage of a position of trust or confidence to commit the offense.

#### MITIGATING CIRCUMSTANCES

- The defendant has no record of criminal convictions punishable by more than 60 days of imprisonment.
- The defendant has made substantial or full restitution.
- The defendant has been a person of good character or has had a good reputation in the community.
- The defendant aided in the apprehension of another felon or testified truthfully on behalf of the prosecution.
- The defendant acted under strong provocation, or the victim was a voluntary participant in the criminal activity or otherwise consented to it.
- The offense was committed under duress, coercion, threat, or compulsion that was insufficient to constitute a defense but that significantly reduced the defendant's culpability.
- At the time of the offense, the defendant was suffering from a mental or physical condition that was insufficient to constitute a defense but that significantly reduced the defendant's culpability.

from the guidelines. Departures were generally expected only in the presence of aggravating or mitigating circumstances—a number of which are specified in the guidelines.[29] Aggravating circumstances may include the possession of a weapon during the commission of a crime, the degree of criminal involvement (whether the defendant was a leader or a follower in the criminal activity), and extreme psychological injury to the victim. Punishments also increase when a defendant violates a position of public or private trust, uses special skills to commit or conceal offenses, or has a criminal history. Defendants who express remorse, cooperate with authorities, or willingly make restitution may have their sentences reduced under the guidelines. Any departure from the guidelines may, however, become the basis for appellate review concerning the reasonableness of the sentence imposed, and judges who deviate from the guidelines were originally required to provide written reasons for doing so.

Federal sentencing guidelines are built around a table containing 43 rows, each corresponding to one offense level. The penalties associated with each level overlap those of the levels above and below to discourage unnecessary litigation. A person convicted of a crime involving $11,000, for example, is unlikely to receive a penalty substantially greater than if the amount had been somewhat less than $10,000—a sharp contrast to the old system. A change of six levels roughly doubles the sentence imposed under the guidelines, regardless of the level at which one starts. Because of their matrix-like quality, federal sentencing provisions have been referred to as *structured.* The federal sentencing table is available at Web Extra 11–4 at cjtoday.com.

**WEB EXTRA**

The sentencing table also contains six rows corresponding to the criminal history category into which an offender falls. Criminal history categories are determined on a point basis. Offenders earn points for previous convictions. Each prior sentence of imprisonment for more than one year and one month counts as three points. Two points are assigned for each prior prison sentence over six months or if the defendant committed the offense while on probation, parole, or work release. The system also assigns points for other types of previous convictions and for offenses committed less than two years after release from imprisonment. Points are added to determine the criminal history category into which an offender falls. Thirteen points or more are required for the highest category. At each offense level, sentences in the highest criminal history category are generally two to three times as severe as for the lowest category.

## Supreme Court Transforms Federal Sentencing Guidelines

The Supreme Court recently transformed federal criminal sentencing by restoring to judges much of the discretion that Congress took away 21 years ago when it put sentencing guidelines in place and told judges to follow them.

The guidelines, intended to make sentences more uniform, should be treated as merely advisory to cure a constitutional deficiency in the system, the court held in an unusual two-part decision produced by two coalitions of justices.

In the first part, five justices declared that the current guidelines system violated defendants' rights to trial by jury by giving judges the power to make factual findings that increased sentences beyond the maximum that the jury's findings alone would support.

That portion of the opinion had been widely anticipated, growing directly out of a similar conclusion the same five justices—John Paul Stevens, Antonin Scalia, David H. Souter, Clarence Thomas and Ruth Bader Ginsburg—reached last June in invalidating the sentencing guidelines system in the state of Washington.

The real question hanging over the case, which the court granted on an expedited basis over the summer and heard in October 2004 on the opening day of its new term, was how the justices would solve the problem.

So it was the second part of the decision—the remedy—that was the surprise and that will shape the continuing debate over sentencing policy. With Justice Ginsburg joining the four justices who dissented from the first part—Stephen G. Breyer, Sandra Day O'Connor, Anthony M. Kennedy and Chief Justice William H. Rehnquist—a separate coalition said the problem could be fixed if the guidelines were treated as discretionary rather than mandatory.

From now on, Justice Breyer said, writing for the majority in this portion of the decision, judges "must consult" the guidelines and "take them into account" in imposing sentences. But at the end of the day the guidelines will be advisory only, with sentences to be reviewed on appeal for "reasonableness." Lawmakers and legal experts predicted Wednesday that the court's decision would renew the struggle between Congress and the judiciary for control over sentencing. On Capitol Hill, some members of Congress made it clear that they were bracing for a fight over how much discretion federal judges should have.

The decision leaves many unanswered questions and much work for the federal courts of appeals. It is in the appeals courts that its real meaning will emerge, as those courts handle sentencing appeals and build a body of law evaluating the "reasonableness" of sentences.

Thousands of federal defendants who have been sentenced since the decision in the Washington State case have effectively been in limbo awaiting clarification of the situation. People whose sentences are still on appeal will be immediately affected by the ruling.

The Albert Bryan Federal Courthouse in Alexandria, Virginia. In 2005, the U.S. Supreme Court transformed criminal sentencing in the federal court system when it held that fact-finding done by a judge under the federal sentencing guidelines violated a defendant's rights to have a jury determine, beyond a reasonable doubt, all the essential facts that relate to the severity of a sentence.

*© Alan Schein Photography, Corbis*

The guidelines provide judges with a grid, with the offense for which the defendant has been convicted on one axis and the offender's history and other details on another. The grid gives the judges a range of possible sentences and the system instructs them to go above that range if they make certain factual findings. It was this mandatory aspect of the system that was at issue in the case.

The remedy devised by Justice Breyer's five-member majority had not been proposed by any party, although the Justice Department suggested a form of advisory guidelines as a fallback position to its defense of the system's constitutionality. Christopher A. Wray, an assistant attorney general, said Wednesday that the department was relieved to see the guidelines remain in place but concerned that sentencing disparities might increase now that they were no longer mandatory.

The decision, *United States* v. *Booker,* No. 04-104, had its roots in a series of intensely disputed sentencing rulings that began with *Apprendi* v. *New Jersey* in 2000. In a series of cases, the court has held that given the Sixth Amendment right to trial by jury, judges cannot impose sentences beyond the "prescribed statutory maximum" unless the facts supporting such an increase are found by a jury beyond a reasonable doubt.

Under that analysis, the constitutional cloud over federal criminal sentencing derived from the mandatory nature of the guidelines, which instruct judges to consider various facts, like a defendant's leadership role in a criminal enterprise, and to increase sentences beyond the guidelines accordingly. The court made it clear in the Washington State case last June that the top of an ordinary guideline range was the equivalent of a statutory maximum.

*(continued)*

## CJ NEWS (continued)

But if judges simply exercise their traditional sentencing discretion, advised by guidelines but not bound by them, the defendant's Sixth Amendment right is not implicated, a conclusion on which all nine justices agreed on Wednesday. In other words, as judges' flexibility grows, defendants' Sixth Amendment protections shrink.

The dispute on the court was not over that paradoxical proposition, but rather over how Congress would have chosen to proceed if it had known of the Sixth Amendment issue when it put the guidelines system in place in the Sentencing Reform Act of 1984. When the Supreme Court finds a statute unconstitutional, the court's next step is to see whether there is a solution consistent with the legislators' original intent.

Dissenting from the remedy portion of the decision, Justice Stevens, with Justices Souter, Scalia and Thomas, said in effect that the last thing Congress would have done would be to give judges back the power that the guidelines were intended to constrain.

Rather, the dissenters said, if the problem was a violation of the right to trial by jury, the solution also lay with the jury: to require prosecutors to make indictments more specific and to present to the jury any factor that would increase a sentence beyond the ordinary range. Justice Stevens said that in avoiding this solution and instead changing the nature of the guidelines themselves, it was "clear that the court's creative remedy is an exercise of legislative, rather than judicial, power," one that "violates the tradition of judicial restraint."

Justice Breyer insisted, however, that his was the solution that "would deviate less radically from Congress's intended system." He said that to make jury findings the basis for sentencing would shift too much power to prosecutors and "undermine the sentencing statute's basic aim of ensuring similar sentences for those who have committed similar crimes in similar ways."

Justice Breyer spoke with some authority; as chief counsel of the Senate Judiciary Committee in the 1970's, he played a leading role in the passage of the Sentencing Reform Act and later was a member of the United States Sentencing Commission. He had been on the losing side of the *Apprendi* decision and the subsequent rulings.

Though the outcome was not one he would have wished—he argued in dissent from the first part of the decision that guidelines were different than statutes and that the analysis of the earlier rulings should not apply—the decision was in some ways a personal triumph. The Sentencing Commission remains intact and the guidelines are still on the books, with the presumption that most judges will follow them most of the time.

The mystery in the case was Justice Ginsburg, who joined the Stevens group, as she consistently has, in applying the Sixth Amendment to the guidelines. She then provided Justice Breyer with his fifth vote to preserve the system's architecture. She did not write a separate opinion to explain herself. The court took considerably longer on the case than had been expected. Many people thought a decision would be out by Thanksgiving, and it is possible that Justice Ginsburg's vote, and therefore the outcome, was in play until late in the process.

The portion of Justice Breyer's opinion that dealt with appeals had the effect of overturning a 2003 congressional amendment to the sentencing law that instructed appeals courts to give no deference to the decisions of trial judges when reviewing sentences shorter than those called for by the guidelines. That provision, known as the Feeney Amendment for its sponsor, Representative Tom Feeney, Republican of Florida, was an expression of congressional impatience with the judiciary and in turn angered many federal judges.

It was not immediately clear whether Freddie J. Booker and Ducan Fanfan, the two defendants in the case before the court, would benefit from the ruling. Mr. Booker, convicted in Federal District Court in Madison, Wisconsin, of possessing 50 grams of cocaine base, received an extra 8 years on a 22-year sentence when the judge found that he had distributed 10 times that amount.

After Mr. Fanfan was found guilty by a jury in Portland, Maine, of distributing 500 grams of cocaine, the judge refused the government's request to increase the sentence, predicting that the Supreme Court would soon find the guidelines unconstitutional. Both defendants will now go back to district court for possible resentencing, with an appeal available to both sides.

For the latest in crime and justice news, visit the Talk Justice news feed at http://www.crimenews.info.

Defendants may also move into the highest criminal history category by virtue of being designated a career offender. Under the sentencing guidelines, a defendant is a career offender if "(1) the defendant was at least 18 years old at the time of the . . . offense, (2) the . . . offense is a crime of violence or trafficking in a controlled substance, and (3) the defendant has at least two prior felony convictions of either a crime of violence or a controlled substance offense."[30]

According to the U.S. Supreme Court, an offender may be adjudged a career offender in a single hearing, even when previous convictions are lacking. In *Deal* v. *U.S.* (1993),[31] the defendant, Thomas Lee Deal, was convicted in a single proceeding of six counts of carrying and using a firearm during a series of bank robberies in the Houston, Texas, area. A federal district court sentenced him to 105 years in prison as a career offender—5 years for the first count and 20 years for each of the five other counts, with sentences to run consecutively. In the words of the Supreme Court, "We see no reason why [the defendant should not receive such a sentence], simply because he managed to evade detection, prosecution, and conviction for the first five offenses and was ultimately tried on all six in a single proceeding."

## Plea Bargaining Under the Guidelines

Plea bargaining plays a major role in the federal judicial system. Approximately 90% of all federal sentences are the result of guilty pleas,[32] and the large majority of those stem from plea negotiations. In the words of former Sentencing Commission Chairman William W. Wilkins, Jr., "With respect to plea bargaining, the Commission has proceeded cautiously. . . . The Commission did not believe it wise to stand the federal criminal justice system on its head by making too drastic and too sudden a change in these practices."[33]

Although the commission allowed plea bargaining to continue, it does require that the agreement (1) be fully disclosed in the record of the court (unless there is an overriding and demonstrable reason why it should not be) and (2) detail the actual conduct of the offense. Under these requirements, defendants are no longer able to hide the actual nature of their offense behind a substitute plea. The thrust of the federal rules concerning plea bargaining is to reduce the veil of secrecy that had previously surrounded the process. Information on the decision-making process itself is available to victims, the media, and the public.

In 1996, in the case of *Melendez* v. *U.S.*,[34] the U.S. Supreme Court held that a government motion requesting that a trial judge deviate from the federal sentencing guidelines as part of a cooperative plea agreement does not permit imposition of a sentence below a statutory minimum specified by law. In other words, under *Melendez*, while federal judges could depart from the guidelines, they could not accept plea bargains that would have resulted in sentences lower than the minimum required by law for a particular type of offense.

## The Legal Environment of Structured Sentencing

A crucial critique of aggravating factors and their use in presumptive sentencing schemes was offered by the U.S. Supreme Court in 2000 in the case of *Apprendi* v. *New Jersey*.[35] In *Apprendi*, the Court questioned the fact-finding authority of judges in making sentencing decisions, ruling that other than the fact of a prior conviction, any fact that increases the penalty for a crime beyond the prescribed statutory maximum is, in effect, an element of the crime, which must be submitted to a jury and proved beyond a reasonable doubt. The case involved Charles Apprendi, a New Jersey defendant who pleaded guilty to unlawfully possessing a firearm—an offense that carried a prison term of five to ten years under state law. Before sentence was imposed, however, the judge found that Apprendi had fired a number of shots into the home of an African-American family living in his neighborhood and concluded that he had done so to frighten the family and convince them to move. The judge held that statements made by Apprendi allowed the offense to be classified as a hate crime, which required a longer prison term under the sentencing enhancement provision of New Jersey's hate crimes statute than did the weapons offense to which Apprendi had confessed. The Supreme Court, in overturning the judge's finding and sentence, took issue with the fact that after Apprendi pleaded guilty, an enhanced sentence was imposed without the benefit of a jury-based fact-finding process. The high court ruled that "under the Due Process Clause of the Fifth Amendment and the notice and jury trial guarantees of the Sixth Amendment, any fact (other than prior conviction) that increases the maximum penalty for a crime must be charged in an indictment, submitted to a jury, and proven beyond a reasonable doubt."

The *Apprendi* case essentially says that *requiring sentencing judges to consider facts not proven to a jury violates the federal Constitution.* It raised the question of whether judges anywhere could legitimately deviate from established sentencing guidelines or apply sentence enhancements based on judicial determinations of aggravating factors that deviate from those guidelines—especially when such deviations are based on findings of fact that might otherwise be made by a jury.[36]

In the 2002 case of *Harris* v. *U.S.*,[37] the Court sidestepped the issue when it found that the brandishing and discharging of a weapon under federal law are sentencing factors to be found by a judge—and not elements of an offense to be found by a jury. The sentence imposed in *Harris* did not extend beyond the statutory maximum for the crime of which the defendant was convicted, and the Court reasoned that incremental changes in the minimum penalty that are specified in the law "are precisely what one would expect to see in provisions meant to identify matters for the sentencing judge's consideration."

A Brief History of Presumptive Sentencing

Similarly, in the case of *U.S.* v. *Cotton* (2002),[38] the Court found that sentences imposed by a federal judge were not improper even though the judge based those sentences on a drug quantity not alleged in the original indictment brought against the defendants. The *Cotton* defendants had been charged with conspiracy to distribute and to possess with intent to distribute a "detectable amount" of cocaine and cocaine base in the city of Baltimore. Under federal law, the penalty for such offenses is "not more than 20 years."[39] After the jury returned a finding of guilt, the judge made an independent finding of drug quantity (more than 500 grams of cocaine base) and then imposed enhanced penalties (up to life) as allowed under federal law. The judge's finding, the Court concluded, was based on "overwhelming and uncontroverted evidence" that the defendants "were involved in a vast drug conspiracy."

In 2004, in the important case of *Blakely* v. *Washington*,[40] the U.S. Supreme Court effectively invalidated any sentencing schema that allow judges rather than juries to determine any factor that increases a criminal sentence, except for prior convictions. The Court found that because the facts supporting Blakely's increased sentence were neither admitted by the defendant himself nor found by a jury, the sentence violated the Sixth Amendment right to trial by jury. The *Blakely* decision required that the sentencing laws of eight states be rewritten.

Finally, in 2005, in the combined cases of *U.S.* v. *Booker*[41] and *U.S.* v. *Fanfan*,[42] attention turned to the constitutionality of federal sentencing practices that relied on extra-verdict determinations of fact in the application of sentencing enhancements. In *Booker*, the U.S. Supreme Court issued what some have called an "extraordinary opinion,"[43] which actually encompasses two separate decisions. The combined cases brought two issues before the Court: (1) whether fact-finding done by judges under federal sentencing guidelines violates the Sixth Amendment right to trial by jury; and (2) if so, whether the guidelines are themselves unconstitutional. As in the preceding cases discussed in this section, the Court found that, on the first question, defendant Freddie Booker's drug-trafficking sentence had been improperly enhanced under the guidelines on the basis of facts found solely by a judge. In other words, the Sixth Amendment right to trial by jury is violated where, under a mandatory guidelines system, a sentence is increased because of an enhancement based on facts found by the judge that were neither admitted by the defendant nor found by the jury.[44] Consequently, Booker's sentence was ruled unconstitutional and invalidated. On the second question, the Court reached a compromise and did not strike down the federal guidelines. Instead, it held that the guidelines could be considered by federal judges during sentencing but that they could no longer be considered mandatory. In effect, the decision in *Booker* and *Fanfan* turned the federal sentencing guidelines on their head, making them merely advisory and giving federal judges wide latitude in imposing punishments. While federal judges must still take the guidelines into consideration in reaching sentencing decisions, they do not have to follow them. Early indications, however, are that federal judges are still following the guidelines to a great degree.[45] It is now up to Congress to reconsider federal sentencing law in light of *Booker*—a process that is under way as this book goes to press. In the meantime, some expect the federal courts to be flooded with inmates appealing their sentences.

# Mandatory Sentencing

**Mandatory sentencing**, another form of structured sentencing, deserves special mention.[46] Mandatory sentencing is just what its name implies: a structured sentencing scheme that mandates clearly enumerated punishments for specific offenses or for habitual offenders convicted of a series of crimes. Mandatory sentencing, because it is truly *mandatory*, differs from presumptive sentencing, which allows at least a limited amount of judicial discretion within ranges established by published guidelines. Some mandatory sentencing laws require only modest mandatory prison terms (for example, three years for armed robbery), while others are much more far-reaching.

Typical of far-reaching mandatory sentencing schemes are "three-strikes" laws, discussed in CJ Today Exhibit 11–2. Three-strikes laws (and, in some jurisdictions, two-strikes laws) require mandatory sentences (sometimes life in prison without the possibility of parole) for offenders convicted of a third serious felony. Such mandatory sentencing enhancements are aimed at deterring known and potentially violent offenders and are intended to incapacitate convicted criminals through long-term incarceration.

Singer Courtney Love being escorted into the Beverly Hills, California, courthouse by a Los Angeles County bailiff. In 2005 Love was sentenced to three years probation and ordered to undergo anger management counseling, pay fines, submit to random drug tests, and perform 100 hours of community service after she pled "no contest" to assault charges. The charges were related to an incident at the home of an ex-boyfriend. Love also pled guilty to a drug charge stemming from an earlier break-in at the same residence.

*AP Wide World Photos*

Three-strikes laws impose longer prison terms than most earlier mandatory minimum sentencing laws. California's three-strikes law, for example, requires that offenders who are convicted of a violent crime and who have had two prior convictions serve a minimum of 25 years in prison. The law doubled prison terms for offenders convicted of a second violent felony.[47] Three-strikes laws also vary in breadth. The laws of some jurisdictions stipulate that both of the prior convictions and the current one be for violent felonies; others require only that the prior convictions be for violent felonies. Some three-strikes laws count only prior adult convictions, while others permit consideration of juvenile crimes.

By passing mandatory sentencing laws, legislators convey the message that certain crimes are deemed especially grave and that people who commit them deserve, and should expect, harsh sanctions. These laws are sometimes passed in response to public outcries following heinous or well-publicized crimes.

Research findings on the impact of mandatory sentencing laws on the criminal justice system have been summarized by British criminologist Michael Tonry.[48] Tonry found that under mandatory sentencing, officials tend to make earlier and more selective arrest, charging, and **diversion** decisions. They also tend to bargain less and to bring more cases to trial. Specifically, Tonry found the following: (1) Criminal justice officials and practitioners (police, lawyers, and judges) exercise discretion to avoid the application of laws they consider unduly harsh. (2) Arrest rates for target crimes tend to decline soon after mandatory sentencing laws take effect. (3) Dismissal and diversion rates increase during the early stages of case processing after mandatory sentencing laws become effective. (4) For defendants whose cases are not dismissed, plea bargain rates decline and trial rates increase. (5) For convicted defendants, sentencing delays increase. (6) When the effects of declining arrests, indictments, and convictions are taken into account, the enactment of mandatory sentencing laws has little impact on the probability that offenders will be imprisoned. (7) Sentences become longer and more severe. Mandatory sentencing laws may also occasionally result in unduly harsh punishments for marginal offenders who nonetheless meet the minimum requirements for sentencing under such laws.

**diversion**

The official suspension of criminal or juvenile proceedings against an alleged offender at any point after a recorded justice system intake, but before the entering of a judgment, and referral of that person to a treatment or care program administered by a nonjustice or private agency. Also, release without referral.

## CJ TODAY EXHIBIT 11-2

### Three Strikes and You're Out: A Brief History of the "Get Tough on Crime" Movement

In the spring of 1994, California legislators passed the state's now-famous "three strikes and you're out" bill. Amid much fanfare, Governor Pete Wilson signed the "three-strikes" measure into law, calling it "the toughest and most sweeping crime bill in California history."[1]

California's law, which is retroactive in that it counts offenses committed before the date the legislation was signed, requires a sentence of 25 years to life for three-time felons with convictions for two or more serious or violent prior offenses. Criminal offenders facing a "second strike" can receive up to double the normal sentence for their most recent offense. Parole consideration is not available until at least 80% of the sentence has been served.

Today, about half of the states have passed three-strikes legislation, and other states may be considering it. At the federal level, the Violent Crime Control and Law Enforcement Act of 1994 contains a three-strikes provision that mandates life imprisonment for federal criminals convicted of three violent felonies or drug offenses.

Questions remain, however, about the effectiveness of three-strikes legislation, and many are concerned about its impact on the justice system. One year after it was signed into law, the California three-strikes initiative was evaluated by the RAND Corporation.[2] RAND researchers found that in the first year, more than 5,000 defendants were convicted and sentenced under the law's provisions. The large majority of those sentenced, however, had committed nonviolent crimes, causing critics of the law to argue that it is too broad. Eighty-four percent of two-strikes convictions and nearly 77% of three-strikes convictions resulted from nonviolent drug or property crimes. A similar 1997 study of three-strikes laws in 22 states, conducted by the Campaign for an Effective Crime Policy (CECP), concluded that such legislation results in clogged court systems and crowded correctional facilities while encouraging three-time felons to take dramatic risks to avoid capture.[3] A 1998 study found that only California and Georgia were making widespread use of three-strikes laws.[4] Other states, the study found, have narrowly written laws that are applicable to repeat offenders only in rare circumstances.

A 2001 study of the original California legislation and its consequences concluded that three-strikes laws are overrated.[5] According to the study, which was conducted by the Washington, D.C.-based Sentencing Project, "California's three-strikes law has increased the number and severity of sentences for nonviolent offenders—and contributed to the aging of the prison population—but has had no significant effect on the state's decline in crime." The study found that declines in California crime rates that are often attributed to the legislation are consistent with nationwide declines in the rate of crime and would mostly have occurred without the law. "Crime had been declining for several years prior to the enactment of the three-strikes law, and what's happening in California is very consistent with what's been happening nationally, including in states with no three-strikes law," said Marc Mauer, an author of the study.

Supporters of three-strikes laws argue that those convicted under them are career criminals who will be denied the opportunity to commit more violent crimes. "The real story here is the girl somewhere that did not get raped," said Mike Reynolds, a Fresno, California, photographer whose 18-year-old daughter was killed by a paroled felon. "The real story is the robbery that did not happen," he added.[6]

Practically speaking, California's three-strikes law has had a dramatic impact on the state's criminal justice system. By 1999, more than 40,000 people had been sentenced under the law. But the law has its critics. "'Three strikes and you're out' sounds great to a lot of people," says Alan Schuman, president of the American Probation and Parole Association. "But no one will cop a plea when it gets to the third time around. We will have more trials, and this whole country works on plea bargaining and pleading guilty, not jury trials," Schuman said at a meeting of the association.[7] According to RAND, full enforcement of the law could cost as much as $5.5 billion annually—or $300 per California taxpayer.

Researchers at RAND conclude that while California's sweeping three-strikes legislation could cut serious adult crime by as much as one-third throughout the state, the high cost of enforcing the law may keep it from ever being fully implemented. In 1996, the California three-strikes controversy became even more complicated following a decision by the state supreme court (in *People* v. *Superior Court of San Diego—Romero*[8]) that California judges retain the discretion to reduce three-strikes sentences and to refuse to count previous convictions at sentencing "in furtherance of justice."

In 2003, however, in two separate cases, the U.S. Supreme Court upheld the three-strikes California convictions of Gary Ewing and Leandro Andrade in California.[9] Ewing, who had four prior felony convictions, had received a 25-year-to-life sentence following his conviction for felony grand theft of three golf clubs. Andrade, who also had a long record, was sentenced to 50 years in prison for two petty theft convictions.[10] In writing for the Court in the *Ewing* case, Justice Sandra Day O'Connor noted that states should be able to decide when repeat offenders "must be isolated from society . . . to protect the public safety," even when nonserious crimes trigger the lengthy sentence. In deciding these two cases, both of which were based on Eighth Amendment claims, the Court found that it is *not* cruel and unusual punishment to impose a possible life term for a nonviolent felony when the defendant has a history of serious or violent convictions.

In 2004, Californians voted down Proposition 66, a ballot initiative that would have changed the state's three-strikes law so that only specified serious or violent crimes could be counted as third strikes. Passage of the proposition would also have meant that only previous convictions for violent or serious felonies, brought and tried separately, would have qualified for second- and third-strike sentence increases.

## CJ TODAY EXHIBIT 11-2 *(continued)*

California's three-strikes law remains firmly in place. In its current form, it punishes anyone who commits a third felony, regardless of its severity, with a mandatory sentence of 25 years to life if the first two felonies were violent or serious.

[1]Michael Miller, "California Gets 'Three Strikes' Anti-Crime Bill," Reuters wire service, March 7, 1994.

[2]Dion Nissenbaum, "Three-Strikes First Year Debated," United Press International wire service, northern edition, March 6, 1995.

[3]Campaign for an Effective Crime Policy, *The Impact of Three Strikes and You're Out Laws: What Have We Learned?* (Washington, DC: Author, 1997).

[4]Walter Dickey and Pam Stiebs Hollenhorst, "Three-Strikes Laws: Massive Impact in California and Georgia, Little Elsewhere," *Overcrowded Times,* Vol. 9, No. 6 (December 1998), pp. 2–8.

[5]Tamar Lewin, "Three-Strikes Law Is Overrated in California, Study Finds," *New York Times,* August 23, 2001.

[6]Bruce Smith, "Crime Solutions," Associated Press wire service, January 11, 1995.

[7]Ryan S. King and Marc Mauer, *Aging behind Bars: "Three Strikes" Seven Years Later* (Washington, DC: Sentencing Project, August 2001).

[8]*People* v. *Superior Court of San Diego—Romero,* 13 Cal. 4th 497, 917 P.2d 628 (1996).

[9]*Ewing* v. *California,* 538 U.S. 11 (2003); and *Lockyer* v. *Andrade,* 538 U.S. 63 (2003).

[10]Under California law, a person who commits petty theft can be charged with a felony if he or she has prior felony convictions. The charge is known as "petty theft with prior convictions." Andrade's actual sentence was two 25-year prison terms to be served consecutively.

In an analysis of federal sentencing guidelines, other researchers found that African-Americans receive longer sentences than whites, not because of differential treatment by judges but because they constitute the large majority of those convicted of trafficking in crack cocaine,[49] a crime Congress has singled out for especially harsh mandatory penalties. This pattern can be seen as constituting a "disparity in results," and partly for this reason, in 1999 the U.S. Sentencing Commission recommended to Congress that it eliminate the legal distinction between crack and regular cocaine for purposes of sentencing (a recommendation that Congress rejected).

> **Punishment, that is justice for the unjust.**
>
> —Saint Augustine (A.D. 354–430)

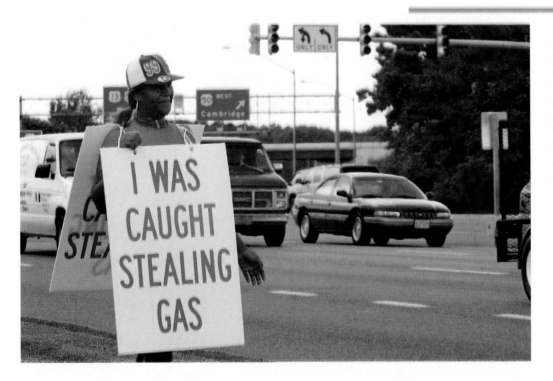

Innovative judges sometimes make use of creative sentences in an attempt to deter offenders from future law violations. Here, Sherelee Purnell, 18, of Salisbury, Maryland, walks along the street in front of a Tiger Mart gas station wearing a sign declaring her offense. On July 30, 2004, Purnell drove away from the station without paying after pumping 2.78 gallons of fuel into her vehicle.

*AP Wide World Photos*

# Innovations in Sentencing

> Legislatures define crimes in terms of the facts that are their essential elements, and Constitutional guarantees attach to these facts. . . . Yet not all facts affecting the defendant's punishment are elements. After the accused is convicted, the judge may impose a sentence within a range provided by statute, basing it on various facts relating to the defendant and the manner in which the offense was committed.
>
> — *Harris* v. *U.S.*[vi]

In an ever-growing number of cases, innovative judges in certain jurisdictions have begun to use the wide discretion in sentencing available to them to impose truly unique punishments. In 2004, for example, 18-year-old Sherelle Purnell was ordered by county judge D. William Simpson to spend three hours walking along the grassy strip between a convenience store and a busy highway in Salisbury, Maryland, wearing a sign that read "I was caught stealing gas."[50] Purnell had been caught on camera by a video surveillance device as she drove away without paying for 2.78 gallons of gas from a Tiger Mart. In Memphis, Tennessee, Judge Joe Brown escorted burglary victims to thieves' homes, inviting them to take whatever they wanted.[51] An Arkansas judge made shoplifters walk in front of the stores they stole from, carrying signs describing their crimes. And in California a purse snatcher was ordered to wear noisy tap dancing shoes whenever he went out in public.[52]

Faced with prison overcrowding, high incarceration costs, and public calls for retribution, other judges have used shaming strategies to deter wrongdoers. At least one Florida court began ordering those convicted of drunk driving to put a "Convicted DUI" sticker on their license plates. In 2001, Coshocton County (Ohio) municipal judge David Hostetler ordered two men to parade down the main street of their hometown dressed as women. The men, Jason Householder, 23, and John Stockum, 21, had been convicted of criminal damage for throwing beer bottles at a woman. The judge told the men that they could either comply with his order or go to jail for 60 days. He also fined them $250 each. Similarly, a few years ago Boston courts began ordering men convicted of sexual solicitation to spend time sweeping streets in Chinatown, an area known for prostitution. The public was invited to watch men sentenced to the city's "John Sweep" program clean up streets and alleyways littered with used condoms and sexual paraphernalia.

There is considerable support in criminal justice literature for shaming as a crime-reduction strategy. Australian criminologist John Braithwaite, for example, found shaming to be a particularly effective strategy because, he said, it holds the potential to enhance moral awareness among offenders, thereby building conscience and increasing inner control.[53] Dan Kahan, a professor at the University of Chicago Law School, points out that "shame supplies the main motive why people obey the law, not so much because they're afraid of formal sanctions, but because they care what people think about them."[54]

Whether public shaming will continue to grow in popularity as an alternative sentencing strategy is unclear. What is clear, however, is that the American public and an ever-growing number of judicial officials are now looking for workable alternatives to traditional sentencing options.

## Questions about Alternative Sanctions

As prison populations continue to rise, alternative sentencing strategies are likely to become increasingly attractive. Many questions must be answered, however, before most alternative sanctions can be employed with confidence. These questions were succinctly stated in a RAND Corporation study authored by Joan Petersilia.[55] Unfortunately, although the questions can be listed, few definitive answers are available yet. Here are some of the questions Petersilia poses:

- Do alternative sentencing programs threaten public safety?
- How should program participants be selected?
- What are the long-term effects of community sanctions on people assigned to these programs?
- Are alternative sanctions cost-effective?
- Who should pay the bill for alternative sanctions?
- Who should manage stringent community-based sanctions?
- How should program outcomes be judged?
- What kinds of offenders benefit most from alternative sanctions?

The Sentencing Environment

# The Presentence Investigation

Before imposing sentence, a judge may request information on the background of a convicted defendant. This is especially true in indeterminate sentencing jurisdictions, where judges retain considerable discretion in selecting sanctions. Traditional wisdom has held that certain factors increase the likelihood of rehabilitation and reduce the need for lengthy prison terms. These fac-

## CJ FUTURES

### Is Chemical Castration a Valid Sentencing Option?

In 2000, convicted Florida sex offender Shannon Coleman circumvented a 21-year prison term by agreeing to undergo chemical castration. Coleman, a self-described sex addict, had used the Internet to contact two Florida girls, ages 12 and 15. He admitted to visiting the 12-year-old at her house, where he fondled her and then masturbated. He had sex with the 15-year-old after she invited him to her house. Coleman and his lawyer asked the judge handling the case to exercise his discretion under Florida's 1997 sex offender law, which gives judges the discretion to order people convicted of sexual battery to undergo drug treatment to stop and/or reduce testosterone production.

The first chemical castration law in the United States was enacted in California in 1996, signed into law by then-Governor Pete Wilson. The California statute requires regular hormone injections for twice-convicted child molesters (where the victim is under 13 years of age) upon their release from prison. Under the law, judges can also mandate injections for first offenders. Treatment is to continue until state authorities determine that it is no longer necessary.

Most chemical castration laws require convicted offenders to receive weekly injections of synthetic female hormones known as Depo-Provera (medroxy-progesterone acetate) and Depo-Lupron. The laboratory-manufactured chemicals reduce blood levels of the sex hormone testosterone and are believed to lower the male sex drive.

To date, California, Florida, Georgia, Texas, and Montana have chemical castration legislation in place, and some other states are considering enacting chemical castration laws. If chemical castration survives continuing court challenges, it may establish itself in the mid-twenty-first century as a widely used form of alternative sentencing. Opposition to chemical castration laws, however, is plentiful. After the California law was enacted, for example, a spokeswoman for the American Civil Liberties Union (ACLU) claimed that the legislation mandates an unproven remedy for child molestation and is therefore a violation of civil rights. "There is no evidence, absolutely no evidence, that chemical castration will alleviate the problem," said Ann Bradley, a Los Angeles ACLU spokeswoman. "We see this as a violation of prisoners' civil liberties," she said.

Proponents of the legislation, on the other hand, cite studies in Canada and Europe in which repeat offender rates of more than 80% were reduced to less than 4% among criminals treated with Depo-Provera. "I would have to say to the ACLU that there is no right to molest a child," Governor Wilson replied.

*References:* Kevin Giordano, "The Chemical Knife," Salon.com, March 1, 2002 Web posted at http://dir.salon.com/health/feature/2000/03/01/castration/index.html; "Castration 1998–2001." Web posted at http://members.aol.com/USCCCN/FAQ-castration.index.html; and Dave Lesher, "Molester Castration Measure Signed: California Becomes the First State to Require That Offenders Get Periodic Injections to Suppress Sex Drive," *Los Angeles Times*, September 18, 1996.

---

tors include a good job record, satisfactory educational attainment, strong family ties, church attendance, no prior arrests for violent offenses, and psychological stability.

Information about a defendant's background often comes to the judge in the form of a **presentence investigation** (PSI) report. The task of preparing presentence reports usually falls to the probation or parole office. Presentence reports take one of three forms: (1) a detailed written report on the defendant's personal and criminal history, including an assessment of present conditions in the defendant's life (often called the *long form*); (2) an abbreviated written report summarizing the information most likely to be useful in a sentencing decision (the *short form*); and (3) a verbal report to the court made by the investigating officer based on field notes but structured according to established categories. A presentence report is much like a résumé, except that it focuses on what might be regarded as negative as well as positive life experiences.

The data on which a presentence report is based come from a variety of sources. The Federal Bureau of Investigation's National Crime Information Center (NCIC), begun in 1967, contains computerized information on people wanted for criminal offenses throughout the United States. Individual jurisdictions also maintain criminal records repositories that can provide comprehensive files on the criminal history of those who have been processed by the justice system.

Sometimes the defendant provides much of the information in the presentence report. In this case, efforts must be made to corroborate the defendant's information. Unconfirmed data are generally marked on the report as "defendant-supplied data" or simply "unconfirmed."

In a presentence report, almost all third-party data are subject to ethical and legal considerations. The official records of almost all agencies and organizations, though often an ideal source of information, are protected by state and federal privacy requirements. In particular, the federal Privacy Act of 1974[56] may limit access to these records. Investigators must first check on

> **presentence investigation**
>
> The examination of a convicted offender's background prior to sentencing. Presentence examinations are generally conducted by probation or parole officers and are submitted to sentencing authorities.

> We will not punish a man because he hath offended, but that he may offend no more; nor does punishment ever look to the past, but to the future; for it is not the result of passion, but that the same thing be guarded against in time to come.
>
> —Seneca (4 B.C.–A.D. 65)

the legal availability of all records before requesting them and must receive in writing the defendant's permission to access the records. Other public laws, among them the federal Freedom of Information Act,[57] may make the presentence report available to the defendant, although courts and court officers have generally been held to be exempt from the provision of such statutes.

The final section of a presentence report is usually devoted to the investigating officer's recommendations. A recommendation may be made in favor of probation, split sentencing, a term of imprisonment, or any other sentencing option available in the jurisdiction. Participation in community service programs or in drug or substance abuse programs may be recommended for probationers. Most judges are willing to accept the report writer's recommendation because they recognize the professionalism of presentence investigators and because they know that the investigator may be assigned to supervise the defendant if he or she is sentenced to a community alternative.

Jurisdictions vary in their use of presentence reports. Federal law mandates presentence reports in federal criminal courts and specifies 15 topical areas that each report must cover. The 1984 federal Determinate Sentencing Act directs report writers to include information on the classification of the offense and of the defendant under the offense-level and criminal history categories established by the statute. Some states require presentence reports only in felony cases, and others require them in cases where the defendant faces the possibility of incarceration for six months or more. Other states have no requirement for presentence reports beyond those ordered by a judge.

Report writing, rarely anyone's favorite task, may seriously tax the limited resources of probation agencies. In 2003, officers from the New York City Department of Probation wrote 32,283 presentence investigation reports for adult offenders and 7,150 reports for juvenile offenders, which averages to more than 40 reports per probation officer per month.[58]

# The Victim—Forgotten No Longer

Thanks to a grassroots resurgence of concern for the plight of victims that began in this country in the early 1970s, the sentencing process now frequently includes consideration of the needs of victims and their survivors.[59] In times past, although victims might testify at trial, the criminal justice system frequently downplayed a victim's experience, including the psychological trauma engendered both by having been a victim and by having to endure the criminal proceedings that bring the criminal to justice. That changed in 1982, when the President's Task Force on Victims of Crime gave focus to a burgeoning victims' rights movement and urged the widespread expansion of victim assistance programs during what was then their formative period.[60] Victim assistance programs today offer services in the areas of crisis intervention and follow-up counseling and help victims secure their rights under the law.[61] Following successful prosecution, some victim assistance programs also advise victims in the filing of civil suits to recoup financial losses directly from the offender. In the mid-1990s, the National Institute of Justice conducted a survey of 319 full-service victim assistance programs based in law enforcement agencies and prosecutors' offices.[62] The survey found that "the majority of individuals seeking assistance were victims of domestic assault and the most common assistance they received was information about legal rights." Other common forms of assistance included help in applying for state victim compensation aid and referrals to social service agencies.

About the same time, voters in California approved Proposition 8, a resolution that called for changes in the state's constitution to reflect concern for victims. A continuing goal of victim advocacy groups is an amendment to the U.S. Constitution, which such groups say is needed to provide the same kind of fairness to victims that is routinely accorded to defendants. In the past, for example, the National Victims' Constitutional Amendment Network (NVCAN) sought to add a phrase to the Sixth Amendment: "likewise, the victim, in every criminal prosecution, shall have the right to be present and to be heard at all critical stages of judicial proceedings." Victims' advocacy groups now propose the addition of an entirely new amendment to the U.S. Constitution. Visit one such group via Web Extra 11–5 at cjtoday.com.

In September 1996, a victims' rights constitutional amendment—Senate Joint Resolution 65— was proposed by a bipartisan committee in the U.S. Congress,[63] but problems of wording and terminology prevented its passage. A revised amendment was proposed in 1998,[64] but its wording was too restrictive for it to gain endorsement from victims' organizations.[65] In 1999, a new amendment was proposed by the Senate Judiciary Committee's Subcommittee on the Constitution, Federalism, and Property, but it did not make it to the Senate floor. The U.S. Department of Justice, which had previously supported the measure, reversed its position due to a provision in the pro-

WEB EXTRA

## CJ TODAY EXHIBIT 11-3

### President Bush Calls for Victims' Rights Amendment

In 2002, President George W. Bush announced his support for a constitutional amendment for victims of violent crime. Bush said, "In the year 2000, Americans were victims of millions of crimes. Behind each of these numbers is a terrible trauma, a story of suffering and a story of lost security. Yet the needs of victims are often an afterthought in our criminal justice system. It's not just, it's not fair, and it must change. As we protect the rights of criminals, we must take equal care to protect the rights of the victims."

The president's remarks were made in support of a Senate Joint Resolution offered by Senators Jon Kyl of Arizona and Dianne Feinstein of California. The bill, which has been repeatedly introduced in the past, never garnered the support of President Bill Clinton during the eight years he was in office. The text of the Kyl–Feinstein resolution follows.

Proposing an amendment to the Constitution of the United States to protect the rights of crime victims:

*Resolved by the Senate and the House of Representatives of the United States of America in Congress assembled (two-thirds of each House concurring therein),* That the following article is proposed as an amendment to the Constitution of the United States, which shall be valid for all intents and purposes as part of the Constitution when ratified by the legislatures of three-fourths of the several States within seven years from the date of its submission by the Congress:

#### ARTICLE

Section 1. A victim of a crime of violence, as these terms may be defined by law, shall have the rights:
- to reasonable notice of, and not to be excluded from, any public proceedings relating to the crime;
- to be heard, if present, and to submit a statement at all such proceedings to determine a conditional release from custody, an acceptance of a negotiated plea, or a sentence;

- to the foregoing rights at a parole proceeding that is not public, to the extent those rights are afforded to the convicted offender;
- to reasonable notice of a release or escape from custody relating to the crime;
- to consideration of the interest of the victim that any trial be free from unreasonable delay;
- to an order of restitution from the convicted offender;
- to consideration for the safety of the victim in determining any conditional release from custody relating to the crime; and
- to reasonable notice of the rights established by this article.

Section 2. Only the victim or the victim's lawful representative shall have standing to assert the rights established by this article. Nothing in this article shall provide grounds to stay or continue any trial, reopen any proceeding or invalidate any ruling, except with respect to conditional release or restitution or to provide rights guaranteed by this article in future proceedings, without staying or continuing a trial. Nothing in this article shall give rise to or authorize the creation of a claim for damages against the United States, a State, a political subdivision, or a public officer or employee.

Section 3. The Congress shall have the power to enforce this article by appropriate legislation. Exceptions to the rights established by this article may be created only when necessary to achieve a compelling interest.

Section 4. This article shall take effect on the 180th day after the ratification of this article. The right to an order of restitution established by this article shall not apply to crimes committed before the effective date of this article.

Section 5. The rights and immunities established by this article shall apply in Federal and State proceedings, including military proceedings to the extent that the Congress may provide by law, juvenile justice proceedings, and proceedings in the District of Columbia and any commonwealth, territory, or possession of the United States.

*Source:* Senate Joint Resolution 3, 106th Congress.

posed amendment that gives crime victims the right to be notified of any state or federal grant of clemency. The U.S. attorney general apparently believed that the provision would impede the power of the president. The legislation also lacked the support of President Clinton and was officially withdrawn by its sponsors in 2000. The amendment may still have a future, however, as President George W. Bush expressed support for the measure in 2002,[66] and 39 state attorneys general have publicly endorsed its adoption.[67] The text of the proposed amendment, known as Senate Joint Resolution 3, is reproduced in CJ Today Exhibit 11–3.

Although a victims' rights amendment to the federal Constitution may not yet be a reality, more than 30 states have passed their own victims' rights amendments,[68] and significant federal legislation has already been adopted. The 1982 Victim and Witness Protection Act

> When our criminal justice system treats victims as irrelevant bystanders, they are victimized for a second time. And because Americans are justifiably proud of our system and expect it to treat us fairly, the second violation of our rights can be traumatic.
>
> —President George W. Bush[vii]

(VWPA),[69] for example, requires judges to consider victim impact statements at federal sentencing hearings and places responsibility for their creation on federal probation officers. In 1984, the federal Victims of Crime Act (VOCA) was enacted with substantial bipartisan support. VOCA authorized federal funding to help states establish victim assistance and victim compensation programs. Under VOCA, the U.S. Department of Justice's Office for Victims of Crime provides a significant source of both funding and information for victim assistance programs. The rights of victims were further strengthened under the Violent Crime Control and Law Enforcement Act of 1994, which created a federal right of allocution, or right to speak, for victims of violent and sex crimes. This gave victims the right to speak at the sentencing of their assailants. The 1994 law also requires sex offenders and child molesters convicted under federal law to pay restitution to their victims and prohibits the diversion of federal victims' funds to other programs. Other provisions of the 1994 law provide civil rights remedies for victims of felonies motivated by gender bias and extend "rape shield law" protections to civil cases and to all criminal cases, which bar inquiries into a victim's sexual history. A significant feature of the 1994 law can be found in a subsection titled the Violence Against Women Act (VAWA). VAWA provides financial support for police, prosecutors, and victims' services in cases involving sexual violence or domestic abuse.

Much of the philosophical basis of today's victims' movement can be found in the restorative justice model, which was discussed briefly earlier in this chapter. Restorative justice emphasizes offender accountability and victim reparation. Restorative justice also provides the basis for victim compensation programs, which are another means of recognizing the needs of crime victims. Today, all 50 states have passed legislation providing for monetary payments to victims of crime. Such payments are primarily designed to compensate victims for medical expenses and lost wages. All existing programs require that applicants meet certain eligibility criteria, and most set limits on the maximum amount of compensation that can be received. Generally disallowed are claims from victims who are significantly responsible for their own victimization, such as those who end up being the losers in fights they provoke. In 2002, California's victim compensation program, the largest in the nation, provided $117 million to more than 50,000 victims for crime-related expenses. A comprehensive California proposal to improve victim's services, with applicability to victim's service programs throughout the nation, can be read at **Library Extra 11–5** at cjtoday.com.

**LIBRARY EXTRA**

In 2001, the USA PATRIOT Act amended the Victims of Crime Act of 1984 to make victims of terrorism and their families eligible for victim compensation payments.[70] It also created an antiterrorism emergency reserve fund to help provide compensation to victims of terrorism. A year earlier, in November 2000, the federal Office for Victims of Crime (OVC) created the Terrorism and International Victims Unit (TIVU) to develop and manage programs and initiatives that help victims of domestic and international terrorism, mass violence, and crimes that have transnational dimensions.[71]

On October 9, 2004, the U.S. Senate passed the Crime Victims' Rights Act,[72] as part of the Justice for All Act of 2004. President Bush signed the act into law three weeks later. Some saw the legislation as at least a partial statutory alternative to a constitutional crime victims' rights amendment. The Crime Victims' Rights Act establishes statutory rights for victims of federal crimes and gives them the necessary legal authority to assert those rights in federal court. The Crime Victims' Rights Act grants the following rights to victims of federal crimes:[73]

1. The right to be reasonably protected from the accused
2. The right to reasonable, accurate, and timely notice of any public proceeding involving the crime or of any release or escape of the accused
3. The right to be included in any such public proceeding
4. The right to be reasonably heard at any public proceeding involving release, plea, or sentencing
5. The right to confer with the federal prosecutor handling the case
6. The right to full and timely restitution as provided by law
7. The right to proceedings free from unreasonable delay
8. The right to be treated with fairness and with respect for the victim's dignity and privacy

In addition to establishing these rights, the legislation expressly requires federal courts to ensure that they are afforded to victims. In like manner, federal law enforcement officials are required to make their "best efforts to see that crime victims are notified of, and accorded" these rights.

# Victim Impact Statements

**victim impact statement**
The in-court use of victim- or survivor-supplied information by sentencing authorities seeking to make an informed sentencing decision.

Another consequence of the national victims' rights movement has been a call for the use of **victim impact statements** before sentencing. A victim impact statement is generally a written document describing the losses, suffering, and trauma experienced by the crime victim or by the victim's survivors. Judges are expected to consider such statements in arriving at an appropriate sanction for the offender.

The drive to mandate inclusion of victim impact statements in sentencing decisions, already required in federal courts by the 1982 Victim and Witness Protection Act, was substantially enhanced by the "right of allocution" provision of the Violent Crime Control and Law Enforcement Act of 1994. Victim impact statements played a prominent role in the sentencing of Timothy McVeigh, who was convicted of the 1995 bombing of the Murrah Federal Building in Oklahoma City and was executed in 2001. Some states, however, have gone further than the federal government. In 1984, the state of California, for example, passed legislation giving victims a right to attend and participate in sentencing and parole hearings.[74] Approximately 20 states now have laws requiring citizen involvement in sentencing, and all 50 states and the District of Columbia "allow for some form of submission of a victim impact statement either at the time of sentencing or to be contained in the presentence investigation reports" made by court officers.[75] Where written victim impact statements are not available, courts may invite the victim to testify directly at sentencing. An alternative to written impact statements and to the appearance of victims at sentencing hearings is the victim impact video.

One study of the efficacy of victim impact statements found that sentencing decisions are rarely affected by them. In the words of the study, "These statements did not produce sentencing decisions that reflected more clearly the effects of crime on victims. Nor did we find much evidence that—with or without impact statements—sentencing decisions were influenced by our measures of the effects of crime on victims, once the charge and the defendant's prior record were taken into account."[76] The authors concluded that victim impact statements have little effect on courts because judges and other officials "have established ways of making decisions which do not call for explicit information about the impact of crime on victims." Learn more about the rights of crime victims and the history of the victims' movement at Web Extra 11–6.

The Constitutionality of Victim Impact Statements

**WEB EXTRA**

# Modern Sentencing Options

Sentencing is fundamentally a risk management strategy designed to protect the public while serving the ends of retribution, incapacitation, deterrence, rehabilitation, and restoration. Because the goals of sentencing are difficult to agree on, so too are sanctions. Lengthy prison terms do little for rehabilitation, while community-release programs can hardly protect the innocent from offenders bent on continuing criminality.

Assorted sentencing philosophies continue to permeate state-level judicial systems. Each state has its own sentencing laws, and frequent revisions of those statutes are not uncommon. Because of huge variation from one state to another in the laws and procedures that control the imposition of criminal sanctions, sentencing has been called "the most diversified part of the Nation's criminal justice process."[77]

There is at least one common ground, however. It can be found in the four traditional sanctions that continue to dominate the thinking of most legislators and judges—fines, probation, imprisonment, and death. Fines and the death penalty are discussed in this chapter, while probation is described in Chapter 12, and imprisonment is covered in Chapters 13 and 14.

In the case of indeterminate sentencing, fines, probation, and imprisonment are widely available to judges. The option selected generally depends on the severity of the offense and the judge's best guess as to the likelihood of the defendant's future criminal involvement. Sometimes two or more options are combined, such as when an offender is fined and sentenced to prison or placed on probation and fined in support of restitution payments.

Jurisdictions that operate under presumptive sentencing guidelines generally limit the judge's choice to only one option and often specify the extent to which that option can be applied. Dollar amounts of fines, for example, are rigidly set, and prison terms are specified for each type of offense. The death penalty remains an option in a fair number of jurisdictions, but only for a highly select group of offenders.

A 2004 report by the Bureau of Justice Statistics on the sentencing practices of trial courts found that state courts convicted 1,051,000 felons in 2002.[78] Another 63,217 felony convictions

Nobody gets rehabilitated. Well, I shouldn't say no one; some of them die.

—Former Los Angeles Police Chief Daryl Gates

**FIGURE 11-1**

**FIGURE 11-1**

**The sentencing of convicted felons in state courts, by type of sentence.**

*Source:* Data from Matthew R. Durose and Patrick A. Langan, *Felony Sentences in State Courts, 2002* (Washington, DC: Bureau of Justice Statistics, 2004).

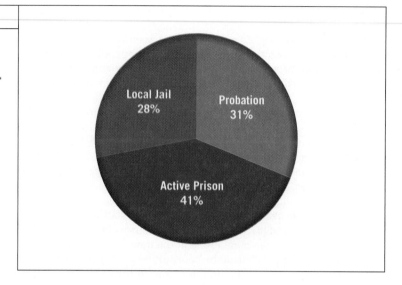

**CJ**  **BLOG**

See the Sentencing Law and Policy Web log available in the cjtoday.com blogspace.

occurred in federal courts. The report also found the following for offenders convicted of felonies in state courts (Figure 11–1):

- Forty-one percent were sentenced to active prison terms.
- The average sentence length for those sent to state prisons has decreased since 1990 (from six years to four and a half years).
- Felons sentenced in 2002 were likely to serve more of their sentence before release (50%) than those sentenced in 1990 (33%).
- Twenty-eight percent received jail sentences, usually involving less than a year's confinement.
- Those sent to jail received an average sentence of seven months.
- Thirty-one percent were sentenced to probation, with no jail or prison time to serve.
- The average probation sentence was 38 months.
- Fines were imposed on 25% of convicted felons.

Although the percentage of felons who receive active sentences may seem low, the number of criminal defendants receiving active prison time has increased dramatically. Figure 11–2 shows that the number of court-ordered prison commitments has increased nearly eightfold in the past 40 years.

**FIGURE 11-2**

**Court-ordered prison commitments, 1960–2002.**

*Source:* Data from Matthew R. Durose and Patrick A. Langan, *Felony Sentences in State Courts, 2002* (Washington, DC: Bureau of Justice Statistics, 2004), and other years.

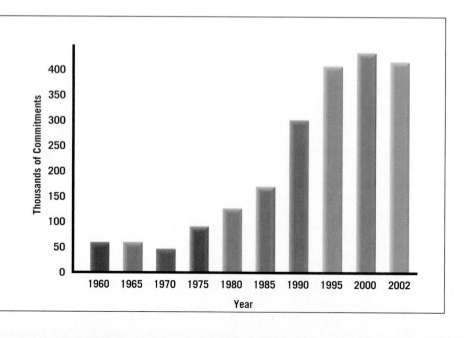

# Fines

While the fine is one of the oldest forms of punishment, until recently, the use of fines as criminal sanctions suffered from built-in inequities and a widespread failure to collect them. Inequities arose when offenders with vastly different financial resources were fined similar amounts. A fine of $100, for example, can place a painful economic burden on a poor defendant but is negligible when imposed on a wealthy offender.

Today, fines are once again receiving attention as a serious sentencing alternative. One reason for the renewed interest is the stress placed on state resources by burgeoning prison populations. The extensive imposition of fines not only results in less crowded prisons but can contribute to state and local coffers and can lower the tax burden of law-abiding citizens. There are other advantages:

- Fines can deprive offenders of the proceeds of criminal activity.
- Fines can promote rehabilitation by enforcing economic responsibility.
- Fines can be collected by existing criminal justice agencies and are relatively inexpensive to administer.
- Fines can be made proportionate to both the severity of the offense and the ability of the offender to pay.

A National Institute of Justice (NIJ) survey found that an average of 86% of convicted defendants in courts of limited jurisdiction receive fines as sentences, some in combination with another penalty.[79] Fines are also widely used in courts of general jurisdiction, where the NIJ study found judges imposing fines in 42% of all cases that came before them for sentencing. Some studies estimate that more than $1 billion in fines are collected nationwide each year.[80]

Fines are often imposed for relatively minor law violations, such as driving while intoxicated, reckless driving, disturbing the peace, disorderly conduct, public drunkenness, and vandalism. Judges in many courts, however, report the use of fines for relatively serious violations of the law, including assault, auto theft, embezzlement, fraud, and the sale and possession of various controlled substances. Fines are most likely to be imposed where the offender has both a clean record and the ability to pay.[81]

Opposition to the use of fines is based on the following arguments:

- Fines allow the release of convicted offenders into the community but do not impose stringent controls on their behavior.
- Fines are a relatively mild form of punishment and are not consistent with the "just deserts" philosophy.
- Fines discriminate against the poor and favor the wealthy. Indigent offenders are especially subject to discrimination since they lack the financial resources with which to pay fines.
- Fines are difficult to collect.

A number of these objections can be answered by procedures that make available to judges complete financial information on defendants. Studies have found, however, that courts of limited jurisdiction, which are the most likely to impose fines, are also the least likely to have adequate information on offenders' financial status.[82] Perhaps as a consequence, judges are sometimes reluctant to impose fines. Two of the most widely cited objections by judges to the use of fines are (1) that fines allow more affluent offenders to "buy their way out" and (2) that poor offenders cannot pay fines.[83]

A solution to both objections can be found in the Scandinavian system of day fines. The day-fine system is based on the idea that fines should be proportionate to the severity of the offense but also need to take into account the financial resources of the offender. Day fines are computed by first assessing the seriousness of the offense, the defendant's degree of culpability, and his or her prior record as measured in "days." The use of days as a benchmark of seriousness is related to the fact that, without fines, the offender could be sentenced to a number of days (or months or years) in jail or prison. The number of days an offender is assessed is then multiplied by the daily wages that person earns. Hence, if two people are sentenced to a five-day fine, but one earns only $20 per day and the other $200 per day, the first would pay a $100 fine and the second $1,000.

In 2004, one of Finland's richest men, 27-year-old Jussi Salonoja, was fined a record 170,000 euros ($217,000) for speeding through the center of Helsinki. Salonoja, heir to his family's international sausage business, was caught driving 80 kilometers per hour (kph) in a 40-kph zone. The fine was based on Salonoja's 2002 earnings, which were estimated at close to 7 million euros.

> Of all the initiatives that this Congress could undertake, few will touch the heart of Americans as dearly as the measure seeking to ensure that the judicial process is just and fair for the victims of crime.
>
> —Senator Orrin Hatch

In the early 1990s, the NIJ reported on experimental day-fine programs conducted by the Richmond County Criminal Court in Staten Island, New York, and by the Milwaukee Municipal Court.[84] Both studies concluded that "the day fine can play a major . . . role as an intermediate sanction"[85] and that "the day-fine concept could be implemented in a typical American limited-jurisdiction court."[86] Those conclusions were supported by a 1996 RAND Corporation report that examined ongoing day-fine demonstration projects in Maricopa County, Arizona; Des Moines, Iowa; Bridgeport, Connecticut; and four counties in Oregon.[87]

# Death: The Ultimate Sanction

A Brief History
of the Death Penalty

Some crimes are especially heinous and seem to cry out for extreme punishment. In 1996, for example, in what some saw as an especially atrocious murder, a Norman, Oklahoma, man decapitated his neighbor and then walked naked down an alleyway to toss the victim's head into a trash dumpster.[88] Witnesses who watched the accused killer, 33-year-old Cameron Smith, throw the head of 44-year-old Roydon Dale Major into the trash called police. Responding officers discovered the rest of Major's body in a room at a boarding house where both Smith and Major had lived. Major had been stabbed repeatedly before his head was severed from his body.

Many states today have statutory provisions that provide for a sentence of **capital punishment** for especially repugnant crimes (known as **capital offenses**). Estimates are that more than 18,800 legal executions have been carried out in the United States since 1608, when records began to be kept on capital punishment.[89] Although capital punishment was widely used throughout the eighteenth and nineteenth centuries, the mid-twentieth century offered a brief respite in the number of offenders legally executed in this country. Between 1930 and 1967, when the U.S. Supreme Court ordered a nationwide stay of pending executions, nearly 3,800 people were put to death. The years 1935 and 1936 were peak years, with nearly 200 legal killings each year. Executions declined substantially every year thereafter. Between 1967 and 1977, a *de facto* moratorium existed, with no executions carried out in any U.S. jurisdiction. Following the lifting of the moratorium, executions resumed (Figure 11–3). In 1993, 38 offenders were put to death, while 56 were executed nationwide in 1995. A modern record for executions was set in 1999, with 98 executions—35 in Texas alone. Substantially fewer offenders (59) were executed in 2004.

Today, 38 of the 50 states and the federal government[90] permit execution for first-degree murder, while treason, kidnapping, aggravated rape, the murder of a police or correctional officer, and murder while under a life sentence are punishable by death in selected jurisdictions.[91] New York, for example, allows for the imposition of a death sentence in cases involving the murder of law enforcement officers, judges, and witnesses and their families and also applies the punishment to serial killers, terrorists, murderers-for-hire, and those who kill while committing another felony, such as robbery or rape.

**capital punishment**

The death penalty. Capital punishment is the most extreme of all sentencing options.

**capital offense**

A criminal offense punishable by death.

---

## FIGURE 11–3

**U.S. executions by state, 1976 through mid-2005.**

Twelve states currently do not have the death penalty: Alaska, Hawaii, Iowa, Maine, Massachusetts, Michigan, Minnesota, North Dakota, Rhode Island, Virginia, West Virginia, and Wisconsin. Executions that occured in those states prior to the abolishment of capital punishment are shown. Data are through June 30, 2005.

*Source:* Data from Death Penalty Information Center.

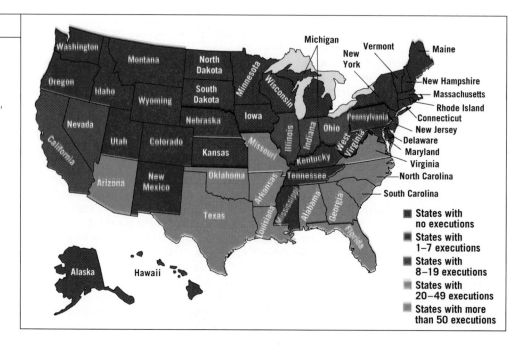

The list of crimes punishable by death under federal jurisdiction increased dramatically with passage of the Violent Crime Control and Law Enforcement Act of 1994 and was expanded still further by the 2001 USA PATRIOT Act, a federal law that focuses on fighting terrorism. The list now includes a total of about 60 offenses. State legislators have also worked to expand the types of crime for which a death sentence can be imposed. In 1997, for example, the Louisiana Supreme Court upheld the state's year-old child rape statute, which allows for the imposition of a capital sentence when the victim is younger than 12 years of age. The case involved an AIDS-infected father who raped his three daughters, ages five, eight, and nine. In upholding the father's death sentence, the Louisiana court ruled that child rape is "like no other crime."[92]

A total of 3,452 offenders were under sentence of death throughout the United States on April 1, 2005.[93] The latest statistics show that 98.5% of those on death row are male, approximately 46% are white, 10% are Hispanic, 42% are African-American, and 2% are of other races (mostly Native American and Pacific Islander).[94]

Methods of imposing death vary by state. The majority of death penalty states authorize execution through lethal injection. Electrocution is the second most common means, while hanging, the gas chamber, and firing squads have survived, at least as options available to the condemned, in a few states. For the most current statistical information on capital punishment, visit the Death Penalty Information Center at Web Extra 11-7 at cjtoday.com.

WEB EXTRA

# *Habeas Corpus* Review

The legal process through which a capital sentence is carried to conclusion is fraught with problems. One serious difficulty centers on the fact that automatic review of all death sentences by appellate courts and constant legal maneuvering by defense counsel often lead to a dramatic delay between the time the sentence is handed down and the time it is carried out. Today, an average of ten years and eleven months passes between the time a sentence of death is imposed and the time it is carried out.[95] Such lengthy delays, compounded by uncertainty over whether an execution will ever occur, directly contravene the generally accepted notion that punishment should be swift and certain.

Delays in the imposition of capital sanctions have been the source of much anguish for condemned prisoners and their victims as well as for the families of both. In 1997, in a final statement just before his client was executed, for example, the attorney for 30-year-old Dorsie Johnson-Bey told witnesses, "If the jury trying this case could see what has happened to him in the 11 years he's been on death row, they would say that he certainly doesn't pose a continuing threat to society."[96] Johnson-Bey was sentenced to die for the March 1986 murder of Jack Huddleston, a 53-year-old convenience store clerk who he had robbed of $161 and cigarettes and then shot in the head with a .25-caliber pistol. During the time that he was imprisoned, he claimed to have found God and said he had been rehabilitated.

In a speech before the American Bar Association in 1989, Chief Justice William Rehnquist called for reforms of the federal *habeas corpus* system, which, at the time, allowed condemned prisoners virtually limitless opportunities for appeal. **Writs of *habeas corpus*** (Latin for "you have the body"), which require that a prisoner be brought into court to determine if he or she is being legally held, form the basis for many federal appeals made by prisoners on state death rows. In 1968, Chief Justice Earl Warren called the right to file *habeas* petitions, as guaranteed under the U.S. Constitution, the "symbol and guardian of individual liberty." Twenty years later, however, Rehnquist claimed that writs of *habeas corpus* were being used indiscriminately by death-row inmates seeking to delay executions even where grounds for delay do not exist. "The capital defendant does not need to prevail on the merits in order to accomplish his purpose," said Rehnquist. "He wins temporary victories by postponing a final adjudication."[97]

In a move to reduce delays in the conduct of executions, the U.S. Supreme Court, in the case of *McCleskey* v. *Zant* (1991),[98] limited the number of appeals a condemned person may lodge with the courts. Saying that repeated filing for the sole purpose of delay promotes "disrespect for the finality of convictions" and "disparages the entire criminal justice system," the Court established a two-pronged criterion for future appeals. According to *McCleskey,* in any petition beyond the first filed with the federal court, a capital defendant must (1) demonstrate good cause why the claim now being made was not included in the first filing and (2) explain how the absence of that claim may have harmed the petitioner's ability to mount an effective defense. Two months later, the Court reinforced *McCleskey* when it ruled, in *Coleman* v. *Thompson* (1991),[99] that state prisoners could not cite "procedural default," such as a defense attorney's failure to meet a state's filing deadline for appeals, as the basis for an appeal to federal court.

**writ of *habeas corpus***

A writ that directs the person detaining a prisoner to bring him or her before a judicial officer to determine the lawfulness of the imprisonment.

I think this country would be much better off if we did not have capital punishment. . . . We cannot ignore the fact that in recent years a disturbing number of inmates on death row have been exonerated.

—U.S. Supreme Court Justice John Paul Stevens[ix]

> There can be no doubt that the taking of the life of the President creates much more societal harm than the taking of the life of a homeless person.
>
> —Tennessee Attorney General Charles Burson, arguing before the U.S. Supreme Court in *Payne* v. *Tennessee*[x]

In 1995, in the case of *Schlup* v. *Delo,*[100] the Court continued to define standards for further appeals from death-row inmates, ruling that before appeals based on claims of new evidence could be heard, "a petitioner must show that, in light of the new evidence, it is more likely than not that no reasonable juror would have found him guilty beyond a reasonable doubt." A "reasonable juror" was defined as one who "would consider fairly all of the evidence presented and would conscientiously obey the trial court's instructions requiring proof beyond a reasonable doubt."

Opportunities for federal appeals by death-row inmates were further limited by the Antiterrorism and Effective Death Penalty Act (AEDPA) of 1996,[101] which sets a one-year postconviction deadline for state inmates filing federal *habeas corpus* appeals. The deadline is six months for state death-row inmates who were provided a lawyer for *habeas* appeals at the state level. The act also requires federal courts to presume that the factual findings of state courts are correct, does not permit the claim of state court misinterpretations of the U.S. Constitution as a basis for *habeas* relief unless those misinterpretations are "unreasonable," and requires that all petitioners must show, prior to obtaining a hearing, facts sufficient to establish by clear and convincing evidence that but for constitutional error, no reasonable fact finder would have found the petitioner guilty. The act also requires approval by a three-judge panel before an inmate can file a second federal appeal raising newly discovered evidence of innocence. In 1996, in the case of *Felker* v. *Turpin,*[102] the U.S. Supreme Court ruled that limitations on the authority of federal courts to consider successive *habeas corpus* petitions imposed by AEDPA are permissible since they do not deprive the U.S. Supreme Court of its original jurisdiction over such petitions.

Some recent statements by Supreme Court justices have indicated that long delays in carrying out executions that are caused by the government may render the punishment unconstitutionally cruel and unusual. One example comes from the 1998 case of *Elledge* v. *Florida,*[103] where the execution of William D. Elledge had been delayed for 23 years. Although the full Court refused to hear the case, Justice Stephen Breyer observed that "[t]wenty-three years under sentence of death is unusual—whether one takes as a measuring rod current practice or the practice in this country and in England at the time our Constitution was written." Moreover, wrote Breyer, execution after such a long delay could be considered cruel because Elledge "has experienced that delay because of the State's own faulty procedures and not because of frivolous appeals on his own part." Elledge remains on death row at the Union Correctional Institution in Florida. As this book goes to press, he has been under sentence of death for 31 years.

Former Illinois Governor George Ryan posing with former death-row inmates Laurence Hayes (left), David Keaton (seated), and Gary Gauger at a film festival. While governor, Ryan declared a moratorium on executions in Illinois and appointed a commission to review the capital punishment system in that state.

*AP Wide World Photos*

---

**FREEDOM OR SAFETY? YOU DECIDE.**

### What Are the Limits of Genetic Privacy?

In 2005, police in Truro, Massachusetts, charged Christopher M. McCowen, a garbage man with a long rap sheet, with the murder of 46-year-old Christa Worthington, a fashion writer who had been raped and stabbed to death in the kitchen of her isolated home in 2002. The case, which had baffled authorities for three years, drew national interest when Truro authorities asked the town's 790 male residents to voluntarily submit saliva-swab DNA samples for analysis. Investigators were hoping to use genetic testing to match semen recovered from the murder scene with the killer. "We're trying to find the person who has something to hide . . . ," said Sgt. David Perry of the Truro Police Department. Although McCowen voluntarily submitted a DNA sample from a cheek swab in early 2004, it took the state crime lab more than a year to analyze it.

As the Massachusetts case shows, DNA profiling can be a powerful forensic tool, although its use in criminal investigations is barely 20 years old. The first well-known DNA forensic analysis occurred in 1986, when British police sought the help of Alec Jeffreys, a geneticist at the University of Leicester who is widely regarded as the father of "DNA fingerprinting." The police were trying to solve the vicious rape and murder of two young schoolgirls. At the center of their investigation was a young man who worked at a mental institution close to where the girls' bodies had been found. Soon after he was questioned, the man confessed to the crimes and was arrested, but police were uncertain of the suspect's state of mind and wanted to be sure that they had the right person.

Jeffreys compared the suspect's DNA to DNA taken from semen samples found on the victims. The samples did not match, leading to a wider police investigation. Lacking any clear leads, the authorities requested that all males living in the area of the killings voluntarily submit to DNA testing so that they might be excluded as suspects. By the fall of 1987 the number of men tested had exceeded 4,500, but the murderer still hadn't been found. Then, however, investigators received an unexpected tip. They learned that a local baker named Colin Pitchfork had convinced another man to provide a DNA sample in his place. Pitchfork was picked up and questioned. He soon confessed, providing details about the crime that only the perpetrator could know. Pitchfork became the 4,583rd man to undergo DNA testing, and his DNA proved a perfect match with that of the killer.

In the last 20 years, the use of DNA testing by police departments has come a long way. Today, the FBI's CODIS (Combined DNA Index System) database makes use of computerized records to match the DNA of individuals previously convicted of certain crimes with forensic samples gathered at crime scenes across the country.

Advocates of genetic privacy, however, question whether anyone—even those convicted of crimes—should be sampled against their wishes and have their genetic profiles added to government databases. The Truro case, in which the ACLU sent letters to the town's police chief and Cape Code prosecutor calling for an end to the "DNA dragnet," highlights what many fear—especially when local police announced that they would pay close attention to those who refused to cooperate. One commentator noted that "if you have nothing to hide, then why not cooperate?" is "a very old trap."

**YOU DECIDE**

What degree of "genetic privacy" should an individual be entitled to? Should the government require routine genetic testing of nonoffenders for identification purposes? How might such information be used in the event of a terrorist attack?

*References:* "Man Charged with 2002 Murder of Cape Cod Writer," *USA Today,* April 15, 2005. Web posted at http://www.usatoday.com/news/nation/2005-04-15-cape-cod-murder_x.htm; "ACLU Slams Mass DNA Collection," CBSNews.com, January 10, 2005. Web posted at http://www.cbsnews.com/stories/2005/01/10/national/main665938.shtml; and Howard C. Coleman and Eric D. Swenson, *DNA in the Courtroom: A Trial Watcher's Guide* (Seattle: Genelex Corporation, web edition 2000). Web posted at http://www.genelex.com/paternitytesting/paternitybook.html.

## Opposition to Capital Punishment

Thirty years ago, David Magris, who was celebrating his twenty-first birthday with a crime spree, shot Dennis Tapp in the back during a holdup, leaving Tapp a paraplegic. Tapp had been working a late-night shift, tending his father's quick-serve gas station. Magris went on to commit more robberies that night, killing 20-year-old Steven Tompkins in a similar crime. Although sentenced to death by a California court, the U.S. Supreme Court overturned the state's death penalty law in 1972, opening the door for Magris to be paroled in 1985. Long before Magris was freed from prison, however, Tapp had already forgiven him. A few minutes after the shooting happened, Tapp regained consciousness, dragged himself to a telephone, and called for help. The next thing he did was ask "God to forgive the man who did this to me."[104] Today, the men—both staunch death penalty opponents—are friends, and Magris is president of the Northern California Coalition to Abolish the Death Penalty. "Don't get me wrong," says Tapp, "What [David] did was wrong. . . . He did something stupid and he paid for it."[105]

Because for many the death sentence is such an emotional issue, attempts have been made to abolish capital punishment since the founding of the United States. The first recorded effort to

> When a juvenile commits a heinous crime, the State can exact forfeiture of some of the most basic liberties, but the State cannot extinguish his life and his potential to attain a mature understanding of his own humanity.
>
> —*Roper v. Simmons* (2005)

eliminate the death penalty occurred at the home of Benjamin Franklin in 1787.[106] At a meeting there on March 9 of that year, Dr. Benjamin Rush, a signer of the Declaration of Independence and a leading medical pioneer, read a paper against capital punishment to a small but influential audience. Although his immediate efforts came to naught, his arguments laid the groundwork for many debates that followed. Michigan, widely regarded as the first abolitionist state, joined the Union in 1837 without a death penalty. A number of other states, including Alaska, Hawaii, Iowa, Maine, Massachusetts, Minnesota, North Dakota, Rhode Island, Vermont, West Virginia, and Wisconsin, have since spurned death as a possible sanction for criminal acts. As noted earlier, it remains a viable sentencing option in 38 of the states and in all federal jurisdictions, so arguments continue to rage over its value.

Today, six main rationales for abolishing capital punishment are heard:

1. The death penalty can be and has been inflicted on innocent people.
2. The death penalty is not an effective deterrent.
3. The imposition of the death penalty is, by the nature of our legal system, arbitrary.
4. The death penalty discriminates against certain ethnic and racial groups.
5. The death penalty is far too expensive to justify its use.
6. Human life is sacred, and killing at the hands of the state is not a righteous act but rather one that is on the same moral level as the crimes committed by the condemned.

> Life is sacred. It's about the only sacred thing on earth—and no one has a right to do away with it.
>
> —Aldona DeVetsco, mother of a murder victim, commenting on the execution of her son's killer

The first five abolitionist claims are pragmatic, that is, they can be measured and verified or disproved by looking at the facts. The last claim is primarily philosophical and therefore not amenable to scientific investigation. Hence, we shall briefly examine only the first five.

The Death Penalty Information Center claims that 113 people in 25 states were freed from death row between 1973 and 2004 after it was determined that they were innocent of the capital crime of which they had been convicted.[107] One study of felony convictions that used analysis of DNA to provide postconviction evidence of guilt or innocence found 28 cases in which defendants had been wrongly convicted and sentenced to lengthy prison terms. The study, *Convicted by Juries, Exonerated by Science,* effectively demonstrated that the judicial process can be flawed.[108] DNA testing can play a critical role in identifying wrongful convictions because, as Barry Scheck and Peter Neufeld, cofounders of the Innocence Project at the Benjamin N. Cardozo School of Law, point out, "Unlike witnesses who disappear or whose recollections fade over time, DNA in biological samples can be reliably extracted decades after the commission of the crime. The results of such testing have invariably been found to have a scientific certainty that easily outweighs the eyewitness identification testimony or other direct or circumstantial proof that led to the original conviction."[109] "Very simply," say Scheck and Neufeld, "DNA testing has demonstrated that far more wrongful convictions occur than even the most cynical and jaded scholars had suspected."[110]

In 2004, for example, David Allen Jones, a 44-year-old mentally disabled janitor, was released from a California prison where he had spent nearly nine years following a wrongful conviction for three slasher-type killings after DNA evidence linked another inmate to the killings.[111] Jones's innocence was discovered when investigators matched DNA from convicted rapist Chester Dwayne Turner, 37, with semen samples gathered at the crime scenes. Jones may not be the only one freed, however, as police now believe that Turner's genetic profile will match evidence they gathered in at least 12 murders of women who were killed in a 30-block area of Los Angeles during the 1990s.

A 2000 study by Columbia Law School professor James Liebman and colleagues examined 4,578 death penalty cases in state and federal courts from 1973 to 1995.[112] They found that appellate courts overturned the conviction or reduced the sentence in 68% of the cases examined. In 82% of the successful appeals, defendants were found to be deserving of a lesser sentence, while convictions were overturned in 7% of such appeals. According to the study's authors, "Our 23 years worth of findings reveal a capital punishment system collapsing under the weight of its own mistakes." You can read the Liebman report in its entirety at Library Extra 11–6 at cjtoday.com.

 **LIBRARY EXTRA**

Claims of innocence are being partially addressed today by recently passed state laws that mandate DNA testing of all death-row inmates in situations where DNA testing might help establish guilt or innocence (that is, in cases where blood or semen from the perpetrator is available for testing).[113] In 2000, Illinois Governor George Ryan announced that he was suspending all executions in his state indefinitely. Ryan's proclamation came after DNA testing showed that 13 Illinois death-row prisoners could not have committed the capital crimes of which they were convicted. Also in 2000, the American Bar Association issued a formal request asking states holding death-row inmates to use DNA tests to minimize the risk that innocent people would be executed.

DNA testing (discussed in more detail in Chapter 18) makes it possible to almost conclusively demonstrate innocence in many cases. In 2004, in recognition of the power that DNA testing holds to exonerate the innocent, President George W. Bush signed the Innocence Protection Act[114] into law. The Innocence Protection Act provides federal funds to eliminate the backlog of unanalyzed DNA samples in the nation's crime laboratories[115] and sets aside money to improve the capacity of federal, state, and local crime laboratories to conduct DNA analyses.[116] The act also facilitates access to postconviction DNA testing for those serving time in state[117] or federal prisons or on death row and sets forth conditions under which a federal prisoner asserting innocence may obtain postconviction DNA testing of specific evidence. Similarly, the legislation requires the preservation of biological evidence by federal law enforcement agencies for any defendant under a sentence of imprisonment or death.

During the 1970s and 1980s, the deterrent effect of the death penalty became a favorite subject for debate in academic circles.[118] Studies of states that had eliminated the death penalty failed to show any increase in homicide rates.[119] Similar studies of neighboring states, in which jurisdictions retaining capital punishment were compared with those that had abandoned it, also failed to demonstrate any significant differences.[120] Although death penalty advocates remain numerous, few still argue for the penalty based on its deterrent effects. One study that has found support for use of the death penalty as a deterrent was reported in 2001 by Hashem Dezhbakhsh and his colleagues at Emory University.[121] According to Dezhbakhsh, "Our results suggest that capital punishment has a strong deterrent effect. . . . In particular, each execution results, on average, in 18 fewer murders."[122] According to Dezhbakhsh, most other studies in the area have not only been methodologically flawed but have failed to consider the fact that a number of states sentence select offenders to death but do not carry out executions. Dezhbakhsh writes, "If criminals know that the justice system issues many death sentences but the executions are not carried out, then they may not be deterred by an increase in probability of a death sentence."[123]

The third abolitionist claim, that the death penalty is arbitrary, is based on the belief that access to effective representation and to the courts themselves is differentially available to people with varying financial and other resources. The notion of arbitrariness also builds on beliefs that differences in jury composition, judges' personal dispositions and backgrounds, varying laws and procedures, and jurisdictional social characteristics may lead to varying sentences and could mean that a person who might be sentenced to die in one place might receive a lesser sentence elsewhere.

Access to the courts, which some see as more dependent on a changing legal environment than on fair standards of due process, is another area in which arbitrariness can play a role. In recent years, access to appellate courts has been restricted by a number of new state and federal laws (discussed in greater detail in Chapter 14). Such restrictions led the American Bar Association (ABA) House of Delegates in 1997 to cite what it called "an erosion of legal rights of death row inmates" and to urge an immediate halt to executions in the United States until the judicial process could be overhauled.[124] ABA delegates were expressing concerns that during the past decade, Congress and the states have unfairly limited death-row appeals through restrictive legislation. The ABA resolution also called for a halt to executions of people under 18 years of age and of those who are mentally retarded.[125]

The claim that the death penalty is discriminatory is harder to investigate. Although past evidence suggests that blacks and other minorities in the United States have been disproportionately sentenced to death,[126] more recent evidence is not as clear. At first glance, disproportionality seems apparent: 45 of the 98 prisoners executed between January 1977 and May 1988 were African-American or Hispanic; 84 of the 98 had been convicted of killing whites.[127] A 1996 Kentucky study found that African-Americans accused of killing whites in that state between 1976 and 1991 had a higher-than-average probability of being charged with a capital crime and of being sentenced to die than did homicide offenders of other races.[128] For an accurate appraisal to be made, however, any claims of disproportionality must go beyond simple comparisons with racial representation in the larger population and must somehow measure both frequency and seriousness of capital crimes between and within racial groups. Following that line of reasoning, the Supreme Court, in the 1987 case of *McCleskey* v. *Kemp*,[129] held that a simple showing of racial discrepancies in the application of the death penalty does not constitute a constitutional violation. A 2001 study of racial and ethnic fairness in federal capital punishment sentences attempted to go beyond mere percentages in its analysis of the role played by race and ethnicity in capital punishment sentencing decisions.[130] Although the study, which closely reviewed 950 capital punishment cases, found that approximately 80% of federal death-row inmates are African-American, researchers found "no intentional racial or ethnic bias in how capital punishment was administered in federal cases."[131] Underrepresented groups were more likely to be sentenced to death, "but only because they are more likely to be arrested on facts that could support a capital

Log on to ResearchNavigator .com, and choose "Criminal Justice" under ContentSelect's Academic Journal Database. Enter the phrase "capital punishment" in the search box, and click "Go." Select three articles that you find especially interesting from the results page. (Choose full-text articles rather than abstracts whenever possible.) Perform the search again, this time using the phrase "death penalty." Select another three articles from the search results. Write a summary of each of the six articles you've identified, including complete source information—that is, article title, author (if available), date of publication, and source. Submit what you have written to your instructor if asked to do so. *Note:* This feature is available only if your instructor has chosen the Research Navigator option available with a new textbook.

There is no evidence of racial bias in the administration of the federal death penalty.

—Former U.S. Attorney General John Ashcroft[xi]

## CJ NEWS

### DNA Tests for Guilty Jam System

Guilty convicts who know they won't be exonerated are joining the innocent to ask courts and prosecutors to order DNA tests, the Justice Department has told Congress.

The DNA tests for the guilty are tying up crime labs and re-traumatizing the victims of rapes and other violent crimes, often years after the crimes occurred, according to a department "views" letter written to sway congressional opinion.

"The creation of a new post-conviction (DNA testing) remedy can readily result in abuse by convicted criminals," wrote William Moschella, assistant attorney general for legislative affairs.

The criminals' motive in seeking tests that will not exonerate them is to "game the system or retaliate against the victims of their crimes," Moschella wrote.

Moschella offered no statistics, and no independent numbers exist on how many DNA appeals are in the courts. But Moschella did cite recent cases from St. Louis. Beginning in 2001, prosecutors there ordered tests on evidence from rapes dating back nearly 20 years. They found that DNA from the crime scenes matched five men who had been convicted of the crimes, though it exonerated two other convicts.

But the testing required rape victims, some of them now elderly, to give DNA samples and to answer questions about their sex lives. Some sobbed and collapsed, while others grew despondent, the memo said. One victim fled the city.

Moschella sent the letter to six key members of Congress, including Senate Judiciary Committee chairman Orrin Hatch, R–Utah, and Rep. James Sensenbrenner, R–Wis., his counterpart in the House of Representatives. Moschella wrote that his goal was to discourage them from supporting a bill that would make it easier for federal convicts to petition courts for DNA tests to challenge their convictions. The bill, which also would authorize more than $1 billion in spending on DNA-based crime fighting programs, passed the House last year and is before the Senate.

DNA, a cellular acid that contains an individual's unique genetic code, has been used since the late 1980s to match biological evidence found at crime scenes to perpetrators. It also has been valuable in challenging convictions because in some cases, DNA tests can show that someone other than the convict committed a crime.

Since 1989, 143 state convicts have been exonerated after DNA tests cast doubt on their convictions, says the Innocence Project, a New York City group that specializes in DNA cases.

In response, 34 states have passed laws making it easier for convicts to petition courts for DNA testing. At issue in the federal legislation is whether a convict seeking a DNA test must show that the test would prove his innocence or only that it would have created reasonable doubt in the minds of a jury.

Sen. Patrick Leahy of Vermont, the ranking Democrat on the Senate Judiciary Committee, supports the "reasonable doubt"

Massachusetts inmate Benjamin LaGuer. In 2002, LaGuer's supporters raised $30,000 to pay for DNA tests they hoped would clear the model inmate of rape charges. Instead, tests confirmed LaGuer's guilt. He now says that prosecutors must have manipulated the results.

*AP Wide World Photos*

standard. He called the Justice Department's letter "misguided" and said it "shows they are still part of the problem."

The state prosecutor's office in Miami has announced plans to review 500 felony convictions obtained before DNA testing of suspects became common and to offer free tests to those who could be exonerated. Since 2000, prosecutors in St. Louis, San Diego and Houston have begun similar programs.

No figures are kept on how often DNA tests reconfirm a convict's guilt. But anecdotal evidence suggests that is often the case.

The Innocence Project does extensive screening to determine a convict's innocence before it takes his case. But one-third to one-half of those tested nevertheless are shown to be guilty, the project reports.

DNA tests have reconfirmed guilt in several high-profile cases.

In Texas in 2000, then-Gov. George W. Bush granted DNA testing to convicted killer Ricky McGinn before his scheduled execution. The tests reconfirmed his guilt in the rape and murder of his 12-year-old stepdaughter and tied McGinn to two other murders for which he had not been tried.

In Massachusetts in 2002, supporters raised $30,000 to pay for DNA tests they hoped would clear model inmate Benjamin LaGuer of a rape 19 years before. LaGuer, who insisted he was innocent, was featured on ABC-TV's *20/20* program and attracted the support of authors, educators and other Massachusetts intellectuals.

The tests confirmed LaGuer's guilt. He says police must have manipulated the tests to obtain that result.

*Source:* Richard Willing, "Justice Dept.: DNA Tests for Guilty Jam System; Authorities Don't Want Petitions to Be Made Easier," *USA Today*, May 13, 2004, page 18A. Copyright © 2004 *USA Today*. Reprinted with permission.

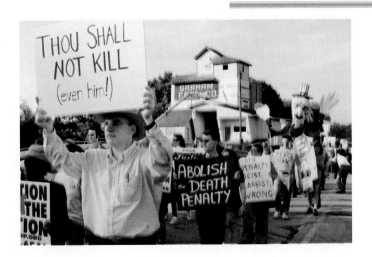

Demonstrators protesting the execution of convicted bomber Timothy McVeigh on June 11, 2001, outside the Terre Haute, Indiana, federal correctional facility only hours before McVeigh was scheduled to die.

*© REUTERS, Jim Bourg, CORBIS*

charge, not because the justice system acts in a discriminatory fashion," the report said.[132] Read the entire report at Library Extra 11–7 at cjtoday.com.

Another 2001 study, this one by New Jersey Supreme Court Special Master David Baime, found no evidence of bias against African-American defendants in capital cases in New Jersey during the period studied (August 1982 through May 2000). The study concluded, "Simply stated, we discern no sound basis from the statistical evidence to conclude that the race or ethnicity of the defendant is a factor in determining which cases advance to a penalty trial and which defendants are ultimately sentenced to death. The statistical evidence abounds the other way—it strongly suggests that there are no racial or ethnic disparities in capital murder prosecution and death sentencing rates."[133]

Evidence of socioeconomic discrimination in the imposition of the death penalty in Nebraska between 1973 and 1999 was found in a 2001 study of more than 700 homicide cases in that state. The study, which had been mandated by the state legislature, found that while race did not appear to influence death penalty decisions, killers of victims with high socioeconomic status received the death penalty four times as often as would otherwise be expected. According to the study: "The data document significant statewide disparities in charging and sentencing outcomes based on the socio-economic status of the victim."[134]

The fifth claim, that the death penalty is too expensive, is difficult to explore. Although the "official" costs associated with capital punishment are high, many death penalty supporters argue that no cost is too high if it achieves justice. Death penalty opponents, on the other hand, point to the huge costs associated with judicial appeals and with the executions themselves. According to the Death Penalty Information Center (DPIC), which maintains a national database on such costs, "The death penalty costs North Carolina $2.16 million per execution over the costs of a non-death penalty murder case with a sentence of imprisonment for life."[135] The DPIC also says that an average execution in Florida costs $3.2 million to carry out and that "in Texas, a death penalty case costs an average of $2.3 million—about three times the cost of imprisoning someone in a single cell at the highest security level for 40 years."

> When I walked out of that execution chamber that night, I felt like I had been given my life back. It could not bring Cary back, but it gave us our life back.
>
> —Charlotte Stout, the mother of an eight-year-old murder victim, after witnessing the killer's execution in 2000[xii]

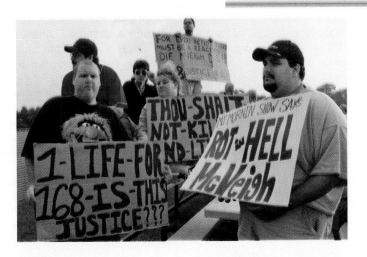

Capital punishment supporters gathering outside the Terre Haute, Indiana, federal correctional facility where convicted bomber Timothy McVeigh awaited execution.

*AP Wide World Photos*

# Justifications for Capital Punishment

On February 11, 2004, 47-year-old Edward Lewis Lagrone was executed by lethal injection in Huntsville, Texas, for the murder of three people in their home. Earlier, Lagrone had molested and impregnated one of the victims, a 10-year-old child, who he shot in the head as she was trying to protect her 19-month-old sister.[136] Lagrone also killed two of the child's great-aunts who were in the house at the time of the attack. One of the women, 76-year-old Caola Lloyd, was deaf, blind, and bedridden with cancer. Prior to the killings, Lagrone had served 7 years of a 20-year prison sentence for another murder and was on parole. "He's a poster child to justify the death penalty," said David Montague, the Tarrant County assistant district attorney who prosecuted Lagrone.

Like many others today, prosecutor Montague feels that "cold-blooded murder" justifies a sentence of death. Justifications for the death penalty are collectively referred to as the *retentionist position.* The three retentionist arguments are (1) revenge, (2) just deserts, and (3) protection. Those who justify capital punishment as revenge attempt to appeal to the idea that survivors, victims, and the state are entitled to "closure." Only after execution of the criminal perpetrator, they say, can the psychological and social wounds engendered by the offense begin to heal.

The just deserts argument makes the simple and straightforward claim that some people deserve to die for what they have done. Death is justly deserved; anything less cannot suffice as a sanction for the most heinous crimes. As U.S. Supreme Court Justice Potter Stewart once wrote, "The decision that capital punishment may be the appropriate sanction in extreme cases is an expression of the community's belief that certain crimes are themselves so grievous an affront to humanity that the only adequate response may be the penalty of death."[137]

The third retentionist claim, that of protection, asserts that offenders, once executed, can commit no further crimes. Clearly the least emotional of the retentionist claims, the protectionist argument may also be the weakest, since societal interests in protection can also be met in other ways, such as incarceration. In addition, various studies have shown that there is little likelihood of repeat offenses among people convicted of murder and later released.[138] One reason for such results, however, may be that murderers generally serve lengthy prison sentences prior to release and may have lost whatever youthful propensity for criminality that they previously possessed. For an intriguing dialogue between two U.S. Supreme Court justices over the constitutionality of the death penalty, see Web Extra 11–8 at cjtoday.com.

WEB EXTRA

# The Courts and the Death Penalty

The U.S. Supreme Court has for some time served as a sounding board for issues surrounding the death penalty. One of the Court's earliest cases in this area was *Wilkerson* v. *Utah* (1878),[139] which questioned shooting as a method of execution and raised Eighth Amendment claims that firing squads constituted a form of cruel and unusual punishment. The Court disagreed, however, contrasting the relatively civilized nature of firing squads with the various forms of torture often associated with capital punishment around the time the Bill of Rights was written.

Similarly, the Court supported electrocution as a permissible form of execution in *In re Kemmler* (1890).[140] In *Kemmler,* the Court defined cruel and unusual methods of execution as follows: "Punishments are cruel when they involve torture or a lingering death; but the punishment of death is not cruel, within the meaning of that word as used in the Constitution. It implies there is something inhuman and barbarous, something more than the mere extinguishing of life."[141] Almost 60 years later, the Court ruled that a second attempt at the electrocution of a convicted person, when the first did not work, did not violate the Eighth Amendment.[142] The Court reasoned that the initial failure was the consequence of accident or unforeseen circumstances and not the result of an effort on the part of executioners to be intentionally cruel.

It was not until 1972, however, in the landmark case of *Furman* v. *Georgia,*[143] that the Court recognized "evolving standards of decency"[144] that might necessitate a reconsideration of Eighth Amendment guarantees. In a 5–4 ruling, the *Furman* decision invalidated Georgia's death penalty statute on the basis that it allowed a jury unguided discretion in the imposition of a capital sentence. The majority of justices concluded that the Georgia statute, which permitted a jury to decide issues of guilt or innocence while it weighed sentencing options, allowed for an arbitrary and capricious application of the death penalty.

Many other states with statutes similar to Georgia's were affected by the *Furman* ruling but moved quickly to modify their procedures. What evolved was the two-step procedure used today in capital cases. In the first stage, guilt or innocence is decided. If the defendant is convicted of a crime for which execution is possible, a second, or penalty, phase ensues. The penalty phase generally permits the introduction of new evidence that may have been irrelevant to the question of guilt but that may be relevant to punishment, such as drug use or childhood abuse. In most death penalty jurisdictions, juries determine the punishment. However, in Arizona, Idaho, Montana, and Nebraska, the trial judge sets the sentence in the second phase of capital murder trials, and Alabama, Delaware, Florida, and Indiana allow juries only to recommend a sentence to the judge.

The Supreme Court specifically approved the two-step trial procedure in *Gregg* v. *Georgia* (1976).[145] In *Gregg,* the Court upheld the two-stage procedural requirements of Georgia's new capital punishment law as necessary for ensuring the separation of the highly personal information needed in a sentencing decision from the kinds of information reasonably permissible in a jury trial where issues of guilt or innocence alone are being decided. In the opinion written for the majority, the Court for the first time recognized the significance of public opinion in deciding on the legitimacy of questionable sanctions.[146] Its opinion cited the strong showing of public support for the death penalty following *Furman* to mean that death was still a socially and culturally acceptable penalty.

Post-*Gregg* decisions set limits on the use of death as a penalty for all but the most severe crimes. In 1977, in the case of *Coker* v. *Georgia,*[147] the Court struck down a Georgia law imposing the death penalty for the rape of an adult woman. The Court concluded that capital punishment under such circumstances would be "grossly disproportionate" to the crime. A year earlier, in the 1976 case of *Woodson* v. *North Carolina,*[148] a law requiring mandatory application of the death penalty for specific crimes was overturned.

In two 1990 rulings, *Blystone* v. *Pennsylvania*[149] and *Boyde* v. *California,*[150] the Court upheld state statutes dictating that death penalties must be imposed where juries find a lack of mitigating factors that could offset obvious aggravating circumstances. In the 1990 case of R. Gene Simmons, an Arkansas mass murderer convicted of killing 16 relatives during a 1987 shooting rampage, the Court granted inmates under sentence of death the right to waive appeals. Prior to the *Simmons* case, any interested party could file a brief on behalf of the condemned—with or without their consent.

Recently, death-row inmates, and those who file cases on their behalf to test the boundaries of statutory acceptability, have been busy challenging state capital punishment laws. Most such challenges focus on the procedures involved in sentencing decisions. In 1994, for example, a challenge to the constitutionality of California's capital sentencing law, which requires the jury to consider details such as the circumstances of the offense, prior violent crimes by the defendant, and the defendant's age, was rejected in *Tuilaepa* v. *California.*[151]

Following *Apprendi* v. *New Jersey* (discussed earlier in this chapter), attorneys for an Arizona death-row inmate successfully challenged that state's practice of allowing judges, sitting without a jury, to make factual determinations necessary for imposition of the death penalty. In *Ring* v. *Arizona* (2002),[152] a jury had found Timothy Stuart Ring guilty of felony murder occurring in the course of an armed robbery for the killing of an armored car driver in 1994, but deadlocked on the charge of premeditated murder. Under Arizona law, Ring could not be sentenced to death, the statutory maximum penalty for first-degree murder, unless a judge made further findings in a separate sentencing hearing. The death penalty could be imposed only if the judge found the existence of at least one aggravating circumstance specified by law that was not offset by mitigating circumstances. During such a hearing, the judge listened to an accomplice who said that Ring planned the robbery and shot the guard. The judge then determined that Ring was the actual killer and found that the killing was committed for financial gain (an aggravating factor). Following the hearing, Ring was sentenced to death. His attorneys appealed, claiming that, by the standards set forth in *Apprendi,* Arizona's sentencing scheme violated the Sixth Amendment's guarantee of a jury trial because it entrusted a judge with fact-finding powers that allowed Ring's sentence to be raised above what would otherwise have been the statutory maximum. The U.S. Supreme Court agreed, finding that "Arizona's enumerated aggravating factors operate as the functional equivalent of an element of a greater offense," and overturned Ring's sentence. *Ring* established that juries, not judges, must decide the facts that lead to a death sentence. The *Ring* ruling called into question at least 150 judge-imposed death sentences[153] in at least five states (Arizona, Colorado, Idaho, Montana, and Nebraska).[154]

In 2003, in the case of *Summerlin* v. *Stewart*[155] the U.S. Court of Appeals for the Ninth Circuit retroactively applied the *Ring* decision and vacated the death sentences of 100 prisoners in three states that fall within its jurisdiction. The court found that inmates in Arizona, Idaho, and Montana had been sent to death row by judges rather than juries in violation of *Ring* and ordered that their sentences be commuted to life in prison. Those sentences were reinstated, however, by the U.S. Supreme Court in the 2004 case of *Schriro* v. *Summerlin,*[156] in which the retroactivity analysis of

Excessive bail shall not be required, nor excessive fines imposed, nor cruel and unusual punishments inflicted.

—Eighth Amendment to the U.S. Constitution

At bottom, then, the Cruel and Unusual Punishments Clause prohibits the infliction of uncivilized and inhuman punishments. The State, even as it punishes, must treat its members with respect for their intrinsic worth as human beings. A punishment is "cruel and unusual," therefore, if it does not comport with human dignity.

—Former U.S. Supreme Court Justice William Brennan, concurring in *Furman* v. *Georgia*[xiii]

the Ninth Circuit Court was invalidated. The rule established in *Apprendi* and *Ring,* said the Court, could not be applied to sentences that had already been imposed because it was merely a new procedural rule and not a substantive change. Only substantive changes, said the Court, are watershed events retroactively applicable to sentences that have already been finalized. Soon after *Ring* was decided, however, the affected states began the process of amending their death penalty laws to bring them into line with the Court's new requirements.

Although questions may arise about sentencing practices, the majority of justices on today's high court seem largely convinced of the fundamental constitutionality of a sentence of death. Open to debate, however, is the constitutionality of *methods* for its imposition. In a 1993 hearing, *Poyner* v. *Murray,*[157] the U.S. Supreme Court hinted at the possibility of revisiting questions first raised in *Kemmler.* The case challenged Virginia's use of the electric chair, calling it a form of cruel and unusual punishment. Syvasky Lafayette Poyner, who originally brought the case before the Court, lost his bid for a stay of execution and was electrocuted in March 1993. Nonetheless, in *Poyner,* Justices David H. Souter, Harry A. Blackmun, and John Paul Stevens wrote, "The Court has not spoken squarely on the underlying issue since *In re Kemmler* . . . and the holding of that case does not constitute a dispositive response to litigation of the issue in light of modern knowledge about the method of execution in question."

In a still more recent ruling, members of the Court questioned the constitutionality of hanging, suggesting that it too may be a form of cruel and unusual punishment. In that case, *Campbell* v. *Wood* (1994),[158] the defendant, Charles Campbell, raped a woman, was released from prison at the completion of his sentence, and then went back and murdered her. His request for a stay of execution was denied since the law of Washington State, where the murder occurred, offered Campbell a choice of various methods of execution and, therefore, an alternative to hanging. Similarly, in 1996, the Court upheld California's death penalty statute, which provides for lethal injection as the primary method of capital punishment in that state.[159] The constitutionality of the statute had been challenged by two death-row inmates who claimed that a provision in the law that permitted condemned prisoners the choice of lethal gas in lieu of injection brought the statute within the realm of allowing cruel and unusual punishments.

Questions about the constitutionality of electrocution as a means of execution again came to the fore in 1997, when flames shot from the head and the leather mask covering the face of Pedro Medina during his Florida execution. Similarly, in 1999, blood poured from behind the mask covering Allen Lee "Tiny" Davis's face as he was put to death in Florida's electric chair. State officials claimed that the 344-pound Davis suffered a nosebleed brought on by hypertension and the blood-thinning medication that he had been taking. Photographs of Davis taken during and immediately after the execution showed him grimacing while bleeding profusely onto his chest and neck. In 2001, the Georgia Supreme Court declared electrocution to be unconstitutional, ending its use in that state.[160] The Georgia court cited testimony from lower court records showing that electrocution may not result in a quick death or in an immediate cessation of consciousness. By the time of the court's decision, however, the Georgia legislature had already passed a law establishing lethal injection as the state's sole method of punishment for capital crimes. Following the decision, only two states, Alabama and Nebraska, still use electrocution as their sole method of execution.[161]

The U.S. Supreme Court has also ruled that certain personal characteristics of the perpetrator, such as age and mental inability, can be a bar to execution. In 2001, for example, in the case of *Penry* v. *Johnson,*[162] the U.S. Supreme Court found that a state trial court in Texas had failed to allow a jury to properly consider a murder defendant's low IQ and childhood abuse as mitigating factors when it found that his crime warranted the death penalty rather than life in prison. This was the second time that the Court had ordered a new sentencing hearing for Johnny Paul Penry, who was first convicted of brutally raping and murdering Pamela Carpenter on October 25, 1979, and had twice been sentenced to die.[163] In both cases, the Court found fault with Texas jury instructions and the system for their implementation, which restricted jurors from effectively weighing Penry's mental retardation as a mitigating circumstance in their sentencing decision. However, shortly after the Court's decision, Texas Governor Rick Perry vetoed legislation that would have banned the execution of mentally retarded death-row inmates throughout the state.[164]

Following *Penry,* the U.S. Supreme Court ruled in the case of *Atkins* v. *Virginia* (2002)[165] that executing mentally retarded people violates the Constitution's ban on cruel and unusual punishments. The Court, following the lead of the federal government and the 18 states that had already banned such executions, noted that "a national consensus has developed against it." According to the Court, the standards by which the practice and imposition of capital punishment are to be judged today are not those that prevailed at the time the Bill of Rights was authored. They are,

Timothy Ring, the Arizona death-row inmate who won a 2002 U.S. Supreme Court case that potentially invalidated the death sentences of at least 150 other prisoners. In that case, *Ring* v. *Arizona,* the Court held that defendants have a Sixth Amendment right to have a jury, and not just a judge, determine whether aggravating factors necessary to impose the death penalty exist.

*AP Wide World Photos*

rather, "the evolving standards of decency that mark the progress of a maturing society."[166] Atkins, whose IQ was measured at 59 (100 is "average"), had been convicted of murdering a man during a robbery when he was 18. In what some thought an unusual turn of events, Johnny Paul Penry, whose case sparked national interest in the execution of mentally retarded offenders, was sentenced to death for a third time only 10 days after the *Atkins* ruling. The Texas jury that sentenced him rejected his claims of mental inadequacy.[167] Nonetheless, *Atkins* called into question the standing of a substantial number of death-row inmates across the country, many of whom are expected to appeal their convictions. The case also ushered in a national debate on how mental retardation should be measured. Finally, some people questioned the Court's wisdom in keeping mentally retarded offenders from facing the death penalty, saying that capital crimes involve moral judgments, not intellectual ones, and that even people of low intelligence should be expected to act morally.[168]

Nor is serious mental illness a bar to execution, unless it affects the condemned inmate's mind such that he doesn't know why he's on death row or the punishment he faces. In 2004, for example Texas Governor Rick Perry rejected a recommendation by the Texas Board of Pardons and Paroles as well as a humanitarian request by the president of the European Union that he commute the sentence of mentally ill killer Kelsey Patterson to life imprisonment.[169] Patterson, who apparently suffered from a particularly severe form of paranoid schizophrenia, frequently spoke of "remote control devices" and "implants" that controlled him and said that he committed acts involuntarily.[170] Patterson was executed shortly after the governor denied clemency. Patterson had been on death row since 1992 for the shooting death of a secretary and her boss at an oil company office in Palestine, Texas.

Age is a bar to execution when the offender committed the crime when he was younger than 18, a standard set forth in the 2005 U.S. Supreme Court case of *Roper* v. *Simmons.*[171] The majority opinion in the case, based on what the Court considered to be evolving standards of decency, was rendered after the justices heard evidence that juveniles are generally impetuous, immature, and vulnerable to negative peer pressure. The ruling invalidated the capital sentences of 72 death-row inmates in 12 states. Among the 962 people put to death between January 1976 and January 2004, 22 had committed their crimes as juveniles.[172]

# The Future of the Death Penalty

Because the question of the death penalty is so emotionally laden, there is little common ground even for discussion between abolitionists and retentionists. Foes of the death penalty hope that its demonstrated lack of deterrent capacity will convince others that it should be

> Evolving standards of human decency will finally lead to the abolition of the death penalty in this country.
>
> —Former U.S. Supreme Court Justice William Brennan

## CJ NEWS

### Death Penalty Gains Unusual Defenders

Robert Blecker sat quietly as other professors ticked off their reasons for opposing the death penalty: It's unfair to blacks. It doesn't really deter crime. Innocent people could be executed.

But Blecker, a professor at New York Law School, was having none of it. When it was his turn to speak at the recent death-penalty forum at New York's John Jay College, he summed up his support for executions in three words: "Barbara Jo Brown."

Blecker then launched into a staccato description of the 11-year-old Louisiana girl's slaying in 1981, how she was abducted, raped and tortured by a man who later was executed. The story drew gasps from a crowd accustomed to dealing in legal theories and academic formulas. "We know evil when we see it, and it's past time that we start saying so," Blecker said later. "When it comes to the death penalty, too many in academia can't face that."

For years, professors and civil rights leaders have led the charge against the death penalty, raising questions about its fairness that caused two states to suspend executions. But now death-penalty supporters have found some unlikely allies: a small but growing number of professors and social scientists who are speaking out in favor of the ultimate sanction.

Challenging themes that have been the foundation of the anti-death penalty movement, about a dozen professors and social scientists have produced unprecedented research arguing that the penalty deters crime. They also are questioning studies that say it is racially biased, and they are attacking one of the anti-death penalty movement's most effective talking points: that more than 100 people released from death row during the past 30 years were "innocent."

The researchers say that only about a third of those released from death row could show they were innocent of murder, and that the rest were released for other reasons, often legal technicalities. The researchers say that those convicts' names have remained on the "innocent" list to exaggerate the case against the death penalty.

The pro-death penalty researchers are still a tiny minority in U.S. academia, which Blecker guesses is "99%-plus" against executions. But the researchers are changing the nature of the death-penalty debate.

Justice Department lawyers have cited their work in legal briefs defending the death penalty. Republican senators have used the new research to try to stave off proposals to make it more difficult to execute inmates. Some death-penalty supporters, noting that more than two-thirds of Americans back capital punishment, say the research validates the views of a relatively silent majority.

And victims' rights groups that have felt excluded from the debate over executions say the professors give them moral support.

"It's been easy for the media to dismiss (death-penalty supporters) as just a rabble that wants to 'hang 'em all,' " says Dudley Sharp, resource director for Justice for All, a victims' rights

Professor Robert Blecker, of New York Law School. Blecker, who has been described as "a lion in a den of Daniels," is a strong supporter of capital punishment.

*John Halpern*

group in Houston. "Now we've got research, respectability—things that have always been conceded to the other side. It's more of a real debate."

### FAIRNESS OF EXECUTIONS QUESTIONED

Some studies have suggested that blacks were more likely than whites to receive death sentences, especially when their victims were white. Other studies compared murder rates in the 38 death-penalty states with lower rates in the 12 states that don't have the penalty and concluded that capital punishment does not deter homicides.

In 1993, a U.S. House of Representatives panel led by a death-penalty foe, Rep. Don Edwards, D–Calif., found that 68 people had been released from wrongfully imposed death sentences during the previous 20 years. The report was the basis for the list of 102 "innocents" that anti-death penalty groups now promote.

The idea that innocent people had been sent to death rows across the nation was politically potent, and capital punishment foes exploited it. The Edwards list was taken over by the Death

Penalty Information Center, which has added to the list 34 death-row inmates who have been exonerated. Among those were 12 who were freed by DNA tests done on evidence years after their convictions.

The center doesn't vouch for the validity of the initial 68 cases. To be added to the center's "innocents" list, a condemned inmate must have his conviction overturned and be acquitted at retrial. Ex-prisoners also are added to the list if prosecutors don't pursue a retrial.

The ongoing campaign against the death penalty has been effective. Analysts say it likely contributed to a dip in the still-strong public support for capital punishment. (Surveys in October said that about 70% of Americans back the death penalty, down from 80% in 1994.)

Meanwhile, the governors of Illinois and Maryland have suspended executions in their states to study whether the death penalty is being imposed fairly.

In 2002, the U.S. Supreme Court ruled that states cannot execute killers who are under 18 when they commit their crimes and that juries, not judges, must impose death sentences. In the latter case, Justice Stephen Breyer called studies of the death penalty's impact on deterring crime "inconclusive."

Also in 2002, a U.S. district court judge here declared the federal death penalty unconstitutional, a decision that applied only in his court and that was appealed by the Justice Department. Judge Jed Rakoff based his ruling on research, including the list of 102 "innocents," that he said suggested there is a high risk that inmates could be wrongly executed. A U.S. appeals court panel reversed that ruling on Dec. 10, saying that the matter should be left to the U.S. Supreme Court. That decision, too, is likely to be appealed.

"There's no way to underestimate the importance of the innocence issue," Dieter says. "It's created an irresolvable concern on the part of the public."

### HOW INNOCENT ARE THEY?

But how innocent are the "innocents"?

Ward Campbell, a deputy attorney general in California, said in a study last year that at least 68 of the 102 ex-death row inmates on the "innocents" list don't belong there. Campbell says some on the list had their convictions reversed because of prosecutors' errors or misconduct but seem certain to have committed the crimes of which they were convicted. Others avoided retrials or were acquitted because witnesses died, evidence was excluded for legal reasons, or because they were in prison for similar crimes.

In some cases, death sentences were overturned because the convict was an accomplice, not the killer. Campbell found that nine "innocents" were exonerated because courts said the evidence against them was valid but did not establish guilt beyond a "reasonable doubt."

Eight of those on the list were not actually on death row when they were exonerated; two others never received a death sentence, Campbell said. In more than a dozen cases, death sentences were overturned only because later Supreme Court rulings invalidated a state's death-penalty statute.

For Campbell, a recent addition to the list shows the problem with its standards: Larry Osborne was convicted of breaking into a Louisville couple's home in 1997 and killing them. He won a new trial because the conviction was based in part on grand jury testimony from an accomplice who died before Osborne's trial. An appeals court said the testimony should not have been admitted as evidence because Osborne's lawyer could not cross-examine the dead witness. Osborne was acquitted in a second trial. He made the "innocents" list in August.

Dieter says convicts whose sentences have been overturned "truly are innocent, in the legal sense." A spokesman for Sen. Patrick Leahy, D–Vt., sponsor of a bill aimed at eliminating wrongful convictions, says that "quibbling over numbers" misses the point.

"Even the staunchest defenders of the status quo must admit that ... innocent people have been sent to death row," Leahy spokesman David Carle says.

Pro-death penalty professors say the number of innocents does matter.

"The idea that 100 innocent people have just missed execution has undermined the public's confidence" in the death penalty, says Barry Latzer, a political scientist at John Jay College. "If it's substantially fewer, it's not nearly as powerful a story."

Latzer and his colleagues are challenging death-penalty foes on other fronts as well.

John McAdams, a political science professor at Marquette University in Milwaukee, acknowledges that African-Americans appear to be overrepresented on death row, where they account for about 42% of the prisoners, compared with about 12% of the U.S. population. (Since 1977, 57% of those executed have been white; 35% have been black.)

McAdams notes the widely held belief that black defendants are more likely to receive the death penalty than whites convicted in similar slayings. But he says that doesn't take into account that blacks make up nearly 50% of all murder victims, and that all but a few are killed by other blacks. Blacks who kill blacks, he argues, are far less likely to get the death penalty than whites, blacks or Hispanics who kill whites.

"Why are the lives of black victims less valued?" McAdams asks. "There's a subtle kind of racism going on here, and it's got to do with the victims of crime, not how we treat the perpetrators." He realizes that his analysis has a provocative implication: that more black killers should be executed. He favors "more executions generally."

But fellow death-penalty supporter Blecker says that the death penalty should be reserved for the "worst of the worst, the ones almost everyone can agree are worthy."

Death-penalty supporters also say there is plenty of evidence that executions deter homicides.

A study last year by researchers at Emory University in Atlanta examined the nearly 6,000 death sentences imposed in the USA from 1977 through 1996. The authors compared

*(continued)*

## CJ NEWS *(continued)*

changes in murder rates in 3,000 U.S. counties to the likelihood of being executed for murder in that county. They found that murder rates declined in counties where capital punishment was imposed. The researchers said a statistical formula suggested that each execution saved the lives of 18 potential victims.

Recent studies at the University of Houston and at the University of Colorado at Denver had similar findings. Blecker, who is researching deterrence, says they square with what he found in interviews with 60 killers. "They are cognizant of whether they are operating in a death-penalty state before they pull the trigger," he says. "They're operating in the real world, not the realm of political theory."

To McAdams, the debate over deterrence is unnecessary. "If you execute a murderer and it stops other murders, you've saved innocent lives," he says. "And if it doesn't, you've executed a murderer. Where's the problem?"

Academics who back executions are gaining some acceptance. Senate Republicans countered Leahy's bill by citing research from pro-death penalty academics. The bill was approved by the Judiciary Committee but is stalled in the Senate.

Meanwhile, Blecker says he's getting asked to more academic conferences on the death penalty—usually as the only voice in favor. " 'A lion in a den of Daniels' is one way I've been introduced," he says.

For the latest in crime and justice news, visit the Talk Justice news feed at http://www.crimenews.info.

*Source:* Richard Willing, "Death Penalty Gains Unusual Defenders," *USA Today,* January 7, 2003, p. 1A. Copyright © 2003, *USA Today.* Reprinted with permission.

---

abandoned. Their stance, based as it is on statistical evidence, appears rational. However, it is doubtful that many capital punishment opponents could be persuaded to support the death penalty even if statistics showed it to be a deterrent. Likewise, the tactics of death penalty supporters are equally instinctive. Retentionists could probably not be swayed by statistical studies that show the punishment's lack of deterrent effect, since their support is bound up with calls for retribution.

The future of the death penalty may rest largely with state legislatures. Short of renewed Supreme Court intervention, the future of capital punishment may depend more on popular opinion than it does on arguments pro or con. Because their careers lie in the hands of their constituencies, legislators are likely to follow the public mandate. Hence, it may be that studies of public attitudes toward the death penalty may be the most useful in predicting the sanction's future. At the moment, it appears that the American public, as a whole, favors the imposition of capital punishment in the case of heinous crimes. Support for the death penalty varies considerably from state to state and from one region of the country to another. The percentage of Americans supporting capital punishment appeared to increase substantially following the events of September 11, 2001.[173] A Gallup poll taken in May 2003 found 79% of those polled in favor of the death penalty under certain circumstances. A similar poll by the same organization found that although most respondents voiced support for the death penalty, that support dropped to 53% when respondents were offered an alternative sentence of life without parole.[174]

The future of the death penalty is likely to be determined in individual states and will probably result in legislatively mandated procedural enhancements meant to guarantee fairness. In 2002, for example, a special commission appointed by Illinois Governor George Ryan to examine the imposition of capital punishment in that state made its report, saying that the system through which capital sentences are imposed should be modified to encompass a number of procedural safeguards. Recommended safeguards include (1) tighter controls on how the police investigate cases, including a requirement that investigators "continue to pursue all reasonable lines of inquiry, whether these point toward or away from the suspect"; (2) controls on the potential fallibility of eyewitness testimony, including lineups where the person in charge is not aware of which person in the lineup is the suspect (to preclude him or her from unconsciously identifying the suspect); and (3) statutory reform so that the death penalty cannot be applied based solely on the testimony of any single accomplice or eyewitness without further corroboration.[175] In April 2003, the state's new governor said that because of his concerns over executing innocent people, he would not lift the ban on executions even if the state's legislature passes a bill aimed at improving the system.[176]

> So justice, while she winks at crimes, stumbles on innocence sometimes.
>
> —Samuel Butler, *Hudibras* (canto II, pt. II, l. 1177)

**SUMMARY**

The goals of criminal sentencing are many and varied, and they include retribution, incapacitation, deterrence, rehabilitation, and restoration. The just deserts model, with its emphasis on retribution and revenge, may be the most influential sentencing philosophy in the United States today. Many citizens, however, still expect sentencing practices to provide for the other general sentencing goals. This ambivalence toward the purpose of sentencing reflects a more basic cultural uncertainty regarding the root causes of crime, the true nature of justice, and the fundamental goals of the criminal justice system.

Structured sentencing, embodied in the Federal Sentencing Guidelines (whose applicability has been called into question by recent U.S. Supreme Court decisions) and in many state sentencing programs today, is a child of the just deserts philosophy. The structured sentencing model, however, while apparently associated with a reduction in biased and inequitable sentencing practices that had characterized previous sentencing models, may not be the panacea it once seemed. Inequitable practices under the indeterminate model may never have been as widespread as opponents of that model claimed them to be. Worse still, the practice of structured sentencing may not reduce sentencing discretion but merely move it out of the hands of judges and into the ever-widening sphere of plea bargaining. Doubly unfortunate, by de-emphasizing parole, structured sentencing weakens incentives for inmates to undergo positive change and tends to swell prison populations until they're overflowing. Even so, as society-wide sentiments and the social policies they support swing further in the direction of social responsibility, the interests of crime victims and the concerns of those who champion them are likely to be increasingly recognized.

**DISCUSSION QUESTIONS**

1. Describe the five goals of contemporary criminal sentencing discussed in this chapter. Which of these goals do you think ought to be the primary goal of sentencing? How might your choice vary with the type of offense? In what circumstances might your choice be less acceptable?

2. Illustrate the difference between indeterminate and structured sentencing. What led some states to abandon indeterminate sentencing?

3. What structured sentencing models are in use today? Which model holds the best promise for long-term crime reduction? Why? In your opinion, is the return to just deserts consistent with structured sentencing? Explain.

4. What is mandatory sentencing? How does it differ from indeterminate sentencing? Why was mandatory sentencing created?

5. What is truth in sentencing? How have states attempted to meet federal truth-in-sentencing requirements?

6. Explain the development of federal sentencing guidelines. What have recent court decisions said about the applicability of those guidelines?

7. What is a presentence investigation? How do presentence investigations contribute to the contents of presentence reports? How are presentence reports used?

8. Describe the history of victims' rights and services in this country. What role does the victim play in criminal justice proceedings today?

9. What are the four traditional sentencing options? Under what circumstances might each be appropriate?

10. Do you support or oppose capital punishment? Outline the arguments on both sides of the issue.

**WEB QUEST**

Visit the U.S. Sentencing Commission (USSC) on the Web at http://www.ussc.gov. Review the most recent publications and reports to Congress available at that site, and identify the current issues in federal sentencing. List and describe these issues. Also view the USSC employment opportunities listed at the site, and read the information about the Judicial Fellows Program.

Now visit the Sentencing Project at http://www.sentencingproject.org. (You can use the Prentice Hall Cybrary to find sites that have moved since this book was published.) What is the mission of the Sentencing Project? How does that mission coincide with the interests of the National Association of Sentencing Advocates? (*Hint:* A link to this organization can be found on the Sentencing Project home page, or you can find it through the Cybrary.) Summarize what you have learned, and submit your findings to your instructor if asked to do so.

To complete this Web Quest online, go to the Web Quest module in Chapter 11 of the *Criminal Justice Today* Companion Website at cjtoday.com.

**NOTES**

i. E-mail communication, Society of Police Futurists International, April 6, 2004.

ii. "The Crime Bust," *U.S. News & World Report,* May 25, 1998.

iii. Lawrence A. Greenfeld, *Prison Sentences and Time Served for Violence,* Bureau of Justice Statistics Selected Findings, No. 4 (Washington, DC: Bureau of Justice Statistics, April 1995).

iv. *Ring* v. *Arizona,* 122 S.Ct. 2428, 153 L.Ed.2d 556 (2002); dissent.

v. "Prepared Remarks of Attorney General Alberto Gonzales," Sentencing Guidelines Speech, Washington, DC, June 21, 2005.

vi. *Harris* v. *U.S.,* 122 S.Ct. 2406, 153 L.Ed.2d 524 (2002).

vii. "President Calls for Crime Victims' Rights Amendment," White House press release, April 16, 2002. Web posted at http://www.whitehouse.gov/news/releases/2002/04/20020416–1.html (accessed September 13, 2002).

viii. "Judge Refuses to Delay McVeigh Execution," *New York Times,* June 6, 2001.

ix. "Fireside chat" with U.S. Supreme Court Justices John Paul Stevens and Stephen Breyer, 53rd annual meeting of the Seventh Circuit Bar Association and Judicial Conference of the Seventh Circuit, Chicago, Illinois, May 9, 2004.

x. *Payne* v. *Tennessee,* 501 U.S. 808 (1991).

xi. *Criminal Justice Newsletter,* Vol. 31, No. 13 (2000), p. 1.

xii. Laura Goodstein, "Death Penalty Falls from Favor as Some Lose Confidence in Its Fairness," *New York Times,* June 17, 2001.

xiii. *Furman* v. *Georgia,* 408 U.S. 238 (1972).

1. Michael Tonry, "Implementing, Changing, and Maintaining Sentencing Guidelines in the Political Climate of the 1990's." Web posted at http://students.washington.edu/ths123/state.htm (accessed January 3, 2002).

2. "Seven Charged in Chicago Beating Deaths," CNN.com, August 3, 2002 (accessed September 12, 2002).

3. "'Brutal Beat-Down' Kills Chicago Men; Deaths Ruled Homicides," *USA Today,* July 31, 2002.

4. Quotations in this paragraph come from John W. Fountain, "Mob Kills Two after Truck Hits Women on a Stoop," *New York Times,* August 1, 2002.

5. For a thorough discussion of the philosophy of punishment and sentencing, see David Garland, *Punishment and Modern Society: A Study in Social Theory* (Chicago: University of Chicago Press, 1990). See also Ralph D. Ellis and Carol S. Ellis, *Theories of Criminal Justice: A Critical Reappraisal* (Wolfeboro, NH: Longwood Academic, 1989); and Colin Summer, *Censure, Politics, and Criminal Justice* (Bristol, PA: Open University Press, 1990).

6. Punishment is said to be required because social order (and the laws that represent it) could not exist for long if transgressions went unsanctioned.

7. "Back to the Chain Gang," *Newsweek,* October 17, 1994, p. 87.

8. Ibid.

9. For an excellent review of the "get tough" attitudes that influenced sentencing decisions during the 1990s, see Tamasak Wicharaya, *Simple Theory, Hard Reality: The Impact of Sentencing Reforms on Courts, Prisons, and Crime* (Albany: State University of New York Press, 1995).

10. For a thorough review of the literature on deterrence, see Raymond Paternoster, "The Deterrent Effect of the Perceived Certainty and Severity of Punishment: A Review of the Evidence and Issues," *Justice Quarterly,* Vol. 4, No. 2 (June 1987), pp. 174–217.

11. Hugo Adam Bedau, "Retributivism and the Theory of Punishment," *Journal of Philosophy,* Vol. 75 (November 1978), pp. 601–620.

12. H. L. A. Hart, *Punishment and Responsibility: Essays in the Philosophy of Law* (Oxford: Clarendon Press, 1968).

13. The definitive study during this period was Douglas Lipton, Robert Martinson, and J. Woks, *The Effectiveness of Correctional Treatment: A Survey of Treatment Valuation Studies* (New York: Praeger Press, 1975).

14. See, for example, Lawrence W. Sherman et al., *Preventing Crime: What Works, What Doesn't, What's Promising* (Washington, DC: National Institute of Justice, 1997).

15. Gordon Bazemore and Mark S. Umbreit, foreword to *Balanced and Restorative Justice: Program Summary* (Washington, DC: Office of Juvenile Justice and Delinquency Prevention, 1994).

16. 18 U.S.C. 3563(a)(2).

17. E-mail communications with the Office of Reparative Programs, Department of Corrections, State of Vermont, July 3, 1995.

18. Donna Hunzeker, "State Sentencing Systems and 'Truth in Sentencing,'" *State Legislative Report,* Vol. 20, No. 3 (Denver, CO: National Conference of State Legislatures, 1995).

19. Paula M. Ditton and Doris James Wilson, *Truth in Sentencing in State Prisons* (Washington, DC: Bureau of Justice Statistics, 1999).

20. "Oklahoma Rapist Gets 30,000 Years," *United Press International* wire service, southwest edition, December 23, 1994.

21. For a historical consideration of alleged disparities, see G. Kleck, "Racial Discrimination in Criminal Sentencing: A Critical Evaluation of the Evidence with Additional Evidence on the Death Penalty," *American Sociological Review,* No. 46 (1981), pp. 783–805; and G. Kleck, "Life Support for Ailing Hypotheses: Modes of Summarizing the Evidence for Racial Discrimination in Sentencing," *Law and Human Behavior,* No. 9 (1985), pp. 271–285.

22. As discussed later in this chapter, federal sentencing guidelines did not become effective until 1987 and still had to meet many court challenges.

23. U.S. Sentencing Commission, *Federal Sentencing Guidelines Manual* (Washington, DC: U.S. Government Printing Office, 1987), p. 2.

24. Inmates can still earn a maximum of 54 days per year of good-time credit.

25. The Parole Commission Phaseout Act of 1996 requires the attorney general to report to Congress yearly as to whether it is cost-effective for the Parole Commission to remain a separate agency or whether its functions (and personnel) should be assigned elsewhere. Under the law, if the attorney general recommends assigning the Parole Commission's functions to another component of the Department of Justice, federal parole will continue as long as necessary.

26. Lawrence A. Greenfeld, *Prison Sentences and Time Served for Violence* (Washington, DC: Bureau of Justice Statistics, April 1995).

27. For an excellent review of the act and its implications, see Gregory D. Lee, "U.S. Sentencing Guidelines: Their Impact on Federal Drug Offenders," *FBI Law Enforcement Bulletin,* May 1995, pp. 17–21.

28. *Mistretta* v. *U.S.,* 488 U.S. 361, 371 (1989).

29. For an engaging overview of how mitigating factors might be applied under the guidelines, see *Koon* v. *U.S.,* 116 S.Ct. 2035, 135 L.Ed.2d 392 (1996).

30. U.S. Sentencing Commission, *Federal Sentencing Guidelines Manual,* p. 207.

31. *Deal* v. *U.S.,* 113 S.Ct. 1993, 124 L.Ed.2d 44 (1993).

32. U.S. Sentencing Commission, *Federal Sentencing Guidelines Manual,* p. 8.

33. National Institute of Justice, *Sentencing Commission Chairman Wilkins Answers Questions on the Guidelines,* NIJ Research in Action Series (Washington, DC: NIJ, 1987), p. 7.

34. *Melendez* v. *U.S.,* 117 S.Ct. 383, 136 L.Ed.2d 301 (1996).

35. *Apprendi* v. *New Jersey,* 120 S.Ct. 2348 (2000).

36. See, for example, Alexandra A. E. Shapiro and Jonathan P. Bach, "Applying 'Apprendi' to Federal Sentencing Rules," *New York Law Journal,* March 23, 2001. Web posted at http://www.lw.com/pubs/articles/pdf/ applyingApprendi.pdf (accessed June 30, 2002); and Freya Russell, "Limiting the Use of Acquitted and Uncharged Conduct at Sentencing: *Apprendi* v. *New Jersey* and Its Effect on the Relevant Conduct Provision of the United States Sentencing Guidelines," *California Law Review,* Vol. 89 (July 2001), p. 1199.

37. *Harris* v. *U.S.,* 122 S.Ct. 2406, 153 L.Ed.2d 524 (2002).

38. *U.S.* v. *Cotton,* 122 S.Ct. 1781, 152 L.Ed.2d 860 (2002).

39. 21 U.S.C. 841(b)(1)(C).

40. *Blakely* v. *Washington,* U.S. Supreme Court, No. 02-1632 (decided June 24, 2004).

41. *U.S.* v. *Booker,* 125 S.Ct. 738 (2005).

42. Combined with *U.S.* v. *Booker* (2005).

43. Stanley E. Adelman, "Supreme Court Invalidates Federal Sentencing Guidelines . . . to an Extent," *On the Line,* the Newsletter of the American Correctional Association, May 2005, p. 1.

44. See *United States* v. *Rodriguez,* 398 F.3d 1291, 1297 (11th Cir. 2005).

45. Ibid., p. 3.

46. Much of the material in this section is derived from Dale Parent et al., *Mandatory Sentencing,* NIJ Research in Action Series (Washington, DC: National Institute of Justice, 1997).

47. In mid-1996, the California Supreme Court ruled the state's three-strikes law an undue intrusion on judges' sentencing discretion,

and California judges now use their own discretion in evaluating which offenses "fit" within the meaning of the law.

48. Michael Tonry, *Sentencing Reform Impacts* (Washington, DC: National Institute of Justice, 1987).

49. D. C. McDonald and K. E. Carlson, *Sentencing in the Courts: Does Race Matter? The Transition to Sentencing Guidelines, 1986–90* (Washington, DC: Bureau of Justice Statistics, 1993).

50. "Public Humiliation," *Lawyer News,* July 31, 2004. Web posted at http://www.lawyernews.com/weblog/2004/08 (accessed July 5, 2005).

51. Much of the information in this section is taken from Haya El Nasser, "Paying for Crime with Shame: Judges Say 'Scarlet Letter' Angle Works," *USA Today,* June 26, 1996, p. 1A.

52. Richard Willing, "Thief Challenges Dose of Shame as Punishment," *USA Today,* August 18, 2004, p. 3A.

53. John Braithwaite, *Crime, Shame, and Reintegration* (Cambridge, England: Cambridge University Press, 1989).

54. Such evidence does, in fact, exist. See, for example, Harold G. Grasmick, Robert J. Bursik, Jr., and Bruce J. Arneklev, "Reduction in Drunk Driving as a Response to Increased Threats of Shame, Embarrassment, and Legal Sanctions," *Criminology,* Vol. 31, No. 1 (1993), pp. 41–67.

55. Joan Petersilia, *House Arrest, A National Institute of Justice Crime File Study Guide* (Washington, DC: National Institute of Justice, 1988).

56. Privacy Act of 1974, 5 U.S.C.A. 522a, 88 Statute 1897, Public Law 93-579, December 31, 1974.

57. Freedom of Information Act, 5 U.S.C. 522, and amendments. The status of presentence investigative reports has not yet been clarified under this act to the satisfaction of all legal scholars.

58. City of New York, Citywide Accountability Program, S.T.A.R.S. (Statistical Tracking, Analysis, and Reporting System). Web posted at http://www.nyc.gov/html/prob/pdf/caps_012004.pdf (accessed May 15, 2005).

59. For a good review of the issues involved, see Robert C. Davis, Arthur J. Lurigio, and Wesley G. Skogan, *Victims of Crime,* 2nd ed. (Thousand Oaks, CA: Sage, 1997); and Leslie Sebba, *Third Parties: Victims and the Criminal Justice System* (Columbus: Ohio State University Press, 1996).

60. President's Task Force on Victims of Crime, *Final Report* (Washington, DC: U.S. Government Printing Office, 1982).

61. Peter Finn and Beverly N. W. Lee, *Establishing and Expanding Victim-Witness Assistance Programs* (Washington, DC: National Institute of Justice, 1988).

62. National Institute of Justice, *Victim Assistance Programs: Whom They Service, What They Offer* (Washington, DC: NIJ, 1995).

63. Senate Joint Resolution (SJR) 65 is a major revision of an initial proposal, SJR 52, which Senators Kyl and Feinstein introduced on April 22, 1996. Representative Henry Hyde introduced House Joint Resolution 174, a companion to SJR 52, and a similar proposal, House Joint Resolution 173, on April 22, 1996.

64. Senate Joint Resolution 44, 105th Congress.

65. See the National Center for Victims of Crime's critique of the 1998 amendment at http://www.ncvc.org/law/Ncvca.htm (accessed January 10, 2000).

66. "President Calls for Crime Victims' Rights Amendment," White House press release, April 16, 2002. Web posted at http://www.whitehouse.gov/news/releases/2002/04/20020416-1.html (accessed September 13, 2002).

67. "Attorneys General Strongly Support S.J. Res. 3," National Victims' Constitutional Amendment Network, April 21, 2000. Web posted at http://www.nvcan.org/news.htm (accessed January 22, 2002).

68. See the National Victims' Constitutional Amendment Network news page at http://www.nvcan.org/news.htm (accessed January 10, 2002).

69. Public Law 97-291.

70. USA PATRIOT Act of 2001, Section 624.

71. Office for Victims of Crime, *Report to the Nation 2003* (Washington, DC: OVC, 2003).

72. S.2329.

73. U.S. Senate, Republican Policy Committee, Legislative Notice No. 63, April 22, 2004.

74. Proposition 8, California's Victim's Bill of Rights.

75. National Victim Center, *Mothers Against Drunk Driving, and American Prosecutors Research Institute, Impact Statements: A Victim's Right to Speak; A Nation's Responsibility to Listen* (Washington, DC: Office for Victims of Crime, July 1994).

76. Robert C. Davis and Barbara E. Smith, "The Effects of Victim Impact Statements on Sentencing Decisions: A Test in an Urban Setting," *Justice Quarterly,* Vol. 11, No. 3 (September 1994), pp. 453–469.

77. Bureau of Justice Statistics, *Report to the Nation on Crime and Justice,* 2nd ed. (Washington, DC: U.S. Government Printing Office, 1988), p. 90.

78. Matthew R. Durose and Patrick A. Langan, *Felony Sentences in State Courts, 2002* (Washington, DC: Bureau of Justice Statistics, 2004). Data for 1990 come from Matthew R. Durose, David J. Levin, and Patrick A. Langan, *Felony Sentences in State Courts,*

*1998* (Washington, DC: Bureau of Justice Statistics, 2001).

79. Durose and Langan, *Felony Sentences in State Courts, 2002,* p. 2.

80. Sally T. Hillsman, Joyce L. Sichel, and Barry Mahoney, *Fines in Sentencing* (New York: Vera Institute of Justice, 1983).

81. Ibid., p. 2.

82. Ibid., p. 4.

83. Ibid.

84. Douglas C. McDonald, Judith Greene, and Charles Worzella, *Day Fines in American Courts: The Staten Island and Milwaukee Experiments* (Washington, DC: National Institute of Justice, 1992).

85. Ibid., p. 56.

86. Laura A. Winterfield and Sally T. Hillsman, *The Staten Island Day-Fine Project* (Washington, DC: National Institute of Justice, 1993), p. 1.

87. S. Turner and J. Petersilia, *Day Fines in Four U.S. Jurisdictions* (Santa Monica, CA: RAND Corporation, 1996).

88. "Man Decapitates Neighbor, Tosses Head in Dumpster," Reuters wire service, May 25, 1996.

89. Capital Punishment Research Project, University of Alabama Law School.

90. Death Penalty Information Center, "State-by-State Death Penalty Information." Web posted at http://www.deathpenaltyinfo.org/FactSheet.pdf (accessed July 12, 2005).

91. Thomas P. Bonczar and Tracy L. Snell, *Capital Punishment 2003* (Washington, DC: Bureau of Justice Statistics, 2004).

92. Richard Willing, "Expansion of Death Penalty to Nonmurders Faces Challenges," *USA Today,* May 14, 1997, p. 6A.

93. NAACP Legal Defense and Educational Fund, *Death Row U.S.A.: Spring 2005.* Web posted at http://www.naacpldf.org/content/pdf/pubs/drusa/DRUSA_Spring_2005.pdf (accessed July 25, 2005).

94. Ibid.

95. *Capital Punishment, 2003,* p. 1.

96. Allan Turner, "Texas Executes Third and Fourth Prisoners in a Week," *Houston Chronicle* via Simon and Schuster's NewsLink service, June 5, 1997.

97. "Chief Justice Calls for Limits on Death Row Habeas Appeals," *Criminal Justice Newsletter,* February 15, 1989, pp. 6–7.

98. *McCleskey* v. *Zant,* 499 U.S. 467, 493–494 (1991).

99. *Coleman* v. *Thompson,* 501 U.S. 722 (1991).

100. *Schlup* v. *Delo,* 115 S.Ct. 851, 130 L.Ed.2d 808 (1995).

101. Public Law 103-322.

102. *Felker* v. *Turpin,* 117 S.Ct. 30, 135 L.Ed.2d 1123 (1996).

103. *Elledge* v. *Florida,* No. 98-5410 (1998).

104. Michelle Locke, "Victim Forgives," Associated Press wire service, May 19, 1996.

105. Ibid.

106. Arthur Koestler, *Reflections on Hanging* (New York: Macmillan, 1956), p. xii.

107. Death Penalty Information Center, "Innocence: Freed from Death Row." Web posted at http://www.deathpenaltyinfo.org/Innocentlist.html (accessed November 1, 2003).

108. Edward Connors et al., *Convicted by Juries, Exonerated by Science: Case Studies in the Use of DNA Evidence to Establish Innocence after Trial* (Washington, DC: National Institute of Justice, 1996).

109. Barry Scheck and Peter Neufeld, "DNA and Innocence Scholarship," in Saundra D. Westervelt and John A. Humphrey, *Wrongly Convicted: Perspectives on Failed Justice* (New Brunswick, NJ: Rutgers University Press, 2001), pp. 248–249.

110. Ibid., p. 246.

111. Details for this story come from "DNA Evidence Links Inmate to 12 Los Angeles Murders," CNN, October 23, 2004. Web posted at http://www.cnn.com/2004/LAW/10/23/ slay.la.ap/index.html (accessed July 6, 2005).

112. James S. Liebman, Jeffrey Fagan, and Simon H. Rifkind, *A Broken System: Error Rates in Capital Cases, 1973–1995* (New York: Columbia University School of Law, 2000). Web posted at http://justice.policy.net/jpreport/finrep.PDF (accessed March 3, 2002).

113. See, for example, Jim Yardley, "Texas Retooling Criminal Justice in Wake of Furor on Death Penalty," *New York Times,* June 1, 2001.

114. Title IV of the Justice for All Act of 2004.

115. At the time the legislation was enacted, Congress estimated that 300,000 rape kits remained unanalyzed in police department evidence lockers across the country.

116. The act also provides funding for the DNA Sexual Assault Justice Act (Title III of the Justice for All Act of 2004), and the Rape Kits and DNA Evidence Backlog Elimination Act of 2000 (42 U.S.C. 14135), authorizing more than $500 million for programs to improve the capacity of crime labs to conduct DNA analysis, reduce non-DNA backlogs, train evidence examiners, support sexual assault forensic examiner programs, and promote the use of DNA to identify missing persons.

117. In those states that accept federal monies under the legislation.

118. Studies include S. Decker and C. Kohfeld, "A Deterrence Study of the Death Penalty in Illinois: 1933–1980," *Journal of Criminal Justice,* Vol. 12, No. 4 (1984), pp. 367–379;

and S. Decker and C. Kohfeld, "An Empirical Analysis of the Effect of the Death Penalty in Missouri," *Journal of Crime and Justice,* Vol. 10, No. 1 (1987), pp. 23–46.

119. See, especially, W. C. Bailey, "Deterrence and the Death Penalty for Murders in Utah: A Time Series Analysis," *Journal of Contemporary Law,* Vol. 5, No. 1 (1978), pp. 1–20; and W. C. Bailey, "An Analysis of the Deterrent Effect of the Death Penalty for Murder in California," *Southern California Law Review,* Vol. 52, No. 3 (1979), pp. 743–764.

120. B. E. Forst, "The Deterrent Effect of Capital Punishment: A Cross-State Analysis of the 1960's," *Minnesota Law Review,* Vol. 61, No. 5 (1977), pp. 743–767.

121. Hashem Dezhbakhsh, Paul Rubin, and Joanna Mehlhop Shepherd, "Does Capital Punishment Have a Deterrent Effect? New Evidence from Post-Moratorium Panel Data," Emory University. Web posted at http://userwww.service.emory.edu/~cozden/Dezhbakhsh_01_01_paper.pdf (January 2001) (accessed November 13, 2001).

122. Ibid., abstract.

123. Ibid., p. 19.

124. "Attorneys Call for Halt to U.S. Executions," Reuters wire service, February 4, 1997.

125. Contrary to some popular beliefs, the term *mental retardation* is still widely used. The American Association for Mental Retardation (AAMR) defines mental retardation as "a disability characterized by significant limitations both in intellectual functioning and in adaptive behavior as expressed in conceptual, social, and practical adaptive skills." See AAMR, "Definition of Mental Retardation." Web posted at http://www.aamr.org/Policies/faq_mental_retardation.shtml (accessed June 6, 2005).

126. As some of the evidence presented before the Supreme Court in *Furman* v. *Georgia,* 408 U.S. 238 (1972), suggested.

127. *USA Today,* April 27, 1989, p. 12A.

128. Thomas J. Keil and Gennaro F. Vito, "Race and the Death Penalty in Kentucky Murder Trials: 1976–1991," *American Journal of Criminal Justice,* Vol. 20, No. 1 (1995), pp. 17–36.

129. *McCleskey* v. *Kemp,* 481 U.S. 279, 107 S.Ct. 1756, 95 L.Ed.2d 262 (1987).

130. *The Federal Death Penalty System: Supplementary Data, Analysis and Revised Protocols for Capital Case Review* (Washington, DC: Department of Justice, 2001).

131. David Stout, "Attorney General Says Report Shows No Racial and Ethnic Bias in Federal Death Sentences," *New York Times,* June 7, 2001. Web posted at http://college1.nytimes.com/guests/articles/2001/06/07/850513.xml.

132. "Expanded Study Shows No Bias in Death Penalty, Ashcroft Says," *Criminal Justice Newsletter,* Vol. 31, No. 13 (June 18, 2001), p. 4.

133. Mary P. Gallagher, "Race Found to Have No Effect on Capital Sentencing in New Jersey," *New Jersey Law Journal* (August 21, 2001), p. 1.

134. "Nebraska Death Penalty System Given Mixed Review in a State Study," *Criminal Justice Newsletter,* Vol. 31, No. 16 (August 2001), pp. 4–5.

135. Death Penalty Information Center website, http://www.deathpenaltyinfo.org (accessed March 20, 2000).

136. Details for this story come from Michael Graczyk, "Killer of Pregnant 10-Year-Old Set to Die Tonight," Associated Press, February 10, 2004; and Texas Execution Information Center, "Edward Lagrone." Web posted at http://www.txexeutions.org/reports/318.asp (accessed May 15, 2004).

137. Justice Potter Stewart, as quoted in *USA Today,* April 27, 1989, p. 12A.

138. Koestler, *Reflections on Hanging,* pp. 147–148; and Gennaro F. Vito and Deborah G. Wilson, "Back from the Dead: Tracking the Progress of Kentucky's *Furman*-Commuted Death Row Population," *Justice Quarterly,* Vol. 5, No. 1 (1988), pp. 101–111.

139. *Wilkerson* v. *Utah,* 99 U.S. 130 (1878).

140. *In re Kemmler,* 136 U.S. 436 (1890).

141. Ibid., p. 447.

142. *Louisiana ex rel. Francis* v. *Resweber,* 329 U.S. 459 (1947).

143. *Furman* v. *Georgia* (1972).

144. A position first adopted in *Trop* v. *Dulles,* 356 U.S. 86 (1958).

145. *Gregg* v. *Georgia,* 428 U.S. 153 (1976).

146. Ibid., p. 173.

147. *Coker* v. *Georgia,* 433 U.S. 584 (1977).

148. *Woodson* v. *North Carolina,* 428 U.S. 280 (1976).

149. *Blystone* v. *Pennsylvania,* 494 U.S. 310 (1990).

150. *Boyde* v. *California,* 494 U.S. 370 (1990).

151. *Tuilaepa* v. *California,* 114 S.Ct. 2630, 129 L.Ed.2d 750 (1994).

152. *Ring* v. *Arizona,* 536 U.S. 584 (2002).

153. "Dozens of Death Sentences Overturned," Associated Press wire service, June 24, 2002.

154. The ruling could also affect Florida, Alabama, Indiana, and Delaware, where juries recommend sentences in capital cases but judges have the final say.

155. *Summerlin* v. *Stewart,* 341 F.3d 1082, 2003.

156. *Schriro* v. *Summerlin,* U.S. Supreme Court, No. 03-526 (decided June 24, 2004).

157. *Poyner* v. *Murray,* 113 S.Ct. 1573, 123 L.Ed.2d 142 (1993).

158. *Campbell* v. *Wood,* 114 S.Ct. 1337, 127 L.Ed.2d 685 (1994).

159. *Director Gomez, et al.* v. *Fierro and Ruiz,* 117 S.Ct. 285 (1996).

160. The court issued its decision after reviewing two cases: *Dawson* v. *State* and *Moore* v. *State.*

161. "Georgia Court Finds Electrocution Unconstitutional," *Criminal Justice Newsletter,* Vol. 31, No. 18 (October 15, 2001), pp. 3–4.

162. *Penry* v. *Johnson,* 532 U.S. 782 (2001).

163. Penry's first death sentence was overturned in *Penry* v. *Lynaugh,* 492 U.S. 302 (1989).

164. Jim Yardley, "Two Groups Help Sway Texas Governor on Veto," *New York Times,* June 19, 2001. Web posted at http://college1.nytimes .com/guests/articles/2001/06/19/852692.xml (accessed November 13, 2001).

165. *Atkins* v. *Virginia,* 122 S.Ct. 2242, 153 L.Ed.2d 335 (2002).

166. The justices were citing *Trop* v. *Dulles,* 356 U.S. 86 (1958), in which Chief Justice Earl Warren created a test that continues to govern interpretations of the cruel and unusual clause of the Eighth Amendment to this day.

167. See "Texas Jury Sentences Penry to Death Once Again," Reuters wire service, July 3, 2002.

168. See, for example, "Letters: Ruling on Retarded Convicts Rests on 'Feeble Foundation,'" *USA Today,* June 25, 2002, p. 22A.

169. The European Union president wrote that "The EU strongly believes that the execution of persons suffering from a mental disorder is contrary to widely accepted human rights norms and in contradiction to the minimum standards of human rights set forth in several international human rights instruments." Read the EU letter to the Texas governor at http:// www.internationaljusticeproject.org/pdfs/ DEMAR1BPatterson.pdf.

170. Details for this story come from the International Justice Project, "Kelsey Patterson." Web posted at http://www .internationaljusticeproject.org/ illnessKPatterson.cfm (accessed July 5, 2005).

171. *Roper* v. *Simmons,* U.S. Supreme Court, No. 03-633 (decided March 1, 2005).

172. Death Penalty Information Center, "Juvenile Offenders Currently on Death Row, or Executed, by State." Web posted at http:// www.deathpenaltyinfo.org/article.php?scid= 27&did=882 (accessed September 10, 2005).

173. See Janet L. Conley, "Execution Protests Wane as Opponents Shift Focus," *Fulton County Daily Report,* August 22, 2002. For the latest information on public opinion polls as they relate to capital punishment, visit the Death Penalty Information Center online at http:// www.deathpenaltyinfo.org.

174. The Gallup Organization on the Web at http:// www.gallup.com. Report dated May 27, 2003.

175. "Illinois Commission Calls for Restrictions on Death Penalty," *Criminal Justice Newsletter,* Vol. 32, No. 7 (April 2002), pp. 1–3.

176. "Death Penalty Freeze to Remain in Illinois," *USA Today,* April 25, 2003, p. 3A.

# PART 4

# Corrections

## RIGHTS OF THE CONVICTED AND IMPRISONED

Common law, constitutional, statutory, and humanitarian rights of the convicted and imprisoned:

- A right against cruel or unusual punishment
- A right to protection from physical harm
- A right to sanitary and healthy conditions of confinement
- A limited right to legal assistance while imprisoned
- A limited right to religious freedom while imprisoned
- A limited right to freedom of speech while imprisoned
- A limited right to due process prior to denial of privileges

These individual rights must be effectively balanced against these public-order concerns:

- Punishment of the guilty
- Safe communities
- The reduction of recidivism
- Secure prisons
- Control over convicts
- The prevention of escape
- Rehabilitation
- Affordable prisons

How does our system of justice work toward balance?

## Punishment—Justice for the Unjust?

The great Christian writer C. S. Lewis (1898–1963) once remarked that if satisfying justice is to be the ultimate goal of Western criminal justice, then the fate of offenders cannot be dictated merely by practical considerations. "The concept of just desert is the only connecting link between punishment and justice," Lewis wrote. "It is only as deserved or undeserved that a sentence can be just or unjust," he concluded.

Once a person has been arrested, tried, and sentenced, the correctional process begins. Unlike Lewis's exhortation, however, the contemporary American correctional system—which includes probation, parole, jails, prisons, capital punishment, and a variety of innovative alternatives to traditional sentences—is tasked with far more than merely carrying out sentences. We also ask of our correctional system that it ensure the safety of law-abiding citizens, that it select the best alternative from among the many available for handling each offender, that it protect those under its charge, and that it guarantee fairness in the handling of all with whom it comes into contact.

This section of *Criminal Justice Today* details the development of probation, parole, community corrections, and imprisonment as correctional philosophies; describes the nuances of prison and jail life; discusses special issues in contemporary corrections (including AIDS, geriatric offenders, and female inmates); and summarizes the legal environment which both surrounds and infuses the modern-day practice of corrections. Characteristic of today's correctional emphasis is a society-wide push for harsher punishments. The culmination of that strategy, however, is dramatically overcrowded correctional institutions, the problems of which are also described. As you read through this section, encountering descriptions of various kinds of criminal sanctions, you might ask yourself, "When would a punishment of this sort be deserved?" In doing so, remember to couple that thought with another question: "What are the ultimate consequences (for society and for the offender) of the kind of correctional program we are discussing here?" Unlike Lewis, you may also want to ask, "Can we afford it?"

12

**Probation, Parole, and Community Corrections**

13

**Prisons and Jails**

14

**Prison Life**

# CHAPTER 12

# Probation, Parole, and Community Corrections

## OUTLINE

- Introduction
- What Is Probation?
- What Is Parole?
- Probation and Parole: The Pluses and Minuses
- The Legal Environment
- The Job of Probation and Parole Officers
- Intermediate Sanctions
- The Future of Probation and Parole

## LEARNING OBJECTIVES

After reading this chapter, you should be able to:

- Explain the differences between probation and parole, and describe the advantages and disadvantages of each.
- Describe in detail the legal environment surrounding the use of probation and parole, and know the names of significant court cases.
- Describe the federal probation system.
- Explain the nature of the job of probation and parole officers.
- List the advantages of intermediate sanctions over more traditional forms of sentencing.
- Describe the likely future of probation and parole.

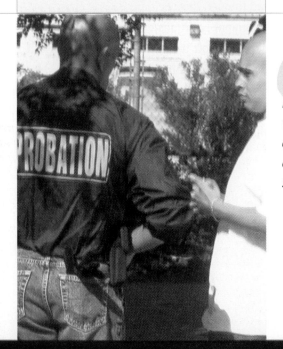

*This year, some 600,000 inmates will be released from prison back into society. We know from long experience that if they can't find work, or a home, or help, they are much more likely to commit crime and return to prison. . . . America is the land of second chance, and when the gates of the prison open, the path ahead should lead to a better life.*

—President George W. Bush[1]

*Community corrections is an integral part of the criminal justice system and should be fully implemented and promoted in order to save expensive and scarce jail and prison space for violent and serious offenders.*

—National Association of Counties, Justice and Public Safety Steering Committee[2]

## KEY CONCEPTS

### TERMS

| | | |
|---|---|---|
| caseload | mixed sentence | probation revocation |
| community corrections | parole | remote location monitoring |
| community service | parole board | restitution |
| conditions of parole (probation) | parole (probation) violation | revocation hearing |
| home confinement | parole revocation | shock incarceration |
| intensive probation supervision (IPS) | prisoner reentry | shock probation |
| intermediate sanctions | probation | split sentence |

### CASES

| | | |
|---|---|---|
| *Bearden* v. *Georgia* | *Griffin* v. *Wisconsin* | *Pennsylvania Board of Probation and* |
| *Escoe* v. *Zerbst* | *Mempa* v. *Rhay* | *Parole* v. *Scott* |
| *Gagnon* v. *Scarpelli* | *Minnesota* v. *Murphy* | *U.S.* v. *Knights* |
| *Greenholtz* v. *Nebraska Penal Inmates* | *Morrissey* v. *Brewer* | |

The original full-text court opinion for each of these cases is available on the CD-ROM that accompanies this book.

# Introduction

Hear the author discuss this chapter at **cjtoday.com**

On February 1, 2004, 11-year-old Carlie Brucia was abducted as she took a shortcut to her home from a slumber party at a friend's house. Video footage of Carlie's abduction was captured by an unattended car wash security camera, which showed the girl being grabbed by an unidentified man and led away.[3] Carlie's body was discovered days later in a church parking lot a few miles from her home. Shortly after her abduction, authorities announced the arrest of Joseph P. Smith, a 37-year-old auto mechanic and father of three who had a lengthy criminal record. Authorities charged Smith with Carlie's murder and said that they would try him for first-degree homicide, kidnapping, and capital sexual battery. It was soon learned that Smith had been arrested at least 13 times in Florida in the 11 years before Carlie's abduction and had previously been charged with kidnapping and false imprisonment. Only a month before Carlie's murder, a probation officer had asked a Florida judge to declare Smith a probation violator because of unpaid fines and court costs that he had been ordered to pay. The probation officer's request was denied and Smith remained free.

In 2005, convicted sex offender John Evander Couey, 46, was arrested and charged with the rape and murder of nine-year-old Jessica Lunsford of Homosassa, Florida.[4] Prosecutors revealed tear-jerking details of the last moments of Jessica's life, saying that she had been tied up and buried alive, kneeling and clutching a purple stuffed dolphin. Like the Smith case, it turns out that Couey had a long record, including 24 arrests for burglary, carrying a concealed weapon, indecent exposure, and other offenses. He had previously been arrested and charged with fondling a child. Although Couey was sentenced to 10 years in prison, he was paroled in 1980 because of prison overcrowding.

In yet another story that came out of Florida in 2005, the body of 13-year-old Sarah Lunde was discovered in a fish pond about a mile from her Hillsborough County home.[5] The man arrested in her killing, 36-year-old David Onstott, has a lengthy criminal record dating back to 1986, including charges of sexual abuse and attempted murder. After his arrest Onstott confessed to choking Lunde and dumping her body near her home.

Stories like those involving Brucia, Lunsford, and Lunde appear all too frequently in the media and cast a harsh light on the early release and poor supervision of criminal offenders. This chapter takes a close look at the realities behind the practice of what we call **community corrections**. Community corrections, also termed *community-based corrections,* is a sentencing style that depends less on traditional confinement options and more on correctional resources available in the community. Community corrections includes a wide variety of sentencing options, such as probation, parole, home confinement, the electronic monitoring of offenders, and other new and developing programs—all of which are covered in this chapter. Learn more about com-

**community corrections**

The use of a variety of officially ordered program-based sanctions that permit convicted offenders to remain in the community under conditional supervision as an alternative to an active prison sentence.

18:21:41 02/01/2004

A car wash surveillance camera in Sarasota, Florida, showing 11-year-old Carlie Brucia being abducted in 2004. Brucia's body was later discovered at a church three miles from the abduction site. Police quickly arrested Joseph P. Smith, 37, a chronic drug abuser with a long arrest record, and charged him with kidnapping and murder. Court records showed that Smith had violated the conditions of his probation and should have been imprisoned at the time of the abduction. In 2005, Smith was tried and convicted of kidnapping, raping, and strangling Brucia.
*AP Wide World Photos*

munity corrections by visiting the International Community Corrections Association via **Web Extra 12–1** at cjtoday.com.

WEB EXTRA

# What Is Probation?

**Probation**, one aspect of community corrections, is "a sentence served while under supervision in the community."[6] Like other sentencing options, probation is a court-ordered sanction. Its goal is to retain some control over criminal offenders while using community programs to help rehabilitate them. Most of the alternative sanctions discussed later in this chapter are, in fact, predicated on probationary sentences in which the offender is ordered to abide by certain conditions—such as participation in a specified program—while remaining free in the community. Although the court in many jurisdictions can impose probation directly, most probationers are sentenced first to confinement but then immediately have their sentences suspended and are remanded into the custody of an officer of the court—the probation officer.

Probation has a long history. By the fourteenth century, English courts had established the practice of "binding over for good behavior,"[7] in which offenders could be entrusted into the custody of willing citizens. American John Augustus (1784–1859) is generally recognized as the world's first probation officer. Augustus, a Boston shoemaker, attended sessions of criminal court in the 1850s and offered to take carefully selected offenders into his home as an alternative to imprisonment.[8] At first, he supervised only drunkards, but by 1857 Augustus was accepting many kinds of offenders and was devoting all his time to the service of the court.[9] Augustus died in 1859, having bailed out more than 2,000 convicts. In 1878, the Massachusetts legislature enacted a statute that authorized the city of Boston to hire a salaried probation officer. Missouri followed suit in 1897, along with Vermont (1898) and Rhode Island (1899).[10] Before the end of the nineteenth century, probation had become an accepted and widely used form of community-based supervision. By 1925, all 48 states had adopted probation legislation. In that same year, the federal government enacted legislation enabling federal district court judges to appoint paid probation officers and to impose probationary terms.[11]

## The Extent of Probation

Today, probation is the most common form of criminal sentencing in the United States. Between 20% and 60% of those found guilty of crimes are sentenced to some form of probation. Figure 12–1 shows that 59% of all offenders under correctional supervision in the United States

**probation**
A sentence of imprisonment that is suspended. Also, the conditional freedom granted by a judicial officer to a convicted offender, as long as the person meets certain conditions of behavior.

Accepting released offenders into the community without a period of supervised release is morally unsatisfying; they have not yet earned their place at our table.

—Jeremy Travis[i]

## CJ NEWS

### Getting Tough on Paroled Sex Offenders

From the moment he enters the sex offender's apartment, North Dakota parole officer Brian Weigel is looking for contraband.

He kicks aside a blanket on the floor, peers down and spies a video game rated for mature players—complete with buxom computer-generated women on the cover. And despite protests from the man who lives here, the video game is coming with Weigel.

In the year since college student Dru Sjodin was abducted from a North Dakota parking lot and killed, allegedly by a convicted sex offender, the state has worked to make its sex offender laws among the strictest in the nation.

Officers such as Weigel have to determine whether an offender is sticking to restrictions that often include a ban on sexual material in the home.

"There's a real threat," said Weigel, one of five sex offender specialists in the state's parole and probation division. "If these guys reoffend, there's going to be another real victim out there."

Weigel's unit is new, part of the state's heightened enforcement since Sjodin's abduction a year ago.

The 22-year-old University of North Dakota student's body was found in 2004 in a ravine in Minnesota.

The man charged with abducting Sjodin and killing her, Alfonso Rodriguez, is a convicted sex offender who had been released from prison six months before she disappeared.

He has pleaded not guilty to a federal charge of kidnapping resulting in death. Prosecutors are seeking the death penalty.

The passage of a year has not softened the blow for Sjodin's family. "Every day weighs heavy in our hearts," said Linda Walker, Sjodin's mother. "There isn't one day that we don't think of her, even from the moment we wake up to the moment we go to sleep."

The case drew national attention as volunteers, National Guard soldiers and law enforcement officers searched the region for months, looking for Sjodin.

Her body wasn't found until after the snow melted.

The U.S. Senate endorsed a bill called "Dru's Law," which would set up a national public database of sex offenders and require strict monitoring of high-risk sex offenders for a year after their release from prison.

The bill was introduced by Sen. Byron Dorgan, D–N.D.

University of North Dakota student Dru Sjodin, 22 (left), was abducted from a shopping mall, raped, and murdered in 2003. Known sex offender Alfonso Rodriguez, Jr., 50 (right),  stands accused of the crimes. He had been released from prison six months before Sjodin disappeared after having served 23 years for stabbing and trying to kidnap a young woman. Sjodin's brutal murder has spurred both North Dakota and Minnesota (where Rodriguez lived) into making their sex offender laws among the toughest in the nation.

*Grand Forks Police Department, Reuters, Landov LLC, and AP Wide World Photos*

## CJ NEWS *(continued)*

"The entire country was looking for Dru Sjodin," Dorgan said.

The case was particularly troubling here and in neighboring Minnesota, where Rodriguez lived. The convicted rapist had been released even though he had been classified as a Level 3 offender, meaning he had the highest risk of committing another sex crime.

Both states have since moved to crack down on sex offenders.

In North Dakota, the new parole unit is partnered with an expanded sex offender program at the state psychiatric hospital in Jamestown for the most serious sexual predators, who are recommended for civil commitment after their release. The number of people civilly committed has doubled to 23 in less than a year.

In Minnesota, two separate commissions have been working on new sentencing guidelines since the Sjodin case.

One plan would double the maximum sentences for sex crimes and impose a life term on any repeat sex offender. It also would set up a board to review the cases of inmates who have served their minimum sentences.

More restrictions may be on the way. When North Dakota lawmakers convene their next session, they will face a list of proposals from a task force launched by Gov. John Hoeven.

Among them are life sentences without parole for gross sexual offenses that result in death, and supervised probation for all other felony sex offenses.

The panel also is seeking a stronger method of tracking sex offenders, using global positioning devices that could alert authorities to an offender's location at all times, said Duane Houdek, an attorney for Hoeven.

Although North Dakota's crime rate remains low, getting tough on sex offenders will help preserve that security, said state Rep. Lois Delmore.

"It means we're not just assuming that we're in North Dakota and everyone's healthy and happy and things like this can't happen," she said.

For the latest in crime and justice news, visit the Talk Justice news feed at http://www.crimenews.info.

as of January 1, 2005, were on probation. Not shown is that the number of offenders supervised yearly on probation has increased from slightly more than 1 million in 1980 to over 4 million today—almost a 300% increase.[12]

Even violent offenders stand about a one in five chance of receiving a probationary term, as Figure 12–2 shows. A Bureau of Justice Statistics study of felony sentences found that 5% of people convicted of homicide were placed on probation, as were 21% of convicted sex offenders.[13] Twelve percent of convicted robbers and 30% of those committing aggravated assault were similarly sentenced to probation rather than active prison time. In one example, 47-year-old Carrie Mote of Vernon, Connecticut, was sentenced to probation for shooting her fiancé in the chest with a .38-caliber handgun after he called off their wedding.[14] Mote, who faced a maximum of 20 years in prison, claimed to be suffering from diminished psychological capacity at the time of the shooting because of the emotional stress brought on by the canceled wedding.

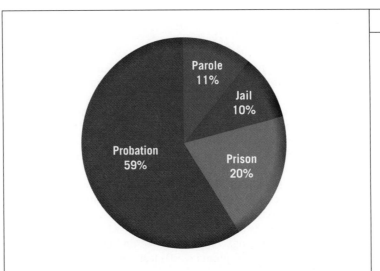

### FIGURE 12–1

**Offenders under correctional supervision in the United States, by type of supervision.**

*Source:* Bureau of Justice Statistics, Correctional Surveys.

## FIGURE 12-2

**Percentage of convicted felony offenders receiving probation, by type of crime.**

*Source:* Jodi M. Brown and Patrick A. Langan, *Felony Sentences in the United States, 1996* (Washington, DC: Bureau of Justice Statistics, 1999).

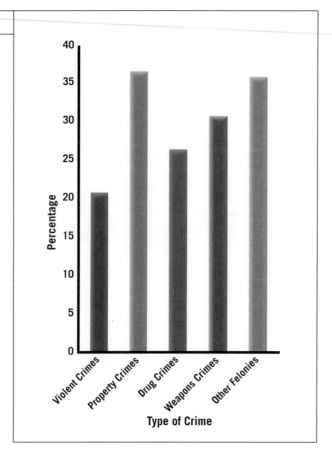

At the beginning of 2005, a total of 4,151,125 adults were on probation throughout the nation.[15] Individual states, however, make greater or lesser use of probation. North Dakota authorities, with the smallest probationary population, supervise only 3,687 people, while Texas reports 428,773 offenders on probation. On a per capita basis, New Hampshire has the lowest rate of probation (431 for every 100,000 residents), while Massachusetts has the highest (3,301 for every 100,000 residents). The national average is 1,884 for every 100,000 residents. Sixty percent of the more than 2.2 million adults discharged from probation in 2004 had successfully met the conditions of their supervision. Approximately 15% of those discharged from supervision, however, were incarcerated because of a rule violation or because they committed a new offense. Another 4% absconded, and 10% had their probation sentence revoked without being ordered to serve time.[16] See more statistics describing community corrections at Library Extra 12–1 at cjtoday.com.

## Probation Conditions

Those sentenced to probation must agree to abide by court-mandated conditions of probation. A violation of conditions can lead to **probation revocation**. Conditions are of two types: general and specific. General conditions apply to all probationers in a given jurisdiction and usually require that the probationer obey all laws, maintain employment, remain within the jurisdiction of the court, possess no firearms, allow the probation officer to visit at home or at work, and so forth. As a general condition of probation, many probationers are also required to pay a fine to the court, usually in a series of installments, that is designed to reimburse victims for damages and to pay lawyers' fees and other court costs.

Special conditions may be mandated by a judge who feels that the probationer is in need of particular guidance or control. Depending on the nature of the offense, a judge may require that the offender surrender his or her driver's license; submit at reasonable times to warrantless and unannounced searches by a probation officer; supply breath, urine, or blood samples as needed for drug or alcohol testing; complete a specified number of hours of community service; or pass the general equivalency diploma (GED) test within a specified time. The judge may also dictate

**probation revocation**

A court order taking away a convicted offender's probationary status and usually withdrawing the conditional freedom associated with that status in response to a violation of the conditions of probation.

Patrick Collier, with his fiancée, Sandy Fabian. Collier was one of five winners in a McDonald's giveaway in 2001. Shortly after winning $1 million, he was arrested and charged with aggravated battery against his 29-year-old fiancée. Collier was released on bail but was soon back in jail, charged with violating probation.

*AP Wide World Photos*

special conditions tailored to the probationer's situation. Such individualized conditions may prohibit the offender from associating with named others (a codefendant, for example), they may require that the probationer be at home after dark, or they may demand that the offender complete a particular treatment program within a set time.

## The Federal Probation System

The federal probation system is nearly 80 years old.[17] In 1916 in the *Killets* case,[18] the U.S. Supreme Court ruled that federal judges did not have the authority to suspend sentences and to order probation. After a vigorous campaign by the National Probation Association, Congress passed the National Probation Act in 1925, authorizing the use of probation in federal courts. The bill came just in time to save a burgeoning federal prison system from serious overcrowding. The prostitution-fighting Mann Act, Prohibition legislation, and the growth of organized crime all led to increased arrests and a dramatic growth in the number of federal probationers in the early years of the system.

Although the 1925 act authorized one probation officer per federal judge, it allocated only $25,000 for officers' salaries. As a consequence, only eight officers were hired to serve 132 judges, and the system came to rely heavily on voluntary probation officers. Some sources indicate that as many as 40,000 probationers were under the supervision of volunteers at the peak of the system.[19] By 1930, however, Congress provided adequate funding, and a corps of salaried professionals began to provide probation services to the U.S. courts. Today, approximately 4,000 federal probation officers are employed through the Administrative Office of the U.S. Courts (AOUSC).[20]

Federal probation officers have statutory authority to arrest probationers for a violation. Under existing policy, however, they are encouraged to obtain an arrest warrant from a court, and the warrant is to be executed by the U.S. Marshals Service. Most federal probation officers may carry a firearm for defensive purposes while on duty. Before doing so, however, they must complete rigorous training and certification requirements, provide objective justification for doing so, and be approved to do so on an individual basis. Some federal districts do not allow any probation officers to carry firearms in the performance of their official duties; these include the Eastern and Western districts of Wisconsin, Eastern Virginia, Eastern Virgin Islands, Middle Tennessee, Massachusetts, Connecticut, and Central California.[21]

> **Texas has one of the toughest parole policies in the country with the most violent offenders serving 50 percent of their sentences in actual time and capital offenders sentenced to life serving 40 years of actual time before parole consideration.**
>
> —Tony Fabelo, Executive Director of the Texas Criminal Justice Policy Council

## MULTICULTURALISM AND DIVERSITY

### Culturally Skilled Probation Officers

A recent article in the journal *Federal Probation* describes the characteristics of "good therapeutic relationships" in probation work and says that "one of the major impediments to building an effective relationship may be found in cross-cultural barriers."

According to the article, probation officers who work with immigrants, or with those whose cultures differ substantially from that of mainstream America, must realize that a client's culture has to be taken into consideration. Doing so can make officers far more effective as both counselors and supervisors.

That's because differences in culture can lead to difficulties in developing the rapport that is necessary to build a helping relationship between an offender and a probation officer. Consequently, effective probation officers work to understand the values, norms, lifestyles, roles, and methods of communicating that characterize their clients.

Culturally skilled probation officers, says the article, are aware and sensitive to their own cultural heritage, and they value and respect differences so long as they do not lead to continued law violation. Culturally skilled officers are also aware of their own preconceived notions, biases, prejudicial attitudes, feelings, and beliefs. They avoid stereotyping and labeling. Skilled officers are comfortable with the cultural differences that exist between themselves and their clients, and they are comfortable referring clients to someone who may be better qualified to help.

Developing multicultural awareness is the first step to becoming culturally skilled, says the article. Developing awareness is an ongoing process—one that culminates in the ability to understand a client's worldview, or *cultural empathy*.

According to the article, developing cultural empathy involves six steps, as follows:

- The counselor must understand and accept the context of family and community for clients from different cultural backgrounds (especially important in working with Hispanic clients where relationships within the extended family are highly valued).
- Counselors should incorporate indigenous healing practices from the client's culture whenever they can (as might be possible when working with Native Americans).
- Counselors must become knowledgeable about the historical and sociopolitical background of clients (especially when clients have fled from repressive regimes in their home countries and might still fear authority figures).
- They must become knowledgeable of the psychosocial adjustment that must be made by clients who have moved from one environment to another (including the sense of loneliness and separation that some immigrants feel on arrival in their adopted country).
- They must be sensitive to the oppression, discrimination, and racism encountered by many people (for example, Kurdish people who suffered discrimination and experienced genocide under Saddam Hussein).
- Counselors must facilitate empowerment for those clients who feel underprivileged and devalued (for example, immigrants who may feel forced to accept menial jobs even though they worked in prestigious occupations in their native countries).

The article concludes that developing cultural awareness provides the probation officer with an effective approach that actively draws the probationer into the therapeutic relationship and which increases the likelihood of a successful outcome.

*Reference:* Robert A. Shearer and Patricia Ann King, "Multicultural Competencies in Probation: Issues and Challenges," *Federal Probation,* Vol. 68, No. 1 (June 2004).

# What Is Parole?

**parole**

The status of a convicted offender who has been conditionally released from prison by a paroling authority before the expiration of his or her sentence, is placed under the supervision of a parole agency, and is required to observe the conditions of parole.

**prisoner reentry**

The managed return to the community of individuals released from prison. Also called *reentry*.

**Parole** is the supervised early release of inmates from correctional confinement. It is a **prisoner reentry** strategy that differs from probation in both purpose and implementation. Whereas probationers generally avoid serving time in prison, parolees have already been incarcerated. Whereas probation is a sentencing option available to a judge who determines the form probation will take, parole results from an administrative decision by a legally designated paroling authority. Whereas probation is a sentencing strategy, parole is a correctional strategy whose primary purpose is to return offenders gradually to productive lives. By making early release possible, parole can also act as a stimulus for positive behavioral change.

States differ as to the type of parole decision-making mechanism they use, as well as the level at which it operates. Two major models prevail: (1) **Parole boards** grant parole based on their judgment and assessment. The parole board's decisions are termed *discretionary parole.* (2) Statutory decrees produce mandatory parole, with release dates usually set near the completion of the inmate's prison sentence, minus time off for good behavior and other special considerations. Fifteen states have entirely abolished discretionary release from prison by a parole board for all offenders (Figure 12–3). Another five states have abolished discretionary parole for certain violent offenses or other crimes against a person. As a result of the movement away from release by parole boards, statutory release has become the most common method of release from prison.[22]

■ no longer have parole boards
■ have parole boards

*Note:* California offenders convicted of some very serious crimes, such as murder or kidnapping for ransom, continue to receive indeterminate sentences and are subject to parole board review. These offenders, however, comprise only a very small percentage of the total California prison population.

FIGURE 12-3

**States that have eliminated parole boards.**

*Source:* Timothy A. Hughes, Doris James Wilson, and Allen J. Beck, *Trends in State Parole, 1990–2000* (Washington, DC: Bureau of Justice Statistics, 2001).

States that do not have parole boards can still have substantial parole populations. For example, California, one of the states that no longer uses parole boards for release decisions, has the largest population of parolees in the country.[23] Although it does not have a parole board, California does have a Board of Prison Terms, which determines when the state's most serious offenders are ready for release from prison. These offenders, however, make up only a very small percentage of the state's prison population.

Parole was a much-heralded tool of nineteenth-century corrections. Its advocates had been looking for a behavioral incentive to motivate youthful offenders to reform. Parole, through its promise of earned early release, seemed the ideal innovation. The use of parole in this country began with New York's Elmira Reformatory in 1876. Indeterminate sentences were then a key part of the rehabilitation philosophy, and they remain so today.

## The Extent of Parole

Parolees make up one of the smallest of the correctional categories shown in Figure 12–1. The growing reluctance to use parole today seems to be due to the realization that correctional routines have generally been ineffective at producing any substantial reformation among many offenders before their release back into the community. The abandonment of the rehabilitation goal, combined with a return to determinate sentencing in many jurisdictions—including the federal judicial system—has substantially reduced the amount of time the average correctional client spends on parole.

Although discretionary parole releases are far less common than they used to be, about 25% of inmates who are freed from prison are still paroled by a paroling authority such as a parole board.[24] States operating under determinate sentencing guidelines, however, often require that inmates serve a short period of time, such as 90 days, on *reentry parole*—a form of mandatory release. Mandatory parole releases have increased 91% since 1990,[25] even though they typically involve either a very small amount of time on parole or no time at all. As a result, determinate sentencing schemes have changed the face of parole in America, resulting in a dramatic reduction in the average time spent under postprison supervision, but having little impact on the actual number of released inmates who experience some form of parole.

At the beginning of 2005, approximately 765,350 people were on parole throughout the United States.[26] As with probation, states vary considerably in the use they make of parole, influenced as they are by the legislative requirements of sentencing schemes. For example, on

**parole board**

A state paroling authority. Most states have parole boards that decide when an incarcerated offender is ready for conditional release. Some boards also function as revocation hearing panels.

We in law enforcement need to recognize that when we locked these guys up, they didn't go away forever. Now, they're coming back, released from prisons and jail systems that our elected officials can't afford to grow anymore. We have to find a way to make sure these people succeed while maintaining the decline in violent crime.

—Chief Dean Esserman, Providence (Rhode Island) Police Department[ii]

**parole (probation) violation**

An act or a failure to act by a parolee (or probationer) that does not conform to the conditions of his or her parole (or probation).

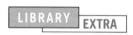

January 1, 2005, Maine, a state that is phasing out parole, reported only 32 people under parole supervision (the lowest of all the states) and Washington had only 120. California (the highest of all) had a parole population in excess of 110,000, and Texas officials were busy supervising more than 102,000 parolees. The per capita rate at which parole is used varies, as well. Only 3 out of every 100,000 Maine residents are on parole, whereas 1,198 out of every 100,000 District of Columbia residents are on parole. The national average is 347 per 100,000.[27]

Nationwide, approximately 46% of parolees successfully complete parole, while about 26% are returned to prison for **parole violations**, and another 11% go back to prison for new offenses during their parole period. (Others may be transferred to new jurisdictions, abscond and not be caught, or die—bringing the total to 100%.)[28] Learn more about trends in parole via Library Extra 12–2 at cjtoday.com.

## Parole Conditions

**conditions of parole (probation)**

The general and special limits imposed on an offender who is released on parole (or probation). General conditions tend to be fixed by state statute, while special conditions are mandated by the sentencing authority (court or board) and take into consideration the background of the offender and the circumstances of the offense.

In those jurisdictions that retain discretionary parole, the **conditions of parole** remain very similar to the conditions agreed to by probationers. General conditions of parole usually include agreement not to leave the state as well as to obey extradition requests from other jurisdictions. Parolees must also periodically report to parole officers, and parole officers may visit parolees at their homes and places of business, often arriving unannounced.

The successful and continued employment of parolees is one of the major concerns of parole boards and their officers, and studies have found that successful employment is a major factor in reducing the likelihood of repeat offenses.[29] Hence, the importance of continued employment is typically stressed on parole agreement forms, with the condition that failure to find employment within 30 days may result in **parole revocation**. As with probationers, parolees who are working can be ordered to pay fines and penalties. A provision for making **restitution** payments is also frequently included as a condition of parole.

As with probation, special parole conditions may be added by the judge and might require the parolee to pay a "parole supervisory fee" (often around $15 to $20 per month). A relatively new innovation, the parole supervisory fee shifts some of the expense of community corrections to the offender.

**parole revocation**

The administrative action of a paroling authority removing a person from parole status in response to a violation of lawfully required conditions of parole, including the prohibition against committing a new offense, and usually resulting in a return to prison.

## Federal Parole

Federal parole decisions are made by the U.S. Parole Commission, which uses hearing examiners to visit federal prisons. Examiners typically ask inmates to describe why, in their opinion, they are ready for parole. The inmate's job readiness, home plans, past record, accomplishments while in prison, good behavior, and previous experiences on probation or parole form the basis for the examiners' report to the parole commission. The 1984 Comprehensive Crime Control Act, which mandated federal fixed sentencing and abolished parole for offenses committed after November 1, 1978, began a planned phaseout of the U.S. Parole Commission. Under the act, the commission was to be abolished by 1992. Various federal legislation has since extended the life of the commission. Visit the commission's website via Web Extra 12–2 at cjtoday.com. Read a detailed history of the federal parole system at Library Extra 12–3.

**restitution**

A court requirement that an alleged or convicted offender pay money or provide services to the victim of the crime or provide services to the community.

# Probation and Parole: The Pluses and Minuses

## Advantages of Probation and Parole

Probation is used to meet the needs of offenders who require some correctional supervision short of imprisonment while providing a reasonable degree of security to the community. Parole fulfills a similar purpose for offenders released from prison. Both probation and parole provide a number of advantages over imprisonment, including these:

■ *Lower cost.* Imprisonment is expensive. Incarcerating a single offender in Georgia, for example, costs approximately $39,501 per year, while the cost of intensive probation is as little as $1,321 per probationer.[30] The expense of imprisonment in some other states may be more than three times as high as it is in Georgia.

- *Increased employment.* Few people in prison have the opportunity for productive employment. Work-release programs, correctional industries, and inmate labor programs operate in most states, but they usually provide only low-paying jobs and require few skills. At best, such programs include only a small portion of the inmates in any given facility. Probation and parole, on the other hand, make it possible for offenders under correctional supervision to work full-time at jobs in the "free" economy. Offenders can contribute to their own and their families' support, stimulate the local economy by spending their wages, and support the government through the taxes they pay.

- *Restitution.* Offenders who are able to work are candidates for court-ordered restitution. Society's interest in restitution may be better served by a probationary sentence or parole than by imprisonment. Restitution payments to victims may help restore their standard of living and personal confidence while teaching the offender responsibility.

- *Community support.* The decision to release a prisoner on parole or to sentence a convicted offender to probation is often partially based on considerations of family and other social ties. Such decisions are made in the belief that offenders will be more subject to control in the community if they participate in a web of positive social relationships. An advantage of both probation and parole is that they allow the offender to continue personal and social relationships. Probation avoids splitting up families, while parole may reunite family members separated from each other by a prison sentence.

- *Reduced risk of criminal socialization.* Criminal values permeate prisons; prison has been called a "school in crime." Probation insulates adjudicated offenders, at least to some degree, from these kinds of values. Parole, by virtue of the fact that it follows time served in prison, is less successful than probation in reducing the risk of criminal socialization.

- *Increased use of community services.* Probationers and parolees can take advantage of services offered through the community, including psychological therapy, substance abuse counseling, financial services, support groups, church outreach programs, and social services. While a few similar opportunities may be available in prison, the community environment itself can enhance the effectiveness of treatment programs by reducing the stigmatization of the offender and by allowing the offender to participate in a more "normal" environment.

- *Increased opportunity for rehabilitation.* Probation and parole can both be useful behavioral management tools. They reward cooperative offenders with freedom and allow for the opportunity to shape the behavior of offenders who may be difficult to reach through other programs.

## Disadvantages of Probation and Parole

Any honest appraisal of probation and parole must recognize that they share a number of strategic drawbacks, such as these:

- *Relative lack of punishment.* The "just deserts" model of criminal sentencing insists that punishment should be a central theme of the justice process. While rehabilitation and treatment are recognized as worthwhile goals, the model suggests that punishment serves both society's need for protection and the victim's need for revenge. Many view probation, however, as practically no punishment at all and it is coming under increasing criticism as a sentencing strategy. Parole is likewise accused of unhinging the scales of justice because (1) it releases some offenders early, even when they have been convicted of serious crimes, while some relatively minor offenders remain in prison, and (2) it is dishonest because it does not require completion of the offender's entire sentence behind bars.

- *Increased risk to the community.* Probation and parole are strategies designed to deal with convicted criminal offenders. The release into the community of such offenders increases the risk that they will commit additional offenses. Community supervision can never be so complete as to eliminate such a possibility, and evaluations of parole have pointed out that an accurate assessment of offender dangerousness is beyond our present capability.[31]

- *Increased social costs.* Some offenders placed on probation and parole will effectively and responsibly discharge their obligations. Others, however, will become social liabilities. In addition to the increased risk of new crimes, probation and parole increase the chance that added expenses will accrue to the community in the form of child support, welfare costs, housing expenses, legal aid, indigent health care, and the like.

The abolition of parole has been tried and has failed on a spectacular scale. . . . The absence of parole means that offenders simply walk out the door of prison at the end of a predetermined period of time, no questions asked.

—American Probation and Parole Association and the Association of Paroling Authorities International

# The Legal Environment

Ten especially significant U.S. Supreme Court decisions provide the legal framework for probation and parole supervision. Among those cases, that of *Griffin* v. *Wisconsin* (1987)[32] may be the most significant. In *Griffin,* the Supreme Court ruled that probation officers may conduct searches of a probationer's residence without either a search warrant or probable cause. According to the Court, "A probationer's home, like anyone else's, is protected by the Fourth Amendment's requirement that searches be 'reasonable.'" However, "[a] State's operation of a probation system . . . presents 'special needs' beyond normal law enforcement that may justify departures from the usual warrant and probable cause requirements." Probation, the Court concluded, is similar to imprisonment because it is a "form of criminal sanction imposed upon an offender after a determination of guilt."

Similarly, in the 1998 case of *Pennsylvania Board of Probation and Parole* v. *Scott,*[33] the Court declined to extend the exclusionary rule to apply to searches by parole officers, even where such searches yield evidence of parole violations. In the words of the Court, "[T]he Court has repeatedly declined to extend the [exclusionary] rule to proceedings other than criminal trials. . . . The social costs of allowing convicted criminals who violate their parole to remain at large are particularly high . . . and are compounded by the fact that parolees . . . are more likely to commit future crimes than are average citizens."

In 2001, the case of *U.S.* v. *Knights*[34] expanded the search authority normally reserved for probation and parole officers to police officers under certain circumstances. Mark James Knights was a California probationer who had signed a standard state probation form agreeing to waive his constitutional protection against warrantless searches as a condition of his probation. The form did not limit such searches to probation officers but instead required that Knights submit to a search at any time, with or without a search or arrest warrant or reasonable cause, by any probation or law enforcement officer. When Knights came under suspicion of setting a fire that caused $1.5 million in damages, police officers searched his home without a warrant. The search uncovered evidence that implicated Knights in the arson. A federal district court granted a motion by Knights' attorneys to suppress the evidence because the search was for police investigatory purposes, rather than for probationary purposes. The Ninth Circuit Court affirmed the lower court's decision. The U.S. Supreme Court disagreed, however, and held that the warrantless search of Knights' residence, "supported by reasonable suspicion and authorized by a probation condition, satisfied the Fourth Amendment . . . as nothing in Knights' probation condition limits searches to those with a 'probationary purpose.'"

Other court cases focus on the conduct of parole or probation **revocation hearings**. Revocation is a common procedure. Annually, about 26% of adults on parole and 25% of those on probation throughout the United States have their conditional release revoked.[35] The supervising officer may request that probation or parole be revoked if a client has violated the conditions of community release or has committed a new crime. The most frequent violations for which revocation occurs are (1) failure to report as required to a probation or parole officer, (2) failure to participate in a stipulated treatment program, and (3) alcohol or drug abuse while under supervision.[36] Revocation hearings may result in an order that a probationer's suspended sentence be made "active" or that a parolee return to prison to complete his sentence in confinement.

In a 1935 decision (*Escoe* v. *Zerbst*[37]) that has since been greatly modified, the U.S. Supreme Court held that probation "comes as an act of grace to one convicted of a crime" and that the revocation of probation without hearing or notice to the probationer is acceptable practice. In 1967, however, in the case of *Mempa* v. *Rhay,*[38] the Warren Court changed direction and declared that both notice and a hearing were required. The Court also held that the probationer should have the opportunity for representation by counsel before a deferred prison sentence could be imposed.[39]

Two of the most widely cited cases affecting parolees and probationers are *Morrissey* v. *Brewer* (1972)[40] and *Gagnon* v. *Scarpelli* (1973).[41] In *Morrissey,* the Court declared a need for procedural safeguards in revocation hearings involving parolees. After *Morrissey,* revocation proceedings would require that (1) the parolee be given written notice specifying the alleged violation; (2) evidence of the violation be disclosed; (3) a neutral and detached body constitute the hearing authority; (4) the parolee have the chance to appear and offer a defense, including testimony, documents, and witnesses; (5) the parolee have the right to cross-examine witnesses; and (6) a written statement be provided to the parolee at the conclusion of the hearing that includes the hearing body's decision, the testimony considered, and reasons for revoking parole, if such occurs.[42]

In 1973, the Court extended the procedural safeguards of *Morrissey* to probationers in *Gagnon* v. *Scarpelli.* Citing its own decision a year earlier in *Morrissey* v. *Brewer,* the Supreme Court ruled that probationers, because they face a substantial loss of liberty, were entitled to two hearings: (1) a preliminary hearing to determine whether there is "probable cause to believe that

---

**revocation hearing**

A hearing held before a legally constituted hearing body (such as a parole board) to determine whether a parolee or probationer has violated the conditions and requirements of his or her parole or probation.

he has committed a violation of his parole" and (2) "a somewhat more comprehensive hearing prior to the making of the final revocation decision." The Court also ruled that probation revocation hearings were to be held "under the conditions specified in *Morrissey* v. *Brewer.*"

In *Gagnon* and later cases, however, the Court reasserted that probation and parole revocation hearings were not a stage in the criminal prosecution process, but a simple adjunct to it, even though they might result in substantial loss of liberty. The difference is a crucial one, for it permits hearing boards and judicial review officers to function, at least to some degree, outside of the adversarial context of the trial court and with lessened attention to the rights of the criminally accused guaranteed by the Bill of Rights.

In 1997, the U.S. Supreme Court extended the rationale found in *Morrissey* and *Gagnon* to inmates set free from prison under early-release programs. In a unanimous decision, the Court held that "an inmate who has been released under a program to relieve prison crowding cannot be reincarcerated without getting a chance to show at a hearing that he has met the conditions of the program and is entitled to remain free."[43]

In 1979, the case of *Greenholtz* v. *Nebraska Penal Inmates*[44] established that parole boards do not have to specify the evidence used in deciding to deny parole. The *Greenholtz* case focused on a Nebraska statute that required that inmates denied parole be provided with reasons for the denial. The Court held that reasons for parole denial might be provided in the interest of helping inmates prepare themselves for future review but that to require the disclosure of evidence used in the review hearing would turn the process into an adversarial proceeding.

The 1983 Supreme Court case of *Bearden* v. *Georgia*[45] established that probation could not be revoked for failure to pay a fine and make restitution if it could not be shown that the defendant was responsible for the failure. The Court also held that alternative forms of punishment must be considered by the hearing authority and must be shown to be inadequate before the defendant can be incarcerated. The Supreme Court decision stated that "[i]f the State determines a fine or restitution to be the appropriate and adequate penalty for the crime, it may not thereafter imprison a person solely because he lacked the resources to pay it."[46] The Court held that if a defendant lacks the capacity to pay a fine or make restitution, then the hearing authority must consider any viable alternatives to incarceration before imposing a prison sentence.

Finally, a probationer's incriminating statements to a probation officer may be used as evidence if the probationer does not specifically claim a right against self-incrimination, according to *Minnesota* v. *Murphy* (1984).[47] According to the Court, the burden of invoking the Fifth Amendment privilege against self-incrimination lies with the probationer.

An important legal issue today surrounds the potential liability of probation officers and parole boards for the criminal actions of offenders they supervise or whom they have released. Some courts have held that officers are generally immune from suit because they are performing a judicial function on behalf of the state.[48] Other courts, however, have indicated that parole board members who do not carefully consider mandated criteria for judging parole eligibility could be liable for injurious actions committed by parolees.[49] In general, however, most experts agree that

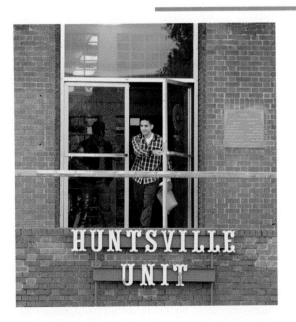

Angel Coronado, 20, rushing through the door of the Huntsville (Texas) Prison Unit after being released due to overcrowding. Coronado, who has been in trouble nearly half his life, had spent nearly two years in a 6- by 10-foot cell by himself. The U.S. Supreme Court has held that "an inmate who has been released under a program to relieve prison crowding cannot be reincarcerated without getting a chance to show at a hearing that he has met the conditions [of his release] and is entitled to remain free."

*Todd Bigelow Photography*

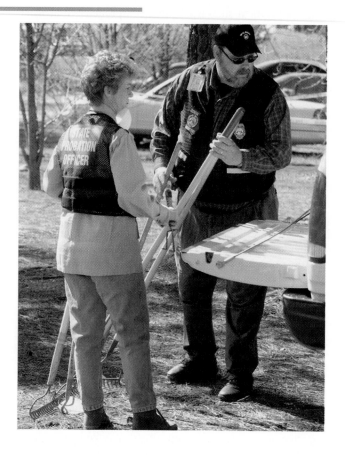

A probation officer's job can involve a wide variety of duties. Here, Georgia probation officers prepare to excavate a site at the Tri-State Crematory in Noble, Georgia, in 2002. Officials found the remains of hundreds of corpses on the crematory's 16-acre grounds. The crematory's operator, Ray Brent Marsh, was charged with 787 felony counts that include theft by deception, abuse of a corpse, and burial service fraud. He was also charged with 47 counts of making false statements to authorities.

*AP Wide World Photos*

> A critical assessment of probation must begin by placing its ailments within the more encompassing and deeper crisis of legitimacy affecting the entire system of justice.
>
> —Reinventing Probation Council

parole board members cannot be successfully sued unless release decisions are made in a grossly negligent or wantonly reckless manner.[50] Discretionary decisions of individual probation and parole officers that result in harm to members of the public, however, may be more actionable under civil law, especially where their decisions were not reviewed by judicial authority.[51]

# The Job of Probation and Parole Officers

The tasks performed by probation and parole officers are often quite similar. Some jurisdictions combine the roles of both into one job. This section describes the duties of probation and parole officers, whether separate or performed by the same individuals. Probation/parole work consists primarily of four functions: (1) presentence investigations, (2) other intake procedures, (3) needs assessment and diagnosis, and (4) client supervision.

Where probation is a possibility, intake procedures may include a presentence investigation, which examines the offender's background to provide the sentencing judge with facts needed to make an informed sentencing decision. Intake procedures may also involve a dispute-settlement process during which the probation officer works with the defendant and the victim to resolve the complaint before sentencing. Intake duties tend to be more common for juvenile offenders than they are for adults, but all officers may eventually have to recommend to the judge the best sentencing alternative for a particular case.

Diagnosis, the psychological inventorying of the probation or parole client, may be done either formally with written tests administered by certified psychologists or through informal arrangements, which typically depend on the observational skills of the officer. Needs assessment, another area of officer responsibility, extends beyond the psychological needs of the client to a cataloging of the services necessary for a successful experience on probation or parole. Supervision of sentenced probationers or released parolees is the most active stage of the probation/parole process, involving months (and sometimes years) of periodic meetings between the officer and the client and an ongoing assessment of the success of the probation/parole endeavor in each case.

All probation and parole officers must keep confidential the details of the presentence investigation, including psychological tests, needs assessment, conversations between the officer and the client, and so on. On the other hand, courts have generally held that communications between

## PROBATION OFFICER

**Name:** Jesse J. Gomes

**Position:** U.S. Probation Officer

**City:** Boston, Massachusetts

**College Attended:** Northeastern University

**Year Hired:** 2000

*I chose a career in probation because it puts me in a position to address issues from both law enforcement and human service perspectives. To work in probation is to quite literally "serve and protect" by serving a population that requires positive intervention while protecting the public from those individuals who choose not to comply.*

*Working for U.S. Probation was the culmination of seven years of case management and offender supervision experience. I started my career as a case manager at a prerelease and intermediate sanctions program in Boston and was then hired as a probation officer for the state of Massachusetts. Federal probation was the next logical step in my career path.*

U.S. probation officers must remain informed and flexible because the nature of the work is ever changing. In general, officers must have strong written and oral skills, be tied into a comprehensive network of treatment and service providers, be able to communicate effectively with a wide array of people, and have a working understanding of applicable laws. Because treatment methodologies, crime, and the laws themselves are all fluid to some extent, officers must be willing and able to implement these changes or anticipate their effects on probationers.

When you do your job well, people's lives are actually improved. That may mean helping an addict establish sobriety, obtaining housing for a homeless person, or ensuring that a dangerous offender is adequately supervised or, if necessary, removed from the community. Much is said about improving people's lives, but in reality that's rarer and more difficult than we would like it to be. But when actual change does occur, it makes up for the many disappointments.

### TYPICAL POSITIONS

A U.S. probation officer has a wide range of duties and responsibilities, including supervising offenders, conducting presentence investigations, and preparing presentence reports. Tasks involve interviewing offenders and their families, investigating offenses, determining prior record and financial status of offenders, and contacting law enforcement agencies, attorneys, and victims of crimes.

### EMPLOYMENT REQUIREMENTS

To qualify for the position of probation officer at the GS-5 level, an applicant must possess a bachelor's degree from an accredited college or university and must have a minimum of two years of general work experience. General experience must have been acquired after obtaining the bachelor's degree and cannot include experience as a police, custodial, or security officer unless the work involved criminal investigative experience. In lieu of general experience, a bachelor's degree from an accredited college or university in an accepted field of study (including criminology,

criminal justice, penology, correctional administration, social work, sociology, public administration, or psychology) will qualify an applicant for immediate employment at the GS-5 level, provided that at least 32 semester hours or 48 quarter hours were taken in one or more of the accepted fields of study. One year of graduate study qualifies applicants for appointment at the GS-7 level, while a master's degree in an appropriate field or a law degree may qualify the applicant for advanced placement.

### OTHER REQUIREMENTS

Applicants must be younger than 37 years of age at the time of hiring and must be in excellent physical health. A full field background investigation by the FBI and preemployment drug testing are also required.

### SALARY

Appointees are typically hired at federal pay grade GS-5 or GS-7, depending on education and prior work history.

### BENEFITS

U.S. probation and pretrial services officers are included in the federal hazardous-duty law enforcement classification and are covered by liberal federal health and life insurance programs. A comprehensive retirement program is available to all federal employees.

### DIRECT INQUIRIES TO:

Administrative Office of the U.S. Courts
Personnel Office
Washington, D.C. 20544

Phone: (202)273–1297

Website: http://www.uscourts.gov

For additional information on employment opportunities in the criminal justice field, view the careers portion of the CD-ROM included with this book.

*Source:* Administrative Office of the United States Courts.

Log on to ResearchNavigator
.com, and choose "Criminal
Justice" under ContentSelect's
Academic Journal Database.
Enter the word "probation" in
the search box, and click "Go."
Select three articles that you find
especially interesting from the
results page. (Choose full-text
articles rather than abstracts
whenever possible.) Perform the
search again, this time using the
word "parole." Select another
three articles from the search
results. Write a summary of
each of the six articles you've
identified, including complete
source information—that is,
article title, author (if available),
date of publication, and source.
Submit what you have written to
your instructor if asked to do so.
*Note:* This feature is available
only if your instructor has
chosen the Research Navigator
option available with a new
textbook.

---

**caseload**

The number of probation or
parole clients assigned to one
probation or parole officer for
supervision.

---

**WEB** EXTRA

---

**intermediate
sanctions**

The use of split sentencing,
shock probation or parole,
shock incarceration,
community service, intensive
supervision, or home confinement in lieu of other, more
traditional, sanctions, such as
imprisonment and fines.

---

the officer and the client are not privileged, as they might be between a doctor and a patient or between a social worker and his or her client.[52] Hence officers can share with the appropriate authorities any incriminating evidence that a client relates.

## The Challenges of the Job

One of the biggest challenges that probation and parole officers face is the need to balance two conflicting sets of duties—one of which is to provide quasi–social work services and the other is to handle custodial responsibilities. In effect, two inconsistent models of the officer's role coexist. The social work model stresses an officer's service role and views probationers and parolees as clients. In this model, officers are caregivers whose goals are to accurately assess the needs of their clients and to match clients with community resources such as job placement, indigent medical care, family therapy, and psychological and substance-abuse counseling. The social work model depicts probation/parole as a "helping profession" wherein officers assist their clients in meeting the conditions imposed on them by their sentence. The other model for officers is correctional. In this model, probation and parole clients are "wards" whom officers are expected to control. This model emphasizes community protection, which officers are supposed to achieve through careful and close supervision. Custodial supervision means that officers will periodically visit their charges at work and at home, often arriving unannounced. It also means that they must be willing to report clients for new offenses and for violations of the conditions of their release.

Most officers, by virtue of their personalities and experiences, identify more with one model than with the other. They consider themselves primarily caregivers or correctional officers. Regardless of the emphasis that each individual officer stresses, however, the demands of the job are bound to generate role conflict at one time or another.

A second challenge of probation and parole work is large **caseloads**. Back in 1973, the President's Commission on Law Enforcement and Administration of Justice recommended that probation and parole caseloads average around 35 clients per officer.[53] However, caseloads of 250 clients are common in some jurisdictions today. Large caseloads combined with limited training and the time constraints imposed by administrative demands culminate in stopgap supervisory measures. "Postcard probation," in which clients mail in a letter or card once a month to report on their whereabouts and circumstances, is an example of one stopgap measure that harried agencies with large caseloads use to keep track of their wards.

Another difficulty with probation and parole work is the frequent lack of opportunity for career mobility within the profession. Probation and parole officers are generally assigned to small agencies serving limited geographic areas, under the leadership of one or two chief probation officers. Unless retirement or death claims a supervisor, there is little chance for other officers to advance.

Learn more about working as a probation or parole officer at the American Probation and Parole Association's website via Web Extra 12–3 at cjtoday.com.

## Intermediate Sanctions

Significant new sentencing options have become available during the past few decades. Many such options are called **intermediate sanctions** because they employ sentencing alternatives that fall somewhere between outright imprisonment and simple probationary release back into the community. They are also sometimes termed *alternative sentencing strategies.* Michael J. Russell, former director of the National Institute of Justice, says that "intermediate punishments are intended to provide prosecutors, judges, and corrections officials with sentencing options that permit them to apply appropriate punishments to convicted offenders while not being constrained by the traditional choice between prison and probation. Rather than substituting for prison or probation, however, these sanctions, which include intensive supervision, house arrest with electronic monitoring (also referred to as *remote location monitoring*), and shock incarceration—programs that stress a highly structured and regimented routine, considerable physical work and exercise, and at times intensive substance abuse treatment—bridge the gap between those options and provide innovative ways to ensure swift and certain punishment."[54]

A number of citizen groups and special-interest organizations are working to widen the use of sentencing alternatives. One organization of special note is the Sentencing Project. The Sentencing Project, based in Washington, D.C., is dedicated to promoting a greater use of alternatives to incarceration. It provides technical assistance to public defenders, court officials, and other community organizations.

The Sentencing Project and other groups like it have contributed to the development of more than 100 locally based alternative sentencing service programs. Most alternative sentencing services work in conjunction with defense attorneys to develop written sentencing plans. Such plans are basically well-considered citizen suggestions as to appropriate sentencing in a given instance. Plans are often quite detailed and may include letters of support from employers, family members, the defendant, and even victims. Sentencing plans may be used in plea bargaining sessions or may be presented to judges following trial and conviction. More than a decade ago, for example, lawyers for country-and-western singer Willie Nelson successfully proposed to tax court officials an alternative option that allowed the singer to pay huge past tax liabilities by performing in concerts for that purpose. Lacking such an alternative, the tax court might have seized Nelson's property or even ordered the singer to be confined to a federal facility.

The basic philosophy behind intermediate sanctions is this: When judges are offered well-planned alternatives to imprisonment, the likelihood of a prison sentence is reduced. An analysis of alternative sentencing plans like those sponsored by the Sentencing Project shows that judges accept them in up to 80% of the cases in which they are recommended and that as many as two-thirds of offenders who receive intermediate sentences successfully complete them.[55]

Intermediate sanctions have three distinct advantages: (1) They are less expensive to operate per offender than imprisonment; (2) they are "socially cost-effective" because they keep the offender in the community, thus avoiding both the breakup of the family and the stigmatization that accompanies imprisonment; and (3) they provide flexibility in terms of resources, time of involvement, and place of service.[56] Some of these new sentencing options are described in the paragraphs that follow.

# Split Sentencing

In jurisdictions where **split sentences** are an option, judges may impose a combination of a brief period of imprisonment and probation. Defendants who are given split sentences are often ordered to serve time in a local jail rather than in a long-term confinement facility. Ninety days in jail, followed by two years of supervised probation, is a typical split sentence. Split sentences are frequently given to minor drug offenders and serve notice that continued law violations may result in imprisonment for much longer periods.

| **split sentence** |
|---|
| A sentence explicitly requiring the convicted offender to serve a period of confinement in a local, state, or federal facility, followed by a period of probation. |

# Shock Probation and Shock Parole

**Shock probation** strongly resembles split sentencing. The offender serves a relatively short period of time in custody (usually in a prison rather than a jail) and is released on probation by court order. The difference is that shock probation clients must *apply* for probationary release from confinement and cannot be certain of the judge's decision. In shock probation, the court in effect makes a resentencing decision. Probation is only a statutory possibility and often little more than an aspiration for the offender as imprisonment begins. If probationary release is ordered, it may well come as a "shock" to the offender. The hope is that the unexpected reprieve will cause the offender to steer clear of future criminal involvement. Shock probation was begun in Ohio in 1965[57] and is used today in about half of the United States.[58] Shock probation lowers the cost of confinement, maintains community and family ties, and may be an effective rehabilitative tool.[59]

Similar to shock probation is shock parole. Whereas shock probation is ordered by judicial authority, shock parole is an administrative decision made by a paroling authority. Parole boards or their representatives may order an inmate's early release, hoping that the brief exposure to prison has reoriented the offender's life in a positive direction.

| **shock probation** |
|---|
| The practice of sentencing offenders to prison, allowing them to apply for probationary release, and enacting such release in surprise fashion. Offenders who receive shock probation may not be aware that they will be released on probation and may expect to spend a much longer time behind bars. |

# Shock Incarceration

**Shock incarceration** programs, which became popular during the 1990s, utilize military-style "boot camp" prison settings to provide highly regimented environments involving strict discipline, physical training, and hard labor.[60] Shock incarceration programs are designed primarily for young first offenders and are of short duration, generally lasting for only 90 to 180 days. Offenders who successfully complete these programs are typically returned to the community under some form of supervision. Program "failures" may be moved into the general prison population for longer terms of confinement.

Georgia established the first shock incarceration program in 1983.[61] Following Georgia's lead, more than 30 other states began their own programs.[62] About half of the states provide for voluntary entry into the program. A few allow inmates to decide when and whether they want to quit. Although

| **shock incarceration** |
|---|
| A sentencing option that makes use of "boot camp"–type prisons to impress on convicted offenders the realities of prison life. |

most states allow judges to place offenders into these programs, some delegate that authority to corrections officials. Two states, Louisiana and Texas, give judges and corrections personnel joint authority in the decision-making process.[63] Some states, including Massachusetts, accept female inmates into boot camp settings. The Massachusetts program, which first accepted women in 1993, requires inmates to spend nearly four months undergoing the rigors of training. The federal government also operates shock incarceration programs.

One of the most comprehensive studies to date of boot camp prison programs focused on eight states: Florida, Georgia, Illinois, Louisiana, New York, Oklahoma, South Carolina, and Texas. The report found that boot camp programs have been popular because "they are . . . perceived as being tough on crime" and "have been enthusiastically embraced as a viable correctional option."[64] The report concluded, however, that "the impact of boot camp programs on offender recidivism is at best negligible."

More limited studies, such as one that focused on shock incarceration in New York State, have found that boot camp programs can be effective money savers. The research indicates that such programs save money in two ways: "first by reducing expenditures for care and custody" (since the intense programs reduce time spent in custody, and participation in them is the only way New York inmates can be released from prison before their minimum parole eligibility dates) and "second, by avoiding capital costs for new prison construction."[65] A 1995 study of Oregon's Summit boot camp program reached a similar conclusion. Although they did not study recidivism, the Oregon researchers found that "the Summit boot camp program is a cost-effective means of reducing prison overcrowding by treating and releasing specially selected inmates earlier than their court-determined minimum period of incarceration."[66]

> **mixed sentence**
>
> A sentence that requires that a convicted offender serve weekends (or other specified periods of time) in a confinement facility (usually a jail) while undergoing probationary supervision in the community.

## Mixed Sentencing and Community Service

Some **mixed sentences** require that offenders serve weekends in jail and receive probation supervision during the week. Other types of mixed sentencing require offenders to participate in treatment or community service programs while on probation. Community service programs be-

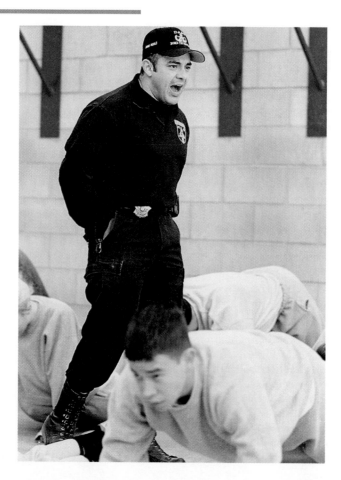

A New Mexico boot camp staff member conducts a push-up drill with young offenders. Boot camps use military-style discipline in an attempt to lessen the chance for recidivism among young and first-time offenders.

*AP Wide World Photos*

## ETHICS AND PROFESSIONALISM

### American Probation and Parole Association Code of Ethics

- I will render professional service to the justice system and the community at large in effecting the social adjustment of the offender.
- I will uphold the law with dignity, displaying an awareness of my responsibility to offenders while recognizing the right of the public to be safeguarded from criminal activity.
- I will strive to be objective in the performance of my duties, recognizing the inalienable right of all persons, appreciating the inherent worth of the individual, and respecting those confidences which can be reposed in me.
- I will conduct my personal life with decorum, neither accepting nor granting favors in connection with my office.
- I will cooperate with my co-workers and related agencies and will continually strive to improve my professional competence through the seeking and sharing of knowledge and understanding.

- I will distinguish clearly, in public, between my statements and actions as an individual and as a representative of my profession.
- I will encourage policy, procedures and personnel practices, which will enable others to conduct themselves in accordance with the values, goals and objectives of the American Probation and Parole Association.
- I recognize my office as a symbol of public faith and I accept it as a public trust to be held as long as I am true to the ethics of the American Probation and Parole Association.
- I will constantly strive to achieve these objectives and ideals, dedicating myself to my chosen profession.

#### THINKING ABOUT ETHICS

1. Which of the ethical principles enumerated here might also apply to correctional officers working in prisons and jails?
2. Which might apply to law enforcement officers?
3. Which might apply to prosecutors and criminal defense attorneys?

*Source:* American Probation and Parole Association. Reprinted with permission.

---

gan in Minnesota in 1972 with the Minnesota Restitution Program, which gave property offenders the opportunity to work and turn over part of their pay as restitution to their victims.[67] Courts throughout the nation quickly adopted the idea and began to build restitution orders into suspended-sentence agreements.

**Community service** is more an adjunct to, rather than a type of, correctional sentence. Community service is compatible with most other forms of innovation in probation and parole. Even with home confinement (discussed below), offenders can be sentenced to community service activities that are performed in the home or at a job site during the hours they are permitted to be away from their homes. Washing police cars, cleaning school buses, refurbishing public facilities, and assisting in local government offices are typical forms of community service. Some authors have linked the development of community service sentences to the notion that work and service to others are good for the spirit.[68] Community service participants are usually minor criminals, drunk drivers, and youthful offenders.

One problem with community service sentences is that authorities rarely agree on what they are supposed to accomplish. Most people admit that offenders who work in the community are able to reduce the costs of their own supervision. There is little agreement, however, on whether such sentences reduce recidivism, act as a deterrent, or serve to rehabilitate offenders.

> **community service**
> A sentencing alternative that requires offenders to spend at least part of their time working for a community agency.

> Probation and parole services are characteristically poorly staffed and often poorly administered.
>
> —President's Commission on Law Enforcement and Administration of Justice

## Intensive Supervision

**Intensive probation supervision (IPS)** has been described as the "strictest form of probation for adults in the United States."[69] IPS is designed to achieve control in a community setting over offenders who would otherwise go to prison. Some states have extended intensive supervision to parolees, allowing the early release of some who would otherwise serve longer prison terms.

Georgia was the first state to implement IPS, beginning its program in 1982. The Georgia program involves a minimum of five face-to-face contacts between the probationer and the supervising officer per week, mandatory curfew, required employment, a weekly check of local arrest records, routine and unannounced alcohol and drug testing, 132 hours of community service, and automatic notification of probation officers via the State Crime Information Network when an IPS client is arrested.[70] The caseloads of probation officers involved in IPS are much lower than the national average. Georgia officers work as a team, with one probation officer and two surveillance officers supervising about 40 probationers.[71]

> **intensive probation supervision (IPS)**
> A form of probation supervision involving frequent face-to-face contact between the probationer and the probation officer.

Electronic supervision in action. Boxing's most notorious middleweight, 38-year-old Tony "El Torito" Ayala, conceals an electronic ankle bracelet under his left sock as he spars during a workout at a gym in San Antonio before a scheduled fight. In 2001, the fighter pleaded guilty to burglary and was sentenced to 90 days in jail and ten years' probation. Ayala had previously served 16 years in a New Jersey prison on a 1983 rape conviction.

*AP Wide World Photos*

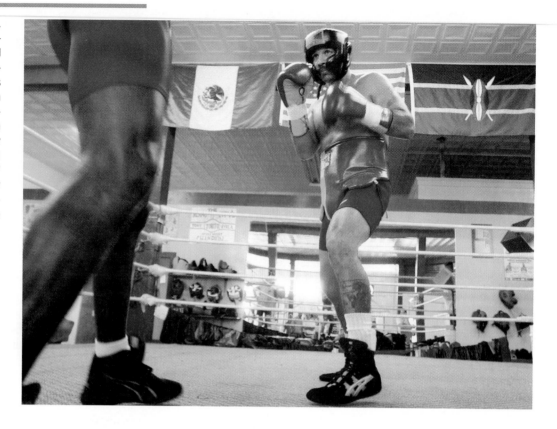

A study published in 2000 shows that IPS programs can be effective at reducing recidivism, especially if the programs are well planned and fully implemented.[72] The study, which examined programs in California's Contra Costa and Ventura Counties, found that the programs worked because, among other things, they used team approaches in their supervision activities and had clear missions and goals.

# Home Confinement and Remote Location Monitoring

**home confinement**

House arrest. Individuals ordered confined to their homes are sometimes monitored electronically to ensure they do not leave during the hours of confinement. Absence from the home during working hours is often permitted.

**remote location monitoring**

A supervision strategy that uses electronic technology to track offenders sentenced to house arrest or those who have been ordered to limit their movements while completing a sentence involving probation or parole.

**Home confinement**, also referred to as *house arrest,* can be defined as "a sentence imposed by the court in which offenders are legally ordered to remain confined in their own residences."[73] Home confinement usually makes use of a system of **remote location monitoring**. Remote location monitoring is typically performed via a computerized system of electronic bracelets. Participants wear a waterproof, shock-resistant transmitting device around the ankle 24 hours a day. The transmitter continuously emits a radio-frequency signal, which is detected by a receiving unit connected to the home telephone. Older systems use random telephone calls that require the offender to insert a computer chip worn in a wristband into a specially installed modem in the home, verifying his or her presence. Some use voice recognition technology and require the offender to verify his or her presence in the home by answering computerized calls. Modern electronic monitoring systems alert the officer when a participant leaves a specific location or tampers with the electronic monitoring equipment, and some systems even make it possible to record the time a supervised person enters or leaves the home.

Much of the electronic monitoring equipment in use today only indicates when participants enter or leave the equipment's range—not where they have gone or how far they have traveled. Newer satellite-supported systems, however, are capable of continuously monitoring an offender's location and tracking him as he moves from place to place (Figure 12–4). Satellite-based systems can alert the officer when participants venture into geographically excluded locations or when they fail to present themselves at required locations at specific times.[74]

Most remotely monitored offenders on home confinement may leave home only to go to their jobs, attend to medical emergencies, or buy household essentials. Because of the strict limits it imposes on offender movements, house arrest has been cited as offering a valuable alternative to prison for offenders with special needs. Pregnant women, geriatric convicts, offenders with special handicaps, seriously or terminally ill offenders, and mentally retarded persons may all be better supervised through home confinement than traditional incarceration.

**FIGURE 12-4**

**Remote location monitoring—how it works.**

*Source:* iSECUREtrac Corporation, 5022 South 114th Street, Omaha, NE 68137; phone: (866)537–0022. Copyright © 2005 iSECUREtrac Corporation. All rights reserved. Used with permission.

One of the best-known people to recently be placed under house arrest using a remote location monitoring system was 63-year-old Martha Stewart, former CEO of Martha Stewart Living Omnimedia, Inc. Stewart served five months in prison for insider stock transactions, and was ordered to serve an additional five months under house arrest at her Bedford, New York, estate.[75] She was allowed daily commutes totaling 48 hours weekly to her office in New York City, 40 miles away.[76]

The Community Justice Assistance Division of the Texas Department of Criminal Justice runs one of the most ambitious home confinement programs in the country. In 1997, 89,095 adults (3.5% of the state's probationers) were being electronically monitored on probation.[77] By 2002, parole offices throughout the state adopted electronic monitoring, and 700 electronic monitoring units were available for parolees.[78]

The electronic monitoring of offenders has increased across the nation. A survey by the National Institute of Justice in 1987, as the use of electronic monitoring was just beginning, showed only 826 offenders being monitored electronically nationwide.[79] By 2000, however, more than 16,000 defendants and offenders under the supervision of U.S. probation and pretrial services officers were on home confinement—most under electronic monitoring programs.[80]

In 1999, South Carolina's Probation and Parole Department began using satellites to track felons recently freed from state prisons. The satellite-tracking plan, which makes use of 21 satellites in the Global Positioning System (GPS), allows the agency's officers to track every move made by convicts wearing electronic bracelets.[81] The system, which also notifies law enforcement officers when a bracelet-wearing offender leaves his assigned area, can electronically alert anyone holding a restraint order whenever the offender comes within two miles of them.

The home confinement program in the federal court system has three components, or levels of restriction.[82] *Curfew* requires program participants to remain at home every day during certain times, usually in the evening. With *home detention*, the participant remains at home at all times except for preapproved and scheduled absences, such as for work, school, treatment, church,

The number of people under criminal justice supervision in this country has reached a record high. As a result, the sentencing policies driving that number, and the field of corrections, where the consequences are felt, have acquired an unprecedented salience. It is a salience defined more by issues of magnitude, complexity, and expense than by any consensus about future directions.

—Julie E. Samuels, Acting Director, National Institute of Justice[iii]

Officials of the New Jersey State Parole Board conduct a parole hearing at their central office in Trenton using video-conferencing technology. Prior to implementation of the technology, board members had to travel between the state's 14 correctional institutions to hear cases. Reviewing the case are board members Thomas Haff and John Paitakes (right).

*Courtesy of the New Jersey State Parole Board*

attorney's appointments, court appearances, and other court-ordered obligations. *Home incarceration,* the highest level of restriction, calls for 24-hour-a-day "lockdown" at home, except for medical appointments, court appearances, and other activities that the court specifically approves.

Many states and the federal government view house arrest as a cost-effective response to the high cost of imprisonment. Georgia, for example, estimates that home confinement costs approximately $1,130 per year per supervised probationer and $2,190 per supervised parolee.[83] Incarceration costs are much higher, running around $18,100 per year per Georgia inmate, with another $43,756 needed to build each cell.[84] Advocates of house arrest argue that it is also socially cost-effective,[85] because it substantially decreases the opportunity for the kinds of negative socialization that occur in prison. Opponents, however, have pointed out that house arrest may endanger the public and that it may provide little or no actual punishment. Critics of Martha Stewart's home confinement, for example, complained that the sentence was more of a reward than a punishment. Stewart's home, a 153-acre multimillion-dollar mansion with guest quarters, lacks few amenities, and the conditions imposed on Stewart allowed her to entertain colleagues, neighbors, friends, and relatives—as long as they didn't have criminal records.

# The Future of Probation and Parole

Probation and parole have essentially shifted from legitimate correctional options in their own right to temporary diversionary strategies that we are using while we are trying to figure out how to get tough on crime, [pay] no new taxes, and not pay for any prisons at all, or to pay as little as we can, or pass it off to another generation.

—Dr. Charles M. Friel,
Sam Houston State University

Parole was widely criticized during the 1980s and 1990s by citizen groups who claimed that it unfairly reduces prison sentences imposed on serious offenders. Official attacks on parole came from some powerful corners. Senator Edward Kennedy called for the abolition of parole, as did former Attorney General Griffin Bell and former U.S. Bureau of Prisons Director Norman Carlson.[86] Academics chimed in, alleging that parole programs can provide no assurance that criminals will not commit further crimes. The media joined the fray, condemning parole for its lack of curbing recidivism and highlighting the so-called revolving prison door as representative of the failure of parole. These criticisms are not without warrant. In 2003, for example, more than 625,000 former prisoners were released into society—most of them on some form of supervised release.[87] Parole violators, however, account for more than half of prison admissions in California (67%), Utah (55%), and Montana and Louisiana (both 53%). Seventy percent of parole violators in prison were arrested or were convicted of a new offense while on parole.[88] Many of these offenses involve drugs.

Prisoners have also challenged the fairness of parole, saying it is sometimes arbitrarily granted and creates an undue amount of uncertainty and frustration in the lives of inmates. Parolees have complained about the unpredictable nature of the parole experience, citing their powerlessness in the parole contract.

Against the pressure of attacks like these, parole advocates struggled to clarify and communicate the value of supervised release in the correctional process. As more and more states moved toward the elimination of parole, advocates called for moderation. A 1995 report by the American Probation and Parole Association (APPA), for example, concluded that states that have eliminated parole "have jeopardized public safety and wasted tax dollars." The researchers wrote, "Getting rid of parole dismantles an accountable system of releasing prisoners back into the community and replaces it with a system that bases release decisions solely on whether a prison term has been completed."[89]

Some jurisdictions responded by creating a different kind of reentry system—one that uses reentry courts and tasks judges to serve the role of reentry managers.[90] Under this model, sentencing judges oversee an offender's sentence from the time of conviction and imprisonment through release into the community under supervision. In 2000, for example, the state of Delaware launched a reentry court pilot project that employs active judicial oversight of offenders during a period of supervised release. The program includes the use of graduated sanctions for violations of release conditions, a broad array of supportive services with community involvement, and positive judicial reinforcement of successful completion of reentry court goals. Learn more about the Delaware reentry court project at Web Extra 12–4 at cjtoday.com. Read about the ideas behind the reentry court movement at Library Extra 12–4.

# Reinventing Parole

By the close of the twentieth century, criticisms of parole had begun to wane, and a number of recent reports have been supportive of well-considered offender reentry and postrelease supervision programs. In 2005, for example, the Re-Entry Policy Council, a bipartisan assembly of almost 100 leading elected officials, policymakers, correctional leaders, and practitioners from community-based organizations around the country, released a report on offender reentry entitled *Charting the Safe and Successful Return of Prisoners to the Community*. The 500-page report pointed out that virtually every person incarcerated in a jail in this country, as well as 97% of those incarcerated in prisons, will eventually be released back into society. This, said the report, results in nearly 650,000 people being released from prisons, and more than 7 million different individuals being released from jails throughout the United States each year—many of them without any form of postrelease supervision.[91]

As the report pointed out, almost two out of every three people released from prison are re-arrested within three years of their release.[92] Report authors noted that while the number of people reentering society has increased fourfold in the past 20 years, and spending on corrections has increased nearly sevenfold in the past two decades, the likelihood of a former prisoner succeeding in the community upon release has not improved.

A host of complex issues create barriers to successful reentry. Three-quarters of those released from prison and jail, for example, have a history of substance abuse; two-thirds have no high school diploma; nearly half of those leaving jail earn less than $600 per month immediately prior to their incarceration, and they leave jail with significantly diminished opportunities for employment. Moreover, said the report, more than a third of jail inmates are saddled with a physical or mental disability, and the rate of serious mental illness among released inmates is at least three times higher than the rate of mental illness among the general population.[93]

According to the report, "the multi-faceted—and costly—needs of people returning to their families and communities require a re-inventing of reentry akin to the reinvention of welfare in the 90s." It requires, the report continued, "a multi-system, collaborative approach that takes into account all aspects of [the] problem." In other words, "the problems faced by re-entering adults are not merely the problems of corrections or community corrections, but also of public health workers, housing providers, state legislators, workforce development staff, and others."

To guide states and local jurisdictions in the creation of successful offender reentry programs, the report provides 35 policy statements, each of which is supported by a series of research highlights. The report is available in its entirety at cjtoday.com as Library Extra 12–5. A 24-page summary is available as Library Extra 12–6.

A second report dealing with the problems of reentry, this one by the Governor's Commission on Criminal Justice Innovation in Massachusetts, was released in 2004.[94] Although the report covered areas of the justice system other than reentry and postrelease supervision, a number of its recommendations focused on creating a seamless continuum of services for offenders leaving jail or prison and increasing the chances of success for offenders leaving incarceration and returning to the community. The commission noted that of the 20,000 offenders released from prison each year in Massachusetts, only 57% of those returning to the community from medium- and maximum-security facilities receive any kind of postrelease supervision.[95] Effective prisoner reentry and postrelease supervision, said the commission, depend on an integrated *corrections continuum* beginning with sentencing and ending with community reintegration. According to the commission, "a successful re-entry and post-release supervision strategy requires the examination of all aspects of the corrections continuum, including sentencing, classification, prerelease programs, release practices and post-release supervision." The commission's recommendations include the following[96]:

- The state legislature should enact laws requiring some form of mandatory supervision for everyone who is released from incarceration, with longer-term mandatory supervision for those offenders who meet criteria focused on potential danger to the community.

By writing parole boards out of the release decision, our sentencing reforms over the past 25 years have eliminated a valuable role they played, namely overseeing the process of preparing prisoners for reentry.

—Jeremy Travis, President, John Jay College of Criminal Justice[iv]

I understand that people want violent criminals locked up. We all do. But not every inmate is violent. We must look to supervised probation, to education. We must overcome the fear and think this out.

—Former Louisiana Governor Edwin Edwards

> The overarching goal of reentry, in my view, is to have returned to our midst an individual who has discharged his legal obligation to society by serving his sentence *and* has demonstrated an ability to live by society's rules.
>
> —Jeremy Travis, President, John Jay College of Criminal Justice

- Parole eligibility should be made available to more prisoners, and intermediate sanctions should be applied, where appropriate.
- A standardized offender assessment process should be established to gather and share information that enables effective placement and programming at every step of the criminal justice process, from arraignment to commitment to release and community reentry.
- Reentry planning should begin early in the period of incarceration.
- Collaboration among the reentry stakeholders (police, probation/parole agencies, charitable organizations, and businesses) at the state, local, county, and community levels must be increased.
- Job training should be increased, and work must be done to remove obstacles to obtaining employment and housing for released offenders.
- Better access to treatment for drug- and alcohol-addicted offenders should be available.
- Tax incentives should be created to encourage the expansion of employment opportunities for those inmates returning to the community who agree to remain in close connection with an organized community-based reentry program.

The report concluded by noting that Massachusetts spends about $43,000 per year to incarcerate an offender, while probation and parole supervision costs the state $520 and $4,000, respectively. "These statistics" said the report, "suggest the need for creative sentencing options that utilize less restrictive settings combined with quality post-incarceration supervision as remedies for an ever-burgeoning correctional budget." The full commission report is available as Library Extra 12–7 at cjtoday.com.

**LIBRARY EXTRA**

## Reinventing Probation

Although probation has generally fared better than parole, it too has its critics. The primary purpose of probation has always been rehabilitation. Probation is a powerful rehabilitative tool because, at least in theory, it allows the resources of a community to be focused on the offender. Unfortunately for advocates of probation, however, the rehabilitative ideal is far less popular today than it has been in the past. The contemporary demand for "just deserts" appears to have reduced society's tolerance for even relatively minor offenders. Also, because it has been too frequently and inappropriately used with repeat or relatively serious offenders, the image of probation has been tarnished. Probation advocates have been forced to admit that it is not a very powerful deterrent because it is far less punishing than a term of imprisonment.

In a series of reports issued in 1999 and 2000, the Reinventing Probation Council, a project of New York's Manhattan Institute, called for the "reinvention of probation."[97] Probation is currently in the midst of a crisis, said the council, because probationers are not being held to even simple

David Duke, the former Ku Klux Klan leader whose case raised eyebrows when he was released on federal parole in 2004. Duke, who served a year in federal prison on fraud charges, was released to a halfway house in Baton Rouge, Louisiana, and met the work requirements of his release by performing duties for the "white civil rights group" that he heads.

*AP Wide World Photos*

## CJ FUTURES

### Probation Kiosks: High-Tech Supervision

In 1997, probation authorities in New York City began experimenting with the use of "probation kiosks" designed to lower probation officer caseloads. Fifteen electronic kiosks, similar in design to automated teller machines, were soon scattered throughout the city. They allow probationers to check in with probation officers by placing their palms on a specially designed surface and by answering questions presented on a flashing screen.

The kiosks identify probationers by the shape and size of their hands, which were previously scanned into the system. Probationers are then prompted to press "yes" or "no" in response to questions like these: "Have you moved recently?" "Have you been arrested again?" "Do you need to see a probation officer?" Meetings with officers can be scheduled directly from the kiosk. Probation officers use a computer to monitor data sent from the kiosks and can zero in on individual probationers who are having problems, prompting more personal attention. By the time the system is fully operational, as many as 30,000 "low-risk" probationers—about one-third of New York City's total—will report through kiosks.

Kiosks have already yielded positive results, according to New York City probation officer Genée Bogans. Before the kiosks, says Bogans, she was swamped by the administrative details required to track the 250 offenders in her caseload. Kiosks allow her to track nonviolent, older offenders with a minimum of time and effort, and she now focuses most of her attention on the relatively few violent youths who are also part of her caseload, meeting with them and their families twice weekly in small group sessions. Bogans even goes to family funerals and graduations, making youthful offenders feel like they are getting special attention. "But it can be done only when you have 30 cases as opposed to 200," says Bogans.

New York's use of kiosks is being watched closely by other probation and parole agencies around the country as they face swelling caseloads and shrinking budgets. Some jurisdictions, like Marion County, Indiana, have installed similar machines. Under its Expedited Caseload Program, Marion County (home to the city of Indianapolis) reports lowering the number of hours required of its probation officers for caseload supervision. "Since its inception," say county officials, the Expedited Caseload Program (which accepts offenders convicted of nonviolent and less serious crimes) "has taken more than 650 cases that would have otherwise gone to the regular probation caseloads. This is a savings of between 15 and 20 cases per casework officer over a two month period." The most recently available statistics show that about 4 million probationers were monitored through kiosks in 2001.

Other jurisdictions have taken different steps to automate their probation systems. Denver and Seattle, for example, are using 900-numbers through which probationers can report.

Critics charge that without personal supervision, probationers are more likely to reoffend—an assertion that is essentially untested. Other opponents say kiosks, 900-numbers, and similar reporting initiatives are far removed from meaningful "punishment" and that offenders deserve stricter treatment. Supporters, on the other hand, say that kiosks and 900-numbers will soon become more commonplace. "New York City had no choice; it had to do something like that," says Todd Clear, professor of criminal justice at New York's John Jay College. Clear assisted the city in restructuring its probation program. "No one wants probationers reporting to kiosks, but the alternative was even more unthinkable—a system in which nobody receives quality service," said Clear.

References: Marion Superior Court Probation Department, "Operation: Probationer Accountability." Web posted at http://www.indygov.org/probation/report/1998/4gh.htm; Isabelle de Pommereau, "N.Y.C. Probation Officers to Get High-Tech Helper," *Christian Science Monitor*, February 8, 1997; Deborah J. Myers, "Take Your Order? Check Probation? Kiosk Use Grows," *Boulder County Business Report*. Web posted at http://www.bcbr.com/display.phtml?VI=P2101&Section=News&Page=2; and the Rice County (Minnesota) website, at http://www.co.rice.mn.us.

standards of behavior and because the field of probation lacks leadership. According to the council, "probation will be reinvented when the probation profession places public safety first, and works with and in the community." Read the council's full reports at Library Extras 12–8 and 12–9 at cjtoday.com.

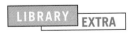

In an intriguing American Society of Criminology task force report on community corrections, Joan Petersilia notes that the "get tough on criminals" attitude that swept the nation during the 1990s resulted in increased funding for prisons but left in its wake stagnating budgetary allotments for probation and parole services.[98] This result has been especially unfortunate, Petersilia says, because "it has been continually shown that there is a 'highly significant statistical relationship between the extent to which probationers received needed services and the success of probation.' . . . As services have dwindled," she says, "recidivism rates have climbed." Some jurisdictions spend only a few hundred dollars per year on each probation or parole client, even though successful treatment in therapeutic settings is generally acknowledged to cost nearly $15,000 per person per year. The investment of such sums in the treatment of correctional clients, argues Petersilia, is potentially worthwhile because diverting probationers and parolees from

> Probation will change when those who run probation departments are held accountable for achieving—or failing to achieve—specific outcomes.
>
> —Reinventing Probation Council

lives of continued crime will save society even more money in terms of the costs of crime and the expenses associated with eventual imprisonment. The solution to the crisis that now exists in community corrections, says Petersilia, is to "first regain the public's trust that probation and parole can be meaningful, credible sanctions." She concludes, "Once we have that in place, we need to create a public climate to support a reinvestment in community corrections. Good community corrections cost money, and we should be honest about that."[99]

## SUMMARY

Probation, simply put, is a sentence of imprisonment that is suspended. Parole, in contrast, is the conditional early release of a convicted offender from prison. Both probation and parole impose conditions on offenders, requiring them to obey the law, meet with probation or parole officers, hold a job, and the like. Failure to abide by the conditions of probation or parole can result in re-arrest and imprisonment.

Viewed historically, probation and parole are two of the most recent major innovations in the correctional field. Both provide opportunities for the reintegration of offenders into the community through the use of resources not readily available in institutional settings. Unfortunately, however, increased freedom for criminal offenders also means some degree of increased risk for other members of society. As a consequence, contemporary "get tough" attitudes have resulted in a decreased use of probation and parole in many jurisdictions—and increased imprisonment. Until and unless we solve the problems of inaccurate risk assessment, increased recidivism, and inadequate supervision, probation and parole will continue to be viewed with suspicion by a public that has become intolerant of crime and criminal offenders.

## DISCUSSION QUESTIONS

1. How do probation and parole differ? How are they alike? What are the advantages and disadvantages of each?

2. Describe the significant court cases that have had an impact on the practice of probation and parole.

3. What is the function of the federal probation system? How did it come into being?

4. What do probation and parole officers do? What role do probation officers play in the sentencing of convicted offenders?

5. What are intermediate sanctions? How do they differ from more traditional forms of sentencing? What advantages (if any) do they have over more traditional forms of sentencing?

6. How are probation and parole changing? What does the future hold for them? Do you agree with those who are trying to eliminate parole? Explain your position.

## WEB QUEST

Use the Cybrary (http://www.cybrary.info) to search the World Wide Web to learn as much as you can about the future of probation and parole. In particular, you might want to focus on the use of satellite technology to monitor offenders placed on probation, the use of home confinement, or public and media attitudes toward probation and parole. Also gather studies on the future of probation and parole. Group your findings under headings (for example, "Innovative Options," "Alternative Sanctions," "Probation in My Home State," and "The Future of Probation and Parole").

Also visit the American Probation and Parole Association at http://www.appa-net.org. (The organization is listed in the Cybrary.) What is the mission of the APPA? What are its goals and objectives? What organizations are affiliated with it? How many of them have websites? Submit your findings to your instructor if asked to do so.

To complete this Web Quest online, go to the Web Quest module in Chapter 12 of the *Criminal Justice Today* Companion Website at cjtoday.com.

i. Jeremy Travis, *But They All Come Back: Rethinking Prisoner Reentry* (Washington, DC: National Institute of Justice, 2000), p. 2.

ii. Re-Entry Policy Council, *Report of the Re-Entry Policy Council: Charting the Safe and Successful Return of Prisoners to the Community—Report Preview* (New York: Council of State Governments, 2005), p. 4.

iii. From the "Director's Message" in Dora Schriro, "Correcting Corrections: Missouri's Parallel Universe," *Sentencing and Corrections Issues for the 21st Century: Papers from the Executive Session on Sentencing and Corrections,* No. 8 (Washington, DC: National Institute of Justice, 2000).

iv. Jeremy Travis, "Thoughts on the Future of Parole," remarks delivered at the Vera Institute of Justice, May 22, 2002, speech transcript, p. 3.

1. State of the Union, 2004.

2. Quotes in *Criminal Justice Newsletter,* January 19, 1993, p. 1.

3. Details for this story come from "Records: Smith Told His Brother," *The Herald Tribune,* June 3, 2004.

4. Details for this story come from "State Prosecutors: 'Jessica Lunsford Was Raped, Buried Alive,'" Associated Press, April 20, 2005.

5. Details for this story come from "Suspected Murderer of Thirteen-Year-Old Sarah Lunde May Face Death Penalty," *Gwinnett Daily Online,* no date. Web posted at http://www.gwinnettdailyonline.com/GDP/archive/articleDF4B74DF8C254FB184D3525E074FF0A6.asp (accessed July 5, 2005).

6. James M. Byrne, *Probation,* National Institute of Justice Crime File Series Study Guide (Washington, DC: U.S. Department of Justice, 1988), p. 1.

7. Alexander B. Smith and Louis Berlin, *Introduction to Probation and Parole* (St. Paul, MN: West, 1976), p. 75.

8. John Augustus, *First Probation Officer: John Augustus' Original Report on His Labors—1852* (Montclair, NJ: Patterson-Smith, 1972).

9. Smith and Berlin, *Introduction to Probation and Parole,* p. 77.

10. Ibid., p. 80.

11. George C. Killinger, Hazel B. Kerper, and Paul F. Cromwell, Jr., *Probation and Parole in the Criminal Justice System* (St. Paul, MN: West, 1976), p. 25.

12. Lauren E. Glaze and Seri Palla, *Probation and Parole in the United States, 2004* (Washington, DC: Bureau of Justice Statistics, November 2005).

13. Jodi M. Brown and Patrick A. Langan, *Felony Sentences in the United States, 1996* (Washington, DC: Bureau of Justice Statistics, 1999).

14. "Woman Gets Probation for Shooting Fiancé," Associated Press wire service, April 16, 1992, p. 9A.

15. Glaze and Palla, *Probation and Parole in the United States, 2004.*

16. Bureau of Justice Statistics, "Probation and Parole Statistics." Web posted at http://www.ojp.usdoj.gov/bjs/pandp.htm (accessed January 10, 2003).

17. This section owes much to Sanford Bates, "The Establishment and Early Years of the Federal Probation System," *Federal Probation* (June 1987), pp. 4–9.

18. *Ex parte United States,* 242 U.S. 27 (1916).

19. Bates, "The Establishment and Early Years of the Federal Probation System," p. 6.

20. Brian A. Reaves and Timothy C. Hart, *Federal Law Enforcement Officers, 2000* (Washington, DC: Bureau of Justice Statistics, 2002), p. 4.

21. See Reaves and Hart, *Federal Law Enforcement Officers, 2000,* p. 4, from which some of the wording in this paragraph has been adapted.

22. Adapted from Timothy A. Hughes, Doris James Wilson, and Allen J. Beck, *Trends in State Parole, 1990–2000* (Washington, DC: Bureau of Justice Statistics, 2001), p. 1.

23. Ibid.

24. Ibid.

25. Ibid.

26. *Probation and Parole in the United States, 2004,* p. 1.

27. Ibid., p. 6.

28. Ibid.

29. "The Effectiveness of Felony Probation: Results from an Eastern State," *Justice Quarterly* (December 1991), pp. 525–543.

30. State of Georgia, Board of Pardons and Paroles, "Adult Offender Sanction Costs for Fiscal Year 2001." Web posted at http://www.pap.state.ga.us/otisweb/corrcost.html (accessed March 1, 2002).

31. See Andrew von Hirsch and Kathleen J. Hanrahan, *Abolish Parole?* (Washington, DC: Law Enforcement Assistance Administration, 1978).

32. *Griffin* v. *Wisconsin,* 483 U.S. 868, 107 S.Ct. 3164 (1987).

33. *Pennsylvania Board of Probation and Parole* v. *Scott,* 524 U.S. 357 (1998).

34. *U.S.* v. *Knights,* U.S. Supreme Court, 534 U.S. 112 (2001).

35. *Probation and Parole in the United States, 2004 .*

36. Robyn L. Cohen, *Probation and Parole Violators in State Prison, 1991* (Washington, DC: Bureau of Justice Statistics, 1995).

**NOTES**

37. *Escoe* v. *Zerbst,* 295 U.S. 490 (1935).

38. *Mempa* v. *Rhay,* 389 U.S. 128 (1967).

39. A deferred sentence involves postponement of the sentencing decision, which may be made at a later time following an automatic review of the defendant's behavior in the interim. A suspended sentence requires no review unless the probationer violates the law or the conditions of probation. Both may result in imprisonment.

40. *Morrissey* v. *Brewer,* 408 U.S. 471 (1972).

41. *Gagnon* v. *Scarpelli,* 411 U.S. 778 (1973).

42. Smith and Berlin, *Introduction to Probation and Parole,* p. 143.

43. See Linda Greenhouse, *New York Times* wire service, March 18, 1997 (no headline). The case is *Young* v. *Harper,* 520 U.S. 143 (1997).

44. *Greenholtz* v. *Nebraska Penal Inmates,* 442 U.S. 1 (1979).

45. *Bearden* v. *Georgia,* 461 U.S. 660, 103 S.Ct. 2064, 76 L.Ed.2d 221 (1983).

46. Ibid.

47. *Minnesota* v. *Murphy,* 465 U.S. 420 (1984).

48. *Harlow* v. *Clatterbuick,* 30 CrL. 2364 (VA S.Ct. 1986); *Santangelo* v. *State,* 426 N.Y.S.2d 931 (1980); *Welch* v. *State,* 424 N.Y.S.2d 774 (1980); and *Thompson* v. *County of Alameda,* 614 P.2d 728 (1980).

49. *Tarter* v. *State of New York,* 38 CrL. 2364 (NY S.Ct. 1986); *Grimm* v. *Arizona Board of Pardons and Paroles,* 115 Arizona 260, 564 P.2d 1227 (1977); and *Payton* v. *U.S.,* 636 F.2d 132 (5th Cir. 1981).

50. Rolando del Carmen, *Potential Liabilities of Probation and Parole Officers* (Cincinnati, OH: Anderson, 1986), p. 89.

51. See, for example, *Semler* v. *Psychiatric Institute,* 538 F.2d 121 (4th Cir. 1976).

52. *Minnesota* v. *Murphy* (1984).

53. National Advisory Commission on Criminal Justice Standards and Goals, *Task Force Report: Corrections* (Washington, DC: U.S. Government Printing Office, 1973).

54. From the introduction to James Austin, Michael Jones, and Melissa Bolyard, *The Growing Use of Jail Boot Camps: The Current State of the Art* (Washington, DC: National Institute of Justice, 1993), p. 1.

55. Sentencing Project, *Changing the Terms of Sentencing: Defense Counsel and Alternative Sentencing Services* (Washington, DC: Sentencing Project, no date).

56. Joan Petersilia, *Expanding Options for Criminal Sentencing* (Santa Monica, CA: RAND Corporation, 1987).

57. Ohio Revised Code, Section 2946.06.1 (July 1965).

58. Lawrence Greenfield, *Probation and Parole, 1984* (Washington, DC: U.S. Government Printing Office, 1986).

59. Harry Allen et al., *Probation and Parole in America* (New York: Free Press, 1985), p. 88.

60. For a good overview of such programs, especially as they apply to juvenile corrections, see Doris Layton MacKenzie et al., *A National Study Comparing the Environments of Boot Camps with Traditional Facilities for Juvenile Offenders* (Washington, DC: National Institute of Justice, 2001).

61. Doris Layton MacKenzie and Deanna Bellew Ballow, "Shock Incarceration Programs in State Correctional Jurisdictions—An Update," *NIJ Reports* (May/June 1989), pp. 9–10.

62. "Shock Incarceration Marks a Decade of Expansion," *Corrections Compendium* (September 1996), pp. 10–28.

63. MacKenzie and Ballow, "Shock Incarceration Programs in State Correctional Jurisdictions."

64. National Institute of Justice, *Multisite Evaluation of Shock Incarceration* (Washington, DC: NIJ, 1995).

65. Cherie L. Clark, David W. Aziz, and Doris L. MacKenzie, *Shock Incarceration in New York: Focus on Treatment* (Washington, DC: National Institute of Justice, 1994), p. 8.

66. "Oregon Boot Camp Is Saving the State Money, Study Finds," *Criminal Justice Newsletter,* May 1, 1995, pp. 5–6.

67. Douglas C. McDonald, *Restitution and Community Service,* National Institute of Justice Crime File Series Study Guide (Washington, DC: U.S. Department of Justice, 1988).

68. Richard J. Maher and Henry E. Dufour, "Experimenting with Community Service: A Punitive Alternative to Imprisonment," *Federal Probation* (September 1987), pp. 22–27.

69. James P. Levine, Michael C. Musheno, and Dennis J. Palumbo, *Criminal Justice in America: Law in Action* (New York: John Wiley, 1986), p. 549.

70. Billie S. Erwin and Lawrence A. Bennett, "New Dimensions in Probation: Georgia's Experience with Intensive Probation Supervision," National Institute of Justice, *Research in Brief* (1987).

71. Probation Division, State of Georgia, "Intensive and Specialized Probation Supervision." Web posted at http://www.dcor.state.ga.us/ProbationDivision/html/ProbationDivision.html (accessed March 2, 2002).

72. Crystal A. Garcia, "Using Palmer's Global Approach to Evaluate Intensive Supervision Programs: Implications for Practice," *Corrections Management Quarterly,* Vol. 4, No. 4 (2000), pp. 60–69.

73. Joan Petersilia, *House Arrest,* National Institute of Justice Crime File Series Study Guide (Washington, DC: U.S. Department of Justice, 1988).

74. Darren Gowen, "Remote Location Monitoring: A Supervision Strategy to Enhance Risk Control," *Federal Probation,* Vol. 65, No. 2, p. 39.

75. An additional year and seven months of supervised confinement was to follow.

76. See "Martha Stewart Starts Home Confinement," Associated Press, March 3, 2005. Web posted at http://moneycentral.msn.com/content/invest/extra/P111258.asp (accessed April 26, 2005).

77. *Electronic Monitoring,* TDCJ-CJAD Agency Brief (Austin, TX: Texas Department of Criminal Justice, March 1999).

78. Texas Department of Criminal Justice, Parole Division, *Specialized Programs.* Web posted at http://www.tdcj.state.tx.us/parole/parole-spclpgms.htm (accessed September 20, 2002).

79. Marc Renzema and David T. Skelton, *The Use of Electronic Monitoring by Criminal Justice Agencies, 1989* (Washington, DC: National Institute of Justice, 1990).

80. U.S. Probation and Pretrial Services, *Court and Community* (Washington, DC: Administrative Office of the U.S. Courts, 2000).

81. "Satellites Tracking People on Parole," Associated Press wire service, April 13, 1999.

82. U.S. Probation and Pretrial Services, "Home Confinement." Web posted at http://www.uscourts.gov/misc/cchome.pdf (accessed March 22, 2002).

83. State of Georgia Board of Pardons and Paroles, "Adult Offender Sanction Costs for Fiscal Year 2001." Web posted at http://www.pap.state.ga.us/otisweb/corrcost.html (accessed September 20, 2002).

84. Construction costs are for cells classified as "medium security."

85. *BI Home Escort: Electronic Monitoring System,* advertising brochure (Boulder, CO: BI Inc., no date).

86. James A. Inciardi, *Criminal Justice,* 2nd ed. (New York: Harcourt Brace Jovanovich, 1987), p. 664.

87. Neely Tucker, "Study Warns of Rising Tide of Released Inmates," *Washington Post,* May 21, 2003, p. A1.

88. BJS, "Forty-Two Percent of State Parole Discharges Were Successful."

89. American Probation and Parole Association and the Association of Paroling Authorities International, *Abolishing Parole: Why the Emperor Has No Clothes* (Lexington, KY: APPA, 1995).

90. See, for example, Jeremy Travis, *But They All Come Back: Rethinking Prisoner Reentry* (Washington, DC: National Institute of Justice, 2000).

91. Much of this information is taken from Re-Entry Policy Council, *Report of the Re-Entry Policy Council: Charting the Safe and Successful Return of Prisoners to the Community—Executive Summary* (New York: Council of State Governments, 2005). Web posted at http://www.reentrypolicy.org/executive-summary.html (accessed July 10, 2005).

92. Patrick A. Langan and David J. Levin, *National Recidivism Study of Released Prisoners: Recidivism of Prisoners Released in 1994* (Washington, DC: Bureau of Justice Statistics, 2002); and *Does Parole Work? Analyzing the Impact of Postprison Supervision on Rearrest Outcomes* (Washington, DC: The Urban Institute, 2005).

93. Esther Griswold, Jessica Pearson, and Lanae Davis, *Testing a Modification Process for Incarcerated Parents* (Denver, CO: Center for Policy Research), pp. 11–12.

94. Governor's Commission on Criminal Justice Innovation, *Final Report* (Boston: The Commission, 2004).

95. Boston Bar Association Task Force on Parole and Community Reintegration, *Parole Practices in Massachusetts and Their Effect on Community Reintegration,* 2002.

96. Ibid., pp. 4, 14.

97. Reinventing Probation Council, *"Broken Windows" Probation: The Next Step in Fighting Crime* (New York: Manhattan Institute, 1999); and Reinventing Probation Council, *Transforming Probation through Leadership: The "Broken Windows" Model* (New York: Center for Civic Innovation at the Manhattan Institute, 2000), from which some of the quoted material in these paragraphs comes.

98. Joan Petersilia, "A Crime Control Rationale for Reinvesting in Community Corrections," in *Critical Criminal Justice Issues: Task Force Reports from the American Society of Criminology* (Washington, DC: National Institute of Justice, 1997).

99. For more about the future of probation and parole, see Joan Petersilia, *Reforming Probation and Parole in the Twenty-First Century* (Lanham, MD: American Correctional Association, 2002).

# CHAPTER 13

# Prisons and Jails

## OUTLINE

- Introduction
- Early Punishments
- The Emergence of Prisons
- Prisons Today
- Jails
- Private Prisons

## LEARNING OBJECTIVES

**After reading this chapter, you should be able to:**

- Describe the nature and history of early punishments and their impact on modern correctional philosophy.
- Outline the historical development of prisons.
- Discuss the major characteristics and purpose of today's prisons.
- Describe the prison population in America today.
- Describe the just deserts model, and explain how it has led to an increased use of imprisonment and to prison overcrowding.
- Discuss how changes in the rate of criminal offending relate to changes in the rate of imprisonment during the last decade.
- Explain the role that jails play in American corrections, and discuss the issues that jail administrators currently face.
- Describe the role of private prisons today, and predict their future.

*To put people behind walls and bars and do little or nothing to change them is to win a battle but lose a war. It is wrong. It is expensive. It is stupid.*

—Former Chief Justice Warren E. Burger (1907–1995)[1]

*Infinite are the nine steps of a prison cell, and endless is the march of him who walks between the yellow brick wall and the red iron gate, thinking things that cannot be chained and cannot be locked.*

—Arturo Giovannitti (1884–1959)

# KEY CONCEPTS

## TERMS

| | | |
|---|---|---|
| ADMAX | *lex talionis* | rated capacity |
| Ashurst-Sumners Act | medical model | recidivism |
| Auburn system | nothing-works doctrine | reformatory style |
| classification system | operational capacity | regional jail |
| design capacity | Pennsylvania system | state-use system |
| direct-supervision jail | prison | warehousing |
| industrial prison | prison capacity | work release |
| jail | private prison | workhouse |
| justice model | privatization | |

## NAMES

| | | |
|---|---|---|
| Zebulon Brockway | Alexander Maconochie | Alexis de Tocqueville |
| Sir Walter Crofton | Robert Martinson | |

# Introduction

Hear the author discuss
this chapter at
**cjtoday.com**

**prison**

A state or federal confinement
facility that has custodial
authority over adults
sentenced to confinement.

In the history of criminal justice, the ten years that have just passed may be remembered as the decade of imprisonment. As concerns with community protection reached a near crescendo, and stiff drug laws and strict repeat offender statutes put more and more people behind bars, rates of imprisonment reached previously unheralded levels. Prison populations approached the breaking point, requiring the construction of many new facilities. Yet the use of **prisons**, as places where convicted offenders serve time as punishment for breaking the law, is a relatively new development in the handling of offenders. In fact, the emphasis on *time served* as the essence of criminal punishment is scarcely 200 years old.

# Early Punishments

Before the development of prisons, early punishments were often cruel and torturous. An example is the graphic and unsettling description of a man broken on the rack in 1721, which is provided by Camden Pelham in his *Chronicles of Crime*.[2] The offender, Nathaniel Hawes, a domestic servant in the household of a wealthy nobleman, had stolen a sheep. When the overseer of the household discovered the offense, Hawes "shot him dead." Pelham's description of what happened next follows: "For these offences, of course, he was sentenced to be broken alive upon the rack, without the benefit of the *coup de grace*, or mercy-stroke. Informed of the dreadful sentence, he composely laid himself down upon his back on a strong cross, on which, with his arms and legs extended, he was fastened by ropes. The executioner, having by now with a hatchet chopped off his left hand, next took up a heavy iron bar, with which, by repeated blows, he broke his bones to shivers, till the marrow, blood, and splinters flew about the field; but the prisoner never uttered a groan nor a sigh! The ropes being next unlashed, I imagined him dead . . . till . . . he writhed himself from the cross. When he fell on the grass . . . he rested his head on part of the timbar, and asked the by-standers for a pipe of tobacco, which was infamously answered by kicking and spitting on him. He then begged his head might be chopped off, but to no purpose." Pelham goes on to relate how the condemned man then engaged in conversation with onlookers, recounting details of his trial. At one point he asked one of those present to repay money he had loaned him, saying, "Don't you perceive, I am to be kept alive." After six hours, Pelham says, Hawes was put out of his misery by a soldier assigned to guard the proceedings. "He was knocked on the head by the . . . sentinel; and having been raised upon a gallows, the vultures were busy picking out the eyes of the mangled corpse, in the skull of which was clearly discernible the mark of the soldier's musket."

This gruesome tale may seem foreign to modern readers—as though it describes an event that happened in a barbarous time long ago or in a place far away. However, a mere 200 years ago, before the emergence of imprisonment, convicted offenders were routinely subjected to physical punishment that often resulted in death. While fines were sometimes levied, corporal punishments were the most common form of criminal punishment and generally fit the doctrine of **lex talionis** (the law of retaliation). Under *lex talionis*, the convicted offender was sentenced to suffer a punishment that closely approximated the original injury. This rule of "an eye for an eye, a tooth for a tooth," generally duplicated the offense. Hence, if a person blinded another, he was blinded in return. Murderers were executed, sometimes in a way tailored to approximate the method they had used in committing the crime.

> **lex talionis**
> The law of retaliation, often expressed as "an eye for an eye" or "like for like."

# Flogging

Historically, the most widely used of physical punishments has been flogging.[3] The Bible mentions instances of whipping, and Christ himself was scourged. Whipping was widely used in England throughout the Middle Ages, and some offenders were said to have been beaten as they ran through streets and towns, hands tied behind their backs. American colonists carried the practice of flogging with them to the New World.

The last officially sanctioned flogging of a criminal offender in the United States was in Delaware on June 16, 1952, when a burglar received 20 lashes,[4] but the practice of whipping continues in other parts of the world. Amnesty International reports its use in various countries for political and other prisoners; in 1994, the flogging in Singapore of Michael Fay, an American teenager convicted of spray-painting parked cars, caused an international outcry from opponents of corporal punishment. But in parts of the United States some people reacted in just the opposite way. After the Fay flogging (called caning in Singapore because it was carried out with a bamboo rod), eight states entertained legislation to endorse whipping or paddling as a criminal sanction. For example, Mississippi legislators proposed paddling graffitists and petty thieves; Tennessee lawmakers considered punishing vandals and burglars by public caning on courthouse steps; and Louisiana looked into the possibility of ordering parents (or a correctional officer if the parents refused) to spank their children in judicial chambers.[5] None of the proposals made it into law.

# Mutilation

While flogging is a painful punishment whose memory might deter repeat offenses, mutilation is primarily a strategy of specific deterrence that makes it difficult or impossible for individuals to commit future crimes. Throughout history, various societies have amputated the hands of thieves and robbers, blinded spies, and castrated rapists. Blasphemers had their tongues ripped out, and pickpockets suffered broken fingers. Extensive mutilation, which included cutting off the ears and ripping out the tongue, was instituted in eleventh-century Britain and imposed on hunters who poached on royal lands.[6]

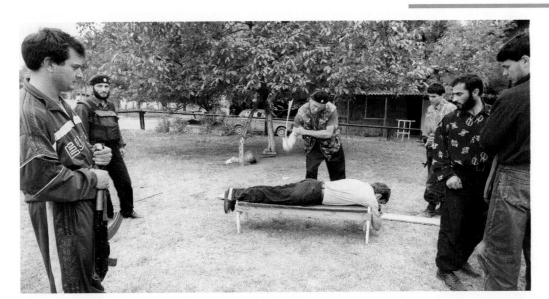

A man undergoing public punishment for a transgression of the Islamic code in Grozny, Chechnya. Other than the death penalty, corporal punishment for crime has been abolished in the United States, but it remains common in some Muslim nations.

*AP Wide World Photos*

Today, some countries in the Arab world, including Iran and Saudi Arabia, still rely on a limited use of mutilation as a penalty to incapacitate selected offenders. Mutilation also creates a general deterrent by providing potential offenders with walking examples of the consequences of crime.

## Branding

Before modern technology and the advent of mechanized record keeping, branding was used to readily identify convicted offenders and to warn others with whom they might come in contact of their dangerous potential.

The Romans, Greeks, French, British, and many other societies have all used branding at one time or another. Harry Barnes and Negley Teeters, early writers on the history of the criminal justice system, report that branding in the American colonies was customary for certain crimes, with first offenders being branded on the hand and repeat offenders receiving an identifying mark on the forehead.[7] Women were rarely marked physically, although they may have been shamed and forced to wear marked clothing. Nathaniel Hawthorne's *The Scarlet Letter* is a report on that practice, where the central figure is required to wear a red letter A embroidered on her dress, signifying adultery.

## Public Humiliation

A number of early punishments were designed to humiliate offenders in public and to allow members of the community an opportunity for vengeance. The stocks and pillory were two such punishments. The pillory closed over the head and hands and held the offender in a standing position, while the stocks kept the person sitting with the head free. A few hundred years ago, each European town had its stocks or pillory, usually located in some central square or alongside a major thoroughfare.

Offenders sent to the stocks or pillory could expect to be heckled and spit on by passersby. Other citizens might gather to throw tomatoes or rotten eggs. On occasion, citizens who were particularly outraged by the magnitude or nature of the offense would throw rocks at the offender, ending his life. Retribution remained a community prerogative, and citizens wielded the power of final sentencing. The pillory was still used in Delaware as late as 1905.[8]

The ducking stool, used in colonial times to punish gossips, provided another form of public humiliation. The offender was tied to it and lowered into a river or lake, turning nearly upside down like a duck searching for food underwater.

## Workhouses

Sixteenth-century Europe suffered severe economic upheaval, caused partly by wars and partly by the growing roots of the Industrial Revolution, which was soon to sweep the continent. By 1550, thousands of unemployed and vagrant people were scouring towns and villages seeking food and shelter. It was not long before they depleted the economic reserves of churches, which were the primary social relief agencies of the time.

In the belief that poverty was caused by laziness, governments were quick to create **workhouses** designed to instill "habits of industry" in the unemployed. The first workhouse in Europe opened in 1557 and taught work habits, not specific skills. Inmates were made to fashion their own furniture, build additions to the facility, and raise gardens. When the number of inmates exceeded the volume of useful work to be done, make-work projects, including treadmills and cranks, were invented to keep them busy.

Workhouses were judged successful, if only because they were constantly filled. By 1576, Parliament decreed that every county in England should build a workhouse. Although workhouses were forerunners of our modern prisons, they did not incarcerate criminal offenders—only vagrants and the economically disadvantaged. Nor were they designed to punish convicts, but served instead to reinforce the value of hard work.

| **workhouse** |
|---|
| An early form of imprisonment whose purpose was to instill habits of industry in the idle. |

## Exile

Many societies have banished criminals. The French sent criminal offenders to Devil's Island, and the Russians used Siberia for centuries for the same purpose. England sent convicts to the American colonies beginning in 1618. The British program of exile, known as *transportation*, served the dual purpose of providing a captive labor force for development of the colonies while assuaging growing English sentiments opposing corporal punishments. In 1776, however, the American Revolution forced the practice to end, and British penology shifted to the use of aging ships, called *hulks*, as temporary prisons. Hulks were anchored in harbors throughout England and served as floating confinement facilities even after transportation (to other parts of the globe) resumed.

In 1787, only 17 years after Captain Cook had discovered the continent, Australia became the new port of call for English prisoners. The name of Captain William Bligh, governor of the New South Wales penal colony, survives today as a symbol of the difficult conditions and the rough men and women of those times.

# The Emergence of Prisons

The identity of the world's first true prison is unknown, but at some point, penalties for crime came to include incarceration. During the Middle Ages, "punitive imprisonment appears to have been introduced into Europe . . . by the Christian Church in the incarceration of certain offenders against canon law."[9] Similarly, debtors' prisons existed throughout Europe during the fifteenth and sixteenth centuries, although they housed inmates who had violated the civil law rather than criminals. John Howard, an early prison reformer, mentions prisons housing criminal offenders in Hamburg, Germany; Bern, Switzerland; and Florence, Italy, in his 1777 book, *State of Prisons*.[10] Early efforts to imprison offenders led to the founding of the Hospice of San Michele, a papal prison that opened in 1704, and the Maison de Force, begun at Ghent, Belgium, in 1773. The Hospice was actually a residential school for delinquent boys and housed 60 youngsters at its opening. Both facilities stressed reformation over punishment and became early alternatives to the use of physical and public punishments.

Near the end of the eighteenth century, the concept of imprisonment as punishment for crime reached its fullest expression in the United States. Soon after they opened, U.S. prisons came to serve as models for European reformers searching for ways to humanize criminal punishment. For that reason, and to better appreciate how today's prisons operate, it is important to understand the historical development of the prison movement in the United States. Figure 13–1 depicts the stages through which American prisons progressed following the introduction around 1790 of the concept of incarceration as a punishment for crime. Each historical era is discussed in the pages that follow. For an online history of early prison development in England, see Web Extra 13–1 at cjtoday.com.

**WEB EXTRA**

# The Penitentiary Era (1790–1825)

In 1790, Philadelphia's Walnut Street Jail was converted into a penitentiary by the Pennsylvania Quakers. As we discussed briefly in Chapter 11, the Quakers viewed incarceration as an opportunity for penance and saw prisons as places wherein offenders might make amends with society and

The Walnut Street Jail, America's first "true" prison, circa 1800.

*Culver Pictures, Inc.*

**Prison Era**

| | The Penitentiary Era | The Mass (Congregate) Prison Era | The Reformatory Era | The Industrial Era | The Punitive Era | The Treatment Era | The Community-based (Decarceration) Era | The Warehousing Era | The Just Deserts Era |
|---|---|---|---|---|---|---|---|---|---|
| Year | 1790 | 1825 | 1876 | 1890 | 1935 | 1945 | 1967 | 1980 | 1995 |
| Philosophy | Rehabilitation, Deterrence | Incapacitation, Deterrence | Rehabilitation | Incapacitation, Restoration | Retribution | Rehabilitation | Restoration, Rehabilitation | Incapacitation | Retribution, Incapacitation, Deterrence |
| Representative Institutions | Philadelphia Penitentiary Eastern Penitentiary (Cherry Hill, PA) Western Penitentiary (Pittsburgh) | New York State Prison (Auburn, NY) | Elmira Reformatory (Elmira, NY) | Auburn (NY) Sing Sing (NY) Statesville (IL) San Quentin (CA) Attica (NY) | Alcatraz (CA) | Marion (IL) | Massachusetts Youth Services Halfway Houses | Most Major Prisons | Characteristic of Many Prisons Today |

**FIGURE 13–1**

Stages of prison development in the United States.

New York's Auburn Prison, shown here in the mid-nineteenth century. A congregate form of imprisonment began here that eventually overshadowed Pennsylvania's penitentiary style.

*Culver Pictures, Inc.*

accept responsibility for their misdeeds. The philosophy of imprisonment begun by the Quakers, heavily imbued with elements of rehabilitation and deterrence, carries over to the present day.[11]

Inmates of the Philadelphia Penitentiary were expected to wrestle alone with the evils they harbored. Penance was the primary vehicle through which rehabilitation was anticipated, and a study of the Bible was strongly encouraged. Solitary confinement was the rule, and the penitentiary was architecturally designed to minimize contact between inmates and between inmates and staff. Exercise was allowed in small high-walled yards attached to each cell. Eventually, handicrafts were introduced into the prison setting, permitting prisoners to work in their cells.

Fashioned after the Philadelphia model, the Western Penitentiary opened in Pittsburgh in 1826, and the Eastern Penitentiary opened in Cherry Hill, Pennsylvania, in 1829. Solitary confinement and individual cells, supported by a massive physical structure with impenetrable walls, became synonymous with the Pennsylvania system of imprisonment. Supporters heralded the **Pennsylvania system** as one that both was humane and provided inmates with the opportunity for rehabilitation. Many well-known figures of the day spoke out in support of the Pennsylvania system, among them Benjamin Franklin and Benjamin Rush—both of whom were influential members of the Philadelphia Society for Alleviating the Miseries of Public Prisons.[12]

## The Mass Prison Era (1825–1876)

Vermont, Massachusetts, Maryland, and New York all built institutions modeled after Pennsylvania's penitentiaries. As prison populations began to grow, however, solitary confinement became prohibitively expensive. One of the first large prisons to abandon the Pennsylvania model was the New York State Prison at Auburn. Auburn introduced the congregate but silent system, under which inmates lived, ate, and worked together in enforced silence. This style of imprisonment, which came to be known as the **Auburn system**, featured group workshops rather than solitary handicrafts and reintroduced corporal punishments into the handling of offenders. Whereas isolation and enforced idleness were inherent punishments under the early Pennsylvania system, Auburn depended on whipping and hard labor to maintain the rule of silence.[13]

Auburn prison was the site of an experiment in solitary confinement, which was the basis of the Pennsylvania system. Eighty-three men were placed in small solitary cells on Christmas Day of 1821 and were released in 1823 and 1824. Five of the 83 died, one went insane, another attempted suicide, and the others became "seriously demoralized."[14] Although the Auburn experiment did not accurately simulate the conditions in Pennsylvania (it allowed for no exercise, placed prisoners in tiny cells, and shunned handicrafts—which had been introduced into Pennsylvania's prisons by the time the experiment began), it provided an effective basis for condemnation of the

**Pennsylvania system**

A form of imprisonment developed by the Pennsylvania Quakers around 1790 as an alternative to corporal punishments. This style of imprisonment made use of solitary confinement and encouraged rehabilitation.

**Auburn system**

A form of imprisonment developed in New York State around 1820 that depended on mass prisons, where prisoners were held in congregate fashion requiring silence. This style of imprisonment was a primary competitor with the Pennsylvania system.

## CJ TODAY EXHIBIT 13-1

### Chaplain James Finley's Letter from the Ohio Penitentiary, 1850

It is true, there are yet two systems of prison discipline still in use, but both claim to have the two parties—the criminal and society—equally in view. The congregate system, going on the supposition that habits of labor and moral character are the chief desiderata among this class of men, set them to work at those trades for which their physical and mental powers, together with the consideration of their former occupations, may more especially adapt them; religious instruction is also given them by men appointed expressly for the purpose; and they are permitted to labor in large communities, where they can see but not converse with each other, as the friends of this system imagine that social intercourse, of some kind and to some extent, is almost as necessary to man as food. The separate system, on the other hand, looking upon all intercourse between criminals as only evil in its tendency, by which one rogue becomes the instructor or accomplice of another, secludes the convicts from each other but, to atone for this defect, it encourages the visits of good men to the cells of the prisoners; and the officers of these prisons make it a particular point of duty to visit the inmates very frequently themselves. The physical habits of the imprisoned are provided for by such trades as can be carried on by individual industry; a teacher is employed to lead them on in the study of useful branches of education; while the Gospel is regularly taught them, not only by sermons on the Sabbath, but by private efforts of the chaplain in his daily rounds.

*Source:* James Finley, *Memorials of Prison Life* (Cincinnati, OH: Swormstedt and Poe, 1855).

Pennsylvania system. Partly as a result of the experiment, the Reverend Louis Dwight, an influential prison reformer of the time and the leader of the prestigious Prison Discipline Society of Boston, became an advocate of the Auburn system, citing its lower cost[15] and more humane conditions.[16] The lower cost resulted from the simpler facilities required by mass imprisonment and from group workshops that provided economies of scale unachievable under solitary confinement. Dwight also believed that the Pennsylvania style of imprisonment was unconscionable and inhumane. As a consequence of criticisms fielded by Dwight and others, most American prisons built after 1825 followed the Auburn architectural style and system of prison discipline.

About the same time, however, a number of European governments sent representatives to study the virtues of the two American systems. Interestingly, most concluded that the Pennsylvania system was more conducive to reformation than the Auburn system, and many European prisons adopted a strict separation of inmates. Two French visitors, Gustave de Beaumont and Alexis de Tocqueville, stressed the dangers of what they called "contamination," whereby prisoners housed in Auburn-like prisons could negatively influence one another.[17]

## The Reformatory Era (1876–1890)

With the tension between the Auburn and Pennsylvania systems, American penology existed in an unsettled state for a half century. That tension was resolved in 1876 with the emergence of the **reformatory style**, which grew out of practices innovated by two especially noteworthy correctional leaders of the mid-1880s: Captain Alexander Maconochie and Sir Walter Crofton.

### Captain Alexander Maconochie and Norfolk Island

During the early 1840s, Captain Alexander Maconochie served as the warden of Norfolk Island, a prison off the coast of Australia for "doubly condemned" inmates. English prisoners sent to Australia who committed other crimes while there were taken to Norfolk to be segregated from less recalcitrant offenders. Prior to Maconochie's arrival, conditions at Norfolk had been atrocious. Disease and unsanitary conditions were rampant on the island, fights among inmates left many dead and more injured, and the physical facilities were not conducive to good supervision. Maconochie immediately set out to reform the island prison by providing incentives for prisoners to participate in their own reformation.

Maconochie developed a system of marks through which prisoners could earn enough credits to buy their freedom. Bad behavior removed marks from the inmate's ledger, while acceptable behavior added marks. The mark system made possible early release and led to a recognition of the

**reformatory style**

A late-nineteenth-century correctional model based on the use of the indeterminate sentence and the belief in the possibility of rehabilitation, especially for youthful offenders. The reformatory concept faded with the emergence of industrial prisons around the turn of the century.

## CJ TODAY EXHIBIT 13-2

### An Early Texas Prison

In 1860, an unknown writer described conditions in the Texas Penitentiary at Huntsville as follows:

By a special enactment of the Legislature, the front of the cell of any prisoner sentenced to solitary confinement for life, is painted black, and his name and sentence distinctly marked thereon. The object would seem to be to infuse a salutary dread into the minds of the other prisoners. Upon the only black-painted cell in the prison was the following inscription, in distinct white letters: William Brown, aged twenty-four years, convicted for murder in Grimes County, spring term, 1858, for which he is now suffering solitary confinement for life. Brown himself, however, was in fact at work in the factory with the other convicts! He entered the Penitentiary in May, 1859, and had been kept in close confinement in his cell, without labor, never being permitted to leave it for any purpose, until about the first of October, when his health was found to have suffered so much that, to preserve his life, he was, under a discretionary power vested in the Directors, released from the rigor of his sentence, and subjected to only the ordinary confinement of the prison. His health has since greatly improved. It is not to be wondered at that his health should decline under the strict enforcement of such a sentence. The cell in which he was confined was the same as to size, ventilation, and light as the rest; and being one of the lower tier of cells, the top of the doorway was some feet below the lower edge of the window upon the opposite side of the corridor in the outside wall. He had even less chance for fresh air than if his cell had been in almost any other location. It is the sight and knowledge of such instances of solitary unemployed confinement as this, and a willful neglect or refusal to inform themselves upon, and recognize, the very wide distinction between the terms separate and solitary, that renders many persons so violently prejudiced against, and opposed to the "Separate System."

*Source: The Journal of Prison Discipline and Philanthropy*, Vol. 15, No. 1 (January 1860), pp. 7–17.

indeterminate sentence as a useful tool in the reformation of offenders. Before Maconochie, inmates had been sentenced to determinate sentences specifying a fixed number of years they had to serve before release. The mark system placed responsibility for winning an early release squarely on the inmate. Because of the system's similarity to the later practice of parole, it won for Maconochie the title "father of parole."

Opinion leaders in England, however, saw Maconochie's methods as too lenient. Many pointed out that the indeterminate sentence made possible new lives for criminals in a world of vast opportunity (the Australian continent) at the expense of the British Empire. Amid charges that he coddled inmates, Maconochie was relieved of his duties as warden in 1844.

## Sir Walter Crofton and the Irish System

Maconochie's innovations soon came to the attention of Sir Walter Crofton, head of the Irish prison system. Crofton adapted the idea of early release to his program of progressive stages. Inmates who entered Irish prisons had to work their way through four stages. The first, or entry level, involved solitary confinement and dull work. Most prisoners in the first level were housed at Mountjoy Prison in Dublin. The second stage assigned prisoners to Spike Island, where they worked on fortifications. The third stage placed prisoners in field units, which worked directly in the community on public-service projects. Unarmed guards supervised the prisoners. The fourth stage depended on what Crofton called the "ticket of leave." The ticket of leave allowed prisoners to live and work in the community under the occasional supervision of a "moral instructor." It could be revoked at any time up until the expiration of the offender's original sentence.

Crofton was convinced that convicts could not be rehabilitated without successful reintegration into the community. His innovations were closely watched by reformers across Europe. But in 1862, a wave of violent robberies swept England and led to the passage of the 1863 Garotters Act, which mandated whipping for robberies involving violence and longer prison sentences for many other crimes, effectively rolling back the clock on Crofton's innovations, at least in Europe.

## The Elmira Reformatory and the Birth of Parole in the United States

In 1865, Gaylord B. Hubbell, warden of Sing Sing Prison in New York, visited Great Britain and studied prisons there. He returned to the United States greatly impressed by the Irish system and recommended that indeterminate sentences be used in American prisons. The New York Prison Association supported Hubbell and called for the creation of a "reformatory" based on the concept of an earned early release if the inmate reformed himself.

When the new National Prison Association held its first conference in 1870 in Cincinnati, Ohio, it adopted a 37-paragraph Declaration of Principles that called for reformation to replace punishment as the goal of imprisonment. The most significant result of the conference, however, was the move to embody those principles in a reformatory built on American soil.

In 1876, the Elmira Reformatory opened in Elmira, New York, under the direction of Zebulon Brockway, a leading advocate of indeterminate sentencing and the former superintendent of the Detroit House of Correction. The state of New York had passed an indeterminate sentencing bill that made possible early release for inmates who earned it. However, because reformation was thought most likely among younger people, the Elmira Reformatory accepted only first offenders between the ages of 16 and 30. A system of graded stages required inmates to meet educational, behavioral, and other goals. Schooling was mandatory, and trade training was available in telegraphy, tailoring, plumbing, carpentry, and other areas.

Unfortunately, the reformatory "proved a relative failure and disappointment."[18] Many inmates reentered lives of crime following their release, which called the success of the reformatory ideal into question. Some authors attributed the failure of the reformatory to "the ever-present jailing psychosis"[19] of the prison staff or to an overemphasis on confinement and institutional security rather than reformation, which made it difficult to implement many of the ideals on which the reformatory had been based.

Even though the reformatory was not a success, the principles it established remain important today. Thus, indeterminate sentencing, parole, trade training, education, and primacy of reformation over punishment all serve as a foundation for ongoing debates about the purpose of imprisonment.

> When a man keeps the key of his own prison, he is soon persuaded to fit it to the lock.
>
> —Captain Alexander Maconochie

## The Industrial Era (1890–1935)

With the failure of the reformatory style of prison, concerns over security and discipline became dominant in American prisons. Inmate populations rose, costs soared, and states began to study practical alternatives. An especially attractive option was found in the potential profitability of inmate labor, and the era of the **industrial prison** in America was born.

Industrial prisons in the northern United States were characterized by thick, high walls, stone or brick buildings, guard towers, and smokestacks rising from within the walls. These prisons smelted steel, manufactured cabinets, molded tires, and turned out many other goods for the open market. Prisons in the South, which had been devastated by the Civil War, tended more toward farm labor and public-works projects. The South, with its labor-intensive agricultural practices, used inmates to replace slaves who had been freed during the war.

The following six systems of inmate labor were in use by the early twentieth century[20]:

- *Contract system.* Private businesses paid to use inmate labor. They provided the raw materials and supervised the manufacturing process inside prison facilities.
- *Piece-price system.* Goods were produced for private businesses under the supervision of prison authorities. Prisons were paid according to the number and quality of the goods manufactured.
- *Lease system.* Prisoners were taken to the work site under the supervision of armed guards. Once there, they were turned over to the private contractor, who employed them and maintained discipline.
- *Public-account system.* This system eliminated the use of private contractors. Industries were entirely prison owned, and prison authorities managed the manufacturing process from beginning to end. Goods were sold on the free market.
- **State-use system.** Prisoners manufactured only goods that could be used by other state offices, or they provided labor to assist other state agencies.
- *Public-works system.* Prisoners maintained roads and highways, cleaned public parks and recreational facilities, and maintained and restored public buildings.

Large prisons that were built or converted to industrialization included San Quentin in California, Sing Sing and Auburn in New York, and the Illinois State Penitentiary at Statesville. Many prison industries were quite profitable and contributed significantly to state treasuries. Reports from 1932 show that 82,276 prisoners were involved in various forms of prison labor that year,

**industrial prison**

A correctional model intended to capitalize on the labor of convicts sentenced to confinement.

**state-use system**

A form of inmate labor in which items produced by inmates may only be sold by or to state offices. Items that only the state can sell include such things as license plates and hunting licenses, while items sold only to state offices include furniture and cleaning supplies.

Church services in Sing Sing Prison in 1906. Note the "ushers" with shotguns.

*Ossining, New York, Underwood Photo Archives*

producing products with a total value of $75,369,471—a huge amount considering the worth of the dollar 70 years ago.[21] Beginning as early as the 1830s, however, workers began to complain of being forced to compete with cheap prison labor. In 1834, mechanics in New York filed a petition with the state legislature asking that prison industries paying extremely low wages be eliminated. Labor unions became very well organized and powerful by the early part of the twentieth century, and the Great Depression of the 1930s, during which jobs were scarce, brought with it a call for an end to prison industries.

In 1929, union influence led Congress to pass the Hawes-Cooper Act, which required prison-made goods to conform to the regulations of the states through which they were shipped. Hence, states that outlawed the manufacture of free-market goods in their own prisons were effectively protected from prison-made goods that might be imported from other states. The death blow to prison industries, however, came in 1935 with the passage of the **Ashurst-Sumners Act**, which specifically prohibited the interstate transportation and sale of prison goods where state laws forbade them. In consort with the Ashurst-Sumners legislation, and because of economic pressures brought on by the Depression, most states soon passed statutes that curtailed prison manufacturing within their borders, and the industrial era in American corrections came to a close.

## Prison Industries Today

Although still hampered by some federal and state laws, prison industries have begun making a comeback. Under the state-use philosophy, most states still permit the prison manufacture of goods that will be used exclusively by the prison system itself or by other state agencies or that only the state can legitimately sell on the open market. An example of the latter is license plates, the sale of which is a state monopoly. North Carolina provides a good example of a modern state-use system. Its Correction Enterprises operates around 20 inmate-staffed businesses, each of which is self-supporting. North Carolina inmates manufacture prison clothing; raise vegetables and farm animals to feed inmates throughout the state; operate an oil refinery, a forestry service, and a cannery; and manufacture soap, license plates, and some office furniture. All manufactured goods other than license plates are for use within the prison system or by other state agencies. North Carolina's Correction Enterprises pays 5% of profits to the state's crime victims' compensation fund.[22]

The federal government also operates a kind of state-use system in its institutions through a government-owned corporation called Federal Prison Industries, Incorporated (also called UNICOR).[23] The corporation was established in 1934 to retain some employment programs for federal inmates in anticipation of the elimination of free-market prison industries. Critics of UNICOR charge that

**Ashurst-Sumners Act**

Federal legislation of 1935 that effectively ended the industrial prison era by restricting interstate commerce in prison-made goods.

Incarceration is a crash course in extortion and criminal behavior.

—Vincent Schiraldi, Executive Director, Justice Policy Institute inmates are paid very low wages and are trained for jobs that do not exist in the free economy.[24] Even so, a long-term study published in 1994 found that federal inmates who participated in UNI-COR "showed better adjustment, were less likely to be revoked at the end of their first year back in the community, and were more likely to find employment in the halfway house and community."[25] The study also found that inmates "earned slightly more money in the community than inmates who had similar background characteristics, but who did not participate in work and vocational training programs."

Free-market money-making prison industries are also staging a comeback, some funded by private-sector investment. In 1981, under the Prison Rehabilitative Industries and Diversified Enterprises, Inc., legislation, commonly called the PRIDE Act, Florida became the first state to experiment with the wholesale transfer of its correctional industry program from public to private control.[26] PRIDE industries include sugar cane processing, construction, and automotive repair. Other states have since followed suit.

Today, the Prison Industry Enhancement Certification Program (PIECP),[27] administered by the Bureau of Justice Assistance (BJA), exempts certified state and local departments of corrections from normal federal restrictions on the sale of inmate-made goods in interstate commerce.[28] In addition, the program lifts restrictions on certified corrections departments, permitting them to sell inmate-made goods to the federal government in amounts exceeding the $10,000 maximum normally imposed on such transactions. The PIECP also allows private industry to establish joint ventures with state and local correctional agencies to produce goods using inmate labor. As of March 2004, 38 jurisdictions were certified to operate under the PIECP. Learn more about the history of federal prison industries at Library Extra 13–1 at cjtoday.com. Visit the National Correctional Industries Association at Web Extra 13–2 to see additional information about the PIECP.

## The Punitive Era (1935–1945)

The moratorium on free-market prison industries initiated by the Ashurst-Sumners Act was to last for more than half a century. Prison administrators, left with few ready alternatives, seized on custody and institutional security as the long-lost central purposes of the correctional enterprise. The punitive era that resulted was characterized by the belief that prisoners owed a debt to society that only a rigorous period of confinement could repay. Writers of the period termed such beliefs the *convict bogey* and the *lock psychosis*,[29] referring to the fact that convicts were to be both shunned and securely locked away from society. Large maximum-security institutions flourished, and the prisoner's daily routine became one of monotony and frustration. The punitive era was a lackluster time in American corrections. Innovations were rare, and an "out of sight, out of mind" philosophy characterized American attitudes toward inmates. The term *stir-crazy* grew out of the experience of many prisoners with the punitive era's lack of educational, treatment, and work programs. In response, inmates created their own diversions, frequently attempting to escape or inciting riots. One especially secure and still notorious facility of the punitive era was the federal penitentiary on Alcatraz Island, which is described in some detail at Web Extra 13–3 at cjtoday.com.

## The Treatment Era (1945–1967)

In the late 1940s, the mood of the nation was euphoric. Memories of World War II were dimming, industries were productive beyond the best hopes of most economic forecasters, and America's position of world leadership was fundamentally unchallenged. Nothing seemed impossible. Amid the bounty of a postwar boom economy, politicians and the public accorded themselves the luxury of restructuring the nation's prisons. A new interest in "corrections" and reformation, combined with the latest in behavioral techniques, ushered in a new era. The treatment era was based on a **medical model** of corrections—one that implied that the offender was sick and that rehabilitation was only a matter of finding the right treatment. Inmates came to be seen more as "clients" or "patients" than as offenders, and terms like *resident* and *group member* replaced *inmate*.

Therapy during the period took a number of forms, many of which are still used today. Most therapeutic models assumed that inmates needed help to mature psychologically and had to be taught to assume responsibility for their lives. Prisons built their programs around both individual treatment and group therapy approaches. In individual treatment, the offender and the therapist develop a face-to-face relationship. Group therapy relies on the sharing of insights, gleaned by members of the therapeutic group, to facilitate the growth process, often by first making clear to offenders the

**medical model**

A therapeutic perspective on correctional treatment that applies the diagnostic perspective of medical science to the handling of criminal offenders.

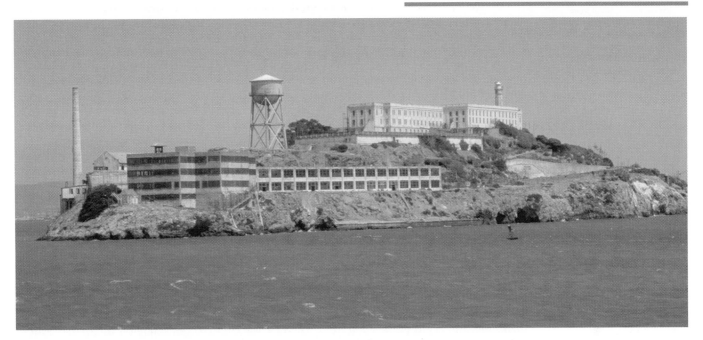

Alcatraz Federal Penitentiary. The island prison closed in 1963, a victim of changing attitudes toward corrections. It survives today as a San Francisco tourist attraction.

*Paul S. Howell, Getty Images, Inc.*

emotional basis of their criminal behavior. Other forms of therapy used in prisons have included behavior therapy, drug therapy, neurosurgery, sensory deprivation, and aversion therapy.

Inmates have not always been happy with the treatment model. In 1972, a group of prisoners at the Marion, Illinois, federal prison joined together and demanded a right to refuse treatment.[30] The National Prison Project of the American Civil Liberties Union (ACLU) supported the inmates' right to refuse personality-altering treatment techniques.[31] Other suits followed. Worried about potential liability, the Law Enforcement Assistance Administration (LEAA) banned the expenditure of LEAA funds to support any prison programs utilizing psychosurgery, medical research, chemotherapy, or behavior modification.[32]

The treatment era also suffered from attacks on the medical model on which it was based. Academics and legal scholars pointed to a lack of evidence in support of the model[33] and began to stress individual responsibility rather than treatment in the handling of offenders. Indeterminate sentencing statutes, designed to reward inmates for improved behavior, fell before the swelling drive to replace treatment with punishment.

Any honest evaluation of the treatment era would conclude that, in practice, treatment was more an ideal than a reality. Many treatment programs existed, some of them quite intensive. Unfortunately, the correctional system in America was never capable of providing any consistent or widespread treatment because the majority of its guards and administrators were oriented primarily toward custody and were not trained to provide treatment. However, although we have identified 1967 as the end of the treatment era, many correctional rehabilitation programs survive to the present day, and new ones are continually being developed.

> The central aim of a true prison system is the protection of society against crime, not the punishment of criminals.
>
> —Zebulon R. Brockway[i]

## The Community-Based Era (1967–1980)

Beginning in the 1960s, the realities of prison overcrowding combined with a renewed faith in humanity and the treatment era's belief in the possibility of behavioral change to inspire a movement away from institutionalized corrections and toward the creation of opportunities for reformation within local communities. The transition to community corrections (also called *deinstitutionalization, diversion*, and *decarceration*) was based on the premise that rehabilitation could not occur in isolation from the free social world to which inmates must eventually return.[34] Advocates of community corrections portrayed prisons as dehumanizing, claiming that they further victimized offenders who had already been negatively labeled by society. Some states strongly embraced the movement toward decarceration. In 1972, for example, Massachusetts drew national attention when it closed all of its reform schools and replaced them with group homes.[35]

Decarceration, which built on many of the intermediate sanctions discussed in the previous chapter, used a variety of programs to keep offenders in contact with the community and out of prison. Among them were halfway houses, work-release programs, and open institutions. Halfway houses have sometimes been called *halfway-in* or *halfway-out houses*, depending on whether offenders were being given a second chance before incarceration or were in the process of gradual release from prison. Boston had halfway houses as early as the 1920s, but they operated for only a few years.[36] It was not until 1961 that the Federal Bureau of Prisons opened a few experimental residential centers in support of its new prerelease programs focusing on juveniles and youthful offenders. Called *prerelease guidance centers*, the first of these facilities were based in Los Angeles and Chicago.[37]

Although the era of community corrections is now in decline, halfway houses and work-release programs still operate in many parts of the country. A typical residential treatment facility today houses 15 to 20 residents and operates under the supervision of a director, supported by a handful of counselors. The environment is nonthreatening, and residents are generally free to come and go during the workday. The building looks more like a motel or a house than it does a prison. Fences and walls are nonexistent. Transportation is provided to and from work or educational sites, and the facility retains a portion of the resident's wages to pay the costs of room and board. Residents are expected to return to the facility after work, and some group therapy may be provided.

Today's work-release programs house offenders in traditional correctional environments—usually minimum-security prisons—but permit them to work at jobs in the community during the day and to return to the prison at night. Inmates are usually required to pay a token amount for their room and board in the institution. The first work-release law was passed by Wisconsin in 1913, but it was not until 1957 that a comprehensive program created by North Carolina spurred the development of work-release programs nationwide.[38] **Work release** for federal prisoners was authorized by the federal Prisoner Rehabilitation Act of 1965.[39] As work-release programs grew, study release—whereby inmates attend local colleges and technical schools—was initiated in most jurisdictions as an adjunct to work release.

Work-release programs are still very much a part of modern corrections. Almost all states have them, and many inmates work in the community as they approach the end of their sentence. Unfortunately, work-release programs are not without their social costs. Some inmates commit new crimes while in the community, and others use the opportunity to escape.

The community-based format led to innovations in the use of volunteers and to the extension of inmate privileges. "Open institutions" routinely provided inmates with a number of opportunities for community involvement and encouraged the community to participate in the prison environment. Some open institutions allowed weekend passes or extended visits by family members and friends, while a few experimented with conjugal visiting and with prisons that housed both men and women ("coeducational incarceration"). In 1968, the California Correctional Institute at Tehachapi initiated conjugal visits, in which inmates who were about to begin parole were permitted to live with their families for three days per month in apartments on the prison grounds. By the late 1960s, conjugal visitation was under consideration in many other states, and the National Advisory Commission on Criminal Justice Standards and Goals recommended that correctional authorities should make "provisions for family visits in private surroundings conducive to maintaining and strengthening family ties."[40] In 1995, however, California, which then allowed about 26,000 conjugal visits a year, eliminated this privilege for those sentenced to death or to life without parole and for those without a parole date. Rapists, sex offenders, and recently disciplined inmates also lost conjugal privileges.

## The Warehousing Era (1980–1995)

During the late 1970s and into the 1980s, public disappointment bred of high **recidivism**[41] rates, coupled with dramatic media stories of inmates who committed gruesome crimes while on release in the community, led many legislatures to curtail the most liberal aspects of educational and work-release programs. Media descriptions of institutions where inmates lounged in relative luxury, enjoyed regular visits from spouses and lovers, and took frequent weekend passes created the image of "prison country clubs." The failure of the rehabilitative ideal in community-based corrections, however, was due as much to changes in the individual sentencing decisions of judges as it was to citizen outrage and restrictive legislative action. Evidence shows that many judges came to regard rehabilitation programs as failures and decided to implement the just deserts model[42] of criminal sentencing. The just deserts model, which we talked about earlier, built on a renewed belief that offenders should "get what's coming to them." It quickly led to a

**work release**

A prison program through which inmates are temporarily released into the community to meet job responsibilities.

**recidivism**

The repetition of criminal behavior. In statistical practice, a recidivism rate may be any of a number of possible counts or instances of arrest, conviction, correctional commitment, or correctional status change related to repetitions of these events within a given period of time.

policy of **warehousing** serious offenders for the avowed purpose of protecting society—and led also to a rapid decline of the decarceration initiative.

Recidivism rates were widely quoted in support of the drive to warehouse offenders. One study, for example, showed that nearly 70% of young adults paroled from prison in 22 states during 1978 were rearrested for serious crimes one or more times within six years of their release.[43] The study group was estimated to have committed 36,000 new felonies within the six years following their release, including 324 murders, 231 rapes, 2,291 robberies, and 3,053 violent assaults.[44] Worse still, observed the study's authors, was the fact that 46% of recidivists would have been in prison at the time of their readmission to prison if they had served the maximum term to which they had originally been sentenced.[45]

The failure of the rehabilitative model in corrections had already been proclaimed emphatically by Robert Martinson in 1974.[46] Martinson and his colleagues had surveyed 231 research studies conducted to evaluate correctional treatments between 1945 and 1967. They were unable to identify any treatment program that substantially reduced recidivism. Although Martinson argued for fixed sentences, a portion of which would be served in the community, his findings were often interpreted to mean that lengthy prison terms were necessary to incapacitate offenders who could not be reformed. About the same time, the prestigious National Academy of Sciences released a report in support of Martinson, saying, "We do not now know of any program or method of rehabilitation that could be guaranteed to reduce the criminal activity of released offenders."[47] This combined attack on the treatment model led to the **nothing-works doctrine**, which, beginning in the late 1970s, cast a pall of doubt over the previously dominant treatment philosophy.

The nothing-works philosophy contributed to new sentencing schemes such as mandatory minimum sentencing provisions and truth-in-sentencing requirements. Together with the growing popularity of "three strikes and you're out" laws, these sentencing rules affected prison populations by substantially increasing the average time served by offenders before release. In the 1990s, prison populations continued to grow substantially because of a rise in the number of parole violators returned to prison; a drop in the annual release rates of inmates; a small number of inmates who would serve long terms or who would never be released; and enhanced punishments for drug offenders.[48] Average time served continues to increase. In 1990, for example, murderers served, on average, 92 months before release. Today, a person convicted of murder can expect to serve 106 months in prison before being released—a 15% increase. During the same period, actual time served in prison for the crime of rape increased 27%, while drug offenders spent 35% more time behind bars.[49]

American prison populations grew dramatically during the warehousing era (Figure 13–2)— and continue to increase. Between 1980 and 2005, state and federal prison populations more than

**warehousing**

An imprisonment strategy that is based on the desire to prevent recurrent crime and that has abandoned all hope of rehabilitation.

**nothing-works doctrine**

The belief, popularized by Robert Martinson in the 1970s, that correctional treatment programs have had little success in rehabilitating offenders.

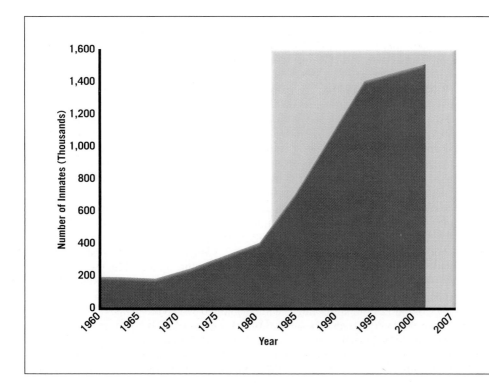

**FIGURE 13–2**

**U.S. prison population, 1960–2005.**

*Source*: Bureau of Justice Statistics.

quadrupled, from 329,000 inmates to almost 1.5 million.[50] Much of the rise in prison populations can be attributed directly to changes in sentencing laws aimed at taking drug offenders off the streets and to the resulting rapid growth in the number of incarcerated drug felons. A warehousing era report by the American Bar Association, for example, directly attributed the huge growth in the number of inmates to what it saw as a system-wide overemphasis on drug-related offenses—an emphasis that tended to imprison mostly poor, undereducated African-American youths who were rarely dangerous.[51] The report pointed out that while the per capita *rate of reported crime* dropped 2.2% across the nation during the 1980s, "the *incarceration rate* increased more than 110 percent."[52]

Warehousing also contributed to numerous administrative difficulties, many of which continue to affect prison systems throughout the nation today. By 1992, when the warehousing era was in full swing, institutions in 40 states and the District of Columbia were operating under court orders to alleviate overcrowding.[53] Entire prison systems in nine states—Alaska, Florida, Kansas, Louisiana, Mississippi, Nevada, Rhode Island, South Carolina, and Texas—had come under court control because overcrowded conditions made it impossible for prison administrators to meet court-supported constitutional requirements related to inmate safety. Today, even more state corrections systems have become subject to federal oversight or are operating under federal consent decrees.[54]

To meet the housing needs of burgeoning prison populations during the 1980s and 1990s, some states constructed "temporary" tent cities within prison yards. Others moved more beds into already packed dormitories, often stacking prisoners three high in triple bunk beds. A few states declared a policy of early release for less dangerous inmates and instituted mandatory diversion programs for first-time nonviolent offenders. Others used sentence rollbacks to reduce the sentences of selected inmates by a fixed amount, usually 90 days. Early parole was similarly employed by numerous states to reduce overcrowded conditions. Most states shifted some of their correctional burden to local jails, and by 2000, 34 states, the District of Columbia, and the federal government were sending prisoners to other jails because of overcrowding at their own long-term institutions.[55]

## The Just Deserts Era (1995–Present)

The Impact of the Just Deserts Philosophy on Corrections

**justice model**

A contemporary model of imprisonment based on the principle of just deserts.

Warehousing and prison overcrowding were primarily the result of both public and official frustration with rehabilitative efforts. In a sense, however, they were also consequences of a strategy without a clear-cut philosophy. Because rehabilitation didn't seem to work, early advocates of warehousing—not knowing what else to do—assumed a pragmatic stance and advocated separating criminals from society by keeping them locked up for as long as possible. Their avowed goal was the protection of law-abiding citizens.

Since the end of the warehousing era, however, a new philosophy based on the second prong of the **justice model**—that is, an emphasis on individual responsibility—has become the operative principle underlying many correctional initiatives. This new philosophy is grounded squarely on the concept of just deserts, in which imprisonment is seen as a fully deserved and proper consequence of criminal and irresponsible behavior rather than just the end result of a bankrupt system unable to reform its charges. Unlike previous correctional eras, which layered other purposes on the correctional experience (the reformatory era, for example, was concerned with reformation, and the industrial era sought economic gain), the current era of just deserts represents a kind of return to the root purpose of incarceration: punishment.

At the start of the just deserts era, state legislatures, encouraged in large part by their constituencies, scrambled to limit inmate privileges and to increase the pains of imprisonment. As with any other era, the exact beginning of the just deserts era is difficult to pinpoint. Noted corrections expert Jeanne B. Stinchcomb says, "The justice model gained momentum throughout the 1980s and 1990s, fueled by political conservatism, media sensationalism, an all-out 'war on drugs,' and public attitudes expressed in 'zero-tolerance' terms."[56] It is safe to say, however, that the just deserts model of criminal punishments was firmly in place by 1995. In that year, Alabama became the first state in modern times to reestablish chain gangs.[57] Under the Alabama system, shotgun-armed guards oversaw prisoners who were chained together by the ankles while they worked the state's roadsides—picking up trash, clearing brush, and filling ditches. The system, intended primarily for parole violators, was tough and unforgiving. Inmates served up to 90 days on chain gangs, during which they worked 12-hour shifts and remained chained even while using portable toilet facilities.

A few months later, Arizona became the second state to field prison chain gangs. Florida jumped on the chain gang bandwagon soon afterward.[58] Alabama chain gangs, which had expanded to include female prisoners, were discontinued in 1996 following a lawsuit against the state. The Florida Department of Corrections continues to use restricted labor squads (its name for chain gangs) at seven correctional institutions. Florida chain gang inmates are shackled at the ankles but are not connected to each other in any way.[59]

Nationally, chain gang proponents, though dwindling in number, continue to be adamant about the purpose this punishment serves. "If a person knows they're going to be out on the highway in chains, they are going to think twice about committing a crime," says former Georgia Prison Commissioner Ron Jones.[60] Opponents of the chain gang, however, like ACLU National Prison Project spokeswoman Jenni Gainsborough, call it "a giant step backward" and "a return to the dark ages."[61]

In another example of the move toward greater punishment indicative of the just deserts era, Virginia abolished parole in 1995, increased sentences for certain violent crimes by as much as 700%, and announced that it would build a dozen new prisons.[62] Changes in Virginia law were intended to move the state further in the direction of truth in sentencing and to appease the state's voters, who—reflecting public opinion nationwide—demanded a "get tough" stance toward criminals.

"Get tough" initiatives can be seen in the "three strikes and you're out" laws that swept through state legislatures in the late 1990s.[63] Three-strikes legislation, which is discussed in more detail in CJ Exhibit 11–2 in Chapter 11, mandates lengthy prison terms for criminal offenders convicted of a third violent crime or felony. Three-strikes laws have been enacted in almost 30 states and by the federal government. Critics of such laws, however, say that they do not prevent crime.[64] Jerome Skolnick, of the University of California at Berkeley, for example, criticizes three-strikes legislation because, he says, such practices almost certainly do not reduce the risk of victimization—especially the risk of becoming a victim of random violence. That is so, says Skolnick, because most violent crimes are committed by young men between the ages of 13 and 23. "It follows," according to Skolnick, "that if we jail them for life after their third conviction, we will get them in the twilight of their careers, and other young offenders will take their place."[65] Three-strikes programs, says Skolnick, are leading to the creation of "the most expensive, taxpayer-supported middle-age and old-age entitlement program in the history of the world," which will provide housing and medical care to older, burned-out law violators. Another author puts it this way: "The question . . . is whether it makes sense to continue to incarcerate aged prisoners beyond the time they would have served under ordinary sentences. This is unnecessary from the standpoint of public safety, and it is expensive."[66]

Criticisms of three-strikes laws fail to appreciate the sentiments underlying the current correctional era. Proponents of "get tough" policies, while no doubt interested in personal safety, lower crime rates, and balanced state and federal budgets, are keenly focused on retribution. And where retribution fuels a correctional policy, deterrence, reformation, and economic considerations play only secondary roles. As more and more states have enacted three-strikes and other "get tough" legislation, prison populations across the nation have continued to swell, eclipsing

> If you don't like the place, don't come here.
>
> —Maricopa County (Arizona) Sheriff Joe Arpaio, offering advice to inmates housed in his desert tent city[iii]

An Alabama chain gang setting out to work on the roads. In 1995, reflecting a renewed society-wide emphasis on punishment, Alabama became the first state in modern times to revive the use of prison chain gangs. Following a lawsuit, however, the state later abandoned the concept.

*AP Wide World Photos*

those of the warehousing era. The just deserts era of correctional philosophy now provides what has become for many an acceptable rationale for continued prison expansion. Some, however, fear that the prevailing retribution-based "lock 'em up" philosophy bodes ill for the future of American corrections. "I am worried there is going to be a disaster in our prisons," says J. Michael Quinlan, who was director of the federal Bureau of Prisons under Presidents Ronald Reagan and George Bush.[67] The combination of burgeoning prison populations and restrictions on inmate privileges could have a catastrophic and disastrous effect—leading to riots, more prison violence, work stoppages, an increased number of inmate suicides, and other forms of prison disorder—says Quinlan.[68]

# Prisons Today

Approximately 1,325 state prisons and 84 federal prisons are in operation across the country today.[69] More are being built as both the states and the federal government continue to fund and construct new facilities. America's prison population has more than quadrupled since 1980, although the growth rate has recently been slowing. On January 1, 2005, the nation's state and federal prisons held 1,496,629 inmates.[70] Seven percent (or 104,848) of those imprisoned were women.[71]

The incarceration rate for state and federal prisoners sentenced to more than a year has reached a record 486 prisoners for every 100,000 U.S. residents. One out of every 109 men and one out of every 1,563 women were sentenced prisoners under the jurisdiction of state or federal authorities in early 2005.[72] If incarceration rates remain unchanged, 6.6% of U.S. residents born in 2001 will go to prison at some time during their lifetime.[73]

Most people sentenced to state prisons are convicted of violent crimes (50.5%), while property crimes (20.4%) and drug crimes (21.4%) are nearly tied as the second most common type of offenses for which offenders are imprisoned.[74] In contrast, prisoners sentenced for drug-law violations are the single largest group of federal inmates (55%), and the increase in the imprisonment of drug offenders accounts for more than three-quarters of the total growth in the number of federal inmates since 1980.[75]

An examination of imprisonment statistics by race highlights the huge disparity between blacks and whites in prison. While only an estimated 1,172 white men are imprisoned in the United States for every 100,000 white men in their late 20s, the latest figures show an incarceration rate of 8,367 black men for every 100,000 black men of the same age—seven times greater than the figure for whites.[76] Worse, the imprisonment rate of African-Americans increased dramatically during the past ten years, while the rate of white imprisonment grew far less. Almost 17% of adult black men in the United States have served time in prison—a rate over twice as high as that for adult Hispanic males (7.7%) and over six times as high as that for adult white males (2.6%).[77] According to the Bureau of Justice Statistics, a black male living in America today has a 32.3% lifetime chance of going to prison, and a black female has a 5.6% lifetime chance of imprisonment. That contrasts sharply with the lifetime chances of imprisonment for white males (5.9%) and white females (0.9%).[78]

The use of imprisonment varies considerably between states, as Figure 13–3 shows. While the average rate of imprisonment in the United States at the start of 2005 was 486 per every 100,000 people in the population,[79] some state rates were nearly double that figure.[80] Louisiana, for example, was holding 816 out of every 100,000 of its citizens in prison on January 1, 2005, while Mississippi was a close second with an incarceration rate of 669. Texas, a state with traditionally high rates of imprisonment, held 694 prisoners per every 100,000 people. Maine had the lowest rate of imprisonment of all the states (148), while other states with low rates were Rhode Island (175), North Dakota (195), and New Hampshire (187). More statistics are available via **Library Extra 13–2** at cjtoday.com.

A recent study by David Greenberg and Valerie West identified factors that contribute to variation in incarceration rates among states.[81] Greenberg and West found that a state's violent crime rate was a significant determinant of its incarceration rate but was not the only factor. Also important were the political leanings of the state's population (more politically conservative states made greater use of imprisonment), the amount of money available to build and maintain prisons (more money led to more imprisonment), the employment rate (unemployment contributed to higher rates of imprisonment), the percentage of African-American men in the state's population (the higher the percentage, the higher the rate of imprisonment), and the level of welfare support available to the poor (higher welfare payments meant less imprisonment). The authors also found that income inequality was not a predictor of imprisonment rates and that the degree of urbanization in a state had no effect on imprisonment.

**LIBRARY EXTRA**

Prisons are no longer a response to increasing crime, and crime does not respond to increasing prisons. The prison system just grows like a weed in the yard.

—Vincent Schiraldi, Executive Director, Justice Policy Institute

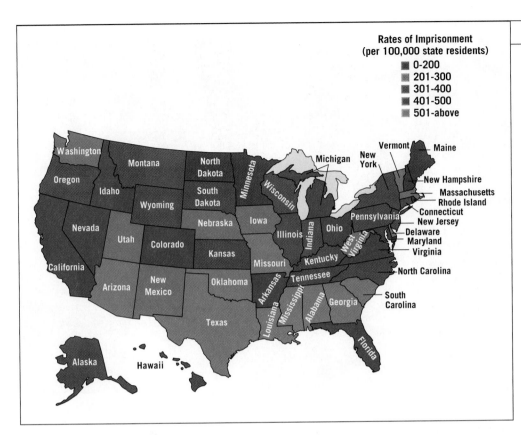

**Rates of Imprisonment
(per 100,000 state residents)**
- 0-200
- 201-300
- 301-400
- 401-500
- 501-above

**FIGURE 13-3**

**Rates of imprisonment
in the United States.**

*Source:* Paige M. Harrison and
Allen J. Beck, *Prisoners in 2004*
(Washington, DC: Bureau of Justice
Statistics, 2005).

The size of prison facilities varies greatly. One out of every four state institutions is a large maximum-security prison, with a population approaching 1,000 inmates. A few exceed that figure, but the typical state prison is small, with an inmate population of fewer than 500. Community-based facilities average around 50 residents. The typical prison system in relatively populous states consists of[82]

- One high-security prison for long-term, high-risk offenders
- One or more medium-security institutions for offenders who are not high risks
- One institution for adult women
- One or two institutions for young adults (generally under age 25)
- One or two specialized mental hospital–type security prisons for mentally ill prisoners
- One or more open-type institutions for low-risk, nonviolent inmates

Incarceration costs average around $62 per inmate per day at both the state and federal levels when all types of adult correctional facilities are averaged together.[83] Prison systems across the nation face spiraling costs as the number of inmates grows and as the age of the inmate population increases. The cost of running the nation's prisons approached $60 billion in 2001.[84]

> Prison and jail populations have skyrocketed during the past two decades, spurring new construction and often generating crowded conditions in our institutions and facilities. Substance abuse is directly and indirectly responsible for a large portion of this population increase.
>
> —James A. Gondles, Jr.,
> Executive Director, the American
> Correctional Association[iv]

# Overcrowding

The just deserts philosophy has led to substantial and continued increases in the American prison population even as crime rates have been dropping. In 1990, for example, the U.S. rate of imprisonment stood at 292 prisoners per every 100,000 residents. By 1995, it had reached 399, and on January 1, 2005, it was 486. While the rate of growth has been slowing, it is still inching higher.[85]

At the same time, crime rates have been falling. As noted in Chapter 2, between 1991 and 2004, the official rate of crime in the United States dropped from 5,897 to 3,983 offenses per every 100,000 residents—a level that had not been seen since 1975.[86] Hence a 32% *decrease* in the national crime rate over a ten-year period was accompanied by a 61% *increase* in the rate of imprisonment. Just deserts advocates, of course, argue that increased rates of incarceration are at least partially responsible for reduced crime rates, since incarceration removes those who are likely to reoffend from the community.

Inmates making collect phone calls at the Davidson County Prison in Tennessee. There are approximately 1,500 state prisons and 84 federal prisons in operation across the country today. Together they hold almost 1.5 million inmates. The prison shown here is run by Corrections Corporation of America.

*A. Ramey, PhotoEdit*

*Rhodes* v. *Chapman*:
Case Background

---

**prison capacity**

The size of the correctional population an institution can effectively hold.[v] There are three types of prison capacity: rated, operational, and design.

---

**rated capacity**

The number of inmates a prison can handle according to the judgment of experts.

---

**operational capacity**

The number of inmates a prison can effectively accommodate based on management considerations.

---

**design capacity**

The number of inmates a prison was intended to hold when it was built or modified.

---

Even though many new prisons have been built throughout the nation during the past 20 years to accommodate the growing number of inmates, prison overcrowding is still very much a reality in many jurisdictions (Figure 13–4 ). Prison overcrowding can be measured along a number of dimensions, including these[87]:

- Space available per inmate (such as square feet of floor space)
- How long inmates are confined in cells or housing units (versus time spent on recreation and other activities)
- Living arrangements (for example, single versus double bunks)
- Type of housing (use of segregation facilities, tents, and so on in place of general housing)

Further complicating the picture is the fact that prison officials have developed three definitions of **prison capacity**. **Rated capacity** refers to the size of the inmate population that a facility can handle according to the judgment of experts. **Operational capacity** is the number of inmates that a facility can effectively accommodate based on an appraisal of the institution's staff, programs, and services. **Design capacity** refers to the inmate population that the institution was originally built to handle. Rated capacity estimates usually yield the largest inmate capacities, while design capacity (on which observations in this chapter are based) typically shows the highest amount of overcrowding.

Overcrowding by itself is not cruel and unusual punishment, according to the U.S. Supreme Court in *Rhodes* v. *Chapman* (1981),[88] which considered the issue of double-bunking along with other alleged forms of "deprivation" at the Southern Ohio Correctional Facility. The Court, reasoning that overcrowding is not necessarily dangerous if other prison services are adequate, held that prison housing conditions may be "restrictive and even harsh," for they are part of the penalty that offenders pay for their crimes.

However, overcrowding combined with other negative conditions may lead to a finding against the prison system. The American Correctional Association believes that such a totality-of-conditions approach requires courts to assess the overall quality of prison life while viewing overcrowded conditions in combination with

- The prison's meeting of basic human needs
- The adequacy of the facility's staff
- The program opportunities available to inmates
- The quality and strength of the prison management

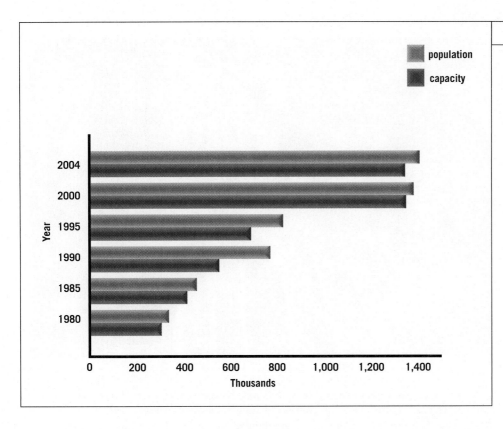

**FIGURE 13–4**

**State prison populations, inmates versus capacity, 1980–2004.**

*Source:* Bureau of Justice Statistics, *Correctional Populations in the United States* (Washington, DC: Author, various years).

## Selective Incapacitation: A Strategy to Reduce Prison Populations

Some authors have identified the central issue of imprisonment as one of selective versus collective incapacitation.[89] Collective incapacitation, a strategy in which almost all serious offenders are imprisoned, is still found today in states that rely on predetermined, or fixed, sentences for given offenses or for a series of specified kinds of offenses (as in the case of three-strikes legislation). Collective incapacitation is, however, prohibitively expensive as well as unnecessary, in the opinion of many experts. Not all offenders need to be imprisoned because not all represent a continuing threat to society, but those who do are difficult to identify.[90]

In most jurisdictions where the just deserts model holds sway, selective incapacitation has become the rule. Selective incapacitation seeks to identify the most dangerous criminals, with the goal of removing them from society. Repeat offenders with records of serious and violent crimes are the most likely candidates for incapacitation—as are those who will probably commit violent crimes in the future, even though they have no records. However, potentially violent offenders cannot be readily identified, and those thought likely to commit crimes cannot be sentenced to lengthy prison terms for things they have not yet done.

In support of selective incapacitation, many states have enacted career offender statutes that attempt to identify potentially dangerous offenders out of known criminal populations. Selective incapacitation efforts, however, have been criticized for yielding a rate of "false positives" of greater than 60%,[91] and some authors have called selective incapacitation a "strategy of failure."[92] Nevertheless, in an analysis of recidivism studies, Canadians Paul Gendreau, Tracy Little, and Claire Goggin found that criminal history, a history of preadult antisocial behavior, and "criminogenic needs"—which were defined as measurable antisocial thoughts, values, and behaviors—were all dependable predictors of recidivism.[93] The article, subtitled "What Works!" was intended as a response to Martinson's nothing-works doctrine, mentioned earlier.

Some state programs designed to reduce prison overcrowding, however, have run afoul of selective incarceration principles. In 1997, for example, the U.S. Supreme Court ordered Florida to release as many as 2,500 inmates—many of whom had been convicted of violent crimes—under a "gain time" program set up by the state in 1983.[94] Provisions of the program allowed inmates to earn as much as two months off their sentences for every month served. Although the program was originally intended to relieve overcrowding, a change in public sentiment led Florida Attorney General Bob Butterworth to revoke gain time that had already been earned. In ordering the inmates' release, however, the U.S. Supreme Court unanimously ruled that Florida had violated

> Today, with an unprecedented number of people behind bars, we are no safer than before. We are, however, much less free.
>
> —American Civil Liberties Union website

Weapons confiscated from inmates at Florida State Prison. The weapons were displayed during a rare media tour of the facility.

*AP Wide World Photos*

constitutional guarantees against *ex post facto* laws and required officials to be bound by the program's original conditions. The release of hundreds of murderers, rapists, robbers, and other felons caused a statewide uproar and media furor.

The Florida experience and others like it have caused states to tighten restrictions on early-release programs. As the just deserts model continues to take center stage, it is likely that we will see the continued sentencing of violent criminals to lengthy prison stays with little possibility of release and the increased use of alternative sanctions for minor offenders.

## Security Levels

Maximum-custody prisons tend to be massive old buildings with large inmate populations. However, some, like Central Prison in Raleigh, North Carolina, are much newer and incorporate advances in prison architecture to provide tight security without sacrificing building aesthetics. Such institutions provide a high level of security characterized by high fences, thick walls, secure cells, gun towers, and armed prison guards. Maximum-custody prisons tend to locate cells and other inmate living facilities at the center of the institution and place a variety of barriers between the living area and the institution's outer perimeter. Technological innovations, such as electric perimeters, laser motion detectors, electronic and pneumatic locking systems, metal detectors, X-ray machines, television surveillance, radio communications, and computer information systems, are frequently used today to reinforce the more traditional maximum-security strategies. These technologies have helped to lower the cost of new prison construction. However, some people argue that prisons may rely too heavily on electronic detection devices that have not yet been adequately tested.[95] Death-row inmates are all maximum-security prisoners, although the level of security on death row exceeds even that experienced by most prisoners held in maximum custody. Prisoners on death row must spend much of the day in single cells and are often permitted a brief shower only once a week under close supervision.

Most states today have one large, centrally located maximum-security institution. Some of these prisons combine more than one custody level and are both maximum- and medium-security facilities. Medium security is a custody level that resembles maximum security in many ways, but medium-security prisoners are generally permitted more freedom to associate with one another and can go to the prison yard, exercise room, library, and shower and bathroom facilities under less intense supervision. An important security tool in medium-security prisons is the count, which is a head count of inmates taken at regular intervals. Counts may be taken four times a day and usually require inmates to report to designated areas to be counted. Until the count has been "cleared," all other inmate activity must cease. Medium-security prisons tend to be smaller than maximum-security institutions and often have barbed-wire-topped chain-link fences instead of the more secure stone or concrete block walls found in many of the older maximum-security facilities. Cells and living quarters typically have more windows and are often located closer to the perimeter of the institution than in maximum-security facilities. Dormitory-style housing, where prisoners live together in wardlike arrangements, is sometimes found in medium-security facilities. There are generally more opportunities for inmates to participate in recreational and other prison programs than in maximum-custody facilities.

In minimum-security institutions, inmates are generally housed in dormitory-like settings and are free to walk the yard and to visit most of the prison facilities. Some newer prisons provide minimum-security inmates with private rooms, which they can decorate (within limits) according to their tastes. Inmates usually have free access to a canteen that sells items such as cigarettes, toothpaste, and candy bars. Minimum-security inmates often wear uniforms of a different color from those of inmates in higher custody levels, and in some institutions they may wear civilian clothes. They work under only general supervision and usually have access to recreational, educational, and skills-training programs on the prison grounds. Guards are unarmed, gun towers do not exist, and fences, if they are present at all, are usually low and gates are sometimes even unlocked. Many minimum-security prisoners participate in some sort of work- or study-release program, and some have extensive visitation and furlough privileges. Counts may be taken, although most minimum-security institutions keep track of inmates through daily administrative work schedules. The primary "force" holding inmates in minimum-security institutions is their own restraint. Inmates live with the knowledge that minimum-security institutions are one step removed from close correctional supervision and that if they fail to meet the expectations of administrators, they will be transferred into more secure institutions, which will probably delay their release. Inmates returning from assignments in the community may be frisked for contraband, but body-cavity searches are rare in minimum custody, being reserved primarily for inmates suspected of smuggling.

The typical American prison today is medium or minimum custody. Some states have as many as 80 or 90 small institutions, which may originally have been located in every county to serve the needs of public works and highway maintenance. Medium- and minimum-security institutions house the bulk of the country's prison population and offer a number of programs and services designed to assist with the rehabilitation of offenders and to create the conditions necessary for a successful reentry of the inmate into society. Most prisons offer psychiatric services, academic education, vocational education, substance-abuse treatment, health care, counseling, recreation, library services, religious programs, and industrial and agricultural training.[96] Learn more about all aspects of contemporary prisons from the Corrections Connection via **Web Extra 13–4** at cjtoday.com.

> **We are the prisoners of the prisoners we have taken.**
>
> —Jennifer Clegg

**WEB** EXTRA

## Prison Classification Systems

Most states use a **classification system** to assign new prisoners to initial custody levels based on their perceived dangerousness, escape risk, and type of offense. A prisoner might be assigned to a minimum-, medium-, or maximum-custody institution. Inmates move through custody levels according to the progress they are judged to have made in self-control and demonstrated responsibility. Serious violent criminals who begin their prison careers with lengthy sentences in maximum custody have the opportunity in most states to work their way up to minimum security, although the process usually takes a number of years. Those who represent continual disciplinary problems are returned to closer custody levels. Minimum-security prisons, as a result, house inmates convicted of all types of criminal offenses.

Once an inmate has been assigned to a custody level, he or she may be reassessed for living and work assignments within the institution. Just as initial (or external) custody classification systems determine security levels, internal classification systems are designed to help determine appropriate housing plans and program interventions within a particular facility for inmates who share a common custody level. In short, initial classification determines the institution in which an inmate is placed, and internal classification determines placement and program assignment within that institution.[97] An overview of the external and internal classification process is shown in Figure 13–5. Learn more about internal prison classification systems via **Library Extra 13–3** at cjtoday.com.

Objective prison classification systems were adopted by many states in the 1980s, but it wasn't until the late 1990s that such systems were refined and validated. Fueled by litigation and overcrowding, classification systems are now viewed as the principal management tool for allocating scarce prison resources efficiently and for minimizing the potential for violence or escape. Classification systems are also expected to provide greater accountability and to forecast future prison

**classification system**

A system used by prison administrators to assign inmates to custody levels based on offense history, assessed dangerousness, perceived risk of escape, and other factors.

**LIBRARY** EXTRA

**FIGURE 13–5**

**The flow of activities in prison classification systems.**

*Source:* Adapted from Patricia L. Hardyman et al., *Internal Prison Classification Systems: Case Studies in Their Development and implementation* (Washington, DC: National Institute of Corrections, 2002), p. 3.

> We spend $60,000 building a prison cell, another $35,000 a year to keep that inmate. They have central heating and air conditioning. At the same time we spend less than $4,000 on each school student. And many of them don't have air-conditioned or centrally heated schools. Let's put the money in education. That's the only answer to crime.
>
> —Louisiana Congressman Cleo Fields

bed-space needs. A properly functioning classification system is the "brain" of prison management, governing and influencing many important decisions, including such fiscal matters as staffing levels, bed space, and programming.[98]

One of the best-known internal classification systems in use today is the adult internal management system (AIMS). AIMS was developed more than 20 years ago to reduce institutional predatory behavior by identifying potential predators and separating them from vulnerable inmates. AIMS assesses an inmate's predatory potential by quantifying aspects of his or her (1) record of misconduct, (2) ability to follow staff directions, and (3) level of aggression toward other inmates.

Before concluding this discussion of classification, it is important to recognize that the criteria used to classify prisoners must be relevant to the legitimate security needs of the institution. In 2005, for example, the U.S. Supreme Court, in the case of *Johnson* v. *California*,[99] invalidated the California Department of Corrections and Rehabilitation's (CDCR) unwritten policy of racially segregating prisoners in double cells for up to 60 days each time they entered a new correctional facility. The policy had been based on a claim that it prevented violence caused by racial gangs. The Court, however, held that the California policy was "immediately suspect" as an "express racial classification" and found that the CDCR was unable to demonstrate that the practice served a compelling state interest.

## The Federal Prison System

In 1895, the federal government opened a prison at Leavenworth, Kansas, for civilians convicted of violating federal law. Leavenworth had been a military prison, and control over the facility was transferred from the Department of the Army to the Department of Justice. By 1906, the Leavenworth facility had been expanded to a capacity of 1,200 inmates, and another federal prison—in Atlanta, Georgia—was built. McNeil Island Prison in Washington State was also func-

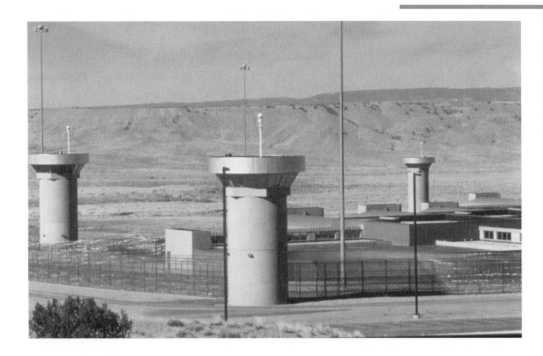

The federal Bureau of Prisons ADMAX facility in Florence, Colorado, which opened in 1995. It is the only ultra-high-security institution in the federal system.

*Agence France Presse, Getty Images*

tioning by the early 1900s. The first federal prison for women opened in 1927 in Alderson, West Virginia. With the increasing complexity of the federal criminal code, the number of federal prisoners grew.[100]

On May 14, 1930, the federal Bureau of Prisons (BOP) was created under the direction of Sanford Bates. The BOP was charged with providing progressive and humane care for federal inmates, professionalizing the federal prison service, and ensuring consistent and centralized administration of the 11 federal prisons in operation at the time.[101] The bureau inherited a system that was dramatically overcrowded. Many federal prisoners were among the most notorious criminals in the nation, and ideals of humane treatment and rehabilitation were all but lacking in the facilities of the 1920s. Bates began a program of improvements to relieve overcrowding and to increase the treatment capacity of the system. In 1933, the Medical Center for Federal Prisoners opened in Springfield, Missouri, with a capacity of around 1,000 inmates. Alcatraz Island began operations in 1934.

Most of the federal prison system's growth since the mid-1980s has been the result of the Sentencing Reform Act of 1984 (which established determinate sentencing, abolished parole, and reduced good time) and federal mandatory minimum sentences enacted in 1986, 1988, and 1990. From 1980 to 1989, the federal inmate population more than doubled, from just over 24,000 to almost 58,000. During the 1990s, the population more than doubled again, and it continued to grow throughout the early years of the twenty-first century, reaching approximately 170,500 prisoners (or 40% over capacity) at the start of 2005.[102]

Today, the federal prison system consists of 104 institutions, six regional offices, the Central Office (headquarters), two staff-training centers, and 28 community corrections offices.[103] The regional offices and the Central Office provide administrative oversight and support to the institutions and to the community corrections offices, which oversee community corrections centers and home-confinement programs.

The BOP classifies its institutions according to five security levels: (1) administrative maximum (**ADMAX**), (2) high security, (3) medium security, (4) low security, and (5) minimum security. High-security facilities are called *U.S. penitentiaries* (USPs); medium- and low-security institutions are both called *federal correctional institutions* (FCIs); and minimum-security prisons are termed *federal prison camps* (FPCs).[104] Minimum-security facilities (like Eglin Air Force Base, Florida, and Maxwell Air Force Base, Alabama) are essentially honor-type camps with barracks-type housing and no fencing. Low-security facilities in the federal prison system are surrounded by double chain-link fencing and employ vehicle patrols around their perimeters to enhance security. Medium-security facilities (like those in Terminal Island, California; Lompoc, California; and Seagoville, Texas) make use of similar fencing and patrols but supplement them with electronic monitoring of the grounds and perimeter areas. High-security facilities (USPs like those in Atlanta, Georgia; Lewisburg, Pennsylvania; Terre Haute, Indiana; and Leavenworth,

**ADMAX**

Administrative maximum. The term is used by the federal government to denote ultra-high-security prisons.

## FIGURE 13-6

**Locations of long-term confinement facilities in the federal correctional system, 2005.**

*Note:* Does not include Bureau of Prisons offices or community corrections management offices.

*Source:* Federal Bureau of Prisons.

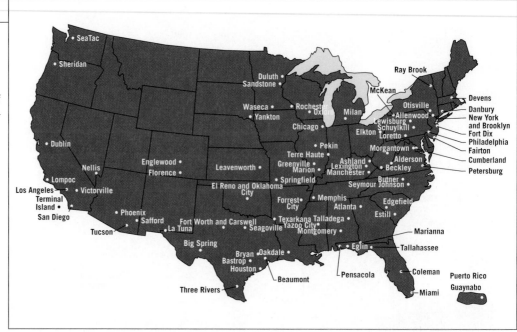

> With the huge expansion of prisons starting in the 1980s, most prison systems gave up believing they had any responsibility for changing offenders or [for] what happened after offenders were released. The objective became that prisons should be just for punishment, and politicians competed to see who could make prisons more unpleasant.
>
> —Todd Clear, John Jay College of Criminal Justice

Kansas) are architecturally designed to prevent escapes and to contain disturbances. They also make use of armed patrols and intense electronic surveillance.

A separate federal prison category is that of administrative facilities, consisting of institutions with special missions that are designed to house all types of inmates. Most administrative facilities are metropolitan detention centers (MDCs). MDCs, which are generally located in large cities close to federal courthouses, are the jails of the federal correctional system and hold defendants awaiting trial in federal court. Another five administrative facilities, medical centers for federal prisoners (MCFPs), function as hospitals.

Federal correctional facilities exist either as single institutions or as federal correctional complexes—that is, sites consisting of more than one type of correctional institution (Figure 13–6). The federal correctional complex at Allenwood, Pennsylvania, for example, consists of a U.S. penitentiary, a federal prison camp, and two federal correctional institutions (one low and one medium security), each with its own warden. Federal institutions can be classified by type as follows: 55 are federal prison camps (holding 35% of all federal prisoners), 17 are low-security facilities (28%), 26 are medium-security facilities (23%), eight are high-security prisons (13%), and one is an ADMAX facility (1%).

One relatively recent addition to the federal system is the $60 million ultra-high-security prison at Florence, Colorado—the federal system's only ADMAX unit. Dubbed "the Alcatraz of the Rockies," the 575-bed facility was designed to be the most secure prison ever built by the government.[105] Opened in 1995, it holds mob bosses, spies, terrorists, murderers, and escape artists. Dangerous inmates are confined to their cells 23 hours per day and are not allowed to see or associate with other inmates. Electronically controlled doors throughout the institution channel inmates to individual exercise sessions, and educational courses, religious services, and administrative matters are conducted via closed-circuit television piped directly into the prisoners' cells. Remote-controlled heavy steel doors within the prison allow correctional staff to section off the institution in the event of rioting, and the system can be controlled from outside if the entire prison is compromised.

In an effort to combat rising expenses associated with a rapidly growing federal prison population, the U.S. Congress passed legislation in 1992 that imposes a "user fee" on federal inmates who are able to pay the costs associated with their incarceration.[106] Under the law, inmates may be assessed a dollar amount up to the cost of a year's incarceration—currently around $22,600.[107] The statute, which was designed so as not to impose hardships on poor offenders or their dependents, directs that collected funds, estimated to total $48 million per year, are to be used to improve alcohol- and drug-abuse programs within federal prisons. To learn more about the federal Bureau of Prisons, visit Web Extra 13–5, or read Library Extras 13–4 and 13–5 at cjtoday.com.

## CJ CAREERS

### FEDERAL BUREAU OF PRISONS

#### TYPICAL POSITIONS

Correctional officer, clinical psychologist, physician, nurse, chaplain, correctional/drug–treatment specialist, safety specialist, teacher, program officer, and vocational instructor.

#### EMPLOYMENT REQUIREMENTS

Applicants for correctional officer positions must (1) be a U.S. citizen, (2) be younger than 37 years of age (although for some hard-to-fill positions, an age waiver may be granted), (3) successfully complete an employee interview, (4) pass a physical examination, (5) pass a field security investigation, and (6) have completed a full four-year course of study in any field leading to a bachelor's degree from an accredited school; possess a bachelor's degree; have the equivalent of at least three years of full-time general experience performing duties such as providing assistance, guidance, and direction to individuals, counseling individuals, responding to emergency situations, supervising or managing, teaching or instructing, or selling products or services; or have a combination of undergraduate education and general experience equivalent to three years of full-time experience.

#### OTHER REQUIREMENTS

Candidates must successfully complete in-service training at the Federal Law Enforcement Training Academy at Glynco, Georgia.

#### SALARY

Correctional officers are appointed at GS-5, but nine semester hours or more of graduate education in criminal justice, criminology, law, or any social science may qualify the applicant for GS-6 or higher. A correctional officer may be advanced to the next higher pay grade after six months of satisfactory service.

#### BENEFITS

Benefits include (1) participation in the Federal Employees' Retirement System, (2) paid annual leave, (3) paid sick leave, (4) low-cost health and life insurance, and (5) paid holidays. Other benefits accrue from what the bureau describes as "strong internal merit promotion practices" and "unlimited opportunities for advancement in one of the fastest-growing government agencies."

#### DIRECT INQUIRIES TO:

Federal Bureau of Prisons
320 First Street, N.W.
Washington, DC 20534

Phone: (202)307–3198

Website: http://www.bop.gov

For additional information on employment opportunities in the criminal justice field, view the careers portion of the CD-ROM included with this book.

*Source:* Federal Bureau of Prisons.

## Recent Improvements

In the midst of frequent lawsuits, court-ordered changes in prison administration, and overcrowded conditions, outstanding prison facilities are being recognized through the American Correctional Association's (ACA's) accreditation program. The ACA Commission on Accreditation has developed a set of standards that correctional institutions can use for conducting self-evaluations. Institutions that meet the standards can apply for accreditation under the program.

Another avenue toward improvement of the nation's prisons can be found in the National Academy of Corrections, the training arm of the National Institute of Corrections. The academy, located in Boulder, Colorado, offers seminars, videoconferencing, and training sessions for state and local corrections managers, trainers, personnel directors, sheriffs, and state legislators.[108] Issues covered include strategies to control overcrowding, community corrections program management, prison programs, gangs and disturbances, security, and public and media relations.[109]

## Jails

**Jails** are locally operated short-term confinement facilities originally built to hold suspects following arrest and pending trial. Today's jails also serve these purposes[110]:

- Receive individuals pending arraignment and hold them awaiting trial, conviction, or sentencing
- Readmit probation, parole, and bail-bond violators and absconders

**jail**

A confinement facility administered by an agency of local government, typically a law enforcement agency, intended for adults but sometimes also containing juveniles, which holds people detained pending adjudication or committed after adjudication, usually those sentenced to a year or less.

- Temporarily detain juveniles, mentally ill persons, and others pending transfer to appropriate facilities
- Hold individuals for the military, for protective custody, for contempt, and for the courts as witnesses
- Release convicted inmates to the community upon completion of their sentence
- Transfer inmates to federal, state, or other authorities
- House inmates for federal, state, or other authorities because of overcrowding in their facilities
- Operate community-based programs with day reporting, home detention, electronic monitoring, or other types of supervision
- Hold inmates sentenced to short terms (generally less than one year)

A 2005 report by the Bureau of Justice Statistics (BJS) found that the nation's jails held 713,990 inmates—12% of whom were women.[111] Juveniles held in local jails numbered 7,083.[112] More than half of jail inmates have been convicted of a crime; a quarter are being detained while awaiting arraignment or trial; and a sixth are being held on a prior sentence but are also awaiting arraignment or trial on a new charge.[113] Jail authorities also supervised an additional 70,548 men and women in the community under programs that included the following: electronic monitoring (11,689), home detention without electronic monitoring (1,173), day reporting (6,627), community service (13,171), and weekender programs (11,589).[114]

A total of 3,365 jails operate throughout the United States, staffed by approximately 207,600 jail employees—the equivalent of about one employee for every three jail inmates.[115] Overall, the nation's jail budget is huge, and facilities are overflowing. State and local governments spend $10 billion every year to operate the nation's jails,[116] with more than $1 billion in additional monies earmarked for new jail construction and for renovation. On average, the housing of one jail inmate costs more than $14,500 per year.[117]

Approximately 20 million people are admitted (or readmitted) to the nation's jails each year. Some jail inmates stay for as little as one day, while others serve extended periods of time. Significantly, one of the fastest-growing sectors of today's jail population consists of sentenced offenders serving time in local jails because overcrowded prisons cannot accept them.

Most people processed through the country's jails are members of minority groups (61%), with 40.1% of jail inmates classifying themselves as African-American, 18.5% as Hispanic, and 2.4% as other minorities. Three percent report being of more than one race and 36% of jail inmates classify themselves as white.[118] Slightly more than 88% are male, and 7.8% are noncitizens.[119] The typical jail inmate is an unmarried black male between 25 and 34 years of age who reports having had some high school education. Typical charges include drug trafficking (12.1%), assault (11.7%), drug possession (10.8%), and larceny (7%).[120]

According to the BJS, about 6% of jail facilities house more than half of all jail inmates in the nation.[121] So, although most jails are small—many were built to house 50 or fewer inmates—most people who spend time in jail do so in larger institutions. Across the country, a handful of "megajails" house thousands of inmates each. The largest such facilities are in Los Angeles; New York City; Cook County, Illinois; Harris County, Texas; and Maricopa County, Arizona. Los Angeles County's 4,000-bed Twin Towers Correctional Facility cost $373 million to build and opened in 1997.[122] The largest employer among these huge jails is Cook County's, with more than 1,200 personnel on its payroll.[123] In 2004, the nation's 50 largest jail jurisdictions held 30.9% (220,556) of all jail inmates. The two jurisdictions with the most jail inmates, Los Angeles County and New York City, together held approximately 34,200 inmates, or 5% of the national total.[124] More jail statistics are available via Library Extra 13–6 at cjtoday.com.

**LIBRARY EXTRA**

## Women and Jail

Although women number only 12% of the country's jail population, they are the largest growth group in jails nationwide.[125] Jailed women face a number of special problems. Only 25.7% of the nation's jails report having a classification system specifically designed to evaluate female inmates,[126] and although many jurisdictions have plans "to build facilities geared to the female offender,"[127] not all jurisdictions today even provide separate housing areas for women. Educational levels are very low among jailed women, and fewer than half are high school graduates.[128] Drug abuse is another significant source of difficulty for jailed women. More than 30% of women who are admitted to jail have a substance-abuse problem at the time of admission, and in some parts of the country, that figure may be as high as 70%.[129]

## CJ NEWS

### Federal Prisons to End Boot-Camp Programs

Prison boot camps are getting the boot. The federal Bureau of Prisons plans to eliminate its "intensive confinement" program after the current batch of 525 inmates completes the military-style course over the next six months at boot camps in California, Pennsylvania and Texas.

In a January 14, 2005, memo to all federal judges, prosecutors and public defenders, Bureau of Prisons Director Harley Lappin said the boot camps, which emphasize physical training and discipline, are no more successful than ordinary incarceration when it comes to preventing released convicts from returning to crime.

By eliminating its three boot camps, the prisons bureau—which oversees about 180,000 inmates at 104 facilities across the nation—will save more than $1 million a year, Lappin said.

Boot camps, so named because they use drill instructors and simulate basic military training, were introduced in 27 states and in the federal prison system beginning in the 1980s.

The federal boot camps and several state programs have had courses in anger management, job skills and English. Many were targeted at young and non-violent offenders, on the theory that a lack of discipline was mostly to blame for their problems. In return for completing programs of 90–180 days, inmates often have been granted early release.

At their peak during the mid-1990s, federal and state boot camps had more than 7,000 inmates, the Justice Department says. More than 7,800 inmates have graduated from the federal program.

But the camps have fallen out of favor amid questions about whether they deter convicts from returning to crime. A federal study in 2003 found that programs in Texas, Georgia, Louisiana, Florida and New York had no significant impact on convicts' tendency to do so. Lappin's memo says the bureau's research into its program reached a similar conclusion.

By 2000, states had closed nearly one-third of the 75 adult boot camps they had been operating five years earlier.

Boot camps also have been sunk by new state policies aimed at easing prison crowding that have led to early releases of non-violent inmates.

Swan Lake, Montana, prison boot camp instructors greet a new inmate. In 2005, the federal Bureau of Prisons announced plans to eliminate its boot camp program. The bureau found that boot camp programs are no more successful than ordinary incarceration in reducing recidivism.

*Eastcott—Momatuik, The Image Works*

The camps continue to have defenders. The executive committee of the Judicial Conference, the federal judges' professional organization, plans to lobby the Justice Department to reconsider its plan.

Timothy Hoover, a federal public defender in Buffalo, says the boot-camp program is "far more beneficial than having someone just sit (in prison) for 24 to 30 months.

"The impact may be slight, but it's there," he says. "I never see any of (my boot-camp clients) again."

Learn more about correctional boot camps, including lessons learned from a decade of research, at Library Extra 13–7 at cjtoday.com.    **LIBRARY EXTRA**

For the latest in crime and justice news, visit the Talk Justice news feed at http://www.crimenews.info.

*Source:* Richard Willing, "U.S. Prisons to End Boot-Camp Program: Ordinary Incarceration Just as Effective, Bureau Reports," *USA Today*, February 4, 2005, p 1A. Copyright © 2005 *USA Today*. Reprinted with permission.

Pregnancy is another problem. Nationally, 4% of female inmates are pregnant when they enter jail,[130] but in urban areas, as much as 10% of the female jail population is reported to be pregnant on any given day.[131] As a consequence, a few hundred children are born in jails each year. However, substantive medical programs for female inmates, such as obstetrics and gynecological care, are often lacking. In planning future medical services for female inmates, some writers have advised jail administrators to expect to see an increasingly common kind of inmate: "an opiate-addicted female who is pregnant with no prior prenatal care having one or more sexually transmitted diseases, and fitting a high-risk category for AIDS (prostitution, IV drug use)."[132]

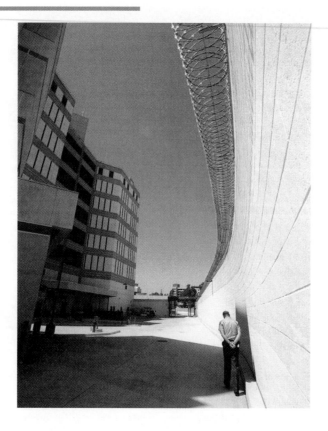

A correctional officer walking along a wall at Los Angeles County's $373 million Twin Towers Correctional Facility. Opened in 1997, it is one of the world's largest jails.

*AP Wide World Photos*

> The first two decades of the [twenty-first] century, at least, will see a major growth in prison populations. We have an opportunity now to start doing a better job of handling the responsibilities of the criminal justice system as well as of society. I hope we take both more seriously in the future than we do currently.
>
> —Dr. Alfred Blumstein, Dean of the School of Urban and Public Affairs, Carnegie Mellon University

Not only are jailed mothers separated from their children, but they may have to pay for their support. Twelve percent of all jails in one study reported requiring employed female inmates to contribute to the support of their dependent children.

When we consider women and jails, female inmates are only half the story. Women who work in corrections are the other half. In one study, Linda Zupan, a noted jail scholar, found that women made up 22% of the correctional officer force in jails across the nation.[133] The deployment of female personnel, however, was disproportionately skewed toward jobs in the lower ranks. Although 60% of all support staff (secretaries, cooks, and janitors) were women, only one in every ten chief administrators was female. Even so, Zupan did find that female correctional employees were significantly committed to their careers and that the attitudes of male workers toward female coworkers in jails were generally positive. Zupan's study uncovered 626 jails in which over 50% of the correctional officer force consisted of women. However, 954 of the nation's 3,316 jails operating at the time of the study had no female officers.[134] Zupan noted that "an obvious problem associated with the lack of female officers in jails housing females concerns the potential for abuse and exploitation of women inmates by male staff."[135]

Jails that do hire women generally accord them equal footing with male staffers. Although cross-gender privacy is a potential area of legal liability, in three-quarters of the jails studied by Zupan, female officers were assigned to supervise male housing areas. Only one in four jails that employed women restricted their access to unscreened shower and toilet facilities used by men or to other areas, such as sexual-offender units.

## The Growth of Jails

Jails have been called the "shame of the criminal justice system." Many are old, poorly funded, scantily staffed by underpaid and poorly trained employees, and given low priority in local budgets. By the end of the 1980s, many of our nation's jails had become seriously overcrowded, and court-ordered caps were sometimes placed on jail populations. One of the first such caps was imposed on the Harris County Jail in Houston, Texas, in 1990. In that year, the jail was forced to release 250 inmates after missing a deadline for reducing its resident population of 6,100 people.[136] A nationwide survey by the Bureau of Justice Statistics, undertaken around the same time, found that 46% of all jails had been built more than 25 years earlier, and of that percentage, over half were more than 50 years old.[137]

| JAIL FACTS | | | | | |
|---|---|---|---|---|---|
| | **1983** | **1988** | **1993** | **2000** | **2004** |
| Number of jails | 3,338 | 3,316 | 3,304 | 3,365 | 3,360* |
| Number of jail inmates | 223,551 | 343,569 | 459,804 | 621,149 | 713,990 |
| Rated capacity of jails | 261,556 | 339,949 | 475,224 | 677,787 | 755,603 |
| Percentage of capacity occupied | 85% | 101% | 97% | 92% | 94% |

TABLE 13–1

*Estimate based on earlier data.
*Source:* Paige M. Harrison and Allen J. Beck, *Prison and Jail Inmates at Midyear 2004* (Washington, DC: Bureau of Justice Statistics, 2005), and other years.

A 1983 national census revealed that jails were operating at 85% of their rated capacity (Table 13–1).[138] In 1990, however, the nation's jails were running at 104% of capacity, and new jails could be found on drawing boards and under construction across the country. By 2004, jail capacity had increased substantially, and overall jail occupancy was reported at 94% of rated capacity. Some individual facilities, however, were still desperately overcrowded.[139] Jail jurisdictions with the largest average daily populations also reported the highest occupancy rates. At midyear 2004, occupancy was 97% of rated capacity in jail jurisdictions with an average daily population of 1,000 or more inmates, compared to 64% in those with fewer than 50 inmates.[140]

Although jail overcrowding is not the issue it was a decade ago, it is still a problem. Overcrowded prisons have taken a toll on jails. In 2004, for example, approximately 74,378 inmates were being held in local jails because of overcrowding in state and federal prisons.[141] Also, the practice of giving jail sentences to offenders who are unable or unwilling to make restitution, alimony, or child-support payments has added to jail occupancy and has made the local lockup, at least partially, a debtors' prison. Symptomatic of problems brought on by huge jail populations, the National Institute of Justice reported 328 suicides in jails across the nation during a recent year.[142] Jail deaths from all causes total about 930 annually.

Other factors conspire to keep jail populations high. They include the following[143]:

- The inability of jail inmates to make bond due to institutionalized bail bond practices and lack of funding sources for indigent defendants
- Unnecessary delays between arrest and final case disposition
- Unnecessarily limited access to vital information about defendants that could be useful in facilitating court-ordered pretrial release
- The limited ability of the criminal justice system to handle cases expeditiously due to a lack of needed resources (judges, assistant prosecuting attorneys, and so on)
- Inappropriate attorney delays in moving cases through court
- Unproductive statutes requiring that specified nonviolent offenders be jailed (including mandatory pretrial jailing of those caught driving while intoxicated, minor drug offenders, second-offense shoplifters, and so on)

Some innovative jurisdictions have successfully contained the growth of jail populations by diverting arrestees to community-based programs. San Diego, California, for example, uses a privately operated detoxification reception program to divert many inebriates from the "drunk tank."[144] Officials in Galveston County, Texas, routinely divert mentally ill arrestees directly to a mental health facility.[145] Other areas use pretrial services and magistrates' offices, which are open 24 hours a day, for setting bail, making release possible. Learn more about jail overcrowding by reading **Library Extra 13–8** at cjtoday.com.

LIBRARY EXTRA

# Direct-Supervision Jails

Some suggest that the problems found in many jails stem from "mismanagement, lack of fiscal support, heterogeneous inmate populations, overuse and misuse of detention, overemphasis on custodial goals, and political and public apathy."[146] Others propose that environmental and organizational aspects of traditional jail architecture and staffing have led to many difficulties.[147]

A History
of Direct-Supervision Jails

**direct-supervision jail**

A temporary confinement facility that eliminates many of the traditional barriers between inmates and correctional staff. Physical barriers in direct-supervision jails are far less common than in traditional jails, allowing staff members the opportunity for greater interaction with, and control over, residents.

Traditional jails, say these observers, were built on the assumption that inmates are inherently violent and potentially destructive. Through the use of thick walls, bars, and other architectural barriers, jails were constructed to give staff maximum control and to restrict inmates' movements. Such institutions, however, also limit the correctional staff's visibility and access to confinement areas. As a consequence, they tend to encourage just the kinds of inmate behavior that jails were meant to control. Today, efficient hallway patrols and expensive video technology help in overcoming the limits that old jail architecture places on supervision.

In an effort to solve many of the problems that dogged jails in the past, a new jail management strategy emerged during the 1970s. Called a **direct-supervision jail**, or podular/direct-supervision (PDS) jail, this approach joined "podular/unit architecture with a participative, proactive management philosophy."[148] Often built in a system of "pods," or modular self-contained housing areas linked to one another, direct-supervision jails are free of the traditional physical barriers that separate staff and inmates. In a number of such "new-generation" jails, large reinforced Plexiglas panels supplant walls and serve to separate activity areas, such as classrooms and dining halls, from one another. Soft furniture is the rule throughout such institutions, and individual rooms take the place of cells, allowing inmates at least a modicum of personal privacy. In today's direct-supervision jails, 16 to 46 inmates typically live in one pod, with correctional staffers present among the inmate population around the clock.

Direct-supervision jails have been touted for their ability to reduce inmate dissatisfaction and to deter rape and violence among the inmate population. By eliminating architectural barriers to staff–inmate interaction, direct-supervision facilities are said to place officers back in control of institutions. A number of studies have demonstrated the success of such jails at reducing the likelihood of inmate victimization. One such study also found that staff morale in direct-supervision jails was far higher than in traditional institutions, that inmates reported reduced stress levels, and that fewer inmate-on-inmate and inmate-on-staff assaults occurred.[149] Similarly, sexual assault, jail rape, suicide, and escape have all been found to occur far less frequently in direct-supervision facilities than in traditional institutions.[150] Significantly, new-generation jails have experienced far fewer lawsuits brought by inmates and negative court-ordered judgments against jail administrators.

While the number of direct-supervision jails has grown rapidly, such facilities are not without their problems. In 1993, for example, the 238-bed Rensselaer County PDS jail in Troy, New York, experienced a disturbance that resulted in "a total loss of control," the removal of officers from the pods, and the escape of two inmates.[151] Somewhat later, the 700-bed San Joaquin County Jail in Stockton, California, experienced numerous problems, including the escape of seven inmates.

Inmates playing cards at the Los Angeles North County Correctional Facility in Saugus, California. The Los Angeles County jail system is the largest in the world, housing more than 20,000 inmates on a given day.

*AP Wide World Photos*

Some authors have recognized that new-generation jails are too frequently run by old-style managers and that correctional personnel sometimes lack the training needed to make the transition to the direct style of supervision.[152] Others have suggested that managers of direct-supervision jails, especially mid-level managers, could benefit from clearer job descriptions and additional training.[153] In the words of one advocate of direct supervision, "Training becomes particularly critical in direct supervision jails where relationships are more immediate and are more complex."[154] Finally, those tasked with hiring have recommended psychological screening and intensive preemployment interviews to determine the suitability of applicants for correctional officer positions in direct-supervision jails.[155]

## Jails and the Future

In contrast to more visible issues confronting the justice system—such as the death penalty, gun control, the war on drugs, terrorism, and big-city gangs—jails have received relatively little attention from the media and have generally escaped close public scrutiny.[156] National efforts are under way, however, to improve the quality of jail life. Some changes involve adding crucial programs for inmates. An American Jail Association (AJA) study of drug-treatment programs in jails, for example, found that "a small fraction (perhaps fewer than 10%) of inmates needing drug treatment actually receive these services."[157]

Jail industries are another growing programmatic area. The best of them serve the community while training inmates in marketable skills.[158] In an exemplary effort to humanize its megajails, for example, the Los Angeles County Sheriff's Department opened an inmate telephone-answering service.[159] Many callers contact the sheriff's department daily, requesting information about the county's 22,000 jail inmates. These requests for information were becoming increasingly difficult to handle due to the growing fiscal constraints facing local government. To handle the huge number of calls effectively without tying up sworn law enforcement personnel, the department began using inmates specially trained to handle incoming calls. Eighty inmates were assigned to the project, with groups of different sizes covering shifts throughout the day. Each inmate staffer went through a training program to learn proper telephone procedures and how to run computer terminals containing routine data on the department's inmates. The new system now handles 4,000 telephone inquiries a day. The time needed to answer a call and to begin to provide information has dropped from 30 minutes under the old system to a remarkable 10 seconds today.

Jail "boot camps," like the one run by the Harris County, Texas, probation department, are also popular. Jail boot camps give offenders who are sentenced to probationary terms a taste of confinement and the rigors of life behind bars. The Harris County Courts Regimented Intensive Probation Program (CRIPP) facility began operation in 1991 and is located in Humble, Texas. Separate CRIPPs are run for about 400 male and 50 female probationers.[160] The most recent comprehensive study of jail boot camps found only ten such jail-based programs in the country,[161] but current numbers are probably higher.

Capturing much recent attention are **regional jails**—that is, jails that are built and run using the combined resources of a variety of local jurisdictions. Regional jails have begun to replace smaller and often antiquated local jails in at least a few locations. Regional jails, which are just beginning to come into their own, may develop quickly in Virginia, where the state, recognizing the economies of consolidation, offers to reimburse localities up to 50% of the cost of building regional jails.

One final element in the unfolding saga of jail development should be mentioned: the emergence of state jail standards. Thirty-two states have set standards for municipal and county jails.[162] In 25 states, those standards are mandatory. The purpose of jail standards is to identify basic minimum conditions necessary for inmate health and safety. On the national level, the Commission on Accreditation for Corrections, operated jointly by the American Correctional Association and the federal government, has developed its own set of jail standards,[163] as has the National Sheriff's Association. Both sets of standards are designed to ensure a minimal level of comfort and safety in local lockups. Increased standards, though, are costly. Local jurisdictions, already hard-pressed to meet other budgetary demands, will probably be slow to upgrade their jails to meet such external guidelines unless forced to do so. In a study of 61 jails that was designed to test compliance with National Sheriff's Association guidelines, Ken Kerle discovered that in many standards areas—especially those of tool control, armory planning, community resources, release preparation, and riot planning—the majority of jails were badly out of compliance.[164] Lack of a written plan was the most commonly cited reason for failing to meet the standards. Learn more about jails by visiting the American Jail Association via Web Extra 13–6 at cjtoday.com.

A Study
of Direct-Supervision Jails

**regional jail**

A jail that is built and run using the combined resources of a variety of local jurisdictions.

WEB EXTRA

## ETHICS AND PROFESSIONALISM

### American Jail Association Code of Ethics for Jail Officers

As an officer employed in a detention/correctional capacity, I swear (or affirm) to be a good citizen and a credit to my community, state, and nation at all times. I will abstain from all questionable behavior which might bring disrepute to the agency for which I work, my family, my community, and my associates. My lifestyle will be above and beyond reproach and I will constantly strive to set an example of a professional who performs his/her duties according to the laws of our country, state, and community and the policies, procedures, written and verbal orders, and regulations of the agency for which I work.

On the job I promise to:

**Keep** The institution secure so as to safeguard my community and the lives of the staff, inmates, and visitors on the premises.

**Work** With each individual firmly and fairly without regard to rank, status, or condition.

**Maintain** A positive demeanor when confronted with stressful situations of scorn, ridicule, danger, and/or chaos.

**Report** Either in writing or by word of mouth to the proper authorities those things which should be reported, and keep silent about matters which are to remain confidential according to the laws and rules of the agency and government.

**Manage** And supervise the inmates in an evenhanded and courteous manner.

**Refrain** At all times from becoming personally involved in the lives of the inmates and their families.

**Treat** All visitors to the jail with politeness and respect and do my utmost to ensure that they observe the jail regulations.

**Take** Advantage of all education and training opportunities designed to assist me to become a more competent officer.

**Communicate** With people in or outside of the jail, whether by phone, written word, or word of mouth, in such a way so as not to reflect in a negative manner upon my agency.

**Contribute** To a jail environment which will keep the inmate involved in activities designed to improve his/her attitude and character.

**Support** All activities of a professional nature through membership and participation that will continue to elevate the status of those who operate our nation's jails. Do my best through word and deed to present an image to the public at large of a jail professional, committed to progress for an improved and enlightened criminal justice system.

#### THINKING ABOUT ETHICS

1. Why does the AJA Code of Ethics require jail officers to "Take advantage of all education and training opportunities designed to assist [them] to become a more competent officer"? What does education have to do with ethics?
2. Are there any features or elements that you might add to this code? Are there any that you might delete?

*Source:* American Jail Association, *Code of Ethics for Jail Officers,* adopted January 10, 1991. Revised May 19, 1993. Reprinted with permission.

Information on Private Prisons

**privatization**

The movement toward the wider use of private prisons.

# Private Prisons

State-run prison systems have always contracted with private industries for food, psychological testing, training, and recreational and other services, and it is estimated that more than three dozen states today rely on private businesses to serve a variety of correctional needs. It follows, then, that states have now turned to private industry for the provision of prison space. The **privatization** movement, which began in the early 1980s, was slow to catch on, but it has since grown at a rapid pace. In 1986, only 2,620 prisoners could be found in privately run confinement facilities.[165] But by 2004, privately operated correctional facilities serving as prisons and jails held over 98,000 state and federal prisoners across 34 states and the District of Columbia.[166]

## CJ FUTURES

### Jails and the Future

A number of trends are beginning to emerge as America's jails meet the needs of the twenty-first century. Among them are these:

- A shift away from traditional publicly run facilities to jails that are operated by private corporations under contract with local government. More information on the privatization of prisons and jails is provided in this chapter.

- An increase in the proportion of inmates who are expected to pay for at least a portion of the expenses associated with their incarceration. In 1996, for example, pretrial inmates in the Broward County, Florida, jail system began paying a $2 per day fee for housing and meals. Charges are deducted from inmates' commissary funds, which are contributed by the inmates themselves or by family members. Inmates who feel they are unable to pay the fee are required to petition jail administrators and to demonstrate why they should not be required to pay.

- The growing use of computer-based inmate information systems that are integrated with networks used for the administration of court schedules, for docket monitoring, and for coordination with other criminal justice agencies. One jail consultant has gone so far as to claim that as a result of efficient and integrated information management systems, "paperwork will [soon] be a thing of the past."[1]

- A movement toward the professionalization of jail facilities, made possible through growing opportunities for accreditation. Accreditation programs, such as those offered through the American Correctional Association, the Commission on Accreditation for Law Enforcement Agencies, and the National Commission on Correctional Health Care, are already helping shield jail administrators and local governments from the threat of lawsuits by demonstrating adherence to professional standards.

- A movement toward the increased professionalization of jail personnel, made possible by certification programs like the Jail Manager Certification Program operated by the American Jail Association (AJA). Certified Jail Manager status has been available since 1997.

- A changing public climate that may soon shift away from the "get tough" policies of the past decade toward a more pragmatic emphasis on the needs of both inmates and administrators. Inmate needs in the areas of mental health counseling, suicide prevention, and opportunities for meaningful employment will be met in an effort to facilitate institutional administration.

- A greater use of direct-supervision jails, resulting in fewer internal problems and easier administration. The increased use of direct-supervision jails will heighten both inmate and staff morale in most locations.

- A growing use of inmate labor, as counties, communities, the nonprofit sector, and corporations begin to more fully recognize the advantages to be gained from the meaningful employment of inmates. As a consequence, more inmates will work, and those who do will be involved in an ever-widening sphere of activities. The increase in inmate labor will lead to a widening of partnerships among jails, their administrators, and other community groups. Corporate employers, for example, will begin to operate more and more training programs in jails with the goal of increasing workforce efficiency.

- A greater use of research in the field of jail operations, which will lead to better informed and more effective programs and strategies. Research showing that a greater number of female officers means fewer assaults overall, for example, should lead to the hiring of more women in the corrections field.

[1]Ron Carroll, "Jails and the Criminal Justice System in the Twenty-First Century," *American Jails* (March/April 1997), p. 31.
*References:* Ron Carroll, "Jails and the Criminal Justice System in the Twenty-First Century," *American Jails* (March/April 1997), pp. 26–31; Susan W. McCampbell, "The Paying Prisoner," *American Jails* (March/April 1997), pp. 37–43; Cindy Malm, "AJA Jail Manager Certification Program," *American Jails* (March/April 1997), p. 99; Rod Miller, "Inmate Labor in the Twenty-First Century," *American Jails* (March/April 1997), pp. 45–49; and Joseph R. Rowan, "Corrections in the Twenty-First Century," *American Jails* (March/April 1997), pp. 32–36.

---

**Private prisons** held 5.6% of all state prisoners and 13.7% of federal prisoners at the start of 2005. One source says that the growth rate of the private prison industry has been around 35% annually[167]—comparable to the highest growth rates anywhere in the corporate sector.

Privately run prisons are operated by Cornell Corrections, Corrections Corporation of America (CCA), Correctional Services Corporation (CSC), Wackenhut Corrections Corporation, and numerous other smaller companies. Most states that use private firms to supplement their prison resources contract with such companies to provide a full range of custodial and other correctional services. State correctional administrators use private companies to reduce overcrowding, lower operating expenses, and avoid lawsuits targeted at state officials and employees.[168] But some studies have shown that private prisons may not bring the kinds of cost savings that had been anticipated.[169] A 1996 study by the U.S. General Accounting Office,[170] for example, found "neither cost savings nor substantial differences in the quality of services" between private and publicly run prisons.[171] Similar findings were reported in a 2001 report by the Bureau of Justice Assistance. That report, entitled *Emerging Issues on Privatized Prisons*, found that "private prisons

**private prison**

A correctional institution operated by a private firm on behalf of a local or state government.

The 2,300-bed California City Correctional Center in the Mojave Desert town of California City. The facility, which opened in December 1999, was built by Corrections Corporation of America (CCA) to provide medium-security correctional services under a contract with the federal Bureau of Prisons. Nashville-based CCA says that it can run prisons as efficiently as the government, and its supporters claim that private prisons are the way of the future.
*AP Wide World Photos*

Log on to ResearchNavigator .com, and choose "Criminal Justice" under ContentSelect's Academic Journal Database. Enter the word "prison" in the search box, and click "Go." Select three articles that you find especially useful in understanding the role that prisons play in our society. (Choose full-text articles rather than abstracts whenever possible.) Perform the search again, this time using the word "jail." Select another three articles from the search results. Write a summary of each of the six articles you've selected, including complete source information—that is, article title, author (if available), date of publication, and source. Submit what you have written to your instructor if asked to do so. *Note:* This feature is available only if your instructor has chosen the Research Navigator option available with a new textbook.

offer only modest cost savings, which are basically a result of moderate reductions in staffing patterns, fringe benefits, and other labor-related costs."[172]

Many hurdles remain before the privatization movement can effectively provide large-scale custodial supervision. Among the most significant barriers to privatization are old state laws that prohibit private involvement in correctional management. Other practical hurdles exist as well. States that do contract with private firms may face the specter of strikes by correctional officers who do not come under state laws restricting the ability of public employees to strike. Moreover, since responsibility for the protection of inmate rights still lies with the state, their liability will not transfer to private corrections.[173] In today's legal climate, it is unclear whether a state can shield itself or its employees through private prison contracting, but it appears that the courts are unlikely to recognize such shielding. To limit their own liability, states will probably have to oversee private operations as well as set standards for training and custody. In 1997, in the case of *Richardson* v. *McKnight*,[174] the U.S. Supreme Court made it clear that correctional officers employed by a private firm are not entitled to qualified immunity from suits by prisoners charging a violation of Section 1983 of Title 42 of the U.S. Code. (See Chapter 8 for more information on Section 1983 lawsuits.) In 2001, however, in the case of *Correctional Services Corporation* v. *Malesko*,[175] the Court found that private corporations acting under color of federal law cannot be held responsible in a *Bivens* action because the purpose of *Bivens* (again, see Chapter 8) "is to deter individual federal officers from committing Constitutional violations."[176]

Perhaps the most serious legal issues confront states that contract to hold inmates outside of their own jurisdiction. In 1996, for example, two inmates escaped from a 240-man sex offender unit run by Corrections Corporation of America (CCA) under contract with the state of Oregon. Problems immediately arose because the CCA unit was located near Houston, Texas—not in Oregon, where the men had originally been sentenced to confinement. Following the escape, Texas officials were unsure whether they even had arrest power over the former prisoners, since they had not committed any crimes in Texas. Moreover, while prison escape is a crime under Texas law, the law applies only to state-run facilities, not to private facilities where correctional personnel are not employed by the state or empowered in any official capacity by state law. Harris County (Texas) Prosecutor John Holmes explained the situation this way: "They have not committed the offense of escape under Texas law . . . and the only reason at all that they're subject to being arrested and were arrested was because during their leaving the facility, they assaulted a guard and took his motor vehicle. That we can charge them with and have."[177]

Opponents of the movement toward privatization cite these and many other issues. They claim that, aside from legal concerns, cost reductions via the use of private facilities can only be achieved by lowering standards. They fear a return to the inhumane conditions of early jails, as private firms seek to turn prisons into profit-making operations. For states that do choose to contract with private firms, the National Institute of Justice (NIJ) recommends a "regular and systematic sampling" of former inmates to appraise prison conditions, as well as annual on-site inspections of each privately run institution. State personnel serving as monitors should be stationed in large facilities, says NIJ, and a "meticulous review" of all services should be conducted before the contract renewal date.[178] You can learn more about prison privatization at Library Extra 13–9 and via Web Extra 13–7 at cjtoday.com.

LIBRARY EXTRA
WEB EXTRA

## CJ TODAY EXHIBIT 13-3

### Arguments For and Against the Privatization of Prisons

**REASONS TO PRIVATIZE**

1. Private operators can provide construction financing options that allow the government to pay only for capacity as needed in lieu of assuming long-term debt.
2. Private companies offer state-of-the-art correctional facility designs that are efficient to operate and that are based on cost–benefit considerations.
3. Private operators typically design and construct a new correctional facility in half the time it takes to build a comparable government project.
4. Private companies provide government with the convenience and accountability of one entity for all compliance issues.
5. Private companies can mobilize rapidly and specialize in unique facility missions.
6. Private companies provide economic development opportunities by hiring and purchasing locally.
7. Government can reduce or share its liability exposure by contracting with private corrections companies.
8. Government can retain flexibility by limiting the contract's duration and by specifying the facility's mission.
9. The addition of alternative service providers injects competition among both public and private organizations.

**REASONS NOT TO PRIVATIZE**

1. There are certain responsibilities that only the government should meet, such as public safety. The government has legal, political, and moral obligations to provide incarceration. Constitutional issues underlie both public and private corrections and involve deprivation of liberty, discipline, and preservation of the rights of inmates. Related issues include use of force, equitable hiring practices, and segregation.
2. Few private companies are available from which to choose.
3. Private operators may be inexperienced with key corrections issues.
4. A private operator may become a monopoly through political ingratiation, favoritism, and so on.
5. Government may, over time, lose the capability to perform the corrections function.
6. The profit motive will inhibit the proper performance of corrections duties. Private companies have financial incentives to cut corners.
7. The procurement process is slow, inefficient, and open to risks.
8. Creating a good, clear contract is a daunting task.
9. The lack of enforcement remedies in contracts leaves only termination or lawsuits as recourse.

*Source:* Dennis Cunningham, "Public Strategies for Private Prisons." Paper presented at the Private Prison Workshop, January 29–30, 1999, at the Institute on Criminal Justice, University of Minnesota Law School.

## SUMMARY

Prisons are long-term secure confinement facilities in which convicted offenders serve time as punishment for breaking the law. Jails, in contrast, are short-term confinement facilities that were originally intended to hold suspects following arrest and pending trial. Differences between the two types of institutions have begun to blur, however, as large and medium-size jails across the country are increasingly being called on to house offenders who have been convicted of relatively minor crimes and to accommodate a portion of our country's overflowing prison population.

The state of today's prisons is largely the result of historical efforts to humanize the treatment of offenders, coupled with recent attempts to have the prison experience reflect prevailing social attitudes toward crime and punishment. "Doing time for crime" is our modern answer to the corporal punishments of centuries past. Even so, contemporary corrections is far from a panacea, and questions remain about the conditions of imprisonment in today's correctional facilities. Many prisons are dangerous places to live and work, others are overcrowded, and new ones are expensive to build. The emphasis on security that characterizes correctional staff members and prison administrators leaves little room for effective treatment programs. Moreover, even with ongoing prison expansion, prison overcrowding is barely held at bay, and a continuing just deserts philosophy strongly influences today's correctional policy. The just deserts philosophy is characterized by a "get tough" attitude that continues to swell prison populations even as it reduces opportunities for change among individual inmates. It is a highly pragmatic philosophy, based at least partially on studies demonstrating the clear likelihood of recidivism among correctional clients, combined with a strong belief that nothing works to rehabilitate criminal offenders.

As a result of these considerations, today's imprisonment practices rest on a policy of frustration. Prisons exist in a kind of limbo, continuing their role as warehouses for those who cannot be trusted or reformed. The heightened interest in efficient technologies of secure imprisonment and the need for court-ordered reforms are signs that society has given up any hope of successful large-scale reformation among inmate populations.

## DISCUSSION QUESTIONS

1. What types of criminal punishments were used before the advent of imprisonment as a criminal sanction? How have early punishments influenced modern correctional philosophy?

2. Trace the historical development of prisons, beginning with the Pennsylvania system. How has correctional practice in America changed over time? What changes do you predict for the future?

3. What are today's prisons like? What purposes do they serve?

4. What are the social characteristics of today's prisoners? What gender and racial disparities, if any, exist in today's prison populations?

5. What is the just deserts model of corrections? Explain the pros and cons of this model. How has it led to an increased use of imprisonment and to prison overcrowding?

6. What is the relationship, if any, between changes in the rate of criminal offending and changes in the rate of imprisonment in America during the last decade? What is the reason for that relationship?

7. What role do jails play in American corrections? What are some of the issues that jail administrators currently face?

8. What is the role of private prisons today? What will be the state of private prisons two or three decades from now?

## WEB QUEST

Visit the Corrections Connection on the World Wide Web (http://www.corrections.com). What are some of the many features available at this site? Explore the Legal Issues bulletin board at the Corrections Connection site to learn about the latest legal issues of concern to corrections professionals. What are some of those issues? Then, participate in one of the Corrections Connections chat rooms. (The "Corrections Lobby" is often a good place to find an ongoing chat.) What topics are being discussed? If no one is in the chat room when you enter, visit the Listserve message boards, and list the most recent topics being discussed. Submit this information to your instructor if asked to do so.

To complete this Web Quest online, go to the Web Quest module in Chapter 13 of the *Criminal Justice Today* Companion Website at cjtoday.com.

## NOTES

i. Zebulon R. Brockway, *The Ideal of a True Prison System for a State* (1865).

ii. Jeff Beard, "The Complex Problem of Offender Reentry," *Corrections Today*, April 2005, p. 8.

iii. Don Myers, "Crime: What Will It Take to Reclaim Our Country?" *USA Today*, May 26, 1995.

iv. James A. Gondles, Jr., "Who Should Be behind Bars?" *Corrections Today*, August 2002. Web posted at http://www.aca.org/admin/pix/ctmagarticles/200208_whoshouldbebehindbars.pdf (accessed September 12, 2002).

v. Bureau of Justice Statistics, *Prisoners in 1998* (Washington, DC: Author, 1999), p. 7.

1. Quoted in Gail S. Funke, *National Conference on Prison Industries: Discussions and Recommendations* (Washington, DC: U.S. Government Printing Office, 1986), p. 23.

2. Camden Pelham, *Chronicles of Crime: A Series of Memoirs and Anecdotes of Notorious Characters* (London: T. Miles, 1887), pp. 28–30.

3. This section owes much to Harry Elmer Barnes and Negley K. Teeters, *New Horizons in Criminology*, 3rd ed. (Englewood Cliffs, NJ: Prentice Hall, 1959).

4. Ibid., p. 290.

5. Ann O'Hanlon, "New Interest in Corporal Punishment: Several States Weigh Get-Tough Measures," *Washington Post* wire service, March 5, 1995.

6. Barnes and Teeters, *New Horizons in Criminology*, p. 292.

7. Ibid.

8. Ibid., p. 293.

9. Arthur Evans Wood and John Barker Waite, *Crime and Its Treatment: Social and Legal Aspects of Criminology* (New York: American Book Company, 1941), p. 488.

10. John Howard, *State of Prisons* (London, 1777; reprint, New York: E. P. Dutton, 1929).

11. Although some writers hold that the Quakers originated the concept of solitary confinement for prisoners, there is evidence that the practice already existed in England before 1789. John Howard, for example, described solitary confinement in use at Reading Bridewell in the 1780s.

12. Vergil L. Williams, *Dictionary of American Penology: An Introduction* (Westport, CT: Greenwood Press, 1979), p. 200.

13. Barnes and Teeters, *New Horizons in Criminology*, p. 348.

14. Williams, *Dictionary of American Penology*, p. 29.

15. With regard to cost, supporters of the Pennsylvania system argued that it was actually less expensive than the Auburn style of imprisonment because it led more quickly to reformation.

16. Williams, *Dictionary of American Penology*, p. 30.

17. Gustave de Beaumont and Alexis de Tocqueville, *On the Penitentiary System in the United States, and Its Application in France* (Philadelphia: Carey, Lea and Blanchard, 1833).

18. Barnes and Teeters, *New Horizons in Criminology*, p. 428.

19. Ibid.

20. Ibid.

21. Wood and Waite, *Crime and Its Treatment*, p. 555, citing U.S. Bureau of Labor statistics.

22. See North Carolina Department of Corrections, Correction Enterprises website, http://www. doc.state.nc.us/eprise (accessed October 20, 2005).

23. See U.S. Department of Justice, Federal Prison Industries, Inc., website, http://www.unicor.gov.

24. Robert Mintz, "Federal Prison Industry—The Green Monster, Part One: History and Background," *Crime and Social Justice*, Vol. 6 (Fall/Winter 1976), pp. 41–48.

25. William G. Saylor and Gerald G. Gaes, "PREP Study Links UNICOR Work Experience with Successful Post-Release Outcome," *Corrections Compendium* (October 1994), pp. 5–6, 8.

26. Criminal Justice Associates, *Private Sector Involvement in Prison-Based Businesses: A National Assessment* (Washington, DC: U.S. Government Printing Office, 1985). See also National Institute of Justice, *Corrections and the Private Sector* (Washington, DC: U.S. Government Printing Office, 1985).

27. The PIE Certification Program was first authorized under the Justice System Improvement Act of 1979 (Public Law 96-157, Sec. 827) and later expanded under the Justice Assistance Act of 1984 (Public Law 98-473, Sec. 819). The Crime Control Act of 1990 (Public Law 101-647) authorizes continuation of the program indefinitely.

28. Domingo S. Herraiz, *Prison Industry Enhancement Certification Program* (Washington, DC: Bureau of Justice Assistance, 2004).

29. Barnes and Teeters, *New Horizons in Criminology*, p. 355.

30. Williams, *Dictionary of Penology*, p. 225.

31. Ibid., p. 64.

32. Ibid., p. 227.

33. Donal E. J. MacNamara, "Medical Model in Corrections: Requiescat in Pace," in Fred Montanino, ed., *Incarceration: The Sociology of Imprisonment* (Beverly Hills, CA: Sage, 1978).

34. For a description of the community-based format in its heyday, see Andrew T. Scull, *Decarceration: Community Treatment and the Deviant—A Radical View* (Englewood Cliffs, NJ: Prentice Hall, 1977).

35. Ibid., p. 51.

36. Williams, *Dictionary of American Penology*, p. 45.

37. Ibid.

38. Clemens Bartollas, *Introduction to Corrections* (New York: Harper and Row, 1981), pp. 166–167.

39. The act also established home furloughs and community treatment centers.

40. National Advisory Commission on Criminal Justice Standards and Goals, Standard 2.17, Part 2c.

41. *Recidivism* can be defined in various ways according to the purpose the term is intended to serve in a particular study or report. Recidivism is usually defined as rearrest (versus reconviction) and generally includes a time span of five years, although some Bureau of Justice Statistics studies have used six years, and other studies one or two years, as definitional criteria.

42. Various advocates of the just deserts, or justice, model can be identified. For a detailed description of rehabilitation and just deserts, see Michael A. Pizzi, Jr., "The Medical Model and the 100 Years War," *Law Enforcement News*, July 7, 1986, pp. 8, 13; and MacNamara, "Medical Model in Corrections."

43. Bureau of Justice Statistics, *Annual Report, 1987* (Washington, DC: BJS, 1988), p. 70.

44. Ibid.

45. Ibid.

46. Robert Martinson, "What Works: Questions and Answers about Prison Reform," *Public Interest*, No. 35 (1974), pp. 22–54. See also Douglas Lipton, Robert M. Martinson, and Judith Wilkes, *The Effectiveness of Correctional Treatment: A Survey of Treatment Evaluation Studies* (New York: Praeger, 1975).

47. L. Sechrest, S. White, and E. Brown, eds., *The Rehabilitation of Criminal Offenders: Problems and Prospects* (Washington, DC: National Academy of Sciences, 1979).

48. U.S. Department of Justice, *Office of Justice Programs Fiscal Year 2000 Program Plan: Resources for the Field* (Washington, DC: Office of Juvenile Justice and Delinquency Prevention, 1999).

49. Timothy A. Hughes, Doris James Wilson, and Allen J. Beck, *Trends in State Parole, 1990–2000* (Washington, DC: Bureau of Justice Statistics, 2001).

50. Ibid.; and Paige M. Harrison and Allen J. Beck, *Prisoners in 2004* (Washington, DC: Bureau of Justice Statistics, 2005). Figures as of January 1 of each year.

51. Lynn S. Branham, *The Use of Incarceration in the United States: A Look at the Present and the Future* (Washington, DC: American Bar Association, 1992).

52. "Reliance on Prisons Is Costly but Ineffective, ABA Panel Says," *Criminal Justice Newsletter*, April 15, 1992, p. 7.

53. *Criminal Justice Newsletter*, February 3, 1992, p. 8.

54. American Correctional Association, *Vital Statistics in Corrections* (Laurel, MD: ACA, 2000).

55. Allen J. Beck and Paige M. Harrison, *Prisoners in 2000* (Washington, DC: Bureau of Justice Statistics, 2002).

56. Jeanne B. Stinchcomb, "From Rehabilitation to Retribution: Examining Public Policy Paradigms and Personnel Education Patterns in Corrections," *American Journal of Criminal Justice*, Vol. 27, No. 1 (2002), p. 3.

57. Although many other states require inmates to work on road maintenance, and though the inmates are typically supervised by armed guards, Alabama became the first state in modern times to shackle prisoners.

58. See "Back on the Chain Gang: Florida Becomes Third State to Resurrect Forced Labor," Associated Press wire service, November 22, 1995.

59. Florida Department of Corrections, *Corrections in Florida: 1998 Opinion Survey*. Web posted at http://www.dc.state.fl.us/pub/survey/index.html (accessed January 24, 2001).

60. Lori Sharn and Shannon Tangonan, "Chain Gangs Back in Alabama," *USA Today*, May 4, 1995, p. 3A.

61. Ibid.

62. See Debra L. Dailey, *Summary of the 1998 Annual Conference of the National Association of Sentencing Commissions*. Web posted at http://www.ussc.gov/states/dailefsr.pdf (accessed October 30, 2001).

63. The state of Washington is generally credited with having been the first state to pass a three-strikes law by voter initiative (in 1993).

64. For a good overview of the topic, see David Shichor and Dale K. Sechrest, *Three Strikes and You're Out: Vengeance as Public Policy* (Thousand Oaks, CA: Sage, 1996).

65. David S. Broder, "When Tough Isn't Smart," *Washington Post* Wire Service, March 24, 1994.

66. "The Klaas Case and the Crime Bill," *Washington Post* wire service, February 21, 1994.

67. Quinlan is now president of Corrections Corporation of America.

68. David Lawsky, "Prison Wardens Decry Overcrowding, Survey Says," Reuters wire service, December 21, 1994.

69. James J. Stephan and Jennifer C. Karberg, *Census of State and Federal Correctional Facilities, 2000* (Washington, DC: Bureau of Justice Statistics, 2003).

70. Harrison and Beck, *Prisoners in 2004*. This number includes state and federal prisoners held in local jails.

71. Ibid.

72. Ibid.

73. Thomas P. Bonczar, *Prevalence of Imprisonment in the U.S. Population, 1974–2001* (Washington, DC: Bureau of Justice Statistics, 2003), p. 1.

74. Harrison and Beck, *Prisoners in 2004*.

75. Bureau of Justice Statistics, *National Corrections Reporting Program, 1998* (Ann Arbor, MI: Interuniversity Consortium for Political and Social Research, 2001).

76. Harrison and Beck, *Prisoners in 2004*.

77. Bonczar, *Prevalence of Imprisonment in the U.S. Population, 1974–2001*, p. 1.

78. Ibid., p. 8.

79. The number includes both state and federal prisoners.

80. Information in this paragraph comes from Harrison and Beck, *Prisoners in 2004.*

81. David F. Greenberg and Valerie West, "State Prison Populations and Their Growth, 1971–1991," *Criminology*, Vol. 39, No. 3 (2001), p. 615.

82. Robert M. Carter, Richard A. McGee, and E. Kim Nelson, *Corrections in America* (Philadelphia: J. B. Lippincott, 1975), pp. 122–123.

83. James J. Stephan, *State Prison Expenditures 2001* (Washington, DC: Bureau of Justice Statistics, 2004); and e-mail correspondence with Susan Allison, Federal Bureau of Prisons, October 29, 2001.

84. Caryl Clarke, "Paying for Life," *York (Pa.) Daily Record*, May 24, 2002; citing Allen Beck at the Bureau of Justice Statistics. Web posted at http://www.ydr.com/main/justice/1justice1.shtml (accessed September 22, 2002).

85. Harrison and Beck, *Prisoners in 2004.*

86. Federal Bureau of Investigation, *Uniform Crime Reports: Crime in the United States, 2004* (Washington, DC: U.S. Government Printing Office, 2005), and other years.

87. Adapted from Bureau of Justice Statistics, *Report to the Nation on Crime and Justice*, 2nd ed. (Washington, DC: U.S. Government Printing Office, 1988), p. 108.

88. *Rhodes* v. *Chapman*, 452 U.S. 337 (1981).

89. D. Greenberg, "The Incapacitative Effect of Imprisonment, Some Estimates," *Law and Society Review*, Vol. 9 (1975), pp. 541–580. See also Jacqueline Cohen, *Incapacitating Criminals: Recent Research Findings,* National Institute of Justice Research in Brief (Washington, DC: National Institute of Justice, December 1983).

90. For information on identifying dangerous repeat offenders, see M. Chaiken and J. Chaiken, "Selecting Career Criminals for Priority Prosecution," final report (Cambridge, MA: Abt Associates, 1987).

91. J. Monahan, *Predicting Violent Behavior: An Assessment of Clinical Techniques* (Beverly Hills, CA: Sage, 1981).

92. S. Van Dine, J. P. Conrad, and S. Dinitz, *Restraining the Wicked: The Incapacitation of the Dangerous Offender* (Lexington, MA: Lexington Books, 1979).

93. Paul Gendreau, Tracy Little, and Claire Goggin, "A Meta-Analysis of the Predictors of Adult Offender Recidivism: What Works!" *Criminology*, Vol. 34, No. 4 (November 1996), pp. 575–607.

94. *Lynce* v. *Mathis*, 519 U.S. 443 (1997).

95. George Camp and Camille Camp, "Stopping Escapes: Perimeter Security," *Prison Construction Bulletin* (Washington, DC: National Institute of Justice, 1987).

96. Adapted from G. A. Grizzle and A. D. Witte, "Efficiency in Collections Agencies," in Gordon P. Whitaker and Charles D. Phillips, eds., *Evaluating the Performance of Criminal Justice Agencies* (Washington, DC: National Institute of Justice, 1983).

97. Patricia L. Hardyman et al., *Internal Prison Classification Systems: Case Studies in Their Development and Implementation* (Washington, DC: National Institutions of Corrections, 2002), from which some of the wording in this section is taken.

98. Ibid.

99. *Johnson* v. *California*, U.S. Supreme Court, No. 03-636 (decided February 23, 2005).

100. U.S. Bureau of Prisons, *Facilities.* Web posted at http://www.bop.gov/map.html (accessed February 2, 2005).

101. Some of the information in this section is derived from Bureau of Prisons, *About the Federal Bureau of Prisons* (Washington, DC: BOP, 2001).

102. Includes federal prisoners held in Bureau of Prisons facilities and privately operated institutions.

103. Bureau of Prisons, "The Bureau in Brief." Web posted at http://www.bop.gov/ipapg/ipabib.html (accessed July 5, 2005).

104. Most of the information in this section comes from telephone conversations with and faxed information from the federal Bureau of Prisons, August 25, 1995.

105. For additional information, see Dennis Cauchon, "The Alcatraz of the Rockies," *USA Today*, November 16, 1994, p. 6A.

106. "Congress OKs Inmate Fees to Offset Costs of Prison," *Criminal Justice Newsletter*, October 15, 1992, p. 6.

107. James J. Stephan, *State Prison Expenditures* (Washington, DC: Bureau of Justice Statistics, 2004), p. 3.

108. National Institute of Corrections website, http://www.nicic.org (accessed March 2, 2002).

109. Ibid.

110. Doris J. James, *Profile of Jail Inmates, 2002* (Washington, DC: Bureau of Justice Statistics, 2004), p. 2.

111. Paige M. Harrison and Allen J. Beck, *Prison and Jail Inmates at Midyear 2004* (Washington, DC: Bureau of Justice Statistics, 2005).

112. Ibid.

113. James, *Profile of Jail Inmates, 2002*, p. 1.

114. Harrison and Beck, *Prison and Jail Inmates at Midyear 2004* (Washington, DC: Bureau of Justice Statistics, 2005).

115. James J. Stephan, *Census of Jails, 1999* (Washington, DC: Bureau of Justice Statistics, 2001).

116. Ibid.

117. Ibid.

118. Three percent of jail inmates report being of more than one race.

119. James, *Profile of Jail Inmates, 2002*, p. 2.

120. Ibid.

121. Stephan, *Census of Jails, 1999*.

122. See Gale Holland, "L.A. Jail Makes Delayed Debut," *USA Today*, January 27, 1997, p. 3A.

123. See Dale Stockton, "Cook County Illinois Sheriff's Office," *Police*, October 1996, pp. 40–43. The Cook County Department of Correction operates ten separate jails, which house approximately 9,000 inmates. The department employs more than 2,800 correctional officers.

124. Ibid.

125. Ibid.

126. William Reginald Mills and Heather Barrett, "Meeting the Special Challenge of Providing Health Care to Women Inmates in the '90's," *American Jails*, Vol. 4, No. 3 (September/October 1990), p. 55.

127. Ibid., p. 21.

128. Ibid.

129. Ibid., p. 55.

130. American Correctional Association, *Vital Statistics in Corrections*.

131. Mills and Barrett, "Meeting the Special Challenge of Providing Health Care," p. 55.

132. Ibid.

133. Linda L. Zupan, "Women Corrections Officers in the Nation's Largest Jails," *American Jails* (January/February 1991), pp. 59–62.

134. Linda L. Zupan, "Women Corrections Officers in Local Jails," paper presented at the annual meeting of the Academy of Criminal Justice Sciences, Nashville, TN, March 1991.

135. Ibid., p. 6.

136. "Jail Overcrowding in Houston Results in Release of Inmates," *Criminal Justice Newsletter*, October 15, 1990, p. 5.

137. Bureau of Justice Statistics, *Census of Local Jails, 1988* (Washington, DC: BJS, 1991), p. 31.

138. Kathleen Maguire and Ann L. Pastore, *Sourcebook of Criminal Justice Statistics, 1994* (Washington, DC: U.S. Government Printing Office, 1995).

139. Paige M. Harrison and Allen J. Beck, *Prison and Jail Inmates at Midyear 2004* (Washington, DC: BJS, 2005).

140. Ibid.

141. Harrison and Beck, *Prisoners in 2004*.

142. Stephan, *Census of Jails, 1999*.

143. George P. Wilson and Harvey L. McMurray, "System Assessment of Jail Overcrowding Assumptions," paper presented at the annual meeting of the Academy of Criminal Justice Sciences, Nashville, TN, March 1991.

144. Andy Hall, *Systemwide Strategies to Alleviate Jail Crowding* (Washington, DC: National Institute of Justice, 1987).

145. Ibid.

146. Linda L. Zupan and Ben A. Menke, "The New Generation Jail: An Overview," in Joel A. Thompson and G. Larry Mays, eds., *American Jails: Public Policy Issues* (Chicago: Nelson-Hall, 1991), p. 180.

147. Ibid.

148. Herbert R. Sigurdson, Billy Wayson, and Gail Funke, "Empowering Middle Managers of Direct Supervision Jails," *American Jails* (Winter 1990), p. 52.

149. Byron Johnson, "Exploring Direct Supervision: A Research Note," *American Jails* (March/April 1994), pp. 63–64.

150. H. Sigurdson, *The Manhattan House of Detention: A Study of Podular Direct Supervision* (Washington, DC: National Institute of Corrections, 1985). For similar conclusions, see Robert Conroy, Wantland J. Smith, and Linda L. Zupan, "Officer Stress in the Direct Supervision Jail: A Preliminary Case Study," *American Jails* (November/December 1991), p. 36.

151. W. Raymond Nelson and Russell M. Davis, "Podular Direct Supervision: The First Twenty Years," *American Jails* (July/August 1995), p. 17.

152. Jerry W. Fuqua, "New Generation Jails: Old Generation Management," *American Jails* (March/April 1991), pp. 80–83.

153. Sigurdson, Wayson, and Funke, "Empowering Middle Managers of Direct Supervision Jails."

154. Duncan J. McCulloch and Tim Stiles, "Technology and the Direct Supervision Jail," *American Jails* (Winter 1990), pp. 97–102.

155. Susan W. McCampbell, "Direct Supervision: Looking for the Right People," *American Jails* (November/December 1990), pp. 68–69.

156. For a good review of the future of American jails, see Ron Carroll, "Jails and the Criminal Justice System in the Twenty-First Century," *American Jails* (March/April 1997), pp. 26–31.

157. Robert L. May II, Roger H. Peters, and William D. Kearns, "The Extent of Drug Treatment Programs in Jails: A Summary Report," *American Jails* (September/October 1990), pp. 32–34.

158. See, for example, John W. Dietler, "Jail Industries: The Best Thing That Can Happen to a Sheriff," *American Jails* (July/August 1990), pp. 80–83.

159. Robert Osborne, "Los Angeles County Sheriff Opens New Inmate Answering Service," *American Jails* (July/August 1990), pp. 61–62.

160. Robert J. Hunter, "A Locally Operated Boot Camp," *American Jails* (July/August 1994), pp. 13–15.

161. James Austin, Michael Jones, and Melissa Bolyard, *The Growing Use of Jail Boot Camps: The Current State of the Art* (Washington, DC: National Institute of Justice, 1993).

162. Tom Rosazza, "Jail Standards: Focus on Change," *American Jails* (November/December 1990), pp. 84–87.

163. American Correctional Association, *Manual of Standards for Adult Local Detention Facilities*, 3rd ed. (College Park, MD: ACA, 1991).

164. Ken Kerle, "National Sheriff's Association Jail Audit Review," *American Jails* (Spring 1987), pp. 13–21.

165. Beck and Harrison, *Prisoners in 2000,* p. 7.

166. Harrison and Beck, *Prisoners in 2004,* p. 7, from which much of the information in this section is taken.

167. Eric Bates, "Private Prisons: Over the Next Five Years Analysts Expect the Private Share of the Prison 'Market' to More Than Double," *The Nation*, Vol. 266, No. 1 (1998), pp. 11–18.

168. Gary Fields, "Privatized Prisons Pose Problems," *USA Today*, November 11, 1996, p. 3A.

169. Dale K. Sechrest and David Shichor, "Private Jails: Locking Down the Issues," *American Jails*, March/April 1997, pp. 9–18.

170. U.S. General Accounting Office, *Private and Public Prisons: Studies Comparing Operational Costs and/or Quality of Service* (Washington, DC: U.S. Government Printing Office, 1996).

171. Sechrest and Shichor, "Private Jails," p. 10.

172. James Austin and Garry Coventry, *Emerging Issues on Privatized Prisons* (Washington, DC: Bureau of Justice Statistics, 2001), p. ix.

173. For a more detailed discussion of this issue, see Austin and Coventry, *Emerging Issues on Privatized Prisons.*

174. *Richardson* v. *McKnight*, 117 S.Ct. 2100, 138 L.Ed.2d 540 (1997).

175. *Correctional Services Corporation* v. *Malesko*, 122 S.Ct. 515 (2001).

176. Ibid.

177. Quoted in Bates, "Private Prisons."

178. Judith C. Hackett et al., "Contracting for the Operation of Prisons and Jails," *National Institute of Justice Research in Brief* (June 1987), p. 6.

# CHAPTER 14

# Prison Life

## OUTLINE

- Introduction
- The Male Inmate's World
- The Female Inmate's World
- The Staff World
- Prison Riots
- Prisoners' Rights
- Issues Facing Prisons Today

## LEARNING OBJECTIVES

After reading this chapter, you should be able to:

- Describe the realities of prison life and prison subculture from the inmate's point of view.
- Explain the concept of prisonization.
- Illustrate the significant differences between men's prisons and women's prisons.
- Describe the realities of prison life from the correctional officer's point of view.
- Describe the causes of prison riots, and list the stages through which most riots progress.
- Explain the nature of the hands-off doctrine, and discuss the status of that doctrine today.
- Discuss the legal aspects of prisoners' rights, and explain the consequences of precedent-setting U.S. Supreme Court cases in the area of prisoners' rights.
- Explain the balancing test established by the U.S. Supreme Court as it relates to the rights of prisoners.
- Explain state-created rights within the context of corrections.
- Describe the major problems and issues that prisons face today.

*Prisons are necessary for punishment. Too often, however, inmates leave them unprepared to take up productive roles in their communities.*

—President George W. Bush[1]

"The degree of civilization in a society can be judged by entering its prisons.

—Fyodor Dostoyevsky

Prison walls do not form a barrier separating prison inmates from the protections of the Constitution.

—*Turner* v. *Safley*, 482 U.S. 78 (1987)"

## KEY CONCEPTS

### TERMS

| | | |
|---|---|---|
| balancing test | hands-off doctrine | security threat group (STG) |
| civil death | prison argot | total institution |
| deliberate indifference | prison subculture | |
| grievance procedure | prisonization | |

### CASES

| | | |
|---|---|---|
| *Block* v. *Rutherford* | *Hudson* v. *Palmer* | *Pell* v. *Procunier* |
| *Bounds* v. *Smith* | *Johnson* v. *Avery* | *Pennsylvania Department of Corrections* v. |
| *Cruz* v. *Beto* | *Jones* v. *North Carolina Prisoners' Labor* | *Yeskey* |
| *Estelle* v. *Gamble* | *Union* | *Ruiz* v. *Estelle* |
| *Helling* v. *McKinney* | *Katz* v. *U.S.* | *Sandin* v. *Conner* |
| *Houchins* v. *KQED, Inc.* | *Overton* v. *Bazzetta* | *Wolff* v. *McDonnell* |

The original full-text court opinion for each of these cases is available on the CD-ROM that accompanies this book.

# Introduction

Hear the author discuss
this chapter at
**cjtoday.com**

For many years, very few citizens cared about prisoners and prison conditions. The philosophy held by most people was "out of sight, out of mind." In the middle of the last century, however, this attitude started to change. Concerned citizens began to offer their services to prison administrations, neighborhoods began accepting work-release prisoners and halfway houses, and social scientists initiated a serious study of prison life.

This chapter describes the realities of prison life today, including prisoner lifestyles, prison subcultures, sexuality in prison, prison violence, and prisoners' rights and grievance procedures. We will discuss both the inmate world and the staff world. A separate section on women in prison details the social structure of women's prisons, daily life in those facilities, and the various types of female inmates. We begin with a brief overview of early research on prison life.

## Research on Prison Life—Total Institutions

In 1935, Hans Reimer, who was then chairman of the Department of Sociology at Indiana University, set the tone for studies of prison life when he voluntarily served three months in prison as an incognito participant-observer.[2] Reimer reported the results of his studies to the American Prison Association, stimulating many other, albeit less spectacular, efforts to examine prison life. Other early studies include Donald Clemmer's *The Prison Community* (1940),[3] Gresham Sykes's *The Society of Captives* (1958),[4] Richard Cloward and Donald Cressey's *Theoretical Studies in Social Organization of the Prison* (1960),[5] and Cressey's edited volume, *The Prison* (1961).[6]

These studies and others focused primarily on maximum-security prisons for men. They treated correctional institutions as formal or complex organizations and employed the analytic techniques of organizational sociology, industrial psychology, and administrative science.[7] As modern writers on prisons have observed, "The prison was compared to a primitive society, isolated from the outside world, functionally integrated by a delicate system of mechanisms, which kept it precariously balanced between anarchy and accommodation."[8]

Another approach to the study of prison life was developed by Erving Goffman, who coined the term **total institutions** in a 1961 study of prisons and mental hospitals.[9] Goffman described total institutions as places where the same people work, recreate, worship, eat, and sleep together daily. Such places include prisons, concentration camps, mental hospitals, seminaries, and other facilities in which residents are cut off from the larger society either forcibly or willingly. Total institutions are small societies. They evolve their own distinctive values and styles of life and pressure residents to fulfill rigidly prescribed behavioral roles.

**total institution**

An enclosed facility separated from society both socially and physically, where the inhabitants share all aspects of their lives daily.

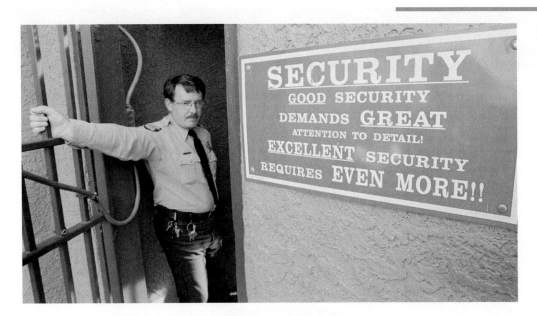

A notice posted on a prison fence. Custody and security remain the primary concerns of prison staffers throughout the country—a fact reinforced by this notice.

*Mike Fiala, Agence France Presse, Getty Images*

Generally speaking, the work of prison researchers built on findings of other social scientists who discovered that any group with similar characteristics confined in the same place at the same time develops its own subculture. Prison subcultures, described in the next section, also provide the medium through which prison values are communicated and expectations are made known. Learn more about prison research via **Library Extra 14–1** at cjtoday.com.

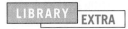

# The Male Inmate's World

Two social realities coexist in prison settings. One is the official structure of rules and procedures put in place by the wider society and enforced by prison staff. The other is the more informal but decidedly more powerful inmate world.[10] The inmate world, best described by how closely it touches the lives of inmates, is controlled by **prison subculture**. The realities of prison life—including a large and often densely packed inmate population that must look to the prison environment for all its needs—mean that prison subculture develops independently of the plans of prison administrators and is not easily subjected to the control of prison authorities.

Inmates entering prison discover a whole new social world in which they must participate or face consequences ranging from dangerous ostracism to physical violence and homicide.[11] The socialization of new inmates into the prison subculture has been described as a process of **"prisonization"**[12]—the new prisoner's learning of convict values, attitudes, roles, and even language. By the time this process is complete, new inmates have become "cons." Gresham Sykes and Sheldon Messinger recognized five elements of the prison code in 1960[13]:

1. Don't interfere with the interests of other inmates. Never rat on a con.
2. Don't lose your head. Play it cool and do your own time.
3. Don't exploit inmates. Don't steal. Don't break your word. Be right.
4. Don't whine. Be a man.
5. Don't be a sucker. Don't trust the guards or staff.

Some criminologists have suggested that the prison code is simply a reflection of general criminal values. If so, these values are brought to the institution rather than created there. Either way, the power and pervasiveness of the prison code require convicts to conform to the worldview held by the majority of prisoners.

Stanton Wheeler, Ford Foundation Professor of Law and Social Sciences at the University of Washington, closely examined the concept of prisonization in an early study of the Washington State Reformatory.[14] Wheeler found that the degree of prisonization experienced by inmates tends to vary over time. He described changing levels of inmate commitment to prison norms and values by way of a U-shaped curve. When an inmate first enters prison, Wheeler said, the conventional values of outside society are of paramount importance. As time passes, inmates adopt the

**prison subculture**

The values and behavioral patterns characteristic of prison inmates. Prison subculture has been found to be surprisingly consistent across the country.

**prisonization**

The process whereby newly institutionalized offenders come to accept prison lifestyles and criminal values. Although many inmates begin their prison experience with only a few values that support criminal behavior, the socialization experience they undergo while incarcerated leads to a much greater acceptance of such values.

## CJ TODAY EXHIBIT 14-1

### Prison Argot: The Language of Confinement

Writers who have studied prison life often comment on prisoners' use of a special language or slang termed *prison argot*. This language generally describes the roles assigned by prison culture to types of inmates as well as to prison activities. This box lists a few of the many words and phrases identified in studies by different authors. The first group of words are characteristic of men's prisons; the second group have been used in women's prisons.

#### MEN'S PRISON SLANG

Ace duce: A best friend

Badge (or bull, hack, the man, or screw): A correctional officer

Banger (or burner, shank, or sticker): A knife

Billy: A white man

Boneyard: The conjugal visiting area

Cat-J (or J-cat): A prisoner in need of psychological or psychiatric therapy or medication

Cellie: A cell mate

Chester: A child molester

Dog: A homeboy or friend

Fag: A male inmate who is believed to be a "natural" or "born" homosexual

Featherwood: A white prisoner's woman

Fish: A newly arrived inmate

Gorilla: An inmate who uses force to take what he wants from others

Homeboy: A prisoner from one's hometown or neighborhood

Ink: Tattoos

Lemon squeezer: An inmate who masturbates frequently

Man walking: A phrase used to signal that a guard is coming

Merchant (or peddler): One who sells when he should give

Peckerwood (or wood): A white prisoner

Punk: A male inmate who is forced into a submissive role during homosexual relations

Rat (or snitch): An inmate who squeals (provides information about other inmates to the prison administration)

Schooled: Knowledgeable in the ways of prison life

Shakedown: A search of a cell or of a work area

Tree jumper: A rapist

Turn out: To rape or make into a punk

Wolf: A male inmate who assumes the dominant role during homosexual relations

#### WOMEN'S PRISON SLANG

Cherry (or cherrie): A female inmate who has not yet been introduced to lesbian activities

Fay broad: A white female inmate

Femme (or mommy): A female inmate who plays the female role during lesbian relations

Safe: The vagina, especially when used for hiding contraband

Stud broad (or daddy): A female inmate who assumes the male role during lesbian relations

*References:* Gresham Sykes, *The Society of Captives* (Princeton, NJ: Princeton University Press, 1958); Rose Giallombardo, *Society of Women: A Study of a Woman's Prison* (New York: John Wiley, 1966); and Richard A. Cloward et al., *Theoretical Studies in Social Organization of the Prison* (New York: Social Science Research Council, 1960). For a more contemporary listing of prison slang terms, see Reinhold Aman, *Hillary Clinton's Pen Pal: A Guide to Life and Lingo in Federal Prison* (Santa Rosa, CA: Maledicta Press, 1996); Jerome Washington, *Iron House: Stories from the Yard* (Ann Arbor, MI: QED Press, 1994); Morrie Camhi, *The Prison Experience* (Boston: Charles Tuttle, 1989); and Harold Long, *Survival in Prison* (Port Townsend, WA: Loompanics, 1990).

**prison argot**

The slang characteristic of prison subcultures and prison life.

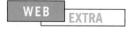

lifestyle of the prison. However, within the half year prior to release, most inmates begin to demonstrate a renewed appreciation of conventional values. Learn more about both the positive and negative impacts of imprisonment at Library Extra 14–2 at cjtoday.com.

Different prisons share aspects of a common inmate culture.[15] **Prison argot**, or language, provides one example of how widespread prison subculture can be. The terms used to describe inmate roles in one institution are generally understood in others. The word *rat*, for example, is prison slang for an informer. Popularized by crime movies of the 1950s, the term is understood today by members of the wider society. Other words common to prison argot are shown in CJ Today Exhibit 14–1. View an online prisoner's dictionary via Web Extra 14–1 at cjtoday.com.

## Prison Subcultures

Prison subcultures, like all subcultures, evolve to reflect the concerns and experiences of the wider culture. John Irwin's 1970 classic study *The Felon*[16] recognized that prison subcultures of the time had begun to reflect the cultural changes sweeping America. A decade later, other investigators of prison subcultures were able to write, "It was no longer meaningful to speak of a single inmate culture or even subculture. By the time we began our field research . . . it was clear that the unified, oppositional convict culture, found in the sociological literature on prisons, no longer existed."[17] Changes in the larger society again affected prison subculture in the 1980s, when the AIDS epidemic brought about changes in prison sexual behavior, at least for a segment of the inmate population.

Charles Stastny and Gabrielle Tyrnauer, describing prison life at Washington State Penitentiary in 1982, discovered four clearly distinguishable subcultures: (1) official, (2) traditional, (3) reform, and (4) revolutionary.[18] Official culture was promoted by the staff and by the administrative rules of the institution. Enthusiastic participants in official culture were mostly correctional officers and other staff members, although inmates were also well aware of the normative expectations that official culture imposed on them. Official culture affected the lives of inmates primarily through the creation of a prisoner hierarchy based on sentence length, prison jobs, and the "perks" that cooperation with the dictates of official culture could produce. Traditional prison culture, described by early writers on the subject, still existed, but its participants spent much of their time lamenting the decline of the convict code among younger prisoners. Reform culture was unique at Washington State Penitentiary. It was the result of a brief experiment with inmate self-government during the early 1970s. Some elements of prison life that evolved during the experimental period survived the termination of self-government and were eventually institutionalized in what Stastny and Tyrnauer called "reform culture." They included inmate participation in civic-style clubs, citizen involvement in the daily activities of the prison, banquets, and inmate speaking tours. Revolutionary culture built on the radical political rhetoric of the disenfranchised and found a ready audience among minority prisoners who saw themselves as victims of society's basic unfairness. Although they did not participate in it, revolutionary inmates understood traditional prison culture and generally avoided running afoul of its rules.

## The Functions of Prison Subcultures

How do social scientists and criminologists explain the existence of prison subcultures? Although people around the world live in groups and create their own cultures, in few cases does the intensity of human interaction approach the level found in prisons. As we discussed in Chapter 13, many of today's prisons are densely crowded places where inmates can find no retreat from the constant demands of staff and the pressures of fellow prisoners. Prison subcultures, according to some authors, are fundamentally an adaptation to deprivation and confinement. In *The Society of Captives,* Sykes called these deprivations the "pains of imprisonment."[19] The pains of imprisonment—the frustrations induced by the rigors of confinement—form the nexus of a deprivation model of prison subculture. Sykes said that prisoners are deprived of (1) liberty, (2) goods and services, (3) heterosexual relationships, (4) autonomy, and (5) personal security and that these deprivations lead to the development of subcultures intended to ameliorate the personal pains that accompany deprivation.

In contrast to the deprivation model, the importation model of prison subculture suggests that inmates bring with them values, roles, and behavior patterns from the outside world. Such external values, second nature as they are to career offenders, depend substantially on the criminal worldview. When offenders are confined, these external elements shape the social world of inmates.

The social structure of the prison—the accepted and relatively permanent social arrangements—is another element that shapes prison subculture. Clemmer's early prison study recognized nine structural dimensions of inmate society. He said that prison society could be described in terms of[20]

- Prisoner–staff dichotomy
- Three general classes of prisoners
- Work gangs and cell-house groups
- Racial groups
- Type of offense
- Power of inmate "politicians"
- Degree of sexual abnormality
- Record of repeat offenses
- Personality differences due to preprison socialization

Clemmer's nine structural dimensions are still descriptive of prison life today. When applied to individuals, they designate an inmate's position in the prison "pecking order" and create

> It is better to prevent crimes than to punish them.
>
> —Cesare Bonesana,
> Marchese di Beccaria

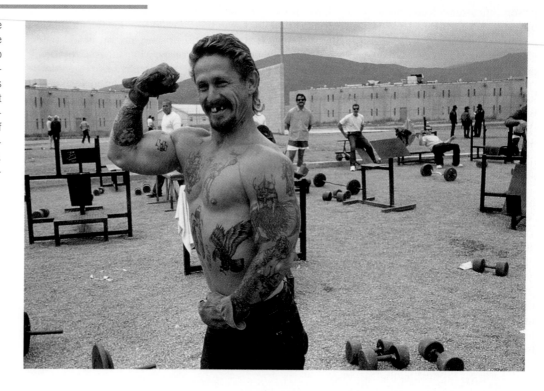

A San Diego, California, inmate showing off his physique. Some inmates attempt to adapt to prison life by acting tough. During the mid-1990s, the states and the federal government moved to ban weight-lifting programs in prison on the belief that they contradict the punishment goal of imprisonment. Nonetheless, many prisons today still retain such facilities.

*Armineh Johannes, SIPA Press*

expectations of the appropriate role for that person. Prison roles serve to satisfy the needs of inmates for power, sexual performance, material possessions, individuality, and personal pleasure and to define the status of one prisoner relative to another. For example, inmate leaders, sometimes referred to as "real men" or "toughs" by prisoners in early studies, offer protection to those who live by the rules. They also provide for a redistribution of wealth inside prison and see to it that the rules of the complex prison-derived economic system—based on barter, gambling, and sexual favors—are observed. For an intimate multimedia portrait of life behind bars, visit Web Extra 14–2 at cjtoday.com.

**WEB EXTRA**

## Prison Lifestyles and Inmate Types

Prison society is strict and often unforgiving. Even so, inmates are able to express some individuality through the choice of a prison lifestyle. John Irwin viewed them (like the subcultures of which they are a part) as adaptations to the prison environment.[21] Other writers have since elaborated on these coping mechanisms. Listed in the paragraphs that follow are some of the types of prisoners that researchers have described.

- *The mean dude.* Some inmates adjust to prison by being violent. Other inmates know that these prisoners are best left alone. The mean dude is frequently written up and spends much time in solitary confinement. This role is most common in male institutions and in maximum-security prisons. For some prisoners, the role of mean dude in prison is similar to the role they played in their life prior to being incarcerated. Certain personality types, such as the psychopath, may feel a natural attraction to this role. Plus, prison culture supports violence in two ways: (1) by expecting inmates to be tough and (2) through the prevalence of the idea that only the strong survive inside prison.

- *The hedonist.* Some inmates build their lives around the limited pleasures available within the confines of prison. The smuggling of contraband, homosexuality, gambling, drug running, and other officially condemned activities provide the center of interest for prison hedonists. Hedonists generally have an abbreviated view of the future, living only for the "now."

- *The opportunist.* The opportunist takes advantage of the positive experiences prison has to offer. Schooling, trade training, counseling, and other self-improvement activities are the focal points of the opportunist's life in prison. Opportunists are generally well liked by prison staff,

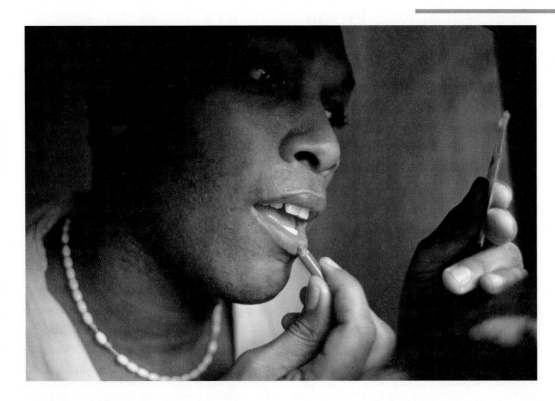

A male inmate dresses as a female in the protective custody wing of the Ferguson Unit in Midway, Texas. Homosexuality is common in both men's and women's prisons.
*© Andrew Lichtenstein, Corbis Sygma*

but other prisoners shun and mistrust them because they come closest to accepting the role that the staff defines as "model prisoner."

- *The retreatist.* Prison life is rigorous and demanding. Badgering by the staff and actual or feared assaults by other inmates may cause some prisoners to attempt psychological retreat from the realities of imprisonment. Such inmates may experience neurotic or psychotic episodes, become heavily involved in drug and alcohol abuse through the illicit prison economy, or even attempt suicide. Depression and mental illness are the hallmarks of the retreatist personality in prison.

- *The legalist.* The legalist is the "jailhouse lawyer." Convicts facing long sentences, with little possibility for early release through the correctional system, are most likely to turn to the courts in their battle against confinement.

- *The radical.* Radical inmates view themselves as political prisoners. They see society and the successful conformists who populate it as oppressors who have forced criminality on many "good people" through the creation of a system that distributes wealth and power inequitably. The inmate who takes on the radical role is unlikely to receive much sympathy from prison staff.

- *The colonizer.* Some inmates think of prison as their home and don't look forward to leaving. They "know the ropes," have many "friends" inside, and may feel more comfortable institutionalized than on the streets. They typically hold positions of power or respect among the inmate population. Once released, some colonizers commit new crimes to return to prison.

- *The religious.* Some prisoners profess a strong religious faith. They may be "born-again" Christians, committed Muslims, or even satanists or witches. Religious inmates frequently attend services, may form prayer groups, and sometimes ask the prison administration to allocate meeting facilities or to create special diets to accommodate their claimed spiritual needs. While it is certainly true that some inmates have a strong religious faith, staff members are apt to be suspicious of the overly religious prisoner.

- *The realist.* The realist sees confinement as a natural consequence of criminal activity and as an unfortunate cost of doing business. This stoic attitude toward incarceration generally leads the realist to "pull his (or her) own time" and to make the best of it. Realists tend to know the inmate code, are able to avoid trouble, and continue in lives of crime once released.

> Whilst we have prisons it matters little which of us occupies the cells.
>
> —George Bernard Shaw (1856–1950)

# Homosexuality in Prison

Homosexual behavior inside prisons is both constrained and encouraged by prison subculture. One Houston woman, whose son is serving time in a Texas prison, explained the path to prison homosexuality this way: "Within a matter of days, if not hours, an unofficial prison welcome wagon sorts new arrivals into those who will fight, those who will pay extortion cash of up to $60 every two weeks, and those who will be servants or slaves. 'You're jumped on by two or three prisoners to see if you'll fight," said the woman. 'If you don't fight, you become someone's girl, until they're tired of you and they sell you to someone else.'"[22]

Sykes's early study of prison argot found many words describing homosexual activity. Among them were the terms *wolf, punk,* and *fag.* Wolves were aggressive men who assumed the masculine role in homosexual relations. Punks were forced into submitting to the female role. The term *fag* described a special category of men who had a natural proclivity toward homosexual activity and effeminate mannerisms. While both wolves and punks were fiercely committed to their heterosexual identity and participated in homosexuality only because of prison conditions, fags generally engaged in homosexual lifestyles before their entry into prison and continued to emulate feminine mannerisms and styles of dress once incarcerated.

Prison homosexuality depends to a considerable degree on the naïveté of young inmates experiencing prison for the first time. Even when newly arrived inmates are protected from fights, older prisoners looking for homosexual liaisons may ingratiate themselves by offering cigarettes, money, drugs, food, or protection. At some future time, these "loans" will be called in, with payoffs demanded in sexual favors. Because the inmate code requires the repayment of favors, the "fish" who tries to resist may quickly find himself face-to-face with the brute force of inmate society.

Prison rape represents a special category of homosexual behavior behind bars. Estimates of the incidence of prison rape are both rare and dated. Survey-based studies vary considerably in their findings. One such study found 4.7% of inmates in the Philadelphia prison system willing to report sexual assaults.[23] Another survey found that 28% of prisoners had been targets of sexual aggressors at least once during their institutional careers.[24]

In 2003, Congress mandated the collection of statistics on prison rape as part of the Prison Rape Elimination Act (PREA).[25] The PREA calls for an evaluation of the problem of prison rape as well as for the development of national standards to prevent prison rape. In 2004, the Bureau of Justice Statistics (BJS) announced plans to implement the data-gathering provisions of the act through a massive project focused on adult and juvenile correctional facilities. The law requires BJS to collect data in federal and state prisons, county and city jails, and juvenile institutions, and the U.S. Census Bureau will act as the collection agent for data as they are collected. Initial results from the surveys will be available shortly after this book goes to press. Look for them at cjtoday.com/prea.

An earlier but comprehensive review of rape inside male prisons was published in 2001 by Human Rights Watch. Entitled *No Escape: Male Rape in U.S. Prisons,*[26] the 378-page report examined three years of research and interviews with more than 200 prisoners in 34 states. Perpetrators of prison rape were found to be young (generally 20 to 30 years old), larger or stronger than their victims, and "generally more assertive, physically aggressive, and more at home in the prison environment" than their victims. Rapists were also found to be "street smart" and were frequently gang members who were well established in the inmate hierarchy and who had been convicted of violent crimes. A large proportion of sexual aggressors are characterized by low education and poverty, having grown up in a broken home headed by the mother, and having a record of violent offenses.[27] Lee H. Bowker, summarizing studies of sexual violence in prison, provides the following observations[28]:

- Most sexual aggressors do not consider themselves homosexuals.
- Sexual release is not the primary motivation for sexual attack.
- Many aggressors must continue to participate in gang rapes to avoid becoming victims themselves.
- The aggressors have themselves suffered much damage to their masculinity in the past.

As in cases of heterosexual rape, sexual assaults in prison are likely to leave psychological scars on the victim long after the physical event is over.[29] Victims of prison rape live in fear, may feel constantly threatened, and can turn to self-destructive activities.[30] Many victims question their masculinity and undergo a personal devaluation. Some victims of prison sexual assault become violent, attacking and sometimes killing the person who raped them. The Human Rights

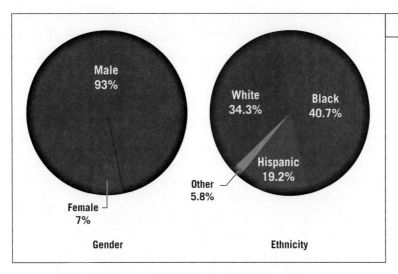

**FIGURE 14–1**

**Prison inmates by gender and ethnicity in state and federal prisons.**

*Source:* Paige M. Harrison and Allen J. Beck, *Prisoners in 2004* (Washington, DC: Bureau of Justice Statistics, 2005).

Watch researchers found that prisoners "fitting any part of the following description" are more likely to become rape victims: "young, small in size, physically weak, white, gay, first offender, possessing 'feminine' characteristics such as long hair or a high voice; being unassertive, unaggressive, shy, intellectual, not street-smart, or 'passive'; or having been convicted of a sexual offense against a minor." The researchers also noted that "prisoners with several overlapping characteristics are much more likely than other prisoners to be targeted for abuse."

The report concluded that to reduce the incidence of prison rape, "prison officials should take considerably more care in matching cell mates, and that, as a general rule, double-celling should be avoided." Learn more about male rape in U.S. prisons at Library Extra 14–3 at cjtoday.com.

# The Female Inmate's World

As Chapter 13 showed, more than 104,800 women were imprisoned in state and federal correctional institutions throughout the United States at the start of 2005, accounting for 7% of all prison inmates.[31] Texas had the largest number of female prisoners (13,958), exceeding even the federal government.[32] Figure 14–1 provides a breakdown of the total American prison population by gender and ethnicity. While there are still far more men imprisoned across the nation than women (approximately 14 men for every woman), the number of female inmates is rising.[33] In 1981, women made up only 4% of the nation's overall prison population, but the number of female inmates nearly tripled during the 1980s and is continuing to grow at a rate greater than that of male inmates.

In 2003, the National Institute of Corrections (NIC) published the results of its three-year project on women offenders in adult correctional settings.[34] Findings from the study produced a national profile of incarcerated women that is shown in Table 14–1.

NIC says that "women involved in the criminal justice system represent a population marginalized by race, class, and gender."[35] African-American women, for example, are overrepresented in correctional populations. While they constitute only 13% of women in the United States, nearly 50% of women in prison are African-American. African-American women are eight times more likely than white women to be incarcerated.

Study authors found that most women offenders are nonviolent and that their crimes are typically less threatening to community safety than those of male offenders. Female offenders, according to the study, are disproportionately low-income women of color who are undereducated and unskilled, with sporadic employment histories. They are less likely than men to have committed violent offenses and more likely to have been convicted of crimes involving drugs or property. Often, their property offenses are economically driven, motivated by poverty and by the abuse of alcohol and other drugs. The majority of offenses committed by women who are in prisons and jails are nonviolent drug and property crimes.

According to NIC, women face life circumstances that tend to be specific to their gender, such as sexual abuse, sexual assault, domestic violence, and the responsibility of being the primary caregiver for dependent children. Research shows that women offenders differ significantly from

| | NATIONAL PROFILE OF WOMEN OFFENDERS |
|---|---|
| **TABLE 14–1** | A profile based on national data for women offenders reveals the following characteristics:<br>• Disproportionately women of color<br>• In their early to mid-30s<br>• Most likely to have been convicted of a drug-related offense<br>• From fragmented families that include other family members who also have been involved with the criminal justice system<br>• Survivors of physical and/or sexual abuse as children and adults<br>• Individuals with significant substance abuse problems<br>• Individuals with multiple physical and mental health problems<br>• Unmarried mothers of minor children<br>• Individuals with a high school or general equivalency diploma (GED) but limited vocational training and sporadic work histories |

*Source:* Barbara Bloom, Barbara Owen, and Stephanie Covington, *Gender-Responsive Strategies: Research, Practice, and Guiding Principles for Women Offenders* (Washington, DC: National Institute of Corrections, 2003).

> I beseech you all to think about these women—to encourage the American people to ask for reforms, both in sentencing guidelines, in length of incarceration for nonviolent first-time offenders, and for those involved in drug-taking. They would be much better served in a true rehabilitation center than in prison where there is no real help, no real programs to rehabilitate, no programs to educate, no way to be prepared for life "out there" where each person will ultimately find herself, many with no skills and no preparation for living.
>
> —Martha Stewart[i]

their male counterparts regarding personal histories and pathways to crime.[36] A female offender, for example, is more likely to have been the primary caretaker of young children at the time of her arrest, more likely to have experienced physical and/or sexual abuse, and more likely to have distinctive physical and mental health needs.

Women's most common pathways to crime, said NIC, involve survival strategies that result from physical and sexual abuse, poverty, and substance abuse. Consequently, the first life circumstance that the NIC study examined closely was physical and sexual abuse. "Not all women who suffer abuse commit crimes, but one of the things most women in prison share is a background of victimization," says Harvard researcher Angel Browne. Supporting data come from BJS findings showing that about half (48%) of women in jail (but only 13% of men) and half (48%) of women in state and federal prisons (but only 12% of men) had been physically or sexually abused before incarceration.[37] Women in prison are three times more likely to have a history of abuse than men in prison.[38] Approximately 37% of women in state prison, 23% of women in federal prison, 37% of women in jail, and 28% of women on probation reported physical or sexual abuse before the age of 18.[39]

Other studies show a much higher rate of abuse than the BJS data. One study, for example, found that 80% of a sample of incarcerated women in California had been physically and/or sexually abused prior to incarceration.[40] A later study found that more than 80% of the women incarcerated in North Carolina's state prisons had been physically and/or sexually abused.[41] In interviews with women at a New York maximum-security prison, Browne found that 70% of incarcerated women reported physical violence, and nearly 60% reported sexual abuse.[42]

The link between female criminality and substance abuse is very strong, and it was the second life circumstance that the NIC study examined. Research shows that women are more likely to be involved in crime if they are drug users.[43] Approximately 80% of women in state prisons have substance abuse problems.[44] About half of women offenders in state prisons had been using alcohol, drugs, or both at the time of their offense. Nearly one in three women serving time in state prisons reported committing the offense to obtain money to support a drug habit. About half described themselves as daily users.[45] To put these statistics into perspective, it is helpful to compare them to statistics on substance abuse among women in the general population. The Substance Abuse and Mental Health Services Administration reports that 2.1% of females in the United States age 12 and older had engaged in heavy alcohol use within the 30 days preceding the survey, 4.1% had used an illicit drug, and 1.2% had used a psychotherapeutic drug for a nonmedical purpose.[46] By contrast, the National Center on Addiction and Substance Abuse found that 54% of women offenders in state prisons had used an illicit drug during the month before they committed their crimes, and 48% were under the influence of either alcohol or another drug when they committed their crimes.[47] Among women offenders in federal prisons, 27% had used an illicit drug in the month before they committed their crimes, and 20% were under the influence when they committed their crimes.

Some complain that many women are being unfairly sent to prison by current federal drug policies for playing only minor roles in drug-related offenses. "We've gone from being a nation of latchkey kids to a nation of locked-up moms, where women are the invisible prisoners of drug laws, serving hard time for someone else's crime,"[48] says Lenora Lapidus, coauthor of the 2005 report *Caught in the Net: The Impact of Drug Policies on Women and Families*.[49] "Even when they have minimal or no involvement whatsoever in the drug trade," the report claims, "women are increasingly caught in the ever-widening net cast by current drug laws." *Caught in the Net* is available at cjtoday.com as Library Extra 14–4.

The third life circumstance that the NIC study examined was physical health. Women inmates face health issues, including pregnancy, that differ from those of men. Women frequently enter jails and prisons in poor health, and they experience more serious health problems than do their male counterparts. Their poor health is often due to poverty, poor nutrition, inadequate health care, and substance abuse.[50] It is estimated that 20% to 35% of women attend prison sick call daily compared with 7% to 10% of men. Women also have more medical problems related to their reproductive systems than do men. About 5% of women enter prison while pregnant. Most of these pregnancies are considered high risk due to a history of inadequate medical care, abuse, and substance abuse.

Sexually transmitted diseases are also a problem among women offenders. Approximately 3.5% of women in prison are HIV positive, and women prisoners are 50% more likely than male prisoners to be HIV positive. The number of women infected with HIV has increased 69% since 1991, while the number of infected male offenders has decreased by 22%.[51] Women offenders are also at greater risk for breast, lung, and cervical cancer. One study, for example, found that incarcerated women who reported sexual abuse before the age of 17 were six times more likely than those who did not experience this abuse to exhibit precancerous cervical lesions.[52]

Women in prison have a higher incidence of mental disorders than do women in the community, and mental health was the fourth focus of the NIC study. One-quarter of women in state prisons have been identified as suffering from mental illness.[53] The major diagnoses of mental illness are depression, post-traumatic stress disorder (PTSD), and substance abuse. Women offenders have histories of abuse that are associated with psychological trauma, and PTSD is a psychiatric condition often seen in women who have experienced sexual abuse and other trauma. Symptoms of PTSD include depression, low self-esteem, insomnia, panic, nightmares, and flashbacks. Approximately 75% of women who have serious mental illness also suffer from substance abuse disorders, and about one in four of all women in state prisons are receiving medication for psychological disorders. A total of 22.3% of women in jail have been diagnosed with PTSD, 13.7% have been diagnosed with a current episode of depression, and about 17% are receiving medication for psychological disorders.[54] Women with serious mental illness and co-occurring disorders experience significant difficulties in jail and prison settings, and the lack of appropriate assessment of and treatment for women with mental health issues is an ongoing problem in correctional settings.[55]

Children and marital status were identified as a fifth important life circumstance by the NIC study. Eighty percent of women entering prison are mothers, and 85% of those women had custody of their children at the time of admission. Approximately 70% of all women under correctional supervision have at least one child younger than age 18. Two-thirds of incarcerated women have minor children; about two-thirds of women in state prisons and half of women in federal prisons had lived with their young children before entering prison. One out of four women entering prison has either recently given birth or is pregnant. Pregnant inmates, many of whom are drug users, malnourished, or sick, often receive little prenatal care—a situation that risks additional complications.

It is estimated that 1.3 million minor children have a mother who is under correctional supervision, and more than 250,000 minor children have mothers in jail or prison.[56] Separation from their children is a significant deprivation for many women. Although husbands or boyfriends may assume responsibility for the children of their imprisoned partners, this outcome is the exception to the rule. Eventually, many children of imprisoned mothers are placed into foster care or are put up for adoption.

Some states do offer parenting classes for female inmates with children. In a national survey of prisons for women, 36 states responded that they provide parenting programs that deal with caretaking, reducing violence toward children, visitation problems, and related issues.[57] Some offer play areas furnished with toys, while others attempt to alleviate difficulties attending mother–child visits. The typical program studied meets for two hours per week and lasts from four to nine weeks.

Of children whose fathers are incarcerated, approximately 90% live with their mothers; only 25% of the children of women offenders live with their fathers. Grandparents are most likely to be the caregivers of the children of female offenders. Approximately 10% of these children are in foster care or group homes. More than half of the children of women prisoners never visit their mothers during the period of incarceration.[58] The lack of visits is due primarily to the remote location of prisons, a lack of transportation, and the inability of caregivers to arrange visitation.

Women under criminal justice supervision are more likely than the general population never to have been married. In one survey, nearly half of the women in jail and prison reported that they had never been married.[59] Forty-two percent of women on probation reported that they had never been married. About 31% of women in prison reported that they were either separated or divorced.

Education and employment were the final life circumstances that the NIC study examined. An estimated 55% of women in local jails, 56% of women in state prisons, and 73% of women in federal prisons have a high school diploma.[60] Approximately 40% of the women in state prisons report that they were employed full-time at the time of their arrest. This compares with almost 60% of males.[61] About 37% of women and 28% of men had incomes of less than $600 per month prior to arrest. Most of the jobs held by women were low-skill entry-level jobs with low pay. Two-thirds of the women reported they had never held a job that paid more than $6.50 per hour. Women are less likely than men to have engaged in vocational training before incarceration. Those who have received vocational training in the community have tended to focus on traditional women's jobs, such as cosmetology, clerical work, and food service.

## Gender Responsiveness

Critics have long charged that female inmates face a prison system designed for male inmates and run by men. Consequently, meaningful prison programs for women are often lacking, often because the ones that are in place were originally based on models adapted from men's prisons or because they are based on traditional views of female roles that leave little room for employment opportunities in the contemporary world. Many trade-training programs still emphasize low-paying jobs, such as cook, beautician, or laundry machine operator, and classes in homemaking are not uncommon.

A central purpose of the NIC report on the female offender was to identify effective gender-responsive approaches for managing women prisoners. The study defined gender responsiveness as "creating an environment . . . that reflects an understanding of the realities of women's lives and addresses the issues of women."[62] The NIC report concluded with a call for recognition of the behavioral and social differences between female and male offenders—especially those that have specific implications for gender-responsive policies and practices. Among the report's recommendations are the following:

■ The creation of an effective system for female offenders that is structured differently from a system for male offenders

■ The development of gender-responsive policies and practices targeting women's pathways to criminality in order to provide effective interventions that address the intersecting issues of substance abuse, trauma, mental health, and economic marginality

■ The modification of criminal justice sanctions and interventions to recognize the low risk to public safety represented by the typical female offender

■ The consideration of women's relationships, especially those with their children, and women's roles in the community in deciding appropriate correctional sanctions

The NIC study concluded that gender-responsive correctional practices can improve outcomes for women offenders by considering their histories, behaviors, and life circumstances. It also suggested that investments in gender-responsive policy and procedures will likely produce long-term dividends for the criminal justice system and the community as well as for women offenders and their families. Read the entire NIC report at Library Extra 14–5 at cjtoday.com.

## Institutions for Women

Most female inmates are housed in centralized state facilities known as women's prisons, which are dedicated exclusively to incarcerating female felons. Many states, however, particularly those with small populations, continue to keep female prisoners in special wings of what are otherwise institutions for men. Although there is not a typical prison for women, the American Correctional Association's 1990 report by the Task Force on the Female Offender found that the institutions that house female inmates could be generally described as follows[63]:

■ Most prisons for women are located in towns with fewer than 25,000 inhabitants.

■ A significant number of facilities were not designed to house female inmates.

A female inmate housed in the segregation unit of a Rhode Island correctional facility because of disciplinary problems. The number of women in prison is growing steadily.
*Richard Falco, Black Star*

- Some facilities that house female inmates also house men.
- Few facilities for women have programs especially designed for female offenders.
- Few major disturbances or escapes are reported among female inmates.
- Substance abuse among female inmates is very high.
- Few work assignments are available to female inmates.

> **We must remember always that the doors of prisons swing both ways.**
>
> **—Mary Belle Harris, first federal female warden**

## Social Structure in Women's Prisons

"Aside from sharing the experience of being incarcerated," says Professor Marsha Clowers of the John Jay College of Criminal Justice, "female prisoners have much in common."[64] Because so many female inmates share social characteristics such as lack of education and a history of abuse, they often also share similar values and behaviors. Early prison researchers found that many female inmates construct organized pseudofamilies. Typical of such studies are D. Ward and G. Kassebaum's *Women's Prison* (1966),[65] Esther Heffernan's *Making It in Prison* (1972),[66] and Rose Giallombardo's *Society of Women* (1966).[67]

Giallombardo, for example, examined the Federal Reformatory for Women at Alderson, West Virginia, spending a year gathering data in the early 1960s. Focusing closely on the social formation of families among female inmates, she entitled one of her chapters "The Homosexual Alliance as a Marriage Unit." In it, she described in great detail the sexual identities assumed by women at Alderson and the symbols they chose to communicate those roles. Hairstyle, dress, language, and mannerisms were all used to signify "maleness" or "femaleness." Giallombardo detailed "the anatomy of the marriage relationship from courtship to 'fall out,' that is, from inception to the parting of the ways, or divorce."[68] Romantic love at Alderson was of central importance to any relationship between inmates, and all homosexual relationships were described as voluntary. Through marriage, the "stud broad" became the husband and the "femme" the wife.

Studies attempting to document how many inmates are part of prison "families" have produced varying results. Some found as many as 71% of female prisoners involved in the phenomenon, while others found none.[69] The kinship systems described by Giallombardo and others, however, extend beyond simple "family" ties to the formation of large, intricately related groups that include many nonsexual relationships. In these groups, the roles of "children," "in-laws," "grandparents," and so on may be explicitly recognized. Even "birth order" within a family can become an issue for kinship groups.[70] Kinship groups sometimes occupy a common household—usually a prison cottage or a dormitory area. The descriptions of women's prisons provided by authors like Giallombardo show a closed society in which social interaction—including expectations, normative forms of behavior, and emotional ties—is regulated by an inventive system of artificial relationships that mirror those of the outside world.

Recent studies provide additional details about the nature of sexual behavior in women's prisons. A 1998 study of the Central California Women's Facility, for example, found that most of the staff and inmates alike claimed that "everybody was involved" in homosexual behavior. When inmates were interviewed individually, however, and asked to provide some details about the extent of their involvement in such behavior, many denied any lesbian activity.

A 2001 study of a women's correctional facility in the southeastern United States found that female inmates asked about their preincarceration sexual orientation gave answers that were quite different than when they were asked about their sexual orientation while incarcerated.[71] In general, before being incarcerated, 64% of inmates interviewed reported being exclusively heterosexual, 28% said they were bisexual, and 8% said that they were lesbians. In contrast, while incarcerated these same women reported sexual orientations of 55% heterosexual, 31% bisexual, and 13% lesbian. Researchers found that same-sex sexual behavior within the institution was more likely to occur in the lives of young inmates who had had such experiences before entering prison. The study also found that female inmates tended to take part in lesbian behavior the longer they were incarcerated.

Finally, a significant aspect of sexual activity far more commonly found in women's prisons than in men's prisons is sexual misconduct between staff and inmates. While a fair amount of such behavior is attributed to the exploitation of female inmates by male correctional officers acting from positions of power, some studies suggest that female inmates may sometimes attempt to manipulate unsuspecting male officers into illicit relationships in order to gain favors.[72]

## Types of Female Inmates

As in institutions for men, the subculture of women's prisons is multidimensional. Esther Heffernan, for example, found that three terms used by the female prisoners she studied—the *square,* the *cool,* and the *life*—were indicative of three styles of adaptation to prison life.[73] Square

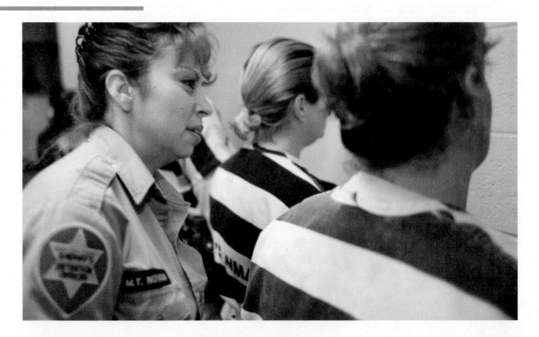

Female inmates in Sheriff Joe Arpaio's "equal opportunity jail" in Maricopa County, Arizona, being inspected by a correctional officer before leaving for chain gang duty. Not all states make use of chain gangs, and only a few use female inmates on chain gangs.

*Jack Kurtz, The Image Works*

inmates had few early experiences with criminal lifestyles and tended to sympathize with the values and attitudes of conventional society. Cool prisoners were more likely to be career offenders. They tended to keep to themselves and generally supported inmate values. Women who participated in the life subculture were quite familiar with lives of crime. Many had been arrested repeatedly for prostitution, drug use, theft, and so on. They were full participants in the economic, social, and familial arrangements of the prison. Heffernan believed that the life offered an alternative lifestyle to women who had experienced early consistent rejection by conventional society. Within the life, women could establish relationships, achieve status, and find meaning in their lives. The square, the cool, and the life represented subcultures to Heffernan because individuals with similar adaptive choices tended to relate closely to one another and to support the lifestyle characteristic of that type.

Recently, the social structure of women's prisons has been altered by the arrival of "crack kids," as they are called in prison argot. Crack kids, whose existence highlights generational differences among female offenders, are streetwise young women with little respect for traditional prison values, for their elders, or even for their own children. Known for frequent fights and for their lack of even simple domestic skills, these young women quickly estrange many older inmates, some of whom call them "animalescents."

## Violence in Women's Prisons

Some authors suggest that violence in women's prisons is less frequent than it is in institutions for men. Lee Bowker observes that "except for the behavior of a few 'guerrillas,' it appears that violence is only used in women's prisons to settle questions of dominance and subordination when other manipulative strategies fail to achieve the desired effect."[74] It appears that few homosexual liaisons are forced, perhaps representing a general aversion among women to such victimization in wider society. At least one study, however, has shown the use of sexual violence in women's prisons as a form of revenge against inmates who are overly vocal in their condemnation of lesbian practices among other prisoners.[75]

Not all abuse occurs at the hands of inmates. In 1992, 14 correctional officers, ten men and four women, were indicted for the alleged abuse of female inmates at the 900-bed Women's Correctional Institute in Hardwick, Georgia. The charges resulted from affidavits filed by 90 female inmates alleging "rape, sexual abuse, prostitution, coerced abortions, sex for favors, and retaliation for refusal to participate" in such activities.[76] One inmate who was forced to have an abortion after becoming pregnant by a male staff member said, "As an inmate, I simply felt powerless to avoid the sexual advances of staff and to refuse to have an abortion."[77]

To address the problems of imprisoned women, including violence, the Task Force on the Female Offender recommended a number of changes in the administration of prisons for women.[78] Among those recommendations were these:

■ Substance-abuse programs should be available to female inmates.

■ Female inmates need to acquire greater literacy skills, and literacy programs should form the basis on which other programs are built.

■ Female offenders should be housed in buildings without male inmates.

■ Institutions for women should develop programs for keeping children in the facility in order to "fortify the bond between mother and child."

■ To ensure equal access to assistance, institutions should be built to accommodate programs for female offenders.

Learn more about women in prison and their special needs via **Library Extras 14–6** and **14–7** at cjtoday.com.

**LIBRARY EXTRA**

## The Staff World

The flip side of inmate society can be found in the world of the prison staff, which includes many people working in various professions. Staff roles encompass those of warden, psychologist, counselor, area supervisor, program director, instructor, correctional officer, and—in some large prisons—physician and therapist.

According to the American Correctional Association (ACA), approximately 350,000 people are employed in corrections,[79] with the majority performing direct custodial tasks in state institutions.

Tom Hanks playing the role of a correctional officer in the movie *The Green Mile*. The job of a correctional officer centers largely on the custody and control of inmates, but growing professionalism is enhancing both personal opportunities and job satisfaction among officers.

*Photofest*

On a per capita basis, the District of Columbia has the most state and local corrections employees (53.3 per every 10,000 residents), followed by Texas (43.8).[80] Across the nation, 70% of correctional officers are white, 22% are black, and slightly over 5% are Hispanic.[81] Women account for 20% of all correctional officers, with the proportion of female officers increasing at around 19% per year.[82] The ACA encourages correctional agencies to "ensure that recruitment, selection, and promotion opportunities are open to women."

Correctional officers, generally considered to be at the bottom of the staff hierarchy, may be divided into cell-block guards and tower guards; others are assigned to administrative offices, where they perform clerical tasks. The inmate-to-staff ratio in state prisons averages around 4.1 inmates for each correctional officer.[83]

Like prisoners, correctional officers undergo a socialization process that helps them function by the official and unofficial rules of staff society. In a now-classic study, Lucien Lombardo described the process by which officers are socialized into the prison work world.[84] Lombardo interviewed 359 correctional personnel at New York's Auburn Prison and found that rookie officers quickly had to abandon preconceptions of both inmates and other staff members. According to Lombardo, new officers learn that inmates are not the "monsters" much of the public makes them out to be. On the other hand, rookies may be seriously disappointed in their experienced colleagues when they realize that the ideals of professionalism, often emphasized during early training, rarely translate into reality. The pressures of the institutional work environment, however, soon force most correctional personnel to adopt a united front when relating to inmates.

One of the leading formative influences on staff culture is the potential threat that inmates pose. Inmates far outnumber correctional personnel in every institution, and the hostility they feel for guards is only barely hidden even at the best of times. Correctional personnel know that however friendly inmates may appear, a sudden change in the institutional climate—from a simple disturbance on the yard to a full-blown riot—can quickly and violently unmask deep-rooted feelings of mistrust and hatred.

As in years past, prison staffers are still most concerned with custody and control. Society, especially under the just deserts philosophy of criminal sentencing, expects correctional staff to

## FREEDOM OR SAFETY? YOU DECIDE.

### Dress Codes and Public Safety

On July 1, 2004, the New York City Commission on Human Rights ordered reinstatement of a New York Police Department (NYPD) officer who had quit the force in 2002 because supervisors would not allow him to wear a turban while working. Jasjit Jaggi is a Sikh, whose religion mandates the wearing of turbans and beards by adult males as a sign of their faith. The order, compelling the police department to grant a Sikh employee a religious accommodation, was the first such ruling in the nation issued to a law enforcement agency.

Although turbaned correctional officers are a rarity, some observers have pointed to the possibility of similar lawsuits in the corrections arena. One way for agencies and businesses to avoid legal action comes from the resolution of a religious bias claim brought against United Airlines by a turban-wearing Sikh employee in 2001. Although airline regulations banned the wearing of headgear by employees while indoors, company officials were able to avoid civil liability by offering the man six alternative jobs where he could wear a turban.

### YOU DECIDE

How might dress codes relate to public safety? Should agencies have the authority to enforce dress codes without fear of civil liability if those codes enhance public safety? What if they merely enforce uniformity of appearance? How do these ideas apply to correctional agencies?

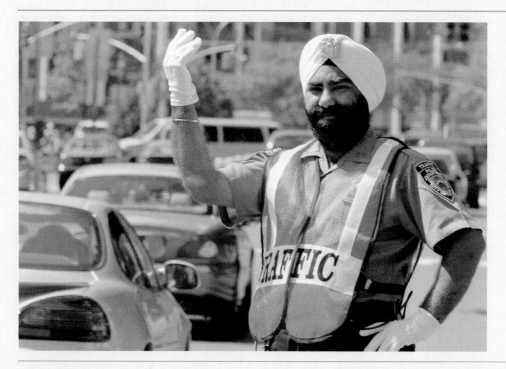

Jasjit Jaggi directs traffic headed toward the Brooklyn Bridge in New York City in 2004. Jaggi, a devout Sikh, quit the NYPD in 2002 because his supervisors would not allow him to wear a turban. His reinstatement by the New York City Commission on Human Rights highlights the clash of cultures for all justice system workers, including correctional officers.

*Todd Maisel, New York Daily News*

*References:* New York City Commission on Human Rights, "Sikh Traffic Enforcement Agent Returns to Work in Landmark Case," *Newsletter,* Summer/Fall 2004, p. 1; Sikh Coalition, Office of Community Relations, "Petition to Mayor Bloomberg: Allow Turbaned Sikhs to Serve as Officers in the NYPD." Web posted at http://www.petitiononline.com/SikhNYPD/petition.html; and Bureau of National Affairs, Inc., "Religious Bias, Indoor Head-Gear Ban, Offering Six Other Jobs to Turban-Wearing Sikh Sufficient Accommodation," *Employment Discrimination Report,* Vol. 18, p. 469. Web posted at http://www.bna.com/current/edr/topa.htm.

keep inmates in custody; this is the basic prerequisite of successful job performance. Custody is necessary before any other correctional activities, such as instruction or counseling, can be undertaken. Control, the other major staff concern, ensures order, and an orderly prison is thought to be safe and secure. In routine daily activities, control over almost all aspects of inmate behavior becomes paramount in the minds of most correctional officers. It is the twin interests of custody and control that lead to institutionalized procedures for ensuring security in most facilities. The enforcement of strict rules; body and cell searches; counts; unannounced shakedowns; the control of dangerous items, materials, and contraband; and the extensive use of bars, locks, fencing, cameras, and alarms all support the staff's vigilance in maintaining security.

## ETHICS AND PROFESSIONALISM

### American Correctional Association Code of Ethics

#### PREAMBLE

The American Correctional Association expects of its members unfailing honesty, respect for the dignity and individuality of human beings and a commitment to professional and compassionate service. To this end, we subscribe to the following principles:

- Members shall respect and protect the civil and legal rights of all individuals.
- Members shall treat every professional situation with concern for the welfare of the individuals involved and with no intent to personal gain.
- Members shall maintain relationships with colleagues to promote mutual respect within the profession and improve the quality of service.
- Members shall make public criticisms of their colleagues or their agencies only when warranted, verifiable, and constructive.
- Members shall respect the importance of all disciplines within the criminal justice system and work to improve cooperation with each segment.
- Members shall honor the public's right to information and share information with the public to the extent permitted by law subject to individuals' right to privacy.
- Members shall respect and protect the right of the public to be safeguarded from criminal activity.
- Members shall refrain from using their positions to secure personal privileges or advantages.
- Members shall refrain from allowing personal interest to impair objectivity in the performance of duty while acting in an official capacity.
- Members shall refrain from entering into any formal or informal activity or agreement which presents a conflict of interest or is inconsistent with the conscientious performance of duties.

- Members shall refrain from accepting any gifts, service, or favor that is or appears to be proper or implies an obligation inconsistent with the free and objective exercise of professional duties.
- Members shall clearly differentiate between personal views/statements and views/statements/positions made on behalf of the agency or association.
- Members shall report to appropriate authorities any corrupt or unethical behaviors in which there is sufficient evidence to justify review.
- Members shall refrain from discriminating against any individual because of race, gender, creed, national origin, religious affiliation, age, disability, or any other type of prohibited discrimination.
- Members shall preserve the integrity of private information; they shall refrain from seeking information on individuals beyond that which is necessary to implement responsibilities and perform their duties; members shall refrain from revealing nonpublic information unless expressly authorized to do so.
- Members shall make all appointments, promotions, and dismissals in accordance with established civil service rules, applicable contract agreements, and individual merit, and not in furtherance of partisan interests.
- Members shall respect, promote, and contribute to a workplace that is safe, healthy, and free of harassment in any form.

Adopted August 1975 at the 105th Congress of Correction. Revised August 1990 at the 120th Congress of Correction. Revised August 1994 at the 124th Congress of Correction.

#### THINKING ABOUT ETHICS

1. How does the American Correctional Association's Code of Ethics differ from the American Jail Association's Code of Ethics found in Chapter 13? How is it similar?
2. Do you think that one code of ethics should cover correctional officers working in both jails and prisons? Why or why not?

*Source:* American Correctional Association. Reprinted with permission. Visit the American Correctional Association at http://www.corrections.com/aca.

# The Professionalization of Correctional Officers

Correctional officers have generally been accorded low occupational status. Historically, the role of prison guard required minimal formal education and held few opportunities for professional growth and career advancement. Such jobs were typically low paying, frustrating, and often boring. Growing problems in our nation's prisons, including emerging issues of legal liability, however, increasingly require a well-trained and adequately equipped force of professionals. As correctional personnel have become better trained and more proficient, the old concept of guard has been supplanted by that of correctional officer.

Many states and a growing number of large-city correctional systems try to eliminate individuals with potentially harmful personality characteristics from correctional officer applicant pools. New Jersey, New York, Ohio, Pennsylvania, and Rhode Island, for example, have all used some form of psychological screening in assessing candidates for prison jobs.[85]

The Arizona State Prison Complex at Lewis, where two inmates held two correctional officers hostage in a watchtower in 2004. One officer, a female, was raped. On April 30, 2004, inmate Steven Coy was sentenced to seven consecutive life sentences for his part in the hostage crisis.

*WP Wide World Photos*

Although only a few states utilize psychological screening, all have training programs intended to prepare successful applicants for prison work. New York, for example, requires trainees to complete six weeks of classroom-based instruction, 40 hours of rifle range practice, and six weeks of on-the-job training. Training days begin around 5 A.M. with a mile run and conclude after dark with study halls for students who need extra help. To keep pace with rising inmate populations, the state has often had to run a number of simultaneous training academies.[86]

# Prison Riots

In 2004, a disturbance took place at the medium- to high-security Arizona State Prison complex—Lewis. Two correctional officers and a staff member were injured in a ruckus that broke out during breakfast preparations, and two other officers were captured and held hostage for 15 days in a watchtower. The episode, which was followed by the major national news services, may have begun as an escape attempt. Officials were able to keep disorder from spreading to the rest of the facility, and the incident ended when inmates released the officers and surrendered. "It could have been a lot worse," said Joe Masella, president of the Arizona Correctional Peace Officers' Association. "Once these inmates get a taste of blood, so to speak, there's no telling what they can do."[87]

Although today's prisons are relatively calm, the ten years between 1970 and 1980 have been called the "explosive decade" of prison riots.[88] The decade began with a massive uprising at Attica Prison in New York State in September 1971, in which 43 deaths occurred and more than 80 men were wounded. The decade ended in 1980 in Santa Fe, New Mexico. There, in a riot at the New Mexico Penitentiary, 33 inmates died, the victims of vengeful prisoners out to eliminate rats and informants. Many of the deaths involved mutilation and torture. More than 200 other inmates were beaten and sexually assaulted, and the prison was virtually destroyed.

While the number of prison riots decreased after the 1970s, they did continue. For 11 days in 1987, the federal penitentiary in Atlanta, Georgia, was under the control of inmates. The institution was heavily damaged, and inmates had to be temporarily relocated while it was rebuilt. The Atlanta riot followed on the heels of a similar, but less intense, disturbance at the federal detention center in Oakdale, Louisiana. Both outbreaks were attributed to the dissatisfaction of Cuban inmates, most of whom had arrived in the mass exodus known as the Mariel boat lift.[89]

Easter Sunday 1993 marked the beginning of an 11-day rebellion at the 1,800-inmate Southern Ohio Correctional Facility in Lucasville, Ohio—one of the country's toughest maximum-security prisons. When the riot ended, nine inmates and one correctional officer were dead. The officer had been hung. The end of the riot—involving a parade of 450 inmates—was televised as prisoners had demanded. Among other demands were (1) no retaliation by officials, (2) review of medical staffing and care, (3) review of mail and visitation rules, (4) review of commissary prices, and (5) better enforcement against what the inmates called "inappropriate supervision."[90]

Riots related to inmate grievances over perceived disparities in federal drug-sentencing policies and the possible loss of weight-lifting equipment occurred throughout the federal prison system in October 1995. Within a few days, the unrest led to a nationwide lockdown of 73 federal prisons. Although fires were set and a number of inmates and guards were injured, no deaths resulted. In February 2000, a riot between 200 black and Hispanic prisoners in California's Pelican Bay State Prison resulted in the death of one inmate. Fifteen other inmates were wounded. Then, in November 2000, 32 inmates took a dozen correctional officers hostage at the privately run Torrance County Detention Facility in Estancia, New Mexico. Two of the guards were stabbed and seriously injured, while another eight were beaten. The riot was finally quelled after an emergency response team threw tear-gas canisters into the area where the prisoners had barricaded themselves.[91]

## Causes of Riots

Researchers have suggested a variety of causes for prison riots.[92] Among them are these:

- An insensitive prison administration and neglected inmates' demands. Calls for "fairness" in disciplinary hearings, better food, more recreational opportunities, and the like may lead to riots when ignored.

- The lifestyles most inmates are familiar with on the streets. It should be no surprise that prisoners use organized violence when many of them are violent people.

- Dehumanizing prison conditions. Overcrowded facilities, the lack of opportunity for individual expression, and other aspects of total institutions culminate in explosive situations of which riots are but one form.

- To regulate inmate society and redistribute power balances among inmate groups. Riots provide the opportunity to "cleanse" the prison population of informers and rats and to resolve struggles among power brokers and ethnic groups within the institution.

- "Power vacuums" created by changes in prison administration, the transfer of influential inmates, or court-ordered injunctions that significantly alter the informal social control mechanisms of the institution.

**security threat group (STG)**

An inmate group, gang, or organization whose members act together to pose a threat to the safety of correctional staff or the public, or who prey upon other inmates, or who threaten the secure and orderly operation of a correctional institution.

Although riots are difficult to predict in specific institutions, some state prison systems appear ripe for disorder. The Texas prison system, for example, is home to a number of gangs [referred to by correctional personnel as **security threat groups (STGs)**], among whom turf violations can easily lead to widespread disorder. Gang membership among inmates in the Texas prison system, practically nonexistent in 1983, was estimated at over 1,200 in 1992.[93] The Texas Syndicate, the Aryan Brotherhood of Texas, and the Mexican Mafia (sometimes known as *La Eme,* Spanish for the letter *M*) are thought to be the largest gangs functioning in the Texas prison system. Each has around 300 members.[94] Other gangs known to operate in some Texas prisons include Aryan Warriors, Black Gangster Disciples (mostly in midwestern Texas), the Black Guerrilla Family, the Confederate Knights of America, and Nuestra Familia, an organization of Hispanic prisoners.

Gangs in Texas grew rapidly in part because of the power vacuum created when a court ruling ended the "building tender" system.[95] Building tenders were tough inmates who were given almost free rein by prison administrators in keeping other inmates in line, especially in many of the state's worst prisons. The end of the building tender system dramatically increased demands on the Texas Department of Criminal Justice for increased abilities and professionalism among its guards and other prison staff.

The real reasons for any riot are specific to the institution and do not allow for easy generalization. However, a clue to prison unrest is provided when we consider that the "explosive decade" of prison riots coincided with the growth of a revolutionary prisoner subculture. As the old convict code gave way to an emerging perception of social victimization among inmates, it was only a matter of time until those perceptions sparked militancy.

## Stages in Riots and Riot Control

Most prison riots are spontaneous, and are typically the result of some relatively minor precipitating event. Generally, riots evolve through five phases: (1) explosion, (2) organization into inmate-led groups, (3) confrontation with authority, (4) termination through negotiation or physical confrontation, and (5) reaction and explanation, usually by investigative commissions.[96] Donald Cressey points out that the early explosive stages of a riot often involve "binges" during which inmates exult in their newfound freedom with virtual orgies of alcohol and drug use or sexual activity.[97] It is during this phase that buildings are burned, facilities are wrecked, and old grudges between individual inmates and inmate groups are settled, often through violence. After this initial explosive stage, leadership changes occur. New leaders emerge who, at least for a time, may effectively organize inmates into a force that can confront and resist officials' attempts to regain control of the institution. Bargaining strategies then develop, and the process of negotiation begins.

In the past, many correctional facilities depended on informal procedures to quell disturbances, often drawing on the expertise of seasoned correctional officers who were veterans of past skirmishes and riots. Given the large size of many of today's institutions, the changing composition of inmate and staff populations, and increasing tensions caused by overcrowding and reduced inmate privileges, the "old guard" system can no longer be depended on to quell disturbances. Hence, most modern facilities have incident-management procedures and systems in place in case a disturbance occurs. Such systems remove the burden of riot control from the individual officer, depending instead on a systematic and deliberate approach developed to deal with a wide variety of correctional incidents.

# Prisoners' Rights

In May 1995, Limestone Prison inmate Larry Hope was handcuffed to a hitching post after arguing with another inmate while working on a chain gang near an interstate highway in Alabama.[98] Hope was released two hours later, after a supervising officer determined that Hope had not instigated the altercation. During the two hours that he was coupled to the post, Hope was periodically offered drinking water and bathroom breaks, and his responses to those offers were recorded on an activity log. Because of the height of the hitching post, however, his arms grew tired, and it was later determined that whenever he tried moving his arms to improve his circulation, the handcuffs cut into his wrists, causing pain.

One month later, Hope was punished more severely after he had taken a nap during the morning bus ride to the chain gang's work site. When the bus arrived, he was slow in responding to an order to exit the vehicle. A shouting match soon led to a scuffle with an officer, and four other guards intervened and subdued Hope, handcuffing him and placing him in leg irons for transportation back to the prison. When he arrived at the facility, officers made him take off his shirt and again put him on the hitching post. He stood in the sun for approximately seven hours, sustaining a sunburn. Hope was given water only once or twice during that time and was provided with no bathroom breaks. At one point, an officer taunted him about his thirst. According to Hope: "[The guard] first gave water to some dogs, then brought the water cooler closer to me, removed its lid, and kicked the cooler over, spilling the water onto the ground."

Eventually Hope filed a civil suit against three officers, claiming that he experienced "unnecessary pain" and that the "wanton infliction of pain . . . constitutes cruel and unusual punishment forbidden by the Eighth Amendment." His case eventually reached the U.S. Supreme Court, and on June 27, 2002, the Court found that Hope's treatment was "totally without penological justification" and constituted an Eighth Amendment violation. The Court ruled, "Despite the clear lack of emergency, respondents knowingly subjected [Hope] to a substantial risk of physical harm, unnecessary pain, unnecessary exposure to the sun, prolonged thirst and taunting, and a deprivation of bathroom breaks that created a risk of particular discomfort and humiliation."

In deciding the *Hope* case, the Court built on almost 40 years of precedent-setting decisions in the area of prisoners' rights. Before the 1960s, American courts had taken a neutral approach—commonly called the **hands-off doctrine**—toward the running of prisons. Judges assumed that prison administrators were sufficiently professional in the performance of their duties to balance institutional needs with humane considerations. The hands-off doctrine rested on the belief that defendants lost most of their rights upon conviction, suffering a kind of **civil death**. Many states defined the concept of civil death through legislation that denied inmates the right to vote, to hold public office, and even to marry. Some states made incarceration for a felony a basis for uncontested divorce at the request of the noncriminal spouse. Aspects of the old notion of civil death are still a reality in a number of jurisdictions today, and the Sentencing Project says that 3.9 million American citizens across the nation are barred from voting because of previous felony convictions.[99]

**hands-off doctrine**

A policy of nonintervention with regard to prison management that U.S. courts tended to follow until the late 1960s. For the past 30 years, the doctrine has languished as judicial intervention in prison administration dramatically increased, although there is now some evidence that a new hands-off era is approaching.

**civil death**

The legal status of prisoners in some jurisdictions who are denied the opportunity to vote, hold public office, marry, or enter into contracts by virtue of their status as incarcerated felons. While civil death is primarily of historical interest, some jurisdictions still limit the contractual opportunities available to inmates.

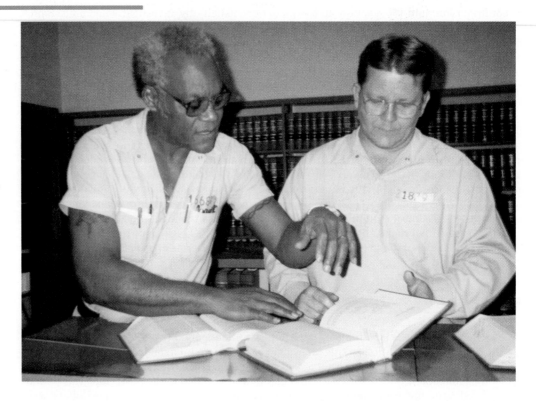

Huttonsville Correctional Center (West Virginia) inmates Thomas Casey (left) and Robert McCabe reviewing statutes in the prison's law library. Casey and McCabe are known to others in the institution as jailhouse lawyers, and they help their peers prepare legal writs. They also represent other inmates in in-house disciplinary actions.

*Courtesy Huttonsville Correctional Center*

The Privilege of the Writ of Habeas Corpus shall not be suspended, unless when in Cases of Rebellion or Invasion the public Safety may require it.

—Article I, Section 9, Clause 2, of the U.S. Constitution

Although the concept of civil death has not entirely disappeared, the hands-off doctrine ended in 1970, when a federal court declared the entire Arkansas prison system to be unconstitutional after hearing arguments that it represented a form of cruel and unusual punishment.[100] The court's decision resulted from what it judged to be pervasive overcrowding and primitive living conditions. Longtime inmates claimed that over the years, a number of inmates had been beaten or shot to death by guards and buried in unmarked graves on prison property. An investigation did unearth some skeletons in old graves, but their origin was never determined.

Detailed media coverage of the Arkansas prison system gave rise to suspicions about correctional institutions everywhere. Within a few years, federal courts intervened in the running of prisons in Florida, Louisiana, Mississippi, New York City, and Virginia.[101] In 1975, in a precedent-setting decision, U.S. District Court Judge Frank M. Johnson issued an order banning the Alabama Board of Corrections from accepting any more inmates. Citing a population that was more than double the capacity of the state's system, Judge Johnson enumerated 44 standards to be met before additional inmates could be admitted to prison. Included in the requirements were specific guidelines on living space, staff-to-inmate ratios, visiting privileges, the racial makeup of staff, and food service modifications.

**balancing test**

A principle, developed by the courts and applied to the corrections arena by *Pell* v. *Procunier* (1974), that attempts to weigh the rights of an individual, as guaranteed by the Constitution, against the authority of states to make laws or to otherwise restrict a person's freedom in order to protect the state's interests and its citizens.

# The Legal Basis of Prisoners' Rights

In 1974, the U.S. Supreme Court case of *Pell* v. *Procunier*[102] established a "balancing test" that, although originally addressing only First Amendment rights, eventually served as a general guideline for all prison operations. In *Pell,* the Court ruled that the "prison inmate retains those First Amendment rights that are not inconsistent with his status as a prisoner or with the legitimate penological objectives of the corrections system."[103] In other words, inmates have rights, much the same as people who are not incarcerated, provided that the legitimate needs of the prison for security, custody, and safety are not compromised. Other courts have declared that order maintenance, security, and rehabilitation are all legitimate concerns of prison administration but that financial exigency and convenience are not. As the **balancing test** makes clear, we see reflected in prisoners' rights a microcosm of the individual-rights versus public-order dilemma found in wider society.

Further enforcing the legal rights of prisoners is the Civil Rights of Institutionalized Persons Act (CRIPA) of 1980.[104] The law, which has been amended over time, applies to all adult and juvenile state and local jails, detention centers, prisons, mental hospitals, and other care facilities (such as those operated by a state, county, or city for the physically challenged or chronically ill). Section 1997a of the act, entitled "Initiation of Civil Actions," reads as follows:

> Whenever the Attorney General has reasonable cause to believe that any State, political subdivision of a State, official, employee, or agent thereof, or other person acting on behalf of a State or political subdivision of a State is subjecting persons residing in or confined to an institution . . . to egregious or flagrant conditions which deprive such persons of any rights, privileges, or immunities secured or protected by the Constitution or laws of the United States . . . and that such deprivation is pursuant to a pattern or practice of resistance to the full enjoyment of such rights, privileges, or immunities, the Attorney General, for or in the name of the United States, may institute a civil action in any appropriate United States district court against such party for such equitable relief as may be appropriate.

Significantly, the most recent version of CRIPA also states[105]:

> No action shall be brought with respect to prison conditions under section 1983 of this title, or any other Federal law, by a prisoner confined in any jail, prison, or other correctional facility until such administrative remedies as are available are exhausted.

Prisoners' rights, because they are constrained by the legitimate needs of imprisonment, can be thought of as conditional rights rather than absolute rights. The Second Amendment to the U.S. Constitution, for example, grants citizens the right to bear arms. The right to arms is, however, necessarily compromised by the need for order and security in prison, and we would not expect a court to rule that inmates have a right to weapons. Prisoner rights must be balanced against the security, order maintenance, and treatment needs of correctional institutions.

Conditional rights, because they are subject to the exigencies of imprisonment, bear a strong resemblance to privileges, which is not surprising since "privileges" were all that inmates officially had until the modern era. The practical difference between a privilege and a conditional right is that privileges exist only at the convenience of granting institutions and can be revoked at any time for any reason. The rights of prisoners, on the other hand, have a basis in the Constitution and in law external to the institution. Although the institution may restrict such rights for legitimate correctional reasons, those rights may not be infringed without cause that can be demonstrated in a court of law. Mere institutional convenience does not provide a sufficient legal basis for the denial of rights.

The past few decades have seen many lawsuits brought by prisoners challenging the constitutionality of some aspect of confinement. As mentioned in Chapter 11, suits filed by prisoners with the courts are generally called writs of *habeas corpus* and formally request that the person detaining a prisoner bring him or her before a judicial officer to determine the lawfulness of the imprisonment. The American Correctional Association says that most prisoner lawsuits are based on "1. the Eighth Amendment prohibition against cruel and unusual punishment; 2. the Fourteenth Amendment prohibition against the taking of life, liberty, or property without due process of law; and 3. the Fourteenth Amendment provision requiring equal protection of the laws."[106] Aside from appeals by inmates that question the propriety of their convictions and sentences, such constitutional challenges represent the bulk of legal action initiated by the imprisoned. State statutes and federal legislation, however, including Section 1983 of the Civil Rights Act of 1871, provide other bases for challenges to the legality of specific prison conditions and procedures.

> The person of a prisoner sentenced to imprisonment in the State prison is under the protection of the law, and any injury to his person, not authorized by law, is punishable in the same manner as if he were not convicted or sentenced.
>
> —Section 2650 of the California Penal Code

# Precedents in Prisoners' Rights

The U.S. Supreme Court has not yet spoken with finality on a number of prisoners' rights questions. Nonetheless, high court decisions of the last few decades and a number of lower-court findings can be interpreted to identify the existing conditional rights of prisoners, as shown in Table 14–2. A number of especially significant Supreme Court decisions are discussed in the pages that follow.

TABLE 14–2

## THE CONDITIONAL RIGHTS OF INMATES[1]

### Communications and Visitation

A right to receive publications directly from the publisher
A right to meet with members of the press[2]
A right to communicate with nonprisoners

### Religious Freedom

A right of assembly for religious services and groups
A right to attend services of other religious groups
A right to receive visits from ministers
A right to correspond with religious leaders
A right to observe religious dietary laws
A right to wear religious insignia

### Access to the Courts and Legal Assistance

A right to have access to the courts[3]
A right to visits from attorneys
A right to have mail communications with lawyers[4]
A right to communicate with legal assistance organizations
A right to consult jailhouse lawyers[5]
A right to assistance in filing legal papers, which should include one of the following:
- Access to an adequate law library
- Paid attorneys
- Paralegal personnel or law students

### Medical Care

A right to sanitary and healthy conditions
A right to medical attention for serious physical problems
A right to required medications
A right to treatment in accordance with "doctor's orders"

### Protection from Harm

A right to food, water, and shelter
A right to protection from foreseeable attack
A right to protection from predictable sexual abuse
A right to protection against suicide

### Institutional Punishment and Discipline

An absolute right against corporal punishments (unless sentenced to such punishments)
A limited right to due process before punishment, including the following:
- A notice of charges
- A fair and impartial hearing
- An opportunity for defense
- A right to present witnesses
- A written decision

[1]All "rights" listed are provisional in that they may be constrained by the legitimate needs of imprisonment.
[2]But not beyond the opportunities afforded for inmates to meet with members of the general public.
[3]As restricted by the Prison Litigation Reform Act of 1996.
[4]Mail communications are generally designated as privileged or nonprivileged. Privileged communications include those between inmates and their lawyers or court officials and cannot legitimately be read by prison officials. Nonprivileged communications include most other written communications.
[5]Jailhouse lawyers are inmates with experience in the law, usually gained from filing legal briefs on their own behalf or on the behalf of others. Consultation with jailhouse lawyers was ruled permissible in the Supreme Court case of *Johnson* v. *Avery,* 393 U.S. 483 (1968), unless inmates are provided with paid legal assistance.

# Communications and Visitation

First Amendment guarantees of freedom of speech are applicable to prisoners' rights in three important areas: (1) the receipt of mail, (2) communications with others (especially those on the outside), and (3) visitation.

Courts have generally not allowed restrictions on the receipt of published mail, especially magazines and newspapers that do not threaten prison security. In 2005, in the case of *Banks* v. *Beard*,[107] for example, the Third Circuit U.S. Court of Appeals held that prison officials in Pennsylvania could not prohibit even the most violent inmates from receiving magazines, photographs, and newspapers sent to them in the mail. Pennsylvania Department of Corrections (DOC) rules had prohibited all inmates classified as disruptive and problematic and who were housed at the Long Term Segregation Unit (LTSU) in LaBelle, Pennsylvania, from receiving newspapers or magazines from all sources, including publishers and the prison library. LTSU inmates were kept alone in their cells for 23 hours a day and were not permitted access to television or radio, although they were allowed to have and read religious literature. Visits from friends and family members were limited to one per month. Prison officials argued that the restrictions on print materials placed on LTSU inmates served legitimate penological interests by controlling materials that could be used to start fires and by providing incentives for improved inmate behavior. The appellate court, however, disagreed, holding that "although we agree that deterrence of future infractions of prison rules can be an appropriate justification for temporarily restricting the rights of inmates, we cannot say that the DOC has shown how the regulations in this case serve such a purpose." The risk of fire was similarly discounted because matches were not permitted within cell blocks.

In the case of *Procunier* v. *Martinez* (1974),[108] the Supreme Court ruled that a prisoner's incoming and outgoing mail may be censored if necessary for security purposes. In *McNamara* v. *Moody* (1979),[109] however, a federal court upheld the right of an inmate to write vulgar letters to his girlfriend in which he made disparaging comments about the prison staff. The court reasoned that the letters may have been embarrassing to prison officials but that they did not affect the security or order of the institution. However, libelous materials have generally not been accorded First Amendment protection in or out of institutional contexts.

Concerning publications produced by inmates, legal precedent holds that prisoners have no inherent right to publish newspapers or newsletters for use by other prisoners, although many institutions do permit and finance such periodicals.[110] Publications originating from outside of prison, such as newspapers, magazines, and special-interest tracts, are generally protected when mailed directly from the publisher, although magazines that depict deviant sexual behavior can be banned, according to *Mallery* v. *Lewis* (1983)[111] and other precedents. Nudity by itself is not necessarily obscene, and federal courts have held that prisons cannot ban nude pictures of inmates' wives or girlfriends.[112]

Visitation and access to the news media are other areas that have come under court scrutiny. Maximum-security institutions rarely permit "contact" visits, and some have on occasion suspended all visitation privileges. In the case of *Block* v. *Rutherford* (1984),[113] the U.S. Supreme Court upheld the policy of the Los Angeles County Central Jail, which prohibited all visits from friends and relatives. The Court agreed that the large jail population and the conditions under which visits might take place could combine to threaten the security of the jail.

In the 2003 case of *Overton* v. *Bazzetta*,[114] the Court held that new visitation restrictions imposed by the Michigan Department of Corrections (DOC) in an effort to counter prison security problems caused by an increasing number of visitors and by substance abuse among inmates were acceptable. The regulations allow routine visits for most inmates but state that prisoners who commit two substance abuse violations while incarcerated may receive visits only from clergy and attorneys. Family members are prohibited from visiting, although substance-abusing inmates can apply for reinstatement of visitation privileges after two years. In upholding the Michigan DOC's visitation regulations, the Court found that "the fact that the regulations bear a rational relation to legitimate penological interests suffices to sustain them."

In *Pell* v. *Procunier* (1974),[115] discussed earlier in regard to the balancing test, the Court found in favor of a California law that denied prisoners the opportunity to hold special meetings with members of the press. The Court reasoned that media interviews could be conducted through regular visitation arrangements and that most of the information desired by the media could be conveyed through correspondence. In *Pell*, the Court also held that any reasonable policy of media access was acceptable so long as it was administered fairly and without bias.

In a later case, the Court ruled that news personnel cannot be denied correspondence with inmates but also ruled that they have no constitutional right to interview inmates or to inspect

Inmate Antonio Ferreria participating in a Catholic worship service at Florida's Everglades Correctional Institution. Florida has established what are called "faith-based" programs at nine of its correctional facilities. Faith-based programs are sponsored by religious organizations and supplement government-sponsored training and rehabilitation programs.

*© Deborah Coleman, Palm Beach Post*

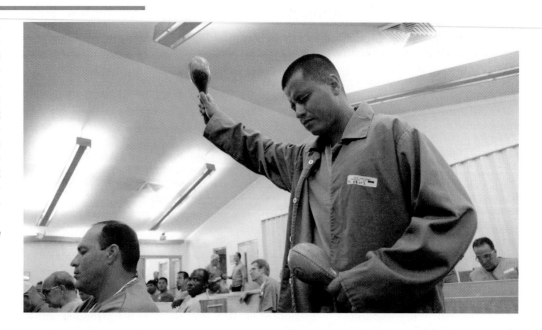

correctional facilities beyond the visitation opportunities available to the public.[116] This equal-access policy was set forth in *Houchins* v. *KQED, Inc.* (1978), by Justice Potter Stewart, who wrote, "The Constitution does no more than assure the public and the press equal access once government has opened its doors."[117]

## Religious Freedom

The First and Fourteenth Amendments provide the basis for prisoners' rights claims in the area of religious freedoms. The U.S. Supreme Court case of *Cruz* v. *Beto* (1972)[118] established that inmates must be given a "reasonable opportunity" to pursue their faith, even if it differs from traditional forms of worship. Meeting facilities must be provided for religious use when those same facilities are made available to other groups of prisoners for other purposes,[119] but no group can claim exclusive use of a prison area for religious reasons.[120] The right to assemble for religious purposes, however, can be denied to inmates who use such meetings to plan escapes or who take the opportunity to dispense contraband. Similarly, prisoners in segregation can be denied the opportunity to attend group religious services.[121]

Although prisoners cannot be made to attend religious services,[122] records of religious activity can be maintained to administratively determine dietary needs and eligibility for passes to religious services outside of the institution.[123] In *Dettmer* v. *Landon* (1985),[124] a federal district court held that an inmate who claimed to practice witchcraft must be provided with the artifacts necessary for his worship services. Included were items such as sea salt, sulfur, a quartz clock, incense, candles, and a white robe without a hood. The district court's opinion was later partially overturned by the U.S. Court of Appeals for the Fourth Circuit. The appellate court recognized the Church of Wicca as a valid religion but held that concerns over prison security could preclude inmates' possession of dangerous items of worship.[125]

Drugs and dangerous substances have not been considered permissible even when inmates claimed they were a necessary part of their religious services.[126] Prison regulations prohibiting the wearing of beards, even those grown for religious reasons, were held acceptable for security reasons in the 1985 federal court case of *Hill* v. *Blackwell.*[127]

A federal law passed in 2000, the Religious Land Use and Institutionalized Persons Act (RLUIPA), has particular relevance to prison programs and activities that are at least partially supported with federal monies. RLUIPA says that "No government shall impose a substantial burden on the religious exercise of a person residing in or confined to an institution even if the burden results from a rule of general applicability, unless the government demonstrates that imposition of the burden on that person (1) is in furtherance of a compelling governmental interest; and (2) is the least restrictive means of furthering that compelling governmental interest." In 2005, in the case of *Benning* v. *State,*[128] the Eleventh Circuit U.S. Court of Appeals found in favor of a Georgia inmate who claimed that RLUIPA supported his right as a "Torah observant Jew" to eat only kosher food and wear a yarmulke at all times.

Also in 2005, in the case of *Cutter* v. *Wilkinson*,[129] the U.S. Supreme Court found in favor of past and present inmates of Ohio's correctional system who claimed that the system failed to accommodate their nonmainstream religious practices. Perhaps the most important aspect of the *Cutter* ruling, however, was the Court's finding that RLUIPA does *not* improperly advance religion in violation of the constitutional requirement of separation of church and state.

## Access to the Courts and Legal Assistance

Access to the courts[130] and to legal assistance is a well-established right of prisoners. The right of prisoners to petition the court was recognized in *Bounds* v. *Smith* (1977),[131] which, at the time, was a far-reaching Supreme Court decision. While attempting to define "access," the Court in *Bounds* imposed on the states the duty of assisting inmates in the preparation and filing of legal papers. Assistance could be provided through trained personnel knowledgeable in the law or via law libraries in each institution, which all states have since built. In 1996, however, in the case of *Lewis* v. *Casey*,[132] the U.S. Supreme Court repudiated part of the *Bounds* decision, saying, "[S]tatements in *Bounds* suggesting that prison authorities must also enable the prisoner to discover grievances, and to litigate effectively once in court . . . have no antecedent in this Court's pre-*Bounds* cases, and are now disclaimed." In *Lewis,* the Court overturned earlier decisions by a federal district court and by the Ninth Circuit Court of Appeals. Both lower courts had found in favor of Arizona inmates who had complained that state prison law libraries provided inadequate legal research facilities, thereby depriving them of their right of legal access to the courts, as established by *Bounds*. In turning back portions of *Bounds,* the majority in *Lewis* wrote that inmates raising such claims need to demonstrate "widespread actual injury" to their ability to access the courts, not merely "isolated instances of actual injury." "Moreover," wrote the justices, "*Bounds* does not guarantee inmates the wherewithal to file any and every type of legal claim, but requires only that they be provided with the tools to attack their sentences . . . and to challenge the conditions of their confinement."

In an earlier case, *Johnson* v. *Avery* (1968),[133] the Court had ruled that prisoners under correctional supervision have a right to consult "jailhouse lawyers" for advice when assistance from trained professionals is not available. Other court decisions have established that inmates have a right to correspond with their attorneys[134] and with legal assistance organizations. Such letters, however, can be opened and inspected for contraband[135] (but not read) by prison authorities in the presence of the inmate. The right to meet with hired counsel for reasonable lengths of time has also been upheld.[136] Indigent defendants must be provided with stamps for the purpose of legal correspondence,[137] and inmates cannot be disciplined for communicating with lawyers or for requesting legal help. Conversations between inmates and their lawyers can be monitored, although any evidence thus obtained cannot be used in court.[138] Inmates do not, however, have the right to an appointed lawyer, even when indigent, if no judicial proceedings have been initiated against them.[139]

## Medical Care

The historic Supreme Court case of *Estelle* v. *Gamble* (1976)[140] specified prison officials' duty to provide for inmates' medical care. In *Estelle,* the Court concerned itself with **deliberate indifference** on the part of the staff toward a prisoner's need for serious medical attention. "Deliberate indifference" can mean a wanton disregard for the health of inmates. Hence, while poor treatment, misdiagnosis, and the like may constitute medical malpractice, they do not necessarily constitute deliberate indifference.[141] In 1992, in *Hudson* v. *McMillan*,[142] the Court clarified the concept of "deliberate indifference" by holding that it requires both actual knowledge and disregard of risk of harm.

Two other cases, *Ruiz* v. *Estelle* (1980)[143] and *Newman* v. *Alabama* (1972),[144] have had a substantial impact on the rights of prisoners to medical attention. In *Ruiz,* the Texas Department of Criminal Justice was found lacking in its correctional medical treatment programs. The court ordered an improvement in record keeping, physical facilities, and general medical care while it continued to monitor the progress of the department. In *Newman,* Alabama's prison medical services were found to be so inadequate as to be "shocking to the conscience."

Part of the issue of medical treatment is the question of whether inmates can be forced to take medication. A 1984 state court held that inmates could be medicated against their will in an emergency.[145] The court did recognize that unwanted medications designed to produce only

**deliberate indifference**

A wanton disregard by correctional personnel for the well-being of inmates. Deliberate indifference requires both actual knowledge that a harm is occurring and disregard of the risk of harm. A prison official may be held liable under the Eighth Amendment for acting with deliberate indifference to inmate health or safety only if he or she knows that inmates face a substantial risk of serious harm and disregards that risk by failing to take reasonable measures to abate it.

## CJ NEWS

### Inmates versus Outsourcing

David Day has a bounce in his step and a glint in his eye unexpected in someone who makes nearly 400 telemarketing calls a day for less than $200 a month. That's because he has a coveted job where few exist: behind bars.

Day, 43, is one of 85 inmates who arrange business meetings from a call center at the Snake River Correctional Institution, an Oregon state penitentiary in this onion- and potato-producing town not far from the Idaho line. "I'm grateful for the opportunity. Many of us end up here because we didn't have jobs and lacked communications skills," he says on a recent morning, ponytail cascading down his state-issued denims.

If not for consulting firm Perry Johnson's aversion to moving jobs offshore, Day, who was convicted of assault, and his cellmates wouldn't be working.

About a dozen states—Oregon, Arizona, California and Iowa, among others—have call centers in state and federal prisons, underscoring a push to employ inmates in telemarketing jobs that might otherwise go to low-wage countries such as India and the Philippines. Arizona prisoners make business calls, as do inmates in Oklahoma. A call center for the DMV is run out of an all-female prison in Oregon. Other companies are keeping manufacturing jobs in the USA. More than 150 inmates in a Virginia federal prison build car parts for Delco Remy International. Previously, some of those jobs were overseas.

At least 2,000 inmates nationwide work in call centers, and that number is rising as companies seek cheap labor without incurring the wrath of politicians and unions. At the same time, prison populations are ballooning, offering U.S. companies another way to slash costs.

"Prisons are prime candidates for low-skill jobs," says Sasha Costanza-Chock, a University of Pennsylvania graduate who last year completed a thesis on call centers at U.S. prisons.

Market conditions seem to favor prisons. After declining for years, call-center jobs in the USA increased several hundred, to about 360,000, last year. At the same time, more white-collar jobs are going offshore than researchers originally thought. About 830,000 U.S. service-sector jobs, from telemarketers to software engineers, will move abroad by the end of 2005, up 41% from previous predictions, says Forrester Research.

About 3.5% of the 2.1 million prisoners in the USA produced goods and services worth an estimated $1.5 billion in 2002.

But the convicted workforce elicits as much dread as interest. Companies flinch at the prospect of a public-relations backlash should news leak out that they employ hardened criminals. Union representatives, meanwhile, call the hiring of prisoners a flagrant violation of minimum-wage laws and unfair competition to free workers.

"Quite literally, they're taking advantage of a captive audience," says Tony Daley, research economist for the Communications Workers of America, which represents 700,000 people nationwide.

Snake River Correctional Institution inmates staff phones and computers at the prison's call center in Ontario, Oregon. The center opened after a yearlong effort by the Oregon Department of Corrections to recruit businesses that would have otherwise moved offshore.
*AP Wide World Photos*

### A SHORT COMMUTE

Tucked away in a corner of Oregon's largest prison, the call center looks like any other, except for the nearby guard stations, razor-wire fences and prison yard.

No more than a football-field-length away, employees commute from their "homes," or cells. The 40-hour workweek is Monday through Friday. A typical workday starts at 7:30 a.m. and ends at 4 p.m. Stellar work earns a half-day on Friday. The pay isn't great—$120 to $185 a month—but for 80 Snake River inmates, it's their first job and a diversion from life in this medium-security prison of 2,900.

"It's a real job: I've learned how to use a computer, make sales pitches and relate to people in the business world," says Willie Wade, 30, who is serving time for robbery. Convicts work for two companies in the Oregon facility. Day and about 60 others pitch Perry Johnson consulting services to American businesses. A group of 20 inmates, including Wade, work for Timlin Industries, an Oregon company that sells promotional items to small businesses.

The center opened last year after a yearlong push by the Oregon Department of Corrections to recruit businesses that would otherwise move offshore. The program reduces by 24% recidivism, the frequency in which released prisoners violate the law and wind up back in jail, and teaches prisoners to work together.

"Guys are sharing business tips rather than talking about their next fix or who to knock off next," says Rob Killgore, administrator of Oregon Corrections Enterprises, a semi-independent state agency that recruits for-profit business to prisons.

"When done properly, it is a vital and important service," says Kara Gotsch, public policy coordinator of the ACLU's National Prison Project. The temptation of call centers behind bars:

## CJ NEWS *(continued)*

■ **Keeping jobs in the USA.** Although inexpensive facilities and English-speaking workers beckon abroad, U.S. companies are unnerved by political backlash.

Consider consulting firm Perry Johnson. It considered moving jobs to India but instead opted for Snake River. "They wanted to keep jobs in the U.S., not take them away," says Ronna Newton, manager at International Marketing Resources, which set up the call center and has fielded calls from other interested companies.

"We're trying to save jobs from going overseas but without hurting the unions," says Philip Glover, president of the National Council of Prison Locals.

But Gordon Lafer, a University of Oregon political science professor, says companies view inmates as an opportunity to skirt the offshore controversy and still save money. "That's as disingenuous as farming jobs overseas," he says.

Besides prisons, companies are relocating call centers and other back-office operations to small towns such as St. Marys, Ga., and Nacogdoches, Texas, where real estate and labor are cheap.

■ **The costs of call centers.** It's hard to retain call-center workers because the job can be demanding, labor experts say. Tethered to a phone up to 10 hours a day, answering hundreds of calls, workers are subjected to peeved callers and dreary work conditions. That has led to dizzying turnover rates of 33%—nearly 10 times the average for other jobs, says Mercer Human Resource Consulting. High turnover has become such a thorny issue for the 7 million-worker industry that Comcast and Comerica have spruced up work spaces and offer specialized training to keep workers, Mercer says.

And it is costly to replace workers. Most companies spend $6,000 to $7,000 to recruit and train each worker, says Jon Anton, a professor at Purdue University's Department of Consumer Sciences.

An official for an Oklahoma-based sales company said if not for its 24-person call center at a state prison, it would have shut down operations or moved jobs to China because of costs. Inmates earn 11 cents to 36 cents an hour, says the Federal Bureau of Prisons.

So far, only six of the 85 inmates in Oregon have quit since the center opened in October, says Mike Reagan, who oversees call-center operations at Snake River. Inmates must have at least a year remaining on their sentences to qualify.

■ **Qualified workers.** There are more inmates—2.1 million in mid-2003, compared with 1.6 million in 1995—because of an influx of convictions for non-violent crimes and longer sentences, says the Justice Policy Institute. As prison populations swell, so has the number of potential qualified workers.

"There isn't as much of a stigma to using prison labor," says Rosemary Batt, a professor at the Cornell University School of Industrial and Labor Relations. "We're sending jobs overseas when there are plenty of qualified people in prison. Why not pay people a wage to rehabilitate them?"

Timlin Industries approached the prison when it became too difficult to find workers in tiny Lakeview, Ore. "Boy, do these guys work hard," says Tim Klosse, who owns Timlin. His crew has performed so well, Timlin recently opened a manufacturing facility in Lakeview to handle an influx of orders.

### GRUNT WORK

Prisons and call centers are nothing new. Best Western phone reservations were logged by female inmates in Arizona in the 1980s and early 1990s before they were replaced by technology. TWA discontinued a phone-reservations program that employed inmates in California in the late 1990s, before the airline went out of business. All got flak for using prison labor. That's not lost on companies considering using inmates instead of exporting jobs. "There is a calculated risk," Killgore admits.

They fear a repeat of the public-relations fiasco that ensnared Dell last year, when it was disclosed that Dell employed prisoners for computer-recycling jobs since late 2002. Dell canceled its contract with Unicor, a branch of the Federal Bureau of Prisons, after an environmental group in California criticized Unicor for improper disposal of toxic waste and unsafe conditions. Dell spokesman Bryant Hilton said moving the jobs to California, Texas and Tennessee was a business decision.

Or worse, executives shudder at the prospects of inmates sharing the personal information of customers with fellow prisoners, as some did in Utah in 2000. That program was scrapped.

Yet advances in technology and common sense have resolved those concerns today, Killgore and others say. At Snake River prison, phone numbers are generated by computer and calls are recorded. Inmates talk to businesses, not consumers. And prisoners convicted of identification theft aren't eligible for jobs.

Ironically, market conditions overseas could return to the U.S. call-center jobs that drifted offshore, says Naren Patni, CEO of Patni Computer Systems, India's sixth-largest software company and a pioneer in outsourcing.

"Costs and turnover for low-skill jobs will increase in India," Patni says. "Who wants to be stuck in a telemarketing job, working odd hours to fit the U.S. time zones, if higher-paying jobs in product development come over? That may force U.S. companies to move call centers, maybe to jails."

Katey Grabenhorst, 42, is eternally grateful one particular call-center job was available at an Oregon prison. She started working for the DMV while imprisoned and remains an employee out of jail.

The job "brought self-esteem, order, skills and a stable income to my life," says Grabenhorst, who served nearly five years for attempted murder. "If this program wasn't available, I would have probably ended up back in prison."

"People can debate the value of prison labor, but I'm living proof it works," she says.

For the latest in crime and justice news, visit the Talk Justice news feed at http://www.crimenews.info.

Inmate Santos Pagon undergoing kidney dialysis at Laurel Highlands Prison in Pennsylvania. Court decisions over the years have established a firm set of inmate rights. Among them is the right to necessary health care.

*Mark Peterson, Corbis/SABA Press Photos, Inc.*

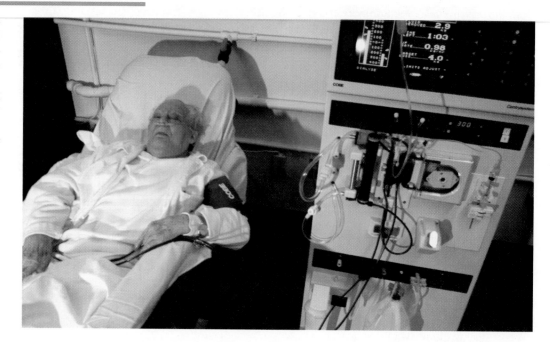

psychological effects, such as tranquilizers, might be refused more readily than life-sustaining drugs.[146] In the 1984 federal court case of *Bee* v. *Greaves,*[147] the Tenth Circuit Court of Appeals ruled that "less restrictive alternatives" should be considered before the administration of antipsychotic drugs to in-custody pretrial detainees. In 1990, in the case of *Washington* v. *Harper,*[148] the U.S. Supreme Court held that prisoners can refuse the involuntary administration of antipsychotic drugs unless government officials can demonstrate an "overriding justification" as to why administration of the drugs is necessary. Under *Washington,* an inmate in a correctional institution "may be treated involuntarily with antipsychotic drugs where there is a determination that the inmate is dangerous to himself or others and the treatment is in the inmate's medical interest."

In 1998, in the case of *Pennsylvania Department of Corrections* v. *Yeskey,*[149] the Supreme Court held that the Americans with Disabilities Act (ADA) of 1990[150] applies to prisons and to prison inmates. In May 1994, Ronald Yeskey was sentenced to serve 18 to 36 months in a Pennsylvania correctional facility. The sentencing court recommended that he be placed in Pennsylvania's Motivational Boot Camp for first-time offenders, the successful completion of which would have led to his release on parole in just six months. When Yeskey was refused admission because of his medical history of hypertension, he sued the Pennsylvania Department of Corrections and several state officials, alleging that his exclusion violated Title II of the ADA, which prohibits a "public entity" from discriminating against a "qualified individual with a disability" on account of that disability. Lawyers for the state of Pennsylvania argued that state prisoners are not covered by the ADA. The Supreme Court ruled, however, that "state prisons fall squarely within Title II's statutory definition of 'public entity,' which includes 'any. . . instrumentality of a State . . . or local government.'"

## Protection from Harm

Claims that inmates have a right to expect prisons to meet their fundamental human needs for food, water, shelter, and reasonable protection from physical and other harm (including potential harm from correctional personnel, other inmates, and oneself) are largely based on Eighth Amendment protection against cruel and unusual punishment. One well-known court decision in this area is the federal district court case of *Holt* v. *Sarver,*[151] in which conditions at two Arkansas state prison farms were found to constitute punishment disproportionate to any offense. Among other things, the court found that inmates have "the right to be fed, housed, and clothed so as not to be subjected to loss of health or life, . . . the right to be free from the abuses of fellow prisoners in all aspects of daily life," and "the right to be free from the brutality of being guarded by fellow inmates." In *Holt,* the state prison system was ordered to correct defects in the conditions of confinement throughout its prisons.

In the case of *Farmer* v. *Brennan* (1994),[152] the U.S. Supreme Court provided substantial protections to prison administration and staff when it found that even when a prisoner is harmed, and even when prison officials knew that a risk of harm existed, they cannot be held liable for that harm if they took appropriate steps to mitigate the risk of its happening. The case involved Dee Farmer, a preoperative transsexual with obvious feminine characteristics who had been incarcerated with other males in the federal prison system. While mixing with other inmates, Farmer was beaten and raped by a fellow prisoner. Subsequently, he sued correctional officials, claiming that they had acted with deliberate indifference to his safety because they knew that the penitentiary had a violent environment as well as a history of inmate assaults and because they should have known that Farmer would be particularly vulnerable to sexual attack. Although both a federal district court and the U.S. Court of Appeals for the Seventh Circuit agreed with Farmer, the U.S. Supreme Court sent Farmer's case back to a lower court for rehearing after clarifying what it said was necessary to establish deliberate indifference. "Prison officials," wrote the justices, "have a duty under the Eighth Amendment to provide humane conditions of confinement. They must ensure that inmates receive adequate food, clothing, shelter, and medical care and must protect prisoners from violence at the hands of other prisoners. However, a constitutional violation occurs only where. . . the official has acted with 'deliberate indifference' to inmate health or safety." The Court continued, "A prison official may be held liable under the Eighth Amendment for acting with 'deliberate indifference' to inmate health or safety only if he knows that inmates face a substantial risk of serious harm and disregards that risk by failing to take reasonable measures to abate it."[153]

In 1993, the U.S. Supreme Court indicated that environmental conditions of prison life that pose a threat to inmate health may have to be corrected. In *Helling* v. *McKinney*,[154] Nevada inmate William McKinney claimed that exposure to secondary cigarette smoke circulating in his cell was threatening his health, in violation of the Eighth Amendment's prohibition against cruel and unusual punishment. The Court, in ordering that a federal district court provide McKinney with the opportunity to prove his allegations, held that "an injunction cannot be denied to inmates who plainly prove an unsafe, life-threatening condition on the ground that nothing yet has happened to them." In effect, the *Helling* case gave notice to prison officials that they are responsible not only for "inmates' current serious health problems," but also for maintaining environmental conditions under which health problems might be prevented from developing.

## Privacy

The Fourth Amendment to the U.S. Constitution guarantees free citizens the right against unreasonable searches and seizures. Courts, however, have not extended this right to prisoners. Many court decisions, including the Tenth Circuit case of *U.S.* v. *Ready* (1978)[155] and the U.S. Supreme Court decisions of *Katz* v. *U.S.* (1967)[156] and *Hudson* v. *Palmer* (1984),[157] have held that inmates do not have a reasonable expectation to privacy while incarcerated. Palmer, an inmate in Virginia, claimed that Hudson, a prison guard, had unreasonably destroyed some of his personal (noncontraband) property following a cell search. Palmer's complaint centered on the lack of due process that accompanied the destruction. The Court disagreed, saying that the need for prison officials to conduct thorough and unannounced searches precludes inmate privacy in personal possessions. In *Block* v. *Rutherford* (1984),[158] mentioned earlier, the Court established that prisoners do not have a right to be present during a search of their cells.

Some lower courts, however, have begun to indicate that body-cavity searches may be unreasonable unless based on a demonstrable suspicion or conducted after prior warning has been given to the inmate.[159] They have also indicated that searches conducted simply to "harass or humiliate" inmates are illegitimate.[160] These cases may be an indication that the Supreme Court will eventually recognize a limited degree of privacy in prison cell searches, especially those that uncover and remove legal documents and personal papers prepared by the prisoner or such documents prepared on his or her behalf.

## Institutional Punishment and Discipline

A major area of inmate concern is the hearing of grievances. Complaints may arise in areas as diverse as food service (quality of food or special diets for religious purposes or health regimens), interpersonal relations between inmates and staff, denial of privileges, and alleged misconduct of an inmate or a guard.

In 1972, the National Council on Crime and Delinquency developed a Model Act for the Protection of Rights of Prisoners, which included the opportunity for grievances to be heard. The 1973 National Advisory Commission on Criminal Justice Standards and Goals called for the

## CJ TODAY EXHIBIT 14-2

### Federal Oversight of the Texas Prison System: A Timeline

1972: Inmate David Ruiz and several other prisoners file a handwritten civil rights suit (*Ruiz* v. *Estelle*) against the Texas Department of Corrections (now called the Texas Department of Criminal Justice), alleging various constitutional violations.

October 2, 1978–September 20, 1979: The *Ruiz* case is tried in Houston.

December 10, 1980: U.S. District Court Judge William Wayne Justice finds that confinement in the Texas prison system constitutes cruel and unusual punishment. He cites overcrowding, understaffing, brutality by guards and inmate-guards known as *building tenders,* substandard medical care, and uncontrolled physical abuse among inmates.

January 12, 1981: The judge orders improvements to be made to the system and sets deadlines.

April 19, 1981: Judge Justice appoints a special master to supervise compliance with his order.

April 1982: The state agrees to halt the building tender system and to hire additional correctional officers.

January–June 1983: The Texas legislature passes laws intended to reduce the prison population.

November 1987: Texas voters authorize $500 million in bonds for prison construction.

March 31, 1990: The special master's office is closed.

November 1990: Texas voters approve $672 million in bonds to build 25,300 prison beds and 12,000 drug- and alcohol-treatment beds.

February 1992: Inmates' attorneys and the Texas Board of Criminal Justice reach an agreement. Texas Attorney General Dan Morales rejects it.

May 1, 1992: Morales offers a settlement proposal.

July 14, 1992: Inmates' attorneys accept the proposal.

December 11, 1992: Judge Justice signs the settlement.

January 21, 1999: Judge Justice begins a hearing to determine whether Texas prisons should be freed of federal court oversight.

March 1, 1999: Judge Justice decides to maintain oversight of the prison system.

March 20, 2001: The 5th U.S. Circuit Court of Appeals reverses Judge Justice's ruling, ending oversight but giving him 90 days to review the matter.

June 18, 2001: Judge Justice says that the Texas prison system has improved but that oversight is still needed in the areas of "conditions of confinement in administrative segregation, the failure to provide reasonable safety to inmates against assault and abuse, and the excessive use of force by correctional officers." Judge Justice discontinues federal oversight of other aspects of the prison system, including health services and staffing.

June 17, 2002: Judge Justice orders an end to federal judicial oversight. The National Institute of Corrections, an arm of the U.S. Department of Justice, was asked to provide further recommendations to the Texas Department of Criminal Justice for a period of two years.

*Source:* Adapted from Ed Timms, "Judge to Lessen Oversight of Texas Prisons," *Dallas Morning News,* June 19, 2001. Reprinted with permission of the *Dallas Morning News.* Web posted at http://www.dallasnews.com/archive (accessed March 12, 2005).

establishment of responsible practices for the hearing of inmate grievances. Finally, in 1977, in the case of *Jones* v. *North Carolina Prisoners' Labor Union,*[161] the Supreme Court held that prisons must establish some formal opportunity for the airing of inmate grievances. Soon, formal grievance plans were established in prisons in an attempt to divert inmate grievances away from the courts.

Today, all sizable prisons have established **grievance procedures** whereby an inmate files a complaint with local authorities and receives a mandated response. Modern grievance procedures range from the use of a hearing board composed of staff members and inmates to a single staff appointee charged with the resolution of complaints. Inmates who are dissatisfied with the handling of their grievance can generally appeal beyond the local prison.

Disciplinary actions by prison authorities may also require a formalized hearing process, especially when staff members bring charges of rule violations against inmates that might result in some form of punishment being imposed on them. In a precedent-setting decision in the case of *Wolff* v. *McDonnell* (1974),[162] the Supreme Court decided that sanctions could not be levied against inmates without appropriate due process. The *Wolff* case involved an inmate who had been deprived of previously earned good-time credits because of misbehavior. The Court established that good-time credits were a form of "state-created right(s)," which, once created, could not be "arbitrarily abrogated."[163] *Wolff* was especially significant because it began an era of court scrutiny that came to be called *state-created liberty interests.* State-created

**grievance procedure**

A formalized arrangement, usually involving a neutral hearing board, whereby institutionalized individuals have the opportunity to register complaints about the conditions of their confinement.

liberty interests were based on the language used in published prison regulations and were held, in effect, to confer due process guarantees on prisoners. Hence, if a prison regulation said that a disciplinary hearing should be held before a prisoner could be sent to solitary confinement and that the hearing should permit a discussion of the evidence for and against the prisoner, courts interpreted that regulation to mean that the prisoner had a state-created right to a hearing and that sending him or her to solitary confinement in violation of the regulation was a violation of a state-created liberty interest. In later court decisions, state-created rights and privileges were called *protected liberties* and were interpreted to include any significant change in a prisoner's status.

In the interest of due process, and especially where written prison regulations governing the hearing process exist, courts have generally held that inmates going before disciplinary hearing boards are entitled to (1) a notice of the charges brought against them, (2) the chance to organize a defense, (3) an impartial hearing, and (4) the opportunity to present witnesses and evidence in their behalf. A written statement of the hearing board's conclusions should be provided to the inmate.[164] In the case of *Ponte* v. *Real* (1985),[165] the Supreme Court held that prison officials must provide an explanation to inmates who are denied the opportunity to have a desired witness at their hearing. The case of *Vitek* v. *Jones* (1980)[166] extended the requirement of due process to inmates about to be transferred from prisons to mental hospitals.

So that inmates will know what is expected of them as they enter prison, the American Correctional Association recommends that "a rulebook that contains all chargeable offenses, ranges of penalties and disciplinary procedures [be] posted in a conspicuous and accessible area; [and] a copy . . . given to each inmate and staff member."[167]

See the Corrections Web logs available in the CJToday.com blogspace.

## A Return to the Hands-Off Doctrine?

Many state-created rights and protected liberties may soon be a thing of the past. In June 1991, an increasingly conservative U.S. Supreme Court signaled what seemed like the beginning of a new "hands-off" era. The case, *Wilson* v. *Seiter et al.*,[168] involved a 1983 suit brought against Richard P. Seiter, director of the Ohio Department of Rehabilitation and Correction, and Carl Humphreys, warden of the Hocking Correctional Facility (HCF) in Nelsonville, Ohio. In the suit, Pearly L. Wilson, a felon incarcerated at HCF, alleged that a number of the conditions of his confinement constituted cruel and unusual punishment in violation of the Eighth and Fourteenth Amendments to the U.S. Constitution. Specifically, Wilson cited overcrowding, excessive noise, insufficient locker storage space, inadequate heating and cooling, improper ventilation, unclean and inadequate restrooms, unsanitary dining facilities and food preparation, and housing with mentally and physically ill inmates. Wilson asked for a change in prison conditions and sought $900,000 from prison officials in compensatory and punitive damages.

Both the federal district court in which Wilson first filed affidavits and the Sixth Circuit Court of Appeals held that no constitutional violations existed because the conditions cited by Wilson were not the result of malicious intent on the part of officials. The U.S. Supreme Court agreed, noting that the "deliberate indifference" standard applied in *Estelle* v. *Gamble* (1976)[169] to claims involving medical care is similarly applicable to other cases in which prisoners challenge the conditions of their confinement. In effect, the Court created a standard that effectively means that all future challenges to prison conditions by inmates, which are brought under the Eighth Amendment, must show "deliberate indifference" by the officials responsible for the existence of those conditions before the Court will hear the complaint.

The written opinion of the Court in *Wilson* v. *Seiter* is telling. Writing for the majority, Justice Antonin Scalia observed that "if a prison boiler malfunctions accidentally during a cold winter, an inmate would have no basis for an Eighth Amendment claim, even if he suffers objectively significant harm. If a guard accidentally stepped on a prisoner's toe and broke it, this would not be punishment in anything remotely like the accepted meaning of the word." At the time that the *Wilson* decision was handed down, critics voiced concerns that the decision could effectively excuse prison authorities from the need to improve living conditions within institutions on the basis of simple budgetary constraints.

In the 1995 case of *Sandin* v. *Conner*,[170] the U.S. Supreme Court took a much more definitive stance in favor of a new type of hands-off doctrine and voted 5 to 4 to reject the argument that any state action taken for a punitive reason encroaches on a prisoner's constitutional due process right to be free from the deprivation of liberty. In *Sandin*, Demont Conner, an inmate at the Halawa Correctional Facility in Hawaii, was serving an indeterminate sentence of 30 years to life for numerous crimes, including murder, kidnapping, robbery, and burglary. In a lawsuit in federal court, Conner alleged that prison officials had deprived him of procedural due process when a hearing committee refused to allow him to present witnesses during a disciplinary hearing and then sentenced him to segregation for alleged misconduct. An appellate court agreed with Conner, concluding that an existing prison regulation that instructed the hearing committee to find guilt in cases where a misconduct charge is supported by substantial evidence meant that the committee could not impose segregation if it did not look at all the evidence available to it.

The Supreme Court, however, reversed the decision of the appellate court, holding that while "such a conclusion may be entirely sensible in the ordinary task of construing a statute defining rights and remedies available to the general public, [i]t is a good deal less sensible in the case of a prison regulation primarily designed to guide correctional officials in the administration of a prison." The Court concluded that "such regulations [are] not designed to confer rights on inmates" but are meant only to provide guidelines to prison staff members.

In *Sandin,* the Court effectively set aside substantial portions of earlier decisions, such as *Wolff* v. *McDonnell* (1974)[171] and *Hewitt* v. *Helms* (1983),[172] which, wrote the justices, focused more on procedural issues than on those of "real substance." As a consequence, the majority opinion held, past cases like these have "impermissibly shifted the focus" away from the nature of a due process deprivation to one based on the language of a particular state or prison regulation. "The *Hewitt* approach," wrote the majority in *Sandin,* "has run counter to the view expressed in several of our cases that federal courts ought to afford appropriate deference and flexibility to state officials trying to manage a volatile environment. . . . The time has come," said the Court, "to return to those due process principles that were correctly established and applied" in earlier times. In short, *Sandin* made it much more difficult for inmates to effectively challenge the administrative regulations and procedures imposed on them by prison officials, even when stated procedures are not explicitly followed.

## The Prison Litigation Reform Act of 1996

Only about 2,000 petitions per year concerning inmate problems were filed with the courts in 1961, but by 1975 the number of filings had increased to around 17,000, and in 1996 prisoners filed 68,235 civil rights lawsuits in federal courts nationwide.[173] Some inmate-originated suits seemed patently ludicrous and became the subject of much media coverage in the mid-1990s.[174] One such suit involved Robert Procup, a Florida State Prison inmate serving time for the murder of his business partner. Procup repeatedly sued Florida prison officials—once because he got only one roll with his dinner; again because he didn't get a luncheon salad; a third time because prison-provided TV dinners didn't come with a drink; and a fourth time because his cell had no television. Two other well-publicized cases involved an inmate who went to court asking to be allowed to exercise religious freedom by attending prison chapel services in the nude and an inmate who, thinking he could become pregnant via homosexual relations, sued prison doctors who wouldn't provide him with birth-control pills. An infamous example of seemingly frivolous inmate lawsuits was one brought by inmates claiming religious freedoms and demanding that members of the Church of the New Song, or CONS, be provided steak and Harvey's Bristol Cream every Friday in order to celebrate communion. The CONS suit stayed in various courts for ten years before finally being thrown out.[175]

The huge number of inmate-originated lawsuits in the mid-1990s created a backlog of cases in many federal courts and was targeted by the media and by some citizens' groups as an unnecessary waste of taxpayers' money. The National Association of Attorneys General, which supports efforts to restrict frivolous inmate lawsuits, estimated that lawsuits filed by prisoners cost states more than $81 million a year in legal fees alone.[176]

In 1996, the federal Prison Litigation Reform Act (PLRA) became law.[177] The PLRA was a legislative effort to restrict inmate filings to worthwhile cases and to reduce the number of suits brought by state prisoners in federal courts. The PLRA

- Requires inmates to exhaust their prison's grievance procedure before filing a lawsuit.
- Requires judges to screen all inmate complaints against the federal government and to immediately dismiss those deemed frivolous or without merit.
- Prohibits prisoners from filing a lawsuit for mental or emotional injury unless they can also show there has been physical injury.
- Requires inmates to pay court filing fees. Prisoners who don't have the needed funds can pay the filing fee over a period of time through deductions to their prison commissary accounts.
- Limits the award of attorneys' fees in successful lawsuits brought by inmates.
- Revokes the credits earned by federal prisoners toward early release if they file a malicious lawsuit.

- Mandates that court orders affecting prison administration cannot go any further than necessary to correct a violation of a particular inmate's civil rights.

- Makes it possible for state officials to have court orders lifted after two years unless there is a new finding of a continuing violation of federally guaranteed civil rights.

- Mandates that any court order requiring the release of prisoners due to overcrowding be approved by a three-member court before it can become effective.

The U.S. Supreme Court has upheld provisions of the PLRA on a number of occasions. In 1997, for example, in the case of *Edwards* v. *Balisok*,[178] the Supreme Court made it harder to successfully challenge prison disciplinary convictions, holding that, under the PLRA, prisoners cannot sue for damages under 42 U.S.C. §1983 for loss of good-time credits until they sue in state court and get their disciplinary conviction set aside.[179] In *Booth* v. *Churner* (2001),[180] the U.S. Supreme Court held that under the PLRA, "an inmate seeking only [monetary] damages must complete any prison administrative process capable of addressing the inmate's complaint and providing some form of relief [before filing his or her grievance with a federal court], even if the process does not make specific provision for monetary relief." Similarly, in the case of *Porter* v. *Nussle* (2002),[181] the U.S. Supreme Court held that a Connecticut inmate had inappropriately brought a Section 1983 complaint directly to federal district court without first having filed an inmate grievance as required by Connecticut Department of Correction procedures. In *Porter*, the Court held that the PLRA's exhaustion requirement applies to all inmate suits about prison life, whether they involve general circumstances or particular episodes and whether they allege excessive force or some other wrong.

According to a 2002 Bureau of Justice Statistics (BJS) study, the PLRA has been effective in reducing the number of frivolous lawsuits filed by inmates alleging unconstitutional prison conditions.[182] The study found that the filing rate of inmates' civil rights petitions in federal courts had been cut in half four years after passage of the act. A similar study by the National Center for State Courts, whose results were published in 2004, found that the "PLRA produced a statistically significant decrease in both the volume and trend of lawsuits . . . nationally and in every [federal court] circuit. . . ."[183]

Opponents of the PLRA fear that it might stifle the filing of meritorious suits by inmates facing real deprivations. According to the American Civil Liberties Union (ACLU), for example, "The Prison Litigation Reform Act . . . attempts to slam the courthouse door on society's most vulnerable members. It seeks to strip the federal courts of much of their power to correct even the most egregious prison conditions by altering the basic rules which have always governed prison reform litigation. The PLRA also makes it difficult to settle prison cases by consent decree, and limits the life span of any court judgment."[184] The ACLU is leading a nationwide effort to have many provisions of the PLRA overturned. So far, however, the effort has borne little fruit.

# Issues Facing Prisons Today

Prisons are society's answer to a number of social problems. They house outcasts, misfits, and some highly dangerous people. While prisons provide a part of the answer to the question of crime control, they also face problems of their own. A few of those special problems are described here.

# AIDS

Chapter 8 discussed the steps that police agencies are taking to deal with health threats from acquired immunodeficiency syndrome (AIDS). In 2004, the Justice Department reported finding 23,864 cases of AIDS among inmates of the nation's prisons[185]—more than a 12-fold increase over 1987, when surveys were first conducted. The most recent survey shows that 3% of all female state prison inmates tested positive for HIV infection, as did 1.9% of male prisoners. Some states have especially high rates of HIV infection among their prisoners. More than 7.5% of New York prison inmates, for example, are HIV-positive.

The incidence of HIV infection among the general population stands at 140 cases per 100,000, according to a recent report by the Centers for Disease Control and Prevention. Among inmates, however, best estimates place the reported HIV-infection rate at 490 cases per 100,000[186]—five times as great. Some years ago, AIDS was the leading cause of death among prison inmates.[187] Today, however, the number of inmates who die from AIDS (or, more precisely, from AIDS-related

> To return to society discharged prisoners unreformed is to poison it with the worst elements possible.
>
> —Zebulon R. Brockway[ii]

Log on to ResearchNavigator .com, and choose "All" under the *New York Times* subject archive section. Enter the word "prison" (without the quotation marks) in the search box and click "Go." Select at least five of the articles that appear by relating them to the ideas discussed in this chapter (for example, prisoners' rights, women's prisons, living behind bars, prison riots). If a particular article is not a clear fit for any idea, then choose another. Send the titles of the articles, along with a brief summary of each and complete source information (that is, author, journal, date of publication), to your instructor if asked to do so. *Note:* This feature is available only if your instructor has chosen the Research Navigator option available with a new textbook.

## CJ CAREERS

### U.S. CUSTOMS AND BORDER PROTECTION (CBP)

**Name:** Jeffrey D. Adami

**Position:** Customs and Border Protection Inspector

**City:** Jamaica, New York

**College Attended:** State University of New York at Brockport

**Year Hired:** 1999

*Customs and Border Protection has given me an excellent working knowledge of the federal justice system along with endless opportunities for advancement.*

#### TYPICAL POSITIONS

Border patrol agent, immigration inspector, immigration officer, immigration agent, deportation officer, detention enforcement officer, and criminal investigator. The primary mission of U.S. Customs and Border Protection is to detect and prevent the smuggling and unlawful entry of undocumented aliens into the United States. It also acts as the primary drug-interdicting agency along U.S. land borders. Entry-level border patrol agents are stationed in Texas, New Mexico, Arizona, and California along the U.S.–Mexico border. Immigration inspector and criminal investigator positions are available nationwide.

#### EMPLOYMENT REQUIREMENTS

Applicants for the position of border patrol agent must meet the general requirements for a federal law enforcement officer and must (1) be a U.S. citizen, (2) pass a background investigation, (3) pass a drug-screening test and a medical exam, (4) hold a valid driver's license, (5) be under age 37 at time of appointment, (6) have one year of qualifying experience or a bachelor's degree, and (7) pass the U.S. Customs and Border Protection entrance exam.

#### OTHER REQUIREMENTS

Border patrol agents must demonstrate proficiency in the Spanish language.

#### SALARY

New agents are hired at the GS-5 or GS-7 level, depending on education and experience, and are paid at the special salary rate for federal law enforcement personnel.

#### BENEFITS

Benefits include paid annual vacation, sick leave, life and health insurance, and a liberal retirement plan.

#### DIRECT INQUIRIES TO:

U.S. Customs and Border Protection
Twin Cities Hiring Center
One Federal Drive, Room 400
Fort Snelling, MN 55111-4055

Website: http://www.cbp.gov

For additional information on employment opportunities in the criminal justice field, view the careers portion of the CD-ROM included with this book.

*Source:* U.S. Office of Personnel Management and http://www.cbp.gov.

complications like pneumonia or Kaposi's sarcoma) is much lower. The introduction of drugs like protease inhibitors and useful combinations of antiretroviral therapies have reduced inmate deaths from AIDS by more than 80% since 1995.[188]

Some inmates are infected in prison, while others carry the HIV virus into prison with them. Authorities say the virus is spread behind bars through homosexual activity (including rape), intravenous drug use, and the sharing of tainted tattoo and hypodermic needles. Those inmates who are infected before entering prison are likely those who have histories of high-risk behavior, especially intravenous drug use.

A report by the National Institute of Justice (NIJ) suggests that correctional administrators can use two types of strategies to reduce the transmission of AIDS.[189] One strategy relies on medical technology to identify seropositive inmates and to segregate them from the rest of the prison population. Mass screening and inmate segregation, however, may be prohibitively expensive. They may also be illegal. Some states specifically prohibit HIV-antibody testing without the informed consent of the person tested.[190] The related issue of confidentiality may be difficult to manage, especially when the purpose of testing is to segregate infected inmates from others. In addition,

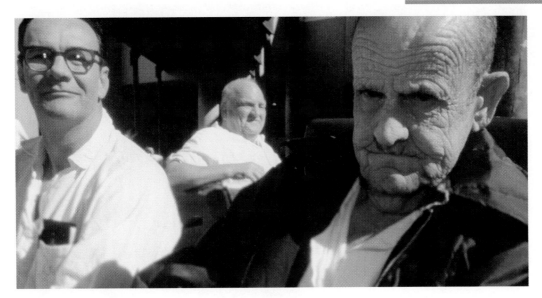

Elderly inmates inside the geriatric unit of Texas's Estelle Prison. Geriatric inmates are becoming an increasingly large part of the inmate population.
*Andrew Lichtenstein, The Image Works*

civil liability may result if inmates are falsely labeled as infected or if inmates known to be infected are not prevented from spreading the disease. Only Alabama and South Carolina still segregate all known HIV-infected inmates,[191] but more limited forms of separation are practiced elsewhere. Many state prison systems have denied HIV-positive inmates jobs, educational opportunities, visitation privileges, conjugal visits, and home furloughs, causing some researchers to conclude that "inmates with HIV and AIDS are routinely discriminated against and denied equal treatment in ways that have no accepted medical basis."[192] In 1994, for example, a federal appeals court upheld a California prison policy that bars inmates who are HIV-positive from working in food-service jobs.[193] In contrast, in 2001, the Mississippi Department of Correction ended its policy of segregating HIV-positive prisoners from other inmates in educational and vocational programs.

The second strategy is prevention through education. Educational programs teach both inmates and staff members about the dangers of high-risk behavior and suggest ways to avoid HIV infection. An NIJ model program recommends the use of simple, straightforward messages presented by knowledgeable and approachable trainers.[194] Alarmism, says NIJ, should be avoided. One survey found that 98% of state and federal prisons provide some form of AIDS/HIV education and that 90% of jails do as well—although most such training is oriented toward correctional staff rather than inmates.[195] Learn more about HIV in prisons and jails via Library Extra 14–8 at cjtoday.com. Inmate medical problems in general are discussed in Library Extra 14–9.

LIBRARY EXTRA

## Geriatric Offenders

In 2003, Eugene Guevara of El Monte, California, shot a physician at Kaiser Permanente's Baldwin Park Medical Center.[196] Surveillance cameras filmed Guevara, who was in his late 70s, fleeing the scene using his walker. Guevara later shot and killed himself outside a fast-food restaurant.

Crimes committed by the elderly, especially violent crimes, have recently been on the decline. Nonetheless, the significant expansion of America's retiree population has led to an increase in the number of elderly people who are behind bars. In fact, crimes of violence are what brings most older people into the correctional system. According to one early study, 52% of inmates who were over the age of 50 when they entered prison had committed violent crimes, compared with 41% of younger inmates.[197] On January 1, 2005, 67,200 inmates age 55 or older were housed in state and federal prisons. The number of prisoners older than 55 increased more than 400% between 1990 and 2005.[198] Similarly, the per capita rate of incarceration for inmates age 55 and over now stands at 231 per 100,000 residents of like age and, until very recently, had steadily increased.

## CJ NEWS

## Death Row Population Is Graying

Like the other 107 convicted killers on Arizona's death row, LeRoy Nash is allowed to leave solitary confinement for an hour each day to exercise in a secure room.

But Nash, 89, seldom does. Hobbled by arthritis, deafness and heart disease, the oldest person under a death sentence in the USA usually just sits in his cell. He reads and writes letters in block print, and sometimes he strains to hear the conversations of other death row inmates through a 1-foot-square glass window and the concrete walls.

"I can't send or receive e-mail, nor make any collect telephone calls," Nash said in a recent letter to a *USA Today* reporter. "Unfortunately, this is one of the tightest death rows in America."

Nash may be held in "solitary," but in another sense he has plenty of company.

A record 110 prisoners aged 60 and older were on death rows across the nation as of Dec. 31, 2003, the U.S. Bureau of Justice Statistics says. That's nearly triple the 39 death row seniors that the bureau counted nine years earlier. During the same period, the total number of convicts under death sentences rose 18.3%, to 3,374.

The rising number of death row seniors is a little-noted phenomenon that is raising new questions for courts, and public relations issues for prison officials.

Nash and another elderly killer have asked federal judges to rule on the constitutionality of executing inmates with dementia, Alzheimer's or other age-related maladies.

And executing a lame, deaf and infirm senior—even one who has committed aggravated murder—is a prospect that few prison wardens relish, according to legal scholars such as Jonathan Turley, a law professor at George Washington University who has worked with older prisoners.

"Dead man walking' is one thing," Turley says. "Dead man being pushed along to the execution chamber in a wheelchair has a different feel."

### "HAVING IT BOTH WAYS"

Death row's elderly population has grown for several reasons.

A few seniors are on death row because they committed aggravated murder at an unusually old age. Nash fatally shot a Phoenix coin store clerk in a holdup in 1982, when he was 67. (Nash insists that it was "a strictly self-defense, live-or-die matter.") Blanche Moore, at 71 the oldest of four elderly women on death row, was convicted of killing a boyfriend with an arsenic-laden milkshake in North Carolina in 1990, when she was 57.

Many others are there because death penalty appeals can stretch for decades. The last senior citizen to be executed, Donald Beardslee of California, was put to death in January at age 61, after 21 years of appeals. North Carolina convict Jerry Cummings began appealing his murder conviction in 1966, when he was 27. It has been set aside and reinstated twice; he's now 65.

Death penalty supporters say it is disingenuous for seniors to prolong their appeals for years and to then argue that they are too old to be executed.

Arizona inmate LeRoy Nash. At 89, Nash is the oldest inmate currently on death row in the United States.

*Arizona Department of Corrections*

"That's having it both ways," says Ken Wallis, legal adviser to Alabama Gov. Bob Riley.

But Nash's attorney, Thomas Phalen, says that foot-dragging by courts often causes appeals to languish. Nash, for example, has had an appeal before the U.S. District Court in Phoenix for more than four years without a ruling. If Nash were to lose, subsequent appeals likely would last for at least four more years—meaning that he likely would not be scheduled for execution until his mid-90s.

"The judges can read the files; they know when they're dealing with an old prisoner," Phalen says. "It's hard not to conclude that they're hoping that natural causes will take an uncomfortable decision out of their hands."

Executing seniors can be an unpopular proposition, even in a prison that houses hardened convicts.

Alabama officials saw an example of that last August, when James Hubbard, 74, was executed. Willie Minor, the old man's neighbor on the state's death row in Donaldson, Ala., filed a petition asking Riley to grant clemency to "this elderly and sick man" as a "matter of justice, mercy and morality."

Executing Hubbard, who suffered from prostate and colon cancer and alleged that he had dementia, was "offensive to every civilized Alabamian," Minor's petition said.

The request was denied.

### CURBING COSTS

Convicts older than 50 represent the fastest-growing group in the general populations of state and federal prisons.

## CJ NEWS (continued)

From 1992 to 2001, the number of state and federal prisoners aged 50 and older jumped from 41,586 to 113,358—or about 170%, according to the Bureau of Justice Statistics. During the same period, the total U.S. prison population increased by 6%, to 2,100,146.

Some states have begun innovations aimed at curbing the rising costs of dealing with older prisoners.

In 35 states, elderly prisoners are housed in geriatric facilities within prisons. Alabama's is across the street from a hospital, saving time and expense when prisoners need critical care. In Ohio, older prisoners are housed in areas that have few stairs.

At least 29 states have begun hospice or other "end of life" programs within prisons, says Ronald Aday, a professor at Middle Tennessee State University in Murfreesboro.

But none of the innovations help the death row elderly. Because of their condemned status, they are segregated from other prisoners and held in special facilities—often in individual cells, as is the case for Nash in Arizona.

Nash is among the death row seniors whose appeals are raising new legal issues.

In 1999, Phalen argued that Nash, then 83, suffered from dementia and thus should not be executed. The attorney cited a 1976 U.S. Supreme Court ruling that forbids executing prisoners who have become mentally incompetent. A federal judge said the appeal was premature because Nash did not have an execution date.

In Alabama last year, attorney Alan Rose Sr. raised the same argument to try to keep Hubbard from being executed. Two of three federal appeals court judges essentially ruled that Hubbard was too late with his appeal.

But U.S. Court of Appeals Judge Rosemary Barkett dissented, noting that Hubbard "could not have brought the claim earlier" because dementia typically begins in old age.

Hubbard was executed. But Phalen says he and other attorneys for death row seniors likely will try to base future arguments on Barkett's reasoning.

Meanwhile, Nash says he has no interest in stretching out his appeal. He first entered prison in 1930, when he was 15, and he has spent nearly half of his 89 years behind bars for robbery, two murders and other crimes. He says he wants his appeal to conclude quickly, so that if he wins he could be resentenced to life in prison and return to the prison's general population.

Keeping old men like him on death row is "idiotic," Nash says. Growing old in prison is "brutish" enough, he says, without being locked up in solitary.

For the latest in crime and justice news, visit the Talk Justice news feed at http://www.crimenews.info.

*Source:* Richard Willing, "Death Row Population Is Graying," *USA Today,* February 10, 2005, p. 3A. Copyright © 2005 *USA Today.* Reprinted with permission.

Not all of today's elderly inmates were old when they entered prison. Because of harsh sentencing laws passed throughout the country in the 1990s, a small but growing number of inmates (10%) will serve 20 years or more in prison, and 5% will never be released.[199] This means that many inmates who enter prison when they are young will grow old behind bars. Hence the "graying" of America's prison population has a number of causes: "(1) the general aging of the American population, which is reflected inside prisons; (2) new sentencing policies such as 'three strikes,' 'truth in sentencing' and 'mandatory minimum' laws that send more criminals to prison for longer stretches; (3) a massive prison building boom that took place in the 1980s and 1990s, and which has provided space for more inmates, reducing the need to release prisoners to alleviate overcrowding; and (4) significant changes in parole philosophies and practices,"[200] with state and federal authorities phasing out or canceling parole programs, thereby forcing jailers to hold inmates with life sentences until they die.

Long-termers and geriatric inmates have special needs. They tend to suffer from handicaps, physical impairments, and illnesses not generally encountered among their more youthful counterparts. Unfortunately, few prisons are equipped to deal adequately with the medical needs of aging offenders. Some large facilities have begun to set aside special sections to care for elderly inmates with "typical" disorders, such as Alzheimer's disease, cancer, or heart disease. Unfortunately, such efforts have barely kept pace with the problems that geriatric offenders present. The number of inmates requiring round-the-clock care is expected to increase dramatically during the next two decades.[201]

The idea of rehabilitation takes on a new meaning where geriatric offenders are concerned. What kinds of programs are most useful in providing the older inmate with the tools needed for success on the outside? Which counseling strategies hold the greatest promise for introducing socially acceptable behavior patterns into the long-established lifestyles of elderly offenders about to be released? There are few answers to these questions. Learn about some of the oldest prisoners in America via Web Extra 14–3 at cjtoday.com.

**WEB EXTRA**

## CJ FUTURES

### Technocorrections

The technological forces that have made cell phones ubiquitous are beginning to converge with the forces of law and order to create what some have called *technocorrections*. Members of the correctional establishment—the managers of the jail, prison, probation, and parole systems and their sponsors in elected office—are seeking more cost-effective ways to increase public safety as the number of people under correctional supervision continues to grow. Technocorrections is being defined by a correctional establishment that seeks to take advantage of all the potential offered by the new technologies to reduce the costs of supervising criminal offenders and to minimize the risk they pose to society.

Emerging technologies in three areas will soon be central elements of technocorrections: electronic tracking and location systems, pharmacological treatments, and genetic and neurobiological risk assessments. While these technologies may significantly increase public safety, we must also be mindful of the threats they pose to democratic principles. The critical challenge will be to learn how to take advantage of new technological opportunities applicable to the corrections field while minimizing their threats.

#### TRACKING AND LOCATION SYSTEMS

Electronic tracking and location systems are the technology perhaps most familiar to correctional practitioners today. Most states use electronic monitoring—either with the older bracelets that communicate through a device connected to telephone lines or with more modern versions based on cellular or satellite tracking. With such technology, corrections officials can continuously track offenders' locations and use that information to supervise their movements. As this technology expands, it will enable corrections officials to define geographic areas from which offenders are prohibited and to furnish tracking devices to potential victims (such as battered spouses). The devices will set "safe zones" that trigger alarms or warning notices when the offender approaches.

Tiny cameras might also be integrated into tracking devices to provide live video of offenders' locations and activities. Miniature electronic devices implanted in the body to signal the location of offenders at all times, to create unique identifiers that trigger alarms, and to monitor key bodily functions that affect unwanted behaviors are under development and are close to becoming reality.[1]

#### PHARMACOLOGICAL TREATMENTS

Pharmacological breakthroughs—new "wonder drugs" being developed to control behavior in correctional and noncorrectional settings—will also be a part of technocorrections. Corrections officials are already familiar with some of these drugs, which are currently used to treat mentally ill offenders. Yet these drugs could also be used to control mental conditions affecting undesirable behaviors even for offenders who are not mentally ill. Research into the relationship between levels of the neurotransmitter serotonin and violent behavior continues to be re-

fined. Findings to date seem to indicate that people who have low levels of serotonin are more prone than others to impulsive, violent acts, especially when they abuse alcohol.[2] Not long ago, the National Academy of Sciences (NAS) recommended a new emphasis in biomedical research on violence as a means to understand the biological roots of violent behavior.[3] The NAS reports that research findings from animal and human studies "point to several features of the nervous system as promising sites" for discovering reliable biological "markers" for violent behavior and designing preventive therapies.[4]

It is only a matter of time before research findings in this area lead to the development of drugs to control neurobiological processes. These drugs could become correctional tools to manage violent offenders and perhaps even to prevent violence. Such advances are related to the third area of technology that will affect corrections: genetic and neurobiological risk-assessment technologies.

#### RISK-ASSESSMENT TECHNOLOGIES

Corrections officials today are familiar with the DNA profiling of offenders, particularly sex offenders. This is just the beginning of the correctional application of gene-related technologies, however. The Human Genome Project, supported by the National Institutes of Health and the Department of Energy, began in 1990 and was completed in 2003. The goal of the Human Genome Project was creation of a map of the 3 billion chemical bases that make up human DNA. The map was constructed by high-powered "sequencer" machines that can analyze human DNA faster than any human researcher can.[5] Emerging as a powerhouse of the high-tech economy, the biotechnology industry will drive developments in DNA-based risk assessment.

Gene "management" technologies are already widely used in agriculture and are increasingly used in medicine. The progression is likely to continue with applications in psychiatric and behavioral management. Researchers are investigating the genetic—or inherited—basis of behavior, including antisocial and criminal behavior. Studies of twins, for example, have revealed similarities in behavior attributable to a genetic effect.[6] Eventually, the genetic roots of human behavior could be profiled.

Neurobiological research is taking the same path, although thus far no neurobiological patterns specific enough to be reliable biological markers for violent behavior have been uncovered. Is it possible that breakthroughs in these areas will lead to the development of risk-assessment tools that use genetic or neurobiological profiles to identify children who have a propensity toward addiction or violence? Might they also be capable of identifying individuals with a propensity for becoming sex offenders? We may soon be able to link genetic and neurobiological traits with social and environmental factors to reliably predict who is at risk for addiction, sex offending, violent behavior, or crime in general.

Attempts will surely be made to develop genetic or neurobiological tests for assessing risks posed by individuals. This is already done for the risk of contracting certain diseases. Demand for risk assessments of individuals will come from corrections officials under pressure to prevent violent recidivism. Once under

## CJ FUTURES (continued)

correctional control, specific offenders could be identified, on the basis of such testing and risk assessment, as likely violent recidivists. The group so classified could be placed under closer surveillance or declared a danger to themselves and society and be civilly committed to special facilities for indeterminate periods. In other words, incarceration could assume a more preventive role.

"Preventive incarceration" is already a reality for some convicted sex offenders. More than a dozen states commit certain sex offenders to special "civil commitment" facilities after they have served their prison sentences because of a behavioral or mental abnormality that makes them dangerous.[7] This happens today with no clear understanding of the nature of the abnormality. It is not difficult to imagine what might be done to justify preventive incarceration if this "abnormal" or criminal behavior could be explained and predicted by genetic or neurobiological profiling.

[1]"Microchip Implants Closer to Reality," *Futurist,* Vol. 33, No. 8 (October 1999), p. 9.
[2]Sheryl Stolberg, "Scientific Studies Are Generating Controversy," *Austin American-Statesman,* January 16, 1994.
[3]Albert J. Reiss, Jr., and Jeffrey A. Roth, eds., *Understanding and Preventing Violence* (Washington, DC: National Academy Press, 1993). Reiss and Roth call for "systematic searches for neurobiologic markers for persons with elevated potentials for violent behavior" (p. 24).
[4]Ibid., p. 12. Reiss and Roth caution, however, that "the generalizability of experimental findings from other animal species to humans is not always straightforward" (p. 116).
[5]Walter Isaacson, "The Biotech Century," *Time,* January 11, 1999, p. 42; and Michael D. Lemonick and Dick Thompson, "Racing to Map Our DNA," *Time,* January 11, 1999, p. 44.
[6]G. Carey and D. Goldman, "The Genetics of Antisocial Behavior," in D. M. Stoff et al., eds., *Handbook of Antisocial Behavior* (New York: John Wiley, 1997), pp. 243–254.
[7]See *Kansas* v. *Hendricks,* 521 U.S. 346 (1997), in which the Court approved such a practice. In the case of *Kansas* v. *Crane* (122 S.Ct. 867 [2002]), however, the U.S. Supreme Court ruled that the Constitution does not permit commitment of certain types of dangerous sexual offenders without a "lack-of-control determination."
*Source:* Adapted from Tony Fabelo, *"Technocorrections": The Promises, the Uncertain Threats* (Washington, DC: National Institute of Justice, 2000); and U.S. Department of Energy, "Human Genome Project Information." Web posted at http://www.ornl.gov/TechResources/Human_Genome/home.html.

# Mentally Ill and Mentally Deficient Inmates

Mentally ill inmates make up another group with special needs. Some mentally ill inmates are neurotic or have personality problems, which increase tension in prison. Others have serious psychological disorders that may have escaped diagnosis at trial or that did not provide a legal basis for the reduction of criminal responsibility. A fair number of offenders develop psychiatric symptoms while in prison.

Inmates suffering from significant mental illnesses account for a substantial number of those imprisoned. A 2002 lawsuit brought by a New York advocacy group on behalf of mentally ill prisoners in New York's penal institutions put the number of inmates suffering from psychiatric illnesses at 16,000 (out of a total state prison population of 67,000). The suit alleges that problem inmates with psychiatric illnesses are often isolated, exacerbating their condition and resulting in a "cycle of torment" for inmates unable to conform to prison regimens.[202]

In contrast to the allegations made by the lawsuit, a 2000 Bureau of Justice Statistics survey of public and private state-level adult correctional facilities (excluding jails) found that 51% of such institutions provide 24-hour mental health care, while 71% provide therapy and counseling by trained mental health professionals as needed.[203] A large majority of prisons distribute psychotropic medications (when such medications are ordered by a physician), and 66% have programs to help released inmates obtain community mental health services. According to BJS, 13% of state prisoners were receiving some type of mental health therapy at the time of the survey, and 10% were receiving psychotropic medications (including antidepressants, stimulants, sedatives, and tranquilizers).

Unfortunately, few state-run correctional institutions have any substantial capacity for the in-depth psychiatric treatment of inmates who are seriously mentally disturbed. A number of states, however, do operate facilities that specialize in psychiatric confinement of convicted criminals. The BJS reports that state governments throughout the nation operate 12 facilities devoted exclusively to the care of mentally ill inmates and that another 143 prisons report psychiatric confinement as one specialty among other functions that they perform.

## FREEDOM OR SAFETY? YOU DECIDE.

### Censoring Prison Communications

On February 28, 2005, NBC News announced that it had learned that Arab terrorists in federal maximum-security prisons had been sending letters to extremists on the outside exhorting them to attack Western interests. The terrorists included Mohammed Salameh, a follower of radical sheik Omar Abdel-Rahman. Salameh had been sentenced to more than 100 years in prison for his part in the 1993 bombing attack on New York's World Trade Center. That attack, which killed six and injured more than 1,000, blew a huge hole in the basement parking garage of one of the towers but failed to topple the buildings.

The men are being held in the federal ADMAX facility in Florence, Colorado—the country's most secure federal prison. While there, NBC News revealed, they sent at least 14 letters to a Spanish terror cell, praised Osama bin Laden in Arabic newspapers, and advocated additional terror attacks. In July 2002, Salameh, a Palestinian with a degree in Islamic law from a Jordanian university, sent a letter to the Al-Quds Arabic daily newspaper, proclaiming that "Osama Bin Laden is my hero of this generation."

Andy McCarthy, a former federal prosecutor who worked to send the terrorists to prison, said that Salameh's letters were "exhorting acts of terrorism and helping recruit would-be terrorists for the *Jihad*." Michael Macko, who lost his father in the Trade Center bombing, posed this question: "If they are encouraging acts of terrorism internationally, how do we know they're not encouraging acts of terrorism right here on U.S. soil?"

Prison officials told reporters that communications involving the imprisoned bombers had not been closely censored because the men hadn't been considered very dangerous. The letters didn't contain any plans for attacks, nor did they name any specific targets. One Justice Department official said that Salameh was "a low level guy," who was not under any special restrictions, and that his letters were seen as "generic stuff" and "no cause for concern."

Rights advocates suggested that inmates should have the right to free speech—even those imprisoned for acts of terrorism—and that advocating terrorism is not the same thing as planning it or carrying it out. After all, they said, calls for a holy war, however repugnant they may be in the current international context, are merely political statements—and politics is not against the law.

**YOU DECIDE**

What kinds of prison communications should be monitored or restricted (letters, telephone calls, e-mail)? Do you believe that communications containing statements like those described here should be confiscated? What kinds of political statements, if any, should be permitted?

*References:* Lisa Myers, "Imprisoned Terrorists Still Advocating Terror," NBC Nightly News, February 28, 2005. Web posted at http://www.msnbc.msn.com/id/7046691 (accessed August 28, 2005); and Lisa Myers, "Bureau of Prisons under Fire for Jihad Letters," March 1, 2005. Web posted at http://www.msnbc.msn.com/id/7053165 (accessed August 28, 2005).

As mentioned previously, the U.S. Supreme Court has ruled that mentally ill inmates can be required to take antipsychotic drugs, even against their wishes.[204] A 1999 study by the BJS found that the nation's prisons and jails hold an estimated 283,800 mentally ill inmates (16% of those confined) and that 547,800 such offenders are on probation.[205] The government study also found that 40% of mentally ill inmates receive no treatment at all. For more details about the report, visit Web Extra 14–4 at cjtoday.com.

**WEB EXTRA**

Mentally deficient inmates constitute still another group with special needs. Some studies estimate the proportion of mentally deficient inmates at about 10%.[206] Inmates with low IQs are less likely than other inmates to complete training and rehabilitative programs successfully. They also evidence difficulty in adjusting to the routines of prison life. As a consequence, they are likely to exceed the averages in proportion of sentence served.[207] Only seven states report special facilities or programs for retarded inmates.[208] Other state systems "mainstream" such inmates, making them participate in regular activities with other inmates.

Texas, one state that does provide special services for retarded inmates, began the Mentally Retarded Offender Program (MROP) in 1984. Inmates in Texas are given a battery of tests that measure intellectual and social adaptability skills, and prisoners who are identified as retarded are housed in special satellite correctional units. The Texas MROP provides individual and group counseling, along with training in adult life skills.

## Terrorism

Today's antiterrorism efforts have brought to light the important role that correctional personnel can play in preventing future attacks on American society and in averting crises that could arise in correctional institutions as a result of terrorist action. In 2005, former New York City Police Commissioner Bernard B. Kerik told participants at the American Correctional Association's winter conference that corrections officers can help in the fight against terrorism through effective intelligence gathering and intelligence sharing. "Intelligence—that's the key to the success of this battle," Kerik said.[209] "You have to be part of that, because when we take the people off the streets in this country that go to jail, they communicate and they talk, they work with other criminals, organized gangs, organized units. You've got to collect that information, you have to get it back to the authorities that need it."

Jess Maghan, director of the Forum for Comparative Corrections and professor of criminal justice at the University of Illinois at Chicago, points to the critical role that intelligence gathering and analysis by correctional agencies can play in providing critical information to prevent terrorist attacks. According to Maghan, "the interaction of all people in a prison (staff, officers, and inmates) can become important intelligence sources."[210] Moreover, says Maghan, the flow of information between inmates and the outside world must be monitored to detect attack plans, especially when prisons house known terrorist leaders or group members. Vital intelligence, according to Maghan, can be passed through legal visits (where people conveying information may have no idea of its significance), sub-rosa communications networks in prisons that can support communications between inmates and the outside world, and prison transportation systems.

The security problems presented by potential information leaks were demonstrated in 2003 at the U.S. Navy's Guantánamo Bay Naval Station prison in Cuba when a translator working with Arab internees was accused of having unlawful possession of classified information, including diagrams of the prison layout and names of the prisoners. Prison administrators responsible for the incarceration of suspected al-Qaeda and Taliban members, like those at Guantánamo, face especially delicate situations as opponents of the government's policies challenge the propriety of using military assets in what they argue is a "law enforcement" role.

Prison administrators must also be concerned about the potential impact of outside terrorist activity on their facility's inmate and staff populations. Of particular concern to today's prison administrators is the possibility of bioterrorism. A concentrated population like that of a prison or jail is highly susceptible to the rapid transmission of biological agents.[211]

The threat of a terrorist act being undertaken by inmates within a prison or jail can be an important consideration in facility planning and management, especially because inmates may be particularly vulnerable to recruitment by terrorist organizations. According to Chip Ellis, research and program coordinator for the National Memorial Institute for the Prevention of Terrorism, "Prisoners are a captive audience, and they usually have a diminished sense of self or a need for identity and protection. They're usually a disenchanted or disenfranchised group of people, [and] terrorists can sometimes capitalize on that situation."[212] Inmates can be radicalized in many ways, including exposure to other radical inmates, the distribution of extremist literature, and through anti-U.S. sermons heard during religious services.

Officials of the Federal Bureau of Investigation (FBI) say al-Qaeda continues to actively recruit members in U.S. prisons and looks especially to the 9,600 Muslims held in the federal prison system. "These terrorists seek to exploit our freedom to exercise religion to their advantage by using radical forms of Islam to recruit operatives," says FBI counterterrorism chief John Pistole. "Unfortunately, U.S. correctional institutions are a viable venue for such radicalization and recruitment."[213] In 2005, the Institute for the Study of Violent Groups, located at Sam Houston State University, charged that the most radical form of Islam, or Wahhabism, was being spread in American prisons by clerics approved by the Islamic Society of North America (ISNA), one of two organizations chosen by the federal Bureau of Prisons (BOP) to select prison chaplains.[214] "Proselytizing in prisons," said the institute, "can produce new recruits with American citizenship." An example might be Jose Padilla, aka Abdullah al-Mujahir, a Chicago thug who converted to Islam after being exposed to radical Islam while serving time in a Florida jail. According to authorities, Padilla, who was arrested in Chicago, intended to contaminate a U.S. city with a radiological dirty bomb. Likewise, British citizen Richard Reid, convicted for attempting to blow up an American Airlines flight from Paris to Miami with explosives in his shoes, had converted to radical Islam in an English prison.[215]

In 2004 the Office of the Inspector General of the U.S. Department of Justice released its review of the federal Bureau of Prisons' practices in selecting Muslim clergy to minister to inmates in BOP facilities. The report concluded that the primary threat of radicalization comes from inmates, not chaplains, contractors, or volunteers. In the words of the report, "inmates from foreign countries politicize Islam and radicalize inmates, who in turn radicalize more inmates when they transfer to other prisons."[216] The report also identified a form of Islam unique to the prison environment called "Prison Islam."[217] Prison Islam, the report said, is a form of Islam that adapts itself to prison values and is used by gangs and radical inmates to further unlawful goals. It was found to be especially common in institutions where religious services are led by lay *mullahs* (spiritual leaders)—a practice made necessary by a lack of Muslim chaplains. The report

## CJ FUTURES

### The Commission on Safety and Abuse in America's Prisons

On March 1, 2005, following the widely publicized scandals at Abu Ghraib prison in Iraq, the Vera Institute of Justice announced formation of the Commission on Safety and Abuse in America's Prisons.[1] The purpose of the commission is to explore the most serious problems inside U.S. correctional facilities and to assess their impact on the incarcerated, correctional personnel, and society at large. "As President Bush was calling the abuse at Abu Ghraib 'un-American,'" says the commission's website, "many Americans raised questions about the treatment of prisoners here at home."

The 21-member nonpartisan panel is cochaired by former U.S. Attorney General Nicholas Katzenbach and the Honorable John J. Gibbons, former chief judge of the U.S. Third Circuit Court of Appeals.

For one year following its formation, the commission will explore the most serious problems facing correctional facilities today, including violence, sexual abuse, the degradation of prisoners, overcrowding, needed treatments for the mentally ill, and the working conditions of correctional officers.

Members of Congress have expressed support for the committee's work, and some seem anxious to read the committee's findings. "How we treat corrections officers and inmates is an issue that goes beyond the walls of our prisons, impacting the families and communities of both corrections officers and inmates," said Senator Patrick Leahy (D–Vt.), the ranking member of the Senate Judiciary Committee when he learned of the commission's formation; "I am looking forward," Leahy continued, "to following the work of the Com-

mission on Safety and Abuse in America's Prisons and to hearing their recommendations and advice for making our prisons safer and less abusive for both prisoners and corrections officers."[2]

The commission is planning four public hearings to be focused on the following concerns:

- Safety failures, abuse, violence, and the use of force
- Institutional determinants of abuse
- Problems identified by correctional officers
- Oversight, standards, and miscellaneous issues

Presenters at the first hearing, which had already taken place by the time this book went to press, included Kenneth Adams, a professor at the University of Central Florida and an expert on prison violence; Douglas Thompkins, a former gang leader and inmate who is now a "convict criminologist" specializing in the sociology of incarceration; Garrett Cunningham, a former Texas inmate who was sexually harassed by a correctional officer; Judith Haney, lead plaintiff in a class-action lawsuit involving thousands of women in Miami-Dade County who were strip-searched in jail; and Scott Hornoff, a former Rhode Island police detective who was wrongfully convicted and incarcerated for six and a half years.

When the hearings conclude, the commission will produce a report built around practical recommendations that local, state, and federal policymakers can use to improve conditions in prisons and jails in their jurisdictions.

For more information about the commission, and to read the commission's report when it becomes available, visit http://www.prisoncommission.org.

[1]Vera Institute of Justice news release, "National Commission to Examine U.S. Prison Conditions: Post-Abu Ghraib, Panel to Study U.S. Prisons and Their Impact on Prisoners, Corrections Officers and Society at Large," March 1, 2005.
[2]Commission on Safety and Abuse in America's Prisons press release, "Federal Policy Makers Support Commission," March 2, 2005.

concluded with a number of recommendations, including one that the BOP should provide staff training on Islam so that correctional officers can recognize radical Islamist messages. The report also recommended that "the BOP can and should improve its process for selecting, screening, and supervising Muslim religious services providers. We recommend," said the report, that "the BOP take steps to examine all chaplains', religious contractors', and religious volunteers' doctrinal beliefs to screen out anyone who poses a threat to security."

The incarceration of convicted terrorists presents new challenges for correctional administrators. Sheik Omar Abdel-Rahman, a blind Muslim cleric and spiritual leader for many Islamic terrorists, including Osama bin Laden, is currently serving a life sentence in a U.S. federal penitentiary for conspiring to assassinate Egyptian President Hosni Mubarak and to blow up five New York City landmarks in the 1990s. Speculation that the sheik continues to motivate terrorist acts against the United States gained credibility when his attorney and three others were indicted in April 2002 for allegedly passing illegal communications between Abdel-Rahman and an Egyptian-based terrorist organization known as the Islamic Group.[218]

The current world situation, and the environment in which correctional agencies operate, is likely to ensure that the issues identified here will take on ever-increasing significance for prison administrators of the future. Learn more about prison issues of all kinds from the Prison Policy Initiative at Web Extra 14–5 at cjtoday.com. Read about concerns over Muslim religious services in correctional institutions from Library Extra 14–10 at cjtoday.com.

**SUMMARY**

Prisons are small self-contained societies that are sometimes described as *total institutions*. Studies of prison life have detailed the existence of prison subcultures, or inmate worlds, replete with inmate values, social roles, and lifestyles. New inmates who are socialized into prison subculture are said to undergo the process of prisonization. This involves, among other things, learning the language of prison, commonly called *prison argot.*

Prison subcultures are very influential, and both inmates and staff must reckon with them. Given the large and often densely packed inmate populations that characterize many of today's prisons, prison subcultures are not easily subject to the control of prison authorities. Complicating life behind bars are numerous conflicts of interest between inmates and staff. Lawsuits, riots, violence, and frequent formal grievances are symptoms of such differences.

For many years, courts throughout the nation assumed a "hands-off" approach to prisons, rarely intervening in the day-to-day administration of prison facilities. That changed in the late 1960s, when the U.S. Supreme Court began to identify inmates' rights mandated by the U.S. Constitution. Rights identified by the Court include the right to physical integrity, an absolute right to be free from unwarranted corporal punishments, certain religious rights, and procedural rights, such as those involving access to attorneys and to the courts. The conditional rights of prisoners, which have repeatedly been supported by the U.S. Supreme Court, mandate professionalism among prison administrators and require vigilance in the provision of correctional services. The era of prisoners' rights was sharply curtailed in 1996 with the passage of the Prison Litigation Reform Act, spurred on by a growing recognition of the legal morass resulting from unregulated access to federal courts by inmates across the nation. The legislation, in concert with other restrictions sanctioned by the U.S. Supreme Court, has substantially limited inmate access to federal courts.

Today's prisons are miniature societies, reflecting the problems and challenges that exist in the larger society of which they are a part. HIV-infected inmates, geriatric offenders, and the mentally ill constitute special groups within the inmate population that require additional attention.

In recent years efforts to combat terrorism have presented new security challenges for America's prisons. Concerns over the spread of ideologies supportive of terrorism have expanded as the number of imprisoned terrorist sympathizers grows. Some believe that terrorist groups might use radical forms of Islam to actively recruit prisoners who see themselves as alienated from the wider society. The opportunity exists for correctional administrators to take a proactive role, however, in monitoring communications and observing behavior that might indicate potential terrorist activity.

**DISCUSSION QUESTIONS**

1. What are prison subcultures, and how do they influence prison life? How do they develop, and what purpose do they serve?

2. What does *prisonization* mean? Describe the U-shaped curve developed by Stanton Wheeler to illustrate the concept of prisonization.

3. How do women's prisons differ from men's? Why have women's prisons been studied less often than institutions for men?

4. What are the primary concerns of prison staff? Do you agree that those concerns are important? What other goals might staff members focus on?

5. What causes prison riots? Through what stages do most riots progress? How might riots be prevented?

6. What is the hands-off doctrine? What is the status of that doctrine today?

7. What are the commonly accepted rights of prisoners in the United States? Where do these rights come from? What U.S. Supreme Court cases are especially significant in this regard? Do inmates have too many rights? Explain.

8. Explain the balancing test established by the Supreme Court in deciding issues of prisoners' rights. How might such a test apply to the emerging area of inmate privacy?

9. What does the term *state-created rights* mean within the context of corrections? What do you predict for the future of state-created rights?

10. What are some of the major problems and issues that prisons face today? What new problems might the future bring?

## WEB QUEST

Visit the Cybrary, and search for "jobs," "careers," and "employment." What criminal justice–related employment sites can you find? Explore some of the sites you find, and consider the possibility of a career in corrections. Document the sources you used, and list the URLs and the date you accessed each. Then answer these questions[219]:

1. What is the difference between a job and a career?
2. What career opportunities are available in corrections?
3. Why is career planning important? How can you develop an effective career plan?
4. What is the difference between education and training?
5. Why are education and training important to building a career in corrections?
6. What role might professionalism play in building your career?
7. What traits must you have to achieve your goals and to be successful in a career in corrections?

E-mail your answers to your instructor if asked to do so.

To complete this Web Quest online, go to the Web Quest module in Chapter 14 of the *Criminal Justice Today* Companion Website at cjtoday.com.

## NOTES

i. Martha Stewart, *An Open Letter from Martha Stewart,* December 22, 2004. Web posted at http://www.marthatalks.com (accessed July 5, 2005).

ii. Zebulon R. Brockway, *The Ideal of a True Prison System for a State* (1865).

1. Web posted at http://www.whitehouse.gov/news/reports/faithbased.html (accessed January 2, 2005).

2. Hans Reimer, "Socialization in the Prison Community," *Proceedings of the American Prison Association, 1937* (New York: American Prison Association, 1937), pp. 151–155.

3. Donald Clemmer, *The Prison Community* (Boston: Holt, Rinehart and Winston, 1940).

4. Gresham M. Sykes, *The Society of Captives: A Study of a Maximum Security Prison* (Princeton, NJ: Princeton University Press, 1958).

5. Richard A. Cloward et al., *Theoretical Studies in Social Organization of the Prison* (New York: Social Science Research Council, 1960).

6. Donald R. Cressey, ed., *The Prison: Studies in Institutional Organization and Change* (New York: Holt, Rinehart and Winston, 1961).

7. Lawrence Hazelrigg, ed., *Prison within Society: A Reader in Penology* (Garden City, NY: Anchor, 1969), preface.

8. Charles Stastny and Gabrielle Tyrnauer, *Who Rules the Joint? The Changing Political Culture of Maximum-Security Prisons in America* (Lexington, MA: Lexington Books, 1982), p. 131.

9. Erving Goffman, *Asylums: Essays on the Social Situation of Mental Patients and Other Inmates* (Garden City, NY: Anchor, 1961).

10. For a firsthand account of the prison experience, see Victor Hassine, *Life without Parole: Living in Prison Today* (Los Angeles: Roxbury, 1996); and W. Rideau and R. Wikberg,

*Life Sentences: Rage and Survival behind Prison Bars* (New York: Times Books, 1992).

11. Gresham M. Sykes and Sheldon L. Messinger, "The Inmate Social System," in Richard A. Cloward et al., eds., *Theoretical Studies in Social Organization of the Prison,* pp. 5–19.

12. The concept of prisonization is generally attributed to Clemmer, *The Prison Community,* although Quaker penologists of the late eighteenth century were actively concerned with preventing "contamination" (the spread of criminal values) among prisoners.

13. Sykes and Messinger, "The Inmate Social System," p. 5.

14. Stanton Wheeler, "Socialization in Correctional Communities," *American Sociological Review,* Vol. 26 (October 1961), pp. 697–712.

15. Sykes, *The Society of Captives,* p. xiii.

16. John Irwin, *The Felon* (Englewood Cliffs, NJ: Prentice Hall, 1970).

17. Stastny and Tyrnauer, *Who Rules the Joint?* p. 135.

18. Ibid.

19. Sykes, *The Society of Captives.*

20. Clemmer, *The Prison Community,* pp. 294–296.

21. Irwin, *The Felon.*

22. Joseph L. Galloway, "Into the Heart of Darkness," *U.S. News* online, March 8, 1999. Web posted at http://www.usnews.com/usnews/issue/990308/8pris.htm (accessed March 20, 2000).

23. Alan J. Davis, "Sexual Assaults in the Philadelphia Prison System and Sheriff's Vans," *Trans-Action,* Vol. 6 (December 1968), pp. 8–16.

24. Daniel Lockwood, "Sexual Aggression among Male Prisoners," unpublished dissertation (Ann Arbor, MI: University Microfilms International, 1978).

25. Public Law 108-79.

26. Joanne Mariner, *No Escape: Male Rape in U.S. Prisons* (New York: Human Rights Watch, 2001). Web posted at http://www.hrw.org/reports/2001/prison/report.html (accessed September 23, 2002).

27. Lee H. Bowker, *Prison Victimization* (New York: Elsevier, 1980).

28. Ibid., p. 42.

29. Ibid., p. 1.

30. Hans Toch, *Living in Prison: The Ecology of Survival* (New York: Free Press, 1977), p. 151.

31. Paige M. Harrison and Allen J. Beck, *Prisoners in 2004* (Washington, DC: Bureau of Justice Statistics, 2005).

32. Ibid.

33. Some of the information in this section comes from the American Correctional Association (ACA) Task Force on the Female Offender, *The Female Offender: What Does the Future Hold?* (Washington, DC: St. Mary's Press, 1990); and "The View from behind Bars," *Time* (Fall 1990, special issue), pp. 20–22.

34. Much of the information and some of the wording in this section come from Barbara Bloom, Barbara Owen, and Stephanie Covington, *Gender-Responsive Strategies: Research, Practice, and Guiding Principles for Women Offenders* (Washington, DC: National Institute of Corrections, 2003).

35. Barbara Bloom, "Triple Jeopardy: Race, Class and Gender as Factors in Women's Imprisonment," paper presented at the American Society of Criminology annual meeting, 1997.

36. Joanne Belknap, *The Invisible Woman: Gender, Crime, and Justice* (Belmont, CA: Wadsworth, 2001).

37. C.W. Harlow, *Prior Abuse Reported by Inmates and Probationers* (Washington, DC: Bureau of Justice Statistics, 1999).

38. Ibid.

39. Ibid.

40. B. Owen and B. Bloom, "Profiling Women Prisoners: Findings from National Survey and California Sample," *The Prison Journal,* Vol. 75, No. 2 (1995), pp. 165–185.

41. B.K. Jordan et al., "Prevalence of Psychiatric Disorders among Incarcerated Women," *Archives of General Psychiatry,* Vol. 53, No. 6 (1996), pp. 513–519.

42. A. Browne, B. Miller, and E. Maguin, "Prevalence and Severity of Lifetime Physical and Sexual Victimization among Incarcerated Women," *International Journal of Law and Psychiatry,* Vol. 22, Nos. 3–4 (1999), pp. 301–322.

43. A. Merlo and J. Pollock, *Women, Law, and Social Control* (Boston: Allyn and Bacon, 1995).

44. Center for Substance Abuse Treatment, *Substance Abuse Treatment for Incarcerated Offenders: Guide to Promising Practices* (Rockville, MD: U.S. Department of Health and Human Services, 1997).

45. Lawrence A. Greenfeld and Tracy L. Snell, *Women Offenders* (Washington, DC: Bureau of Justice Statistics, 1999).

46. Substance Abuse and Mental Health Services Administration, *National Household Survey on Drug Abuse: Population Estimates 1992* (Rockville, MD: U.S. Department of Health and Human Services, 1993).

47. National Center on Addiction and Substance Abuse, *Behind Bars: Substance Abuse and America's Prison Population* (New York: Columbia University Press, 1998).

48. Quoted in "Report Cites Unfair Treatment of Female Drug Offenders," *Corrections Journal,* March 22, 2005, p. 4.

49. Lenora Lapidus et al., *Caught in the Net: The Impact of Drug Policies on Women and Families* (New York: American Civil Liberties Union, 2005).

50. L. Acoca, "Defusing the Time Bomb: Understanding and Meeting the Growing Health Care Needs of Incarcerated Women in America," *Crime and Delinquency,* Vol. 44, No. 1 (1998), pp. 49–70; and D.S. Young, "Contributing Factors to Poor Health among Incarcerated Women: A Conceptual Model," *Affilia,* Vol. 11, No. 4, (1996), pp. 440–461.

51. Acoca, "Defusing the Time Bomb."

52. A. L. Coker et al., "Childhood Forced Sex and Cervical Dysplasia among Women Prison Inmates," *Violence Against Women,* Vol. 4, No. 5 (1998), pp. 595–608.

53. Allen J. Beck and Laura M. Maruschak, *Mental Health Treatment in State Prisons, 2000* (Washington, DC: Bureau of Justice Statistics, 2001).

54. L. A. Teplin et al., "Prevalence of Psychiatric Disorders among Incarcerated Women," *Archives of General Psychiatry,* Vol. 53, No. 6 (1996), pp. 505–512.

55. B. M. Veysey, *Specific Needs of Women Diagnosed with Mental Illnesses in U.S. Jails* (Delmar, NY: National GAINS Center, 1997); and M. Singer et al., "The Psychosocial Issues of Women Serving Time in Jail," *Social Work,* Vol. 40 No. 1 (1995), pp. 103–113.

56. Greenfeld and Snell, *Women Offenders;* and Mary K. Shilton, *Resources for Mother–Child Community Corrections* (Washington, DC: Bureau of Justice Assistance, 2001), p. 3.

57. Mary Jeanette Clement, "National Survey of Programs for Incarcerated Women," paper presented at the annual meeting of the Academy of Criminal Justice Sciences, Nashville, TN, March 1991, pp. 8–9.

58. B. Bloom and D. Steinhart, *Why Punish the Children? A Reappraisal of the Children of Incarcerated Mothers in America* (San Francisco: National Council on Crime and Delinquency, 1993).

59. Greenfeld and Snell, *Women Offenders*

60. Ibid.

61. Ibid.

62. Barbara Bloom and Stephanie Covington, "Gendered Justice: Programming for Women in Correctional Settings," paper presented at the American Society of Criminology annual meeting, San Francisco, CA, November 2000, p. 11.

63. American Correctional Association, *The Female Offender.*

64. Marsha Clowers, "Dykes, Gangs, and Danger: Debunking Popular Myths about Maximum Security Life," *Journal of Criminal Justice and Popular Culture,* Vol. 9, No. 1 (2001), pp. 22–30.

65. D. Ward and G. Kassebaum, *Women's Prison: Sex and Social Structure* (London: Weidenfeld and Nicolson, 1966).

66. Esther Heffernan, *Making It in Prison: The Square, the Cool, and the Life* (London: Wiley-Interscience, 1972).

67. Rose Giallombardo, *Society of Women: A Study of Women's Prisons* (New York: John Wiley, 1966).

68. Ibid., p. 136.

69. For a summary of such studies (including some previously unpublished), see Lee H. Bowker, *Prisoner Subcultures* (Lexington, MA: Lexington Books, 1977), p. 86.

70. Giallombardo, *Society of Women,* p. 162.

71. Mary Koscheski and Christopher Hensley, "Inmate Homosexual Behavior in a Southern Female Correctional Facility," *American Journal of Criminal Justice,* Vol. 25, No. 2 (2001), pp. 269–277.

72. See, for example, Margie J. Phelps, "Sexual Misconduct between Staff and Inmates," *Corrections Technology and Management,* Vol. 12 (1999).

73. Heffernan, *Making It in Prison.*

74. Bowker, *Prison Victimization,* p. 53.

75. Giallombardo, *Society of Women.*

76. "Georgia Indictments Charge Abuse of Female Inmates," *USA Today,* November 16, 1992, p. 3A.

77. Ibid.

78. American Correctional Association, *The Female Offender,* p. 39.

79. American Correctional Association, "Correctional Officers in Adult Systems," in *Vital Statistics in Corrections* (Laurel, MD: ACA, 2000).

80. Sidra Lea Gifford, *Justice Expenditure and Employment in the United States, 1999* (Washington, DC: Bureau of Justice Statistics, 2002), p. 8.

81. Ibid. "Other" minorities round out the percentages to a total of 100%.

82. Ibid.

83. American Correctional Association, "Correctional Officers in Adult Systems."

84. Lucien X. Lombardo, *Guards Imprisoned: Correctional Officers at Work* (New York: Elsevier, 1981), pp. 22–36.

85. Leonard Morgenbesser, "NY State Law Prescribes Psychological Screening for CO Job Applicants," *Correctional Training* (Winter 1983), p. 1.

86. "A Sophisticated Approach to Training Prison Guards," *Newsday,* August 12, 1982.

87. "Two Guards Taken Hostage by Inmates at Arizona Prison," *USA Today,* January 18, 2004. Web posted at http://www.usatoday.com/news/nation/2004-01-18-prison-hostage_x.htm (accessed July 12, 2004).

88. Stastny and Tyrnauer, *Who Rules the Joint?* p. 1.

89. See Frederick Talbott, "Reporting from behind the Walls: Do It before the Siren Wails," *The Quill* (February 1988), pp. 16–21.

90. "Ohio Prison Rebellion Is Ended," *USA Today,* April 22, 1993, p. 2A.

91. "Guards Hurt in Prison Riot," Associated Press wire service, November 11, 2000.

92. See, for example, Reid H. Montgomery and Gordon A. Crews, *A History of Correctional Violence: An Examination of Reported Causes of Riots and Disturbances* (Lanham, MD: American Correctional Association, 1998); Bert Useem and Peter Kimball, *States of Siege: U.S. Prison Riots 1971–1986* (New York: Oxford University Press, 1991); and Michael Braswell et al., *Prison Violence in America,* 2nd ed. (Cincinnati, OH: Anderson, 1994).

93. Robert S. Fong, Ronald E. Vogel, and S. Buentello, "Prison Gang Dynamics: A Look inside the Texas Department of Corrections," in A. V. Merlo and P. Menekos, eds., *Dilemmas and Directions in Corrections* (Cincinnati, OH: Anderson, 1992).

94. Ibid.

95. *Ruiz* v. *Estelle,* 503 F.Supp. 1265 (S.D. Texas, 1980).

96. Vernon Fox, "Prison Riots in a Democratic Society," *Police,* Vol. 26, No. 12 (December 1982), pp. 35–41.

97. Donald R. Cressey, "Adult Felons in Prison," in Lloyd E. Ohlin, ed., *Prisoners in America* (Englewood Cliffs, NJ: Prentice Hall, 1972), pp. 117–150.

98. The facts in this story are taken from *Hope* v. *Pelzer,* 122 S.Ct. 2508, 153 L.Ed.2d 666 (2002).

99. "Convictions Bar 3.9 Million from Voting," Associated Press wire service, September 22, 2000.

100. *Holt* v. *Sarver,* 309 F.Supp. 362 (E.D. Ark. 1970).

101. Vergil L. Williams, *Dictionary of American Penology: An Introduction* (Westport, CT: Greenwood Press, 1979), pp. 6–7.

**102.** *Pell* v. *Procunier,* 417 U.S. 817, 822 (1974).

**103.** Ibid.

**104.** Title 42 U.S.C.A. 1997, Public Law 104-150.

**105.** Section 1997e.

**106.** American Correctional Association, *Legal Responsibility and Authority of Correctional Officers: A Handbook on Courts, Judicial Decisions and Constitutional Requirements* (College Park, MD: ACA, 1987), p. 8.

**107.** *Banks* v. *Beard,* No. 03-1245 (3d Cir. 2005).

**108.** *Procunier* v. *Martinez,* 416 U.S. 396 (1974).

**109.** *McNamara* v. *Moody,* 606 F.2d 621 (5th Cir. 1979).

**110.** *Luparar* v. *Stoneman,* 382 F.Supp. 495 (D. Vt. 1974).

**111.** *Mallery* v. *Lewis,* 106 Idaho 227 (1983).

**112.** See, for example, *Pepperling* v. *Crist,* 678 F.2d 787 (9th Cir. 1981).

**113.** *Block* v. *Rutherford,* 486 U.S. 576 (1984).

**114.** *Overton* v. *Bazzetta,* 539 U.S. 126 (2003).

**115.** *Pell* v. *Procunier.*

**116.** *Houchins* v. *KQED, Inc.,* 438 U.S. 11 (1978).

**117.** Ibid.

**118.** *Cruz* v. *Beto,* 405 U.S. 319 (1972).

**119.** *Aziz* v. *LeFevre,* 642 F.2d 1109 (2d Cir. 1981).

**120.** *Glasshofer* v. *Thornburg,* 514 F.Supp. 1242 (E.D. Pa. 1981).

**121.** See, for example, *Smith* v. *Coughlin,* 748 F.2d 783 (2d Cir. 1984).

**122.** *Campbell* v. *Cauthron,* 623 F.2d 503 (8th Cir. 1980).

**123.** *Smith* v. *Blackledge,* 451 F.2d 1201 (4th Cir. 1971).

**124.** *Dettmer* v. *Landon,* 617 F.Supp. 592, 594 (D.C. Va. 1985).

**125.** *Dettmer* v. *Landon,* 799 F.2d 929 (4th Cir. 1986).

**126.** *Lewellyn (L'Aquarius)* v. *State,* 592 P.2d 538 (Okla. Crim. App. 1979).

**127.** *Hill* v. *Blackwell,* 774 F.2d 338, 347 (8th Cir. 1985).

**128.** *Benning* v. *State,* No. 04-10979 (11th Cir. 2005).

**129.** *Cutter* v. *Wilkinson,* U.S. Supreme Court, No. 03-987 (decided May 31, 2005).

**130.** For a Supreme Court review of the First Amendment right to petition the courts, see *McDonald* v. *Smith,* 105 S.Ct. 2787 (1985).

**131.** *Bounds* v. *Smith,* 430 U.S. 817, 821 (1977).

**132.** *Lewis* v. *Casey,* 516 U.S. 804 (1996).

**133.** *Johnson* v. *Avery,* 393 U.S. 483 (1968).

**134.** *Bounds* v. *Smith.*

**135.** *Taylor* v. *Sterrett,* 532 F.2d 462 (5th Cir. 1976).

**136.** *In re Harrell,* 87 Cal. Rptr. 504, 470 P.2d 640 (1970).

**137.** *Guajardo* v. *Estelle,* 432 F.Supp. 1373 (S.D. Texas, 1977).

**138.** *O'Brien* v. *U.S.,* 386 U.S. 345 (1967); and *Weatherford* v. *Bursey,* 429 U.S. 545 (1977).

**139.** *U.S.* v. *Gouveia,* 104 S.Ct. 2292, 81 L.Ed.2d 146 (1984).

**140.** *Estelle* v. *Gamble,* 429 U.S. 97 (1976).

**141.** Ibid., pp. 105–106.

**142.** *Hudson* v. *McMillan,* 503 U.S. 1 (1992).

**143.** *Ruiz* v. *Estelle,* 503 F.Supp. 1265 (S.D. Tex. 1980); aff'd in part, rev'd in part, 679 F.2d 1115 (5th Cir. 1982); amended in part, vacated in part, 688 F.2d 266 (5th Cir. 1982); cert. denied, 460 U.S. 1042 (1983).

**144.** *Newman* v. *Alabama,* 349 F.Supp. 278 (M.D. Ala. 1972).

**145.** *In re Caulk,* 35 CrL 2532 (New Hampshire S.Ct. 1984).

**146.** Ibid.

**147.** *Bee* v. *Greaves,* 744 F.2d 1387 (10th Cir. 1984).

**148.** *Washington* v. *Harper,* 494 U.S. 210 (1990).

**149.** *Pennsylvania Department of Corrections* v. *Yeskey,* 524 U.S. 206, 209 (1998).

**150.** 42 U.S.C. §12132.

**151.** *Holt* v. *Sarver,* 309 F.Supp. 362 (E.D. Ark. 1970).

**152.** *Farmer* v. *Brennan,* 114 S.Ct. 1970, 128 L.Ed.2d 811 (1994).

**153.** Ibid.

**154.** *Helling* v. *McKinney,* 113 S.Ct. 2475, 125 L.Ed.2d 22 (1993).

**155.** *U.S.* v. *Ready,* 574 F.2d 1009 (10th Cir. 1978).

**156.** *Katz* v. *U.S.,* 389 U.S. 347, 88 S.Ct. 507, 19 L.Ed.2d 576 (1967).

**157.** *Hudson* v. *Palmer,* 468 U.S. 517 (1984).

**158.** *Block* v. *Rutherford,* 104 S.Ct. 3227, 3234–35 (1984).

**159.** *U.S.* v. *Lilly,* 576 F.2d 1240 (5th Cir. 1978).

**160.** *Palmer* v. *Hudson,* 697 F.2d 1220 (4th Cir. 1983).

**161.** *Jones* v. *North Carolina Prisoners' Labor Union,* 433 U.S. 119, 53 L.Ed.2d 629, 641 (1977).

**162.** *Wolff* v. *McDonnell,* 94 S.Ct. 2963 (1974).

**163.** Ibid.

**164.** Ibid.

**165.** *Ponte* v. *Real,* 471 U.S. 491, 105 S.Ct. 2192, 85 L.Ed.2d 553 (1985).

**166.** *Vitek* v. *Jones,* 445 U.S. 480 (1980).

**167.** American Correctional Association, Standard 2-4346. See ACA, *Legal Responsibility and Authority of Correctional Officers,* p. 49.

**168.** *Wilson* v. *Seiter et al.,* 501 U.S. 294 (1991).

**169.** *Estelle* v. *Gamble,* 429 U.S. 97, 106 (1976).

**170.** *Sandin* v. *Conner,* 63 U.S.L.W. 4601 (1995).

**171.** *Wolff* v. *McDonnell,* 94 S.Ct. 2963 (1974).

**172.** *Hewitt* v. *Helms,* 459 U.S. 460 (1983).

173. Laurie Asseo, "Inmate Lawsuits," Associated Press wire service, May 24, 1996; and Bureau of Justice Statistics, "State and Federal Prisoners Filed 68,235 Petitions in U.S. Courts in 1996," press release, October 29, 1997.

174. See, for example, "The Great Prison Pastime," *20/20*, ABC News, September 24, 1993, which is part of the video library available to instructors using this textbook.

175. Ibid.

176. Asseo, "Inmate Lawsuits."

177. Public Law 104-134. Although the PLRA was signed into law on April 26, 1996, and is frequently referred to as the Prison Litigation Reform Act of 1996, the official name of the act is the Prison Litigation Reform Act of 1995.

178. *Edwards* v. *Balisok,* 520 U.S. 641 (1997).

179. American Civil Liberties Union (ACLU), *Prisoners' Rights—An ACLU Position Paper,* Fall 1999. Web posted at http://www.aclu.org/library/PrisonerRights.pdf (accessed March 5, 2002).

180. *Booth* v. *Churner,* 532 U.S. 731 (2001).

181. *Porter* v. *Nussle,* 534 U.S. 516 (2002).

182. John Scalia, *Prisoner Petitions Filed in U.S. District Courts, 2000, with Trends 1980–2000* (Washington, DC: Bureau of Justice Statistics, 2002).

183. F. Cheesman, R. Hanson, and B. Ostrom, *A Tale of Two Laws Revisited: Investigating the Impact of the Prison Litigation Reform Act and the Antiterrorism and Effective Death Penalty Act* (Williamsburg, VA: National Center for State Courts, 2004).

184. ACLU, *Prisoners' Rights.*

185. Laura M. Maruschak, *HIV in Prisons and Jails, 2002* (Washington, DC: Bureau of Justice Statistics, 2004).

186. Ibid., p. 4.

187. Dennis Cauchon, "AIDS in Prison: Locked Up and Locked Out," *USA Today,* March 31, 1995, p. 6A.

188. Maruschak, *HIV in Prisons and Jails, 2002,* p. 6.

189. Theodore M. Hammett, *AIDS in Correctional Facilities: Issues and Options,* 3rd ed. (Washington, DC: National Institute of Justice, 1988), p. 37.

190. At the time of this writing, California, Massachusetts, New York, Wisconsin, and the District of Columbia were among those jurisdictions.

191. "Mississippi Eases Policy of Separating Inmates with HIV," *Corrections Journal,* Vol. 5, No. 6 (2001), p. 5.

192. Cauchon, "AIDS in Prison."

193. See "Court Allows Restriction on HIV-Positive Inmates," *Criminal Justice Newsletter,* Vol. 25, No. 23 (December 1, 1994), pp. 2–3.

194. Ibid.

195. Darrell Bryan, "Inmates, HIV, and the Constitutional Right to Privacy: AIDS in Prison Facilities," *Corrections Compendium,* Vol. 19, No. 9 (September 1994), pp. 1–3.

196. Alexandria Sage, "Doctor Shot at Los Angeles-Area Hospital," Associated Press wire service, September 20, 2003.

197. Lincoln J. Fry, "The Older Prison Inmate: A Profile," *Justice Professional,* Vol. 2, No. 1 (spring 1987), pp. 1–12.

198. Harrison and Beck, *Prisoners in 2004.*

199. Bureau of Justice Statistics, "The Nation's Prison Population Grew by 60,000 Inmates Last Year," press release, August 15, 1999.

200. Jim Krane, "Demographic Revolution Rocks U.S. Prisons," APB online, April 12, 1999. Web posted at http://www.apbonline.com/safestreets/oldprisoners/mainpris0412.html (accessed January 5, 2000).

201. Ronald Wikbert and Burk Foster, "The Longtermers: Louisiana's Longest Serving Inmates and Why They've Stayed So Long," paper presented at the annual meeting of the Academy of Criminal Justice Sciences, Washington, DC, 1989, p. 51.

202. *Disability Advocates, Inc.* v. *New York State Office of Mental Health,* Complaint, No. 02 CV 4002 (SDNY, May 28, 2002).

203. Allen J. Beck and Laura M. Maruschak, *Mental Health Treatment in State Prisons, 2000,* BJS Special Report (Washington, DC: Bureau of Justice Statistics, 2001), p. 1, from which most of the information in this paragraph and the next is derived.

204. *Washington* v. *Harper,* 494 U.S. 210 (1990).

205. Paula M. Ditton, *Mental Health and Treatment of Inmates and Probationers* (Washington, DC: Bureau of Justice Statistics, 1999).

206. Robert O. Lampert, "The Mentally Retarded Offender in Prison," *Justice Professional,* Vol. 2, No. 1 (Spring 1987), p. 61.

207. Ibid., p. 64.

208. George C. Denkowski and Kathryn M. Denkowski, "The Mentally Retarded Offender in the State Prison System: Identification, Prevalence, Adjustment, and Rehabilitation," *Criminal Justice and Behavior,* Vol. 12 (1985), pp. 55–75.

209. "Opening Session: Kerik Emphasizes the Importance of Corrections' Protective Role for the Country." Web posted at http://www.aca.org/conferences/Winter05/updates05.asp (accessed July 22, 2005).

210. Jess Maghan, "Intelligence-Led Penology: Management of Crime Information Obtained from Incarcerated Persons," paper presented at the Investigation of Crime World Conference, 2001, p. 6.

211. Keith Martin, *Corrections Prepares for Terrorism,* Corrections Connection News Network, January 21, 2002. Web posted at http://www.corrections.com (accessed June 15, 2005).

212. Quoted in Meghan Mandeville, "Information Sharing Becomes Crucial to Battling Terrorism Behind Bars," Corrections.com, December 8, 2003. Web posted at http://database.corrections.com/news/results2.asp?ID_8988 (accessed July 11, 2005).

213. "FBI: Al-Qaida Recruiting in U.S. Prisons," United Press International wire service, January 7, 2004. Web posted at http://database.corrections.com/news/results2.asp?ID_9148 (accessed July 1, 2005).

214. Institute for the Study of Violent Groups, "Land of Wahhabism," *Crime and Justice International,* March/April 2005, p. 43.

215. Office of the Inspector General, *A Review of the Federal Bureau of Prisons' Selection of Muslim Religious Services Providers* (Washington, DC: U.S. Department of Justice, 2004).

216. Ibid., p. 8.

217. Ibid.

218. Associated Press, "Attorney, Three Others Indicted for Alleged 'Support of Terrorism,'" *Dallas Morning News,* April 9, 2002. Web posted at http://www.dallasnews.com/latestnews/ stories/040902dnnatterrorindictment.66910.html (accessed July 25, 2003).

219. The questions in this Web Quest were adapted from "Building Your Career in Corrections," *Keeper's Voice,* Vol. 18, No. 1. Web posted at http://www.oict.org/public/toc.efm?series-KV (accessed February 20, 2002).

# PART 5

# Special Issues

## ISSUES FOR THE FUTURE

Common law, constitutional, statutory, and humanitarian rights of the accused that may be threatened by technological advances and other developments:

- A right to privacy
- A right to be assumed innocent
- A right against self-incrimination
- A right to equal protection of the laws
- A right against cruel and unusual punishment

These individual rights must be effectively balanced against these present and emerging community concerns:

- Widespread drug abuse among youth
- The threat of juvenile crime
- Urban gang violence
- High-technology, computer, and Internet crime (cybercrime)
- Terrorism and narco-terrorism
- Occupational and white-collar crime

How does our system of justice work toward balance?

## The Future Comes One Day at a Time

No one can truly say what the future holds. Will the purveyors of individual rights or the advocates of public order ultimately claim the day? We cannot say for sure. This much is certain, however: Things change. The future system of American criminal justice will not be quite the same system we know today. Many of the coming changes, however, are now discernible—and hints of what is to come appear on the horizon with increasing frequency and growing clarity. Some of the more obvious of the coming changes are already upon us. They include (1) a restructuring of the juvenile justice system in the face of growing concerns about violent juvenile crime and spreading youth gang warfare; (2) the increased bankruptcy of a war against drugs whose promises seem increasingly hollow; (3) a growing recognition of America's international role as both victim and purveyor of worldwide criminal activity; (4) the war on terrorism, including its substantial potential consequences for individual rights in America; and (5) the quickly unfolding potential of cybercrimes, those which both employ high technology in their commission and target the fruits of such technology.

This last part of *Criminal Justice Today* discusses each of these issues in the chapters that follow. It also draws your attention back to the bedrock underlying the American system of justice: the Constitution, the Bill of Rights, and the demands of due process, all of which will continue to structure the justice system well into the future.

# 15
**Juvenile Justice**

# 16
**Drugs and Crime**

# 17
**Terrorism and Multinational Criminal Justice**

# 18
**The Future of Criminal Justice**

# CHAPTER 15

# Juvenile Justice

## OUTLINE

- Introduction
- Juvenile Justice throughout History
- The Problems of Children Today
- The Legal Environment
- The Juvenile Justice Process Today
- The Post–Juvenile Court Era

## LEARNING OBJECTIVES

**After reading this chapter, you should be able to:**

- Describe the history and evolution of the juvenile justice system in the Western world.
- List and define the categories of children in today's juvenile justice system.
- Describe the nature of the problems that juveniles face in the United States today.
- Name the important U.S. Supreme Court decisions of relevance to juvenile justice, and describe their impact on the handling of juveniles by the system.
- Explain the similarities and differences between the juvenile and adult systems of justice.

*America's best hope for reducing crime is to reduce juvenile delinquency and youth crime.*

—President's Commission on Law Enforcement and Administration of Justice (1967)

> *Our society's fearful of our kids. I think we don't know how to set limits on them. They begin to behave in severely outrageous ways, and nobody stops them.*
>
> —David York, cofounder of Toughlove International[1]

## KEY CONCEPTS

### TERMS

| | | |
|---|---|---|
| abused child | intake | social ecology |
| adjudicatory hearing | juvenile disposition | status offender |
| cohort | juvenile justice system | status offense |
| delinquency | juvenile petition | teen court |
| delinquent child | neglected child | undisciplined child |
| dependent child | opportunity theory | |
| dispositional hearing | *parens patriae* | |

### CASES

| | | |
|---|---|---|
| *Breed* v. *Jones* | *In re Winship* | *McKeiver* v. *Pennsylvania* |
| *In re Gault* | *Kent* v. *U.S.* | *Schall* v. *Martin* |

The original full-text court opinion for each of these cases is available on the CD-ROM that accompanies this book.

# Introduction

Hear the author discuss this chapter at **cjtoday.com**

In September 2001, 12-year-old Tavaris Knight was convicted by a criminal court jury in Tampa, Florida, of kidnapping and raping a 43-year-old woman. Prosecutors proved that Knight had used a silver toy gun to force the woman away from her four young children at a playground and into the surrounding woods. Knight raped the woman twice and beat her with the gun.[2] His fingerprints were found on the toy gun to which the victim led police. In closing arguments, prosecutor Michael Sinacore pointed to Knight, saying, "That young man is not a child. He stopped being a child when he forced [his victim] into the woods and raped her."[3] Following conviction, Knight was sentenced to 15 years in prison by Florida Circuit Judge Jack Espinosa, Jr. Knight will likely be held at a youth facility for sexual offenders until he is 21, at which time he could be transferred to another youth offender facility until the age of 25, followed by adult prison.[4]

Crimes committed by preteens are not that unusual. In 2000, for example, two Kennesaw, Georgia, elementary school students, ages seven and ten, were caught by police officers ransacking a house. The pair had smashed the owner's possessions with a baseball bat and were in the process of stealing $1,000 worth of jewelry, a Samurai sword, and handgun ammunition when police arrived.[5] In another example, two 12-year-old St. Lucie County, Florida, girls were charged in 2001 with trying to drown a classmate in a lake near her home. The victim, 12-year-old Nicole Maines, had refused to surrender her swimming mask and flippers—leading the other girls to jump in the water, grab her gear, and beat her.[6] When the attackers shoved Maines's head underwater, a witness, 16-year-old Hosea Rivers, jumped into the lake and pulled the girls apart. A police report showed that Maines suffered cuts and bruises all over her body.

A key finding of the Office of Juvenile Justice and Delinquency Prevention's (OJJDP's) Study Group on Serious and Violent Juvenile Offenders is that most chronic juvenile offenders begin their delinquency careers before age 12, and some as early as age 10.[7] The most recent national data show that in 2004 police arrested about 128,000 children ages 12 and younger.[8] These very young offenders (known as *child delinquents*) represent almost 10% of the total number of juvenile arrestees (those up to age 18).

Although states vary as to the age at which a person legally enters adulthood, statistics on crime make it clear that young people are disproportionately involved in certain offenses. A recent report, for example, found that nearly 15% of all violent crimes and 30% of all property crimes are committed by people younger than 18, though this age group makes up only 26% of the population of the United States.[9] On average, about 17% of all arrests in any year are of juveniles,[10] and people younger than 18 have a higher likelihood of being arrested for

There was nothing to do.

—Terrance Wade, 15, on why he and his friends allegedly raped, stomped, stabbed, and ultimately murdered a Boston woman

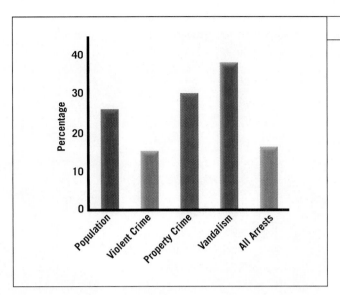

**FIGURE 15-1**

**Juvenile involvement in crime versus system totals, 2004.**

*Note:* The term *juvenile* refers to people younger than 18 years of age.

*Source:* Federal Bureau of Investigation, *Uniform Crime Reports: Crime in the United States, 2004* (Washington, DC: U.S. Government Printing Office, 2005).

robbery and other property crimes than do people in any other age group. Figure 15–1 shows *Uniform Crime Report* statistics on juvenile arrests for selected offense categories.

OJJDP is a primary source of information on juvenile justice in the United States. A sweeping OJJDP overview of juvenile crime and the juvenile justice system in America reveals the following[11]:

■ About 1.6 million juveniles (under 18) are arrested annually in America.

■ Violent crime by juveniles is decreasing.

■ Younger juveniles account for a substantial proportion of juvenile arrests and the juvenile court caseload.

■ Female delinquency has grown substantially, increasing 76% in the last ten years.

■ The number of juveniles held in public facilities has increased sharply.

■ Minority juveniles are greatly overrepresented in the custody population.

■ Crowding is a serious problem in juvenile facilities.

Learn more about OJJDP via Web Extra 15–1 at cjtoday.com.

This chapter has four purposes. First, we will look at the history of the **juvenile justice system**. The juvenile justice system has its roots in the adult system. In the juvenile system, however, we find a more uniform philosophical base and a generally clear agreement about the system's purpose. These differences may be due to the system's relative newness and to the fact that society generally agrees that young people who have gone wrong are worth salvaging. However, the philosophy that underlies the juvenile justice system in America is increasingly being questioned by "get tough" advocates of law and order, many of whom are fed up with violent juvenile crime.

Our second purpose is to compare the juvenile and adult systems as they currently operate. The reasoning behind the juvenile justice system has led to administrative and other procedures that, in many jurisdictions, are not found in the adult system. The juvenile justice process, for example, is frequently not as open as the adult system. Hearings may be held in secret, the names of offenders are not published, and records of juvenile proceedings may later be destroyed.[12]

Our third purpose is to describe in detail the agencies, processes, and problems of the juvenile justice system itself. Although each state may have variations, a common system structure is shared by all.

Near the end of this chapter, we will turn to our fourth focus and will consider some of the issues raised by critics of the current system. As conservative attitudes began to bring changes in the adult criminal justice system during the last few decades, the juvenile justice system remained relatively unchanged. Based on premises quite different from those of the adult system, juvenile justice has long been a separate decision-making arena in which the best interests of the child have been accorded great importance. As we will see, substantial changes are now afoot.

**juvenile justice system**

Government agencies that function to investigate, supervise, adjudicate, care for, or confine youthful offenders and other children subject to the jurisdiction of the juvenile court.

In 2002, Robert Iler, 17, who played the role of Anthony (A. J.) Soprano on the HBO television series *The Sopranos*, pleaded guilty to a misdemeanor charge of petty larceny in connection with a real-life New York City robbery that took place a year earlier. To some, Iler (who was arrested along with three other teenagers and who was also charged with possession of marijuana and drug paraphernalia) came to symbolize the problems of youth today. Iler could have been sentenced to 15 years' imprisonment on the original charges, but instead he received three years' probation as part of a plea agreement.

*© Brad Rickerby, Reuters NewMedia, Inc., CORBIS*

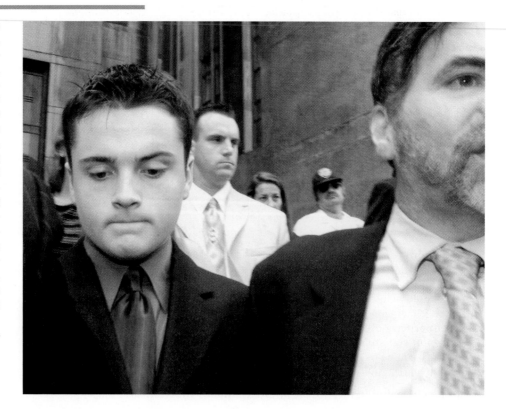

# Juvenile Justice throughout History

## Earliest Times

Before the modern era, children who committed crimes in the Western world received no preferential treatment because of their youth. They were adjudicated and punished alongside adults and a number of recorded cases have come down through history of children as young as six being hung or burned at the stake. Children were also imprisoned alongside adults; no segregated juvenile facilities existed. Neither the development of gaols (an old English word for "jails") in the thirteenth century nor the early English prisons provided any leniency on the basis of age.[13] In like fashion, little distinction was made between criminality and **delinquency** or other kinds of undesirable behavior. Problems such as epilepsy, insanity, retardation, and poverty were seen in the same light as crime,[14] and people suffering from these conditions were shut away in facilities shared by juvenile and adult offenders.

Court philosophy in dealing with juveniles derived from an early Roman principle called *patria postestas*. Under Roman law (circa 753 B.C.), children were members of their family, but the father had absolute control over children, and they in turn had an absolute responsibility to obey his wishes. Roman understanding of the social role of children strongly influenced English culture and eventually led to the development of the legal principle of ***parens patriae***. *Parens patriae* allowed the king, or the English state, to take the place of parents in dealing with children who broke the law. *Parens patriae* held that the king was father of the country and thus had parental rights over all his citizens.

By the Middle Ages, social conceptions of children had become strongly influenced by Christian churches. Church doctrine held that children under the age of seven had not yet reached the age of reason and could not be held liable for spiritual transgressions. In adopting the perspective of the Church, English law of the period excepted children under the age of seven from criminal responsibility. Juveniles ages 7 to 14 were accorded a special status, being tried as adults only if it could be demonstrated that they fully understood the nature of their criminal acts.[15] Adulthood was considered to begin at age 14, when marriage was also allowed.[16]

Early English institutions placed a large burden of responsibility on the family, and especially the father, who, as head of the household, was held accountable for the behavior of all family

**delinquency**

In the broadest usage, juvenile actions or conduct in violation of criminal law, juvenile status offenses, and other juvenile misbehavior.

***parens patriae***

A common law principle that allows the state to assume a parental role and to take custody of a child when he or she becomes delinquent, is abandoned, or is in need of care that the natural parents are unable or unwilling to provide.

members, even their wives. When the father failed in his responsibility to control family members, the king, through the concept of *parens patriae,* could intervene.

The inexorable power of the king, often marked by his personal and unpredictable whims, combined with a widespread fear of the dismal conditions in English institutions made many families hide their problem kin. The retarded, insane, and epileptic were kept in attics or basements, sometimes for their entire lives. Delinquent children were confined to the home or, if their families were wealthy enough, sent overseas to escape the conditions of asylums and gaols.

## Juveniles in Early America

Early American solutions to the problems of delinquency were much like those of the English. Puritan influence in the colonies, with its heavy emphasis on obedience and discipline, led to frequent use of jails and prisons for both juveniles and adults. Legislation reflected the Ten Commandments and often provided harsh punishments for transgressors of almost any age. For example, one seventeenth-century Massachusetts law provided, in part, that[17]

> if a man have a stubborn or rebellious son of sufficient years of understanding, viz. sixteen, which will not obey the voice of his father or the voice of his mother, and that when they have chastened him will not harken to them, then shall his father and mother, being his natural parents, lay hold on him and bring him to the magistrates assembled in Court, and testify to them by sufficient evidence that this their son is stubborn and rebellious and will not obey their voice and chastisement, but lives in sundry notorious crime. Such a son shall be put to death.

Severe punishment was consistent with the Puritan belief that unacknowledged social evils might bring the wrath of God down upon the entire colony. In short, disobedient children had no place in a social group committed to a spiritual salvation understood as strict obedience to the wishes of the Divine.

By the end of the eighteenth century, social conditions in Europe and America began to change. The Enlightenment, a highly significant intellectual and social movement, focused on human potential. It was accompanied by the growth of an industrialized economy, with a corresponding move away from farming. English poor laws (which preceded welfare legislation), lower infant death rates, and social innovations born of the Enlightenment led to a reassessment of the place of children in society. In this new age, children were recognized as the only true heirs to the future, and society became increasingly concerned about their well-being.

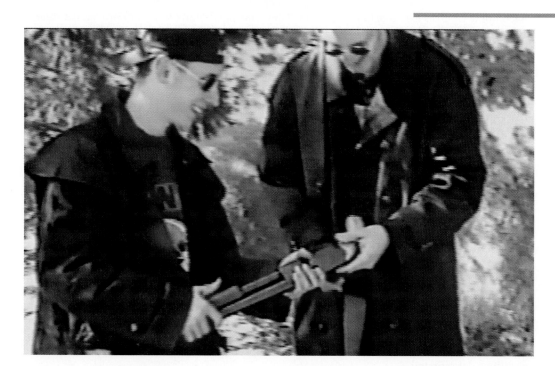

Columbine (Colorado) High School shooters Eric Harris (left) and Dylan Klebold examine a sawed-off shotgun in a still image taken from a videotape made at a makeshift shooting range in 1999. About six weeks after the video was made, Klebold (17) and Harris (18) shot and killed 15 people and injured 20 more at the school. Learn more about the shootings via Web Extra 15–2 at cjtoday.com.

*Getty Images, Inc.*

Young New York City pickpockets in custody, circa 1900. Beginning in the late nineteenth century, juvenile courts had to consider what was in the child's best interests.

*© Underwood & Underwood, CORBIS*

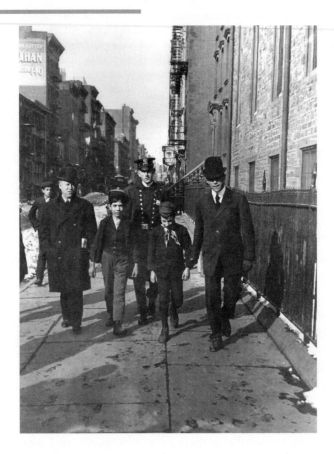

# The Institutional Era

The nineteenth century was a time of rapid social change in the United States. The population was growing dramatically, cities were burgeoning, and the industrial era was in full swing. Industrial tycoons, the new rich, and frontier-bound settlers lived elbow to elbow with immigrants eking out a living in the sweatshops of the new mercantile centers. In this environment, children took on new value as a source of cheap labor. They fueled assembly lines and proved invaluable to shop owners who could not or would not pay fair wages. Parents were gratified by the income-producing opportunities available to their offspring. On the frontier, settlers and farm families put their children to work clearing land and seeding crops.

Unfortunately, economic opportunities and the luck of the draw were not equally favorable to all. Some immigrant families became victims of the cities that drew them, settling in squalor in hastily formed ghettos. Many families, seeing only the economic opportunities represented by their children, neglected to provide them with anything but a rudimentary education. Children who did work labored for long hours and had little time for family closeness. Other children, abandoned by families unable to support them, were forced into lives on the streets, where they formed tattered gangs—surviving off the refuse of the glittering cities.

## The House of Refuge

An 1823 report by the Society for the Prevention of Pauperism in the City of New York called for the development of "houses of refuge" to save children from lives of crime and poverty. The society also cited the problems caused by locking up children with mature criminals. Houses of refuge were to be places of care and education, where children could learn positive attitudes about work.

In 1824, the first house of refuge opened in New York City.[18] The New York House of Refuge was intended only for those children who could still be "rescued," and it sheltered mostly young thieves, vagrants, and runaways. Other children, especially those with more severe delinquency problems, were placed in adult prisons and jails. Houses of refuge became popular in New York, and other cities quickly copied them. It was not long before overcrowding developed and living conditions deteriorated.

The 1838 case of *Ex parte Crouse* clarified the power that states had in committing children to institutions.[19] The case involved Mary Ann Crouse, who had been committed to the Philadelphia House of Refuge by a lower court over the objections of her father. The commitment was based on allegations made by the girl's mother that she was incorrigible—that is, beyond the control of her parents. Mary Ann's father petitioned the court to release his daughter on the grounds that she had been denied the right to trial by jury.

The decision by the appeals court upheld the legality of Mary Ann's commitment. It pointed to the state's interest in assisting children and denied that punishment or retribution played any part in her treatment. The court also focused on parental responsibilities in general and stressed the need for state intervention to provide for the moral development of children whose parents had failed them. Most important of all, the court built its decision around the doctrine of *parens patriae,* taking what had previously been an English judicial concept and applying it to the American scene. The court wrote,[20]

> The object of the charity is reformation, by training its inmates to industry; by imbuing their minds with principles of morality and religion; by furnishing them with means to earn a living; and above all, by separating them from the corrupting influence of improper associates. To this end, may not the natural parents, when unequal to the task of education, or unworthy of it, be superseded by the *parens patriae,* or common guardianship of the community?

## The Chicago Reform School

Around the middle of the nineteenth century, the child-savers movement began. Child savers espoused a philosophy of productivity and eschewed idleness and unprincipled behavior. Anthony Platt, a modern writer who recognizes the significance of the child-savers movement, suggests that the mid-nineteenth century provided an ideological framework combining Christian principles with a strong emphasis on the worth of the individual.[21] It was a social perspective that held that children were to be guided and protected.

One product of the child-savers movement was the reform school—a place for delinquent juveniles that embodied the atmosphere of a Christian home. By the middle of the nineteenth century, the reform school approach to handling juveniles was well under way. The Chicago Reform School, which opened in the 1860s, provided an early model for the reform school movement. The movement focused primarily on predelinquent youths who showed tendencies toward more serious criminal involvement. Reform schools attempted to emulate wholesome family environments to provide the security and affection thought necessary in building moral character.

The reform school movement also emphasized traditional values and the worth of hard work, idealizing country living. Some early reform schools were built in rural settings, and many were farms. A few programs even tried to relocate problem children to the vast open expanses of the Western states.

The reform school movement was not without its critics. As Platt writes, "If institutions sought to replicate families, would it not have been better to place the predelinquents directly in real families?"[22] As with houses of refuge, reform schools soon became overcrowded. What began as a meaningful attempt to help children ended in routinized institutional procedures devoid of the reformers' original zeal.

In the 1870s, the Illinois Supreme Court handed down a decision that practically ended the reform school movement. The case of *People ex rel. O'Connell* v. *Turner*[23] centered on Daniel O'Connell, who had been committed to the Chicago Reform School under an Illinois law that permitted confinement for "misfortune." Youngsters classified as "misfortunate" had not necessarily committed any offense. They were, rather, ordered to reform school because their families were unable to care for them or because they were seen as social misfits. Because O'Connell had not been convicted of a crime, the Illinois Supreme Court ordered him released. The court reasoned that the power of the state under *parens patriae* could not exceed the power of the natural parents except in punishing crime. The *O'Connell* case is remembered today for the lasting distinction it made between criminal and noncriminal acts committed by juveniles.

## The Juvenile Court Era

In 1870, an expanding recognition of children's needs led the state of Massachusetts to enact legislation that required separate hearings for juveniles.[24] New York followed with a similar law in 1877,[25] which also prohibited contact between juvenile and adult offenders. Rhode Island enacted juvenile court legislation in 1898, and in 1899 the Colorado School Law became the first comprehensive

> The current [juvenile justice] system, a relic from a more innocent time, teaches youthful offenders that crime pays and that they are totally immune and insulated from responsibility.
>
> —National Policy Forum

legislation designed to adjudicate problem children.[26] It was, however, the 1899 codification of Illinois juvenile law that became the model for juvenile court statutes throughout the nation.

The Illinois Juvenile Court Act created a juvenile court, separate in form and function from adult criminal courts. To avoid the lasting stigma of criminality, the law applied the term *delinquent* rather than *criminal* to young adjudicated offenders. The act specified that the best interests of the child were to guide juvenile court judges in their deliberations. In effect, judges were to serve as advocates for juveniles, guiding their development. Determining guilt or innocence took second place to the betterment of the child. The law abandoned a strict adherence to the due process requirements of adult prosecutions, allowing informal procedures designed to scrutinize the child's situation. By sheltering the juvenile from the punishment philosophy of the adult system, the Illinois Juvenile Court emphasized reformation in place of retribution.[27]

In 1938, the federal government passed the Juvenile Court Act, which embodied many of the features of the Illinois statute. By 1945, every state had enacted special legislation focusing on the handling of juveniles, and the juvenile court movement became well established.[28]

The juvenile court movement was based on five philosophical principles that can be summarized as follows[29]:

- The state is the "higher or ultimate parent" of all the children within its borders.
- Children are worth saving, and nonpunitive procedures should be used to save the child.
- Children should be nurtured. While the nurturing process is under way, they should be protected from the stigmatizing impact of formal adjudicatory procedures.
- To accomplish the goal of reformation, justice needs to be individualized; that is, each child is different, and the needs, aspirations, living conditions, and so on, of each child must be known in their individual particulars if the court is to be helpful.
- Noncriminal procedures are necessary to give primary consideration to the needs of the child. The denial of due process can be justified in the face of constitutional challenges because the court acts not to punish, but to help.

 Learn more about the history of juvenile justice and the juvenile court via Library Extra 15–1 at cjtoday.com.

## Categories of Children in the Juvenile Justice System

By the time of the Great Depression, most states had expanded juvenile statutes to include the following six categories of children. These categories are still used today in most jurisdictions to describe the variety of children subject to juvenile court jurisdiction.

- **Delinquent children** are those who violate the criminal law. If they were adults, the word *criminal* would be applied to them.
- **Undisciplined children** are said to be beyond parental control, as evidenced by their refusal to obey legitimate authorities, such as school officials and teachers. They need state protection.
- **Dependent children** typically have no parents or guardians to care for them. Their parents are deceased, they were placed for adoption, or they were abandoned in violation of the law.
- **Neglected children** are those who do not receive proper care from their parents or guardians. They may suffer from malnutrition or may not be provided with adequate shelter.
- **Abused children** are those who suffer physical abuse at the hands of their custodians. This category was later expanded to include emotional and sexual abuse.
- **Status offenders** is a special category that embraces children who violate laws written only for them. In some states, status offenders are referred to as persons in need of supervision, or PINS.

**Status offenses** include behavior such as truancy, vagrancy, running away from home, and incorrigibility. The youthful "status" of juveniles is a necessary element in such offenses. Adults, for example, may "run away from home" and not violate any law. Runaway children, however, are subject to apprehension and juvenile court processing because state laws require that they be subject to parental control.

Status offenses were a natural outgrowth of juvenile court philosophy. As a consequence, however, juveniles in need of help often faced procedural dispositions that treated them as though they were delinquent. Rather than lowering the rate of juvenile incarceration, the juvenile court movement led to its increase. Critics of the juvenile court movement quickly focused on the abandonment of due process rights, especially in the case of status offenders, as a major source of problems. Detention and incarceration, they argued, were inappropriate options where children had not committed crimes.

### delinquent child

A child who has engaged in activity that would be considered a crime if the child were an adult. The term *delinquent* is used to avoid the stigma associated with the term *criminal*.

### undisciplined child

A child who is beyond parental control, as evidenced by his or her refusal to obey legitimate authorities, such as school officials and teachers.

### dependent child

A child who has no parents or whose parents are unable to care for him or her.

### neglected child

A child who is not receiving the proper level of physical or psychological care from his or her parents or guardians or who has been placed up for adoption in violation of the law.

### abused child

A child who has been physically, sexually, or mentally abused. Most states also consider a child who is forced into delinquent activity by a parent or guardian to be abused.

### status offender

A child who commits an act that is contrary to the law by virtue of the offender's status as a child. Purchasing cigarettes, buying alcohol, and being truant are examples of such behavior.

# Explanation of Delinquency

As states implemented innovative programs to handle problem children, researchers began to investigate the causes of juvenile misbehavior. One of the first comprehensive social science explanations for delinquency, advanced by University of Chicago social scientists Clifford Shaw and Henry McKay in the 1920s, was known as **social ecology**.[30] The social ecology approach focused on the misbehavior of lower-class youth and saw delinquency primarily as the result of social disorganization. Whereas social order is the condition of a society characterized by social integration, consensus, smooth functioning, and lack of interpersonal and institutional conflicts, social disorganization exists when a group is faced with social change, uneven development, maladaptation, disharmony, conflict, and lack of consensus. Geographic areas characterized by economic deprivation had high rates of population turnover and cultural heterogeneity, both of which were seen as contributors to social disorganization. Social disorganization weakened otherwise traditional societal controls, such as family life, church, jobs, and schools, making delinquency more likely.

The first large-scale delinquency-prevention program grew out of the work of Shaw and McKay. Known as the Chicago Area Project, the program, which began in the 1930s, established self-help neighborhood centers staffed by community volunteers. Each center offered counseling services, educational programs, camps, recreational activities, and discussion groups. Programs were intended to reduce social disorganization by bringing members of the community together to work toward common goals and by providing community members with the skills needed for success.

Shaw and McKay's social ecology explanation of delinquency was replaced in the 1960s by a perspective known as **opportunity theory**. Richard Cloward and Lloyd Ohlin and other opportunity theorists saw delinquency as the result of the lack of legitimate opportunities for success available to most lower-class youth.[31] Others have claimed that delinquency is a natural consequence of participation in lower-class culture. Even stable lower-class communities, these authors suggest, produce delinquency as a matter of course.[32] A combination of both approaches is found in the work of Albert Cohen, who held that delinquency, especially gang-related activity, is a response to the frustration lower-class youth experience when they find they cannot share in the rewards of a middle-class lifestyle.[33] According to Cohen, vengeance and protest are major motivators among deprived youth and may account for vandalism and other seemingly senseless acts.

Opportunity theory gave rise to treatment models designed to increase chances for legitimate success among lower-class youth. Programs like New York City's Mobilization for Youth, founded in 1961, provided education, skills training, and job-placement services to young men and women. Mobilization for Youth, through the federal funds it received, hired hundreds of unemployed neighborhood youths to work on community projects, such as parks conservation and building renovation.

One contemporary research method that attempts to unveil the underlying causes of juvenile delinquency is **cohort** analysis. Cohort analysis usually begins at birth and traces the development of members of a population who share common characteristics until they reach a certain age. One well-known analysis of a birth cohort, undertaken by Marvin Wolfgang during the 1960s, found that a small nucleus of chronic juvenile offenders accounted for a disproportionately large share of all juvenile arrests.[34] Wolfgang studied males born in Philadelphia in 1945 until they reached age 18. He concluded that a relatively small number of violent offenders were responsible for most of the crimes committed by the cohort. Eighteen percent of cohort members accounted for 52% of all arrests. A follow-up study found that the seriousness of offenses among the cohort increased in adulthood but that the actual number of offenses decreased as the cohort aged.[35] Wolfgang's analysis has been criticized for its lack of a second cohort, or "control group," against which the experiences of the cohort under study could be compared.[36]

Perhaps the most comprehensive study to date that has looked at the causes of juvenile delinquency was begun in 1986. Results of this research are still being reported. The study, named the Program of Research on the Causes and Correlates of Juvenile Delinquency, is sponsored by the U.S. Department of Justice's OJJDP.[37] The study, which we looked at in Chapter 3, draws together data on 4,000 youths from three distinct but coordinated projects in Denver, Pittsburgh, and Rochester. The survey sampled youngsters at high risk for serious delinquency and drug use and found that (1) "the more seriously involved in drugs a youth was, the more seriously that juvenile was involved in delinquency," (2) "greater risks exist for violent offending when a child is physically abused or neglected early in life," (3) "students who were not highly committed to school had higher rates of delinquency," (4) "poor family life exacerbates delinquency and drug use," and (5) affiliation with street gangs and illegal gun ownership are both predictive of delinquency. The study also found that "peers who were delinquent or used drugs had a great impact on [other] youth."

---

**status offense**

An act or conduct that is declared by statute to be an offense, but only when committed by or engaged in by a juvenile, and that can be adjudicated only by a juvenile court.

**social ecology**

A criminological approach that focuses on the misbehavior of lower-class youth and sees delinquency primarily as the result of social disorganization.

**opportunity theory**

A perspective that sees delinquency as the result of limited legitimate opportunities for success available to most lower-class youth.

**cohort**

A group of individuals sharing similarities of age, place of birth, and residence. Cohort analysis is a social science technique that tracks cohorts over time to identify the unique and observable behavioral traits that characterize them.

Other studies have also indicated the importance of regular school attendance and commitment to success at school.[38] One report by OJJDP, for example, found that "chronic absenteeism is the most powerful predictor of delinquent behavior."[39] A comprehensive task force report by the American Society of Criminology similarly concluded that "strong evidence links early problem behavior to later adolescent delinquency and serious adult criminality" and suggested that early intervention is the key to preventing the development of chronic patterns of criminal behavior.[40] Authors of the task force report wrote, "There is clear indication that problem behavior often begins early in life, and there is strong evidence of substantial continuity between problem behavior in early childhood and later adolescent delinquency and serious adult criminality. 'An ounce of prevention is worth more than a pound of cure' is more than an old adage. Not only can early prevention and intervention reduce future crime and delinquency, but waiting until the mid-to-late teenage years to intervene in serious, persistent delinquency commonly results in an uphill and all too frequently fruitless battle."[41]

Library Extra 15–2 at cjtoday.com provides an overview of OJJDP's Causes and Correlates of Delinquency Program. Read the latest report from the Causes and Correlates Studies at Library Extra 15–3 at cjtoday.com.

**LIBRARY** **EXTRA**

# The Problems of Children Today

> If a child cannot go to school without fear of being raped, robbed, or even murdered, then nothing else the government does really matters.
>
> —National Policy Forum

Today's children face a vast array of problems that contribute to delinquency. One general problem that many youth grapple with is frustration. Poor urban children and teens in particular wrestle with anger and dissatisfaction. Sometimes frustration turns to rage. In 2004, for example, in a scene that would make even the experienced viewers of the FOX Broadcasting Company's popular prime-time show *Nanny 911* cringe, an 11-year-old Barstow, California, girl attacked her 34-year-old babysitter with a machete during a struggle that began with an argument over feeding a dog.[42] Refusing a demand to care for the pet, the girl turned angry and started to choke and beat the animal. The sitter had to pry the girl off of the dog, and the scuffle spilled out into the front yard of the girl's home where she grabbed a shovel, then a baseball bat, and finally a BB gun and tried to use them on the sitter, who was able to deflect the attacks. Finally, however, the girl grabbed a machete lying in the yard and chased the sitter into a bathroom, where she locked the door and called for help. The girl fled on a bicycle before deputies arrived but was apprehended an hour later and taken into custody. "Angry adolescents," or preadolescents in the case of the 11-year-old described here, have been described as sharing these traits: (1) aggressiveness, (2) immaturity, (3) susceptibility to peer pressure, and (4) a lack of accountability.[43]

How did angry youth come to be a problem in America? More than half a century ago, many young people gained a sense of personal worth as day laborers in sweatshops and factories. The economic prosperity that followed World War II, however, was based on a less labor-intensive form of production, and meaningful jobs for young people started to disappear. Complicating matters still further was the need for the national economy to absorb millions of women who were entering the labor force. Juveniles, no longer needed for their labor, were thrown into a cultural limbo. Some, unable to meaningfully participate in the long educational process that was becoming necessary for future success, turned to delinquency and vandalism. For these disenfranchised youths, criminal activity became an alternative avenue to excitement and some limited sense of purpose.

By the 1960s, a self-indulgent ethic had replaced a sense of personal responsibility among many American youths. For some lower-class youths, this ethic led to violence, theft, and increased participation in gangs. Middle-class youths, because they were more affluent, focused on what some authors at the time called the "automobile-alcohol-sex combination,"[44] rejecting middle-class values of social duty and personal restraint. There is also evidence that upper-class youths commit a fair number of delinquent acts. A study of the "lifetime delinquency" of Ivy League college students, for example, found "substantial levels of involvement in a variety of serious offenses."[45] According to the study, 167 students admitted to 4,100 past offenses ranging from public intoxication to forcible rape.

Regardless of class background, juveniles today face a number of common problems. They are described in the sections that follow.

## Drug and Alcohol Abuse

Many of today's adolescents have experimented with illegal drugs, and statistics documenting both long-term use and experimentation are available from many sources. The Department of Health and Human Services Monitoring the Future (MTF) survey,[46] one of the most comprehensive sources of information on juvenile drug use, annually measures self-reported illegal drug use among high school and college students. Conducted by the University of Michigan's Institute for Social Research, the MTF survey began in 1975 as a long-term study of drug use throughout the 50 states.

The 2004 MTF survey found that illicit drug use remains widespread among American young people. Today, 51% of teenagers have tried an illicit drug by the time they finish high school. If inhalant use is included in the definition of *illicit drug,* 30% of students have done so as early as the eighth grade. Twenty-nine percent of in-school students have tried some illicit drug *other* than marijuana by the end of twelfth grade, and 21% of twelfth graders used some illicit drug other than marijuana in the past year. It is important to note that the MTF survey of high school seniors "may underrepresent drug use among youth of that age because high school dropouts and truants are not included, and these groups may have more involvement with drugs than those who stay in school."[47]

The 2004 MTF survey provides a nearly 30-year overview of self-reported drug-use habits throughout the country. Survey results show that marijuana continues to be the most widely used illicit drug among high school students. Annual marijuana usage peaked at 51% among twelfth graders in 1979, following a rise that began during the 1960s. After that, use declined steadily for 13 years, bottoming at 22% in 1992. The 1990s, however, saw a resurgence of use. After a considerable increase in the 1990s, usage rates peaked in 1996 and 1997. From 2002 through 2004, reported rates of abuse fell appreciably in all grades. In 2004, approximately 37% of high school seniors reported having used marijuana in the past 12 months.

According to the long-term data from twelfth graders surveyed by the MTF, inhalant use rose gradually between 1976 and 1987. The use of inhalants also rose among eighth and tenth graders from 1991 through 1995, and it rose among twelfth graders from 1992 to 1995. All grades then exhibited a fairly steady and substantial decline in inhalant use through 2002. In 2003 the decline continued for tenth and twelfth graders, but there was a significant increase in use among eighth graders. By 2004 all grades were showing some evidence of an increase in the use of inhalants, and 11% of eighth graders reported having used inhalants during the past year.

The annual prevalence of LSD use among twelfth graders has been below 10% since the study began in 1975. Reported usage levels had been level in the latter half of the 1980s but, as was true for a number of other drugs, rose in all three grades between 1991 and 1996. After significant declines in all three grades, particularly between 2001 and 2003, annual prevalence in 2003 reached the lowest point since data collection began. Little further change occurred in 2004, when approximately 2% of students in twelfth grade reported using LSD in the past year. There have been some important changes in the levels of overall cocaine use (which includes crack) over the life of the MTF study. Cocaine use among twelfth graders swelled in the late 1970s and then remained nearly stable through the first half of the 1980s, before starting a steep decline after 1986. Between 1992 and 1999, use reversed course and doubled to 6.2%, before declining to 5% by 2000—a level at which it has remained ever since.

Amphetamine usage rose in the last half of the 1970s and reached a peak in 1981. After 1981, a long and steady decline in amphetamine use by twelfth graders began but ended in 1992. As with many other illicit drugs, amphetamine use experienced a resurgence in the 1990s, partially due to the popularity of ecstasy. Usage peaked in the lower two grades by 1996 and in twelfth grade by 1997. Since those peak years, use has steadily declined, with about 10% of high school seniors reporting having used amphetamines in the past year.

The annual prevalence of heroin use among twelfth graders fell by half between 1975 and 1979, from 1% to less than half a percent. The rate then held steady until 1993, when it began to rise. The increase in use slowed in 1996 and stabilized in 2000. No systematic change has been observed since 2001, with about 1% of students reporting past-year heroin use in the eighth, tenth, and twelfth grades.

Some young people abuse a wide variety of mind- and mood-altering substances. Surveys show that 9% of eighth graders have used inhalants at least once during the past year, while 28% of seniors, 21% of tenth graders, and 13% of eighth graders report binge drinking (defined as consuming five or more alcoholic drinks in a row).[48] According to a RAND Corporation Drug Policy Research Center study, (1) about one out of every six high school seniors averages at least one alcoholic drink every other day; (2) more than a quarter of all teenagers experience a drinking-related problem (such as missing school) on at least three occasions in any given year—or a more serious problem (such as a fight) at least once; and (3) about 25% of teenagers engage in two or more high-risk drinking activities (combining alcohol with other drugs, driving while drinking, and so on) at least once per year.[49]

As Figure 15–2 shows, drug-related arrests of juveniles have risen significantly during the past 30 years, nearly doubling between 1970 and 2002. The rise, however, has not been consistent, with peaks occurring around 1976 and 1996, with declines in between.[50] While some of the increase in the number of arrests may be due to "get tough" enforcement policies, evidence indicates that a juvenile arrested today is far more likely to be using methamphetamines ("crystal meth"), ecstasy, GHB, Rohypnol, and cocaine or crack cocaine than were juveniles in earlier

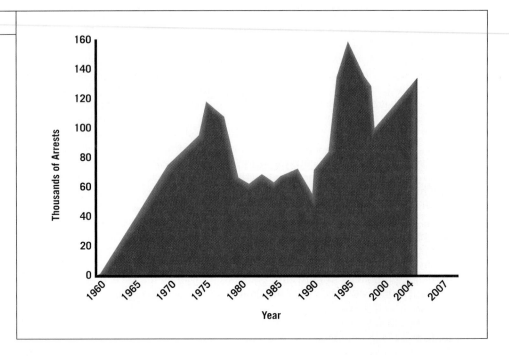

**FIGURE 15–2**

**Drug-related arrests of juveniles, 1960–2004.**

*Source:* Federal Bureau of Investigation, *Uniform Crime Reports: Crime in the United States* (Washington, DC: U.S. Government Printing Office, various years).

> For the foreseeable future, American youngsters will be aware of the psychoactive potential of many drugs and, in general, will have relatively easy access to them. In the absence of reasons not to use, many are going to try them and a significant number will get into trouble with them.
>
> —Monitoring the Future survey

periods. Likewise, heroin use has made a small but noticeable comeback. In contrast, the most commonly abused drug among young people in 1975 was marijuana.

Drug abuse can lead to other types of crime. One study, for example, found that seriously delinquent youths were regular drug users.[51] The National Institute of Justice concludes, "The involvement of adolescent users in other destructive behavior is strongly associated with the number and types of harmful substances they use; the more substances they use, the greater their chance of being involved in serious destructive or assaultive behavior."[52]

## Violence

In 2005, members of the Red Lake band of Chippewas were shocked when a young member of their Minnesota tribe, 16-year-old Jeff Weise, killed nine people in an attack at the local high school before taking his own life.[53] Five of the dead were students. A week after the shootings, Louis Jourdain, the 16-year-old son of tribal leader Floyd Jourdain, Jr., was taken into custody by federal authorities in connection with the incident. His arrest was said to be part of an investigation into a potentially larger plot.

The Red Lake shootings were sadly reminiscent of the Columbine High School shootings in Littleton, Colorado, in 1999, which claimed the lives of 12 students and a teacher. In that incident the shooters, 18-year-old Eric Harris and 17-year-old Dylan Klebold, took their own lives as police surrounded the school.

While the numbers are small (juveniles commit approximately 800 homicides annually), violence committed both by and against children is a serious national problem. The National Center for Health Statistics lists homicide as the third leading cause of death for children ages 1 to 4 and 5 to 14, and the second leading cause for young people 15 to 24.[54] Of the 1,365 juvenile murder victims in 2004—an average of three per day—24% were under age 5.[55] Thirty-two percent were female, and 45% were African-American.[56] Sixty-two percent of all juvenile murder victims and 57% of murdered youth who were 13 or older were killed with a firearm.[57] Forty percent were killed by family members, 45% by acquaintances, and only 15% by strangers.[58] The older juvenile victims, compared with those under age 13, were more likely to be male and African-American.[59] Younger victims were more likely to be killed by family members.

These statistics reflect only juvenile victimizations that were reported to the police. Only about half of the serious violent victimizations of juveniles in this country—including aggravated assault, murder, forcible rape, and robbery—are reported to police or other authorities, such as teachers and school principals.[60] Violent crimes that occur in schools, those that result in injury, and those that involve an adult rather than a juvenile perpetrator are the most likely to be reported.[61] Learn more about juvenile offenders and victims from OJJDP via **Library Extra 15–4** at cjtoday.com.

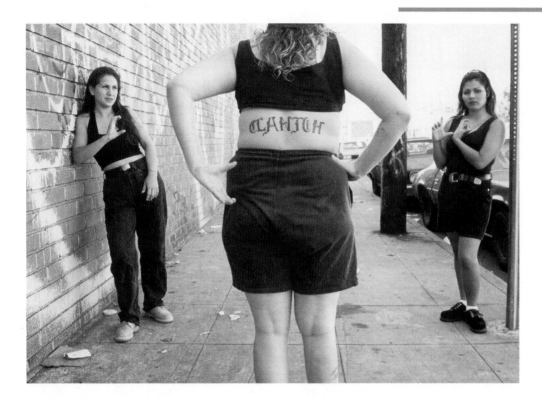

Female gang members. The values and experiences of many children today are far different from those of the past.

*Robert Yager, Getty Images, Inc.— Stone Allstock*

# Gangs

Juvenile gangs have been an inner-city phenomenon for decades. Detailed descriptions of gang activities in the United States date from the 1920s.[62] Contemporary gang activities, however, differ substantially from those early reports, reflecting, perhaps, the influence of the rapid growth of cocaine markets. Whereas membership in early gangs served to provide some sense of personal identity in the immigrant's culturally diverse world, many of today's juvenile gangs have developed into financial enterprises. Their activities may center on drug running and on the acquisition and sale of stolen goods. Today's gangs rarely hesitate to use ruthless violence to protect their financial opportunities. One study of an East Coast gang of the 1930s found that the weapons of choice included milk bottles, flowerpots, and banana tree stalks.[63] In contrast, members of some large-city gangs today brandish semiautomatic weapons and Uzi submachine guns.[64]

The National Youth Gang Survey, conducted annually by OJJDP in conjunction with the National Youth Gang Center (NYGC) in Tallahassee, Florida, estimates that approximately 21,500 gangs and more than 731,500 gang members were active in the United States during 2002.[65] Survey results show that, in 2002, youth gangs were active in more than 2,300 cities with a population of 2,500 or more, and in more than 550 jurisdictions served by county law enforcement agencies. Responding to the NYGC survey, officials in Chicago and Los Angeles reported a total of 655 gang-related homicides. When compared with the more than 1,300 total homicides recorded in Chicago and Los Angeles in 2002, these findings suggest that approximately half of all homicides in those cities were gang related.

Fifty percent of gang members are between the ages of 18 and 24,[66] while the race-ethnicity composition of the nation's gangs is as follows: Hispanic (47%), African-American (31%), white (13%), Asian (7%), and other (2%). Forty-seven percent of gangs are multiethnic or multiracial.

In the National Youth Gang Survey, law enforcement agencies were asked to identify gang members by social class. Fifty percent of gang members were reported to be underclass, followed by working class (35%), middle class (12%), and upper middle class (3%). Responding jurisdictions were asked to estimate the proportion of their youth gang members who engage in specific types of serious and violent crimes. They reported that the offense types most prevalent among gang members are larceny/theft, aggravated assault, and burglary/breaking and entering. Respondents also estimated that 46% of youth gang members are involved in street drug sales to generate money for their gangs. The percentage of youth gangs that are considered drug gangs (that is, organized specifically for the purpose of trafficking in drugs) was around 40%.

## CJ NEWS

### Mean Streets Once Again: Gang Activity Surging

A decade after police crackdowns on drug gangs helped lead to historically low crime rates in cities across the nation, gangs suddenly are re-emerging in waves of violence that have jolted officials in Tulsa, the Virginia suburbs of Washington, D.C., and many other communities well beyond the groups' traditional big-city bases.

The resurgence of gangs whose names became symbols of the turf wars over crack cocaine during the 1980s—the Crips, the Bloods, the Mexican Mafia, the Gangster Disciples and others—is helping to lift homicide rates in several cities at a time when overall crime rates remain low.

Some police officials—including those in Tulsa, where federal, state and local authorities now keep an intelligence database on suspected gang members—say they can trace the recent violence to the releases of senior gang members from prison. Others note that the violence has flared as police agencies, facing budget cuts and increased concerns about terrorism, gradually have dismantled anti-gang units. Now, officials from Durham, N.C., to Los Angeles are scrambling to assign more cops and prosecutors to deal with gangs. "We had a chance to pull the weeds out of our communities for good a few years ago," says Tim Twining, director of gang prosecutions in Denver, where budget cuts forced the elimination of the district attorney's anti-gang unit in 2002 before it was re-established last year. "We didn't do it; we got distracted. Now, the weeds are back."

Nationwide, gang-related homicides jumped by 50% from 1999 to 2002, according to a report commissioned by Fight Crime: Invest in Kids, a coalition of big-city police chiefs. In 2002, the most recent year analyzed in the study by Northeastern University professor James Alan Fox, 1,034 of the 16,204 homicides across the nation were linked to gangs—the most since 1995, when there were 1,237 gang-related slayings.

A separate Justice Department review this year found that 42% of the 2,182 cities that responded to the 2002 National Youth Gang Survey reported that gang activity was "getting worse," up from 27% the previous year. In the same survey, 87% of U.S. cities with populations of at least 100,000 reported problems with gangs.

Recently, the U.S. House of Representatives responded to increased reports of gang violence by approving the creation of a National Gang Intelligence Center. If approved by the Senate, the center would provide additional federal agents and prosecutors to track gang members involved in crimes.

Authorities say that in many cases, gangs have branched out from their traditional homes in Los Angeles, Chicago and New York City because they have found new drug markets—and less scrutiny from police—in smaller communities. In a few instances, authorities say, youths from troubled urban neighborhoods who were sent to live with relatives in safer, smaller towns have wound up starting new criminal groups.

A group portrait of some members of the 18th Street Gang, an Hispanic gang in the Rampart area of Los Angeles. The 18th Street Gang is said to be one of the most violent and fastest-growing gangs in the United States.

*A. Ramey, PhotoEdit*

### CLAMPING DOWN ON GANGS

Gangs have operated in Tulsa since the late 1980s. Like many other cities, Tulsa was slow to respond to them. But during the early 1990s, Tulsa police formed a squad to clamp down on gang turf wars and illegal drug sales.

Nearly a dozen officers were assigned to the unit at its peak during the late 1990s. As crime declined, several officers were reassigned to more pressing priorities. That all began to change last year, when Tulsa had a record 70 slayings, 17 of which police linked to gangs. Then came a flurry of violence late last spring, after a local gang leader was released from prison.

"We knew he was coming back," says police Capt. Walter Busby, who asked that the gang leader not be identified because he is a focus of several pending investigations. "When he did, (violence) started to spike significantly."

Tulsa authorities now suspect that the gang leader has been involved in as many as a half-dozen killings since his release from prison in late March. Meanwhile, police in this city of

## CJ NEWS *(continued)*

393,049 estimate that more than 3,300 residents have at least some tie to a gang, and that the number is rising by about 200 people a year.

Tulsa's murder rate is down this year; there have been 24 slayings. But police have linked about one-third of the killings to gangs, a higher percentage than last year.

For many Tulsa residents, the escalating danger posed by gangs became vivid in late February, when police were called to the modest, North Side home of Ples and Shelly Vann. The couple had been executed, apparently because their sons had been involved in a dispute with Crips members, police say. Philip Summers, a suspected Crips member, was charged in the slayings and is awaiting trial.

The Vann slayings shocked the city and reinvigorated Tulsa's anti-gang efforts. Police Major Mark McCrory says the brutality of the slayings was "an eye-opener" that led city officials to put unprecedented pressure on gangs and to conduct almost-daily raids on suspected safe houses.

A new police team of a dozen officers has joined Tulsa's existing anti-gang unit on 92 raids. Authorities routinely have recovered drugs and bundles of cash and guns, including several assault weapons. More than 100 people, most of them alleged gang members, have been arrested.

### "HITTING THEM AS HARD AS WE CAN"

McCrory, a burly officer who oversees the raid teams in the manner of an enthusiastic football coach, says he believes the aggressive tactics by police have helped to slow the violence. "We're hitting them as hard as we can," he says. "Our goal is to make life as miserable as possible for these people."

In Tulsa, a coalition of local, state and federal law enforcement agencies has been formed to chart gang membership. Each week, representatives of the FBI, the federal Bureau of Alcohol, Tobacco, Firearms and Explosives, the Tulsa police, Oklahoma's state prison system and the Tulsa County Sheriff's Office meet to examine the spread of gang membership in the area.

The officials keep track of gang members with a database that includes information from patrol officers, informants and other sources. The idea is to learn who is joining gangs and to find out more about gangs' crime networks.

Tulsa's process of designating people as possible gang members is based on a range of factors, officials say. Those in the database—about 3,300 residents—might have criminal records or tattoos or brands on their skin that claim an allegiance to specific gangs. Or they might be frequent associates of known gang members.

Tulsa officials say that to avoid violating privacy rights, the intelligence files are restricted to suspected gang members and do not include information on others.

Two years ago, Denver police dropped a broader database effort after residents accused the department of compiling "spy files" against innocent people. The Denver database included information about thousands of residents, including some who had been involved in lawful protests or demonstrations. Denver officials disbanded the database and issued public apologies.

In Tulsa, McCrory says, authorities have used the database to track gang members' movements through the community and state prisons. Last month, some of the intelligence led McCrory's officers to the brick home of a 27-year-old admitted Crips member and suspected cocaine dealer. The man had been released from prison two months earlier after serving 18 months for a drug conviction.

Police say that when they broke through the man's door, the last of his cocaine supply was swirling down the toilet. Police salvaged some of the evidence when an officer yanked the toilet from its foundation and fought through a gusher of water to retrieve a small amount of crack.

Police hope the seizure will give investigators enough leverage to turn the suspect into an informant.

### BUSY WITH ANTI-TERRORISM EFFORTS

Since the September 11, 2001, attacks, U.S. authorities have been consumed by the threat of terrorism. But this year, a spate of violence in the Virginia suburbs of Washington, D.C., that involved suspected members of the Mara Salvatrucha (MS-13) gang caught the attention of U.S. Attorney General John Ashcroft.

In a February meeting with Paul McNulty, the U.S. attorney in Alexandria, Va., Ashcroft expressed concern that gangs were threatening several communities a short drive from the nation's capital.

In a follow-up memo, McNulty called the gang threat "serious" and "growing" and said U.S. authorities had begun to help local police deal with an estimated 2,700 gang members and their associates in northern Virginia's mostly affluent suburbs. A string of recent attacks has underscored the increasing gang activity there.

In May, a suspected MS-13 member was charged in a machete attack on a 16-year-old boy in Alexandria. Three weeks ago, U.S. authorities who are investigating MS-13 announced charges against four of the gang's members in the slaying of a pregnant, 17-year-old member who had become a government informant.

Meanwhile, gang violence has exploded in Durham, N.C., where police Sgt. Howard Alexander says there were three gang-related slayings and "too many shootings to count" just last week. The city of 187,035 had a record low 22 homicides last year. Already there have been 18 this year, and more than half have been linked to gangs, Alexander says.

"We've got murders, armed robberies, home invasions and witness intimidation," says Alexander, who says Durham's gang wars, like those elsewhere, are rooted in disputes over turf and the local market for illegal drugs.

The violence has led Durham police to increase the city's anti-gang unit from seven to 20 officers.

The resurgence of gangs, some law enforcement analysts say, can be traced to police departments' post-9/11 emphasis

*(continued)*

## CJ NEWS *(continued)*

on preventing terrorism. Analysts say such efforts have drawn attention from basic community problems.

"This (gang) problem has been around for a long time, but we've taken our eye off the ball since 9/11," said John Moore, director of the National Youth Gang Center. Funded by the Justice Department, the center monitors gang activity across the nation.

As gang violence spreads, it also is surging in places where it has long been a problem. In southern California, authorities estimate that there are 100,000 gang members in Los Angeles County, home to about 9.8 million people. Gang membership has been stable during the past two years, but

Los Angeles Police Chief William Bratton says gang-related killings have contributed to a 5% increase in homicides in the city this year.

"This thing is growing, but it has been masked to a great extent by reports about how overall crime has been coming down," Bratton says. "Not a lot of people are paying attention to this. But the way it's going, it has the potential to explode as it did in the early '90s."

For the latest in crime and justice news, visit the Talk Justice news feed at http://www.crimenews.info.

*Source:* Kevin Johnson, "Mean Streets Once Again: Gang Activity Surging," *USA Today,* July 21, 2004, p. 1A. Copyright © 2004 *USA Today.* Reprinted with permission.

Males were reported to be substantially more involved in gang activity than females, as females constituted only 10% of gang members throughout the country. This contrasts, however, with several recent self-report studies in which females represented approximately one-fourth to one-third of all gang members in urban adolescent samples. Read a summary of the latest National Youth Gang Survey at Library Extra 15–5 on cjtoday.com.

A large-scale project of the National Gang Crime Research Center (NGCRC), known as Project Gangfact, also provides a profile of gangs and gang members nationwide. The most recent Gangfact report, based on data collected by 28 researchers in 17 states, shows that (1) "gang members were sig-

**LIBRARY EXTRA**

Los Angeles gang members displaying signs of membership in front of a street mural. The National Youth Gang Survey estimates that there are around 21,500 gangs and 731,500 active gang members in the United States.

*A. Reininger, Woodfin Camp & Associates*

## CJ TODAY EXHIBIT 15-1

### What Is a Gang?

Gangs and gang violence are of great concern today to many of our nation's citizens, law enforcement planners, and legislators. But just what is a gang? Section 186.22(f) of the California penal code provides one definition. It says a gang is

> any ongoing organization, association, or group of three or more persons, whether formal or informal, having as one or more of its primary activities the

commission of one or more of the enumerated criminal acts [defined elsewhere as assault with a deadly weapon, robbery, homicide, drug trafficking, shooting at an occupied dwelling or occupied motor vehicle, arson, and intimidation of witnesses], which has a common name or common identifying sign or symbol, [and] whose members individually or collectively engage in or have engaged in a pattern of criminal activity.

nificantly more likely than non-gang members to have . . . sold crack cocaine, and to be involved in organized drug dealing," (2) "gang members were less likely to come from an intact family" and more often came from a "dysfunctional family," (3) "gang members were significantly less likely than non-gang members to complete high school," and (4) gang members tended to be more predatory (that is, to be bullies in school and to be risk takers).[67] Among its dozens of intriguing findings, Gangfact also found that (1) the average age nationally for joining a gang is 12.8 years; (2) over half who joined gangs have tried to quit; (3) more than two-thirds of gangs have written rules for members to follow; (4) over half of all gangs hold regular weekly meetings; (5) nearly 30% of gangs require their members to pay dues; (6) about 55% of gang members were recruited by other gang members, while the remainder sought out gang membership; (7) more than three-fourths of all gang members said they would leave the gang if given a "second chance in life"; (8) four-fifths of gang members reported that their gang sold crack cocaine; (9) 70% of gangs are not racially exclusive and consist of members of various ethnic groups; (10) one-third of gang members report that they have been able to conceal their gang membership from their parents; (11) 83% of the gangs report having female members, but few allow female members to assume leadership roles; and (12) 40% of gang members reported knowing male members of their gangs who have raped females. Visit the National Gang Crime Research Center via Web Extra 15–3 at cjtoday.com.

WEB EXTRA

Some years ago, the city of Chicago attempted to disrupt gang activity by passing a city ordinance prohibiting public association between criminal street gang members. The ordinance provided that people in the company of a gang member shall be ordered to disperse if their purpose is not apparent to a police officer. In 1999, however, in the case of *Chicago* v. *Morales,*[68] the U.S. Supreme Court invalidated Chicago's gang congregation ordinance, ruling that it was impermissibly vague and failed to provide adequate standards to guide police discretion. Learn more about gangs from the National Youth Gang Center via Web Extras 15–4 at cjtoday.com. Examine one of the most comprehensive Web-based compilations of gang research ever assembled at Library Extra 15–6.

WEB EXTRA

LIBRARY EXTRA

## Runaways

The 2002 National Incidence Study of Missing, Abducted, Runaway, and Thrownaway Children (NISMART) says that the number of children reported missing each year is more than 800,000.[69] NISMART says that runaways constitute the largest subgroup of missing children, while a sizable proportion are "throwaways"—children no longer wanted by their parents.[70] Family abductions and children who are lost through accident, injury, or misadventure make up the remainder of all missing children. Although most runaway children eventually return home, there is evidence that runaway and thrownaway children are beginning to contribute to the increasing number of homeless on city streets.

Children run away for a variety of reasons. Some come from homes where there is little love and affection. Others clash with their parents over disputed activities within the home, problems in school, and difficulties with friends. Some are lured away from home by the promise of drugs or the money that drugs might bring. Official statistics show that one-third of runaways leave home because of sexual abuse,[71] while half leave because of beatings.

Whatever the reason, runaway children have become a huge problem. OJJDP estimates that the vast majority of the children "who remain at large for a few weeks will resort to theft or prostitution

We know that many [youths] who are on the streets are there as a result of sound rational choices they have made for their own safety and welfare, such as avoiding physical abuse, sexual abuse, or extreme neglect at home.

—National Council of Juvenile and Family Court Judges

An adolescent runaway living under a highway overpass in Hollywood, California. In recent years, the number of runaway children has become a problem of near-epidemic proportions.

*Dorothy Littell, Stock Boston*

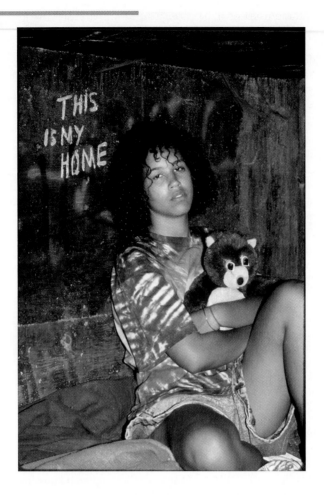

as a method of self-support."[72] Of all children who do run away, only about 20% ever come into official contact with police or social service agencies.[73]

The juvenile justice system is hampered by statute in its ability to deal effectively with runaways. Running away from home is not a criminal act. Under the 1974 Juvenile Justice and Delinquency Prevention Act (as amended in 1992), runaways are designated *status offenders.* As a result, although some runaway children are placed in unguarded group homes by police officers and social service workers, neither shelter workers nor the police have any legal authority to force a child to stay in the facility.

Short-term solutions to the problem of runaways are being sought in clearinghouses for cataloging and disseminating information about missing and located children. The Missing Children Act of 1982 mandates that the parents, the legal guardians, or the next of kin of missing children may have information about a missing child entered into the FBI's National Crime Information Center (NCIC). The essence of these informational strategies is speed. The fast dissemination of information and the rapid reunion of family members with runaway children may provide the best hope that distraught children can be persuaded to return home.

Unless and until the Juvenile Justice and Delinquency Prevention Act is amended to provide states and local jurisdictions with the needed authority to take runaway children into custody and safely control them, however, the problem of runaways will remain. Learn more about missing children from the National Center for Missing and Exploited Children via Web Extra 15–5 at cjtoday.com.

**WEB EXTRA**

## Sexual Abuse

Some parents exploit their children for personal gain. In recent years, the sexual exploitation of children has repeatedly made headlines. In a famous case of more than a decade ago, a mother living in Fort Lauderdale, Florida, was sentenced to a year in prison and two years of house arrest for forcing her 17-year-old daughter to work as a topless dancer.[74] The daughter committed suicide. All states have laws circumscribing the procuring of minor children for sexual performances.

In some parts of the country, day-care center operators have been charged with the sexual molestation of their charges, and many grade schools now routinely train young children to resist and report the inappropriate advances of adults.

The commercial sexual exploitation of children is a crime in all U.S. jurisdictions. A 2001 report by the University of Pennsylvania's Center for the Study of Youth Policy found that "child sexual abuse (CSA), child sexual assault (CSA) and child sexual exploitation (CSE) are not isolated events that are committed by a discrete group of perpetrators against a more or less clearly definable and restricted group of children. Rather, these sexual crimes against children are perpetrated by a broad segment of the American population and virtually any American child potentially can fall victim to one or another form of these abuses."[75] The report emphasizes the existence of a *continuum of abuse* associated with child sexual abuse, child sexual assault, child sexual exploitation, and the commercial sexual exploitation of children. "While the faces of the children victimized by each form of abuse may differ," says the report, "the underlying socio-emotional-cultural dynamics responsible for all forms of child sexual abuse are the same, i.e., in every case the abuse is initiated by a more powerful offender(s), usually an adult, who exerts his or her will over [that of the] children in order to secure some sexual, economic or other benefit of value to the offender."[76] The report, which can be read at **Library Extra 15–7** at cjtoday.com, also offers a series of recommendations for responding to the needs of sexually exploited children and youth.

## Other Forms of Abuse

According to the U.S. Department of Health and Human Services, an estimated 2.9 million referrals alleging child abuse or neglect were received by state and local child protective services agencies during 2003 (Figure 15–3).[77] Of these, approximately 906,000 children were determined to be victims of abuse or neglect. Overall, 60.9% of victims suffered neglect, 18.9% were physically abused, 9.9% were sexually abused, 4.9% were emotionally or psychologically maltreated, and 2.3% were medically neglected. In addition, 16.9% of child victims experienced such "other" types of maltreatment as "abandonment," "threats of harm to the child," and "congenital drug addiction."[78]

All forms of abuse are damaging to children and may contribute to their becoming delinquent. A study conducted by the Child Welfare League of America found that "two of the surest predictors of a child likely to commit a crime [are] a child who has previously committed a crime and a child who has been victimized by child abuse and/or neglect."[79] According to the league, "9 to 12 year old youth known to the child welfare system are 67 times more likely to be arrested than 9 to 12 year old youth from the general population of children."

> The number of abused and neglected children has special significance for the juvenile justice system because many of these children end up in the system.
>
> —Federal Advisory Committee on Juvenile Justice[i]

Problems Facing Juveniles: Teen Suicide

**LIBRARY EXTRA**

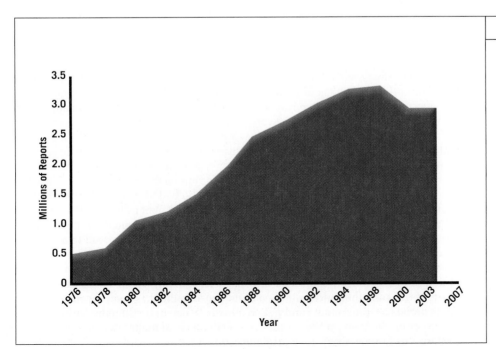

**FIGURE 15–3**

Reports of child abuse and neglect to child protective services agencies, 1976–2003.

*Source:* Based on information from the National Child Abuse and Neglect Data System, and the National Clearinghouse on Child Abuse and Neglect.

## CJ TODAY EXHIBIT 15-2

### Parents on Trial

Faced with a significant increase in crime among juveniles, a number of jurisdictions have responded with laws that place responsibility for children's behavior squarely on the parents. California's Street Terrorism Enforcement and Prevention Act, one of the first of its kind in the nation, subjects parents of wayward youths to arrest. Gloria Williams, the first person arrested under the law, was charged with neglecting her parental duties after her 15-year-old son was charged with rape.[1] Police said photo evidence proved that she knew her son was a gang member. Charges against her were dropped when she was able to show that she had taken a parenting course in an effort to gain better control over her son.

A number of other states have similar laws. Florida imposes a five-year prison term and a $5,000 fine on the parents of children who find and use guns left around the house, and Wisconsin makes both sets of grandparents financially liable for a child born to unmarried minor children. Wisconsin also has a law that can cause welfare parents to lose their benefits if their children are habitually truant from school.

Local jurisdictions are beginning to follow suit. In 1995, the town of Silverton, Oregon (population 6,710), began enforcing an ordinance that holds parents responsible when their children break the law. Parents of wayward children in Silverton can be fined up to $1,000. The Silverton ordinance, which is called a *parental duty law*, reads,

> A person commits the offense of failing to supervise a minor if the person is the parent, legal guardian or

person with legal responsibility . . . of a child under 18 years of age and the child violates Silverton municipal code.

Soon after the Silverton law was passed, communities across the nation began asking for a copy of the ordinance.[2] Six months later, the Oregon state legislature adopted a parental responsibility law that stipulated that, after a warning, parents of delinquent children could be fined up to $1,000 and be required to attend parenting classes.[3]

Local parental duty laws are being tailored to the specific needs of individual communities. After 25 youngsters were killed in two years of gang violence, for example, Atlanta passed an 11 P.M. curfew for anyone under 17, enforceable by a $1,000 fine with which the parents of violators can be saddled.[4] Washington, D.C., faced with a juvenile crime problem spiraling out of control, enacted a similar curfew. The law requires teenagers found in public places during curfew hours to be held at designated police-run truancy centers until a parent or guardian can claim them. Parents who are found to be permitting or aiding teens to break the curfew law are subject to fines and community service.

Supporters of these laws say they are trying to force parents to be parents. Critics claim that the statutes go "well beyond the pale of traditional law."[5] The American Civil Liberties Union (ACLU), for example, objects strenuously to the idea that people can go to prison for a crime committed by someone else. "The crime is having a kid who commits a crime," says Jay Jacobson, Director of the Arkansas section of the ACLU.

[1]"Now, Parents on Trial," *Newsweek,* October 2, 1989, pp. 54–55.
[2]Deeann Glamser, "Communities Seek to Stem Youth Crime," *USA Today,* February 21, 1995, p. 1A.
[3]"Oregon Will Punish Delinquents' Parents," *USA Today,* July 18, 1995, p. 3A.
[4]*ABC Nightly News,* December 17, 1990.
[5]"Now, Parents on Trial," p. 55.

Some forms of abuse, such as the instance of sexual procurement mentioned earlier, may lead directly to the child's involvement in delinquency. Parents who are already engaged in criminal activities may encourage delinquency among their children. Prostitutes, for example, sometimes encourage their daughters to learn their work. In families where the theft and sale of stolen goods is a way of life, children may be recruited for shoplifting or for burglaries that require wriggling into tight spaces where an adult might not fit. Research shows that children who are encouraged in delinquency by adults tend to become criminals when they reach maturity.[80]

Research finds that abused children have a similar tendency toward adult criminality. A National Institute of Justice survey found that children "who had been abused or neglected . . . were more likely to be arrested as juveniles, as adults, and for a violent crime."[81] Although some studies have questioned the strength of the relationship, maltreatment and delinquency appear to be intertwined.[82] If so, early intervention into abusive environments may lead to an overall reduction in future criminality.

In an effort to support vigorous prosecution of child abuse cases, the National Center for the Prosecution of Child Abuse was formed in 1985.[83] The center, which serves as a national clearinghouse for legal and other information on child abuse, publishes comprehensive training manuals and materials for prosecutors and police officers to use in battling the child abuse problem. Visit the center on the Web via Web Extra 15–6. Federal child maltreatment reports are available on the Internet as Library Extra 15–8 at cjtoday.com.

# The Legal Environment

Throughout the first half of the twentieth century, the U.S. Supreme Court followed a hands-off approach to juvenile justice, much like its early approach to prisons (see Chapter 14). The adjudication and further processing of juveniles by the system were left mostly to specialized juvenile courts or to local appeals courts. Although one or two early Supreme Court decisions[84] dealt with issues of juvenile justice, it was not until the 1960s that the Court began close legal scrutiny of the principles underlying the system itself. In the pages that follow, we will discuss some of the most important U.S. Supreme Court cases relating to juvenile justice.

## *Kent* v. *U.S.* (1966)

The U.S. Supreme Court case that ended the hands-off era in juvenile justice was *Kent* v. *U.S.,*[85] decided in 1966. The *Kent* case, which focused on the long-accepted concept of *parens patriae,* signaled the beginning of the Court's systematic review of all lower-court practices involving delinquency hearings.

Morris Kent, Jr., age 14, was apprehended in the District of Columbia in 1959 and was charged with several house burglaries and an attempted purse snatching. Kent was placed on juvenile probation and was released into the custody of his mother. In 1961, an intruder entered a woman's apartment, took her wallet, and raped her. At the scene, police found fingerprints that matched those on file belonging to Morris Kent. At the time, Kent was 16 years old and, according to the laws of the District of Columbia, was still under the exclusive jurisdiction of the juvenile court.

Kent was taken into custody and interrogated. He volunteered information about the crime and spoke about other offenses involving burglary, robbery, and rape. Following interrogation, his mother retained counsel on his behalf. Kent was kept in custody for another week, during which time psychological and psychiatric evaluations were conducted. The professionals conducting the evaluations concluded that Kent was a "victim of severe psychopathology." Without conferring with Kent, his parents, or his lawyers, the juvenile court judge ruled that Kent should be remanded to the authority of the adult court system. He was eventually tried in U.S. District Court for the District of Columbia. The judge gave no reasons for assigning Kent to the adult court.

Kent was indicted in criminal court on eight counts of burglary, robbery, and rape. Citing the psychological evaluations performed earlier, Kent's lawyers argued that his behavior was the product of mental disease or defect. Their defense proved fruitless, and Kent was found guilty on six counts of burglary and robbery. He was sentenced to 5 to 15 years in prison on each count. Kent's lawyers ultimately appealed to the U.S. Supreme Court. They argued that Kent should have been entitled to an adequate hearing at the level of the juvenile court and that, lacking such a hearing, his transfer to adult jurisdiction was unfair.

The Supreme Court, reflecting the Warren Court ideologies of the times, agreed with Kent's attorneys, reversed the decision of the district court, and ordered adequate hearings for juveniles being considered for transfer to adult court. At these hearings, the Court ruled, juveniles are entitled to representation by attorneys who must have access to their records.

Although it focused only on a narrow issue, the *Kent* decision was especially important because for the first time it recognized the need for at least minimal due process in juvenile court hearings. The *Kent* decision set the stage for what was to come, but it was the *Gault* decision, which we look at next, that turned the juvenile justice system upside down.

## *In re Gault* (1967)

In 1964, Gerald Gault and a friend, Ronald Lewis, were taken into custody by the sheriff of Gila County, Arizona, on the basis of a neighbor's complaint that the boys had telephoned her and made lewd remarks. At the time, Gault was on probation for having been in the company of another boy who had stolen a wallet.

When Gault was apprehended, his parents were both at work. No notice was posted at their house to indicate that their son had been taken into custody, a fact that they later learned from Lewis's parents. The authorities gave Gault's parents little information. Although they were notified when their son's initial hearing would be held, the Gaults were not told the nature of the complaint against him or the identity of the complainant, who was not present at the hearing.

At the hearing, the only evidence presented was statements made by young Gault and testimony given by the juvenile officer as to what the complainant had alleged. Gault was not represented by counsel. He admitted to having made the phone call but stated that after dialing the

> Established in the 1960s, status offender systems were created to help parents, schools, and communities get disobedient, but not delinquent, children back on track by providing treatment, counseling, and supervision. Yet despite their good intentions, many status offender systems across the country have had the opposite effect.
>
> —The Vera Institute of Justice[ii]

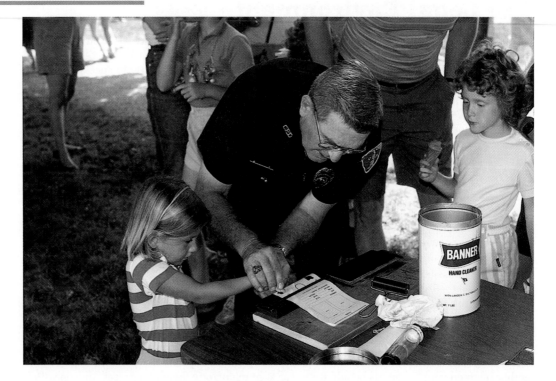

A Concord, Massachusetts, policeman fingerprinting a young girl. Many parents, driven by a significant increase in crimes against children, make special efforts to assist in the identification of their offspring.

*Bruce M. Wellman, Stock Boston*

number he had turned the phone over to his friend, Lewis. After hearing the testimony, Judge McGhee ordered a second hearing, to be held a week later. At the second hearing, Mrs. Gault requested that the complainant be present so that she could identify the voice of the person making the lewd call. Judge McGhee ruled against her request. Finally, young Gault was adjudicated delinquent and remanded to the State Industrial School until his twenty-first birthday.

On appeal, eventually to the U.S. Supreme Court, Gault's attorney argued that his constitutional rights were violated because he had been denied due process. The appeal focused specifically on six areas:

- *Notice of charges.* Gault was not given enough notice to prepare a reasonable defense to the charges against him.
- *Right to counsel.* Gault was not notified of his right to an attorney or allowed to have one at his hearing.
- *Right to confront and to cross-examine witnesses.* The court did not require the complainant to appear at the hearing.
- *Protection against self-incrimination.* Gault was never advised that he had the right to remain silent, nor was he informed that his testimony could be used against him.
- *Right to a transcript.* In preparing for the appeal, Gault's attorney was not provided a transcript of the adjudicatory hearing.
- *Right to appeal.* At the time, the state of Arizona did not give juveniles the right to appeal.

The Supreme Court ruled in Gault's favor on four of the six issues raised by his attorneys. The majority opinion read, in part, as follows[86]:

In *Kent* v. *United States,* we stated that the Juvenile Court Judge's exercise of the power of the state as *parens patriae* was not unlimited. . . . Notice, to comply with due process requirements, must be given sufficiently in advance of scheduled court proceedings so that reasonable opportunity to prepare will be afforded. . . . The probation officer cannot act as counsel for the child. His role in the adjudicatory hearing, by statute and in fact, is as arresting officer and witness against the child. There is no material difference in this respect between adult and juvenile proceedings of the sort here involved. . . . A proceeding where the issue is whether the child will be found to be "delinquent" and subjected to the loss of his liberty for years is comparable in seriousness to a felony prosecution. The juvenile needs the assistance of counsel to cope with the problems of law, to make skilled inquiry into the facts, to insist upon regularity of the proceedings, and to ascertain whether he has a defense and to prepare and submit it.

The Court did not agree with the contention of Gault's lawyers relative to appeal or with their arguments in favor of transcripts. Right to appeal, where it exists, is usually granted by statute or by state constitution—not by the Constitution of the United States. Similarly, the Court did not require a transcript because (1) there is no constitutional right to a transcript, and (2) no transcripts are produced in the trials of most adult misdemeanants.

Today, the impact of *Gault* is widely felt in the juvenile justice system. Juveniles are now guaranteed many of the same procedural rights as adults. Most precedent-setting Supreme Court decisions that followed *Gault* further clarified the rights of juveniles, focusing primarily on those few issues of due process that it had not explicitly addressed.

> There are no illegitimate children—only illegitimate parents.
>
> —U.S. District Court Judge Leon R. Yankwich, in *Zipkin* v. *Mozon* (1928)

## *In re Winship* (1970)

At the close of the 1960s, a New York Family Court judge found a 12-year-old boy named Samuel Winship delinquent on the basis of a petition that alleged that he had illegally entered a locker and stolen $112 from a pocketbook. The judge acknowledged to those present at the hearing that the evidence in the case might not be sufficient to establish Winship's guilt beyond a reasonable doubt. Statutory authority, however, in the form of the New York Family Court Act, required a determination of facts based only on a preponderance of the evidence—the same standard required in civil suits. Winship was sent to a training school for 18 months, subject to extensions until his eighteenth birthday.

Winship's appeal to the U.S. Supreme Court centered on the lower court's standard of evidence. His attorney argued that Winship's guilt should have been proved beyond a reasonable doubt—the evidentiary standard of adult criminal trials. The Court agreed, ruling that[87]

> the constitutional safeguard of proof beyond a reasonable doubt is as much required during the adjudicatory stage of a delinquency proceeding as are those constitutional guards applied in *Gault*. . . . We therefore hold . . . that where a 12 year old child is charged with an act of stealing which renders him liable to confinement for as long as six years, then, as a matter of due process . . . the case against him must be proved beyond a reasonable doubt.

As a consequence of *Winship,* allegations of delinquency today must be established beyond a reasonable doubt. The Court allowed, however, the continued use of the lower evidentiary standard in adjudicating juveniles charged with status offenses. Even though both standards continue to exist, most jurisdictions have chosen to use the stricter burden-of-proof requirement for all delinquency proceedings.

## *McKeiver* v. *Pennsylvania* (1971)

Cases like *Winship* and *Gault* have not extended all adult procedural rights to juveniles charged with delinquency. For example, juveniles do not have the constitutional right to trial by a jury of their peers. The case of *McKeiver* v. *Pennsylvania* (1971)[88] reiterated what earlier decisions had established and legitimized some generally accepted practices of juvenile courts.

Joseph McKeiver, age 16, was charged with robbery, larceny, and receiving stolen property, all felonies in Pennsylvania. McKeiver had been involved with 20 to 30 other juveniles who chased three teenage boys and took 25 cents from them. He had no previous arrests and was able to demonstrate a record of gainful employment. McKeiver's attorney requested that his client be allowed a jury trial. The request was denied. McKeiver was adjudicated delinquent and committed to a youth development center. McKeiver's attorney pursued a series of appeals and was finally granted a hearing before the U.S. Supreme Court. There he argued that his client, even though a juvenile, should have been allowed a jury trial as guaranteed by the Sixth and Fourteenth Amendments to the Constitution.

The Court, although recognizing existent problems in the administration of juvenile justice, held to the belief that the Constitution did not mandate jury trials for juveniles. In the opinion of the Court,

> [t]he imposition of the jury trial on the juvenile court system would not strengthen greatly, if at all, the fact-finding function, and would contrarily, provide an attrition of the juvenile court's assumed ability to function in a unique manner. It would not remedy the defects of the system. . . . If the jury trial were to be injected into the juvenile court system as a matter of right, it would bring with it into that system the traditional delay, the formality, and the clamor of the adversary system and, possibly, the public trial. . . . If the formalities of

the criminal adjudicative process are to be superimposed upon the juvenile court system, there is little need for its separate existence.

*McKeiver* v. *Pennsylvania* did not set any new standards. Rather, it reinforced the long-accepted practice of conducting juvenile adjudicatory hearings in the absence of certain due process considerations, particularly those pertaining to trial by jury. It is important to note, however, that the *McKeiver* decision did not specifically prohibit jury trials for juveniles. As a consequence, approximately 12 states today allow the option of jury trials for juveniles.

## *Breed* v. *Jones* (1975)

In 1971, a delinquency complaint was filed against Jones, age 17, alleging that he committed robbery while armed with a deadly weapon. At the adjudicatory hearing, Jones was declared delinquent. A later dispositional hearing determined that Jones was "unfit for treatment as a juvenile," and he was transferred to superior court for trial as an adult. The superior court found Jones guilty of robbery in the first degree and committed him to the custody of the California Youth Authority.

In an appeal eventually heard by the U.S. Supreme Court, Jones alleged that his transfer to adult court, and the trial that ensued, placed him in double jeopardy because he had already been adjudicated in juvenile court. Double jeopardy is prohibited by the Fifth and Fourteenth Amendments to the Constitution. The state of California argued that the superior court trial was only a natural continuation of the juvenile justice process and, as a consequence, did not fall under the rubric of double jeopardy. The state further suggested that double jeopardy existed only where an individual ran the risk of being punished more than once. In the case of Jones, no punishment had been imposed by the juvenile court.

The U.S. Supreme Court did not agree that the possibility of only one punishment negated double jeopardy.[89] The Court pointed to the fact that the double jeopardy clause speaks in terms of "potential risk of trial and conviction—not punishment" and concluded that two separate adjudicatory processes were sufficient to warrant a finding of double jeopardy. Jones's conviction was vacated, clearing the way for him to be returned to juvenile court. However, by the time the litigation had been completed, Jones was beyond the age of juvenile court jurisdiction, and he was released from custody.

The *Jones* case severely restricted the conditions under which transfers from juvenile to adult courts may occur. In effect, the high court mandated that such transfers as do occur must be made before an adjudicatory hearing in juvenile court.

## *Schall* v. *Martin* (1984)

Gregory Martin, age 14, was arrested in New York City, charged with robbery and weapons possession, and detained in a secure detention facility for more than two weeks until his hearing. The detention order drew its authority from a New York preventive detention law that allowed for the jailing of juveniles thought to represent a high risk of continued delinquency.

Martin was adjudicated delinquent. His case eventually reached the U.S. Supreme Court, where his lawyer argued that the New York detention law had effectively denied Martin's freedom before conviction and that it was therefore in violation of the Fourteenth Amendment to the U.S. Constitution.

The Supreme Court, however, upheld the constitutionality of the New York statute, ruling that pretrial detention of juveniles based on "serious risk" does not violate the principle of fundamental fairness required by due process.[90] In so holding, the Court recognized that states have a legitimate interest in preventing future delinquency by juveniles thought to be dangerous. Preventive detention, the Court reasoned, is nonpunitive in its intent and is therefore not a "punishment."

While the *Schall* decision upheld the practice of preventive detention, it seized on the opportunity provided by the case to impose procedural requirements on the detaining authority. Consequently, preventive detention today cannot be imposed without (1) prior notice, (2) an equitable detention hearing, and (3) a statement by the judge setting forth the reason or reasons for detention.

## *Illinois* v. *Montanez* (1996)

In 1996, in the case of *Illinois* v. *Montanez,*[91] the U.S. Supreme Court let stand a state court ruling that threw out a voluntary confession made by a juvenile suspect who had been tried as an adult. The confession was held inadmissible because it had not been made in the presence of a parent or other "concerned adult." The Chicago case involved 15-year-old Jacqueline Montanez, who admitted to participating in two execution-style slayings of rival gang members in May 1992.

According to an eyewitness, Montanez and two female companions were laughing and giggling as Montanez forced a young male member of a rival gang into a men's room at Humbolt Park. The witness described hearing a "noise like a firecracker" and seeing Montanez emerge from the men's room alone. The witness also saw the two other girls kill a second rival gang member, according to court records. Montanez was seen to then kick the body, and the three girls ran off. Both boys, members of the Latin Kings, had been shot in the back of the head at close range.

Police later arrested Montanez, who claimed to be a leader of the Maniac Latin Disciples street gang, "and two of her female gang underlings."[92] Montanez was charged as an adult and was advised of her right to remain silent and to have a lawyer present during questioning. Her mother was not allowed into the interrogation room. Montanez refused a lawyer and made three incriminating statements to police during the course of an eight-hour late-night interrogation. A videotape prepared for a local news program showed Montanez leaving the interrogation room the next morning flashing gang signs and repeating the phrase K.K. According to police, *K.K.* meant "King Killer," a status Montanez was said to have claimed.

Montanez was tried as an adult. Her confession was admitted at trial, and she was convicted of homicide. The Illinois Court of Appeals, however, reversed the judge's ruling, holding that since the girl's mother, a "concerned adult," was not allowed to be present at her daughter's interrogation, the confession obtained by police should have been suppressed. In refusing to hear the case, the U.S. Supreme Court indicated its agreement with the appellate court's finding.

Because the decision of the U.S. Supreme Court not to review the lower court's ruling in *Illinois* v. *Montanez* did not result in a written opinion, the case may be accorded less weight by jurists than the other cases cited here. Within the contemporary context of growing concern over violent juvenile crime, however, and given the ever-increasing number of minors throughout the nation now being charged as adults, the *Montanez* case may prove especially important in the future.

# Legislation Concerning Juvenile Justice

In response to the rapidly increasing crime rates of the late 1960s, Congress passed the Omnibus Crime Control and Safe Streets Act of 1968. The act provided money and technical assistance for states and municipalities seeking to modernize their justice systems. The Safe Streets Act provided funding for youth services bureaus, which had been recommended by the 1967 presidential commission report *The Challenge of Crime in a Free Society*. These bureaus were available to police, juvenile courts, and probation departments and acted as a centralized community resource for handling delinquents and status offenders. Youth services bureaus also handled juveniles referred by schools and young people who referred themselves. Unfortunately, within a decade after their establishment, most youth services bureaus succumbed to a lack of continued federal funding.

In 1974, recognizing the special needs of juveniles, Congress passed the Juvenile Justice and Delinquency Prevention (JJDP) Act. Employing much the same strategy as the 1968 bill, the JJDP Act provided federal grants to states and cities seeking to improve their handling and disposition of delinquents and status offenders. Nearly all the states chose to accept federal funds through the JJDP Act. Participating states had to meet two conditions within five years:

- They had to agree to a "separation mandate," under which juveniles would not be held in institutions where they might come into regular contact with adult prisoners.
- Status offenders had to be deinstitutionalized, with most being released into the community or placed in foster homes.

Within a few years, institutional populations were cut by more than half, and community alternatives to juvenile institutionalization were rapidly being developed. Jailed juveniles were housed in separate wings of adult facilities or were removed from adult jails entirely.

When the JJDP Act was reauthorized for funding in 1980, the separation mandate was expanded to require that separate juvenile jails be constructed by the states. Studies supporting reauthorization of the JJDP Act in 1984 and 1988, however, found that nearly half the states had failed to come into "substantial compliance" with the new mandate. As a consequence, Congress modified the requirements of the act, continuing funding for states making "meaningful progress" toward removing juveniles from adult jails.[93] In 1996, however, in the face of pressures toward punishment and away from treatment for violent juvenile offenders, the Office of Juvenile Justice and Delinquency Prevention proposed new rules for jailing juveniles. The new rules allow an adjudicated delinquent to be detained for up to 12 hours in an adult jail before a court appearance and make it easier for states to house juveniles in separate wings of adult jails.[94]

## The Legal Rights of Juveniles

Most jurisdictions today have statutes designed to extend the *Miranda* provisions to juveniles. Many police officers routinely offer *Miranda* warnings to juveniles in their custody before questioning them. It is unclear, however, whether juveniles can legally waive their *Miranda* rights. A 1979 U.S. Supreme Court ruling held that juveniles should be accorded the opportunity for a knowing waiver when they are old enough and sufficiently educated to understand the consequences of a waiver.[95] A later high court ruling upheld the murder conviction of a juvenile who had been advised of his rights and waived them in the presence of his mother.[96]

One important area of juvenile rights centers on investigative procedures. In 1985, for example, the U.S. Supreme Court ruled in *New Jersey* v. *T.L.O.*[97] that schoolchildren have a reasonable expectation of privacy in their personal property. The case involved a 14-year-old girl who was accused of violating school rules by smoking in a high school bathroom. A vice principal searched the girl's purse and found evidence of marijuana use. Juvenile officers were called, and the girl was eventually adjudicated in juvenile court and found delinquent.

On appeal to the New Jersey Supreme Court, the girl's lawyers were successful in having her conviction reversed on the grounds that the search of her purse, as an item of personal property, had been unreasonable. The state's appeal to the U.S. Supreme Court resulted in a ruling that prohibited school officials from engaging in unreasonable searches of students or their property. A reading of the Court's decision leads to the conclusion that a search could be considered reasonable if it (1) is based on a logical suspicion of rule-breaking actions; (2) is required to maintain order, discipline, and safety among students; and (3) does not exceed the scope of the original suspicion.

> Today we are living with a juvenile justice system that was created around the time of the silent film.
>
> —Former Attorney General John Ashcroft

# The Juvenile Justice Process Today

Juvenile court jurisdiction rests on the offender's age and conduct. The majority of states today define a child subject to juvenile court jurisdiction as a person who has not yet turned 18. A few states set the age at 16, and several use 17. Figure 15–4 shows the upper ages of children subject to juvenile court jurisdiction in delinquency matters, by state. When they reach their eighteenth birthday, children in most states become subject to the jurisdiction of adult criminal courts.

**FIGURE 15–4**

Limit of juvenile court jurisdiction over young offenders, by state.

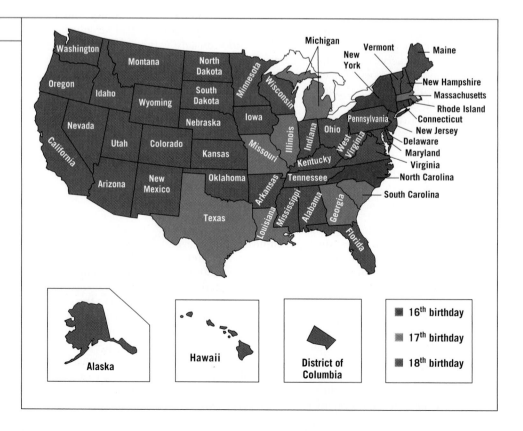

■ 16th birthday
■ 17th birthday
■ 18th birthday

In 2005, OJJDP reported that U.S. courts with juvenile jurisdiction annually handle slightly more than 1.6 million delinquency cases.[98] Depending on the laws of the state and the behavior involved, the jurisdiction of the juvenile court may be exclusive. Exclusive jurisdiction applies when the juvenile court is the only court that has statutory authority to deal with children for specified infractions. For example, status offenses like truancy normally fall within the exclusive jurisdiction of juvenile courts. Delinquency, which involves violation of the criminal law, however, is often not within the juvenile court's exclusive jurisdiction. All 50 states, the District of Columbia, and the federal government have provisions that allow juveniles who commit serious crimes to be bound over to criminal court. Forty-six states give juvenile court judges the power to waive jurisdiction over cases involving juveniles so that they can be transferred to criminal court.[99] Fifteen states have "direct file" provisions that authorize the prosecutor to decide where to file certain kinds of serious cases—in juvenile or criminal court. The minimum age for transfer to criminal court in the various states is shown in Figure 15–5.

Juveniles who commit violent crimes or who have prior records are among the most likely to be transferred to adult courts.[100] In a case that made national headlines a few years ago, for example, Lionel Tate, who was 12 years old when he killed a 6-year-old playmate while imitating wrestling moves he had seen on TV, was tried as an adult in Fort Lauderdale, Florida; found guilty of first-degree murder and sentenced to life in prison without the possibility of parole. In 2004, after intense public debate, Tate was released from prison and ordered to serve 11 years on probation. At the time of his release, he had spent three years behind bars. In 2005, however, 18-year-old Tate was again arrested and charged with pulling a gun on a pizza delivery man at a friend's apartment and beating up the friend.[101]

Where juvenile court authority is not exclusive, the jurisdiction of the court may be original or concurrent. Original jurisdiction means that a particular offense must originate, or begin, with juvenile court authorities. Juvenile courts have original jurisdiction over most delinquency petitions and all status offenses. Concurrent jurisdiction exists where other courts have equal statutory authority to originate proceedings. If a juvenile has committed a homicide, rape, or other serious crime, for example, an arrest warrant may be issued by the adult court.

Some states specify that juvenile courts have no jurisdiction over certain excluded offenses. Delaware, Louisiana, and Nevada, for example, allow no juvenile court jurisdiction over children charged with first-degree murder. Twenty-nine states have statutes that exclude certain serious, violent, and/or repeat offenders from the juvenile court's jurisdiction.

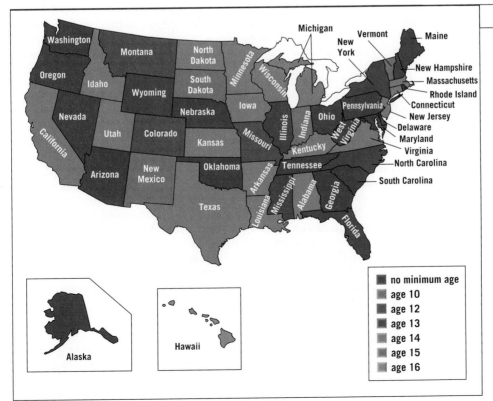

**FIGURE 15–5**

Minimum age for transfer to adult criminal court, by state.

- no minimum age
- age 10
- age 12
- age 13
- age 14
- age 15
- age 16

## CJ TODAY EXHIBIT 15-3

### The Juvenile Justice System versus Criminal Case Processing

| CRIMINAL PROCEEDINGS | JUVENILE PROCEEDINGS |
|---|---|
| Focus on criminality | Focus on delinquency and a special category of "status offenses" |
| Comprehensive rights against unreasonable searches of person, home, and possessions | Limited rights against unreasonable searches |
| A right against self-incrimination; a knowing waiver is possible | A right against self-incrimination; waivers are questionable |
| Assumed innocent until proven guilty | Guilt and innocence are not primary issues; the system focuses on the interests of the child |
| Adversarial setting | Helping context |
| Arrest warrants form the basis for most arrests | Petitions or complaints legitimize apprehension |
| Right to an attorney | Right to an attorney |
| Public trial | Closed hearing; no right to a jury trial |
| System goals are punishment and reformation | System goals are protection and treatment |
| No right to treatment | Specific right to treatment |
| Possibility of bail or release on recognizance | Release into parental custody |
| Public record of trial and judgment | Sealed records; may sometimes be destroyed by specified age |
| Possible incarceration in adult correctional facility | Separate facilities at all levels |

## Adult and Juvenile Justice Compared

The court cases of relevance to the juvenile justice system that we've discussed in this chapter have two common characteristics. They all turn on due process guarantees specified by the Bill of Rights, and they all make the claim that adult due process should serve as a model for juvenile proceedings. Due process guarantees, as interpreted by the U.S. Supreme Court, are clearly designed to ensure that juvenile proceedings are fair and that the interests of juveniles are protected. However, the Court's interpretations do not offer any pretense of providing juveniles with the same kinds of protections guaranteed to adult defendants. While the high court has tended to agree that juveniles are entitled to due process protection, it has refrained from declaring that juveniles have a right to all the aspects of due process afforded adult defendants.

Juvenile court philosophy brings with it other differences from the adult system. Among them are (1) a reduced concern with legal issues of guilt or innocence and an emphasis on the child's best interests; (2) an emphasis on treatment rather than punishment; (3) privacy and protection from public scrutiny through the use of sealed records, laws against publishing the names of juvenile offenders, and so forth; (4) the use of the techniques of social science in dispositional decision making rather than sentences determined by a perceived need for punishment; (5) no long-term confinement, with most juveniles being released from institutions by their twenty-first birthday, regardless of offense; (6) separate facilities for juveniles; and (7) broad discretionary alternatives at all points in the process.[102] This combination of court philosophy and due process requirements has created a unique justice system for juveniles that takes into consideration the special needs of young people while attempting to offer reasonable protection to society. The juvenile justice process is diagrammed in Figure 15–6.

## How the System Works

The juvenile justice system can be viewed as a process that, when carried to completion, moves through four stages: intake, adjudication, disposition, and postadjudicatory review. Though organizationally similar to the adult criminal justice process, the juvenile system is far more likely

# THE JUVENILE JUSTICE SYSTEM

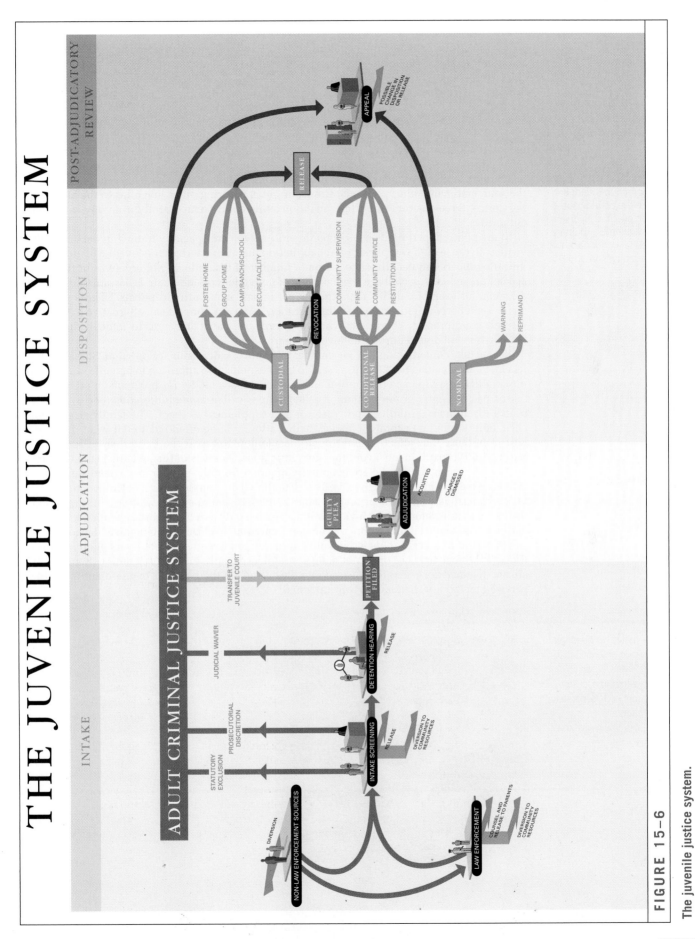

FIGURE 15–6

The juvenile justice system.

to maximize the use of discretion and to employ diversion from further formal processing at every point in the process. Each stage is discussed in the pages that follow.

## Intake and Detention Hearings

Delinquent juveniles may come to the attention of the police or juvenile court authorities either through arrest or through the filing of a **juvenile petition** by an aggrieved party. Juvenile petitions are much like criminal complaints in that they allege illegal behavior. They are most often filed by teachers, school administrators, neighbors, store managers, or others who have frequent contact with juveniles. Parents who are unable to control the behavior of their teenage children are the source of many other petitions. Crimes in progress bring other juveniles to the attention of the police; three-quarters of all referrals to juvenile court come directly from law enforcement authorities.[103]

Many police departments have juvenile officers who are specially trained in dealing with juveniles. Because of the emphasis on rehabilitation that characterizes the juvenile justice process, juvenile officers can usually choose from a number of discretionary alternatives in the form of special programs, especially in the handling of nonviolent offenders. In Delaware County, Pennsylvania, for example, police departments participate in "youth aid panels." These panels are composed of private citizens who volunteer their services to provide an alternative to the formal juvenile court process. Youngsters who are referred to a panel and agree to abide by the decision of the group are diverted from the juvenile court.

Real justice conferencing (RJC) is another example of a diversionary program. Started in Bethlehem, Pennsylvania, in 1995, RJC is said to be a cost-effective approach to juvenile crime, school misconduct, and violence prevention and has served as a model for programs in other cities. It makes use of family group conferences (sometimes called *community conferences*) in lieu of school disciplinary or judicial processes or as a supplement to them. The family group conference, built around a restorative justice model, allows young offenders to tell what they did, to hear from those they affected, and to help decide how to repair the harm their actions caused. Successful RJC participants avoid the more formal mechanisms of the juvenile justice process.

However, even youth who are eventually diverted from the system may spend some time in custody. One juvenile case in five involves detention before adjudication.[104] Unlike the adult system, where jail is seen as the primary custodial alternative for people awaiting a first appearance, the use of secure detention for juveniles is acceptable only as a last resort. Detention hearings investigate whether candidates for confinement represent a "clear and immediate danger to themselves and/or to others." This judgment is normally rendered within 24 hours of apprehension. Runaways, since they are often not dangerous, are especially difficult to confine. Juveniles who are not detained are generally released into the custody of their parents or guardians or into a supervised temporary shelter, like a group home.

A teenager hangs his head in a cell in a juvenile detention facility in Austin, Texas. When young people are taken into custody, they are confined separately from adult offenders.
*Bob Daemmrich, The Image Works*

**Detention Hearing** Detention hearings are conducted by the juvenile court judge or by an officer of the court, such as a juvenile probation officer who has been given the authority to make **intake** decisions. Intake officers, like their police counterparts, have substantial discretion. Along with detention, they can choose diversion and outright dismissal of some or all of the charges against the juvenile. Diverted juveniles may be sent to job-training programs, mental health facilities, drug-treatment programs, educational counseling, or other community service agencies. When caring parents are present who can afford private counseling or therapy, intake officers may release the juvenile into their custody with the understanding that they will provide for treatment. The National Center for Juvenile Justice estimates that more than half of all juvenile cases disposed of at intake are handled informally, without a petition, and are dismissed or diverted to a social service agency.[105]

**Preliminary Hearing** A preliminary hearing may be held in conjunction with the detention hearing. The purpose of the preliminary hearing is to determine if there is probable cause to believe that the juvenile committed the alleged act. At the hearing, the juvenile, along with the child's parents or guardians, will be advised of his or her rights as established by state legislation and court precedent. If probable cause is established, the juvenile may still be offered diversionary options, such as an "improvement period" or "probation with adjudication." These alternatives usually provide a one-year period during which the juvenile must avoid legal difficulties, attend school, and obey his or her parents. Charges may be dropped at the end of this informal probationary period, provided the juvenile has met the conditions specified.

When a serious offense is involved, statutory provisions may allow for transfer of the case to adult court at the prosecuting attorney's request. Transfer hearings are held in juvenile court and focus on (1) the applicability of transfer statutes to the case under consideration and (2) whether the juvenile is amenable to treatment through the resources available to the juvenile justice system. Exceptions exist where statutes mandate transfer (as is sometimes the case with first-degree murder).

## Adjudication

**Adjudicatory hearings** for juveniles are similar to adult trials, with some notable exceptions. Similarities derive from the fact that the due process rights of children and adults are essentially the same. Differences include the following:

- *Emphasis on privacy.* An important distinctive characteristic of the juvenile system is its concern with privacy. Juvenile hearings are not open to the public or to the mass media. Witnesses are permitted to be present only to offer testimony and may not stay for the rest of the hearing.

> **intake**
>
> The first step in decision making regarding a juvenile whose behavior or alleged behavior is in violation of the law or could otherwise cause a juvenile court to assume jurisdiction.

> **adjudicatory hearing**
>
> The fact-finding process wherein the juvenile court determines whether there is sufficient evidence to sustain the allegations in a petition.

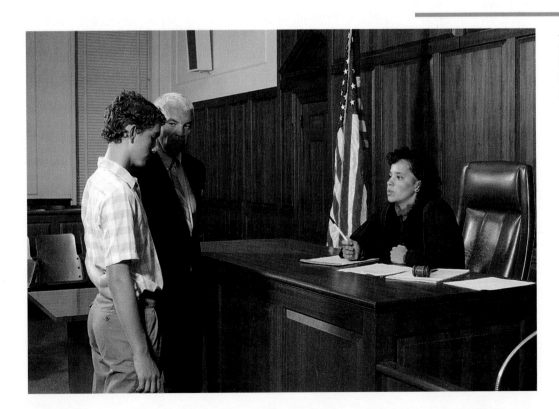

Juvenile court in action. Juvenile courts are expected to act in the best interests of the children who come before them.

*Billy Barnes, Stock Boston*

## CJ TODAY EXHIBIT 15-4

### Juvenile Courts versus Adult Courts

The language used in juvenile courts is less harsh than that used in adult courts. For example, juvenile courts

- Accept "petitions of delinquency" rather than criminal complaints.

- Conduct "hearings," not trials.
- "Adjudicate" juveniles to be "delinquent" rather than find them guilty of a crime.
- Order one of a number of available "dispositions" rather than sentences.

---

> Eventually, the justice system may need to adapt to a new environment in which all criminal matters are referred to a single system, regardless of the offender's age.
>
> —Jeffrey Butts and Ojmarrh Mitchell[iii]

No transcript of the proceedings is created. One purpose of the emphasis on privacy is to prevent juveniles from being negatively labeled by the community.

- *Informality.* Whereas the adult criminal trial is highly structured, the juvenile hearing is more informal and less adversarial. The juvenile court judge takes an active role in the fact-finding process rather than serving as arbitrator between prosecution and defense.

- *Speed.* Informality, the lack of a jury, and the absence of an adversarial environment promote speed. While the adult trial may run into weeks or even months, the juvenile hearing is normally completed in a matter of hours or days.

- *Evidentiary standard.* On completion of the hearing, the juvenile court judge must weigh the evidence. If the charge involves a status offense, the judge may adjudicate the juvenile as a status offender upon finding that a preponderance of the evidence supports this finding. A preponderance of the evidence exists when evidence of an offense is more convincing than evidence offered to the contrary. If the charge involves a criminal-type offense, the evidentiary standard rises to the level of reasonable doubt.

- *Philosophy of the court.* Even in the face of strong evidence pointing to the offender's guilt, the judge may decide that it is not in the child's best interests to be adjudicated delinquent. The judge also has the power, even after the evidence is presented, to divert the juvenile from the system. Juvenile court statistics indicate that only about half of all cases disposed of by juvenile courts are processed formally.[106] Formal processing involves the filing of a petition requesting an adjudicatory or transfer hearing. Informal cases, on the other hand, are handled without a petition. Among informally handled (nonpetitioned) delinquency cases, almost half were dismissed by the court. Most of the remainder resulted in voluntary probation (33%) or other dispositions (27%), but a small number (less than 1%) involved voluntary out-of-home placements.[107] Residential treatment was ordered 24% of the time in cases where the youth was adjudicated delinquent.[108]

- *No right to trial by jury.* As we discussed in our review of the U.S. Supreme Court decision in the case of *McKeiver* v. *Pennsylvania*,[109] juveniles do not have a constitutional right to trial by jury, and most states do not provide juveniles with a statutory opportunity for jury trial.[110]

Some jurisdictions, however, allow juveniles to be tried by their peers. The juvenile court in Columbus County, Georgia, for example, began experimenting with peer juries in 1980.[111] In Georgia, peer juries are composed of youths under the age of 17 who receive special training by the court. Jurors are required to be successful in school and may not be under the supervision of the court or have juvenile petitions pending against them. Training consists of classroom exposure to the philosophy of the juvenile court system, Georgia's juvenile code, and Supreme Court decisions affecting juvenile justice.[112] The county's youthful jurors are used only in the dispositional (or sentencing) stage of the court process, and then only when adjudicated youths volunteer to go before the jury.

Today, hundreds of **teen court** programs are in operation across the country. OJJDP notes that teen courts are "an effective intervention in many jurisdictions where enforcement of misdemeanor charges is sometimes given low priority because of heavy caseloads and the need to focus on more serious offenders."[113] Teen courts, says OJJDP, "present communities with opportunities to teach young people valuable life and coping skills and promote positive peer influence for youth who are defendants and for volunteer youth who play a variety of roles in the teen court process." Learn more about teen courts via Web Extra 15–7 at cjtoday.com.

**teen court**
An alternative approach to juvenile justice in which alleged offenders are judged and sentenced by a jury of their peers.

# Disposition

Once a juvenile has been found delinquent, the judge will set a **dispositional hearing**, which is similar to an adult sentencing hearing. Dispositional hearings are used to decide what action the court should take relative to the child. As in adult courts, the judge may order a presentence investigation before making a dispositional decision. These investigations are conducted by special court personnel, sometimes called *juvenile court counselors,* who are, in effect, juvenile probation officers. Attorneys on both sides of the issue will also have the opportunity to make recommendations concerning dispositional alternatives.

The juvenile justice system typically gives the judge a much wider range of sentencing alternatives than does the adult system. Two major classes of **juvenile disposition** exist: to confine or not to confine. Because rehabilitation is still the primary objective of the juvenile court, the judge is likely to select the least restrictive alternative that meets the needs of the juvenile while recognizing the legitimate concerns of society for protection.

Most judges decide not to confine juveniles. Statistics indicate that in nearly two-thirds (62%) of all adjudicated delinquency cases, juveniles are placed on formal probation.[114] Probationary disposition usually means that juveniles will be released into the custody of a parent or guardian and ordered to undergo some form of training, education, or counseling. As in the adult system, juveniles placed on probation may be ordered to pay fines or to make restitution. In 11% of adjudicated delinquency cases, courts order juveniles to pay restitution or a fine, to participate in some form of community service, or to enter a treatment or counseling program—dispositions that require minimal continuing supervision by probation staff.[115] Because juveniles rarely have financial resources or jobs, most economic sanctions take the form of court-ordered work programs, as in refurbishing schools or cleaning school buses.

The Lehigh County (Pennsylvania) Juvenile Probation Office runs an innovative probation program that places juvenile probation officers in public schools. The officers function much like school counselors, paying special attention to the needs of their charges in areas like tutoring, attendance, and grades. In-school probation officers work at addressing problems as diverse as getting students to school on time (by developing personal schedules), raising grades (through improving study skills, tutoring, and sitting in on classes), and successful involvement in extracurricular activities. The program, which began more than a decade ago, has since been expanded through a federal grant to 29 other Pennsylvania counties.[116]

Of course, not all juveniles who are adjudicated delinquent receive probation. Nearly one-quarter (24%) of adjudicated cases in 1999 resulted in the youth being placed outside the home in a residential facility. In a relatively small number of cases (4%), the juvenile was adjudicated delinquent, but the case was then dismissed or the youth was otherwise released.[117]

**Secure Institutions for Juveniles** Juveniles who demonstrate the potential for serious new offenses may be ordered to participate in rehabilitative programs within a secure environment, such as a youth center or a training school. As of January 2002, approximately 104,400 young people were being held under custodial supervision in the United States.[118] Of these, 25% were being held for personal crimes like murder, rape, or robbery; 29% were being held for property crimes; 9% were locked up for drug offenses; 23% were held for public-order offenses (including weapons offenses); and 4% were held for status offenses. Probation and parole violations accounted for another 14% of those confined.[119]

Most confined juveniles are held in semisecure facilities designed to look less like prisons and more like residential high school campuses. Most states, however, operate at least one secure facility for juveniles that is intended as a home for the most recalcitrant youthful offenders. Halfway houses, "boot camps,"[120] ranches, forestry camps, wilderness programs, group homes, and state-hired private facilities also hold some of the juveniles reported to be under confinement. Children placed in group homes continue to attend school and live in a family-like environment in the company of other adjudicated children, shepherded by "house parents." Figure 15–7 shows juvenile custody rates by state. Learn more about the juvenile justice systems of each state from the National Center for Juvenile Justice's State Juvenile Justice Profiles at Web Extra 15–8.

The operative philosophy of custodial programs for juveniles focuses squarely on the rehabilitative ideal. Juveniles are usually committed to secure facilities for indeterminate periods of time, with the typical stay being less than one year. Release is often timed to coincide with the beginning or the end of the school year.

Most juvenile facilities are small, with 80% designed to hold 40 residents or fewer.[121] Many institutionalized juveniles are held in the thousand or so homelike facilities across the nation that are limited to ten residents or fewer.[122] At the other end of the scale are the nation's 70 large juvenile institutions, each designed to hold more than 200 hard-core delinquents.[123] Residential

**dispositional hearing**

The final stage in the processing of adjudicated juveniles in which a decision is made on the form of treatment or penalty that should be imposed on the child.

**juvenile disposition**

The decision of a juvenile court, concluding a dispositional hearing, that an adjudicated juvenile be committed to a juvenile correctional facility; be placed in a juvenile residence, shelter, or care or treatment program; be required to meet certain standards of conduct; or be released.

**WEB** EXTRA

## FIGURE 15-7

**Juvenile custody rates, by state.**

*Source:* Office of Juvenile Justice and Delinquency Prevention.

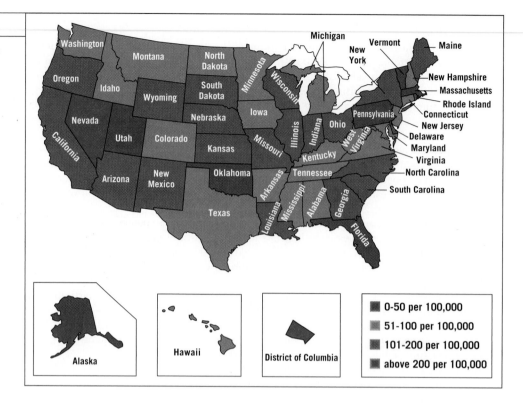

facilities for juveniles are intensively staffed. One study found that staff members outnumber residents ten to nine on the average in state-run institutions, and by an even greater ratio in privately run facilities.[124]

Jurisdictions vary widely in their use of secure detention for juveniles. In 2001, juvenile custody populations ranged from a low of 62 in Vermont to a high of 18,145 in California.[125] This variance reflects population differences as well as economic realities and philosophical beliefs. Some jurisdictions, like California, expect rehabilitative costs to be borne by the state rather than by families or local government agencies. Hence, California shows a higher rate of institutionalization than many other states. Similarly, some states have more firmly embraced the reformation ideal and are more likely to use diversionary options for juveniles.

**Characteristics of Juveniles in Confinement**  Institutionalized juveniles are a small but special category of young people with serious problems. A recent report on institutionalized youth by the Bureau of Justice Statistics found five striking characteristics[126]:

■ 85.5% were male.

■ 38.9% were black, 39.4% were white, and 17.3% were Hispanic.

■ 6.5% were institutionalized for having committed a status offense, such as being truant, running away, or violating curfew.

■ 42.4% were in residential facilities for a serious personal or property offense.

■ 1% were charged with homicide.

**Overcrowding in Juvenile Facilities**  As in adult prisons, overcrowding exists in many juvenile institutions. In a recent survey, half of all states reported overcrowding in juvenile facilities, and 22 states were operating facilities at more than 50% over capacity.[127]

A national study of the conditions of confinement in juvenile detention facilities conducted by OJJDP found that "there are several areas in which problems in juvenile facilities are substantial and widespread—most notably living space, health care, security, and control of suicidal behavior."[128] Using a variety of evaluative criteria, the study found that 47% of juveniles were confined in facilities whose populations exceeded their reported design capacity and that 33% of residents had to sleep "in rooms that were smaller than required by nationally recognized standards." To address the problem, the authors of the study recommended the use of alternative placement options so that only juveniles judged to be the most dangerous to their

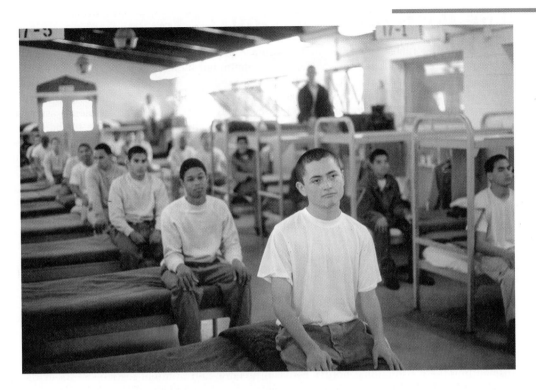

communities would be confined in secure facilities. Similarly, because it found that injuries to residents were most likely to occur within large dormitory-like settings, the OJJDP study recommended that "large dormitories be eliminated from juvenile facilities." Finally, the study recommended that "all juveniles be screened for risk of suicidal behavior immediately upon their admission to confinement" and that initial health screenings be "carried out promptly at admission." Other problems that OJJDP found "still important enough to warrant attention" included education and treatment services. Further study of both areas is needed, OJJDP said.

A number of states use private facilities. A survey found that 13 states contract with 328 private facilities—most of which were classified as halfway houses—for the custody of adjudicated juveniles.[129] In the past few years, admissions to private facilities (comprised primarily of halfway houses, group homes, shelters, and ranches, camps, or farms) have increased by more than 100%, compared with an increase of only about 10% for public facilities (mostly detention centers and training schools).[130] The fastest-growing category of detained juveniles comprises drug and alcohol offenders. Approximately 12% of all juvenile detainees are being held because of alcohol and drug-related offenses.[131] Reflecting widespread socioeconomic disparities, an OJJDP report found that "a juvenile held in a public facility . . . was most likely to be black, male, between 14 and 17 years of age, and held for a delinquent offense such as a property crime or a crime against a person. On the other hand, a juvenile held in custody in a private facility . . . was most likely to be white, male, 14 to 17 years of age, and held for a nondelinquent offense such as running away, truancy, or incorrigibility."[132] The report also noted that "juvenile corrections has become increasingly privatized."

## Postadjudicatory Review

The detrimental effects of institutionalization on young offenders may make the opportunity for appellate review more critical for juveniles than it is for adults. However, federal court precedents have yet to establish a clear right to appeal from juvenile court. Even so, most states do have statutory provisions that make such appeals possible.[133]

From a practical point of view, however, juvenile appeals may not be as consequential as are appeals of adult criminal convictions. Most juvenile complaints are handled informally, while only a relatively small proportion of adjudicated delinquents are placed outside the family. Moreover, because sentence lengths are short for most confined juveniles, appellate courts hardly have time to complete the review process before the juvenile is released.

# The Post–Juvenile Court Era

Three decades of reform have largely dissolved the traditional juvenile court, and the system that remains is rapidly losing political viability. Policy makers may soon need to devise an entirely new process for handling young offenders.

—Jeffrey Butts and Adele Harrell[iv]

Beginning in the 1990s, extensive media coverage of violent juvenile crime across the United States fueled public perceptions that violence committed by teenagers had reached epidemic proportions and that no community was immune to random acts of violence committed by young people—especially crimes involving a weapon. In response, the American public became vitally concerned with juvenile crime and with the seemingly increased levels of violence associated with those crimes. Many saw the apparent "professionalization" of delinquency, the hallmark of which is the repeated and often violent criminal involvement of juveniles in drug-related gang activity, as representing a major challenge to the idealism of the juvenile justice system. By the turn of the twenty-first century, the issue of youth violence was at or near the top of nearly every state legislature and governor's agenda. Most states took some form of legislative or executive action to stem what was seen as an escalating level of dangerous crime by juveniles. As OJJDP observed, "This level of [legislative and political] activity has occurred only three other times in our nation's history: at the outset of the juvenile court movement at the turn of the [twentieth] century; following the U.S. Supreme Court's *Gault* decision in 1967; and with the enactment of the Juvenile Justice and Delinquency Prevention Act in 1974."[134]

Jeffrey Butts and Ojmarrh Mitchell, members of the Program on Law and Behavior at the Urban Institute in Washington, D.C., and experts on juvenile justice, say that today, "policymakers throughout the United States have greatly dissolved the border between juvenile and criminal justice. Young people who violate the law are no longer guaranteed special consideration from the legal system. Some form of juvenile court still exists in every state, but the purposes and procedures of juvenile courts are becoming indistinguishable from those of criminal courts."[135] Butts and Mitchell also claim that "Changes in juvenile law and juvenile court procedure are slowly dismantling the jurisdictional border between juvenile and criminal justice."[136] As evidence, Butts and Mitchell note that juvenile courts across the United States are becoming increasingly similar to criminal courts in the methods they use to reach conclusions and to process cases, as well as in the general atmosphere that characterizes them.

As a result of ongoing changes, some say that many states have substantially "criminalized" juvenile courts by effectively mandating the transfer of serious juvenile offenders to adult criminal courts and by reducing the confidentiality of juvenile court proceedings. In March 2000, for example, California voters endorsed sweeping changes in the state's juvenile justice system by passing Proposition 21, the Gang Violence and Juvenile Crime Prevention Act. The law reduces confidentiality in the juvenile court, limits the use of probation for young offenders, and increases the power of prosecutors to send juveniles to adult court and to put them in adult prisons. Public support for the measure was undiminished by projections that it would increase operational costs in the California juvenile justice system by $500 million annually.[137] Because laws like California's Proposition 21 are being passed at a growing rate throughout the country, a leading expert on juvenile justice notes that "the similarities of juvenile and adult courts are becoming greater than the differences between them."[138]

Cindy Lederman, presiding judge of the Miami-Dade Juvenile Court, refers to the changes as the "adultification" of the juvenile justice system.[139] The juvenile court, says Lederman, has undergone significant change since it was created. In the early twentieth century, the juvenile court focused on social welfare and was primarily concerned with acting in a child's best interest. By the mid-twentieth century, it had seized on the issue of children's due process rights as an important guiding principle. The court today, says Lederman, has turned its focus to accountability and punishment.

An OJJDP analysis of the sea change sweeping the juvenile justice system found five common themes in new state laws intended to target serious and violent juvenile offenders: (1) changes in jurisdictional authority, such as legislation that enables violent juvenile offenders to be prosecuted as adults in criminal court; (2) changes in sentencing authority that mandate the imposition of specified minimum sentences, extend juvenile court jurisdiction beyond the age of majority, and allow for the imposition of "blended sentences" that mix both juvenile and adult sanctions; (3) increased pressure on correctional administrators to develop programs to serve violent juveniles; (4) revision of traditional confidentiality provisions in favor of more open juvenile proceedings and court records; and (5) inclusion of victims of juvenile crime as "active participants" in the juvenile justice process.[140]

Proposals for further change abound. In 2001, the Task Force on Juvenile Justice Reform (TFJJR) of the American Academy of Child and Adolescent Psychiatry issued a report on juvenile justice reform. The report covered many areas, including competence to stand trial, forensic evaluations of children and adolescents, recommended standards for juvenile detention and confinement facilities, health care in the juvenile justice system, females in the juvenile justice system, disproportionate minority confinement, the educational needs of youth in juvenile justice facilities, and the transfer of juvenile cases to criminal court. Read the entire report at Library Extra 15–9 at cjtoday.com.

The Department of Justice Authorization Act for Fiscal Year 2003[141] set dramatic new accountability standards for federally funded programs for juveniles who violate the law.[142] The law built on the premise that young people who violate criminal laws should be held accountable for their offenses through the swift and consistent application of sanctions that are proportionate to the offense.[143] Lawmakers made it clear that it was their belief that enhanced accountability and swift sanctions were both a matter of basic justice and a way to combat delinquency and improve the quality of life in our nation's communities.

The flood of new federal and state legislation, mandated by surging public demand for greater responsibility among adolescents, is leading to significant changes in the American juvenile justice system. Hence, the juvenile justice system of the mid-twenty-first century may in many respects be quite different than the one we have known for the past hundred years. Learn more about likely changes to the juvenile justice system via Library Extra 15–10 at cjtoday.com. For an overview of the issues being debated, see Web Extra 15–9.

## SUMMARY

Children are the future hope of each mature generation, and under today's laws they occupy a special status. That status is tied closely to cultural advances that occurred in the Western world during the past 200 years, resulting in a reevaluation of the child's role.

Many children today lead privileged lives that would have been unimaginable several decades ago. Others are not as lucky, and the problems they face are as diverse as they are staggering. Some problems are a direct consequence of increased national wealth and the subsequent removal of children from the economic sphere, which has lessened expectations for responsible behavior during childhood. Other problems grow from the easy availability of illicit drugs—a condition that has dramatically altered the early life experiences of many children, especially in the nation's large cities. Finally, the decline of traditional institutions, the plethora of broken homes throughout our country, and the immoral excesses of adult sexual predators have led to an early loss of childhood innocence. Gang involvement, child abuse and neglect, juvenile runaways and suicides, and serious incidents of delinquency have been the result.

In the face of these massive challenges, the juvenile justice system's commitment to a philosophy of protection and restoration has begun to crumble. The present juvenile system, for the most part, still differs substantially from the adult system in the multitude of opportunities it provides for diversion and in the emphasis it places on rehabilitation rather than punishment. The "professionalization" of delinquency, however, the hallmark of which is the repeated and often violent criminal involvement of juveniles in drug-related gang activity, represents a major challenge to the idealism of the juvenile justice system. Addressing that challenge may well prove to be the most significant determinant of system change in coming years.

## DISCUSSION QUESTIONS

1. Describe the history and evolution of the juvenile justice system in the Western world.

2. Describe the six categories of children recognized by the laws of most states.

3. What problems do juveniles face in the United States today? Do these problems necessitate the development of new legal categories for some children handled by the courts? If so, what categories are needed? If not, how can existing categories adequately address illicit drug use by juveniles or the repeated and vicious delinquency of some inner-city gang members?

4. What was the impact of the *Gault* decision on juvenile justice in America? What adult rights were not accorded to juveniles by *Gault?* What other U.S. Supreme Court decisions have had a substantial impact on the handling of juvenile offenders by the justice system?

5. What are the major similarities and differences between the juvenile and adult systems of justice? In your opinion, should children continue to receive what many regard as preferential treatment from the courts? Explain.

**WEB QUEST**

Visit the National Council on Crime and Delinquency (NCCD) at http://www.nccd-crc.org. What are some of the areas in which NCCD is working to prevent and understand delinquency? What other areas do you think it should be exploring?

Use the Cybrary to identify other juvenile justice research and delinquency-prevention sites on the Web. Which sites contain information about school shootings? What, if anything, do they suggest can be done to reduce the incidence of these crimes? Submit your findings to your instructor if asked to do so.

To complete this Web Quest online, go to the Web Quest module in Chapter 15 of the *Criminal Justice Today* Companion Website at cjtoday.com.

**NOTES**

i. Federal Advisory Committee on Juvenile Justice, *Annual Report 2004* (Washington, DC: U.S. Government Printing Office, 2005), p. 16.

ii. Tina Chiu and Sara Mogulescu, *Changing the Status Quo for Status Offenders: New York State's Efforts to Support Troubled Teens* (New York: Vera Institute of Justice, 2005).

iii. Jeffrey A. Butts and Ojmarrh Mitchell, "Brick by Brick: Dismantling the Border between Juvenile and Adult Justice," in Phyllis McDonald and Janice Munsterman, eds., *Criminal Justice 2000, Vol. 2: Boundary Changes in Criminal Justice Organizations* (Washington, DC: National Institute of Justice, 2000), pp. 167–213.

iv. Jeffrey A. Butts and Adele V. Harrell, *Delinquents or Criminals: Policy Options for Young Criminals* (Washington, DC: Urban Institute, 1998).

1. Elliot Grossman, "Toughlove Parents Scared," *Allentown (Pa.) Morning Call,* March 7, 1995, p. B1.

1. Elliot Grossman, "Toughlove Parents Scared," *Allentown (Pa.) Morning Call,* March 7, 1995, p. B1.

2. Many of the details for this story come from David Karp, "Boy, 13, Found Guilty of Rape," *St. Petersburg (Fla.) Times,* September 8, 2001.

3. Ibid.

4. "Judge Sentences 13-Year-Old to 15 Years for Daytime Park Rape," Associated Press wire service, November 9, 2001.

5. Randy Wyles, "Boys, 7 and 10, Busted for Burglary," APB News, November 1, 2000.

6. "Florida Girls Charged with Attempting to Drown Classmate," Associated Press wire service, March 14, 2001.

7. Office of Juvenile Justice and Delinquency Prevention, *OJJDP Research, 2000* (Washington, DC: OJJDP, 2001).

8. Federal Bureau of Investigation, *Uniform Crime Reports: Crime in the United States, 2004* (Washington, DC: U.S. Government Printing Office, 2005).

9. Ibid.; and U.S. Census Bureau, *Age, 2000: A Census 2000 Brief* (Washington, DC: U.S. Census Bureau, 2001). Web posted at

http://www.census.gov/prod/2001pubs/c2kbr01-12.pdf (accessed January 12, 2002).

10. The term *juvenile* refers to people under 18 years of age.

11. H. Snyder, C. Puzzanchera, and W. Kang, *Easy Access to FBI Arrest Statistics 1994–2002* (Washington, DC: Office of Juvenile Justice and Delinquency Prevention, 2005). Web posted at http://ojjdp.ncjrs.org/ojstatbb/ezaucr (accessed November 11, 2005).

12. A reform movement, now under way, may soon lead to changes in the way juvenile records are handled.

13. For an excellent review of the handling of juveniles through history, see Wiley B. Sanders, ed., *Juvenile Offenders for a Thousand Years* (Chapel Hill: University of North Carolina Press, 1970).

14. Robert M. Mennel, *Thorns and Thistles: Juvenile Delinquents in the United States, 1925–1940* (Hanover, NH: University Press of New England, 1973).

15. Thomas A. Johnson, *Introduction to the Juvenile Justice System* (St. Paul, MN: West, 1975), p. 1.

16. Charles E. Springer, *Justice for Juveniles,* 2nd ed. (Washington, DC: Office of Juvenile Justice and Delinquency Prevention, 1987), p. 18.

17. Ibid., p. 50.

18. See Sanford Fox, "Juvenile Justice Reform: An Historical Perspective," in Sanford Fox, ed., *Modern Juvenile Justice: Cases and Materials* (St. Paul, MN: West, 1972), pp. 15–48.

19. *Ex parte Crouse,* 4 Whart. 9 (Pa., 1838).

20. Fox, "Juvenile Justice Reform," p. 27.

21. Anthony Platt, *The Child Savers: The Invention of Delinquency,* 2nd ed. (Chicago: University of Chicago Press, 1977).

22. Ibid., p. 29.

23. *People ex rel. O'Connell* v. *Turner,* 55 Ill. 280, 8 Am. Rep. 645 (1870).

24. Johnson, *Introduction to the Juvenile Justice System,* p. 3.

25. Ibid.

26. Ibid.

27. Fox, "Juvenile Justice Reform," p. 47.

28. Ibid., p. 5.

29. Principles adapted from Robert G. Caldwell, "The Juvenile Court: Its Development and Some Major Problems," in Rose Giallombardo, ed., *Juvenile Delinquency: A Book of Readings* (New York: John Wiley, 1966), p. 358.

30. Clifford Shaw et al., *Delinquency Areas* (Chicago: University of Chicago Press, 1929).

31. Richard A. Cloward and Lloyd E. Ohlin, *Delinquency and Opportunity: A Theory of Delinquent Gangs* (New York: Free Press, 1960).

32. Walter B. Miller, "Lower Class Culture as a Generating Milieu of Gang Delinquency," *Journal of Social Issues,* Vol. 14, No. 3 (1958), pp. 5–19.

33. Albert K. Cohen, *Delinquent Boys: The Culture of the Gang* (New York: Free Press of Glencoe, 1955).

34. Marvin Wolfgang, Robert Figlio, and Thorsten Sellin, *Delinquency in a Birth Cohort* (Chicago: University of Chicago Press, 1972).

35. Marvin Wolfgang, Terence Thornberry, and Robert Figlio, *From Boy to Man, from Delinquency to Crime* (Chicago: University of Chicago Press, 1987).

36. Steven P. Lab, "Analyzing Change in Crime and Delinquency Rates: The Case for Cohort Analysis," *Criminal Justice Research Bulletin,* Vol. 3, No. 10 (Huntsville, TX: Sam Houston State University, 1988), p. 2.

37. Katharine Browning et al., "Causes and Correlates of Delinquency Program," *Office of Juvenile Justice and Delinquency Prevention Fact Sheet,* April 1999.

38. For further information on the causes of juvenile delinquency, along with suggestions for the control of delinquency, see *Critical Criminal Justice Issues: Task Force Reports from the American Society of Criminology* (Washington, DC: National Institute of Justice, 1997).

39. Eileen M. Garry, "Truancy: First Step to a Lifetime of Problems," *Juvenile Justice Bulletin* (Washington, DC: Office of Juvenile Justice and Delinquency Prevention, 1996).

40. Marcia Chaiken and David Huizinga, "Early Prevention of and Intervention for Delinquency and Related Problem Behavior," in *Critical Criminal Justice Issues.*

41. Ibid.

42. "Cops: 11-Year-Old Attacked Baby Sitter with Machete," *USA Today,* October 8, 2004.

43. Marco R. della Cava, "The Societal Forces That Push Kids Out of Control," *USA Today,* April 27, 1989, p. 6D.

44. Ruth Shonle Cavan, *Juvenile Delinquency: Development, Treatment, Control,* 2nd ed. (Philadelphia: J. B. Lippincott, 1969), p. 152.

45. Alexis M. Durham III, "Ivy League Delinquency: A Self-Report Analysis," *American Journal of Criminal Justice,* Vol. 12, No. 2 (Spring 1988), p. 188.

46. U.S. Department of Health and Human Services, *Monitoring the Future Survey, 2004* (Washington, DC: HHS, 2005).

47. Ibid.

48. Ibid.

49. Phyllis L. Ellickson et al., "Teenagers and Alcohol Misuse in the United States," *Addiction,* Vol. 91, No. 10 (1996), pp. 1489–1503.

50. Federal Bureau of Investigation, *Uniform Crime Reports: Crime in the United States, 1996* (Washington, DC: U.S. Government Printing Office, 1997).

51. Cheryl Carpenter et al., *Kids, Drugs, and Crime* (Lexington, MA: Lexington Books, 1988).

52. M. R. Chaiken and B. D. Johnson, *Characteristics of Different Types of Drug-Involved Offenders* (Washington, DC: National Institute of Justice, 1988), p. 9, citing Delbert S. Elliott, David Huizinga, and Barbara Morse, "Self-Reported Violent Offending: A Descriptive Analysis of Juvenile Violent Offenders and Their Offending Careers," *Journal of Interpersonal Violence,* Vol. 1, No. 4 (1986), pp. 472–514.

53. Amy Forliti, "Tribal Leader Confirms Son's Arrest," *USA Today,* March 29, 2005.

54. S. L. Murphy, *Deaths: Final Data for 1998, National Vital Statistics Reports,* Vol. 48, No. 11 (Washington, DC: U.S. Department of Health and Human Services, Centers for Disease Control and Prevention, National Center for Health Statistics, 2000), p. 8.

55. FBI, *Uniform Crime Reports, 2004.*

56. Ibid.

57. Bureau of Justice Statistics, *Sourcebook of Criminal Justice Statistics, 1999* (Washington, DC: BJS, 2000), p. 297.

58. Office of Juvenile Justice and Delinquency Prevention, *Children as Victims* (Washington, DC: OJJDP, 2000).

59. BJS, *Sourcebook of Criminal Justice Statistics, 1999,* p. 302.

60. OJJDP, *Children as Victims,* p. 7.

61. Ibid., p. 11.

62. See, for example, Frederick M. Thrasher, *The Gang* (Chicago: University of Chicago Press, 1927); and William Foote Whyte, *Street Corner Society: The Social Structure of an Italian Slum* (Chicago: University of Chicago Press, 1943).

63. "Young Urban Terrorists," *Ohio State University Quest* (Fall 1988), p. 11.

64. For a good overview of the topic, see C. Ronald Huff, *Gangs in America,* 2nd ed. (Thousand Oaks, CA: Sage, 1996).

65. Arlen Egley, Jr., and Aline K. Major, *Highlights of the 2002 National Youth Gang Survey* (Washington, DC: Office of Juvenile Justice and Delinquency, 2004).

66. Office of Juvenile Justice and Delinquency Prevention, *1999 National Youth Gang Survey* (Washington, DC: OJJDP, 2001).

67. National Gang Crime Research Center, *Achieving Justice and Reversing the Problem of Gang Crime and Gang Violence in America Today: Preliminary Results of the Project Gangfact Study* (Chicago: NGCRC, 1996).

68. *Chicago* v. *Morales*, 527 U.S. 41 (1999).

69. Andrea J. Sedlak et al., "National Estimate of Missing Children: An Overview," in *NISMART: National Incidence Studies of Missing, Abducted, Runaway, and Thrownaway Children* (Washington, DC: Office of Juvenile Justice and Delinquency Prevention, 2002).

70. Heather Hammer, David Finkelhor, and Andrea J. Sedlak, "Runaway/Thrownaway Children: National Estimates and Characteristics," in *NISMART*, pp. 1–12.

71. "Runaway Children and the Juvenile Justice and Delinquency Prevention Act: What Is Its Impact?" *Juvenile Justice Bulletin* (Washington, DC: Office of Juvenile Justice and Delinquency Prevention, no date).

72. Ibid., p. 1.

73. Ibid., p. 2.

74. "Teen Stripper's Mom Gets Year in Jail," United Press International wire service, January 22, 1988.

75. Richard J. Estes and Neil Alan Weiner, *The Commercial Sexual Exploitation of Children in the U.S., Canada and Mexico* (Philadelphia: University of Pennsylvania Press, 2001), p. 67.

76. Ibid., p. 68.

77. U.S. Department of Health and Human Services, Administration on Children, Youth and Families. *Child Maltreatment 2003* (Washington, DC: U.S. Government Printing Office, 2005), p. xiv.

78. Ibid., p. 22.

79. Child Welfare League of America, *Sacramento County Community Intervention Program: Findings from a Comprehensive Study by Community Partners in Child Welfare, Law Enforcement, Juvenile Justice, and the Child Welfare League of America* (Washington, DC: CWLA, 1997).

80. National Committee for Prevention of Child Abuse, *Child Abuse: Prelude to Delinquency?* (Washington, DC: Office of Juvenile Justice and Delinquency Prevention, 1986).

81. Charles B. DeWitt, *The Cycle of Violence* (Washington, DC: National Institute of Justice, 1992), p. 2.

82. Matthew T. Zingraff et al., "Child Maltreatment and Youthful Problem Behavior," *Criminology*, Vol. 31, No. 2 (May 1993), pp. 173–202.

83. See "The Role of the National Center for the Prosecution of Child Abuse," *Prosecutors Perspective*, Vol. 2, No. 1 (January 1988), p. 19.

84. See, for example, *Haley* v. *Ohio*, 332 U.S. 596 (1948).

85. *Kent* v. *U.S.*, 383 U.S. 541 (1966).

86. *In re Gault*, 387 U.S. 1 (1967).

87. *In re Winship*, 397 U.S. 358 (1970).

88. *McKeiver* v. *Pennsylvania*, 403 U.S. 528 (1971).

89. *Breed* v. *Jones*, 421 U.S. 519 (1975).

90. *Schall* v. *Martin*, 467 U.S. 253 (1984).

91. *Illinois* v. *Montanez*, No. 95–1429 (1996), *cert. denied*.

92. Michael Kirkland, "Court Rejects Juvenile Confession Case," United Press International wire service, June 10, 1996.

93. "Drug Bill Includes Extension of OJJDP, with Many Changes," *Criminal Justice Newsletter*, Vol. 19, No. 22 (November 15, 1988), p. 4.

94. See "OJJDP Eases Rules on Juvenile Confinement," *Corrections Compendium* (November 1996), p. 25.

95. *Fare* v. *Michael C.*, 442 U.S. 707 (1979).

96. *California* v. *Prysock*, 453 U.S. 355 (1981).

97. *New Jersey* v. *T.L.O.*, 105 S.Ct. 733 (1985).

98. Charles Puzzanchera et al., *Juvenile Court Statistics, 2000* (Washington, DC: Office of Juvenile Justice and Delinquency Prevention, 2005), p. 52.

99. National Center for Juvenile Justice, *State Juvenile Justice Profiles*. Web posted at http://www.ncjj.org/stateprofiles (accessed August 10, 2005).

100. Charles M. Puzzanchera, *Delinquency Cases Waived to Criminal Court, 1990–1999* (Washington, DC: Office of Juvenile Justice and Delinquency Prevention, 2003).

101. "Young Killer Lionel Tate Held in Pizza Delivery Robbery," Associated Press, May 24, 2005.

102. Adapted from Peter Greenwood, *Juvenile Offenders, a Crime File Study Guide* (Washington, DC: National Institute of Justice, no date).

103. Bureau of Justice Statistics, *Report to the Nation on Crime and Justice*, 2nd ed. (Washington, DC: U.S. Government Printing Office, 1988), p. 78.

104. Ibid.

105. Ibid.

106. Charles Puzzanchera et al., *Juvenile Court Statistics, 2000*, p. 52.

107. Ibid.

108. Ibid.

109. *McKeiver* v. *Pennsylvania.*

110. Some states, like West Virginia, do provide juveniles with a statutory right to trial.

111. Other early peer juries in juvenile courts began operating in Denver, Colorado; Duluth, Minnesota; Deerfield, Illinois; Thompkins County, New York; and Spanish Fork City, Utah, at about the same time. See Philip Reichel and Carole Seyfrit, "A Peer Jury in the Juvenile Court," *Crime and Delinquency,* Vol. 30, No. 3 (July 1984), pp. 423–438.

112. Ibid.

113. Tracy M. Godwin, *A Guide for Implementing Teen Court Programs* (Washington, DC: Office of Juvenile Justice and Delinquency Prevention, 1996).

114. Charles M. Puzzanchera, *Juvenile Delinquency Probation Caseload, 1990–1999* (Washington, DC: Office of Juvenile Justice and Delinquency Prevention, 1999).

115. Charles Puzzanchera et al., *Juvenile Court Statistics, 2000,* p. 52.

116. Bethany Gardner, "Successful Pennsylvania School-Based Probation Expands," *Corrections Compendium,* Vol. 19, No. 8 (August 1994), pp. 1–3.

117. Puzzanchera, *Juvenile Delinquency Probation Caseload, 1990–1999,* p. 1.

118. Melissa Sickmund, T. J. Sladky, and Wei Kang, *Census of Juveniles in Residential Placement Databook,* 2004. Web posted at http:// www.ojjdp.ncjrs.org/ ojstatbb/cjrp (accessed July 5, 2005).

119. Office of Juvenile Justice and Delinquency Prevention, *Census of Juveniles in Residential Placement 2001* (Washington, DC: OJJDP, 2005).

120. See, for example, Blair B. Bourque et al., "Boot Camps for Juvenile Offenders: An Implementation Evaluation of Three Demonstration Programs," *NIJ Research in Brief* (Washington, DC: National Institute of Justice, 1996).

121. Melissa Sickmund, *Juvenile Offenders in Residential Placement, 1997* (Washington, DC: Office of Juvenile Justice and Delinquency Prevention, 2002), p. 110.

122. Ibid.

123. Ibid.

124. Ibid.

125. Sickmund, Sladky, and Kang, *Census of Juveniles in Residential Placement Databook.*

126. Ibid.

127. "Juvenile Offenders in Residential Placement, 1997," *Office of Juvenile Justice and Delinquency Prevention Fact Sheet,* (Washington, DC: OJJDP, 1999).

128. Dale G. Parent et al., *Conditions of Confinement: Juvenile Detention and Corrections Facilities* (Washington, DC: Office of Juvenile Justice and Delinquency Prevention, 1994).

129. *Corrections Compendium* (December 1993), p. 14.

130. Ibid.

131. Ibid., p. 22.

132. Office of Juvenile Justice and Delinquency Prevention, *National Juvenile Custody Trends, 1978–1989* (Washington, DC: U.S. Department of Justice, 1992), p. 2.

133. Section 59 of the Uniform Juvenile Court Act recommends the granting of a right to appeal for juveniles (National Conference of Commissioners on Uniform State Laws, Uniform Juvenile Court Act, 1968).

134. Patricia Torbet et al., *State Responses to Serious and Violent Juvenile Crime* (Washington, DC: Office of Juvenile Justice and Delinquency Prevention, 1996).

135. Jeffrey A. Butts and Ojmarrh Mitchell, "Brick by Brick: Dismantling the Border between Juvenile and Adult Justice," in Phyllis McDonald and Janice Munsterman, eds., *Criminal Justice 2000, Vol. 2: Boundary Changes in Criminal Justice Organizations* (Washington, DC: National Institute of Justice, 2000), p. 207.

136. Ibid., p. 167.

137. Ibid., pp. 167–213.

138. Barry C. Feld, "Abolish the Juvenile Court: Youthfulness, Criminal Responsibility, and Sentencing Policy," *Journal of Criminal Law and Criminology* (Winter 1998).

139. Cindy S. Lederman, "The Juvenile Court: Putting Research to Work for Prevention," *Juvenile Justice,* Vol. 6, No. 2 (Washington, DC: Office of Juvenile Justice and Delinquency Prevention, 1999), p. 23.

140. Feld, "Abolish the Juvenile Court."

141. Public Law 107-273.

142. Activities funded under the legislation fall under Juvenile Accountability Block Grants (JABG) program.

143. See Chryl Andrews and Lynn Marble, "Changes to OJJDP's Juvenile Accountability Program," *A Juvenile Justice Bulletin* (Washington, DC: OJJDP, 2003).

# CHAPTER 16

# Drugs and Crime

## OUTLINE

- Introduction
- What Is a Drug?
- A History of Drug Abuse in America
- The Most Common Drugs— And Who Is Using Them
- Costs of Abuse
- Solving the Drug Problem

## LEARNING OBJECTIVES

After reading this chapter, you should be able to:

- Discuss the history of drug abuse in America.
- Discuss the history of antidrug legislation in America.
- Identify the different types of drugs that are illegally used in this country, as well as the effects and legal classifications of each.
- Explain the link between drugs and other social problems, including different forms of criminal activity.
- Describe the various efforts to respond to the drug problem, and assess the effectiveness of each.

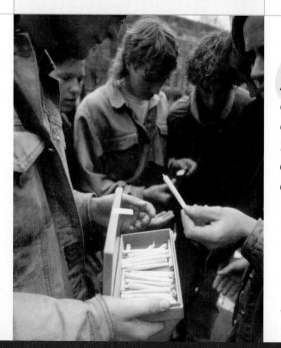

*As the Republican governor of New Mexico, I'm neither soft on crime nor pro-drugs in any sense. I believe a person who harms another person should be punished. But as a successful businessman, I also believe that locking up more and more people who are nonviolent drug offenders, people whose real problem is that they are addicted to drugs, is simply a waste of money and human resources.*

—Former Governor Gary E. Johnson[1]

> "The myth that anti-drug efforts do not work is refuted by the tireless, everyday efforts of our partners in this struggle: parents, teachers, coaches, and community leaders throughout the nation. They are a tribute to what works and what has kept these levels from skyrocketing."
>
> —"Drug Czar" John P. Walters[2]

# KEY CONCEPTS

## TERMS

club drug

controlled substance

Controlled Substances Act (CSA)

curtilage

decriminalization

drug

drug abuse

drug court

drug czar

drug trafficking

forfeiture

Harrison Narcotics Act

interdiction

legalization

money laundering

pharmaceutical diversion

physical dependence

psychoactive substance

psychological dependence

Racketeer Influenced and Corrupt
   Organizations (RICO)

recreational drug user

## CASES

*Alexander* v. *U.S.*

*Austin* v. *U.S.*

*California* v. *Greenwood*

*Oliver* v. *U.S.*

*Ratzlaf* v. *U.S.*

*U.S.* v. *Dunn*

*U.S.* v. *92 Buena Vista Ave.*

*U.S.* v. *Oakland Cannabis Buyers'
   Cooperative*

*U.S.* v. *Ursery*

The original full-text court opinion for each of these cases is available on the CD-ROM that accompanies this book.

# Introduction

Hear the author discuss
this chapter at
**cjtoday.com**

**drug abuse**

Illicit drug use that results in
social, economic,
psychological, or legal
problems for the user.[i]

**Drug abuse** is pervasive in American society, and the values that support it have become entrenched among large segments of the American population. In December 2004, a Police Foundation national survey of 300 police chiefs across the country found that drug abuse is the most serious law enforcement problem facing communities today.[3] Sixty-three percent of the chiefs, who represented large and medium-sized cities and small towns, cited drug abuse as an "extremely serious" or "very serious" problem. Other serious problems that the chiefs identified were domestic violence (50%), property crime (48%), violent crime (18%) and the threat of terrorism (17%). As the chiefs knew well, the last four decades have seen a dramatic increase in drug-related crime relative to other offenses, and a corresponding expansion of both drug laws and efforts at enforcement.

The resulting impact on the criminal justice system has been nothing less than phenomenal. In some parts of the country, court dockets have become so clogged with drug cases that criminal case processing has almost ground to a halt. Prison populations also reflect the huge increase in drug crimes (Figure 16–1). Today, three-quarters of the growth in the number of federal prison inmates is due to drug crimes,[4] and about 70% of all first offenders in the federal prisons are serving drug sentences. This is also true of 85% of the noncitizens and 66% of women who are imprisoned. And drug offenders are rarely violent. More than half (55.7%) of federal prisoners sentenced for a drug offense fall into the lowest criminal history category of the federal sentencing guidelines, and in 87% of cases no weapon is involved.[5] Although drug crimes account for only about 20% of state prison populations, the number of men held in state prisons as a result of drug crimes has increased by almost 50% since 1990, while the number of women incarcerated for drug crimes has risen by 108%.[6] Even though we are incarcerating more drug offenders than ever before, a strong majority of the chiefs who were surveyed in 2004 said that today's drug problem is greater than it was in the mid-1990s.[7] Only 1% of the surveyed chiefs scored the police response to drug abuse as "very successful."[8]

## Drug Abuse: More Than an Individual Choice

While in many texts drug-related crime is looked at briefly as one of several social-order or victimless crimes, in this book we will take an in-depth look at drug crime because of its pervasive and far-reaching impact, not only on the criminal justice system, but on all aspects of society.

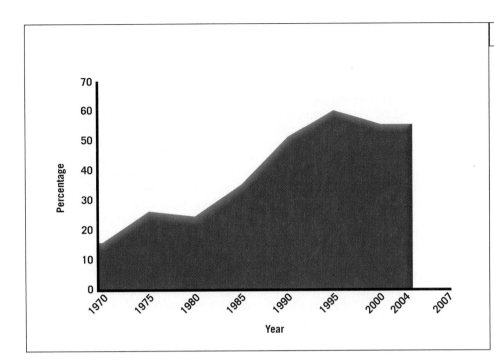

**FIGURE 16-1**

**Percentage of federal prisoners sentenced for drug offenses, 1970–2004.**
*Source: Sourcebook of Criminal Justice Statistics Online,* Table 6.54.

Drug abuse accounts for a large proportion of present-day law violations. It contributes to other types of criminal activity, such as smuggling, theft, robbery, and murder, and leads to a huge number of arrests, clogged courtrooms, and overcrowded prisons. As a consequence, drug abuse places tremendous strain on the criminal justice system, and the fight against it is one of the most expensive activities ever undertaken by federal, state, and local governments.

Because drug abuse is one of a great number of social-order offenses, it shares a number of characteristics with other "victimless" crimes, like prostitution and gambling. A hallmark of such crimes is that they involve willing participants. In the case of drug-law violations, buyers, sellers, and users willingly purchase, sell, and consume illegal drugs. They do not complain to the authorities of criminal injuries to themselves or to others resulting from the illegal use of drugs. Few victimless crimes, however, are truly without an injured party. Even where the criminal participant does not perceive an immediate or personal injury, the behavior frequently affects the legitimate interests of nonparticipants. In many victimless crimes, it is society that is the ultimate victim. Prostitution, for example, lowers property values in areas where it regularly occurs, degrades the status of women, and may victimize the customers and their families through the spread of AIDS and other venereal diseases.

Drug abuse has many of its own destructive consequences, including lost productivity, an inequitable distribution of economic resources among the poorest members of society, disease, wasted human potential, fragmented families, violence, and other crimes. Some evidence has even linked drug trafficking to international terrorism and to efforts to overthrow the democratic governments of the West. Each of these consequences will be discussed in some detail in this chapter. We begin now with an analysis of what constitutes a drug, explore the history of drug abuse in America, and then describe the various categories of major **controlled substances**. Finally, we will look at the link between drugs and other forms of crime, and possible solutions to the problem of drug abuse will be described. See Web Extra 16–1 at cjtoday.com to learn more about drugs and crime.

**controlled substance**

A specifically defined bioactive or psychoactive chemical substance proscribed by law.

**drug**

Any chemical substance defined by social convention as bioactive or psychoactive.

WEB EXTRA

# What Is a Drug?

Before we begin any comprehensive discussion of drugs, we must first grapple with the concept of what a drug is. In common usage, a **drug** may be any ingestible substance that has a noticeable effect on the mind or body. Drugs may enter the body via injection, inhalation, swallowing, or even direct absorption through the skin or mucous membranes. Some drugs, like penicillin and tranquilizers, are useful in medical treatment, while others, like heroin and cocaine, are attractive only to **recreational drug users**[9] or to those who are addicted to them.

**recreational drug user**

A person who uses drugs relatively infrequently and primarily with friends and in social contexts that define drug use as pleasurable. Most addicts begin as recreational users.

I keep in my house a letter from Bill O'Dwyer, who once was the mayor of New York, and who wrote to me, "There is no power on earth to match the power of the poor, who, just by sitting in their hopelessness, can bring the rest of us down." It always sounded right, but I never saw it happen until crack came along. And with it, there are no more rules in American crime. The implied agreements on which we were raised are gone. You now shoot women and children. A news reporter is safe as long as he is not there. A cop in his uniform means nothing.

—Jimmy Breslin, *Crack*

**psychoactive substance**

A chemical substance that affects cognition, feeling, or awareness.

In determining which substances should be called "drugs," it is important to recognize the role that social definitions of any phenomenon play in our understanding of it. Hence, what Americans today consider to be drugs depends more on social convention or agreed-on definitions than it does on any inherent property of the substances themselves. The history of marijuana provides a case in point. Before the early twentieth century, marijuana was freely available in the United States. Although alcohol was the recreational drug of choice at the time, marijuana found a following among some artists and musicians. Marijuana was also occasionally used for medical purposes to "calm the nerves" and to treat hysteria. Howard Becker, in his classic study of the early Federal Bureau of Narcotics (forerunner of the Drug Enforcement Administration, or DEA), demonstrates how federal agencies worked to outlaw marijuana in order to increase their power.[10] Federally funded publications voiced calls for laws against the substance, and movies like *Reefer Madness* led the drive toward classifying marijuana as a dangerous drug. The 1939 Marijuana Tax Act was the result, and marijuana has been thought of as a drug worthy of federal and local enforcement efforts ever since.

Both the law and social convention make strong distinctions between drugs that are socially acceptable and those that are not. Some substances with profound effects on the mind and body are not even thought of as drugs. Gasoline fumes, chemical vapors of many kinds, perfumes, certain vitamins, sugar-rich foods, and toxic chemicals may all have profound effects. Even so, most people do not think of these substances as drugs, and they are rarely regulated by the criminal law.

Recent social awareness has reclassified alcohol, caffeine, and nicotine as "drugs," although before the 1960s it is doubtful that most Americans would have applied that word to these three substances. Even today, alcohol, caffeine, and nicotine are readily available throughout the country, with only minimal controls on their manufacture and distribution. As a result, these three drugs continue to enjoy favored status in both our law and culture. Nonetheless, alcohol abuse and addiction are commonplace in American society, and anyone who has tried to quit smoking knows the power that nicotine can wield.

Occupying a middle ground on the continuum between acceptability and illegality are substances that have a legitimate medical use and are usually available only with a prescription. Antibiotics, diet pills, and, in particular, tranquilizers, stimulants, and mood-altering chemicals (such as the popular drug Prozac®) are culturally acceptable but typically can only be attained legally with a physician's prescription. These substances are clearly recognized as drugs, albeit useful ones, by the majority of Americans.

Powerful drugs, those with the ability to produce substantially altered states of consciousness and with a high potential for addiction, occupy the "high ground" in social and legal condemnation. Among them are **psychoactive substances** such as heroin, peyote, mescaline, LSD, and cocaine. Even here, however, legitimate uses for such drugs may exist. Cocaine is used in the treatment of certain medical conditions and can be applied as a topical anesthetic during medical interventions. LSD has been employed experimentally to investigate the nature of human consciousness, and peyote and mescaline may be used legally by members of the Native American Church in religious services. Even heroin has been advocated as beneficial in relieving the suffering associated with some forms of terminal illness. Hence, answers to the question of "What is a drug?" depend to a large extent on the social definitions and conventions operating at a given time and in a given place. Some of the clearest definitional statements relating to controlled substances can be found in the law, although informal strictures and definitions guide much of everyday drug use.

## Alcohol Abuse

Although the abuse of alcohol is rarely described in the same terms as the illegal use of controlled substances, alcohol misuse can lead to serious problems with grim consequences. Ten years ago, for example, a pickup truck driven by Gallardo Bermudes, 35, of Cathedral City, California, rear-ended a car carrying 11 people—two adults and nine children—near Beaumont, California.[11] Most of the children in the car were the sons and daughters of Jose Luis Rodriquez and Mercedes Diaz. Eight of the children burned to death when the car flipped and caught fire after being hit. Bermudes, who fled from the scene, had been convicted of drunk driving on three previous occasions. He later told police investigators that he had 10 to 15 beers before the crash.

Most states define a blood-alcohol level of 0.08% to 0.10% or more as intoxication and hold that anyone who drives with that amount of alcohol in his or her blood is driving under the influence (DUI) of alcohol.[12] In October 2000, however, an amendment to a federal highway construction bill[13] required that states lower their blood-alcohol limits for drunk driving to 0.08% by the year 2004 or lose a substantial percentage of the federal highway construction funds allocated to them.[14] Any state that adopts the new standard by 2007 will be permitted to recover any previously forfeited highway funds.

Drunk driving has been a major social concern for some time. Groups like Mothers against Drunk Driving (MADD) and Remove Intoxicated Drivers (RID) have given impetus to enforcement efforts to curb drunk drivers. Today, approximately 1.4 million drunk driving arrests are made annually—more than for any offense other than drug abuse.[15] The average driver arrested for DUI is substantially impaired. Studies show that he or she has consumed an average of six ounces of pure alcohol (the equivalent of a dozen bottles of beer) in the four hours preceding arrest.[16] Twenty-six percent of arrestees have consumed nearly twice that amount. Approximately 40% of all vehicle crashes resulting in death are alcohol related.[17] The National Highway Traffic Safety Administration estimates that alcohol caused 17,013 traffic fatalities in 2003—the first year since 1999 that showed a decline from the previous year in alcohol-related fatalities.[18] (Visit MADD via Web Extra 16–2 at cjtoday.com.)

Another offense directly related to alcohol consumption is public drunkenness. During the late 1960s and early 1970s, some groups fought to decriminalize drunkenness and to treat it as a health problem. Although the number of arrests for public drunkenness reached 550,795 in 2004,[19] law enforcement officers retain a great deal of discretion in handling these offenders. Many people who are drunk in public, unless they are assaultive or involved in other crimes, are likely to receive an "official escort" home rather than face arrest.

The use of alcohol may also lead to the commission of other, very serious crimes. Some experts have found that use of alcohol lowers inhibitions and increases the likelihood of aggression.[20] A report by the National Institute of Justice (NIJ) concluded that "of all psychoactive substances, alcohol is the only one whose consumption has been shown to commonly increase aggression."[21] As Figure 16–2 shows, approximately 37% of offenders consume alcohol immediately before committing a crime.[22] In cases of violent crime, the percentage of offenders under the influence of alcohol at the time of the crime jumps to 42%—and is highest for murder (44.6%).[23]

Lawmakers appear willing to deal with the problems caused by alcohol only indirectly. The American experience with Prohibition is not one that legislators are anxious to repeat. In all likelihood, future efforts to reduce the damaging effects of alcohol will continue to take the form of educational programs, legislation to raise the drinking age, and enforcement efforts designed to deter the most visible forms of abuse. Struggles in other areas may also have some impact. For example, lawsuits claiming civil damages are now being brought against some liquor companies and taverns in behalf of accident victims, cirrhosis patients, and others. We can anticipate, however, that while concern over alcohol abuse will continue, few sweeping changes in either law or social custom will occur anytime soon.

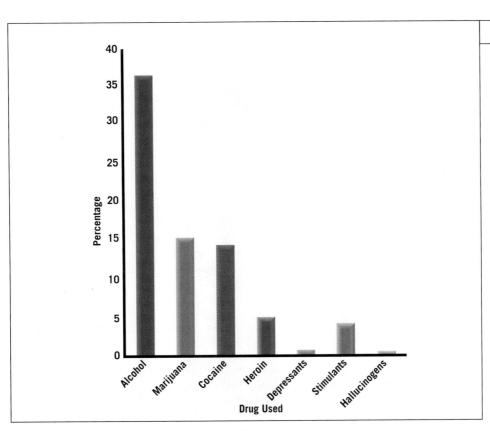

**FIGURE 16–2**

**Percentage of state prisoners admitting drug use immediately before crime commission, by type of drug.**

*Source:* Christopher J. Mumola, *Substance Abuse and Treatment, State and Federal Prisoners, 1997* (Washington, DC: Bureau of Justice Statistics, 1999).

# A History of Drug Abuse in America

> The drug problem did not develop overnight; it took years and years to get to this point as a result of misguided attitudes and a mindset that drug usage, at least using cocaine and marijuana, was all right. Dealing with the drug problem involves changing attitudes, and that takes time.
>
> —Judge Reggie B. Walton

Alcohol is but one example of the many conflicting images of drug use prevalent in contemporary American society. The "war on drugs," initiated during the latter part of the twentieth century, portrayed an America fighting for its very existence against the scourge of drug abuse. While many of the negative images of drugs that emanated from the "war period" may be correct, they have not always been a part of the American worldview.

Opium and its derivatives, for example, were widely available in patent medicines of the nineteenth and early twentieth centuries. Corner drugstores stocked mixtures of opium and alcohol, and traveling road shows extolled the virtues of these magical curatives. These elixirs, purported to offer relief from almost every malady, did indeed bring about feelings of well-being in most users. Although no one is certain just how widespread opium use was in the United States a hundred years ago, some authors have observed that baby formulas containing opium were fed to infants born to addicted mothers.[24]

Opium was also widely used by Chinese immigrants who came to the West Coast in the nineteenth century, often to work on the railroads. Opium dens—in which the drug was smoked—flourished, and the use of opium quickly spread to other ethnic groups throughout the West. Some of the more affluent denizens of West Coast cities ate the substance, and avant-garde poetry was written extolling the virtues of the drug.

Morphine, an opium derivative, has a similar history. Although it was legally available in this country almost since its invention, its use as a painkiller on the battlefields of the Civil War dramatically heightened public awareness of the drug.[25] In the late nineteenth century, morphine was widely prescribed by physicians and dentists, many of whom abused the substance themselves. By 1896, per capita morphine consumption peaked, and addiction to the substance throughout the United States was apparently widespread.[26]

Heroin, the most potent derivative of opium ever created, was invented as a substitute for morphine in 1874. It was commercially marketed as a new pain remedy and cough suppressant beginning in 1898.[27] When first introduced, heroin's addictive properties were unknown, and it was said to be useful in treating morphine addiction.[28]

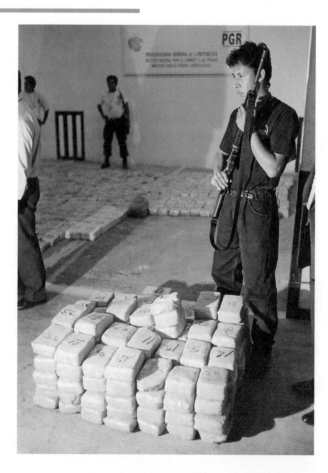

A Mexican federal policeman guarding a shipment of high-grade cocaine seized near Mexico City. Drug abuse is one of the most significant problems facing the criminal justice system and society today.

*Miguel Castillo, MIC Photo Press, Corbis/Sygma*

Marijuana, which is considerably less potent than heroin, has a relatively short history in this country. Imported by Mexican immigrants around the turn of the twentieth century, the drug quickly became associated with nonmainstream groups. By 1930, most of the states in the Southwest had passed legislation outlawing marijuana, and some authors have suggested that antimarijuana laws were primarily targeted at Spanish-speaking immigrants who were beginning to challenge whites in the economic sector.[29] As mentioned earlier, other writers have suggested that the rapidly growing use of marijuana throughout the 1920s and 1930s provided a rationale for the development of drug legislation and the concomitant expansion of drug-enforcement agencies.[30] By the 1960s, public attitudes regarding marijuana had begun to change. The hippie generation popularized the drug, touting its "mellowing" effects on users. In a short time, marijuana use became epidemic across the country, and books on marijuana cultivation and preparation flourished.

Another drug that found adherents among some youthful idealists of the 1960s and 1970s was LSD. LSD, whose chemical name is lysergic acid diethylamide, was first synthesized in Switzerland in 1938 and was used occasionally in this country in the 1950s for the treatment of psychiatric disorders.

Many drugs, when first "discovered," were touted for their powerful analgesic or therapeutic effects. Cocaine was one of them. An early leading proponent of cocaine use, for example, was Sigmund Freud, who prescribed it for a variety of psychological disorders. Freud was himself a user and wrote a book, *The Cocaine Papers,* describing the many benefits of the drug. The cocaine bandwagon reached the United States in the late nineteenth century, and various medicines and beverages containing cocaine were offered to the American public. Prominent among them was Coca-Cola, which combined seltzer water, sugar, and cocaine in a new soft drink advertised as providing a real "pick-me-up." Cocaine was removed from Coca-Cola in 1910 but continued to be used by jazz musicians and artists. Beginning in the 1970s, cocaine became associated with exclusive parties, the well-to-do, and the jet set. It was not long before an extensive drug underworld developed, catering to the demands of affluent users. Crack cocaine, a derivative of powdered cocaine that is smoked, became popular in the 1980s and is sold today in the form of "rocks," "cookies," or "biscuits" (large pieces of crack).

## Drug Use and Social Awareness

Although drugs have long been a part of American society, there have been dramatic changes during the last century in the form drug use takes and in the social consequences associated with drug involvement. Specifically, six elements have emerged that today cast drug use in a far different light than in the past:

- The conceptualization of addiction as a physical condition
- The understanding that drug use is associated with other kinds of criminal activity
- Generally widespread social condemnation of drug use as a waste of economic resources and human lives
- Comprehensive and detailed federal and state laws regulating the use or availability of drugs
- A large and perhaps still growing involvement with illicit drugs among the urban poor and the socially disenfranchised, both as an escape from the conditions of life and as a path to monetary gain
- The view that drug abuse is a law enforcement issue rather than primarily a medical problem

In an insightful work that clarifies the ideational basis of modern antidrug sentiments, criminologists Franklin Zimring and Gordon Hawkins examine three schools of thought that, they say, form the basis for current drug policy in the United States.[31] The first is "public health generalism," a perspective that holds that all controlled substances are potentially harmful and that drug abusers are victimized by the disease of addiction. This approach views drugs as medically harmful and argues that effective drug control is necessary as a matter of public health. The second approach, "cost–benefit specifism," proposes that drug policy be built around a balancing of the social costs of drug abuse (crime, broken families, drug-related killings, and so on) with the costs of enforcement. The third approach, the "legalist," suggests that drug-control policies are necessary to prevent the collapse of public order and of society itself. Advocates of the legalist perspective say that drug use is "defiance of lawful authority that threatens the social fabric."[32] According to Zimring and Hawkins, all recent and contemporary antidrug policies have been based on one or the other of these three schools of thought. Unfortunately, say these authors, it may not be possible to base successful antidrug policy on

An early advertisement for cocaine-laced wine. Cocaine, a controlled substance today, was commonly found in late-nineteenth-century medicines and consumer products.

*Corbis/Bettmann*

such beliefs, since they do not necessarily recognize the everyday realities of drug use. Nonetheless, antidrug legislation and activities undertaken in the United States today are accorded political and ideational legitimacy via all three perspectives.

## Antidrug Legislation

Antidrug legislation in the United States dates back to around 1875, when the city of San Francisco enacted a statute prohibiting the smoking of opium.[33] A number of western states were quick to follow the city's lead. The San Francisco law and many that followed it, however, clearly targeted Chinese immigrants and were rarely applied to other ethnic groups involved in the practice.

The first major piece of federal antidrug legislation came in 1914, with the enactment of the **Harrison Narcotics Act**. The Harrison Act required anyone dealing in opium, morphine, heroin, cocaine, and specified derivatives of these drugs to register with the federal government and to pay a tax of $1 per year. The only people permitted to register were physicians, pharmacists, and members of the medical profession. Nonregistered drug traffickers faced a maximum fine of $2,000 and up to five years in prison.

Because the Harrison Act allowed physicians to prescribe controlled drugs for the purpose of medical treatment, heroin addicts and other drug users could still legally purchase the drugs they needed. All the law required was a physician's prescription. By 1920, however, court rulings had established that drug "maintenance" only prolonged addiction and did not qualify as "treatment."[34] The era of legally available heroin had ended.

> **Harrison Narcotics Act**
>
> The first major piece of federal antidrug legislation, passed in 1914.

Marijuana was not included in the Harrison Act because it was not considered a dangerous drug.[35] By the 1930s, however, government attention became riveted on marijuana. At the urging of the Federal Bureau of Narcotics, Congress passed the Marijuana Tax Act in 1937. As the title of the law indicates, the act simply placed a tax of $100 per ounce on cannabis. Those who did not pay the tax were subject to prosecution. With the passage of the Boggs Act in 1951, however, marijuana, along with a number of other drugs, entered the class of federally prohibited controlled substances. The Boggs Act also removed heroin from the list of medically useful substances and required the removal, within 120 days, of any medicines containing heroin from pharmacies across the country.[36]

The Narcotic Control Act of 1956 increased penalties for drug trafficking and possession and made the sale of heroin to anyone under age 18 a capital offense. However, on the eve of the massive explosion in drug use that was to begin in the mid-1960s, the Kennedy administration began a shift in emphasis from the strict punishment of drug traffickers and users to rehabilitation. A 1963 presidential commission recommended the elimination of the Federal Bureau of Narcotics, recommended shorter prison terms for drug offenders, and stressed the need for research and social programs in dealing with the drug problem.[37]

## The Comprehensive Drug Abuse Prevention and Control Act of 1970

By 1970, America's drug problem was clear, and legislators were anxious to return to a more punitive approach to controlling drug abuse. Under President Richard Nixon, legislation designed to encompass all aspects of drug abuse and to permit federal intervention at all levels of use was enacted. Termed the Comprehensive Drug Abuse Prevention and Control Act of 1970, the legislation still forms the basis of federal enforcement efforts today. Title II of the Comprehensive Drug Abuse Prevention and Control Act is the **Controlled Substances Act (CSA)**. The CSA sets up five schedules that classify psychoactive drugs according to their degree of psychoactivity and abuse potential[38]:

> **Controlled Substances Act (CSA)**
>
> Title II of the Comprehensive Drug Abuse Prevention and Control Act of 1970, which established schedules classifying psychoactive drugs according to their degree of psychoactivity.

- Schedule I controlled substances have no established medical usage, cannot be used safely, and have great potential for abuse.[39] Federal law requires that any research employing Schedule I substances be fully documented and that the substances themselves be stored in secure vaults. Included under this category are heroin, LSD, mescaline, peyote, methaqualone (Quaaludes), psilocybin, marijuana,[40] and hashish, as well as other specified hallucinogens. Penalties for first-offense possession and sale of Schedule I controlled substances under the federal Narcotic Penalties and Enforcement Act of 1986 include up to life imprisonment and a $10 million fine. Penalties increase for subsequent offenses.

- Schedule II controlled substances are drugs with high abuse potential for which there is a currently accepted pharmacological or medical use. Most Schedule II substances are also considered to be addictive.[41] Drugs that fall into this category include opium, morphine, codeine, cocaine, phencyclidine (PCP), and their derivatives. Certain other stimulants, such as methylphenidate (Ritalin®) and phenmetrazine (Preludin®), and a few barbiturates with high abuse potential also come under Schedule II. Legal access to Schedule II substances requires written nonrefillable prescriptions, vault storage, and thorough record keeping by vendors. Penalties for first-offense possession and sale of Schedule II controlled substances include up to 20 years' imprisonment and a $5 million fine under the federal Narcotic Penalties and Enforcement Act. Penalties increase for subsequent offenses.

- Schedule III controlled substances have lower abuse potential than do those in Schedules I and II. They are drugs with an accepted medical use but that may lead to a high level of **psychological dependence** or to moderate or low **physical dependence**.[42] Schedule III substances include many of the drugs found in Schedule II but in derivative or diluted form. Common low-dosage antidiarrheals, such as opium-containing paregoric, and cold medicines and pain relievers with low concentrations of codeine fall into this category. Anabolic steroids, whose abuse by professional athletes has been subject to scrutiny, were added to the list of Schedule III controlled substances in 1991. Legitimate access to Schedule III drugs is through a doctor's prescription (written or oral), with refills authorized in the same manner. Maximum penalties associated with first-offense possession and sale of Schedule III controlled substances under federal law include five years' imprisonment and fines of up to $1 million.

> **psychological dependence**
>
> A craving for a specific drug that results from long-term substance abuse. Psychological dependence on drugs is marked by the belief that drugs are needed to achieve a feeling of well-being.[ii]

> **physical dependence**
>
> A biologically based craving for a specific drug that results from frequent use of the substance. Physical dependence on drugs is marked by a growing tolerance of a drug's effects, so that increased amounts of the drug are needed to obtain the desired effect, and by the onset of withdrawal symptoms over periods of prolonged abstinence.[iii]

- Schedule IV controlled substances have a relatively low potential for abuse (when compared to higher schedules), are useful in established medical treatments, and involve only a limited risk of psychological or physical dependence.[43] Depressants and minor tranquilizers such as Valium, Librium, and Equanil fall into this category, as do some stimulants. Schedule IV substances are medically available in the same fashion as Schedule III drugs. Maximum penalties

Former Oakland Athletic and Texas Ranger baseball player Mark McGwire is sworn in before testifying at a hearing on Capitol Hill on the use of steroids in major league baseball in Washington, March 17, 2005. Sammy Sosa, of the Baltimore Orioles, is at the far left; the Orioles' Rafael Palmiero is to the right of McGwire, and Curt Schilling of the Boston Red Sox is at far right. Anabolic steroids were added to the list of Schedule III controlled substances in 1991.

*AP Wide World Photos*

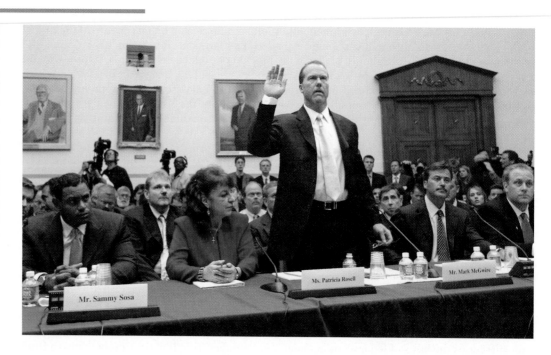

> **Wake up, America. The drug war is over. We lost.**
>
> —David Nyhan, *Boston Globe* columnist

associated with first-offense possession and sale of Schedule IV substances under federal law include three years in prison and fines of up to $1 million.

■ Schedule V controlled substances are prescription drugs with a low potential for abuse and with only a very limited possibility of psychological or physical dependence.[44] Cough medicines (antitussives) and antidiarrheals containing small amounts of opium, morphine, or codeine are found in Schedule V. A number of Schedule V medicines may be purchased through retail vendors with only minimal controls or upon the signature of the buyer (with some form of identification required). Maximum federal penalties for first-offense possession and sale of Schedule V substances include one year in prison and a $250,000 fine.

Pharmacologists, chemists, and botanists regularly create new drugs. Likewise, street-corner "chemists" in clandestine laboratories churn out inexpensive *designer drugs*—laboratory-created psychoactive substances with widely varying effects and abuse potential. Designer drugs include substances with names like Ecstasy (MDMA), GHB, ketamine, and methamphetamine (meth), which will be discussed in greater detail later in this chapter. The Controlled Substances Act includes provisions for determining which new drugs should be controlled and into which schedule they should be placed. Under the CSA, criteria for assigning a new drug to one of the existing schedules include (1) the drug's actual or relative potential for abuse; (2) scientific evidence of the drug's pharmacological effects; (3) the state of current scientific knowledge regarding the substance; (4) its history and current pattern of abuse; (5) the scope, duration, and significance of abuse; (6) risk, if any, to the public health; (7) the drug's psychic or physiological dependence liability; and (8) whether the substance is an immediate precursor of a substance already controlled.[45] Proceedings to add a new chemical substance to the list of those controlled by law or to delete or change the schedule of an existing drug may be initiated by the chief administrator of the Drug Enforcement Administration, the Department of Health and Human Services, or by a petition from any interested party, including manufacturers, medical societies, or public-interest groups.[46] Access the CSA via **Library Extra 16–1** at cjtoday.com.

**LIBRARY** EXTRA

## The Anti-Drug Abuse Act of 1988

In 1988, the country's Republican leadership, under President Ronald Reagan, capitalized on the public's frustration with rampant drug abuse and stepped up the "war on drugs." The president created a new cabinet-level post, naming a "drug czar" who would be in charge of federal drug-fighting initiatives through the Office of National Drug Control Policy (ONDCP). William Bennett, a former secretary of education, was appointed to fill the post. At the same time, Congress passed the Anti-Drug Abuse Act. The overly optimistic tenor of the act is clear from its preamble, which reads, "It is the declared policy of the United States Government to create a Drug-Free America by 1995."[47] That goal, which reflected far more political rhetoric than realistic planning, was incredibly naive.

## CJ CAREERS

### DRUG ENFORCEMENT ADMINISTRATION

**Name:** James L. Capra

**Position:** Chief of Domestic Operations

**City:** Arlington, Virginia

**Colleges Attended:** Marist College and Seton Hall University

**Year Hired:** 1987

*Although I was influenced by my father, a retired New York City police officer, I didn't choose this career; it chose me. I truly believe that individuals who seek out careers as law enforcement professionals are answering a calling in their lives. They have a desire to serve others, and they embody the finest attributes of what it means to be a public servant. . . . One of the greatest challenges I have is ensuring that DEA uses every resource available to disrupt and dismantle those drug-trafficking organizations that impact the United States. What raises the stakes on this challenge is that there are now terrorist organizations that rely on drug proceeds to finance their terrorist activity against our nation and its citizens. . . . DEA is a single-mission agency; it takes drugs off the street and puts bad guys in jail, and we do this very creatively, with great distinction and honor. One of the greatest rewards is witnessing the incredible impact we have in making our towns, cities, states, and, for that matter, our nation a safer place to live, work, and play.*

#### TYPICAL POSITIONS

Special agent, criminal investigator, chemist, diversion investigator, and intelligence research specialist. Special agents conduct clandestine surveillance, infiltrate drug-trafficking organizations, conduct investigations, arrest violators, confiscate controlled substances, collect and prepare evidence, and testify in criminal court cases.

#### EMPLOYMENT REQUIREMENTS

Applicants for the GS-5 level must (1) be a U.S. citizen, (2) be between the ages of 21 and 36 at time of hiring, (3) hold a four-year college degree, (4) be in good health, (5) pass a comprehensive background investigation, (6) hold a valid driver's license, (7) possess effective oral and written communications skills, and (8) have three years of general job experience. Applicants for the GS-7 level must also demonstrate *one* of the following: (1) a 2.95 overall college grade point average, (2) a 3.5 grade point average in the applicant's major field of study, (3) a standing in the upper one-third of the applicant's graduating class, (4) membership in a national honorary scholastic society, (5) one year of successful graduate study, or (6) one year of specialized experience (defined as "progressively responsible investigative experience").

#### OTHER REQUIREMENTS

Applicants must (1) be willing to travel frequently, (2) submit to a urinalysis test designed to detect the presence of controlled substances, and (3) successfully complete a two-month formal training program at the FBI's Training Center in Quantico, Virginia. Special-agent applicants must be in excellent physical condition, possess sharp hearing, and have uncorrected vision of at least 20/200 and corrected vision of 20/20 in one eye and at least 20/40 in the other. (Radial keratotomy is disqualifying.) They must also possess normal color vision and be capable of heavy lifting (including carrying 45 pounds or more).

#### SALARY

Entry-level positions for individuals with four-year college degrees begin at GS-7. Appointments are made at higher pay grades for individuals possessing additional education and experience.

#### BENEFITS

Benefits include (1) 13 days of sick leave annually, (2) two and a half to five weeks of paid vacation and ten paid federal holidays each year, (3) federal health and life insurance, and (4) a comprehensive retirement program.

#### DIRECT INQUIRIES TO:

Drug Enforcement Administration
Special Agent Recruitment Unit
Office of Personnel
700 Army Navy Drive
Alexandria, VA 22202

Phone: (800)DEA-4288

Website: http://www.dea.gov

For additional information on employment opportunities in the criminal justice field, view the careers portion of the CD-ROM included with this book.

*Source:* Drug Enforcement Administration.

Even so, the Anti-Drug Abuse Act of 1988 carries much weight. Under the law, penalties for "recreational" drug users increased substantially,[48] and weapons purchases by suspected drug dealers became more difficult. The law also denies federal benefits, ranging from loans (including student loans) to contracts and licenses, to convicted drug offenders.[49] Earned benefits, such as Social Security, retirement, and health and disability benefits, are not affected by the legislation, nor are welfare payments or existing public-housing arrangements (although separate legislation does provide for termination of public-housing tenancy for drug offenses[50]). Under the law, civil penalties of up to $10,000 may be assessed against convicted "recreational" users for possession of even small amounts of drugs.

The legislation also allows capital punishment for drug-related murders. The killing of a police officer by offenders seeking to avoid apprehension or prosecution is specifically cited as carrying a possible sentence of death, although other murders by major drug dealers also fall under the capital punishment provision.[51] In May 1991, 37-year-old David Chandler, an Alabama marijuana kingpin, became the first person to be sentenced to die under the law.[52] Chandler was convicted of ordering the murder of a police informant in 1990.

One especially interesting aspect of the Anti-Drug Abuse Act is its provision for designating selected areas as high-intensity drug-trafficking areas (HIDTAs), making them eligible for federal drug-fighting assistance so that joint interagency operations can be implemented to reduce drug problems. Using the law, former **drug czar** William Bennett declared Washington, D.C., a "drug zone" in 1989. His designation was based in part on what was then the city's reputation as the murder capital of the country. At the time of the declaration, more than 60% of Washington's murders were said to be drug related,[53] and legislators and tourists were clamoring for action. Bennett's plan called for more federal investigators and prosecutors and for specially built prisons to handle convicted drug dealers. Visit ONDCP via Web Extra 16–3, and learn more about HIDTAs via Web Extra 16–4 at cjtoday.com.

## Other Federal Antidrug Legislation

Other significant federal antidrug legislation exists in the form of the Crime Control Act of 1990, the Violent Crime Control and Law Enforcement Act of 1994, and the Drug-Free Communities Act of 1997.[54] The Crime Control Act of 1990 (1) doubled the appropriations authorized for drug-law enforcement grants to states and local communities; (2) enhanced drug-control and -education programs aimed at the nation's schools; (3) expanded specific drug-enforcement assistance to rural states; (4) expanded regulation of precursor chemicals used in the manufacture of illegal drugs; (5) sanctioned anabolic steroids under the Controlled Substances Act; (6) included provisions to enhance control over international money laundering; (7) created "drug-free school zones" by enhancing penalties for drug offenses occurring in proximity to schools; and (8) enhanced the ability of federal agents to seize property used in drug transactions or purchased with drug proceeds.

The Violent Crime Control and Law Enforcement Act of 1994 provided $245 million for rural anticrime and drug efforts; set aside $1.6 billion for direct funding to localities around the country for anticrime efforts, including drug-treatment programs; budgeted $383 million for drug-treatment programs for state and federal prisoners; created a treatment schedule for all drug-addicted federal prisoners; required postconviction drug testing of all federal prisoners upon release; allocated $1 billion for drug-court programs for nonviolent offenders with substance-abuse problems; and mandated new stiff penalties for drug crimes committed by gangs. The act also tripled penalties for using children to deal drugs and enhanced penalties for drug dealing in drug-free zones near playgrounds, school yards, video arcades, and youth centers. Finally, the law also expanded the federal death penalty to cover offenders involved in large-scale drug trafficking and mandated life imprisonment for criminals convicted of three violent felonies or drug offenses.

The Drug-Free Communities Act of 1997 provided support to local communities to reduce substance abuse among youth. It helped enhance broad-based community antidrug coalitions, which were previously shown to be successful at driving down casual drug use. Under the law, neighborhoods with successful antidrug programs became eligible to apply for federal grants to assist in their continued development.

## The Investigation of Drug Abuse and Manufacturing

Investigation of the illegal production, transportation, sale, and use of controlled substances is a major police activity. Investigation of drug-manufacturing activities has given rise to an area of case law that supplements the plain-view doctrine discussed in Chapter 7. Two legal concepts, abandonment and curtilage, have taken on special significance in drug investigations.

Abandonment refers to the fact that property, once it has been clearly thrown away or discarded, ceases to fall under Fourth Amendment protections against unreasonable search and

**drug czar**

The popular name for the head of the Office of National Drug Control Policy (ONDCP), a federal cabinet-level position that was created during the Reagan presidency to organize federal drug-fighting efforts.

**WEB EXTRA**

If I were king, I would find a civil way to allow citizens to sue the drug dealer for selling drugs to their children.

—Samuel F. Saxton, Director, Prince George's County (Maryland) Department of Corrections

## FREEDOM OR SAFETY? YOU DECIDE.

### Drug-Related Criminal Activity and Public Housing

Seventy-nine-year-old Herman Walker lives in a public-housing development in Oakland, California. Walker, who suffers from severe arthritis and complications from a stroke he suffered five years ago, is facing eviction from his apartment because federal housing authority officials determined that his full-time caretaker had hidden crack pipes in his home. Authorities admit that Walker likely had no knowledge of his caretaker's illegal actions, but they say that Walker's eviction will serve notice to other residents that they must carefully oversee the activities of people who live with them.

Walker's problems stem from federal law[1] and from a rule based on that law that was adopted by the Department of Housing and Urban Development (HUD) in 1991. Both the law and the HUD rule were upheld by a unanimous U.S. Supreme Court decision in 2002.[2] The rule provides that "any drug-related criminal activity on or off [federally assisted low-income housing] premises, engaged in by a public housing tenant, any member of the tenant's household, or any guest or other person under the tenant's control, shall be cause for termination of tenancy." The decision opened the door for the eviction of poor, elderly, and sick public-housing residents for drug use of which they had no personal knowledge. Tenant rights advocates con-

demned the ruling, saying that it allows harsh punishments to be imposed on the innocent. Supporters of the Court's decision saw it as affirmation of their belief that drug-free public housing is an important priority.

In a related issue, the U.S. Supreme Court upheld a Richmond, Virginia, public-housing trespass law in 2003.[3] The law makes it illegal for nonresidents to be on public-housing premises without a legitimate reason. The case grew out of efforts by the Richmond Redevelopment and Housing Authority (RRHA) to combat "rampant crime and drug dealing" at its Whitcomb Court development, where "open-air drug markets" had been commonplace.

RRHA closed the streets of the development to nonresidents and posted "No Trespassing" signs, warning that "unauthorized persons will be subject to arrest and prosecution." Police were authorized to arrest any nonresidents who refused to leave or who returned after being warned that they were trespassing. Critics charged that housing authority streets were public avenues and that members of the public should have access to them.[4]

### YOU DECIDE

In your opinion, does the goal of reducing drug-related criminal activity in public housing justify evicting residents who have no knowledge of such activities? Does it justify restricting access to public housing and criminalizing the acts of nonresident trespassers?

[1] Title 42 U.S.C. §1437d(I)(6).

[2] *Department of Housing and Urban Development* v. *Rucker,* 122 S.Ct. 1230, 152 L.Ed.2d 258 (2002).

[3] *Virginia* v. *Hicks,* 539 U.S. 113 (2003).

[4] The argument before the Court was actually more complex. RRHA, which had assumed control of the Whitcomb Court development from the city of Richmond some years previously, is not regarded as a public agency. Lawyers representing nonresidents argued that the area's streets had served as a "traditional public forum," although from a strict legal viewpoint they may no longer be public.

*References:* Evelyn Nieves, "Drug Ruling Worries Some in Public Housing," *New York Times,* March 28, 2002; Tom Schoenberg, "Supremes Examine Trespassing Policy," Law.com, May 1, 2003; and "U.S. Supreme Court Upholds Public Housing Trespass Law," *Criminal Justice Newsletter,* July 1, 2003, p. 4.

---

seizure. The U.S. Supreme Court case of *California* v. *Greenwood* (1988)[55] began when Officer Jenny Stracner of the Laguna Beach (California) Police Department arranged with a neighborhood trash collector to receive garbage collected at a suspect's residence. The refuse was later found to include items "indicative of narcotics use."[56] Based on this evidence, Stracner applied for a search warrant, which was used in a search of the defendant's home. The search uncovered controlled substances, including cocaine and hashish. The defendant, Billy Greenwood, was arrested. Upon conviction, Greenwood appealed, arguing that the trash had been placed in opaque bags and could reasonably be expected to remain unopened until it was collected and disposed of. His appeal emphasized his right to privacy with respect to his trash.

The Supreme Court disagreed, saying that "[a]n expectation of privacy does not give rise to Fourth Amendment protection unless society is prepared to accept that expectation as objectively reasonable. . . . [I]t is common knowledge that plastic garbage bags left on or at the side of a public street are readily accessible to animals, children, scavengers, snoops, and other members of the public." Hence, the Court concluded, the property in question had been abandoned, and no reasonable expectation of privacy can attach to trash left for collection "in an area accessible to the public." The concept of abandonment extends beyond trash that is actively discarded. In *Abel* v. *U.S.* (1960),[57] for example, the Court found that the warrantless search of a motel room by an FBI agent immediately after it had been vacated was acceptable.

**Curtilage**, a concept that the Supreme Court clearly recognized in the case of *Oliver* v. *U.S.* (1984),[58] refers to the fact that household activity generally extends beyond the walls of a residence. People living in a house, for example, spend some of their time in their yard. Property within the

**curtilage**

In legal usage, the area surrounding a residence that can reasonably be said to be a part of the residence for Fourth Amendment purposes.

## CJ TODAY EXHIBIT 16-1

### Drugs: What's in a Name?

Drug names have been a source of confusion for many people who have attempted to grapple with the drug problem. A single drug may have a dozen or more names. Drugs may be identified according to brand name, generic name, street name, or psychoactive category.

#### BRAND NAME

The name given to a chemical substance by its manufacturer is the *brand name.* Brand names are registered and are often associated with trademarks. They identify a drug in the pharmaceutical marketplace and may not be used by other manufacturers. Psychoactive substances with no known medical application or experimental use are not produced by legitimate companies and have no brand name.

#### GENERIC NAME

The chemical or other identifying name of a drug is the *generic name.* Generic names are often used by physicians in writing prescriptions because generic drugs are often less costly than brand-name drugs. Generic names are also used in most drug-abuse legislation at the federal and state levels to specify controlled substances. Generic names are sometimes applicable only to the psychoactive chemical substances in drugs and not to the drugs themselves. With marijuana, for example, the chemical tetrahydrocannabinol, or THC, is the active substance.

#### STREET NAME

*Street names* are slang terms. Many of them originated with the pop culture of the 1960s, and others continue to be produced by modern-day drug subculture. For example, street names for cocaine include coke, flake, and snow; heroin is known as horse, smack, or H. Learn more about street names currently in use via Web Extra 16–5 at cjtoday.com.

#### PSYCHOACTIVE CATEGORY

Psychoactive drugs are categorized according to the effects they produce on the human mind. Narcotics, stimulants, depressants, and hallucinogens are typical psychoactive categories.

#### AN EXAMPLE

PCP and angel dust are the street names for a veterinary anesthetic marketed under the brand name Sernylan. Sernylan contains the psychoactive chemical phencyclidine, which is classified as a depressant under the Controlled Substances Act.

---

curtilage of a residence has generally been accorded the same Fourth Amendment guarantees against search and seizure as areas within the walls of a house or an apartment. But just how far does the curtilage of a residence extend? Does it vary according to the type or location of the residence? Is it necessary for an area to be fenced for it to fall within residential curtilage?

A collateral area of concern is that of activity conducted in fields. The open fields doctrine began with the case of *Hester* v. *U.S.* (1924),[59] in which the Supreme Court held that law enforcement officers could search an open field without a warrant. The *Oliver* case extended that authority to include secluded and fenced fields posted with *No Trespassing* signs.

In *U.S.* v. *Dunn* (1987),[60] the U.S. Supreme Court considered a Houston-area defendant's claim that the space surrounding a barn, which was located approximately 50 yards from the edge of a fence surrounding a farmhouse, was protected against intrusion by the Fourth Amendment. The Court rejected the defendant's arguments and concluded that even though an area may be fenced, it is not within the curtilage of a residence if it is sufficiently distant from the area of household activity that attends the residence.

Other related decisions have supported seizures based on warrantless aerial observation of marijuana plants growing in the backyard of a defendant's home[61] and those based on naked-eye sightings from helicopters of the contents of a greenhouse.[62] The Court's reasoning in such cases is that flights within navigable airspace are common. Where no comprehensive efforts to secure privacy have been made, there can be no reasonable expectation of privacy—even within areas that might normally be considered curtilage. Were sophisticated surveillance techniques to be employed by law enforcement authorities, however—such as the use of drone aircraft, satellite, or infrared photography—the Court's decision would be in doubt because such devices extend beyond the realm of "normal flight."

# The Most Common Drugs—And Who Is Using Them

The 2003 National Survey on Drug Use and Health (NSDUH), formerly called the National Household Survey on Drug Abuse (NHSDA), an annual publication of the federal Substance Abuse and Mental Health Services Administration (SAMHSA), estimates that 19.5 million Americans age 12 and older

**PERCENTAGE OF NSDUH RESPONDENTS REPORTING USE OF SPECIFIC DRUGS IN LIFETIME, PAST YEAR, AND PAST MONTH, BY AGE GROUP, 2003**

| Age | Lifetime | Past Year | Past Month |
|---|---|---|---|
| **Cocaine** | | | |
| 12–17 | 2.6 | 1.8 | 0.6 |
| 18–25 | 15.0 | 6.6 | 2.2 |
| 26 and older | 16.3 | 1.9 | 0.8 |
| **Crack** | | | |
| 12–17 | 0.6 | 0.4 | 0.1 |
| 18–25 | 3.8 | 0.9 | 0.2 |
| 26 and older | 3.6 | 0.6 | 0.3 |
| **Methamphetamine** | | | |
| 12–17 | 1.3 | 0.7 | 0.3 |
| 18–25 | 5.2 | 1.6 | 0.6 |
| 26 and older | 5.7 | 0.4 | 0.2 |
| **Marijuana** | | | |
| 12–17 | 19.6 | 15.0 | 7.9 |
| 18–25 | 53.9 | 28.5 | 17.0 |
| 26 and older | 41.2 | 6.9 | 4.0 |
| **Heroin** | | | |
| 12–17 | 0.3 | 0.1 | 0.1 |
| 18–25 | 1.6 | 0.3 | 0.1 |
| 26 and older | 1.7 | 0.1 | 0.0 |
| **MDMA** | | | |
| 12–17 | 2.4 | 1.3 | 0.4 |
| 18–25 | 14.8 | 3.7 | 0.7 |
| 26 and older | 3.1 | 0.3 | 0.1 |
| **LSD** | | | |
| 12–17 | 1.6 | 0.6 | 0.2 |
| 18–25 | 14.0 | 1.1 | 0.2 |
| 26 and older | 10.8 | 0.0 | 0.0 |
| **PCP** | | | |
| 12–17 | 0.8 | 0.4 | 0.1 |
| 18–25 | 3.0 | 0.4 | 0.1 |
| 26 and older | 3.3 | 0.0 | * |

*Low precision; no estimate reported.

*Source:* U.S. Department of Health and Human Services, Substance Abuse and Mental Health Services Administration, *National Survey on Drug Use and Health 2003.*

**TABLE 16–1**

are "current" users of illegal drugs—defined as those who have used an illicit drug in the month preceding the survey[63] (Table 16–1). Nearly 15 million people were estimated to be using marijuana, and 5 million of those were thought to be "frequent" marijuana users (defined as those who used the drug on 20 or more days during the past month). An estimated 2.3 million persons (1%) were current cocaine users, 604,000 of whom used crack during the same time period. Hallucinogens were used by 1 million persons, including 470,000 users of Ecstasy. There were an estimated 119,000 current heroin users. An estimated 6.3 million persons were current nonmedical users of prescription-type psychotherapeutic drugs. This includes 4.7 million using pain relievers, 1.8 million using tranquilizers, 1.2 million using stimulants, and 0.3 million using sedatives. In 2003, approximately 2.8 million persons age 12 or older had used OxyContin nonmedically at least once in their lives.

These figures represent a considerable decline from 1979, the year in which the highest levels of drug abuse in the United States were reported, although figures for recent years have shown a

> We cannot define what victory is. We cannot tell you which objectives to look at. We can only try to have policymakers at all levels of government working together to do what is right for this nation: reduce the impact of drug abuse and increase the strength of our families and communities. If we do that, we may still have a drug use issue, but we will have a healthier nation that can absorb that issue, that will reduce the harm of drug abuse.
>
> —Ross Deck, Office of National Drug Control Policy

> The 11th Commandment: Thou shalt not end the war on drugs.
>
> —Anonymous

**FIGURE 16–3**

**Past-month illicit drug use by age in the United States, 2003.**

*Source:* Department of Health and Human Services, Substance Abuse and Mental Health Services Administration, *Overview of Findings from the 2003 National Survey on Drug Use and Health* (Washington, DC: Author, 2004), p. 13.

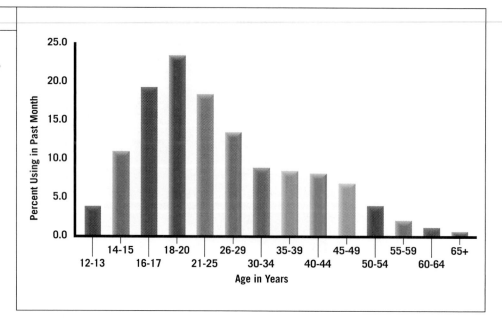

gradual increase in drug use (especially "occasional use"). As the Office of National Drug Control Policy points out, however, federal studies typically underestimate the number of hard-core drug abusers in the country because they fail to survey the homeless, prisoners, people living at colleges, active-duty military personnel, and those in mental and other institutions. ONDCP estimates that there are 2.1 million hard-core cocaine addicts and up to 1 million heroin addicts in the country[64]—figures well above those provided by the survey.

Rates of drug use show substantial variation by age. For example, in 2003, 3.8 percent of American youths ages 12 or 13 reported current illicit drug use compared with 10.9 percent of youths ages 14 or 15 and 19.2 percent of youths ages 16 or 17 (Figure 16–3). As in other years, illicit drug use in 2003 tended to increase with age among young persons, peaking among 18- to 20-year-olds (23.3 percent) and declining steadily after that point with increasing age. Current employment status is also highly correlated with rates of current illicit drug use in 2003. An estimated 18.2% of unemployed adults ages 18 or older were current illicit drug users in the United States in 2003, compared with 7.9% of those employed full-time and 10.7% of those employed part-time. Although the rate of drug use was higher among unemployed persons compared with those from other employment groups, most drug users were employed. Of the 16.7 million illicit drug users ages 18 or older in 2003, 12.4 million (74.3%) were employed either full- or part-time. The use of drugs is also more prevalent in some parts of the country than in others (Figure 16–4). Read a summary of the latest findings from the National Survey on Drug Use and Health via Library Extra 16–2 at cjtoday.com.

# Drug Trafficking

A number of agencies report on the amount and types of illicit drugs that enter the country or are produced here. One such group, the National Drug Intelligence Center (NDIC) based in Johnstown, Pennsylvania, was established in 1993 and is a component of the U.S. Department of Justice and a member of the national intelligence community. The federal General Counterdrug Intelligence Plan,[65] implemented in February 2000, designated NDIC as the nation's principal center for strategic domestic counterdrug intelligence and planning.[66] Each year, the NDIC publishes the *National Drug Threat Assessment,* a comprehensive report on **drug trafficking** and abuse trends within the United States. The assessment identifies the most serious drug threats, monitors fluctuations in national consumption levels, tracks drug availability by geographic area, and analyzes trafficking and distribution patterns. The report also includes the most current information on illicit drug availability, demand, production, cultivation, transportation, and distribution, as well as the effects of particular drugs on abusers and society as a whole. NDIC and DEA data for each of the major drug categories are described in the paragraphs that follow. Learn more about the DEA via Web Extra 16–6 at cjtoday.com. You can reach the NDIC via Web Extra 16–7. The latest *National Drug Threat Assessment,* which contains detailed trafficking information, can be read in its entirety at Library Extra 16–3. The entire General Counterdrug Intelligence Plan is available at Library Extra 16–4.

**drug trafficking**

Trading or dealing in controlled substances, to include the transporting, storage, importing, exporting, or sale of a controlled substance.

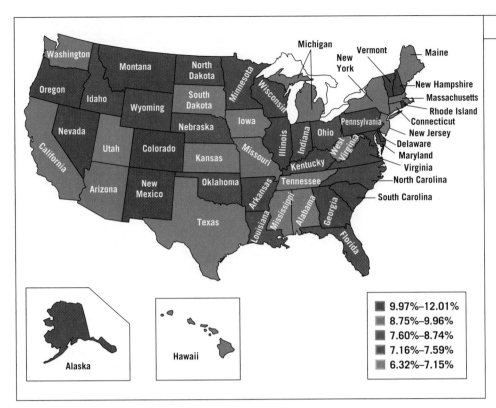

**FIGURE 16–4**

**Drug use by state.**

*Source:* Originally appeared in Donna Leinwand, "Extensive New Study Details States' Drug, Alcohol Use: Binge Drinking Is Big Problem," *USA Today,* February 14, 2005, p. 1A. Copyright © *USA Today.* Reprinted with permission.

■ 9.97%–12.01%
■ 8.75%–9.96%
■ 7.60%–8.74%
■ 7.16%–7.59%
■ 6.32%–7.15%

# Marijuana

Marijuana, whose botanical name is *Cannabis sativa L.,* grows wild throughout most of the tropic and temperate regions of the world.[67] Marijuana commonly comes in loose form, as the ground leaves and seeds of the hemp plant. Also available to street-level users are stronger forms of the drug, such as sinsemilla (the flowers and the leaves of the female cannabis plant), hashish (the resinous secretions of the hemp plant), and hash oil (a chemically concentrated form of delta-9-tetrahydrocannabinol, or THC, the psychotropic agent in marijuana).

> Antidrug strategies must be supported by knowledge gained from research.
>
> —The National Drug Control Strategy

Michael Sullivan, left, and David Shull of San Francisco sharing a pipe of marijuana in a smoking lounge. Both men have AIDS, and smoking pot makes them feel better. In 1996, voters in California and Arizona passed ballot initiatives legalizing the use of marijuana for medical purposes when approved or prescribed by a doctor. In 2001, and again in 2005, however, the U.S. Supreme Court effectively invalidated California's Compassionate Use Act when it held that Congress has the authority to prohibit all marijuana cultivation and use.

*Fred Mertz*

TABLE 16–2

## MAJOR CONTROLLED SUBSTANCES: THEIR USES AND EFFECTS

| Substance | Legitimate Use | Street Use |
|---|---|---|
| **Narcotics**, including opium, morphine, heroin, codeine, Dilaudid | Pain relief, antidiarrheal, cough suppressant | To produce pleasure, euphoria, lack of concern, general feeling of well-being |
| **Stimulants**, including amphetamines, such as Dexedrine and Benzedrine, and other drugs like cocaine, crack, crank, methamphetamine, ice | Increased alertness, reduced fatigue, weight control | To produce excitability, feelings of competence and power |
| **General depressants**, including sedatives and tranquilizers, such as Nembutal, Seconal, phenobarbital, Quaalude, sopor, Valium, , Librium Thorazine, Equanil | Release from anxiety, mood elevation, treatment of psychological problems | In high doses to produce intoxication; also used to counter the effects of other drugs or in the self treatment of withdrawal |
| **Marijuana**, including hashish, cannabis, sinsemilla, hashish oil | None fully recognized; possible use in treating nausea from chemotherapy | To produce euphoria, relaxation, intoxication, time distortion, memory alteration, focused awareness |
| **Hallucinogens**, including LSD, mescaline, psilocybin, peyote, MDMA | None recognized | To produce hallucinations and distortions of reality |
| **Inhalants**, including nitrous oxide, gasoline, toluene, amyl nitrite, butyl nitrite | Some are used as medical sedatives | To produce a "rush" or sense of light-headedness |
| **Anabolic steroids**, including nandrolone, oxandrolone, oxymetholone, stanozolol | Weight gain; treatment of anemia, breast cancer, angioedema | To build muscle mass and increase strength (in weight lifters, professional athletes, others) |

*Note:* Each drug may have a variety of effects or may produce different effects on individual users. Drugs used in combination may have unpredictable effects.

*Sources:* Adapted from Drug Enforcement Administration, *Drugs of Abuse* (Washington, DC: U.S. Department of Justice, 1999); and U.S. Pharmacopeial Convention, *USP DI Drug Information for the Healthcare Professional,* 23rd ed. (Greenwood Village, CO: Thomson Micromedex, 2003).

Marijuana is usually smoked, although it may be eaten or made into a "tea." Low doses of marijuana create restlessness and an increasing sense of well-being, followed by dreamy relaxation and a frequent craving for sweets. Sensory perceptions may be heightened by the drug, while memory and rational thought are impaired (see Table 16–2). Marijuana's effects begin within a few minutes following use and may last for two to three hours.

Although marijuana has no officially sanctioned medical use, it may sometimes serve as a supplemental medication in cases of ongoing chemotherapy (where it often reduces nausea), glaucoma (where it may reduce pressure within the eye), anorexia and "AIDS wasting" (where it may increase appetite and lead to weight gain), and sleep disorders.[68] To support such use, voters in California and Arizona passed ballot initiatives in 1996 legalizing the use of marijuana for medical purposes when approved or prescribed by a doctor. California's medical marijuana law was overturned, however, by a unanimous U.S. Supreme Court in the 2001 case of *U.S.* v. *Oakland Cannabis Buyers' Cooperative.*[69] In that case, the Court found that the activities of the Oakland (California) Cannabis Buyers' Cooperative, which distributed marijuana to qualified patients for medical purposes, were in violation of the U.S. Controlled Substances Act—regardless of what state law said. The Court also held that there is no medical necessity exception to the federal act's prohibitions on manufacturing and distributing marijuana.[70] In 2005, in the case of *Gonzales* v. *Raich*,[71] the Court reinforced its earlier holding, ruling that Congress holds the final authority, under the Commerce Clause of the U.S. Constitution, to prohibit the cultivation and use of marijuana.

Most illicit marijuana users, however, do not use cannabis for medical purposes. The majority of users are young people, many younger than 20 years old. In 2004, for example, the U.S. Department of Health and Human Services reported that past-year use of marijuana was 11.8% for eighth graders, 27.5% for tenth graders, and 34.3% for twelfth graders.[72]

Intelligence shows that domestic production accounts for about 19% of all marijuana in the United States. Most marijuana brought into the United States comes from Mexico, Jamaica, and Colombia.[73] Of all the marijuana entering the country or produced domestically, approximately one-quarter, or 4,000 metric tons, is seized or lost in transit.[74]

# Cocaine

Cocaine (cocaine hydrochloride [HCL]) is the most potent central nervous system stimulant of natural origin.[75] Cocaine is extracted from the leaves of the coca plant (whose botanical name is *Erythroxylon coca*). Since ancient times, the drug has been used by native Indians throughout the highlands of Central and South America, who chew the leaves of the coca plant to overcome altitude sickness and to sustain the high levels of physical energy needed for strenuous mountain farming.

Cocaine has some medical value as a topical anesthetic for use on sensitive tissues, such as the eyes and mucous membranes. Throughout the early twentieth century, physicians valued cocaine for its ability to anesthetize tissue while simultaneously constricting blood vessels and reducing bleeding. Recently, more effective products have replaced cocaine in many medical applications.

A report by ONDCP classifies cocaine users into three groups: "(1) the younger, often minority crack user; (2) the older injector who is combining cocaine HCL with heroin in a speedball; and (3) the older, more affluent user who is snorting cocaine HCL."[76] Cocaine generally reaches the United States in the form of a much-processed white crystalline powder. It is often diluted with a variety of other ingredients, including sugar and anesthetics such as lidocaine. Dilution allows sellers to reap high profits from small amounts of the drug.

Cocaine produces intense psychological effects, including a sense of exhilaration, superabundant energy, hyperactivity, and extended wakefulness.[77] Irritability and apprehension may be unwanted side effects. Excessive doses may cause seizures and death from heart failure, cerebral hemorrhage, and respiratory collapse. Some studies show that repeated use of cocaine may heighten sensitivity to these toxic side effects of the drug.[78]

National Narcotics Intelligence Consumers Committee (NNICC) data indicate that cocaine has become the country's most dangerous commonly used drug. During a recent year, nearly 100,000 hospital emergencies involving cocaine abuse were reported across the country.[79] In 1998, at the time of the NNICC report, cocaine was available in all major American metropolitan areas and in most small communities. The cocaine derivative crack, manufactured by numerous street-level laboratories, was available primarily in large urban areas. A DEA survey in the mid-1990s, however, found that "crack dealers are expanding their markets to target potential users in small towns and rural areas across the United States" because "crack distribution and use appear to have reached the saturation point in large urban areas."[80] The Federal Drug Seizure System reports the seizure of around 300,000 pounds of cocaine throughout the United States annually.[81]

Most cocaine enters the United States from Peru, Bolivia, or Colombia. Together, these three countries have an estimated annual production capability of around 555 tons of pure cocaine.[82] During the 1980s, most cocaine coming into the United States was controlled by the Medellín Cartel, based in Medellín, Colombia. Multinational counterdrug efforts had crippled the cartel by the start of the 1990s, however, and the Cali Cartel (based in Cali, Colombia), a loose organization of five semi-independent trafficking organizations, took over as the major illegal supplier of cocaine to this country. Arrests of the Cali Cartel's top leaders, Gilberto Rodriguez and his brother, Miguel, however, are said to have sounded the death knell for what may have been the world's most successful drug-trafficking organization ever.[83]

We cannot go into tomorrow with the same formulas that are failing today. We must not blindly add to the body count and the terrible cost of the War on Drugs, only to learn . . . 30 years from now, that what we've been doing is wrong, terribly wrong.

—Walter Cronkite

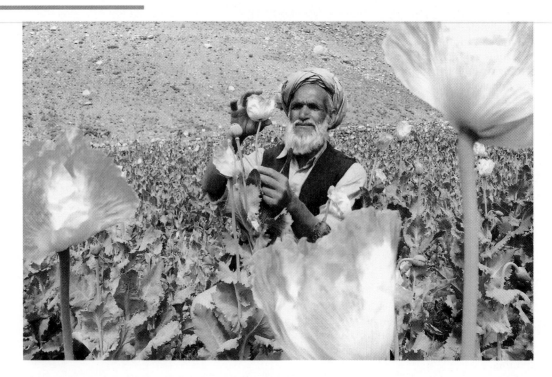

Sayed Mohammed checks his poppy field at a village in Bagh-e-Afghan, about 70 miles north-west of Kabul, Afghanistan. Despite U.S. efforts to curtail poppy cultivation in the country, Afghanistan remains the world's largest producer of heroin. Much of the money that Mohammed earns comes from the United States—where the sale of illicit drugs constitutes a multibillion-dollar industry.

*© Ahmad Sear, Reuters, Corbis*

# Heroin

Classified as a narcotic, heroin is a derivative of opium—itself the product of the milky fluid found in the flowering poppy plant (*Papaver somniferum*). Opium poppies have been grown in the Mediterranean region since 300 B.C.[84] and are now produced in many other parts of the world as well. Although heroin is not used medicinally in this country, many of the substances to which it is chemically related—such as morphine, codeine, hydrocodone, naloxone, and oxymorphone—do have important medical uses as pain relievers.

Heroin is a highly seductive and addictive drug that, when smoked, injected underneath the skin ("skin popping"), or shot directly into the bloodstream ("mainlining"), produces euphoria. Because tolerance for the drug increases with use, larger and larger doses of heroin must be taken to achieve the pleasurable effects desired by addicts. Heroin deprivation causes withdrawal symptoms that initially include watery eyes, runny nose, yawning, and perspiration. Further deprivation results in restlessness, irritability, insomnia, tremors, nausea, and vomiting. Stomach cramps, diarrhea, chills, and other flulike symptoms are also common. Most withdrawal symptoms disappear within seven to ten days[85] or when the drug is readministered.

Street-level heroin varies widely in purity. It is often cut with powdered milk, food coloring, cocoa, or brown sugar. Most heroin sold in the United States is only 5% pure.[86] Because of dosage uncertainties, overdosing is common. Mild overdoses produce lethargy and stupor, while larger doses may cause convulsions, coma, and death. Other risks, including infectious hepatitis and AIDS, are associated with using contaminated needles from other users. The Centers for Disease Control and Prevention (CDC) estimates that almost one-third of AIDS cases are associated with intravenous drug use.[87]

Heroin abuse has remained fairly constant during the past few decades. Some indicators point to an increased availability of heroin in the last few years.[88] Street-level heroin prices have declined in recent years, while nationwide heroin-related emergency room admissions have reached almost 40,000 per year.

Most heroin in the United States comes from South America, Southwest Asia (Afghanistan, Pakistan, and Iran), Southeast Asia (Burma, Laos, and Thailand), and Mexico. According to data from the Heroin Signature Program (HSP), which uses chemical analysis of the trace elements in heroin supplies to identify source countries, 65% of all heroin entering the United States comes from South America.[89] The Federal Drug Seizure System reports the seizure of approximately 2,500 pounds of heroin throughout the United States annually.[90]

Evidence indicates that the heroin abuse picture is changing. Although older users still dominate heroin markets in all parts of the country,[91] increasing numbers of non-inner-city young

## CJ NEWS

### Club Drugs Sending More Young People to Hospitals

Club drugs, including Ecstasy and GHB, are sending increasing numbers of young people to the hospital with toxic reactions and overdoses, emergency-room data shows.

Emergency rooms in 21 metropolitan areas tracked by the Drug Abuse Warning Network reported 4,511 emergency visits involving Ecstasy in 2000. That's a 58% increase over 1999.

The network, part of a federal agency that tracks hospital admissions, also reported 4,969 visits involving the "date-rape drug" GHB, which is a 56% increase over the previous year's 3,178 cases.

Club drugs still account for only a fraction of emergency-room visits. However, the numbers indicate the drugs are becoming more widespread.

Club-drug users began arriving at emergency rooms in 1994. The drugs, including Ecstasy, GHB, an anesthetic called Ketamine and the so-called date-rape drug, Rohypnol, had grown popular at all-night rave parties and in dance clubs. That year, emergency rooms reported 56 visits for GHB and 253 visits for Ecstasy. People ages 25 and younger account for almost a third of drug emergencies, the data show. Their share is much higher for club-drug emergencies: People 25 and younger make up 80% of Ecstasy emergencies and 60% of those involving GHB.

"We are concerned about the continued increase of club drugs among young people, which seems to be contributing to the overall increase of young people ending up in emergency rooms," says Mark Weber, spokesman for the Substance Abuse and Mental Health Services Administration in Rockville, Md., which collects the data from 466 hospitals.

For the latest in crime and justice news, visit the Talk Justice news feed at http://www.crimenews.info.

A fire juggler lighting up the night at a rave party attended by thousands in the French village of Paule, Brittany. Rave parties typically involve abundant drugs, particularly the designer drug Ecstasy.

*AP Wide World Photos*

*Source:* Donna Leinwand, "Club Drugs Sending More Young People to Hospitals," *USA Today,* July 25, 2001, p. 3A. Copyright © 2001, *USA Today.* Reprinted with permission.

---

users (under 30 years of age) are turning to the drug. Additionally, because high-purity powdered heroin is widely available in most parts of the country, new users seem to be experimenting with heroin inhalation, which often appears to lead to injection as addiction progresses. Treatment programs report that the typical heroin user is male, is over 30 years old, and has been in treatment previously.[92] Alcohol, cocaine, and marijuana remain concurrent problems for heroin users in treatment. Learn more about heroin, including statistics on use, production, and trafficking, at **Library Extra 16–5** at cjtoday.com.

## Club Drugs

In 1997, DEA officials recommended that the "date rape drug" Rohypnol (also discussed in Chapters 2 and 4) be added to the list of Schedule I controlled substances. Rohypnol is a powerful sedative manufactured by Hoffmann-LaRoche Pharmaceuticals.[93] Rohypnol is among the new "club drugs" that became popular in the mid- to late-1990s. **Club drug** is a general term used to refer primarily to synthetic psychoactive substances often found at nightclubs, bars, and "raves"

**club drug**

A synthetic psychoactive substance often found at nightclubs, bars, "raves," and dance parties. Club drugs include MDMA (Ecstasy), ketamine, methamphetamine (meth), GBL, PCP, GHB, and Rohypnol.

## FIGURE 16-5

**Estimated emergency room mentions for selected club drugs, 1994–2000.**

*Source:* Drug Abuse Warning Network (DAWN).

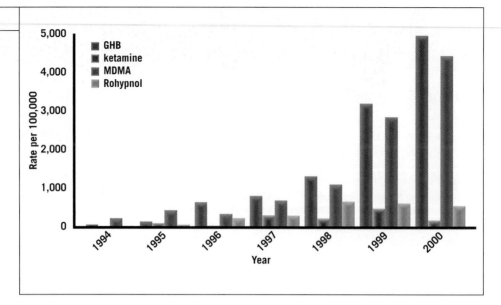

(all-night dance parties). In addition to Rohypnol, club drugs include GHB, GBL, MDMA (Ecstasy), methamphetamine (meth), ketamine, and PCP. According to the Drug Enforcement Administration, the use of club drugs is increasing rapidly. (See Figure 16–5.)

A few years ago, the growing use of Rohypnol at fraternity parties, raves, bars, and dance clubs gave rise to the phrase *chemically assisted date rape,* a term now generically applied to rapes in which sexual predators use drugs to incapacitate unsuspecting victims. Rohypnol (a brand name for flunitrazepam) is a member of the benzodiazepine family of depressants and is legally prescribed in 64 countries for insomnia and as a preoperative anesthetic. Seven to 10 times more powerful than Valium, Rohypnol has become popular with some college students and with "young men [who] put doses of Rohypnol in women's drinks without their consent in order to lower their inhibitions."[94] Available on the black market, it dissolves easily in drinks and can leave anyone who unknowingly consumes it unconscious for hours, making them vulnerable to sexual assault. The drug is variously known as *roples, roche, ruffles, roofies,* and *rophies* on the street.

Penalties for trafficking in flunitrazepam were increased under the Drug-Induced Rape Prevention and Punishment Act of 1996,[95] effectively placing it into a Schedule I category for sentencing purposes. Under the act, it is a crime to give someone a controlled substance without the person's knowledge and with intent to commit a violent crime.

GHB (gamma-hydroxybutyrate), another date rape drug, has effects similar to Rohypnol. GHB, a central nervous system depressant, is now designated as a Schedule I drug but was once sold in health food stores as a performance enhancer for use by bodybuilders. Rumors that GHB stimulates muscle growth were never proven. The intoxicating effects of GHB, however, soon became obvious. In 1990, the Food and Drug Administration (FDA) banned the use of GHB except under the supervision of a physician. In 2001, federal sentencing guideline changes removed the upper limit, or cap, on GHB sentences in cases where large amounts of the drug were sold or distributed.[96]

GBL (gamma-butyrolactone) is a chemical used in many industrial cleaners and is the precursor chemical for the manufacture of GHB. Several Internet businesses offer kits that contain GBL and the proper amount of sodium hydroxide or potassium hydroxide, along with litmus paper and directions for the manufacture of GHB. The process is quite simple and does not require complex laboratory equipment. Like GHB, GBL can be added to water and is nearly undetectable. GBL is synthesized by the body to produce GHB. As a consequence, some users drink small quantities of unmodified GBL. This often causes a severe physical reaction, usually vomiting. GBL increases the effects of alcohol and can cause respiratory distress, seizure, coma, and death.

MDMA (Ecstasy), the most popular of the club drugs, is primarily manufactured in and trafficked from Europe. DEA reports indicate widespread abuse of this drug within virtually every city in the United States. Estimates from the Drug Abuse Warning Network (DAWN) show that hospital emergency department mentions for MDMA quadrupled over three years, from 1,143 in 1998 to 4,511 in 2000.[97] A redesigned DAWN survey, known as the *New DAWN,* found that

4,442 MDMA-related emergency department visits were reported in 2003.[98] Although it is primarily found in urban settings, abuse of this substance also has been noted in rural communities. Prices in the United States generally range from $20 to $30 per dosage unit; however, prices as high as $50 per dosage unit have been reported in Miami. MDMA (3, 4-methylenedioxymethamphetamine) is a synthetic, psychoactive substance possessing stimulant and mild hallucinogenic properties. Known as the "hug drug" or the "feel good drug," it reduces inhibitions, produces feelings of empathy for others, eliminates anxiety, and produces extreme relaxation. In addition to chemical stimulation, the drug reportedly suppresses the need to eat, drink, or sleep. This enables club goers to endure all-night and sometimes two- to three-day parties. MDMA is taken orally, usually in tablet form, and its effects last approximately four to six hours. Often taken in conjunction with alcohol, the drug destroys both dopamine and serotonin cells in the brain. When taken at raves, the drug often leads to severe dehydration and heatstroke, since it has the effect of "short-circuiting" the body's temperature signals to the brain. An MDMA overdose is characterized by a rapid heartbeat, high blood pressure, faintness, muscle cramping, panic attacks, and, in more severe cases, seizures or loss of consciousness. Side effects of the drug are jaw muscle tension and teeth grinding. As a consequence, MDMA users will often use pacifiers to help relieve the tension. The most critical life-threatening response to MDMA is hyperthermia, or excessive body heat. Many rave clubs now have cooling centers or cold showers designed to allow participants to lower their body temperatures. MDMA is a Schedule I drug under the Controlled Substances Act.

The Ecstasy Anti-Proliferation Act of 2000[99] directed the U.S. Sentencing Commission to increase penalties for the manufacture, importation, exportation, and trafficking of MDMA. Under resulting emergency amendments to the U.S. Sentencing Guidelines, MDMA trafficking became a crime with serious consequences. As a result of this penalty enhancement, which became permanent in 2001, a violator convicted of trafficking 200 grams of MDMA (approximately 800 tablets) can receive a five-year prison sentence.

Another designer drug is methamphetamine. Known on the street as *speed, chalk, meth, crank,* and *fire,* methamphetamine is a stimulant drug chemically related to other amphetamines (like MDMA) but with stronger effects on the central nervous system. Methamphetamine is taken in pill form or is used in powdered form by snorting or injecting.[100] Crystallized methamphetamine (known as *ice, crystal,* or *glass*) is a smokable and still more powerful form of the drug. Effects of methamphetamine use include increased heart rate and blood pressure, increased wakefulness, insomnia, increased physical activity, decreased appetite, and anxiety, paranoia, or violent behavior. The drug is easily made in simple home "laboratories" ("meth labs") from readily available chemicals, and recipes describing how to produce the substance circulate on the Internet. Methamphetamine appeals to the abuser because it increases the body's metabolism, produces euphoria and alertness, and gives the user a sense of increased energy. An increasingly popular drug at raves, it is not physically addictive but can be psychologically addictive. High doses or chronic use of the drug increases nervousness, irritability, and paranoia. In recent years, drug store companies and state legislators have joined forces to control over-the-counter sales of common decongestants containing the ingredient pseudoephedrine, after it was learned that criminals were buying large quantities of the cold remedies to make methamphetamines. In 2005, the National Association of Chain Drug Stores announced that most national retailers would begin restricting the sale of those medicines and might require buyers to show driver's licenses and to sign logs at pharmacies.[101]

Ketamine (known as *K, special K,* and *cat valium*) produces effects that include mild intoxication, hallucinations, delirium, catatonia, and amnesia. Low doses of the drug create an experience called *K-Land,* a mellow, colorful "wonder world." Higher doses produce an effect referred to as *K-Hole,* an "out-of-body" or "near-death" experience. Use of the drug can cause delirium, amnesia, depression, long-term memory and cognitive difficulties, and fatal respiratory problems.[102]

Marketed as a dissociative general anesthetic for human and veterinary use, the only known street source of ketamine is **pharmaceutical diversion**. A significant number of veterinary clinics are being robbed specifically for their ketamine stock. Ketamine liquid can be injected, applied to smokable material, or consumed in drinks. The powdered form is made by allowing the solvent to evaporate, leaving a white or slightly off-white powder that, once pulverized, looks very similar to cocaine. The powder can be put into drinks, smoked, or injected. Pharmaceutical diversion and illicit Internet pharmacies are major sources of supply for *pharming parties,* which have been called "the newest venue for teenage prescription-drug abuse."[103]

Learn more about club drugs at Web Extra 16–8, and discover more about drug abuse among young people via Library Extra 16–6 at cjtoday.com.

> If we fail, it means that what we have been saying is true—that drugs may represent to our civilization, to many of our cities, a life-or-death situation. If we don't get control of this drug problem, we may not go into the twenty-first century intact.
>
> —William Bennett,
> the first "drug czar"

**pharmaceutical diversion**

The transfer of prescription medicines controlled by the Controlled Substance Act by theft, deception, and/or fraudulent means for other than their intended legitimate therapeutic purposes.

# Costs of Abuse

The societal costs of drug abuse can be categorized as direct and indirect. *Direct costs* are those costs immediately associated with drug crimes themselves, such as the dollar losses incurred by a homeowner from a burglary committed to support a drug habit. The value of stolen property, damage to the dwelling, and the costs of clean-up and repair figure into any calculation of direct costs. *Indirect costs,* which are harder to measure, include such things as the homeowner's lost wages from time off at work needed to deal with the burglary's aftermath, the value of time spent filling out police reports, going to court, and so on. Other indirect costs, such as the mental stress and feelings of violation and personal insecurity that often linger in the wake of criminal victimization are much harder to measure.

## The Indirect Costs of Abuse

A December 2004 report by the Office of National Drug Control Policy entitled *The Economic Costs of Drug Abuse in the United States*[104] placed the annual national cost of illicit drug use in the United States at a staggering $180.9 billion. That total includes costs from three areas: (1) lost productivity, (2) health care, and (3) justice system and social welfare expenditures needed to prevent drug abuse and to deal with its consequences.

The ONDCP says that the largest proportion of indirect costs, or $128.6 billion, comes from lost worker productivity. In contrast to the other indirect costs of drug abuse (which entail expenditures for goods and services), this value reflects a loss of potential—specifically, lost work in the labor market and in household production that was never performed, but could reasonably be expected to have been performed absent the impact of drug abuse. The greatest share of productivity loss comes from drug-related criminal activities that directly lead to the incarceration of approximately 660,000 offenders each year. The ONDCP study also includes the impact that an estimated 23,500 annual drug use–related accidental deaths have on productivity. Estimates of lost worker productivity based on premature death from drug use, lost time at work due to criminal victimization, and institutionalization for drug treatment and dependency also enter the totals. The study found that the legitimate U.S. economy loses about 1 million person years of effort every 12 months as the result of drug-related crimes.

Annual health-related costs associated with illicit drug use are estimated to total $15.8 billion and include costs associated with emergency room care, ongoing medical treatment for drug abuse–related illnesses and dependence, institutionalization, and hospitalization. A major component of health care costs related to drug abuse consists of spending on care for HIV/AIDS patients whose infections are directly attributable to drug-related activities (for example, the sharing of needles). Also included are expenses stemming from the annual estimated 23,500 drug-related deaths from overdose, poisoning, homicide, HIV, and hepatitis B and C.

The third major indirect drug cost is justice system–related expenses, which ONDCP estimates total about $36.4 billion annually, $14.2 billion of which is spent incarcerating drug offenders. Another $9.8 billion is spent on state and local drug abuse–related police protection, followed by $6.2 billion for federal supply-reduction initiatives. Additional monies are spent on jails, for the adjudication of drug offenders ($2.3 billion), for the cost of private legal defense attributable to drug abuse ($647 million), and for the administration of those components of the social welfare system that are forced to compensate for worker productivity lost to drugs. Federal justice system expenditures on drug-control activities stood at $12.4 billion in fiscal year 2006 and were expected to increase during the next few years.[105]

## Drug-Related Crime

The direct costs of drug-related crime have at least three dimensions: (1) economic losses from crimes committed by drug users to obtain money for drugs or from crimes committed by users whose judgment is altered by drugs; (2) the costs associated with drug transactions themselves (for example, what people spend to buy drugs); and (3) economic losses due to organized criminal activities in support of the drug trade (including money laundering).

ONDCP says that about 382,000 individuals suffer drug abuse–attributable violent crimes every year and that about 5.2% of all homicides are related to narcotic drug-law violations.[106] Additionally, an estimated 5 million property offenses are committed annually in order to pay for illicit drugs. ONDCP estimates that over a quarter of the total number of property offenses in any

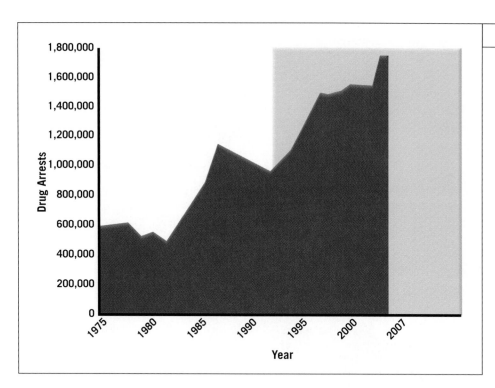

**FIGURE 16–6**

**Drug arrests in the United States, 1975–2004.**

*Source:* Federal Bureau of Investigation, *Uniform Crime Reports: Crime in the United States* (Washington, DC: U.S. Government Printing Office, various years).

given year are directly attributable to drug abuse.[107] Other crimes committed by those seeking to pay for drugs include prostitution, identity theft, fraud, and robbery.

As Figure 16–6 shows, more than 1.7 million people were arrested for drug-law violations (excluding alcohol) in the United States in 2004.[108] Eighty percent of all arrests nationally were for possession of controlled substances; most of the remainder were for sale or manufacture.[109] Arrests for heroin or cocaine possession accounted for 22% of all possession arrests, while 39.2% of such arrests were for marijuana possession.[110] Possession of PCP, LSD, amphetamines, and tranquilizers accounted for only a relatively small number of arrests.

Crimes committed by drug-dependent offenders can run the gamut from serious to relatively minor. A National Institute of Justice study of 201 heroin users in Central and East Harlem (New York City), for example, found that each daily user committed on average about 1,400 crimes per year. Of these offenses, 1,116 were directly drug related, involving primarily drug sales and use.[111] Another 75 were relatively minor crimes, such as shoplifting, but the remaining 209 offenses committed by each user involved relatively serious violations of the law, such as robbery, burglary, theft, forgery, fraud, and the fencing of stolen goods. Another study, which examined the daily activities of 354 Baltimore heroin addicts over a nine-year period, found that they had committed a total of nearly 750,000 criminal offenses.[112] Learn more about the dynamics of the drug–crime relationship via **Library Extra 16–7** at cjtoday.com.

The sale of illegal drugs is a $57 billion industry in the United States, and that's the amount that ONDCP estimates that Americans spend annually on illicit drugs.[113] Some perspective on this figure can be gained by recognizing that each year Americans spend approximately $44 billion on alcohol products and another $37 billion on tobacco products.[114]

Organized criminal activities in support of the drug trade represent a third area of indirect costs. Cash can flow into the hands of dealers in such huge amounts that it can be difficult for them to spend. Few people buy houses, cars, and other big-ticket items with cash, and cash transactions arouse suspicion. **Money laundering** is the name given to the process used by drug dealers to hide the source of their revenues, to avoid taxes, and to disguise the financial evidence of drug dealing. Drug profits are laundered by converting them into other assets, such as real estate, stocks and bonds, racehorses, jewels, gold, and other valuables. The Bureau of Justice Statistics says that many millions of dollars in drug monies are laundered through commercial banks and other financial institutions each year.[115] Under the federal Money Laundering Strategy Act of 1998,[116] particular regions have been designated as high-intensity financial crimes areas (HIFCAs). HIFCAs can be found in Chicago, New York, New Jersey, San Juan, Los Angeles, San Francisco, and the

**money laundering**

The process by which criminals or criminal organizations seek to disguise the illicit nature of their proceeds by introducing them into the stream of legitimate commerce and finance.[iv]

Sergeant Jeff Yurkiewicz of the Pennsylvania State Police K-9 unit leads his dog, Jake, through a search for drugs and contraband at the Allegheny County Jail in Pittsburgh. More than 20 dogs were brought in to sweep through the entire jail for drugs. Strict enforcement of antidrug laws is one of six strategies for attacking the drug problem that this chapter discusses.

*AP Wide World Photos*

> **Each of us has a responsibility to work toward reducing the demand for drugs in this country. We should expect nothing less from our government. The Congress, the media, communities, schools, churches, families, and every single citizen in this country must make living in a drug-free society their top priority.**
>
> —Dr. Lee P. Brown, Former Director, Office of National Drug Control Policy

southwestern border region, including Arizona and Texas. During 2001, 1,477 defendants were charged in U.S. district courts with money laundering as their most serious offense.[117]

In an effort to catch money launderers, U.S. banking law requires financial institutions to report deposits in excess of $10,000.[118] Traffickers attempt to avoid the law through two techniques known as *smurfing* and *structuring*.[119] Smurfers repeatedly purchase bank checks in denominations of less than $10,000, which are then sent to accomplices in other parts of the country, who deposit them in existing accounts. Once the checks have cleared, the funds are transferred to other banks or moved out of the country. Structuring is very similar and involves cash deposits to bank accounts in amounts of less than $10,000 at a time. After accounts are established, the money is withdrawn and deposited in increments elsewhere, making it difficult to trace. Countries that have secrecy laws protecting depositors are favorites for drug traffickers. Among them are Switzerland, Panama, Hong Kong, the United Arab Emirates, and the Bahamas.[120]

In 1994, in the case of *Ratzlaf* v. *U.S.*,[121] the U.S. Supreme Court made the task of catching money launderers more difficult. The Court ruled that no one can be convicted of trying to evade bank-reporting requirements unless authorities can prove that offenders knew they were violating the law.

In 2001, in an effort to enhance the amount of information received by federal regulators from banks about potential money-laundering activities, Congress passed the International Money Laundering Abatement and Anti-Terrorist Financing Act of 2001, which is Title III of the USA PATRIOT Act.[122] The law requires banks to make considerable effort in determining the source of monies held in individual overseas accounts and provides for sanctions to be placed on nations that hinder this reporting.

Although federal law prohibits the laundering of money, relatively few states have had strict laws against the practice. As a consequence, many local enforcement agencies were reluctant to investigate money-laundering activities in their jurisdictions. To counteract this reluctance and to facilitate interagency cooperation, the federal government created the Financial Crimes Enforcement Network (FINCEN). Partially as a result of FINCEN leadership, 36 states had adopted money-laundering legislation as of June 2003.[123] You can access the FINCEN website via Web Extra 16–9 at cjtoday.com. Learn more about money laundering and efforts to combat it via Library Extra 16–8 at cjtoday.com.

# Solving the Drug Problem

American drug-control strategies seem caught in a kind of limbo between conservative approaches advocating supply reduction through strict enforcement and interdiction, and innovative strategies proposing demand reduction through education, treatment, and counseling. In 2005, the Office of National Drug Control Policy released its latest *National Drug Control Strategy*,[124] a yearly publication outlining the current drug-abuse situation in the United States and detailing a strategy intended to guide the nation's criminal justice agencies in the continuing battle against drugs. The 2005 *National Drug Control Strategy* set as its first priority "stopping drug use before it starts."[125] The strategy said that it is critical to teach young people how to avoid drug use because of the damage drugs can inflict on their health and on their future. A major portion of the strategy was built on the $2 billion five-year National Youth Anti-Drug Media Campaign, which the *Strategy* claims "has had an impact on improving youth anti-drug attitudes and intentions."[126] The campaign is an integrated effort that combines media advertising with public communications outreach. It uses television and newspaper advertisements intended to coach parents in monitoring teen behavior and to promote quick parental intervention against signs of early drug use.

Although the federal strategy's primary focus is on education and prevention, the White House report maintains that no single solution can suffice to deal with the multifaceted challenge that drug abuse represents. Hence, the strategy also views law enforcement as essential to reducing drug use in the United States and sees policing as the first line of defense against drug trafficking. The strategy stresses the need to protect borders from drug incursion and to cut drug supply more effectively in domestic communities, seeks to curtail illegal drug trafficking via the interdiction of illicit drugs, focuses on supply-reduction operations at the source, and supports international efforts to curtail drug production and trafficking. Read the latest *National Drug Control Strategy* in its entirety at Library Extra 16–9 at cjtoday.com.

Politics aside, six general types of strategies can be identified among the many methods proposed for attacking the drug problem: (1) strict law enforcement, (2) asset forfeiture, (3) interdiction, (4) domestic and international crop control, (5) prevention and treatment, and (6) legalization and decriminalization. Each of these strategies is discussed in the following pages.

# Strict Enforcement

Trafficking in controlled substances is, of course, an illegal activity in the United States—and has been for a long time. Conservative politicians generally opt for a strict program of antidrug law enforcement and costly drug sentences, with the goal of removing dealers from the streets, disrupting supply lines, and eliminating sources of supply. Unfortunately, legal prohibitions appear to have done little to discourage widespread drug abuse. Those who look to strict law enforcement as a primary drug-control strategy usually stress the need for secure borders, drug testing to identify users, and stiff penalties to discourage others from drug involvement. The U.S. Coast Guard policy of "zero tolerance," for example, which was highly touted in the late 1980s, led to widely publicized seizures of multimillion-dollar vessels when even small amounts of drugs (probably carried aboard by members of the crew) were found.

But strict enforcement measures may be only a stopgap strategy and may eventually lead to greater long-term problems. As James Q. Wilson observes, "It is not clear that enforcing the laws against drug use would reduce crime. On the contrary, crime may be caused by such enforcement because it keeps drug prices higher than they would otherwise be."[127]

Some U.S. enforcement strategies attempt to enlist the help of foreign officials. However, because drug exports represent extremely lucrative sources of revenue and may even be thought of as valuable "foreign trade" by the governments of some nations, effective international antidrug cooperation is hard to come by. In 1991, for example, partly in response to pressures from cocaine-producing cartels within the country, Colombia outlawed the extradition of Colombian citizens for any purpose—making the extradition and trial of Colombian cocaine kingpins impossible.

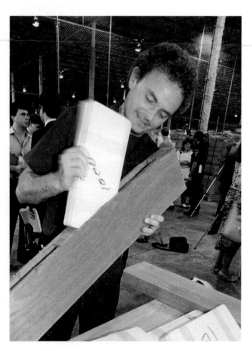

U.S. Customs officers with seized cocaine. Officer Rick Dallent (right) shows how four tons of packaged cocaine were hidden in hardwood boards designed for picnic tables and shipped from Honduras to Florida. Some drug seizures—like this one—involve huge amounts of drugs.

*Bob Sherman and UPI, Corbis/Bettmann*

A number of international drug-control treaties do, however, exist. In 2005, in actions supported by such treaties, the DEA announced that its Operation Cyber Chase, which had targeted e-traffickers who used more than 200 websites to illicitly distribute pharmaceutical controlled substances, had led to more than 20 arrests in the United States, Australia, Costa Rica, and India.[128] Among substances being sold by the cybertraffickers through illegal storefront pharmacies set up on the Internet were the drugs Vicodin, Xanax, and OxyContin. International cooperation resulted in the forfeiture of 41 bank accounts linked to the storefronts worth over $6 million.[129] One important group concerned with ensuring compliance with United Nations drug-control conventions is the International Narcotics Control Board (INCB). Visit the INCB via Web Extra 16–10 at cjtoday.com.

**WEB** EXTRA

## Asset Forfeiture

**forfeiture**

The authorized seizure of money, negotiable instruments, securities, or other things of value. Under federal antidrug laws, judicial representatives are authorized to seize all cash, negotiable instruments, securities, or other things of value furnished or intended to be furnished by any person in exchange for a controlled substance, as well as all proceeds traceable to such an exchange.

**Forfeiture**, an enforcement strategy that federal statutes and some state laws support, bears special mention. Antidrug forfeiture statutes authorize judges to seize "all monies, negotiable instruments, securities, or other things of value furnished or intended to be furnished by any person in exchange for a controlled substance . . . [and] all proceeds traceable to such an exchange."[130] Forfeiture statutes are based on the relation-back doctrine. This doctrine assumes that because the government's right to illicit proceeds relates back to the time they are generated, anything acquired through the expenditure of those proceeds also belongs to the government.[131]

The first federal laws to authorize forfeiture as a criminal sanction were passed in 1970. They were the Continuing Criminal Enterprise (CCE) statute and the Organized Crime Control Act. A section of the Organized Crime Control Act known as the **Racketeer Influenced and Corrupt Organizations (RICO)** statute was designed to prevent criminal infiltration of legitimate businesses and has been extensively applied in federal drug-smuggling cases. In 1978, Congress authorized civil forfeiture of any assets acquired through narcotics trafficking in violation of federal law. Many states modeled their own legislation after federal law and now have similar statutes.

The newer civil statutes have the advantage of being relatively easy to enforce. Civil forfeiture requires proof only by a preponderance of the evidence, rather than proof beyond a reasonable doubt, as in criminal prosecution. In civil proceedings based on federal statutes, there is no need to trace the proceeds in question to a particular narcotics transaction. It is enough to link them to narcotics trafficking generally.[132]

Forfeiture amounts can be huge. In one 15-month period, for example, the South Florida–Caribbean Task Force, composed of police agencies from the federal, state, and local levels, seized

**Racketeer Influenced and Corrupt Organizations (RICO)**

A federal statute that allows for the federal seizure of assets derived from illegal enterprise.

$47 million in airplanes, vehicles, weapons, cash, and real estate.[133] In a single investigation involving two brothers convicted of heroin smuggling, the federal government seized a shopping center, three gasoline stations, and seven homes worth over $20 million in New York City.[134]

Although almost all states now have forfeiture statutes, prosecutions built on them have met with less success than prosecutions based on federal law. The Police Executive Research Forum attributes the difference to three causes: (1) the fact that federal law is more favorable to prosecutors than are most state laws, (2) the greater resources of the federal government, and (3) the difficulties imposed by statutory requirements that illegal proceeds be traced to narcotics trafficking.[135]

In 1993, in *U.S.* v. *92 Buena Vista Ave.,*[136] the U.S. Supreme Court established an "innocent owner defense" in forfeiture cases, whereby the government was prohibited from seizing drug-transaction assets that were later acquired by a new and innocent owner. In the same year, in the case of *Austin* v. *U.S.,*[137] the Court placed limits on the government's authority to use forfeiture laws against drug criminals, finding that seizures of property must not be excessive when compared to the seriousness of the offense charged. Otherwise, the justices wrote, the Eighth Amendment's ban on excessive fines could be contravened. The justices, however, refused to establish a rule by which excessive fines could be judged. The *Austin* ruling was supported by two other 1993 cases, *Alexander* v. *U.S.* and *U.S.* v. *James Daniel Good Real Property.*[138] In *Alexander,* the Court found that forfeitures under the RICO statute must be limited according to the rules established in *Austin,* while in *Good,* the Court held that "absent exigent circumstances, the Due Process Clause requires the Government to afford notice and a meaningful opportunity to be heard before seizing real property subject to civil forfeiture."

In 1996, the U.S. Supreme Court upheld the seizure of private property used in the commission of a crime, even though the property belonged to an innocent owner not involved in the crime. The case, *Bennis* v. *Michigan,*[139] involved the government's taking of a car that had been used by the owner's husband when procuring the services of a prostitute. In effect, the justices ruled, an innocent owner is not protected from criminal conviction–related property forfeiture.

Also in 1996, in the case of *U.S.* v. *Ursery,*[140] the U.S. Supreme Court rejected claims that civil forfeiture laws constitute a form of double jeopardy. In *Ursery,* the defendant's house had been seized by federal officials who claimed that it had been used to facilitate drug transactions. The government later seized other personal items owned by Guy Jerome Ursery, saying that they had been purchased with the proceeds of drug sales and that Ursery had engaged in money-laundering activities to hide the source of his illegal income. The court of appeals, however, reversed Ursery's drug conviction and the forfeiture judgment, holding that the double jeopardy clause of the U.S. Constitution prohibits the government from both punishing a defendant for a criminal offense and forfeiting his property for that same offense in a separate civil proceeding. In reaffirming Ursery's conviction, however, the U.S. Supreme Court concluded that "civil forfeitures are neither 'punishment' nor criminal for purposes of the Double Jeopardy Clause." In distinguishing civil forfeitures and criminal punishments, the majority opinion held that "Congress has long authorized the Government to bring parallel criminal actions and . . . civil forfeiture proceedings based upon the same underlying events . . . , and this Court consistently has concluded that the Double Jeopardy Clause does not apply to such forfeitures because they do not impose punishment."

Civil forfeiture laws have come under considerable fire recently as being fundamentally unfair. More than 200 forfeiture laws have been enacted across the country in recent years, many requiring only mere suspicion before items of value can be seized by government agents. Once property has been seized, getting it back can be a nightmare, even when no crime was committed. A few years ago, Illinois U.S. Representative Henry Hyde reported that 80% of people whose property was seized by the federal government under drug laws were never formally charged with any crime.[141]

To address problems with federal forfeiture provisions, Congress passed the Civil Asset Forfeiture Reform Act of 2000. Under the law, federal prosecutors must meet a new burden-of-proof standard in forfeiture cases. They are required to establish by a *preponderance of the evidence* that the property in question was subject to forfeiture. The property owner has five years in which to make a claim on the property after the government has claimed it, but a claimant's status as a fugitive from justice is grounds for dismissal of the case contesting the forfeiture of the property. Under the new law, it is a crime to remove or destroy property to prevent seizure for forfeiture.

# Interdiction

In 1989, a single Los Angeles drug bust amazed investigators with the size of their catch. In a warehouse in a quiet section of the city, police seized 20 tons of cocaine, then valued at $20 billion on the street.[142] Found along with the cocaine was $10 million in cash. Since then, other large

The drug policy process in the United States is permeated with ideology, impervious to the lessons of history, and addicted to debating polar abstractions rather than focusing on practical alternatives to current policy.

—Franklin E. Zimring and Gordon Hawkins

Customs inspectors James McDermott and Jessica Quiles searching travelers' belongings at Newark International Airport in New Jersey. Drug interdiction, which involves efforts aimed at stopping drugs from entering a country, is an international strategy.

*Todd Plitt*

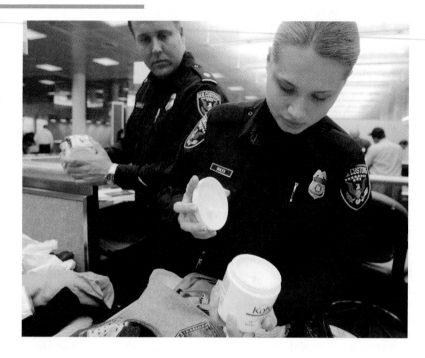

caches have also been uncovered, including 9 tons of cocaine in a house in Harlingen, Texas; 6 tons on a ship in the Gulf of Mexico; and more than 5 tons hidden in barrels of lye in New York City.[143] The 2001 seizure by the Coast Guard of 13 tons of cocaine found aboard a Belize-registered fishing boat south of San Diego, California, resulted in the biggest cocaine seizure in U.S. maritime history.[144] Annual seizures of cocaine in the United States total about 140 tons (with an estimated wholesale value of $50 billion).

**Interdiction** involves efforts aimed at stopping drugs from entering the United States. The Coast Guard, the Border Patrol, and Customs agents have played the most visible roles in interdiction efforts during the last few decades. Interdiction strategies in the fight against drugs, however, are almost doomed to failure by the sheer size of the task. Although most enforcement efforts are focused on international airports and major harbors, the international boundary of the United States extends over 12,000 miles. Rough coastline, sparsely populated desert, and dense forests provide natural barriers to easy observation and make detection of controlled substances entering the country very difficult. Add to this the fact that over 420 billion tons of goods and more than 270 million people cross over the American border annually, and the job of interdiction becomes more complicated still.[145] Because most drugs can be highly potent in even minute quantities, the interdiction strategy suffers from the proverbial "needle in the haystack" predicament.

## Crop Control

Crop control strategies attempt to limit the amount of drugs available for the illicit market by targeting foreign producers. Crop control in source countries generally takes one of two forms. In the first, government subsidies (often with U.S. support) are made available to farmers to induce them to grow other kinds of crops. Sometimes illegal crops are bought and destroyed. The second form of control involves aerial spraying or ground-level crop destruction.

Source country crop control suffers from two major drawbacks.[146] First, the potentially large profits that can be made from illegal acreage encourage farmers in unaffected areas to take up the production of crops that have been destroyed elsewhere. Second, it can be difficult to get foreign governments to cooperate in eradication efforts. In some parts of the world, opium and coca are major cash crops, and local governments are reluctant to undertake any action directed against them.

## Prevention and Treatment

As the population of incarcerated drug offenders swelled, some state legislatures began to question the necessity of imprisoning nonviolent substance abusers who were not involved in drug sale or distribution. In 1996, as a consequence of such thinking, Arizona voters approved Proposition 200,

---

**interdiction**

The interception of drug traffic at the nation's borders. Interdiction is one of the many strategies used to stem the flow of illegal drugs into the United States.

---

One of the most promising means of reducing the supply of drugs is a strong source country strategy.

*—The National Drug Control Strategy*

the Drug Medicalization, Prevention, and Control Act. A central purpose of the act was to expand drug-treatment and education services for drug offenders and to utilize probation for nonviolent drug offenders, thereby potentially diverting many arrested drug abusers from prison. To fund the program, the Arizona law established the state's Drug Treatment and Education Fund, administered by Arizona's Office of the Courts; the fund draws revenues from the state's luxury tax on liquor.

A study by Arizona's Administrative Office of the Courts concluded that the Arizona law is "resulting in safer communities and more substance abusing probationers in recovery."[147] Moreover, said the report, the law has saved the state millions of dollars and has helped more than 75% of program participants to remain drug free.[148] In 2000, the state of California followed Arizona's lead when voters approved Proposition 36 (also known as the California Substance Abuse and Crime Prevention Act of 2000), a sweeping initiative requiring treatment instead of imprisonment for nonviolent drug users throughout the state.[149] Similar legislation became law in Kansas in 2003 when Governor Sebelius signed Senate Bill 123, the First Time Non-Violent Drug Offenders Act. The law requires Kansas judges to place nonviolent offenders convicted of nothing more than drug possession in community-based or faith-based drug-treatment programs for up to 18 months.[150]

Many different kinds of prevention and treatment programs are available for drug offenders. Michael Goodstadt of the Addiction Research Foundation groups drug-prevention and drug-treatment programs into three categories: (1) those that provide factual information about drugs; (2) those that address feelings, values, and attitudes; and (3) those that focus directly on behavior.[151] Most modern programs contain elements of all three approaches, and most experts agree that drug-prevention programs, if they are to be successful, must include a wide array of components, including components for individuals, families, schools, the media, health care providers, law enforcement officials, and other community agencies and organizations.[152]

Antidrug education programs can be found in schools, churches, and youth groups and may be provided by police departments, social service agencies, hospitals, and private citizens' groups. Project DARE (the Drug Abuse Resistance Education program) falls into Goodstadt's second category. DARE, the nation's most visible school-based antidrug education program, began as a cooperative effort between the Los Angeles Police Department and the Los Angeles Unified School District in 1983. Using uniformed law enforcement officers to conduct classes in elementary schools, the program focuses on decision-making skills, peer pressure, and alternatives to drug use.

A 1994 study cast the effectiveness of the DARE program into doubt, and officials in the Clinton administration were charged with refusing to recognize the study's results. The study, published in the *American Journal of Public Health,* reviewed DARE programs in six states and British Columbia and found that "the popular drug prevention program does not work well and is less effective than other drug prevention efforts targeted at students."[153] Defending the DARE program, Justice Department officials questioned the study's methodology and published their own version of the study's results, which showed that "user satisfaction" with the DARE program is high. The study, according to Justice Department interpreters, found substantial grassroots support for the DARE program and led to the conclusion that DARE "has been extremely successful at placing substance abuse education in the nation's schools."[154]

Later studies again questioned Project DARE's effectiveness. A 1997 review of numerous DARE studies concluded that the program's "effects on drug use, except for tobacco use, are nonsignificant."[155] Finally, a 1999 University of Kentucky study tracked over 1,000 Midwestern students who participated in Project DARE in the sixth grade in order to see if the level of drug abuse among them differed from those who had not been exposed to the program.[156] The study found no difference in actual drug use immediately following exposure to the program or ten years later, when most of the former students were 20 years old.

Other studies also show that there is little evidence to support the belief that school-based anti-substance-abuse education will produce the desired effect on problem drug users or those at risk of beginning drug use.[157] Studies analyzing state-by-state spending on school-based drug education, for example, show little relationship between the amount of money spent on drug education and the number of hard-core cocaine users.[158] To be effective, programs will probably have to acknowledge the perceived positive aspects of the drug experience, as well as cultural messages that encourage drug use.[159] Until they do, many recipients of today's messages may discount them as conflicting with personal experience. Read more about the debate over DARE at Web Extra 16–11 at cjtoday.com.

Other kinds of drug-education programs may be effective, however. A recent study by the RAND Corporation's Drug Policy Research Center (DPRC), for example, found education to be the most efficacious alternative for dealing with drug abuse.[160] DPRC researchers focused on the use of alternative strategies for reducing cocaine abuse. Visit RAND's DPRC via Web Extra 16–12 at cjtoday.com.

> A key response to drug use and drug trafficking is an aggressive and coordinated law enforcement effort. Americans have the right to feel safe in their homes and secure in their communities.
>
> —*The National Drug Control Strategy*

WEB EXTRA

WEB EXTRA

A young woman shooting up with help from friends. Drug abuse extends to all social groups and can be found among all ages.

*Dennis MacDonald, PhotoEdit*

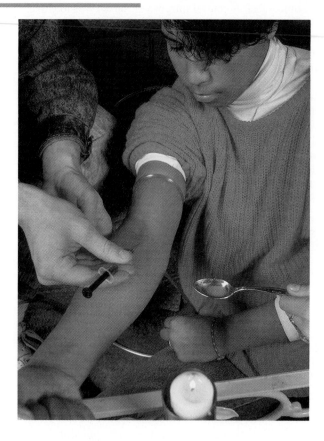

## Drug Courts

> **drug court**
>
> A special state, county, or municipal court that offers first-time substance-abuse offenders judicially mandated and court-supervised treatment alternatives to prison.

One of the most widely accepted antidrug programs operating today is the **drug court**. Drug courts focus on promoting public safety and employ a nonadversarial approach that provides defendants with easy access to a continuum of alcohol, drug, and other related treatment and rehabilitation services. Drug courts also monitor abstinence from the use of drugs on an individual basis through frequent alcohol and other drug testing. Failing to comply with court-ordered treatment, or returning to drug use, results in harsher punishments, including imprisonment.

Modern drug courts are modeled after a Dade County, Florida, innovation that became known as the *Miami Drug Court model.* An early evaluation of Miami's drug court found a high rate of success: Few clients were rearrested, incarceration rates were lowered, and the burden on the criminal justice system was lessened.[161] The success of the drug-court model led to $1 billion worth of funding under the Violent Crime Control and Law Enforcement Act of 1994 for the establishment of similar courts throughout the nation. Since then, the growth in the number of drug courts serving the nation has been huge. In 2005, the National Association of Drug Court Professionals (NADCP) reported that nearly 1,500 drug courts were in existence or were being planned.[162] The federal budget for fiscal year 2006 includes $70.1 million in continuation funding for such courts, although states and local governments also contribute to the support of drug courts.[163] The Congress of State Drug Courts, part of the NADCP, is working to support and nurture drug-court leadership at local levels in anticipation of the day when federal funding for drug courts runs out.

There are special drug courts for juveniles and for drunk drivers (sometimes called DUI courts). The National Drug Court Institute, in conjunction with the National Association of Drug Court Professionals, provides training for judges and professional courtroom staff interested in today's drug-court movement.[164] Learn more about drug courts via Web Extra 16–13 and Library Extras 16–10 and 16–11 at cjtoday.com.

**WEB** EXTRA

**LIBRARY** EXTRA

## Legalization and Decriminalization

Some years ago at an annual conference on controversies in criminal justice, Ross Deck, senior policy analyst at the Office of National Drug Control Policy, opened his remarks to a yearly conference on controversies in criminal justice with these words: "First of all, we are not fighting a

Cher Fisher (left) of England and Henny Fou of Holland posing before the start of the sixth annual beauty pageant for inmates at the Santa Monica Women's Prison in Lima, Peru. Most women incarcerated at the Peruvian penitentiary previously worked as drug "mules" and were caught trying to smuggle cocaine out of Peru.

*Jaime Razuri, Agence France Presse, Getty Images*

drug war anymore. To have a war you must have enemies. In this situation, we are our own enemy."[165] Such realizations have led a number of well-meaning people to question the wisdom of current laws and to seek alternatives to existing U.S. drug-control policies. For them, it has become clear that the fight against drug abuse through the application of strict criminal justice sanctions is bound to fail. Arrest, incarceration, and a national prison system filled with drug-law violators do not seem to hold the answer to winning the drug-control battle.

More than one-third (37%) of the police chiefs who participated in the survey mentioned at the start of this chapter state that our nation's drug policy needs a fundamental overhaul, and 47% think that it needs major changes. Only 2% of responding chiefs said that they would maintain the status quo.[166]

Often regarded as the most "radical" approach to solving the drug problem, legalization and decriminalization have been proposed repeatedly, and in recent years, these ideas seem to be gaining at least a modicum of respectability. Although the words *legalization* and *decriminalization* are often used interchangeably, there is a significant difference. **Legalization** refers to the removal of all legal strictures from the use or possession of the drug in question. Manufacture and distribution might still be regulated. **Decriminalization**, on the other hand, substantially reduces penalties associated with drug use but may not eliminate them entirely. States like Oregon, which have decriminalized marijuana possession, for example, treat simple possession of small amounts of the substance as a ticketable offense similar to jaywalking or improper parking.[167] Hence, decriminalization of a controlled substance might mean that the drug "would remain illegal but the offense of possession would be treated like a traffic violation, with no loss of liberty involved for the transgressor."[168]

The following arguments have been offered in support of both legalization and decriminalization[169]:

- Legal drugs would be easy to track and control. The involvement of organized criminal cartels in the drug-distribution network could be substantially curtailed.

- Legal drug sales could be taxed, generating huge revenues.

- Legal drugs would be cheap, significantly reducing the number of drug-related crimes committed to feed expensive drug habits.

- Since some people are attracted to anything taboo, legalization could, in fact, reduce the demand for drugs.

- The current war on drugs is already a failure and will be remembered as one of history's follies.[170] Prohibiting drugs is too expensive in terms of tax dollars, sacrificed civil liberties, and political turmoil.

- Drug dealers and users care little about criminal justice sanctions. They will continue their illegal activities no matter what the penalties.

- Drug use should ultimately be a matter of personal choice.

Advocates of legalization are primarily motivated by cost–benefit considerations, weighing the social costs of prohibition against its results.[171] The results, they say, have been meager at best, while the costs have been almost more than society can bear.

**legalization**

Elimination of the laws and associated criminal penalties associated with certain behaviors—usually the production, sale, distribution, and possession of a controlled substance.

**decriminalization**

The redefinition of certain previously criminal behaviors into regulated activities that become "ticketable" rather than "arrestable."

Opponents of legalization argue from both a moral and a practical stance. Some, like former New York City Mayor Rudolph Giuliani, believe that legalization would only condone a behavior that is fundamentally immoral.[172] Others argue that under legalization, drug use would increase, causing more widespread drug-related social problems than exist today. Robert DuPont, former head of the National Institute on Drug Abuse, for example, estimates that up to ten times the number of people who now use cocaine would turn to the substance if it were legal.[173]

A compromise approach has been suggested in what some writers call the *limitation model*. The limitation model "would make drugs legally available, but with clearly defined limits as to which institutions and professions could distribute the drugs."[174] Hence, under such a model, doctors, pharmacists, and perhaps licensed drug counselors could prescribe controlled substances under appropriate circumstances, and the drugs themselves might be taxed. Some claim that a more extreme form of the limitation model might be workable. Under that model, drugs would be sold through designated "drugstores" with distribution systems structured much like those of liquor stores today. Controlled substances would be sold to those of suitable age but taxed substantially, and the use of such substances under certain circumstances (such as when operating a car) might still be illegal. The regulation and taxation of controlled substances would correspond to today's handling of alcoholic beverages.

Another example of the limitation model, already tried in some countries, is the two-market system.[175] The two-market approach would allow inexpensive and legitimate access to controlled substances for registered addicts. Only maintenance amounts (the amounts needed to forestall symptoms of drug withdrawal) of the needed drugs, however, would be available. The two-market approach would purportedly reduce the massive profits available to criminal drug cartels while simultaneously discouraging new drug use among those who are not addicted. Great Britain provides an example of the two-market system. During the 1960s and 1970s, British heroin addicts who registered with the government received prescriptions for limited amounts of heroin, which was dispensed through medical clinics. Because of concern about system abuses, clinics in the late 1970s began to dispense reduced amounts of heroin, hoping to wean addicts away from the drug.[176] By 1980, heroin was replaced by methadone,[177] a synthetic drug designed to prevent the physical symptoms of heroin withdrawal. Methadone, in amounts sufficient to prevent withdrawal, does not produce a heroin-like high.

It is doubtful that the two-market system will be adopted in the United States anytime soon. American cultural condemnation of major mind-altering drugs has created a reluctance to accept the legitimacy of drug treatment using controlled substances. In addition, cocaine is much more of a problem in the United States than is heroin. The large number of drug abusers in the country, combined with the difficulty of defining and measuring addiction to drugs like cocaine, would make any maintenance program impractical.

One group advocating for a change in current drug laws, including the possible decriminalization of some controlled substances, is Law Enforcement Against Prohibition (LEAP). LEAP members are current and former law enforcement officers, and the group describes itself as "an organization made up of former drug warriors speaking out about the excesses and abuses of current drug policy and the utter failure of the war on drugs." The group originated with Peter Christ, a retired police captain living in New York City. Christ believed that an organization modeled after Vietnam Veterans Against the War would catch the attention of the media and appeal to other law enforcement officers. Visit LEAP on the Web at Web Extra 16–14.

**WEB** EXTRA

---

## SUMMARY

Drug crimes and drug-related crimes account for a substantial proportion of all crimes committed in this country. While the manufacture, importation, sale, and use of illegal drugs account for a substantial number of law violations, many other offenses are also linked to drug use. Among them are thefts of all kinds, burglary, assault, and murder.

Drug-related crimes occur because drugs are both expensive for users and extremely profitable for suppliers. The high cost of drugs forces many users, some of whom have little legitimate income, to commit property crimes to make money to continue their drug habit. On the other hand, users of illicit drugs who have substantial legitimate incomes may indirectly shift the cost of drug use to society through lowered job productivity, psychological or family problems, and medical expenses.

The widespread use of illegal drugs in America today carries with it other social costs. Many criminal enterprises, for example, are supported by the street-level demand for drugs. Some of these illegitimate businesses are massive international cartels that will stop at nothing to protect their financial interests. Bribery, extortion, kidnapping, torture, and murder are tools of the trade among drug kingpins in their battle to continue reaping vast profits.

Any realistic appraisal of the current situation must admit that the resources of the criminal justice system in dealing with drug crime are strained to the limit. There are simply not enough agents, airplanes, equipment, and money to entirely remove illegal drugs from American communities. The justice system faces the added problem of corruption—a problem inherent in any social-control situation in which large amounts of money frequently change hands. Until attitudes that support drug use are modified or are replaced, law enforcement professionals can only hope to keep the problem of drug abuse in America from becoming worse—and to keep from losing sight of their fundamental mandates in the process.

**DISCUSSION QUESTIONS**

1. How long have substances that today would be considered illicit been used in the United States? For what purposes?

2. List and describe some of the most important pieces of federal drug-control legislation.

3. What are the major types of drugs that are illegally used in this country? Describe the effects and legal classification of each.

4. What is the relationship between drug use and other social problems? What kinds of crimes might be linked to drug use?

5. What strategies have been used or suggested as ways of responding to the drug problem? Which of these strategies seem to hold the most potential?

**WEB QUEST**

Research drug and alcohol abuse using the Cybrary (http://www.cybrary.info) as a starting point. Search the Cybrary listings to find sites that contain suggestions and ideas on how to solve the drug problems facing this country.

What sources did you find? (*Hint:* Don't forget the *National Drug Control Strategy* available from ONDCP.) Describe the various strategies you've found. Which do you think are the most useful? Why? Submit your findings to your instructor if asked to do so.

To complete this Web Quest online, go to the Web Quest module in Chapter 16 of the *Criminal Justice Today* Companion Website at cjtoday.com.

**NOTES**

i. Bureau of Justice Statistics, *Drugs, Crime, and the Justice System* (Washington, DC: Author, 1992), p. 20.

ii. Ibid., p. 21.

iii. Ibid.

iv. U.S. Department of Treasury, *2000–2005 Strategic Plan* (Washington, DC: U.S. Government Printing Office, 2000), p. 1.

1. Gary E. Johnson, "Bad Investment," a Mother Jones.com Special Report, July 10, 2001. Web posted at http://www.motherjones.com/prisons/investment.html (accessed January 30, 2002).

2. "New Drug Czar Targets 'Unacceptably High' Rates of Drug Use among Students," Office of National Drug Control Policy press release, December 19, 2001. Web posted at http://www.whitehousedrugpolicy.gov/news/press01/121901.html (accessed February 3, 2002).

3. Peter D. Hart Research Associates, *Drugs and Crime across America: Police Chiefs Speak Out—A National Survey among Chiefs of Police* (Washington, DC: The Police Foundation, December 2004).

4. National Association of Drug Court Professionals, *The Facts: Facts on Drug Courts* (Alexandria, VA: NADCP, 2001).

5. The Sentencing Project, *The Federal Prison Population: A Statistical Analysis* (Washington, DC: The Sentencing Project, 2005).

6. Paige M. Harrison and Allen J. Beck, *Prisoners in 2003* (Washington, DC: Bureau of Justice Statistics, 2004). See also Barbara Owen, "Women in Prison," Drug Policy Alliance, 2005. Web posted at http://www.drugpolicy.org/communities/women/womeninprison/ (accessed May 14, 2005).

7. Peter D. Hart Research Associates, *Drugs and Crime across America*, pp. 1–2.

8. Ibid.

9. The term *recreational user* is well established in the literature of drug abuse. Unfortunately, it tends to minimize the seriousness of drug abuse by according the abuse of even hard drugs the status of a hobby.

10. Howard Becker, *Outsiders: Studies in the Sociology of Deviance* (New York: Free Press, 1963).

11. Jay Tokasz, "Eight of 11 People in Car Die in Crash," *USA Today,* June 20, 1995, p. 2A.

12. In most states, individuals may also be arrested for driving under the influence of other drugs and controlled substances, including prescription medicines.

13. Fiscal year 2001 Transportation Appropriations Bill (H.R. 4475), signed by the president on October 23, 2000.

14. "Drunk Driving Limit Lowered," *Lawyers Weekly USA,* October 16, 2000.

15. Federal Bureau of Investigation, *Uniform Crime Reports: Crime in the United States, 2004* (Washington, DC: U.S. Government Printing Office, 2005).

16. James B. Jacobs, *Drinking and Crime,* NIJ Crime File Study Guide (Washington, DC: National Institute of Justice, no date).

17. Rajesh Subramanian, *Alcohol Involvement in Fatal Motor Vehicle Traffic Crashes, 2003* (Washington, DC: National Highway Traffic Safety Administration, 2005).

18. Ibid.

19. FBI, *Uniform Crime Reports, 2004.*

20. Bureau of Justice Statistics, *Report to the Nation on Crime and Justice,* 2nd ed. (Washington, DC: Department of Justice, 1988), p. 50.

21. Jeffrey A. Roth, *Psychoactive Substances and Violence,* NIJ Research in Brief (Washington, DC: National Institute of Justice, February 1994), p. 1.

22. Christopher J. Mumola, *Substance Abuse and Treatment, State and Federal Prisoners, 1997* (Washington, DC: Bureau of Justice Statistics, 1999).

23. Ibid.

24. Howard Abadinsky, *Drug Abuse: An Introduction* (Chicago: Nelson-Hall, 1989), p. 32.

25. Charles E. Terry and Mildred Pellens, *The Opium Problem* (New York: Committee on Drug Addiction, 1928).

26. Ibid.

27. Office of National Drug Control Policy, *Heroin,* ONDCP Fact Sheet (Washington, DC: ONDCP, 2003), p. 1.

28. Terry and Pellens, *The Opium Problem,* p. 76.

29. David Musto, *The American Disease: Origins of Narcotic Control* (New Haven, CT: Yale University Press, 1973).

30. Becker, *Outsiders.*

31. Franklin E. Zimring and Gordon Hawkins, *The Search for Rational Drug Control* (New York: Cambridge University Press, 1992).

32. Ibid., p. 9.

33. President's Commission on Organized Crime, *Organized Crime Today* (Washington, DC: U.S. Government Printing Office, 1986).

34. *Webb* v. *U.S.,* 249 U.S. 96 (1919).

35. Michael D. Lyman and Gary W. Potter, *Drugs in Society: Causes, Concepts, and Control* (Cincinnati, OH: Anderson, 1991), p. 359.

36. Drug Enforcement Administration, *Drug Enforcement: The Early Years* (Washington, DC: DEA, 1980), p. 41.

37. White House Conference on Drug Abuse, *Commission Report* (Washington, DC: U.S. Government Printing Office, 1963).

38. For a good summary of the law, see Drug Enforcement Administration, *Drugs of Abuse* (Washington, DC: U.S. Government Printing Office, 1997).

39. Drug Enforcement Administration, *Drug Enforcement Briefing Book* (Washington, DC: DEA, no date), p. 3.

40. A number of states now recognize that marijuana may be useful in the treatment of nausea associated with cancer chemotherapy, glaucoma, and other medical conditions.

41. DEA, *Drug Enforcement Briefing Book,* p. 3.

42. Ibid.

43. Ibid., p. 4.

44. Ibid.

45. DEA, *Drugs of Abuse.*

46. Ibid.

47. Anti-Drug Abuse Act of 1988, P.L. 100-690, Sec. 5251.

48. This provision became effective on September 1, 1989.

49. "Congress Gives Final OK to Major Antidrug Bill," *Criminal Justice Newsletter,* Vol. 19, No. 21 (November 1, 1988), pp. 1–4.

50. The U.S. Supreme Court upheld that legislation in the 2002 case of *Department of Housing and Urban Development* v. *Rucker,* 122 S.Ct. 1230, 152 L.Ed.2d 258 (2002).

51. "Congress Gives Final OK to Major Antidrug Bill," p. 2.

52. "Drug Lord Sentenced to Death," *USA Today,* May 15, 1991, p. 3A.

53. Ibid.

54. Public Laws 101-647, 103-322, and 105–20.

55. *California* v. *Greenwood,* 486 U.S. 35, 108 S.Ct. 1625 (1988).

56. Ibid.

57. *Abel* v. *U.S.,* 363 U.S. 217 (1960).

58. *Oliver* v. *U.S.,* 466 U.S. 170 (1984).

59. *Hester* v. *U.S.,* 265 U.S. 57, 44 S.Ct. 445 (1924).

60. *U.S.* v. *Dunn,* 480 U.S. 294, 107 S.Ct. 1134 (1987).

61. *California* v. *Ciraolo,* 476 U.S. 207, 106 S.Ct. 1809 (1986).

62. *Florida* v. *Riley,* 488 U.S. 445, 109 S.Ct. 693, 102 L.Ed.2d 835 (1989).

63. Substance Abuse and Mental Health Services Administration, *Overview of Findings from the 2003 National Survey on Drug Use and Health* (Rockville, MD; Office of Applied Studies, NHSDA, 2004). Web posted at http://www.oas.samhsa.gov/NHSDA/2k3NSDUH/2k3OverviewW.pdf (accessed October 21, 2005).

64. ONDCP, *Heroin,* p. 1.

65. Office of National Drug Control Policy, *General Counterdrug Intelligence Plan* (Washington, DC: ONDCP, 2000). Web posted at http://www.fas.org/irp/ops/le/docs/gcip/index.html.

66. Information in this section comes from the National Drug Intelligence Center, http://www.usdoj.gov/ndic.

67. Office of National Drug Control Policy, *Pulse Check: National Trends in Drug Abuse—Marijuana* (Washington, DC: ONDCP, 2002). Web posted at http://www.whitehousedrugpolicy.gov/publications/drugfact/pulsechk/nov02/marijuana.html (accessed August 4, 2003).

68. See Anita Manning and Andrea Stone, "How States Will Face Regulating Marijuana as Medicine," *USA Today,* November 7, 1996, p. 3D.

69. *U.S.* v. *Oakland Cannabis Buyers' Cooperative,* 532 U.S. 483 (2001).

70. Ibid., syllabus.

71. *Gonzales* v. *Raich,* U.S. Supreme Court, No. 03-1454 (decided June 6, 2005).

72. Department of Health and Human Services, "Trends in Annual Prevalence of Use of Various Drugs, for Eighth, Tenth, and Twelfth Graders." Web posted at http://www.monitoringthefuture.org/data/04data/pr04t2.pdf (accessed May 30, 2005).

73. National Narcotics Intelligence Consumers Committee, *The NNICC Report, 1998* (Washington, DC: Drug Enforcement Administration, 2000), preface.

74. Ibid.

75. Ibid.

76. ONDCP, *Pulse Check.*

77. NNICC, *The NNICC Report, 1998.*

78. Ibid.

79. Ibid.

80. Drug Enforcement Administration, *Crack Cocaine Drug Intelligence Report, 1994* (Washington, DC: DEA, 1995).

81. National Institute of Justice, JUSTINFO Online, July 5, 1995.

82. NNICC, *The NNICC Report, 1998.*

83. Sam Vincent Meddis, "Arrests 'Last Rites' for Cali Cartel," *USA Today,* August 7, 1995, p. 1A.

84. DEA, *Drugs of Abuse,* p. 14.

85. Ibid., p. 12.

86. Ibid., p. 15.

87. Office of National Drug Control Policy, *The National Drug Control Strategy: Executive Summary* (Washington, DC: ONDCP, 1995), p. 13.

88. DEA, *Drugs of Abuse.*

89. NNICC, *The NNICC Report, 1998.*

90. National Institute of Justice, JUSTINFO Online, July 5, 1995.

91. ONDCP, *Pulse Check.*

92. Ibid.

93. Much of the information on club drugs in this section comes from Drug Enforcement Administration, "An Overview of Club Drugs," *Drug Intelligence Brief, February 2000.* Web posted at http://www.usdoj.gov/dea/pubs/intel/20005intellbrief.pdf (accessed March 2, 2002).

94. "'Rophies' Reported Spreading Quickly throughout the South," *Drug Enforcement Report,* June 23, 1995, pp. 1–5.

95. Public Law 104-305.

96. Sentencing enhancement information in this section comes from the congressional testimony of Asa Hutchinson, administrator of the Drug Enforcement Administration, before the Senate Caucus on International Narcotics Control, December 4, 2001. Web posted at http://www.usdoj.gov/dea/pubs/cngrtest/ct120401.html (accessed February 3, 2002).

97. Substance Abuse and Mental Health Services Administration, *The DAWN Report.* Web posted at http://www.samhsa.gov/oas/dawn.htm (accessed March 10, 2002).

98. Substance Abuse and Mental Health Services Administration, *Drug Abuse Warning Network 2003: Interim National Estimates of Drug-Related Emergency Department Visits* (Washington, DC: U.S. Department of Health and Human Services, December, 2004), p. 34. Numbers extrapolated by author from available data.

99. Public Law 106-310.

100. Much of the information in this section comes from the National Institute on Drug Abuse's website at http://www.nida.nih.gov.

101. Margaret Webb Pressler, "Retailers Restrict Some Cold Medicines," *The Washington Post,* May 14, 2005, p. A1.

102. DEA, "An Overview of Club Drugs," from which some of the wording in this section is taken.

103. Carolyn Banta, "Trading for a High: An Inside Look at a 'Pharming Party,'" *Time,* August 1, 2005, p. 35.

104. Office of National Drug Control Policy, *The Economic Costs of Drug Abuse in the United States 1992–2002* (Washington, DC: ONDCP, December 2004).

105. Office of National Drug Control Policy, *The National Drug Control Strategy, 2005* (Washington, DC: U.S. Government Printing Office, February 2005), p. 5.

106. Office of National Drug Control Policy, *The National Drug Control Strategy 2003: Executive Summary* (Washington, DC: ONDCP, 2003), p. 12.

107. ONDCP, *The Economic Costs of Drug Abuse in the United States 1992–2002,* p. iii–18.

108. FBI, *Uniform Crime Reports, 2004.*

109. Ibid.

110. Ibid. Unfortunately, UCR data combine arrests for heroin and cocaine possession into one category. They do the same for sale and manufacture arrests.

111. Bernard A. Gropper, *Probing the Links between Drugs and Crime,* NIJ Research in Brief (Washington, DC: National Institute of Justice, February 1985), p. 4.

112. J. C. Ball, J. W. Shaffer, and D. N. Nurco, *Day to Day Criminality of Heroin Addicts in Baltimore: A Study in the Continuity of Offense Rates* (Washington, DC: National Institute of Justice, 1983).

113. Office of National Drug Control Policy, "ONDCP Finds Americans Spent $57 Billion in One Year on Illegal Drugs," press release, 1997.

114. Office of National Drug Control Policy, *What America's Users Spend on Illegal Drugs* (Washington, DC: ONDCP, 1991), p. 4.

115. Mark Motivans, *Money Laundering Offenders, 1994–2001* (Washington, DC: Bureau of Justice Statistics, 2003).

116. Public Law 105-310.

117. Motivans, *Money Laundering Offenders,* p. 1.

118. 18 U.S.C. §1957.

119. NNICC, *The NNICC Report, 1998.*

120. Ibid.

121. *Ratzlaf* v. *U.S.,* 114 S.Ct. 655, 126 L.Ed.2d 615 (1994).

122. Public Law 107-56.

123. Motivans, *Money Laundering Offenders,* p. 10.

124. ONDCP, *The National Drug Control Strategy, 2005.*

125. Ibid., p. 33.

126. Ibid., p. 3.

127. James Q. Wilson, "Drugs and Crime," in Michael Tonry and James Q. Wilson, eds., *Drugs and Crime* (Chicago: University of Chicago Press, 1990), p. 522.

128. Drug Enforcement Administration Web log, "DEA Announces Major Takedown of Online Drug Dealers," April 20, 2005. Web posted at http://www.pushingback.com/archives/042005_2.html (accessed July 4, 2005).

129. "20 Arrested in Crackdown on Internet Pharmacies," CNN.com, April 20, 2005. Web posted at http://www.cnn.com/2005/LAW/04/20/internet.drugs.ap (accessed July 4, 2005).

130. 21 U.S.C. §881(a)(6).

131. Michael Goldsmith, *Civil Forfeiture: Tracing the Proceeds of Narcotics Trafficking* (Washington, DC: Police Executive Research Forum, 1988), p. 3.

132. *U.S.* v. *$4,255,625.39 in Currency,* 762 F.2d 895, 904 (1982).

133. Bureau of Justice Assistance, *Asset Forfeiture Bulletin* (October 1988), p. 2.

134. Ibid.

135. Goldsmith, *Civil Forfeiture.*

136. *U.S.* v. *92 Buena Vista Ave.,* 113 S.Ct. 1126, 122 L.Ed.2d 469 (1993).

137. *Austin* v. *U.S.,* 113 S.Ct. 2801, 15 L.Ed.2d 448 (1993).

138. *Alexander* v. *U.S.,* 113 S.Ct. 2766, 125 L.Ed.2d 441 (1993); and *U.S.* v. *James Daniel Good Real Property,* 114 S.Ct. 492, 126 L.Ed.2d 490 (1993).

139. *Bennis* v. *Michigan,* 116 S.Ct. 1560, 134 L.Ed.2d 661 (1996).

140. *U.S.* v. *Ursery,* 116 S.Ct. 2135, 135 L.Ed.2d 549 (1996).

141. Statement by the Honorable Henry J. Hyde, "Civil Asset Forfeiture Reform Act." Web posted at http://www.house.gov/judiciary/161.htm (accessed March 10, 2002).

142. "Drug Raid Called Biggest Ever," Associated Press wire service, September 30, 1989, p. 1A.

143. "Cocaine Found Packed in Toxic Chemical Drums," *Fayetteville (N.C.) Observer-Times,* November 5, 1989.

144. "Raid on Boat in Pacific Seizes 13 Tons of Cocaine," Associated Press, May 15, 2001.

145. Mark Moore, *Drug Trafficking,* NIJ Crime File Study Guide (Washington, DC: National Institute of Justice, 1988), p. 3.

146. Ibid.

147. Ibid.

148. Ibid.

149. In 2003, a California appellate court ruled that Proposition 36 does not apply to inmates in the state's correctional system. See *People* v. *Ponce,* Court of Appeals of California, First Appellate District, Division Five, No. A096707, March 7, 2003.

150. "Governor Signs Final Round of Bills," Kansas Governor's Office, April 21, 2003. Web posted at http://www.ksgovernor.org/news/docs/news_rel042103.html (accessed August 3, 2003).

151. Michael S. Goodstadt, *Drug Education,* NIJ Crime File Study Guide (Washington, DC: National Institute of Justice, no date), p. 1.

152. See Federal Advisory Committee, *Methamphetamine Interagency Task Force: Final Report* (Washington, DC: Office of National Drug Control Policy, 2000), p. 5, from which some of the wording in this paragraph is adapted.

153. "DARE Not Effective in Reducing Drug Abuse, Study Finds," *Criminal Justice Newsletter,* October 3, 1994, pp. 6–7.

154. The government version of the study was first reported as *The DARE Program: A Review of Prevalence, User Satisfaction, and Effectiveness,* NIJ Update (Washington, DC: National Institute of Justice, October 1994). The full study, as published by NIJ, is Christopher L. Ringwalt et al., *Past and Future Directions of the DARE Program: An Evaluation Review* (Washington, DC: National Institute of Justice, 1995).

155. Fox Butterfield, no headline, *New York Times* wire service, April 16, 1997, citing Office of Justice Programs, *Preventing Crime: What Works, What Doesn't, What's Promising* (Washington, DC: U.S. Department of Justice, 1997).

156. Donald R. Lynam et al., "Project DARE: No Effects at 10-Year Follow-Up," *Journal of Consulting and Clinical Psychology,* Vol. 67, No. 4 (1999).

157. Goodstadt, *Drug Education,* p. 3.

158. *USA Today,* September 6, 1990, p. 8A, citing a report by the U.S. Senate Judiciary Committee.

159. Ibid.

160. RAND Corporation, *Drug Policy Research Center: Are Mandatory Minimum Drug Sentences Cost-Effective?* (Santa Monica, CA: RAND, 1997).

161. John S. Goldkamp and Doris Weiland, *Assessing the Impact of Dade County's Felony Drug Court,* NIJ Research in Brief (Washington, DC: National Institute of Justice, December 1993).

162. National Association of Drug Court Professionals, *Facts on Drug Courts.* Web posted at http://www.nadcp.org/whatis/facts.html (accessed July 10, 2005).

163. ONDCP, *The National Drug Control Strategy, 2005,* p. 37.

164. Ibid.

165. Ross Deck, "A New Way of Looking at the Drug War," in *Enhancing Capacities and Confronting Controversies in Criminal Justice—Proceedings of the 1993 National Conference of the Bureau of Justice Statistics and the Justice Research and Statistics Association* (Washington, DC: Bureau of Justice Statistics, 1994), p. 12.

166. Peter D. Hart Research Associates, *Drugs and Crime Across America,* p. 5.

167. Paul H. Blachy, "Effects of Decriminalization of Marijuana in Oregon," *Annals of the New York Academy of Sciences,* Vol. 282 (1976), pp. 405–415. For more information on the decriminalization of marijuana, see James A. Inciardi, "Marijuana Decriminalization Research: A Perspective and Commentary," *Criminology,* Vol. 19, No. 1 (May 1981), pp. 145–159.

168. Arnold S. Trebach, "Thinking through Models of Drug Legalization," *Drug Policy Letter* (July/August 1994), p. 10.

169. For a more thorough discussion of some of these arguments, see Ronald Hamowy, ed., *Dealing with Drugs: Consequences of Government Control* (Lexington, MA: Lexington Books, 1987).

170. See Kurt Schmoke, "Decriminalizing Drugs: It Just Might Work," *Washington Post,* May 15, 1988.

171. "Should Drugs Be Legal?" *Newsweek,* May 30, 1988, p. 36.

172. Ibid., p. 37.

173. Ibid., pp. 37–38.

174. Trebach, "Thinking through Models of Drug Legalization," p. 10.

175. For a more detailed discussion of the two-market system, see John Kaplan, *Heroin,* NIJ Crime File Study Guide (Washington, DC: National Institute of Justice, no date).

176. Ibid., p. 3.

177. Ibid., p. 4.

# CHAPTER 17

# Terrorism and Multinational Criminal Justice

## OUTLINE

- Introduction
- Islamic Criminal Justice
- International Criminal Justice Organizations
- Transnational Crime
- Terrorism

## LEARNING OBJECTIVES

After reading this chapter, you should be able to:

- Describe the nature of comparative criminal justice, and identify the potential benefits of, and problems inherent in, cross-cultural comparisons of crime.
- Describe the principles that inform Islamic law.
- Identify important international criminal justice organizations, and explain their role in fighting international crime.
- Explain transnational crime, and explicate its possible relationship to terrorism.
- Define *terrorism,* and identify two major types of terrorism.
- Discuss the causes of terrorism and the U.S. government's attempts to prevent and control the spread of terrorism.
- Explain why terrorism is a law enforcement concern and how it is a form of criminal activity.

*America's response to globalization in the criminal justice arena will necessitate major changes in both law and policy, placing greater emphasis on the education and training of practitioners at all levels of government. In addition to culture and language, tomorrow's criminal justice practitioner must have a broader understanding of the legal systems of other countries and respect for the customs and practices of immigrants, as well as an increasing number of international visitors.*

—Richard H. Ward, Dean and Director, Criminal Justice Center, Sam Houston State University[1]

## KEY CONCEPTS

### TERMS

comparative criminologist
cyberterrorism
domestic terrorism
ethnocentric
European Police Office (Europol)
extradition

foreign terrorist organization (FTO)
globalization
*Hudud* crime
infrastructure
International Criminal Police Organization
   (INTERPOL)

international terrorism
Islamic law
narcoterrorism
*Tazir* crime
terrorism
transnational crime

# Introduction

Hear the author discuss
this chapter at
**cjtoday.com**

In 2005, 70-year-old British businessman and suspected international arms dealer Hemant Lakhani was found guilty of terrorism-related crimes and sentenced to 47 years in prison for attempting to sell 50 shoulder-fired antiaircraft missiles to undercover officers during an FBI sting operation in Newark, New Jersey.[3] Lakhani, a British citizen born in India, had tried to sell missiles known as MANPADS (Man Portable Air Defense Systems) to federal agents posing as well-heeled terrorists. The undercover officers told Lakhani they wanted to use the missiles to shoot down commercial aircraft. Also arrested in the operation were Moinuddeen Ahmed Hameed, a Malaysian resident, and Yehuda Abraham, 76, of New York City. Hameed and Abraham were charged with conspiring to operate a money-laundering operation in support of the missile sales. The Russian-made MANPADS, which are about the size of a golf bag and weigh between 35 and 70 pounds, have been a source of continuing concern for law enforcement and security officials. The 18-month investigation that resulted in Lakhani's arrest and ultimate conviction was conducted jointly by agents from the FBI's Joint Terrorism Task Force, Britain's MI-5 and MI-6 intelligence agencies, and Russia's Federal Security Service (FSB), and proved to be an exemplary instance of international police cooperation.

Criminologists who study crime and criminal justice on a cross-national level are referred to as **comparative criminologists**, and their field is called *comparative criminal justice, comparative criminology,* or *cross-national criminal justice.* Comparative criminal justice is becoming increasingly valued for the insights it provides. By contrasting native institutions of justice with similar institutions in other countries, procedures and problems in one system can be reevaluated in the light of world experience. As technological advances effectively "shrink" the world, we are able to learn firsthand about the criminal justice systems of other countries and to use that information to improve our own.

This chapter explains the value of comparative criminal justice, points to the problems that arise in comparing data from different nations, and explains international terrorism within the context of cross-national crime. By way of example, this chapter also briefly examines criminal justice systems based on Islamic principles. International police agencies are described, and the role of the United Nations in the worldwide fight against crime and terror is discussed. Additional information on the justice systems of many countries can be found in the *World Factbook of Criminal Justice Systems,* available via **Library Extra 17–1** at cjtoday.com. Another place to visit for international criminal justice information is the National Institute of Justice's International Center, which is accessible via **Web Extra 17–1** at cjtoday.com.

**comparative
criminologist**

One who studies crime and
criminal justice on a cross-
national level.

# Ethnocentrism and the Study of Criminal Justice

**ethnocentric**

Holding a belief in the
superiority of one's own social
or ethnic group and culture.

The study of criminal justice in the United States has been largely **ethnocentric**. Because people are socialized from birth into a particular culture, they tend to prefer their own culture's way of doing things over that of any other. Native patterns of behavior are seen as somehow "natural" and therefore better than foreign ones. The same is true for values, beliefs, and customs. People tend to think that their religion holds a spiritual edge over other religions, that their values and ethical sense are superior to those of others, and that the fashions they wear, the language they speak, and the rituals of daily life in which they participate are somehow better than comparable practices elsewhere. Ethnocentric individuals do not consider that people elsewhere in the world cling to their own values, beliefs, and standards of behavior with just as much fervor as they do.

Only in recent years have American students of criminal justice begun to examine the justice systems of other cultures. Unfortunately, not all societies are equally open, and it is not always easy to explore them. In some societies, even the *study* of criminal justice is taboo. As a result, data-gathering strategies taken for granted in Western culture may not be well received elsewhere. One author, for example, has observed that in China, "the seeking of criminal justice information through face-to-face questioning takes on a different meaning in Chinese officialdom than it does generally in the Western world. While we accept this method of inquiry because we prize thinking on our feet and quick answers, it is rather offensive in China because it shows lack of respect and appreciation for the information given through the preferred means of prepared questions and formal briefings."[4] Hence most of the information available about Chinese criminal justice comes by way of bureaucracy, and routine Western social science practices like door-to-door interviews, participant observation, and random surveys would produce substantial problems for researchers who attempt to use these techniques in China.

# Problems with Data

Similar difficulties arise in the comparison of crime rates from one country to another. The crime rates of different nations are difficult to compare because of (1) differences in the way a specific crime is defined, (2) diverse crime-reporting practices, and (3) political and other influences on the reporting of statistics to international agencies.[5]

Definitional differences create what may be the biggest problem. For cross-national comparisons of crime data to be meaningful, it is essential that the reported data share conceptual similarities. Unfortunately, that is rarely the case. Nations report offenses according to the legal criteria by which arrests are made and under which prosecution can occur. Switzerland, for example, includes bicycle thefts in its reported data on what we call "auto theft" because Swiss data gathering focuses more on the concept of personal transportation than it does on the type of vehicle stolen. The Netherlands has no crime category for robberies, counting them as thefts. Japan classifies an assault that results in death as an assault or an aggravated assault, not as a homicide. Greek rape statistics include crimes of sodomy, "lewdness," seduction of a child, incest, and prostitution. China reports only robberies and thefts that involve the property of citizens; crimes against state-owned property fall into a separate category.

Social, cultural, and economic differences among countries compound these difficulties. Auto theft statistics, for example, when compared between countries like the United States and China, need to be placed in an economic as well as demographic context. While the United States has two automobiles for every three people, China has only one car per every 100 of its citizens. For the Chinese auto theft rate to equal that of the United States, every automobile in the country would have to be stolen nearly twice each year!

Reporting practices vary substantially between nations. The International Criminal Police Organization (INTERPOL) and the United Nations (UN) are the only international organizations that regularly collect crime statistics from a large number of countries.[6] Both agencies can only request data and have no way of checking on the accuracy of the data reported to them. Many countries do not disclose the requested information, and those that do often make only partial reports. In general, small countries are more likely to report than are large ones, and nonsocialist countries are more likely to report than are socialist nations.[7]

International reports of crime are often delayed. Complete, up-to-date data are rare since the information made available to agencies like the United Nations (UN) and INTERPOL is reported at different times and according to schedules that vary from nation to nation. In addition, official United Nations world crime surveys are conducted infrequently. To date, only eight such surveys have been undertaken.[8]

Crime statistics also reflect political biases and national values. Some nations do not accurately admit to the frequency of certain kinds of culturally reprehensible crimes. Communist countries, for example, appear loathe to report crimes like theft, burglary, and robbery because the very existence of such offenses demonstrates felt inequities within the Communist system. After the breakup of the Soviet Union, Alexander Larin, a criminal justice scholar who worked as a Russian investigator during the 1950s and 1960s, revealed that "inside the state security bureaucracy, where statistics were collected and circulated, falsification of crime figures was the rule, not the exception. The practice was self-perpetuating," said Larin. "Supervisors in the provinces were under pressure to provide Moscow with declining crime rates. And no self-respecting investigator wanted to look worse than

An Iraqi man holds a picture of top Shiite cleric Ayatollah Ali Sistani during a protest favoring an Islamic constitution. The traditions and legal systems of many Middle Eastern countries are strongly influenced by Islamic law, which is based on the teachings of the Koran and the sayings of the Prophet Muhammad.

*AP Wide World Photos*

It may be only a matter of time before al-Qaeda or other groups attempt to use chemical, biological, radiological or nuclear weapons. We must focus on that.

—CIA Director Porter Goss[i]

WEB **EXTRA**

LIBRARY **EXTRA**

The Chinese Justice System

his neighbor. . . . From the top to the bottom, the bosses depended on their employees not to make them look bad with high crime statistics."[9]

On the other hand, observers in democratic societies showed similar biases in their interpretation of statistics following the end of the cold war. Some Western analysts, for example, reporting on declines in the prison populations of Eastern and Central Europe during that period, attributed the decline to lessened frustration and lowered crime rates brought about by democratization. In one country, Hungary, prison populations declined from 240 inmates per 100,000 residents in 1986 to 130 per 100,000 in 1993, with similar decreases in other nations.[10] The more likely explanation, however, is the wholesale post-Soviet release of political dissidents from prisons formerly run by Communist regimes. Learn more about world crime via the United Nations *Global Report on Crime and Justice,* which is available via **Library Extra 17–2** at cjtoday.com. View data from the Eighth United Nations Survey on Crime Trends at **Web Extra 17–2**, and read some detailed cross-national studies in crime and justice at **Library Extra 17–3**.

# Islamic Criminal Justice

Islamic law has been the subject of much discussion in the United States since the September 11, 2001, terrorist attacks on the World Trade Center and the Pentagon. It is important for American students of criminal justice to recognize, however, that Islamic law refers to legal ideas (and sometimes entire legal systems) based on the teachings of Islam—and that it bears no intrinsic relationship to acts of terrorism committed by misguided zealots with Islamic backgrounds. Similarly, Islamic law is by no means the same thing as *jihad* (Muslim holy war) or Islamic fundamentalism. Although Americans are now much better informed about the concept of Islamic law than they were in the past, some may not be aware that various interpretations of Islam still form the basis of laws in many countries and that the entire legal systems of some nations are based on Islamic principles. Islamic law holds considerable sway in a large number of countries, including Syria, Iran, Iraq (where a new constitution is being voted on as this book goes to press), Pakistan, Afghanistan, Yemen, Saudi Arabia, Kuwait, the United Arab Emirates, Bahrain, Algeria, Jordan, Lebanon, Libya, Ethiopia, Gambia, Nigeria, Oman, Qatar, Senegal, Tunisia, Tajikistan, Uzbekistan, and Turkey (which practices official separation of church and state).

Islamic law descends directly from the teachings of the Prophet Muhammad, whom the *Cambridge Encyclopedia of Islam* describes as a "prophet-lawyer."[11] Muhammad rose to fame in the city of Mecca (in what is now Saudi Arabia) as a religious reformer. Later, however, he traveled to Medina, where he became the ruler and lawgiver of a newly formed religious society. In his role as lawgiver, Muhammad enacted legislation whose aim was to teach men what to do and how to behave in order to achieve salvation. As a consequence, Islamic law today is a system of duties and rituals founded on legal and moral obligations—all of which are ultimately sanctioned by the authority of a religious leader (or leaders) who may issue commands (known as *fatwas* or *fatwahs*) that the faithful are bound to obey.

Criminal justice professor Sam Souryal and his coauthors describe four aspects of justice in Arab philosophy and religion. Islamic justice, they say, means the following[12]:

- A sacred trust, a duty imposed on humans to be discharged sincerely and honestly. As such, these authors say, "justice is the quality of being morally responsible and merciful in giving everyone his or her due."

- A mutual respect of one human being by another. From this perspective, a just society is one that offers equal respect for individuals through social arrangements made in the common interest of all members.

- An aspect of the social bond that holds society together and transforms it into a brotherhood in which everyone becomes a keeper of everyone else and each is held accountable for the welfare of all.

- A command from God. Whosoever violates God's commands should be subject to strict punishments according to Islamic tradition and belief.

As Souryal and his coauthors observe, "The third and fourth meanings of justice are probably the ones most commonly invoked in Islamic jurisprudence" and form the basis of criminal justice practice in many Middle Eastern countries.

# The *Hudud* Crimes

**Islamic law** (or *Shari'ah* in Arabic, which means "path of God") forms the basis of theocratic judicial systems in Kuwait, Saudi Arabia, the Sudan, Iran, and Algeria. Other Arabic nations, such as Egypt, Jordan, and Iraq, recognize substantial elements of Islamic law in their criminal justice systems but also make wide use of Western and nontheocratic legal principles. Islamic law is based on four sources. In order of importance, these sources are (1) the Koran (also spelled *Quran* and *Qur'an*), or Holy Book of Islam, which Muslims believe is the word of God, or Allah; (2) the teachings of the Prophet Muhammad; (3) a consensus of the clergy in cases where neither the Koran nor the prophet directly addresses an issue; and (4) reason or logic, which should be used when no solution can be found in the other three sources.[13]

Islamic law recognizes seven **Hudud** crimes—or crimes based on religious strictures. *Hudud* (sometimes called *Hodood* or *Huddud*) crimes are essentially violations of "natural law" as interpreted by Arab culture. Divine displeasure is thought to be the basis of crimes defined as *Hudud,* and *Hudud* crimes are often said to be crimes against God (or, more specifically, God's rights). The Koran specifies punishments for four of the seven *Hudud* crimes: (1) making war on Allah and His messengers, (2) theft, (3) adultery or fornication, and (4) false accusation of fornication or adultery. The three other *Hudud* offenses are mentioned by the Koran, but no punishment is specified: (1) "corruption on earth," (2) drinking alcohol, and (3) highway robbery—and the punishments for these crimes are determined by tradition.[14] The *Hudud* offenses and associated typical punishments are shown in Table 17–1. "Corruption on earth" is a general category of religious offense, not well understood in the West, which includes activities like embezzlement, revolution against lawful authority, fraud, and "weakening the society of God." In 2004, for example, Mehdi Hassan, a 36-year-old Pakistani was sentenced to life in prison by a court in Lahore for burning a copy of the Koran. Hassan was convicted and sentenced under Pakistan's laws covering offenses against Islam.[15]

Islamic law mandates strict punishment of moral failure. Sexual offenders, even those who engage in what would be considered essentially victimless crimes in Western societies, are subject to especially harsh treatment. The Islamic penalty for sexual intercourse outside of marriage, for example, is 100 lashes. Men are stripped to the waist, women have their clothes bound tightly, and flogging is carried out with a leather whip. Adultery carries a much more severe penalty: flogging and stoning to death.

**Islamic law**

A system of laws, operative in some Arab countries, based on the Muslim religion and especially the holy book of Islam, the Koran.

**Hudud crime**

A serious violation of Islamic law that is regarded as an offense against God. *Hudud* crimes include such behavior as theft, adultery, sodomy, alcohol consumption, and robbery.

With criminals' ability to cross international borders in a few hours, and the advances of our modern age, such as the Internet and telecommunications, crime can no longer be viewed as just a national issue.

—Assistant U.S. Attorney General Laurie Robinson

## CRIME AND PUNISHMENT IN ISLAMIC LAW: THE IRANIAN EXAMPLE

Islamic law looks to the Koran and to the teachings of the Prophet Muhammad to determine which acts should be classified as crimes. The Koran and tradition specify punishments to be applied to designated offenses, as the following verse from the Koran demonstrates: "The only reward of those who make war upon Allah and His messenger and strive after corruption in the land will be that they will be killed or crucified, or have their hands and feet on alternate sides cut off, or will be expelled out of the land" (*Surah* V, Verse 33). Other crimes and punishments include the following:

| Offense | Punishment |
| --- | --- |
| Theft | Amputation of the hand |
| Adultery | Stoning to death |
| Fornication | One hundred lashes |
| False accusation (of fornication or adultery) | Eighty lashes |
| Corruption on earth | Death by the sword or by burning |
| Drinking alcohol | Eighty lashes; death if repeated three times |
| Robbery | Cutting off of hands and feet on alternate sides, exile, or execution |

*Note:* For more information, see Sam S. Souryal, Dennis W. Potts, and Abdullah I. Alobied, "The Penalty of Hand Amputation for Theft in Islamic Justice," *Journal of Criminal Justice,* Vol. 22, No. 3 (1994), pp. 249–265; and Parviz Saney, "Iran," in Elmer H. Johnson, ed., *International Handbook of Contemporary Developments in Criminology* (Westport, CT: Greenwood Press, 1983), pp. 356–369.

Under Islamic law, even property crimes are firmly punished. Thieves who are undeterred by less serious punishments may eventually suffer amputation of the right hand. In a reputedly humane move, Iranian officials recently began the use of an electric guillotine, specially made for the purpose, which can sever a hand at the wrist in one-tenth of a second. For amputation to be imposed, the item stolen must have value in Islam. Pork and alcohol, for example, are regarded as being without value, and their theft is not subject to punishment. Islamic legal codes also establish a minimum value for stolen items that could result in a sentence of amputation. Likewise, offenders who have stolen because they are hungry or are in need are exempt from the punishment of amputation and receive fines or prison terms.

Slander and the consumption of alcohol are both punished by 80 lashes. Legal codes in strict Islamic nations also specify whipping for the crimes of pimping, lesbianism, kissing by an unmarried couple, cursing, and failure of a woman to wear a veil. Islamic law provides for the execution, sometimes through crucifixion, of robbers. Laws stipulate that anyone who survives three days on the cross may be spared. Depending on the circumstances of the robbery, however, the offender may suffer the amputation of opposite hands and feet or may be exiled.

Rebellion, or revolt against a legitimate political leader or established economic order, which is considered an aspect of "corruption on earth," is punishable by death. The offender may be killed outright in a military or police action or, later, by sentence of the court. The last of the *Hudud* crimes is rejection of Islam. The penalty, once again, is death and can be imposed for denying the existence of God or angels, denying any of the prophets of Islam, or rejecting any part of the Koran.

Souryal and coauthors observe that *Hudud* crimes can be severely punished because "punishment serves a three-tiered obligation: (1) the fulfillment of worship, (2) the purification of society, and (3) the redemption of the individual." However, they add, the interests of the individual are the least valuable component of this triad and may have to be sacrificed "for the wholesomeness and integrity of the encompassing justice system."[16]

**Tazir crime**

A minor violation of Islamic law that is regarded as an offense against society, not God.

# The *Tazir* Crimes

All crimes other than *Hudud* crimes fall into an offense category called *tazirat*. **Tazir crimes** are regarded as any actions not considered acceptable in a spiritual society. They include crimes against society and against individuals, but not against God. *Tazir* crimes may call for *quesas* (retribution) or *diya* (compensation or fines). Crimes requiring *quesas* are based on the Arabic principle of "an eye for an eye," and generally require physical punishments up to and including death. *Quesas* offenses may include murder, manslaughter, assault, and maiming. Under Islamic law, such crimes may require the victim or his representative to serve as prosecutor. The state plays a role only in providing the forum for the trial and in imposing punishment. Sometimes victims' representatives dole out punishment. In 1997, for example, 28-year-old taxi driver Ali Reza Khoshruy, nicknamed "The Vampire" because he stalked, raped, and killed women at night after picking them up in his cab, was hung from a yellow crane in the middle of Tehran, the Iranian capital.[17] Before the hanging, prison officials and male relatives of the victims cursed Khoshruy and whipped him with thick leather belts as he lay tied to a metal bed. The whipping was part of a 214-lash sentence.

## Islamic Courts

Islamic courts typically exist on three levels.[18] The first level hears cases involving the potential for serious punishments, including death, amputation, and exile. The second level deals with relatively minor matters, such as traffic offenses and violations of city ordinances. Special courts, especially in Iran, may hear cases involving crimes against the government, narcotics offenses, state security, and corruption. Appeals within the Islamic court system are only possible under rare circumstances and are by no means routine. A decision rendered by second-level courts will generally stand without intervention by higher judicial authorities.

Under Islamic law, men and women are treated very differently. Testimony provided by a man, for example, can be heard in court. The same evidence, however, can only be provided by two virtuous women; one female witness is not sufficient.

While Islamic law may seem archaic or even barbaric to many Westerners, Islamic officials defend their system by pointing to low crime rates at home and by pointing to what they consider near anarchy in Western nations. An early criticism of Islamic law was offered by Max Weber at the start of the twentieth century.[19] Weber said that Islamic justice is based more on the moral conceptions of individual judges than on any rational and predictable code of laws. He found that the personality of each judge, what he called "charisma," was more important in reaching a final legal result than was the written law. Weber's conclusion was that a modern society could not develop under Islamic law because enforcement of the law was too unpredictable. Complex social organizations, he argued, could only be based on a rational and codified law that is relatively unchanging from place to place and over time.[20]

More recent observers have agreed that "Islamic justice is based on philosophical principles that are considered alien, if not unconscionable, to the Western observer." However, these same writers note, strict punishments such as hand amputation "may not be inconsistent with the fundamentals of natural law or Judeo-Christian doctrine. The imposition of the penalty in specific cases and under rigorous rules of evidence—as the principle requires—may be indeed justifiable, and even necessary, in the Islamic context of sustaining a spiritual . . . society."[21]

# International Criminal Justice Organizations

The first international conference on criminology and criminal justice met in London in 1872.[22] It evolved out of emerging humanitarian concerns about the treatment of prisoners. Human rights, the elimination of corporal punishment, and debates over capital punishment occupied the conference participants. Although other meetings were held from time to time, little agreement could be reached among the international community on criminal etiology, justice paradigms, or the philosophical and practical bases for criminal punishment and rehabilitation. Finally, in 1938, the International Society for Criminology (ISC) was formed to bring together people from diverse cultural backgrounds who shared an interest in social policies relating to crime and justice. In its early years, membership in the ISC consisted mostly of national officials and academics with close government ties.[23] As a consequence, many of the first conferences (called *international congresses*) sponsored by the ISC strongly supported the status quo and were devoid of any significant recommendations for change or growth.

Throughout the 1960s and 1970s, the ISC was strongly influenced by a growing worldwide awareness of human rights. About the same time, a number of international organizations began

> At the beginning of the third millennium, the criminal phenomenon not only does not care about borders, but it also participates in globalization.
>
> —Andre Bossard, former Secretary General of INTERPOL[ii]

to press for an understanding of the political and legal processes through which deviance and crime come to be defined. Among them were the Scandinavian Research Council for Criminology (formed in 1962), the Criminological Research Council (created in 1962 by the Council of Europe), and other regional associations concerned with justice issues.

A number of contemporary organizations and publications continue to focus world attention on criminal justice issues. Perhaps the best-known modern center for the academic study of cross-national criminal justice is the International Center of Comparative Criminology at the University of Montreal. Established in 1969, the center serves as a locus of study for criminal justice professionals from around the world and maintains an excellent library of international criminal justice information. The International Police Executive Symposium (IPES) was founded in 1994 to bring international police researchers and practitioners together and to facilitate cross-cultural and international exchanges between criminal justice experts around the world. IPES, which is associated with the Human Rights and Law Enforcement Institute (HRALEI) at the State University of New York at Plattsburg, publishes *Police Practice and Research: An International Journal.* The Office of International Criminal Justice (OICJ), with offices in Illinois, Indiana, and Texas, has also become a well-known contributor to the study of comparative criminal justice. In conjunction with Sam Houston State University's Criminal Justice Center (in Huntsville, Texas), OICJ publishes the magazine *Crime and Justice International* and sponsors study tours of various nations. Visit OICJ via Web Extra 17–3 at cjtoday.com.

In 1995, Mitre Corporation in McLean, Virginia, began an Internet service that provides information about the United Nations Crime Prevention Branch. The United Nations Crime and Justice Information Network (UNCJIN) holds much promise as an online provider of international criminal justice information. Visit UNCJIN via Web Extra 17–4 at cjtoday.com. Similarly, the World Justice Information Network (WJIN), sponsored by the National Institute of Justice and the U.S. Department of State, provides a members-only forum for the discussion of justice issues around the globe. Apply for membership in WJIN via Web Extra 17–5 at cjtoday.com. Finally, the United Nations Center for International Crime Prevention, in conjunction with the World Society of Victimology, sponsors the International Victimology website, available via Web Extra 17–6 at cjtoday.com.

## The Role of the United Nations in Criminal Justice

The United Nations, composed of 185 member states and based in New York City, is the largest and most inclusive international body in the world. From its inception in 1945, the United Nations has been very interested in international crime prevention and world criminal justice systems. A UN resolution entitled the International Bill of Human Rights supports the rights and dignity of everyone who comes into contact with a criminal justice system.

One of the best-known specific UN recommendations on criminal justice is its Standard Minimum Rules for the Treatment of Prisoners. The rules call for the fair treatment of prisoners, including recognition of the basic humanity of all inmates, and set specific standards for housing, nutrition, exercise, and medical care. Follow-up surveys conducted by the United Nations have shown that the rules have had a considerable influence on national legislation and prison regulations throughout the world.[24] Although the rules do not have the weight of law unless adopted and enacted into local legislation, they carry the strong weight of tradition, and at least one expert claims that "there are indeed those who argue that the rules have entered the *corpus* of generally customary human rights law, or that they are binding . . . as an authoritative interpretation of the human rights provisions of the UN charter."[25]

A more recent and potentially significant set of recommendations can be found in the UN Code of Conduct for Law Enforcement Officials. The code calls on law enforcement officers throughout the world to be cognizant of human rights in the performance of their duties. It specifically proscribes the use of torture and other abuses.

The UN World Crime Surveys, which report official crime statistics from nearly 100 countries, provide a global portrait of criminal activity. Seen historically, the surveys have shown that crimes against property are most characteristic of nations with developed economies (where they constitute approximately 82% of all reported crime), while crimes against the person occur much more frequently in developing countries (where they account for 43% of all crime).[26] Complementing the official statistics of the World Crime Surveys are data from the International Victim Survey (IVS), which is conducted in approximately 50 countries. To date, three surveys have been conducted—in 1989, 1992, and 1996–1997.

Through its Office for Drug Control and Crime Prevention (ODCCP), the United Nations continues to advance the cause of crime prevention and to disseminate useful criminal justice information. The program provides forums for ongoing discussions of justice practices around the world. It has regional links throughout the world, sponsored by supportive national governments that have agreed to fund the program's work. The European Institute for Crime Prevention and Control (HEUNI), for example, provides the program's regional European link in a network of institutes operating throughout the world. Other network components include the UN Interregional Crime and Justice Research Institute (UNICRI) in Rome; an Asian regional institute (UNAFEI) in Tokyo; ILANUE, based in San Jose, Costa Rica, which focuses on crime problems in Latin America and the Caribbean; an African institute (UNAFRI) in Kampala, Uganda; Australia's AIC in Canberra; an Arabic institute (ASSTC) in Riyadh, Saudi Arabia; and other centers in Siracusa, Italy, and in Vancouver and Montreal, Canada.[27] Visit the United Nations Office for Drug Control and Crime Prevention via Web Extra 17–7 at cjtoday.com.

In 1995, the United States signed an agreement with the United Nations Crime Prevention and Criminal Justice Branch that is intended to facilitate the international sharing of information and research findings.[28] Under the agreement, the National Institute of Justice joined 11 other criminal justice research organizations throughout the world as an associate UN institute.

Continuing a tradition begun in 1885 by the former International Penal and Penitentiary Commission, the United Nations holds an international congress on crime every five years. The first UN crime congress, the 1955 Congress on the Prevention of Crime and the Treatment of Offenders met in Geneva, Switzerland. Crime congresses provide a forum through which member states can exchange information and experiences, compare criminal justice practices between countries, find solutions to crime, and take action at an international level. The Tenth United Nations crime congress was held in Vienna, Austria, in 2000. Topics discussed at the meeting included (1) promoting the rule of law and strengthening the criminal justice systems of various nations, (2) the need for international cooperation in combating transnational crime, and (3) the need for a fair, ethical, and effective system of criminal justice in the promotion of economic and social development. CJ Today Exhibit 17–1 in this chapter contains the UN declaration on criminal justice that resulted from the Vienna meeting.

The meeting also led to passage of the 2000 United Nations Protocol to Prevent, Suppress and Punish Trafficking in Persons, Especially Women and Children, which supplements the United Nations Convention against Transnational Organized Crime.[29] Nations that are parties to the protocol must criminalize the offense of human trafficking, prevent trafficking, protect and assist victims of trafficking, and promote international cooperation to combat the problem of trafficking.[30] Learn more about the crime of human trafficking via the Protection Project at Web Extra 17–8 at cjtoday.com, and read the U.S. Department of State's 2003 *Trafficking in Persons Report* at Library Extra 17–4.

Young girls working in a brothel in Thailand. Human trafficking is common in some parts of the third world and even impacts developed countries such as our own. The 2003 federal Trafficking Victims Protection Reauthorization Act focuses on the illegal practice of sex trafficking and on the illegal "obtaining of a person for labor services."

© Way Gary, Corbis Sygma

## Vienna Declaration on Crime and Justice

We the Member States of the United Nations,

Concerned about the impact on our societies of the commission of serious crimes of a global nature and convinced of the need for bilateral, regional and international cooperation in crime prevention and criminal justice,

Concerned in particular about transnational organized crime and the relationships between its various forms,

Convinced that adequate prevention and rehabilitation programmes are fundamental to an effective crime control strategy, and that such programmes should take into account social and economic factors which may make people more vulnerable to, and likely to engage in criminal behaviour,

Stressing that a fair, responsible, ethical and efficient criminal justice system is an important factor in the promotion of economic and social development and of security,

Aware of the promise of restorative approaches to justice that aim to reduce and promote the healing of victims, offenders and communities,

Having assembled at the Tenth United Nations Congress on the Prevention of Crime and the Treatment of Offenders in Vienna from 10 to 17 April 2000 to decide to take effective concerted action, in a spirit of cooperation, to combat the world crime problem,

Declare as follows:

- We emphasize the responsibility of each State to establish and maintain a fair, responsible, ethical and efficient criminal justice system.
- We recognize the necessity of closer coordination and cooperation among States in combating the world crime problem, bearing in mind that action against it is a common and shared responsibility. . . .
- We undertake to strengthen international cooperation in order to create a conducive environment for the fight against organized crime, promoting growth and sustainable development and eradicating poverty and unemployment.
- We also commit ourselves to the development of action-oriented policy recommendations based on the special needs of women as criminal justice practitioners, victims, prisoners and offenders.
- We commit ourselves to the development of more effective ways of collaborating with one another with a view to eradicating the scourge of trafficking in persons, especially women and children, and the smuggling of migrants. . . .
- We also commit ourselves to the enhancement of international cooperation and mutual legal assistance to curb illicit manufacturing of and trafficking in firearms, their parts and components and ammunition, and we establish 2005 as the target year for achieving a significant decrease in their incidence worldwide.
- We reaffirm that combating money-laundering and the criminal economy constitutes a major element of the strategies against organized crime. . . .

- We decide to develop action-oriented policy recommendations on the prevention and control of computer-related crime. . . . We also commit ourselves to working towards enhancing our ability to prevent, investigate and prosecute high-technology and computer-related crime.
- We note that acts of violence and terrorism continue to be of grave concern. In conformity with the Charter of the United Nations and taking into account all the relevant General Assembly resolutions, we will together, in conjunction with our other efforts to prevent and to combat terrorism, take effective, resolute and speedy measures with respect to preventing and combating criminal activities carried out for the purpose of furthering terrorism in all its forms and manifestations. . . .
- We also note that racial discrimination, xenophobia and related forms of intolerance continue and we recognize the importance of taking steps to incorporate into international crime prevention strategies and norms measures to prevent and combat crime associated with racism, racial discrimination, xenophobia and related forms of intolerance.
- We affirm our determination to combat violence stemming from intolerance on the basis of ethnicity and resolve to make a strong contribution, in the area of crime prevention and criminal justice. . . .
- We also recognize the importance of prison reform, the independence of the judiciary and the prosecution authorities, and the International Code of Conduct for Public Officials. . . .
- We shall endeavour, as appropriate, to use and apply the United Nations standards and norms in crime prevention and criminal justice in national law and practice. . . .
- We further recognize with great concern that juveniles in difficult circumstances are often at risk of becoming delinquent or easy candidates for recruitment by criminal groups, including groups involved in transnational organized crime, and we commit ourselves to undertaking countermeasures to prevent this growing phenomenon. . . .
- We recognize that comprehensive crime prevention strategies at the international, national, regional and local levels must address the root causes and risk factors related to crime and victimization through social, economic, health, educational and justice policies. . . .
- We commit ourselves to according priority to containing the growth and overcrowding of pre-trial and detention prison populations, as appropriate, by promoting safe and effective alternatives to incarceration.
- We decide to introduce, where appropriate, national, regional and international action plans in support of victims of crime, such as mechanisms for mediation and restorative justice. . . .
- We encourage the development of restorative justice policies, procedures and programmes that are respectful of the rights, needs and interests of victims, offenders, communities and all other parties. . . .

*Source:* Excerpted from the Tenth United Nations Congress on the Prevention of Crime and the Treatment of Offenders, *Vienna Declaration on Crime and Justice: Meeting the Challenges of the Twenty-First Century,* Vienna, Austria, April 10–17, 2000.

# INTERPOL and Europol

The **International Criminal Police Organization (INTERPOL)**, headquartered in Lyons, France, traces its origins back to the first International Criminal Police Congress of 1914, which met in Monaco.[31] The theme of that meeting was international cooperation in the investigation of crimes and the apprehension of fugitives. INTERPOL, however, did not officially begin operations until 1946, when the end of World War II brought about a new spirit of international harmony.

Today, 182 nations belong to INTERPOL.[32] The U.S. INTERPOL unit is called the U.S. National Central Bureau (USNCB) and is a separate agency within the U.S. Department of Justice. USNCB is staffed with personnel from 12 federal agencies, including the Drug Enforcement Administration, the Secret Service, and the Federal Bureau of Investigation. Through USNCB, INTERPOL is linked to all major U.S. computerized criminal records repositories, including the FBI's National Crime Information Index, the State Department's Advanced Visa Lookout System, and the Department of Homeland Security's Master Index.

INTERPOL's primary purpose is to act as a clearinghouse for information on offenses and suspects who are believed to operate across national boundaries. The organization is committed to promoting "the widest possible mutual assistance between all criminal police authorities within the limits of laws existing in . . . different countries and in the spirit of the Universal Declaration of Human Rights."[33] Historically, INTERPOL pledged itself not to intervene in religious, political, military, or racial disagreements in participant nations. As a consequence, a number of bombings and hostage situations that were related to these types of disagreements were not officially investigated until 1984, when INTERPOL officially entered the fight against international terrorism.

In late 2001, INTERPOL's Seventieth General Assembly unanimously adopted the Budapest Anti-Terrorism Resolution. The resolution calls for greater police cooperation in fighting international terrorism. In 2005, delegates attending INTERPOL's first Global Conference on Preventing Bio-Terrorism met in Lyon, France, and agreed on a series of measures aimed at preventing or effectively responding to bio-terror attacks.[34] As this book goes to press, INTERPOL continues to expand its activities, and is in the process of developing a centralized international forensic DNA database and is creating an international framework for disaster victim identification.[35]

INTERPOL does not have its own field investigators. The agency has no powers of arrest or of search and seizure in member countries. Instead, INTERPOL's purpose is to facilitate, coordinate, and encourage police cooperation as a means of combating international crime. It draws on the willingness of local and national police forces to lend support to its activities. The headquarters staff of INTERPOL consists of around 250 individuals, many with prior police experience, who direct data-gathering efforts around the world and who serve to alert law enforcement organizations to the movement of suspected offenders within their jurisdiction. Visit INTERPOL headquarters via Web Extra 17–9, and read the organization's latest annual activity report at Library Extra 17–5 at cjtoday.com.

The members of the European Union agreed to the establishment of the **European Police Office (Europol)** in the Maastricht Treaty of February 7, 1992. Based in The Hague, the Netherlands, Europol started limited operations in 1994 in the form of the Europol Drugs Unit. Over time, other important law enforcement activities were added to the Europol agenda. The Europol Convention was ratified by all member states in 1998, and Europol commenced full operations the next year. Europol's mission is to improve the effectiveness and cooperation of law enforcement agencies within the member states of the European Union (EU) with the ultimate goal of preventing and combating terrorism, illegal drug trafficking, illicit trafficking in radioactive and nuclear substances, illegal money laundering, trafficking in human beings, and other serious forms of international organized crime. Europol is sometimes described as the "European Union (EU) police clearing house."[36] Following the July 2005 London underground and bus bombings, in which more than 50 people died and hundreds were injured, German Interior Minister Otto Schilly asked his European Union counterparts meeting in Brussels to give Europol executive powers to conduct EU-wide investigations.[37]

Europol and INTERPOL are committed to interagency cooperation, and they work with one another in developing information on international terrorism, drug trafficking, and trafficking in human beings.[38] Learn more about Europol via Web Extra 17–10 at cjtoday.com.

## International Criminal Police Organization (INTERPOL)

An international law enforcement support organization that began operations in 1946 and today has 182 members.

## European Police Office (Europol)

The integrated police-intelligence gathering and dissemination arm of the member nations of the European Union.

# The International Criminal Court

Log on to ResearchNavigator .com, and select "criminal justice" from the "Link Library" drop-down menu. Click "Go," and select the "I" category from the next screen. As you will see, items that start with the letter I include "INTERPOL." Click on "INTERPOL," and visit each of the websites that describe the organization. Write down what you learn from your Web-based visits, and submit it to your instructor if asked to do so. *Note:* This feature is available only if your instructor has chosen the Research Navigator option available with a new textbook.

On April 12, 2000, the International Criminal Court (ICC) was created under the auspices of the United Nations. The ICC, whose operations are only now beginning, is intended to be a permanent criminal court for trying individuals (not countries) who commit the most serious crimes of concern to the international community, such as genocide, war crimes, and crimes against humanity—including the wholesale murder of civilians, torture, and mass rape. The ICC intends be a global judicial institution with international jurisdiction complementing national legal systems around the world. Support for the ICC was developed through the United Nations, where more than 90 countries approved the court's creation by ratifying what is known as the Rome Statute of the International Criminal Court. The ICC's first prosecutor, Luis Moreno Ocampo of Argentina, was elected in April 2003.[39]

The ICC initiative began after World War II, with unsuccessful efforts to establish an international tribunal to try individuals accused of genocide and other war crimes.[40] In lieu of such a court, military tribunals were held in Nuremberg, Germany, and Tokyo, Japan, to try those accused of war crimes. The 1948 UN Genocide Convention[41] identified the crimes of (1) genocide, (2) conspiracy to commit genocide, (3) direct and public incitement to commit genocide, (4) attempt to commit genocide, and (5) complicity in genocide, and called for the creation of an international criminal court to punish genocide-related offenses. Efforts to establish a permanent court, however, were delayed for decades by the cold war and by the refusal of some national governments to accept the court's proposed international legal jurisdiction.

In December 1948, the UN General Assembly adopted the Universal Declaration of Human Rights and the Convention on the Prevention and Punishment of the Crime of Genocide. It also called for criminals to be tried "by such international penal tribunals as may have jurisdiction." A number of member states soon asked the United Nation's International Law Commission (ILC) to study the possibility of establishing an ICC.

Development of an ICC was delayed by the cold war that took place between the world's superpowers, who were not willing to subject their military personnel or commanders to international criminal jurisdiction in the event of a "hot" war. In 1981, however, the United Nations General Assembly asked the International Law Commission to consider creation of an international Code of Crimes.

The 1992 War in Bosnia-Herzegovina, which involved clear violations of the Genocide and Geneva Conventions, heightened world interest in the establishment of a permanent ICC. A few years later, 160 countries participated in the Conference of Plenipotentiaries on the Establishment of an International Criminal Court,[42] which was held in Rome. At the end of that conference, member states voted overwhelmingly in favor of the Rome Statute,[43] calling for establishment of an ICC. Effective July 1, 2002, the Rome Statute criminalized trafficking in persons, categorizing it as a crime against humanity.

A few years ago, in what became a stumbling block on the road to the court's creation, the United States expressed concern about the ICC, saying that members of the American military could become subject to ICC jurisdiction. That concern led to U.S. efforts to delay the court's creation. The issue was resolved in 2002 when the United Nations Security Council voted to exempt members of the American military from prosecution by the court's War Crimes Tribunal.[44] The Security Council resolution, however, must be renewed annually if it is to remain in force.[45]

In 2005, in one of the court's first official actions, a panel of ICC judges decided to allow independent Dutch investigators to carry out forensic tests in the Democratic Republic of Congo (DRC) as part of an ongoing investigation into the deaths of thousands of people in genocidal violence throughout central Africa.[46] Learn more about these efforts and other activities of the ICC by visiting the Coalition for an International Criminal Court via Web Extra 17–11 at cjtoday.com.

**WEB EXTRA**

Before the ICC came into existence, Belgium made its courts available to the rest of the world for the prosecution of alleged crimes against humanity.[47] The country's legal system, in essence, took on the role of global prosecutor for these kinds of crimes. Under a 1993 Belgian law, which is regarded by many as the world's most expansive statute against genocide and other crimes against humanity, Belgian justices were called on to enforce substantial portions of the country's criminal laws on a global scale. Belgian courts also focused on enforcing the 1949 Geneva Convention governing the conduct of war and the treatment of refugees. Belgian law specifically provides for the criminal prosecution of individuals who are not Belgian citizens, and it provides no immunity to prosecution for foreign leaders. In 2001, for example, a Brussels jury convicted four people, including two Catholic nuns, of contributing to ethnic violence in the central African nation of Rwanda in 1994.

Belgian authorities have investigated more than a dozen complaints involving current and former state officials, including Ariel Sharon (prime minister of Israel), Saddam Hussein (former Iraqi leader), Hissene Habre (former dictator of Chad), Hashemi Rafsanjani (former president of Iran), Driss Basri (former interior minister of Morocco), Denis Sassou Nguesso (president of Congo-Brazzaville), and Fidel Castro (leader of Cuba). In the case of the Cuban leader, Cuban exiles charged Castro in Brussels's criminal court in October 2001 with false imprisonment, murder, torture, and other crimes against humanity. As a result of such investigations, Belgium has experienced strained relationships with a number of countries, and some in the nation have questioned the wisdom of charging sitting heads of state with violations of the criminal law.

> The effects of globalization have created a growing phenomenon of globalized crime that is threatening the stability and values of the entire world community.
>
> —Daniel Mabrey, Sam Houston State University[iv]

# Transnational Crime

**Transnational crime** and the internationally organized criminal groups that support it promise to be one of the most pressing challenges of the early twenty-first century. In a recent conference in Seoul, Korea, Assistant Attorney General Laurie Robinson addressed the issue of transnational crime, saying, "The United States recognizes that we cannot confront crime in isolation. . . . It is clear crime does not respect international boundaries. It is clear crime is global. As recent economic trends demonstrate, what happens in one part of the world impacts all the rest. And crime problems and trends are no different."[48]

The post–cold war world is more dangerous and less stable than when power was balanced among superpowers. The power vacuum created in many parts of the world by the fall of the Soviet Union and growing instability in the Middle East has led to a number of new threats. According to Robert Gelbard, U.S. assistant secretary for International Narcotics and Law Enforcement Affairs, "The main threat now is transnational organized crime. It comes in many forms: drug trafficking, money laundering, terrorism, alien smuggling, trafficking in weapons of mass destruction, [human trafficking, often involving forced prostitution], fraud and other forms of corruption. These problems all have one critical element in common," says Gelbard. "They threaten the national security of all states and governments—from our closest allies to those that we find most repugnant. No country is safe. International criminal organizations all seek to establish pliant governments that can be manipulated through bribery and intimidation. They respect no national boundaries and already act with virtual impunity in many parts of the world."[49]

Worse still, entire nations may become rogue countries, or quasi-criminal regimes where criminal activity runs rampant and wields considerable influence over the national government. Russia, for example, appears to be approaching this status through an intertwining of the goals of organized criminal groups and official interests that run to the top levels of government. The number of organized criminal groups operating in Russia is estimated to be more than 12,000.[50] Emilio Viano, professor of criminology at American University and an expert on Russian organized crime, notes that "what we have is an immense country practically controlled by organized crime. These groups are getting stronger and stronger and using Russia as a base for their global ventures—taking over everything from drugs and prostitution to currency exchange and stealing World Bank and IMF [International Monetary Fund] loans."[51] In 1999, federal authorities discovered that more than $10 billion had passed through the Bank of New York in a major money-laundering scheme run by Russian organized crime.[52] Much of the money may have come from loans made to Russia by the IMF almost a year earlier.

| transnational crime |
| --- |
| Unlawful activity undertaken and supported by organized criminal groups operating across national boundaries. |

# Globalization and Crime

Transnational crime is partly the result of an ongoing process of globalization. **Globalization** refers to the internationalization of trade, services, investments, information, and other forms of human social activity, including crime. The process of globalization is fed by modern systems of transportation and communication, including air travel, television, and the Internet. Globalization contributes to growing similarities in the way people do things and in the beliefs and values that they hold. The lessening of differences brought about by globalization is highlighted by a definition from one authoritative source, which says that globalization is "a process of social homogenization by which the experiences of everyday life, marked by the diffusion of commodities and ideas, can foster a standardization of cultural expressions around the world."[53] The adoption of English as the *de facto* standard language on the Internet and of

| globalization |
| --- |
| The internationalization of trade, services, investment, information, and other forms of human social activity. |

the global software community, for example, has exposed many around the world to literature and ideas that they might not otherwise have encountered, and has influenced the way they think. Consequently, globalization is opposed in many parts of the world by those who would hold to traditional ways of thinking and doing. Instead of uniting humanity, as some had hoped, globalization has also made people aware of differences—and led many to reject people and ideas not their own.

The first steps toward globalization occurred long before the modern era and were taken by nation-states seeking to expand their spheres of influence. The banner of globalization today is carried by multinational corporations whose operations span the globe. The synergistic effects of rapid travel, instantaneous communication, and national economies that are tied closely to one another have led to an increasingly rapid pace of the globalization process, which some refer to as *hyperglobalization.* Criminal entrepreneurs and terrorists are among those with a global vision, and at least some of them think and plan like the CEOs of multinational businesses. Today's international criminal community consists of terrorists, drug traffickers, pornography peddlers, identity thieves, copyright violators, and those who traffic in human beings, body parts, genetic material, and military weapons. The recent globalization of crime and terrorism, which is sometimes termed the *globalization of insecurity,* has necessitated enhanced coordination of law enforcement efforts in different parts of the world as well as the expansion of American law enforcement activities beyond national borders. In 2003, for example, the U.S. Congress passed the Trafficking Victims Protection Reauthorization Act[54] (TVPA) to further protect victims of human trafficking, regardless of their country of origin. Trafficking offenses under the law, which is aimed primarily at international offenders, include (1) sex trafficking, in which a commercial sex act is induced by force, fraud, or coercion, or in which the person induced to perform such act has not attained 18 years of age[55]; and (2) the recruitment, harboring, transportation, provision, or obtaining of a person for labor services, through the use of force, fraud, coercion, for the purpose of subjection to involuntary servitude, peonage, debt bondage, or slavery. The TVPA also provides funds for training U.S. law enforcement personnel at international police academies, and U.S. police agencies routinely send agents to assist law enforcement officers in other countries who are involved in transnational investigations.

Another tool in the fight against transnational crime is **extradition.** Not all countries, however, are willing to extradite suspects wanted in the United States. Consequently, as Kevin Ryan observes, "The globalization of United States law enforcement policy has also entailed the abduction of fugitives from abroad to stand trial when an asylum nation refuses an extradition request."[56] While certainly not a common practice, the kidnapping and forcible removal of criminal suspects from foreign jurisdiction appears more likely with suspected terrorists than with other types of criminals. For additional information on transnational organized crime and the globalization phenomenon, see Web Extra 17–12 at cjtoday.com.

**extradition**

The surrender by one state or jurisdiction to another of an individual accused or convicted of an offense in the second state or jurisdiction.

WEB EXTRA

# Terrorism

**terrorism**

A violent act or an act dangerous to human life in violation of the criminal laws of the United States or of any state committed to intimidate or coerce a government, the civilian population, or any segment thereof, in furtherance of political or social objectives.[v]

**Terrorism** as a criminal activity and the prevention of further acts of terrorism became a primary concern of American political leaders and justice system officials following the September 11, 2001, attacks on the World Trade Center and the Pentagon. There is, however, no single uniformly accepted definition of terrorism that is applicable to all places and all circumstances. Some definitions are statutory in nature, while others were created for such practical purposes as gauging success in the fight against terrorism. Still others relate to specific forms of terrorism, such as cyberterrorism (discussed later in this section), and many legislative sources speak only of "acts of terrorism" or "terrorist activity" rather than terrorism itself because the nature of Western jurisprudence is to legislate against acts rather than against concepts.

The federal Foreign Relations Authorization Act[57] defines *terrorism* in terms of four primary characteristics. The act says that terrorism is (1) premeditated, (2) politically motivated (3) violence (4) committed against noncombatant targets.[58] The FBI offers a nonstatutory working definition of terrorism as "a violent act or an act dangerous to human life in violation of the criminal laws of the United States or of any state to intimidate or coerce a government, the civilian population, or any segment thereof, in furtherance of political or social objectives."[59] Among the laws that define certain forms of human *activity* as terrorism, the Immigration and Nationality Act provides one of the most comprehensive and widely used definitions. That definition is shown in CJ Today Exhibit 17–2.

## CJ TODAY EXHIBIT 17-2

### What Is Terrorist Activity?

Federal law enforcement efforts directed against agents of foreign terrorist organizations derive their primary authority from the Immigration and Nationality Act, found in Title 8 of the U.S. Code. The act defines *terrorist activity* as follows:

(ii) "Terrorist activity" defined

As used in this chapter, the term "terrorist activity" means any activity which is unlawful under the laws of the place where it is committed (or which, if committed in the United States, would be unlawful under the laws of the United States or any State) and which involves any of the following:

(I) The hijacking or sabotage of any conveyance (including an aircraft, vessel, or vehicle).

(II) The seizing or detaining, and threatening to kill, injure, or continue to detain, another individual in order to compel a third person (including a governmental organization) to do or abstain from doing any act as an explicit or implicit condition for the release of the individual seized or detained.

(III) A violent attack upon an internationally protected person (as defined in section 1116(b)(4) of title 18) or upon the liberty of such a person.

(IV) An assassination.

(V) The use of any—

(a) biological agent, chemical agent, or nuclear weapon or device, or

(b) explosive or firearm (other than for mere personal monetary gain), with intent to endanger, directly or indirectly, the safety of one or more individuals or to cause substantial damage to property.

(VI) A threat, attempt, or conspiracy to do any of the foregoing.

(iii) "Engage in terrorist activity" defined

As used in this chapter, the term "engage in terrorist activity" means to commit, in an individual capacity or as a member of an organization, an act of terrorist activity or an act which the actor knows, or reasonably should know, affords material support to any individual, organization, or government in conducting a terrorist activity at any time, including any of the following acts:

(I) The preparation or planning of a terrorist activity.

(II) The gathering of information on potential targets for terrorist activity.

(III) The providing of any type of material support, including a safe house, transportation, communications, funds, false documentation or identification, weapons, explosives, or training, to any individual the actor knows or has reason to believe has committed or plans to commit a terrorist activity.

(IV) The soliciting of funds or other things of value for terrorist activity or for any terrorist organization.

(V) The solicitation of any individual for membership in a terrorist organization, terrorist government, or to engage in a terrorist activity.

---

According to criminologist Gwynn Nettler, all forms of terrorism share six characteristics[60]:

- *No rules.* There are no moral limitations on the type or degree of violence that terrorists can use.

- *No innocents.* No distinctions are made between soldiers and civilians. Children can be killed as easily as adults.

- *Economy.* Kill one, frighten 10,000.

- *Publicity.* Terrorists seek publicity, and publicity encourages terrorism.

- *Meaning.* Terrorist acts give meaning and significance to the lives of terrorists.

- *No clarity.* Beyond the immediate aim of destructive acts, the long-term goals of terrorists are likely to be poorly conceived or impossible to implement.

Moreover, notes Nettler, "Terrorism that succeeds escalates."[61]

## Types of Terrorism

It is important to distinguish between two major forms of terrorism: domestic and international. Distinctions between the two forms are made in terms of the origin, base of operations, and objectives of a terrorist organization. In the United States, **domestic terrorism** refers to the unlawful use of force or violence by a group or an individual who is based and operates entirely within this country and its territories without foreign direction and whose acts are directed at elements of the U.S. government or population.[62] **International terrorism**, in contrast, is the unlawful use of force or violence by a group or an individual who has some connection to a foreign power, or

**domestic terrorism**

The unlawful use of force or violence by a group or an individual who is based and operates entirely within the United States and its territories without foreign direction and whose acts are directed at elements of the U.S. government or population.[vi]

**international terrorism**

The unlawful use of force or violence by a group or an individual who has some connection to a foreign power, or whose activities transcend national boundaries, against people or property in order to intimidate or coerce a government, the civilian population, or any segment thereof, in furtherance of political or social objectives.[vii]

whose activities transcend national boundaries, against people or property in order to intimidate or coerce a government, the civilian population, or any segment thereof, in furtherance of political or social objectives.[63] International terrorism is sometimes mistakenly called *foreign terrorism,* a term that, strictly speaking, refers only to acts of terrorism that occur outside of the United States.

## Domestic Terrorism

Throughout the 1960s and 1970s, domestic terrorism in the United States required the expenditure of considerable criminal justice resources. The Weathermen, Students for a Democratic Society, the Symbionese Liberation Army, the Black Panthers, and other radical groups routinely challenged the authority of federal and local governments. Bombings, kidnappings, and shoot-outs peppered the national scene. As overt acts of domestic terrorism declined in frequency in the 1980s, international terrorism took their place. The war in Lebanon; terrorism in Israel; bombings in France, Italy, and Germany; and the many violent offshoots of the Iran-Iraq war and the first Gulf War occupied the attention of the media and of much of the rest of the world. Vigilance by the FBI, the Central Intelligence Agency (CIA), and other agencies largely prevented the spread of terrorism to the United States.

Worrisome today are domestic underground survivalist and separatist groups and potentially violent special-interest groups, each with its own vision of a future America. In 1993, for example, a confrontation between David Koresh's Branch Davidian followers and federal agents left 72 Davidians (including Koresh) and four federal agents dead in Waco, Texas.

Exactly two years to the day after the Davidian standoff ended in a horrific fire that destroyed the compound, a powerful truck bomb devastated the Alfred P. Murrah Federal Building in downtown Oklahoma City. One hundred sixty-eight people died, and hundreds more were wounded. The targeted nine-story building had housed offices of the Social Security Administration; the Drug Enforcement Administration; the Secret Service; the Bureau of Alcohol, Tobacco, and Firearms; and a day-care center called America's Kids. The fertilizer-and-diesel-fuel device used in the terrorist attack was estimated to have weighed about 1,200 pounds and had been left in a rental truck on the Fifth Street side of the building. The blast, which left a crater 30 feet wide and 8 feet deep and spread debris over a ten-block area, demonstrated just how vulnerable the United States is to terrorist attack.

In 1997, a federal jury found 29-year-old Timothy McVeigh guilty of 11 counts, ranging from conspiracy to first-degree murder, in the Oklahoma City bombing. Jurors concluded that McVeigh had conspired with Terry Nichols, a friend he had met while both were in the Army, and with unknown others to destroy the Murrah Building. Prosecutors made clear their belief that the attack was intended to revenge the 1993 assault on the Branch Davidian compound. McVeigh was sentenced to death and was executed by lethal injection at the U.S. penitentiary in Terre Haute, Indiana, in 2001.[64] McVeigh was the first person under federal jurisdiction to be put to death since 1963. In 2004, Terry Nichols was convicted of 161 counts of first-degree murder by an Oklahoma jury and sentenced to 161 life terms for his role in the bombings.[65] He had previously been convicted of various federal charges.

> No group or nation should mistake America's intentions: We will not rest until terrorist groups of global reach have been found, have been stopped, and have been defeated.
>
> —President George W. Bush

Sport utility vehicles destroyed in a New Year's Day fire at a Ford Lincoln Mercury dealership in Girard, Pennsylvania. The Earth Liberation Front (ELF), a domestic terrorist organization with an environmentalist agenda, claimed responsibility for the fire.

*AP Wide World Photos*

## CJ NEWS

### Domestic Terrorism: New Trouble at Home

Since 9/11, the nation's attention has been focused on possible threats from Islamic terrorists. But home-grown terrorists have been steadily plotting and carrying out attacks in unrelated incidents across the nation, according to federal authorities and two organizations that monitor hate groups.

None of the incidents over the past few years matched the devastation of 9/11 or even the 1995 bombing of the Oklahoma City federal building, which killed 168 and remains the deadliest act of terrorism against the nation by a U.S. citizen.

But some of the alleged domestic terrorists who have been arrested had ambitious plans. The people and groups range from white supremacists, anti-government types and militia members to eco-terrorists and people who hate corporations. They include violent anti-abortionists and black and brown nationalists who envision a separate state for blacks and Latinos. And they have been busy.

"Not a lot of attention is being paid to this, because everybody is concerned about the guy in a turban. But there are still plenty of angry, Midwestern white guys out there," says U.S. Marshals Service chief inspector Geoff Shank.

Shank, who is based in the Chicago area, says the concerns about domestic terrorism range from anti-abortion extremists who threaten to attack clinics and doctors to some violent biker gangs that may be involved in organized crime. And the FBI said in June that eco-terrorism—acts of violence, sabotage or property damage motivated by concern for animals or the environment—was the nation's top domestic terrorism threat. The bureau said then that eco-terrorists had committed more than 1,100 criminal acts and caused property damage estimated at least $110 million since 1976.

Alleged terrorist plots by U.S. citizens are not new, but many of the recent conspiracies were overshadowed by 9/11 and the hunt for terrorists abroad. Most of the foiled plots didn't get very far. And few got much publicity. But there were some potentially close calls, such as the scheme by William Krar, an east Texas man who stockpiled enough sodium cyanide to gas everyone in a building the size of a high school basketball gymnasium before he was arrested in 2002.

Shank, whose unit mainly searches for fugitives, including some wanted on domestic terror-related charges, led the manhunt for Clayton Lee Waagner, 48, of Kennerdell, Pa. Waagner was convicted in December of mailing hundreds of threat letters containing bogus anthrax to abortion clinics in 24 states. During his trial in Philadelphia, prosecutors documented Waagner's ties to the Army of God, an extremist group that believes violence against abortion providers is an acceptable way to end abortion.

"There's been a very, very heavy focus nationally on foreign terrorism since 9/11," says Mark Potok of the Southern Poverty Law Center in Montgomery, Ala., which has tracked hate groups since 1971. "The reality is that, meanwhile, domestic terrorism has hummed along at quite a steady clip. It . . . still poses a very serious threat."

William Krar, 63, left, and his common-law wife, Judith Bruey, 55, right, are escorted by authorities following their sentencing at the U.S. courthouse in Tyler, Texas, on May 4, 2004, after pleading guilty to illegally stockpiling an array of dangerous chemical weapons and conspiracy to possess illegal chemical weapons. Krar received a sentence of 11 years in prison, while Bruey was ordered to serve 5 years.
*AP Wide World Photos*

Among the incidents since 9/11:

- In Tennessee, the FBI recently arrested a man who agents say hated the federal government and was attempting to acquire chemical weapons and explosives to blow up a government building. Demetrius "Van" Crocker, 39, of McKenzie, Tenn., pleaded not guilty on November 5, 2004. His attorney, public defender Stephen Shankman, did not return calls.

- In May, Krar, 63, of Noonday, Texas, was sentenced to more than 11 years in prison after he stockpiled enough sodium cyanide to kill everyone inside a 30,000-square-foot building. Krar, described by federal prosecutors as a white supremacist, also had nine machine guns, 67 sticks of explosives and more than 100,000 rounds of ammunition. Investigators and the federal prosecutor said they didn't know what Krar intended to do with the potentially deadly chemicals. Krar's common-law wife, Judith Bruey, 55, pleaded guilty to conspiracy to possess illegal weapons and was sentenced to nearly five years.

- In 2004, two Utah men described by the U.S. attorney there as "domestic terrorists" pleaded guilty to setting separate arson fires related to eco-terrorism. Justus Ireland, 23, admitted starting a fire that caused $1.5 million damage at a West Jordan lumber company and spray-painting "ELF" at the site. The Earth Liberation Front has been connected to dozens of acts of vandalism and arson around the country

*(continued)*

## CJ NEWS *(continued)*

since 1996. Joshua Demmitt, 18, of Provo, pleaded guilty to starting a fire at Brigham Young University's Ellsworth Farm, where animal experiments are conducted, in the name of the Animal Liberation Front. A third man, Harrison Burrows, 18, also of Provo, pleaded guilty earlier.

■ In May, 2004, the FBI's domestic terrorism unit charged seven members of an animal rights group with terrorism after investigating what they said was a marked increase in crimes to stop the use of animals for product-testing. The activists, arrested in New York, New Jersey, California and Washington state, are members of Stop Huntingdon Animal Cruelty. The group seeks to shut down Huntingdon Life Sciences, a New Jersey product-testing company.

Prosecutors allege that the activists set fire to Huntingdon employees' cars, vandalized shareholders' homes and threatened their families. They are charged with conspiring to commit terrorism against an enterprise that uses animals for research and could face up to three years in prison if convicted.

■ In mid-2004, a Brookfield, Wisconsin, man labeled a domestic terrorist by federal prosecutors received an eight-year prison sentence for interfering with Madison police radio frequencies. Rajib Mitra, 26, had blocked police radio signals and later broadcast sex sounds over police radios. His attorney argued that the transmissions were an accident.

Mitra was one of the first defendants sentenced under guidelines changed after the Sept. 11 terrorist attacks. The changes, effective November 5, 2003, impose stiffer penalties for domestic terrorism. Under the previous sentencing guidelines, Mitra probably would have been sentenced to 18 to 24 months.

Mitra's attorney, Chris Van Wagner, says his client was not a terrorist and should have received a lesser punishment. "It's clear that (the guidelines) were put in place to punish those who seek to subvert our government and not intended to increase the punishment for people who simply engage in criminal mischief but had no terrorist angle or connection whatsoever," Van Wagner says. "He was just a dolphin caught in a tuna net."

Mitra was charged under provisions of the USA PATRIOT Act that make it a crime to cause such public-safety problems, even if there were no monetary damages. "This is a vivid example of how the PATRIOT Act has been used in cases that clearly have nothing to do with terrorism and that are far removed from what Congress was concerned about when it passed the PATRIOT Act," says Timothy Edgar of the American Civil Liberties Union.

During the 1990s, anti-government groups sprang up all over the country, according to the Southern Poverty Law Center and the Anti-Defamation League, which was founded in 1913 to combat anti-Semitism and now monitors hate groups. Many formed militias to prepare for large-scale resistance to the government, which the groups blamed for the Randy Weaver siege

at Ruby Ridge, Idaho, in 1992 and the Branch Davidian confrontation in Waco, Texas, in 1993.

Many of these group members believed the federal government was secretly setting up concentration camps for dissident Americans and was planning a takeover of the United States by United Nations troops as part of a "new world order." Many also said that mysterious black helicopters were conducting surveillance in the West, according to the ADL.

"The 'black helicopter' crowd is still out there," says Wisconsin federal prosecutor Tim O'Shea, referring to extremists who distrust and abhor the federal government.

Potok says the Southern Poverty Law Center identified 751 hate groups last year, a 6% increase over the 708 such organizations it counted in 2002.

Potok, director of the center's Intelligence Project, which monitors hate groups, says, "I don't mean to minimize the work of groups with ties to al-Qaeda. Obviously, there's a huge external threat as well. But there's a tendency to want to externalize the threat and say the people who want to hurt us don't look like us, they don't worship the same god and don't have the same skin color."

In 2004, the National District Attorneys Association, which has about 7,000 members, held a first-ever conference on domestic terrorism in Washington, D.C., to help local prosecutors identify potential terrorist groups.

"It was very well received," says the association's vice president, Robert Honecker, a prosecutor in Monmouth County, N.J. "They were appreciative of getting the information and the knowledge so they would be prepared should something happen in their jurisdiction."

Some of the alleged efforts by domestic terrorists are chilling.

According to an FBI affidavit in the Tennessee case, Crocker had inquired last spring about where he could obtain nuclear waste or nuclear materials. An informant told the FBI that Crocker, who had "absolute hatred" for the government, wanted "to build a bomb to be detonated at a government building, particularly a courthouse, either federal or state."

In September, 2004, according to the affidavit, Crocker told an undercover FBI agent "it would be a good thing if somebody could detonate some sort of weapon of mass destruction in Washington, D.C.," while both houses of Congress "were in session." Crocker allegedly told the agent he admired Adolf Hitler and the Nazi Party. He said "establishing a concentration camp for Jewish insurance executives would be a desirable endeavor."

Crocker later bought what he thought was Sarin nerve gas and a block of C-4 explosive from the undercover agent, the affidavit says.

Authorities arrested Crocker last month.

For the latest in crime and justice news, visit the Talk Justice news feed at http://www.crimenews.info.

Some experts believe that the Oklahoma City attack was modeled after a similar bombing described in the *Turner Diaries,* a novel used by extremist groups to map their rise to power.[66] Just as Hitler's biography *Mein Kampf* served as a call to arms for Nazis in Europe during the 1930s, the *Turner Diaries* describes an Aryan revolution that occurs in the United States during the 1990s in which Jews, blacks, and other minorities are removed from positions of influence in government and society.

In 2005, 38-year-old Eric Robert Rudolph pled guilty to a string of bombing attacks in Alabama and Georgia, including a blast at Atlanta's Centennial Park during the 1996 Olympics in which one person died and 111 were injured.[67] Rudolph, who was sentenced to life in prison without the possibility of parole, had eluded law enforcement officers for years.

Active fringe groups include those espousing a nationwide "common law movement," under which the legitimacy of elected government officials is not recognized. An example is the Republic of Texas separatists who took neighbors hostage near Fort Davis, Texas, in 1997 to draw attention to their claims that Texas was illegally annexed by the United States in 1845. While not necessarily bent on terrorism, such special-interest groups may turn to violence if thwarted in attempts to reach their goals.

Sometimes individuals can be as dangerous as organized groups. In 1996, for example, 52-year-old Theodore Kaczynski, a Lincoln, Montana, recluse, was arrested and charged in the Unabomber case. The Unabomber (so called because the bomber's original targets were universities and airlines) had led police and FBI agents on a 17-year-long manhunt through a series of incidents that involved as many as 16 bombings, resulting in three deaths and 23 injuries. Kaczynski pleaded guilty to federal charges in 1998 and was sentenced to life in prison without possibility of parole.

> Those who employ terrorism . . . strive to subvert the rule of law and effect change through violence and fear.
>
> —*National Strategy for Combating Terrorism*, 2003

## International Terrorism

In 1988 Pan American's London–New York Flight 103 was destroyed over Scotland by a powerful two-stage bomb as it reached its cruising altitude of 30,000 feet, killing all of the 259 passengers and crew members aboard. Another 11 people on the ground were killed, and many others injured as flaming debris from the airplane crashed down on the Scottish town of Lockerbie. It was the first time Americans were undeniably the target of international terrorism. Any doubts about this being the case were dispelled by the 1996 truck bomb attack on U.S. military barracks in Dhahran, Saudi Arabia. Nineteen U.S. Air Force personnel were killed and more than 250 others injured in the blast, which destroyed the Khobar Towers housing complex.

The 1993 bombing of the World Trade Center in New York City and the 1995 conviction of Sheik Omar Abdel-Rahman and eight other Muslim fundamentalists on charges of plotting to start a holy war and of conspiring to commit assassinations and bomb the United Nations[68] indicated to many that the threat of international terrorism could soon become a part of daily life in America. According to some terrorism experts, the 1993 explosion at the World Trade Center, which killed four people and created a 100-foot hole through four subfloors of concrete, ushered in an era of international terrorist activity in the United States. In 1999, the Second U.S. Circuit Court of Appeals upheld the convictions of the sheik and his co-conspirators, and they remain in federal prison.

In 2001, Muslim terrorist Osama bin Laden showed the world how easy it can be to strike at American interests on U.S. soil when members of his organization allegedly attacked the World Trade Center and the Pentagon using commandeered airliners, killing approximately 3,000 people. Earlier, in 1998, bin Laden's agents struck American embassies in Nairobi, Kenya, and Dares Salaam, Tanzania, killing 257 people, including 12 Americans. In 2003, a coordinated attack by Islamic extremists on a residential compound for foreigners in Riyadh, Saudi Arabia, killed 34 people (nine attackers died), including eight Americans, and wounded many more.[69] Similar attacks are continuing in the Middle East and elsewhere.

Some believe that the wars in Afghanistan and Iraq, as well as a coordinated international effort against al-Qaeda, may have substantially weakened that organization's ability to carry out future strikes outside of the Middle East. Those who study international terrorism, however, note that Jihadism, or the Islamic holy war movement, survives independent of any one organization and appears to be gaining strength around the world.[70] Jihadist principles continue to serve as the organizing rationale for extremist groups in much of the Muslim world.

A still frame taken from a security video camera records the instant a bomb detonates in Atocha railway station in Madrid, Spain, on March 11, 2004. The bomb was one in a series of terrorist explosions that went off within seconds of one other on Madrid's trains and killed 191 people. Hundreds more were injured by the blasts, which were blamed on Muslim extremists operating in Spain with links to al-Qaeda.

© Reuters, Corbis

## Cyberterrorism

A new kind of terrorism, called **cyberterrorism**, makes use of high technology, especially computers and the Internet, in the planning and carrying out of terrorist attacks. The term was coined in the 1980s by Barry Collin, a senior research fellow at the Institute for Security and Intelligence in California, who used it to refer to the convergence of cyberspace and terrorism.[71] It was later popularized by a 1996 RAND report that warned of an emerging "new terrorism" distinguished by how terrorist groups organize and by how they use technology. The report warned of a coming "netwar" or "infowar" consisting of coordinated cyberattacks on our nation's economic, business, and military **infrastructure**.[72] A year later, FBI agent Mark Pollitt offered a working definition of *cyberterrorism,* saying that it is "the premeditated, politically motivated attack against information, computer systems, computer programs, and data which results in violence against noncombatant targets by subnational groups or clandestine agents."[73]

Scenarios describing cyberterrorism possibilities are imaginative and diverse. Some have suggested that a successful cyberterrorist attack on the nation's air traffic control system might cause airplanes to collide in midair or that an attack on food- and cereal-processing plants that drastically altered the levels of certain nutritional supplements might sicken or kill a large number of our nation's children. Other such attacks might cause the country's power grid to collapse or could muddle the records and transactions of banks and stock exchanges. Possible targets in such attacks are almost endless.

In 1998, the Critical Infrastructure Assurance Office (CIAO) was created by a presidential directive to coordinate the federal government's initiatives on critical infrastructure protection and to provide a national focus for cyberspace security. In 2001, the White House formed the President's Critical Infrastructure Protection Board (PCIPB) and tasked it with recommending policies in support of critical infrastructure protection.[74] In September 2002, the PCIPB released an important document entitled *The National Strategy to Secure Cyberspace,*[75] which is available as Library Extra 17–6 at cjtoday.com. In 2003 CIAO functions were transferred to the National Cyber Security Division (NCSD) of the Directorate of Information Analysis and

## FREEDOM OR SAFETY? YOU DECIDE.

### Should Violent Speech Be Free Speech?

In 2005, a state jury in Alexandria, Virginia, convicted Muslim scholar Ali al-Timimi of a number of offenses—including the crime of incitement, in what prosecutors said was a call for his followers to join in a war against the United States. The spiritual advisor had verbally encouraged his followers to train with terrorist organizations and to engage in violent Jihad, or Holy War. As this book goes to press, al-Timimi is facing a mandatory sentence of life in prison without parole.

The al-Timimi case raises a number of interesting issues—among them the issue of when violent speech crosses the line from free expression into criminal advocacy.

The First Amendment to the U.S. Constitution guarantees the right to free speech. It is a fundamental guarantee of our democratic way of life. So, for example, the speech of those who advocate a new form of government in the United States is protected, even though their ideas may appear anti-American and ill considered.

In the 1957 case of *Roth* v. *United States,* the U.S. Supreme Court held that "The protection given speech and press was fashioned to assure unfettered interchange of ideas for the bringing about of political and social changes desired by the people."

It is important to remember, however, that constitutional rights are not without limit—that is, they have varying applicability under differing conditions. Some forms of speech are too dangerous to be allowed even under our liberal rules.

Freedom of speech does not mean, for example, that you have a protected right to stand up in a crowded theater and yell "Fire!" That's because the panic that would follow such an exclamation would likely cause injuries and put members of the public at risk of harm.

Hence, the courts have held that although freedom of speech is guaranteed by the Constitution, there are limits to it.

(Shouting "Fire!" in a public park would likely not be considered an actionable offense.)

Similarly, saying "The president deserves to die," horrific as it may sound, may be merely a matter of personal opinion. Anyone who says "I'm going to kill the president," however, can wind up in jail because threatening the life of the president is a crime—as is the act of communicating threats of imminent violence in most jurisdictions.

Al-Timimi's mistake may have been the timing of his remarks, which were made to a public gathering in Virginia five days after the 9/11 attacks. In his speech, al-Timimi called for a "holy war" and "violent Jihad" against the West. He was later quoted by converts with whom he met as referring to American forces in Afghanistan as "legitimate targets."

Critics of al-Timimi's conviction point to a seeming double standard under which people can be arrested for unpopular speech, but not for popular speech—regardless of the degree of violence it implies. They note, for example, that conservative columnist Ann Coulter has suggested in writing that "we should invade (Muslim) countries, kill their leaders and convert them to Christianity," but was never arrested for what she said. More recently, Oklahoma Sen. Tom Coburn's chief of staff, upset over decisions returned by the federal bench, proclaimed, "I don't want to impeach judges. I want to impale them!" Should he have been arrested for threatening the lives of judges?

The al-Timimi conviction, which is being appealed as this box is being written, may be more about the nature of a free society than about al-Timimi himself, or what he said.

**YOU DECIDE**
Should al-Timimi's advocacy of violence be unlawful? Why or why not? Might we have more to fear from the suppression of speech (even speech like al-Timimi's) than from its free expression? If so, how?

*References:* "Virginia Man Convicted of Urging War on U.S.," *USA Today,* April 27, 2005, p. 3A; and Jonathan Turley, "When Is Violent Speech Still Free Speech?" *USA Today,* May 3, 2005, p. 13A.

Infrastructure Protection (IAIP) within the Department of Homeland Security (DHS). According to DHS, the creation of NCSD improved protection of critical cyber assets by "maximizing and leveraging the resources" of previously separate offices.[76] NCSD coordinates its activities with the United States Computer Emergency Response Team (US-CERT), which runs a National Cyber Alert System. Visit US-CERT, which is also a part of the Department of Homeland Security, at Web Extra 17–13. Another group, the Secret Service National Threat Assessment Center (NTAC), is developing its Critical Systems Protection Initiative (CSPI) and will soon offer advanced cyber security prevention and response capabilities to the nation's business community. Visit NTAC at Web Extra 17–14.

## Narcoterrorism

Some authors have identified a link between major drug traffickers and terrorist groups.[77] In mid-2005, for example, Afghan drug lord Bashir Noorzai was arrested in New York and held without bond on charges that he tried to smuggle more than $50 million worth of heroin into the United

## CJ NEWS

### Intelligence Chiefs: Terrorists Intent on U.S. Attack

Al-Qaeda and other extremist groups continue to pose the most serious threat to the United States, and "it may be only a matter of time" before they try to attack Americans with chemical, biological, radiological or nuclear weapons, CIA Director Porter Goss said recently.

Goss testified publicly before the Senate's Intelligence Committee for the first time since he was confirmed in September 2004. He said that despite "serious blows" to al-Qaeda since the September 11 terrorist attacks, the group remains "intent on finding ways to circumvent U.S. security enhancements to strike Americans and the homeland."

FBI Director Robert Mueller, who testified on a panel that also included representatives from the departments of State, Homeland Security and Defense, said he has three main concerns:

■ The threat from long-term "sleeper" operatives or recently arrived terrorists "who may be inside the United States" planning an attack. "Finding them is a top priority for the FBI, but it is also one of the most difficult challenges," he said.

■ The "growing body" of evidence that shows al-Qaeda's "clear intention to obtain and ultimately use" weapons of mass destruction.

■ The potential for al-Qaeda to enlist other extremists for "attack planning or logistical support."

At a separate hearing, Defense Secretary Donald Rumsfeld told the House Armed Services Committee that terrorists are planning their next strike. "The extremists continue to plot to attack again," he said. "They are at this moment recalibrating and reorganizing. And so are we."

Many of the warnings about al-Qaeda echoed those at last year's Senate Intelligence Committee hearing on worldwide threats, when George Tenet, who was then CIA director, warned that al-Qaeda was still capable of "catastrophic attacks" and was trying to obtain chemical, biological and radiological weapons.

The hearing is designed to help give Congress and the public a broad view of threats against the United States. This year's was the first since the committee pledged to more closely monitor and investigate the government's intelligence operations.

"This committee learned from our Iraq weapons of mass destruction inquiry that we cannot and should not always take the intelligence community's assessments at face value," Chairman Pat Roberts, R-Kan., said, referring to mistakes that preceded the war in Iraq.

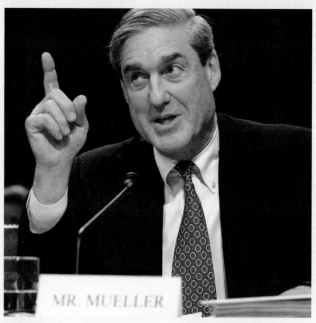

FBI director Robert Mueller testifying on national security threats to the United States before a Senate Select Committee hearing on intelligence on Capitol Hill in Washington, D.C. in 2005. Not shown is CIA Director Porter Goss, who supported Mueller's testimony.

*Shaun Heasley, Getty Images, Inc.*

Roberts said the committee will be watching closely to make sure the intelligence community does a better job of investigating the threat of nuclear terrorism and Iran's nuclear bomb program.

Among other warnings at the hearing:

■ Iran is pursuing long-range ballistic missiles while saying it won't abandon its nuclear program. Iran says the program is only for energy production, but the Bush administration says it intends to build a bomb.

■ North Korea, which has announced it intends to increase its nuclear arsenal, has a long-range missile "capable of reaching the United States with a nuclear-weapon-sized payload," Goss said.

■ The officials don't know whether poorly secured material at Russian nuclear facilities has made it into terrorists' hands.

■ Three countries in Southeast Asia—Indonesia, the Philippines and Thailand—need to be closely monitored as hotbeds for terrorists and other extremists.

■ Neglected African states are breeding grounds for terrorists.

For the latest in crime and justice news, visit the Talk Justice news feed at http://www.crimenews.info.

States.[78] Noorzai, who was on the DEA's list of most-wanted drug kingpins, had apparently operated with impunity under the protection of the Taliban between 1990 and 2004. According to the DEA, Noorzai's organization "provided demolitions, weapons and manpower to the Taliban." In exchange, the Taliban were said to have protected Noorzai's opium crops and transit routes through Afghanistan and Pakistan.

The link between drug traffickers and insurgents has been termed **narcoterrorism**.[79] Narcoterrorism, simply defined, is the involvement of terrorist organizations and insurgent groups in the trafficking of narcotics.[80] The relationship that exists between terrorist organizations and drug traffickers is mutually beneficial. Insurgents derive financial benefits from their supporting role in drug trafficking, while the traffickers receive protection and benefit from the use of terrorist tactics against foes and competitors.

The first documented instance of an insurgent force financed at least in part with drug money came to light during an investigation of the virulent anti-Castro Omega 7 group in the early 1980s.[81] Clear-cut evidence of modern narcoterrorism, however, is difficult to obtain. Contemporary insurgent organizations with links to drug dealers probably include the 19th of April Movement (M-19) operating in Colombia, Sendero Luminoso (Shining Path) of Peru, the Revolutionary Armed Forces of Colombia, and the large Farabundo Marti National Liberation Front (FMLN), which has long sought to overthrow the elected government of El Salvador.[82]

Narcoterrorism raises a number of questions. Drug researcher James Inciardi summarizes them as follows[83]:

- What is the full threat posed by narcoterrorism?
- How should narcoterrorism be dealt with?
- Is narcoterrorism a law enforcement problem or a military one?
- How might narcoterrorism be affected by changes in official U.S. policy toward drugs and drug use?
- Is the international drug trade being used as a tool by anti-U.S. and other interests to undermine Western democracies in a calculated way?

Unfortunately, in the opinion of some experts, the United States is ill prepared to combat this type of international organized crime. Testifying before the Senate's Foreign Relations Subcommittee on Terrorism, Narcotics, and International Operations, William J. Olson, a senior fellow at the National Strategy Information Center, told Congress that more than $1 trillion (equivalent to one-sixth of the U.S. gross national product) is generated yearly by organized criminal activities like those associated with narcoterrorism. "We must recognize that the rules of the crime game have changed," said Olson. "International criminal organizations are challenging governments, permeating societies. They're running roughshod over weak institutions and exploiting gaps in the U.S. and international response. They have the upper hand at the moment and they know it," he said.[84] Other experts testified that a comprehensive national strategy—one that goes far beyond law enforcement and criminal prosecution to include diplomacy and organized international efforts—is needed to combat international organized criminal enterprises before they can co-opt global markets and worldwide financial institutions.[85]

Even more potentially damaging are efforts being made by some criminal groups to wrest control of political institutions in various parts of the world. As transnational organized crime expert Emilio C. Viano points out, "powerful drug constituencies influence the electoral process more and more, seeking to gain actual political representation and consequently weaken the rule of law in a number of countries."[86]

# Causes of Terrorism

According to the U.S. government,[87] international terrorist organizations build on a process shown in Figure 17–1. The federal government's *National Strategy for Combating Terrorism*,[88] from which this figure is derived, says that the *underlying conditions* that lead to terrorism include poverty, political corruption, religious and ideational conflict, and ethnic strife. Such conditions provide terrorists with the opportunity to legitimize their cause and to justify their actions. Feeding on the social disorganization fostered by poverty, ethnic strife, and so on, terrorists position themselves to demand political change.

---

**narcoterrorism**

A political alliance between terrorist organizations and drug-supplying cartels. The cartels provide financing for the terrorists, who in turn provide quasi-military protection to the drug dealers.

---

Powerful international criminal groups now work outside national or international law. They include traffickers in drugs, money laundering, the illegal trade in arms—including trade in nuclear materials—and the smuggling of precious metals and other commodities. These criminal elements exploit both the new liberal international economic order and the different approaches and practices of States. They command vast sums of money, which they use to suborn State officials. Some criminal "empires" are richer than many poorer States. These problems demand a concerted, global response.

—Former United Nations Secretary-General Boutros Boutros-Ghali[ix]

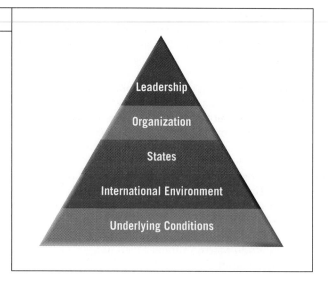

The second level in Figure 17–1, the *international environment,* refers to the geopolitical boundaries within which terrorist organizations form and through which they operate. If international borders are free and open, then terrorist groups can readily establish safe havens, hone their capabilities, practice their techniques, and provide support and funding to distant members and collaborators. Either knowingly or unwittingly, nations (*states*) can provide the physical assets and bases needed for the terrorist *organization* to grow and function. Finally, the terrorist *leadership,* at the top of the pyramid, provides the overall direction and strategy that give life to the organization's terror campaign.

# Combating Terrorism

Terrorism represents a difficult challenge to all societies. The open societies of the Western world, however, are potentially more vulnerable than are totalitarian regimes like dictatorships. Western democratic ideals restrict police surveillance of likely terrorist groups and curtail luggage, vehicle, and airport searches. Press coverage of acts of terrorism encourage copycat activities by other fringe groups and communicate information on workable techniques. Laws designed to limit terrorist access to technology, information, and physical locations are stopgap measures at best. The federal Terrorist Firearms Detection Act of 1988 is an example. Designed to prevent the development of plastic firearms by requiring handguns to contain at least 3.7 ounces of detectable metal,[89] it applies only to weapons manufactured within U.S. borders.

In 1996, the Antiterrorism and Effective Death Penalty Act (AEDPA) became law. The act includes these provisions:

- Bans fund-raising and financial support within the United States for international terrorist organizations.
- Provides $1 billion for enhanced terrorism-fighting measures by federal and state authorities.
- Allows foreign terrorism suspects to be deported or to be kept out of the United States without the disclosure of classified evidence against them.
- Permits a death sentence to be imposed on anyone committing an international terrorist attack in the United States in which a death occurs.
- Makes it a federal crime to use the United States as a base for planning terrorist attacks overseas.
- Orders identifying chemical markers known as *taggants* to be added to plastic explosives during manufacture.
- Orders a feasibility study on marking other explosives (except gunpowder).

More than a year before the events of September 11, 2001, the National Commission on Terrorism released a report titled *Countering the Changing Threat of International Terrorism.*[90] The commission, created by House and Senate leaders in 1998 in response to the bombings of the U.S. embassies in Kenya and Tanzania, was led by former U.S. Ambassador-at-Large for

Counter-Terrorism L. Paul Bremer. The commission's report, which we now see presaged the attacks on the World Trade Center and the Pentagon, began with these words: "International terrorism poses an increasingly dangerous and difficult threat to America." The report identified Afghanistan, Iran, Iraq, Sudan, and Syria as among state sponsors of terrorism and concluded that "the government must immediately take steps to reinvigorate the collection of intelligence about terrorists' plans, use all available legal avenues to disrupt and prosecute terrorist activities and private sources of support, convince other nations to cease all support for terrorists, and ensure that federal, state, and local officials are prepared for attacks that may result in mass casualties." A number of the commission's recommendations were implemented only *after* the terrorist attacks of 2001.

Following the 2001 attacks, Congress enacted, and the president signed, the USA PATRIOT Act. The act, which is discussed in some detail in other chapters, created a number of new crimes, such as terrorist attacks against mass transportation and harboring or concealing terrorists. Those crimes were set forth in Title VIII of the act, titled "Strengthening the Criminal Laws Against Terrorism." Title VIII can be found in CJ Today Exhibit 17–3.

> In this kind of conflict, where the enemy is hard to identify, the increased interest in civil liberties can be a problem for the government.
>
> —Lee Casey, Washington lawyer[x]

## Antiterrorism Committees and Reports

A number of important antiterrorism reports and studies have been released during the last seven or eight years by various groups, including those by the Advisory Panel to Assess Domestic Response Capabilities for Terrorism Involving Weapons of Mass Destruction (also known as the Gilmore Commission), the National Commission on Terrorism, the U.S. Commission on National Security in the Twenty-First Century, the New York–based Council on Foreign Relations (CFR), and the National Commission on Terrorist Attacks upon the United States (aka the 9/11 Commission).

Some pre–September 11, 2001, reports offered valuable suggestions that, if followed, might have helped prevent the events that took place on that day. Some of the subsequent reports have been voices of reason in the rush to strengthen the nation's antiterrorism defenses at potentially high costs to individual freedoms. The 2002 CFR report, for example, notes that "systems such as those used in the aviation sector, which start from the assumption that every passenger and every bag of luggage poses an equal risk, must give way to more intelligence-driven and layered security approaches that emphasize prescreening and monitoring based on risk-criteria." The report of the 9/11 Commission, released on July 22, 2004, which many saw as especially valuable, said that the September 11, 2001, attacks should have come as no surprise because the U.S. government had received clear warnings that Islamic terrorists were planning to strike at targets within

Palestinian boys hold toy rifles as a girl displays a poster of Osama bin Laden in Gaza City during a demonstration at Al Azhar University to honor suicide bombers. The school was organized by members of the Islamic Jihad. The 9/11 Commission report, released in 2004, pointed to the radical ideology underpinning international Islamic terrorism today and bemoaned the fact that too many Middle Eastern children are being socialized into a culture of terrorism.

*AP Wide World Photos*

## CJ TODAY EXHIBIT 17-3

### The USA PATRIOT Act of 2001

Title VIII of the USA PATRIOT Act of 2001 created two new federal crimes of terrorist activity: (1) terrorist attacks against mass transportation systems and (2) harboring or concealing terrorists. The following excerpts from the act describe these offenses.

#### TITLE VIII—STRENGTHENING THE CRIMINAL LAWS AGAINST TERRORISM

#### Sec. 801. Terrorist Attacks and Other Acts of Violence Against Mass Transportation Systems.

Chapter 97 of title 18, United States Code, is amended by adding at the end the following:

#### § 1993. Terrorist attacks and other acts of violence against mass transportation systems

(a) GENERAL PROHIBITIONS.—Whoever willfully—

(1) wrecks, derails, sets fire to, or disables a mass transportation vehicle or ferry;

(2) places or causes to be placed any biological agent or toxin for use as a weapon, destructive substance, or destructive device in, upon, or near a mass transportation vehicle or ferry, without previously obtaining the permission of the mass transportation provider, and with intent to endanger the safety of any passenger or employee of the mass transportation provider, or with a reckless disregard for the safety of human life;

(3) sets fire to, or places any biological agent or toxin for use as a weapon, destructive substance, or destructive device in, upon, or near any garage, terminal, structure, supply, or facility used in the operation of, or in support of the operation of, a mass transportation vehicle or ferry, without previously obtaining the permission of the mass transportation provider, and knowing or having reason to know such activity would likely derail, disable, or wreck a mass transportation vehicle or ferry used, operated, or employed by the mass transportation provider;

(4) removes appurtenances from, damages, or otherwise impairs the operation of a mass transportation signal system, including a train control system, centralized dispatching system, or rail grade crossing warning signal without authorization from the mass transportation provider;

(5) interferes with, disables, or incapacitates any dispatcher, driver, captain, or person while they are employed in dispatching, operating, or maintaining a mass transportation vehicle or ferry, with intent to endanger the safety of any passenger or employee of the mass transportation provider, or with a reckless disregard for the safety of human life;

(6) commits an act, including the use of a dangerous weapon, with the intent to cause death or serious bodily injury to an employee or passenger of a mass transportation provider or any other person while any of the foregoing are on the property of a mass transportation provider;

(7) conveys or causes to be conveyed false information, knowing the information to be false, concerning an attempt or alleged attempt being made or to be made, to do any act which would be a crime prohibited by this subsection; or

(8) attempts, threatens, or conspires to do any of the aforesaid acts,

shall be fined under this title or imprisoned not more than twenty years, or both, if such act is committed, or in the case of a threat or conspiracy such act would be committed, on, against, or affecting a mass transportation provider engaged in or affecting interstate or foreign commerce, or if in the course of committing such act, that person travels or communicates across a State line in order to commit such act, or transports materials across a State line in aid of the commission of such act.

(b) AGGRAVATED OFFENSE.—Whoever commits an offense under subsection

(a) in a circumstance in which—

(1) the mass transportation vehicle or ferry was carrying a passenger at the time of the offense; or

(2) the offense has resulted in the death of any person, shall be guilty of an aggravated form of the offense and shall be fined under this title or imprisoned for a term of years or for life, or both.

### Sec. 803. Prohibition Against Harboring Terrorists.

(a) In General.—Chapter 113B of title 18, United States Code, is amended by adding after section 2338 the following new section:

#### § 2339. Harboring or concealing terrorists

(a) Whoever harbors or conceals any person who he knows, or has reasonable grounds to believe, has committed, or is about to commit, an offense under section 32 (relating to destruction of aircraft or aircraft facilities), section 175 (relating to biological weapons), section 229 (relating to chemical weapons), section 831 (relating to nuclear materials), paragraph (2) or (3) of section 844(f) (relating to arson and bombing of government property risking or causing injury or death), section 1366(a) (relating to the destruction of an energy facility), section 2280 (relating to violence against maritime navigation), section 2332a (relating to weapons of mass destruction), or section 2332b (relating to acts of terrorism transcending national boundaries) of this title, section 236(a) (relating to sabotage of nuclear facilities or fuel) of the Atomic Energy Act of 1954 (42 U.S.C. 2284(a)), or section 46502 (relating to aircraft piracy) of title 49, shall be fined under this title or imprisoned not more than ten years, or both.

(b) A violation of this section may be prosecuted in any Federal judicial district in which the underlying offense was committed, or in any other Federal judicial district as provided by law.

(b) TECHNICAL AMENDMENT.—The chapter analysis for chapter 113B of title 18, United States Code, is amended by inserting after the item for section 2338 the following: "2339. Harboring or concealing terrorists."

## CJ TODAY EXHIBIT 17-4

### The Report of the National Commission on Terrorist Attacks upon the United States

On July 22, 2004, the National Commission on Terrorist Attacks upon the United States (better known as the 9/11 Commission) released its report. The Commission had been created by the president and Congress on November 27, 2002, and was charged with investigating the "facts and circumstances relating to the terrorist attacks of September 11, 2001, including those relating to intelligence agencies, law enforcement agencies, diplomacy, immigration issues and border control, the flow of assets to terrorist organizations, commercial aviation, the role of congressional oversight and resource allocation, and other areas determined relevant by the Commission."

In preparing their report, Commission members reviewed more than 2.5 million pages of documents and interviewed more than 1,200 people in ten countries. The final 585-page report touched on a variety of topics. Central to the report, however, is a "global strategy" to defeat terrorism.

"The enemy is not just 'terrorism,' some generic evil," said the Commission. A generic response to "terrorism" would blur the need for a focused U.S. anti-terrorism response. "The catastrophic threat at this moment in history," said the Commission, "is more specific. It is the threat posed by *Islamist* terrorism—especially the al Qaeda network, its affiliates, and its ideology."

The Commission noted that Islam is not the enemy, and that Islam is not synonymous with terror. "Nor does Islam teach terror," said the Commission. "America and its friends oppose a perversion of Islam, not the great world faith itself."

The following few paragraphs, taken directly from the report of the Commission, identify the radical ideology underpinning much of international terrorism today, and lay out a long term but important strategy for dealing with the continuing terrorist threat.

> Osama Bin Ladin and other Islamist terrorist leaders, draw on a long tradition of extreme intolerance within one stream of Islam (a minority tradition). . . . That stream is motivated by religion and does not distinguish politics from religion, thus distorting both. It is further fed by grievances stressed by Bin Ladin and widely felt throughout the Muslim world—against the U.S. military presence in the Middle East, policies perceived as anti-Arab and anti-Muslim, and support

of Israel. Bin Ladin and Islamist terrorists mean exactly what they say: to them America is the fount of all evil, the "head of the snake," and it must be converted or destroyed.

It is not a position with which Americans can bargain or negotiate. With it there is no common ground—not even respect for life—on which to begin a dialogue. It can only be destroyed or utterly isolated.

Because the Muslim world has fallen behind the West politically, economically, and militarily for the past three centuries, and because few tolerant or secular Muslim democracies provide alternative models for the future, Bin Ladin's message finds receptive ears. It has attracted active support from thousands of disaffected young Muslims and resonates powerfully with a far larger number who do not actively support his methods. The resentment of America and the West is deep, even among leaders of relatively successful Muslim states. Tolerance, the rule of law, political and economic openness, the extension of greater opportunities to women—these cures must come from within Muslim societies themselves. The United States must support such developments.

But this process is likely to be measured in decades, not years. It is a process that will be violently opposed by Islamist terrorist organizations, both inside Muslim countries and in attacks on the United States and other Western nations. The United States finds itself caught up in a clash *within* a civilization. That clash arises from particular conditions in the Muslim world, conditions that spill over into expatriate Muslim communities in non-Muslim countries.

Our enemy is twofold: al Qaeda, a stateless network of terrorists that struck us on 9/11; and a radical ideological movement in the Islamic world, inspired in part by al Qaeda, which has spawned terrorist groups and violence across the globe. The first enemy is weakened, but continues to pose a grave threat. The second enemy is gathering, and will menace Americans and American interests long after Osama Bin Ladin and his cohorts are killed or captured. Thus our strategy must match our means to two ends: dismantling the al Qaeda network and prevailing in the longer term over the ideology that gives rise to Islamist terrorism.

*Source:* National Commission on Terrorist Attacks upon the United States, *The 9/11 Commission Report: Final Report of the National Commission on Terrorist Attacks on the United States* (Washington, DC: U.S. Government Printing Office, 2004), pp. 362–363.

the United States (see CJ Today Exhibit 17–4). The report also said that the United States is still not properly prepared to adequately deal with terrorist threats and called for the creation of a new federal intelligence-gathering center to unify the more than a dozen federal agencies currently gathering terrorism-related intelligence at home and abroad. While it is impossible to discuss each of the reports mentioned here in detail in this textbook, they are available in their entirety as **Library Extras 17–7** through **17–16** at cjtoday.com.

**LIBRARY** EXTRA

Members of the National Commission on Terrorist Attacks upon the United States (aka the 9/11 Commission), from left: Thomas H. Kean, Lee H. Hamilton, Fred F. Fielding, Bob Kerrey, John F. Lehman, and Richard Ben-Veniste. The commission's report, released on July 22, 2004, called for a major overhaul of U.S. intelligence agencies and for a realignment of federal expenditures on homeland security.

*Doug Mills,* The New York Times

## The Department of Homeland Security

The Homeland Security Act of 2002, enacted to protect America against terrorism, created the federal Department of Homeland Security, which is also charged with protecting the nation's critical infrastructure against terrorist attack. The new department began operations on March 1, 2003, with former Pennsylvania governor Tom Ridge as its first director. The director is a member of the cabinet, whose official title is Secretary of Homeland Security. In 2005 Michael Chertoff became the new secretary of homeland security. A former federal prosecutor, Chertoff previously served as assistant attorney general for the Criminal Division at the U.S. Department of Justice and helped trace the 9/11 terrorist attacks to the al-Qaeda network.

Experts say that the creation of DHS is the most significant transformation of the U.S. government since 1947, when President Harry S. Truman merged the various branches of the armed forces into the Department of Defense in an effort to better coordinate the nation's defense against military threats.[91] DHS coordinates the activities of 22 disparate domestic agencies by placing administration of those agencies under five "directorates," or departmental divisions:

1. *Border and Transportation Security (BTS).* BTS is responsible for maintaining security of the nation's borders and transportation systems. The largest of the directorates, it is home to the Transportation Security Administration, the U.S. Customs Service, the border security functions of the former Immigration and Naturalization Service,[92] the Animal and Plant Health Inspection Service, and the Federal Law Enforcement Training Center.

2. *Emergency Preparedness and Response (EPR).* EPR works to ensure that the nation is prepared for, and able to recover from, terrorist attacks and natural disasters.

3. *Science and Technology (S&T).* This directorate coordinates the department's efforts in research and development, including preparing for and responding to the full range of terrorist threats involving weapons of mass destruction.

4. *Information Analysis and Infrastructure Protection (IAIP).* IAIP merges under one roof the functions of identifying and assessing a broad range of intelligence information concerning threats to the homeland, issuing timely warnings, and taking appropriate preventive and protective actions.

5. *Management.* The Management Directorate is responsible for budgetary, managerial, and personnel issues within DHS.

Several other critical agencies have been folded into the new department or have been created under the five directorates[93]:

■ *United States Coast Guard (USCG).* The commandant of the Coast Guard reports directly to the secretary of DHS. However, the USCG also works closely with the undersecretary of BTS and maintains its existing identity as an independent military service. Upon declaration of war or when the president so directs, the Coast Guard will operate as an element of the Department of Defense, consistent with existing law.

■ *United States Secret Service (USSS).* The primary mission of the Secret Service is the protection of the president and other government leaders, as well as security for designated national events. The Secret Service is also the primary agency responsible for protecting U.S. currency from counterfeiters and safeguarding Americans from credit card fraud.

■ *Bureau of Citizenship and Immigration Services (CIS).* A new agency, CIS (also known as U.S. Citizenship and Immigration Services, or USCIS) dedicates its energies to providing efficient immigration services and easing the transition to American citizenship.

■ *Bureau of Customs and Border Protection (CBP).* CBP is the unified border control agency of the United States and has as its mission the protection of our country's borders and the American people.

■ *Bureau of Immigration and Customs Enforcement (ICE).* Also known as U.S. Immigration and Customs Enforcement, ICE (along with CIS) has roots in the now-defunct U.S. Immigration and Naturalization Service (INS). ICE is the largest investigative arm of the Department of Homeland Security and is responsible for identifying and eliminating vulnerabilities in the nation's border, economic, transportation, and infrastructure security.

■ *Office of State and Local Government Coordination.* This office ensures close coordination between local, state, and federal governments to ensure an effective terrorism-prevention effort and to provide quick responses to terrorist incidents.

■ *Office of Private Sector Liaison.* The Office of Private Sector Liaison provides the business community with a direct line of communication to DHS. The office works directly with individual businesses and through trade associations and other nongovernmental organizations to foster dialogue between the private sector and DHS on the full range of issues and challenges that America's businesses face today.

■ *Office of Inspector General.* The Office of Inspector General serves as an independent and objective inspection, audit, and investigative body to promote effectiveness, efficiency, and economy in DHS's programs and operations and to prevent and detect fraud, abuse, mismanagement, and waste.

All the agencies described here can be found in the Cybrary at http://www.cybrary.info. You can reach DHS on the Web via Web Extra 17–15 at cjtoday.com. Learn what DHS is doing to keep America safe at Web Extra 17–16.

WEB EXTRA

## The National Strategy for Combating Terrorism

In 2003, the White House released its official *National Strategy for Combating Terrorism.*[94] The strategy includes a multipronged initiative aimed at reducing both the threat severity and international reach of international terrorist organizations. The avowed goals of the *National Strategy* are as follows:

■ Defeat terrorists and their organizations by identifying, locating, and destroying them.

■ Deny sponsorship, support, and sanctuary to terrorists by helping other nations fulfill their responsibilities and obligations to combat terrorism.

■ Diminish the underlying conditions that terrorists seek to exploit by resolving regional disputes; by fostering economic, social, and political development; by encouraging market-based economies; by supporting good governance and the rule of law; and by "winning the war of ideas" to ensure that ideologies that promote terrorism do not find fertile ground in any nation.

■ Defend U.S. citizens and interests at home and abroad by implementing strong and effective security measures and by enhancing measures intended to ensure the integrity, reliability, and availability of critical physical and information-based infrastructures (including transportation and information systems).

The nation's highest-ranking officials in the fight against terrorism. Top left: Director of National Intelligence John Negroponte; top right: FBI Director Robert Mueller; middle left: CIA Director Porter Goss; middle right: National Security Agency head Michael Hayden; and bottom: Secretary of Homeland Security Michael Chertoff. All answer directly to the president of the United States.

© Kevin Lamarque, Reuters, Corbis; © Brooks Craft, Corbis; AP Wide World Photos; U.S. Air Force; and U.S. Department of Homeland Security

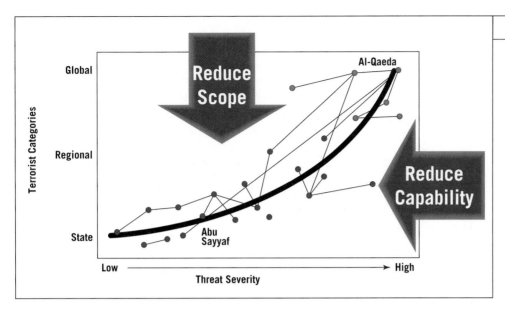

**FIGURE 17–2**

**Reducing the scope and capability of terrorist organizations.**

*Source: National Strategy for Combating Terrorism* (Washington, DC: White House, 2003), p. 13.

Figure 17–2, which is taken from the *National Strategy,* shows the assessed threat severity and geopolitical reach of two terrorist groups at the time of the report. The figure illustrates the federal government's two-pronged strategy of reducing the scope and the capability of such organizations. Learn more about countering terrorist threats at Library Extra 17–17 at cjtoday.com. The *National Strategy* is available in its entirety at Library Extra 17–18.

# Foreign Terrorist Organizations

The Immigration and Nationality Act (INA)[95] and the Intelligence Reform and Terrorism Prevention Act of 2004 (IRTPA)[96] provide the U.S. Department of State with the authority to designate any group outside the United States as a **foreign terrorist organization (FTO)**. The process involves an exhaustive interagency review process in which all evidence of a group's activity, from

**Foreign terrorist organization (FTO)**

A foreign organization that engages in terrorist activity that threatens the security of U.S. nationals or the national security of the United States and that is so designated by the U.S. secretary of state.

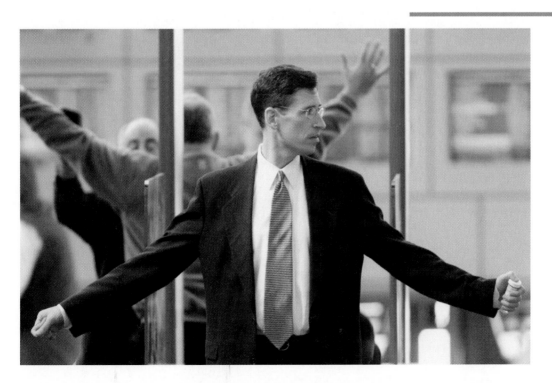

Transportation Security Administration screeners at work in Chicago's O'Hare International Airport. The hijackings of four airplanes by Islamic terrorists on September 11, 2001, led to tightened security controls over air travel nationwide and abroad.

*Sue Ogrocki, Corbis/Bettman*

both classified and open sources, is scrutinized. The State Department, working closely with the Justice and Treasury Departments and the intelligence community, prepares a detailed "administrative record" that documents the organization's terrorist activity.

Federal law requires that any organization considered for FTO designation must meet three criteria: (1) It must be foreign; (2) it must engage in terrorist activity as defined in Section 212 (a)(3)(B) of the Immigration and Nationality Act[97]; and (3) the organization's activities must threaten the security of U.S. nationals or the national security (national defense, foreign relations, or economic interests) of the United States. Table 17–2 lists 40 FTOs, as designated by the U.S.

**TABLE 17–2**

## DESIGNATED FOREIGN TERRORIST ORGANIZATIONS

1. Abu Nidal Organization (ANO)
2. Abu Sayyaf Group
3. Al-Aqsa Martyrs Brigade
4. Ansar al-Islam
5. Armed Islamic Group (GIA)
6. Asbat al-Ansar
7. Aum Shinrikyo
8. Basque Fatherland and Liberty (ETA)
9. Communist Party of the Philippines/New People's Army (CPP/NPA)
10. Continuity Irish Republican Army
11. Gama'a al-Islamiyya (Islamic Group)
12. HAMAS (Islamic Resistance Movement)
13. Harakat ul-Mujahidin (HUM)
14. Hizballah (Party of God)
15. Islamic Movement of Uzbekistan (IMU)
16. Jaish-e-Mohammed (JEM) (Army of Mohammed)
17. Jemaah Islamiya organization (JI)
18. al-Jihad (Egyptian Islamic Jihad)
19. Kahane Chai (Kach)
20. Kongra-Gel (KGK) (formerly Kurdistan Workers' Party, PKK, KADEK)
21. Lashkar-e Tayyiba (LT) (Army of the Righteous)
22. Lashkar i Jhangvi
23. Liberation Tigers of Tamil Eelam (LTTE)
24. Libyan Islamic Fighting Group (LIFG)
25. Mujahedin-e Khalq Organization (MEK)
26. National Liberation Army (ELN)
27. Palestine Liberation Front (PLF)
28. Palestinian Islamic Jihad (PIJ)
29. Popular Front for the Liberation of Palestine (PFLP)
30. PFLP-General Command (PFLP-GC)
31. al-Qaeda
32. Real IRA
33. Revolutionary Armed Forces of Colombia (FARC)
34. Revolutionary Nuclei (formerly ELA)
35. Revolutionary Organization 17 November
36. Revolutionary People's Liberation Party/Front (DHKP/C)
37. Salafist Group for Call and Combat (GSPC)
38. Shining Path (Sendero Luminoso, SL)
39. Tanzim Qa'idat al-Jihad fi Bilad al-Rafidayn (QJBR) (al-Qaida in Iraq) (formerly Jama'at al-Tawhid wa'al-Jihad, JTJ, al-Zarqawi Network)
40. United Self-Defense Forces of Colombia (AUC)

*Source:* U.S. Department of State. Current as of June 30, 2005.

Department of State. For more detailed descriptions of these organizations, see the State Department publication *Patterns of Global Terrorism,* which can be accessed via Library Extra 17–19 at cjtoday.com.

Under federal law, FTO designations are subject to judicial review. In the event of a challenge to a group's FTO designation in federal court, the U.S. government relies on the administrative record to defend the designation decision. These administrative records contain intelligence information and are therefore classified. FTO designations expire in two years unless renewed.

Once an organization has been designated as an FTO, a number of legal consequences follow. First, it becomes unlawful for a person in the United States or subject to the jurisdiction of the United States to provide funds or other material support to a designated FTO. Second, representatives and certain members of a designated FTO, if they are aliens, can be denied visas or kept from entering the United States. Finally, U.S. financial institutions must block funds of designated FTOs and their agents and must report the blockage to the Office of Foreign Assets Control within the U.S. Department of the Treasury.

The State Department also has the authority to designate selected foreign governments as state sponsors of international terrorism. As of mid-2005, Cuba, Iran, Libya, North Korea, Sudan, and Syria were designated as state sponsors of international terrorism. According to the State Department, Iran remains the most active state sponsor of terrorism.[98] The State Department says that the Iranian government provides continuing support to numerous terrorist groups, including the Lebanese Hizballah, HAMAS, and the Palestinian Islamic Jihad (PIJ), all of which seek to undermine the Middle East peace process through the use of terrorism. Syria provides safe haven and support to several terrorist groups, some of which oppose Middle East peace negotiations. The State Department notes, however, that Libya is attempting to mend its international image following its surrender in 1999 of two Libyan suspects for trial in the Pan Am Flight 103 bombing. In early 2001, one of those suspects was convicted of murder, and judges in the case found that he had acted "in furtherance of the purposes of . . . Libyan Intelligence Services." Also, in 2003 Libya agreed to foreswear its well-developed nuclear arms program in an effort to attract foreign investment. Cuba, however, continues to provide safe haven to several terrorists and U.S. fugitives, and maintains ties to other state sponsors of terrorism and to Latin American insurgents. North Korea harbored several hijackers of a Japanese Airlines flight to North Korea in the 1970s and maintains links to terrorist groups. It also continues to sell ballistic missile technology to countries designated by the United States as state sponsors of terrorism, including Syria and Libya. Finally, Sudan continues to provide a safe haven for members of various terrorist groups, including the Lebanese Hizballah, Gama'a al-Islamiyya, Egyptian Islamic Jihad, the PIJ, and HAMAS, although it has been engaged in a counterterrorism dialogue with the United States since mid-2000. Learn more about terrorism from the Terrorism Research Center via Web Extra 17–17 at cjtoday.com. Visit the State Department's Counterterrorism Office via Web Extra 17–18.

# The Future of International Terrorism

Terrorist groups are active throughout the world (Figure 17–3), and the United States is not their only target. Terrorist groups operate in South America, Africa, the Middle East, Latin America, the Philippines, Japan, India, England, Nepal, and some of the now independent states of the former Soviet Union. The Central Intelligence Agency reports that "between now and 2015 terrorist tactics will become increasingly sophisticated and designed to achieve mass casualties."[99] The CIA also notes that nations "with poor governance; ethnic, cultural, or religious tensions; weak economies; and porous borders will be prime breeding grounds for terrorism."[100] In the area of Islamic terrorism, the CIA expects that "by 2020 Al-Qaeda will have been superseded by similarly inspired but more diffuse Islamic extremist groups."[101] Read two CIA reports on the global trends that are likely to increase the risk of terrorism via Library Extras 17–20 and 17–21 at cjtoday.com.

The current situation leads many observers to conclude that the American justice system is not fully prepared to deal with the threat represented by domestic and international terrorism. Prior intelligence-gathering efforts that focused on such groups have largely failed or were not quickly acted on, leading to military intervention in places like Afghanistan and Iraq. Intelligence failures are at least partially understandable, given that many terrorist organizations are tight-knit and very difficult for intelligence operatives to penetrate.

**AL QAEDA**
Global
**ACTIVITIES**
*Funding, planning, and conducting terrorism*
**MEMBERS**
*Unknown*
Founded by Osama bin Laden in the 1980s, al Qaeda first supported the *mujahidin* fighting Soviets in Afghanistan. Today the group wages war on the world, through a global Islamist insurgency.

**1. UNITED SELF-DEFENSE FORCES OF COLOMBIA**
Colombia
**ACTIVITIES**
*Massacres, narcotics*
**MEMBERS**
*12,000 to 15,000*
This right-wing coalition of paramilitaries was formed to fight leftist insurgents but often targets civilians.

**1. REVOLUTIONARY ARMED FORCES OF COLOMBIA (FARC)**
Colombia
**ACTIVITIES**
*Bombing, kidnapping, narcotics*
**MEMBERS**
*15,000 to 18,000*
These communist insurgents use kidnapping and mass murder in their fight to overthrow the Colombian government and redistribute wealth.

**1. NATIONAL LIBERATION ARMY (ELN)**
Colombia
**ACTIVITIES**
*Kidnapping, bombing, extortion*
**MEMBERS**
*3,000*
This leftist group is one of the leading practitioners of kidnapping for ransom. It also attacks government oil pipelines and energy infrastructure.

**2. ■ SALAFIST GROUP FOR CALL AND COMBAT**
Algeria
**ACTIVITIES**
*Attacks on government and military*
**MEMBERS**
*Several hundred*
This newly powerful Islamist group aims to topple Algeria's secular government, expel foreign influences, and advance al Qaeda's agenda in Africa and Europe.

**3. ■ MOROCCAN ISLAMIC COMBATANT GROUP**
Morocco
**ACTIVITIES**
*Bombing, arms, forgery*
**MEMBERS**
*Unknown*
This Moroccan Islamist group, reportedly linked to al Qaeda, is accused of recent mass-casualty bombings in Madrid and Casablanca.

**HOT SPOT COLOMBIA**

As communist insurgents battle right-wing militias—and each other—for territory and drug profits, locals are caught in the crossfire. The government is now fighting to regain control of the countryside.

The latest wave of international terrorism has focused the world's attention on a tactic that uses death and destruction as political tools. But terrorism itself, with roots deep in history and geography, is hardly new.

**HOT SPOT ISRAEL & THE OCCUPIED TERRITORIES**

Fueled by nationalism and mistrust, the cycle continues: Palestinian insurgents use terrorism against Israeli troops, settlers, and civilians in the occupied territories and Israel—while Israeli forces target militants, often inflicting civilian casualties.

**6. ISLAMIC RESISTANCE MOVEMENT (HAMAS)**
Israel, West Bank, Gaza Strip
**ACTIVITIES**
*Suicide attacks*
**MEMBERS**
*Several thousand*
Seeking to destroy Israel and extend Muslim rule across the Middle East, Hamas has mounted dozens of suicide attacks against Israeli civilians.

**6. PALESTINE ISLAMIC JIHAD**
Israel, West Bank, Gaza Strip
**ACTIVITIES**
*Suicide attacks*
**MEMBERS**
*Several dozen*
Led by operatives based in Lebanon and Syria, this radical group aims to replace Israel with a Palestinian Islamic state.

**6. AL AQSA MARTYRS' BRIGADES**
Israel, West Bank, Gaza Strip
**ACTIVITIES**
*Shootings, suicide attacks*
**MEMBERS**
*Unknown*
This group, linked to Palestinian leader Yasser Arafat's Fatah movement, arose during a Palestinian intifada in 2000.

**6. KACH AND KAHANE CHAI**
Israel, West Bank
**ACTIVITIES**
*Shootings, assaults*
**MEMBERS**
*Several dozen*
Outlawed since the massacre of 29 Muslims at Hebron in 1994, these groups seek to expand Israel by driving Palestinians from the West Bank and Gaza Strip.

**6. HEZBOLLAH**
Lebanon
**ACTIVITIES**
*Bombing, hijacking, suicide attacks*
**MEMBERS**
*Several hundred*
Formed in 1982 after the Israeli invasion of Lebanon, this Iran-backed group claimed victory when Israel pulled out in 2000. Its goal: destruction of the Jewish state.

**6. ■ ASBAT AL ANSAR**
Lebanon
**ACTIVITIES**
*Assassination, bombing*
**MEMBERS**
*About 300*
These al Qaeda-linked extremists attack both domestic and international targets within Lebanon.

# FIGURE 17–3

**International terrorist groups and areas of operation.**

*Source:* Walter Laqueur, "World of Terror" (National Geographic Maps), *National Geographic*, November 2004, pp. 72–74.

**4. BASQUE FATHERLAND AND LIBERTY (ETA)**
Spain, France
**ACTIVITIES**
*Assassination, bombing, extortion*
**MEMBERS**
*Dozens*
Founded in 1959, this group has targeted Spanish officials and security forces in its fight for an independent Basque state in northern Spain and southwestern France.

**5. REAL IRA**
Northern Ireland
**ACTIVITIES**
*Assassination, bombing, robbery*
**MEMBERS**
*100 to 200*
An offshoot that formed after the Irish Republican Army declared a cease-fire in 1997, the RIRA has killed dozens in its fight for a united Ireland, free from British rule.

# WHERE THEY ARE

This map shows a sample of the many groups that use terror to achieve their goals, attracting an array of nationalists, political ideologues, and religious zealots. Some groups are multifaceted, incorporating politics and social programs along with violence; others are purely brutal. Today one type of group—related to a movement called Islamism—has earned an especially high profile for its drive to impose theocracy on Muslim lands and excise "impure" Western influences. According to the CIA, the deadliest of these groups—al Qaeda—operates in 68 countries worldwide.

**HOT SPOT**
**INDIA & PAKISTAN**

Nuclear rivals India and Pakistan duel over the region of Kashmir, a flash point for conflict between Indian troops and Pakistan-based terrorist groups. Attacks against the pro-U.S. government of Pakistan are also on the rise.

ASIA

**5. ULSTER DEFENCE ASSOCIATION**
Northern Ireland
**ACTIVITIES**
*Bombing, narcotics, shootings, intimidation*
**MEMBERS**
*Several hundred*
Largest of the Protestant paramilitary groups that favor retaining British rule. Though bound by a cease-fire, the group often engages in violence against Catholics.

**8. KURDISTAN WORKERS' PARTY (PKK)**
Turkey
**ACTIVITIES**
*Assassination, bombing*
**MEMBERS**
*More than 5,000*
Also known as Kongra-Gel, this separatist group operates from northern Iraq and targets Turkish security forces and civilians in its fight for an independent Kurdish state.

**9. ■ CHECHEN SEPARATISTS**
Russia
**ACTIVITIES**
*Bombing, kidnapping, murder*
**MEMBERS**
*Several thousand*
Seeking independence from Russia, rebels have killed Moscow-backed Chechen officials, including Chechnya's president, and killed and kidnapped Russian civilians.

**9. ■ ISLAMIC MOVEMENT OF UZBEKISTAN**
Central Asia
**ACTIVITIES**
*Bombing, kidnapping*
**MEMBERS**
*More than 1,000*
This homegrown Islamist coalition seeks to replace Uzbekistan's secular regime and advance the regional goals of al Qaeda.

**10. ■ LASHKAR E-JHANGVI**
Pakistan
**ACTIVITIES**
*Massacres, bombing*
**MEMBERS**
*Fewer than a hundred*
A small but brutally effective Sunni group, LEJ has attacked Shiite mosques and foreigners in a bid to destabilize Pakistan. Also linked to the 2002 murder of journalist Daniel Pearl.

**HOT SPOT**
**INDONESIA & PHILIPPINES**

Recent acts of terrorism have claimed hundreds of lives in Indonesia, prime target for indigenous groups like Jemaah Islamiyah that are now affiliated with al Qaeda. In the Philippines, Muslim and Marxist rebels are an ongoing threat to stability.

MALAYSIA 12 PHILIPPINES
INDONESIA

AUSTRALIA

**10. ■ JAISH-E-MOHAMMED**
Pakistan
**ACTIVITIES**
*Massacres, bombing*
**MEMBERS**
*Several hundred*
This Islamist group is blamed for the bombing of an Indian state legislature in Kashmir that killed 38. Now split into two factions, this groups, like others, fights to make predominantly Muslim Kashmir part of

**10. LASHKAR E-TAIBA**
Pakistan
**ACTIVITIES**
*Massacres, bombing*
**MEMBERS**
*Several hundred*
With training camps in Afghanistan, LET specializes in daredevil missions with devastating results, directed mainly against Indian troops and civilians in

**11. LIBERATION TIGERS OF TAMIL EELAM**
Sri Lanka
**ACTIVITIES**
*Assassination, bombing*
**MEMBERS**
*10,000 to 15,000*
Favoring suicide attacks, members seek an independent Tamil state in Sri Lanka. A precarious cease-fire is now in place.

**12. ■ JEMAAH ISLAMIYAH**
Southeast Asia
**ACTIVITIES**
*Bombing*
**MEMBERS**
*Unknown*
Responsible for a series of deadly bombings across Southeast Asia—including the Bali night-club attacks in 2002—al Qaeda's local partner seeks an Islamic superstate spanning the region.

**7. TAWHID W' AL JIHAD**
Iraq
**ACTIVITIES**
*Kidnapping, bombing*
**MEMBERS**
*Unknown*
Jordanian Abu Musab al Zarqawi leads this loose network of jihadists, most of whom are Iraqi. Their common goal: to expel U.S. forces and create a Sunni Islamic state in Iraq. Many of its fighters are veterans of an older group, Ansar al Islam.

**12. ABU SAYYAF**
Philippines
**ACTIVITIES**
*Kidnapping, bombing, piracy*
**MEMBERS**
*300 to 500*
High-profile kidnappings of foreigners for ransom keep this group well financed—though the profit motive may be clouding Abu Sayyaf's founding vision of an Islamic state in the

**12. ■ MORO ISLAMIC LIBERATION FRONT**
Philippines
**ACTIVITIES**
*Bombing*
**MEMBERS**
*Around 12,000*
Though it officially disavows terrorism, this insurgent group is linked to attacks on Philippine cities through its support for Jemaah Islamiyah. Now in peace talks with the government, the MILF aims for ethnic autonomy.

# LEGEND

■ **Countries where al Qaeda cells are known to be operating**
■ **Countries where al Qaeda cells may be operating**
■ **Group affiliated with al Qaeda**

Karim Koubriti, 24, of Detroit, left, and Abdel-llah Elmardoudi, 37, of Minneapolis—convicted members of a radical Islamic terrorist "sleeper" cell. The men, Muslim immigrants who had been living in the United States, were convicted in federal court in 2003 of conspiring to support terrorism and of conspiring to commit document and visa fraud. Not all terrorists are adjudicated by the criminal justice system. If Koubriti and Elmardoudi had been assigned the status of "foreign combatants," they would have faced trial by military tribunal. Enemy combatants, such as those held at the American naval base at Guantánamo Bay, Cuba, following the wars in Afghanistan and Iraq have no right to an attorney and can be held indefinitely.

*AP Wide World Photos*

## SUMMARY

The international perspective has much to contribute to the study of American criminal justice. Law enforcement agencies, court personnel, and corrections officials in the United States can benefit from learning about innovative crime-prevention, investigative, and treatment techniques used in other parts of the world. By studying foreign legal codes and the routine practice of criminal justice in other countries, policymakers can acquire a fresh perspective on the issues and decisions they face.

A number of barriers continue to limit the applicability of cross-national studies, however. One is the continuing unavailability of sufficiently detailed, up-to-date, and reliable international information on crime rates, victimization, and adjudication. Another, more difficult, barrier is imposed by ethnocentrism. Ethnocentrism, a culturally determined hesitancy on the part of some people to consider any personal or professional viewpoints other than their own, reduces the likelihood of serious analysis of even the limited international information that is available.

Transnational crime, brought about in part by globalization of the world's economy and by advances in technologies supporting communications and transportation, may be one of the most significant challenges of the twenty-first century. Organized international criminal cartels recognize no boundaries and engage in activities like drug trafficking, money laundering, human trafficking, and international weapons smuggling.

Terrorism, which today is the focus of significant criminal justice activity, brings with it the threat of massive destruction and large numbers of casualties. Cyberterrorism and attacks on information management segments of our nation's critical infrastructure could theoretically shut down or disable important infrastructure services like electricity, food processing, military activity, and even state and federal governments. The vigilance required to prevent terrorism, both domestic and international, consumes a significant number of law enforcement resources and has resulted in new laws that restrict a number of freedoms that many Americans have previously taken for granted.

Given enough time, most barriers can be overcome. Although political, economic, and ideological differences will remain dominant throughout the world for many years, the globe is shrinking. Advances in communications, travel, and the exchange of all types of information are combining with a huge growth in technology to produce an interdependence among nations. As new international partnerships are forged, barriers to understanding should continue to fall.

1. What are the potential benefits of studying criminal justice systems in other countries? What problems are inherent in such study?

2. What are the principles that inform Islamic law? How do these principles contribute to the structure and activities of the criminal justice systems of Muslim nations that follow Islamic law?

3. What important international criminal justice organizations does this chapter discuss? Describe the role of each in fighting international crime.

4. What is transnational crime? What possible relationships might exist between transnational crime and terrorism?

5. What is terrorism? What are two major types of terrorism?

6. What causes terrorism? What efforts is the U.S. government making to prevent and control the spread of terrorism?

7. Why is terrorism a law enforcement concern? How is terrorism a violation of the criminal law? What can the American criminal justice system do to better prepare itself for future terrorist crimes?

Use the Cybrary (http://www.cybrary.info) to identify countries other than the United States that make information on their criminal justice system available on the Web. (You might want to begin by clicking on the "International" category.) List the sites that you find, and describe the justice system of each nation.

Then use the Cybrary to identify countries other than the United States that make crime statistics available on the Web. List the statistics sites that you find for each country, and include a summary of the statistics available for each. Submit your findings to your instructor if asked to do so.

To complete this Web Quest online, go to the Web Quest module in Chapter 17 of the *Criminal Justice Today* Companion Website at cjtoday.com.

i. Testimony of Director of Central Intelligence Porter J. Goss before the Senate Select Committee on Intelligence, February 16, 2005.

ii. Andre Bossard, "Crime and Globalization," *Crime and Justice International,* Vol. 19, No. 71 (March 2003), p. 38.

iii. Ibid.

iv. Daniel Mabrey, "Human Smuggling from China," *Crime and Justice International,* Vol. 19, No. 71 (March 2003), p. 5.

v. Federal Bureau of Intelligence, Counterterrorism Section, *Terrorism in the United States, 1987* (Washington, DC: FBI, 1987).

vi. Adapted from Federal Bureau of Investigation, *FBI Policy and Guidelines: Counterterrorism.* Web posted at http://www.fbi.gov/contact/fo/jackson/cntrterr.htm (accessed March 4, 2002).

vii. Ibid.

viii. Adapted from Dictionary.com. Web posted at http://dictionary.reference.com/search?q=infrastructure (accessed January 10, 2003).

ix. UN Department of Public Information, "The United Nations versus Transnational Crime," April 1995. Web posted at http://www.un.org/ecosocdev/geninfo/crime/dpi1744e.htm (accessed January 15, 2000).

x. As quoted in Joan Biskupic, "Attention Turns Back to Liberty," *USA Today,* November 1, 2002, p. 17A.

1. Richard H. Ward, "The Internationalization of Criminal Justice," in Phyllis McDonald and Janice Munsterman, eds., *Criminal Justice 2000: Vol. 2 Boundary Changes in Criminal Justice Organizations* (Washington, DC: National Institute of Justice, 2000), p. 267.

2. Office for Victims of Crime, *Report to the Nation 2003* (Washington, DC: OVC, 2003), p. 83.

3. Details for this story come from "50-Missile Deal Was in the Works," *Straits Times Interactive,* August 15, 2003. Web posted at straitstimes.asia1.com.sg/topstories/story/0,4386,204768,00.html (accessed August 21, 2003); "Man Gets 47 Years in Missile-Launcher Case," *USA Today,* September 13, 2005, p. 3A; and "Man Who Tried to Sell Missiles Found Guilty," *USA Today,* April 28, 2005, p. 3A.

4. Robert Lilly, "Forks and Chopsticks: Understanding Criminal Justice in the PRC," *Criminal Justice International* (March/April 1986), p. 15.

5. Adapted from Carol B. Kalish, *International Crime Rates,* BJS Special Report (Washington, DC: Bureau of Justice Statistics, 1988).

6. Ibid.

7. Ibid.

8. For information about the latest survey, see *The Eighth United Nations Survey on Crime Trends and the Operations of Criminal Justice* (New York: United Nations, 2005). Web posted at http://www.unodc.org/unodc/en/crime_cicp_survey_eighth.html (accessed July 10, 2005).

9. As quoted in Lee Hockstader, "Russia's War on Crime: A Lopsided, Losing Battle," *Washington Post* wire service, February 27, 1995.

10. Roy Walmsley, *Developments in the Prison Systems of Central and Eastern Europe,* HEUNI papers no. 4 (Helsinki, 1995).

11. J. Schact, "Law and Justice," *The Cambridge Encyclopedia of Islam,* Vol. II, p. 539, from which most of the information in this paragraph comes.

12. Sam S. Souryal, Dennis W. Potts, and Abdullah I. Alobied, "The Penalty of Hand Amputation for Theft in Islamic Justice," *Journal of Criminal Justice,* Vol. 22, No. 3 (1994), pp. 249–265.

13. Parviz Saney, "Iran," in Elmer H. Johnson, ed., *International Handbook of Contemporary Developments in Criminology* (Westport, CT: Greenwood Press, 1983), p. 359.

14. This section owes much to Matthew Lippman, "Iran: A Question of Justice?" *Criminal Justice International* (1987), pp. 6–7.

15. "Life Sentence for Burning Koran," BBC News, October 18, 2004. Web posted at http://news.bbc.co.uk/1/hi/world/south_asia/3754276.stm (accessed May 21, 2005).

16. Souryal, Potts, and Alobied, "The Penalty of Hand Amputation for Theft in Islamic Justice."

17. Afshin Valinejad, "Iran Flogs, Hangs Serial Killer Known as 'The Vampire,'" *USA Today,* August 14, 1997, p. 11A.

18. For additional information on Islamic law, see Adel Mohammed el Fikey, "Crimes and Penalties in Islamic Criminal Legislation," *Criminal Justice International* (1986), pp. 13–14; and Sam S. Souryal, "Shariah Law in Saudi Arabia," *Journal for the Scientific Study of Religion,* Vol. 26, No. 4 (1987), pp. 429–449.

19. Max Weber, in Max Rheinstein, ed., *On Law in Economy and Society* (New York: Simon and Schuster, 1967), translated from the 1925 German edition.

20. Ibid.

21. Souryal, Potts, and Alobied, "The Penalty of Hand Amputation for Theft in Islamic Justice."

22. Paul Friday, "International Organization: An Introduction," in Johnson, *International Handbook of Contemporary Developments in Criminology,* p. 31.

23. Ibid., p. 32.

24. Gerhard O. W. Mueller, "The United Nations and Criminology," in Johnson, *International Handbook of Contemporary Developments in Criminology,* pp. 74–75.

25. Roger S. Clark, *The United Nations Crime Prevention and Criminal Justice Program: Formulation of Standards and Efforts at Their Implementation* (Philadelphia: University of Pennsylvania Press, 1994).

26. Ibid., pp. 71–72.

27. "International News," *Corrections Compendium* (June 1995), p. 25.

28. Khaled Dawoud, "U.N. Crime Meeting Wants Independent Jail Checks," Reuters wire service, May 6, 1995.

29. "Protocol to Prevent, Suppress, and Punish Trafficking in Persons, Especially Women and Children, Supplementing the United Nations Convention against Transnational Organized Crime," *Report of the Ad Hoc Committee on the Elaboration of a Convention against Transnational Organized Crime on the Work of Its First to Eleventh Sessions,* U.N. GAOR, 55th Sess., Agenda Item 105, U.N. Document Number A/55/383 (2000), Annex II.

30. For additional information, see Mohamed Y. Mattar, "Trafficking in Persons, Especially Women and Children, in Countries of the Middle East: The Scope of the Problem and the Appropriate Legislative Response," *Fordham International Law Journal,* Vol. 26 (March 2003), p. 721. Web posted at http://209.190.246.239/article.pdf (accessed August 2, 2003).

31. See "INTERPOL: Extending Law Enforcement's Reach around the World," *FBI Law Enforcement Bulletin* (December 1998), pp. 10–16.

32. "Interpol Member Countries." Web posted at http://www.interpol.int/Public/Icpo/Members/default.asp (accessed June 19, 2005).

33. "INTERPOL at Forty," *Criminal Justice International* (November/December 1986), pp. 1, 22.

34. "INTERPOL Conference Agrees on Measures to Fight Bio-Terrorism," INTERPOL media release No. 11/2005, March 2, 2005.

35. INTERPOL General Secretariat, *INTERPOL at Work: 2003 Activity Report* (Lyons, France, 2004).

36. Marc Champion, Jeanne Whalen, and Jay Solomon, "Terror in London: Police Make One Arrest after Raids in North England," *Wall Street Journal,* July 12, 2005. Web posted at http://online.wsj.com/article/0,, SB112116092902883194,00.html?mod= djemTAR (accessed August 5, 2005).

37. Ibid.

38. ICPO-Interpol General Assembly Resolution No. AG-2001-RES-07.

39. See the Coalition for an International Criminal Court, "Building the Court." Web posted at http://www.iccnow.org/buildingthecourt.html (accessed July 10, 2003).

40. Much of the information and some of the wording in this section are adapted from "The ICC International Criminal Court Home Page." Web posted at http://www.iccnow.org/index.html; and the ICC "Timeline." Web posted at http://www.iccnow.org/html/timeline.htm (accessed April 12, 2002).

41. *Convention on the Prevention and Punishment of the Crime of Genocide,* adopted by Resolution 260 (III) A of the U.N. General Assembly on December 9, 1948. Web accessible at http://www.preventgenocide.org/law/convention/text.htm.

42. Plenipotentiary is another word for "diplomat."

43. Rome Statute of the International Criminal Court, United Nations Diplomatic Conference of Plenipotentiaries on the Establishment of an International Criminal Court, Rome, Italy, June 15–July 16, 1998. U.N. Document Number A/CONF.183/9 (1998), art. 7. Web posted at http://www.un.org/law/icc/statutw/romefra.htm.

44. Jan M. Olsen, "EU Welcomes U.S. Compromise on War Crimes Tribunal," Associated Press, July 13, 2002.

45. United Nations Security Council Resolution No. 1422 (July 1, 2002).

46. "Decision of Pre-Trial Chamber I on the Prosecutor's Request under Article 56 of the Rome Statute," ICC Press Release, April 26, 2005. Web posted at http://www.icc-cpi.int/press/pressreleases/105.html (accessed May 20, 2005).

47. Much of the information in this paragraph and the next comes from David J. Lynch, "Belgium Plays Global Prosecutor," *USA Today,* July 16, 2001, p. 7A; and Katie Nguyen, "Cubans Use Belgian Law to File Case against Castro," Reuters wire service, October 4, 2001.

48. Laurie Robinson, address given at the Twelfth International Congress on Criminology, Seoul, Korea, August 28, 1998.

49. Robert S. Gelbard, "Foreign Policy after the Cold War: The New Threat—Transnational Crime," address at St. Mary's University, San Antonio, Texas, April 2, 1996.

50. Barbara Starr, "A Gangster's Paradise," ABC News Online, September 14, 1998. Web posted at http://more.abcnews.go.com/sections/world/dailynews/russiacrime980914.html (accessed January 22, 2000).

51. As quoted in Starr, "A Gangster's Paradise."

52. Raymond Bonner and Timothy L. O'Brien, "Activity at Bank Raises Suspicions of Russia Mob Tie," *New York Times,* August 19, 1999, p. 1A.

53. Adapted from "Globalization," *Encyclopedia Britannica, 2003.* Encyclopedia Britannica Premium Service. Web posted at http://www.britannica.com/eb/article?eu=369857 (accessed July, 23, 2003).

54. Public Law 108-193.

55. Sex trafficking is defined separately under 22 U.S.C. § 7102 (8); (9); (14) as "the recruitment, harboring, transportation, provision, or obtaining of a person for the purpose of a commercial sex act."

56. Kevin F. Ryan, "Globalizing the Problem: The United States and International Drug Control," in Eric L. Jensen and Jurg Gerber, eds., *The New War on Drugs: Symbolic Politics and Criminal Justice Policy* (Cincinnati, OH: Anderson, 1997).

57. Foreign Relations Authorization Act, 22 U.S.C. 2656 f (d)(2).

58. In the words of the act: "The term 'terrorism' means premeditated, politically motivated violence perpetrated against noncombatant targets by subnational groups or clandestine agents." 22 U.S.C. 2656 f (d)(2).

59. Federal Bureau of Investigation, *Counterterrorism Section, Terrorism in the United States, 1987* (Washington, DC: FBI, 1987), in which the full definition offered here can be found. See also *FBI Policy and Guidelines: Counterterrorism.* Web posted at http://www.fbi.gov/contact/fo/jackson/cntrterr.htm (accessed January 15, 2002), which offers a somewhat less formal definition of the term.

60. Gwynn Nettler, *Killing One Another* (Cincinnati, OH: Anderson, 1982).

61. Ibid., p. 253.

62. Adapted from *FBI Policy and Guidelines.*

63. Ibid.

64. The death penalty was imposed for the first-degree murders of eight federal law enforcement agents who were at work in the Murrah Building at the time of the bombing. While all of the killings violated Oklahoma law, only the killings of the federal agents fell under federal law, which makes such murders capital offenses.

65. "Terry Nichols Receives Life Sentences for Each of 161 Victims in 1995 Oklahoma City Bombing," Associated Press, August 9, 2004.

66. Michael E. Wiggins, "Rationale and Justification for Right-Wing Terrorism: A Politico-Social Analysis of the Turner Diaries," paper presented at the annual meeting of the American Society of Criminology, Atlanta, GA, October 1986.

67. "Rudolph Agrees to Plea Agreement," CNN Law Center, April 12, 2005. Web posted at http://www.cnn.com/2005/LAW/04/08/ rudolph.plea (accessed May 21, 2005).

68. Bruce Frankel, "Sheik Guilty in Terror Plot," *USA Today,* October 2, 1995, p. 1A. Sheik Abdel-Rahman and codefendant El Sayyid Nosair were both sentenced to life in prison. Other defendants received sentences of between 25 and 57 years in prison. See Sascha Brodsky, "Terror Verdicts Denounced," United Press International wire service, January 17, 1996.

69. "Qaeda Suspect Dead, Suicide Eyed," CBSNews.com, July 3, 2003. Web posted at http://www.cbsnews.com/stories/2003/06/ 26/world/main560618.shtml (accessed July 10, 2003).

70. Philip Stephens, "All Nostalgia Is Futile at the Beginning of History," *Financial Times,* May 27, 2005, p. 13.

71. See Barry Collin, "The Future of Cyberterrorism," *Crime and Justice International* (March 1997), pp. 15–18.

72. John Arquilla and David Ronfeldt, *The Advent of Netwar* (Santa Monica, CA: RAND Corporation, 1996).

73. Mark M. Pollitt, "Cyberterrorism: Fact or Fancy?" *Proceedings of the Twentieth National Information Systems Security Conference,* October 1997, pp. 285–289.

74. The White House Office of the Press Secretary, "Executive Order on Critical Infrastructure Protection," October 16, 2001. Web posted at http://www.whitehouse.gov/ news/releases/2001/10/20011016-12.html (accessed May 21, 2005).

75. President's Critical Infrastructure Protection Board, *The National Strategy to Secure Cyberspace* (Washington, DC: U.S. Government Printing Office, September 18, 2002).

76. Department of Homeland Security, "Ridge Creates New Division to Combat Cyber Threats," press release, June 6, 2003. Web posted at http://www.dhs.gov/dhspublic/ display?content=916 (accessed May 21, 2005).

77. Daniel Boyce, "Narco-terrorism," *FBI Law Enforcement Bulletin* (October 1987), p. 24; and James A. Inciardi, "Narcoterrorism: A Perspective and Commentary," in Robert O. Slater and Grant Wardlaw, eds., *International Narcotics* (London: Macmillan/St. Martins, 1989).

78. Details for this story come from "Alleged Afghan Drug Kingpin Arrested," *USA Today,* April 26, 2005, p. 3A.

79. A term reportedly invented by former Peruvian President Fernando Belaunde Terry; see James A. Inciardi, "Narcoterrorism," paper presented at the 1988 annual meeting of the Academy of Criminal Justice Sciences, San Francisco, p. 8.

80. Boyce, "Narco-terrorism," p. 24.

81. Ibid., p. 25.

82. U.S. Department of State, *Terrorist Group Profiles* (Washington, DC: U.S. Government Printing Office, 1989).

83. Inciardi, "Narcoterrorism."

84. "U.S. Government Lacks Strategy to Neutralize International Crime," *Criminal Justice International,* Vol. 10, No. 5 (September/October 1994), p. 5.

85. *National Strategy for Combating Terrorism* (Washington, D.C: White House, 2003).

86. Emilio C. Viano, Jose Magallanes, and Laurent Bridel, "Transnational Organized Crime: Myth, Power, and Profit," *Crime and Justice International,* May/June 2005, p. 23.

87. *National Strategy for Combating Terrorism,* p. 6.

88. Ibid.

89. The actual language of the act sets a standard for metal detectors through the use of a "security exemplar" made of 3.7 ounces of stainless steel in the shape of a handgun. Weapons made of other substances might still pass the test provided that they could be detected by metal detectors adjusted to that level of sensitivity. See "Bill Is Signed Barring Sale or Manufacture of Plastic Guns," *Criminal Justice Newsletter,* Vol. 19, No. 23 (December 1, 1988), pp. 4–5.

90. National Commission on Terrorism, *Countering the Changing Threat of International Terrorism* (Washington, DC: U.S. Department of State, 2000).

91. U.S. Department of Homeland Security, "DHS Organization: Building a Secure Homeland." Web posted at http://www.dhs.gov/dhspublic/ theme_home1.jsp (accessed August 2, 2003).

92. On March 1, 2003, the Immigration and Naturalization Service became part of the U.S. Department of Homeland Security, and its functions were divided into various bureaus within that department.

93. The information in this section comes from U.S. Department of Homeland Security, "DHS Organization: Department Components." Web posted at http://www.dhs.gov/dhspublic/ display?theme=9&content=858 (accessed August 2, 2003).

94. *National Strategy for Combating Terrorism.*

95. 8 U.S.C. 1-1599.

96. Public Law 108-408.

97. 8 U.S.C. 219.

98. Information in this paragraph comes from U.S. Department of State, *Patterns of Global Terrorism 2002.* Web posted at http://www.state.gov/s/ct/rls/pgtrpt/2002/ (accessed August 2, 2005).

99. Central Intelligence Agency, National Foreign Intelligence Council, *Global Trends, 2015: A Dialogue about the Future with Nongovernment Experts* (Washington, DC: U.S. Government Printing Office, 2000).

100. Ibid.

101. Central Intelligence Agency, National Foreign Intelligence Council, *Mapping the Global Future: Report of the National Intelligence Council's 2020 Project* (Washington, DC: U.S. Government Printing Office, 2005).

# 18

# CHAPTER

# The Future of Criminal Justice

## OUTLINE

- Introduction
- Technology and Crime
- Technology and Crime Control
- Criminalistics: Past, Present, and Future
- Technology and Individual Rights

## LEARNING OBJECTIVES

After reading this chapter, you should be able to:

- Describe the historical relationship between technological advances and social and cultural changes.
- Explain the nature of high-technology crime, and list some forms that such crimes have taken in the past and that they might take in the future.
- Explain the important role that technology has played, and will continue to play, in the fight against crime and the quest for justice.
- Explain why laws defining criminal activity must change to keep pace with advancing technologies.
- Provide an overview of criminalistics, and explain how evolving technology contributes to advances in that field.
- Identify the threats to individual rights inherent in the ever-increasing use of advanced technology.

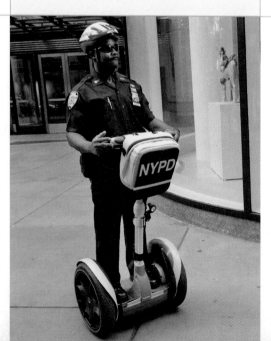

*At some point, we can do away with cybercrime laws because most crimes will involve computers in some way, and all crime will be cybercrime.*

—Computer crime expert Donn Parker[1]

"The rise of a new kind of America requires a new kind of law enforcement system.

—Alvin Toffler

He that will not apply new remedies must expect new evils; for time is the greatest innovator."

—Sir Francis Bacon, 1601

# KEY CONCEPTS

## TERMS

| | | |
|---|---|---|
| augmented reality (AR) | criminalistics | malware |
| ballistics | *Daubert* standard | protected computer |
| biocrime | DNA profiling | smart card |
| biometrics | expert system | social engineering |
| bioterrorism | forensic anthropology | software piracy |
| computer crime | forensic entomology | spam |
| computer virus | hacker | technocrime |
| criminalist | identity management | weapon of mass destruction (WMD) |

## CASES

*Daubert* v. *Merrell Dow Pharmaceuticals, Inc.*     *Frye* v. *U.S.*     *Reno* v. *ACLU*

The original full-text court opinion for each of these cases is available on the CD-ROM that accompanies this book.

# Introduction

Hear the author discuss this chapter at **cjtoday.com**

At 9 P.M. on October 24, 2004, Secret Service assistant director Brian K. Nagel issued a "go" order for the arrest of suspected members of the ShadowCrew, an international gang of computer hackers adept at pillaging bank accounts, stealing identities, and laundering money over the Internet.[2] The arrests, which netted 28 cyber criminals in eight states and a dozen countries, were the culminating step in Operation Firewall, a month-long international effort involving federal, state, and local law enforcement agencies, along with Britain's National High-Tech Crimes Unit, the Royal Canadian Mounted Police, and the Bulgarian Interior Ministry. Agents in participating countries struck simultaneously in a coordinated effort to prevent gang members from warning one another. By the time the raid ended, investigators had confiscated 1.7 million stolen credit card numbers, 18 million pilfered e-mail addresses and passwords, and identity data for thousands of people in the United States and abroad. The accused ring leaders, Andrew Mantovani, 23, a part-time community college student from Arizona, and David Appleyard, 45, a former New Jersey mortgage broker, are alleged to have run a website called ShadowCrew.com, which served as an international clearinghouse for stolen credit card numbers and identity information. Affidavits filed by the Secret Service say that the ShadowCrew website served the nefarious needs of 4,000 gang members who used it to buy and sell stolen information and merchandise. Dozens of companies were targeted by the cyber offenders, including those operated by Bank of America and MasterCard, Inc. The ShadowCrew site, which director Nagel called a "criminal bazaar," also posted tips on how to avoid arrest, including pages of information on how to use stolen credit cards and fake IDs at large retail stores and online shopping services. As this book goes to press, arrests based on intelligence obtained through Operation Firewall are still being carried out. "We will be arresting people for months and months and months," said Nagel.

New technologies can make life easier for those who use them. They can also provide novel criminal opportunities to those looking for ill-gotten gains. The tools of the trade used by cyber criminals like the ShadowCrew members, for example, did not exist a mere generation ago. Because technology is one of the most important instruments of change in the modern world, this chapter focuses on the opportunities and threats that contemporary technology represents to the justice system. Learn more about technology and its role in social change via Library Extra 18–1 at cjtoday.com.

**LIBRARY EXTRA**

> Computers can be broken into. If they're on the Internet, [they] might as well have a welcome mat.
>
> —Kevin Mitnick[i]

# Technology and Crime

Rapid advances in the biological sciences and electronic technologies during the past few decades, including genetic mapping, nanotechnology, computer networking, the Internet, wireless services of all kinds, artificial intelligence (AI), and geopositioning devices, have ushered in

A Muslim traveler arriving in Saudi Arabia for the annual Hajj, or pilgrimage to Mecca, undergoes an iris scan to authenticate his identity. Technology is an important tool in the worldwide fight against identity manipulation and criminal acts of terrorism.

*Nicole Bengiveno,* The New York Times

a wealth of new criminal opportunities. Crimes that employ advanced or emerging technologies in their commission are referred to as **technocrimes**.

New York State police captain and law enforcement visionary Thomas Cowper says that "it is important for police officers and their agencies to understand emerging technologies" for three reasons[3]: (1) to anticipate their use by terrorists and criminals and thereby thwart their use against our nation and citizens, (2) to incorporate their use into police operations when necessary, and (3) to deal effectively with the social changes and cultural impact that inevitably result from technological advances. According to Cowper, "Continued police apathy and ignorance of nanotech, biotech and AI, and the potential changes they will bring to our communities and way of life, will only add to the turmoil, making law enforcement a part of the problem and not part of the solution."[4]

| **technocrime** |
| --- |
| A criminal offense that employs advanced or emerging technology in its commission. |

## Biocrime

In 2005, the World Health Organization (WHO) raised alarms when it said that some samples of a potentially dangerous influenza virus that had been sent to thousands of laboratories in 18 countries had been lost and could not be located. Bio-kits containing the influenza A (H2N2) virus, which caused the flu pandemic of 1957–1958, were sent to 4,614 laboratories for use in testing the labs' ability to identify flu viruses. Meridian Bioscience Inc. of Cleveland, Ohio, sent the kits on behalf of the College of American Pathologists (CAP) and three other U.S. organizations that set testing standards for laboratories. Although most of the laboratories were in the United States, some were in Latin America, and a few were in the Arab world—raising fears that Islamic terrorists might use the viral material, against which most people living today have no immunity, to create a pandemic. The H2N2 scare ended on May 2, 2005, when the U.S. Centers for Disease Control and Prevention issued a press release saying that the last remaining sample of the virus outside the United States had been found and destroyed at the American University of Beirut in Lebanon.[5] The Lebanese sample had been misplaced by a local delivery service but was discovered in a warehouse at the Beirut airport. Although the incident came to a successful conclusion, it heightened concerns about the spread of highly pathogenic avian influenza (HPAI) viruses and the possible appropriation by criminals of reverse-genetics research on the 1918 pandemic flu virus that killed millions worldwide.

Biological crime, or **biocrime**, is a criminal offense perpetrated through the use of biologically active substances, including chemicals and toxins, disease-causing organisms, altered genetic material, and organic tissues and organs. Biocrimes unlawfully affect the metabolic, biochemical, genetic, physiological, or anatomical status of living organisms. A major change in such status can, of course, produce death.

Biocrimes can be committed with simple poisons, but the biocrimes of special concern today involve technologically sophisticated delivery and dispersal systems and include the use of

| **biocrime** |
| --- |
| A criminal offense perpetrated through the use of biologically active substances, including chemicals and toxins, disease-causing organisms, altered genetic material, and organic tissues and organs. Biocrimes unlawfully affect the metabolic, biochemical, genetic, physiological, or anatomical status of living organisms. |

substances that have been bioengineered to produce the desired effect. Biocrime becomes a high-technology offense when it involves the use of purposefully altered genetic material or advanced bioscientific techniques.

Although many people think of terrorist-related biocrimes, including biological attacks on agricultural plants and animals (agroterrorism) and on human beings, many other kinds of potential biocrimes lurk on the horizon. They include the illegal harvesting of human organs for medical transplantation, human cloning, and the direct alteration of the DNA of living beings to produce a mixing of traits between species. Stem cell harvesting, another area that faces possible criminalization, is currently the subject of hot debate. As this book goes to press, the situation in the United States with regard to stem cell harvesting is one of funding restrictions, not legal or criminal restrictions. Although the federal government has yet to enact comprehensive legislation curtailing, regulating, or forbidding many of the kinds of activities mentioned here, there are indications that legislative action may soon come.

In 2004, Korean scientists became the first to announce that they had successfully cloned a human embryo and extracted embryonic stem cells from it.[6] In 2005 those same scientists used the process to make stem cells tailored to match an individual patient, meaning that medical treatments for diseases like diabetes might be possible without fear of cellular rejection. Similarly, in 2005, British scientists working at Newcastle University in England disclosed that they had created a cloned human embryo. Cloning is a cellular reproductive process that does not require the joining of a sperm and an egg, but that occurs when the nucleus of an egg is replaced with the nucleus of another cell.

Currently, President Bush favors a ban on all research into human cloning in the United States,[7] and he threatened to veto proposed federal legislation in 2005 that would have provided federal support for cloning research.[8] Similarly, in 2003, the U.S. House of Representatives voted to criminalize all human cloning activities and research.[9] The proposed legislation, known as the Human Cloning Research Prohibition Act, would have made it a crime to transfer the nucleus of an ordinary human cell into an unfertilized human egg whose own nucleus has been removed.[10] It also would have made it a crime to "receive or import a cloned human embryo or any product derived from a cloned human embryo." The scientific technique targeted by the bill, known as *nuclear transfer*, is the process that was used to clone Dolly the sheep in 1996.[11] A similar bill, known as the Human Cloning Prohibition Act of 2005, was introduced in the 109th Congress by Senator Sam Brownback (R–Kans.).[12] The bill, if passed, would have prohibited both reproductive cloning and the use of cloning technology to derive stem cells. In other words, the legislation aimed to thwart not just reproductive cloning, in which a copy of a living organism might be made, but also therapeutic cloning.[13] Therapeutic cloning is a healing technique in which a person's own cells can be used to grow a new organ such as a heart, liver, or lungs to replace diseased or damaged ones. Opponents feared that the proposed legislation, which specified punishments of up to a $1 million fine and ten years in prison, would have significantly retarded biomedical progress in the United States, relegating America to a kind of technological backwater in the world's burgeoning biotechnology industry.[14]

## Cybercrime

**computer crime**

Any crime perpetrated through the use of computer technology. Also, any violation of a federal or state computer-crime statute. Also called *cybercrime*.

**hacker**

A computer hobbyist or professional, generally with advanced programming skills. Today, the term *hacker* has taken on a sinister connotation, referring to hobbyists who are bent on illegally accessing the computers of others or who attempt to demonstrate their technological prowess through computerized acts of vandalism.

The dark side of new technologies, as far as the justice system is concerned, is the potential they create for committing old crimes in new ways or for committing new crimes never before imagined. In 2003, for example, technologically savvy scam artists replicated the website of the Massachusetts State Lottery Commission.[15] The scammers, believed to be operating out of Nigeria, sent thousands of e-mails and cell phone text messages telling people that they had won $30,000 in the Massachusetts State Lottery. People who received the messages were told to sign on to an official-looking website to claim their prize. The site required that users enter their Social Security and credit card numbers and pay a $100 processing fee before the winnings could be distributed.

A person's online activities occur in a virtual world comprised of bits and bytes. That's why we said in Chapter 2 that "true" computer criminals engage in behavior that goes beyond the theft of hardware. **Computer crime**, or cybercrime, focuses on the information stored in electronic media, which is why it is sometimes referred to as *information technology crime* or *infocrime*. A decade ago, for example, the activities of computer expert Kevin Mitnick, then known as the "FBI's most wanted **hacker**,"[16] alarmed security experts because of the potential for harm that Mitnick's electronic intrusions represented. The 31-year-old Mitnick broke into an Internet service provider's computer system and stole more than 20,000 credit card numbers. Tsutoma Shimomura, whose home computer Mitnick had also attacked, helped FBI experts track Mitnick through telephone lines and computer networks to the computer in his Raleigh, North Carolina, apartment, where he was arrested. In March 1999, Mitnick pleaded guilty to seven federal counts of computer and wire fraud. He was sentenced to 46 months in prison but was released on parole in January 2000. Under the terms of his release, Mitnick was barred from access to computer hardware and software and from any form of wireless communication for a period of three years.[17] In an interview after his release, Mitnick pointed out that "malicious hackers don't need to use stealth computer techniques to break into a network. . . . Often they just trick someone into giving them passwords and other information."[18] According to Mitnick, "People are the weakest link. . . . You can have the best technology, firewalls, intrusion-detection systems, biometric devices . . . and somebody can call an unsuspecting employee. . . . [and] they [get] everything."

Neil Barrett, a digital crime expert at International Risk Management, a London-based security consultancy, agrees. "The most likely way for bad guys to break into the system is through **social engineering**. This involves persuading administrators or telephonists to give details of passwords or other things by pretending to be staff, suppliers or trusted individuals—even police officers. They could be even masquerading as a computer repair man to get access to the premises."[19] Social engineering is a devastating security threat, says Barrett, because it targets and exploits a computer network's most vulnerable aspect—people.

## Transnational Cybercrime

An especially important characteristic of cybercrime is that it can easily be cross-jurisdictional or transnational. A cyberoffender sitting at a keyboard in Australia, for example, can steal money from a bank in Russia and then transfer the digital cash to an account in Chile. For investigators, the question may be "What laws were broken?" Complicating matters is the fact that Australia and Chile have fragmented computer-crime laws, and Russia[20] has laws that are particularly ineffective.

According to researchers at McConnell International, a consulting firm based in Washington, D.C., of 52 developing countries surveyed in 2000, only the Philippines had effective computer-crime legislation in effect.[21] The Philippines enacted new cybercrime laws in 2000 after the creator of the highly damaging "Love Bug" computer virus, a 23-year-old Philippine student named Onel de Guzman, could not be prosecuted under the country's existing computer-crime laws.[22] De Guzman was finally charged with theft and violation of a law that had been enacted to deter credit card fraud. The country's new cybercrime law could not be applied to him retroactively.

In an effort to enhance similarities in the computer-crime laws of different countries and to provide a model for national law-making bodies concerned with controlling cybercrimes, the 43-nation Council of Europe approved a cybercrime treaty in November 2001.[23] The treaty outlaws specific online activities, including fraud and child pornography, and outlines what law enforcement officials in member nations may and may not do in enforcing computer-crime laws. The goal of the treaty is to standardize both legal understandings of cybercrime and cybercrime laws in member nations. It also allows police officers to detain suspects wanted in other countries for cybercrimes and facilitates the gathering of information on such crimes across national borders. In addition to the council's member states, the treaty was also signed by the United States, Canada, Japan, and South Africa.[24] Visit the Council of Europe's Treaty Office via **Web Extra 18–1** at cjtoday.com, and click on "New Treaties" to find the full text of the council's cybercrime treaty. Learn more about cybercrime from the President's Working Group on Unlawful Conduct on the Internet via **Library Extra 18–2** at cjtoday.com.

## Types of Cybercrime

Although a generally accepted comprehensive typology of computer crime has yet to be developed,[25] Peter Grabosky of the Australian Institute of Criminology suggests that most such crimes fall into one of the following broad categories[26]: (1) theft of services, such as telephone or long-distance access; (2) communications in furtherance of criminal conspiracies—for example, the e-mail communications said to have taken place between members of Osama bin Laden's al-Qaeda terrorist network[27]; (3) information piracy and forgery—that is, the stealing of trade secrets or copyrighted information; (4) the dissemination of offensive materials such as child pornography, or high volumes of unwanted commercial material such as bulk e-mail (spam), or extortion threats, like those made against financial institutions by hackers claiming the ability to destroy a company's electronic records; (5) electronic money laundering and tax evasion (through electronic funds transfers that conceal the origin of financial proceeds); (6) electronic vandalism and terrorism, including computer viruses, worms, Trojan horses, and cyberterrorism (see Chapter 17); (7) telemarketing fraud (including investment frauds and illegitimate electronic auctions); (8) illegal interception of telecommunications—that is, illegal eavesdropping; and (9) electronic funds–transfer fraud (specifically, the illegal interception and diversion of legitimate transactions).

> The future comes one day at a time.
>
> —Dean Acheson

**social engineering**
A nontechnical kind of cyber intrusion that relies heavily on human interaction and often involves tricking people into breaking normal security procedures.

The 2004 Computer Crime and Security Survey, conducted annually by the Computer Security Institute (CSI) and the FBI, found that 53% of the large businesses, medical institutions, universities, and government agencies participating in the survey reported detecting security-related breaches of their computer networks in 2003.[28] The survey also found that only about half of all reported breaches originated outside of the organization. Other researchers have determined that some of the most serious corporate computer security threats come from employees, including 70% of all unauthorized access to information systems incidents and 95% of all network intrusions that result in significant financial loss.[29] The CSI/FBI report found that the highest average annual computer security expenditure per employee ($608) in 2003 was reported by organizations in the transportation sector. The federal government reported spending $261 per federal employee to secure its computers in 2003, and the telecommunications industry reported annual computer security expenditures averaging $209 per employee.[30]

Also in 2004, the Bureau of Justice Statistics (BJS) released initial results from its 2001 Computer Security Survey (CSS), which had been conducted in collaboration with the U.S. Census Bureau.[31] The 2004 report summarized findings from a pilot survey of 500 companies nationwide. Nearly three-fourths of businesses surveyed reported detecting at least one computer security incident during the previous 12-month period. Computer viruses were the most common type of incident reported (65%), followed by denial-of-service attacks (25%) and vandalism or sabotage of computer equipment or computer networks (19%). Other crimes, such as fraud, theft of proprietary information, and embezzlement, were also reported. Not surprisingly, the largest companies experienced the greatest number of incidents. When fully implemented, the CSS will provide the first official national statistics on the extent and consequences of cybercrime against the nation's 5.3 million businesses. You may access the initial BJS report in its entirety as Library Extra 18–3 at cjtoday.com. The Computer Crime and Security Survey can be found online as Library Extra 18–4.

**Computer viruses** are a special concern of computer users everywhere. Computer viruses were first brought to public attention in 1988, when the Pakistani virus (or Pakistani brain virus) became widespread in personal and office computers across the United States.[32] The Pakistani virus was created by Amjad Farooq Alvi and his brother, Basit Farooq Alvi, two cut-rate computer software dealers in Lahore, Pakistan. The Alvi brothers made copies of costly software products and sold them at low prices, mostly to Western shoppers looking for a bargain. Motivated by convoluted logic, the brothers hid a virus on each disk they sold to punish buyers for seeking to evade copyright laws.

A more serious virus incident affected sensitive machines in the National Aeronautics and Space Administration (NASA) nuclear weapons labs, federal research centers, and universities across the United States in late 1988.[33] The virus did not destroy data. Instead, it made copies of itself and multiplied so rapidly that it clogged and effectively shut down computers within hours after invading them. Robert Morris, creator of the virus, was sentenced in 1990 to 400 hours of community service, three years' probation, and a fine of $10,000.[34] Since then, many other virus attacks have made headlines, including the infamous Michelangelo virus in 1992; the intentional distribution of infected software on an AIDS-related research CD-ROM distributed about the same time; the Kournikova virus in 2000; and the Sircam, Nimda, W32, NastyBrew, Berbew, Mydoom, and Code Red worms—all of which made their appearance or were substantially modified by their creators between 2001 and 2005.

Technically speaking, most of today's malicious software falls under the category of worms or Trojan horses—called **malware** by technophiles. Malware has become increasingly sophisticated. Although early viruses were relatively easy to detect with hardware or software scanning devices that looked for virus "signatures," new malicious software using stealth and polymorphic computer codes change form with each new "infection" and are much more difficult to locate and remove. Moreover, while older viruses infected only executable programs, or those that could be run, newer malware (such as the Word for Windows Macro virus, also called the Concept virus) attaches itself to word-processing documents and to computer codes that are routinely distributed via the World Wide Web (including Java and Active-X components used by Web browsers). In 1998, the world's first HTML virus was discovered. The virus, named HTML.Internal, infects computers whose users are merely viewing Web pages.[35] Later that year, the first JAVA-based malware, named Strange Brew, made its appearance,[36] and in 2004 malware capable of infecting digital images using the Joint Photographic Experts Group (JPEG) format was discovered.[37] Evolving forms of malware are even able to infect cellular phones (Figure 18–1) and other wireless-enabled handheld devices.

**LIBRARY EXTRA**

**computer virus**

A computer program designed to secretly invade systems and either modify the way in which they operate or alter the information they store. Viruses are destructive software programs that may effectively vandalize computers of all types and sizes.

**malware**

Malicious computer programs such as viruses, worms, and Trojan horses.

**STEP 1: APPROACH**
A virus-spreader enters Heathrow Airport toting a briefcase with a laptop and an external antenna. The rig can sniff Bluetooth signals from up to 20 feet away—and with just a bit of hacking, it can be modified to send and receive signals over much greater distances.

**STEP 2: DISCOVER**
Using a program like bluesnarf, the laptop automatically finds Bluetooth phones with firmware vulnerable to remote takeover. This process is completed in less than 15 seconds.

**STEP 3: TAKE OVER**
The laptop sends a program to all the vulnerable phones. Disguised as a game or a marketing promotion, the program is really a Trojan horse hiding a nasty virus. Once the user launches it, the virus hijacks the phone's operating system, taking over basic functions like dialing and messaging.

**STEP 4: PROPAGATE**
The target phone is now infected, and it reacts by broadcasting the virus to other vulnerable Bluetooth phones within 20 feet. Within minutes, thousands of phones can be infected.

**STEP 5: STEAL**
Commandeering the phones' SMS system, the virus uses a popular European micropayment system called reverse SMS to transfer 10 euros from each phone to a temporary account in Estonia. The virus requests the transfer and stays in control until it can confirm the order. The account is closed long before any user sees the charge reflected on the monthly bill.

**FIGURE 18–1**

**The great cell phone robbery.**
*Source:* blanddesigns.co.uk. Originally published in *Wired Magazine*, December 2004, p. 94. Reprinted with permission.

One form of cybercrime that relies primarily on social engineering to succeed is *phishing* (pronounced *fishing*). Phishing is a relatively new form of high-technology fraud that uses official-looking e-mail messages to elicit responses from victims, directing them to phony websites. Microsoft Corporation says that phishing is "the fastest-growing form of online fraud in the world today."[38] Phishing e-mails typically instruct recipients to validate or update account information before their accounts are canceled. Phishing schemes, which have targeted most major banks, the Federal Deposit Insurance Corporation, IBM, eBay, PayPal, and some major health care providers, are designed to steal valuable information such as credit card numbers, Social Security numbers, user IDs, and passwords. In 2004, Gartner Inc., a leading provider of research and analysis on the global information technology industry, released a report estimating that some 57 million adult Americans received phishing e-mails during the spring of 2004 and that 11 million recipients clicked on the link contained in the messages.[39] Gartner estimated that 1.78 million recipients actually provided personal information to the thieves behind the phishing schemes.

Another form of cybercrime, the unauthorized copying of software programs, also called **software piracy**, appears to be rampant. According to the Software and Information Industry Association (SIIA), global losses from software piracy total nearly $12.2 billion annually.[40] The SIIA says that 38% of all software in use in the world today has been copied illegally. Some countries have especially high rates of illegal use. Of all the computer software in use in Vietnam, for example, SIIA estimates that 97% has been illegally copied, while 95% of the software used in China and 92% of the software used in Russia are thought to be pirated—resulting in a substantial loss in manufacturers' revenue.

Software pirates seem to be especially adept at evading today's copy-protection schemes, including those that involve software "keys" and Internet authentication. Similar to software piracy, peer-to-peer Internet file-sharing services (which directly connect users' computers with one another via the Internet) have been criticized for allowing users to download copyright-protected e-music and digital video files free of charge. Lawsuits involving the music-sharing service Napster resulted in the site's near closure, and similar websites, such as KaZaA, Morpheus, and Grokster, are the targets of ongoing music industry lawsuits. In 2003, however, a U.S. district court in New York held that many music-swapping services and their operators could not be held accountable for the actions of their users, although individual users who download copyrighted materials *can* be held liable for copyright infringements.[41] That same year, a federal judge in Los Angeles ruled that peer-to-peer network software providers Grokster and StreamCast Networks could not be held liable for the copyright infringements of their users.[42] In 2004, the 9th

Our "can-do" spirit as Americans generates tremendous fascination with technology and what it can do for us [as a society]. But at the same time we have an innate and healthy skepticism, perhaps even a fear, of what technology can do to us as individuals.

—Mark H. Gitenstein,
Executive Director of the
Foundation for Change

**software piracy**
The unauthorized duplication of software or the illegal transfer of data from one storage medium to another. Software piracy is one of the most prevalent computer crimes in the world.

U.S. Circuit Court of Appeals upheld that ruling,[43] but in 2005 the U.S. Supreme Court agreed to hear an appeal from the music industry, and in the landmark case of *MGM* v. *Grokster*,[44] the Court found that online file sharing services may be held liable for copyright infringement if they promote their services explicitly as a way for users to download copyrighted music and other content. The *Grokster* decision contrasts with the 1984 case of *Sony Corporation of America* v. *Universal City Studios, Inc.*, in which the Court held that a distributor/operator of a copying tool cannot be held liable for users' copyright infringements so long as the tool in question is capable of substantial noninfringing uses.[45] Attempts to legislatively criminalize the downloading of digitized music and movies began on Capitol Hill in 2003. If the proposed legislation is enacted, illegal downloaders could face prison terms of up to five years.[46]

Also in 2003, federal legislators acted to criminalize the sending of unsolicited commercial e-mail, or **spam**. The federal CAN-SPAM Act (Controlling the Assault of Non-Solicited Pornography and Marketing), which took effect on January 1, 2004, regulates the sending of "commercial electronic mail messages."[47] The law, which applies equally to mass mailings and to individual e-mail messages, defines commercial electronic mail messages as electronic mail whose *primary purpose* is the "commercial advertisement or promotion of a commercial product or service." The CAN-SPAM law requires that a commercial e-mail message include the following three features: (1) a clear and conspicuous identification that the message is an advertisement or solicitation, (2) an opt-out feature, allowing recipients to opt out of future mailings, and (3) a valid physical address identifying the sender.

Some experts estimate that 80% of all e-mail today is spam,[48] and a number of states have enacted their own antispam laws. Virginia's 2003 antispam statute,[49] for example, imposes criminal penalties of from one to five years for anyone convicted of falsifying electronic mail transmission information or other routing information during the sending of unsolicited commercial bulk e-mail (UCBE). The law applies to anyone sending more than 10,000 UCBEs in a 24-hour period or anyone who generates more than $1,000 in revenue from a UCBE transmission. The law also applies to anyone who uses fraudulent practices to send bulk e-mail to or from Virginia, a state that is home to a number of large Internet service providers, including America Online. In 2005, in the nation's first felony prosecution of a spammer, Jeremy Jaynes, 30, one of the world's most active spammers, received a nine-year prison sentence under Virginia's law after he was convicted of using false Internet addresses and aliases to send mass e-mailings to America Online subscribers. Prosecutors were able to prove that Jaynes, a Raleigh, North Carolina, resident, earned as much as $750,000 a month by sending as many as 10 million illegal messages a day using computers operating in Virginia.[50] Learn more about cybercrime and efforts to combat it at Web Extra 18–2 at cjtoday.com.

**spam**

Unsolicited commercial bulk e-mail (UCBE), whose *primary purpose* is the commercial advertisement or promotion of a commercial product or service.

**WEB EXTRA**

Tennis superstar Anna Kournikova. Kournikova served as inspiration for Jan de Wit, 20, of Sneek, Netherlands, creator of the Kournikova computer virus. In 2001, Wit was convicted of violating Holland's law against spreading data into a computer network with the intention of causing damage. He was sentenced to 150 hours of community service.

*AP Wide World Photos*

## CJ NEWS

# Terrorists' Use of the Internet Spreads

Cyberfraud, ranging from credit card theft to money laundering, is the latest wrinkle in terrorists' use of the Internet.

It's "the new cash cow" for terrorists to finance operations, says John Pironti, a security consultant at tech consultant Unisys. Online scams are harder to trace because they are relayed through a sophisticated network of individuals and Web sites worldwide, he says. And many schemes originate from abroad, where cyberlaws don't exist or law enforcement is lax.

In dozens of incidents during the past few months, groups linked to terrorism have stolen credit card numbers over the Internet, laundered money and hijacked Web sites, security experts say.

The recent surge in activity has given counterterrorism specialists, already concerned with threats to physical structures, another worry. Like their colleagues in the FBI, Secret Service, the Treasury Department and elsewhere, they must bone up on Internet technology to match wits with the criminals.

For several years, groups including al-Qaeda have used cyberspace for communications, recruiting and propaganda. Now they've branched into other areas. Credit card numbers are often swiped through hacking attacks and phishing, fraudulent e-mails that trick consumers into surrendering personal information.

There are indications terrorists may next steal trade secrets from U.S. companies as their computer skills improve and they begin to work with organized crime in Eastern Europe. The stolen documents could then be sold to rogue foreign businesses or held for ransom, security experts say.

## TERRORISM.ORG

A few months ago, Imam Samudra, convicted of masterminding the bombing that killed 202 in Bali, Indonesia, in 2002, wrote a jailhouse manifesto on the funding of terrorism through cyberfraud.

A chapter in his obscure autobiography—titled "Hacking, Why Not?"—directs fellow Muslim radicals to Indonesian-language Web sites and chat rooms for instructions on online credit card fraud and money laundering. "Any man-made product contains weakness because man himself is a weak creature," Samudra writes. "So it is with the Americans, who boast they are a strong nation."

Evidence collected from Samudra's laptop showed he tried to finance the bombing through cyberfraud, law-enforcement officials say.

In October, a suspected Palestinian supporter of Middle Eastern terrorist groups posted several credit card numbers online and instructions for stealing databases of other active credit card numbers from the Web sites of U.S. businesses.

Internet use by terrorists mirrors that of criminals. While some security experts fear a cyberstrike could disrupt power supplies to millions of homes, disrupt air traffic control systems and shut down water supplies, most agree terror groups are more likely to exploit the Internet for financial gain and to

Imam Samudra, convicted of masterminding terrorist bombings in Bali, Indonesia, that killed 202 people in 2002, shouts "Allah Akbar" (God is great) after being sentenced to death by firing squad. Following his capture, Samudra wrote a jailhouse manifesto on the funding of terrorism through cyberfraud. He is awaiting execution in Indonesia.

*AP Wide World Photos*

spread propaganda. The number of terrorist-related Web sites has rocketed to 4,350 from a dozen in 1997.

Terrorist organizations have graduated to the Internet to steal because it reaches more potential victims and is harder to trace, says Evan Kohlmann, an international terrorism consultant who runs the Web site Globalterroralert.com.

Previously, militants used more conventional ways for funding, Kohlmann says. The Roubaix gang in France robbed armored cars to help fund terrorist activities in the mid-1990s. And the group behind the abortive millennium attack on the Los Angeles airport robbed supermarkets in Canada and engaged in traditional credit card fraud, he says.

"It is a paradox: Those movements who criticize Western technology and modernity are using the West's most advanced communication technology, the Internet, to spread their message," Gabriel Weimann, a professor in Israel who follows cyberterrorism, said in an e-mail.

But the U.S. government should not dismiss the possibility of a large-scale electronic attack by terrorists against the nation's computer systems, says Richard Clarke, the former White House head of counterterrorism. He made the comments at the RSA security conference in San Francisco last week.

## DIGITAL CAT AND MOUSE

Federal investigators are locked in an escalating game of digital cat-and-mouse with cyberterrorists. "The FBI understands that some terrorist organizations, like criminals, could exploit the Internet to further their goals," FBI spokeswoman Megan Baroska says. FBI policy prohibits it from discussing ongoing investigations, she says.

*(continued)*

## CJ NEWS *(continued)*

The departments of Justice, State, Treasury and Homeland Security and intelligence agencies have identified a broad range of potential Internet vulnerabilities and are constantly developing policies. They compare the fight against terrorist financing to the war against money-laundering drug traffickers.

"As Internet technologies become more advanced, so do those who use them for illicit and illegal activities," says Dexter Ingram, director of information-security policy for the Business Software Alliance and a former analyst for the House Committee on Homeland Security's cybersecurity subcommittee. "Security must remain a continuous process. It's a never-ending cycle."

Still, the feds' ranks are in flux. Robert Liscouski, assistant director of the Department of Homeland Security, resigned in January after the Bush administration nominated a federal judge to head the department.

In October, Amit Yoran, director of the department's cybersecurity division, resigned amid criticism from the tech community that he lacked clout.

Clarke has called for the appointment of a cybersecurity czar in the White House to coordinate actions between the FBI, CIA and other government agencies.

"After 911, the emphasis has clearly been on physical infrastructure rather than cybersecurity," says Paul Kurtz, executive director of the Cyber Security Industry Alliance, a non-profit trade group of software and hardware companies. "That's understandable. But cyberspace is where the bad guys are going."

For the latest in crime and justice news, visit the Talk Justice news feed at http://www.crimenews.info.

*Source:* Jon Swartz, "Terrorists' Use of the Internet Spreads," *USA Today*, February 21, 2005, p. 3B. Copyright © 2005 *USA Today*. Reprinted with permission.

# Terrorism and Technology

The technological sophistication of state-sponsored terrorist organizations is rapidly increasing. Handguns and even larger weapons are now being manufactured out of plastic polymers and ceramics. Capable of firing Teflon-coated armor-piercing hardened ceramic bullets, such weapons are extremely powerful and impossible to uncover with metal detectors. Evidence points to the black market availability of other sinister items, including liquid metal embrittlement (LME). LME is a chemical that slowly weakens any metal it contacts. It could easily be applied with a felt-tipped pen to fuselage components in domestic aircraft, causing delayed structural failure.[51] Backpack-type electromagnetic pulse generators may soon be available to terrorists. Such devices could be carried into major cities, set up next to important computer installations, and activated to wipe out billions of items of financial, military, or other information now stored on magnetic media. International terrorists, along with the general public, have easy access to maps and other information that could be used to cripple the nation. The approximately 500 extremely high-voltage (EHV) transformers on which the nation's electric grid depends, for example, are largely undefended, but in the recent past were specified with extreme accuracy on easily available Web-based power network maps.

> **weapon of mass destruction (WMD)**
>
> A chemical, biological, or nuclear weapon that has the potential to cause mass casualties.

It is now clear that at least some terrorist organizations are seeking to obtain **weapons of mass destruction (WMDs)**, involving possible chemical, biological, radiological, and nuclear threats. A Central Intelligence Agency (CIA) report recently made public warned that al-Qaeda's "end goal" is to use WMDs. The CIA noted that the group had "openly expressed its desire to produce nuclear weapons" and that sketches and documents recovered from an al-Qaeda facility in Afghanistan contained plans for a crude nuclear device.[52]

The collapse of the Soviet Union in the late 1980s led to very loose internal control over nuclear weapons and weapons-grade fissionable materials held in the former Soviet republics. Evidence of this continues to surface. In 2003, for example, a cab driver in the Eastern European nation of Georgia was arrested while transporting containers of cesium-137 and strontium-90, materials that could be used to make a "dirty" bomb (a radiological dispersal device, or RDD[53]) that would use conventional explosives to spread nuclear contamination over a wide area.[54] A month later, officials arrested a traveler in Bangkok, Thailand, who had a canister of cesium-137 in his possession. Although the Thai traveler told police that he had acquired the cesium in Laos, scientists were able to determine that it had originated in Russia.

A study by Harvard University researchers found that the United States and other countries are moving too slowly in efforts to help Russia and other former Soviet-bloc nations destroy poorly protected nuclear material and warheads left over from the cold war.[55] The study also warned that most civilian nuclear reactors in Eastern Europe are "dangerously insecure." Experts say the amount of plutonium needed to make one bomb can be smuggled out of a supposedly secure area in a briefcase or even in the pocket of an overcoat.

Biological weapons were banned by the 1975 international Biological Weapons Convention (BWC),[56] but biological terrorism (or bioterrorism), which seeks to disperse destructive or disease-producing biologically active agents among civilian or military populations, is of considerable concern today. **Bioterrorism**, one form of biocrime, is defined by the Centers for Disease Control and Prevention (CDC) as the "intentional or threatened use of viruses, bacteria, fungi, or toxins from living organisms to produce death or disease in humans, animals, or plants."[57] The infamous anthrax letters mailed to at least four people in the United States in 2001 provide an example of a bioterrorism incident intended to create widespread fear among Americans. Five people, including mail handlers, died, and 23 others were infected.[58] Other possible bioterror agents include botulism toxin, brucellosis, cholera, glanders, plague, ricin, smallpox, tularemia Q fever, and a number of viral agents capable of producing diseases such as viral hemorrhagic fever and severe acute respiratory syndrome (SARS). As the "biocrimes" section of this chapter pointed out, experts fear that technologically savvy terrorists could create their own novel bioweapons through bioengineering, a process that uses snippets of made-to-order DNA, the molecular code on which life is based.[59] Learn more about biological agents via the CDC website at Web Extra 18–3, and visit the Center for the Study of Bioterrorism via Web Extra 18–4 at cjtoday.com. Read the CDC's overview of bioterrorism at Library Extra 18–5.

> **bioterrorism**
>
> The intentional or threatened use of viruses, bacteria, fungi, or toxins from living organisms to produce death or disease in humans, animals, or plants.[iii]

# Technology and Crime Control

Technology, while it has increased criminal opportunity, has also been a boon to police investigators and other justice system personnel. We will now look at technology's impact on the arsenal of crime-fighting and administrative techniques available to criminal justice practitioners.

Law enforcement access to high-technology investigative tools has produced enormous amounts of information on crimes and suspects, and the use of innovative investigative tools like DNA fingerprinting, keystroke captures, laser and night vision technologies, digital imaging, and thermography are beginning to shape many of the practical aspects of the twenty-first-century criminal justice system (Table 18–1). Today, some laptop computers and vehicles are programmed to contact police when they are stolen and provide satellite-based tracking information so authorities can

> The crucial component of effective policing in a rapidly changing world is the ability to think creatively about emerging technologies and how they can be used successfully within the constitutional limits of a free society.
>
> —Thomas J. Cowper, New York State Police[iv]

**TABLE 18–1**

| | SPECIAL TECHNOLOGIES USED BY LOCAL POLICE DEPARTMENTS, BY SIZE OF POPULATION SERVED, 2000 | | | | | | | | |
|---|---|---|---|---|---|---|---|---|---|
| | **Percentage of Agencies Using** | | | | | | | | |
| | **Night Vision/Electro-Optic** | | | **Vehicle Stopping/Tracking** | | | **Digital Imaging** | | |
| **Population Served** | **Infrared (Thermal) Imagers** | **Image Intensifiers** | **Laser Range Finders** | **Tire Deflation Spikes** | **Stolen Vehicle Tracking** | **Electrical/ Engine Disruption** | **Mug Shots** | **Suspect Composites** | **Fingerprints** |
| All sizes | 11% | 6% | 6% | 26% | 5% | —%[a] | 29% | 16% | 11% |
| 1,000,000 or more | 73 | 53 | 40 | 47 | 73 | 20 | 87 | 60 | 80 |
| 500,000–999,999 | 47 | 36 | 26 | 38 | 62 | 9 | 83 | 53 | 79 |
| 250,000–499,999 | 58 | 33 | 23 | 60 | 35 | 5 | 63 | 45 | 68 |
| 100,000–249,999 | 40 | 17 | 19 | 56 | 37 | 2 | 70 | 55 | 66 |
| 50,000–99,999 | 27 | 17 | 19 | 52 | 25 | 1 | 71 | 41 | 52 |
| 25,000–49,999 | 28 | 14 | 15 | 45 | 22 | 0 | 58 | 43 | 29 |
| 10,000–24,999 | 16 | 10 | 9 | 40 | 10 | — | 50 | 27 | 13 |
| 2,500–9,999 | 11 | 4 | 5 | 27 | 3 | 0 | 28 | 13 | 5 |
| Under 2,500 | 4 | 3 | 2 | 15 | 1 | — | 13 | 7 | 6 |

[a]— = less than 0.5%.

*Source:* Matthew J. Hickman and Brian A. Reaves, *Local Police Departments, 2000* (Washington, DC: Bureau of Justice Statistics, 2003), p. 22.

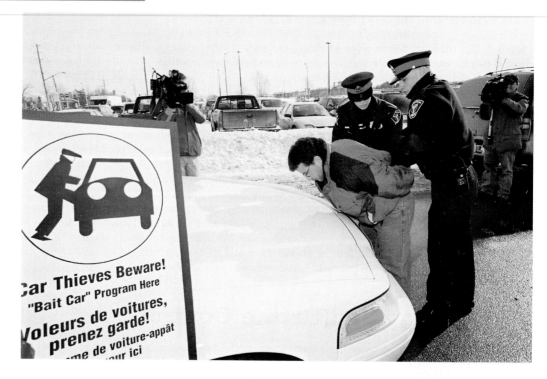

Police officers in Ottawa, Canada, arrest a car thief snared in a bait car program while news cameras roll. Bait cars, now in use in more than 100 cities across the United States and in some other countries, demonstrate how advancing technology can serve law enforcement needs.

*Michael Houston, Ottawa Police Service*

Log on to ResearchNavigator .com, and choose "All" under the *New York Times* subject archive section. Enter the phrase "computer crime" (without the quotation marks) in the search box, and click "Go." From the results page, select four articles related to criminal justice that you find interesting. Write a summary of each article, including complete source information—that is, article title, author (if available), date of publication, and source (in this case, the *New York Times*). Submit what you have written to your instructor if asked to do so. *Note:* This feature is available only if your instructor has chosen the Research Navigator option available with a new textbook.

determine their whereabouts. A number of rental car companies, for example, now have cars equipped with systems that can receive instruction from a central location. These instructions can be used to prevent the car from starting and thus being stolen. The system can also track the car as it moves. Likewise, some police departments are using high-technology bait cars to catch auto thieves.[60] Bait cars can signal when stolen, send digitized images of perpetrators to investigators, radio their position to officers, be remotely immobilized, and lock their doors on command, trapping thieves inside.

Another crime-fighting technology making headway in the identification of stolen vehicles is automatic plate recognition (APR) technology. In December 2004, for example, the Ohio State Highway Patrol completed a four-month evaluation of an APR system using infrared cameras mounted at strategic points along the state's highways and connected to computers to alert troopers to the possible presence of stolen vehicles or wanted persons. During the four-month test period, the system led to the apprehension of 23 criminal suspects and the recovery of 24 stolen vehicles.[61]

Car thieves, however, have made some technological advances of their own, including the "laundering" of vehicle identification numbers (VINs), which allows stolen cars to be sold as legitimate vehicles. In mid-2005, for example, the National Insurance Crime Bureau reported that about 600 luxury cars and SUVs had been seized during the previous 12 months whose VIN numbers had been removed and replaced with numbers copied from nonstolen vehicles.[62] Stolen cars with "cloned" VIN numbers are usually not discovered until an insurance claim is filed, and investigators learn that there are two or more vehicles registered with the same VIN numbers to people in different locals.

As these stories indicate, the future will no doubt see a race between technologically sophisticated offenders and law enforcement authorities to determine who can wield the most advanced technical skills in the age-old battle between crime and justice.[63]

# Leading Technical Organizations in Criminal Justice

The National Law Enforcement and Corrections Technology Center (NLECTC) performs yearly assessments of key technological needs and opportunities facing the justice system. The center is responsible for helping to identify, develop, manufacture, and adopt new products and technologies designed for law enforcement, corrections, and other criminal justice applications.[64] NLECTC concentrates on four areas of advancing technology: (1) communications and electronics, (2) forensic science, (3) transportation and weapons, and (4) protective equipment.[65] Once opportunities for improvement are identified in any area, referrals are made to the Law Enforcement Standards Laboratory—a part of the National Bureau of Standards—for the testing of available hardware. The Justice Technology Information Network (JUSTNET), a service of NLECTC, acts as an information gateway for law enforcement, corrections, and criminal justice technology and notifies the justice community of the latest technological advances. JUSTNET, accessible via the World Wide Web, lists the websites of technology providers and makes them easy to access.

Another important organization is the Society of Police Futurists International (PFI). PFI members are a highly select group of forward-thinking international police professionals. The group employs prediction techniques developed by other futures researchers to make reasonable forecasts about the likely role of the criminal justice system in the future. Recently, PFI and the Federal Bureau of Investigation collaborated to form a Futures Working Group (FWG) to examine and promote innovation in policing. Consisting of approximately 15 members from PFI and staff members from the FBI Academy, the FWG has implemented a variety of projects in collaboration with other organizations and academic institutions engaged in futures research. The group intends to continue to pursue opportunities for further cooperative efforts between American and international law enforcement agencies and organizations such as the Foresight Institute (a British-based futures think tank).

While justice technology assessment programs concentrate primarily on facilitating suspect apprehension and the protection of enforcement personnel, other authors have pointed to the potential held by emerging technologies in the area of offender treatment. Some have suggested, for example, that novel forms of biomedical intervention, building on the earlier practices of castration, psychosurgery, and drug treatment, will continue to be adapted from advances in the biological sciences and will serve as innovative treatment modalities.[66] Chemical substances to reform the offender, drugs to enhance the memories of witnesses and victims, recombinant DNA behavioral therapy, and microchip extensions of the personality all appear to be on the horizon.[67]

Keep abreast of technological, cultural, and other changes affecting justice systems worldwide by visiting the Society of Police Futurists International at Web Extra 18–5 and the Foresight Institute via Web Extra 18–6 at cjtoday.com.

**WEB EXTRA**

# Criminalistics: Past, Present, and Future

Technological advances throughout history have signaled both threats and opportunities for the justice field. By the turn of the twentieth century, for example, police call boxes were standard features in many cities, utilizing the new technology of telephonic communications to pass along information on crimes in progress or to describe suspects and their activities. A few years later, police departments across the nation adapted to the rapid growth in the number of private automobiles and the laws governing their use. Over the years, motorized patrol, VASCAR speed-measuring devices, radar, laser speed detectors, and police helicopters and aircraft were all called into service to meet the need for a rapid response to criminal activity. Today's citizens band radios, often monitored by local police and highway patrol agencies, and cell phones with direct numbers to police dispatchers are continuing the trend of adapting advances in communications technology to police purposes. In-field computers (that is, laptop or handheld computers, typically found in police vehicles) are commonplace (Figure 18–2), and many local police departments now provide their officers with access to computer databases from the field.

The use of technology in the service of criminal investigation is a subfield of criminal justice referred to as **criminalistics**. Criminalistics applies scientific techniques to the detection and evaluation of criminal evidence. Police crime-scene analysts and laboratory personnel who use these techniques are referred to as **criminalists**. Modern criminalistics began with the need for the certain identification of individuals. Early methods of personal identification were notoriously inaccurate. In the nineteenth century, for instance, one day of the week was generally dedicated to a "parade" of newly arrested offenders; experienced investigators from distant jurisdictions would scrutinize the convicts, looking for recognizable faces.[68] By the 1840s, the Quetelet system of anthropometry was making itself known.[69] The Quetelet system depended on precise measurements of various parts of the body to give an overall "picture" of a person for use in later identification.

The first "modern" system of personal identification was created by Alphonse Bertillon.[70] Bertillon was the director of the Bureau of Criminal Identification of the Paris Police Department during the late nineteenth century. The Bertillon system of identification was based on the idea that certain bodily aspects, such as eye color, skeletal size and shape, and ear form, did not change

**criminalistics**

The use of technology in the service of criminal investigation; the application of scientific techniques to the detection and evaluation of criminal evidence.

**criminalist**

A police crime-scene analyst or laboratory worker versed in criminalistics.

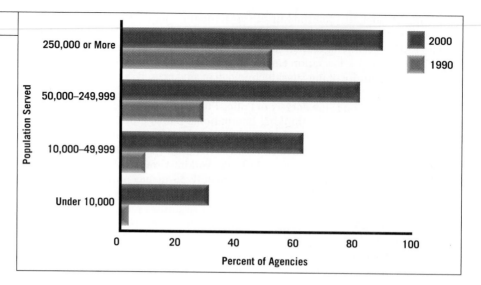

**FIGURE 18-2**

**Local police departments using in-field computers or terminals, 1990 and 2000.**

*Source:* Matthew J. Hickman and Brian A. Reaves, *Local Police Departments, 2000* (Washington, DC: Bureau of Justice Statistics, 2003), p. iv.

substantially after physical maturity. The system combined physical measurements with the emerging technology of photography. Although photography had been used previously in criminal identification, Bertillon standardized the technique by positioning measuring guides beside suspects so that their physical dimensions could be calculated from their photographs and by taking both front views and profiles.

Fingerprints, produced by contact with the ridge patterns in the skin on the fingertips, became the subject of intense scientific study in the mid-1840s. While their importance in criminal investigation today seems obvious, it was not until the 1880s that scientists began to realize that each person's fingerprints were unique and unchangeable over a lifetime. Both discoveries appear to have come from the Englishmen William Herschel and Henry Faulds, who were working in Asia.[71] Some writers, observing that Asiatic lore about finger ridges and their significance extends back to antiquity, suggest that Herschel and Faulds must have been privy to such information.[72] As early as the Tang Dynasty (A.D. 618–906), inked fingerprints were being used in China as personal seals on important documents, and there is some evidence that the Chinese had classified patterns of the loops and whorls found in fingerprints and were using them for the identification of criminals as far back as 1,000 years ago.[73]

The use of fingerprints in identifying offenders was popularized by Sir Francis Galton[74] and was officially adopted by Scotland Yard in 1901. By the 1920s, fingerprint identification was in use in police departments everywhere, having quickly replaced Bertillon's anthropometric system. Suspects were fingerprinted, and their prints were compared with those lifted from a crime scene. Those comparisons typically required a great deal of time and a bit of luck to produce a match. Over time, as fingerprint inventories in the United States grew huge, including those of everyone in the armed services and in certain branches of federal employment, researchers looked for a rapid and efficient way to compare large numbers of prints. Until the 1980s, most effective comparison schemes depended on manual classification methods that automatically eliminated large numbers of prints from consideration. As late as 1974, one author lamented, "Considering present levels of technology in other sciences . . . [the] classification of fingerprints has profited little by technological advancements, particularly in the computer sciences. [Fingerprint comparisons are] limited by the laborious inspection by skilled technicians required to accurately classify and interpret prints. Automation of the classification and comparison process would open up fingerprinting to its fullest potential."[75]

Within a decade, advances in computer hardware and software made possible CAL-ID, the automated fingerprint identification system (AFIS) of the California State Department of Justice. The system used optical scanning and software pattern matching to compare suspects' fingerprints. Such computerized systems have grown rapidly in capability, and links between systems operated by different agencies are now routine. Modern technology employs proprietary electro-optical scanning systems that digitize live fingerprints, eliminating the need for traditional inking and rolling techniques.[76] Other advances in fingerprint identification and matching are also being made. The use of lasers in fingerprint lifting, for example, allowed the

**TABLE 18-2**

## USE OF AUTOMATED FINGERPRINT IDENTIFICATION SYSTEMS (AFIS) IN LOCAL POLICE DEPARTMENTS, BY SIZE OF POPULATION SERVED, 2000

| Population Served | Percentage of Agencies with AFIS Ownership or Remote Access | | |
|---|---|---|---|
| | Total with Access | Exclusive or Shared Ownership | Access Terminal Only |
| All sizes | 20% | 5% | 15% |
| 1,000,000 or more | 100 | 93 | 7 |
| 500,000–999,999 | 85 | 59 | 26 |
| 250,000–499,999 | 95 | 60 | 35 |
| 100,000–249,999 | 85 | 41 | 44 |
| 50,000–99,999 | 58 | 25 | 33 |
| 25,000–49,999 | 39 | 13 | 26 |
| 10,000–24,999 | 26 | 8 | 18 |
| 2,500–9,999 | 17 | 2 | 15 |
| Under 2,500 | 13 | 2 | 11 |

*Source:* Matthew J. Hickman and Brian A. Reaves, *Local Police Departments, 2000* (Washington, DC: Bureau of Justice Statistics, 2003), p. 24.

FBI to detect a 50-year-old fingerprint of a Nazi war criminal on a postcard.[77] Other advances now make it possible, in at least some cases, to lift latent fingerprints from the skin of crime victims and even from bodies that have been submerged underwater for considerable periods of time.[78]

Computerization and digitization have improved accuracy and reduced the incidence of "false positives" in fingerprint comparisons.[79] The Los Angeles Police Department, which uses an automated fingerprint identification system, estimates that fingerprint comparisons that in the past would have taken as long as 60 years can now be performed in a single day or less.[80] Computerized fingerprint identification systems took a giant step forward in 1986 with the introduction of a new electronic standard for fingerprint data exchange.[81] This standard makes it possible to exchange data between different automated fingerprint identification systems. Before its invention, the comparison of fingerprint data among AFISs was often difficult or impossible. Using the standard, cities across the nation can share and compare fingerprint information over the Internet or secure networks linking their AFISs (see Table 18–2).[82] Recently, the FBI announced plans to develop an integrated automated fingerprint identification system (IAFIS) as part of the National Crime Information Center (see Chapter 5). IAFIS will integrate state fingerprint databases and automate search requests from police agencies throughout the country.

Fingerprinting provides an example of an early form of biometric technology used to positively identify individuals. Modern **biometrics** typically employs hardware and software in combination to provide identity verification for specific purposes. Today's biometric devices include retinal and iris scanners, facial recognition systems, keyboard rhythm recognition units, voice authentication systems, hand geometry and digital fingerprint readers, facial thermography, and body odor sniffers. Some universities are now using hand geometry units to allow resident access to secure dormitories. In a significant adaptation of biometric technology, the Liberian International Ship and Corporate Registry, one of the largest shipping registries in the world, announced in 2003 that it was implementing a digital fingerprint recognition system to prevent known terrorists from infiltrating the cargo ship industry.[83] Multimodal biometric systems utilize more than one physiological or behavioral characteristic for identification (preventing, for example, the use of a severed finger to gain access to a controlled area). Learn more about security-related biometrics via Web Extra 18–7.

Modern criminalistics also depends heavily on **ballistics** to analyze weapons, ammunition, and projectiles; medical pathology, to determine the cause of injury or death; **forensic anthropology**, to reconstruct the likeness of a decomposed or dismembered body; **forensic entomology**, to determine issues such as the time of death; forensic dentistry, to help identify deceased victims and offenders; the photography of crime scenes (now often done with video or digital

**biometrics**
The science of recognizing people by physical characteristics and personal traits.

**ballistics**
The analysis of firearms, ammunition, projectiles, bombs, and explosives.

**forensic anthropology**
The use of anthropological principles and techniques in criminal investigation.

WEB EXTRA

**forensic entomology**
The study of insects to determine such matters as a person's time of death.

## CJ CAREERS

### CRIMINALIST

**Name:** J. Sippa Pardo-Hastings

**Position:** Senior Criminalist

**City:** Richmond, California

**College Attended:** University of California, Berkeley

**Year Hired:** 1994

*After studying ballet from childhood through my twenties, I felt the need to pursue my very early love of all things scientific. I returned to my early fictional role models, Nancy Drew and Sherlock Holmes, and realized that what interested me most was using science to solve mysteries—specifically, to solve crimes. After graduation I assumed a criminalist position with the San Francisco City and County Crime Laboratory, a full-service forensic lab where I gained my initial professional experience. This included crime-scene processing (recognition and collection of potential evidence samples), serology (analysis of biological evidence), controlled substance analysis, as well as trial testimony in these same areas. Working with detectives and attorneys was especially compelling, as was learning about the "big picture" with respect to the criminal justice system and the role of the criminalist within this context. I then accepted a position as a criminalist with the California Department of Justice DNA lab, which was located in Berkeley. It was at this lab that I became immersed in forensic DNA analysis, a subsection of both serology and trace evidence. After several years of performing forensic DNA analyses, which often included court testimony throughout the state, I was promoted to the position of senior criminalist.*

### TYPICAL POSITIONS

Criminalist, forensic analyst, missing and unidentified persons (MUPS) specialist, and DNA databank/CODIS analyst. The criminalist is called on to render scientific opinions in written form as well as in court testimony. The criminalist may also visit violent crime scenes to collect potential evidence. Senior criminalists perform the most complex types of evidence examination and analyses of physical evidence associated with complex criminal investigations. The senior criminalist generally performs casework and/or research in areas of criminalistics such as crime-scene investigation, biological evidence, firearms and toolmark examinations, and trace evidence.

### EMPLOYMENT REQUIREMENTS

Education equivalent to graduation from college with a major in one of the physical or biological sciences, including the equivalent of eight semester hours of general chemistry and three semester hours of quantitative analysis; or four years of professional experience in a physical or biological science laboratory performing independent research related to forensic science. (Possession of a master's degree in a physical or biological science may be substituted for one year of experience, and possession of a Ph.D. in a physical or biological

science for two years of the required experience.) Successful completion of criminalist examination, and completion of a successful interview. Senior criminalist positions require two years of experience in the California state service performing the duties of a criminalist, or four years of professional experience beyond the trainee level in a physical or biological science laboratory setting performing the duties of a chemist, biochemist, or a related position.

### OTHER REQUIREMENTS

Personal qualities of successful applicants will include attention to detail, meticulous work habits, ability to focus, integrity, analytical ability, keenness of observation, patience, tact, ability to work independently, openness of mind, creative thinking, and good communication skills. The senior criminalist should be able to independently devise experiments and conduct research to address complex forensic science questions. Candidates must possess a state of health consistent with the ability to perform the assigned duties. A medical examination may be required. California Department of Justice regulations require preemployment investigations consisting of fingerprinting; inquiry to local, state, and national files to disclose criminal records; verification of minimum qualifications (college

## CJ CAREERS *(continued)*

transcripts), financial status; previous employment background checks; and personal interviews to determine applicant's suitability for employment.

### SALARY
Range A: $2,674–$3,132; Range B: $3,499–$4,320; Range C: $4,215–$5,208; senior criminalist: $4,857–$6,012 monthly.

### BENEFITS
Benefits include (1) participation in the California Public Employee's Retirement System (CALPERS), (2) participation in the state health insurance and vision programs, (3) availability of dental insurance, and (4) earned vacation and sick leave.

### DIRECT INQUIRIES TO:
California Department of Justice
Testing and Selection Unit
1300 "I" Street, 7th Floor
Sacramento, CA 95815
Attn: Criminalist Exam

Phone: (916)324–5039

For additional information on employment opportunities in the criminal justice field, view the careers portion of the CD-ROM included with this book.

*Source:* State of California, Department of Justice.

---

cameras); plaster and polymer castings of tire tracks, boot prints, and marks made by implements; polygraph (the "lie detector") and voiceprint identification (used by the CIA and National Security Agency to authenticate voice recordings made by known terrorists); as well as a plethora of other techniques. Many criminal investigative practices have been thoroughly tested and are now accepted by most courts for the evidence they offer. Polygraph[84] and voiceprint identification techniques are still being refined, however, and have not won the wide acceptance of the other techniques mentioned.

> That's what happens in a free society. With rights come responsibilities.
>
> —U.S. Representative J. D. Hayworth (R—Ariz.)[v]

Forensic anthropologist Frank Bender explaining how he makes forensic models at his studio in Philadelphia. Bender, who describes himself as "the recomposer of the decomposed," has helped police identify dozens of murder victims and, in some cases, find their killers.

*AP Wide World Photos*

# New Technologies in Criminalistics

Law enforcement practitioners of the future will be aided in their work by a number of technologies, some of which are still in their infancy. These technologies include the following:

- DNA profiling and new serological/tissue identification techniques, many of which have already received widespread acceptability
- Online databases for the sharing of in-depth and timely criminal justice information
- Computer-aided investigations
- Computer-based training

Brief descriptions of these technologies, including their current state of development and the implications they hold for the future, are provided in the paragraphs that follow.

## DNA Profiling

In March 2000, a man known only by his genetic makeup was indicted and charged with a series of sexual assaults in Manhattan.[85] Authorities said that it was the first indictment based solely on a DNA profile. The man, dubbed the "East Side Rapist" and named in the indictment as "John Doe, an unidentified male," followed by his DNA profile, was charged with two sexual assaults in 1995 and one in 1997. He is alleged to have sexually attacked 16 women since 1994. No arrest has yet been made.

Three years later, New York City Mayor Michael Bloomberg announced that his city would begin using DNA to seek hundreds of indictments in unsolved sexual attacks.[86] Bloomberg said that the DNA-based indictments would effectively "stop the clock" on the state's ten-year statute of limitations, which bars prosecution of even known felons if they have not been charged with the crime after a decade has passed.

DNA analysis (also discussed in Chapter 11) is nearly infallible from a scientific point of view and is increasingly preferred by criminal justice experts as a method of identification. It can prove innocence as well as demonstrate guilt. In December 2001, for example, Marvin Lamond Anderson, a Virginia parolee, was cleared of rape charges stemming from a 1982 crime for which he had served 15 years in prison.[87] Anderson received assistance from the Innocence Project, a volunteer organization specializing in the use of DNA technology to investigate and challenge what it regards as dubious convictions. A Virginia law passed in 2000, which allows felons to seek exoneration and expungement of their convictions on the basis of modern DNA testing, helped Anderson prove that he could not have committed the crime of which he had been convicted. DNA taken from a 19-year-old cotton swab was compared to the state's DNA database of more than 100,000 convicted felons and conclusively demonstrated that Anderson had not committed the crime. Learn more about the Innocence Project via Web Extra 18–8 at cjtoday.com.

**DNA profiling**

The use of biological residue, found at the scene of a crime, for genetic comparisons in aiding in the identification of criminal suspects.

The U.S. Department of Justice notes that "DNA evidence is playing a larger role than ever before in criminal cases throughout the country, both to convict the guilty and to exonerate those wrongly accused or convicted."[88] **DNA profiling**, also termed *DNA fingerprinting*, makes use of human DNA for purposes of identification. DNA (deoxyribonucleic acid) is a nucleic acid found in the center of cells. It is the principal component of chromosomes, the structures that transmit hereditary characteristics between generations. Each DNA molecule is a long two-stranded chain made up of subunits called *nucleotides*, coiled in the form of a double helix. Because genetic material is unique to each individual (except in the case of identical twins or clones), it can provide a highly reliable source of suspect identification. DNA profiling was originally used as a test for determining paternity.

DNA profiling requires only a few human cells for comparison. One drop of blood, a few hairs, a small amount of skin, or a trace of semen usually provides sufficient genetic material. Because the DNA molecule is very stable, genetic tests can be conducted on evidence taken from crime scenes long after fingerprints have disappeared. The process, diagrammed in Figure 18–3, involves the use of a highly technical procedure called electrophoresis. As of mid-2004, most states were building forensic DNA databases, and 32 states and the federal government required collection of DNA samples from all convicted felons.[89]

Forensic use of DNA technology in criminal cases began in 1986 when British police asked Dr. Alec J. Jeffreys (who coined the term *DNA fingerprints*[90]) of Leicester University to verify a suspect's confession that he was responsible for two rape-murders in the English Midlands. DNA tests proved that the suspect could not have committed the crimes. Police then began obtaining blood samples from several thousand male inhabitants in the area in an attempt to identify a new suspect.[91]

**FIGURE 18-3**

**The DNA fingerprinting process.**

*Source:* Cellmark Diagnostics. Reprinted with permission.

In a 1987 British case, 32-year-old Robert Melias became the first person ever convicted of a crime on the basis of DNA evidence.[92] Melias was convicted of raping a 43-year-old disabled woman, and the conviction came after genetic tests of semen left on the woman's clothes positively identified him as the perpetrator.[93]

In the civil case of *Daubert* v. *Merrell Dow Pharmaceuticals, Inc.* (1993),[94] the Supreme Court revised the criteria for the admissibility of scientific evidence by rejecting a previous admissibility standard established in the 1923 case of *Frye* v. *U.S.*[95] The *Daubert* Court ruled that the older *Frye* standard requiring "general acceptance" of a test or procedure by the relevant scientific

> Technology throughout history has been a double-edged sword, equally capable of enhancing or endangering democratic values.
>
> —John H. Gibbons, Director of the Office of Technology Assessment, U.S. Congress

**Daubert standard**

A test of scientific acceptability applicable to the gathering of evidence in criminal cases.

community "is not a necessary precondition to the admissibility of scientific evidence." The baseline rule for the admissibility of scientific evidence, said the Court, is established by Rule 402 of the *Federal Rules of Evidence*, which was published after *Frye* and supersedes it. Rule 402 says that, in a trial, "all relevant evidence is admissible, except as otherwise provided by the Constitution of the United States, by Act of Congress, by these Rules, or by other rules prescribed by the Supreme Court pursuant to statutory authority." The Court went on to say that although "the Frye test was displaced by the Rules of Evidence, [that] does not mean . . . that the Rules themselves place no limits on the admissibility of purportedly scientific evidence. Nor is the trial judge disabled from screening such evidence. To the contrary, under the Rules the trial judge must ensure that any and all scientific testimony or evidence admitted is not only relevant, but reliable." The real test for the admissibility of scientific expert testimony, said the Court, is for the trial judge to decide "at the outset . . . whether the expert is proposing to testify to (1) scientific knowledge that (2) will assist the trier of fact to understand or determine a fact in issue." The Court concluded that the task of the trial judge is one of "ensuring that an expert's testimony both rests on a reliable foundation and is relevant to the task at hand. Pertinent evidence based on scientifically valid principles," said the Court, "will satisfy those demands."

The plaintiffs in *Daubert* did not argue the merits of DNA testing but claimed, instead, that the drug Bendectin caused birth defects. Nonetheless, the **Daubert standard** eased the criteria for the introduction of scientific evidence at both civil and criminal trials, effectively clearing the way for the use of DNA evidence in the courtroom.[96] Specifically, the *Daubert* Court found that the following factors may be used to determine whether any form of scientific evidence is reliable[97]:

- Whether it has been subject to testing
- Whether it has been subject to peer review
- Known or potential rates of error
- The existence of standards controlling application of the techniques involved

In 1994, the DNA Identification Act[98] provided substantial funding to improve the quality and availability of DNA analyses for law enforcement identification. The act also provided for the establishment of a "Combined DNA Index" for law enforcement purposes (see Chapter 5 for more information). The index, which held 1 million profiles by mid-2002,[99] allows investigators to produce quick matches with DNA samples already on file. The law limits accessibility of DNA samples to investigators, court officials, and personnel authorized to evaluate such samples for the purposes of criminal prosecution and defense.

In 1996, the most comprehensive report to date on the applicability of DNA testing to criminal case processing was released by the National Institute of Justice (NIJ). The report, entitled *Convicted by Juries, Exonerated by Science*,[100] called DNA testing "the most important technological breakthrough of twentieth-century forensic science" and provided a detailed review of 28 cases in which postconviction DNA evidence exonerated defendants who had been sentenced to lengthy prison terms. The cases were selected on the basis of a detailed examination of records that indicated that the convicted defendants might have actually been innocent. The men in the study had served, on average, seven years in prison, and most had been tried and sentenced before the widespread availability of reliable DNA testing.

In each of the cases, which involved 14 states and the District of Columbia, the imprisoned defendant obtained, through an attorney, case evidence for DNA testing and consented to a comparison to his own DNA sample. In each case, the results conclusively showed the lack of matching DNA, and the defendant was ultimately set free. Sexual assault was the most frequent crime for which the defendants had been sentenced. In six of the cases, the victims had also been murdered. All but one case involved a jury trial.[101] Of the cases where the time required for jury deliberations was known, most verdicts had been returned in less than a day.

The 28 wrongful conviction cases shared several common themes in the evidence presented during and after trial, including (1) eyewitness identification—all cases, except for homicides, involved identification by the victim both prior to and at trial; (2) an alibi defense—most defendants had presented an alibi defense, frequently corroborated by family or friends; (3) the use of forensic evidence other than DNA testing, including the examination of nonvictim specimens of blood, semen, or hair at the crime scene; (4) the testimony of prosecution experts who explained the reliability and scientific strength of non-DNA evidence to the jury; and (5) alleged government malfeasance or misconduct, including perjured testimony at trial, police and prosecutors who intentionally kept exculpatory evidence from the defense, and intentionally erroneous laboratory tests and expert testimony admitted at trial as evidence.

One provocative finding of the NIJ report was that "every year since 1989, in about 25% of the sexual assault cases referred to the FBI where results could be obtained (primarily by State and local law enforcement), the primary suspect has been excluded by forensic DNA testing. . . . The fact that these percentages have remained constant for seven years, and that the National Institute of Justice's informal survey of private laboratories reveals a strikingly similar 26% exclusion rate, strongly suggests that postarrest and postconviction DNA exonerations are tied to some strong, underlying systemic problems that generate erroneous accusations and convictions."

As standards develop, DNA identification techniques continue to evolve. Notably, the amount of DNA needed for accurate identification continues to grow smaller. In 1997, for example, Australian forensic scientists reported success in obtaining useful amounts of DNA from the surface of objects that people touched for as little as five seconds as long ago as one year. In their tests, researchers at the Victoria Forensic Science Center in Victoria, Australia, used swabs to recover DNA-laden material from partial fingerprints found on gloves, glasses, mugs, pens, car keys, briefcases, knives, locker handles, and telephone handsets. Moreover, in one in four cases, they also were able to recover DNA that was transferred from one person to another while shaking hands. The technique developed by Australian forensic scientists uses "naked DNA," such as that found on the surface of skin, rather than the DNA found inside of cells.[102]

In 1998, in an effort to enhance the use of DNA evidence as a law enforcement tool, the U.S. attorney general established the National Commission on the Future of DNA Evidence. The task of the commission was to submit recommendations to the U.S. Department of Justice to help ensure more effective use of DNA as a crime-fighting tool and to foster its use throughout the criminal justice system. The commission addressed issues in five specific areas: (1) the use of DNA in postconviction relief cases; (2) legal concerns, including *Daubert* challenges and the scope of discovery in DNA cases; (3) criteria for training and technical assistance for criminal justice professionals involved in the identification, collection, and preservation of DNA evidence at the crime scene; (4) essential laboratory capabilities in the face of emerging technologies; and (5) the impact of future technological developments on the use of DNA in the criminal justice system. Each topic became the focus of in-depth analysis by separate working groups comprised of prominent professionals. The work of the commission culminated in the National Law Enforcement Summit on DNA Technology, held in Washington, D.C., on July 27–28, 2000. The proceedings of the summit, as well as transcripts of commission meetings, are available as **Web Extra 18–9** at cjtoday.com.

**WEB EXTRA**

The commission's work led the White House to sponsor an *Advancing Justice through DNA Technology* initiative. The initiative culminated in passage of federal legislation designed to take advantage of the opportunities offered by DNA testing. That legislation, the DNA Sexual Assault Justice Act of 2004 and the Innocence Protection Act of 2004 (also discussed in Chapter 11)—both of which are parts of the Justice for All Act of 2004[103]—was signed into law by President Bush on October 30, 2004. The Innocence Protection Act established new procedures for applications for DNA testing by inmates in the federal prison system. Those new procedures require a court to order DNA testing if (1) the inmate applicant asserts that he or she is actually innocent of a qualifying offense, (2) the proposed DNA testing would produce new material evidence that would support such an assertion, and (3) it would create a reasonable probability that the applicant did not commit the offense. The court must grant the applicant's motion for a new trial or resentencing if DNA testing indicates that a new trial would likely result in acquittal. The act also seeks to preserve DNA evidence by prohibiting the destruction of biological evidence in a federal criminal case while a defendant remains incarcerated. The law established the Kirk Bloodsworth Post-Conviction DNA Testing Program, which provides millions of dollars in grants to states for postconviction DNA testing. It also provided money for states to train prosecutors in the appropriate use of DNA evidence, and to train defense counsel to ensure effective representation in capital cases. A provision of the Innocence Protection Act increased the maximum amount of damages an individual may be awarded for being wrongfully imprisoned in the federal system from $5,000 to $50,000 per year in noncapital cases and $100,000 per year in capital cases.

The DNA Sexual Assault Justice Act authorized (1) $10 million per year for five years for grants to states and local governments to eliminate forensic science backlogs; (2) $12.5 million per year for five years to provide grants for training and education relating to the identification, collection, preservation, and analysis of DNA evidence for law enforcement officers, correctional personnel, and court officers; (3) $42.1 million in additional funds for the FBI to enhance its DNA programs, including the Combined DNA Index System; (4) $30 million per year for five years to create a grant program to provide training, technical assistance, education, equipment, and information to medical personnel relating to the identification, collection, preservation, analysis, and use of DNA evidence; and (5) $15 million per year for five years to establish a National Forensic Science Commission to be appointed by the attorney general to provide recommendations for maximizing the use of forensic science technology in the criminal justice system.

Finally, the Justice for All Act also amended the federal statute of limitations[104] by adding the following words to existing law: "In a case in which DNA testing implicates an identified person

## CJ NEWS

### Study: Untested DNA Allows Crime

At least 150 rapes, murders and other crimes since 1993 could have been prevented if states took DNA samples from burglars and other non-violent criminals before they moved on to more serious crimes, a new Justice Department study says.

The study, given to members of Congress in 2004, also found that local police and crime labs have evidence from more than 540,000 unsolved crimes—including 52,000 homicides and 169,000 rapes—that has not been subjected to DNA or other tests that could help identify suspects. Local agencies often do not perform tests, the study found, because of personnel and funding shortages and a lack of understanding about DNA technology.

The report was done for the Justice Department by Washington State University and a Tacoma, Washington, law firm that represents a DNA equipment manufacturer. It outraged women's and victims' rights groups, which called on Congress to pass a proposal to increase spending on DNA tests and expand the reach of the nation's DNA database.

DNA, a cellular acid that carries an individual's unique genetic code, can be used to solve crimes such as rape and murder in which biological evidence is left at the crime scene. Since 1992, the FBI has kept a database that matches DNA taken from convicted criminals with DNA from the scenes of unsolved crimes. As of March 2004, the system had about 1.7 million DNA profiles and had scored about 11,800 matches.

But the system relies on states to collect DNA from criminals and suspects, and the rules for collecting DNA vary among the states. When the study was done last year, 31 states took DNA from all felons, while 19 took samples only from those convicted of violent crimes.

Massachusetts was one of the 19. In late 1997 and early 1998, four Springfield, Mass., women were found raped and killed in their homes or in nearby alleys. A DNA sample provided voluntarily by a suspect in the case linked him to all four slayings. The suspect had felony convictions in 1996 for breaking and entering and larceny, but had been sentenced to community supervision.

If Massachusetts had required him to give a DNA sample after either of the 1996 convictions, the report said, "a DNA

Lance Gima, chief of the California Bureau of Forensic Services, is shown with a team of technicians at a forensics laboratory in Berkeley, California. The facility analyzes and records DNA samples taken from convicted felons.

*AP Wide World Photos*

match could have been obtained after the first rape/murder, thereby preventing the subsequent three."

The study found similar cases in the other 18 states that did not take DNA from all felons. Since the study was completed, one of those states, West Virginia, has passed a law that requires anyone convicted of a felony to provide a DNA sample.

Barry Steinhardt, a lawyer for the American Civil Liberties Union in New York City, warned against a "headlong rush" into drawing DNA from all felons. "We know that expanding the reach of the (DNA) databases increases the number of crimes solved, but at what cost, both financial and to our liberty?" said Steinhardt, who specializes in privacy law. "Sooner or later somebody is going to test (DNA) for a purpose other than what it is there for."

For the latest in crime and justice news, visit the Talk Justice news feed at http://www.crimenews.info.

*Source:* Richard Willing, "Study: Untested DNA Allows Crime—Samples Not Taken from Many Felons," *USA Today,* April 2, 2004, p. 3A. Copyright © 2004 *USA Today.* Reprinted with permission.

in the commission of a felony ... no statute of limitations that would otherwise preclude prosecution of the offense shall preclude such prosecution until a period of time following the implication of the person by DNA testing has elapsed that is equal to the otherwise applicable limitation period." The wording allows for prosecutions where DNA analysis reveals the identity of "cold case" perpetrators in investigations that might have otherwise been abandoned. Learn more about the impact of forensic DNA on American criminal justice via Library Extra 18–6 at cjtoday.com.

### Online Databases

Computerized information systems and the personnel who operate them are an integral part of most police departments today. Police department computers assist with such routine tasks as word processing, filing, record keeping, report printing, and personnel, equipment, and facilities scheduling. Computers that serve as investigative tools, however, have the greatest potential to affect criminal justice in the near future. The automated fingerprint technology discussed earlier is but one example of information-based systems designed to help in identifying offenders and solving crimes. Others include the nationwide National Crime Information Center (NCIC) and the Violent Criminal Apprehension Program (ViCAP) databases; state-operated police identification networks; specialized services like METAPOL, an information-sharing network run by the Police Executive Research Forum; and the FBI's Combined DNA Index System (CODIS), which allows law enforcement agencies to compare DNA profiles in their possession with other DNA profiles that have been entered into local, state, and national databases in order to identify a suspect or to link serial crimes. NCIC and police information networks furnish a 24-hour channel with information on suspects, stolen vehicles, and other data that can be accessed through computers installed in patrol cars.

Increasingly, law enforcement agencies are making criminal database information available to the public via the Internet. Among the most common forms of information available are sex offender registries, although the FBI's "Most Wanted" list and the "Most Wanted" lists of various states can also be viewed online. In 1998, Texas became the first state to make its entire criminal convictions database available on the Internet.[105] View the sex offender registries for a number of states via Web Extra 18–10 at cjtoday.com, and see the FBI's "Most Wanted" list at Web Extra 18–11.

WEB EXTRA

## Computer-Aided Investigations

Some police agencies use large computer databases that can cross-reference specific information about crimes to determine patterns and to identify suspects. One of the earliest of these programs was HITMAN, developed by the Hollywood (California) Police Department in 1985. HITMAN has since evolved into a department-wide database that helps detectives in the Los Angeles Police Department (LAPD) solve violent crimes. The LAPD uses a similar computer program to track a target population of approximately 60,000 gang members.[106]

The developing field of artificial intelligence uses computers to make inferences based on available information and to draw conclusions or to make recommendations to the system's operators. **Expert systems**, as these computer models are often called, depend on three components: (1) a user interface or terminal, (2) a knowledge base containing information on what is already known in the area of investigation, and (3) a computer program known as an *inference engine* that compares user input and stored information according to established decision-making rules.

A number of expert systems exist today. One is used by the FBI's National Center for the Analysis of Violent Crime (NCAVC) in a project designed to profile violent serial criminals. The NCAVC system depends on computer models of criminal profiling to provide a theoretical basis for the development of investigative strategies. A number of other systems have been developed, including some that focus on serological (blood serum) analysis, narcotics interdiction, serial murder and rape, and counterterrorism.[107]

Similar to expert systems are relational databases, which permit fast and easy sorting of large records. Perhaps the best known early criminal justice database of this sort was called Big Floyd. It was developed in the 1980s by the FBI in conjunction with the Institute for Defense Analyses. Big Floyd was designed to access the more than 3 million records in the FBI's Organized Crime Information System and to allow investigators to decide which federal statutes apply in a given situation and whether investigators have enough evidence for a successful prosecution.[108] In the years since Big Floyd, other "bad-guy" relational databases targeting malfeasants of various types have been created, including computer systems to track deadbeat parents and quack physicians. In 1996, President Bill Clinton ordered the Department of Justice to create a computerized national registry of sex offenders.[109] The national sex offender registry, developed as part of an overhaul of the FBI's computer systems, went online in 1999.

Some systems are even more problem specific. For example, ImAger, a product of Face Software, Inc., uses computer technology to artificially age photographs of missing children. The program has been used successfully to identify and recover a number of children. One of them was only six months old when he disappeared and was found after ImAger created a photo of what the child would look like at age five. The child was recognized by viewers who called police after the photo was broadcast on television.[110] Another composite-imaging program, Compusketch by Visatex Corporation, is used by police artists to create simulated photographs of criminal suspects.[111]

The most advanced computer-aided investigation systems are being touted by agencies such as NASA and the Defense Advanced Research Projects Agency (DARPA) as having the ability to prevent crime. DARPA, for example, announced its new Total Information Awareness (TIA) Program in 2003.[112] The five-year development project uses information-sorting and pattern-matching software to sift through vast numbers of existing business and government databases in an effort to identify possible terror threats. The software will attempt to detect suspicious patterns

**expert system**

Computer hardware and software that attempts to duplicate the decision-making processes used by skilled investigators in the analysis of evidence and in the recognition of patterns that such evidence might represent.

A screen shoot of ImageWare Systems' digital mugbook software. The software, which can store snapshots and detailed demographic information on criminal suspects, can also be used to scan mugshot databases for likely matches.

*Image courtesy of ImageWare Systems, Inc.*

of activity, identify the people involved, and locate them so that investigations can be conducted. Suspected insurgents might be identified when the software detects a series of credit card, bank, and official transactions that form a pattern that resembles preparations for an insurgency attack. The process, which is known as *data mining*, will generate computer models in an attempt to predict terrorists' actions. Privacy advocates have raised concerns about DARPA's plans, but the agency has tried to defuse concerns by assuring the public that the project "is not an attempt to build a supercomputer to snoop into the private lives or track the everyday activities of American citizens." The agency claims that "all TIA research complies with all privacy laws, without exception."

Another DARPA project that is potentially applicable to the needs of American law enforcement agencies but is currently being developed for military use overseas is called Combat Zones That See (CZTS).[113] The CZTS program will build a huge surveillance system by networking existing cameras from department stores, subway platforms, banks, airports, parking lots, and other points of surveillance, and by feeding images to supercomputer-like processors capable of recognizing suspects by face, gait, and mannerisms as they move from one place to another. The data can be fed via satellite to remote locations across the globe, allowing the agency to track suspects on the move—either within cities or between countries. Vehicles could also be tracked. CZTS is being introduced gradually in selected locations, beginning with areas in and around American military bases. Future implementations of CZTS may involve nanocameras equipped with microminiaturized transmitters that can be spread over a city like grains of dust but which have the power to communicate relatively detailed information to local cellular-like installations for entry into the CZTS network. The civil rights implications of local adaptations of DARPA's TIA and CZTS technology within the United States and its use by domestic law enforcement agencies must be considered by any law enforcement agency considering the use of similar kinds of technologies.

## Computer-Based Training

Computers provide an ideal training medium for criminal justice agencies. They allow users to work at their own pace, and they can be made available around the clock to provide off-site instruction to personnel whose job requirements make other kinds of training difficult to imple-

A "radar flashlight" in use. Using this new technology, police officers can "see" through walls—even those made of concrete. As technological advances provide additional criminal opportunity, technologies that serve the justice system will improve, as well.

*Gary Meek, Georgia Institute of Technology*

ment. Computer-based training (CBT) is already well established as a management training tool and is used extensively in law enforcement. CBT has the added advantage of familiarizing personnel with computers so that they will be better able to use them in other tasks.

Some of the more widely used computer-training programs include shoot/no-shoot decision-based software and police-pursuit driving simulators. The Atari Mobile Operations Simulator (AMOS), firearms training simulation (FATS), and Robbec's JUST (Judgment Under Stress Training) are just a few of the products available to police-training divisions. Recent innovations in the field of virtual reality (a kind of high-tech-based illusion) have led to the creation of realistic computer-based virtual environments in which law enforcement agents can test their skills.[114]

We have looked at just some of the most prominent uses of technology in criminal justice. Laser fingerprint-lifting devices, space age photography, video camera–equipped patrol cars, satellite and computerized mapping,[115] advanced chemical analysis techniques, chemical sniffers, and hair and fiber identification are all contemporary crime-fighting techniques. Field test kits for drug analysis, chemical sobriety checkers, and handheld ticket-issuing computers have also made the transition from costly high technology to widespread and relatively inexpensive use. As one expert has observed, "Police agencies throughout the world are entering an era in which high technology is not only desirable but necessary in order to combat crime effectively."[116] Learn more about information technology innovations in criminal justice via **Library Extra 18–7** and **Web Extra 18–12** at cjtoday.com.

> Some people fail to understand that security is designed to secure something, and what we are securing are the rights of individuals.
>
> —Former Attorney General John Ashcroft

## On the Horizon

In mid-2003, the Department of Homeland Security (DHS) submitted its first semiannual report to Congress.[117] The report, which is available in its entirety at **Library Extra 18–8**, provides insight into some of the intrusion-detection technologies being used to help secure the nation's borders.

The DHS report recognizes existing concerns that weapons of mass destruction and other contraband or implements of terrorism can enter the country through our nation's seaports. Shipping containers are too numerous for each to be opened and visually inspected. Millions of such containers enter the country every year from ports around the world. DHS recognizes, however, that shipping containers are "highly vulnerable to exploitation by terrorists" and has begun to focus on the need to enhance container inspection efforts.

Since the terrorist attacks of September 11, 2001, border security has expanded to include the use of high-technology equipment to search for radioactive materials, explosives, toxic chemicals, and dangerous biological materials. These pieces of equipment—which include various vehicle and rail X-ray systems, radiation-detection units, trace-detection devices, video systems, and the like—permit officers to inspect cargo and conveyances for contraband without having to perform the costly and time-consuming process of unloading cargo or drilling through or dismantling containers.

Trace-detection technology, which focuses on cargo, luggage, packages, containers, and vehicles, gathers and analyzes the minute amounts of vapors given off and the microscopic particles left behind when narcotics and explosives contraband are packaged and handled. Current technology provides security screeners with nonintrusive search capabilities

Radiation-detection equipment is used at the nation's ports and border crossings to detect attempts to smuggle radioactive materials into the United States. Detection devices range from personal radiation detectors, which are somewhat limited in capability and not very costly, to more sophisticated, capable, and expensive portable radiation-detection systems.

Passengers, cargo handlers, seamen, and flight crews must also be screened to determine the level of risk they represent. The Advance Passenger Information System (APIS) is a border enforcement tool used at our nation's airports to identify and detain high-risk travelers on flights bound for the United States. The system is intended to collect biographical information such as name, date of birth, and country of residence from international airline passengers and crew members entering the United States at airports around the country. Before arrival, travelers are matched against law enforcement databases to identify people who should be detained and examined for violation of U.S. law. All airlines serving the United States are required to provide APIS information to the Department of Homeland Security.

The Remote Video Inspection System (RVIS) used at border crossings is designed to expedite the clearance of low-risk travelers and to enhance security at remote border areas, including parts of the U.S.–Canadian border. RVIS transmits images of a driver, vehicle, documents, and passengers to an inspector located miles away at a main monitoring 24-hour port of entry.

Other security technologies now being employed sound like science fiction. Recently, for example, officials at NASA told security specialists that the agency is developing "noninvasive neuro-electric sensors," or brain-monitoring devices, that can receive and analyze brain-wave and heartbeat patterns from a distance.[118] The data are fed into a computer, which scrutinizes it in order to "detect passengers who potentially might pose a threat."[119]

Especially intriguing technological advances can be found in the field of **augmented reality (AR)**.[120] Whereas virtual reality (VR) systems generate audio and visual stimuli predicated on fictional scenarios and usually experienced by relatively passive viewers in situations not requiring interpersonal interaction, AR technology provides users with real-time fact-based information that can be accessed in the midst of real-world activity. Wearable AR systems, such as those being developed by the U.S. military under the name Battlefield Augmented Reality System (BARS), provide visual, audio, and tactile overlays that can give the user critical information about the people he or she is facing and the situation in which he or she is involved. AR systems supply the user with data presented in a fashion similar to the science fiction visual readouts shown in *Terminator* films. There, the main character's computer-like brain automatically and continuously computes threat assessments by accessing stored databases and displays them in the character's visual field as easy-to-read schematics that are overlaid on the immediate surroundings. In the near future, it is anticipated that AR systems will be available to police personnel and that they will be able to provide "wired" officers with capabilities such as these:

- Real-time intelligence about crime and criminals in the surrounding area
- Facial, voiceprint, and other biometric recognition data of known criminals, allowing for instantaneous identification
- Automated scans for chemical, biological, and explosive threats in the immediate area
- Real-time language translation to assist interaction with non-English-speaking people
- Three-dimensional maps, complete with building floor plans, sewer system schematics, and possible access and escape routes
- Advanced optics, including digital zoom and audio amplification for seeing and hearing at a distance
- Identification Friend or Foe (IFF) technology to allow immediate recognition of "good guys"
- Coordinated deployment of robots and unmanned aerial vehicles (UAVs), including the ability to "see" and "hear" what the robots or UAVs encounter

Augmented reality systems incorporating at least some of the features mentioned here are already a reality in police work. Xybernaut Corporation, for example, a leading provider of wearable computers, has teamed up with ZNQ3, a company that specializes in secure communications and dynamic identification, to provide wearable computers that enhance tactical awareness. According to Jeffrey Stutzman, founder and CEO of ZNQ3, "The secure communications and point-

**augmented reality (AR)**

The real-time and accurate overlay of digital information on a user's real-world experience, through visual, aural, and/or tactile interfaces.[vi] The computer readouts superimposed on the visual fields of the fictional cyborgs in the various *Robocop* and *Terminator* movies provide an example.

The X-45A Unmanned Combat Air Vehicle (UCAV) in flight during a test at Edwards Air Force Base, California. Miniaturized unmanned aerial vehicles (UAVs)—offshoots of military technology—can be used to gather law enforcement intelligence, follow suspects, and patrol borders. UAVs frequently offer long-range capabilities and transmit aerial images back to controllers. Guided by the Global Positioning System and ground controllers, some UAVs are less than six inches in size.

*Jim Ross, NASA, Dryden Flight Research Center*

of-task computing power afforded by the joint Xybernaut/ZNQ3 solution allow first responders complete access to information providing critical situational awareness during a crisis."[121]

Thomas Cowper, who we mentioned earlier in this chapter, poses some important questions about the practicality of augmented-reality applications in police work. How would "wired" officers be accepted by the public, given that their appearance would differ substantially from that of other officers? How cost-effective would AR technology be in police work? Who will pay for such systems, especially in smaller agencies? How can the accuracy of AR databases be ensured? What legal issues might arise?

Nanotechnology, or engineering and creating useful products on a molecular level, is another cutting-edge technology whose application to policing and the justice system is still largely in the realm of science fiction. Nonetheless, the National Science Foundation predicts that the field could potentially grow into a $1 trillion industry annually by 2015. Nanotechnology may produce practical investigative applications in the near future. Microscopic cameras, motors, solar cells, recording devices, and high-frequency transmitters built with nanotechnology may have already resulted in the production of classified spy hardware like a maneuverable mechanical mosquito able to fly into buildings and vehicles, providing its controllers with "fly on the wall" observation capabilities.[122] Super sensors on such ultraminiaturized devices are said to be able to literally read over a person's shoulder and transmit visual, audio, Global Positioning System (GPS), infrared, and other data to remote recording and viewing devices, all the while remaining nearly invisible to those being targeted. The Institute of Nanotechnology says that miniaturized machines will soon be used to enhance tamper-prevention devices; bolster anticounterfeiting efforts; provide labs on a chip (sometimes called dipstick technology) for drug, food, explosives, and DNA testing; permit easy product tracking; and contribute to futuristic intruder-detection and -identification systems.[123]

Recently, the Japanese news agency Kyodo reported that Hitachi Corporation is involved in talks with the European Central Bank to control counterfeiting and money laundering by embedding radio tags much smaller than a grain of sand in European bank notes (Euros).[124] Radio-frequency identification (RFID) tags built with nanotechnology cannot be seen with the naked eye nor felt by fingertips. The devices, called Mu-Chips, can authenticate bank notes that carry them and can even record details about the transactions in which they have been involved. RFID devices, which act much like digital watermarks, are queried by radio and use the energy of the incoming signal to generate a reply. Applicability of the technology was demonstrated at Japan's 2005 International Expo—a gathering that used RFID-tagged admission tickets. The Expo, which ran for five months, involved participants from 125 countries and drew nearly 15 million visitors.[125]

## Problems in Implementing New Technologies

Technological innovations are not always easy to integrate into standard systems. First, the speed with which justice agencies successfully adapt to the opportunities offered by technology may be limited. Some writers have observed that "law enforcement has been slow to utilize new

> The industry that most lags in the distribution of computing is government, and the most needy is probably the criminal justice system.
>
> —Dr. Alfred Blumstein, Dean of the School of Urban and Public Affairs, Carnegie Mellon University

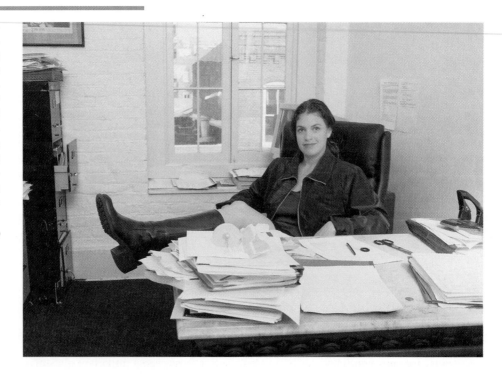

Criminal defense lawyer Jennifer Granick in her San Francisco office. Granick specializes in defending computer hackers and crackers. Tougher cybercrime laws are keeping her busy, and her desk is cluttered with software piracy and unauthorized access cases. She also directs the public interest law and technology clinic at Stanford University law school's Center for Internet and Society in Stanford, California.

*Douglas Adesko, Douglas Adesko Photography*

technology,"[126] and an early study by the International Association of Chiefs of Police found that only 10% of police departments were innovative in their use of computers.[127] Line staff and decision makers within police departments may lack the personal experience and knowledge to use technology effectively. Equally significant, the future legal acceptability and social applicability of specific technologies are uncertain.[128]

A second area of concern arises from the "supersleuth" capabilities of some high-technology items. As high-tech gadgetry becomes more commonplace in criminal justice agencies, we can be sure that the courts will watch for potential violations of individual rights. The use of photographic techniques developed for the space program, for example, which permit enlargement of details never before thought possible, and the use of supersensitive listening devices, like those now used to isolate and amplify the voices of referees and quarterbacks on televised football games, may extend investigative capabilities beyond previous understandings of limited search and seizure.

## Prosecution of Computer and High-Technology Crime

A generation ago, computer crimes were virtually unheard of, and as recently as a decade ago, few states had computer-crime laws. People who committed crimes using computer technology had to be prosecuted, if at all, under laws intended for other purposes. Burglary laws sometimes served to prosecute illegal entry into computer systems, laws against theft were applied to the stealing of digitized information, and embezzlement statutes were applied to illegal electronic fund transfers. Forty years ago, for example, an employee of Texas Instruments Corporation who stole more than 50 typewritten copies of software programs was convicted of theft under Texas law.[129] Had the software been stolen in electronic form or through the use of a modem, prosecution under the state larceny statute would have been much more difficult. In another early case, Wisconsin authorities found themselves at a loss as to how to prosecute the "414 gang"—a teenage group of computer hackers based in Milwaukee who had infiltrated the computers of 60 businesses and other organizations, including government computer systems, the Los Alamos National Laboratory, the Sloan-Kettering Cancer Center, and the Security Pacific National Bank in Los Angeles.[130] At the time of the offense (1983), neither Wisconsin nor the federal government had specific legislation applicable to the hackers' activity, and they had to be arraigned under a law pertaining to telephone mischief.

Because existing laws were often not adequate in the prosecution of computer crimes, most states and the federal government moved rapidly to create computer and high-technology criminal statutes. In 1984, the first federal computer-crime law was enacted.[131] The Computer Fraud and Abuse Act (CFAA) criminalized unauthorized access to government computers or to com-

## FREEDOM OR SAFETY? YOU DECIDE.

### Religion and Public Safety

In 2003, Florida Judge Janet Thorpe ruled that a Muslim woman could not wear a veil while being photographed for a state driver's license. The woman, Sultaana Freeman, claimed that her religious rights were violated when the state department of motor vehicles required that she reveal her face for the photograph. She offered to show her eyes, but not the rest of her face, to the camera.

Judge Thorpe said, however, that a "compelling interest in protecting the public from criminal activities and security threats" did not place an undue burden on Freeman's ability to practice her religion.

After the hearing, Freeman's husband, Abdul-Maalik Freeman, told reporters, "This is a religious principle; this is a prin-

ciple that's imbedded in us as believers. So, she's not going to do that. We'll take the next step, and this is what we call the American way." Howard Marks, the Freemans' attorney, said that he would file an appeal in a higher court.

### YOU DECIDE

Do the demands of public safety justify the kind of restriction on religious practice described here? Should photo IDs, such as driver's licenses, be replaced with other forms of identification (such as an individual's stored DNA profile) in order to accommodate the beliefs of individuals like the Freemans?

*Reference:* "Judge: No Veil in Driver's License Photo," Associated Press wire services, June 6, 2003.

puters containing information protected under the Federal Privacy Act.[132] It also made unauthorized interstate entry into any computer illegal. In 1986, Congress modified the Computer Fraud and Abuse Act,[133] expanding the penalty for illegal access to federal-interest computers—or those that represent a "unique federal interest." (The term *federal-interest computer* has since been replaced by **protected computer**.) Under the CFAA, which has been revised a number of times since it was first enacted, convicted offenders face penalties of up to ten years' imprisonment and fines of up to twice the amount of any "unlawful gain."

Today, high-tech criminals may be prosecuted under a variety of other federal statutes. In addition to the Computer Fraud and Abuse Act, applicable federal statutes include the Computer Abuse Amendments Act of 1994 (a part of the Violent Crime Control and Law Enforcement Act); the Cyber Security Enhancement Act of 2002[134] (part of the Homeland Security Act); aspects of the Electronic Communications Privacy Act of 1986; the National Stolen Property Act[135]; the Federally Protected Property Act[136]; the federal Trade Secrets Act[137]; the amended Copyright Act of 1980[138]; the No Electronic Theft Act of 1997 (NETA)[139]; the Digital Millennium Copyright Act of 1998[140]; the Digital Theft Deterrence and Copyright Damages Improvement Act of 1999[141]; the federal Wiretap Act of 1968[142]; and various federal wire, mail, and bank fraud statutes.[143] All can support prosecutions of high-tech offenders.

In December 2000, the Computer Crime Enforcement Act was signed into law. The act established a grant program within the U.S. Department of Justice to help state and local law enforcement officers and prosecutors improve education, training, enforcement, and prosecution of computer crimes. The funds could be used to assist state and local law enforcement agencies enforce laws relating to computer crime; educate and train law enforcement officers and prosecutors to conduct investigations, forensic analyses of evidence, and prosecutions of computer crime; acquire computers and other equipment to conduct investigations and forensic analysis of evidence of computer crimes; and facilitate and promote the sharing of federal law enforcement expertise and information about the investigation, analysis, and prosecution of computer crimes with state and local law enforcement officers and prosecutors, including the use of multijurisdictional task forces.

Following the lead of the federal government, most states developed their own computer-crime laws. New York's Computer Crime Act is an example of such legislation.[144] Enacted in 1986, it created six crime categories involving software and computer misuse. The law specifically prohibits the duplication of copyrighted software and makes the possession of illegally duplicated software a felony. Other activities defined as illegal under the law include the unauthorized use of a computer, computer trespass, and theft of computer services. The New York law also created sweeping amendments to existing laws. Theft laws were modified to specifically include "computer program" and "computer data" under the definition of "property," and computer terminology was incorporated into forgery laws. Most state computer-crime laws impose punishments proportional to the damage done, although California bases penalties on the number of violations.

### protected computer

Under federal law, (1) a computer used exclusively by a financial institution or the U.S. government, (2) a computer used by or for a financial institution or the U.S. government, or (3) a computer used in interstate or foreign commerce or communication.

# Secure Identity Management

As noted in Chapter 2, one of the fastest growing crimes in the United States is identity theft. According to the Federal Trade Commission, identity theft directly impacts as many as 10 million victims annually, although most do not report the crime[145]—and the number is rising at a breathtaking rate. Most identity thieves seek personal gain, using stolen identities to acquire charge cards, purchase personal items, and so on. They hunt for discarded credit card receipts, steal personal identification numbers, and purchase Social Security cards from purse snatchers and robbers.

The theft and manipulation of identities, however, can take on a far more sinister character when committed by terrorists or by those who use assumed identities or identity deception to hide from security and enforcement officials. In October 2001, for example, Luis Martinez-Flores, an illegal immigrant from El Salvador, was arraigned in federal court and charged with identity fraud for allegedly helping some of the September 11 hijackers procure Virginia driver's licenses just six weeks before the hijackings.[146] About the same time, Kenys Galicia, a legal secretary and notary public, was arrested and charged with notarizing falsified documents for the hijackers. Apparently neither was aware that the men they were dealing with were terrorists.

The need for secure **identity management** and for a comprehensive and workable identity management system is more apparent today than ever before. The crux of any such system is accurate and dependable identity authentication or verification. A number of foreign countries have moved toward the adoption of national identification cards—an idea that, at least to date, has proved unpopular in the United States. Citizens and visitors can carry the identification cards in lieu of other documents, such as driver's licenses, visas, passports, and birth certificates. One of the most interesting techniques for effective and secure identity management is the smart card. **Smart cards** are technologically advanced credit card–like devices that can store a considerable amount of unalterable information about the cardholder. Smart cards were developed independently in Germany in 1967, in Japan in 1970, in the United States in 1972, and in France in 1974.[147] The term *smart card* was not coined, however, until 1980, when France initiated a major campaign to export smart card technology.

Smart cards can be used for a variety of purposes. They can store detailed records of a person's medical history or banking transactions. They can enable the holder to purchase goods

**identity management**

The comprehensive management and administration of a user's individual profile information, permissions, and privileges across a variety of social settings.[viii]

**smart card**

A plastic card or similar device, containing a computer chip and other sources of nonalterable information (such as a hologram or a laser-encoded memory strip), that is used to provide highly secure personal identification.

Smart cards and smart card readers. These bank cards contain microchips allowing for enhanced security and ease of use. The chips in these cards keep track of how much money is available in the holder's account and permit a wide variety of secure transactions tied to that account. Smart cards are being developed for many different purposes. They can store details of a person's medical history, allow the holder access to restricted areas (both real and virtual), authenticate the holder's identity (through embedded DNA code, stored and unalterable retinal images, and so on), or be tracked from orbiting satellites, which can report a card's location to within a few feet anywhere on the earth's surface. Most of today's smart cards, however, are tailored for more limited uses.

*AP Wide World Photos*

# FREEDOM OR SAFETY? YOU DECIDE.

## A National ID: An Idea Whose Time Has Come?

In 2005, the National Institute of Standards and Technology announced a new Federal Information Processing Standard (FIPS) intended to improve the procedures used to authenticate the identity of federal employees and contractors seeking access to federal facilities and federal information systems.

The new FIPS came in response to a Homeland Security Presidential Directive issued by the White House on August 27, 2004, calling for a secure and reliable government-wide personal identification standard.

U.S. government offices nationwide and overseas have mandated the use of the new identification system, which is based on a credit card–sized Personal Identification Verification (PIV) smart card containing integrated circuit chips. Those chips store an identification number, personal information, and biometric data, including two digitized fingerprints and a photograph.

Critics of the system see the PIV card as the first step toward a mandatory national ID. In fact, with plans already in place for the use of digital photographs stored in enhanced state driver's licenses and federal passports, the future of biometric recognition technology appears to be quickly growing.

The Intelligence Reform and Terrorism Prevention Act of 2004, which set national standards for driver's licenses, Social Security cards, and birth certificates, may be another step in this direction. Under the law, state-issued driver's licenses will have to conform to federal requirements or will not be accepted for certain federally mandated identification requirements such as the screening of airline passengers.

One aspect of biometric technology, facial recognition systems, has already been used to scan crowds at Super Bowls, and camera-equipped taxicabs and public transportation facilities are making it easier to identify suspected terrorists and wanted criminals. Passive scanning of PIV cards can be used to conduct clandestine identity verification without the bearer's knowledge or participation.

What many fear is the creation of a national identification system that would require anyone living in this country to carry some form of electronic biometric identification with them at all times. Supporters say that such a system would provide for far greater security on public transportation systems, in public buildings, on highways, and at border crossings than is available today.

Critics say, however, that under such a system personal privacy would quickly become a thing of the past and that government intrusion into the lives of individuals would be potentially overwhelming.

### YOU DECIDE

Do you think that creation of a mandatory national ID, such as a smart card, is a good idea? Why or why not? Under what circumstances should citizens and others living in the United States be required to present identification materials for inspection by enforcement authorities?

*References:* Alan Beckley, "The Future of Privacy in Law Enforcement," *FBI Law Enforcement Bulletin*, September, 2004, pp. 16–23; Duncan Graham-Rowe, "ID Row Is Bad News for Transatlantic Travellers," *New Scientist*, April 16, 2005, pp. 23–24; "Commerce Secretary Announces New ID Standard for Federal Agencies," NIST news release, February 25, 2005; and NIST PIV Project website, http://csrc.nist.gov/piv-project/index.html.

and services, to enter restricted areas (both real and virtual), or to perform other operations. Smart cards can even be designed so that they can be tracked from orbiting satellites, which can report a card's location to within ten feet anywhere on the earth's surface. Most of today's smart cards are tailored for a variety of limited uses, however. A number of universities, for example, have adopted modified versions of smart cards for use as student identification cards. Credit card companies have also begun to make use of at least certain aspects of smart card technology. One of the most widely carried smart cards today is Blue, an "intelligent" credit card available through American Express.

Today's smart cards may feature a tamper-resistant hologram of the intended bearer, along with a miniature computer memory chip containing unalterable digitized information, such as name, home address, Social Security number, birth date, gender, ethnicity, telephone number, e-mail address, office address, frequent flyer numbers, or bank account and credit card numbers. Some cards also include a plastic strip encoded with read-only laser-imprinted information that may contain something as complex as the intended bearer's DNA code. None of today's smart cards hold all of the information described here, although cards capable of doing so can readily be made. Currently being tested by the U.S. military and by governments in Italy and Singapore, smart cards are already used in some industries to enhance access security in the workplace.[148] See a visual presentation of smart card technology via Web Extra 18–13 at cjtoday.com.

# Technology and Individual Rights

> The correct question is not "What rights does the Constitution give to the American people," but rather "What powers does the Constitution grant to the government?"
>
> —Jacob Hornberger

The Office of Technology Assessment of the U.S. Congress notes that "what is judicially permissible and socially acceptable at one time has often been challenged when technology changes."[149] Barring global war or world catastrophe, advances in technology will continue to occur. When agencies of the justice system use cutting-edge technology, it inevitably provokes fears of a future in which citizens' rights are abrogated in favor of advancing technology. Individual rights, equal treatment under the law, and due process issues all require constant reinterpretation as technology improves.

In 1996, for example, amidst fierce debate, the U.S. Congress passed and President Clinton signed a law intended to control the availability of obscene materials on the Internet. Entitled the Communications Decency Act (CDA),[150] the new law was part of the Telecommunications Act of 1996. The CDA made it a federal offense for anyone to distribute "indecent" or "patently offensive" material to minors (anyone under 18 years of age) over computer networks like the Internet or commercial online services. The law provided for prison terms of up to two years and a $250,000 fine for breaking the law. Opponents of the law claimed that it unconstitutionally restricted free speech because it is not technologically possible for providers of access or content on the Internet to prevent minors from obtaining indecent materials intended for adults. A federal court agreed and soon found portions of the CDA unconstitutional. In 1997, the U.S. Supreme Court upheld the lower court's decision in the landmark case of *Reno* v. *ACLU*.[151] In 2003, however, a split Supreme Court upheld a federal law that denied federal funds to libraries that refused to install pornography filters on computers that provide patrons with Internet access.[152] Emily Sheketoff, executive director of the American Library Association, decried the ruling, saying that it "forces libraries to choose between federal funding and censorship."[153]

The Second Amendment to the U.S. Constitution reads, "A well regulated Militia, being necessary to the security of a free State, the right of the people to keep and bear Arms, shall not be infringed." Many interpret the words of this amendment as a complete and total ban on gun control by the federal government. Control advocates, however, are now suggesting the adoption of international treaties requiring gun manufacturers to embed special transponder chips in each weapon made for civilian use so that it can be tracked anywhere in the world. Such miniaturized computer chips, which draw their energy from background electromagnetic radiation (like passing radio or TV signals), would be detectable by a variety of high-tech means, as well as through a network of geosynchronous satellites circling the earth, which could pinpoint the location of a specific weapon to within ten feet. Tampering with embedded transponders might carry penalties similar to those now imposed for altering or removing a weapon's serial number.

The Fourth Amendment to the U.S. Constitution guarantees "[t]he right of the people to be secure in their persons, houses, papers, and effects, against unreasonable searches and seizures." Given the electronic network that permeates contemporary society, today's "houses" are far less secure from prying eyes than were those of the eighteenth century. Modern dwellings are linked to the outside world through phone lines, modems, fax machines, electronic mail, broadband connections, and even direct radio and television communications. Wireless computer networks can also provide anyone who knows how to "listen" with substantial insight into what is occurring within the home. One highly significant question centers on where the "security" of the home ends and the public realm begins.

Complicating matters still further are today's "supersnoop" technologies, which provide investigators with the ability to literally hear through walls (using vibration detectors), listen to conversations over tremendous distances (with parabolic audio receivers), record voices in distant rooms (via laser readings of windowpane vibrations), and even look through walls using forward-looking infrared (FLIR) devices, which can detect temperature differences of as little as two-tenths of one degree. (The use of FLIR for certain kinds of investigative purposes was discussed in Chapter 7.)

Another question concerns the Fourth Amendment's guarantee of secure "papers and effects." The phrase "papers and effects" takes on a much wider meaning when we enter the world of modern technology. Although the framers of the Constitution could not envision electronic documents and databases, their admonition would seem to apply to such records. Electronic tax listings, records of draft registrants, Social Security rolls, health reports, criminal histories, credit bureau ratings, and government and bank logs all contain billions of items of information on almost every man, woman, and child in the country. Most agree that official access to such information should be limited. A separate question centers on the privacy of various kinds of information, the proper legal steps to be used in acquiring information for investigative purposes, and the types of information that can appropriately be stored in criminal justice data repositories (and for how long). In a 2003 civil case that may prove prophetic, the New Hampshire Supreme

Identix Corporation's CEO Joseph Atick demonstrates use of a digital handprint scanner. As personal identification technologies continue to develop, some people are concerned that terrorism and other criminal threats have seriously eroded personal liberties.

*Steve Woit*

Court ruled that the family of a young woman who was killed by an obsessed stalker could sue the Internet data broker that he hired to locate his victim.[154]

Finally, Section One of the Fourteenth Amendment concludes with the phrase, "No State shall . . . deny to any person within its jurisdiction the equal protection of the laws." Modern technology, because it is expensive and often experimental, is not always equally available. Criminal justice programs that depend on technology that is limited in its availability may contravene this Fourteenth Amendment provision. Court-ordered confinement, for example, which utilizes electronic monitoring and house arrest, is an alternative to imprisonment that offenders greatly prefer. The technology supporting this kind of confinement is expensive, however, which dramatically limits its availability. Although the Supreme Court has yet to address this particular topic, it has ruled that programs that require the offender to bear a portion of the cost of confinement are unconstitutional when their availability is restricted to only those offenders who can afford them.[155]

## SUMMARY

Old concepts of crime and criminality have undergone significant revision as a result of emerging technologies. Science fiction–like products that are now readily available either legally or on the black market have brought with them a plethora of possibilities for new high-stakes crimes. The well-equipped, technologically advanced offender in tomorrow's world will be capable of attempting crimes involving dollar amounts undreamed of only a few decades ago, and the potential for crime-caused human suffering will rise astronomically. The relentless advance of globalization will combine with powerful technologies to produce a new world of challenges for criminal justice agencies. Domestic and international terrorism, highly organized transnational criminal cartels, and changing social values will evolve into a challenging complex tangle of legal, technological, and social issues.

In response, the crime-fighting abilities of police agencies will be substantially enhanced by cutting-edge surveillance and enforcement technologies and by international and interagency cooperation. A massive infusion of funds will be needed to support the adoption of new crime-fighting technologies, and the hiring and training of sophisticated personnel able to operate in multicultural environments will be necessary to allow tomorrow's enforcement agencies to compete with technologically adept criminals of global reach.

Although the crimes it faces may change, American criminal justice will remain recognizable through its backbone of subsystems: the police, the courts, and corrections. It will continue to rest on constitutional mandates and will be responsive to court precedent. Deterrence, apprehension, and reformation will continue to serve as the philosophical triad guiding the day-to-day operations of criminal justice agencies. New issues will arise, but most of them will be resolved within the context of the question that has guided American criminal justice since its inception: How do we ensure public order and safety while guaranteeing individual rights and social justice in a free society? Learn more about what the American criminal justice system of the future may be like via Library Extra 18–9 at cjtoday.com.

**LIBRARY EXTRA**

---

## DISCUSSION QUESTIONS

1. Historically speaking, how have advances in technology affected society and culture? Is the same relationship between technology and society likely to persist into the future?

2. What is high-technology crime? What new kinds of crimes have technological advances made possible? Distinguish between new types of crimes produced by advancing technology and new ways of committing "old crimes" that have been facilitated by emerging technologies.

3. How has technology affected the practice of criminal justice in America during the past century? How has it affected the criminal law?

4. Why do criminal laws have to change to keep up with changes in technology? What modifications in current laws defining criminal activity might soon be necessary to meet the criminal possibilities inherent in new technologies?

5. What is criminalistics? Explain the interplay between advancing technology and methods used to gather evidence in the fight against crime.

6. What threats to individual rights might advanced technology create? Will our standards as to what constitutes admissible evidence, what is reasonable privacy, and so on undergo a significant reevaluation as a result of emerging technologies?

---

## WEB QUEST

Use the Cybrary (http://www.cybrary.info) to learn about computer and high-technology crimes and their link to international terrorism. Specifically, answer the following questions:

1. How can terrorists use computer technology to attack the United States?
2. How likely is such an attack?
3. What might be the potential consequences of a cyberterrorism attack? (See Chapter 17 for more information.)
4. How well prepared is the United States to defend itself against cyberterrorism?
5. What other forms of computer crime might international organized criminal groups engage in?

Summarize the information you've found, and submit it to your instructor if asked to do so.

To complete this Web Quest online, go to the Web Quest module in Chapter 18 of the *Criminal Justice Today* Companion Website at cjtoday.com.

---

## NOTES

i. Jonathan Littmann, "In the Mind of Most Wanted Hacker, Kevin Mitnick," *Computer World*, January 15, 1996, p. 87.

ii. "President Bush Calls on Senate to Back Human Cloning Ban," White House press release, April 10, 2002.

iii. Centers for Disease Control and Prevention, *Bioterrorism: An Overview*. Web posted at

http://www.bt.cdc.gov/documents/ PPTResponse/laboverview.pdf (accessed August 5, 2003).

iv. Thomas J. Cowper and Michael E. Buerger, *Improving Our View of the World: Police and Augmented Reality Technology* (Police Futurists International/Federal Bureau of Investigation, 2003), p. 5.

**v.** *Imus in the Morning*, MSNBC, May 10, 2005.

**vi.** Thomas J. Cowper and Michael E. Buerger, *Improving Our View of the World: Police and Augmented Reality Technology* (Washington, DC: Federal Bureau of Investigation, 2003). Web posted at http://www.fbi.gov/ publications/realitytech/realitytech.pdf (accessed October 7, 2003).

**vii.** Ayn Rand, "The Lessons of Vietnam," *The Ayn Rand Letter*, August 26, 1974.

**viii.** Adapted from Entrust, Inc., "Secure Identity Management: Challenges, Needs, and Solutions," p. 1. Web posted at http://www .entrust.com (accessed August 5, 2003).

---

1. Quoted in Susan W. Brenner, "Is There Such a Thing as 'Virtual Crime'?" *California Criminal Law Review*, Vol. 4 (June 2001).

2. Information for this story comes from "Hacker Hunters: An Elite Force Takes on the Dark Side of Computing," *Business Week*, May 30, 2005, pp. 74–82.

3. Thomas J. Cowper, "Foresight Update 49." Web posted at http://www.foresight.org/ Updates/ Update49/Update49.4.html (accessed August 5, 2003).

4. Ibid.

5. University of Minnesota Center for Infectious Disease Research and Policy (CIDRAP), "All H2N2 Flu Virus Samples, Destroyed, CDC Says," May 3, 2005. Web posted at http:// www.cidrap.umn.edu/cidrap/content/ influenza/general/news/may0305h2n2.html (accessed July 10, 2005).

6. "Stem Cells Extracted from Human Clone," MSNBC News, February 12, 2004. Web posted at http://www.msnbc.msn.com/id/4244988 (accessed July 8, 2005).

7. "President Bush Calls on Senate to Back Human Cloning Ban," White House press release, April 10, 2002.

8. "Bush Condemns Embryonic Cloning," Fox News, May 21, 2005. Web posted at http:// www.foxnews.com/story/0,2933,157163,00 .html (accessed July 8, 2005).

9. H.R. 222, Human Cloning Research Prohibition Act.

10. Many other countries, such as England, permit therapeutic cloning, although they often criminalize or severely restrict human cloning efforts.

11. Dolly was euthanized in 2003 after falling ill with lung disease.

12. S. 658, The Human Cloning Prohibition Act of 2005.

13. House Committee on Energy and Commerce, Subcommittee on Health, "Prepared Witness Testimony," June 20, 2001. Web posted at http://energycommerce.house.gov/107/hearins / 06202001Hearing291/Allen449.htm (accessed August 5, 2003).

14. "Bush Backs Total Ban on Human Cloning: Declares Life Is a 'Creation, Not a Commodity,'" April 10, 2002. Web posted at http://usgovinfo.about.com/library/weekly/ aa041102a.htm (accessed August 10, 2003).

15. Linda Rosencrance, "Cyberscam Strikes Massachusetts State Lottery," *Computerworld*, July 24, 2003.

16. "Are You Vulnerable to Cybercrime?" *USA Today*, February 20, 1995, p. 3B.

17. "Most Wanted Hacker Released from Prison," *USA Today* online, January 21, 2000. Web posted at http://www.usatoday.com/news/ ndsfri02.htm (accessed January 21, 2000).

18. Elinor Abreu, "Kevin Mitnick Bares All," *Industry Standard*, September 28, 2000. Web posted at http://www.nwfusion.com/news/ 2000/0928mitnick.html (accessed January 26, 2002).

19. Pia Turunen, "Hack Attack: How You Might Be a Target," CNN.com, April 12, 2002. Web posted at http://www.cnn.com/2002/TECH/ ptech/04/12/hack.dangers (accessed August 3, 2003).

20. Nikola Krastev, "East: Many Nations Lack Effective Computer Crime Laws," *Radio Free Europe*, December 19, 2000. Web posted at http://www.rferl.org/nca/features/2000/12/ 15122000153858.asp (accessed April 8, 2002).

21. Ibid.

22. "'Love Bug' Prompts New Philippine Law," *USA Today*, June 14, 2000.

23. "Cybercrime Treaty Gets Green Light," BBC News Online, November 12, 2001.

24. Details for this section come from the Council of Europe, Convention on Cybercrime signatories website, http://conventions.coe.int (accessed April 8, 2002).

25. For suggested computer crime categories, see Peter Grabosky, "Computer Crime: A Criminological Overview," paper presented at the Workshop on Crimes Related to the Computer Network, Tenth United Nations Congress on the Prevention of Crime and the Treatment of Offenders, Vienna, Austria, April 15, 2000. Web posted at http://www .aic.gov.au/conferences/other/compcrime/ computercrime.pdf (accessed January 12, 2002). Also see David L. Carter, "Computer Crime Categories: How Techno-Criminals Operate," *FBI Law Enforcement Journal*, July 1995, pp. 21–26.

26. Grabosky, "Computer Crime."

27. Kevin Johnson, "Hijackers' E-Mails Sifted for Clues," *USA Today*, October 11, 2001.

28. Computer Security Institute, *2004 CSI/FBI Computer Crime and Security Survey* (Southampton, PA: Computer Security Institute, 2004), p. 9. Web posted at http:// i.cmpnet.com/gocsi/db_area/pdfs/fbi/FBI2004 .pdf (accessed August 1, 2005).

29. "Focus on Physical Security, Too," *eWeek*, January 27, 2003, p. 6a.

30. Ibid., p. 5.

31. Ramona R. Rantala, *Cybercrime against Businesses: Pilot Test Results, 2001 Computer Security Survey* (Washington, DC: Bureau of Justice Statistics, 2004).

32. "Invasion of the Data Snatchers!" *Time*, September 26, 1988, pp. 62–67.

33. "Virus Infects NASA, Defense, University Computer Systems," *Fayetteville (N.C.) Observer-Times*, November 4, 1988, p. 19A.

34. *Raleigh News and Observer*, April 27, 1990.

35. "First HTML Virus Detected," Andover News Network. Web posted at http://www. andovernews.com/cgi-bin/ news_story.pl?95529/topstories (accessed January 6, 2000).

36. Sophos Antivirus, "The First JAVA Virus." Web posted at http://www.sophos.com/ virusinfo/articles/java.html (accessed January 5, 2002).

37. Net IQ, "Virus Protection." Web posted at http://marshal.netiq.com/0195/ solutions_virusprotection.html (accessed August 1, 2005).

38. Gregg Keizer, "Microsoft Says Phishing Bad, Offers Little New for Defense," *TechWeb News*, March 15, 2005. Web posted at http://www.techweb.com/wire/159900391 (accessed July 7, 2005).

39. Avivah Litan, "Phishing Victims Likely Will Suffer Identity Theft Fraud," Gartner, Inc., May 14, 2004. Web posted at http://www .gartner.com/DisplayDocument?ref=g_ search&id=448 11 (accessed July 6, 2005).

40. Software Information Industry Association, *Report on Global Software Piracy, 2000*. Web posted at http://www.siia.net/piracy/pubs/ piracy2000.pdf (accessed August 1, 2003).

41. See the music industry's reaction to the court's decision at http://www.nmpa.org/pr/ NMPAPressRelease.doc (accessed August 1, 2003).

42. *Metro-Goldwyn-Mayer Studios, Inc.* v. *Grokster, Ltd.*, 259 F.Supp. 2d 1029 (C.D. Cal. 2003).

43. Motion to dismiss denied, 243 F.Supp. 2d 1073 (C.D. Cal. 2003).

44. *MGM* v. *Grokster*, U.S. Supreme Court, No. 04-480 (decided June 27, 2005).

45. *Sony Corporation of America* v. *Universal City Studios, Inc.*, 464 U.S. 417 (1984).

46. Pending federal legislation, known as the Conyers-Berman bill, would allow felony charges to be brought against users of illegal peer-to-peer services and would provide for a maximum prison term of five years.

47. Public Law 108-187.

48. Peter Firstbrook, "META Trend Update: The Changing Threat Landscape," The Meta Group, March 24, 2005. Web posted at http://www.metagroup.com/us/ displayArticle.do?oid=51768 (accessed July 5, 2005).

49. Virginia Statutes, Section 18.2-152.3:1.

50. Jack McCarthy, "Spammer Sentenced to Nine Years in Prison," *InfoWorld*, April 11, 2005.

51. Some of the technological devices described in this section are discussed in G. Gordon Liddy, "Rules of the Game," *Omni*, January 1989, pp. 43–47, 78–80.

52. CIA Directorate of Intelligence, *Terrorist CBRN: Materials and Effects* (Washington, DC: Central Intelligence Agency, 2003).

53. Radiological Weapons Working Group, Harvard Project on Managing the Atom.

54. The information in this paragraph comes from a June 30, 2003, General Accounting Office report. See "Continuing Radioactive Materials Seizures," Nuclear Threat Initiative website. Web posted at http://www.nti.org/ e_research/cnwm/overview/cnwm_home.asp (accessed August 1, 2003).

55. Matthew Bunn, Anthony Wier, and John P. Holden, *Controlling Nuclear Warheads and Materials: A Report Card and Action Plan* (Cambridge, MA: Nuclear Threat Initiative and Harvard University, 2003).

56. "Fact Sheet: The Biological Weapons Convention" (Washington, DC: Bureau of Arms Control, 2002). Web posted at http://www.state.gov/t/ac/rls/fs/10401.htm (accessed August 8, 2003).

57. Ali S. Kahn et al., *Biological and Chemical Terrorism: Strategic Plan for Preparedness and Response* (Atlanta, GA: Centers for Disease Control and Prevention, April 21, 2000). Web posted at http://www.cdc.gov/ mmwr/preview/ mmwrhtml/rr4904a1.htm (accessed August 2, 2003).

58. Council on Foreign Relations, "Terrorism: Questions and Answers—The Anthrax Letters." Web posted at http://www .terrorismanswers.com/weapons/ anthraxletters.html (accessed August 3, 2003).

59. See Rick Weiss, "DNA by Mail: A Terror Risk," *Washington Post*, July 18, 2002.

60. Peter Eisler, "High-Tech 'Bait Cars' Catch Unsuspecting Auto Thieves," *USA Today*, November 29, 2004, p. 1A.

61. Paul McClellan, "Automatic Plate Recognition Evaluation Ends with Positive Results," Ohio State Highway Patrol, December 22, 2004. Web posted at http://www.statepatrol.ohio.gov/ colcolumn/2004/AutoScanner-2.htm (accessed July 9, 2005).

62. Toni Locy, "Thieves Target Auto Identification," *USA Today*, May 20, 2005, p. 1A.

63. For an excellent overview of technology in criminal justice, see Laura J. Moriarty and David L. Carter, eds., *Criminal Justice Technology in the Twenty-First Century* (Springfield, IL: Charles C. Thomas, 1998).

64. National Law Enforcement and Corrections Technology Center, electronic press release, April 7, 1995.

65. Lester D. Shubin, *Research, Testing, Upgrading Criminal Justice Technology,* National Institute of Justice Reports (Washington, DC: U.S. Government Printing Office, 1984), pp. 2–5.

66. Simon Dinitz, "Coping with Deviant Behavior through Technology," *Criminal Justice Research Bulletin,* Vol. 3, No. 2 (1987).

67. See, for example, Laurence P. Karper et al., "Antipsychotics, Lithium, Benzodiazepines, Beta-Blockers," in Marc Hillbrand and Nathaniel J. Pallone, eds., *The Psychobiology of Aggression: Engines, Measurement, Control* (New York: Haworth Press, 1994), pp. 203–222.

68. Harry Soderman and John J. O'Connell, *Modern Criminal Investigation* (New York: Funk and Wagnalls, 1945), p. 41.

69. The system was invented by Lambert Adolphe Jacques Quetelet (1796–1874), a Belgian astronomer and statistician.

70. For more on Bertillon's system, see Alphonse Bertillon, *Signaletic Instructions* (New York: Werner, 1896).

71. Robert D. Foote, "Fingerprint Identification: A Survey of Present Technology, Automated Applications, and Potential for Future Development," *Criminal Justice Monograph Series,* Vol. 5, No. 2 (Huntsville, TX: Sam Houston State University Press, 1974), pp. 3–4.

72. Soderman and O'Connell, *Modern Criminal Investigation,* p. 57.

73. Ibid.

74. Francis Galton, *Finger Prints* (London: Macmillan, 1892).

75. Foote, "Fingerprint Identification," p. 1.

76. Office of Technology Assessment, *Criminal Justice: New Technologies and the Constitution: A Special Report* (Washington, DC: U.S. Government Printing Office, 1988), p. 18. Electro-optical systems for live fingerprint scanning were developed by Fingermatric, Inc., of White Plains, New York.

77. T. F. Wilson and P. L. Woodard, *Automated Fingerprint Identification Systems— Technology and Policy Issues* (Washington, DC: U.S. Department of Justice, 1987), p. 5.

78. Kristi Gulick, "Latent Prints from Human Skin," *Law and Order Magazine* Online. Web posted at http://www.lawandermag .com/magazine/current/latentprints.html.htm (accessed September 26, 1998).

79. Los Angeles Police Department, *Annual Report, 1985–1986,* p. 26.

80. Ibid., p. 27.

81. American National Standards Institute, *American National Standard for Information Systems—Fingerprint Identification—Data Format for Information Interchange* (New York: ANSI, 1986). Originally developed as the Proposed American National Standard Data Format for the Interchange of Fingerprint Information by the National Bureau of Standards (Washington, DC: NBS, 1986).

82. Dennis G. Kurre, "On-Line Exchange of Fingerprint Identification Data," *FBI Law Enforcement Bulletin,* December 1987, pp. 14–16.

83. Jon Swartz, "Ins and Outs of Biometrics," *USA Today,* January 27, 2003, p. 3B.

84. In 1998, ruling for the first time on polygraph examinations, the U.S. Supreme Court upheld the military's ban on the use of polygraph tests in criminal trials. In refusing to hear a case, Justice Clarence Thomas wrote, "[T]he aura of infallibility attending polygraph evidence can lead jurors to abandon their duty to assess credibility and guilt."

85. Details for this story come from *USA Today,* Nationline, March 16, 2000, p. 3A.

86. "NYC Seeks to Indict Rapists by DNA Alone," *USA Today,* August 5, 2003, p. 3A.

87. Francis X. Clines, "DNA Clears Virginia Man of 1982 Assault," *New York Times,* December 10, 2001.

88. U.S. Department of Justice, *Understanding DNA Evidence: A Guide for Victim Service Providers* (Washington, DC: DOJ, 2001).

89. Tim Schellberg and Lisa Hurst, *DNA Resource Report,* March 19, 2004. Web posted at http://www.dnaresource.com/ 03-192004%20Summary.pdf (accessed July 4, 2005).

90. See Alec J. Jeffreys, Victoria Wilson, and Swee Lay Thein, "Hypervariable 'Minisatellite' Regions in Human Nature," *Nature,* No. 314 (1985), p. 67; and "Individual-Specific 'Fingerprints' of Human DNA," *Nature,* No. 316 (1985), p. 76.

91. Peter Gill, Alec J. Jeffreys, and David J. Werrett, "Forensic Application of DNA Fingerprints," *Nature,* No. 318 (1985), p. 577. See also Craig Seton, "Life for Sex Killer Who Sent Decoy to Take Genetic Test," *London Times,* January 23, 1988, p. 3. A popular account of this case, *The Blooding,* was written by crime novelist Joseph Wambaugh (New York: William Morrow, 1989).

92. Bureau of Justice Statistics, *Forensic DNA Analysis: Issues* (Washington, DC: BJS, 1991).

93. "Genetic Fingerprinting Convicts Rapist in U.K.," *Globe and Mail,* November 14, 1987, p. A3.

**94.** *Daubert* v. *Merrell Dow Pharmaceuticals, Inc.,* 509 U.S. 579, 113 S.Ct. 2786 (1993).

**95.** *Frye* v. *U.S.,* 54 App. D.C. 46, 47, 293 F. 1013, 1014 (1923).

**96.** For the application of *Daubert* to DNA technology, see Barry Sheck, "DNA and Daubert," *Cardozo Law Review,* Vol. 15 (1994), p. 1959.

**97.** In 1999, in the case of *Kumho Tire Co.* v. *Carmichael,* 526 U.S. 137 (1999), the Court held that *Daubert* factors may also apply to the testimony of engineers and other experts who are not, strictly speaking, "scientists" and that a trial judge determining the admissibility of an engineering expert's testimony may consider one or more of the specific *Daubert* factors.

**98.** Violent Crime Control and Law Enforcement Act of 1994, Section 210301.

**99.** "National DNA Index System Reaches 1,000,000 Profiles," FBI National Press Office, June 14, 2002.

**100.** Edward Connors et al., *Convicted by Juries, Exonerated by Science: Case Studies in the Use of DNA Evidence to Establish Innocence after Trial* (Washington, DC: National Institute of Justice, 1996).

**101.** The nonjury case involved a guilty plea from a defendant who had mental disabilities.

**102.** Stephen Strauss, "Fingerprints Leaving Fingerprints of Their Own," Simon and Schuster NewsLink, June 20, 1997.

**103.** Public Law No. 108-405.

**104.** Chapter 213 of Title 18, U.S. Code, Section 3297.

**105.** "Time Line '98," *Yahoo! Internet Life,* January 1999, p. 90. To access the database, visit http:// www.publicdata.com.

**106.** William S. Sessions, "Criminal Justice Information Services: Gearing Up for the Future," *FBI Law Enforcement Bulletin,* February 1993, pp. 181–188.

**107.** OTA, *Criminal Justice,* p. 29.

**108.** Ibid.

**109.** For more on the system, see Craig Stedman, "Feds to Track Sex Offenders with Database," *Computerworld,* September 2, 1996, p. 24.

**110.** "Saving Face," *PC Computing,* December 1988, p. 60.

**111.** See Dawn E. McQuiston and Roy S. Malpass, "Use of Facial Composite Systems in U.S. Law Enforcement Agencies." Web posted at http://eyewitness.utep.edu/Documents/McQuiston%20APLS%202000.pdf (accessed March 5, 2002).

**112.** "Security or Privacy? DARPA's Total Information Awareness Program Tests the Boundaries," InformationWeek.com. Web posted at http://www.informationweek.com/story/showArticle.jhtml?articleID=10000184 (accessed August 2, 2003). John Poindexter, who was in charge of the TIA program, resigned his position on August 1, 2003, and the future of the program is in doubt.

**113.** Information in this paragraph comes from "U.S. Sensors Could Track Any Car, All Passengers in Foreign Cities," WorldTribune.com, July 30, 2003. Web posted at http://www.worldtribune.com/worldtribune/breaking_8.html (accessed August 5, 2003).

**114.** See, for example, Jeffrey S. Hormann, "Virtual Reality: The Future of Law Enforcement Training," *FBI Law Enforcement Bulletin,* July 1995, pp. 7–12.

**115.** See, for example, Thomas F. Rich, *The Use of Computerized Mapping Crime Control and Prevention Programs* (Washington, DC: National Institute of Justice, 1995).

**116.** Matt L. Rodriguez, "The Acquisition of High Technology Systems by Law Enforcement," *FBI Law Enforcement Bulletin,* December 1988, p. 10.

**117.** Office of the Inspector General, Department of Homeland Security, *Semiannual Report to the Congress* (Washington, DC: DHS, 2003).

**118.** Frank J. Murray, "NASA Plans to Read Terrorists' Minds at Airports," *Washington Times,* August 17, 2002.

**119.** Ibid.

**120.** The information in this section comes from Thomas J. Cowper and Michael E. Buerger, *Improving Our View of the World: Police and Augmented Reality Technology* (Washington, DC: Federal Bureau of Investigation, 2003). Web posted at http://www.fbi.gov/publications/realitytech/realitytech.pdf (accessed October 7, 2003).

**121.** "Xybernaut and ZNQ3, Inc. Team to Deliver Secure Mobile Wearable Computing Solutions to State and Local Governments," *Business Wire,* July 29, 2003.

**122.** See the fictional discussion of such an advanced device in Dan Brown, *Deception Point* (New York: Simon and Schuster, 2002).

**123.** See "Nanotechnology in Crime Prevention and Detection," Institute of Nanotechnology. Web posted at http://www.nano.org.uk/crime2.htm (accessed August 5, 2003).

**124.** Winston Chai, "Radio ID Chips May Track Banknotes," CNET News.com, May 23, 2003. Web posted at http://news.com.com/2100-1019-1009155.html (accessed August 12, 2003).

**125.** The 2005 World Exposition website. Web posted at http://www1.expo2005.or.jp/en/whatexpo/index.html (accessed August 3, 2005).

**126.** William L. Tafoya, "Law Enforcement beyond the Year 2000," *Futurist* (September/October 1986), pp. 33–36.

**127.** Ibid.

128. See Rodriguez, "The Acquisition of High Technology Systems by Law Enforcement," pp. 11–12.

129. *Hancock* v. *State*, 402 S.W.2d 906 (Tex. Crim. Appl. 1966).

130. Stanley S. Arkin et al., *Prevention and Prosecution of Computer and High Technology Crime* (New York: Matthew Bender, 1988), §3.05.

131. The Computer Fraud and Abuse Act (Public Law 98-473, Title II, Section 2102 [a], October 12, 1984). The act was substantially revised in 1986 and again in 1988.

132. William J. Hughes, "Congress versus Computer Crime," *Information Executive*, Vol. 1, No. 1 (Fall 1988), pp. 30–32.

133. Because of significant modifications introduced into the legislation in 1986, the law is often referred to as the Computer Fraud and Abuse Act of 1986.

134. Section 225 of the Homeland Security Act, Public Law 107-296.

135. 18 U.S.C. 2311.

136. 18 U.S.C. 641.

137. 18 U.S.C. 1905.

138. 17 U.S.C. 101, 117.

139. Public Law 106-160.

140. Public Law 105-304.

141. Public Law 105-147.

142. 18 U.S.C. § 2510.

143. 18 U.S.C. § 1341, 1343, and 1344.

144. N.Y. Penal Law, sections 156.30 and 156.35.

145. Christine Dugas, "Federal Survey: Identity Theft Hits 1 in 4 U.S. Households; Scope of Crime Much Worse Than Previously Thought," *USA Today*, September 4, 2003, p. B10.

146. Information in this paragraph comes from "Two Arraigned on False ID Charges Involving Hijackers," CNN.com, October 3, 2001. Web posted at http://www.cnn.com/ 2001/US/ 10/03/inv.virginia.hearing (accessed August 6, 2003).

147. eEurope, One World: Smart Cards, p. 2. Web posted at http://eeurope-smartcards.org/ Smart20Cards.pdf.

148. Eric Duprat, "Smart Cards, Payment Terminals and the Point-of-Transaction," *Hyperline*, 1 (2003), p. 6.

149. OTA, *Criminal Justice*, p. 51.

150. 47 U.S.C. 151 et seq.

151. *Reno* v. *ACLU* (1997), 117 S.Ct. 2329.

152. *United States* v. *American Library Association*, U.S. Supreme Court, No. 02-361 (2003).

153. "Supreme Court Upholds Use of Porn Filters in Libraries," Associated Press, June 23, 2003.

154. *Helen Remsburg, Administratrix of the Estate of Amy Lynn Boyer* v. *Docusearch, Inc.*, No. 2002-255 (D.N.H., 1993).

155. *Bearden* v. *Georgia*, 461 U.S. 660 (1983).

# THE BILL OF RIGHTS

The first ten amendments to the U.S. Constitution are known as the Bill of Rights. These amendments, ratified in 1791, have special relevance to criminal justice and are reproduced here. The entire U.S. Constitution can be found online at this book's Companion Website (http://www.cjtoday.com). You can save the file to your desktop or easily print it.

## AMENDMENT I

Congress shall make no law respecting an establishment of religion, or prohibiting the free exercise thereof; or abridging the freedom of speech, or of the press; or the right of the people peaceably to assemble, and to petition the Government for a redress of grievances.

## AMENDMENT II

A well regulated Militia, being necessary to the security of a free State, the right of the people to keep and bear Arms, shall not be infringed.

## AMENDMENT III

No Soldier shall, in time of peace be quartered in any house, without the consent of the Owner, nor in time of war, but in a manner to be prescribed by law.

## AMENDMENT IV

The right of the people to be secure in their persons, houses, papers, and effects, against unreasonable searches and seizures, shall not be violated, and no Warrants shall issue, but upon probable cause, supported by Oath or affirmation, and particularly describing the place to be searched, and the persons or things to be seized.

## AMENDMENT V

No person shall be held to answer for a capital, or otherwise infamous crime, unless on a presentment or indictment of a Grand Jury, except in cases arising in the land or naval forces, or in the Militia, when in actual service in time of War or public danger; nor shall any person be subject for the same offence to be twice put in jeopardy of life or limb; nor shall be compelled in any criminal case to be a witness against himself, nor be deprived of life, liberty, or property, without due process of law; nor shall private property be taken for public use, without just compensation.

## AMENDMENT VI

In all criminal prosecutions, the accused shall enjoy the right to a speedy and public trial, by an impartial jury of the State and district wherein the crime shall have been committed, which district shall have been previously ascertained by law, and to be informed of the nature and cause of the accusation; to be confronted with the witnesses against him; to have compulsory process for obtaining witnesses in his favor, and to have the Assistance of Counsel for his defence.

## AMENDMENT VII

In suits of common law, where the value in controversy shall exceed twenty dollars, the right of trial by jury shall be preserved, and no fact tried by a jury, shall be otherwise reexamined in any court of the United States, than according to the rules of the common law.

## AMENDMENT VIII

Excessive bail shall not be required, nor excessive fines imposed, nor cruel and unusual punishments inflicted.

## AMENDMENT IX

The enumeration in the Constitution, of certain rights, shall not be construed to deny or disparage others retained by the people.

## AMENDMENT X

The powers not delegated to the United States by the Constitution, nor prohibited by it to the States, are reserved to the States respectively, or to the people.

| | | | |
|---|---|---|---|
| AACAP | American Academy of Child and Adolescent Psychiatry | CCA | Corrections Corporation of America |
| ABA | American Bar Association | CCE | Continuing Criminal Enterprise (statute) |
| ACA | American Correctional Association | CCIPS | Computer Crime and Intellectual Property Section (FBI) |
| ACJS | Academy of Criminal Justice Sciences | CCJJDP | Coordinating Council on Juvenile Justice and Delinquency Prevention |
| ACLU | American Civil Liberties Union | | |
| ADA | Americans with Disabilities Act | CDA | Communications Decency Act (1996) |
| ADAM | Arrestee Drug Abuse Monitoring | CDC | Centers for Disease Control and Prevention |
| ADD | attention deficit disorder | | |
| ADMAX | administrative maximum | CFAA | Computer Fraud and Abuse Act (1986) |
| AEDPA | Antiterrorism and Effective Death Penalty Act (1996) | CFO | chief financial officer |
| | | CFR | Council on Foreign Relations |
| AFDA | Association of Federal Defense Attorneys | CIA | Central Intelligence Agency |
| AFIS | automated fingerprint identification system | CIAO | Critical Infrastructure Assurance Office |
| | | CIC | children in custody |
| AI | artificial intelligence | CIO | chief information officer |
| AIDS | acquired immunodeficiency syndrome | CJA | Criminal Justice Act (England) |
| AIMS | adult internal management system | CJDLC | Criminal Justice Distance Learning Consortium |
| AJA | American Jail Association | | |
| ALI | American Law Institute | CJIS | Criminal Justice Information Services (FBI) |
| AMOS | Atari Mobile Operations Simulator | CALEA | Commission on Accreditation for Law Enforcement Agencies |
| ANS | autonomic nervous system | | |
| AOUSC | Administrative Office of the United States Courts | CLET | Certified Law Enforcement Trainer |
| | | CODIS | Combined DNA Index System (FBI) |
| APIS | Advance Passenger Information System | COPE | Citizen Oriented Police Enforcement |
| APPA | American Probation and Parole Association | COPS | Community Oriented Policing Services |
| | | CPO | certified protection officer |
| AR | augmented reality | CPOP | Community Police Officer Program (New York City) |
| ASC | American Society of Criminology | | |
| ASIS | ASIS International (formerly the American Society for Industrial Security) | CPP | certified protection professional |
| | | CPR | cardiopulmonary resuscitation |
| ASLET | American Society for Law Enforcement Training | CPTED | crime prevention through environmental design |
| ATF | Bureau of Alcohol, Tobacco, and Firearms | CRIPA | Civil Rights of Institutionalized Persons Act |
| AWDWWITK | assault with a deadly weapon with intent to kill | CRIPP | Courts Regimented Intensive Probation Program |
| BARS | Battlefield Augmented Reality System | CSA | Controlled Substances Act (1970) |
| BCS | British Crime Survey | CSC | Correctional Services Corporation |
| BJA | Bureau of Justice Assistance | CSE | child sexual exploitation |
| BJS | Bureau of Justice Statistics | CSO | chief security officer |
| BOP | Bureau of Prisons | CZTS | Combat Zones That See |
| BTS | Border and Transportation Security | DARE | Drug Abuse Resistance Education |
| BWC | Biological Weapons Convention | DARPA | Defense Advanced Research Projects Agency |
| BWS | battered women's syndrome | | |
| CAD | computer-assisted dispatch | DART | Directed Area Responsibility Teams (Houston) |
| CAFA | Class Action Fairness Act | | |
| CALEA | Commission on Accreditation for Law Enforcement Agencies | DAWN | Drug Abuse Warning Network |
| | | DCA | district court of appeals |
| CAN-SPAM | Controlling the Assault of Non-Solicited Pornography and Marketing | DCCTAP | Drug Court Clearinghouse and Technical Assistance Project (American University) |
| CAPRA | clients, acquired/analyzed, partnerships, respond, assess | DEA | Drug Enforcement Administration |
| | | DES | data encryption standard |
| CAPS | Chicago's Alternative Policing Strategy | DHS | Department of Homeland Security |
| CAT | computer-aided transcription | DIRPPA | Drug-Induced Rape Prevention and Punishment Act (1996) |
| CBT | computer-based training | | |

| | | | |
|---|---|---|---|
| DNA | deoxyribonucleic acid | ICC | International Criminal Court |
| DOJ | U.S. Department of Justice | IDRA | Insanity Defense Reform Act (1984) |
| DPIC | Death Penalty Information Center | IFF | Identification Friend or Foe |
| DPRC | Drug Policy Research Center (RAND Corporation) | ILC | International Law Commission |
| | | ILEA | International Law Enforcement Academy |
| DUF | Drug Use Forecasting | ILP | intelligence-led policing |
| DUI | driving under the influence (of alcohol or drugs) | INCB | International Narcotics Control Board |
| | | INTERPOL | International Criminal Police Organization |
| DWI | driving while intoxicated | IPES | International Police Executive Symposium |
| ECPA | Electronic Communications Privacy Act (1986) | IPS | intensive probation supervision |
| | | IRS | Internal Revenue Service |
| EPI | Executive Protection Institute | ISC | International Society for Criminology |
| EPR | emergency preparedness and response | IVS | International Victim Survey (UN) |
| ESI | Executive Security International | JCPT | Joint Community Police Training |
| Europol | European Police Office | JIC | Justice Information Center |
| FACTS | Factual Analysis Criminal Threat Solution (software application) | JJDP | Juvenile Justice and Delinquency Prevention Act (1974) |
| FATS | firearms training simulation | JTTF | Joint Terrorism Task Force |
| FBI | Federal Bureau of Investigation | JUST | Judgment Under Stress Training |
| FCC | federal correctional complex | JUSTNET | Justice Technology Information Network |
| FCI | federal correctional institution | KKK | Ku Klux Klan |
| FDA | Food and Drug Administration | LAPD | Los Angeles Police Department |
| FDSS | Federal-wide Drug Seizure System | LASD | Los Angeles County Sheriff's Department |
| FGC | family group conference | LEAA | Law Enforcement Assistance Administration |
| FINCEN | Financial Crimes Enforcement Network | | |
| FLETC | Federal Law Enforcement Training Center | LEAP | law enforcement availability pay |
| FLIR | forward-looking infrared | LEEP | Law Enforcement Education Program |
| FMLN | Farabundo Marti National Liberation Front | LESL | Law Enforcement Standards Laboratory |
| FOP | Fraternal Order of Police | LESTN | Law Enforcement Satellite Training Network |
| FPC | federal prison camp | | |
| FSB | Federal Security Service (Russia) | LME | liquid metal embrittlement |
| FTCA | Federal Tort Claims Act | M-19 | 19th of April Movement |
| FTO | foreign terrorist organization | MADD | Mothers Against Drunk Driving |
| FWG | Futures Working Group | MANPADS | Man Portable Air Defense Systems |
| GBL | gamma-butyrolactone | MATRIX | Multistate Anti-Terrorism Information Exchange |
| GBMI | guilty but mentally ill | | |
| GED | general equivalency diploma | MBO | management by objectives |
| GGI | guided group interaction | MCFP | medical center for federal prisoners |
| GHB | gamma-hydroxybutyrate | MDC | metropolitan detention center |
| HCL | cocaine hydrochloride | MPC | Model Penal Code |
| HEUNI | European Institute for Crime Prevention and Control | MROP | Mentally Retarded Offender Program |
| | | MSBP | Munchausen syndrome by proxy |
| HIDTA | high-intensity drug-trafficking area | MTF | Monitoring the Future (survey) |
| HIFCA | high-intensity financial crime area | NAACP | National Association for the Advancement of Colored People |
| HIV | human immunodeficiency virus | | |
| HRALEI | Human Rights and Law Enforcement Institute | NACDL | National Association of Criminal Defense Lawyers |
| HSP | Heroin Signature Program | NADCP | National Association of Drug Court Professionals |
| IACP | International Association of Chiefs of Police | | |
| IAD | internal affairs division | NADDIS | Narcotics and Dangerous Drugs Information System |
| IAFIS | integrated automated fingerprint identification system (FBI) | | |
| | | NAP | National Assessment Program |
| IAIP | Information Analysis and Infrastructure Protection | NASA | National Aeronautics and Space Administration |

| | | | |
|---|---|---|---|
| NCAVC | National Center for the Analysis of Violent Crime | OIG | Office of the Inspector General (Department of Justice) |
| NCCD | National Council on Crime and Delinquency | OJARS | Office of Justice Assistance, Research, and Statistics |
| NCCS | National Computer Crime Squad (FBI) | OJJDP | Office of Juvenile Justice and Delinquency Prevention |
| NCEA | National Center on Elder Abuse | | |
| NCIC | National Crime Information Center (FBI) | OLES | Office of Law Enforcement Standards |
| NCIC 2000 | National Crime Information Center 2000 (FBI) | OLETC | Office of Law Enforcement Technology Commercialization |
| NCIS | National Criminal Intelligence Service (England) | ONDCP | Office of National Drug Control Policy |
| NCISP | National Criminal Intelligence Sharing Plan | OSCA | Office of the State Courts Administrator |
| NCJC | National Criminal Justice Commission | PCC | Police Cadet Corps (New York City) |
| NCJRS | National Criminal Justice Reference Service | PCCIP | President's Commission on Critical Infrastructure Protection |
| NCSC | National Center for State Courts | PCIPB | President's Critical Infrastructure Protection Board |
| NCTP | National Cybercrime Training Partnership | | |
| NCVS | National Crime Victimization Survey | PCP | phencyclidine |
| NCWP | National Center for Women and Policing | PCR | police–community relations |
| NDAA | National District Attorneys Association | PDS | podular/direct supervision |
| NDIC | National Drug Intelligence Center | PERF | Police Executive Research Forum |
| NDIS | National DNA Index System (FBI) | PFI | Police Futurists International |
| NETA | No Electronic Theft Act (1997) | PHDCN | Project on Human Development in Chicago Neighborhoods |
| NGCRC | National Gang Crime Research Center | | |
| NIBRS | National Incident-Based Reporting System (FBI) | PIJ | Palestine Islamic Jihad |
| | | PINS | Persons in Need of Supervision (status offenders) |
| NIDA | National Institute on Drug Abuse | | |
| NIJ | National Institute of Justice | PLRA | Prison Litigation Reform Act (1996) |
| NIPC | National Infrastructure Protection Center | PMS | premenstrual syndrome |
| NISMART | National Incidence Study of Missing, Abducted, Runaway, and Thrownaway Children | PORAC | Peace Officer's Research Association of California |
| | | POST | police officer standards and training |
| NLADA | National Legal Aid and Defender Association | PPS | personal protection specialist |
| | | PRC | People's Republic of China |
| NLECTC | National Law Enforcement and Corrections Technology Center | PREA | Prison Rape Elimination Act (2003) |
| | | PSI | presentence investigation |
| NNICC | National Narcotics Intelligence Consumers Committee | RAS | reticular-activating system |
| | | RESTTA | Restitution Education, Specialized Training, and Technical Assistance (program) |
| NOBLE | National Organization of Black Law Enforcement Executives | | |
| NRA | National Rifle Association | RFID | radio-frequency identification |
| NSA | National Sheriffs Association | RICO | Racketeer Influenced and Corrupt Organizations (statute) |
| NSDUH | National Survey on Drug Use and Health | | |
| NVAWS | National Violence Against Women Survey | RID | Remove Intoxicated Drivers |
| NVC | National Victims Center | RISE | Reintegrative Shaming Experiments (Australian Institute of Criminology) |
| NVCAN | National Victims' Constitutional Amendment Network | | |
| | | RISS-ATIX | Regional Information Sharing Systems Anti-Terrorism Information Exchange Program |
| NWCCC | National White Collar Crime Center | | |
| NYGC | National Youth Gang Center | | |
| NYPD | New York Police Department | RJC | Real Justice Conferencing (Pennsylvania) |
| OBTS | offender-based transaction statistics | RLUIPA | Religious Land Use and Institutionalized Persons Act |
| ODCCP | Office for Drug Control and Crime Prevention (UN) | | |
| | | ROR | release on recognizance |
| OICJ | Office of International Criminal Justice (University of Illinois at Chicago) | RTTF | Regional Terrorism Task Force |
| | | RVIS | Remote Video Inspection System |

| | | | |
|---|---|---|---|
| SAMHSA | Substance Abuse and Mental Health Services Administration | UCR | Uniform Crime Reports |
| SARA | scanning, analysis, response, and assessment | UN | United Nations |
| | | UNICRI | United Nations Interregional Crime and Justice Research Institute |
| SARS | severe acute respiratory syndrome | UNOJUST | United Nations Online Justice Information System |
| SBI | State Bureau of Investigation | | |
| SCU | Street Crimes Unit (New York City) | USBP | United States Border Patrol |
| SEARCH | National Consortium for Justice Information and Statistics | U.S.C. | United States Code |
| | | USCG | United States Coast Guard |
| SIIA | Software and Information Industry Association | USNCB | United States National Central Bureau (INTERPOL) |
| SLATT | State and Local Anti-Terrorism Training Program | USP | United States penitentiary |
| | | USSC | United States Sentencing Commission |
| SPECDA | School Program to Educate and Control Drug Abuse | VAWA | Violence Against Women Act (1994) |
| | | VCAN | Victims' Constitutional Amendment Network |
| STG | security threat group | | |
| SWAT | special weapons and tactics | VCF | virtual case file |
| TFJJR | Task Force on Juvenile Justice Reform | ViCAP | Violent Criminal Apprehension Program (FBI) |
| TIA | Total Information Awareness | | |
| TIVU | Terrorism and International Victims Unit (Office for Victims of Crime) | VOCA | Victims of Crime Act (1984) |
| | | VR | virtual reality |
| TWGECSI | Technical Working Group for Electronic Crime Scene Investigation | VWPA | Victim and Witness Protection Act (1982) |
| | | WAR | White Aryan Resistance |
| TWGEDE | Technical Working Group for the Examination of Digital Evidence | WJIN | World Justice Information Network |
| | | WMD | weapon of mass destruction |
| UAV | unmanned aerial vehicle | WTC | World Trade Center |
| UCBE | unsolicited commercial bulk e-mail | WWW | World Wide Web |

The 18 chapters of *Criminal Justice Today* contain hundreds of terms commonly used in the field of criminal justice. This glossary contains many more. All concepts, wherever they appear in the book, are explained whenever possible according to definitions provided by the Bureau of Justice Statistics under a mandate of the Justice System Improvement Act. That mandate was to create a consistent terminology set for use by criminal justice students, practitioners, and planners. It found its most complete expression in the *Dictionary of Criminal Justice Data Terminology*,[1] the second edition of which provides many of our definitions. Others (especially those in Chapter 2) are derived from the FBI's Uniform Crime Reporting Program and are taken from the *Uniform Crime Reporting Handbook*.[2]

Standardization is becoming increasingly important because American criminal justice agencies, justice practitioners, and involved citizens now routinely communicate between and among themselves, and often over considerable distances, about the criminal justice system and about justice-related issues. For communications to be meaningful and efficient, a shared terminology is necessary. Standardization, however desirable, is not easy to achieve—sometimes because of legal and technical distinctions between jurisdictions, or because of variations in customary usage. In the words of the Bureau of Justice Statistics, "It is not possible to construct a single national standard criminal justice data terminology where every term always means the same thing in all of its appearances. However, it is possible and necessary to standardize the language that represents basic categorical distinctions."[3] Although this glossary should be especially valuable to the student who will one day work in the criminal justice system, it should also prove beneficial to anyone seeking a greater insight into that system.

**1983 lawsuit** A civil suit brought under Title 42, Section 1983, of the U.S. Code against anyone who denies others their constitutional right to life, liberty, or property without due process of law.

**abused child** A child who has been physically, sexually, or mentally abused. Most states also consider a child who is forced into delinquent activity by a parent or guardian to be abused.

**acquittal** The judgment of a court, based on a verdict of a jury or a judicial officer, that the defendant is not guilty of the offense or offenses for which he or she was tried.

***actus reus*** An act in violation of the law. Also, a guilty act.

**adjudication** The process by which a court arrives at a decision regarding a case. Also, the resultant decision.

**adjudicatory hearing** The fact-finding process wherein the juvenile court determines whether there is sufficient evidence to sustain the allegations in a petition.

**ADMAX** Administrative maximum. The term is used by the federal government to denote ultra-high-security prisons.

**administration of justice** The performance of any of the following activities: detection, apprehension, detention, pretrial release, post-trial release, prosecution, adjudication, correctional supervision, or rehabilitation of accused persons or criminal offenders.[4]

**admission** In corrections, the entry of an offender into the legal jurisdiction of a correctional agency or into the physical custody of a correctional facility.

**adult** A person who is within the original jurisdiction of a criminal court, rather than a juvenile court, because his or her age at the time of an alleged criminal act was above a statutorily specified limit.

**adversarial system** The two-sided structure under which American criminal trial courts operate that pits the prosecution against the defense. In theory, justice is done when the most effective adversary is able to convince the judge or jury that his or her perspective on the case is the correct one.

**aftercare** In juvenile justice usage, the status or program membership of a juvenile who has been committed to a treatment or confinement facility, conditionally released from the facility, and placed in a supervisory or treatment program.

**aggravated assault (UCR)** The unlawful, intentional inflicting, or attempted or threatened inflicting, of serious injury upon the person of another. While *aggravated assault* and *simple assault* are standard terms for reporting purposes, most state penal codes use labels like *first-degree* and *second-degree* to make such distinctions.

**aggravating circumstances** Circumstances relating to the commission of a crime that make it more grave than the average instance of that crime. See also **mitigating circumstances.**

**alias** Any name used for an official purpose that is different from a person's legal name.

**alibi** A statement or contention by an individual charged with a crime that he or she was so distant when the crime was committed, or so engaged in other provable activities, that his or her participation in the commission of that crime was impossible.

**alter ego rule** In some jurisdictions, a rule of law that holds that a person can only defend a third party under circumstances and only to the degree that the third party could act on his or her own behalf.

**alternative sanctions** See **intermediate sanctions.**

**anomie** A socially pervasive condition of normlessness. Also, a disjunction between approved goals and means.

**Antiterrorism Act** See **USA PATRIOT Act of 2001.**

**appeal** Generally, the request that a court with appellate jurisdiction review the judgment, decision, or order of a lower court and set it aside (reverse it) or modify it.

**appearance (court)** The act of coming into a court and submitting to its authority.

**appellant** The person who contests the correctness of a court order, judgment, or other decision and who seeks review and relief in a court having appellate jurisdiction. Also, the person on whose behalf this is done.

**appellate court** A court whose primary function is to review the judgments of other courts and of administrative agencies.

**appellate jurisdiction** The lawful authority of a court to review a decision made by a lower court.

**arraignment** Strictly, the hearing before a court having jurisdiction in a criminal case, in which the identity of the defendant is established, the defendant is informed of the charge and of his or her rights, and the defendant is required to enter a plea. Also, in some usages, any appearance in criminal court prior to trial.

**arrest** The act of taking an adult or juvenile into physical custody by authority of law for the purpose of charging the person with a criminal offense, a delinquent act, or a status offense, terminating with the recording of a specific offense. Technically, an arrest occurs whenever a law enforcement officer curtails a person's freedom to leave.

**arrest (UCR)** In Uniform Crime Reports terminology, each separate instance in which a person is taken into physical custody or is notified or cited by a law enforcement officer or agency, except those relating to minor traffic violations.

**arrest rate** The number of arrests reported for each unit of population.

**arrest warrant** A document issued by a judicial officer that directs a law enforcement officer to arrest an identified person who has been accused of a specific offense.

**arson (UCR)** The burning or attempted burning of property, with or without the intent to defraud. Some instances of arson result from malicious mischief, some involve attempts to claim insurance moneys, and some are committed in an effort to disguise other crimes, such as murder, burglary, or larceny.

**Ashurst-Sumners Act** Federal legislation of 1935 that effectively ended the industrial prison era by restricting interstate commerce in prison-made goods.

**assault (UCR)** An unlawful attack by one person upon another. Historically, *assault* meant only the attempt to inflict injury on another person; a completed act constituted the separate offense of battery. Under modern statistical usage, however, attempted and completed acts are grouped together under the generic term *assault.*

**assault on a law enforcement officer** A simple or aggravated assault, in which the victim is a law enforcement officer engaged in the performance of his or her duties.

**atavism** A condition characterized by the existence of features thought to be common in earlier stages of human evolution.

**attendant circumstances** The facts surrounding an event.

**attorney** A person trained in the law, admitted to practice before the bar of a given jurisdiction, and authorized to advise, represent, and act for others in legal proceedings. Also called *lawyer; legal counsel.*

**Auburn system** A form of imprisonment developed in New York State around 1820 that depended on mass prisons, where prisoners were held in congregate fashion requiring silence. This style of imprisonment was a primary competitor with the Pennsylvania system.

**augmented reality (AR)** The real-time and accurate overlay of digital information on a user's real-world experience, through visual, aural, and/or tactile interfaces.[5] The computer readouts superimposed on the visual fields of the fictional cyborgs in the various *Robocop* and *Terminator* movies provide an example.

**backlog (court)** The number of cases awaiting disposition in a court that exceeds the court's capacity for disposing of them within the period of time considered appropriate.

**bail** The money or property pledged to the court or actually deposited with the court to effect the release of a person from legal custody.

**bail bond** A document guaranteeing the appearance of a defendant in court as required and recording the pledge of money or property to be paid to the court if he or she does not appear, which is signed by the person to be released and anyone else acting on his or her behalf.

**bail bondsman** A person, usually licensed, whose business it is to effect release on bail for people charged with offenses and held in custody, by pledging to pay a sum of money if the defendant fails to appear in court as required.

**bail revocation** A court decision withdrawing the status of release on bail that was previously conferred on a defendant.

**bailiff** The court officer whose duties are to keep order in the courtroom and to maintain physical custody of the jury.

**balancing test** A principle, developed by the courts and applied to the corrections arena by *Pell* v. *Procunier* (1974), that attempts to weigh the rights of an individual, as guaranteed by the Constitution, against the authority of states to make laws or to otherwise restrict a person's freedom in order to protect the state's interests and its citizens.

**ballistics** The analysis of firearms, ammunition, projectiles, bombs, and explosives.

**battered women's syndrome (BWS)** 1. A series of common characteristics that appear in women who are abused physically and psychologically over an extended period of time by the dominant male figure in their lives. 2. A pattern of psychological symptoms that develops after somebody has lived in a battering relationship. 3. A pattern of responses and perceptions presumed to be characteristic of women who have been subjected to continuous physical abuse by their mates.[6]

**behavioral conditioning** A psychological principle that holds that the frequency of any behavior can be increased or decreased through reward, punishment, and association with other stimuli.

**bench warrant** A document issued by a court directing that a law enforcement officer bring a specified person before the court. A bench warrant is usually issued for a person

who has failed to obey a court order or a notice to appear.

**bias crime** See **hate crime.**

**Bill of Rights** The popular name given to the first ten amendments to the U.S. Constitution, which are considered especially important in the processing of criminal defendants.

**bind over** To require by judicial authority that a person promise to appear for trial, appear in court as a witness, or keep the peace. Also, the decision by a court of limited jurisdiction requiring that a person charged with a felony appear for trial on that charge in a court of general jurisdiction, as the result of a finding of probable cause at a preliminary hearing held in the court of limited jurisdiction.

**biocrime** A criminal offense perpetrated through the use of biologically active substances, including chemicals and toxins, disease-causing organisms, altered genetic material, and organic tissues and organs. Biocrimes unlawfully affect the metabolic, biochemical, genetic, physiological, or anatomical status of living organisms.

**Biological School** A perspective on criminological thought that holds that criminal behavior has a physiological basis.

**biological weapon** A biological agent used to threaten human life (for example, anthrax, smallpox, or any infectious disease).[7]

**biometrics** The science of recognizing people by physical characteristics and personal traits.

**bioterrorism** The intentional or threatened use of viruses, bacteria, fungi, or toxins from living organisms to produce death or disease in humans, animals, or plants.[8]

***Bivens* action** A civil suit, based on the case of *Bivens* v. *Six Unknown Federal Agents,* brought against federal government officials for denying the constitutional rights of others.

**bobbies** The popular British name given to members of Sir Robert (Bob) Peel's Metropolitan Police Force.

**booking** A law enforcement or correctional administrative process officially recording an entry into detention after arrest and identifying the person, the place, the time, the reason for the arrest, and the arresting authority.

**Bow Street Runners** An early English police unit formed under the leadership of Henry Fielding, magistrate of the Bow Street region of London.

**broken windows thesis** A perspective on crime causation that holds that physical deterioration in an area leads to higher crime rates and an increased concern for personal safety among residents.

**Bureau of Justice Statistics (BJS)** A U.S. Department of Justice agency responsible for the collection of criminal justice data, including the annual National Crime Victimization Survey.

**burglary** By the narrowest and oldest definition, trespassory breaking and entering of the dwelling house of another in the nighttime with the intent to commit a felony.

**burglary (UCR)** The unlawful entry of a structure to commit a felony or a theft (excludes tents, trailers, and other mobile units used for recreational purposes). For the UCR, the crime of burglary can be reported if (1) an unlawful entry of an unlocked structure has occurred, (2) a breaking and entering (of a secured structure) has taken place, or (3) a burglary has been attempted.

**capacity (legal)** The legal ability of a person to commit a criminal act. Also, the mental and physical ability to act with purpose and to be aware of the certain, probable, or possible results of one's conduct.

**capacity (prison)** See **prison capacity.**

**capital offense** A criminal offense punishable by death.

**capital punishment** The death penalty. Capital punishment is the most extreme of all sentencing options.

**career criminal** In prosecutorial and law enforcement usage, a person who has a past record of multiple arrests or convictions for serious crimes or who has an unusually large number of arrests or convictions for crimes of varying degrees of seriousness. Also called *professional criminal.*

**carnal knowledge** Sexual intercourse, coitus, sexual copulation. Carnal knowledge is accomplished "if there is the slightest penetration of the sexual organ of the female by the sexual organ of the male."[9]

**case law** The body of judicial precedent, historically built on legal reasoning and past interpretations of statutory laws, that serves as a guide to decision making, especially in the courts.

**caseload** The number of probation or parole clients assigned to one probation or parole officer for supervision.

**caseload (corrections)** The total number of clients registered with a correctional agency or agent on a given date or during a specified time period, often divided into active supervisory cases and inactive cases, thus distinguishing between clients with whom contact is regular and those with whom it is not. Also, the number of probation or parole clients assigned to one probation or parole officer for supervision.

**caseload (court)** The number of cases requiring judicial action at a certain time. Also, the number of cases acted on in a given court during a given period.

*certiorari* See **writ of** *certiorari.*

**chain of command** The unbroken line of authority that extends through all levels of an organization, from the highest to the lowest.

**change of venue** The movement of a trial or lawsuit from one jurisdiction to another or from one location to another within the same jurisdiction. A change of venue may be made in a criminal case to ensure that the defendant receives a fair trial.

**charge** An allegation that a specified person has committed a specific offense, recorded in a functional document such as a record of an arrest, a complaint, an information or indictment, or a judgment of conviction. Also called *count.*

**Chicago School** A sociological approach that emphasizes demographics (the characteristics of population groups) and geographics (the mapped location of such groups relative to one another) and that sees the social disorganization that characterizes delinquency areas as a major cause of criminality and victimization.

**child abuse** The illegal physical, emotional, or sexual mistreatment of a child by his or her parent or guardian.

**child neglect** The illegal failure by a parent or guardian to provide proper nourishment or care to a child.

**circumstantial evidence** Evidence that requires interpretation or that requires a judge or jury to reach a conclusion based on what the evidence indicates. From the proximity of the defendant to a smoking gun, for example, the jury might conclude that she pulled the trigger.

**citation (to appear)** A written order issued by a law enforcement officer directing an alleged offender to appear in a specific court at a specified time to answer a criminal charge, and not permitting forfeit of bail as an alternative to court appearance.

**citizen's arrest** The taking of a person into physical custody by a witness to a crime other than a law enforcement officer for the purpose of delivering him or her to the physical custody of a law enforcement officer or agency.

**civil death** The legal status of prisoners in some jurisdictions who are denied the opportunity to vote, hold public office, marry, or enter into contracts by virtue of their status as incarcerated felons. While civil death is primarily of historical interest, some jurisdictions still limit the contractual opportunities available to inmates.

**civil justice** The civil law, the law of civil procedure, and the array of procedures and activities having to do with private rights and remedies sought by civil action. Civil justice cannot be separated from social justice because the kind of justice enacted in our nation's civil courts is a reflection of basic American understandings of right and wrong.

**civil law** The branch of modern law that governs relationships between parties.

**civil liability** Potential responsibility for payment of damages or other court-ordered enforcement as a result of a ruling in a lawsuit. Civil liability is not the same as criminal liability, which means "open to punishment for a crime."[10]

**class-action lawsuit** A lawsuit filed by one or more people on behalf of themselves and a larger group of people "who are similarly situated."[11]

**Classical School** An eighteenth-century approach to crime causation and criminal responsibility that grew out of the Enlightenment and that emphasized the role of free will and reasonable punishments. Classical thinkers believed that punishment, if it is to be an effective deterrent, has to outweigh the potential pleasure derived from criminal behavior.

**classification system** A system used by prison administrators to assign inmates to custody levels based on offense history, assessed dangerousness, perceived risk of escape, and other factors.

**clearance (UCR)** The event in which a known occurrence of a Part I offense is followed by an arrest or another decision which indicates that the crime has been solved.

**clearance rate** A traditional measure of investigative effectiveness that compares the number of crimes reported or discovered to the number of crimes solved through arrest or other means (such as the death of the suspect).

**clemency** An executive or legislative action in which the severity of punishment of a single person or a group of people is reduced, the punishment is stopped, or the person or group is exempted from prosecution for certain actions.

**closing argument** An oral summation of a case presented to a judge, or to a judge and jury, by the prosecution or by the defense in a criminal trial.

**club drug** A synthetic psychoactive substance often found at nightclubs, bars, "raves," and dance parties. Club drugs include MDMA (Ecstasy), ketamine, methamphetamine (meth), GBL, PCP, GHB, and Rohypnol.

**codification** The act or process of rendering laws in written form.

**cohort** A group of individuals sharing similarities of age, place of birth, and residence. Cohort analysis is a social science technique that tracks cohorts over time to identify the unique and observable behavioral traits that characterize them.

***comes stabuli*** A nonuniformed mounted law enforcement officer of medieval England. Early police forces were small and relatively unorganized but made effective use of local resources in the formation of posses, the pursuit of offenders, and the like.

**commitment** The action of a judicial officer in ordering that a person subject to judicial proceedings be placed in a particular kind of confinement or residential facility for a specific reason authorized by law. Also, the result of the action—that is, the admission to the facility.

**common law** Law originating from usage and custom rather than from written statutes. The term refers to an unwritten body of judicial opinion, originally developed by English courts, that is based on nonstatutory customs, traditions, and precedents that help guide judicial decision making.

**community-based corrections** See community corrections.

**community corrections** The use of a variety of officially ordered program-based sanctions that permit convicted offenders to remain in the community under conditional supervision as an alternative to an active prison sentence. Also called *community-based corrections.*

**community court** A low-level court that focuses on quality-of-life crimes that erode a neighborhood's morale, that emphasizes problem solving rather than punishment, and that builds on restorative principles such as community service and restitution.

**community policing** "A collaborative effort between the police and the community that identifies problems of crime and disorder and involves all elements of the community in the search for solutions to these problems."[12]

**community service** A sentencing alternative that requires offenders to spend at least part of their time working for a community agency.

**comparative criminologist** One who studies crime and criminal justice on a cross-national level.

**compelling interest** A legal concept that provides a basis for suspicionless searches when public safety is at issue. (Urinalysis tests of train engineers are an example.) It is the concept on which the U.S. Supreme Court cases of *Skinner* v. *Railway Labor Executives' Association* (1989) and *National Treasury Employees Union* v. *Von Raab* (1989) turned. In those cases, the Court held that public safety may sometimes provide a sufficiently compelling interest to justify limiting an individual's right to privacy.

**compensatory damages** Damages recovered in payment for an actual injury or economic loss.

**competent to stand trial** A finding by a court, when the defendant's sanity at the time of trial is at issue, that the defendant has sufficient present ability to consult with his or her attorney with a reasonable degree of rational understanding and that the defendant has a rational as well as factual understanding of the proceedings against him or her.

**complaint** Generally, any accusation that a person has committed an offense, received by or originating from a law enforcement or prosecutorial agency or received by a court. Also, in judicial process usage, a formal document submitted to the court by a prosecutor, law enforcement officer, or other person, alleging that a specified person has committed a specific offense and requesting prosecution.

**CompStat** A crime-analysis and police-management process built on crime mapping that was developed by the New York City Police Department in the mid-1990s.

**computer crime** Any crime perpetrated through the use of computer technology. Also, any violation of a federal or state computer-crime statute. Also called *cybercrime.*

**computer virus** A computer program designed to secretly invade systems and either modify the way in which they operate or alter the information they store. Viruses are destructive software programs that may effectively vandalize computers of all types and sizes.

**concurrence** The coexistence of (1) an act in violation of the law and (2) a culpable mental state.

**concurrent sentence** One of two or more sentences imposed at the same time, after conviction for more than one offense, and served at the same time. Also, a new sentence for a new conviction, imposed upon a person already under sentence for a previous offense, served at the same time as the previous sentence.

**concurring opinion** An opinion written by a judge who agrees with the conclusion reached by the majority of judges hearing a case but whose reasons for reaching that conclusion differ. Concurring opinions, which typically stem from an appellate review, are written to identify issues of precedent, logic, or emphasis that are important to the concurring judge but that were not identified by the court's majority opinion.

**conditional release** The release by executive decision of a prisoner from a federal or state correctional facility who has not served his or her full sentence and whose freedom is contingent on obeying specified rules of behavior.

**conditions of parole (probation)** The general and special limits imposed on an offender who is released on parole (or probation). General conditions tend to be fixed by state statute, while special conditions are mandated by the sentencing authority (court or board) and take into consideration the background of the offender and the circumstances of the offense.

**confinement** In corrections terminology, the physical restriction of a person to a clearly defined area from which he or she is lawfully forbidden to depart and from which departure is usually constrained by architectural barriers, guards or other custodians, or both.

**conflict model** A criminal justice perspective that assumes that the system's components function primarily to serve their own interests. According to this theoretical framework, justice is more a product of conflicts among agencies within the system than it is the result of cooperation among component agencies.

**conflict perspective** A theoretical approach that holds that crime is the natural consequence of economic and other social inequities. Conflict theorists highlight the stresses that arise among and within social groups as they compete with one another for resources and for survival. The social forces that result are viewed as major determinants of group and individual behavior, including crime.

**consecutive sentence** One of two or more sentences imposed at the same time, after conviction for more than one offense, and served in sequence with the other sentence. Also, a new sentence for a new conviction, imposed upon a person already under sentence for a previous offense, which is added to the previous sentence, thus increasing the maximum time the offender may be confined or under supervision.

**consensus model** A criminal justice perspective that assumes that the system's components work together harmoniously to achieve the social product we call *justice.*

**constitutive criminology** The study of the process by which human beings create an ideology of crime that sustains the notion of crime as a concrete reality.

**containment** The aspects of the social bond and of the personality that act to prevent individuals from committing crimes and that keep them from engaging in deviance.

**contempt of court** Intentionally obstructing a court in the administration of justice, acting in a way calculated to lessen the court's authority or dignity, or failing to obey the court's lawful orders.

**controlled substance** A specifically defined bioactive or psychoactive chemical substance proscribed by law.

**Controlled Substances Act (CSA)** Title II of the Comprehensive Drug Abuse Prevention and Control Act of 1970, which established schedules classifying psychoactive drugs according to their degree of psychoactivity.

**conviction** The judgment of a court, based on the verdict of a jury or judicial officer or on the guilty plea or *nolo contendere* plea of the defendant, that the defendant is guilty of the offense with which he or she has been charged.

**corporate crime** A violation of a criminal statute by a corporate entity or by its executives, employees, or agents acting on behalf of and for the benefit of the corporation, partnership, or other form of business entity.[13]

*corpus delicti* The facts that show that a crime has occurred. The term literally means "the body of the crime."

**correctional agency** A federal, state, or local criminal or juvenile justice agency, under a single administrative authority, whose principal functions are the intake screening, supervision, custody, confinement, treatment, or presentencing or predisposition investigation of alleged or adjudicated adult offenders, youthful offenders, delinquents, or status offenders.

**corrections** A generic term that includes all government agencies, facilities, programs, procedures, personnel, and techniques concerned with the intake, custody, confinement, supervision, treatment, and presentencing and predisposition investigation of alleged or adjudicated adult offenders, youthful offenders, delinquents, and status offenders.

**corruption** See **police corruption**.

**Cosa Nostra** A secret criminal organization of Sicilian origin. Also called *Mafia.*

**counsel (legal)** See **attorney**.

**count (offense)** See **charge**.

**court** An agency or unit of the judicial branch of government, authorized or established by statute or constitution and consisting of one or more judicial officers, which has the authority to decide cases, controversies in law, and disputed matters of fact brought before it.

**court calendar** The court schedule; the list of events comprising the daily or weekly work of a court, including the assignment of the time and place for each hearing or other item of business or the list of matters that will be taken up in a given court term. Also called *docket*.

**court clerk** An elected or appointed court officer responsible for maintaining the written records of the court and for supervising or performing the clerical tasks necessary for conducting judicial business. Also, any employee of a court whose principal duties are to assist the court clerk in performing the clerical tasks necessary for conducting judicial business.

**court disposition** 1. For statistical reporting purposes, generally, the judicial decision terminating proceedings in a case before judgment is reached. 2. The judgment. 3. The outcome of judicial proceedings and the manner in which the outcome was arrived at.

**court-martial** A military court convened by senior commanders under the authority of the Uniform Code of Military Justice for the purpose of trying a member of the armed forces accused of a violation of the code.

**court of last resort** The court authorized by law to hear the final appeal on a matter.

**court of record** A court in which a complete and permanent record of all proceedings or specified types of proceedings is kept.

**court order** A mandate, command, or direction issued by a judicial officer in the exercise of his or her judicial authority.

**court probation** A criminal court requirement that an offender fulfill specified conditions of behavior in lieu of a sentence to confinement, but without assignment to a probation agency's supervisory caseload.

**court reporter** A person present during judicial proceedings who records all testimony and other oral statements made during the proceedings.

**courtroom work group** The professional courtroom actors, including judges, prosecuting attorneys, defense attorneys, public defenders, and others who earn a living serving the court.

**credit card fraud** The use or attempted use of a credit card to obtain goods or services with the intent to avoid payment.

**crime** Conduct in violation of the criminal laws of a state, the federal government, or a local jurisdiction, for which there is no legally acceptable justification or excuse.

**crime-control model** A criminal justice perspective that emphasizes the efficient arrest and conviction of criminal offenders.

**Crime Index** An inclusive measure of the violent and property crime categories, or Part I offenses, of the Uniform Crime Reports. The Crime Index has been a useful tool for geographic (state-to-state) and historical (year-to-year) comparisons because it employs the concept of a crime rate (the number of crimes per unit of population). However, the addition of arson as an eighth index offense and the new requirements with regard to the gathering of hate-crime statistics could result in new Crime Index measurements that provide less-than-ideal comparisons.

**crime prevention** The anticipation, recognition, and appraisal of a crime risk and the initiation of action to eliminate or reduce it.

**crime rate** The number of Crime Index offenses reported for each unit of population.

**crime scene** The physical area in which a crime is thought to have occurred and in which evidence of the crime is thought to reside.

**crime-scene investigator** An expert trained in the use of forensics techniques, such as gathering DNA evidence, collecting fingerprints, photography, sketching, and interviewing witnesses.

**crime typology** A classification of crimes along a particular dimension, such as legal categories, offender motivation, victim behavior, or the characteristics of individual offenders.

**criminal homicide (UCR)** The act of causing the death of another person without legal justification or excuse.

**criminal incident** In National Crime Victimization Survey terminology, a criminal event involving one or more victims and one or more offenders.

**criminal intelligence** Information compiled, analyzed, and/or disseminated in an effort to anticipate, prevent, or monitor criminal activity.[14]

**criminal investigation** "The process of discovering, collecting, preparing, identifying, and presenting evidence to determine *what happened and who is responsible*"[15] when a crime has occurred.

**criminal justice** In the strictest sense, the criminal (penal) law, the law of criminal procedure, and the array of procedures and activities having to do with the enforcement of this body of law. Criminal justice cannot be separated from social justice because the kind of justice enacted in our nation's criminal courts is a reflection of basic American understandings of right and wrong.

**criminal justice system** The aggregate of all operating and administrative or technical support agencies that perform criminal justice functions. The basic divisions of the operational aspects of criminal justice are law enforcement, courts, and corrections.

**criminal law** The branch of modern law that concerns itself with offenses committed against society, its members, their property, and the social order. Also called *penal law*.

**criminal negligence** Behavior in which a person fails to reasonably perceive substantial and unjustifiable risks of dangerous consequences.

**criminal proceedings** The regular and orderly steps, as directed or authorized by statute or a court of law, taken to determine whether an adult accused of a crime is guilty or not guilty.

**criminalist** A police crime-scene analyst or laboratory worker versed in criminalistics.

**criminalistics** The use of technology in the service of criminal investigation; the application of scientific techniques to the detection and evaluation of criminal evidence.

**criminology** The scientific study of the causes and prevention of crime and the rehabilitation and punishment of offenders.

**cruel and unusual punishment** Punishment involving torture or a lingering death or the infliction of unnecessary and wanton pain.

**culpability** Blameworthiness; responsibility in some sense for an event or situation deserving of moral blame. Also, in Model Penal Code usage, a state of mind on the part of one who is committing an act that makes him or her potentially subject to prosecution for that act.

**cultural defense** A defense to a criminal charge in which the defendant's culture is taken into account in judging his or her culpability.

**cultural pluralism** See **multiculturalism**.

**curtilage** In legal usage, the area surrounding a residence that can reasonably be said to be a part of the residence for Fourth Amendment purposes.

**custody** The legal or physical control of a person or a thing. Also, the legal, supervisory, or physical responsibility for a person or a thing.

**cybercrime** See **computer crime**.

**cyberstalking** The use of the Internet, e-mail, and other electronic communication technologies to stalk another person.[16]

**cyberterrorism** A form of terrorism that makes use of high technology, especially computers and the Internet, in the planning and carrying out of terrorist attacks.

**danger law** A law intended to prevent the pretrial release of criminal defendants judged to represent a danger to others in the community.

**dangerousness** The likelihood that a given individual will later harm society or others. Dangerousness is often measured in terms of recidivism, or the likelihood of additional crime commission within five years following arrest or release from confinement.

**dark figure of crime** Crime that is not reported to the police and that remains unknown to officials.

**data encryption** The encoding of computerized information.

**date rape** Unlawful forced sexual intercourse with a female against her will that occurs within the context of a dating relationship. Date rape, or acquaintance rape, is a subcategory of rape that is of special concern today.

**Daubert standard** A test of scientific acceptability applicable to the gathering of evidence in criminal cases.

**deadly force** Force likely to cause death or great bodily harm. Also, "the intentional use of a firearm or other instrument resulting in a high probability of death."[17]

**deadly weapon** An instrument designed to inflict serious bodily injury or death or capable of being used for such a purpose.

**deconstructionist theory** One of the emerging approaches that challenges existing criminological perspectives to debunk them and that works toward replacing them with concepts more applicable to the postmodern era.

**decriminalization** The redefinition of certain previously criminal behaviors into regulated activities that become "ticketable" rather than "arrestable."

**defendant** A person formally accused of an offense by the filing in court of a charging document.

**defense (to a criminal charge)** Evidence and arguments offered by a defendant and his or her attorney to show why the defendant should not be held liable for a criminal charge.

**defense attorney** See **defense counsel**.

**defense counsel** A licensed trial lawyer hired or appointed to conduct the legal defense of a person accused of a crime and to represent him or her before a court of law. Also called *defense attorney*.

**defensible space theory** The belief that an area's physical features may be modified and structured so as to reduce crime rates in that area and to lower the fear of victimization that residents experience.

**deliberate indifference** A wanton disregard by correctional personnel for the well-being of inmates. Deliberate indifference requires both actual knowledge that a harm is occurring and disregard of the risk of harm. A prison official may be held liable under the Eighth Amendment for acting with deliberate indifference to inmate health or safety only if he or she knows that inmates face a substantial risk of serious harm and disregards that risk by failing to take reasonable measures to abate it.

**delinquency** In the broadest usage, juvenile actions or conduct in violation of criminal law, juvenile status offenses, and other juvenile misbehavior.

**delinquent** A juvenile who has been adjudged by a judicial officer of a juvenile court to have committed a delinquent act.

**delinquent act** An act committed by a juvenile for which an adult could be prosecuted in a criminal court, but for which a juvenile can be adjudicated in a juvenile court or prosecuted in a court having criminal jurisdiction if the juvenile court transfers jurisdiction. Generally, a felony- or misdemeanor-level offense in states employing those terms.

**delinquent child** A child who has engaged in activity that would be considered a crime if the child were an adult. The term *delinquent* is used to avoid the stigma associated with the term *criminal*.

**dependent child** A child who has no parents or whose parents are unable to care for him or her.

**design capacity** The number of inmates a prison was intended to hold when it was built or modified. Also called *bed capacity*.

**detainee** Usually, a person held in local, very short-term confinement while awaiting consideration for pretrial release or a first appearance for arraignment.

**detention** The legally authorized confinement of a person subject to criminal or juvenile court proceedings, until the point of commitment to a correctional facility or until release.

**detention hearing** In juvenile justice usage, a hearing by a judicial officer of a juvenile court to determine whether a juvenile is to be detained, is to continue to be detained, or is to be released while juvenile proceedings are pending.

**determinate sentencing** A model of criminal punishment in which an offender is given a fixed term that may be reduced by good time or gain time. Under the model, for example, all offenders convicted of the same degree of burglary would be sentenced to the same length of time behind bars. Also called *fixed sentencing*.

**deterrence** A goal of criminal sentencing that seeks to inhibit criminal behavior through the fear of punishment.

**deviance** A violation of social norms defining appropriate or proper behavior under a particular set of circumstances. Deviance often includes criminal acts. Also called *deviant behavior*.

**digital criminal forensics** The lawful seizure, acquisition, analysis, reporting and safeguarding of data from digital devices that may contain information of evidentiary value to the trier of fact in criminal events.[18]

**diminished capacity** A defense based on claims of a mental condition that may be insufficient to exonerate the defendant of guilt but that may be relevant to specific mental elements of certain crimes or degrees of crime. Also called *diminished responsibility*.

**direct evidence** Evidence that, if believed, directly proves a fact. Eyewitness testimony and videotaped documentation account for the majority of all direct evidence heard in the criminal courtroom.

**direct-supervision jail** A temporary confinement facility that eliminates many of the traditional barriers between inmates and correctional staff. Physical barriers in direct-supervision jails are far less common than in traditional jails, allowing staff members the opportunity for greater interaction with, and control over, residents. Also called *new-generation jail; podular direct jail*.

**directed patrol** A police management strategy designed to increase the productivity of patrol officers through the scientific analysis and evaluation of patrol techniques.

**discharge** To release from confinement or supervision or to release from a legal status imposing an obligation upon the subject person.

**discretion** See **police discretion**.

**disposition** The action by a criminal or juvenile justice agency which signifies that a portion of the justice process is complete and that jurisdiction is terminated or transferred to another agency or which signifies that a decision has been reached on one aspect of a case and a different aspect comes under consideration, requiring a different kind of decision.

**dispositional hearing** The final stage in the processing of adjudicated juveniles in which a decision is made on the form of treatment or penalty that should be imposed on the child.

**dispute-resolution center** An informal hearing place designed to mediate interpersonal disputes without resorting to the more formal arrangements of a criminal trial court.

**district attorney (DA)** See **prosecutor**.

**diversion** The official suspension of criminal or juvenile proceedings against an alleged offender at any point after a recorded justice system intake, but before the entering of a judgment, and referral of that person to a treatment or care program administered by a nonjustice or private agency. Also, release without referral.

**DNA profiling** The use of biological residue, found at the scene of a crime, for genetic comparisons in aiding in the identification of criminal suspects.

**docket** See **court calendar**.

**domestic terrorism** The unlawful use of force or violence by a group or an individual who is based and operates entirely within the United States and its territories without foreign direction and whose acts are directed at elements of the U.S. government or population.[19]

**double jeopardy** A common law and constitutional prohibition against a second trial for the same offense.

**drug** Any chemical substance defined by social convention as bioactive or psychoactive.

**drug abuse** Illicit drug use that results in social, economic, psychological, or legal problems for the user.[20]

**drug court** A special state, county, or municipal court that offers first-time substance-abuse offenders judicially mandated and court-supervised treatment alternatives to prison.

**drug czar** The popular name for the head of the Office of National Drug Control Policy (ONDCP), a federal cabinet-level position that was created during the Reagan presidency to organize federal drug-fighting efforts.

**drug-law violation** The unlawful sale, purchase, distribution, manufacture, cultivation, transport, possession, or use of a controlled or prohibited drug. Also, the attempt to commit one of these acts.

**drug trafficking** Trading or dealing in controlled substances, to include the transporting, storage, importing, exporting, or sale of a controlled substance.

**due process** A right guaranteed by the Fifth, Sixth, and Fourteenth Amendments of the U.S. Constitution and generally understood, in legal contexts, to mean the due course of legal proceedings according to the rules and forms established for the protection of individual rights. In criminal proceedings, due process of law is generally understood to include the following basic elements: a law creating and defining the offense, an impartial tribunal having jurisdictional authority over the case, accusation in proper form, notice and opportunity to defend, trial according to established procedure, and discharge from all restraints or obligations unless convicted.

**due process model** A criminal justice perspective that emphasizes individual rights at all stages of justice system processing.

**Electronic Communications Privacy Act (ECPA)** A law passed by Congress in 1986 establishing the due process requirements that law enforcement officers must meet in order to legally intercept wire communications.

**electronic evidence** Information and data of investigative value that are stored in or transmitted by an electronic device.[21]

**element (of a crime)** In a specific crime, one of the essential features of that crime, as specified by law or statute.

**embezzlement** The misappropriation, or illegal disposal, of legally entrusted property by the person to whom it was entrusted, with the intent to defraud the legal owner or the intended beneficiary.

**emergency search** A search conducted by the police without a warrant, which is justified on the basis of some immediate and overriding need, such as public safety, the likely escape of a dangerous suspect, or the removal or destruction of evidence.

**entrapment** An improper or illegal inducement to crime by agents of law enforcement. Also, a defense that may be raised when such inducements have occurred.

**equity** A sentencing principle, based on concerns with social equality, that holds that similar crimes should be punished with the same degree of severity, regardless of the social or personal characteristics of the offenders.

**espionage** The "gathering, transmitting, or losing"[22] of information related to the national defense in such a manner that the information becomes available to enemies of the United States and may be used to their advantage.

**ethnocentric** Holding a belief in the superiority of one's own social or ethnic group and culture.

**ethnocentrism** The phenomenon of "culture-centeredness," by which one uses one's own culture as a benchmark against which to judge all other patterns of behavior.

**European Police Office (Europol)** The integrated police-intelligence gathering and dissemination arm of the member nations of the European Union.

**evidence** Anything useful to a judge or jury in deciding the facts of a case. Evidence may take the form of witness testimony, written documents, videotapes, magnetic media, photographs, physical objects, and so on.

**evidence-based policing** The use of best available research on the outcomes of police work to implement guidelines and evaluate agencies, units, and officers.[23]

**ex post facto** Latin for "after the fact." The Constitution prohibits the enactment of *ex post facto* laws, which make acts committed before the laws in question were passed punishable as crimes.

**excessive force** The application of an amount and/or frequency of force greater than that required to compel compliance from a willing or unwilling subject.[24]

**exclusionary rule** The understanding, based on U.S. Supreme Court precedent, that incriminating information must be seized according to constitutional specifications of due process or it will not be allowed as evidence in a criminal trial.

**excuse** A legal defense in which the defendant claims that some personal condition or circumstance at the time of the act was such that he or she should not be held accountable under the criminal law.

**exemplary damages** See **punitive damages**.

**Exemplary Projects Program** An initiative, sponsored by the Law Enforcement Assistance Administration, designed to recognize outstanding innovative efforts to combat crime and to provide assistance to crime victims.

**expert system** Computer hardware and software that attempt to duplicate the decision-making processes used by skilled investigators in the analysis of evidence and in the recognition of patterns that such evidence might represent.

**expert witness** A person who has special knowledge and skills recognized by the court as relevant to the determination of guilt or innocence. Unlike lay witnesses, expert witnesses may express opinions or draw conclusions in their testimony.

**extradition** The surrender by one state or jurisdiction to another of an individual accused or convicted of an offense in the second state or jurisdiction.

**federal court system** The three-tiered structure of federal courts, comprising U.S. district courts, U.S. courts of appeal, and the U.S. Supreme Court.

**federal law enforcement agency** A U.S. government agency or office whose primary functional responsibility is the enforcement of federal criminal laws.

**felony** A criminal offense punishable by death or by incarceration in a prison facility for at least one year.

**feminist criminology** A developing intellectual approach that emphasizes gender issues in criminology.

**filing** The initiation of a criminal case by formal submission to the court of a charging document, alleging that a named person has committed a specified criminal offense.

**fine** The penalty imposed on a convicted person by a court, requiring that he or she pay a specified sum of money to the court.

**first appearance** An appearance before a magistrate during which the legality of the defendant's arrest is initially assessed and the defendant is informed of the charges on which he or she is being held. At this stage in the criminal justice process, bail may be set or pretrial release arranged. Also called *initial appearance*.

**first plea** See **initial plea**.

**fixed sentencing** See **determinate sentencing**.

**fleeting-targets exception** An exception to the exclusionary rule that permits law enforcement officers to search a motor vehicle based on probable cause but without a warrant. The fleeting-targets exception is predicated on the fact that vehicles can quickly leave the jurisdiction of a law enforcement agency.

**force** See **police use of force**.

**forcible rape (UCR)** The carnal knowledge of a female forcibly and against her will. For statistical reporting purposes, the FBI defines *forcible rape* as "unlawful sexual intercourse with a female, by force and against her will, or without legal or factual consent." Statutory rape differs from forcible rape in that it generally involves nonforcible sexual intercourse with a minor. See also **carnal knowledge** and **rape**.

**foreign terrorist organization (FTO)** A foreign organization that engages in terrorist activity that threatens the security of U.S. nationals or the national security of the United States and that is so designated by the U.S. secretary of state.

**forensic anthropology** The use of anthropological principles and techniques in criminal investigation.

**forensic entomology** The study of insects to determine such matters as a person's time of death.

**forfeiture** The authorized seizure of money, negotiable instruments, securities, or other things of value. Under federal antidrug laws, judicial representatives are authorized to seize all cash, negotiable instruments, securities, or other things of value furnished or intended to be furnished by any person in exchange for a controlled substance, as well as all proceeds traceable to such an exchange. Also called *asset forfeiture*.

**forgery** The creation or alteration of a written or printed document, which if validly executed would constitute a record of a legally binding transaction, with the intent to defraud by affirming it to be the act of an unknowing second person. Also, the creation of an art object with intent to misrepresent the identity of the creator.

**fraud** An offense involving deceit or intentional misrepresentation of fact, with the intent of unlawfully depriving a person of his or her property or legal rights.

**frivolous suit** A lawsuit with no foundation in fact. Frivolous suits are generally brought by lawyers and plaintiffs for reasons of publicity, politics, or other non-law-related issues and may result in fines against plaintiffs and their counsel.

**fruit of the poisoned tree doctrine** A legal principle that excludes from introduction at trial any evidence later developed as a result of an illegal search or seizure.

**gain time** The amount of time deducted from time to be served in prison on a given sentence as a consequence of participation in special projects or programs.

**general deterrence** A goal of criminal sentencing that seeks to prevent others from committing crimes similar to the one for which a particular offender is being sentenced by making an example of the person sentenced.

**globalization** The internationalization of trade, services, investments, information, and other forms of human social activity. Also, a process of social homogenization by which the experiences of everyday life, marked by the diffusion of commodities and ideas, can foster a standardization of cultural expressions around the world.[25] Globalization involves the progressive erosion of the influence of nation-states and the rise in influence of global decision makers at both public and private levels.

**good-faith exception** An exception to the exclusionary rule. Law enforcement officers who conduct a search or who seize evidence on the basis of good faith (that is, when they believe they are operating according to the dictates of the law) and who later discover that a mistake was made (perhaps in the format of the application for a search warrant) may still use the seized evidence in court.

**good time** The amount of time deducted from time to be served in prison on a given sentence as a consequence of good behavior.

**grand jury** A group of jurors who have been selected according to law and have been sworn to hear the evidence and to determine whether there is sufficient evidence to bring the accused person to trial, to investigate criminal activity generally, or to investigate the conduct of a public agency or official.

**grievance procedure** A formalized arrangement, usually involving a neutral hearing board, whereby institutionalized individuals have the opportunity to register complaints about the conditions of their confinement.

**gross negligence** The intentional failure to perform a manifest duty in reckless disregard of the consequences as affecting the life or property of another.[26]

**guilty but mentally ill (GBMI)** A verdict, equivalent to a finding of "guilty," that establishes that the defendant, although mentally ill, was in sufficient possession of his or her faculties to be morally blameworthy for his or her acts.

**guilty plea** A defendant's formal answer in court to the charge or charges contained in a complaint, information, or indictment, claiming that he or she did commit the offense or offenses listed.

**guilty verdict** See **verdict**.

*habeas corpus* See **writ of** *habeas corpus*.

**habitual offender** A person sentenced under the provisions of a statute declaring that people convicted of a given offense, and shown to have previously been convicted of another specified offense, shall receive a more severe penalty than that for the current offense alone.

**hacker** A computer hobbyist or professional, generally with advanced programming skills. Today, the term *hacker* has taken on a sinister connotation, referring to hobbyists who are bent on illegally accessing the computers of others or who attempt to demonstrate their technological prowess through computerized acts of vandalism.

**hands-off doctrine** A policy of nonintervention with regard to prison management that U.S. courts tended to follow until the late 1960s. For the past 40 years, the doctrine has languished as judicial intervention in prison administration dramatically increased, although there is now some evidence that a new hands-off era is approaching.

**Harrison Narcotics Act** The first major piece of federal antidrug legislation, passed in 1914.

**hate crime** A criminal offense in which the motive is "hatred, bias, or prejudice, based on the actual or perceived race, color, religion, national origin, ethnicity, gender, or sexual orientation of another individual or group of individuals."[27] Also called *bias crime*.

**hearing** A proceeding in which arguments, witnesses, or evidence is heard by a judicial officer or an administrative body.

**hearsay** Something that is not based on the personal knowledge of a witness. Witnesses who testify about something they have heard, for example, are offering hearsay by repeating information about a matter of which they have no direct knowledge.

**hearsay rule** The long-standing precedent that hearsay cannot be used in American courtrooms. Rather than accepting testimony based on hearsay, the court will ask that the person who was the original source of the hearsay information be brought in to be questioned and cross-examined. Exceptions to the hearsay rule may occur when the person with direct knowledge is dead or is otherwise unable to testify.

**hierarchy rule** A standard Uniform Crime Reports scoring practice in which only the most serious offense is counted in a multiple-offense incident.

**high-technology crime** Violations of the criminal law whose commission depends on, makes use of, and often targets sophisticated and advanced technology. See also **computer crime**.

**home confinement** House arrest. Individuals ordered confined to their homes are sometimes monitored electronically to ensure they do not leave during the hours of confinement. Absence from the home during working hours is often permitted.

**homicide** See **criminal homicide**.

*Hudud* **crime** A serious violation of Islamic law that is regarded as an offense against God. *Hudud* crimes include such behavior as theft, adultery, sodomy, alcohol consumption, and robbery.

**hung jury** A jury that, after long deliberation, is so irreconcilably divided in opinion that it is unable to reach any verdict.

**hypothesis** An explanation that accounts for a set of facts and that can be tested by further investigation. Also, something that is taken to be true for the purpose of argument or investigation.[28]

**identity management** The comprehensive management and administration of a user's individual profile information, permissions, and privileges across a variety of social settings.[29]

**identity theft** A crime in which an impostor obtains key pieces of information, such as Social Security and driver's license numbers, to obtain credit, merchandise, and services in the name of the victim. The victim is often left with a ruined credit history and the time-consuming and complicated task of repairing the financial damages.[30]

**illegal search and seizure** An act in violation of the Fourth Amendment of the U.S. Constitution, which reads, "The right of the people to be secure in their persons, houses, papers, and effects, against unreasonable searches and seizures, shall not be violated, and no Warrants shall issue, but upon probable cause, supported by Oath or affirmation, and particularly describing the place to be searched, and the persons or things to be seized."

**illegally seized evidence** Evidence seized without regard to the principles of due process as described by the Bill of Rights. Most illegally seized evidence is the result of police searches conducted without a proper warrant or of improperly conducted interrogations.

**incapacitation** The use of imprisonment or other means to reduce the likelihood that an offender will commit future offenses.

**inchoate offense** An offense not yet completed. Also, an offense that consists of an action or conduct that is a step toward the intended commission of another offense.

**incident-based reporting** Compared with summary reporting, a less restrictive and more expansive method of collecting crime data in which all of the analytical elements associated with an offense or arrest are compiled by a central collection agency on an incident-by-incident basis.

**included offense** An offense that is made up of elements that are a subset of the elements of another offense having a greater statutory penalty, and the occurrence of which is established by the same evidence or by some portion of the evidence that has been offered to establish the occurrence of the greater offense.

**incompetent to stand trial** In criminal proceedings, a finding by a court that as a result of mental illness, defect, or disability, a defendant is incapable of understanding the nature of the charges and proceedings against him or her, of consulting with an attorney, and of aiding in his or her own defense.

**indeterminate sentence** A type of sentence to imprisonment in which the commitment, instead of being for a precise length of time, is for a range of time, such as two to five years or five years maximum and zero minimum.

**indeterminate sentencing** A model of criminal punishment that encourages rehabilitation through the use of general and relatively unspecific sentences (such as a term of imprisonment of from one to ten years).

**index crime** See **Crime Index**.

**indictment** A formal, written accusation submitted to the court by a grand jury, alleging that a specified person has committed a specified offense, usually a felony.

**individual rights** The rights guaranteed to all members of American society by the U.S. Constitution (especially those found in the first ten amendments to the Constitution, known as the *Bill of Rights*). These rights are particularly important to criminal defendants facing formal processing by the criminal justice system.

**individual-rights advocate** One who seeks to protect personal freedoms within the process of criminal justice.

**industrial prison** A correctional model intended to capitalize on the labor of convicts sentenced to confinement.

**information** A formal written accusation submitted to the court by a prosecutor, alleging that a specified person has committed a specific offense.

**infraction** A minor violation of state statute or local ordinance punishable by a fine or other penalty or by a specified, usually limited, term of incarceration.

**infrastructure** The basic facilities, services, and installations that a country needs to function. Transportation and communications systems, water and power lines, and institutions that serve the public, including banks, schools, post offices, and prisons, are all part of a country's infrastructure.[31]

**inherent coercion** The tactics used by police interviewers that fall short of physical abuse but that nonetheless pressure suspects to divulge information.

**initial appearance** See **first appearance**.

**initial plea** The first plea to a given charge entered in the court record by or for the defendant. The acceptance of an initial plea by the court unambiguously indicates that the arraignment process has been completed. Also called *first plea*.

**insanity defense** A legal defense based on claims of mental illness or mental incapacity.

**institutional capacity** The official number of inmates that a confinement or residential facility is housing or was intended to house.

**intake** The first step in decision making regarding a juvenile whose behavior or alleged behavior is in violation of the law or could otherwise cause a juvenile court to assume jurisdiction.

**intelligence-led policing** The collection and analysis of information to produce an intelligence end product designed to inform police decision making at both the tactical and strategic levels.[32]

**intensive probation supervision (IPS)** A form of probation supervision involving frequent face-to-face contact between the probationer and the probation officer.

**intent** The state of mind or attitude with which an act is carried out. Also, the design, resolve, or determination with which a person acts to achieve a certain result.

**interdiction** The interception of drug traffic at the nation's borders. Interdiction is one of the many strategies used to stem the flow of illegal drugs into the United States.

**interdisciplinary theory** An approach that integrates a variety of theoretical viewpoints in an attempt to explain crime and violence.

**intermediate appellate court** An appellate court whose primary function is to review the judgments of trial courts and the decisions of administrative agencies and whose decisions are, in turn, usually reviewable by a higher appellate court in the same state.

**intermediate sanctions** The use of split sentencing, shock probation or parole, shock incarceration, community service, intensive supervision, or home confinement in lieu of other, more traditional, sanctions, such as imprisonment and fines. Also called *alternative sanctions*.

**internal affairs** The branch of a police organization tasked with investigating charges of wrongdoing involving members of the department.

**International Criminal Police Organization (INTERPOL)** An international law enforcement support organization that began operations in 1946 and today has 182 members.

**international terrorism** The unlawful use of force or violence by a group or an individual who has some connection to a foreign power, or whose activities transcend national boundaries, against people or property in order to intimidate or coerce a government, the civilian population, or any segment thereof, in furtherance of political or social objectives.[33]

**interrogation** The information-gathering activity of police officers that involves the direct questioning of suspects.

**Islamic law** A system of laws, operative in some Arab countries, based on the Muslim religion and especially the holy book of Islam, the Koran.

**jail** A confinement facility administered by an agency of local government, typically a law enforcement agency, intended for adults but sometimes also containing juveniles, which holds people detained pending adjudication or committed after adjudication, usually those sentenced to a year or less.

**jail commitment** A sentence of commitment to the jurisdiction of a confinement facility system for adults that is administered by an agency of local government and whose custodial authority is usually limited to people sentenced to a year or less of confinement.

**judge** An elected or appointed public official who presides over a court of law and who is authorized to hear and sometimes to decide cases and to conduct trials.

**judgment** The statement of the decision of a court that the defendant is acquitted or convicted of the offense or offenses charged.

**judgment suspending sentence** A court-ordered sentencing alternative that results in the convicted offender being placed on probation.

**judicial officer** Any person authorized by statute, constitutional provision, or court rule to exercise the powers reserved to the judicial branch of government.

**judicial review** The power of a court to review actions and decisions made by other agencies of government.

**jural postulates** Propositions developed by the famous jurist Roscoe Pound that hold that the law reflects shared needs without which members of society could not coexist. Pound's jural postulates are often linked to the idea that the law can be used to engineer the social structure to ensure certain kinds of outcomes. In capitalist societies, for example, the law of theft protects property rights.

**jurisdiction** The territory, subject matter, or people over which a court or other justice agency may exercise lawful authority, as determined by statute or constitution. See also **venue**.

**jurisprudence** The philosophy of law. Also, the science and study of the law.

**juror** A member of a trial or grand jury who has been selected for jury duty and is required to serve as an arbiter of the facts in a court of law. Jurors are expected to render verdicts of "guilty" or "not guilty" as to the charges brought against the accused, although they may sometimes fail to do so (as in the case of a hung jury).

**jury panel** The group of people summoned to appear in court as potential jurors for a particular trial. Also, the people selected from the group of potential jurors to sit in the jury box, from which those acceptable to the prosecution and the defense are finally chosen as the jury.

**jury selection** The process whereby, according to law and precedent, members of a trial jury are chosen.

**just deserts** A model of criminal sentencing that holds that criminal offenders deserve the punishment they receive at the hands of the law and that punishments should be appropriate to the type and severity of the crime committed.

**justice** The principle of fairness; the ideal of moral equity.

**justice model** A contemporary model of imprisonment based on the principle of just deserts.

**justification** A legal defense in which the defendant admits to committing the act in question but claims it was necessary in order to avoid some greater evil.

**juvenile** A person subject to juvenile court proceedings because a statutorily defined event or condition caused by or affecting that person was alleged to have occurred while his or her age was below the statutorily specified age limit of original jurisdiction of a juvenile court.

**juvenile court** A court that has, as all or part of its authority, original jurisdiction over matters concerning people statutorily defined as juveniles.

**juvenile court judgment** The juvenile court decision, terminating an adjudicatory hearing, that the juvenile is a delinquent, a status offender, or a dependent or that the allegations in the petition are not sustained.

**juvenile disposition** The decision of a juvenile court, concluding a dispositional hearing, that an adjudicated

juvenile be committed to a juvenile correctional facility; be placed in a juvenile residence, shelter, or care or treatment program; be required to meet certain standards of conduct; or be released.

**juvenile justice** The policies and activities of law enforcement and the courts in handling law violations by youths under the age of criminal jurisdiction.[34]

**juvenile justice agency** A government agency, or subunit thereof, whose functions are the investigation, supervision, adjudication, care, or confinement of juvenile offenders and nonoffenders subject to the jurisdiction of a juvenile court. Also, in some usages, a private agency providing care and treatment.

**juvenile justice system** Government agencies that function to investigate, supervise, adjudicate, care for, or confine youthful offenders and other children subject to the jurisdiction of the juvenile court.

**juvenile petition** A document filed in juvenile court alleging that a juvenile is a delinquent, a status offender, or a dependent and asking that the court assume jurisdiction over the juvenile or that an alleged delinquent be transferred to a criminal court for prosecution as an adult.

**Kansas City experiment** The first large-scale scientific study of law enforcement practices. Sponsored by the Police Foundation, it focused on the practice of preventive patrol.

**kidnapping** The transportation or confinement of a person without authority of law and without his or her consent, or without the consent of his or her guardian, if a minor.

**Knapp Commission** A committee that investigated police corruption in New York City in the early 1970s.

**labeling theory** A social process perspective that sees continued crime

as a consequence of the limited opportunities for acceptable behavior that follow from the negative responses of society to those defined as offenders.

**landmark case** A precedent-setting court decision that produces substantial changes in both the understanding of the requirements of due process and in the practical day-to-day operations of the justice system.

**larceny-theft (UCR)** The unlawful taking or attempted taking, carrying, leading, or riding away of property, from the possession or constructive possession of another. Motor vehicles are excluded. Larceny is the most common of the eight major offenses, although probably only a small percentage of all larcenies are actually reported to the police because of the small dollar amounts involved.

**latent evidence** Evidence of relevance to a criminal investigation that is not readily seen by the unaided eye.

**law** A rule of conduct, generally found enacted in the form of a statute, that proscribes or mandates certain forms of behavior. Statutory law is often the result of moral enterprise by interest groups that, through the exercise of political power, are successful in seeing their valued perspectives enacted into law.

**law enforcement** The generic name for the activities of the agencies responsible for maintaining public order and enforcing the law, particularly the activities of preventing, detecting, and investigating crime and apprehending criminals.

**law enforcement agency** A federal, state, or local criminal justice agency or identifiable subunit whose principal functions are the prevention, detection, and investigation of crime and the apprehension of alleged offenders.

**Law Enforcement Assistance Administration (LEAA)** A now-defunct federal agency established under

Title I of the Omnibus Crime Control and Safe Streets Act of 1968 to funnel federal funding to state and local law enforcement agencies.

**law enforcement intelligence** See **criminal intelligence**.

**law enforcement officer** An officer employed by a law enforcement agency who is sworn to carry out law enforcement duties.

**lawyer** See **attorney**.

**lay witness** An eyewitness, character witness, or other person called on to testify who is not considered an expert. Lay witnesses must testify to facts only and may not draw conclusions or express opinions.

**learning organization** "An organization skilled at creating, acquiring, and transferring knowledge and at modifying its behavior to reflect new knowledge and insights."[35]

**legal cause** A legally recognizable cause. A legal cause must be demonstrated in court in order to hold an individual criminally liable for causing harm.

**legal counsel** See **attorney**.

**legalistic style** A style of policing marked by a strict concern with enforcing the precise letter of the law. Legalistic departments may take a hands-off approach to disruptive or problematic behavior that does not violate the criminal law.

**legalization** Elimination of the laws and associated criminal penalties associated with certain behaviors—usually the production, sale, distribution, and possession of a controlled substance.

**less-lethal weapon** A weapon that is designed to disable, capture, or immobilize—but not kill—a suspect. Occasional deaths do result from the use of such weapons, however.

**lex talionis** The law of retaliation, often expressed as "an eye for an eye" or "like for like."

**life course perspective** An approach to explaining crime and deviance that investigates developments and turning points in the course of a person's life over time.

**line operations** In police organizations, the field activities or supervisory activities directly related to day-to-day police work.

**Mafia** See **Cosa Nostra**.

**major crimes** See **Part I offenses**.

**mala in se** Acts that are regarded, by tradition and convention, as wrong in themselves.

**mala prohibita** Acts that are considered wrong only because there is a law against them.

**malware** Malicious computer programs such as viruses, worms, and Trojan horses.

**mandatory sentence** A statutorily required penalty that must be set and carried out in all cases upon conviction for a specified offense or series of offenses.

**mandatory sentencing** A structured sentencing scheme that allows no leeway in the nature of the sentence required and under which clearly enumerated punishments are mandated for specific offenses or for habitual offenders convicted of a series of crimes.

**MATRIX** An acronym for the Multistate Anti-Terrorism Information Exchange, an Internet-based proof-of-concept pilot program funded by the Department of Justice and the Department of Homeland Security to increase and enhance the exchange of sensitive information about terrorism and other criminal activity between enforcement agencies at the local, state, and federal levels.

**maximum sentence** In legal usage, the maximum penalty provided by law for a given criminal offense, usually stated as a maximum term of imprisonment or a maximum fine. Also, in corrections usage in relation to a given offender, any of several quantities (expressed in days, months, or years) that vary according to whether calculated at the point of sentencing or at a later point in the correctional process and according to whether the time period referred to is the term of confinement or the total period under correctional jurisdiction.

**medical model** A therapeutic perspective on correctional treatment that applies the diagnostic perspective of medical science to the handling of criminal offenders.

**mens rea** The state of mind that accompanies a criminal act. Also, a guilty mind.

**Miranda rights** The set of rights that a person accused or suspected of having committed a specific offense has during interrogation and of which he or she must be informed prior to questioning, as stated by the U.S. Supreme Court in deciding *Miranda* v. *Arizona* (1966) and related cases.

**Miranda triggers** The dual principles of custody and interrogation, both of which are necessary before an advisement of rights is required.

**Miranda warnings** The advisement of rights due criminal suspects by the police before questioning begins. *Miranda* warnings were first set forth by the U.S. Supreme Court in the 1966 case of *Miranda* v. *Arizona*.

**misdemeanor** An offense punishable by incarceration, usually in a local confinement facility, for a period whose upper limit is prescribed by statute in a given jurisdiction, typically one year or less.

**mistrial** A trial that has been terminated and declared invalid by the court because of some circumstance which created a substantial and uncorrectable prejudice to the conduct of a fair trial or which made it impossible to continue the trial in accordance with prescribed procedures.

**mitigating circumstances** Circumstances relating to the commission of a crime that may be considered to reduce the blameworthiness of the defendant. See also **aggravating circumstances**.

**mixed sentence** A sentence that requires that a convicted offender serve weekends (or other specified periods of time) in a confinement facility (usually a jail) while undergoing probationary supervision in the community.

**M'Naghten rule** A rule for determining insanity, which asks whether the defendant knew what he or she was doing or whether the defendant knew that what he or she was doing was wrong.

**Model Penal Code (MPC)** A generalized modern codification considered basic to criminal law, published by the American Law Institute in 1962.

**money laundering** The process by which criminals or criminal organizations seek to disguise the illicit nature of their proceeds by introducing them into the stream of legitimate commerce and finance.[36]

**moral enterprise** The process undertaken by an advocacy group to have its values legitimated and embodied in law.

**motion** An oral or written request made to a court at any time before, during, or after court proceedings, asking the court to make a specified finding, decision, or order.

**motive** A person's reason for committing a crime.

**motor vehicle theft (UCR)** The theft or attempted theft of a motor vehicle. *Motor vehicle* is defined as a self-propelled road vehicle that runs on land surface and not on rails. The stealing of trains, planes, boats, construction equipment, and most farm machinery is classified as larceny under the UCR Program, not as motor vehicle theft.

**multiculturalism** The existence within one society of diverse groups that maintain unique cultural identities while frequently accepting and participating in the larger society's legal and political systems.[37] *Multiculturalism* is often used in conjunction with the term *diversity* to identify many distinctions of social significance.

**municipal police department** A city- or town-based law enforcement agency; also known as *local police*.

**murder** The unlawful killing of a human being. *Murder* is a generic term that in common usage may include first- and second-degree murder, manslaughter, involuntary manslaughter, and other similar offenses.

**murder and nonnegligent manslaughter (UCR)** Intentionally causing the death of another without legal justification or excuse. Also, causing the death of another while committing or attempting to commit another crime.

**narcoterrorism** A political alliance between terrorist organizations and drug-supplying cartels. The cartels provide financing for the terrorists, who in turn provide quasi-military protection to the drug dealers.

**National Crime Victimization Survey (NCVS)** An annual survey of selected American households conducted by the Bureau of Justice Statistics to determine the extent of criminal victimization—especially unreported victimization—in the United States.

**National Incident-Based Reporting System (NIBRS)** An incident-based reporting system that collects data on every single crime occurrence. NIBRS data will soon supersede the kinds of traditional data provided by the FBI's Uniform Crime Reports.

**natural law** Rules of conduct inherent in human nature and in the natural order that are thought to be knowable through intuition, inspiration, and the exercise of reason, without the need for reference to created laws.

**NCVS** See **National Crime Victimization Survey**.

**neglected child** A child who is not receiving the proper level of physical or psychological care from his or her parents or guardians or who has been placed up for adoption in violation of the law.

**negligence** In legal usage, generally, a state of mind accompanying a person's conduct such that he or she is not aware, though a reasonable person should be aware, that there is a risk that the conduct might cause a particular harmful result.

**negligent manslaughter (UCR)** Causing the death of another by recklessness or gross negligence.

**neoclassical criminology** A contemporary version of classical criminology that emphasizes deterrence and retribution and that holds that human beings are essentially free to make choices in favor of crime and deviance or conformity.

**new police** A police force formed in 1829 under the command of Sir Robert Peel. It became the model for modern-day police forces throughout the Western world. Also called *Metropolitan Police Force*.

**night watch** An early form of police patrol in English cities and towns.

**no true bill** The decision by a grand jury that it will not return an indictment against the person accused of a crime on the basis of the allegations and evidence presented by the prosecutor.

***nolle prosequi*** A formal entry in the record of the court indicating that the prosecutor declares that he or she will proceed no further in the action. The terminating of adjudication of a criminal charge by the prosecutor's decision not to pursue the case requires the approval of the court in some jurisdictions.

***nolo contendere*** A plea of "no contest." A no-contest plea is used when the defendant does not wish to contest conviction. Because the plea does not admit guilt, however, it cannot provide the basis for later civil suits that might follow a criminal conviction.

**not guilty by reason of insanity** The plea of a defendant or the verdict of a jury or judge in a criminal proceeding that the defendant is not guilty of the offense charged because at the time the crime was committed, the defendant did not have the mental capacity to be held criminally responsible for his or her actions.

**nothing-works doctrine** The belief, popularized by Robert Martinson in the 1970s, that correctional treatment programs have had little success in rehabilitating offenders.

**occupational crime** Any act punishable by law that is committed through opportunity created in the course of a legitimate occupation.

**offender** An adult who has been convicted of a criminal offense.

**offense** A violation of the criminal law. Also, in some jurisdictions, a minor crime, such as jaywalking, that is sometimes described as *ticketable*.

**offenses known to police (UCR)** Reported occurrences of offenses that have been verified at the police level.

**opening statement** The initial statement of the prosecution or the defense, made in a court of law to a judge, or to a judge and jury, describing the facts that he or she intends to present during trial to prove the case.

**operational capacity** The number of inmates a prison can effectively accommodate based on management considerations.

**opinion** The official announcement of a decision of a court, together with the reasons for that decision.

**opportunity theory** A perspective that sees delinquency as the result of limited legitimate opportunities for success available to most lower-class youth.

**organized crime** The unlawful activities of the members of a highly organized, disciplined association engaged in supplying illegal goods and services, including gambling, prostitution, loan-sharking, narcotics, and labor racketeering, and in other unlawful activities.[38]

**original jurisdiction** The lawful authority of a court to hear or to act on a case from its beginning and to pass judgment on the law and the facts. The authority may be over a specific geographic area or over particular types of cases.

*parens patriae* A common law principle that allows the state to assume a parental role and to take custody of a child when he or she becomes delinquent, is abandoned, or is in need of care that the natural parents are unable or unwilling to provide.

**Parliament** The British legislature, the highest law-making body of the United Kingdom.

**parole** The status of a convicted offender who has been conditionally released from prison by a paroling authority before the expiration of his or her sentence, is placed under the supervision of a parole agency, and is required to observe the conditions of parole.

**parole board** A state paroling authority. Most states have parole boards that decide when an incarcerated offender is ready for conditional release. Some boards also function as revocation hearing panels. Also called *parole commission*.

**parole (probation) violation** An act or a failure to act by a parolee (or probationer) that does not conform to the conditions of his or her parole (or probation).

**parole revocation** The administrative action of a paroling authority removing a person from parole status in response to a violation of lawfully required conditions of parole, including the prohibition against committing a new offense, and usually resulting in a return to prison.

**parole supervision** Guidance, treatment, or regulation of the behavior of a convicted adult who is obligated to fulfill conditions of parole or conditional release. Parole supervision is authorized and required by statute, is performed by a parole agency, and occurs after a period of prison confinement.

**parole supervisory caseload** The total number of clients registered with a parole agency or officer on a given date or during a specified time period.

**parolee** A person who has been conditionally released by a paroling authority from a prison prior to the expiration of his or her sentence, is placed under the supervision of a parole agency, and is required to observe conditions of parole.

**paroling authority** A board or commission that has the authority to release on parole adults committed to prison, to revoke parole or other conditional release, and to discharge from parole or other conditional release status.

**Part I offenses** A set of UCR categories used to report murder, rape, robbery, aggravated assault, burglary, larceny-theft, motor vehicle theft, and arson, as defined under the FBI's Uniform Crime Reporting Program. Also called *major crimes*.

**Part II offenses** A set of UCR categories used to report arrests for less serious offenses.

**PATRIOT Act** See **USA PATRIOT Act of 2001**.

**peace officer standards and training (POST) program** The official program of a state or legislative jurisdiction that sets standards for the training of law enforcement officers. All states set such standards, although not all use the term *POST*.

**peacemaking criminology** A perspective that holds that crime-control agencies and the citizens they serve should work together to alleviate social problems and human suffering and thus reduce crime.

**penal code** The written, organized, and compiled form of the criminal laws of a jurisdiction.

**penal law** See **criminal law**.

**penitentiary** A prison. See also **Pennsylvania system**.

**Pennsylvania system** A form of imprisonment developed by the Pennsylvania Quakers around 1790 as an alternative to corporal punishments. This style of imprisonment made use of solitary confinement and encouraged rehabilitation.

**peremptory challenge** The right to challenge a potential juror without disclosing the reason for the challenge. Prosecutors and defense attorneys routinely use peremptory challenges to eliminate from juries individuals who, although they express no obvious bias, are thought to be capable of swaying the jury in an undesirable direction.

**perjury** The intentional making of a false statement as part of the testimony by a sworn witness in a judicial proceeding on a matter relevant to the case at hand.

**perpetrator** The chief actor in the commission of a crime; that is, the person who directly commits the criminal act.

**petit jury** See **trial jury**.

**petition** A written request made to a court asking for the exercise of its judicial powers or asking for permission to perform some act that requires the authorization of a court.

**pharmaceutical diversion** The transfer of prescription medicines controlled by the Controlled Substance Act by theft, deception, and or fraudulent means for other than their intended legitimate therapeutic purposes.

**phrenology** The study of the shape of the head to determine anatomical correlates of human behavior.

**physical dependence** A biologically based craving for a specific drug that results from frequent use of the substance. Physical dependence on drugs is marked by a growing tolerance of a drug's effects, so that increased amounts of the drug are needed to obtain the desired effect, and by the onset of withdrawal symptoms over periods of prolonged abstinence.[39] Also called *physical addiction*.

**piracy** See **software piracy**.

**plain view** A legal term describing the ready visibility of objects that might be seized as evidence during a search by police in the absence of a search warrant specifying the seizure of those objects. To lawfully seize evidence in plain view, officers must have a legal right to be in the viewing area and must have cause to believe that the evidence is somehow associated with criminal activity.

**plaintiff** A person who initiates a court action.

**plea** In criminal proceedings, the defendant's formal answer in court to the charge contained in a complaint, information, or indictment that he or she is guilty of the offense charged, is not guilty of the offense charged, or does not contest the charge.

**plea bargaining** The process of negotiating an agreement among the defendant, the prosecutor, and the court as to an appropriate plea and associated sentence in a given case. Plea bargaining circumvents the trial process and dramatically reduces the time required for the resolution of a criminal case.

**police–community relations (PCR)** An area of police activity that recognizes the need for the community and the police to work together effectively and that is based on the notion that the police derive their legitimacy from the community they serve. Many police agencies began to explore PCR in the 1960s and 1970s.

**police corruption** The abuse of police authority for personal or organizational gain.[40]

**police discretion** The opportunity of law enforcement officers to exercise choice in their daily activities.

**police ethics** The special responsibility to adhere to moral duty and obligation that is inherent in police work.

**police management** The administrative activities of controlling, directing, and coordinating police personnel, resources, and activities in the service of preventing crime, apprehending criminals, recovering stolen property, and performing regulatory and helping services.[41]

**police professionalism** The increasing formalization of police work and the accompanying rise in public acceptance of the police.

**police subculture** A particular set of values, beliefs, and acceptable forms of behavior characteristic of American police. Socialization into the police subculture begins with recruit training and continues thereafter. Also called *police culture*.

**police use of force** The use of physical restraint by a police officer when dealing with a member of the public.[42]

**police working personality** All aspects of the traditional values and patterns of behavior evidenced by police officers who have been effectively socialized into the police subculture. Characteristics of the police personality often extend to the personal lives of law enforcement personnel.

**political defense** An innovative defense to a criminal charge that claims that the defendant's actions stemmed from adherence to a set of political beliefs and standards significantly different from those on which the American style of government is based. A political defense questions the legitimacy and purpose of all criminal proceedings against the defendant.

**Positivist School** An approach to criminal justice theory that stresses the application of scientific techniques to the study of crime and criminals.

**POST** See **peace officer standards and training (POST) program**.

**postconviction remedy** The procedure or set of procedures by which a person who has been convicted of a crime can challenge in court the lawfulness of a judgment of conviction, a penalty, or a correctional agency action and thus obtain relief in situations where this cannot be done by a direct appeal.

**postmodern criminology** A branch of criminology that developed after World War II and that builds on the tenets inherent in postmodern social thought.

**precedent** A legal principle that ensures that previous judicial decisions are authoritatively considered and incorporated into future cases.

**preliminary hearing** A proceeding before a judicial officer in which three matters must be decided: (1) whether a crime was committed, (2) whether the crime occurred within the territorial jurisdiction of the court, and (3) whether there are reasonable grounds to believe that the defendant committed the crime.

**preliminary investigation** All of the activities undertaken by a police officer who responds to the scene of a crime, including determining whether a crime has occurred, securing the crime scene, and preserving evidence.

**presentence investigation** The examination of a convicted offender's background prior to sentencing. Presentence examinations are generally conducted by probation or parole officers and are submitted to sentencing authorities.

**presentment** Historically, unsolicited written notice of an offense provided to a court by a grand jury from their own knowledge or observation. In current usage, any of several presentations of alleged facts and charges to a court or a grand jury by a prosecutor.

**presumptive sentencing** A model of criminal punishment that meets the following conditions: (1) The appropriate sentence for an offender convicted of a specific charge is presumed to fall within a range of sentences authorized by sentencing guidelines that are adopted by a legislatively created sentencing body, usually a sentencing commission. (2) Sentencing judges are expected to sentence within the range or to provide written justification for departure. (3) There is a mechanism for review, usually appellate, of any departure from the guidelines.

**pretrial detention** Confinement occurring between the time of arrest or of being held to answer a charge and the conclusion of prosecution.[43]

**pretrial discovery** In criminal proceedings, disclosure by the prosecution or the defense prior to trial of evidence or other information that is intended to be used in the trial.

**pretrial release** The release of an accused person from custody, for all or part of the time before or during prosecution, on his or her promise to appear in court when required.

**prison** A state or federal confinement facility that has custodial authority over adults sentenced to confinement.

**prison argot** The slang characteristic of prison subcultures and prison life.

**prison capacity** The size of the correctional population an institution can effectively hold.[44] There are three types of prison capacity: rated, operational, and design.

**prison commitment** A sentence of commitment to the jurisdiction of a state or federal confinement facility system for adults whose custodial authority extends to offenders sentenced to more than a year of confinement, to a term expressed in years or for life, or to await execution of a death sentence.

**prison subculture** The values and behavioral patterns characteristic of prison inmates. Prison subculture has been found to be surprisingly consistent across the country.

**prisoner** A person in physical custody in a state or federal confinement facility or in the personal physical custody of a criminal justice official while being transported to or between confinement facilities.

**prisoner reentry** The managed return to the community of individuals released from prison. Also called *reentry*.

**prisonization** The process whereby newly institutionalized offenders come to accept prison lifestyles and criminal values. Although many inmates begin their prison experience with only a few values that support criminal behavior, the socialization experience they undergo while incarcerated leads to a much greater acceptance of such values.

**private prison** A correctional institution operated by a private firm on behalf of a local or state government.

**private protective services** Independent or proprietary commercial organizations that provide protective services to employers on a contractual basis.

**private security** Self-employed individuals and privately funded business entities and organizations providing security-related services to specific clientele for a fee, for the individual or entity that retains or employs them, or for themselves, in order to protect people, private property, or interests from various hazards.[45]

**private security agency** See **private protective services**.

**privatization** The movement toward the wider use of private prisons.

**probable cause** A set of facts and circumstances that would induce a reasonably intelligent and prudent person to believe that a particular other person has committed a specific crime. Also, reasonable grounds to make or believe an accusation. Probable cause refers to the necessary level of belief that would allow for police seizures (arrests) of individuals and full searches of dwellings, vehicles, and possessions.

**probation** A sentence of imprisonment that is suspended. Also, the conditional freedom granted by a judicial officer to a convicted offender, as long as the person meets certain conditions of behavior.

**probation revocation** A court order taking away a convicted offender's probationary status and usually withdrawing the conditional freedom associated with that status in response to a violation of the conditions of probation.

**probation termination** The ending of the probation status of a given person by routine expiration of the probationary period, by special early termination by the court, or by revocation of probation.

**probation violation** An act or a failure to act by a probationer that does not conform to the conditions of his or her probation.

**probation workload** The total set of activities required to carry out the probation agency functions of intake screening of juvenile cases, referral of cases to other service agencies, investigation of juveniles and adults for the purpose of preparing predisposition or presentence reports, supervision or

treatment of juveniles and adults granted probation, assistance in the enforcement of court orders concerning family problems, such as abandonment and nonsupport cases, and other such functions assigned by statute or court order.

**probative value** The degree to which a particular item of evidence is useful in, and relevant to, providing something important in a trial.

**problem police officer** A law enforcement officer who exhibits problem behavior, as indicated by high rates of citizen complaints and use-of-force incidents and by other evidence.[46]

**problem-solving policing** A type of policing that assumes that crimes can be controlled by uncovering and effectively addressing the underlying social problems that cause crime. Problem-solving policing makes use of community resources, such as counseling centers, welfare programs, and job-training facilities. It also attempts to involve citizens in crime prevention through education, negotiation, and conflict management. Also called *problem-oriented policing*.

**procedural defense** A defense that claims that the defendant was in some significant way discriminated against in the justice process or that some important aspect of official procedure was not properly followed in the investigation or prosecution of the crime charged.

**procedural law** The part of the law that specifies the methods to be used in enforcing substantive law.

**profession** An organized undertaking characterized by a body of specialized knowledge acquired through extensive education and by a well-considered set of internal standards and ethical guidelines which hold members of the profession accountable to one another and to society.

**professional criminal** See **career criminal**.

**property bond** The setting of bail in the form of land, houses, stocks, or other tangible property. In the event that the defendant absconds prior to trial, the bond becomes the property of the court.

**property crime** A UCR offense category that includes burglary, larceny-theft, motor vehicle theft, and arson.

**proportionality** A sentencing principle that holds that the severity of sanctions should bear a direct relationship to the seriousness of the crime committed.

**prosecution agency** A federal, state, or local criminal justice agency or subunit whose principal function is the prosecution of alleged offenders.

**prosecutor** An attorney whose official duty is to conduct criminal proceedings on behalf of the state or the people against those accused of having committed criminal offenses. Also called *county attorney; district attorney (DA); state's attorney; U.S. attorney.*

**prosecutorial discretion** The decision-making power of prosecutors, based on the wide range of choices available to them, in the handling of criminal defendants, the scheduling of cases for trial, the acceptance of negotiated pleas, and so on. The most important form of prosecutorial discretion lies in the power to charge, or not to charge, a person with an offense.

**prostitution** The act of offering or agreeing to engage in, or engaging in, a sex act with another in return for a fee.

**protected computer** Under federal law, (1) a computer used exclusively by a financial institution or the U.S. government, (2) a computer used by or for a financial institution or the U.S. government, or (3) a computer used in interstate or foreign commerce or communication.

**psychoactive substance** A chemical substance that affects cognition, feeling, or awareness.

**psychoanalysis** A theory of human behavior, based on the writings of Sigmund Freud, that sees personality as a complex composite of interacting mental entities.

**psychological dependence** A craving for a specific drug that results from long-term substance abuse. Psychological dependence on drugs is marked by the belief that drugs are needed to achieve a feeling of well-being.[47] Also called *psychological addiction*.

**psychological manipulation** Manipulative actions by police interviewers, designed to pressure suspects to divulge information, that are based on subtle forms of intimidation and control.

**psychological profiling** The attempt to categorize, understand, and predict the behavior of certain types of offenders based on behavioral clues they provide.

**Psychological School** A perspective on criminological thought that views offensive and deviant behavior as the product of dysfunctional personalities. Psychological thinkers identify the conscious, and especially the subconscious, contents of the human psyche as major determinants of behavior.

**psychopath** A person with a personality disorder, especially one manifested in aggressively antisocial behavior, which is often said to be the result of a poorly developed superego. Also called *sociopath*.

**psychopathology** The study of pathological mental conditions—that is, mental illness.

**psychosis** A form of mental illness in which sufferers are said to be out of touch with reality.

**public defender** An attorney employed by a government agency or subagency, or by a private organization under contract to a government body, for the purpose of providing defense services to indigents, or an attorney who has volunteered such service.

**public defender agency** A federal, state, or local criminal justice agency or subunit whose principal function is to represent in court people accused or convicted of a crime who are unable to hire private counsel.

**public-order advocate** One who believes that under certain circumstances involving a criminal threat to public safety, the interests of society should take precedence over individual rights.

**public safety department** A state or local agency that incorporates various law enforcement and emergency service functions.

**punitive damages** Damages requested or awarded in a civil lawsuit when the defendant's willful acts were malicious, violent, oppressive, fraudulent, wanton, or grossly reckless.[48] Also called *exemplary damages*.

**quality-of-life offense** A minor violation of the law (sometimes called a *petty crime*) that demoralizes community residents and business-people. Quality-of-life offenses involve acts that create physical disorder (for example, excessive noise or vandalism) or that reflect social decay (for example, panhandling and prostitution).

**racial profiling** "Any police-initiated action that relies on the race, ethnicity, or national origin rather than [1] the behavior of an individual, or [2] . . . information that leads the police to a particular individual who has been identified as being, or having been, engaged in criminal activity."[49]

**Racketeer Influenced and Corrupt Organizations (RICO)** A federal statute that allows for the federal seizure of assets derived from illegal enterprise.

**radical criminology** A conflict perspective that sees crime as engendered by the unequal distribution of wealth, power, and other resources, which adherents believe is especially characteristic of capitalist societies. Also called *critical criminology; Marxist criminology*.

**rape** Unlawful sexual intercourse, achieved through force and without consent. Broadly speaking, the term *rape* has been applied to a wide variety of sexual attacks and may include same-sex rape and the rape of a male by a female. Some jurisdictions refer to same-sex rape as *sexual battery*. See also **forcible rape; sexual battery**.

**rated capacity** The number of inmates a prison can handle according to the judgment of experts.

**rational choice theory** A perspective on crime causation that holds that criminality is the result of conscious choice. Rational choice theory predicts that individuals will choose to commit crime when the benefits of doing so outweigh the costs of disobeying the law.

**reaction formation** The process whereby a person openly rejects that which he or she wants or aspires to but cannot obtain or achieve.

**real evidence** Evidence that consists of physical material or traces of physical activity.

**reasonable doubt** In legal proceedings, an actual and substantial doubt arising from the evidence, from the facts or circumstances shown by the evidence, or from the lack of evidence.[50] Also, the state of a case such that, after the comparison and consideration of all the evidence, jurors cannot say they feel an abiding conviction of the truth of the charge.[51]

**reasonable doubt standard** The standard of proof necessary for conviction in criminal trials.

**reasonable force** A degree of force that is appropriate in a given situation and is not excessive. Also, the minimum degree of force necessary to protect oneself, one's property, a third party, or the property of another in the face of a substantial threat.

**reasonable suspicion** The level of suspicion that would justify an officer in making further inquiry or in conducting further investigation. Reasonable suspicion may permit stopping a person for questioning or for a simple pat-down search. Also, a belief, based on a consideration of the facts at hand and on reasonable inferences drawn from those facts, that would induce an ordinarily prudent and cautious person under the same circumstances to conclude that criminal activity is taking place or that criminal activity has recently occurred. Reasonable suspicion is a *general* and reasonable belief that a crime is in progress or has occurred, whereas probable cause is a reasonable belief that a *particular* person has committed a *specific* crime. See also **probable cause**.

**recidivism** The repetition of criminal behavior. In statistical practice, a recidivism rate may be any of a number of possible counts or instances of arrest, conviction, correctional commitment, or correctional status change related to repetitions of these events within a given period of time.

**recidivist** A person who has been convicted of one or more crimes and who is alleged or found to have subsequently committed another crime or series of crimes.

**reckless behavior** Activity that increases the risk of harm.

**recreational drug user** A person who uses drugs relatively infrequently and primarily with friends and in social contexts that define drug use as pleasurable. Most addicts begin as recreational users.

**reformatory style** A late-nineteenth-century correctional model based on the use of the indeterminate sentence and the belief in the possibility of rehabilitation, especially for youthful of-

fenders. The reformatory concept faded with the emergence of industrial prisons around the turn of the century.

**regional jail** A jail that is built and run using the combined resources of a variety of local jurisdictions.

**rehabilitation** The attempt to reform a criminal offender. Also, the state in which a reformed offender is said to be.

**release on recognizance (ROR)** The pretrial release of a criminal defendant on his or her written promise to appear in court as required. No cash or property bond is required.

**remote location monitoring** A supervision strategy that uses electronic technology to track offenders sentenced to house arrest or those who have been ordered to limit their movements while completing a sentence involving probation or parole.

**reprieve** An executive act temporarily suspending the execution of a sentence, usually a death sentence. A reprieve differs from other suspensions of sentence not only in that it almost always applies to the temporary withdrawing of a death sentence, but also in that it is usually an act of clemency intended to provide the prisoner with time to secure amelioration of the sentence.

**research** The use of standardized, systematic procedures in the search for knowledge.

**resident** A person required, by official action or by his or her acceptance of placement, to reside in a public or private facility established for purposes of confinement, supervision, or care.

**residential commitment** A sentence of commitment to a correctional facility for adults, in which the offender is required to reside at night, but from which he or she is regularly permitted to depart during the day, unaccompanied by any official.

**response time** A measure of the time that it takes for police officers to respond to calls for service.

**restitution** A court requirement that an alleged or convicted offender pay money or provide services to the victim of the crime or provide services to the community.

**restoration** A goal of criminal sentencing that attempts to make the victim "whole again."

**restorative justice** A sentencing model that builds on restitution and community participation in an attempt to make the victim "whole again."

**retribution** The act of taking revenge on a criminal perpetrator.

**revocation hearing** A hearing held before a legally constituted hearing body (such as a parole board) to determine whether a parolee or probationer has violated the conditions and requirements of his or her parole or probation.

**rights of defendant** The powers and privileges that are constitutionally guaranteed to every defendant.

**robbery (UCR)** The unlawful taking or attempted taking of property that is in the immediate possession of another by force or violence and/or by putting the victim in fear. Armed robbery differs from unarmed, or strong-arm, robbery with regard to the presence of a weapon. Contrary to popular conceptions, highway robbery does not necessarily occur on a street—and rarely in a vehicle. The term *highway robbery* applies to any form of robbery that occurs outdoors in a public place.

**routine activities theory** A neoclassical perspective that suggests that lifestyles contribute significantly to both the volume and the type of crime found in any society.

**rule of law** The maxim that an orderly society must be governed by established principles and known codes that are applied uniformly and fairly to all of its members.

**rules of evidence** Court rules that govern the admissibility of evidence at criminal hearings and trials.

**runaway** A juvenile who has been adjudicated by a judicial officer of juvenile court as having committed the status offense of leaving the custody and home of his or her parents, guardians, or custodians without permission and of failing to return within a reasonable length of time.

**schizophrenic** A mentally ill individual who suffers from disjointed thinking and possibly from delusions and hallucinations.

**scientific jury selection** The use of correlational techniques from the social sciences to gauge the likelihood that potential jurors will vote for conviction or for acquittal.

**scientific police management** The application of social science techniques to the study of police administration for the purpose of increasing effectiveness, reducing the frequency of citizen complaints, and enhancing the efficient use of available resources.

**search incident to an arrest** A warrantless search of an arrested individual conducted to ensure the safety of the arresting officer. Because individuals placed under arrest may be in possession of weapons, courts have recognized the need for arresting officers to protect themselves by conducting an immediate search of arrestees without obtaining a warrant.

**search warrant** A document issued by a judicial officer that directs a law enforcement officer to conduct a search at a specific location, for specified property or person relating to a crime, to seize the property or person if found, and to account for the results of the search to the issuing judicial officer.

**security** The restriction of inmate movement within a correctional facility, usually divided into maximum, medium, and minimum levels.

**security threat group (STG)** A inmate group, gang, or organization whose members act together to pose a threat to the safety of correctional staff or the public, or who prey upon other inmates, or who threaten the secure and orderly operation of a correctional institution.

**self-defense** The protection of oneself or of one's property from unlawful injury or from the immediate risk of unlawful injury. Also, the justification that the person who committed an act that would otherwise constitute an offense reasonably believed that the act was necessary to protect self or property from immediate danger.

**sentence** 1. The penalty imposed by a court on a person convicted of a crime. 2. The court judgment specifying the penalty imposed on a person convicted of a crime. 3. Any disposition of a defendant resulting from a conviction, including the court decision to suspend execution of a sentence.

**sentencing** The imposition of a criminal sanction by a judicial authority.

**sentencing disposition** 1. A court disposition of a defendant after a judgment of conviction, expressed as a penalty, such as imprisonment or payment of a fine. 2. Any of a number of alternatives to actually executed penalties, such as a suspended sentence, a grant of probation, or an order to perform restitution. 3. Various combinations of the foregoing.

**sentencing hearing** In criminal proceedings, a hearing during which the court or jury considers relevant information, such as evidence concerning aggravating or mitigating circumstances, for the purpose of determining a sentencing disposition for a person convicted of an offense.

**sequestered jury** A jury that is isolated from the public during the course of a trial and throughout the deliberation process.

**service style** A style of policing marked by a concern with helping rather than strict enforcement. Service-oriented police agencies are more likely to use community resources, such as drug-treatment programs, to supplement traditional law enforcement activities, than are other types of agencies.

**sex offense** In current statistical usage, any of a broad category of varying offenses, usually consisting of all offenses having a sexual element, except forcible rape and commercial sex offenses. The category includes all unlawful sexual intercourse, unlawful sexual contact, and other unlawful behavior intended to result in sexual gratification or profit from sexual activity.

**sex offense (UCR)** Any of various "offenses against chastity, common decency, morals, and the like," except forcible rape, prostitution, and commercialized vice.

**sexual battery** Intentional and wrongful physical contact with a person, without his or her consent, that entails a sexual component or purpose.

**sheriff** The elected chief officer of a county law enforcement agency. The sheriff is usually responsible for law enforcement in unincorporated areas and for the operation of the county jail.

**sheriff's department** A local law enforcement agency, directed by a sheriff, that exercises its law enforcement functions at the county level, usually within unincorporated areas, and that operates the county jail in most jurisdictions.

**shock incarceration** A sentencing option that makes use of "boot camp"–type prisons to impress on convicted offenders the realities of prison life.

**shock probation** The practice of sentencing offenders to prison, allowing them to apply for probationary release, and enacting such release in surprise fashion. Offenders who receive shock probation may not be aware that they will be released on probation and may expect to spend a much longer time behind bars.

**simple assault (UCR)** The unlawful threatening, attempted inflicting, or inflicting of less-than-serious bodily injury, without a deadly weapon.

**smart card** A plastic card or similar device, containing a computer chip and other sources of nonalterable information (such as a hologram or a laser-encoded memory strip), that is used to provide highly secure personal identification.

**smuggling** The unlawful movement of goods across a national frontier or state boundary or into or out of a correctional facility.

**"sneak and peek" search** A search that occurs in the suspect's absence and without his or her prior knowledge. Also known as *delayed notification search.*

**social control** The use of sanctions and rewards within a group to influence and shape the behavior of individual members of that group. Social control is a primary concern of social groups and communities, and it is their interest in the exercise of social control that leads to the creation of both criminal and civil statutes.

**social debt** A sentencing principle that holds that an offender's criminal history should objectively be taken into account in sentencing decisions.

**social development theory** An integrated view of human development that points to the process of interaction among and between individuals and society as the root cause of criminal behavior.

**social disorganization** A condition said to exist when a group is faced with social change, uneven development of culture, maladaptiveness, disharmony, conflict, and lack of consensus.

**social ecology** A criminological approach that focuses on the misbehavior of lower-class youth and sees delinquency primarily as the result of social disorganization.

**social engineering** A nontechnical kind of cyberintrusion that relies heavily on human interaction and often involves tricking people into breaking normal security procedures.

**social justice** An ideal that embraces all aspects of civilized life and that is linked to fundamental notions of fairness and to cultural beliefs about right and wrong.

**social learning theory** A psychological perspective that says that people learn how to behave by modeling themselves after others whom they have the opportunity to observe.

**social order** The condition of a society characterized by social integration, consensus, smooth functioning, and lack of interpersonal and institutional conflict. Also, a lack of social disorganization.

**social process theory** A perspective on criminological thought that highlights the process of interaction between individuals and society. Most social process theories highlight the role of social learning.

**social-psychological theory** A perspective on criminological thought that highlights the role played in crime causation by weakened self-esteem and meaningless social roles. Social-psychological thinkers stress the relationship of the individual to the social group as the underlying cause of behavior.

**sociopath** See **psychopath.**

**software piracy** The unauthorized duplication of software or the illegal transfer of data from one storage medium to another. Software piracy is one of the most prevalent computer crimes in the world.

**solvability factor** Information about a crime that forms the basis for determining the perpetrator's identity.

**somatotyping** The classification of human beings into types according to body build and other physical characteristics.

**spam** Unsolicited commercial bulk e-mail (UCBE), whose *primary purpose* is the commercial advertisement or promotion of a commercial product or service.

**span of control** The number of police personnel or the number of units supervised by a particular commander.

**specific deterrence** A goal of criminal sentencing that seeks to prevent a particular offender from engaging in repeat criminality.

**speedy trial** A trial that is held in a timely manner. The right of a defendant to have a prompt trial is guaranteed by the Sixth Amendment of the U.S. Constitution, which begins "In all criminal prosecutions, the accused shall enjoy the right to a speedy and public trial."

**Speedy Trial Act** A 1974 federal law requiring that proceedings against a defendant in a federal criminal case begin within a specified period of time, such as 70 working days after indictment. Some states also have speedy trial requirements.

**split sentence** A sentence explicitly requiring the convicted offender to serve a period of confinement in a local, state, or federal facility, followed by a period of probation.

**staff operations** In police organizations, activities (such as administration and training) that provide support for line operations.

**stalking** Repeated harassing and threatening behavior by one individual against another, aspects of which may be planned or carried out in secret. Stalking might involve following a person, appearing at a person's home or place of business, making harassing phone calls, leaving written messages or objects, or vandalizing a person's property. Most stalking laws require that the perpetrator make a credible threat of violence against the victim or members of the victim's immediate family.

***stare decisis*** A legal principle that requires that in subsequent cases on similar issues of law and fact, courts be bound by their own earlier decisions and by those of higher courts having jurisdiction over them. The term literally means "standing by decided matters."

**state-action doctrine** The traditional legal principle that only government officials or their representatives in the criminal justice process can be held accountable for the violation of an individual's constitutional civil rights.

**state court administrator** A coordinator who assists with case-flow management, operating funds budgeting, and court docket administration.

**state court system** A state judicial structure. Most states have at least three court levels: generally, trial courts, appellate courts, and a state supreme court.

**state highway patrol** A state law enforcement agency whose principal functions are preventing, detecting, and investigating motor vehicle offenses and apprehending traffic offenders.

**state police** A state law enforcement agency whose principal functions usually include maintaining statewide police communications, aiding local police in criminal investigations, training police, and guarding state property. The state police may include the highway patrol.

**state-use system** A form of inmate labor in which items produced by inmates may only be sold by or to state offices. Items that only the state can sell include such things as license plates and hunting licenses, while items sold only to state offices include furniture and cleaning supplies.

**status offender** A child who commits an act that is contrary to the law by virtue of the offender's status as a child. Purchasing cigarettes, buying alcohol, and being truant are examples of such behavior.

**status offense** An act or conduct that is declared by statute to be an offense, but only when committed by or engaged in by a juvenile, and that can be adjudicated only by a juvenile court.

**Statute of Winchester** A law, written in 1285, that created a watch and ward system in English cities and towns and that codified early police practices.

**statutory law** Written or codified law; the "law on the books," as enacted by a government body or agency having the power to make laws.

**statutory rape** Sexual intercourse with a person who is under the legal age of consent.

**stay of execution** The stopping by a court of the implementation of a judgment—that is, of a court order previously issued.

**stolen property offense** The unlawful receiving, buying, distributing, selling, transporting, concealing, or possessing of the property of another by a person who knows that the property has been unlawfully obtained from the owner or other lawful possessor.

**stop and frisk** The detaining of a person by a law enforcement officer for the purpose of investigation, accompanied by a superficial examination by the officer of the person's body surface or clothing to discover weapons, contraband, or other objects relating to criminal activity.

**stranger violence** Seemingly random violence perpetrated by assailants who were previously unknown to their victims. Stranger violence often results from rage, opportunity, or insanity.

**strategic policing** A type of policing that retains the traditional police goal of professional crime fighting but enlarges the enforcement target to include nontraditional kinds of criminals, such as serial offenders, gangs and criminal associations, drug-distribution networks, and sophisticated white-collar and computer criminals. Strategic policing generally makes use of innovative enforcement techniques, including intelligence operations, undercover stings, electronic surveillance, and sophisticated forensic methods.

**street crime** A class of offenses, sometimes defined with some degree of formality as those which occur in public locations and are visible and assaultive, that are a special risk to the public and a special target of law enforcement preventive efforts and prosecutorial attention.

**strict liability** Liability without fault or intention. Strict liability offenses do not require *mens rea*.

**structured sentencing** A model of criminal punishment that includes determinate and commission-created presumptive sentencing schemes, as well as voluntary/advisory sentencing guidelines.

**subculture of violence** A cultural setting in which violence is a traditional and often accepted method of dispute resolution.

**subpoena** A written order issued by a judicial officer or grand jury requiring an individual to appear in court and to give testimony or to bring material to be used as evidence. Some subpoenas mandate that books, papers, and other items be surrendered to the court.

**substantive criminal law** The part of the law that defines crimes and specifies punishments.

**supermale** A human male displaying the XYY chromosome structure.

**superpredator** A juvenile who is coming of age in actual and "moral poverty" without the benefits of parents, teachers, coaches, and clergy to teach right from wrong[52] and who turns to criminal activity. The term is often applied to inner-city youths, socialized in violent settings without the benefit of wholesome life experiences, who hold considerable potential for violence.

**supervised probation** Guidance, treatment, or regulation by a probation agency of the behavior of a person who is subject to adjudication or who has been convicted of an offense, resulting from a formal court order or a probation agency decision.

**suspect** An adult or a juvenile who has not been arrested or charged but whom a criminal justice agency believes may be the person responsible for a specific criminal offense.

**suspended sentence** The court decision to delay imposing or executing a penalty for a specified or unspecified period. Also, a court disposition of a convicted person pronouncing a penalty of a fine or a commitment to confinement but unconditionally discharging the defendant or holding execution of the penalty in abeyance upon good behavior. Also called *sentence withheld.*

**suspicionless search** A search conducted by law enforcement personnel without a warrant and without suspicion. Suspicionless searches are permissible only if based on an overriding concern for public safety.

**sworn officer** A law enforcement officer who is trained and empowered to perform full police duties, such as making arrests, conducting investigations, and carrying firearms.[53]

***Tazir* crime** A minor violation of Islamic law that is regarded as an offense against society, not God.

**team policing** The reorganization of conventional patrol strategies into "an integrated and versatile police team assigned to a fixed district."[54]

**technocrime** A criminal offense that employs advanced or emerging technology in its commission.

**teen court** An alternative approach to juvenile justice in which alleged offenders are judged and sentenced by a jury of their peers.

**TEMPEST** A standard developed by the U.S. government that requires that electromagnetic emanations from computers designated as "secure" be below levels that would allow radio receiving equipment to "read" the data being computed.

**terrorism** A violent act or an act dangerous to human life in violation of the criminal laws of the United States or of any state committed to intimidate or coerce a government, the civilian population, or any segment thereof, in furtherance of political or social objectives.[55]

**testimony** Oral evidence offered by a sworn witness on the witness stand during a criminal trial.

**theft** Generally, any taking of the property of another with intent to deprive the rightful owner of possession permanently.

**theory** A set of interrelated propositions that attempt to describe, explain, predict, and ultimately control some class of events. A theory gains explanatory power from inherent logical consistency and is "tested" by how well it describes and predicts reality.

**three-strikes laws** Statutes that require mandatory sentences (sometimes life in prison without the possibility of parole) for offenders convicted of a third felony. Such mandatory sentencing enhancements are aimed at deterring known and potentially violent offenders and are intended to incapac-itate convicted criminals through long-term incarceration.

**tort** A wrongful act, damage, or injury not involving a breach of contract. Also, a private or civil wrong or injury.

**total institution** An enclosed facility separated from society both socially and physically, where the inhabitants share all aspects of their lives daily.

**transfer to adult court** The decision by a juvenile court, resulting from a transfer hearing, that jurisdiction over an alleged delinquent will be waived and that he or she should be prosecuted as an adult in a criminal court.

**transnational crime** Unlawful activity undertaken and supported by organized criminal groups operating across national boundaries.

**treason** A U.S. citizen's actions to help a foreign government overthrow, make war against, or seriously injure the United States.[56] Also, the attempt to overthrow the government of the society of which one is a member.

**trial** In criminal proceedings, the examination in court of the issues of fact and relevant law in a case for the purpose of convicting or acquitting the defendant.

**trial *de novo*** Literally, "new trial." The term is applied to cases that are retried on appeal, as opposed to those that are simply reviewed on the record.

**trial judge** A judicial officer who is authorized to conduct jury and nonjury trials but who may not be authorized to hear appellate cases. Also, the judicial officer who conducts a particular trial.

**trial jury** A statutorily defined number of people selected according to law and sworn to determine, in accordance with the law as instructed by the court, certain matters of fact based on evidence presented in a trial and to render a verdict. Also called *petit jury*.

**truth in sentencing** A close correspondence between the sentence imposed on an offender and the time actually served in prison.[57]

**UCR** See **Uniform Crime Reports (UCR)**.

**unconditional release** The final release of an offender from the jurisdiction of a correctional agency. Also, a final release from the jurisdiction of a court.

**undisciplined child** A child who is beyond parental control, as evidenced by his or her refusal to obey legitimate authorities, such as school officials and teachers.

**Uniform Crime Reports (UCR)** An annual FBI publication that summarizes the incidence and rate of reported crimes throughout the United States.

**USA PATRIOT Act of 2001** A federal law (Public Law 107–56) enacted in response to terrorist attacks on the World Trade Center and the Pentagon on September 11, 2001. The law, officially titled the Uniting and Strengthening America by Providing Appropriate Tools Required to Intercept and Obstruct Terrorism Act, substantially broadened the investigative authority of law enforcement agencies throughout America and is applicable to many crimes other than terrorism.

**use of force** See **police use of force**.

**vagrancy (UCR)** An offense related to being a suspicious person, including vagrancy, begging, loitering, and vagabondage.

**vandalism (UCR)** The destroying or damaging, or attempting to destroy or damage, of public property or the property of another without the owner's consent. This definition of vandalism does not include burning.

**venue** The particular geographic area in which a court may hear or try a case. Also, the locality within which a particular crime was committed. See also **jurisdiction**.

**verdict** The decision of the jury in a jury trial or of a judicial officer in a nonjury trial.

**victim** A person who has suffered death, physical or mental anguish, or loss of property as the result of an actual or attempted criminal offense committed by another person.

**victim assistance program** An organized program that offers services to victims of crime in the areas of crisis intervention and follow-up counseling and that helps victims secure their rights under the law.

**victim impact statement** The in-court use of victim- or survivor-supplied information by sentencing authorities seeking to make an informed sentencing decision.

**victimization** In National Crime Victimization Survey terminology, the harming of any single victim in a criminal incident.

**victimology** The scientific study of crime victims and the victimization process. Victimology is a subfield of criminology.

**vigilantism** The act of taking the law into one's own hands.

**violation** 1. The performance of an act forbidden by a statute, or the failure to perform an act commanded by a statute. 2. An act contrary to a local government ordinance. 3. An offense punishable by a fine or other penalty but not by incarceration. 4. An act prohibited by the terms and conditions of probation or parole.

**violent crime** A UCR offense category that includes murder, rape, robbery, and aggravated assault.

**voluntary/advisory sentencing guidelines** Recommended sentencing policies that are not required by law.

**warden** The official in charge of the operation of a prison, the chief administrator of a prison, or the prison superintendent.

**warehousing** An imprisonment strategy that is based on the desire to prevent recurrent crime and that has abandoned all hope of rehabilitation.

**warrant** In criminal proceedings, a writ issued by a judicial officer directing a law enforcement officer to perform a specified act and affording the officer protection from damages if he or she performs it.

**watchman style** A style of policing marked by a concern for order maintenance. Watchman policing is characteristic of lower-class communities where police intervene informally into the lives of residents to keep the peace.

**weapon of mass destruction (WMD)** A chemical, biological, or nuclear weapon that has the potential to cause mass casualties.

**weapons offense** The unlawful sale, distribution, manufacture, alteration, transportation, possession, or use, or the attempted unlawful sale, distribution, manufacture, alteration, transportation, possession, or use, of a deadly or dangerous weapon or accessory.

**white-collar crime** Violations of the criminal law committed by a person of respectability and high social status in the course of his or her occupation. Also, nonviolent crime for financial gain utilizing deception and committed by anyone who has special technical and professional knowledge of business and government, irrespective of the person's occupation.

**Wickersham Commission** The National Commission on Law Observance and Enforcement. In 1931, the commission issued a report stating that Prohibition was unenforceable and carried a great potential for police corruption.

**witness** Generally, a person who has knowledge of the circumstances of a case. Also, in court usage, one who testifies as to what he or she has seen, heard, or otherwise observed or who has expert knowledge.

**work release** A prison program through which inmates are temporarily released into the community to meet job responsibilities.

**workhouse** An early form of imprisonment whose purpose was to instill habits of industry in the idle. Also called *bridewell*.

**writ** A document issued by a judicial officer ordering or forbidding the performance of a specified act.

**writ of *certiorari*** A writ issued from an appellate court for the purpose of obtaining from a lower court the record of its proceedings in a particular case. In some states, this writ is the mechanism for discretionary review. A request for review is made by petitioning for a writ of *certiorari,* and the granting of review is indicated by the issuance of the writ.

**writ of *habeas corpus*** A writ that directs the person detaining a prisoner to bring him or her before a judicial officer to determine the lawfulness of the imprisonment.

**youthful offender** A person, adjudicated in criminal court, who may be above the statutory age limit for juveniles but is below a specified upper age limit, for whom special correctional commitments and special record-sealing procedures are made available by statute.

---

1. Bureau of Justice Statistics, *Dictionary of Criminal Justice Data Terminology*, 2nd ed. (Washington, DC: U.S. Government Printing Office, 1982).

2. Federal Bureau of Investigation, *Uniform Crime Reporting Handbook* (Washington, DC: U.S. Department of Justice, 1984).

3. BJS, *Dictionary of Criminal Justice Data Terminology*, p. 5.

4. Adapted from U.S. Code, Title 28, Section 20.3 (2[d]). Title 28 of the U.S. Code defines the term *administration of criminal justice*.

5. Thomas J. Cowper and Michael E. Buerger, *Improving Our View of the World: Police and Augmented Reality Technology* (Washington, DC: Federal Bureau of Investigation, 2003). Web posted at http://www.fbi.gov/publications/realitytech/realitytech.pdf (accessed October 7, 2003).

6. *People* v. *Romero,* 8 Cal. 4th 728, 735 (1994).

7. Technical Working Group on Crime Scene Investigation, *Crime Scene Investigation: A Guide for Law Enforcement* (Washington, DC: National Institute of Justice, 2000), p. 12.

8. Centers for Disease Control and Prevention, *Bioterrorism: An Overview.* Web posted at http://www.bt.cdc.gov/documents/ PPTResponse/laboverview. pdf (accessed August 5, 2003).

9. *State* v. *Cross,* 200 S.E.2d 27, 29 (1973).

10. Adapted from Gerald Hill and Kathleen Hill, *The Real Life Dictionary of the Law.* Web posted at http://www.law.com (accessed June 11, 2003).

11. Ibid (accessed February 21, 2005).

12. Community Policing Consortium, *What Is Community Policing?* (Washington, DC: Community Policing Consortium, 1995).

13. Michael L. Benson, Francis T. Cullen, and William J. Maakestad, *Local Prosecutors and Corporate Crime* (Washington, DC: National Institute of Justice, 1992), p. 1.

14. Office of Justice Programs, *The National Criminal Intelligence Sharing Plan* (Washington, DC: U.S. Department of Justice, 2005), p. 27.

15. Wayne W. Bennett and Karen M. Hess, *Criminal Investigation,* 6th ed. (Belmont, CA: Wadsworth, 2001), p. 3. Italics in original.

16. Violence against Women Office, *Stalking and Domestic Violence: Report to Congress* (Washington, DC: U.S. Department of Justice, 2001).

17. Sam W. Lathrop, "Reviewing Use of Force: A Systematic Approach," *FBI Law Enforcement Bulletin,* October 2000, p. 18.

18. Adapted from Larry R. Leibrock, "Overview and Impact on 21st Century Legal Practice: Digital Forensics and Electronic Discovery," no date. Web posted at http://www.courtroom21.net/FDIC.pps (accessed July 5, 2005).

19. Adapted from Federal Bureau of Investigation, *FBI Policy and Guidelines: Counterterrorism.* Web posted at http://www.fbi.gov/contact/fo/jackson/cntrterr.htm (accessed March 4, 2004).

20. Bureau of Justice Statistics, *Drugs, Crime, and the Justice System* (Washington, DC: BJS, 1992), p. 20.

21. Adapted from Technical Working Group for Electronic Crime Scene Investigation, *Electronic Crime Scene Investigation: A Guide for First Responders* (Washington, DC: National Institute of Justice, 2001), p. 2.

22. Henry Campbell Black, Joseph R. Nolan, and Jacqueline M. Nolan-Haley, *Black's Law Dictionary,* 6th ed. (St. Paul, MN: West, 1990), p. 24.

23. Lawrence W. Sherman, *Evidence-Based Policing* (Washington, DC: Police Foundation, 1998), p. 3.

24. International Association of Chiefs of Police, *Police Use of Force in America 2001* (Alexandria, VA: IACP, 2001), p. 1.

25. Adapted from "Globalization," *Encyclopedia Britannica, 2003.* Encyclopedia Britannica Premium Service. Web posted at http:// www.britannica.com/eb/article?eu=369857 (accessed July, 23, 2003).

26. Black, Nolan, and Nolan-Haley, *Black's Law Dictionary,* p. 1003.

27. H.R. 4797, 102d Cong. 2d Sess. (1992).

28. *The American Heritage Dictionary and Electronic Thesaurus* on

*CD-ROM* (Boston: Houghton Mifflin, 1987).

29. Adapted from Entrust, Inc., "Secure Identity Management: Challenges, Needs, and Solutions," p. 1. Web posted at http://www.entrust.com (accessed August 5, 2003).

30. Identity Theft Resource Center website, http://www.idtheftcenter. org (accessed April 4, 2005).

31. Adapted from Dictionary.com. Web posted at http://dictionary .reference. com/search?q= infrastructure (accessed January 10, 2005).

32. Angus Smith, ed., *Intelligence-Led Policing* (Richmond, VA: International Association of Law Enforcement Intelligence Analysts, 1997), p. 1.

33. Adapted from Federal Bureau of Investigation, *FBI Policy and Guidelines: Counterterrorism.* Web posted at http://www.fbi.gov/ contact/fo/jackson/cntrterr.htm (accessed March 4, 2005).

34. Jeffrey A. Butts and Ojmarrh Mitchell, "Brick by Brick: Dismantling the Border between Juvenile and Adult Justice," in Phyllis McDonald and Janice Munsterman, eds., *Criminal Justice 2000,* Vol. 2: *Boundary Changes in Criminal Justice Organizations* (Washington, DC: National Institute of Justice, 2000), p. 207.

35. David A. Garvin, "Building a Learning Organization," *Harvard Business Review* (1993), pp. 78–91.

36. U.S. Department of Treasury, *2000–2005 Strategic Plan* (Washington, DC: U.S. Government Printing Office, 2000), p. 1.

37. Adapted from Robert M. Shusta et al., *Multicultural Law Enforcement,* 2nd ed. (Upper Saddle River, NJ: Prentice Hall, 2002), p. 443.

38. The Organized Crime Control Act of 1970 (Public Law 91–451).

39. BJS, *Drugs, Crime, and the Justice System,* p. 20.

40. Carl B. Klockars et al., *The Measure- ment of Police Integrity,* National Institute of Justice Research in Brief (Washington, DC: NIJ, 2000), p. 1.

41. This definition draws on the classic work by O. W. Wilson, *Police Administration* (New York: McGraw- Hill, 1950), pp. 2–3.

42. National Institute of Justice, *Use of Force by Police: Overview of National and Local Data* (Washington, DC: NIJ, 1999).

43. National Council on Crime and Delinquency, *National Assessment of Structured Sentencing* (Washington, DC: Bureau of Justice Statistics, 1996), p. xii.

44. Bureau of Justice Statistics, *Prisoners in 1998* (Washington, DC: BJS, 1999), p. 7.

45. *Private Security: Report of the Task Force on Private Security* (Washington, DC: U.S. Government Printing Office, 1976), p. 4.

46. Samuel Walker, Geoffrey P. Albert, and Dennis J. Kenney, *Responding to the Problem Police Officer: A National Study of Early Warning Systems* (Washington, DC: National Institute of Justice, 2000).

47. BJS, *Drugs, Crime, and the Justice System,* p. 21.

48. Gerald Hill and Kathleen Hill, *The Real Life Dictionary of the Law* (Santa Monica, CA: General Publishing Group, 2000). Web posted at http://dictionary.law.com/ lookup2.asp (accessed February 21, 2004).

49. Deborah Ramierz, Jack McDevitt, and Amy Farrell, *A Resource Guide on Racial Profiling Data Collection Systems: Promising Practices and Lessons Learned* (Washington, DC: U.S. Department of Justice, 2000), p. 3.

50. *Victor v. Nebraska,* 114 S.Ct. 1239, 127 L.Ed.2d 583 (1994).

51. As found in the California jury instructions.

52. The term *superpredator* is generally attributed to John J. DiIulio, Jr. See John J. DiIulio, Jr., "The Question of Black Crime," *Public Interest* (Fall 1994), pp. 3–12.

53. Adapted from Darl H. Champion and Michael K. Hooper, *Introduction to American Policing* (New York: McGraw-Hill, 2003), p. 166.

54. Sam S. Souryal, *Police Administration and Management* (St. Paul, MN: West, 1977), p. 261.

55. Federal Bureau of Intelligence, Counterterrorism Section, *Terrorism in the United States, 1987* (Washington, DC: FBI, 1987).

56. Daniel Oran, *Oran's Dictionary of the Law* (St. Paul, MN: West, 1983), p. 306.

57. Lawrence A. Greenfeld, "Prison Sentences and Time Served for Violence," *Bureau of Justice Statistics Selected Findings,* No. 4 (April 1995).

# CASE INDEX

## A

Abel v. U.S., 633, 656
Aguillar v. Texas, 268, 286
Ake v. Oklahoma, 147
Alabama v. Shelton, 347, 366
Alabama v. White, 268
Alexander v. U.S., 649, 658
Allen v. U.S., 392, 399
Anders v. California, 349, 366
Andersen v. U.S., 76
Anderson v. General Motors Corp., 124
Apodaca v. Oregon, 399
Apprendi v. New Jersey, 411, 413, 435, 443
Argersinger v. Hamlin, 347, 366
Arizona v. Evans, 250, 251
Arizona v. Fulminante, 251, 270, 286, 399
Arizona v. Hicks, 252, 284
Arizona v. Mauro, 275, 286
Arizona v. Roberson, 270, 286
Arkansas v. Sanders, 258, 285
Ashcroft v. Tennessee, 269, 286
Atkins v. Virginia, 436–437, 447
Atwater v. Lago Vista, 285
Austin v. U.S., 649, 658
Aziz v. LeFevre, 573

## B

Banks v. Beard, 549, 573
Banks v. Dretke, 366
Barker v. Wingo, 382, 398
Batson v. Kentucky, 386, 399
Bearden v. Georgia, 463, 478, 741
Beckwith v. U.S., 251
Bee v. Greaves, 554, 573
Benning v. State, 550, 573
Bennis v. Michigan, 649, 658
Beno v. ACLU, 279
Berchardt v. U.S., 251
Berger v. New York, 277, 286
Biscoe v. Arlington County, 316, 323
Bivens v. Six Unknown Federal Agents,
        318, 323
Black v. Rutherford, 549
Blakely v. Washington, 414, 443
Blanton v. City of North Las Vegas, 19, 30
Block v. Rutherford, 555, 573
Blystone v. Pennsylvania, 435, 446
Board of the County Commissioners of
        Bryan County, Oklahoma v. Brown,
        317, 323
Bond v. U.S., 264, 285
Booth v. Churner, 284, 559, 574
Bounds v. Smith, 551, 573
Boyde v. California, 284, 435, 446
Boykin v. Alabama, 398
Brady v. Maryland, 345, 366
Brecht v. Abrahamson, 275, 286, 399
Breed v. Jones, 602, 618
Brewer v. Williams, 273, 286
Brown v. Mississippi, 269, 286
Brown v. Texas, 257, 285
Buck v. Bell, 90, 113
Burns v. Reed, 345, 366

## C

California Department of Corrections v.
        Morales, 154
California v. Acevedo, 251, 284, 285
California v. Carney, 251, 263, 285
California v. Ciraolo, 251, 657
California v. Green, 367
California v. Greenwood, 251, 633, 656
California v. Hodari D., 258, 285
California v. Prysock, 618
Campbell v. Cauthron, 573
Campbell v. Louisiana, 387, 399
Campbell v. Wood, 436, 446
Caribbean International News Corporation
        v. Puerto Rico, 362, 367
Carroll v. City of Westminster, 321
Carroll v. U.S., 251, 259, 285
Center for National Security Studies v.
        U.S. Department of Justice, 30
Chambers v. Florida, 269, 286
Chandler v. Florida, 367
Chapman v. California, 270, 286
Chavez v. Martinez, 275, 286
Chicago v. Morales, 595
Chimel v. California, 247, 251, 284
City of Canton, Ohio v. Harris, 317, 323
Coker v. Georgia, 435, 446
Coleman v. Thompson, 284, 427, 445
Colorado v. Bertine, 259, 285
Colorado v. Connelly, 274, 286
Colorado v. Spring, 273, 286
Coolidge v. New Hampshire, 251, 284
Correctional Services Corporation v.
        Malesko, 516
County of Riverside v. McLaughlin,
        371, 397
Coy v. Iowa, 390, 399
Crosby v. U.S., 361, 367
Crown v. Dudly & Stephen, The, 139, 154
Cruz v. Beto, 550, 573
Cutter v. Wilkinson, 551, 573

## D

Daubert v. Merrell Dow Pharmaceuticals,
        Inc., 721, 740
Davis v. Dallas, 225
Davis v. Minnesota, 399
Davis v. U.S., 270, 286
Dawson v. State, 447
Deal v. U.S., 412, 443
Delaware v. Prouse, 265
Demarest v. Manspeaker et al., 357, 367
Department of Housing and Urban
        Development v. Rucker, 633
Dettmer v. Landon, 550, 573
Dickerson v. New Banner Institute,
        Inc., 398
Dickerson v. U.S., 286
Director Gomez et al. v. Fierro and
        Ruiz, 447
Disability Advocates, Inc. v. New York
        State Office of Mental Health, 574
Doggett v. U.S., 383, 398

Doyle v. Ohio, 275, 286
Durham v. U.S., 146, 154

## E

Edmonson v. Leesville Concrete Co., Inc.,
        386, 399
Edwards v. Arizona, 270, 286
Edwards v. Balisok, 284, 559, 574
Elder v. Holloway, 323
Elledge v. Florida, 428, 445
Escobedo v. Illinois, 270, 286
Escoe v. Zerbst, 462, 478
Estelle v. Gamble, 551, 557, 573
Ewing v. California, 284, 416, 417
Ex parte Crouse, 585
Ex parte United States, 477

## F

Fare v. Michael C., 618
Faretta v. California, 349, 366
Farmer v. Brennan, 555, 573
F.D.I.C. v. Meyer, 323
Felker v. Turpin, 284, 428, 445
Fex v. Michigan, 383, 398
Florida v. Bostick, 264, 285
Florida v. Jimeno, 238, 261, 285
Florida v. J.L., 268, 286
Florida v. Riley, 251, 657
Florida v. Wells, 259, 285
Ford v. Georgia, 386, 399
Ford v. Wainwright, 147, 155
Foucha v. Louisiana, 147, 155
Frye v. U.S., 721, 740
Furman v. Georgia, 434, 436, 442, 446

## G

Gagnon v. Scarpelli, 462, 478
Georgia v. McCollum, 386, 399
Gideon v. Wainwright, 22, 347, 350, 366
Glasshofer v. Thornburg, 573
Gonzales v. Raich, 639, 657
Gordon v. State, 154
Graham v. Connor, 306, 322
Greenholtz v. Nebraska Penal Inmates,
        463, 478
Gregg v. Georgia, 435, 446
Griffin v. California, 390, 399
Griffin v. Wisconsin, 462, 477
Grimm v. Arizona Board of Pardons and
        Paroles, 478
Guajardo v. Estelle, 573

## H

Haley v. Ohio, 618
Hancock v. State, 741
Harlow v. Clatterbuick, 478
Harris v. U.S., 250, 251, 268, 284, 418,
        442, 443
Hayes v. Florida, 275, 286
Helling v. McKinney, 555, 573
Henderson v. Morgan, 379, 398
Henderson v. U.S., 155

# CASE INDEX

Herrera v. Collins, 334, 364
Hester v. U.S., 251, 284, 634, 657
Hewitt v. Helms, 558, 573
Hiibel v. Sixth Judicial District Court of Nevada, 251, 257, 285
Hill v. Blackwell, 550, 573
Holt v. Sarver, 554, 572, 573
Hope v. Pelzer, 572
Horton v. California, 251, 252, 258, 284
Houchins v. KQED, Inc., 550, 573
Hudson v. McMillan, 551, 573
Hudson v. Palmer, 555, 573
Hudson v. U.S., 155
Hunter v. Bryant, 318, 323

## I

Idaho v. Horiuchi, 318, 323
Idaho v. Wright, 391, 399
Illinois v. Caballes, 262, 285
Illinois v. Gates, 268
Illinois v. Krull, 249, 251, 284
Illinois v. Lidster, 263, 285
Illinois v. McArthur, 253, 284
Illinois v. Montanez, 602–603, 618
Illinois v. Perkins, 251, 274, 286
Illinois v. Rodriguez, 249–250, 284
Illinois v. Wardlow, 285
Illinois v. White, 286
Imbler v. Pachtman, 345, 366
In re Caulk, 573
In re Gatti, 344
In re Gault, 347, 366, 618
In re Harrell, 573
In re Kemmler, 434, 446
In re Oliver, 399
In re Winship, 601, 618
Indianapolis v. Edmond, 263, 265, 285

## J

Jaffee v. Redmond, 366
J.E.B. v. Alabama, 385, 386, 399
Johnson v. Avery, 548, 551, 573
Johnson v. California, 504, 521
Johnson v. Louisiana, 399
Johnson v. Zerbst, 347, 366
Jones v. North Carolina Prisoners' Labor Union, 556, 573
Jones v. U.S., 147, 155

## K

Kansas v. Crane, 565
Kansas v. Hendricks, 565
Kaplan v. Lloyd's Insurance Co., 323
Katz v. U.S., 277, 284, 286, 555, 573
Keeney v. Tamayo-Reyes, 334, 364
Kent v. U.S., 599, 618
Ker v. California, 284
Kercheval v. U.S., 398
Killets, 457
Kirk v. Louisiana, 254, 285
Klopfer v. North Carolina, 382, 398
Knowles v. Iowa, 261, 285
Koon v. U.S., 443

Kotteakos v. U.S., 286, 399
Kuhlmann v. Wilson, 251, 274, 286
Kumho Tire v. Carmichael, 740
Kyllo v. U.S., 267, 286

## L

Lee v. Florida, 278, 286
Lee v. U.S., 277, 286
Lewellyn (L'Aquarius) v. State, 573
Lewis v. Casey, 551, 573
Lewis v. U.S., 367
Leyra v. Denno, 269, 286
Lockyer v. Andrade, 284
Lopez v. U.S., 286
Louisiana ex rel. Francis v. Resweber, 446
Luparar v. Stoneman, 573
Lynce v. Mathis, 521

## M

Mabry v. Johnson, 398
Mallery v. Lewis, 549
Malley v. Briggs, 316, 323
Mapp v. Ohio, 246–247, 284, 339, 365
Marbury v. Madison, 339, 365
Maryland v. Buie, 251, 253, 284
Maryland v. Craig, 390, 399
Maryland v. Garrison, 249, 284
Maryland v. Wilson, 261, 285
Massachusetts v. Sheppard, 249, 284
Maughs v. Commonwealth, 154
Maurice Turner v. Fraternal Order of Police, 298, 321
McCleskey v. Kemp, 284, 431, 446
McCleskey v. Zant, 284, 427, 445
McDonald v. Smith, 573
McKeiver v. Pennsylvania, 601–602, 610, 618
McNabb v. U.S., 371, 397
McNamara v. Moody, 549, 573
Melendez v. U.S., 413, 443
Mempa v. Rhay, 462, 478
MGM v. Grokster, 710, 738
Michigan Dept. of State Police v. Sitz, 262, 285
Michigan v. Lucas, 389, 399
Michigan v. Sitz, 265
Miller-El v. Cockrell, 387, 399
Mincey v. Arizona, 253, 284
Minnesota v. Carter, 248, 284
Minnesota v. Dickerson, 257, 285
Minnesota v. Murphy, 463, 478
Minnesota v. Olson, 248, 284
Minnick v. Mississippi, 270, 286
Miranda v. Arizona, 17, 30, 243, 271–275, 284, 286
Missouri v. Seibert, 276
Mistretta v. U.S., 409, 443
Montana v. Egelhoff, 154
Moore v. State, 447
Moran v. Burbine, 273, 286
Morrissey v. Brewer, 462, 478
Mullery v. Lewis, 573
Mu'Min v. Virginia, 383–384, 399
Murphy v. Florida, 398

## N

National Treasury Employees Union v. Von Raab, 263, 285, 321
Nebraska Press Association v. Stuart, 361, 367
New Jersey v. T.L.O., 604, 618
New York v. Belton, 251
New York v. Quarles, 251, 274, 286
Newman v. Alabama, 551, 573
Nix v. Whiteside, 352, 366
Nix v. Williams, 251, 274, 286

## O

O'Brien v. U.S., 573
Ohio v. Reiner, 390, 399
Oliver v. U.S., 251, 633, 656
Olmstead v. U.S., 277, 286
Oregon v. Harberts, 398
Oregon v. Mathiason, 286
Ornelas v. U.S., 251, 259, 261, 285
Overton v. Bazzetta, 549, 573

## P

Palmer v. Hudson, 573
Payne v. Tennessee, 423, 428, 442
Payton v. New York, 254, 264, 285
Payton v. U.S., 478
Pell v. Procunier, 546, 549, 573
Pennsylvania Board of Probation and Parole v. Scott, 462, 477
Pennsylvania Department of Corrections v. Yeskey, 554, 573
Pennsylvania v. Mimms, 285
Penry v. Johnson, 447
Penry v. Lynaugh, 447
People ex rel. O'Connell v. Turner, 585
People v. Deutsch, 266–267, 286
People v. Hall, 154
People v. Ponce, 658
People v. Robbins, 366
People v. Superior Court of San Diego—Romero, 416, 417
People v. Wende, 349
Pepperling v. Crist, 573
Philip Caruso, President of P.B.A. v. Benjamin Ward, Police Commissioner, 298, 321
Ponry v. Johnson, 436
Ponte v. Real, 557, 573
Porter v. Nussle, 284, 559, 574
Powell v. Alabama, 347, 366
Powers v. Ohio, 385, 386, 399
Poyner v. Murray, 436, 446
Press Enterprise Company v. Superior Court of California, 367
Preston v. U.S., 259, 285
Procunier v. Martinez, 549, 573

## R

Ratzlaf v. U.S., 646, 658
Reno v. ACLU, 287, 734, 741
Rhodes v. Chapman, 500, 521
Richards v. Wisconsin, 251, 253, 284

Richardson v. McKnight, 516, 523
Ring v. Arizona, 413, 435, 437, 442, 446
Rock v. Zimmerman, 274, 286
Roper v. Simmons, 428, 437, 447
Roth v. United States, 681
Ruiz v. Estelle, 551, 556, 572, 573

## S

Sandin v. Conner, 557, 558, 573
Santangelo v. State, 478
Santiago-Martinez v. U.S., 399
Santobello v. New York, 398
Schall v. Martin, 602, 618
Schlup v. Delo, 284, 428, 445
Schmerber v. California, 277, 286
Schriro v. Summerlin, 435, 446
Sell v. U.S., 377, 398
Semler v. Psychiatric Institute, 478
Silverthorne Lumber Co. v. U.S., 245–246, 276, 284
Skinner v. Railway Labor Executives' Association, 263, 264, 285
Smith v. Blackledge, 573
Smith v. Coughlin, 573
Smith v. Ohio, 258, 285
Smith v. Robbins, 349, 366
Smith v. Texas, 367
Sony Corporation of America v. Universal City Studios, Inc., 710, 738
South Dakota v. Neville, 275, 286
South Dakota v. Opperman, 259, 285
Stansbury v. California, 251, 254, 285
State of New Jersey v. Pedro Sato et al., 323
State of New York v. Smith, 122
State of Tennessee v. Charles Arnold Ballinger, 154
State v. Blocker, 154
State v. Fulminante, 286
State v. Kindle, 137, 154
State v. Stephenson, 154
State v. Stiffler, 154
Strauder v. West Virginia, 399
Strunk v. U.S., 382, 398
Sullivan v. Louisiana, 399
Summerlin v. Stewart, 435, 446
Swain v. Alabama, 399

## T

Tarter v. State of New York, 478
Taylor v. Sterrett, 573
Taylor v. Taintor, 397
Tennessee v. Garner, 306, 322
Terry v. Ohio, 251, 256, 285
Texas v. Cobb, 349–350, 366
Thiel v. Southern Pacific Co., 360, 367
Thompson v. County of Alameda, 478

Thompson v. Keohane, 251, 285
Thornton v. U.S., 251, 261, 285
Trop v. Dulles, 446, 447
Tuilaepa v. California, 435, 446
Turner v. Safley, 525

## U

United States v. American Library Association, 741
United States v. Booker, 411
United States v. Rodriguez, 443
U.S. Dept. of Justice v. Landano, 268, 286
U.S. v. 92 Buena Vista Ave., 649, 658
U.S. v. $4,255,625.39 in Currency, 658
U.S. v. Armstrong, 155
U.S. v. Arvizu, 257, 285
U.S. v. Bagley, 345, 366
U.S. v. Baldacchino, 398
U.S. v. Banks, 251, 255, 285
U.S. v. Barnes, 251
U.S. v. Booker, 414, 443
U.S. v. Borchardt, 259, 285
U.S. v. Brady, 246
U.S. v. Brainer, 398
U.S. v. Brawner, 146, 155
U.S. v. Brignoni-Ponce, 285
U.S. v. Carter, 155
U.S. v. Cotton, 414, 443
U.S. v. Dickerson, 272, 286
U.S. v. Dinitz, 399
U.S. v. Donahey, 398
U.S. v. Drayton, 264, 266, 286
U.S. v. Dunn, 251, 634, 657
U.S. v. Edwards, 251
U.S. v. Fanfan, 414
U.S. v. Felix, 150, 155
U.S. v. Flores-Montano, 266, 286
U.S. v. Gouveia, 573
U.S. v. Halper, 155
U.S. v. Harris, 286
U.S. v. Hazzard, 376, 398
U.S. v. Hill, 263, 285
U.S. v. Irizarry, 252
U.S. v. James Daniel Good Real Property, 649
U.S. v. Karo, 278, 286
U.S. v. Knights, 462, 477
U.S. v. Lee, 284
U.S. v. Lefkowitz, 284
U.S. v. Leon, 249, 251, 284
U.S. v. Lilly, 573
U.S. v. Martinez-Fuerte, 262, 285
U.S. v. Mendenhall, 251, 254, 285
U.S. v. Montalvo-Murillo, 376, 398
U.S. v. Montoya de Hernandez, 277, 286
U.S. v. Motamedi, 398
U.S. v. Nachtigal, 19, 30

U.S. v. Oakland Cannabis Buyers' Cooperative, 638, 657
U.S. v. Patane, 251, 276
U.S. v. Pohlot, 155
U.S. v. Rabinowitz, 247–248, 251, 284
U.S. v. Ready, 555, 573
U.S. v. Reardon, 398
U.S. v. Robinson, 256, 285
U.S. v. Ross, 251, 261, 285
U.S. v. Scott, 278, 287
U.S. v. Shabam, 154
U.S. v. Smith, 122
U.S. v. Sokolow, 257, 285
U.S. v. Steagald, 285
U.S. v. Taylor, 383, 398
U.S. v. Ursery, 649
U.S. v. Villamonte-Marquez, 263, 285
U.S. v. White, 278, 286

## V

Virginia v. Hicks, 633
Vitek v. Jones, 557, 573

## W

Warden v. Hayden, 251, 253, 284
Washington v. Harper, 554, 573, 574
Washington v. LeTourneau, 74
Watson v. U.S., 285
Weeks v. U.S., 244–245, 284
Welch v. State, 478
White v. Illinois, 391, 399
White v. Maryland, 397
Whren v. U.S., 261, 285
Wilkerson v. Utah, 434, 446
Wilson v. Arkansas, 251, 253, 261, 284
Wilson v. Seiter et al., 557, 573
Winston v. Lee, 276, 286
Witherspoon v. Illinois, 383, 398
Wolf v. Colorado, 247, 284
Wolff v. McDonnell, 556, 558, 573
Wong Sun v. U.S., 276
Woodson v. North Carolina, 435, 446
Wyler v. U.S., 323
Wyoming v. Houghton, 261, 285

## Y

Yarborough v. Alvarado, 251, 254, 285
Young v. Harper, 478

## Z

Zafiro v. U.S., 361, 367
Zipkin v. Mozan, 601

## A

Abadinsky, Howard, 656
Abdel-Rahman, Omar, 350, 351, 566, 568, 679
Abel, David, 323
Abraham, Yehuda, 662
Abrahamsen, David, 94, 114
Abreu, Elinor, 737
Acheson, Dean, 707
Acoca, L., 571
Adami, Jeffrey D., 560
Adams, Eric, 265, 266
Adams, Kenneth, 304–305, 568
Adams, Lorraine, 155
Aday, Ronald, 563
Adelman, Stanley E., 443
Adem, Khalid, 141
Adler, Freda, 109
Akers, Ronald L., 102, 115
Akhenaton, 406
al-Mujahir, Abdullah, 567
Al-Timimi, Ali, 681
Alexander, Howard, 593
Alfini, James, 399
Allen, Harry, 478
Alobied, Abdullah I., 665, 666
Alpert, Geoffrey P., 235, 305, 320, 322
Alvi, Amjad Farooq, 708
Alvi, Basit Farooq, 708
Aman, Reinhold, 528
Anderson, Marvin Lamond, 720
Anderson, Patricia, 125
Andrade, Leandro, 416
Andrews, Chryl, 619
Anshel, Mark H., 322
Anton, Jon, 553
Appleyard, David, 704
Arenella, Peter, 147, 155
Ares, C., 397
Arkin, Stanley S., 741
Armey, Dick, 124
Arnekley, Bruce J., 444
Arpaio, Joe, 497, 538
Arquilla, John, 700
Artest, Ron, 48
Ashcroft, John, 63, 174, 426, 431, 593, 604, 727
Asplen, Christopher H., 188
Asseo, Laurie, 574
Atassi, Karema, 26
Atick, Joseph, 735
Atkins, Laura, 127
Atta, Mohammed, 43
Atwater, Gail, 254
Augustus, John, 453, 477
Ault, Richard L., 115
Austin, James, 478, 523
Auten, Joe, 322
Ayala, Tony "El Torito," 470
Aziz, David W., 478

## B

Babcock, Charles L., 367
Babineck, Mark, 74
Babwin, Don, 364
Bach, Jonathan P., 443

Backover, Andrew, 73
Bacon, Sir Francis, 16, 703
Baden, Michael, 356
Bailey, W. C., 446
Baime, David, 433
Baird, Jeffrey W., 295
Baker, John S., Jr., 154
Bakley, Bonny Lee, 370, 371
Ball, J. C., 658
Ballinger, Charles, 142
Ballow, Deanna Bellew, 478
Banks, Delma, 345
Banks, Lashawn, 255
Banta, Carolyn, 658
Barker, Thomas, 293, 320
Barkett, Rosemary, 563
Barnes, Harry, 484
Barnes, Harry Elmer, 519
Barnes, Julie, 372
Barnes, Rowland, 328, 329
Baroska, Megan, 711
Barot, Dhiren, 214
Barrett, Heather, 522
Barrett, Kevin, 321
Barrett, Neil, 707
Bartollas, Clemens, 284, 519
Barton, Antigone, 311
Basri, Driss, 673
Bates, Eric, 523
Bates, Sanford, 477, 505
Batt, Rosemary, 553
Baum, Dan, 73
Baum, Katrina, 75
Bayley, David H., 186, 187, 189, 234, 297, 320
Bazemore, Gordon, 406
Bean, Roy, 162, 163
Beard, Jeff, 494, 518
Beardslee, Donald, 562
Beaumont, Gustave de, 488
Beccaria, Cesare, 86
Beck, Allen J., 477, 511, 520–523, 533, 571, 574, 655
Becker, Howard, 103, 116, 624, 656
Beckley, Alan, 733
Beckwith, Byron De La, 151
Bedau, Hugo Adam, 404, 442
Belknap, Joanne, 116, 571
Bell, Griffin, 472
Bell, Marsha, 311
Bellows, Randy, 130
Ben-Veniste, Richard, 688
Bender, Frank, 719
Bennett, C. Lee, 237
Bennett, Lawrence A., 478
Bennett, Richard, 320
Bennett, Wayne W., 232, 234
Bennett, William, 630, 632, 643
Benson, Michael L., 73, 365
Bentham, Jeremy, 86, 118, 120
Benton, Claudia, 43
Berk, Richard A., 188
Berkowitz, David, 43
Berkson, Larry, 399
Berlin, Louis, 477, 478
Bermudes, Gallardo, 624
Bernard, Thomas J., 48

Berry, Shawn Allen, 63
Bertillon, Alphonse, 715
Betterly, Laura, 127
Bible, Bobby, 6
Biden, Joseph R., Jr., 38
Big L., 80
bin Laden, Osama, 679, 685
Bioulac, B., 114
Birchmeister, Jason, 113
Biskupic, Joan, 155, 364
Bittner, Egon, 208, 209, 234
Bjeck, William, 188
Blachy, Paul H., 659
Black, Henry Campbell, 153, 154, 155
Black, Hugo, 338
Black, Morris, 358
Blake, Robert, 370, 371
Blecker, Robert, 438–440
Bligh, William, 485
Block, Sherman, 108, 314
Bloodsworth, Kirk, 723
Bloom, Barbara, 534, 571, 572
Bloomberg, Michael R., 196, 265, 720
Blumstein, Alfred, 510, 729
Bobbitt, John Wayne, 145
Bobbitt, Lorena, 145
Bogans, Genée, 475
Bohm, Robert M., 213, 235
Boland, Barbara, 398
Bolyard, Melissa, 478
Bonczar, Thomas P., 445, 520
Bonesana, Cesare, 529
Bonger, Willem, 107
Bonner, Raymond, 699
Booker, Freddie J., 412, 414
Bork, Robert, 243
Borland, Barbara, 366
Bossard, Andre, 667, 672, 697
Botsis, Alexander, 114
Bourque, Blair B., 619
Boutros-Ghali, Boutros, 683
Bowens, Matthew, 299
Bowker, Lee H., 532, 539, 571, 572
Bowles, Jennifer, 367
Boyce, Daniel, 700
Boyd, David G., 24
Boylard, Melissa, 523
Bradley, Donald, 75
Brady, Sarah, 76
Braithwaite, John, 418, 444
Brandau, Julie Ann, 328, 329
Branham, Lynn S., 520
Brannon, Joan G., 366
Braswell, Michael, 572
Bratton, William J., 196, 197, 295, 594
Bremer, L. Paul, 685
Brennan, William, 437
Brenner, Susan W., 737
Breslin, Jimmy, 624
Brewer, Lawrence Russell, 63
Breyer, Stephen G., 376, 411, 412, 428, 439, 442
Bridel, Laurent, 700
Brill, William, 100
Briseno, Theodore, 241
Brockway, Zebulon R., 490, 493, 518, 559, 570

Broder, David S., 520
Broder, John M., 30
Broderick, Mary, 348
Brown, Dan, 740
Brown, E., 520
Brown, Jodi M., 322, 456, 477
Brown, Joe, 418
Brown, Lee P., 646
Brown, Michael, 320
Brown, Nicole, 392
Brown, Robert, 81
Brown, Serena-Lynn, 114
Brownback, Sam, 706
Browne, A., 571
Browne, Angel, 534
Browne, Paul J., 266
Browning, Katharine, 116, 617
Brownmiller, Susan, 46, 74
Brucia, Carlie, 45, 452, 453
Bruder, Jessica, 179
Bruey, Judith, 677
Bryan, Darrell, 574
Bryant, Dot, 396
Bryant, Kobe, 389
Buckley, R. E., 114
Bucqueroux, Bonnie, 234
Buentello, S., 572
Buerger, Michael E., 736, 737, 740
Bugliosi, Vincent, 414
Bulzomi, Michael J., 741
Bundy, Ted, 43
Bunn, Matthew, 738
Burger, Warren E., 249, 335, 480
Burgess, Alan E., 115
Burgess, Ernest, 97, 115
Burgess, Robert L., 102, 115
Burnett, D. Graham, 368, 397
Burns, Tom, 310, 312
Burrell, Sharon, 321
Bursik, Robert J., Jr., 444
Burton, Preston, 130
Busby, Walter, 592
Bush, George H. W., 8, 63, 498
Bush, George W., 9, 10, 30, 44, 64, 66, 78,
        124, 128, 167, 340, 421, 431, 432,
        450, 524, 568, 676, 706, 723
Butler, Samuel, 440
Butterfield, Fox, 659
Butterworth, Bob, 501
Butts, Jeffrey A., 610, 614, 616, 619
Buzawa, Carl G., 76
Buzawa, Eve S., 76
Byrd, James, Jr., 63, 64
Byrne, James M., 477
Byrne, William, Jr., 272

### C

Cacheris, Plato, 130
Caldwell, Robert G., 617
Callahan, L. A., 154
Camp, Camille, 521
Camp, George, 521
Campbell, Terry, 387
Campbell, Ward, 439
Canedo, Rufina, 150
Cantor, Joanne, 113
Capra, James L., 631

Caracappa, Stephen, 292–293
Carbon, Susan, 399
Cardozo, Benjamin, 245
Carey, G., 565
Caringella-MacDonald, S., 116
Carlson, K. E., 444
Carlson, Norman, 472
Carollo, Joe, 345
Carpenter, Cheryl, 617
Carroll, Eric, 297–298
Carroll, Ron, 515, 522
Carte, Gene Edward, 31
Carter, David L., 218, 236, 237, 293, 320,
        737, 739
Carter, Lief H., 126, 153
Carter, Robert M., 521
Caruso, David, 359
Casey, Lee, 685
Casey, Thomas, 546
Casso, Anthony "Gaspipe," 292–293
Castro, Fidel, 673
Catalano, Shannan M., 75
Cattell, R. B., 114
Cauchon, Dennis, 521, 574
Cavan, Ruth Shonle, 617
Cavender, Gary, 113
Chai, Winston, 740
Chaiken, J. M., 76, 521
Chaiken, Marcia R., 76, 521, 617
Chambers, Breanna, 195
Chambers, James Paul, 195
Chambers, Robert, 139
Chambliss, William J., 107, 114, 116
Champion, Darl H., 187, 233
Champion, Marc, 699
Chandler, David, 632
Chandler, Raymond, 122
Chapman, Duane "Dog," 374
Chapman, Robert E., 232
Cheesman, F., 574
Chemerinsky, Erwin, 321
Chen, Dong Lu, 142
Chermak, Steven, 188
Cherry, Bobby Frank, 148
Chertoff, Michael, 688, 690
Chesney-Lind, Meda, 109
Chikatilo, Andrei, 43
Chiu, Tina, 616
Christ, Peter, 654
Christiansen, Karl, 114
Christopher, Liz, 70, 71
Cicero, 434
Clark, Cherie L., 478
Clark, Jacob R., 68
Clark, Ramsey, 295
Clark, Roger S., 698
Clark, Tom C., 343
Clarke, Caryl, 521
Clarke, Richard, 711
Clarke, Ronald V., 113
Clear, Todd, 506
Cleckley, Hervey M., 95, 114
Clegg, Jennifer, 503
Clemens, Kristi, 26
Clement, Mary Jeanette, 571
Clemmer, Donald, 526, 529, 570
Clines, Francis X., 739

Clinton, Bill, 66, 421, 725, 734
Cloward, Richard A., 100, 115, 526, 528,
        570, 587, 617
Clowers, Marsha, 537, 572
Clynch, Edward J., 365
Coburn, Tom, 681
Cohen, Albert K., 100, 115, 587, 617
Cohen, Anne, 307, 322
Cohen, David, 217, 218
Cohen, Howard, 236
Cohen, Jacqueline, 521
Cohen, L. E., 113
Cohen, Lawrence, 87
Cohen, Richard, 144, 153
Cohen, Robyn L., 477
Cohen, Thomas H., 153
Coke, Sir Edward, 139, 154
Coker, A. L., 571
Cole, David D., 265, 313, 323
Coleman, Howard C., 429
Coleman, Shannon, 419
Coles, Catherine M., 233
Collier, Patrick, 457
Collin, Barry, 680, 700
Collins, Larry, 239, 283
Conklin, John E., 115
Conley, Janet L., 447
Connor, Eugene "Bull," 228
Connors, Edward, 445, 740
Conrad, J. P., 521
Conroy, Robert, 522
Cook, Thomas J., 399
Cooper, Tab W., 323
Copeland, Larry, 678
Cornish, Derek B., 113
Coronado, Angel, 463
Correla, Mark E., 235
Cosby, William, 330
Costanza-Chock, Sasha, 552
Couey, John Evander, 452
Coulter, Ann, 681
Coventry, Garry, 523
Covington, Stephanie, 534, 571, 572
Cowper, Thomas J., 705, 713, 729, 736,
        737, 740
Cressey, Donald R., 321, 526, 545, 570, 572
Crews, Gordon A., 572
Cribbs, Arthur L., Jr., 81, 113
Crocker, Demetrius "Van," 677, 678
Crofton, Sir Walter, 489
Cronkite, Walter, 639
Crossen, Cynthia, 181
Culkin, Macaulay, 6
Cullen, Francis T., 73, 113
Cummings, Jerry, 562
Cunningham, Dennis, 517
Cunningham, Garrett, 568
Cunningham, William C., 184, 189

### D

Dabbs, J. M., Jr., 114
Dahmer, Jeffrey, 43
Dailey, Debra L., 520
Daley, Richard M., 13, 210, 235
Daley, Tony, 552
Dallent, Rick, 648
Daly, Kathleen, 109

Dardan, Christopher, 345
Darrow, Clarence, 382
Darwin, Charles, 89
Dash, Eric, 52
Dass, Ram, 116
Daufenbach, Donald, 67
Daunt, Tina, 321
Davies, Dani, 311
Davies, John G., 393
Davis, Alan J., 570
Davis, Allen Lee "Tiny," 436
Davis, Edward F., 321, 322
Davis, Kenneth Culp, 221, 236, 366
Davis, Kim L., 53
Davis, Lanae, 479
Davis, Robert C., 444
Davis, Russell M., 522
Dawoud, Khaled, 698
Day, David, 552
de Beaumont, Gustave, 519
de Guzman, Onel, 707
de Pommereau, Isabelle, 475
de Wit, Jan, 710
Deakin, Thomas J., 188
Deck, Ross, 635, 652, 659
Decker, S., 445, 446
DeFrances, Carol J., 350, 365, 366
del Carmen, Rolando V., 323, 478
DeLamatre, Mary, 106
della Cava, Marco R., 617
Delmore, Lois, 455
DeLorean, John, 149–150, 150
Delucchi, Alfred, 340, 342
Demjanjuk, John, 151
Demmitt, Joshua, 678
Denkowski, George C., 574
Denkowski, Kathryn M., 574
Denny, Reginald, 393
Dershowitz, Alan, 370
DesPortes, Betty Layne, 359
Deters, Joe, 142
Deutsch, Linda, 321
DeVetsco, Aldona, 430
Devine, Elizabeth, 359
DeWitt, Charles B., 618
Dezhbakhsh, Hashem, 431, 446
di Beccaria, Marchese, 529
Diallo, Amadou, 240, 241
Diaz, Mercedes, 624
Dickey, Walter, 417
Dietler, John W., 522
Dietz, Park, 144
DiGuido, Al, 127
DiIulio, John J., Jr., 74
Dinitz, Simon, 521, 739
DiPietro, A. Louis, 285
Disraeli, Benjamin, 14, 325
Distaso, Rick, 344
Ditton, Paula M., 408, 443, 574
Dix, George, 144
Dixon, Janice, 236
Dobson, Mark, 255
Dole, Bob, 87
Dolnick, Bernard, 320
Dorgan, Byron, 454, 455
Dorn, Roosevelt, 208
Doshi, Anil, 114

Dotson, Gary, 381
Douglas, Chuck, 250
Douglas, John E., 115
Douglas, William O., 338
Dowd, Michael, 294
du Pont, John E., 147
Duffy, Robert J., 234
Dufour, Henry E., 478
Dugas, Christine, 52, 741
Dugdale, Richard Louis, 90, 113
Duke, David, 474
Duncan, Gary, 359
Dunham, Roger G., 305, 322
Dunworth, Terence, 188
DuPont, Robert, 654
Duprat, Eric, 741
Duran, Victoria, 113
Durham, Alexis M., III, 617
Durkheim, Émile, 97, 115
Durose, Mathew R., 305, 322, 424, 444, 445
Durst, Robert, 358
Dwight, Louis, 488

### E

Earp, Wyatt, 163
Edgar, Timothy, 678
Edwards, Don, 438
Edwards, Edwin, 473
Edwards, Rob, 298
Eggen, Dan, 73, 74
Egger, Steven A., 74
Egley, Arlen, Jr., 617
Ehrenhalt, Samuel, 43
Einstadter, Werner, 113
Eisenstein, James, 365
Eisler, Peter, 738
el Fikey, Adel Mohammed, 698
El Nasser, Haya, 444
Elledge, William D., 428
Ellickson, Phyllis L., 617
Ellis, Carol S., 442
Ellis, Chip, 567
Ellis, Ralph D., 442
Elmardoudi, Abdel-Ilah, 696
Elwork, Amiram, 399
Engel, Robert Shepard, 236
Eppolito, Louis, 292
Epstein, Cynthia Fuchs, 237
Erickson, William H., 284
Erwin, Billie S., 478
Espinosa, Jack, Jr., 580
Esserman, Dean, 459
Estabrook, Arthur A., 90
Estes, Richard J., 618
Estey, Joseph G., 235
Etheridge, Jeffrey, 178
Etzioni, Amitai, 313, 323
Evers, Medgar, 151
Exum, David, 366

### F

50 Cent (Curtis Jackson), 80, 81
Fabelo, Tony, 17, 457, 565
Fabian, Sandy, 457
Fagan, Jeffrey, 445
Fairstein, Linda, 60

Fanfan, Ducan, 412
Faris, Lyman, 97
Farmer, Dee, 555
Farragher, Thomas, 323
Farrell, Amy, 320, 323
Farrell, Dan, 178
Farris, Edward A., 236
Faulds, Henry, 716
Fay, Michael, 483
Feeney, Tom, 412
Feinstein, Dianne, 421, 444
Feld, Barry C., 619
Feldman, M. P., 115
Felson, Marcus, 87, 113
Ferguson, Colin, 349
Ferracuti, Franco, 100, 115
Ferreira, Antonio, 550
Fessler, Donald R., 235
Fettig, Jennifer, 299
Fiatal, Robert A., 287
Field, Stephen J., 338
Fielding, Fred F., 688
Fielding, Henry, 162
Fields, Cleo, 504
Fields, Gary, 523
Figlio, Robert, 617
Filipazzo, Chris, 37
Finkelhor, David, 618
Finley, James, 488
Finn, Peter, 444
Firstbrook, Peter, 738
Fishbein, Diana H., 114
Fisher, Barry, 359
Fisher, Cher, 653
Flango, Carol R., 364
Fleissner, Dan, 100
Flemming, Roy B., 365
Flowers, Ronald Berri, 74
Flynn, Daniel W., 235
Fong, Robert S., 572
Foote, Robert D., 739
Fordice, Kirk, 403
Forliti, Amy, 617
Forst, B. E., 446
Forsyth, Robert, 298
Foster, Burk, 574
Fou, Henny, 653
Fountain, John W., 442
Fowler, Orson Squire, 113
Fowler, Tiffany, 50
Fox, James Alan, 39, 40, 44, 74, 592
Fox, Sanford, 616
Fox, Vernon, 572
France, Mike, 124
Frankel, Bruce, 700
Franklin, Benjamin, 430, 487
Free, Marvin, Jr., 47, 48
Freeman, Abdul-Maalik, 731
Freeman, Sultaana, 731
Freud, Sigmund, 93–94, 114, 627
Friday, Paul, 698
Fridell, Lorie, 320
Friedman, Leon, 29
Friedman, Robert, 37
Friel, Charles M., 472
Fritsch, Jane, 366
Fry, Lincoln J., 574

Fualuaau, Vili, 46
Fuhrman, Mark, 151–152
Fukuyama, Francis, 151, 155
Funke, Gail S., 518, 522
Fuqua, Jerry W., 522
Fyfe, James, 307, 322

## G

Gaes, Gerald G., 519
Gaffigan, Stephen J., 321
Galicia, Kenys, 732
Gall, Franz Joseph, 88
Gallagher, Mary P., 446
Galloway, Joseph L., 570
Galton, Sir Francis, 716, 739
Gandolfini, James, 66
Garcia, Crystal A., 478
Garczynski, John T., Jr., 307
Gardner, Bethany, 619
Garland, David, 442
Garner, Joel H., 322
Garrett, James, 148
Garrett, Pat, 163
Garrison, Carole G., 237
Garry, Eileen M., 617
Gates, Daryl, 241, 243, 423
Gatright, Mandell, 242
Gauger, Gary, 428
Gelbard, Robert S., 673, 699
Geller, William, 322
Gelsthorpe, Loraine, 75, 116
Gendreau, Paul, 501, 521
Geragos, Mark, 340, 342, 349
Gerber, Jurg, 699
Gertz, Marc G., 398
Giallombardo, Rose, 528, 537, 572
Giannangelo, Stephen J., 74
Gibbons, Don C., 116
Gibbons, John H., 722
Gibbons, John J., 568
Gibson, Gail, 320
Gifford, Sidra Lea, 572
Gill, Peter, 739
Gima, Lance, 724
Gingrich, Newt, 92, 403
Ginsburg, Ruth Bader, 411
Giordano, Kevin, 419
Giovannitti, Arturo, 481
Girard, Stephen, 163
Gitenstein, Mark H., 709
Giuliani, Rudolph W., 11, 214, 654
Glamser, Deeann, 598
Glaze, Lauren E., 477
Glover, Philip, 553
Glover, Scott, 321
Goddard, Henry Herbert, 90, 113
Godwin, Tracy M., 619
Goffman, Erving, 526, 570
Goggin, Claire, 501, 521
Goldberg, Andrew L., 236, 237
Golden, Tisjé, 178
Goldkamp, John S., 659
Goldman, D., 565
Goldman, Roger, 284
Goldman, Ronald, 392
Goldsmith, Michael, 658
Gomes, Jesse J., 465

Gondles, James A., Jr., 499, 518
Gonzales, Alberto, 27, 30, 413
Goodbody, William L., 235
Goodstadt, Michael S., 651, 659
Goodstein, Laura, 442
Goos, Eugene, 296
Gordon, Corey L., 100
Goring, Charles, 89
Gorman, P., 116
Goss, Porter J., 664, 682, 690, 697
Gotsch, Kara, 552
Gottfredson, Michael, 115
Gowen, Darren, 478
Grabenhorst, Katey, 553
Grabosky, Peter, 707, 737
Graczyk, Michael, 446
Graham, Fred P., 30
Graham-Rowe, Duncan, 733
Gramm, Phil, 9
Grammer, Lon, 50
Granick, Jennifer, 730
Grant, Nancy K., 237
Grasmick, Harold G., 444
Grebmeier, Joe, 262
Green, John, 48
Green, Tom, 24–25
Greenberg, David F., 107, 115, 116, 498, 521
Greene, Jack R., 235
Greene, Judith, 445
Greenfeld, Lawrence A., 442, 443, 571, 572
Greenhouse, Linda, 286, 398, 412, 478
Greenstein, Theodore, 320
Greenwood, Billy, 633
Gresso, Tom, 70, 71
Grey, Robert, 354
Grey, Robert J., Jr., 360
Griswold, Esther, 479
Grizzle, G. A., 521
Gropper, Bernard A., 658
Gross, Mortimer, 91
Gross, Samuel R., 381, 398
Grossman, Elliot, 616
Groth, A. Nichols, 74
Groves, W. Byron, 116
Gruhl, John, 366
Grunwell, Rachel, 77
Guevara, Eugene, 561
Gugliociello, Taralee, 179
Guinier, Lani, 47
Gulick, Kristi, 739

## H

Haarr, Robin N., 322
Habre, Hissene, 673
Hackett, Judith C., 523
Haff, Thomas, 472
Hagan, Frank, 58, 73, 75
Hagan, John, 47, 48
Hale, C. D., 233, 234
Hall, Andy, 522
Hall, John C., 322
Hall, Mimi, 682
Hall, Nathan, 136
Hameed, Moinuddeen Ahmed, 662
Hamilton, Alexander, 339
Hamilton, Andrew, 330
Hamilton, James, 266

Hamilton, Lee H., 688
Hammer, Heather, 618
Hamowy, Ronald, 659
Hampton, Tracy, 356
Handelman, Dan, 311
Haney, Judith, 568
Hanks, Tom, 540
Hanrahan, Kathleen J., 477
Hanson, R., 574
Hanssen, Robert, 129, 130
Harberts, Scott Dean, 382
Harcourt, Bernard E., 233
Harden, Blaine, 323
Hardenbergh, Don, 364
Hardyman, Patricia L., 504, 521
Harlow, Caroline Wolf, 76, 366, 571
Harper, Larry, 354
Harrell, Adele V., 100, 616
Harris, Dave, 344
Harris, David, 323
Harris, Eric, 583
Harris, John F., 124
Harris, Mary Belle, 537
Harrison, David, 48
Harrison, Paige M., 511, 520–523, 533, 571, 574, 655
Harrison, Tracie, 210
Hart, H. L. A., 404, 442
Hart, Timothy C., 177, 321, 477
Hartmann, Francis X., 234
Hartnett, S. M., 234
Hassan, Mehdi, 665
Hassine, Victor, 570
Hatch, Orrin, 425, 432
Hawkins, Gordon, 627, 656
Hawley, C., 114
Hawthorne, Nathaniel, 484
Hayden, Michael, 690
Hayes, Laurence, 428
Hayeslip, David W., 322
Haynes, Terrance, 277
Hayworth, J. D., 719
Hazelrigg, Lawrence, 570
Hazelwood, Robert R., 115
Heffernan, Esther, 537–539, 572
Heinzelmann, Fred, 100
Held, James, 178, 179
Helihy, Jim, 320
Heller, Emily, 153
Hemmett, Theodore M., 574
Henderson, Thomas A., 332–333, 364, 399
Henry, Stuart, 111, 113
Henry, Vincent E., 233
Hensley, Christopher, 572
Herman, Madelynn, 396
Herrnstein, Richard J., 92, 113, 114
Herschel, William, 716
Hess, Karen M., 187, 188, 232, 234
Hickman, Matthew J., 189, 226, 227, 235, 236, 237, 321, 713, 716, 717
Hickok, "Wild Bill," 163
Higgins, Christopher S., 217–218
Hill, D., 113
Hill, Gerald, 153, 320
Hill, John, 323
Hill, Kathleen, 153, 320
Hillbrand, Marc, 114, 739

Hillsman, Sally T., 445
Hilton, Bryant, 553
Hirschhorn, Robert, 358
Hirschi, Travis, 102, 115
Hitler, Adolf, 96
Hockstader, Lee, 698
Hodgson, Jim, 232
Hoeven, John, 455
Hoffer, Abram, 92, 114
Holden, John P., 738
Holland, Gale, 522
Hollenhorst, Pam Stiebs, 417
Holmes, John, 516
Holmes, Oliver Wendell, Jr., 90, 132, 154
Holms, Stephen T., 235
Homant, Robert J., 322
Hone, Brian, 114
Honecker, Robert, 678
Hooper, Michael K., 187, 233
Hooton, Earnest A., 89
Hoover, J. Edgar, 131
Hoover, Timothy, 509
Hope, Larry, 545
Hopkins, Anthony, 87
Horan, David, 181
Hormann, Jeffrey S., 740
Hornberger, Jacob, 734
Hornoff, Scott, 568
Hornych, Kristina Lynn, 382
Horraiz, Domingo S., 519
Hostetler, David, 418
Houdek, Duane, 455
Householder, Jason, 418
Howard, John, 485, 519
Howell, Lamar, 140
Howlett, Debbie, 13
Hubbard, James, 562
Hubbell, Gaylord B., 489–490
Huberman, Ron, 13
Huddleston, Jack, 427
Hudson, Donald C., 379
Huff, C. Ronald, 617
Hughes, Charles Evans, 350
Hughes, Timothy A., 459, 477, 520
Hughes, William J., 741
Huizinga, David, 617
Hume, David, 24
Humphrey, John A., 445
Humphries, D., 116
Hunt, Jim, 9
Hunter, Robert J., 522
Hunzeker, Donna, 443
Hurst, Lisa, 739
Hussein, Saddam, 120, 673
Hyde, Henry, 444, 649

**I**

Iler, Robert, 582
Inciardi, James A., 479, 659, 700
Ingram, Dexter, 712
Irwin, John, 528, 570
Isaacson, Walter, 565
Israel, Fred L., 29

**J**

Jackson, Bryant, 48
Jackson, Curtis "50 Cent," 80, 81

Jackson, Jesse L., 27, 30
Jackson, Melodie, 40
Jackson, Michael, 6
Jackson, Robert H., 17, 345
Jackson, Stephen, 48
Jacobs, James B., 656
Jacobs, K. J., 113
Jacobs, Patricia, 91, 113
Jacobs, Pearl, 237
Jacobson, Jay, 598
Jaggi, Jasjit, 541
Jam Master Jay, 80
James, Doris J., 521, 522
Janklow, Bill, 121, 123
Jaschan, Sven, 71
Jay, John, 343
Jefferson, Thomas, 10, 726
Jeffreys, Alec J., 429, 720, 739
Jensen, Eric L., 699
Johnson, Anna, 367
Johnson, Anthony, 48
Johnson, B. D., 617
Johnson, Byron, 522
Johnson, Elmer H., 665, 666
Johnson, Frank M., 546
Johnson, Gary E., 620, 655
Johnson, Jeffrey, 113
Johnson, Kevin, 26, 320, 594, 737
Johnson, Tamara N., 260
Johnson, Thomas A., 616
Johnson-Bey, Dorsie, 427
Jones, David Allen, 430
Jones, Michael, 478, 523
Jones, Ron, 497
Jones, Tim R., 321
Jordan, B. K., 571
Jordan, Lamar, 76
Jordan, Robert J., 236
Jurik, Nancy C., 230, 237

**K**

Kaczynski, Theodore, 43, 679
Kahan, Dan, 418
Kahn, Ali S., 738
Kalish, Carol B., 698
Kallikak, Martin, 90
Kang, Wei, 619
Kaplan, John, 659
Kappeler, Victor E., 233, 320, 398
Karberg, Jennifer C., 520
Karp, David, 616
Karper, Laurence P., 739
Kassebaum, G., 537, 572
Katzenbach, Nicholas, 568
Kean, Thomas H., 688
Kearns, William D., 522
Keenan, Kate, 106
Keil, Thomas J., 446
Keizer, Gregg, 738
Kelley, Barbara Tatem, 106
Kelley, Douglas M., 223
Kelley, Richard, 314
Kelling, George L., 100, 188, 210, 233, 234
Kellner, R., 114
Kelly, Raymond W., 196, 197, 218, 265
Kelly, Tom, 265

Kendrick, Kevin, 172
Kennedy, Anthony M., 411
Kennedy, Daniel B., 322
Kennedy, David M., 188
Kennedy, Edward, 472
Kennedy, John F., 122, 153
Kenney, Dennis Jay, 320, 322
Kerik, Bernard B., 566, 567
Kerle, Ken, 513, 523
Kerper, Hazel B., 477
Kerrey, Bob, 688
Kershaw, Sarah, 312
Kessler, David, 188
Kevorkian, Jack, 349
Khoshruy, Ali Reza, 667
Killgore, Rob, 552, 553
Killinger, George C., 477
Kimball, Peter, 572
King, John William, 63, 64
King, Martin Luther, Jr., 129, 153
King, Patricia Ann, 458
King, Rodney, 8, 15, 207, 240–241, 392
King, Ryan S., 417
Kingston, Kimberly A., 284
Kirkland, Michael, 399, 618
Klaus, Patsy, 75
Klebold, Dylan, 583
Kleck, G., 443
Klockars, Carl B., 293, 320
Klosse, Tim, 553
Knight, Tavaris, 580
Knights, Mark James, 462
Knoller, Marjorie, 136
Knopp, F. H., 116
Koestler, Arthur, 445, 446
Kohfeld, C., 445, 446
Kohlmann, Evan, 711
Koon, Stacey, 241
Koop, C. Everett, 59
Koresh, David, 8–9, 676
Koscheski, Mary, 572
Koubriti, Karim, 696
Kournikova, Anna, 710
Kozlowski, L. Dennis, 64
Krajick, Kevin, 188
Kramer, Robert, 127
Krane, Jim, 574
Krar, William, 677
Krastev, Nikola, 737
Krisberg, Barry, 98
Kurland, Philip B., 29
Kurre, Dennis G., 739
Kurtz, Paul, 712
Kyl, Jon, 421

**L**

Lab, Steven P., 233, 617
Lacayo, Richard, 284
Lafer, Gordon, 553
LaFree, Gary, 19, 59
Lagrone, Edward Lewis, 434
LaGuer, Benjamin, 432
Lait, Matt, 321
Lake, Anthony, 11
Lakhani, Hemant, 662
Lambreth, John, 323
Lampert, Robert O., 574

# NAME INDEX

Langan, Patrick A., 322, 424, 444, 445, 456, 477, 479
Langer, William, 96
Langworthy, Robert H., 195, 233
Lapidus, Lenora, 535, 571
Lapierre, Dominique, 239, 283
Lappin, Harley, 509
Laqueur, Walter, 694
Larin, Alexander, 663
Larkin, Dan, 70
Latessa, Edward J., 113
Lathrop, Sam W., 320, 322
Latzer, Barry, 439
Laub, John H., 104, 116
Laws, D. R., 114
Lawsky, David, 520
Leahy, Patrick, 432, 439, 440, 568
Lederer, Fred, 394
Lederman, Cindy S., 614, 619
Lee, Beverly N. W., 444
Lee, Chisun, 366
Lee, Gregory D., 443
Lee, Matthew T., 30
Lefkow, Joan Humphrey, 328
Lehman, John F., 688
Leibrock, Larry R., 283
Leinwand, Donna, 637, 641
Lemert, Edwin M., 116
Lemonick, Michael D., 565
Leno, Jay, 6
Lersch, Kim Michelle, 320
Lesher, Dave, 419
LeTourneau, Mary Kay, 46
Levesque, Thomas, 372
Levin, Bernard H., 219, 236, 403
Levin, David J., 444, 479
Levin, Jennifer, 139
Levine, James P., 478
Levine, Ned, 233
Lewin, Tamar, 417
Lewis, C. S., 449
Lewis, Chris, 127
Lewis, Judith, 202
Lewis, Peter, 189
Libeskind, Daniel, 7
Lieberman, Donna, 265
Liebman, James, 430, 445
Liewellyn, Barbara, 359
Lilly, Robert, 698
Lincoln, Abraham, 293, 356
Lindlaw, Scott, 76
Lippman, Matthew, 698
Liptak, Adam, 365
Lipton, Douglas, 443
Liscouski, Robert, 712
Litan, Avivah, 738
Litras, Marika F. X., 366
Little, Tracy, 501, 521
Littmann, Jonathan, 736
Lloyd, Caola, 434
Locke, Michelle, 445
Lockwood, Daniel, 570
Locy, Toni, 235, 738
Loeber, Rolf, 106
Lomax, William, 311, 312
Lombard, Louis, 88
Lombardo, Lucien X., 540, 572

Lombroso, Cesare, 88–89
Long, Harold, 528
Lott, George, 353
Love, Courtney, 415
Lovrich, Nicholas P., 235
Lowery, Henry Berry, 163
Lucas, Henry Lee, 43
Lunde, Sarah, 452
Lunsford, Jessica, 452
Lurigio, Arthur J., 444
Lyman, Michael D., 656
Lynam, Donald R., 659
Lynch, David J., 699
Lynch, Michael J., 116

## M

Maakestad, William J., 73
Mabrey, Daniel, 673, 697
Mackay, Peta, 320
MacKenzie, Doris L., 478
Macko, Michael, 566
Maclin, Tracey, 265
MacNamara, Donal E. J., 519, 520
Maconochie, Alexander, 488–489, 490
Madigan, Nick, 30
Magallanes, Jose, 700
Maghan, Jess, 567, 574
Magris, David, 429
Maguin, E., 571
Maguire, Kathleen, 522
Maher, Richard J., 478
Mahoney, Barry, 377, 397, 445
Maines, Nicole, 580
Major, Aline K., 617
Major, Roydon Dale, 426
Malm, Cindy, 515
Malpass, Roy S., 740
Malveaux, Suzanne, 73
Malvo, Lee Boyd, 43
Mandeville, Meghan, 575
Maniscalco, Salvatore, 175
Mann, Coramae Richey, 47, 48
Mann, Lisa Pollock, 127
Manning, Anita, 657
Mannion, Kevin, 179
Manson, Charles, 43, 79, 95
Mantovani, Andrew, 704
Maple, Jack, 196
Marasis, Etienne, 320
Marble, Lynn, 619
Mariner, Joanne, 571
Markon, Jerry, 154
Marks, Howard, 731
Marquardt, Philip, 343
Marquez, Ethan, 189
Marquis, Joshua, 359
Marsh, Ray Brent, 464
Marshall, Eric, 299
Marshall, John, 338
Marshall, Thurgood, 341
Martin, Glenn, 218
Martin, John S., Jr., 233
Martin, Keith, 575
Martin, Susan Ehrlich, 230, 237
Martinez, Ramiro, Jr., 30
Martinez, Roberto, 272
Martinez-Flores, Luis, 732

Martinson, Robert M., 443, 495, 520
Maruschak, Laura M., 571, 574
Marx, Karl, 107
Masella, Joe, 543
Masters, Brooke A., 76
Masters, Roger D., 114
Masterson, Bat, 163
Mattar, Mohamed Y., 698
Matza, David, 103, 116
Mauer, Marc, 416, 417
Mauli, Samuel, 76
Mawson, A. R., 113
Maxwell, Christopher D., 322
May, Robert L., II, 522
Mayne, Richard, 163
Mayo, Louis A., 166
Mays, G. Larry, 522
Mazerolle, Lorraine, 233
McAdams, John, 439, 440
McBride, D., 76
McBride, Stirling, 70
McCabe, Robert, 546
McCall, Nathan, 113
McCampbell, Susan W., 515, 522
McCarthy, Andy, 566
McCarthy, Jack, 738
McClellan, Paul, 738
McCloskey, Patrick L., 154, 155, 367
McCorkle, Richard C., 59, 75
McCormack, William U., 323, 398
McCowen, Christopher M., 429
McCrory, Mark, 593
McCulloch, Duncan J., 522
McDermott, James, 650
McDevitt, Jack, 320, 323
McDonald, Douglas C., 444, 445, 478
McDonald, Phyllis P., 321, 616, 619
McDonough, Molly, 399
McDoweel, Bryan, 70
McEwen, Thomas, 188
McFarland, Sheena, 75
McGarrell, Edmund F., 188
McGee, Jim, 155
McGee, Richard A., 521
McGinn, Ricky, 432
McGwire, Mark, 630
McIlvaney, William, 325
McInnis, Mac, 403
McKay, Henry D., 97, 115, 587
McKee, Mike, 366
McKinney, William, 555
McLaren, Roy Clinton, 237
McMahon, Patrick, 208
McMurray, Harvey L., 522
McNulty, Paul, 593
McQuillan, Laurence, 30
McQuiston, Dawn E., 740
McVeigh, Timothy, 43, 193, 348, 349, 423, 433, 676
Mead, George Herbert, 111
Meddis, Sam Vincent, 235, 657
Medina, Petro, 436
Mednick, Sarnoff, 92
Mefford, Larry, 218
Melias, Robert, 721
Melton, Terry, 359
Menke, Ben A., 522

Mennel, Robert M., 616
Merlo, A., 571
Merton, Robert K., 97–98, 115
Messinger, Sheldon L., 527, 570
Michaelson, Dick, 300
Michalowski, Raymond J., 109, 116
Miethe, Terance D., 59, 75
Miller, B., 571
Miller, Charles E., III, 322
Miller, Laurence, 114
Miller, Michael, 417
Miller, Rod, 515
Miller, Sarah, 136
Miller, Thomas, 312
Miller, Walter B., 100, 115, 617
Mills, Gregory, 188
Mills, Shari, 114
Mills, William Reginald, 522
Milovanovic, Dragan, 111
Minor, Willie, 562
Mintz, Robert, 519
Miranda, Ernesto, 272
Mirowsky, John, 98, 115
Miscikowski, Cindy, 295
Mitchell, Ojmarrh, 610, 614, 619
Mitnick, Kevin, 704, 706–707
Mitra, Rajib, 678
Mixon, Taquita, 402
Mizell, Jason "Jam Master Jay", 80
Moffitt, Bob, 43
Mogulescu, Sara, 616
Mohammed, Sayed, 640
Mohr, Kevin, 352
Mollen, Milton, 294
Monahan, John, 81, 521
Monahan, Tom, 312
Montague, David, 434
Montesquieu, 119
Montgomery, Reid H., 572
Moore, Blanche, 562
Moore, John, 594
Moore, Mark, 658
Moore, Mark H., 197, 234, 235
Morash, Marry, 322
Morgenbesser, Leonard, 572
Moriarty, Laura J., 739
Morris, Allison, 75, 116
Morris, Norval, 35, 73, 114, 188
Morris, Robert, 708
Morse, Jeffrey, 379
Moschella, William, 432
Moss, Desda, 235
Mote, Carrie, 455
Motivans, Mark, 658
Moua, Thai Chia, 141
Moussaoui, Zacarias, 349
Mubarak, Hosni, 568
Mueller, Gerhard O. W., 698
Mueller, Robert S., III, 171, 174–176, 188,
    219, 682, 690
Muhammad, 665
Muhammad, John Allen, 43
Mullins, Ed, 37
Mumola, Christopher J., 625, 656
Munsterman, Janice, 616, 619
Murphy, Kim, 365

Murphy, Patrick V., 104, 157, 170,
    180, 318
Murphy, S. L., 617
Murray, Frank J., 740
Murrow, Edward R., 307
Musgrave, Jane, 320
Musheno, Michael C., 478
Musto, David, 656
Myers, Don, 518
Myers, Lisa, 566

N

Nagel, Brian K., 704
Nardulli, Peter F., 365
Nash, LeRoy, 562, 563
Negroponte, John, 690
Neighbors, William D., 284
Nelson, E. Kim, 521
Nelson, Shawn, 52
Nelson, W. Raymond, 522
Nettler, Gwynn, 94, 112, 114, 115, 675, 700
Neubauer, David W., 365
Neuborne, Burt, 327
Neufeld, Peter, 430, 445
Newman, G., 116
Newton, Jim, 321
Newton, Ronna, 553
Nichols, Brian, 328, 329
Nichols, Terry, 676
Nicholson, Jack, 87
Niesse, Mark, 37
Nieves, Evelyn, 633
Niles, Lorenzo, 113
Nissenbaum, Dion, 417
Nixon, Richard, 629
Noel, Robert, 136
Nolan, Joseph R., 153, 154, 155
Nolan-Haley, Jacqueline M., 153, 154, 155
Noorzai, Bashir, 681, 682
Norris, Edward T., 291–292
Notorious B.I.G., 80, 295
Novak, Viveca, 284
Nowell, Paul, 52
Nunn, Annetta, 228
Nurco, D. N., 658
Nyhan, David, 630

O

Obert, Ron, 398
O'Brien, Timothy L., 699
Ocampo, Luis Moreno, 672
O'Connell, Daniel, 585
O'Connell, John J., 739
O'Connor, Sandra Day, 11, 332, 364, 411,
    413, 416
O'Driscoll, Patrick, 31
O'Grady, Ellen, 164
O'Hanlon, Ann, 519
Ohlin, Lloyd E., 100, 115, 587, 617
O'Keefe, Michael, 277, 283
Oliver, Willard M., 234
Olson, Theodore B., 68
Olson, William J., 683
O'Neal, Jermaine, 48
Onstott, David, 452
Oran, Daniel, 153, 385

Orcutt, James D., 115
O'Rourke, P. J., 420
Osborne, Erma, 200
Osborne, Larry, 439
Osborne, Robert, 522
O'Shea, Tim, 678
Ostrom, B., 574
Ottley, Ted, 233
Ouderkirk, John, 393
Ovando, Javier Francisco, 295
Owen, Barbara, 534, 571
Owens, Compton, 321
Owens, Dan, 407–408

P

Packer, Herbert L., 23, 31, 34
Padilla, Jose, 567
Pagon, Santos, 554
Paitakes, John, 472
Palla, Seri, 477
Paller, Alan, 70
Pallone, Nathaniel J., 114, 739
Palmiero, Rafael, 630
Palmiotto, Michael J., 293, 320
Pardo-Hastings, J. Sippa, 718
Parent, Dale G., 443, 619
Park, Robert E., 97, 115
Parker, Alisha, 125
Parker, Donn, 702
Parker, Laura, 154
Parker, William H., 24
Parks, Bernard, 295
Parks, Roger B., 235
Parks, William R., II, 211
Parris, Edward A., 31
Pastore, Ann L., 522
Patni, Naren, 553
Patrick, Sarah, 70
Patterson, Kelsey, 437
Paulsen, Derek J., 100
Pavlov, Ivan, 93
Pearson, Jessica, 479
Pearson, Karl, 89
Pease, Susan E., 114
Peay, Jill, 115
Peel, Sir Robert, 160, 162, 163, 192,
    198, 289
Pelham, Camdem, 187, 482, 518
Pellens, Mildred, 656
Pellicano, Anthony, 152
Pennington, Richard, 37
Pepinsky, Harold E., 108, 116
Perez, Jacob, 375
Perez, Rafael, 295
Perrotta, Tom, 367
Perry, David, 429
Perry, Frank L., 293, 320
Perry, Rick, 436, 437
Peternoster, Raymond, 442
Peters, Roger H., 522
Petersilia, Joan, 418, 444, 445, 475, 478, 479
Peterson, Joseph L., 366
Peterson, Laci, 44, 340, 342
Peterson, Ruth D., 47, 48
Peterson, Scott, 14, 340, 342
Phalen, Thomas, 562, 563

Phelps, Margie J., 572
Phillips, Charles D., 521
Pichardo, Ernesto, 141
Pike, Albert, 341
Pinizzotto, Anthony J., 321, 322
Pino, Jorge, 192
Pironti, John, 711
Pitchfork, Colin, 429
Piutau, Taufui, 141
Pizzi, Michael A., Jr., 520
Platt, Anthony, 585, 616
Pollak, Otto, 109
Pollitt, Mark M., 680, 700
Pollock, J., 571
Potok, Mark, 677, 678
Potter, Gary W., 656
Potts, Dennis W., 665, 666, 698
Powell, Laurence, 241
Poydasheff, Bob, 304
Prenzler, Tim, 320
Pressler, Margaret Webb, 657
Preszler, Alan, 322
Price, Barbara R., 187
Procup, Robert, 558
Provine, Doris Marie, 365
Pryor, Donald E., 398
Purnell, Sherelle, 417, 418
Puro, Steven, 284
Puzzanchera, Charles M., 618, 619

## Q

Qazi, Khalid, 26
Quetelet, Lambert Adolphe Jacques, 739
Quigley, John, 37
Quiles, Jessica, 650
Quinlan, J. Michael, 498, 520
Quinney, Richard, 107, 108, 116

## R

Rabin, Albert I., 115
Rada, R. T., 114
Rader, Dennis, 43
Rafsanjani, Hashemi, 673
Rafter, Nicole, 88, 112
Rai, Mukesh, 142
Raine, Adrian, 114
Rainille, Gerald, 375
Rainville, Gerard, 36, 397
Rakoff, Jed, 439
Ramirez, Deborah, 320, 323
Ramshaw, Emily, 40
Rand, Ayn, 732, 737
Rankin, A., 397
Rantala, Ramona R., 738
Rashbaum, William K., 197, 218, 234
Ratner, Michael, 351
Rauch, Janine, 320
Reagan, Mike, 553
Reagan, Ronald, 8, 66, 146, 498, 630
Reaves, Brian A., 36, 177, 189, 226, 227,
    235, 236, 237, 321, 375, 397, 477,
    713, 716, 717
Reckless, Walter C., 102, 115
Reese, James T., 115
Regan, Brian P., 129
Rehnquist, William H., 340, 411, 413, 427

Reichel, Philip, 619
Reid, Richard, 567
Reimer, Hans, 526, 570
Reisig, Michael D., 235
Reiss, A., 114
Reiss, Albert J., Jr., 565
Remsburg, Helen, 741
Reno, Janet, 9, 231, 422
Renteln, Alison Dundes, 141, 142
Renzema, Marc, 479
Resendiz, Angel Maturino, 43
Reynolds, Dan, 198
Reynolds, K. Michael, 235
Reynolds, Mike, 416
Rheinstein, Max, 698
Rich, Thomas F., 740
Rideau, W., 570
Rider, A. O., 115
Ridge, Tom, 214, 688
Ridgway, Gary L., 43
Rifkind, Simon H., 445
Rigas, John, 64
Rigas, Timothy, 64
Riggs, Joanne, 179
Riley, Bob, 562
Riley, Jack, 40
Rinaldi, Catherine A., 265
Ring, Timothy, 437
Ringwalt, Christopher L., 659
Rivers, Hosea, 580
Robel, Christy, 53
Robel, Jake, 53
Roberts, John G., Jr., 250, 340
Roberts, Pat, 682
Roberts, Thad, 50
Robinson, Charles Scott, 408
Robinson, Laurie, 76, 665, 673, 699
Robinson, Matthew B., 100
Rodriguez, Alfonso, Jr., 454–455
Rodriguez, Gilberto, 639
Rodriguez, Jose Luis, 624
Rodriguez, Matt L., 235, 740
Rodriguez, Miguel, 639
Roen, Sara, 237
Rogers, Raymond "Freaky Tah," 80
Ronfeldt, David, 700
Roosevelt, Eleanor, 16
Roosevelt, Teddy, 164
Rosazza, Tom, 523
Rose, Alan, Sr., 563
Rosencrance, Linda, 737
Rosenthal, Harry F., 367
Rosenwald, Michael S., 40
Roske, Randall, 255
Ross, Bart, 328
Ross, Catherine E., 98, 115
Rossi, Richard Michael, 343
Roth, J., 114
Roth, Jeffrey A., 565, 656
Rothwax, Harold J., 30, 355, 392, 399
Rottman, David B., 364
Rowan, Charles, 163
Rowan, Joseph R., 515
Rowland, John G., 121, 123
Rozek, Dan, 398

Rubin, H. Ted, 364
Rubin, Paul, 446
Rubin, Rita, 76
Rudolph, Eric Robert, 380, 679
Rumsfeld, Donald, 682
Rush, Benjamin, 430, 487
Russell, Freya, 443
Russell, Katheryn K., 47, 48
Russell, Michael J., 465
Rutledge, Devallis, 285
Ryan, George, 428, 430, 440
Ryan, Kevin, 674, 699

## S

Sack, Kevin, 155
Sage, Alexandria, 574
Saint Augustine, 417
Salameh, Mohammed, 566
Sales, Bruce D., 399
Salnick, Michael, 316
Salonoja, Jussi, 425
Sampson, Robert J., 104, 116
Samudra, Imam, 711
Samuels, Julie E., 471
Sanders, Wiley B., 616
Saney, Parviz, 665, 666, 698
Santiago-Martinez, Luis, 386
Sapp, Allen D., 237
Sargent, W., 113
Sassou, Denis, 673
Sauls, John Gales, 284
Savage, David G., 74
Saxton, Samuel F., 632
Saylor, William G., 519
Scalia, Antonin, 411, 412
Scalia, John, 375, 397, 574
Schact, J., 698
Schafer, Stephen, 86, 113
Schauss, Alexander, 114
Scheb, John M., 30, 398
Scheb, John M., II, 30, 398
Scheck, Barry, 430, 445
Scheider, Matthew C., 213, 232
Schell, Donald, 126
Schellberg, Tim, 739
Schilling, Curt, 630
Schilly, Otto, 671
Schmidt, Erica L., 322
Schmidt, Howard, 71
Schmoke, Kurt, 659
Schoenberg, Ronald L., 154, 155, 367.
Schoenberg, Tom, 633
Schofield, Daniel L., 323
Schuler, Peter, 233
Schulz, Dorothy Moses, 164, 187
Schuman, Alan, 416
Scott, Michael S., 199, 232, 233, 234
Scull, Andrew T., 519
Searcey, Dionne, 76
Sechrest, Dale K., 520, 523
Sechrest, L., 520
Sedlak, Andrea J., 618
Seelman, Michael F., 232
Seidman, Robert B., 116
Selby, Hugh, 394

Sellin, Thorsten, 107, 116, 617
Seneca, 419
Sengupta, Somini, 323
Sensenbrenner, James, 432
Serpico, Frank, 294
Serra, Tony, 361
Sessions, William S., 740
Seton, Craig, 739
Seyfrit, Carole, 619
Shabani, Reshat, 131
Shaffer, J. W., 658
Shaffi, Qaisar, 214
Shakur, Tupac, 80, 295
Shank, Geoff, 677
Shankman, Stephen, 677
Shapiro, Alexandra A. E., 443
Sharn, Lori, 520
Sharon, Ariel, 673
Sharp, Dudley, 438
Shaw, Clifford R., 97, 115, 587, 617
Shaw, George Bernard, 531
Shearer, Robert A., 458
Shearing, Clifford D., 186, 187, 189
Sheck, Barry, 740
Sheldon, William, 90
Shepherd, Joanna Mahlhop, 446
Sherman, Lawrence W., 169, 170, 187,
    188, 443
Shichor, David, 520, 523
Shipley, Wes, 113
Shirley, Michael, 120
Shubin, Lester D., 739
Shull, David, 637
Shusta, Robert M., 30, 292
Sichel, Joyce L., 445
Sickmund, Melissa, 619
Siegel, Norman, 233
Siegfried, Michael, 236
Sigurdson, Herbert R., 522
Silberman, Charles E., 29
Silverman, Eli B., 197
Simmons, R. Gene, 435
Simon, Rita, 109
Simon, Thomas, 75
Simpson, D. William, 418
Simpson, Kevin S., 135
Simpson, O. J., 15, 151, 333, 356, 392
Simpson, Sally S., 116
Sims, William, 402
Sinacore, Michael, 580
Singer, M., 571
Singh, Jasbir, 142
Sistani, Ali, 664
Sjodin, Dru, 454
Skelton, David T., 479
Skogan, Wesley G., 234, 444
Skolnick, Jerome H., 16, 30, 210, 234,
    290, 292, 297, 320, 497
Skove, Anne Endress, 396
Sladky, T. J., 619
Slater, Robert O., 700
Slater, Stephanie, 322
Sluder, Richard D., 320
Smeal, Eleanor, 68
Smith, Alexander B., 477, 478
Smith, Angus, 232, 236
Smith, Ashley, 328

Smith, Barbara E., 444
Smith, Bruce, 417
Smith, Cameron, 426
Smith, Joseph, 45
Smith, Joseph P., 452, 453
Smith, Latasha, 252
Smith, Melissa A., 321
Smith, Steven K., 350, 366
Smith, Susan, 362
Smith, Walter F., 398
Smith, Wantland J., 522
Snelgrove, Victoria, 309
Snell, Tracy L., 445, 571, 572
Sobol, James J., 236
Soderman, Harry, 739
Sokoloff, Natalie J., 187
Sokolow, Andrew, 257
Solomon, Jay, 699
Sosa, Sammy, 630
Souryal, Sam S., 232, 665, 666, 698
Souter, David H., 243, 255, 411, 412
Sparrow, Malcolm K., 211, 235
Spinoza, Baruch, 160
Spohn, Cassia, 366
Springer, Charles E., 616
Spurzheim, Johann Gaspar, 88
Stalenheim, E. G., 114
Stanko, Elizabeth, 75
Starr, Barbara, 699
Stastny, Charles, 529, 570, 572
Steadman, Greg W., 365
Stearns, Matt, 75
Stedman, Craig, 740
Steinhardt, Barry, 724
Steinhart, D., 571
Stephan, James J., 520, 521, 522
Stephens, Darrel W., 237
Stephens, Gene, 207, 234, 236, 283,
    317, 320
Stephens, Philip, 700
Stevens, Dennis J., 46, 74
Stevens, John Paul, 411, 412, 427, 442
Stewart, Lynne, 350, 351
Stewart, Martha, 9, 65, 471, 534, 570
Stewart, Potter, 434, 446, 550
Stiles, Tim, 522
Stincelli, Rebecca, 307, 322
Stinchcomb, Jeanne B., 496, 520
Stockton, Dale, 522
Stockum, John, 418
Stolberg, Sheryl, 565
Stone, Andrea, 657
Stone, Christopher, 9, 313, 323
Stout, Charlotte, 433
Stout, David, 446
Stracner, Jenny, 633
Strauchs, John J., 184, 189
Strauss, Stephen, 740
Streeter, Kurt, 234
Strentz, Thomas, 115
Stupak, Bart, 82
Sturz, H., 397
Stutman, Suzanne, 81, 113
Stutzman, Jeffrey, 728
Subramanian, Rajesh, 656
Sudnow, David, 398
Sullivan, Michael, 637

Summerlin, Warren, 343
Susswein, Ronald, 265
Sutherland, Edwin H., 64, 76, 101, 115,
    295, 321
Sutor, Andrew P., 233
Swanson, Charles R., 197, 233, 234,
    315, 323
Swartz, Jon, 71, 553, 712
Swartz, Mark H., 64
Sweetingham, Lisa, 397
Swenson, Eric D., 429
Sykes, Gary W., 187, 207, 222, 234, 236
Sykes, Gresham M., 103, 116, 526, 527,
    528, 529, 532, 570

## T

Tafoya, William L., 740
Taiji, Erik Y., 322
Talarico, Susette M., 398
Talbott, Frederick, 572
Tangonan, Shannon, 520
Tannenbaum, Frank, 103, 116
Tapp, Dennis, 429
Tarde, Gabriel, 101
Tarmohamed, Nadeem, 214
Tate, Lionel, 605
Tate, Sharon, 43
Tavernise, Sabrina, 320
Taylor, Anthony Lemar, 51
Taylor, Philip, 11
Taylor, Ralph B., 100
Taylor, Robert W., 233, 234
Teasley, Hoyt, 328
Teeters, Negley K., 484, 519
Teevan, James, 320
Tenet, George, 682
Teplin, L. A., 571
Territo, Leonard, 233, 234, 323
Terry, Charles E., 656
Terry, Fernando Belaunde, 700
Thein, Swee Lay, 739
Thoennes, Nancy, 76
Thomas, Clarence, 243, 411, 412, 739
Thompkins, Douglas, 568
Thompson, Devin, 125
Thompson, Dick, 565
Thompson, Jack, 125
Thompson, Joel A., 522
Thompson, Robert, 359
Thornberry, Mac, 71
Thornberry, Terence, 617
Thorpe, Janet, 731
Thrasher, Frederick M., 617
Thurman, Quint, 235
Tigar, Michael E., 346
Timms, Ed, 556
Tjaden, Patricia, 76
Tjoflat, Gerald, 304
Toch, Hans, 571
Tocqueville, Alexis de, 344, 488, 519
Toffler, Alvin, 162, 703
Tokasz, Jay, 656
Tompkins, Steven, 429
Tonry, Michael, 114, 188, 400, 415,
    442, 444
Toole, Ottis, 43
Torbet, Patricia, 619

Torres, Gamaliel, 179
Townsend, Bruce, 71
Townsend, Paula, 195
Traficant, James, 121, 123
Travis, Jeremy, 453, 473, 474, 479
Travis, Lawrence P., III, 233
Trebach, Arnold S., 659
Troisi, Joseph, 343
Trojanowicz, Robert C., 210, 213, 234, 235
True, Edmond J., 398
Truman, Harry S., 688
Tucker, Neely, 479
Turek, Bart, 254
Turk, Austin T., 107, 116
Turley, Jonathan, 54, 73, 562, 681
Turner, Allan, 445
Turner, Chester Dwayne, 430
Turner, S., 445
Turunen, Pia, 737
Tuttle, Steve, 312
Twain, Mark, 362
Tyrnauer, Gabrielle, 529, 570, 572

## U

Ulmer, Jeffrey T., 365
Ulpian, 118
Umbreit, Mark S., 406
Urlacher, Gordon F., 234
Useem, Bert, 572

## V

Valdez, Joel, 140
Valdmanis, Thor, 235
Valinejad, Afshin, 698
Van Dine, S., 521
Van Meter, Clifford W., 184, 189
Van Praag, Herman M., 114
Van Wagner, Chris, 678
Van Zandt, Clinton R., 193
VandeHei, Jim, 124
Vaughan-Nichols, Steven J., 75
Vaughn, Joseph B., 398
Vaughn, Michael S., 323
Verniero, Peter, 323
Veysey, B. M., 571
Viano, Emilio C., 673, 683, 700
Vila, Bryan, 303, 322
Vilsack, Tom, 296
Vito, Gennaro F., 446
Vogel, Ronald E., 572
Volavka, Jan, 114
Vold, George B., 107, 116
Vollmer, August, 23, 237
von Hirsch, Andrew, 477
von Knorring, L., 114

## W

Waagner, Clayton Lee, 677
Wade, Terrance, 580
Wade, Willie, 552
Waggoner, John, 52

Waite, John Barker, 519
Walker, Herman, 633
Walker, Linda, 454
Walker, N., 115
Walker, Samuel, 37, 320, 322
Wallace, Henry Louis, 94
Wallace, Kelly, 127
Wallis, Ken, 562
Walmsley, Roy, 698
Walters, John P., 621
Walton, Reggie B., 626
Wamp, Zach, 82
Want, Ting-Li, 25
Ward, D., 537, 572
Ward, Richard H., 660, 697
Wardlaw, Grant, 700
Wardlow, William, 258
Warren, Earl, 21, 242, 246, 427
Wasby, Stephen L., 365
Washington, Jerome, 528
Wasserman, Robert, 235
Wattenberg, Ben, 47
Wayne, William, 556
Wayson, Billy, 522
Weber, Mark, 641
Weber, Max, 667, 698
Webster, Daniel, 3
Webster, William, 171
Weigel, Brian, 454
Weiland, Doris, 659
Weimann, Gabriel, 711
Weiner, Neil Alan, 618
Weise, Jeff, 590
Weiss, Alexander, 188
Weiss, Rick, 738
Weissenstein, Michael, 235
Welch, Susan, 366
Wells, Alice Stebbins, 164
Werrett, David J., 739
West, Valerie, 498, 521
Westervelt, Saundra D., 445
Weston, Paul B., 234
Whalen, Jeanne, 699
Wheeler, Stanton, 527, 570
Whipple, Diane, 136
Whitaker, Gordon P., 521
White, Ben, 76
White, S., 520
Whittens, Bill, 343
Whyte, William Foote, 617
Wicharaya, Tamasak, 442
Wickersham, George W., 165
Wide, L., 114
Widom, Cathy Spatz, 109
Wier, Anthony, 738
Wiggins, Michael E., 700
Wikberg, R., 570
Wikbert, Ronald, 574
Wilbanks, William, 47, 48
Wild, Jonathan, 162
Wildeman, John, 116
Wildhorn, Sorrel, 399
Wilhelm, David, 328

Wilkes, Judith, 520
Wilkins, William W., Jr., 413
Williams, Alexander "Clubber," 240
Williams, Gloria, 598
Williams, Hubert, 159, 194
Williams, Vergil L., 519, 572
Williams, Vicki, 12
Willing, Richard, 142, 255, 286, 359, 364, 432, 440, 444, 445, 509, 563, 724
Wilson, Charles, 266
Wilson, Christopher P., 320
Wilson, Deborah G., 446
Wilson, Doris James, 408, 443, 459, 477, 520
Wilson, George P., 522
Wilson, James Q., 7, 32, 73, 92, 100, 114, 207, 233, 234, 407, 647, 658
Wilson, O. W., 24, 227, 232, 234, 237
Wilson, Pete, 416, 419
Wilson, T. F., 739
Wilson, Victoria, 739
Wind, Timothy, 241
Winfrey, Oprah, 357
Winterfield, Laura A., 445
Witte, A. D., 521
Woks, J., 443
Wolfgang, Marvin, 100, 587, 617
Wolle, Charles, 127
Wood, Arthur Evans, 519
Woodard, P. L., 739
Woods, Tiger, 51
Wooldredge, John D., 113
Woolsey, R. James, 66, 76
Worden, Robert E., 236
Worthington, Christa, 429
Worzella, Charles, 445
Wray, Christopher A., 411
Wright, Jonathan, 113
Wright, Martin, 364
Wrobleski, Henry M., 187, 188
Wyles, Randy, 616

## Y

Yardley, Jim, 445, 447
Yates, Andrea, 143–144
Yohnka, Ed, 13
Yoran, Amit, 712
York, David, 579
Young, D. S., 571
Young, Robert M., Jr., 308
Yuan, Li, 76
Yurkiewicz, Jeff, 646

## Z

Zeisel, H., 397
Zeller, Tom, 52
Zenger, John, 330
Zhao, Jihong, 235
Zimring, Franklin E., 627, 649, 656
Zingraff, Matthew T., 618
Zoubek, Paul, 323
Zupan, Linda L., 510, 522

# SUBJECT INDEX

## A

ABA Code of Professional Responsibility, 352
absolute liability offenses, 132
Abu Sayyae, 695
abuse of police power, 240–241
abused children, 586
ACA accreditation program, 507
ACA code of ethics, 542
accounting fraud, 63–64
accreditation, 224
*Actus reus,* 130–131
Adelphia Communications, 64
adjudication
    arraignment, 378
    courts, 326–367. *See also* courts
    first appearance, 371–372
    grand jury, 376
    motions, 388. *See also* motion
    plea bargaining, 378–379
    preliminary hearing, 376–378
    pretrial release, 372–376, 377
    sentencing. *See* sentencing
    trial. *See* criminal trial
ADMAX facility (Florence, Colorado), 505, 506
administration of justice, 14
administrative law, 126
Administrative Office of the United States Courts (AOUSC), 335
adolescent development, 105
adult internal management system (AIMS), 504
Advance Passenger Information System (APIS), 728
*Advancing Justice through DNA Technology,* 723
adversarial process, 333
adversarial system, 381
African Americans. *See* race and ethnicity
aggravated assault, 48–49
aggravating circumstances, 409, 410
AIDS, 300–302, 559–561
AJA code of ethics, 514
akathisia, 126
Al Aqsa Martyrs' Brigades, 694
al-Qaeda, 26, 97, 175, 214, 567, 664, 678, 679, 680, 682, 688, 692, 693, 694, 707, 712, 711
Alcatraz Federal Penitentiary, 493
alcohol abuse, 624–625
ALI rule, 146
alibi, 138
*Allen* charge, 392
alter ego rule, 138
alternative sentencing strategies, 466–467
American Probation and Parole Association code of ethics, 469
American Sign Language, 396
American Society for Law Enforcement Training (ASLET), 224
anabolic steroids, 638
Animal Liberation Front, 678
animalescents, 539
anomie, 97
anomie theory, 97–98

Anti-Drug Abuse Act of 1988, 630, 632
antidrug legislation, 628–632
antistalking statutes, 131
antiterrorism, 174–175, 216–221. *See also* terrorism
Antiterrorism and Effective Death Penalty Act (AEDPA), 428, 684
antiterrorism committees/reports, 685–687
appeal, 333
appellate courts
    federal, 337–338
    state, 333–334
appellate jurisdiction, 331
arraignment, 18–19, 378
arrest, 17, 253–258
arson, 53
Arthur Andersen, 64
Asbat Al Ansar, 694
Ashurst-Sumners Act, 491
ASIS International, 181–182
ASIS International Code of Ethics, 182, 183
ASIS Security Toolkit, 182
assault weapons, 68
asset forfeiture, 648–649
assigned counsel, 347
atavism, 88–89
ATF employee, 308
attendant circumstances, 134
Auburn system, 487
augmented reality (AR), 728
authority conflict pathway, 104
auto theft, 41, 52–53
automated fingerprint identification system (AFIS), 716–717
automatic plate recognition (APR), 714
automatic release, 377
autonomic nervous system (ANS), 92

## B

bail, 373–376
bail bond, 373–375
bail bond office, 373
bail bondsman, 373, 377
bail forfeiture, 373
Bail Reform Act, 376
bail schedules, 377
bailiff, 353
bait cars, 714
balancing test, 546
ballistics, 717
barrister, 330
Basque Fatherland and Liberty (ETA), 695
Battlefield Augmented Reality System (BARS), 728
behavioral conditioning, 93
bench trial, 19
Beretta AR-70, 68
Bertillon system of identification, 89, 715–716
bias crime, 63
Big Floyd, 725
bilingual courtroom, 396
bill of particulars, 388
Bill of Rights, 21, 242
biochemical factors/imbalances, 91
biocrime, 705–706

biological incident law enforcement concerns, 300–302
biological school, 87
biological theories, 87–90
biological weapon, 300
biometrics, 717
bioterrorism, 713
*Bivens* action, 318
blacks. *See* race and ethnicity
bloodborne diseases, 300–301
Bloodborne Pathogens Act, 301
Blue, 733
bobbies, 162
body-cavity search, 277
Boggs Act, 629
booking, 17
boot camp, 467–468, 509, 613
Border and Transportation Security (BTS), 688
boundaryless policing, 221
bounty hunters, 374
Bow Street Runners, 162
Brady Handgun Violence Prevention Act, 66
brain chemistry, 92
Branch Davidian cult, 8–9, 676
branding, 484
Brawner rule, 146
broken windows thesis, 99, 197
BTK strangler, 43
Bureau of Citizenship and Immigration Services (CIS), 689
Bureau of Customs and Border Protection (CBP), 689
Bureau of Immigration and Customs Enforcement (ICE), 689
Bureau of Justice Statistics (BJS), 35, 166
Bureau of Prisons (BOP), 505–507
Burger Court, 249
burglary, 49–50

## C

California City Correctional Center, 516
calling the cops, 198
camera-equipped police cars, 208
cameras (in court), 361–363
CAN-SPAM Act, 710
capable guardian, 87
capital offense, 426
capital punishment, 426–440
    courts, 434–437
    future of, 437–440
    *habeas corpus* review, 427–428
    pros/cons, 429–434, 438–440
careers. *See* CJ careers
case law, 126
caseload, 466
*Caught in the Net: The Impact of Drug Policies on Women and Families,* 535
causation, 133
CBP employee, 560
*certiorari,* 245, 340
chain gang, 496–497
chain of command, 203–204
challenge for cause, 383

*Challenge of Crime in a Free Society, The,* 165, 603
challenge to the array, 383
change of venue, 362, 388
charge to jury, 392
Charting the Safe and Successful Return of Prisoners to the Community, 473
Chechen separatists, 695
chemically assisted date rape, 642
Chicago Area Project, 587
Chicago Reform School, 585
Chicago School, 96
Chicago surveillance camera program, 13
chief judge, 341
child abuse and neglect, 596–598
child delinquency. *See* juvenile justice
child witness, 390–391
Christian burial speech, 273
Christopher Commission, 213, 305–306
chromosome theory, 91
*Chronicles of Crime* (Pelham), 482
circuit courts, 333, 337
circumstantial evidence, 387
Cisco Systems, 50
Civil Asset Forfeiture Reform Act, 649
civil death, 545
civil forfeiture, 648–649
civil justice, 14
civil law, 123–126
civil liability, 314–318
civil rights era, 10
Civil Rights of Institutionalized Persons Act (CRIPA), 547
CJ careers
    Bureau of Alcohol, Tobacco, Firearms, and Explosives, 308
    Bureau of Immigration and Customs Enforcement, 260
    criminalist, 718–719
    Customs and Border Protection, 560
    Drug Enforcement Administration, 631
    FBI, 172
    Federal Bureau of Prisons, 507
    probation officers, 465
    Secret Service—Uniformed Division, 135
    U.S. Marshals Service, 354
CJIS Division, 174
class-action lawsuits, 124
classical school, 86–87
classification systems, 503–504
clearance rate, 41
clearances by exceptional means, 42
clerk of court, 354–355
cloning research, 706
closing arguments, 391
club drugs, 641–643
Coca-Cola, 627
cocaine, 8, 627, 628, 635, 639
*Cocaine Papers, The* (Freud), 627
coeducational incarceration, 494
coercion, 140
cohort, 587
cohort analysis, 587
collateral estoppel, 150
collective incapacitation, 501

colonizer, 531
Colt AR-15, 68
Combat Zones That See (CZTS), 726
Combined DNA Index System (CODIS), 173
comes stabuli, 161
commission-based presumptive sentencing guidelines, 408
Commission on Accreditation for Law Enforcement Agencies (CALEA), 224
Commission on Safety and Abuse in America's Prisons, 568
common law, 121
common peacemakers, 330
commonwealth attorney, 343
Communications Assistance for Law Enforcement Act (CALEA), 278
Communications Decency Act (CDA), 279, 734
community conferences, 608
community corrections, 452, 493–494
community courts, 336
community mediation programs, 335–336
community policing, 209–214, 219
Community Policing Act, 212
Community Policing Consortium, 212
community reparative boards, 406
community service, 468–469
comparative criminal justice, 662–674
    Europol, 691
    globalization and crime, 673–674
    International Criminal Court (ICC), 692–693
    international criminal justice organization, 667–668
    INTERPOL, 691
    Islamic criminal justice, 664–667
    problems with data, 663–664
    terrorism. *See* terrorism
    transnational crime, 673
    United Nations (UN), 668–669
    Vienna Declaration, 690
comparative criminologist, 662
compassionate criminology, 108
compelling interest, 263
compensatory damages, 125
competency to stand trial, 148–149, 377, 388
Comprehensive Crime Control Act, 460
Comprehensive Drug Abuse Prevention and Control Act of 1970, 629
CompStat, 195, 196–197
Compusketch, 725
computer-aided investigations, 725–726
computer-based training (CBT), 726–727
computer crime, 67, 70–71, 706–711
Computer Crime Enforcement Act, 731
Computer Fraud and Abuse Act (CFAA), 173, 730–731
computer virus, 708
computerized information systems, 724–725
con artists, 62
Concept virus, 708
Conch Republic, 181
concurrence, 132

concurrent jurisdiction, 605
concurrent sentence, 20
conditional release, 375
conditioning, 93
conditions of parole, 460
conditions of probation, 456–457, 460
condom rapist case, 140
conflict model, 16
conflict perspective, 106
conflict theories, 106–109
conformists, 98
consecutive sentence, 20
consensus model, 16
consent, 139–140
Consortium for State Council Interpreter Certification, 396
conspiracy, 130, 131
constitutional amendments. *See* U.S. Constitution
constitutive criminology, 111
containment, 102
containment theory, 102
contamination, 488
continuance, 388
contract attorney programs, 348
contract system, 490
controlled substance, 623
Controlled Substances Act (CSA), 629–630
convict bogey, 492
*Convicted by Juries, Exonerated by Science,* 430, 722
cool prisoners, 539
COPLINK, 196
COPS Office, 212, 224
corporate crime, 64
corporate fraud, 63–64
*corpus delicti,* 136–137
correctional officers, 539–543
corrections, 448–575
    AIDS, 559–561
    correctional officers, 539–543
    geriatric offenders, 561–563
    historical overview, 482–498
    incarceration rates, 495–496, 498, 499
    jail, 507–514. *See also* jail
    juveniles, 611–613
    mentally ill inmates, 565–566
    overcrowding, 499–502, 510–511
    parole. *See* parole
    prison. *See* prison
    private prisons, 514–517
    probation. *See* probation
    recent improvements, 507
    riots, 543–545
    security levels, 502–503, 505
    selective incapacitation, 501–502
    technological advancements, 564–565
    terrorism, 566–568
    women, 508–510, 533–539
Corrections Corporation of America (CCA), 516
corruption, 291–296
*Cosa Nostra,* 65
cost-benefit specificism, 627
*Countering the Changing Threat of International Terrorism,* 684

county attorney, 343
county clerk, 354
court. *See* courts
court administrator, 353
court-appointed defense attorneys, 347–348
Court Interpreters Act, 396
court of appeals, 333, 337–338
Court of International Trade, 336
court reporter, 353–354
court-watch citizens' groups, 393
Courtroom 21, 394–395
courtroom participants, 341–363. *See also* criminal trial
    bailiff, 353
    clerk of court, 354–355
    court reporter, 353–354
    defendant, 361
    defense counsel, 346–352
    expert witness, 355–356
    judge, 341–343
    juror, 357–360
    lay witness, 356–357
    local court administrator, 353
    press (media), 361–363
    prosecuting attorney, 343–346
    spectators, 361
    victim, 360–361
courtroom work group, 340–341
courts, 326–367
    bilingual courtroom, 396
    courtroom participants. *See* courtroom participants
    courtroom work group, 340–341
    federal court system, 330, 336–340
    historical overview, 326–327
    state court system, 331, 332–336
    technologically advanced courtroom, 394–395
courts of last resort, 333
covert pathway, 104
crack cocaine, 627
crack kids, 539
cranioscopy, 88
crime
    biocrime, 705–706
    computer, 67, 70–71, 706–711
    defined, 7
    drug, 67
    elements, 134
    features, 130–134
    gun, 66–67
    hate, 63
    organized, 65–66
    petty, 195, 197
    property, 41
    transnational, 673
    violent, 41
    white-collar, 63–65
crime against the elderly, 62
crime against women, 59–62
*Crime and Human Nature* (Wilson/Herrnstein), 92
*Crime and the Nation's Households,* 56
Crime Awareness and Campus Security Act, 55
crime clock, 40, 41

crime congresses, 669
Crime Control Act of 1990, 632
crime-control model, 23
crime index, 38
crime prevention, 194
crime prevention through environmental design (CPTED), 99
crime scene, 201
crime-scene investigation process, 201
crime-scene investigators, 202
crime statistics, 32–77
    campus security reports, 55
    NCVS, 56, 57
    NIBRS, 54–55
    problems with, 57–59
    UCR. *See* Uniform Crime Reports (UCR)
Crime Stoppers International, 194
Crime Stoppers USA, 194
crime typology, 59
Crime Victims' Rights Act, 422
*Crimes and Punishment* (Beccaria), 86
criminal defense attorney, 347
criminal families, 90
criminal intelligence, 216–219
criminal investigation, 199, 200–202
criminal justice, 14
Criminal Justice Information Services (CJIS) Division, 174
criminal justice system, 15–16
criminal justice theory. *See* criminology theory
criminal law, 122–123
criminal negligence, 132
criminal offenses, 129
criminal procedure laws, 128
criminal trial, 380. *See also* jury trial
    closing arguments, 391
    judge's charge to jury, 392
    jury deliberation, 392
    jury selection, 383–387
    nature/purpose, 380–381
    opening statements, 387
    participants. *See* courtroom participants
    presentation of evidence, 387–391
    stages, 381, 382
    trial initiation, 382–383
    verdict, 392
*Criminal Victimization,* 56
criminalist, 715, 718–719
criminalistics, 715
*Criminality of Woman, The* (Pollak), 109
criminaloids, 89
Criminological Research Council, 668
criminology, 24
criminology theory, 78–116
    anomie theory, 97–98
    atavism, 88–89
    behavioral conditioning, 93
    biochemical factors/imbalances, 91
    biological theories, 87–90
    chromosome theory, 91
    classical school, 86–87
    conflict theories, 106–109
    constitutive criminology, 111
    containment theory, 102

criminal families, 90
differential association theory, 101–102
feminist criminology, 109–110
Freudian psychoanalysis, 93–94
heredity, 92
labeling theory, 103–104
life course perspective, 104–106
neutralization technique, 103
overview, 84–85
peacemaking criminology, 107–108
phrenology, 87–88
postmodern criminology, 111
psychobiological theories, 91–93
psychological theories, 93–96
psychopathology, 94–95
radical criminology, 107
restraint theories, 102–103
social control theory, 102–103
social ecology theory, 97
social process theory, 101–102
sociological theories, 96–100
somatotype, 90
subcultural theory, 98–100
critical incidents, 200
Critical Infrastructure Assurance Office (CIAO), 680
Critical Infrastructure Protection Board (CIPB), 680
Critical Systems Protection Initiative (CSPI), 681
cross-examination, 357, 390
cross-national criminal justice, 662. *See also* comparative criminal justice
*CSI: Crime Scene Investigation,* 34, 35, 358–359
*CSI effect,* 358–359
cultural defense, 140–142
*Cultural Defense, The* (Renteln), 141
cultural diversity. *See* race and ethnicity
culturally skilled probation officers, 458
curfew, 471
curtilage, 633
cybercrime, 67, 70–71, 706–711
cyberfraud, 711–712
cybersleuths, 70
cyberstalking, 62
cyberterrorism, 680–681

### D

danger laws, 375
dangerousness, 96
dangers of police work, 298–303
DARE program, 651
data mining, 726
date rape, 45
date rape drug, 641–642
*Daubert* standard, 722
day-fine, 426
deadly force, 138, 306–307
death penalty, 426–440
death-row inmates, 504, 562–563
death wish, 94
decarceration, 493–494
decisional model, 333
deconstructionist, 111
deconstructionist theories, 111

decriminalization, 653
defendant, 125, 361
defendant's refusal to testify, 390
defense. *See* defenses
defense counsel, 346–352
defense of a third person, 138
defense of home and property, 139
defense of infancy, 140, 142
defense of others, 138–139
defenses, 137–152
    age, 140, 142
    alibi, 138
    collateral estoppel, 150
    consent, 139–140
    defense of home and property, 139
    defense of others, 138–139
    defined, 137
    denial of speedy trial, 151
    diminished capacity, 147–148
    double jeopardy, 150
    duress, 140
    entrapment, 149–150
    excuses, 140–149
    insanity, 143–147
    involuntary intoxication, 143
    justification, 138–140
    mental incompetence, 148–149
    mistake, 142–143
    necessity, 139
    overview, 137
    police fraud, 151–152
    procedural, 149–152
    prosecutorial misconduct, 151
    provocation, 143
    resisting unlawful arrest, 140
    selective prosecution, 151
    self-defense, 138
    unconsciousness, 143
defensible space theory, 99
deinstitutionalization, 493
delayed notification search, 282
deliberate indifference, 551
delinquency, 582. *See also* juvenile justice
delinquent children, 586
denial of speedy trial, 151
Department of Homeland Security (DHS),
    688–689
Department of Justice (DOJ), 297
dependent children, 586
deposit bail, 374–375
design capacity, 500
designer drugs, 630
desk appearance tickets, 377
detection devices, 728
detective, 201
detention hearing, 376, 609
determinate sentencing, 408
Determinate Sentencing Act, 420
deterrence, 404
differential association-reinforcement
    theory, 102
differential association theory, 101–102
digital criminal forensics, 282
digital mugbook software, 726
diminished capacity, 147–148
diminished responsibility, 147
direct evidence, 387

direct examination, 390
direct file provisions, 605
direct-supervision jail, 511–513
directed patrol, 167
discretionary parole, 458
discretionary police activity, 221–223
dispositional hearing, 611
dispute-resolution centers, 335–336
district attorney, 343–346
district courts, 336–337
diversion, 415, 493
diversity. *See* race and ethnicity; women
DNA Identification Act, 722
DNA profiling, 173, 720–724
DNA Sexual Assault Justice Act, 723
DNA testing, 429, 431, 432
documentary evidence, 388
domestic terrorism, 676–679
Domestic Violence Offender Gun Ban, 68
double jeopardy, 150
driving under the influence (DUI) of
    alcohol, 624–625
driving while black, 309
drug, 623
drug court, 652
drug crime, 67
drug czar, 632
drug-education programs, 651
Drug-Free Communities Act, 632
Drug-Induced Rape Prevention and
    Punishment Act, 642
drug names, 634
drug-related crime, 644–647
drug testing of police employees,
    297–298
drug trafficking, 636
drugs and crime, 620–659
    alcohol abuse, 624–625
    antidrug legislation, 628–632
    asset forfeiture, 648–649
    club drugs, 641–643
    cocaine, 639
    costs of abuse, 644–647
    crop control, 650
    drug court, 652
    drug-related crime, 644–647
    drug trafficking, 636
    heroin, 640–641
    historical overview, 626–627
    interdiction, 649–650
    juveniles, 588–590
    legalization/decriminalization,
        652–654
    marijuana, 637–639
    prevention/treatment, 650–652
    public housing, 633
    social awareness, 627–628
    solving the drug problem, 647–652
drunk driving, 624–625
drunkenness, 143
dual-court system, 329
ducking stool, 484
due process, 21
due process model, 23
due process requirements, 244
duress, 140
*Durham* rule, 146

## E

early-intervention programs, 372
Earth Liberation Front (ELF), 676, 677
*Economic Costs of Drug Abuse in the
    United States, The,* 644
Ecstasy, 641, 642–643
Ecstasy Anti-Proliferation Act, 643
ectomorphs, 90
*Edmond*-type stops, 263
ego, 93
Eighth Amendment, 243, 435
elderly persons
    prison, in, 561–563
    victims, as, 62
Electronic Communications Privacy Act
    (ECPA), 278
*Electronic Crime Scene Investigation: A
    Guide for First Responders,* 282
electronic eavesdropping, 277–279
electronic evidence, 282
electrophoresis, 720
element of a crime, 134
Elk Grove (California) Police
    Department, 204
Elmira Reformatory, 490
Emergency Preparedness and Response
    (EPR), 688
emergency response, 199, 200
emergency search of persons, 258–259
emergency search of property, 253
*Emerging Issues on Privatized
    Prisons,* 515
endomorphs, 90
Enron, 64
entrapment, 149–150
epileptic seizure, 143
Equal Justice for Women in the Courts
    Act, 61
equity, 408
espionage, 129
ethnocentrism, 662–663
European Police Office (Europol),
    671, 691
evidence
    admissibility of, 391, 721–722
    circumstantial, 387
    defined, 387
    direct, 387
    documentary, 388
    evaluation of, 389
    real, 388
    rules of, 380
    scientific, 721–722
evidence-based policing, 170
*ex post facto,* 133
exceptional clearances, 42
excessive force, 304–306
exclusionary rule, 244–246
excuses, 140–149
Exemplary Projects Program, 166
exhibits, 388
exigent circumstances searches, 253
exile, 484–485
expert systems, 725
expert witness, 355–356
extradition, 674

## F

factual guilt, 381
fatigue, 303
FBI. *See* Federal Bureau of Investigation
FBI automated messaging system
    (FAMS), 176
FBI crime clock, 40, 41
FBI employee, 172
FBI intelligence information reports
    dissemination system (FIDS), 176
FBI Laboratory Division, 174
federal appellate courts, 337–338
Federal Bureau of Investigation (FBI),
    170–176
Federal Bureau of Prisons, 507
Federal Communications Act, 278
federal correctional institutions (FCIs), 505
federal court system, 330, 336–340
federal deadly force policy, 306–307
Federal district courts, 336–337
federal investigative case management
    solution (FICMS), 176
federal law enforcement agencies, 170–175
Federal Law Enforcement Training Center
    (FLETC), 224
federal prison camps (FPCs), 505
Federal Prison Industries
    Incorporated, 491
federal prison system, 504–506
Federal Rules of Appellate Procedure, 338
Federal Rules of Criminal Procedure, 128
Federal Rules of Evidence, 128, 380
federal sentencing table, 410
Federal Tort Claims Act (FTCA), 318
*Felon, The* (Irwin), 528
felony, 128
female officers, 228–231
feminist criminology, 109–110
Fifth Amendment, 243, 390
fine, 425–426
fingerprinting, 716–717
firearms, 66–67, 68
First Amendment, 681
first appearance, 371–372
first-degree murder, 134, 136
first responders, 201
fleeting-targets exception, 261
flogging, 483
flunitrazepam, 642
force, 138, 303–309. *See also* police use
    of force
forcible rape, 44–46
foreign terrorist organization (FTO),
    691–695
forensic anthropology, 717
forensic entomology, 717
Forfeiture, 648–649
forward-looking infrared (FLIR), 734
414 gang, 730
Fourteenth Amendment, 243, 735
Fourth Amendment, 243, 244, 734. *See
    also* search and seizure
Fraternal Order of Police (FOP),
    164, 224
Freedom of Information Act, 420
freedom of speech, 681

Freemen, 360
Freudian psychoanalysis, 93–94
fruit of the prisoned tree doctrine, 245–246
FTAA protest (Miami, 2003), 192, 193
Futures Working Group (FWG), 715

## G

gain time, 407
gangs, 591–595
general condition of probation, 456
General Court, 330
general depressants, 638
general deterrence, 404
General Schedule (GS) pay, 23
genetic privacy, 429
geriatric offenders, 561–563
get tough legislation, 497
Global Crossing, 64
*Global Report on Crime and Justice,* 664
globalization and crime, 673–674
globalization of insecurity, 674
good-faith exception, 249–250
good time, 407
grand jury, 18, 376, 378
grass eating, 294
*Green Mile, The,* 540
Green River strangler, 43
grievance procedure, 556
Grokster, 709–710
gross negligence, 125, 136
group homes, 611
GS pay, 23
guilty but mentally ill (GBMI), 146–147
guilty plea, 18–19, 378, 379
gun control, 68
gun crime, 66–67
guns, 66–67, 68

## H

H2N2 scare, 705
*habeas corpus* review, 427–428, 547
hacker, 706
halfway house, 494, 613
*Hallcrest Report II,* 184
hallucinogens, 635, 638
Hamas, 694
hands-off doctrine, 545, 546, 557–559
harm, 133
harmless error rule, 389
Harrison Narcotics Act, 628
hate crime, 63
Hate Crime Statistics Act, 63
Hawes-Cooper Act, 491
hedonist, 530
hedonistic calculus, 86
hemophobic homicide, 63
heredity, 92
heroin, 626, 635, 640–641
Hezbollah, 694
Hidden Cameras Project, 166
hierarchy rule, 41
high-courts, 333
high-intensity drug-trafficking areas
    (HIDTAs), 632
high-security facilities, 505
high-speed chase, 316
high-tech search, 266–267

Hispanics. *See* race and ethnicity
Hitachi Corporation, 729
HITMAN, 725
HIV-infected inmates, 559–561
home confinement, 470–472
home detention, 471
home incarceration, 472
hormones, 92
Hospice of San Michele, 485
house arrest, 470–472
house of refuge, 584
houseboats, 263
*Hudud* crimes, 665–666
hulks, 485
human cloning, 706
Human Cloning Research Prohibition
    Act, 706
Human Rights and Law Enforcement
    Institute (HRALEI), 668
hung jury, 392
hyperglobalization, 674
hypothesis, 82

## I

ICE employee, 260
id, 93
Identification Friend or Foe (IFF)
    technology, 728
identity management, 732–733
identity theft, 51, 732
Identity Theft Penalty Enhancement
    Act, 51
IFF technology, 728
illegally seized evidence, 244
ImAger, 725
imminent danger standard, 306
incapacitation, 404
incarceration rates, 495–496, 498, 499,
    508, 533
inchoate offense, 130
incompetent to stand trial, 148
indeterminate sentencing, 406–408
indictment, 18
indigent defense, 347–350
individual rights, 8
individual-rights advocates, 11
individual rights versus public order, 10–12
industrial prison, 490
inevitable-discovery exception to
    *Miranda,* 273–274
infancy, 140, 142
infected evidence, 300–302
inference engine, 725
infocrime, 706
informants, 267–268
information, 18, 376
Information Analysis and Infrastructure
    Protection (IAIP), 688
information-technology crime, 67, 706
infraction, 129
infrastructure, 680
inhalants, 638
inherent coercion, 269
initial appearance, 371
inmate labor, 490
inmate rights. *See* prisoners' rights
inmate types, 530–531

inner containment, 102
innovators, 98
insanity, 143–147
insanity defense, 143–147
Insanity Defense Reform Act (IDRA), 147
intake, 609
integrated automated fingerprint
        identification system (IAFIS),
        174, 717
integrity, 296–297
intelligence function, 267–282
intelligence-led policing (ILP), 216–219
Intelligence Reform and Terrorism
        Prevention Act, 733
intelligent waiver, 273
intensive probation supervision (IPS),
        469–470
intentional action, 131
interdiction, 649–650
interdisciplinary theories, 83
intermediate sanctions, 466–472
        community service, 468–469
        defined, 466
        home confinement, 470–472
        intensive probation supervision (IPS),
            469–470
        mixed sentence, 468
        shock incarceration, 467–468
        shock parole, 467
        shock probation, 467
        split sentencing, 467
internal affairs, 297
International Association of Chiefs of
        Police (IACP), 215, 297
International Bill of Human Rights, 668
International Center of Comparative
        Criminology, 668
International Criminal Court (ICC), 672
international criminal justice. See
        comparative criminal justice
international criminal justice
        organization, 667–668
International Law Enforcement Academy
        (ILEA), 173
International Police Executive
        Symposium (IPES), 668
International Society for Criminology
        (ISC), 667
international terrorism, 679, 693
international terrorist groups, 691–695
INTERPOL, 691
interpreter, 396
interrogation, 268–275
intoxications, 143
Intratec TEC-9/DC-9, 68
investigative data warehouse (IDW), 176
involuntary intoxication, 143
Irish system of prisons, 489
irresistible impulse, 145–146
Islamic courts, 667
Islamic criminal justice, 664–667
Islamic law, 665
Islamic Movement of Uzbekistan, 695
Islamic Resistance Movement
        (Hamas), 694
"I've Killed That Man Ten Thousand
        Times" (Cohen), 307

## J

jail, 507–514
        boot camps, 513
        defined, 507
        direct-supervision, 511–513
        factoids, 511
        future of, 513, 515
        officers (code of ethics), 514
        overcrowding, 510–511
        purposes, 507–508
        regional, 513
        women, 508–510
jail administrators, 377
jail boot camps, 513
jail officers, 514
jail overcrowding, 510–511
jail standards, 513
Jaish-E-Mohammed, 695
Jemaah Islamiyah, 695
JJDP Act, 603
jobs. See CJ careers
Joe Brown, 332
"John Sweep" program, 418
Joint Terrorism Task Force (JTTF),
        175, 216
judge, 341–343
Judge Judy, 332
judge's charge to jury, 392
Judicial Councils Reform and Judicial
        Conduct and Disability Act, 343
judicial election, 342–343
judicial misconduct, 343
judicial qualifications, 343
judicial review, 339
jurisdiction, 329
juror, 357–360
jury deliberation, 392
jury selection, 383–387
jury trial
        charge to jury, 392
        deliberation, 392
        problems with jury system, 392–393
        segmentation, 385
        selection of jury, 383–387
        verdict, 392
just deserts era of correctional
        philosophy, 496–498
justice, 14
justice model, 496
justice of the people, 330
Justice Technology Information Network
        (JUSTNET), 715
justification, 138–140
Juvenile Court Act, 586
juvenile court counselors, 611
juvenile court era, 585–586
juvenile custody rates, 612
juvenile disposition, 611
juvenile gangs, 591–595
juvenile jurisdiction, 605
juvenile justice, 578–619
        adult system, compared, 606
        categories of children, 586
        child abuse and neglect, 596–598
        court cases, 599–603
        custody rates, 612

disposition, 611–613
drug and alcohol abuse, 588–590
gangs, 591–595
historical overview, 582–586
intake and detention hearing,
        608–609
legislation, 603
post-juvenile court era, 614–615
postadjudicatory review, 613
preliminary hearing, 609–610
research studies, 587–588
rights of juveniles, 604
runaway, 595–596
secure detention, 611–612
sexual abuse, 596–597
teen court, 610
transfer to adult court, 605
violence, 590
Juvenile Justice and Delinquency
        Prevention (JJDP) Act, 603
juvenile petition, 608

## K

K-Hole, 643
Kach and Kahane Chai, 694
Kansas City experiment, 167
Kansas City Gun experiment, 169
Kansas City studies, 167–169
ketamine, 643
khat, 141
Kmart, 64
Knapp Commission, 294
knowing behavior, 131
knowing waiver, 273
Koran, 665
Kournikova computer virus, 710
Kurdistan Workers' Party (PKK), 695

## L

labeling theory, 103–104
Laci and Conner's Law, 44
landmark cases, 244
language-skilled interpreters, 396
larceny—theft, 50–52
Lashkar E-Jhangvi, 695
Lashkar E-Taiba, 695
latent evidence, 282
law
        administrative, 126
        case, 126
        civil, 123–126
        common, 121
        criminal, 122–123
        defined, 120
        procedural, 126–128
        statutory, 121
Law & Order, 359
Law Enforcement Against Prohibition
        (LEAP), 654
Law Enforcement Assistance
        Administration (LEAA), 165, 166
law enforcement code of ethics, 223
law enforcement intelligence, 216–219
Law Enforcement Intelligence: A Guide
        for State, Local, and Tribal Law
        Enforcement Agencies, 216–218
law enforcement oath of honor, 297

Law Enforcement Standards Laboratory, 715
laws of limitation, 101
lay witness, 356–357
leading questions, 390
lease system, 490
legal cause, 133
legal guilt, 381
legalist, 531
legalistic style, 207
legality, 133
legalization, 653–654
less-lethal weapons, 309, 310–312
*lex talionis,* 483
Liberation Tigers of Tamil Eelam, 695
Liberian International Ship and Corporate Registry, 717
life course perspective, 104–106
life subculture, 539
limitation model, 654
line operations, 203
linked lives, 104
liquid metal embrittlement (LME), 712
local court administrator, 353
local law enforcement agencies, 179–180
local lockups, 513
lock psychosis, 20, 492
Los Angeles (L.A.) County Jail System, 180
Los Angeles County Sheriff's Department (LASD), 205
low-security facilities, 505
lower courts, 332
LSD, 627, 635
lust murderers, 96

## M

Mafia, 65
*Mafiya,* 65
magistrate, 330
magistrate judges, 337
magistrate's review, 371
Maison de Force, 485
*Making It in Prison* (Heffernan), 537
malice aforethought, 136
malware, 708
mandatory sentencing, 414–415
Manhattan Bail Project, 374
MANPADS, 662
manslaughter, 136
*Manual of Law Enforcement Records,* 37
Mariel boat lift, 543
marijuana, 627, 635, 637–639
Marijuana Tax Act, 629
*Mask of Sanity, The* (Cleckley), 95
mass murder, 43
mass prison era (1825-76), 487–488
MATRIX, 220, 221
maximum-security institutions, 502
McDade-Murtha Law, 344
mean dude, 530
meat eaters, 294
media coverage (of court cases), 361–363
mediation centers, 335–336
medical model of corrections, 492
medium-security institutions, 502–503, 505
*Mens rea,* 131–132

mental incompetence, 148–149
mentally ill inmates, 565–566
merit plan of judicial selection, 343
mesomorphs, 90
Metabolife, 64
METAPOL, 725
methamphetamine, 635, 643
metropolitan detention centers (MDCs), 506
Miami Drug Court model, 652
minimum-security institutions, 503, 505
Minneapolis Domestic Violence Experiment, 169
Minnesota Restitution Program, 469
*Miranda* triggers, 275
*Miranda* warnings, 271–276
misdemeanor, 128–129
Missouri Plan, 342–343
mistake of fact, 142–143
mistake of law, 142
mistrial, 19, 388
mitigating circumstances, 409, 410
Mitre Corporation, 668
mixed sentence, 468
M'Naghten rule, 145
Mobilization for Youth, 587
Mollen Commission, 294–295
money laundering, 645
money-making prison industries, 491–492
moral enterprise, 103
Moro Islamic Liberation Front, 695
Moroccan Islamic Combatant Group, 694
morphine, 626
"Most Wanted" lists, 725
motion, 388
    arrest of judgment, 388
    bill of particulars, 388
    change of venue, 388
    continuance, 388
    discovery, 388
    dismiss charges, 388
    mistrial, 388
    new trial, 388
    present sanity, 388
    severance of defendants, 388
    severance of offenses, 388
    suppress evidence, 388
motive, 132
motor home, 263
motor vehicle checkpoint, 262–263
motor vehicle theft, 52–53
MPC rule, 146
Mu-Chips, 729
multiculturalism, 25–27. *See also* race and ethnicity
multinational criminal justice. *See* comparative criminal justice
municipal police departments, 179–180
murder, 41, 42–44, 134, 136
mutilation, 483–484
*Myth of a Racist Criminal Justice System, The* (Wilbanks), 47

## N

naked DNA, 723
*Nanny 911,* 588
nanotechnology, 729
Napster, 709

narcoterrorism, 681–683
Narcotic Control Act of 1956, 629
narcotics, 638
National Academy of Corrections, 507
National Academy Program, 174
National Advisory Commission on Criminal Justice Standards and Goals, 165
National Center for State Courts (NCSC), 334–335
National Center for the Analysis of Violent Crime (NCAVC), 725
National Center for Women and Policing (NCWP), 229
National Commission on Crime Prevention and Control, 165
National Computer Crime Squad (NCCS), 173
National Crime Information Center (NCIC), 725
National Criminal Intelligence Sharing Plan (NCISP), 220
National Criminal Justice Reference Service (NCJRS), 166
National Cyber-Forensics & Training Alliance (NCFTA), 70
National Cyber Security Division (NCSD), 680–681
National DNA Index System (NDIS), 173
*National Drug Control Strategy,* 647, 651
National Drug Intelligence Center (NDIC), 636
*National Drug Threat Assessment,* 636
national ID, 733
National Incident-Based Reporting System (NIBRS), 54–55
National Institute of Justice (NIJ), 166
National Law Enforcement and Corrections Technology Center (NLECTC), 24, 714
National Liberation Army (ELN), 694
*National Strategy for Combating Terrorism,* 689, 691
*National Strategy to Secure Cyberspace, The,* 680
National Threat Assessment Center (NTAC), 681
necessary attendant circumstances, 134
necessity, 139
neglected children, 586
neighborhood watch, 194
neoclassical criminology, 86–87
neurological dysfunction, 143
neutralization technique, 103
New DAWN, 642
new police, 162–163
*New Structure of Policing, The,* 182
New York City Police Department (NYPD), 179, 215
New York House of Refuge, 584
New York State Field Code, 331
night watch, 161
*NIJ Journal,* 166
*NIJ Research in Review,* 166
9-1-1 systems, 198
1983 lawsuit, 317

NISMART, 595
*No Escape: Male Rape in U.S. Prisons,* 532
no knock entry, 253
*nolo contendere,* 378
nonjudicial pretrial release decisions, 377
nontestimonial evidence, 275–277
Norfolk Island, 488
Norinco MAK-90, 68
nothing-works doctrine, 404, 495
nuclear transfer, 706
NYPD. *See* New York City Police
Department

## O

oath of honor, 297
offense, 129
Office for Domestic Preparedness
(ODP), 219
Office of Inspector General, 689
Office of International Criminal Justice
(OICJ), 668
Office of Justice Programs (OJP), 166
Office of Juvenile Justice and
Delinquency Prevention
(OJJDP), 104
Office of Private Sector Liaison, 689
Office of State and Local Government
Coordination, 689
officer fatigue, 303
O.J. Simpson trial, 151–152, 392
omission to act, 131
online databases, 724–725
open institutions, 494
opening statements, 387
Operation Ceasefire, 169
Operation Cyber Chase, 648
Operation Identification, 194
Operation Losing Proposition, 178–179
Operation Nexus, 217
operational capacity, 500
opium, 626
opportunist, 530–531
opportunity theory, 587
organized crime, 63–65
original jurisdiction, 331, 605
outer containment, 102
overcrowding, 499–502, 510–511, 612
overt pathway, 104
OxyContin, 635

## P

pains of imprisonment, 529
Pakistani virus, 708
Palestine Islamic Jihad, 694
paranoid schizophrenic, 96
*parens patriae,* 582
parental duty law, 598
parole
advantages/disadvantages, 460–461
civil liability, 463–464
conditions, 460
defined, 458
future of, 472–473
officer, 464–466
reinventing, 473–474
revocation hearings, 462–463
shock, 467

statistics, 459–460
parole board, 458, 459
parole officer, 458, 464–466
parole violation, 460
part I offenses
aggravated assault, 48–49
arson, 53
burglary, 49–50
crime clock, 41
forcible rape, 44–46
larceny—theft, 50–52
motor vehicle theft, 52–53
murder, 42–44
robbery, 46–48
part II offenses, 53–54
*patria postestas,* 582
*Patterns of Global Terrorism,* 693
Paxil, 126
PDS jail, 512
peace officer standards and training
(POST) program, 224
peacemaking criminology, 107–108
penal code, 121
penitentiary era (1790-1825), 485–487
Pennsylvania Constabulary, 176
Pennsylvania system, 487
People Assisting Victims, 222
peremptory challenge, 383–385
perjury, 390
personality-altering treatment techniques,
493
petition, 388
petty crimes, 195, 197
pharmaceutical diversion, 643
pharming parties, 643
Philadelphia Penitentiary, 487
phishing, 709
photographs, 389
phrenology, 87–88
physical dependence, 629
physical environment and crime, 99–100
physical evidence, 388
piece-price system, 490
pillory, 484
PIV card, 733
plain feel exception, 257
plain view, 250
plain-view doctrine, 250–252
plaintiff, 125
plea, 378
plea bargaining, 378–379, 413
police. *See* policing
police civil liability, 314–318
police-community relations (PCR), 208
police corruption, 291–296
Police Development Fund, 166
police discretion, 221–223
police ethics, 223
police fraud, 151–152
police informants, 267–268
police integrity, 296–297
*Police Integrity: Public Serving with
Honor,* 296
police interrogation, 268–275
police management, 203
police mission, 192–198
police organization and structure, 203–205

police professionalism, 223
police-pursuit driving simulators, 727
police subculture, 213
police training, 224
Police Training Network, 224
Police Training Officer (PTO)
program, 224
Police TV, 208
police use of force, 303–309
deadly force, 306–307
defined, 303
excessive force, 304–306
less-lethal weapons, 309, 310–312
police working personality, 290
policing, 156–323
abuse of power, 240–241
accreditation, 224
boundaryless, 221
chain of command, 203–204
civil liability, 314–318
community, 209–214, 219
corruption, 291–296
criminal investigation, 199, 200–202
dangers of police work, 298–303
discretion, 221–223
drug testing, 297–298
emergency response, 199, 200
ethics training, 223
evidence-based, 170
fatigue, 303
federal agencies, 170–175
female officers, 228–231
force, 303–309. *See also* police use
of force
historical overview, 161–166,
204–207
informants, 267–268
integrity, 296–297
intelligence function, 267–282
interrogation, 268–275
local agencies, 179–180
multicultural society, 292, 309–314
oath of honor, 297
organizational structure, 203–205
preventive patrol, 198, 199
private protective services, 180–186
problem officers, 305–306
problem-oriented, 169, 202
problem solving, 199, 202–203
professional organization, 224
purposes, 192–198
race/ethnicity, 228–231
racial bias, 309–314
recruitment and selection, 226–227
risk of disease/infection, 300–302
routine incident response, 198–200
salary, 226, 295–296
scientific studies, 166–169
slain officers, 299–300
state agencies, 175–177
strategic, 210
stress, 302–303
styles of, 207–208
support services, 199, 203
team, 209
technological advances, 196–197, 208
terrorism, 214–221

policing (*continued*)
    training, 224–225
    violence in line of duty, 299–300
    wages, 226, 295–296
    women officers, 228–231
policing styles, 207–208
Positivist School, 89
postmodern criminology, 111
precedent, 126
preliminary hearing, 376–378, 609–610
preliminary investigation, 202
preppy murder case, 139
prerelease guidance centers, 494
present sanity, 388
presentence investigation (PSI), 418–420
presentence report, 419–420
press reports, 361–363
presumptive sentencing, 408–409
pretrial detention, 372, 376
pretrial release, 372–376, 377
pretrial service agencies, 377
preventive patrol, 198, 199
PRIDE Act, 492
Principles for Juries and Jury Trials, 360
Principles for Promoting Police
    Integrity, 297
*Principles of Criminology*
    (Sutherland), 101
prison, 524–575
    AIDS, 559–561
    civil death, 545
    classification system, 503–504
    correctional officers, 539–543
    defined, 482
    federal system, 504–506
    geriatric offenders, 561–563
    hands-off doctrine, 545, 546,
        557–559
    historical overview, 485–488
    homosexuality, 532–533
    inmate rights. *See* prisoners' rights
    inmate types, 530–531
    overcrowding, 499–502
    private, 514–517
    recent improvements, 507
    riots, 543–545
    security levels, 502–503, 505
    state systems, 499
    women, 533–539
prison argot, 528
prison capacity, 500
*Prison Community, The* (Clemmer), 526
prison homosexuality, 532–533
prison industry enhancement
    certification program (PIECP), 492
prison Islam, 567
Prison Litigation Reform Act (PLRA),
    558–559
prison overcrowding, 499–502
Prison Rape Elimination Act (PREA), 532
prison riots, 543–545
prison subculture, 527–530
prisoner reentry, 458
prisoners' rights, 545–559
    access to courts, 551
    communications and visitation,
        549–550

hands-off doctrine, 545, 546,
    557–559
legal assistance, 551
medical care, 551, 554
overview, 548
privacy, 555
protection from harm, 554–555
punishment/discipline, 555–557
religious freedom, 550–551
prisonization, 527
privacy, 275–277
private attorney, 347
private prisons, 514–517
private protective services, 181
private security agencies, 180–186
privatization, 514
probable cause, 18, 249, 257
probable cause hearing, 371
probation
    advantages/disadvantages, 460–461
    civil liability, 463–464
    conditions, 456–457
    defined, 453
    federal system, 457
    future of, 472–473
    officer, 458, 464–466
    reinventing, 474–476
    revocation hearings, 462–463
    shock, 467
    statistics, 453–456
probation officer, 464–466
probation violation, 460
probative value, 389
problem-oriented policing, 169, 202
problem police officers, 305–306
problem solving, 199, 202–203
problem-solving policing, 210
procedural defenses, 149–152
procedural law, 126–128
procedural model, 333
professional organization, 224
Program of Research on the Causes and
    Correlates of Delinquency, 104
Program of Research on the Causes and
    Correlates of Juvenile Delinquency,
    104, 587
prohibition, 164–165
Project DARE, 651
Project Gangfact, 594
Project on Human Development in
    Chicago Neighborhoods (PHDCN),
    106
property bonds, 374
property crime, 41
proportionality, 408
prosecuting attorney, 343–346
prosecutor, 343
prosecutorial discretion, 345–346
prosecutorial misconduct, 151
protected computer, 731
protected liberties, 557
provocation, 143
psychoactive substance, 624
psychoanalysis, 93–94
psychobiological theories, 91–93
psychobiology, 91
psychological dependence, 629

psychological manipulation, 269–270
psychological profiling, 96
Psychological School, 93
psychological theories, 93–96
psychopath, 95
psychopathology, 94–95
psychopathy, 94
psychosis, 95
PTO program, 224
public-account system, 490
public defender, 348
public drunkenness, 625
public health generalism, 627
public humiliation, 484
public-order advocates, 11
public-safety exception to *Miranda,* 274
Public Safety Partnership and
    Community Policing Act, 212
public shaming, 418
public-works system, 490
punishment, 133
punitive damages, 125
purposeful action, 131

## Q

qualified immunity, 318
quality-of-life offenses, 195, 197
Quetelet system, 715

## R

race and ethnicity, 25–27
    academic review, 47–48
    death sentence, 427
    incarceration rates, 498, 508, 533
    jails, 508
    jury selection, 385, 386–387
    juvenile confinement, 612
    juvenile murder victims, 590
    peremptory challenges, 385
    police officers, 228–231
    probation, 458
    racial profiling, 309–311
    racially biased policing, 313–314
    sentencing, 417
racial profiling, 309–311
racially biased policing, 313–314
*Racially Biased Policing: A Principled
    Response,* 313
Racketeer Influenced and Corrupt
    Organizations (RICO), 648
radar flashlight, 727
radiation-detection equipment, 728
radical, 531
radical criminology, 107
radio-frequency identification (RFID)
    tags, 729
Rampart scandal, 293, 295
rape, 44–46
rape shield law, 60
rated capacity, 500
rational choice theory, 86
rave parties, 641
reaction formation, 100
real evidence, 388
Real IRA, 695
real justice conferencing (RJC), 608
realist, 531

reality principle, 93
reasonable force, 138
reasonable person, 132
reasonable suspicion, 256–257
rebels, 98
recidivism, 494, 501
reckless behavior, 131
recreational drug user, 623
redirect examination, 390
reentry, 458
reform school movement, 585
reformatory era (1876-90), 488–490
reformatory style, 488
regional jail, 513
regional terrorism task force
    (RTTF), 216
rehabilitation, 404–405
Rehnquist Court, 249–250
reinforcement, 102
release on recognizance (ROR), 374
release under supervision, 375
religious (prisoners), 531
remote location monitoring, 470, 471
Remote Video Inspection System
    (RVIS), 728
*Report on the Enforcement of the
    Prohibition Laws of the United
    States,* 165
research, 82
resident agencies, 173
resisting unlawful arrest, 140
response time, 200
restitution, 460
restoration, 405
restorative justice, 405, 406
restraint theories, 102–103
retained counsel, 346, 347
retentionist position, 434
retreatists, 98, 531
retributive justice, 406
revocation hearings, 462–463
Revolutionary Armed Forces of Colombia
    (FARC), 694
RFID tags, 729
right to remain silent, 390
rights, 243
rights to privacy, 275–277
riots (prison), 543–545
RISS ATIX, 221
ritualists, 98
roadblock, 262–263
robbery, 46–48
Rohypnol, 143, 641–642
Rome Statute, 672
rough-sex defense, 139
routine activities theory, 87
routine incident response, 198–200
rule of law, 121–122
rules of evidence, 380
run-down city street, 99
runaway children, 595–596
rustling, 50

## S

Safe Streets Act, 603
Salafist Group for Call and Combat, 694
Sarbanes-Oxley Act, 9, 64

Scandinavian Research Council for
    Criminology, 668
*Scarlett Letter, The* (Hawthorne), 484
schedule I controlled substances, 629
schedule II controlled substances, 629
schedule III controlled substances, 629
schedule IV controlled substances, 629
schedule V controlled substances, 630
schizophrenic, 96
school in crime, 461
Science and Technology (S&T), 688
scientific jury selection, 384
scientific police management, 166
search and seizure, 244–267
    body-cavity search, 277
    Burger Court, 249
    emergency search of persons,
        258–259
    emergency search of property, 253
    exclusionary rule, 244–246
    fleeting-targets exception, 261
    fruit of the prisoned tree doctrine,
        245–246
    good-faith exception, 249–250
    high-tech search, 266–267
    motor home, 263
    motor vehicle checkpoint, 262–263
    plain-view doctrine, 250–252
    Rehnquist Court, 249–250
    roadblock, 262–263
    searches incident to arrest, 247–248,
        256–258
    sneak and peak search, 280–281, 282
    subways, searches in, 265–266
    suspicionless search, 263–266
    vehicle search, 259–263
    Warren Court, 246–248
    watercraft, 263
searches incident to arrest, 247–248,
    256–258
*Searching and Seizing Computers and
    Obtaining Electronic Evidence in
    Criminal Investigations,* 282
Second Amendment, 734
second-degree murder, 136
Secret Service—Uniformed Division, 135
secure identity management, 732–733
*Security Management,* 182
security threat group (STG), 544
selective incapacitation, 501–502
selective prosecution, 151
self-defense, 138
sentencing, 19–20, 400–447
    consecutive/concurrent sentence, 20
    death penalty, 426–440. *See also*
        capital punishment
    defined, 402
    fine, 425–426
    goals, 403–406
    guidelines, 409–413
    indeterminate, 406–408
    innovations, 418
    intermediate sanctions, 466–472
    mandatory, 414–415
    presentence investigation (PSI),
        418–420
    presumptive, 408–409

statistics, 424
    structured, 408–409
    three-strikes law, 414–417
    victim, 420–423
Sentencing Commission, 409
sentencing guidelines, 409–413
Sentencing Project, 466
Sentencing Reform Act of 1984, 409, 505
Sentinel, 176
September 11 terrorist attacks, 7
sequestered jury, 385
serial murder, 43
serotonin, 92
service style, 207–208
severance of defendants, 388
severance of offenses, 388
sexual battery, 44
shadow juries, 384
ShadowCrew, 704
shaming, 418
sheriff, 179–180
*Shining, The,* 87
shock incarceration, 467–468
shock parole, 467
shock probation, 467
shoot/no-shoot decision-based
    software, 727
signature bonds, 375
*Silence of the Lambs, The,* 87
*Sisters in Crime* (Adler), 109
Sixth Amendment, 243, 383, 386
slain officers, 299–300
sleepwalking, 143
smart cards, 732–733
smurfing, 646
sneak and peak search, 280–281, 282
social control, 23
social control theory, 102–103
social debt, 408
social development theory, 104
social ecology, 587
social ecology theory, 97
social engineering, 707
social justice, 14
social learning theory, 102
social-order offenses, 58
social policy
    biological theories, 90
    classical theories, 87
    conflict theories, 108–109
    crime data, 34–35
    psychobiological theories, 93
    psychological theories, 96
    sociological theories, 100
social process theory, 101–102
*Society of Captives, The* (Sykes), 526, 529
Society of Police Futurists International
    (PFI), 715
*Society of Women* (Giallombardo), 537
sociological theories, 96–100
software piracy, 709
solicitor, 343
solvability factor, 202
somatotype, 90
Son of Sam, 43
*Sopranos, The,* 66
Sotheby's, 64

*Sourcebook of Criminal Justice Statistics,* 35
sovereign immunity, 318
spam, 710
span of control, 204
special condition of probation, 456–457
specific deterrence, 404
spectators (in courtroom), 361
speedy drug raid, 255
Speedy Trial Act, 382–383
speedy trial acts, 151
split sentencing, 467
spree killing, 43
square inmates, 538–539
staff operations, 203
stalking, 59–62
Standard Minimum Rules for the Treatment of Prisoners, 668
*Stare decisis,* 126
state appellate courts, 333–335
state court administration, 334
state court system, 331, 332–336
state-created liberty interests, 556–557
state law enforcement agencies, 175–177
*State of Prisons* (Howard), 485
state supreme court, 333
state trial courts, 332–333
state-use system, 490
state's attorney, 343–346
statistics. *See* crime statistics
status offenders, 586
status offense, 586
Statute of Winchester, 161
statutory law, 121
statutory rape, 44
stem cell harvesting, 706
stimulants, 638
stir-crazy, 492
stocks (pillory), 484
Stop Huntingdon Animal Cruelty, 678
Strange Brew, 708
strategic intelligence, 218
strategic policing, 210
StreamCast Networks, 709
Streetsweeper, 68
streetwise cops, 290
stress, 302–303
strict liability, 132
structured sentencing, 408–409
structuring, 646
subcultural theory, 98–100
subculture of violence, 100
sublimation, 94
subpoena, 357
substantive criminal law, 122
subways, searches in, 265–266
suicide by cop, 307
*Suicide by Cop: Victims from Both Sides of the Badge* (Stincelli), 307
superego, 93, 94
superior courts, 333
supermale, 91
supersnoop technologies, 734
support services, 199, 203
supremacy of law, 121

Supreme Court of the United States, 338–340
suspicionless search, 263–266
sworn officer, 170
symbolic interaction, 111
systems model of criminal justice, 16

## T

tactical intelligence, 218
tagging, 103
*Taking Command Initiative,* 215
Targeted Outreach, 100
Taser gun, 310–312
Tawhid W' Al Jihad, 695
*Tazir* crimes, 666–667
team policing, 209
technocorrections, 564–565
technocrime, 705
technologically advanced courtroom, 394–395
technology, 702–741
   biocrime, 705–706
   computer-aided investigations, 725–726
   computer-based training (CBT), 726–727
   crime control, 713–727
   cybercrime, 706–711
   DNA profiling, 720–724
   fingerprinting, 716–717
   future advances, 727–729
   individual rights, 734–735
   legislation, 730–731
   nanotechnology, 729
   online databases, 724–725
   secure identity management, 732–733
   smart cards, 732–733
   terrorism, 711–713
teen court, 610
Telecommunications Act of 1996, 279
television coverage (of court cases), 361–363
television shows, 34, 358–359
temporary insanity, 147
terrorism, 69, 674–695
   antiterrorism committees/reports, 685–687
   bioterrorism, 713
   causes, 683–684
   combating, 684–691
   community policing, 219
   cyberterrorism, 680–681
   defined, 674–675
   Department of Homeland Security, 688–689
   domestic, 676–679
   FBI, 174–175
   foreign terrorist organization (FTO), 691–695
   future of, 693
   intelligence-lead policing (ILP), 216–219
   information sharing, 219–221
   international, 679
   Internet, 711–712

   narcoterrorism, 681–683
   *National Strategy for Combating Terrorism,* 689, 691
   policing, 214
   prisons, 566–568
   technology, 711–713
   U.S. highest ranking officials, 690
   USA PATRIOT Act, 279–282, 686
Terrorism and International Victims Unit (TIVU), 422
*Terry*-type stops, 256
testimony, 390
Texas Rangers, 177
Thanatos, 94
theft, 50–52
theme of this book, 10–12
*Theoretical Studies in Social Organization of the Prison* (Cloward/Cressey), 526
theory, 82. *See also* criminology theory
therapeutic cloning, 706
third-party custody, 375
threatening to act, 131
3-1-1 system, 198
three-strikes law, 414–417, 497
thrownaway children, 595
ticket of leave, 489
tort, 123
Total Information Awareness (TIA), 724–725
total institution, 526
trace-detection technology, 728
Trafficking Victims Protection Reauthorization Act (TVPA), 674
transferred intent, 131
transitions, 104
transnational crime, 673
transnational cybercrime, 707
transnational organized crime, 65
transportation, 484
treason, 129
treatment era of corrections, 492–493
trial. *See* criminal trial
trial courts of general jurisdiction, 333
trial courts of limited jurisdiction, 332
trial *de novo,* 333
trial initiation, 382–383
trilogy, 176
truth in sentencing, 409
Truth in Sentencing Incentive Funds, 409
*Turner Diaries,* 679
TV shows, 34, 358–359
TWGECSI guide (electronic evidence), 282
two-market system, 654
Tyco International, 64

## U

UCR. *See* Uniform Crime Reports (UCR)
Ulster Defence Association, 695
Unabomber, 43, 679
Unborn Victims of Violence Act, 44
unconsciousness, 143
undisciplined children, 586
*Uniform Crime Reporting Handbook,* 37

Uniform Crime Reports (UCR)
  clearance rate, 41
  hierarchy rule, 41
  historical overview, 36–40
  NCVS, compared, 57, 58
  NIBRS, compared, 55
  part I offenses. *See* part I offenses
  part II offenses, 53–54
  problems with, 57–59
  terminology, 40–42
UN. *See* United Nations
UN Code of Conduct for Law
  Enforcement Officials, 668
UN World Crime Surveys, 668
United Nations, 668–669
United Nations Crime and Justice
  Information Network (UNCJIN),
  668
United Self-Defense Forces of Colombia,
  694
United States Coast Guard (USCG), 689
United States Secret Service (USSS), 689
unmanned aerial vehicle (UAV), 316, 729
unsecured bonds, 375
unsolicited commercial bulk e-mail
  (UCBE), 710
U.S. attorneys, 344
U.S. Citizenship and Immigration
  Services (USCIS), 689
U.S. Constitution
  Bill of Rights, 21, 242
  Eighth Amendment, 243, 435
  Fifth Amendment, 243, 390
  First Amendment, 681
  Fourteenth Amendment, 243, 735
  Fourth Amendment, 243, 244, 734.
    *See also* search and seizure
  guaranteed rights, 21
  overview, 243
  Second Amendment, 734
  Sixth Amendment, 243, 383, 386
  technology, 734–735
U.S. Court of Federal Claims, 336
U.S. courts of appeal, 337–338
U.S. district courts, 336–337
U.S. magistrates, 337
U.S. Marshals Service, 354
U.S. Parole Commission, 460
U.S. penitentiaries (USPs), 505
U.S. Supreme Court, 338–340
US-CERT, 681
USA PATRIOT Act, 9, 12, 279–282,
  646, 686
utilitarianism, 86

## V

vagrancy laws, 131
vehicle identification number (VIN), 714
vehicle search, 259–263
verdict, 392
vertical rule, 126
victim, 360–361, 420–423
Victim and Witness Protection Act
  (VWPA), 421–422
victim-assistance program, 357
victim impact statements, 423
victimless crimes, 58
victims' assistance groups, 222
Victim's Assistance Network, 222
Victims of Crime Act (VOCA), 422
Vienna Declaration on Crime, 670
vigilantism, 163
VIN numbers, 714
Violence Against Women Act (VAWA),
  60, 61, 422
violence in line of duty, 299–300
violent crime, 41
Violent Crime Control and Law
  Enforcement Act, 68, 409, 422, 632
Violent Gang and Terrorist Organization
  File (VGTOF), 26
virtual case file (VCF), 176
virtual reality (VR), 728
vitamins, 92
Vivendi Universal, 64
*voir dire,* 383
voluntary/advisory sentencing
  guidelines, 408
voluntary intoxication, 143

## W

wages, 226, 295–296
Waiver of *Miranda* rights, 271, 273
Walnut Street Jail, 485
war on drugs, 626
warehousing, 495
warehousing era, 494–495
warrant, 17
Warren Court, 21, 242–243, 246–248
watchman style, 207
watercraft, 263
weapon of mass destruction (WMD), 712
Westfall Act, 318
"What Works!" (Gendreau et al.), 501
*Where the Jobs Are: The Continuing
  Growth of Federal Job
  Opportunities,* 22
white-collar crime, 63–65

Wickersham Commission, 165, 225, 296
wiretapping, 275–277
witness
  child, 390
  expert, 355–356
  lay, 356–357
  testimony, 390
witness for the defense, 390
witness for the prosecution, 390
women
  crime statistics, 110
  feminist criminology, 109–110
  incarceration rates, 533
  jail, 508–510, 533–539
  police officers, 228–231
  prison slang, 528
  Violence Against Women Act
    (VAWA), 60, 61, 422
  victims, as, 59–62
*Women and Crime* (Simon), 109
women police officers, 228–231
*Women's Prison* (Ward/Kassebaum), 537
Word for Windows Macro virus, 708
work release, 494
workhouse, 484
workplace stress, 302–303
*World Factbook of Criminal Justice
  Systems,* 662
World Justice Information Network
  (WJIN), 668
WorldCom, 64
writ of *certiorari,* 245, 340
writ of *habeas corpus,* 427, 547
wrongful convicting cases, 722

## X

Xybernaut Corporation, 728

## Y

*yakuza,* 65
young offenders. *See* juvenile justice
youth aid panels, 608
youth gangs, 591–595

## Z

ZNQ3, 728

**Pearson Education, Inc.**

## YOU SHOULD CAREFULLY READ THE TERMS AND CONDITIONS BEFORE USING THE CD-ROM PACKAGE. USING THIS CD-ROM PACKAGE INDICATES YOUR ACCEPTANCE OF THESE TERMS AND CONDITIONS.

Pearson Education, Inc. provides this program and licenses its use. You assume responsibility for the selection of the program to achieve your intended results, and for the installation, use, and results obtained from the program. This license extends only to use of the program in the United States or countries in which the program is marketed by authorized distributors.

### LICENSE GRANT

You hereby accept a nonexclusive, nontransferable, permanent license to install and use the program ON A SINGLE COMPUTER at any given time. You may copy the program solely for backup or archival purposes in support of your use of the program on the single computer. You may not modify, translate, disassemble, decompile, or reverse engineer the program, in whole or in part.

### TERM

The License is effective until terminated. Pearson Education, Inc. reserves the right to terminate this License automatically if any provision of the License is violated. You may terminate the License at any time. To terminate this License, you must return the program, including documentation, along with a written warranty stating that all copies in your possession have been returned or destroyed.

### LIMITED WARRANTY

THE PROGRAM IS PROVIDED "AS IS" WITHOUT WARRANTY OF ANY KIND, EITHER EXPRESSED OR IMPLIED, INCLUDING, BUT NOT LIMITED TO, THE IMPLIED WARRANTIES OR MERCHANTABILITY AND FITNESS FOR A PARTICULAR PURPOSE. THE ENTIRE RISK AS TO THE QUALITY AND PERFORMANCE OF THE PROGRAM IS WITH YOU. SHOULD THE PROGRAM PROVE DEFECTIVE, YOU (AND NOT PRENTICE-HALL, INC. OR ANY AUTHORIZED DEALER) ASSUME THE ENTIRE COST OF ALL NECESSARY SERVICING, REPAIR, OR CORRECTION. NO ORAL OR WRITTEN INFORMATION OR ADVICE GIVEN BY PRENTICE-HALL, INC., ITS DEALERS, DISTRIBUTORS, OR AGENTS SHALL CREATE A WARRANTY OR INCREASE THE SCOPE OF THIS WARRANTY.

SOME STATES DO NOT ALLOW THE EXCLUSION OF IMPLIED WARRANTIES, SO THE ABOVE EXCLUSION MAY NOT APPLY TO YOU. THIS WARRANTY GIVES YOU SPECIFIC LEGAL RIGHTS AND YOU MAY ALSO HAVE OTHER LEGAL RIGHTS THAT VARY FROM STATE TO STATE.

Pearson Education, Inc. does not warrant that the functions contained in the program will meet your requirements or that the operation of the program will be uninterrupted or error-free.

However, Pearson Education, Inc. warrants the diskette(s) or CD-ROM(s) on which the program is furnished to be free from defects in material and workmanship under normal use for a period of ninety (90) days from the date of delivery to you as evidenced by a copy of your receipt.

The program should not be relied on as the sole basis to solve a problem whose incorrect solution could result in injury to person or property. If the program is employed in such a manner, it is at the user's own risk and Pearson Education, Inc. explicitly disclaims all liability for such misuse.

### LIMITATION OF REMEDIES

Pearson Education, Inc.'s entire liability and your exclusive remedy shall be:

1. the replacement of any diskette(s) or CD-ROM(s) not meeting Pearson Education, Inc.'s "LIMITED WARRANTY" and that is returned to Pearson Education, or

2. if Pearson Education is unable to deliver a replacement diskette(s) or CD-ROM(s) that is free of defects in materials or workmanship, you may terminate this agreement by returning the program.

IN NO EVENT WILL PRENTICE-HALL, INC. BE LIABLE TO YOU FOR ANY DAMAGES, INCLUDING ANY LOST PROFITS, LOST SAVINGS, OR OTHER INCIDENTAL OR CONSEQUENTIAL DAMAGES ARISING OUT OF THE USE OR INABILITY TO USE SUCH PROGRAM EVEN IF PRENTICE-HALL, INC. OR AN AUTHORIZED DISTRIBUTOR HAS BEEN ADVISED OF THE POSSIBILITY OF SUCH DAMAGES, OR FOR ANY CLAIM BY ANY OTHER PARTY.

SOME STATES DO NOT ALLOW FOR THE LIMITATION OR EXCLUSION OF LIABILITY FOR INCIDENTAL OR CONSEQUENTIAL DAMAGES, SO THE ABOVE LIMITATION OR EXCLUSION MAY NOT APPLY TO YOU.

### GENERAL

You may not sublicense, assign, or transfer the license of the program. Any attempt to sublicense, assign or transfer any of the rights, duties, or obligations hereunder is void.

This Agreement will be governed by the laws of the State of New York.

Should you have any questions concerning this Agreement, you may contact Pearson Education, Inc. by writing to:

Director of New Media
Higher Education Division
Pearson Education, Inc.
One Lake Street
Upper Saddle River, NJ 07458

**Should you have any questions concerning technical support, you may contact:**

**Product Support Department: Monday–Friday 8:00 A.M. –8:00 P.M. and Sunday 5:00 P.M.-12:00 A.M. (All times listed are Eastern). 1-800-677-6337**

**You can also get support by filling out the web form located at http://247.prenhall.com**

YOU ACKNOWLEDGE THAT YOU HAVE READ THIS AGREEMENT, UNDERSTAND IT, AND AGREE TO BE BOUND BY ITS TERMS AND CONDITIONS. YOU FURTHER AGREE THAT IT IS THE COMPLETE AND EXCLUSIVE STATEMENT OF THE AGREEMENT BETWEEN US THAT SUPERSEDES ANY PROPOSAL OR PRIOR AGREEMENT, ORAL OR WRITTEN, AND ANY OTHER COMMUNICATIONS BETWEEN US RELATING TO THE SUBJECT MATTER OF THIS AGREEMENT.

# Welcome
## to the
# EXPLORING
# CRIMINAL JUSTICE
# TODAY
# CD-ROM!

Up-to-date, with a new design, this exciting and engaging CD-ROM is loaded with interactive scenarios, practice questions for every chapter, resources and much, much more.

**Interactive Multimedia Scenarios:** Experience the world of criminal justice by stepping into the role of a police officer, a judge, a probation officer, and a corrections officer in real-life scenarios. Based on actual US Supreme Court cases, each scenario confronts you with situations that require you to make critical decisions.

Illustrating important aspects from the criminal justice system, these scenarios bring your textbook to life. Look for the "What Would You Do?" icon in every chapter to connect each scenario to information covered specifically in that chapter.

**Career Profiles:** Provide in-depth job descriptions highlighting various careers in the field. Each profile includes a video interview with a professional from the real world of Criminal Justice.

**Study Review Games:** Vocabulary-building interactive games help you master key criminal justice terms.

**Electronic Study Guide:** Test your understanding of the material covered in each chapter with self-scoring practice quizzes.

**Glossary:** A dictionary of criminal justice terms.